THE OXFORD HANDBOOK OF

SPORT AND
SOCIETY

THE OXFORD HANDBOOK OF

SPORT AND SOCIETY

Edited by

LAWRENCE A. WENNER

OXFORD
UNIVERSITY PRESS

OXFORD
UNIVERSITY PRESS

Oxford University Press is a department of the University of Oxford. It furthers
the University's objective of excellence in research, scholarship, and education
by publishing worldwide. Oxford is a registered trade mark of Oxford University
Press in the UK and certain other countries.

Published in the United States of America by Oxford University Press
198 Madison Avenue, New York, NY 10016, United States of America.

CIP data is on file at the Library of Congress
ISBN 978–0–19–751901–1

DOI: 10.1093/oxfordhb/9780197519011.001.0001

1 3 5 7 9 8 6 4 2
Printed by Marquis, Canada

CONTENTS

INTRODUCTION

PART I. SOCIETY AND VALUES

PART IV. LIFESPAN AND CAREERS

PART V. INCLUSION AND EXCLUSION

PART VI. SPECTATOR ENGAGEMENT AND MEDIA

About the Editor

Lawrence A. Wenner (Ph.D., University of Iowa, 1977) is the Von der Ahe Professor of Communication and Ethics in the College of Communication and Fine Arts and the School of Film and Television at Loyola Marymount University in Los Angeles. His earlier notable appointments include serving as the William Evans Fellow at the University of Otago, the Diederich Distinguished Visiting Scholar at Marquette University, the Louise Davies Professor of Contemporary Values in America at the University of San Francisco, and a University Fellow at the University of Iowa. Wenner's research includes 10 books and approximately 140 scholarly journal articles and book chapters. He has been featured in Intellect Books' *Who's Who in Research: Media Studies*, and the University of Nebraska Press's *Journal of Sports Media* has characterized him as such a "heavy hitter in the world of sport research" that he "may be the most prolific and accomplished scholar in the field."

Wenner was founding editor-in-chief of the bimonthly scholarly journal *Communication & Sport* and has served as two-term editor-in-chief of both the *International Review for the Sociology of Sport* and the *Journal of Sport and Social Issues*. He has edited special issues of *American Behavioral Scientist* and the *Journal of Sport Management* on sport communication and has served on numerous journal editorial boards in media and communication studies, sport studies, sociology, and management. With Andrew Billings and Marie Hardin he edits the Communication, Sport, and Society book series for the Peter Lang Publishing Group.

Wenner has lectured in more than 30 countries on research focusing on critical assessments of media content, ethical dimensions of race and gender portrayals in advertising, audience experiences with television in the family context, and the values and consumption of mediated sports. His recent books include *American Sport in the Shadow of a Pandemic: Communicative Insights* (2022, with Andrew Billings and Marie Hardin) and *Sport, Media and Mega-Events* (2017, with Andrew Billings). His other books on sport include *Fallen Sports Heroes, Media, and Celebrity Culture* (2013), *Sport, Beer, and Gender: Promotional Culture and Contemporary Social Life* (2009, with Steven Jackson), *MediaSport* (1998), and *Media, Sports, and Society* (1989).

Wenner's honors include a commemorative panel featured at the annual conference of the International Association for Communication and Sport recognizing the 25th anniversary of the publication of his anthology *Media, Sports, and Society* for being foundational in establishing the scholarly study of communication and sport. In 2018, he received the PROSE Award as editor of *Communication & Sport*, which was recognized as the Best New Journal in the Social Sciences; he received the inaugural Legacy Scholar Award from the

International Communication Association's Sport Communication Interest Group; he was named a research fellow of the North American Society for the Sociology of Sport; and he received the LMU Rains Award for Excellence in Scholarship and Creative Activity. In 2019, Wenner received the Honorary Member Award from the International Sociology of Sport Association for lifetime scholarly contributions to the sociology of sport, and the Emerging Scholar Award of the National Communication Association's Communication and Sport Division was named in his honor. Media reports on his research and interviews have been featured widely across broadcast, print, and web outlets.

About the Contributors

Daryl Adair is an associate professor of sport management in the Business School of the University of Technology in Sydney. His research has encompassed sport history, sociology, politics, media, and management, and his recent interests are gender relations in sport, race and ethnicity in sport, and drugs in sport. His books include *Sport: Race, Ethnicity, and Identity* (2011), *Embodied Masculinities in Global Sport* (2014, with Jorge Knijnik), *Managing the Football World Cup* (2014, with Stephen Frawley), and *Global Sport-for-Development: Critical Perspectives* (2014, with Nico Schulenkorf). Adair writes regularly for *The Conversation* under the column "The Bounce of the Ball."

Eric Anderson is a professor of sport, health and social sciences at the University of Winchester. He holds degrees in health, psychology, and sociology and has published 25 books and 75 peer-reviewed scientific papers. Anderson's research excellence has been recognized by the British Academy of Social Sciences, and he is a full fellow of the International Academy of Sex Research and a chartered psychologist.

David L. Andrews is a professor in the physical cultural studies research area in the Department of Kinesiology at the University of Maryland. He is also an affiliate faculty member in the Department of American Studies and the Department of Sociology. Andrews's research interests center on contextualizing sport and physical culture in relation to the intersecting cultural, political, economic, and technological forces shaping contemporary society. Recent books include *Making Sport Great Again? The Uber-Sport Assemblage, Neoliberalism, and the Trump Conjuncture* (2019) and *Sport, Physical Culture, and the Moving Body: Materialisms, Technologies, Ecologies* (2020, edited with Joshua Newman and Holly Thorpe).

Michael Atkinson is a professor of physical cultural studies in the Faculty of Kinesiology and Physical Education at the University of Toronto. His research and teaching interests focus on the social experience of suffering and pain in sport cultures, invisible disabilities, the phenomenology of insomnia, animal welfare in physical cultures, and ethnographic research methods. Atkinson is the author or editor of 11 books, is past editor of the *Sociology of Sport Journal*, and is currently the coeditor of *Qualitative Research in Sport, Exercise, and Health*.

Zoë Avner is a lecturer in the Department of Sport, Exercise and Rehabilitation at Northumbria University. Her current research draws on poststructuralist and feminist methodologies to explore athlete and coach learning and coaching ethics. Her work has appeared in various journals, including *Sports Coaching Review* and *Sport, Education and Society*.

Richard Bailey is based in the Centre for Academic Partnerships & Engagement at the University of Nottingham Malaysia. After working as a schoolteacher, he carried out graduate studies in epistemology, psychiatry, and evolutionary anthropology. Current research includes a Europe-wide study of the relationship between physical activity and educational achievement, cross-context inclusive education, and the philosophy of the Austrian psychiatrist and Holocaust survivor Viktor Frankl.

Alan Bairner is a professor of sport and social theory at Loughborough University, having previously worked at Ulster University. He serves on several editorial boards. His work focuses on the relationship between sport and politics, with a particular emphasis on sport, nations, and national identities. Recent edited books include the *Routledge Handbook of Sport and Politics* (2017, with John Kelly and Jung Woo Lee), *Sport and Body Cultures in East and South East Asia* (2017, with Friederike Trotier), and *Sport and Secessionism* (2020, with Mariann Vaczi).

Adam S. Beissel is an assistant professor of sport leadership and management at Miami University, Ohio.. His scholarship and teaching critically examine the cultural and political economies of global sport. He is currently working on a research project exploring the political economy of the 2026 FIFA Men's World Cup, jointly hosted by the United States, Mexico, and Canada.

Andrew C. Billings is the Ronald Reagan Chair of Broadcasting and executive director of the Alabama Program in Sports Communication at the University of Alabama in Tuscaloosa. With 22 books and over 200 journal articles and book chapters, he is one of the most published sports media scholars in the world. His works typically focus on the intersection of sport, media, and issues of identity.

Raymond Boyle is a professor of communication and the director of the Centre for Cultural Policy Research at the University of Glasgow. He has written widely on media and sport and is the author and coauthor of a number of books on media issues, the latest being *The Talent Industry*, published in 2018. He is also co–managing editor of the journal *Media, Culture and Society*.

Ian Brittain is an associate professor (research) in the Centre for Business in Society, Coventry University. His area of research interest is sociological, historical, and sports management aspects of disability and Paralympic sport. He has published seven books in this field, including *The Paralympic Games Explained* (2009), *The Palgrave Handbook of Paralympic Studies* (2018, with Aaron Beacom) and *The Disability Sport in Europe: Policy, Structure, and Participation—A Cross-National Perspective* (2020, with Caroline van Lindert and Jeroen Scheerder).

Daniel D. Buckley is a lecturer in life sciences at the University of Hertfordshire, where he currently teaches on the Sport, Health and Exercise programs. He is completing his doctorate, which aims to provide insight into different types of therapies for people living with dementia, with a particular focus on reminiscence therapy.

Michael L. Butterworth is the Governor Ann W. Richards Chair for the Texas Program in Sports and Media, a professor in the Department of Communication Studies, and director of the Center for Sports Communication & Media at the University of Texas at Austin. His research focuses on rhetoric, democracy, and sport, with particular interests in national identity, militarism, and public memory. He is the author or editor of *Baseball and Rhetorics of Purity* (2010); *Communication and Sport: Surveying the Field* (2021, fourth edition with Andrew Billings); *Sport and Militarism* (2017); *Sport, Rhetoric, and Political Struggle* (2019); *Rhetorics of Democracy in the Americas* (2021); and *Handbook of Communication and Sport* (2021).

Nicholas R. Buzzelli is a doctoral candidate in the University of Alabama's Communication & Information Sciences graduate program. After earning a bachelor's degree in communication from Robert Morris University (2015), Buzzelli matriculated to Kent State University, where he graduated with a master's degree in magazine journalism (2017). His primary research interests are rooted in sports journalism processes and norms and the media's coverage of race- and gender-based issues in sport.

Ben Carrington teaches sociology and journalism in the Annenberg School for Communication and Journalism at the University of Southern California. His books on sport include *Sport and Politics: The Sporting Black Diaspora* (2010); *Marxism, Cultural Studies and Sport* (2008, edited with Ian McDonald); and the *Blackwell Companion to Sport* (2013, edited with David Andrews). He has written widely on topics focused on the sociology of race, gender and culture, post/colonial theory, Marxism and culture, sport studies, media studies, and youth culture and music.

Laurence Chalip is a professor in and director of the School of Sport, Recreation, and Tourism Management at George Mason University. He was the founding editor of *Sport Management Review*, later edited *Journal of Sport Management*, and has served on editorial boards of 19 other journals. He has published and consulted widely in sport management, for which he earned the Earl F. Ziegler Award from the North American Society for Sport Management and a Distinguished Service Award from the Sport Management Association of Australia and New Zealand. He also served as the international chair of Olympism for the IOC and the Olympic Studies Centre.

Matej Christiaens is a lecturer of sport and event management at the School of Marketing and Management, Coventry University. His research interests are sports participation, gender in sport, and sports management aspects of disability. His recent work includes a book chapter titled "United Kingdom: An Inclusionary Approach to Sport" (with Ian Brittain and Christopher Brown) in *Disability Sport in Europe: Policy, Structure, and Participation—A Cross-National Perspective* (2020).

Jay Coakley is Professor Emeritus of Sociology at the University of Colorado at Colorado Springs. He was the founding editor of the *Sociology of Sport Journal* and is an internationally recognized scholar. His textbook, *Sports in Society: Issues and Controversies* (13th edition, 2021), along with adaptations and translations, is used in universities worldwide. He coedited *Inside Sports* (1999) with Peter Donnelly and the *Handbook of Sports Studies* (2000) with Eric Dunning. He continues to do research and consulting focused primarily on making sports more democratic and humane for people of all ages and abilities.

Cheryl Cooky is a professor of American studies and women's, gender, and sexuality studies at Purdue University. She is the coauthor of *No Slam Dunk: Gender, Sport and the Unevenness of Social Change* (2018). Her research is published in a diverse array of journals, including *Communication & Sport, Gender & Society, Journal of Sex Research, Sex Roles,* and *Sociology of Sport Journal.* She is the editor of *Sociology of Sport Journal.* Committed to making research accessible to general audiences, Cooky has been quoted in over 100 national and international news media outlets.

T. Bettina Cornwell (PhD in marketing, University of Texas) is the Philip H. Knight Chair in the Lundquist College of Business and head of the Department of Marketing at the University of Oregon. Her research has recently appeared in the *Journal of the Academy of Marketing Science, Journal of Marketing,* and *Academy of Management Review.* Cornwell's research focuses on marketing communications and consumer behavior and often includes international and public policy emphases. The second edition of her book *Sponsorship in Marketing* was published 2020, and *Influencer: The Science behind Swaying Others,* with co-author Helen Katz, was published in 2021.

Seán Crosson is a senior lecturer in film in the Huston School of Film & Digital Media, leader of the Sport & Exercise Research Group, and co-director of the MA in Sports Journalism and Communication at the University of Galway. His previous publications include the monographs *Gaelic Games on Film: From Silent Films to Hollywood Hurling, Horror and the Emergence of Irish Cinema* (2019) and *Sport and Film* (2013) and the collections *Sport, Film and National Culture* (2020) and (as coeditor) *Sport, Representation and Evolving Identities in Europe* (2010).

Jim Denison is a professor in the Faculty of Kinesiology, Sport, and Recreation at the University of Alberta. A sport sociologist and coach educator, his research examines the formation of coaches' practices through a poststructuralist lens. Along with his numerous book chapters and referred articles, he edited *Coaching Knowledges: Understanding the Dynamics of Performance Sport* (2007) and coedited *Moving Writing: Crafting Movement in Sport Research* (2003). He serves on the editorial board of *Sports Coaching Review* and was coeditor of *The Routledge Handbook of Sports Coaching* (2013).

Paul Dimeo is an associate professor in the Faculty of Health Sciences and Sport, University of Stirling. He is co-director of the International Network of Doping Research and has published widely on various subjects, including antidoping history and policy. His books include *The Anti-Doping Crisis in Sport: Causes, Consequences, Solutions* (2018, with Vernon Møller,), *Elite Sport, Doping and Public Health* (2009, with Vernon Møller and Michael McNamee), and *Drugs, Alcohol and Sport* (2006).

Kevin Dixon is a senior lecturer in sport management at Northumbria University. He is the author or coauthor of five books and over 40 research papers and book chapters. His research largely focuses on the topic of sport and civic responsibility, which covers the role of sport in social inclusion, prejudice and stigma, identity formation and maintenance, consumerism, public health, criminal justice, and education, among other important social issues.

Guillaume Dumont is an assistant professor at OCE Research Center, EMLyon Business School. He studied ethnographically the work of professional rock climbers in the USA and Europe, and his recent books include *Professional Climbers: Creative Work on the Sponsorship Labor Market* (2018).

Adam Epstein is department chair and professor of finance and law at Central Michigan University. He has written four textbooks, including *Sports Law* (2002), and has published over 60 law articles. He has received numerous teaching and research awards and has been inducted into the Sport and Recreation Law Association (SRLA) as a research fellow. Epstein has also received SRLA's Betty van der Smissen Leadership Award. His work (with Paul Anderson) was quoted by the Seventh Circuit Court of Appeals. He serves on several editorial boards, including the *Journal of Legal Aspects of Sport*.

Sheranne Fairley is an associate professor in the School of Business at the University of Queensland. Fairley's research focuses on three major streams: sport and event tourism, volunteerism, and the globalization of sport. Her books include *Rebranding and Positioning Australian Rules Football in the American Market* (2009) and *Renegotiating the Shanghai Formula One Event* (2009, with K. D'Elia). She is editor-in-chief of the research journal *Sport Management Review*.

Brian T. Gearity is the director and an associate professor of sport coaching and on-line sport graduate certificate programs at the University of Denver. In addition to over 50 peer-reviewed publications, he coedited the book *Coach Education and Development in Sport: Instructional Strategies* (2020) and coauthored *Understanding Strength and Conditioning as Sport Coaching: Bridging the Biophysical, Pedagogical and Sociocultural Foundations of Practice* (2020). He is editor-in-chief for the National Strength and Conditioning Association's practitioner journal, *NSCA Coach*, and is on the editorial board for *Sport Coaching Review, International Sport Coaching Journal, Qualitative Research in Sport, Exercise, and Health*, and *Strength & Conditioning Journal*.

Bill Gerrard is a professor of business management at Leeds University Business School. He has published academic papers on the methodology of economics, Keynesian economics, sports economics, and sport management. His sports-based research has included the soccer players' transfer market, measuring team quality, coaching efficiency, stadium naming rights, the sporting and financial performance of pro sports teams, and the importance of shared team experience. He is a former editor of the *European Sport Management Quarterly*. His principal focus in recent years has been developing data analysis as an evidence-based approach to coaching in soccer and rugby union.

Heather J. Gibson is a professor of tourism at the University of Florida. Her work cuts across the fields of leisure, tourism, and sport, with a focus on understanding behavioral choices in the context of gender, life span, and well-being. She authored some of the seminal papers in sport tourism and incorporated her focus on women and mid- and later life into the study of active sport tourism. She is a former managing editor of *Leisure Studies* and is an associate editor for the *Annals of Tourism Research* and the *Journal of Sport & Tourism*, among others.

Kass Gibson is an associate professor at Plymouth Marjon University, where he teaches research methods, social theory, and pedagogy. His research uses a range of sociological theories and research methodologies to understand experiences and practices in research, public health, and physical culture. He has published in journals such as *British Journal of Sports Medicine, Journal of Public Health, Psychology of Sport & Exercise*, and *Qualitative Research in Sport, Exercise and Health*, for the latter of which he serves on the editorial board.

Iva Glibo is a research associate and PhD candidate at the Chair of Sport and Health Management, Technical University of Munich. She has an educational background in physical education and sport management. Her current work focuses on sustainable development in international sport policy and practice, with occasional detours into the area of mental health inclusion in sport, in particular for youth.

Ken Green is a professor of sociology of physical education and youth sport and the head of the Faculty of Sport and Exercise Sciences at the University of Chester, as well as a visiting professor at Inland University of Applied Sciences in Norway. He is editor-in-chief of the *European Physical Education Review,* and his books include *Understanding Physical Education* (2008), *Key Themes in Youth Sport* (2010), *The Routledge Handbook of Youth Sport* (2016, coedited with Andy Smith), and *Sport in Scandinavia and the Nordic Countries* (2019, coedited with Thorsteinn Sigurjónsson and Eivind Skille). His main research interests revolve around physical education and youth sport.

Jennifer Guiliano is an associate professor in the Department of History and affiliated faculty in both Native American and Indigenous studies and American studies at IUPUI in Indianapolis. She received a Bachelor of Arts in English and History from Miami University (2000), a Master of Arts in History from Miami University (2002), and a Master of Arts in American History from the University of Illinois (2004) before completing her PhD in History at the University of Illinois (2010).

Edward T. Hall is a senior lecturer in sport coaching at Northumbria University. His scholarship is focused on the relational, (micro)political, and emotional complexities of sports work. Recent and ongoing research explores how networks of social relations influence the thoughts, feelings, and (inter)actions of sport professionals, and how sense is made of experiences, relationships, and the self.

Peizi Han is a PhD student in the School of Sport, Exercise and Health Sciences at Loughborough University, majoring in the sociology of sport. Having graduated from Beijing Sport University, he was awarded an MSc in Sport Management at Loughborough University. His current work focuses on sport, nationalism, national identity, and naturalization in China.

Michael J. Hartill is a professor in the sociology of sport and director of the Centre for Child Protection and Safeguarding in Sport at Edge Hill University. In addition to research articles and book chapters, Hartill authored *Sexual Abuse in Youth Sport: A Sociocultural Analysis* (2016). He recently co-led the EU-funded project VOICE, enabling direct engagement between the sport sector and individuals with personal experience of sexual abuse in sport. Alongside colleagues from across Europe he is currently investigating the scale and character of abuse experienced by athletes in different national contexts.

Douglas Hartmann is a professor of sociology at the University of Minnesota. His research and media work focuses on race, sports, social movements, and public culture. He is the author of *Midnight Basketball: Race, Sports, and Neoliberal Social Policy* and *Race* (2016), *Culture, and the Revolt of the Black Athlete: The 1968 Olympic Protests and Their Aftermath* (2004). Hartmann also coedits (with Mike Messner) the Critical Issues in Sport and Society book series at Rutgers University Press.

April Henning has a PhD in Sociology and is a lecturer in sport studies at the University of Stirling. Henning has published widely on topics related to health and substance use in sport. Her recent book (2021, with Jesper Andreasson), *Performance Cultures and Doped Bodies,* focuses on doping in sport and fitness, gender, and antidoping policy. She is a director of the International Network of Doping Research and an associate editor at the journal *Performance Enhancement and Health.*

John Horne is currently a visiting professor of sport and social theory at Waseda University in Tokyo. He is past chair of the British Sociological Association, fellow of the Academy of Social Sciences, and research fellow of the North American Society for the Sociology of Sport. He is the editor of two book series, Globalizing Sport Studies and Sociological Futures, and the author, coauthor, editor, and coeditor of several books, articles, and book chapters, including *Understanding the Olympics* (2020, with Garry Whannel) and *Mega-Events and Globalization* (2016, edited with Richard Gruneau).

Steven J. Jackson is a professor in the School of Physical Education, Sport & Exercise Sciences at the University of Otago. A past president of the International Sociology of Sport Association, he has published widely in the areas of sport, media, and advertising, globalization, sport and national identity, and sport and masculinity. His recent books include *Sport, Promotional Culture and the Crisis of Masculinity* (2017, with Sarah Gee), *Sport Policy in Small States* (2016, with Michael Sam), and *Globalization, Sport and Corporate Nationalism: The New Cultural Economy of the New Zealand All Blacks* (2011, with Jay Scherer).

Ruth Jeanes is an associate professor in the Faculty of Education at Monash University. Jeanes is a social scientist whose research interests focus on the use of sport and active recreation as a community development resource, particularly to address social exclusion of marginalized groups. She has published over 100 scholarly journal articles and book chapters and five books. She has successfully gained a range of research funding for her work, including two highly competitive Australian Research Council–funded projects. The most recent of these examines informal sport as a health and social resource within diverse communities.

Patrick Foss Johansen is a PhD student and part-time lecturer at Inland University of Applied Sciences, Norway. His research interests adopt sociological perspectives on youth sport and leisure, youth transitions, and public health in Norway. His publications include coauthored works on parents, children, and sport published in *Sport, Education and Society* and a chapter on sports participation in Norway in the book *The Business and Culture of Sports* (2019).

Lauren M. Kamperman is a PhD candidate at Durham University in the Department of Sport and Exercise Sciences, cofunded by the Talented Athlete Scholarship Scheme. She is currently researching experiences of inclusion and exclusion in dual-career sport systems. Kamperman holds an MA in Women's Studies from the University of York. She has previously worked at the Women's Sports Foundation in New York City.

Tara Keegan is an early career scholar. She received her PhD in history from the University of Oregon in 2021, where she won various research and teaching awards. Her work has been supported by such organizations as the American Historical Association, the Oregon

Humanities Center, Oregon's Center for the Study of Women in Society, and the Bancroft Library. She studies Native modernity, popular culture, and sports, with a particular emphasis on Indigenous running.

Lisa A. Kihl is an associate professor of sport management in the School of Kinesiology at the University of Minnesota and the director of the Global Institute for Responsible Sport Organizations. She has research expertise in the interconnections of sport ethics, policy, and governance in fostering responsible sport organizations. She has published extensively on the topics of corruption in sport, sport social responsibility, and athlete representation. She is a research fellow and past president of the North American Society of Sport Management.

Sigmund Loland is a professor of sport philosophy and ethics at the Norwegian School of Sport Sciences in Oslo (NSSS). He has published extensively on topics such as fair play and sports justice, the ethics of performance-enhancing technologies in sport and society, and epistemological issues in the sport sciences. He is a former pro-chancellor of the NSSS, former president of the European College of Sport Science, and a current member of WADA's Ethics Board.

Ryan Lucas is currently undertaking doctoral studies at Monash University, his research focusing on the sport for development policies targeting Indigenous Australians. Lucas's research interest is drawn from his professional experience, which has predominantly focused on the management of youth development programs in remote Indigenous communities of the Northern Territory of Australia. He previously worked in the field of international sport for development, undertaking a long-term volunteering role promoting cricket development in the Solomon Islands. His research interests include sport for development policy, organizational effectiveness in sport for development, and approaches to Indigenous youth development.

Rory Magrath is an associate professor of sociology at Solent University. He is the author of *Inclusive Masculinities in Contemporary Football* (2016) and coauthor of *Out in Sport: The Experiences of Openly Gay and Lesbian Athletes in Contemporary Sport* (2016). He has edited three books and authored or coauthored 25 journal articles. His research focuses on declining homophobia and the changing nature of contemporary masculinities, with a specific focus on elite sport.

Dominic Malcolm is a reader in the sociology of sport at Loughborough University. During the 2000s his research increasingly focused on sociological aspects of sport, health, and medicine, and latterly turned to the social and structural dimensions of concussion and sport. In particular, he has examined the concussion-related experiences of athletes and clinicians, the relationship between concussion and wider public debates about sports safety, and proposed recommendations for enhancing safeguarding practices for sports injury. He is the author of *The Concussion Crisis in Sport* (2019) and the current editor-in-chief of the *International Review for the Sociology of Sport*.

Pirkko Markula is a professor of sociocultural studies of physical activity at the University of Alberta, Edmonton. Her research interests include poststructuralist analyses of dance, exercise, and sport. She is the author of *Deleuze and the Physically Active Body* (2019), coauthor, with Michael Silk, of *Qualitative Research for Physical Culture* (2011), and coauthor, with Richard Pringle, of *Foucault, Sport and Exercise: Power, Knowledge and Transforming the Self* (2006). She is a former editor of the *Sociology of Sport Journal*.

Daniel S. Mason is a professor with the faculty of Kinesiology, Sport, and Recreation at the University of Alberta in Edmonton. His research examines the business of sport and the relationships between all levels of government, sports teams and leagues, and host communities. His research has been funded by the Social Sciences and Humanities Research Council of Canada, and he has published over 100 scholarly journal articles, books, and book chapters. In 2004 he was named a research fellow by the North American Society of Sport Management and is currently an associate editor of the *Journal of Sport Management*.

Elspeth J. Mathie is a senior research fellow at the Centre for Research in Public Health and Community Care at the University of Hertfordshire. She has over 30 years of health and social care research experience, with a focus on older people and dementia. She is co-lead for the National Institute for Health Research, Applied Research Collaboration (East of England), Inclusive Involvement in Research theme, which explores how best to involve members of the public and patients in shaping, designing, and prioritizing research.

Mary G. McDonald is the Homer C. Rice Chair of Sports and Society in the School of History and Sociology at the Georgia Institute of Technology. Her research explores inequality as related to gender, race, class, and sexuality. McDonald has published over 50 journal articles and book chapters. She is coeditor of *Sports, Society, and Technology: Bodies, Practices, and Knowledge* with Jennifer Sterling (2020) and *Sociocultural Examinations of Sports Concussions* with Matt Ventresca (2020). At Georgia Tech, she also directs the Ivan Allen College of Liberal Arts' Sports, Society, and Technology Program.

Toby Miller is Stuart Hall Professor of Cultural Studies, Universidad Autónoma Metropolitana–Cuajimalpa and Sir Walter Murdoch Distinguished Collaborator, Murdoch University. The author and editor of over 50 books, his work has been translated into Spanish, Chinese, Portuguese, Japanese, Turkish, German, Italian, Farsi, French, Urdu, and Swedish. His most recent volumes are *Violence* (2021), *The Persistence of Violence: Colombian Popular Culture* (2020), *How Green Is Your Smartphone?* (coauthored, 2020), *El trabajo cultural* (2018), *Greenwashing Culture* (2018), *Greenwashing Sport* (2018), and *The Routledge Companion to Global Cultural Policy* (coedited, 2018). *A COVID Charter, a Better Future* is in press.

Győző Molnár is a principal lecturer in sport studies at the University of Worcester. His current publications revolve around migration, the Olympics, gender, and populist politics. His current research, with Yoko Kanemasu, has focused on the migratory and gendered aspects of Fiji rugby. He is coeditor of *The Politics of the Olympics* (2010), *Ethnographies in Sport and Exercise Research* (2016), and *Women, Sport and Exercise in the Asia-Pacific Region* (2018) and coauthor of *Sport, Exercise and Social Theory: An Introduction* (2012).

Stuart Murray is an associate professor in international relations at Bond University, Global Fellow of the Academy of Sport at University of Edinburgh, and an associate editor of the journals *Diplomacy & Foreign Policy* and the *Journal of Public Diplomacy*. The author of 32 peer-reviewed publications, Murray recently published *Sports Diplomacy: Origins, Theory and Practice* (2018), the first major book on the role sport plays in international diplomacy. He is also the founding director of the Sports Diplomacy Alliance, a global institution that regularly advises governments, nonstate actors, and sportspeople how to harness the power of sport for positive outcomes.

Adam J. Nichol is a senior research assistant in the Department of Sport, Exercise and Rehabilitation at Northumbria University and a teaching fellow in the Department of Sport and Exercise Sciences at Durham University. His research interests focus on the critical sociological study of (non)influence and (micro)political astuteness in sport.

Catherine Ordway is an assistant professor of sports management at University of Canberra. She is a sports lawyer with degrees from the University of Adelaide and a Graduate Diploma in Investigations Management. Ordway's PhD thesis was titled "Protecting Sports Integrity: Sport Corruption Risk Management Strategies." Her edited book *Restoring Trust in Sport: Corruption Cases and Solutions* was published in 2021. She is a senior fellow with the University of Melbourne Law School, an affiliated scholar with the Global Institute for Responsible Sport Organizations, and an expert consultant with Sports Integrity & Governance Partners.

Catherine Palmer is a professor of sociology at Northumbria University. Her research marries empirical and theoretical insight across a range of topics, including sport and alcohol, and fitness philanthropy. Her work has appeared in *Qualitative Research in Sport, Exercise & Health, International Review for the Sociology of Sport, Sport in Society, Journal of Gender Studies, Social & Cultural Geography,* and *Sociology of Sport Journal,* and she has received significant funding for her research from national and international funding bodies. Her most recent book is *Sports Charity and Gendered Labour* (2021).

Andrew Parker is a professor of sports ministry at Ridley Hall, Cambridge, where his research interests focus on the connections between sport, spirituality, and social identity. Published outputs reflect these interests and have appeared in periodicals such as *Practical Theology* and *Studies in World Christianity.* He has served on the editorial boards of the *Sociology of Sport Journal* and *Qualitative Research.* He is a former coeditor of the *International Journal of Religion and Sport.*

Elizabeth C. J. Pike is a professor and head of the Faculty of Sport, Health and Exercise at the University of Hertfordshire. Her research focuses on the potential of sport and physical activity to address issues of equality and diversity, with particular attention to improving opportunities for females and older adults in and through sport. She has more than 50 research publications and has delivered keynote presentations at international conferences on six continents. She is cofounder of the Anita White Foundation and past president of the International Sociology of Sport Association.

Paul A. Potrac is a professor in the Department of Sport, Exercise and Rehabilitation at Northumbria University. He also holds visiting professorships at University College Dublin and Cardiff Metropolitan University. His research and teaching interests focus on the micropolitical, dramaturgical, and emotional demands of sports work, especially coaching and coach education.

Emma Pullen (@DrEmmaPullen) is a lecturer in the sociology of sport and sport management at Loughborough University. Her research is primarily focused on sport, social inclusion, and disability. Pullen has published articles in a range of journals, such as *Media, Culture & Society, Cultural Studies,* and *Qualitative Research in Sport, Exercise and Health.*

Katherine Raw is an academic course advisor and lecturer in sport development at Western Sydney University. Her research focuses on the use and management of sport as a vehicle to foster a variety of community outcomes, including social cohesion, inclusion, health, gender equity, and diplomacy. Her work has been conducted in partnership with a number of organizations, including Tennis Australia, the NRL, Netball Australia, North Melbourne Football Club, Tennis NSW, and the Commonwealth Secretariat. Raw's fieldwork has been completed across a range of locations both locally and internationally, including Fiji, Vanuatu, Tonga, and Timor Leste.

Martin Roderick is a professor in and head of the Department of Sport and Exercise Sciences at Durham University. His research focuses on professional athletes' lived experiences; work, identity, and well-being in sport; and the roles of space and place in mental health in sport. His books include *Sport in Films* (2008, with Emma Poulton), and he serves on the editorial board of *Qualitative Research in Sport, Exercise, and Health*.

David Rowe is Emeritus Professor of Cultural Research, Institute for Culture and Society, Western Sydney University; Honorary Professor, Faculty of Humanities and Social Sciences, University of Bath; and research associate, Centre for International Studies and Diplomacy, SOAS University of London. His books include *Popular Cultures* (1995); *Sport, Culture and the Media* (2003); *Sport beyond Television* (2012, authored with Brett Hutchins); and *Sport, Public Broadcasting, and Cultural Citizenship* (2014, edited with Jay Scherer). A frequent expert media commentator, his work has been translated into nine languages. His book *Global Media Sport* was a 2018 Outstanding Book Selection of the National Academy of Sciences, Republic of Korea.

Suzanne Ryder is a PhD candidate and casual lecturer in the Institute of Health and Sport at Victoria University, Melbourne. Her ethnographic research focuses on gender and labor relations in professional women's road cycling.

Parissa Safai is an associate professor in the School of Kinesiology and Health Science in the Faculty of Health at York University. Her research interests focus on the critical study of sport at the intersection of risk, health, and healthcare, including the social determinants of athletes' health. Her interests also center on sport and social inequality, with attention to the impact of gender, socioeconomic, and ethnocultural inequities on accessible physical activity for all.

Michael P. Sam is an associate professor in the School of Sport and Exercise Sciences at the University of Otago. His research comprises areas of policy, politics, and administration as they relate to the governance of sport. He has published widely in both sport studies and policy journals and has coedited three books: *Sport in the City: Cultural Connections* (2011), *Sport Policy in Small States* (2016), and *Case Studies in Sport and Diplomacy* (2017). Sam currently serves as co-director of the New Zealand Centre for Sport Policy and Politics and is the president of the International Sociology of Sport Association.

Jimmy Sanderson is an assistant professor in the Department of Kinesiology and Sport Management at Texas Tech University. His research centers on social media and its intersection with sport, along with health and family communication in sport. He is the author of several books related to sport and social media and has authored or coauthored over 80 journal articles and book chapters.

Emma Sherry is a professor of management at Swinburne University of Technology in Melbourne. She is an internationally regarded expert in the area of sport for development and is one of the founding editors of the *Journal of Sport for Development*. She currently sits on the editorial boards of leading sport management journals, including *Sport Management Review*, *Journal of Sport Management*, and *European Sport Management Quarterly*. Sherry publishes widely in sport management and sociology, where her work focuses on sport for development and social inclusion, access, equity, and diversity in sport.

Barry Smart is a research professor of sociology at the University of Portsmouth. He is the author of 10 books, including *The Sport Star: Modern Sport and the Cultural Economy of Sporting Celebrity* (2005) and *Consumer Society: Critical Issues and Environmental Consequences* (2010), nine edited volumes and reference works, and over 100 journal articles and book chapters. His work ranges across a number of fields, including critical social theory and political economy, and in the field of sports studies his focus has been on cultural and economic aspects.

Andy Smith is a professor of sport and physical activity at Edge Hill University. He is managing editor of *Leisure Studies* and former founding coeditor of the *International Journal of Sport Policy and Politics*, for which he now serves on the editorial board. He is also on the editorial boards of *Qualitative Research in Sport, Exercise and Health*, and *European Physical Education Review*. Smith is the coauthor of eight books, including the *Routledge Handbook of Youth Sport* (2016, with Ken Green), and his work focuses on youth, sport, physical activity, and mental health in community and professional sport and leisure.

Ramón Spaaij is a professor in the Institute for Health and Sport at Victoria University, Australia. He also holds a Professorial Chair in Sociology of Sport at the University of Amsterdam. His work focuses on sport, diversity, social change, and violence, and his books include *The Palgrave International Handbook of Football and Politics* (2018), *The Age of Lone Wolf Terrorism* (2017), *Routledge Handbook of Football Studies* (2016), *Mediated Football: Representations and Audience Receptions of Race/Ethnicity, Nation and Gender* (2015), and *Sport and Social Exclusion in Global Society* (2014).

Emily S. Sparvero is an assistant professor of instruction at the University of Texas at Austin, where she is the faculty director of the online Sport Management Master's program. Her research focuses on the ways in which sport assets can be leveraged to generate economic, social, and tourism benefits for host communities. Her recent work has examined the financial management of professional sport team charitable foundations and the public health impact of corporate social responsibility programs.

Jennifer J. Sterling is a lecturer in sport studies in the Department of American Studies at the University of Iowa. Her research interests revolve around the disciplinary intersections of sport studies, science and technology studies, digital humanities, and visual culture. In particular, her research explores how technoscientific practices, including data analytics and visualization, shape understandings of active bodies and affect sporting inequalities. She teaches courses focused on diversity, equity, and inclusion in sport, international sport and globalization, and technoscientific cultures of sport.

Minhyeok Tak is a lecturer in the School of Sport, Exercise and Health Sciences at Loughborough University. His research interests include governance issues around sports betting and institutional designs of sport development systems behind integrity issues such as match-fixing, corruption, and abuse. His work has been published in the *International Review for the Sociology of Sport, Journal of Criminological Research, Policy and Practices,* and *Crime, Law and Social Change.*

Holly Thorpe is a professor at Te Huataki Waiora School of Health at the University of Waikato. Her research, published in over 100 articles and chapters, focuses on informal and action sports, youth culture, gender, female athlete health, and sport for development and recovery. Her recent books include the coedited anthology *Sport, Physical Culture and the Moving Body: Materialisms, Technologies, Ecologies* (2020, with Joshua Newman and David Andrews), the coauthored *Feminist New Materialisms, Sport and Fitness: A Lively Entanglement* (2021, with Julie Brice and Marianne Clark) and *Action Sports and the Olympic Games: Past, Present, Future* (2021, with Belinda Wheaton).

Alan Tomlinson is a professor of leisure studies at the University of Brighton. He has served as editor of the journals *Leisure Studies* and the *International Review for the Sociology of Sport,* edited and authored more than 40 books and volumes, and published over 150 scholarly journal articles and book chapters. Recent interdisciplinary studies include *Sir Stanley Rous and the Growth of World Football* and *Populism in Sport, Leisure and Popular Culture* (2020, with Bryan C. Clift).

Travers is a professor of sociology at Simon Fraser University. They are the author of *The Trans Generation: How Trans Kids (and Their Parents) Are Creating a Gender Revolution* (2019). In addition to a focus on transgender issues in general, they have published widely on issues related to sport, gender, sexuality, and social justice. Travers is currently deputy editor of the journal *Gender and Society.*

Nick J. Watson is chief operating officer of the Archbishop of York Youth Trust and founder of the Global Congress on Sports and Christianity. Formerly, he was an associate professor in sport and social justice at York St John University. Watson has also coached soccer in the United States, Spain, and the United Kingdom.

Lawrence A. Wenner is Von der Ahe Professor of Communication and Ethics at Loyola Marymount University in Los Angeles. He was founding editor of the research journal *Communication & Sport,* and former editor-in-chief of both the *International Review for the Sociology of Sport* and the *Journal of Sport & Social Issues.* In 10 books and over 140 scholarly journal articles and book chapters, his work focuses on sport, media, gender, and commodity culture. His recent books include *American Sport in the Shadow of a Pandemic: Communicative Insights* (2022, with Andrew Billings and Marie Hardin) and *Sport, Media, and Mega-Events* (2017, with Andrew Billings).

Sharon Wheeler is a senior lecturer in public health and well-being and program leader for the BSc (Hons) Public Health and Wellbeing and MSc Health, Mental Health and Wellbeing at Wrexham Glyndŵr University. Drawing predominantly on the disciplines of sociology and psychology, her research expertise and interests span a number of areas, including developing active lifestyles, green exercise and well-being, and health inequalities and social justice.

John Williams is an associate professor in sociology in the School of Media, Communication and Sociology at the University of Leicester and co-director of the unit for Diversity, Inclusion and Community Engagement at Leicester. He began his research career exploring fan hooliganism but has since been involved in research and writing on sports cultures, fandom, and issues of fairness and equality in sport. His books include *Offside? Women and Football* (1999), *Passing Rhythms* (2001), *Into the Red* (2001), *Groove Armada* (2006), *Football Nation* (2009, with Andrew Ward), *Red Men* (2010), and *The Game* (2018, with Stuart Clarke).

Kevin Young is a professor of sociology at the University of Calgary. His research and teaching interests bridge criminology and sociology of sport. He has published widely on matters relating to violence, gender, body and health, and the use of animals in sport. Young is a former vice president of the International Sociology of Sport Association and has served on the editorial boards of several recognized journals. He is an award-winning teacher and a regular graduate student supervisor. His recent books include *Sport, Violence and Society* (2019, second edition).

FOREWORD

THE *Oxford English Dictionary* defines a "handbook" as a reference work that provides useful information on a topic. In higher education, academic handbooks are traditionally viewed as authoritative collections of chapters that highlight the current state of knowledge on key topics and provide a glimpse into the relevance and future of a discipline or subdiscipline. Ideally, handbook editors are identified and chosen for their broad grasp of research and knowledge across the content area encompassed by the anthology and by their familiarity with recognized experts on key topics in a field of study. In most cases, handbooks are intended to be accessible resources for a broad audience of scholars, students, and interested laypersons.

Academic handbooks, apart from those using the "handbook" moniker as a marketing hook, are state-of-the-art summaries of a discipline or subdiscipline at a particular point in time. Ideally, the chapters are written with context and continuity so that readers can develop a sense of the breadth and depth of knowledge in a field and anticipate future research topics. Those of us who study sports as social phenomena enjoy access to the following seven English-language handbooks, listed by publication date:

> Lüschen, G., & Sage, G. (Eds.). (1981). *Handbook of social science of sport*. Champaign IL: Stipes Publishing Company.
>
> Coakley, J., & Dunning, E. (Eds.). (2000). *Handbook of sports studies*. London: Sage.
>
> Giulianotti, R. (Ed.). (2015). *Routledge handbook of the sociology of sport*. London: Routledge.
>
> Bairner, A., Kelly, J., & Lee, J. W. (Eds.). (2017). *Routledge handbook of sport and politics*. New York: Routledge.
>
> Silk, M. L, Andrews, D. L., & Thorpe, H. (Eds.). (2017). *Routledge handbook of physical cultural studies*. New York: Routledge.
>
> Pike, E. C. J. (Ed.). (2021). *Research handbook on sports and society*. New York: Edgar Eiger Publishing.
>
> Wenner, L. A. (Ed.). (2023) *Oxford handbook of sport and society*. Oxford: Oxford University Press.

Each of these handbooks is an edited collection of chapters that presents or summarizes research and knowledge on the social and cultural dimensions of sports. Bairner et al. (2017), Silk et al. (2017), and Pike (2021) focus, respectively, on politics, physical cultural studies, and research on seven central topics in the field. The other four—Lüschen and Sage

(1981), Coakley and Dunning (2000), Giulianotti (2015), and Wenner (2023)—focus on the broader field of sport and society. Together, this collection of handbooks chronicles the development of an increasingly expanding body of scholarly work on sport and society over the past six decades.

As the quantity and quality of research on sport and society have increased since the early 1960s, so have new and more well-defined research questions been asked by scholars from multiple disciplines in the social sciences and humanities. This trend goes hand in hand with increased visibility of the field, additional scholars concerned with sports as social phenomena, the use of multiple theories and research methods in published work, and more journals publishing research on the social dimensions of sports and their social and cultural relevance.

The growth of this field, often identified as the "sociology of sport" to give it the legitimacy of a disciplinary home, is documented in the content of the listed handbooks. For example, the 25 chapters in the 1981 *Handbook of Social Science of Sport* served as a status report on the formation and institutionalization of an emerging field of study focused on producing knowledge about sport and society; the inclusion of a 146-page bibliography further documented that play, games, and sports were research-worthy and that the boundaries of the field encompassed multiple topic categories. The 44 chapters in the 2000 *Handbook of Sports Studies* emphasized that scholarly work on sport and society was part of an increasingly respected field of study that utilized multiple theoretical perspectives and attracted scholars worldwide from a range of disciplines. The 40 chapters in the 2015 *Routledge Handbook of the Sociology of Sport* edited by Richard Giulianotti provided a content update that highlighted new topics of research and theoretical perspectives characterizing the field during the first 15 years of the 21st century. The 57 chapters in this *Oxford Handbook of Sport and Society* edited by Lawrence Wenner bring continuity and comparability to knowledge in the field by focusing on the issues, approaches, and debates associated with each of the research topics that are central to the study of sports as social phenomena as we move into the 2020s.

Content differences among these seven handbooks reflect recent historical changes and the choices made by editors and the scholars they consulted. Those choices are primarily based on what they considered to be the goal of the handbook at a specific point in time. In 1981, Lüschen and Sage were concerned with the perceived legitimacy of research on sports as social phenomena and used their handbook to present discussions of the cross-cultural analysis of games and sports, relationships between sports and major social institutions, the social structures and social processes associated with sports, the groups and organizations that control and regulate sports, social problems and deviance in sports, and the social psychology of play and sport. Most of the chapters focused on clarifying concepts and identifying the extent to which sport had come to be a social institution worthy of scientific study.

In their 2000 handbook, Coakley and Dunning organized content to highlight the global expansion of sport and society research and provide "a comprehensive, up-to-date and authoritative reference book for scholars" in the field. Increasing international travel combined with access to the internet during the 1990s expanded relationships and research networks that transcended national borders, facilitating collaboration on research projects and encouraging the formation of sport studies departments worldwide. At the same time, the expansion of communications media and technology increased the global visibility and cultural relevance of national and international sport events, especially those driven by state and commercial interests during the late and post–Cold War years. As a result, this handbook was also conceptualized as "a stocktaking exercise" that involved critical self-reflection in the field as it experienced the challenges and conflicts that came with expansion and increased intellectual diversity.

In the 2015 handbook, editor Richard Giulianotti described the sociology of sport as "a core discipline within the academic study of sport." As many sports studies programs prioritized a physical science approach to studying human performance in which competitive success was a goal, the focus of this collection reaffirmed the importance of the sociology of sport by highlighting its "theoretical and substantive diversity" and its commitment to critical analysis. As the scale and social significance of sport grew rapidly worldwide during the early years of the century, this diversity enabled sociologists and scholars in related fields to produce useful knowledge about the multiple social and cultural dimensions of sport in a global context.

For this 2023 *Oxford Handbook of Sport and Society*, editor Lawrence Wenner, with assistance from 10 consulting editors, chose chapter topics highlighting the expansion and increasingly diverse scope of research in a field characterized by porous disciplinary boundaries and an emphasis on the inclusion of topics and disciplinary perspectives. As explained in the editor's general introduction, each chapter focuses on a pair of sport-related concepts and is organized around an outline that provides continuity to the collection. Topic choices were guided by recognition of the social, cultural, political, and economic importance of sports in the 21st century and the need to utilize diverse lenses to understand the multifaceted relationships between sport and society. Collectively, the 57 chapters emphasize the breadth, depth, and relevance of knowledge in the field at a time when social science research in sport studies is being excluded, marginalized, and woefully underfunded at the departmental and university levels and regularly ignored in sport organizations.

Challenges to the status and importance of research and knowledge on sport and society led Wenner and his consulting editors to stress continuity in the field while also showing that it encompasses "history, political science, human geography, anthropology, social psychology, and economics" viewed through the perspectives of sociology along with "cultural studies, media studies, and gender studies." As "handbooks" have become a prevalent and heavily marketed segment of academic publishing, a goal of the *Oxford Handbook* was to avoid a collection of chapters little different from a giant journal issue and to provide a state-of-the-art synthesis of existing knowledge and informed explanations focused on sport and society.

Those of us who teach, do research, and act as public intellectuals in this field now have seven thoughtfully organized broad handbooks that meet the definition of what handbooks are supposed to be. This will be helpful as we confront challenges to our status and role in departments, degree programs, and higher education. For that reason, keep this *Oxford Handbook of Sport and Society* handy as a source of support when you are called on to justify your teaching, research, and service as it is related to sport and society and the mission of higher education.

Jay Coakley
Fort Collins, Colorado

Acknowledgments

THE timeline for a project of the magnitude of a project such as the *Oxford Handbook of Sport and Society* is considerable even in the best of times. While much planning for the project took place prior to the COVID-19 pandemic of 2020 and 2021, the stresses that the pandemic put on the lives of the over 80 elite scholars who were recruited to contribute to this volume have been substantial. These stresses, which included illness from viral infection, challenges from working at home, increased childcare and other caregiving responsibilities, and new demands for online teaching modalities, wreaked much havoc and fractured focus not only in the scholarly community but across social life. In aiding this project getting over the finish line, I would like to thank both the scholars who have contributed to the volume and those who have enabled and influenced the project.

At Oxford University Press, I would like to thank James Cook, the publishing editor for sociology and many other areas, for his encouragement, support, and patience for this work. I would also like to recognize his assistant editor Emily Benitez for her "hands on" management of the many changes in the authorial lineup that were necessitated in response to the disruptions in scholarly life brought on by the pandemic. As one might expect, the diverse scope of projects like this expands well beyond the "wheelhouse" of any one scholar. I would like to thank ten seminal figures in the study of sport and society who advised me as informal consulting editors on framing the topics included in the volume and the identifying the best contributors to address them. Here, my heartfelt thanks go to my long-time colleagues and friends: Alan Bairner (Loughborough University), Laurence Chalip (George Mason University), John Horne (Waseda University), Steven Jackson (University of Otago), Pirkko Markula (University of Alberta), Mary McDonald (Georgia Institute of Technology), Catherine Palmer (Northumbria University), Elizabeth Pike (University of Hertfordshire), David Rowe (Western Sydney University), and Brian Wilson (University of British Columbia).

Finally, for a project that has seemingly moved into our house and stayed a bit too long, I would like to thank my wife Susan Rice for her love, encouragement, support, patience, and counsel. Susan's long engagement in my professional projects that have made a case for the importance of the study of sport and society, including her notable contributions as Editorial Operations Manager at two scholarly journals that I edited, the *International Review for the Sociology of Sport* and *Communication and Sport*, has both helped shape and increased the profile of sport studies. Lastly, let me give a tip of my hat to my late father Sam Wenner who made clear the importance of sport in his life by teaching me to appreciate just about any ball (or puck) in play on our living room television set. I think that Sam would be impressed that sport, as the baseball legend Minnie Miñoso (also known as "Mr. White Sox" and the "Cuban Comet") once said, has been very very good to me.

INTRODUCTION

CHAPTER 1

··

SPORT, SOCIETY, AND SCHOLARLY INQUIRY

··

LAWRENCE A. WENNER

WHAT I most likely share with both the readers of and the contributors to this *Oxford Handbook of Sport and Society* is the sense that, in contemporary times, sport matters perhaps more than has been the case in earlier eras. Indeed, sport as a cultural and media product has never cast a longer social and political-economic shadow. The seemingly oppositional trends of ever-increasing corporatized bidding by media giants for the broadcast, cable, and streaming rights to sports product (from the biggest mega-events to the more mundane everyday sports time-fillers) and the rise of athlete activism (in and seemingly at odds with such corporatized spheres) show both how malleable and powerful sport on our cultural main stages can be.

Culturally, politically, and economically, sport matters. Fueled not only by its main-stage prominence, the effects of sport are ubiquitous. Indeed, the reach of sporting logics, alternatively characterized as "sportification" or "sportization" (Heere, 2018; Maguire, 2013), have seepages into virtually all corners of social life. This is true even if one is not a sports fan or participant. One of the largest and most vibrant cultural industries, the contemporary global sports market, recently peaking at U.S.$459 billion in 2019 (prior to a "blip" decline in 2020 due to the lockdowns and social distancing responses to the COVID-19 pandemic), is projected to grow about 7% a year to reach U.S.$826 billion by 2030. While the market is largest in North America, followed by the Asia-Pacific and Western European markets, the fastest growth is expected in South America and the Middle East. And while media coverage may lead us to believe that the spectator sports market, dominated by elite team, club, and individual sports, is most significant, the participatory sports market segment, where engagement in recreational sport and fitness along with much merchandising and services reside, accounts for over 70% of marketplace valuation (Business Research Company, 2021).

While it is easy to make a case that sport matters broadly, both globally and locally, it is important to step back and recognize its limits. Much media focus is generated by attention on the results of sporting competitions, the "who wins" and "who loses." Yet, while this may drive a good deal of why we watch or pay attention, in the big picture of life, this doesn't really matter much. One can bask in the "thrill of victory" or be set back by the "agony of defeat" in watching or even playing sport, but the pathways of one's life largely go on unaltered in substantive ways. As I have argued elsewhere, the power of sport

> rests on a conundrum, much like Kundera's (1999) "lightness of being" where we know life matters but we often act as though it is insignificant. With sport, we may act as though it matters, but in the end we know it is insignificant. (Wenner, 2009, p. 91)

This is not to say that sports don't matter whatsoever; they do, in no small part because of this dynamic, which might be called the "heaviness of sport." Sports are an essential part of many people's lives, as a diversion, a preoccupation, or an aesthetic pleasure. For others, engagement with sport becomes a professionalized endeavor, a "job," a career, or an enterprise to be managed. As well, there is much evidence that engagement in sport and exercise plays an integral role in the physical and mental well-being of many. Given the diversity of these and other indicants, understanding sport as a social phenomenon necessarily entails using a diversity of lenses to consider important intersections that sport has both with society and for those who engage with and experience its cultures. And fundamentally, that is what this *Handbook* tries to do. Featured throughout this volume are leading international scholars who consider the most important ways that we should take sport, broadly defined, seriously. Explored are essential social, cultural, and political-economic dynamics that engage with sport.

SITUATING SCHOLARLY INQUIRY

Just as is the case with producing wine, the production of scholarly inquiry about sport and society depends on its terroir, a host of factors that make up its natural environments. As with wine, factors such as soil, topography, and climate all affect what is (or can be) produced. And just as has been the case with wine, certain regions are cultivated first, setting de facto standards or norms. Yet, tastes and their evaluation vary. Other areas, with different climatic features, with fields planted later or plowed differently, can produce fine wines or scholarship. These can surpass "old vines" and stimulate the rise of new varietals and the invention of new hybrids that can be well received in the marketplace, whether that be for wine or scholarly inquiry about something like sport and society.

The Scope of Sport Studies

Integral to variant assessments about the scope of sport studies, as well as the study of sport and society, is the question of what is meant by "sport." Seemingly an easy definitional issue, there was considerable early debate about this (Snyder & Spreitzer, 1974), and matters of scope are still wrestled with to this day (Malcolm, 2012). Early debate focused on the "game" versus "sport" issue and hinged on questions about "competition" and whether it entailed the "physical." For instance, chess was clearly a competitive endeavor. Yet, its physicality, limited to moving pieces on the board, was deemed insufficient by most to be characterized as sport.

Other, more nuanced discussions concerned activities that were more clearly physical—such as gymnastics, ice skating, diving, and even dance contests—but where "competition," the "winning" and "losing," entailed judgments of performance "aesthetics" rather than objective measures. For the most part, definitional "spitting matches" abated, aided by distinctions such as those made by Best (1978) between "purposive" and "aesthetic" sports, and such concerns largely devolved in (sometimes resigned) recognition that "sport" as a term and concept was inherently "elastic" (Coakley, 2021b).

Yet, as can be seen in ongoing debates, such as those over whether eSports—whose very name invokes sport but is actually competitive, organized video gaming—is an endeavor that should be constituted as sport (Evans, 2019), it is clear that while such concerns may have devolved, they have not dissolved. Even with continued wrestling over whether emergent new "sportish" activities may technically qualify as sport, it is fair to say that contemporary sport studies have a fundamental commitment to inclusivity and have long ago made peace with being what Geertz (1973) has called a "blurred genre."

Other debates about the scope of what might be called sport studies are conflated by assessments about the bounds and focus of inquiry. Although it may be obvious, the scope of sport studies extends beyond sociocultural inquiry or what might be construed as the relationship between sport and society (and/or culture). Indeed, a good deal of scholarly inquiry about sport tends to be insouciant on matters of societal impact, cultural dynamics, and political and economic contexts. Here, sport is largely approached from a "received" view, taken as a given. This has allowed for and facilitated a focus on "performance" and "efficiency." This tendency has not happened by accident, and in some sense it should not be viewed as a matter of neglect. Rather, here there has been an essential focus on the "science" at the nexus of the "physical" and the "body." In many ways, this is a considerable and valuable undertaking.

However, this core focus and its more dominant position in the academy has, perhaps not intentionally, served to relegate and disperse the study of sport and society. That the focus on a different kind of "performance" and "efficiency" in sport has risen in other quarters of academia has further stretched understandings and articulations of sport studies. This has been most notable in long-burgeoning programs in sport management and marketing and is evident as well in the more recently blooming focus on "professional" sport communication—from strategic sport communication to the doing of sport journalism, broadcasting, and production in local and national settings. Fueled by ready career entailments, such pragmatic and professional focus on performance and efficiency in the sport marketplace and its communication has shifted much of the scholarly "gaze" on sport away from sociocultural inquiry.

Scholarly Playing Fields: Naming, Homes, and Homelessness

As in life, "names," the shorthand by which we refer to something or someone, matter. Names too, like those popular for children in a given epoch, go in and out of fashion. They not only signal preferences but can sign priorities and sensitivities. Some names are wildly popular, others little seen. Certainly, the latter is true for "sport studies," a name applied surprisingly infrequently to characterize a scholarly playing field in academic formations.

In academia, sport is most centrally studied in what most "nonacademics" familiarly think of as "physical education." As the unfortunately common joke "Those who can't do, teach, and that those who can't teach, teach P.E." suggests, in much of the world the discipline of physical education has long experienced struggles to become a worthy and legitimate, let alone elite, endeavor on the scholarly playing field. This is evidenced by what has seemed at times thesaurus-driven attempts to upgrade characterizations of what the field entails. Here, a diverse set of efforts was made to recast the field (either alone or in combination) as kinesiology, human kinetics, sport sciences, exercise science, human performance, human movement studies, and the like. While this state of affairs has been characterized as "chaos," with at least 70 naming variants documented (Newell, 1990), the overriding trend was recognized as signaling a "science movement" in the field, responding to the perceived lack of scientific rigor in the discipline formerly known as "physical education" (Corbin & Cardinal, 2008).

While many physical education programs had a place, albeit often a modest one, for the sociocultural study of sport, this scientific movement served to push such concerns further to the margins of a field in the midst of redefining its core to advance academic legitimacy. This was in line with an overarching tendency in academia, as Coakley (2021b) has wryly observed, to relegate the focus on the physical body (something integral to sport) to "repair shops" in the physical sciences (including scientized articulations reimagining physical education) and medical schools. Even as repair shop functions (as seen in foci on recovery from injury and physical therapy) could be seen in these new articulations of physical education, their characterization as "hot rod shops," where after-market tweaks are made, may be even more apropos given the increasing focus on performance optimization in athletics and physical activity.

Regardless, as these new articulations were increasingly housed in science (and, even more specific, health sciences) colleges, the study of sport and society, which is necessarily reliant on a diverse set of sociocultural lenses more naturally at home in the social sciences and humanities, was often more accommodated than prioritized. Structural biases toward funded research, at play in "scientific" study but more elusive in supporting a "social problems" focus underlying the study of sport and society, also contributed to making these new articulations less than satisfactory academic homes for the sociocultural study of sport.

Thus, in fundamental ways, the scholarly study of sport and society can be seen, if not as "homeless," than as "an itinerant scholarly endeavor" continually seeking "safe houses" in the academy. Yet, a "diaspora" of scholars, spread across the terroirs of the academic landscape, persists in the study of sport and society, and not surprisingly, the endeavor has been a notably interdisciplinary and intersectional affair. Still, it is indisputable that the dominant place where the study of sport and society has found an academic home has been in a remarkably accommodating sociology of sport, which ironically has itself struggled to find its "homeland" (Coakley, 2021a). In further irony, much of the work done under the banner of the sociology of sport comes from those situated in scientized articulations of physical education, not by "card-carrying" sociologists. And although much of the study of sport and culture can be seen as "sociological" (or at least emanating from a "sociological impulse"), the study of sport remains a minor strain seen in academic departments of sociology, where it resides as one of many areas of study about culture.

CROSSROADS: SOCIOLOGY OF SPORT

It is not happenstance that, more than any of the diverse disciplinary areas that have contributed to the study of sport and society, the sociology of sport has long fostered inclusivity and interdisciplinarity. Because of its malleability and willingness to be inclusive, the sociology of sport sits at the main crossroads of scholarly inquiry about sport and society. In some sense, this has been both intentional and pragmatic. As a comparatively small area of inquiry on the academic landscape, the viability of the sociocultural study of sport depended on a broad reach across the social sciences and humanities. That sport was global helped as well. While comparatively few scholars may study sport and society in a given locale, when taken collectively international interest facilitated a critical mass of scholars forming to undergird its legitimacy. Because of the larger (and continuing) challenges in finding a "one nation" solution, a "natural" or even stable academic home for the sociocultural study of sport, the sociology of sport, while not exactly serving as a "home for the homeless," has served as a refuge providing sanctuary for those, "card-carrying" sociologists or not, seeking legitimacy to study sport and society.

Contexts

The story of what today is recognized as the sociology of sport has been told many times over (cf. Andrews & Carrington, 2013; Coakley, 2021b; Coakley & Dunning, 2000; Greendorfer, 1981; Giulianotti, 2015; Malcolm, 2012, 2014; Pike, 2021; Pike, Jackson, & Wenner, 2015). Emerging with formative coherence in the 1960s in Europe and North America, early scholarly priorities charted basic grounds with empirically driven descriptive research. These often featured structural-functionalist approaches to how sport was organized and governed and how sport transacted with other institutional sectors (e.g., education, government, business, media). An important early turning point was stimulated by Elias and Dunning's (1986) foundational work advocating for a figurational sociology focused on the processual roles that sport, and those engaged with it, played in the "civilizing process."

Over time the inclination to study the dynamic processes of sport and society, rather than to assess sport at discrete moments of stasis, stimulated moving the scholarly center of the sociology of sport to interpretive and critical research and served to prioritize qualitative methods over empirical inquiry using survey and experimental research tools. Even as the functionalist paradigm faded and was "replaced by a Millsian-informed Marxist approach, and subsequently Gramscian-informed cultural studies" (Dart, 2014, p. 647) and, increasingly, poststructuralist and Continental critical theory, debates over epistemology remained vibrant during the 1990s (Ingham & Donnelly, 1997). Still, the sociology of sport, perhaps because of its need to maintain a critical mass of scholars for its continued viability and legitimacy, remained largely an egalitarian enclave with regard to both theory and method, sensibilities that remain to this day.

As sport has grown in cultural importance, its use-value in the marketplace has been amplified by media "partnerships," and this visibility (and the socially constructed neoliberal meanings that have accompanied this) have stimulated both politicians and the corporate sphere to piggyback on its power and popularity in advancing strategic goals. Concomitant with this, as media attention given to sport has moved beyond game coverage and the reporting of scores, social issues in sport and the metaphoric resonances they reveal about problems in the larger society have received increased attention. Amid these competing contexts, interest in the sociology of sport has grown systematically across the globe.

An interlocking set of substantial international, regional, and national societies and scholarly journals dot its scholarly landscape (Pike, Jackson, & Wenner, 2015). The oldest and most global of these, the International Sociology of Sport Association, along with its companion research journal, the *International Review for the Sociology of Sport (IRSS)*, was founded in the mid-1960s by a core group of mostly European scholars. Formal inquiry followed in North America, first with the late 1970s publication of the *Journal of Sport and Social Issues (JSSI)* by Northeastern University's Center for the Study of Sport in Society, and then by the formation of the North American Society for the Sociology of Sport (NASSS), which began publication of its signature *Sociology of Sport Journal (SSJ)* in the mid-1980s. In the early 1990s, notable national scholarly societies, such as the Korean Society for the Sociology of Sport and the Japan Society of Sport Sociology, each with a companion research journal, signaled growing interest in Asia and globally. Mirroring NASSS in the European region, the European Association for Sociology of Sport and its *European Journal for Sport and Society*, began in the early 2000s. Shortly following this, the Latin American Association of Sociocultural Studies of Sport (better known as ALESDE, the Asociacion Latinoamerican de Estudios Socioculturales del Deporte) was established and began publication of its *Journal of the Latin American Sociocultural Studies of Sport*.

Priorities and Themes

There have been many attempts at both characterizing and assessing the core concerns of the sociology of sport (cf. Coakley, 2021b; Dart, 2014; Malcolm, 2012; Seippel, 2018; Tian & Wise, 2020). Collectively, such well-meaning attempts at stocktaking what is atop the research agenda of the sociology of sport have yielded an "apples and oranges" set of dominant priorities and themes. Using variant but systematic approaches to take stock of the field, the resultant "mash-up" characterizations do indeed reveal more similarities than differences. Yet, perhaps not surprisingly, operational differences in these stocktaking efforts have resulted in different Rorschach blots resolving for the sociology of sport that they wish to describe, proving yet again that how you ask a question affects what kind of answers result.

For example, Dart (2014), Seippel (2018), and Tian and Wise (2020) all attempt to determine the most dominant themes and topics published in the three leading sociology of sport journals (*IRSS, SSJ, JSSI*) from the late 1970s until recently. Dart assessed 25 years of research content (nearly 2,000 articles) as characterized in article titles, abstracts, keywords, and subject terms. Rising to the top of his Wordie-based visualization analysis of approximately 45 dominant themes was a collective focus on gender (aggregating sex/sexuality, feminism, masculinity, etc.), followed in order by themes encompassing "*race/ethnicity, education, media, politics and economy,* and *globalization*" (Dart, 2014, p. 652).

Seippel's (2018) approach is distinguished by using a more granular "topic models method" that considered the entirety of the content in articles published in the three journals over

30 years (1984–2014). Using both inductive assessments and contextual interpretations, Seippel's more complex "slicing and dicing" yielded 20 multidimensional and overlapping content categories. Seippel finds that "culture" (encompassing descending foci on the body, gender, disability, nationalism, globalization, and media) was by far the dominant topic featured. Mirroring Dart's findings, football (soccer) and the Olympics led sport-centered foci, and these too featured highly in considerations of culture.

Tian and Wise (2020) use yet another method, employing CiteSpace bibliometric citation software. Their mappings of research proclivities melds assessments of total keyword frequencies with Freeman's "betweenness centrality" measure, which assesses "co-citation networks" to determine the research influence strength of each topic. By both measures, consensus "hot topics" leading the top 10 keywords in both North American and European research are "gender, identity, body, politics (including power) and masculinity" (p. 1038). The total keyword frequencies for "media" rivaled these topics but were found less centrally in co-citation networks. Tian and Wise found regional differences, with more emphasis on race, women, and politics in North America and with football (soccer), identity, culture, and globalization prioritized in Europe.

Even as these three systematic attempts to characterize the proclivities of the sociology of sport reveal offsets, largely as a result of "shaking the jar" differently, they substantively align with broad scholarly assessments of key topics as featured in foundational works such as Giulianotti (2015) and Malcolm (2012). It is worth noting that issues of gender, race/ethnicity, the body (including disability), and other matters of identity (and the politics that surround them) come to the fore in all of these assessments. Collectively, these speak to a field undergirded by concerns over equity and opportunity as they are set amid cultural and political dynamics.

Yet, of these topics, a good case may be made that issues concerning gender deserve foremost attention. As many scholars have observed (Cahn, 1994; Hargreaves, 1994; Messner, 1992, 2002), gender remains the great divide of sport, distinct for an interlocking set of essential reasons. Modern sport was founded as a male domain, a place integral to socializing boys to become men amid the softening influences of industrialization and domestication. Even today, most sport is distinguished by gender segregation. Men and women almost never (even recognizing occasional exceptions such as mixed-doubles tennis) play on the same team or take the field together, while those from different races, ethnicities, and classes commonly work together and compete in events. Even as participation and interest in women's sports has risen, institutional support and devoted resources lag behind, and media coverage continues to "symbolically annihilate" its importance (Cooky, Council, Mears, & Messner, 2021). While it is crucial to note this gender caveat, the overarching takeaway remains that issues concerning gender, race/ethnicity, and other matters of identity, inclusion/exclusion, and equity have become fundamental to the sociology of sport project and may be seen to fuel the field's stimulative inclinations.

Stimulative Inclinations

Putting aside these checkerboarded assessments of which themes and topics rise as chief concerns of the sociology of sport, it may be more useful to engage in a little bit of rearview mirror reductionism in characterizing two foundational dispositions that underlie much inquiry in the sociology of sport. As has been suggested, the sociology of sport may be characterized by being anchored in questions about fairness, equity, and the humaneness and the very decency of engagement with sport. In basic ways, these concerns may be traced to two foundational stimulative inclinations: (1) a fundamental challenging of the assumptions underlying what Coakley (2015) has called "the Great Sport Myth" (GSM) and (2) a related disposition toward activism (Edwards, 1969, 1973; Scott, 1969, 1971) and an affinity, too little realized, for a public sociology of sport (Donnelly, 2015).

Coakley's conception of the GSM speaks to the rise of modern sport as a remedy to the aforementioned worries over the softening of men, which was attributed to the decline of manual labor and fed into fears over domestication and the influence of women in boy's lives (Messner, 1992). Embedded in response to these concerns was the notion of sport as an antidote to modern society's ills. In simple terms, the GSM hoists sport as a panacea. Coakley (2015, p. 404), reflecting on his "four decades of studying sports in society," remains "awed" by the impacts of a foundational myth anchored in a "pervasive and nearly unshakable belief in the inherent purity and goodness of sport."

Supporting this seemingly primordial belief are two often repeated, but unsubstantiated and easily debunked, corollary assertions that are embedded in hegemonically naturalized assumptions about the connection of sport to the creation of common good. These pose that (1) "the purity and goodness of sport is transmitted to those who play or consume it" and (2) "sport inevitably leads to individual and community development" (Coakley, 2015, pp. 404–405). For Coakley, these pervasive logics combine, not only to create the GSM but to support the conclusion that "there is NO need to study and analyze sport critically, because it already is as it should be" (p. 405).

As Coakley (2015, p. 403) argues, in a Gramscian twist of fate, the popular appeal of sport (facilitated by sport and sport media reinforcement of the GSM) has made the public more gullible to these beliefs, and this has enabled ruling elites to "camouflage personal interests related to projects in which sport is presented as a tool for solving problems and contributing to individual and collective development." The cultural force of the GSM continues to create resistance to research in the sociology of sport that provides clear counter evidence about sport and the common good; faith in the GSM trumps facts.

As a result, the GSM is enlisted by political and corporate sectors to "sell through sport." And while evidence about the value of much of what is sold—sports mega-events, publicly financed stadiums, the purported educational or character benefits of sports, remedies for young people at risk, engines for community development, and many more—is at best mixed, sport plays a key role in advancing power and profit for those doing the selling. Seen in this way, much of what has stimulated research in the sociology of sport can be considered a critical test of the received assumptions of the GSM. Here, there is recognition that sport is not magic. Sport can do good things, but as a social elixir, it can be flawed, and there may be better solutions to advance both individual and common good. As is revealed in a common joke among sport sociologists, "we know that sports builds character, we're just not sure what kind."

For many—girls and women, people of color, those not able-bodied, and others—sport has not been a level playing field, and the professional project of the sociology of sport has long been animated by this (Malcolm, 2012). Indeed, much in the foundational disposition of the sociology of sport may be seen to be fueled by the early work of Edwards (1969, 1973) and Scott (1969, 1971) that was both attuned to and actively engaged in public advocacy for racial justice and gender equity in sport. Cognizant of the endemic fallacies in the GSM, the stimulative resonance of this work was considerable. Coakley (1987, p. 67) sees the emergence of the field in no small part as "a response to the awareness of problems generated by muckrakers, and to the call for changes by reformers." In a broader assessment, Malcolm (2014, p. 6) argues that the intellectual raison d'être driving much of the critical disposition of the sociology of sport may be attributed to those "who felt their scholarship could make a significant and positive impact on the social world."

Thus, in an era when athletes are increasingly kneeling to protest racial injustice and support for Black Lives Matter has been integrated into the brand identities of sport teams and leagues, it is not surprising that this disposition continues to resonate. Such events, companioned by foundational activist inclinations, stimulate the need for an effective "public sociology of sport" (Bairner, 2009; Coakley, 2021a; Donnelly, 2015). So notably essential is this, given the prevalence of the GSM and the rise of the "sportification" of culture, that Donnelly (2015, pp. 419–420) argues for "a more engaged, relevant and *practical* approach" to knowledge production "for the sake of humanity" and the need to publicly show "whose side we are on" in order to accelerate public understandings of sport and to influence "policy changes that can help make sport a more equitable and humane place."

Joining these "stimulative inclinations," to challenge the GSM and for knowledge production to engage public advocacy are two tendencies foundational to the sociology of sport. As has been suggested in characterizing its malleability and willingness to be inclusive, the sociology of sport is in some sense misnamed. As Malcolm (2012, 2014) notes, its scope of analysis extends broadly beyond sport to physical culture, and its disciplinary breadth is exemplified by a necessary multidisciplinarity rather than sociological "purity." As I have written elsewhere (Wenner, 2017), the sociology of sport inherently entails both "more than sociology" and "more than sport." Because of its role at the crossroads of sociocultural inquiry about sport, through which diverse disciplines across the social sciences and humanities continue to pass, it has become increasingly clear that characterizing the area of inquiry as the "sociology of sport," while satisfactory for some, may be inadequate for many. As will be seen in the sections ahead, the sociocultural study of sport is marked by a host of influences that both complement and challenge the sociology of sport as a professional project.

INTERSECTIONS: COMPLEMENTARY AND COMPROMISED

In recognition of the broad seepages of sport across society, a diverse set of long-standing complementary articulations focused on sport is evident across the social sciences and humanities. While many of these discipline-seated intersections with sport have been institutionalized, the undertaking can be seen as structurally peripheral, and often decidedly optional, in relation to these disciplines' cores, often functioning much like an eccentric elective course in a more sober academic major. Ahead, select consideration is given to engagement with sport in fields such as history, religion, philosophy, politics, and psychology. Noted more cursorily is the attention that sport is given in diverse area and identity studies (foremost those concerning gender, race, ethnicity, and disability) and specialty fields such as those focused on the body, tourism, leisure, urban development, the environment, and popular culture.

Such discipline-seated engagement with sport has both strengthened and expanded the agenda for the sociocultural study of sport. Yet, the benefits often pertain less to the individual home disciplines than to fueling intersectional concerns in the broader study of sport and society as they are manifest in the large, inclusive tent of a necessarily interdisciplinary sociology of sport. Beyond these dynamics, attention is given to three scholarly articulations—physical cultural studies, communication and sport, and sport management—which have more recently brought particularized resonances to the study of sport and society. By posing both opportunities and threats to the sociology of sport, they may be seen as both complementary and compromised in how they may affect future study.

Long-Standing Intersections

With scholarly societies in North America, Europe, and other regions of the world, foundational research journals such as the *International Journal of the History of Sport*, the *Journal of Sport History*, and *Sport History Review*, and an impressive parade of scholarly books, including two recent handbooks (Edelman & Wilson, 2017; Phillips, Booth, & Adams, 2021), the history of sport is both complementary and integral to the sociology of sport and the broader contemporary area of sport and society which is considered in this volume. In theorizing and taking long looks at specific dimensions in the etiology of sport and society, there are many points of comparison with the sociology of sport (Pringle, 2022). As sport history may be seen in essential ways to engage many sociology of sport issues in the rearview mirror, it is not surprising that there is a good deal of crossover among their scholarly communities. Most integrally related to sport history, the study of sport and religion has long legs in the sociology of sport as well. Key works (e.g., Adogame, Watson, & Parker, 2017, Alpert, 2015; Scholes & Sassower, 2014; Watson & Parker, 2014) explore the long-standing dynamics of sport *in* and *as* religion and their sacred and profane characteristics in socialization and moral development.

Also fundamentally concerned with the role of sport in moral development and the ethics *of* and *in* sport is scholarly inquiry on the philosophy of sport. With established international and national scholarly societies, robust journals such as the *Journal of the Philosophy of Sport* and *Sport, Ethics and Philosophy*, and comprehensive research handbooks (McNamee & Morgan, 2017; Torres, 2015), the area interrogates fundamental assertions and articulations of sport's role and functioning in society. Featured are overarching concerns with ethics and fairness, and foundational questions about matters such as metaphysics, epistemologies, aesthetics, and ideology in theorizing sport and its purported *value* and *values*.

As philosophy provides much undergirding about ideals for human behavior in sport, the study of sport, politics, and policy in a basic sense assesses and interrogates those ideals amid the pragmatic realities of sport governance and leadership. Focused on power relations and ideology, issues and tensions between nationalized priorities and nongovernmental organizations, the roles of sport in diplomacy and sport for development (and peace), sport mega-events and the omnipresent demands of commodification, and the impacts of sport on local communities and the environment, the study of the sport-politics nexus is essential to understanding sport and society. Featuring focused research journals, such as the *International Journal of Sport Policy and Politics*, and a host of major works and handbooks (Bairner, Kelly, & Lee, 2017; Henry & Ko, 2014; Murray, 2018; Wagg & Pollock, 2021), the area has grown in importance. It has become increasingly obvious that sport, rather than existing separately from politics, is inherently infused with questions about athlete activism, social justice, and human rights.

Pragmatism of a different sort is a key feature as well in much of the research agenda of sport psychology. Much work has a ready applied bent, focused on both individual and social psychological processes in performance. Concerns about personality, cognition, motivation, emotion, group dynamics, and leadership strategies are all key features of a research agenda that focuses on motivation and optimization. Closer to the nexus of sport and society, the social psychology of sport engages a range of issues that includes socialization in youth sport, recovery from injury, athletic careers and retirement, and clinical, counseling, and coaching issues in sport. The area features a panoply of handbooks (Anchel, 2019; Murphy, 2012; Schinke, McGannon, & Smith, 2016; Tenenbaum & Eklund, 2020) and a list of major research journals that dwarfs the number of outlets featured in the sociology of sport/sport and society space. Focused more on performance optimization and exercise psychology than the sociocultural ramifications of sport, it is fair to say that cross-fertilization between the social psychology of sport and the sociology of sport research communities has been less robust than might be expected and the area has more firm affinities with the sport sciences.

Beyond the aforementioned disciplinary standpoints, disciplinary intersections with sport and society are found across a wide swath of the social sciences and humanities. Select scholars seated in particularized area studies, such as those focused on gender, race, ethnicity, and disability, regularly engage with core questions about sport, identities, and cultural power. Other disciplinary vantage points, spanning the sociology of the body, tourism and leisure studies, urban and environmental studies, literary and film studies, and many more, have shed light on sport's social and cultural impacts. While all necessarily intersect with the sociology of sport, no disciplinary disposition has done so more than cultural studies.

Physical Cultural Studies

Perhaps the most overt and robust "answer" to the focus, dimensionality, and demeanor of the sociology of sport has been the relatively recent posing of physical cultural studies (PCS) as a distinct field (Andrews, 2008, 2015; Andrews & Silk, 2011; Silk & Andrews, 2011; Silk, Andrews, & Thorpe, 2017). Yet, in relation to the sociology of sport, PCS is both complementary and compromised. Just why PCS has emerged as its own "brand" is complex. At a base level, its emergence was predicated on core problems seen in both kinesiology and the sociology of sport. The critique of kinesiology focused on its epistemological anchor in the physical sciences and its antipathy to critical engagement. The critique of the sociology of sport takes cognizance, on one hand, of its being "more than" both sociology and sport (notably concerning body cultures broadly defined) and its parochialism in responding to and resisting the threats of rising neoliberalism on critical inquiry in the academy.

Indeed, in embracing social and cultural inquiry about the body, PCS has been more overtly welcoming to the study of exercise, fitness, and other bodily cultures that, in a sense, "don't fit" a disciplinary characterization, such as the sociology of sport, that marks its fence posts only with the word "sport." However, in invoking this, PCS is ironically inspired more by a "kinesiological" impulse (even though it rejects its epistemological foundations) than a sport-centered one as it focuses on diverse implications of bodies in motion. In doing so, it marks its terrain with a modifier, "physical," which of course includes sport but implicitly goes beyond exercise and fitness or even dance to include physicality in other settings, including presumably manual labor. More important, the "physical" construct modifies its core in "cultural studies," which may be seen as a critically disposed mash-up of sociology, literary, and media studies (Bennett & Frow, 2008; Carrington & McDonald, 2009; Durham & Kellner, 2012; Miller, 2001).

Yet, cultural studies, with its anchor in critical cultural theory, excludes and, in many quarters, devalues and segregates itself from other approaches to inquiry, most particularly those that engage empiricism and hypothesis-testing that remain widely embraced across the social sciences. While there is much to dislike about the wanton adoption of logical empiricism, and the limits of measurement and deduction are both obvious and considerable, other problems can arise from an unnecessarily delimited epistemological construction set in self-imposed theoretical and methodological segregation (even as it touts a diversity of subject matter focus). Further, it is difficult from an egalitarian perspective to support an approach to knowledge that rules out diverse ways of knowing along with the possibility that empirical inquiry can complement and "test" critical assessments and advance understanding of their generalizability. While the "shoe fits" on the other foot as well, in that empirically oriented scholars are often negligent in engaging critical understandings, most especially about the power relations and political-economic dynamics at play in their "scientized" inquiries, this too does not make a good argument for segregation in inquiries about sport or physical cultures.

While one can see that there is a real dilemma embedded in an inclusive sociology of sport that is both more than sociology and more than sport, the notion of PCS, although more overtly inclusive of exercise, fitness, and other body cultures, has been framed in a way that excludes (or is implicitly dismissive of or unwelcoming to) much inquiry seated in theoretical and methodological traditions other than critical-cultural inquiry. The blanket rejection of some useful dosing of normative empirical social sciences approaches that can add dimensionality and breadth to sociocultural inquiry about sport positions the PCS "answer" more as a political project than a satisfactory solution to problems in the sociology of sport that do, in fact, exist. Presently, much functioning of PCS resides within the large (if problematically named) tent of the sociology of sport. It may be that a more delicately nuanced conceptual mash-up, such as "sport, physical culture, and society" (Coakley, 2021a, p. 388), that overtly expands the gaze to physical culture without delimiting itself by signing an allegiance to cultural studies, will emerge. Should something of this sort shake out on the disciplinary playing field, the PCS "challenge" to both kinesiology and the sociology of sport could be particularly fruitful for the study of sport and society.

Communication and Sport

While the study of the role of media has been long recognized in the sociology of sport (Birrell & Loy, 1979), it is fair to say that early on sociologists of sport, whether working out of the emergent physical education variants or sociology, had little foundational understanding of communication processes or the literature of what was then mass communication research. Perhaps compounded by the sense that mediated sport and its tendencies toward spectacle and commodification were somehow debasing sport (or at least the idealized GSM version of it), surprisingly little early research focused on what would come to be characterized as the media/sport/culture production complex (Jhally, 1984) or, more economically, by the neologism "MediaSport" (Wenner, 1998) to signify a uniquely powerful sociocultural and political-economic fusing of two of Althusser's (1971) ideological state apparatuses. Yet, with the realization that there could be no (increasingly ubiquitous) big-time sport without big-time media (Wenner, 2006), and that cultural understandings of sport and sporting cultures (even at distinctly small-time recreational and community levels) were being structurally changed by the effects of mediatization (Frandsen, 2019), the focus on media in the sociology of sport grew from the mid-1980s onward to become by some accounts the dominant area of inquiry (Messner & Musto, 2014).

Much about the coming of media studies to the sociology of sport was complementary, expanding what was already on the docket in areas ranging from fandom to mega-events to representations of sporting stars and celebrities. The "cultural turn" in media studies, as it evolved from the structural functionalism of "mass communication research," with a critical focus on questions of identities (manifest through the political-economies of gender, race, class, and nation), both accelerated and mirrored the adoption of critical-interpretive lenses and qualitative methods in the sociology of sport. Early important works both signaled this turn and cross-fertilized efforts from the two fields (such as Real, 1975; Whannel, 1983; and evident in edited works such as Lawrence & Rowe, 1986; Wenner, 1989). Yet, it remained true that naïveté in both scholarly communities, about communication and media in the sociology of sport, and about the sociology of sport in communication and media studies, compromised early efforts. As the legitimacy trendlines advanced for sport in communication and media studies, beginning in the early 1990s and accelerating in the new millennium, cross-fertilization with the sociology of sport regularized.

Adding to this, a broadened frame of communication and sport reached past the more truncated focus on MediaSport to advance inquiry about sport in interpersonal, group, organizational, and other "nonmediated" communication contexts (Kassing et al., 2004; Wenner, 2021) in ways that had clear relevance for the sociocultural study of sport. By the second decade of the new millennium, the infrastructure for sport inquiry in communication and media studies had matured. The formation of a new scholarly society, the International Association for Communication and Sport, stimulated organizational legitimacy for sport in a swath of long-resistant legacy organizations; three research journals—*Journal of Sports Media*, the *International Journal of Sport Communication*, and *Communication and Sport*—commenced publication; and texts and substantial handbooks of the area were published (Billings & Butterworth, 2021; Butterworth, 2021, Pedersen, 2013).

Sport Management

If there is an increasingly large presence in a sport and society "room" where it may not really belong, it is the field of sport management. Fueled in no small part by the mediatization of sport, the growth of the professionalized elite (sometimes called "prolympic") sport marketplace has been considerable (Donnelly, 1996). This, in tandem with the recognition that there were huge untapped upsides to building more vibrant markets in youth, community, recreational sport, fitness, and "athleisure" contributed to the field of sport management blooming notably in the 1990s and beyond. In upgraded professionalized guise as "management" (much attuned to marketing), this surge gave a shot in the arm to the typically less strategic earlier framings as sport "administration" seen in physical education units and their scientized articulations. As well, the "shiny penny" of sport captivated many a business school, where sport management was seen as an attractive specialty. There was much goodness of fit as the underlying core disposition of sport management, to take sport as a received social force, something to be built upon to universalize virtues as embraced by the GSM and make it bigger and "better," was consonant with seatings in both the physical education variants and business schools. Yet, for the sociocultural study of sport, this has been both a blessing and a curse.

It was a blessing in that the expansion and success of sport management opened up opportunities in academic units to focus on "nonphysical" aspects of sport beyond the physical functioning and performance focus at the heart of the sport sciences. Still, in this process, finite resources, which had previously supported sociocultural inquiry about sport, were often devoted to advancing sport management, which more comfortably shared a received view of sport common across the sport sciences. With the prioritization of sport management, it was not uncommon to see sociocultural inquiry about sport "housed" with "strange bedfellows" in sport management. Increasingly, those looking for academic appointments focused on the sociology of sport found that their "opportunities" were in sport management. Thus, this blessing was in some sense a curse as the compromises fostered by such structural pragmatics should not be underestimated.

While the critical inquiry is not unheard of in the field of sport management (Nauright & Pope, 2009), it remains the exception and not the rule. The press for sociocultural scholars to "fit" into sport management academic cultures meant fitting into the "mantra" of the marketplace. This is seen in some simple ways, for example, in the "bending" of research on sport and development toward a focus on prosocial outcomes, such as advancing peace and improving disadvantaged communities (Collison, Darnell, Giulianotti, & Howe, 2019; Houlihan & Green, 2011). In recent years, sociocultural inquiry about sport has been increasingly situated amid the "logics" of sport management scholarly communities.

These logics are anchored in "real-world" sensitivities to pragmatics and application, a received neoliberal worldview construction, where a "normal" and "natural" marketplace is both valued and preeminent. While understandings of sociocultural processes may be engaged, they are often compromised by overarching concerns with "effectiveness" and marketplace growth. Thus, it is not surprising that frequent rationales to justify inquiry, as seen in the area's major journals, such as the *Sport Management Review* and the *Journal of Sport Management*, center—often exclusively so—on the goal of helping sport managers and marketers advance the reach and reception of their wares, in achieving a more enjoyable

or "better" spectator, fan, or customer experience. At one with a little-questioned political worldview and advancing the yield of those holding power in the sport marketplace,
this "has, hegemonically, resulted in many scholars willingly serving as *de facto* unpaid
research assistants" (Wenner, 2021, p. 32), even with little evidence that their research has
been either asked for or used by the sport industries. Yet, this is the water that increasing
numbers of sociocultural scholars of sport are necessarily swimming in. While this does
not preclude their ability to do meaningful research on sport and society, priorities valued
in management-focused scholarly cultures can compromise the agenda to make this more
challenging.

Approaching Sport and Society

The approach taken in fashioning this *Oxford Handbook of Sport and Society* has been
influenced by a long list of earlier efforts to showcase sociocultural inquiry about sport
(Andrews & Carrington, 2013; Coakley, 2021b; Coakley & Dunning, 2000; Giulianotti,
2004, 2005, 2015; Horne, Tomlinson, Whannel, & Woodward, 2013; Houlihan & Malcolm,
2016; Jarvie, 2017; Karen & Washington, 2015; Maguire, 2014, 2019; Malcolm, 2012; Pike,
2021; Snyder & Spreitzer, 1974; Young, 2016). Reflecting on confluences and tendencies in
these works, much effort was made to distinctly structure this volume in a way that breaks
thoughtfully on occasion from familiar characterizations of key themes and topics to stimulate new ways of thinking about the sport-and-society relationship.

The organizational scheme for the volume and the tactical approach to chapters was
arrived upon in consultation with a distinguished team of 10 consulting editors from across
the globe with diverse expertise and understandings of contemporary trends and needs
in the field. I would like to thank this team of consulting editors—Alan Bairner, Laurence
Chalip, John Horne, Steven Jackson, Pirkko Markula, Mary McDonald, Catherine Palmer,
Elizabeth Pike, David Rowe, and Brian Wilson—who were integral in helping to shape the
topics considered and identify a diverse set of area experts who have graciously contributed
thoughtful assessments of key areas of scholarly inquiry.

As you will see in the chapters ahead, each treatment considers sport in light of two societal "intersections." To ease readers in negotiating a diverse plethora of topical intersections
that sport has with society, authors were asked to structure the treatment of their topics
into three main sections: (1) Issues (select key issues, themes, areas, major findings),
(2) Approaches (select matters of theory, method, and disposition), and (3) Debates (select
matters under debate, pending, and/or unresolved). The volume is divided into six sections
that consider sport in terms of (1) society and values, (2) enterprise and capital, (3) participation and cultures, (4) lifespan and careers, (5) inclusion and exclusion, and (6) spectator
engagement and media.

Society and Values. This section leads with noted philosopher Sigmund Loland's ethical
appraisal of values and character in sport. Next, theorist Ben Carrington assesses the roles
of ideology and the exercise of power in sport. Political values in sport are interrogated
in the next four chapters, with Michael Sam dissecting the tensions between politics and
policy, Alan Bairner and Peizi Han considering articulations of nationalism and national
identities, Stuart Murray assessing the employ of diplomacy and rapprochement, and

Michael Butterworth pondering embedded roles of militarism and its signification. The section concludes with Adam Epstein's focus on where ethical lines are legally drawn and Andrew Parker and Nick Watson's situating the role of religion and beliefs in sport.

Enterprise and Capital. The impacts of "prolympic" sport are featured in the first four chapters in this section, with Adam Beissel and David Andrews considering their roles in globalization and glocalization, John Horne's broad drawing of spectacle in sports mega-events, Alan Tomlinson's deconstruction of the realities of Olympic ideals, and Lisa Kihl and Catherine Ordway's piercing look at corruption and fraud in sport. The ways sport has affected where we live are explored in Daniel Mason's chapter on the impacts on cities and communities and Toby Miller's look at geopolitical logics and environmental ramifications. The tenor and strategies of the sport marketplace are considered in the final four chapters, beginning with Emily Sparvero and Laurence Chalip's appraisal of organizational leadership and social responsibility, followed by Bill Gerrard's assessment of economic and finance dynamics in professional sport and Bettina Cornwell's drawing of inherent tensions between sport marketing and consumer culture, and closing with Heather Gibson and Sheranne Fairley's look at the social impacts of sport tourism.

Participation and Cultures. Three chapters focused on how health in sport is facilitated and challenged lead this section, opening with Parissa Safai's assessment of sport, health, and well-being, followed by Kevin Young's analysis of the effects of aggressive play and violence and Dominic Malcolm and Emma Pullen's consideration of emerging norms for medical intervention for injury. This is followed by Mary McDonald and Jennifer Sterling's critical take on the increased roles of science and technology in sport. Substance use and abuse is considered in the next two chapters: Paul Dimeo and April Henning's consideration of key issues about drugs and doping and Catherine Palmer's cultural analysis of alcohol rituals in sport. Athletic optimization is critically engaged by Jim Denison and Zoë Avner in appraising relations between coaching and performance, and the role of emotion in athlete engagement is assessed by Paul Potrac, Brian Gearity, Adam Nichol, and Edward Hall. Culturally embedded but morally wayward problems in sport are next considered along two fronts, first in Mike Hartill's exploration of the dynamics of child maltreatment and sexual violence and then in David Rowe and Catherine Palmer's assessment of sport scandal and social morality. Righteousness in sport cultures is considered by Douglas Hartmann in charting the relationship between athlete activism and social movements. Ethical quandaries too little considered—surrounding the relationship between animals and humans in sport—are interrogated by Michael Atkinson and Kass Gibson.

Lifespan and Careers. The cultures of early engagement with sport are considered along three fronts: Ken Green, Sharon Wheeler, and Patrick Foss Johansen explore key issues in the socialization of children into sport; Andy Smith engages debates about the elite development of young athletes; and Richard Bailey and Iva Glibo assess evidence about sport's role in education and advancing opportunity. Athletic career and lifecycle issues are featured in the next four chapters, with Ramón Spaaij and Suzanne Ryder appraising how elite athletics may facilitate social mobility, Győző Molnár considering sport labor and migration dynamics, Martin Roderick and Lauren Kamperman assessing the arc of athletic careers and struggles over retirement, and Elizabeth Pike, Elspeth Mathie, and Daniel Buckley analyzing how athletes adapt to aging. The section closes with consideration of alternative pathways for careers in lifestyle sports by Holly Thorpe and Guillaume Dumont.

Inclusion and Exclusion. Two chapters overviewing the dynamics of creating and challenging unlevel playing fields in sport frame this section, with Emma Sherry and Katherine Raw first considering the roles of sport in social inclusion and development, followed by Ruth Jeanes and Ryan Lucas examining the obverse processes of social exclusion and discrimination. Chapters that follow round out this section's focus on "othering" dynamics in sport. Daryl Adair's analysis of race and ethnicity in sport is followed by Tara Keegan and Jennifer Guiliano's interrogation of Indigenous peoples' identities and their appropriation in sport, Pirkko Markula's exploration of tensions between obesity and ideals of the sporting body, Ian Brittain and Matej Christiaens's consideration of how opportunities for inclusion are manifest for disabled athletes, Rory Magrath and Eric Anderson's accounting of stasis and change in heteronormative expectations of masculinities in sport, Cheryl Cooky's drawing of how norms of femininity intersect with women's experiences in sport, and Travers's examination of transgender and nonbinary experience in sport.

Spectator Engagement and Media. This section opens by considering the appeal of sport along two axes; first, Barry Smart considers the allure and manufacture of sport heroes and their celebrityhood, and this is followed by Kevin Dixon's analysis of what undergirds sport fandom and spectatorship. Dysfunctional aspects of engagement are considered along related fronts, first by John Williams in a football-centered analysis of fan violence and hooliganism, and then by Minyeok Tak, who considers the dynamics of gambling and match-fixing in sport. The last five chapters in the volume consider the state of media in sport. Here, David Rowe and Raymond Boyle consider how the norms of sport journalism are foundational in how sport is socially reproduced. Andrew Billings and Nicholas Buzzelli deconstruct the central role that sport on television has had in structuring how we see and understand sport. Seán Crosson examines how feature and documentary film have contributed to a fantasized cultural imaginary about sport. Steven Jackson explores another "imaginary," the roles of advertising and promotional culture in advancing the powerful role that sport plays in the consumer economy. The volume closes with Jimmy Sanderson's consideration of the increasingly large roles that digital and social media have in the circulation of our understandings about sport.

Collectively the treatments featured in this volume speak to the considerable roles that sport plays in contemporary society and culture. As you will see, the vantage points taken and the impacts that are considered are both diverse and substantial. While an overarching goal of a volume like this is to comprehensively cover the bases of social research on sport, even the notable breadth featured in this treatment must necessarily leave out important matters. In this light, I join the authors in our research community in hoping that what you find here will open new doors to thinking about the role and impacts of sport in society.

References

Adogame, A., Watson, N. J., & Parker, A. (Eds.). (2017). *Global perspectives on sport and religion*. London: Routledge.

Alpert, R. T. (2015). *Religion and sports: An introduction and case studies*. New York: Columbia University Press.

Althusser, L. (1971). *Lenin and philosophy and other essays* (Ben Brewster, Trans.). New York: Monthly Review Press.

Anchel, M. H. (Ed.). (2019). *APA handbook of sport and psychology*. Washington, D.C.: American Psychological Association.

Andrews, D. L. (2008). Kinesiology's inconvenient truth and the physical cultural studies imperative. *Quest, 60*(1), 45–62.

Andrews, D. L. (2015). Assessing the sociology of sport: On the hopes and fears for the sociology of sport in the U.S. *International Review for the Sociology of Sport, 50*(4–5), 368–374.

Andrews, D. L., & Carrington, B. (Eds.). (2013). *A companion to sport*. Malden, MA: Wiley-Blackwell.

Andrews, D. L. & Silk, M. (2011). Physical cultural studies: Engendering a productive dialogue. *Sociology of Sport Journal, 28*(1), 1–3.

Bairner, A. (2009). Sport, intellectuals and public sociology: Obstacles and opportunities. *International Review for the Sociology of Sport, 44*(2–3), 115–129.

Bairner, A., Kelly, J., & Lee, J. W. (Eds.). (2017). *Routledge handbook of sport and politics*. New York: Routledge.

Bennett, T., & Frow, J. (Eds.). (2008). *The Sage handbook of cultural analysis*. Thousand Oaks, CA: Sage.

Best, D. (1978). *Philosophy and human movement*. Boston: Allyn & Unwin.

Billings, A. C., & Butterworth, M. L. (2021). *Communication and sport: Surveying the field* (4th ed.). Thousand Oaks, CA: Sage.

Birrell, S., & Loy, J. W. (1979). Media sport: Hot and cool. *International Review for the Sociology of Sport, 14*(1), 5–19.

Business Research Company. (2021, May). *Global sports market—by type (participatory sports, spectator sports), by revenue (media rights, sponsorship, merchandising and tickets), and by region, opportunities, and strategies—global forecast to 2030*. https://www.thebusinessresearchcompany.com/report/sports-market.

Butterworth, M. L. (Ed.). (2021). *Handbook of communication and sport*. Berlin: Mouton de Gruyter Publishers.

Cahn, S. (1994). *Coming on strong: Gender and sexuality in twentieth century women's sport*. New York: Free Press.

Carrington, B., & McDonald, I. (Eds.). (2009). *Marxism, cultural studies and sport*. London: Routledge.

Coakley, J. (1987). Sociology of sport in the United States. *International Review for the Sociology of Sport, 22*(1), 63–79.

Coakley, J. (2015). Assessing the sociology of sport: On cultural sensibilities and the great sport myth. *International Review for the Sociology of Sport, 50*(4–5), 402–406.

Coakley, J. (2021a). The future of sports and society: A reflection and call to action. In E. C. J. Pike (Ed.), *Research handbook on sports and society* (pp. 380–392). Cheltenham, U.K.: Edward Elgar Publishing.

Coakley, J. (2021b). Sociology of sport: Growth, diversification, and marginalization, 1982–2021. *Kinesiology Review, 10*, 292–300. https://doi.org/10.1123/kr.2021-0017.

Coakley, J., & Dunning, E. (Eds.). (2000). *Handbook of sport studies*. London: Sage Publications.

Collison, H., Darnell, S. C., Giulianotti, R., & Howe, P. D. (Eds.). (2019). *Routledge handbook of sport development and peace*. London: Routledge.

Cooky, C., Council, L. D., Mears, M. A., & Messner, M. A. (2021). One and done: The long eclipse of women's televised sports, 1989–2919. *Communication & Sport, 9*, 347–371.

Corbin, C. B., & Cardinal, B. J. (2008). Conceptual physical education: The anatomy of an innovation. *Quest, 60*, 467–487.

Dart, J. (2014). Sports review: A content analysis of the *International Review for the Sociology of Sport*, the *Journal of Sport and Social Issues* and the *Sociology of Sport Journal* across 25 years. *International Review for the Sociology of Sport, 49*(6), 645–668.

Donnelly, P. (1996). Prolympism: Sport monoculture as crisis and opportunity. *Quest, 48*, 25–42.

Donnelly, P. (2015). Assessing the sociology of sport: On public sociology of sport and research that makes a difference. *International Review for the Sociology of Sport, 50*(4–5), 419–423.

Durham, M. G., & Kellner, D. M. (Eds.). (2012). *Media and cultural studies: Key works* (2nd ed.). Malden, MA: Wiley-Blackwell.

Edelman, R., & Wilson, W. (Eds.). (2017). *The Oxford handbook of sports history.* Oxford: Oxford University Press.

Edwards, H. (1969). *The revolt of the Black athlete.* New York: Free Press.

Edwards, H. (1973). *Sociology of sport.* Chicago: Dorsey Press.

Elias, N., & Dunning, E. (1986). *Quest for excitement: Sport and leisure in the civilizing process.* Oxford: Blackwell.

Evans, M. (2019, September 19). A question of sport: Is eSports a real sport? *The Drum.* https://www.thedrum.com/opinion/2019/09/13/question-sport-esports-real-sport.

Frandsen, K. (2019). *Sport and mediatization.* London: Routledge.

Geertz, C. (1973). *The interpretation of cultures.* New York: Basic Books.

Giulianotti, R. (Ed.). (2004). *Sport and modern social theorists.* New York: Palgrave Macmillan.

Giulianotti, R. (2005). *Sport: A critical sociology.* Cambridge, U.K.: Polity.

Giulianotti, R. (Ed.). (2015). *The Routledge handbook of sociology of sport.* London: Routledge.

Greendorfer, S. (1981). Emergence and future prospects for sociology of sport. In G. Brooks (Ed.), *Perspectives on the academic discipline of physical education: A tribute to G. Lawrence Rarick* (pp. 379–398). Champaign, IL: Human Kinetics.

Hargreaves, J. (1994). *Sporting females: Critical issues in the history and sociology of women's sports.* London: Routledge.

Heere, B. (2018). Embracing the sportification of society: Defining e-sports through a polymorphic view on sport. *Sport Management Review, 21*, 21–24.

Henry, I., & Ko, L.-M. (Eds.). (2014). *Routledge handbook of sport policy.* London: Routledge.

Horne, J., Tomlinson, A., Whannel, G., & Woodward, K. (2013). *Understanding sport: A sociocultural analysis* (2nd ed.). London: Routledge.

Houlihan, B., & Green, M. (Eds.). (2011). *Routledge handbook of sports development.* London: Routledge.

Houlihan, B., & Malcolm, D. (Eds.). (2016). *Sport and society: A student introduction* (3rd ed.). London: Sage.

Ingham, A., & Donnelly, P. (1997). A sociology of North American sociology of sport: Disunity in unity, 1965 to 1996. *Sociology of Sport Journal, 14*(4), 362–418.

Jarvie, G. (2017). *Sport, culture, and society: An introduction* (3rd ed.). London: Routledge.

Jhally, S. (1984). The spectacle of accumulation: Material and cultural factors in the evolution of the sports/media complex. *Insurgent Sociologist, 3*, 41–57.

Karen, D., & Washington, R. E. (Eds.). (2015). *Sociological perspectives on sport: The game outside the games.* New York: Routledge.

Kassing, J. W., Billings, A. C, Brown, R. S., Halone, K. K., Harrison, K., Krizek, R., Meân, L., & Turman, P. D. (2004). Communication in the community of sport: The process of enacting, (re)producing, consuming, and organizing sport, *Communication Yearbook, 28*, 373–410.

Kundera, M. (1999). *The unbearable lightness of being.* New York: Perennial.

Lawrence, G., & Rowe, D. (Eds.). (1986). *Power play: The commodification of Australian sport.* Sydney: Hall & Iremonger.

Maguire, J. (2013). Sportization. In G. Ritzer (Ed.), *The Blackwell encyclopedia of sociology* (online). London: Blackwell. doi:10.1002/9781405165518.wbeoss242.pub2.

Maguire, J. (Ed.). (2014). *Social sciences in sport.* Champaign, IL: Human Kinetics.

Maguire, J. (Ed.). (2019). *The business and culture of sports: Society, politics, economy, environment.* Farmington Hills, MI: Gale Centage.

Malcolm, D. (2012). *Sport and sociology.* London: Taylor and Francis.

Malcolm, D. (2014). The social construction of the sociology of sport: A professional project. *International Review for the Sociology of Sport, 49*(1), 3–21.

McNamee, M., & Morgan, W. (Eds.). (2017). *Routledge handbook of the philosophy of sport.* London: Routledge.

Messner, M. A. (1992). *Power at play: Sports and the problem of masculinity.* Boston: Beacon Press.

Messner, M. A. (2002). *Taking the field: Women, men, and sports.* Minneapolis: University of Minnesota Press.

Messner, M. A. & Musto, M. (2014). Where are the kids? *Sociology of Sport Journal, 31,* 102–122.

Miller, T. (Ed.). (2001). *A companion to cultural studies.* Malden, MA: Wiley-Blackwell.

Murphy, S. M. (Ed.). (2012). The Oxford handbook of sport and performance. Oxford: Oxford University Press.

Murray, S. (2018). *Sports diplomacy: Origins, theory and practice.* London: Routledge.

Nauright, J., & Pope, S. (2009). *The new sport management reader.* Morgantown, WV: Fitness Information Technology.

Newell, K. M. (1990). Physical education in higher education: Chaos out of order. *Quest, 42,* 227–242.

Pedersen, P. M. (Ed.). (2013). *Routledge handbook of sport communication.* London: Routledge.

Phillips, M. G., Booth, D., & Adams, C. (Eds.). (2021). *Routledge handbook of sport history.* London: Routledge.

Pike, E. C. J. (Ed.). (2021). *Research handbook on sports and society.* Cheltenham, U.K.: Edward Elgar Publishing.

Pike, E. C. J., Jackson, S. J., & Wenner, L. A. (Eds.) (2015). Assessing the trajectory and challenges of the sociology of sport. *International Review for the Sociology of Sport, 50*(4–5), Special 50th anniversary issue.

Pringle, R. (2022). The last comparative review of sport history and sport sociology? In M. G. Phillips, D. Booth, & C. Adams (Eds.), *Routledge handbook of sport history* (pp. 24–31). London: Routledge.

Real, M. R. (1975). Super Bowl: Mythic spectacle. *Journal of Communication, 25*(1), 31–43.

Schinke, R. J., McGannon, K. R., & Smith, B. (Eds.). (2016). *The Routledge international handbook of sport psychology.* London: Routledge.

Scholes, J., & Sassower, R. (2014). *Religion and sports in American culture.* London: Routledge.

Scott, J. (1969). *Athletics for athletes.* Oakland, CA: An Other Ways Book.

Scott, J. (1971). *The athletic revolution.* New York: Free Press.

Seippel, Ø. (2018). Topics and trends: 30 years of sociology of sport. *European Journal for Sport and Society, 15*(3), 288–307.

Silk, M. L., & Andrews, D. L. (2011). Toward a physical cultural studies. *Sociology of Sport Journal, 28*(1), 4–35.

Silk, M. L, Andrews, D. L., & Thorpe, H. (Eds.). (2017). *Routledge handbook of physical cultural studies.* New York: Routledge.

Snyder, E., & Spreitzer, E. (1974). Sociology of sport: An overview. *Sociological Quarterly*, 15, 467–487.

Tenenbaum, G., & Eklund, R. C. (Eds.). (2020). *Handbook of sport psychology* (4th ed.). Malden, MA: Wiley-Blackwell.

Tian, E., & Wise, N. (2020). An Atlantic divide? Mapping the knowledge domain of European and North American–based sociology of sport, 2008–2018. *International Review for the Sociology of Sport*, 55(8), 1029–1055.

Torres, C. R. (Ed.). (2015). *The Bloomsbury companion to the philosophy of sport*. London: Bloomsbury.

Wagg, S., & Pollock, A. M. (Eds.). (2021). *The Palgrave handbook of sport, politics and harm*. New York: Palgrave Macmillan.

Watson, N. J., & Parker, A. (2014). *Sport and the Christian religion: A systematic review of literature*. Newcastle-upon-Tyne, U.K.: Cambridge University Press.

Wenner, L. A. (Ed.). (1989). *Media, sports, and society*. Thousand Oaks, CA: Sage.

Wenner, L. A. (Ed.). (1998). *MediaSport*. London: Routledge.

Wenner, L. A. (2006). Sports and media through the super glass mirror: Placing blame, breast-beating, and a gaze to the future. In J. Bryant & A. A. Raney (Eds.), *Handbook of sports media* (pp. 45–60). Hillsdale, NJ: Erlbaum.

Wenner, L. A. (2009). The unbearable dirtiness of being: On the commodification of mediasport and the need for ethical criticism. *Journal of Sports Media*, 4(1), 85–94.

Wenner, L. A. (2017). On the *International Review for the Sociology of Sport*, the field of play, and six years of more "more than less." *International Review for the Sociology of Sport*, 52(8), 903–909.

Wenner, L. A. (2021). Playing on the communication and sport field: Dispositions, challenges, and priorities. In M. L. Butterworth (Ed.), *Handbook of communication and sport* (pp. 23–42). Berlin: Mouton de Gruyter Publishers.

Whannel, G. (1983). *Blowing the whistle: The politics of sport*. London: Pluto.

Young, K. (Ed.). (2016). *Sociology of sport: A global discipline in review*. Bingley, U.K.: Emerald.

PART I

SOCIETY
AND VALUES

CHAPTER 2

···

SPORT, VALUES, AND CHARACTER

···

SIGMUND LOLAND

To Pierre de Coubertin, the founding father of the International Olympic Committee, sport represented the ideal, meritocratic society in which participants competed under fair conditions enabling physical, mental, and moral progress (Chatziefstathiou, 2011). Albert Camus, French author and youth soccer goalkeeper, claimed late in life that all he knew about morality and duty he owed to sport (Owen, 2019). In contrast, in an article in *Tribune* and reflecting upon a soccer match, his contemporary George Orwell (1945/2022) saw sport very differently: as a "war minus the shooting." Philosopher Torbjörn Tännsjö (1998) goes even further, claiming that the public fascination with elite sport is fascistoid: its core is a cult of the strong and contempt for weakness. And, from a critical feminist perspective, current hegemonic sports culture is characterized by the values and repressive normativity of colonialism, white supremacy, and cisgender heteropatriarchy (Travers, this volume).

What is to be made of these polarized positions? What are the values *in* sport, that is, within the practice of sport itself? And what are the values *of* sport in the larger social and cultural contexts in which sport is played? Moreover, what are the relationships, if any, *between* the values *in* and *of* sport? In this chapter, and from selected social science and philosophy perspectives, I will suggest some answers.

My understanding of "sport" here is traditional. "Sport" refers to the training for and practicing of rule-governed, competitive games in which bodily movement plays a constitutive and meaning-producing part. In Coakley's (2001, p. 20) more extensive definition, sports are "institutionalized competitive activities that involve rigorous physical exertion or the use of relatively complex physical skills by participants motivated by personal enjoyment and external rewards." Typical examples are the activities organized as Olympic sports: team ball games such as soccer and basketball and individual sports such as athletics and skiing.

Sports are played in many and diverse social and cultural contexts and by a diversity of people: children and youth as well as the middle-aged and old, men and women, amateurs, elite professional performers, able-bodied and disabled people. Obviously, the values of sport are understood in a diversity of ways. Simplistically speaking, a key aim of the social sciences of sport is to describe, interpret, and explain this diversity. In the philosophy of sport, there is further interest in shared normative patterns between sports, in the possibility of defining sport as a human practice, and also in the possibility of weighing sporting values according to their moral significance.

In what follows, and after some initial conceptual groundwork, I will give examples of what I see as some of the main issues in and approaches to the study of sporting values. In the final section of the chapter, I will look in more detail at two current controversies: the use of performance-enhancing drugs and the expectations on sport of meeting requirements on sustainable development.

ISSUES

Conceptualizing Values and Character

In general terms, values are conceptualizations of "the good," of something that is worth striving for. Dictionary definitions (Macmillan Dictionary Online, 2021b) refer to values in several ways, among them "the amount that something is worth, measured especially in money," for instance, in the sense of the commercial value to a broadcasting company of a sporting event; "the degree to which someone or something is important or useful," for instance, soccer players' love of playing; and "the principles and beliefs that influence behavior and way of life of a particular group or community," for instance, principles of fairness or the belief in the value of sport in character formation or in democratic grassroots sports as a means to strengthen civil society.

Values can be further categorized. A distinction can be made between *subjective* and *objective* values. My personal preference for skiing is subjective. Skiing is important *to me*. Skiing pioneers, on the other hand, such as polar explorer, scientist, and 1922 Nobel Peace Prize laureate Fridtjof Nansen (1952), viewed their position as objective: more than any other sport, skiing ("the sport of sports") cultivates and hardens the individual and, if practiced by the masses, can cure the maladies of modern society.

In the social sciences and humanities, there is an interest in both subjective and alleged objective conceptualizations of value. One main question is how such views have emerged and developed within the social and cultural contexts in which sports occur. I was born and raised in a skiing-loving family. For me, primary socialization made its mark. Nansen skied and wrote in the late 19th- and early 20th-century context of "manliness" and national identity construction (Goksøyr, 2013). For him, skiing became a signifier for "true," Norwegian values.

Values can be further differentiated into *moral* and *nonmoral*. Moral values are intrinsic values; that is, they are ends in themselves, in addition to being considered necessary constituents of a good life for all. Examples are justice, truth, freedom, happiness, love, and human flourishing. Moral values are often held as axioms in more detailed systems of values, as in the form of normative systems. For example, the United Nations' (2021) Declaration on Human Rights departs from the axiom of "the inherent dignity and of the equal and inalienable rights of all members of the human family," leading to a series of rights, among them the right to "life, liberty and security of person."

Nonmoral values, on the other hand, can be important to me, to a group, or to a society and a culture but come with no claims on universality. Skills in a sport, such as mastery of tennis techniques or tactical skills in soccer, are not necessary parts of a good life (although tennis and soccer enthusiasts may think so) but can offer significant contributions hereto. In a narrow physical sense, health is a significant value as it is closely linked to a good life but is not strictly necessary for the experience of life as good and meaningful. And the other way round, as exemplified by sporting narratives from totalitarian sports systems such as the one of the former German Democratic Republic (Spitzer, 2006), there is also the possibility of physically healthy but deeply unhappy individuals.

A further distinction is the one between *values* and *norms*. Values serve to justify norms, and norms are guidelines for actions. Norms can be seen as *operationalizations of values*. In sport, values such as justice, fairness, and mutual respect give rise to norms of fair play: keep the rules, do your best, and show dignity in victory as well as in defeat (Serrano-Durá, Molina, & Martínez-Baena, 2020). Interpretations of these norms in specific contexts, however, vary. Holding another player's shirt might be accepted as fair to a certain extent in English Premier League soccer but is considered unfair in children's games. Trash talking might be an accepted strategy in some sport cultures and rejected in others.

A final concept to be clarified is that of *character*. Dictionaries point to a definition of "good personal qualities, especially the qualities of being brave and determined when doing something difficult" (Macmillan Dictionary Online, 2021a). The following exemplifications routinely involve sports, such as "The team showed real character in coming back from two goals down." Character building is definitionally exemplified by posing "the idea of competitive sport as a character-building activity." More generally, a person's *moral character* can be judged by the person's stable dispositions to judge and act in morally sound ways, particularly in situations of value conflict.

The idea of sport as character building has deep historical roots, originating in ancient Greece and the view of the Olympic athlete as embodying Greek identity at its best (Reid, 2012). With the rise of modern sport, the 19th-century British educational ideology of Muscular Christianity is a paradigmatic example. Sporting toughness, team spirit, and winning mentality were considered efficient means in the construction of the future defenders of the British Empire (Mangan, 2000).

This idea is by no means dead. Coakley (2015) articulates the Great Sport Myth, which postulates the ubiquitous view that sport is inherently pure and good, and its purity and goodness are automatically transmitted to its practitioners and spectators. In this logic, moral improvement of the individual leads to improvement of the community and, in Olympic versions, to the improvement of society and even the global community. Coakley's critique and deconstruction of the Great Sport Myth, in particular his arguments on its more or less tacit impact in the social sciences of sport, are illuminating.

The nature of and relationships between ideas of sporting values, norms, and character and the social and cultural contexts in which sport occurs are key issues in the scholarly study of sport. First, let me look at some selected issues from a social science perspective.

Social Science Issues

From a social-psychological point of view, there is an interest in the nature and variability of *individual sporting values and norms* and sport's potential in *moral education and character development* (Shields & Bredemeier, 2008, 2014). A significant body of research looks into the effects of motivation and goal orientation on developing and forming individual values and attitudes, such as about the notion of fair play (Ring & Kavussanu, 2018; Shields, Funk, & Bredemeier, 2016). In this vein, a related series of studies anchored in so-called self-determination theory explores differences between performance- and result-oriented climates and those stressing mastery and intrinsic values (Ntoumanis & Standage, 2009; Shields & Bredemeier, 2007). Not surprisingly, the former is associated with the acceptance of antisocial behavior and rule violations, and the latter with respect for opponents and fair play. One core message is that, if conducted in a mastery-oriented motivational climate, sport *can* cultivate good character. But, just as obviously, in a result-oriented climate, sport can hinder moral character development and lead to the opposite: cynical and amoral character traits. Psychological studies demonstrate *the normative ambiguity* of sport. Simply put, sport is a "moral laboratory" (McFee, 2004, pp. 129ff.), with outcomes that can go either way, depending upon the "experimental" setup.

From the perspective of sociology, there is an interest in how normative interpretations of sport find their form in the interchange with more general social and cultural contexts. One hypothesis is that there is no such thing as universally shared values and norms connected to sports; sport is an empty shell or "signifier" to be filled with whatever meaning and value make sense in the contexts in which sport is practiced. Although less radical, common to much social science sport research is skepticism of normative generalizations and claims on universality. Let me take three examples of studies exploring value diversity.

A pioneering study in social anthropology is that of Trobriand cricket. The Trobriand Islands are part of Papua New Guinea and well known to anthropologists due to Malinowski's classic studies conducted between 1915 and 1918. The Trobriand version of cricket, a hybrid of the British game introduced in the early 1900s by the colonists and Methodist missionaries, and local Trobriand precolonial warlike ritual and dance, was portrayed in the celebrated early 1970s ethnographic documentary *Trobriand Cricket*. Although a contested interpretation (Foster, 2006), Trobriand cricket still stands as a classic example of merging a hegemonic practice paradigm with local values, norms, and practices; of what anthropologists call *cultural syncretism* (Stewart, 1999).

Archetti's (1999) study of Argentinian nationalism and masculinity is another demonstration of the dynamic interchange among social, cultural, and sporting values. To Archetti, Argentinian masculinity is constructed and expressed in three core practices: (1) football played by the poor immigrants and the working class; (2) the rural upper-class sport of polo (totally dependent upon the equine expertise of the Argentinian cowboy, the *gaucho*); and (3) the tango, which, in opposition to football and polo, is seen as a pure, Argentinian invention and in which the display of masculinity is contrasted to images of femininity. To a sports scholar, the narrative of the rise from the poor Buenos Aires neighborhoods in the 1980s of *el pibe del oro* (the golden kid) and "soccer god" Diego Maradona is of particular interest. Archetti's emphasis on the impact of early 20th-century immigration of one million Europeans to Buenos Aires provides fertile ground in developing the theoretical concept of *hybridization*: popular cultural practices such as sports are creative free zones that can challenge hegemonic discourses on identity, gender, and morality and produce mixed and complementary hybrid understandings.

Wacquant's (2003) three-year participant-observation study as an apprentice boxer in a Chicago South Side Black ghetto boxing club is the story of how a sport cultivating physical confrontation and combat can frame a strong and caring masculine community. The study is original and innovative, with the intellectual and white Wacquant immersing himself in the racialized social world of young, underprivileged Black men. To its participants, boxing offered "an island of order and virtue" (p. 17) in a world of chaos. Wacquant presents a combination of urban and sport sociology and an embodied phenomenology of boxing. Using Bourdieu's ideas of *habitus* and trying to grasp "the taste and ache" of the sport, Wacquant aims at developing an embodied *carnal sociology* equipped for understanding the characteristic values and norms in and of sporting practice.

Whereas these examples aim to describe and interpret the diversity of sporting values, critical social theory has the additional aims of revealing and challenging power structures and stimulating social change and empowerment of marginalized groups. One example from sport studies is the critique of the binary sex classification systems found in most sports. One of the most discussed cases is that of South African middle-distance runner and World and Olympic Champion Caster Semenya. After being ruled ineligible in the women's class by World Athletics due to alleged high testosterone levels, Semenya challenged the system, ending in a 2019 ruling in the Court of Arbitration for Sport (CAS). In a split decision, the CAS acknowledged the case as involving a dilemma of rights, pitting the right to fair competition of competitors within the statistical female normal range of testosterone values against the right of competitors outside of this range but with legal status as females to compete in the women's class. In what emerged as a "lesser evil" approach (Loland, 2020), the CAS weighed the former above the latter and provided World Athletics with conditional support. From a critical perspective, the treatment of noncis athletes such as Semenya is considered an expression of reductionist biological essentialism and Eurocentric, heteropatriarchal sex and gender systems (Travers, this volume). The view is that binary sex classification works as repressively *gender-conforming* systems as opposed to empowering *gender-transforming* inclusion strategies and should, in fairness, be overturned (Travers, 2006).

Studies of this latter kind have a clear normative dimension as their interest in weighing values also has ready practical implications. In the section ahead, I move from consideration of social science perspectives to the underpinnings of normative analysis as situated primarily in the fields of philosophy and ethics.

APPROACHES

Normative Analyses

Where there is a particular interest in the diversity of sporting values in social sciences, the philosopher will pursue somewhat different questions. In this diversity, are there common and demarcating characteristics or values? Can sports be essentially defined? Definitional efforts are linked to *the normative* question about whether some values and norms are to be preferred above others and whether normative rankings can be justified rationally, with intersubjective and even universally valid reasons. Is skiing, de facto, the sport of sports? Is the ruling on the noneligibility of Semenya, de facto, morally wrong?

As a cultural practice, sport offers experiential qualities of many kinds: fun, joy, excitement, pleasure and pain, winning and losing, a sense of community, of conflict, and of mastery and failure. Huizinga's (1971) classic study of play, *Homo Ludens*, departs from the idea that the very raison d'être of play is to be found in the activity itself. Play is further characterized by a clear order as defined by rules, both written and unwritten. The characteristics resonance well with sporting games. Basketball teams operate within a strict rule framework, with the goal of shooting a ball through a hoop defended by another team. Golf is defined by hitting a ball with clubs into a specified number of holes with a minimum number of shots. Play opens a distinct world in locality and duration which is different from ordinary life. Play finds its meaning in the very process of playing. Play is an autotelic activity: its values are both internal and self-contained.

Suits (2014, p. 54) presents similar ideas as he defines the demarcating logic of game playing as "the voluntary attempt to overcome unnecessary obstacles." Games stand out as autotelic contrasts to the instrumentality of everyday life. Moreover, Suits argues, most sports can be considered games as they are defined by this logic. In basketball, there are rigid rules on how a player can move with the ball. The premise of hurdle racing is that participants accept the difficulty of going over the hurdles before reaching the finishing line. Slalom skiers must move through the course gates instead of taking the faster route straight down the hill. The constitutive rules of a sport define "unnecessary" obstacles and make sense only within the practice of these activities in themselves. This, says Suits, demonstrates a lusory, or playful, attitude.

The idea of a demarcating social logic of games, or that game rules make sense primarily within the context of game playing, has been fertile in the sport philosophy literature. Some studies examine in more detail the normative structures of the rules, for instance, as underpinned by ideals of equality of opportunity and of fair play (Loland, 2002). Similarly, there is an interest in the internal values in terms of the experiential qualities of movement expertise. One example is Montero's (2016) study of the proprioceptive sense giving kinesthetic information about bodily positions and movements. Elite performances have a constitutive sensual-aesthetic dimension, and the primary value and joy of mastery lie in the experience of executing it. A related example comes from positive sports psychology, which is inspired in part by Csikszentmihályi's (1990) concept of "flow": a total absorption in a task facilitated by an optimal balance between challenge and mastery.

Such ideas about the internal values of sports beg further questions: What is the normative status of sport as compared to other human practices? And how are we to prioritize in potential conflicts between values in and of sport?

Neo-Aristotelian Ethics: The Internal and External Goods of Sport

One traditional view is that noninstrumental activities such as art, music, dance, and sport are important and cultivating elements in an all-around education. The view has aristocratic and elitist roots, as is obvious in the English upper-class amateur ideology (Mangan, 2000) and in Coubertin's Olympism (Loland, 1995). As the saying goes, a good game of pool is a sign of all-around education, whereas excellence in the game is a sign of an ill-spent youth. Emphasis on the cultivating force of activities such as sport is, however, also found in more reflective, critical frameworks such as in the neo-Aristotelian approach of Alasdair MacIntyre (2007; McNamee, 2008).

In MacIntyre's (2007) analysis, social practices are understood in terms of internal and external goods or, in our terminology, internal and external values. MacIntyre talks of a social practice as a coherent, complex, cooperative and social human activity. Internal goods are realized by embracing the internal standards of excellence embedded in the practice. When a tennis player executes a stroke with technical and tactical finesse, or when a diver performs in line with the relevant aesthetical standards, internal goods of these sports are realized. At this point, internal goods have the status of nonmoral values. If, however, the standards of excellence cultivate more general human virtues such as fairness, courage, resilience, and respect for others, they have moral significance. We necessarily deal here with developing not just sporting but human excellence and character. This then indicates a potential moral justification with a primary emphasis on values *in* sport. Finally, at a third and societal level, and if practiced according to standards of excellence that cultivate virtue, social practices can become building blocks of a good and flourishing society.

At first glance, this might sound like an overly idealistic image of the potential of sport. However, MacIntyre's philosophy has a clear, critical edge. First, in terms of basic philosophical premises, MacIntyre rejects modern rationalist and universalist approaches. In neo-Aristotelian ethics, moral values and norms are developed and shaped within particular historical, social, and cultural contexts. Evaluating them according to some external, objective standard is impossible. Second, standards of excellence in a particular practice do not necessarily make them morally relevant. Quite to the contrary, social practices can have morally problematic standards. For instance, the hidden and complex systems of performance-enhancing drug use in late 20th-century professional cycling followed a "mafialike" standard of excellence in terms of *omerta:* a code of silence and secrecy (Waddington & Smith, 2009).

Third, there is tension between internal and external goods. External goods are those linked to a social practice by "the accident of social circumstances" (MacIntyre, 2007, p. 181). These are values toward which a social practice is considered a means. External goods can be of moral significance. Sport organizations and public authorities and governments can use sports to enhance public health or to promote human rights and civic society. Often, this is done with emphasis on the social practice and its internal goods. The institutional pursuit of other external goods, however, such as power and profit or political prestige, tend to challenge internal goods and lead to instrumentalization. One current example is the efforts of some political regimes to enhance their international image with win at all costs strategies through the powers of "sportswashing" (Chadwick, 2018). Whereas realizing the internal goods and standards of excellence benefits the whole practicing community, external goods typically are distributed in zero-sum games. The wins of one party lead to losses of another.

In the setting of heterogeneous and multicultural modern societies, the neo-Aristotelian approach can be challenged. Most sporting communities consist of members with diverse backgrounds. Sharing the same values and standards of excellence can be difficult. Is the practice of play-acting to fake rule violations in soccer an acceptable part of soccer tactics? Should boys and girls practice swimming at the same time and in the same pool? Ought the national Olympic team boycott the Olympic Games in totalitarian political or religious regimes? In situations like these, where there may be no apparent way of rationally deciding whether one option is better than another, how are we to proceed?

Morgan's (2020) solution is to move from "vulgar ethnocentrism" to "deep convention-alism." Here, there is no external criterion or Archimedean mean point from which moral conflict can be solved. In line with a MacIntyrean understanding, what must be protected in sport are its internal goods. And, in line with Suits (2014), Morgan (1994) points to "the gratuitous logic" of sport: its ludic qualities. Sports invite (but do not guarantee) the development of morally relevant standards of excellence. The impact of strong external commercial and political interests, in combination with weak and even corrupt sports leadership, leads to mismanagement and trivialization. The possibility lies in informed and critical discourse among practitioners, or as Morgan (1994, 2020) advises, in deliberative practice communities.

Interestingly, during the past several decades, athletes and fans have "awakened" to challenge the established sport system. Among illustrative examples are individual actions such as U.S. National Football League quarterback Colin Kaepernick's on-field protest against racial inequality and police violence, and collective responses, as in public referendums turning down Olympic bids, or the intense public debates on mega-event boycotts due to alleged human rights violations in organizing states as in the case of the 2022 Beijing Winter Games and the 2022 Soccer World Cup in Qatar. In his work on "the new sports diplomacy," Murray (2018) portrays the current political fields surrounding sport as a diverse network of interests and power structures with a critical public exerting a stronger impact than seen earlier.

Deontology: Sport and Principles of Fairness

As is evident from the protests, sport is not an isolated island of internal standards of excellence. Public expectations on sports as a vehicle in promoting human rights point to possibilities for departing from more general principles and norms. In the view of "the continuity thesis" (Russell, 2018) or of "broad internalism" (Simon, 2000), specific and "internal" sporting values are connected to and can be justified with reference to more extensive social and moral values. These positions relate to rationalist and universalist traditions in ethics.

With the rise of modern science in the 18th and 19th centuries, ethics went through a process of secularization. One core question was this: How can we distinguish between the morally right and wrong and good and bad when religion is no longer the authoritative source?

German Enlightenment philosopher Immanuel Kant is the main representative of a long-standing tradition in modern ethics: deontological ethics (from Greek *to deon*: duty). Kant's premise is that, independent of historical, social, and cultural contexts, each human being has inherently infinite and inviolable worth. One main universal norm, or a categorical imperative in Kant's terminology, prescribes that we are never to treat others as means only, but always as ends in themselves and in respect of their special moral status as *persons*. Our duty is to act in a way that, if universalized, would be in the best interests of humankind. Kantian ethics is the main source of an ethics of rights and duties, as exemplified in the UN's Declaration of Human Rights and our duty to respect them.

The deontological ideas of respect for persons and human rights have had an enormous impact on the normative foundation of modern, democratic welfare societies, including their sub-practices such as sport (Donnelly, 2008). Kantian ethics holds a basic premise for current interpretations of justice and fairness (Rawls, 1971). One overriding idea is expressed in a fair equality of opportunity norm (FEON): in the distribution of basic goods and burdens, we should eliminate or compensate for inequalities upon which individuals cannot exert impact or control. And indeed, this goal is evident in welfare societies which are premised on the notion that if enough pressure can be exerted on the inequitable distribution of basic goods such as income, education, and healthcare, then we can eliminate or compensate for structural inequalities anchored in differences in matters such as sex and sexual orientation, age, and socioeconomic, ethnic, cultural, and religious background.

Ideals of fairness in sport are practice-specific operationalizations of FEON (Loland, 2002). When it comes to classification, inequalities in biological sex are compensated for in sports in which power and speed are crucial and we do so with regard to body size in combat sports and weightlifting for similar reasons. There are rules to compensate, too, for inequalities in external conditions, for instance, by drawing starting positions as when the referee flips the coin at the start of a soccer match, or by standardizing schemes to reduce inequalities in equipment and technology.

As with neo-Aristotelian approaches, deontological ethics have a critical edge. First, in many sports, and even if a deliberative sporting community accept them, some handling of inequalities (or the lack of it) emerges as simply unfair and wrong. Why distinguish between the sexes in sailing, pistol shooting, and, for that matter, chess? Why accept radical inequalities in technology between competitors in skiing? Why, by looking at the Olympic national medal statistics, accept the obvious impact in elite sport of global inequalities in resources? These are additional challenges for an international sport system under pressure.

Typically, deontological theories of fairness and justice cover questions of *the morally right*. In ethics, there is also the question of *the morally good*. A fair sporting game is not necessarily experienced as good and does not necessarily contribute to advancing moral value and character development. Are there other ways of dealing with values than what has been discussed so far?

The etymology of "fairness" provides some leads (Online Etymology Dictionary, 2021). "Fair," from Old English *fæger* and Old Norse *fagr,* refers to what is just and also to what is admirable and beautiful, as used in expressions such as "a fair sky," "a fair lady." What, then, can be relevant theories of "the good" in this respect?

Utilitarianism: Good Sport

Teleological ethical theory, or consequentialism, or, more specifically, as the most common version of the consequentialist tradition, *utilitarianism,* provides an answer. Utilitarianism found its form in the early 19th century. Inspired by the emergence of mechanistic natural science, a key figure such as Jeremy Bentham and later his student John Stuart Mill pointed to one basic moral currency toward which all moral issues should be measured: *individual happiness.* Bentham dreamed of a future, empirical ethics in which happiness could be quantified in units, so-called *hedons.* When in doubt about future actions and policies, extensive cost-benefit analyses could point to the solution that minimizes unhappiness or pain and, if possible, creates the greatest happiness (and hopefully the greatest good) for the greatest number.

The impact of utilitarianism in both current ethical theory and the pragmatics of policymaking is considerable. For instance, most professional ethical codes include elements of utilitarian thinking. Take research ethics as an example. In addition to the de-ontological requirement of informed consent to respect the rights of human subjects, re-search must meet expectations of greater and more broadly spread social value. In exercise science studies, participants' discomfort and risk of harm must be weighed against the po-tential positive impacts of new knowledge. Similarly, in sport policy, the use of resources on children's sport has to be justified with reference to expected positive outcomes such as the learning of values and the promotion of health.

Can utilitarian cost-benefit analyses complement deontological fairness concepts and provide further and more specific criteria to assess the values *in* sport, that is, in their em-ploy in *good* sporting games? At first glance, the answer seems to be no. Games have a nonutilitarian logic. Their rules prescribe "unnecessary" obstacles to reach a goal which is the basis of realizing their internal goods. Upon closer examination, however, utilitarian perspectives seem to have something to offer. Popular and good games offer valuable blends of experiential qualities and endure, sometimes with astonishing stability, over generations. From a utilitarian perspective, a good sporting game is a game that maximizes happiness, or in a more technical term from preference-utilitarians such as Richard Hare (1982), maximizes average preference-satisfaction among all parties concerned. Good games make people happy.

There is an obvious catch in utilitarian reasoning. In the quest for the greatest happiness for the greatest number, we might end up with a majority of sensation-hungry spectators outnumbering the preferences of a few athletes and sport aficionados, leading to a revival of the ancient brutal gladiator games (which with events such as Mixed Martial Arts (MMA) is already a reality?). One response is to distinguish between two levels of moral reasoning: act and rule utilitarianism (Hare 1982).

Single-act calculations are fit only for the most difficult moral dilemmas. The acceptance of a rule allowing the exploitation of a few athletes to satisfy the many can have problem-atic long-term consequences such as when a lack of respect for persons leads to an overall reduction of happiness in society. An alternative, as exemplified with research ethics, is to combine utilitarian schemes with deontological ones. In Loland's (2002) theory of fair play, a deontological framework of *fairness* and FEON is combined with a utilitarian-based norm on *playing* to win, that is, on doing one's best. Adhering to the fairness norm provides a stable framework, whereas the play norm provides uncertainty and tension. Sport at its best seems to include an optimal blend of fairness and predictability together with play and un-predictability, giving rise to experiential qualities with the characteristic phenomenological structure that philosopher Warren Fraleigh referred to as "the sweet tension of uncertainty of outcome" (as cited in Kretchmar, 1975, p. 26).

The fair play argument represents what we may call a mild form of essentialism in its claim that sport, when played at its best, is no empty signifier but requires fairness and honest and sincere efforts to make sense.

DEBATES

In what follows, I interrogate two debates on sport values. The first relates primarily to values *in* sport and concerns the use of performance-enhancing drugs (PEDs). The second matter under debate relates to expectations from larger society on the value *of* sport in contributing to sustainable development.

PEDs and "the Spirit of Sport"

Being typical expressions of the values of modernity, including a strong belief in quantifiable progress and records, elite sport, in particular, implies a constant quest for a competitive edge. Medicalization processes together with a significant societal increase in the use of nonprescription and prescription drugs have blurred the distinction between therapeutic and nontherapeutic use, also in sport (Malcolm, 2017). Being formalized in the mid- and late 1960s, sports organizations such as the International Olympic Committee enforced the first rules banning some PEDs (Gleaves & Llewellyn, 2014). Banned PEDs were referred to as "doping means" and the practice of using them as "doping." As of today, doping is considered among the main threats to the values of sport. Since 1999, the PED ban is enforced by the World Anti-Doping Agency (WADA) and is financed by the combined support of the Olympic movement and governments and public authorities (Houlihan, Hanstad, Loland, & Waddington, 2019).

The critical question in this context is *why* the use of PEDs is considered a problem in the first place. In what way and against what values is PED use a threat? What is the rationale for the PED ban?

An immediate response is that doping is cheating: the intentional violation of sporting rules to get an unfair advantage. This is a deontological gut reaction. Doping is unfair. Indeed, the reaction is relevant. As long as the use of a specified PED is banned, using it is cheating. However, referring to fairness is not a satisfactory response to the basic question about the rationale for the ban. The argument can be turned around: legalize PED use, and the cheating problem is solved. Justifying rules with reference to the wrongness of breaking them is a circular argument and gets us nowhere.

A second response is that the use of specified PEDs should be banned due to the risk of harm. Doping is a threat to the value of health. This is a consequentialist or utilitarian response. Extensive use of PEDs such as anabolic-androgenic steroids and synthetic erythropoietin can lead to serious illness and even death. However, the health argument can be challenged, too.

Competitive sport, in particular at elite levels, represents a health hazard in and of itself. Hard and intensive training implies a constant risk for fatigue injuries and burnout. In competition, there is the risk of acute injuries and even death, at least in so-called risk sports such as downhill skiing and combat sports. A principled application of the health argument would lead to a strong revision of many sports and perhaps to abandoning elite sport as a whole.

As an alternative, some scholars argue that the best harm-reduction strategy is regulated legalization (Kayser, Mouron, & Miah, 2007; Kayser & Tolleneer, 2017). In the current situation, secret and black-market doping dominates the scene. The argument then is that athletes should be able to use whatever PED they prefer but under impartial medical control. In practice, however, there are challenges even here. First, impartial and continuous medical control of elite athletes would require far more resources than the current antidoping testing regime. Second, legalizing PED use could exert a problematic coercive effect on athletes (Murray, 1983). With the premise that PEDs actually work, successful careers would depend upon the willingness to use PED with the risk of becoming guinea pigs in more extensive sport systems' quest for success. In Hoberman's (1992) words, extensive PED use is a sign of a "dehumanization of sport."

Another line of reasoning would be to distinguish between different kinds of health risks. This is a regular exercise in the ruling bodies of sport. In female gymnastics, some moves requiring extreme lower back flexibility are banned. In some downhill skiing events, jumps are taken down to reduce the risk of falling. To a large extent, these are risks that are outside of athlete control. Similarly, most PEDs are administered by external expertise and with risk assessments outside of the execution of skills and more or less outside of athletes' impact competence. The risk can be considered irrelevant, whereas athletes' assessment and taking of risk in the execution of their sport are part of the relevant sporting challenge. Such risk differentiation, however, depends upon a more explicit normative view of sport. Thus, in the end, the PED ban hinges on a question of values.

WADA has acknowledged this point. There are three criteria for substances and methods to be evaluated for the prohibited list: evidence of performance enhancement, evidence of potential harm to athletes, and arguments that the means/methods challenge what is referred to as "the spirit of sport" (World Anti-Doping Agency, 2021, pp. 33–34). The first two criteria are descriptive, and the third criterion is normative. However, WADA's definition of "the spirit of sport" is general and vague and open for interpretation. In a culturally heterogeneous sports world, detailed definitions would challenge the consensus. In tight situations of controversial line drawing, on the other hand, there is the need for stronger operational force.

One solution departs from the sketch above of a normative view of sport (Loland & McNamee, 2019). FEON prescribes the elimination of or compensation for inequalities upon which athletes exert little or no impact or control and for which they cannot be claimed responsible. This is the rationale for rules on equality in external conditions, in system strength, and in certain individual characteristics such as age, sex, and body size. The further FEON rationale is found in values, in particular, as suggested by Murray (2019), in values of sporting and human excellence. To Murray, and echoing perspectives from neo-Aristotelian ethics, sporting performances, being the virtuous development of natural talent over time with hard training and effort, signify moral character: courage, resilience, and perfectionism. At its best, elite sport is about admirable enhancement and not just enhancement per se.

Based on these premises, PED use becomes problematic. Different from training, PED interacts with the organism in ways that overrule human "natural" systemic adaptation and can provide a competitive advantage without athlete effort and hard work (Loland, 2018). The responsibility for performance is moved from the athlete to an external support system. This reduces athlete potential for developing human excellence and sport performance as a source of admiration. If this value-based rationale for antidoping is accepted, arguments from fairness and health are revitalized. Doping implies violating justified rules and is cheating, and risks of harm due to doping are to be considered irrelevant as they threaten sporting values.

These premises however can be challenged. One line of critique would pose that the PED ban is based on a reductionist view of human and sporting excellence and a failed vision of being able to distinguish between "natural" and technological performance enhancement (Fouché, 2017). There is no sound rationale for the ban (Savulescu, Foddy, & Clayton, 2004). A further argument is that the use of performance-enhancing biomedical means represents not only a possibility but, at least in some situations, a moral obligation Savulescu (2006). In the future, we have the chance—via innovative technology to enhance our health, our intelligence, our physical and mental capabilities, perhaps our ability of empathy—of living longer, more meaningful, and happier lives. Why should we not take that chance? Elite sport is in many ways in the forefront: the Formula 1 in the race of human enhancement. Provided informed consent and responsible medical support, PED-enhanced athletic performance is recommendable and admirable. Antidoping, just as amateurism, is an anachronistic and paternalistic normative position of the past.

With the rapid development of biomedical means and methods, and with blurred lines between therapeutic and nontherapeutic use, the discourse on PEDs in sport will no doubt continue and pose even tougher challenges when it comes to justification and line drawing than is the case today.

Sport and Sustainability

As is evident by the growing volume of scholarly publications in the past decade (Dingle & Mallon, 2020; McCullough & Kellison, 2017; Wilson & Millington, 2020), an emerging field of value inquiry in sport is that of sport and sustainability. Since the early 1960s, and with the publication of groundbreaking works such as Rachel Carson's (1962) *Silent Spring*, protection of the natural environment has become a public and political priority. With the World Commission on Environment and Development's (1987, p. 8) definition of a sustainable environmental, social, and economic development as one that "meets the needs of the present without compromising the ability of future generations to meet their own needs," the concept was given a mainstream position. In 2015, the UN General Assembly adopted a program of 17 sustainable development goals to be attained by 2030, ranging from extinguishing hunger and poverty via gender equality and 'green' economic growth to climate action on land and sea (United Nations, 2021). Sporting institutions and communities have addressed these goals and developed various sustainability policies and priorities (McCullough, Pfahl, & Nguyen, 2016).

The most challenged field is those of sporting mega-events such as the FIFA World Cup and the Olympic Summer and Winter Games. Mega-events require extensive logistics and construction of infrastructure and exert significant and problematic environmental, social, and economic impacts. International sport organizations such as the International Olympic Committee (2018) respond with elaborate sustainability plans without really convincing their critics (Geeraert & Gauthier, 2018). With the help of a sustainability index, Müller et al. (2021) examined sixteen Olympic events between 1992 and 2000. Overall, no Olympic event scored particularly well. The 2014 Sochi Winter Games and the 2015 Rio Summer Games were at the low end of the scale, whereas the Winter Games in Albertville (1992) and Salt Lake City (2002) were the most sustainable. Interestingly, the 2010 Vancouver Winter Games and the 2012 London Summer Games, promoted as sustainable events and used as showcases for future organizers, scored relatively low.

However, elite sport is not without sustainability possibilities (Barker, Barker-Ruchti, Wals, & Tinning, 2014). Stricter adherence to FEON could enhance inclusion and social justice. Müller et al. (2021) suggest several possibilities for further environmental improvement. A first step is downsizing, primarily by reducing the number of people attending and developing interactive digital spectatorship. A second step is to rotate between organizing cities. One possibility could be that mega-events take place in cities and countries with particular historical roots and legacies: the Summer Olympic Games in Greece, perhaps in ancient Olympia; the Winter Games in Lillehammer, Norway; the soccer World Cup in England, where the game was invented; and so on. To avoid organizational monopoly and disseminate sport expertise and competence globally, there is the possibility, too, of a rotation system of organizing cities over 5- to 10-year cycles.

Sustainability issues are perhaps less discussed but are no less relevant when it comes to amateur and mass sports activities. Their environmental impact is obvious. Transportation to and from training and events (Triantafyllidis, 2018; Triantafyllidis and Darvin, 2021), construction of infrastructure, and an extensive and nonsustainable sporting goods consumer culture pose challenges (Tricarico & Simms, 2021). Post et al.'s (2018) study from the United States is illuminating. Parents pay an annual average of U.S.$1,500 for children's sport club activities, and the higher parents' income and education, the higher likelihood of children's sport club membership. Millington and Wilson's (2016) review of golf demonstrates that adult amateur sports fare no better. With 60 million active players worldwide and more than 30,000 courses in 140 countries, primarily in warm climates with water supply shortages, the ecological footprint is immense.

To borrow an expression from Eriksen (2016): the unlimited sporting quest of growth in participants, sporting goods consumption, performances and records, spectatorship, as well as in profit and prestige, is a sign of *overheating*. Without cooling down with regulations , nonsustainable *runaway processes* will lead to system collapse. Moreover, philosophically inclined critics argue that traditional sustainability definitions are narrowly anthropocentric and build on the impossible premise of sustainable economic and material growth (Hopwood, Mellor, & O'Brien, 2005; Naess, 1993; Stables, 2013). There is the need for radical change guided by non-anthropocentric conceptions that relate to all living beings (biocentrism) and even to all ecosystems, that is the ecosphere (ecocentrism).

An example of a biocentric position is found in Naess's (1989) deep ecological principle of "biospheric egalitarianism." To the deep ecologist, all life forms have equal intrinsic value and an equal right to flourish. If human activities threaten other life forms, from extensive ecosystems, such as the rainforest, to a particular subspecies of insects, human beings have an obligation to withdraw. Or, framed in a sporting context: if Olympic winter sports events challenge local ecosystems, there should be no such events. To the deep ecologist, sustainability implies acting and living in ways that uphold and enhance the richness, diversity, and unity of life.

What are the further implications on non-anthropocentric positions when it comes to sport? Close contact with nature is considered important in the development of ecological consciousness and the disposition to act in sustainable ways. Everyday local leisure physical activity such as cycling, hiking, and running emerge as environmentally friendly, offering the same activity possibilities to future generations as to the current one. Welters's (2019) careful analysis of the ecology of cycling provides a good case study. Cyclists can be eco-movers who, on zero-emission premises, interact in deep and meaningful ways with their environment.

Skill and performance development can be framed within the non-anthropocentric vision of sustainability as well. Traditional sporting rhetoric is often one of struggle and opposition: the skier "overcomes" the force of gravity and "conquers" the mountain, the swimmer struggles to minimize water resistance, the marathoner "fights" fatigue. Andrieu, Parry, Porrovecchio, and Sirost (2018) elaborate on the potential for "ecologization" in human movement: experiences of transcendence of distinctions between mind, body, and the environment. Competent skiers, swimmers, and runners know that mastery is not about combating but rather collaborating with the environment: playing with gravity, gliding through water, and listening to the body.

Another main sustainability critique is related to competition and to the very logic of sport itself. This is a traditional criticism voiced by, among others, Kohn (1992): competition leads to unhealthy individualism, self-esteem is sabotaged, and social relationships are compromised. What can be said of sports in this respect? Loland (2001, 2006) points to two kinds of competitive logic. Record sports are problematic from a sustainability point of view, whereas games are sound. The former kind is defined by performance evaluation in physical-mathematical entities (time, weight, distance) under standardized conditions enabling abstract comparisons independent of time and place: *sports records*. Examples are the running and throwing events in athletics, swimming, and weightlifting. Provided external conditions are kept identical, every new record represents a lost resource for future generations of athletes. Every tenth-of-a-second improvement on a swimming race or a track-and-field running distance is a reduction of the available resources (time) for the next generation of athletes who will have to perform better in objective terms. Record sports are vulnerable to runaway processes and build on the nonsustainable logic of infinite growth in a finite system.

The alternative logic of games is found in netball games and ball games such as tennis and soccer. Performances are not evaluated in exact quantities but in sport-specific and de facto inaccurate units: points, games, sets, or goals. Requirements on standardized conditions are not as strict. Tennis takes place on varied surfaces; soccer pitches can vary in both size and surface. In their outdoor versions, there are no requirements on wind conditions, as in track-and-field record performances. An individual athlete or team performance is always relative to the opposition, and performances are not accurate and comparable above and beyond time and space. There are entertaining discussions on the best tennis player and the best soccer team ever, but there is no objective standard to reach a correct answer. Games offer each new generation of athletes the same possibilities for athletic success as the previous one. The game logic is sustainable.

This does not mean that typical record sports such as track and field should be abandoned. We deal here with classic events based on basic movement patterns: the stride, the jump, the throw. There is the possibility, however, to convert the nonsustainable record logic into the logic of games. Running distances and surfaces can vary from event to event, performance can be measured with a point system related to position as runners pass the finishing line, and the events can be elements of a season series, as in ball games. What is at stake, then, is not the nonsustainable quest for the best *performance* ever, but who wins today and who is the faster *performer* in each particular event or over a season. Within this game logic, future generations will have the same possibilities of meeting their sporting needs as the current generation.

The cooling down of overheated sporting systems takes radical measures but needs in no way to reduce sporting values. On the contrary, and in line with the Suitsian idea of the voluntary acceptance of "unnecessary" obstacles, intelligent constraints are the very core logic of sports. With the current strong impact of external political and commercial interests and with a sports leadership that does not seem to support its internal goods and standards of excellence, the system seems to suffer from the same logic as is found in the record idea: a quest for infinite growth in finite systems.

Studies such as those of Müller et al. (2020) portray a pessimistic image. However, hope, albeit in the context of urgency, remains. There is an environmental slogan pointing out that, given the current state of the world, it is too late to be a pessimist! With sports activism and public concern with sport on the rise, radical change can (and must) come about sooner than we may expect.

CONCLUSION

Sport is a value-driven cultural practice. I have defined and categorized various values *in* and *of* sport and discussed how these values are interpreted within the social and cultural contexts in which sport takes place. A basic distinction runs between what I have called internal values departing from the logic and experiential qualities in the sport itself, and external values, that is, the actual and potential values of sport in society.

A core idea is that the playful logic of sporting games opens for internal, experiential values: fun, joy, excitement, mastery and failure, collaboration and opposition. Sport practice and performance development in line with fair play ideals can facilitate character development and sporting excellence as concrete and embodied expressions of human excellence. In addition, sports have the potential of realizing external values, among them health and well-being, a sense of community and belonging, and sustainable development.

Sport, however, is contested terrain. Sports can be realized as zero-sum games in which whatever is lost by one side is gained by another. Result and performance orientation is associated with immoral and antisocial behavior. In its most explicit entertainment versions, elite sport can express chauvinism, sexism, racism, and violence and can be used politically to "whitewash" the images of problematic political regimes and environmental practices.

Hence, from a value point of view, sports are basically *ambiguous*. Value outcomes depend upon how sports are interpreted and practiced. In a MacIntyrean understanding of social practices, internal values are primary, and external values are secondary. The value potential *of* sport is to be found *in* sport itself.

ACKNOWLEDGMENTS

Thanks to Lawrence Wenner for valuable comments and for all his help in the development of this chapter.

REFERENCES

Andrieu, B., Parry, J., Porrovecchio, A., & Sirost, O. (2018). *Body ecology and emersive leisure*. London: Routledge. https://doi.org/10.4324/9780203704059.

Archetti, E. P. (1999). *Masculinities: Football, polo, and the tango in Argentina*. London: Taylor & Francis.

Barker, D., Barker-Ruchti, N., Wals, A., & Tinning, R. (2014). High performance sport and sustainability: A contradiction of terms? *Reflective Practice, 15*(1), 1–11. https://www.tand fonline.com/doi/abs/10.1080/14623943.2013.868799.

Carson, R. (1962). *Silent spring*. Boston: Houghton-Mifflin.

Chadwick, S. (2018). Can international events really clean up a country's tarnished image? *APPS Policy Forum*. https://www.policyforum.net/sport-washing-soft-power-and-scrubb ing-the-stains/.

Chatziefstathiou, D. (2011). Paradoxes and contestations of Olympism in the history of the modern Olympic Movement. *Sport in Society, 14*(3), 332–344. https://doi.org/10.1080/17430 437.2011.557269.

Coakley, J. (2001). *Sports in society: Issues and controversies (7th ed.)*. New York: McGraw Hill.

Coakley, J. (2015). Assessing the sociology of sport: On cultural sensibilities and the Great Sport Myth. *International Review for the Sociology of Sport 50*(4–5), 402–406. https://doi. org/10.1177/1012690214538864.

Csikszentmihályi, M. (1990). *Flow: The psychology of optimal experience*. New York: Harper and Row.

Dingle, G., & Mallen, C. (Eds.). (2020). *Sport and environmental sustainability*. London: Routledge.

Donnelly, P. (2008). Sport and human rights. *Sport in Society, 11*(4), 381–394. https://doi.org/ 10.1080/17430430802019326.

Eriksen, T. H. (2016). *Overheating. An anthropology of accelerated change*. London: Pluto Press.

Foster, R. J. (2006). From Trobriand cricket to rugby nation: The mission of sport in Papua New Guinea. *International Journal of the History of Sport, 23*(5), 739–758. https://doi.org/ 10.1080/09523360600673138.

Fouché, R. (2017). *Game changer: The techno-scientific revolution in sports*. Boston: Johns Hopkins University Press.

Geeraert, A., & Gauthier, R. (2018). Out-of-control Olympics: Why the IOC is unable to en sure an environmentally sustainable Olympic Games. *Journal of Environmental Policy & Planning, 20*(1), 16–30. https://doi.org/10.1080/1523908X.2017.1302322.

Gleaves, J., & Llewellyn, M. (2014). Sport, drugs and amateurism: Tracing the real cultural origins of anti-doping rules in international sport. *International Journal of the History of Sport, 31*(8), 839–853. https://doi.org/10.1080/09523367.2013.831838.

Goksøyr, M. (2013). Taking ski tracks to the north: The invention and reinvention of Norwegian polar skiing: Sportisation, manliness and national identities. *International Journal of the History of Sport, 30*(6), 563–579. https://doi.org/10.1080/09523367.2012.760998.

Hare, R. M. (1982). *Moral thinking. Its levels, method, and point*. Oxford: Oxford University Press.

Hoberman, J. (1992). *Mortal engines: The science of performance and the dehumanization of sports*. New York: Free Press.

Hopwood, B., Mellor, M., & O'Brien, G. (2005). Sustainable development: Mapping different approaches. *Sustainable Development, 13*, 38–52. https://doi.org/10.1002/sd.244.

Houlihan, B., Hanstad, D. V., Loland, S., & Waddington, I. (2019). The World Anti-Doping Agency at 20: Progress and challenges. *International Journal of Sport Policy and Politics 11*(2), 193–201. https://doi.org/10.1080/19406940.2019.1617765.

Huizinga, J. (1971). *Homo ludens: A study of the play element in culture*. London: Beacon Press.

International Olympic Committee. (2018). Manual on sport and the environment. https://still med.olympic.org/Documents/Commissions_PDFfiles/manuel_sport_environment_en.pdf.

Kayser, B., Mauron, A., & Miah, A. (2007). Current anti-doping policy: A critical appraisal. *BMC Medical Ethics*, *8*(2). https://doi.org/10.1186/1472-6939-8-2.

Kayser, B., & Tolleneer, J. (2017). Ethics of a relaxed antidoping rule accompanied by harm-reduction measures. *Journal of Medical Ethics*, *43*(5), 282–286. https://doi.org/10.1136/medethics-2015-102659.

Kohn, A. (1992). *No contest: The case against competition* (2nd ed.). New York: Houghton Mifflin.

Kretchmar, R. S. (1975). From test to contest: An analysis of two kinds of counterpoint in sport. *Journal of the Philosophy of Sport*, *2*(1), 23–30. https://doi.org/10.1080/00948705.1975.10654094.

Loland, S. (1995). Pierre de Coubertin's Olympism from the perspective of the history of ideas. *Olympika*, *4*, 49–78.

Loland, S. (2001). Record sports: An ecological critique and a reconstruction *Journal of the Philosophy of Sport*, *28*(2), 127–139. https://doi.org/10.1080/00948705.2001.9714608.

Loland, S. (2002). *Fair play in sport: A moral norm system*. London: Routledge.

Loland, S. (2006). Olympic sport and the ideal of sustainable development. *Journal of the Philosophy of Sport*, *33*(2), 144–156. https://doi.org/10.1080/00948705.2006.9714698.

Loland, S. (2018). Performance-enhancing drugs, sport, and the ideal of natural, athletic performance. *American Journal of Bioethics*, *18*(6), 8–15. https://doi.org/10.1080/15265161.2018.1459934.

Loland S. (2020). Caster Semenya, athlete classification, and fair equality of opportunity in sport. *Journal of Medical Ethics*, *46*(9), 584–590. https://jme.bmj.com/content/46/9/584.

Loland, S., & McNamee, M. J. (2019). The "spirit of sport," WADA's code review, and the search for an overlapping consensus. *International Journal of Sport Policy and Politics*, *11*(2), 325–339. https://doi.org/10.1080/19406940.2019.1581646.

MacIntyre, A. (2007). *After virtue: A study in moral theory*. Notre Dame, IN: University of Notre Dame Press.

Macmillan Dictionary Online. (2021a). Character. https://www.macmillandictionary.com/dictionary/british/character#character__25.

Macmillan Dictionary Online. (2021b). Value. https://www.macmillandictionary.com/dictionary/british/value_1?q=values.

Malcolm, D. (2017). *Sport, medicine, and health. The medicalisation of sport?* London: Routledge.

Mangan, A. J. (2000). *Athleticism in the Victorian and Edwardian public schools*. London: Routledge.

McCullough, B. O., Pfahl, M. E., & Nguyen, S. N. (2016). The green waves of environmental sustainability in sport. *Sport in Society*, *19*(7), 1040–1065. https://doi.org/10.1080/17430437.2015.1096251.

McCullough, B. P., & Kellison, T. B. (Eds.). (2017). *Routledge handbook of sport and the environment*. London: Routledge.

McFee, G. 2004. *Sport, rules and values: Philosophical investigations into the nature of sports*. London: Routledge.

McNamee, M. J. (2008). *Sport, virtues, and vices: Morality plays*. London: Routledge.

Millington, B., & Wilson, B. (2016). *The greening of golf: Sport, globalization and the environment*. Manchester, U.K.: Manchester University Press.

Montero, B. J. (2016). *Thought in action: Expertise and the conscious mind*. Oxford: Oxford University Press.

Morgan W. J. (1994). *Leftist theories of sport: A critique and a reconstruction.* Champaign: University of Illinois Press.

Morgan, W. J. (2020). *Sport and moral conflict.* Philadelphia, PA: Temple University Press.

Müller, M., Wolfe, S. D., Gaffney, C., Gogishvili, D., Hug, M., & Leick, A. (2021). An evaluation of the sustainability of the Olympic Games. *Nature Sustainability, 4,* 340–348. https://doi.org/10.1038/s41893-021-00696-5.

Murray, S. (2018). *Sports diplomacy: Origins, theory and practice.* London: Routledge.

Murray, T. H. (1983). The coercive effect of drugs in sport. *Hastings Center Report, 13*(4), 24–30. https://www.jstor.org/stable/3561718.

Murray, T. H. (2019). What's the point of sport? *International Journal of Sport Policy and Politics, 11*(2), 355–364. https://doi.org/10.1080/19406940.2019.1581647.

Naess, A. (1989). *Ecology, community and lifestyle.* Cambridge: Cambridge University Press.

Naess, A. (1993). Sustainability: The integral approach. *Paradigms, 7*(1), 66–72.

Nansen, F. (1952). *På ski over Grønland.* Oslo: Aschehoug.

Ntoumanis, N., & Standage, M. (2009). Morality in sport: A self-determination theory perspective. *Journal of Applied Sport Psychology, 21*(4), 365–380. https://doi.org/10.1080/10413200903036040.

Online Etymology Dictionary. (2021). Fair. https://www.etymonline.com/word/fair.

Orwell, G. (1945/2022). *The sporting spirit.* London: The Orwell Foundation. https://www.orwellfoundation.com/the-orwell-foundation/orwell/essays-and-other-works/the-sporting-spirit/.

Owen, M. M. (10 April 2019). *How Albert Camus found solace in the absurdity of football.* The Independent. https://www.mmowen.me/camus-absurd-love-of-football.

Post, E. G., Green, N. E., Schaefer, D. A., Trigsted, S. M., Brooks, M. A., McGuine, T. A., Watson, A. M., & Bell, D. R. (2018). Socioeconomic status of parents with children participating on youth club sport teams. *Physical Therapy in Sport, 32,* 126–132. doi:10.1016/j.ptsp.2018.05.014.

Rawls, J. (1971). *A theory of justice. Cambridge.* Mass: Harvard University Press.

Reid, H. (2012). The soul of an Olympian: Olympism and the ancient philosophical ideal of Aretē. In H. Reid & M. Austin (Eds.), *The Olympics and Philosophy* (pp. 86–98). Lexington: University Press of Kentucky.

Ring, C., & Kavussanu, M. (2018). The impact of achievement goals on cheating in sport. *Psychology of Sport and Exercise, 35,* 98–103. https://doi.org/10.1016/j.psychsport.2017.11.016.

Russell, J. S. (2018). A critique of conventionalist broad internalism. *Sport, Ethics and Philosophy, 12*(4), 453–467. https://doi.org/10.1080/17511321.2018.1497079.

Savulescu, J. (2006). Justice, fairness, and enhancement. *Annals of the New York Academy of Sciences, 1093*(1), 321–338. https://doi.org/10.1196/annals.1382.021.

Savulescu, J., Foddy, B., & Clayton, M. (2004). Why we should allow performance enhancing drugs in sport. British Journal of Sports Medicine, *38*(6), 666–670. http://dx.doi.org/10.1136/bjsm.2003.005249.

Serrano-Durá, J., Molina, P., & Martínez-Baena, A. (2020). Systematic review of research on fair play and sporting competition. *Sport, Education and Society, 26*(6), 648–662, https://doi.org/10.1080/13573322.2020.1786364

Shields, D. L., & Bredemeier, B. L. (2007). Advances in sport morality research. In G. Tenenbaum & R. C. Eklund (Eds.), Handbook of sport psychology (pp. 662–684). John Wiley & Sons, Inc.

Shields, D. L., & Bredemeier, B. L. (2008). Sport and the development of character. In L. P. Nucci, T. Krettenauer, & D. Narvaez (Eds.), *Handbook of moral and character education* (pp. 500–519). New York: Routledge.

Shields, D. L., & Bredemeier, B. L. (2014). Promoting morality and character development. In A. G. Papaioannou & D. Hackfort (Eds.), *Routledge companion to sport and exercise psychology: Global perspectives and fundamental concepts* (pp. 636–649). London: Routledge.

Shields, D. L., Funk, C. D., & Bredemeier, B. L. (2016). Testing contesting theory: Conceptual metaphors and prosocial behavior. *Psychology of Sport and Exercise, 27*, 213–221. https://doi.org/10.1016/j.psychsport.2016.09.001.

Simon, R. L. (2000). Internalism and internal values in sport. *Journal of the Philosophy of Sport, 27*(1), 1–16. https://doi.org/10.1080/00948705.2000.9714586.

Spitzer, G. (2006). A case study of state-sponsored mandatory doping in East Germany. In S. Loland, B. Skirstad, & I. Waddington (Eds.), *Pain and injury in sport: Social and ethical perspectives* (pp. 109–126). London: Routledge.

Stables, A. (2013). The unsustainability imperative? Problems with "sustainability" and "sustainable development" as regulative ideals. *Environmental Education Research, 19*(2), 177–186. https://doi.org/10.1080/13504622.2012.729813.

Stewart, C. (1999). Syncretism and its synonyms: Reflections on cultural mixture. *Diacritics, 29*(3), 40–62. http://www.jstor.org/stable/1566236.

Suits, B. (2014). *The grasshopper: Games, life, and utopia.* Peterborough, CA: Broadview Press.

Tännsjö, T. (1998). Is our admiration for sports heroes fascistoid? *Journal of the Philosophy of Sport, 25*(1), 23–34. https://doi.org/10.1080/00948705.1998.9714566.

Travers, A. (2006). Queering sport: Lesbian softball leagues and the transgender challenge. *International Review for the Sociology of Sport, 41*(3–4), 431–446.

Trendafilova, S., & McCullough, B. P. (2018). Environmental sustainability scholarship and the efforts of the sport sector: A rapid review of literature. *Cogent Social Sciences, 4*(1). https://doi.org/10.1080/23311886.2018.1467256.

Triantafyllidis, S. (2018). Carbon dioxide emissions research and sustainable transportation in the sports industry. *Carbon, 4*(4), 57. https://www.mdpi.com/2311-5629/4/4/57.

Triantafyllidis, S., & Darvin, L. (2021). Mass-participant sport events and sustainable development: Gender, social bonding, and connectedness to nature as predictors of socially and environmentally responsible behavior intentions. *Sustainable Science, 16*, 239–253. https://doi.org/10.1007/s11625-020-00867-x.

Tricarico, E., & Simms, A. (2021). *Badvertising: Sweat not oil: Why sport should drop advertising and sponsorship from high-carbon producers.* New Weather Institute, KR Foundation, Rapid Transition Alliance. https://static1.squarespace.com/static/5ebd0080238e863d04911b51/t/605b60b09a957c1b05f433e2/1616601271774/Sweat+Not+Oil+-+why+Sports+should+drop+advertising+from+high+carbon+polluters+-+March+2021v3.pdf.

United Nations. (2021). United Nations' sustainable development goals. https://www.un.org/sustainabledevelopment.

Wacquant, L. (2003). *Body and soul: Notebook of an apprentice boxer.* New York: Oxford University Press.

Waddington, I., & Smith, A. (2009). *An introduction to drugs in sport: Addicted to winning?* London: Taylor and Francis.

Welters, R. (2019). *Towards a sustainable philosophy of endurance sport: Cycling for life.* Cham, Switzerland: Springer Nature.

Wilson, B., & Millington, B. (2020). *Sport and the environment: Politics and preferred futures.* Bingley, U.K.: Emerald Publishing.

World Anti-Doping Agency. (2021). World anti-doping code. https://www.wada-ama.org/sites/default/files/resources/files/2021_wada_code.pdf.

World Commission on Environment and Development. (1987). *Our common future.* New York: Oxford University Press.

CHAPTER 3

SPORT, IDEOLOGY, AND POWER

BEN CARRINGTON

ON the front cover of the March 11, 2013, edition of the American magazine *Sports Illustrated*, the National Football League (NFL) commissioner Roger Goodell is seen dressed in a suit, sitting on a throne made of swords, his two hands tightly grasped around a silver sword that is pointing down and into the ground. Goodell looks powerful as he stares directly at the reader. Next to the commissioner, and with a nod to the popular HBO series *Game of Thrones*, the accompanying text reads, "No. 1 Roger Goodell: Sits atop The Throne of Games." In the accompanying lead article, the journalist Steve Rushin (2013, p. 42) noted:

> The power that runs through sports isn't physical, despite all those power hitters and power forwards, power plays and power alleys. . . . So, what constitutes power in the 21st century? Where does it come from? And why aren't our most powerful sportsmen the men who actually play sports?

In addition to Goodell, the other top five "most powerful people in sport" (which was, more accurately, largely focused on American sports) were David Stern, then National Basketball Association (NBA) commissioner; the billionaire, founder and owner of Anschutz Entertainment Group Philip Anshultz; John Skipper, then president of ESPN; and Bud Selig, then commissioner of Major League Baseball. The rest of the top 50 included Nike chairman Phil Knight (#9); Robert Kraft, owner of the NFL New England Patriots (#12); then Fédération Internationale de Football Association president Sepp Blatter (#16); Bernie Ecclestone, then president and CEO of Formula One (#22); and Mark Cuban, owner of the NBA's Dallas Mavericks (#48).

Tellingly, the list contained not a single active athlete. There were only three women on the list: Alison Lewis and Sharon Byers, heads of marketing for Coca-Cola North America, who collectively shared the 41st spot, and Cindy Davis, then president of Nike Golf, at 46. There were just three African Americans on the list, which included President Barack Obama at 44 and Michael Jordan, as the owner of the NBA Charlotte Bobcats, filling out the list at 50. In fact, there were more white men named Mark in the top 50 than women of any race or African Americans. Although *Sports Illustrated* intimated in 2013 that this would be an annual list, they have never, to date, repeated this power accounting exercise. Neither did they redundancy explicitly answer the sociological questions the magazine promised to address, namely: What constitutes power in the 21st century, where does power come from, and how much power do athletes have compared to those who run, organize, own, and shape the present and future of sports? This chapter takes up the charge to define the concept of power and the important and related idea of ideology in the context of sports.

As the *Sports Illustrated* quote above alludes to, we are used to associating sports with powerful *bodies*, that is, the muscular, athletic, and, at times, poetic forms of physical movement and human performance that define our perceptions of sports. What is sometimes referred to as "embodiment" is the idea that our sense of selfhood—who we understand ourselves to be, our "identities"—are formed in and through our bodies (see Hargreaves & Vertinsky, 2007). Think, for example, of how we categorize people into racial categories, based largely upon the ways in which we "read" other bodies and certain observable physical markers, and how those racial categories are themselves internalized and performed and become part of our own racial identities. The chapter also considers the idea of sporting bodies, not just in the (individual) corporeal sense of the physical bodies just described, but in terms of institutions and bureaucracies, the *corporate bodies* and wider structures of sport that are sometimes more powerful than even the most physically powerful and gifted individual athlete in shaping the goals, values, and practices of sport. The chapter briefly surveys key foundational texts within sports studies that have sought to situate sporting bodies in relation to wider social structures and processes, such as the state, sports media, and political economy, and highlights more recent studies that show how sports are shaped by wider discourses, especially those associated with race, class, and gender. Sport, as Michael Messner (2002, p. 137) puts it, "is a dynamic story of power at play," and it is the details of that dramatic story the chapter seeks to explore.

ISSUES

Defining Power

Before looking at how theorists of sport have analyzed the relationship between sport, ideology, and power, it is necessary to better understand the key terms "power" and "ideology." Let's take "power" first. Power is one of the most important concepts in the social sciences. It is also a term, unlike "ideology," that many people use in their everyday lives. We typically think of power as both something that people *possess* and also a *relational* attribute *between* people, groups, or individuals. Thus, we might refer to somebody, a celebrity perhaps, or a politician or our boss at work as "*having* power" or "*holding* power." This implies that such people possess power, almost like an object, that they can then use or wield over those with less or no power. Everyday language thus expresses this idea of *power as an object* that some people have or own and that others do not and, perhaps also, the idea that there is an unequal *distribution of power*, with some having more of it than others. In a hierarchical and spatial sense, we often refer to "those *in power*" (typically politicians and senior administrators working within bureaucracies, for example), or sometimes power is used as a collective descriptor for such people (i.e., "*the* powerful").

In all of these senses, there is an implication that those *with* power or *in* power are able to dictate and shape the lives of others. In this context, *authority*, especially when those people "in positions of authority" are seen to be there legitimately, is also a form of power. There is, perhaps, an implicit normative assumption that those "with power" do not always wield their power in a fair and equitable manner. That is to say, those with power seek to keep it, and those without power (the "powerless") have a life of struggle against "the powerful" as a result of this imbalance. Such terms also suggest that the powerful, regardless of whether they are involved in politics or the military or big business or the media or the legal system, have shared interests, come from similar backgrounds, go to the same schools and universities, join the same private clubs, marry and befriend each other, and become further isolated from the rest of society. "The powerful" thus increasingly act in ways that solidify their own power at the expense of others and have formed, as the American sociologist C. Wright Mills (1956) argued many decades ago, a "power elite." For Mills, the power elite "occupy the strategic command posts of the social structure, in which are now centered the effective means of the power and the wealth and the celebrity which they enjoy" (p. 4).

A number of questions emerge at this point, questions that have concerned the minds of intellectuals for centuries. Given the vast array of writings on power, I will simply highlight some of the key issues in this section, so that we can see, later in the chapter, how these different approaches have informed contemporary debates and approaches to thinking about power within sports studies. The first observation is that some definitions of power imply that power is a zero-sum game, meaning that there is a finite amount of power that exists and that one person or group having more necessarily means that the other person or group has less. Further, we might want to consider whether power is about the ability and capacity to control and organize one's own life or the ability to dictate and shape (and perhaps control) the lives of others—or both? The discussion becomes further complicated when we try to locate power, to understand where power is, that is, to ask where power *resides*. Is it located *in* particular places or parts of society, and if power is *situated*, how did it get there? We sometimes refer, for example, to the "seat of power," which we generally associate with government, that is to say, the formal, institutionalized operation of state power, where the important social and economic issues of the day are debated, where bills are passed and laws enacted that govern how populations live and behave.

As the last example suggests, there is one very obvious source of power: *politics*. We might think of politics as the formalized arena in which various actors within civil society, such as political parties, candidates running for office, and social movements, contest for access to power, that is, the ability to use the power of the state to secure their desired goals. In addition to *political* power, the centralized mechanisms of state power that regulate and govern social life within a particular territory, the sociologist Michael Mann (2013) argues that there are three other major sources of power: *economic* power, *military* power, and *ideological* power. *Economic* power derives from the human need to produce, transform, and distribute the raw materials of nature that become the manufactured goods and services that sustain human life and the complex social systems we abstractly call "society." The interconnected (global) division of labor, trade between and within nations, as well as the circulation of capital, media, services, and goods produce intense forms of economic power. This form of power, industrial capitalism, shapes everything from the power of markets to the power and role of trade unions, the power of multinational corporations, and the power of capital markets. *Military* power relates to the social organization of concentrated and often lethal violence (as well as the *threat* of lethal force), perhaps one of the ultimate and most recognizable forms of power. Nation-states often have influence in the world in direct proportion to their military strength (Japan and Germany being two exceptions to this general rule). Political commentators refer to certain countries as "superpowers" not just due to their population size or the strength of their economy but also due to the size and sophistication of a particular country's military apparatus, actual or imagined, such as a country's possession of nuclear armaments. *Ideological* power, for Mann, can be understood in relation to the human desire to find meaning in life, the ritualistic practices that then shape and give public expression to our societal values, and the ethics by which we conduct our lives. Ideologies, Mann suggests, become especially salient and important during uncertain times when ideologies come to embody our hopes, fears, and desires. I will come back to the question of ideology shortly.

Another way to think about power is less from a top-down, or macro, perspective, but rather to think about the agency that people have over their own lives and in their communities, and how people, potentially, are active in shaping history, regardless of whether or not they hold formal "positions of power" within their societies, such as judges, politicians, military leaders, or CEOs of major corporations. Further, rather than thinking about power as an object or property that some have more of than others or that is used, like an instrument, we might consider how power is productive (rather than regressive), a dimension of all social relations and interactions. Mann (2013), for example, defines power succinctly as the capacity to get others to do things that they would not otherwise do; thus in order to achieve our goals we enter into power relations involving both cooperation and conflict. Such a conception of power suggests that power is capacious, not just centrally located, say, "in the state," but ever present in our daily micro practices. Power, to return to the idea of embodiment, is not just external but "internal" too, found in and exercised through our bodies, or what we might call "biopolitics" (Foucault 2010). The idea here is that power is constantly being made and remade and always "at play," even if we do not always recognize this and see it as such.

We might also consider, for example, that even within what Erving Goffman (1968) called "total institutions," people still have some degree of agency over the meanings they give to their daily routines. Within these institutions, such as prisons and psychiatric hospitals ("asylums"), where there is near constant surveillance of those inside, where inhabitants are largely cut off from the outside world and have their every behavior controlled and heavily restricted, individuals still have the ability to resist power. Here, resistance often takes the form of symbolic gestures or radical refusals to accept the legitimacy of the institution's power. Thus, even under the most extreme cases of institutional domination, namely slavery, humans can still exert power by rebelling, working more slowly, stealing from and mocking their owners, using mimicry and gossip, engaging in fantasy, and even, ultimately, employing suicide as an act of rebellion in order to deny the slave master their "property rights" over the bodies of the enslaved.

Why do people accept unequal power relations, especially if, by doing so, they are exploited? Is it possible that one of the effects of power is its ability to deny its own existence? It seems likely that those who are dominated fail to see the reality of such imbalances because those in power are able to persuade those without power either that this state of affairs is natural (the way things should be) or that the unequal distribution of resources, a consequence of power inequalities, is justified and morally defensible, perhaps on religious

(God-ordained orders) or biological (genetic inferiority) grounds. As Steven Lukes (2005, pp. 143–144) puts it, a dimension of power is "the capacity to secure compliance to domination through the shaping of beliefs and desires, by imposing internal constraints under historically changing circumstances." This brings us to the question of "ideology."

Defining Ideology

If "power" turns out to be a complicated term, then trying to define "ideology" is equally tricky. The British sociologist Anthony Giddens (1983) once remarked that ideology is one of the most contested terms within social theory. Giddens adds, "If there are such things as contested concepts, and if there were a prize for the most contested concept, the concept of ideology would very nearly rank first. Nobody can even decide on how to pronounce it!" (p. 18). Whether one says *i*-de-ology or *id*-e-ology, the term encompasses a broad range of meanings and definitions, some not compatible with others. According to the literary theorist Terry Eagleton (2007), the most common definitions include (but are not limited to) the process of production of meanings, signs, and values in social life; a body of ideas characteristic of a particular group or class; ideas which help to legitimate a dominant political power; false ideas which help to legitimate a dominant political power; systematically distorted communication; that which offers a position for a subject; forms of thought motivated by social interests; identity thinking; socially necessary illusions; the conjuncture of discourse and power; the medium in which conscious social actors make sense of their world; action-oriented sets of beliefs; the confusion of linguistic and phenomenal reality; semiotic closure; the indispensable medium in which individuals live out their relations to a social structure; and the process whereby social life is converted to a natural reality (pp. 1–2).

As Eagleton alludes to in this list, a key aspect of ideology is the idea that it refers, generally, to the ways in which we see, understand, and interpret the world around us, our beliefs about society and our place within it. Or, put even more succinctly, how we think society works. In some contexts, ideology has a negative connotation, implying mistaken beliefs or perhaps a worldview driven by partisan political beliefs rather than an objective, realist view. Think, for example, of how, in an argument, someone might try to discredit the opposing position by accusing them of being "ideological", which, of course, assumes that the person making such a charge is free from ideology, at least when understood as bias. All worldviews and our claims about society are "ideological" to the extent that they rely upon assumptions concerning how the world works (or should work) and that such claims are clearly shaped by our own direct experiences, social background and upbringing, education, consumption of media and political values (even if that is denied).

As the last point suggests, a further complication to the question of ideology concerns how ideology is formed. Do we each, as individuals, form our own interpretations of the world, through direct, firsthand experience, in a way that is largely autonomous from outside influences, or is our worldview fundamentally shaped by the communities and societies we grow up in and the media that we consume? If the latter is the case, and if those communities and societies are unequal in some way, and if the media too are immersed in structures of domination, then might those power relations also shape and inform how we see the world? Or put more starkly, might the worldview we have (and perhaps even our consciousness, who we *think* we are) be the product *not* of our own, autonomous experiences of the world, but a compromised version of how the dominant classes in society *want us* to see the world? That is to say, "knowledge," rather than emerging unfiltered from an individual's own mind, is itself linked to wider power dynamics; thus knowledge may even be understood as an *effect of power*. A good example of how supposedly scientific expertise and impartial knowledge can often become intertwined with power is explored in Edward Said's (2003, p. 5) *Orientalism,* where he shows how the "Orient" as an idea was invented within the Occidental imagination as a precursor and justification for Western imperialism: "The relationship between Occident and Orient is a relationship of power, of domination, of varying degrees of a complex hegemony" (on the question of the Western geopolitics of knowledge and how modernity is intertwined with coloniality, see Mignolo & Walsh, 2018).

In *The German Ideology* Karl Marx (Marx & Engels, 1970, p. 64) provocatively argued that

> the ideas of the ruling class are in every epoch the ruling ideas: i.e., the class which is the ruling material force of the society, is at the same time its ruling intellectual force. The class which has the means of material production at its disposal, has control at the same time over the means of mental production, so that thereby, generally speaking, the ideas of those who lack the means of mental production are subject to it.

What has been termed the "dominant ideology thesis" (see Abercrombie & Turner, 1978) is the radical proposal that the worldview of the dominant group or class in a society becomes the default window through which everybody else makes sense of the world. The ideas of the ruling class become "common sense" for everyone. Thus, it is argued, such views inevitably validate the existing unequal system by either denying inequalities exist (the system is fair and meritocratic!) or by convincing the dominated that such conditions are justified and necessary (you deserve to be punished, live a lowly life because you did not work hard enough and have poor morals and self-destructive behavior as a result).

Although this approach has merit, many scholars question this "top-down" theory of ideology, implying, as it does, that many people suffer from a *false consciousness* in being unable to see the world as it really is and who are seemingly incapable of articulating, let alone fighting for, their own self-interests. Instead, scholars have argued that ideology should be seen as a contested terrain, in which the dominant group's worldview and interests are not simply imposed upon the rest of society, but that the subordinate group's interests and needs have to be acknowledged and even met to some degree if dominant logics are to be (partially) accepted (Hall, 1983). This more nuanced attempt to understand the production and reproduction of ideology highlights that people often challenge, mock, and confront the ideas and views of elites, and rarely simply accept them *en bloc*. While it may be true that dominant groups attempt to impose their worldview onto others, this attempt is not always successful. In fact, history is replete with symbolic, cultural, and linguistic forms of resistance, the weapons of the weak, as anthropologist James Scott (1987) puts it, that suggest ideological formations are marked by ongoing and constant struggles between various blocs to achieve a "commonsense" view of the world. The outcomes of such struggles cannot be known in advance, but only delineated through careful research and historical analysis.

As this brief overview has shown, the relationship between power and ideology is complicated. We might say that ideology is the mechanism through which power is reproduced. Ideology enables power to shape our lives, influence our behavior and even our very subjectivity and consciousness. But ideology might also be understood as the site where power is confronted, challenged, and resisted. This approach, which has been popular in sports studies, draws upon the ideas of Antonio Gramsci (2005) and his suggestion that ideological struggle can best be understood as a battle for "hegemony." The dominant economic ruling class tries to produce a "commonsense" view of the world and to have this accepted by the working classes. This process is never final but always in flux. Rather than viewing ideology as false belief, a more refined definition would see ideology as a mix of partial truths and partial distortions; it is our only way to "access" the world, but one that is not always reliable. We might further suggest that for the power elites (in Mills's terms) to be challenged, there must first be a contestation at the level of ideology, wherein the very legitimacy of the existing system and the associated hierarchies are called into question, perhaps when the "gap" between lived experiences and how we are told the world works becomes too big. It is in this context that culture, and popular culture in particular, becomes important to theorize. Culture is where meaning making, identity production, communication of shared beliefs and values, and the varied practices of everyday life occur. In the following sections, I outline how scholars have studied and theorized sports in relation to these questions of culture, power, and ideology.

Approaches

Theorizing Sport, Power, and Ideology

Not surprisingly, given its central focus on theorizing power and inequality, some of the earliest critiques of sport, power, and ideology emerged from critical thinkers associated with Marxism (Carrington & McDonald, 2009). In the late 19th and early 20th century, socialist political leaders in Europe were concerned with what they perceived to be the depoliticizing effects of popular culture, including sports, on the critical consciousness of the working class. Of worry was the emerging role of commercial entertainment, or what Theodor Adorno (2001) would later call "the cultural industries." Socialist leaders saw the commercial provision of leisure, of which sport was a central part, as a capitalist ploy to deaden the revolutionary spirit by promoting blind allegiance to non-class identities, be they the local factory or town or nationally based identifications (Carrington & Andrews, 2013). For late 19th-century socialists, the leisure industries, noted Chris Waters (1990, p. 29),

> exploited workers who provided entertainment for the masses; it directly threatened the livelihood of those who produced leisure activities in less-commercial ways; it encouraged homogeneity; it threatened older, radical ways of organizing leisure; it fostered a dependence on its products, thereby blocking the development of socialist cultural alternatives; and, finally, it began to redefine recreation as a mere purchasable commodity.

Worse, sport's very logic, which celebrates individual success over collective endeavor, competition over solidarity, and violence and aggression over contemplation and reflection, was seen as capitalist ideology made manifest. As Karl Kautsky (1902, p. 102) argued, the English working class rejected revolutionary struggle as their class emancipation "appears to them as a foolish dream. Consequently, it is football, boxing, horse racing and opportunities for gambling which move them the deepest and to which their entire leisure time, their individual powers, and their material means are devoted." Rather than being a realm of freedom, sport, the French situationist Jean-Marie Brohm (1976) famously claimed, is a *prison of measured time* that leads to alienation of the sporting body, as athletes are encouraged to view their own bodies as tools, a place where sports crowds are turned into fascistic cheering machines, and the creative spirit of play transformed into corporatized and commodified modes of highly rationalized production for capital accumulation and profit maximization. In short, according to orthodox Marxists, sport in capitalist societies serves the ideological interests of the ruling, economic class. The power of the capitalists is maintained via the distorting prism of sports, which proclaims to show how sports (like society) are governed by meritocratic values, that everyone is treated equally, and that those who get to the top, or win, deservedly did so, due to their own hard work, perseverance, and talent. In reality, such ideals are just that, idealizations that do not correspond to the lived reality of sports, which, Marxists argue, is actually saturated with violence and cheating that necessarily create great harm to the human body and to society more widely. As Richard Gruneau (2017, p. 150) notes, Marxist critiques highlight sport's ideological "dark side," specifically, how the

> intensity of training in high-level sport enables sadistic bodily regimes and their sadomasochistic acceptance. . . . As archaic models for mass rallies, and in their rigid hierarchies of organization and production, sports contain anti-democratic and authoritarian principles and promote blind obedience to authority.

As considered in the previous section, while the dominant ideology thesis undoubtedly reveals the hidden dimensions of sport's relationship to structures of power and practices of inequality, it has been accused of fueling a one-dimensional, overly pessimistic reading of sport that both overstates the degree of domination and underplays the forms of creative resistance, joy, and agency of those involved in sports. Rather than reading the cultural industries (and sport as a part of that) as simply serving the ideological needs of capitalism, scholars influenced by the field of cultural studies have instead understood popular culture (and sport within this), as a site of struggle. That is to say, culture is understood to be a contested terrain wherein dominant ideologies are indeed found but where they are also resisted, a site where people in their daily lives create alternative ways of being and meaning making that challenge capitalism (Carrington, 2009). Cultural studies emerged out of adult and workers' educational associations in Britain during the 1940s and 1950s and latterly became more widely known through the writings of scholars such as Richard Hoggart, E. P. Thompson, Raymond Williams, and Stuart Hall (Carrington, 2001). Cultural studies approaches attempt to construct a more nuanced and nonmechanistic reading of (popular) culture, power, and ideology. Raymond Williams (1977, p. 68) notes that cultural studies set out to challenge the "dogmatic retention" of an account of ideology as simply "false consciousness" toward a formulation that acknowledged the complexity of how ideology was actually reproduced. As Stuart Hall (1981, pp. 232–233) put it in his seminal essay, "Notes on Deconstructing 'The Popular,'" and that draws upon a Gramscian hegemony approach:

> The study of popular culture keeps shifting between these two, quite unacceptable, poles: pure "autonomy" or total incapsulation. . . . I think there is a continuous and necessarily uneven

and unequal struggle, by the dominant culture, constantly to disorganize and reorganize popular culture; to enclose and confine its definitions and forms within a more inclusive range of dominant forms. There are points of resistance; there are also moments of supersession. This is the dialectic of cultural struggle. In our times, it goes on continuously, in the complex lines of resistance and acceptance, refusal and capitulation, which make the field of culture a sort of constant battlefield. A battlefield where no once-for-all victories are obtained but where there are always strategic positions to be won and lost.

In the 1980s and early 1990s, numerous scholars attempted to apply and extend these approaches to popular culture and more specifically to the study of sports and leisure (Carrington & McDonald, 2009). Key texts in this period include Jennifer Hargreaves's (1982) edited collection *Sport, Culture and Ideology*, Richard Gruneau's (1983/1999) *Class, Sports and Social Development*, Garry Whannel's (1983) *Blowing the Whistle: The Politics of Sport*, John Hoberman's (1984) *Sport and Political Ideology*, John Clarke and Chas Critcher's (1985) *The Devil Makes Work: Leisure in Capitalist Britain*, John Hargreaves's (1986) *Sport, Power and Culture*, Stephen Jones's (1988) *Sport, Politics and the Working Class*, and George Sage's (1990) *Power and Ideology in American Sport*. Although there were theoretical differences in approach among these writers, some—like Clarke and Critcher, Jennifer Hargreaves, and Whannel, for example—would likely have identified their work within the cultural studies tradition, while others, like Gruneau, are situated closer to the political economy tradition of critical Marxist thought, and Hoberman and Sage arguably embrace a more classical liberal position; these texts shared a broad commitment to developing historically grounded and complex theorizations of the ways in which sports could be understood as sites for the play of power and ideology, a cultural practice where agency and resistance, constraints, and domination could often be found occurring at the same time.

This "turn to hegemony theory" enabled sports studies scholars to avoid both the naïve idealism of conservative accounts of sport that posited the inherently integrative and positive functionality of sports on the one hand, and, on the other, the economic determinism of orthodox Marxist approaches that tended, as discussed earlier, to read sport solely through the negative prism of bodily alienation of athletes, false class consciousness on the part of working-class fans, and sport's general ideological capitulation to the values and norms of capitalism. As Critcher (1986, p. 335) notes, "the way out of the dichotomy between liberal idealism and vulgar Marxism lies in a model of sport as a relatively autonomous cultural practice within more general hegemonic class relations." Sport, in short, was viewed as a contested terrain wherein the play of power could be found, a cultural site of *attempted* class domination "from above" as well as the location for *potential* forms of symbolic resistance "from below." John Hargreaves (1986, pp. 6–7) summarizes this point by arguing that "sport was significantly implicated in the process whereby the growing economic and political power of the bourgeoisie in nineteenth-century Britain was eventually transformed into that class's hegemony in the later part of the century." In other words, as Hargreaves's book title (*Sport, Power and Culture*) indicates, sport was to be located as a central and contested facet of culture, one that was immersed within the broader circuits of (predominantly although not exclusively) classed power relations.

Similarly, for Gruneau, the interrelationship of sport and class needs to be situated in the context of the study of social development. "Put most simply," Gruneau (1983/1999, p. xxix) states, "I argue that any examination of the changing nature of human possibilities in social development must be drawn ineluctably to a very old sociological problem: the problem of class inequality and domination. It was this problem that defined many of the

personal troubles and public issues of citizens in the earliest stages of liberal democracy."
Tracing the dialectical relationship between freedom and autonomous play on the one hand
and domination and cultural constraint on the other, Gruneau theorizes sport as a potentially liberatory space for self-actualization. He brings to the fore the "fundamental paradox" (p. 3) of play, namely that it appears as both an *independent and spontaneous* as well
as a *dependent and regulated* aspect of human agency. By extension, sport is viewed as a
relatively autonomous institutionalized form that embodies play's central paradox: it is a
space of freedom, creativity, and human expression that can come into being only in the
context of formalized rules that govern and delimit its boundaries, ethically, spatially, and
temporally. Gruneau argues for a materialist account of sport that is "sensitive to the dialectical relationships between socially structured possibilities and human agency" (p. 27).
This requires an understanding and analysis of the historical conditions within which these
dialectical relationships have taken shape in order to map, in precise detail, the nature
and consequences of these moments of freedom and limitation. Thus, as with Hargreaves,
Gruneau utilizes hegemony to think through the play of power *within* sport: "the concept
of hegemony allows for the idea of reflexive human agency in a manner not shared by functionalist models of inculcation or socialization" (p. 60).

Hargreaves, Gruneau, and other hegemony theorists demonstrate that sport is a potential modality for freedom and human actualization, even if this is not always or is rarely
fully realized. Sport is understood as a contested terrain wherein competing ideologies
of domination and resistance can be found. Nothing is guaranteed in terms of political
outcomes. Sport is neither a freely chosen leisure pursuit somehow divorced from the material conditions of its existence nor reducible to those very same economic determinants
that would otherwise, and in the last instance, collapse all forms of culture-making back
into the logic of capital accumulation. Coercion as well as consent is ever-present. As John
Hargreaves (1986, p. 7) puts it:

> Power resides more in the ability of the hegemonic group to win consent to, and support for,
> its leadership, and on its ability to pre-empt and disorganize opposition, so that the major
> forces in society are unified behind the hegemonic group and forceful, coercive measures
> against opposition to the pattern of hegemony acquire legitimacy as well. Hegemony is
> achieved through a continuous process of work: potential resistance is anticipated, organized
> opposition is over-come and disarmed by broadening and deepening the base of support.

Following this line of argument, Gruneau (1983/1999, p. 17) suggests that sports are "active
constitutive features of human experience" that should be analyzed in the context of the
struggles over the limits and possibilities of the rules and resources through which they are
themselves defined. Thus, depending "on their association with divergent material interests,
the meanings of sports, like all cultural creations, have the capacity to be either reproductive or oppositional, repressive or liberating" (p. 17).

While much of the earlier work on sport centered around questions of class and capitalism,
sports are clearly an important domain for the production and reproduction of gender relations. (For a fuller discussion of the limited engagement with race from the authors discussed
above and the lack of a critical analysis of colonialism as a key form of Western power, see
Carrington, 2010.) In fact, some have argued that as a site of popular culture, sport is perhaps the key social institution for the production and maintenance of gender ideologies. As
Messner (1992) notes in *Power at Play: Sports and the Problem of Masculinity*, sports are seen
as a "male preserve," a bulwark against wider "feminizing" changes in society, associated

with the impact of feminist social movements and increased women's rights. By equating force and aggression with physical strength, Messner argues, "modern sport naturalized the equation of maleness with power, thus legitimizing a challenged and faltering system of masculine domination" (p. 15). In this context, the entry of women into sports and even the idea of the "athletic woman" challenges dominant ideas and hegemonic ideals about masculinity and femininity. Jennifer Hargreaves (1989, p. 135) observes:

> "Femininity" in sport is not a static phenomenon, but a concept encompassing varied images of women which can be understood as manifestations of struggles over meanings which are in a constant state of flux and negotiation. By their entry into more sports, and through the successes of competitive athletes, women are themselves changing "common-sense" thinking about their biology and potential in sport.

Along these lines, Birrell (2000) identifies four key areas that feminist scholars of sport, working broadly within this Gramscian and cultural studies–inspired critique of sport, have focused on, namely (1) the production of an ideology of masculinity and male power through sport; (2) the media practices through which dominant notions of women are reproduced; (3) physicality, sexuality, and the body as sites for defining gender relations; and (4) the resistance of women to dominant sport practices. In the next section I look at some specific examples of this work.

An ongoing debate within much of this work has been whether the entry of women into male-dominated sports does in fact challenge extant dominant gender ideologies or whether it further entrenches gender binaries and hierarchies. Put another way, is the goal, from a (liberal) feminist perspective to simply get more women into (heteronormative) sports, or to challenge *and change* the existing cultures of sport, with sport's traditional emphasis on aggression, violence, competition, and an often dehumanizing ethic of win-at-all-costs? As Paul Willis (1982, p. 128) has argued,

> To accept that it is a worthwhile endeavor to push female performance closer to that of a male, even to surpass it, admits at a stroke the stigma of femininity and the legacy of that male eminence which coined the standards. So, no matter how the actual gap is closed, there is an equal and opposite reaction which expands the cultural and ideological resonance of that gap. Put another way, "the battle" so to speak, is conceded as soon as it is started by starting it.

Instead, Willis suggests, sports should be developed which emphasize "[h]uman similarity and not dissimilarity, a form of activity which isn't competitive and measured, a form of activity which expresses values which are indeed immeasurable, a form of activity which is concerned with individual well-being and satisfaction rather than comparison" (p. 128). In the next section I look in more detail at contemporary debates and highlight research in these areas.

Debates

Sports studies has a rich array of research that has sought to explore the concepts of power and ideology across the traditional sociological domains of race, gender, sexuality, nation, and class, and more recently areas concerning the environment, trans and nonbinary identities, diaspora, and disability. The "power of sport" as a force for social good, sport's ability to reproduce dominant power relations or to act as a site of contestation, as well as the potential of sport to serve as a space for identity formation, human creativity, and joy

have been carefully investigated. I selectively survey some of this literature below and conclude with some of the ongoing debates within the fields.

Media

The media have been a key subject for much of the research on sport and power, especially given the centrality of the mediated sports complex (Wenner, 1989) to how sports are
consumed and the immense power of the sports media industries in reshaping sports themselves. As Boyle and Haynes (2000, p. 15) note in *Power Play: Sport, the Media and Popular
Culture*, "the media are becoming increasingly powerful in driving the form and content of
modern sport and its relationship with its supporters." As a result, they argue, it is vital to

> recognize the importance of the political economy of media sport as well as the ideological
> and political dimension to media coverage of sporting forms. By political in this context, we
> mean the ways in which power is organized in society, and the ways in which formulations of
> power are both maintained and often challenged by groups and individuals. (p. 21)

These arguments have been taken up by other scholars of sports media, tracing, variously, the political economy of global sports media, the impact of sports mega-events,
questions of aesthetics and media texts, market differentiation, advertising and promotional culture, the cultural economy of sports celebrity and spectacle, the cultural politics of representation, audience consumption and fandom, and the profound changes
to the sports media landscape that social media, fantasy sports, sports gambling, and
eSports have brought about (for example, see Jackson, 2015, Rowe, 2015; Smart, 2005;
Wenner, 1998, 2013; Wenner & Billings, 2017; Whannel, 2009). Sport, as Rowe (2015,
p. 578) notes, "through its combination of popular exposure and claimed political innocence, became deeply insinuated into the politics of discourse and representation, its
treatment in the media always invoking, overtly or covertly, regimes and mechanisms of
power." For example, McKay and Rowe (1987) have examined the ideological effects of
the Australian sports media in legitimizing hegemonic masculinity, capitalist rationality,
and nationalistic militarism, while marginalizing and trivializing alternative ideologies
of how sport might be made and played. Delgado (2003) also explores the issue of politics and representation and the ways various media "fuse" sport with politics by framing
sporting contests with wider political meanings and symbolism, in the case study of the
1998 football World Cup game between the U.S.A. and Iran. Scholars in this area have
demonstrated not just the power of the media industries in affecting sports but the crucial ways in which all sports are *mediated*. That is to say, the ways in which our engagement with and understanding of sports at all levels are powerfully shaped by the prism
of the sports media complex and the role of the media as an especially significant site for
the reproduction of ideologies of race and gender in particular, some examples of which
I highlight below.

Race

Sports remain an important space for the reproduction of racialized ideologies
(Carrington, 2012). The idea that humanity can be divided into biologically distinct
subgroups, called "races," and that there is a hierarchy among the Races of Man, has

been one of the most destructive ideologies for human civilization. Sports, due to the seemingly obvious "facts of difference" that we see when certain racial groups excel at particular sports, has, at times, helped to reinforce the pernicious "idea of race," or, as the anthropologist Ashley Montagu (1997) titles his book, "man's most dangerous myth." The world of sports, as Hoberman (1997, p. xxiii) suggests, has become "an image factory that disseminates and even intensifies our racial preoccupations." Sports have been segregated by race in many Western countries, often formally and explicitly in countries like the U.S.A. and more informally in countries like Great Britain. And yet, as writers like the Trinidadian intellectual C. L. R. James (1963) has shown, sports have also been a site of politics, of struggles for freedom from colonial domination, and a space of empowerment for racial and ethnic minorities in the face of racial discrimination. Sports can be understood as a racial project that makes and remakes race not just within sports but within wider society as well; sport sometimes challenges racial ideologies, and sometimes it reproduces them, depending on the political and social circumstances of the moment. The racial signification of sports means that sporting arenas are always engaged in race making (Carrington, 2010).

Many authors have tried to better understand the racial signification of sports (Carrington, 2010) in various contexts and historical periods. For example, Daniel Burdsey (2011) shows how the embrace of color-blind ideology in sport (he uses the example of cricket in England) works to deny the existence of extant racism, particularly directed at British Asians, by reframing forms of racial abuse among teammates as just "banter" and "jokes." Haslerig, Vue, and Grummert (2020), in their discussion of racialized media discourse of American college football players, provide an analysis of the differential narratives produced by commentators when describing Black and white players. They show that inhuman abilities and characteristics are encoded onto the bodies of Blacks, further reinforcing white supremacist ideology. Foy and Ray (2019), in a similar study of American college basketball players, focus on the power of "colorism," that is, the processes of discriminating against darker-skin people and the positive associations with lighter skin tone, even within Black populations. Foy and Ray show that sports announcers were more likely to positively discuss the performance and mental abilities of lighter-skin players and to focus on the physical characteristics of darker-skin players.

Parry, Cleland, and Kavanagh (2020) have found similar evidence of "racial folklores" and dominant racial ideologies being reproduced by both the media and fans when discussing Black athletes in the Australian media, while Harrison (2013) has shown how structural and symbolic forces in skiing produce racialized discourses of belonging and geographies of exclusion that restrict the participation and representation of Black skiers. Developing on from arguments concerning the white Eurocentrism of the Winter Olympics made earlier by King (2007), Harrison demonstrates how skiing's "hegemony of whiteness" results in a form of racial segregation in the leisure-sports-tourism industries that reflects wider patterns of segregation within U.S. society. The regulation, surveillance, and controlling of Black athletic bodies have been analyzed by researchers who have demonstrated how the policing of Black bodies has been reproduced in sports such as the NBA and the NHL through dress codes, often invoking Black criminality as the pretext for the new rules and sanctions (see also Leonard, 2006; Lorenz & Murray, 2014). Schultz (2005) has similarly analyzed the differential ways in which the sports media have treated and discussed Black female athletes such as Serena Williams in ways that ultimately reproduce the dominant racialized order of women's tennis.

Gender

Scholars have shown how women's sports has been central to the wider feminist movement to enable women to control their own bodies and physicality. As such, sports are deeply immersed in wider gender relations of cultural power. As Jennifer Hargreaves (1994, p. 289) notes:

> [T]here are no authentic, absolutely autonomous sports for women; but neither are women simply passive recipients of culture, duped by men, or impossibly constrained by circumstances. Although a strong tendency exists for sports to reproduce dominant culture, the potential also is present to transform it. Women are involved in the dialectic of cultural struggle—they are manipulated *and* resistant, determined by circumstances *and* active agents in the transformation of culture.

Messner (2011), in his work on youth sports, shows there has been a shift since the 1970s away from the "hard essentialism" of hegemonic gender ideologies that prohibited girls' and women's entry into sports, toward what he calls a "soft essentialism" that allows for a liberal feminist language of "choice" for girls but not for boys, who are still expected to conform to more traditional gender roles in which sport remains axiomatic.

Washington and Economides (2016) in their essay "'Strong Is the New Sexy': Women, CrossFit, and the Postfeminist Ideal," argue that new sports and leisure spaces offer a broader range of possibilities for how the female body is represented, yet even here, certain archetypes of attractive heteronormative femininity abound. Schrijnder, Amsterdam, and McLachlan's (2021) study of a CrossFit gym in Holland seems to confirm these findings. Schrijnder et al. suggest that the new fitness movements are nominally more gender neutral and provide equal opportunities for men and women to engage in sporting activities without the "hard essentialism" of traditional sports cultures that scholars like Hargreaves and Messner discuss. In fact, CrossFit allows and encourages women to engage in behavior that was typically reserved for men. Yet the researchers found that traditional gender norms, such as compulsory heterosexuality and the male gaze, continue within these spaces, limiting the ability of such spaces to "undo gender."

As these examples show, sports studies scholarship continues to examine the power struggles of female athletes in gaining access to sports as well as shifting gender and sex identities. This is a discussion not just about more "flexible" notions of femininity and masculinity; increasingly sport is the space where debates around the very category of "woman" (and by extension "man") itself are taking place. From deliberations about the standing and status of intersex athletes to the highly politicized discussions regarding trans athletes competing in recreational and elite sports and scientific and ethical arguments over appropriate levels of testosterone in female athletes, sport has become the primary modality through which gender and sex are understood and publicly discussed, demonstrating the power of sport in remaking ideologies of gender and sex (and their interrelationship) more generally.

CONCLUSION

"Who Runs the Game? Where the Real Power Lies" was the February 2021 front cover lead of *The Cricketer* magazine. Under the headline a cricket ball was displayed, with the world's continents etched into the red leather, the ball itself turned into a globe. The accompanying articles noted the geopolitical shift in power (from the "West" to the "East"), away from England and the traditional centers of cricket power (the England and Wales Cricket Board and the Marylebone Cricket Club) and toward the South Asian subcontinent, and to India in particular, where "powerful politicians" and "heavyweight businessmen" are shaping the game in the 21st century. Another article focused on the rising "star power" of celebrity cricketers like India's Virat Kohli, while another examined the lack of current and former cricket players in formal positions of power within the institutions of cricket, reflecting, in some ways, the list produced by *Sports Illustrated* back in 2013. The best professional cricketers, like elite athletes around the world, have gained power in terms of visibility, media exposure, and financial reward, yet they remain, like most fans, on the outside when it comes to making decisions about how sports are structured, organized, and run. Having powerful athletic bodies, we might conclude, does not necessarily translate into broader dimensions of power in being able to directly shape the conditions under which those athletic bodies perform.

This chapter has highlighted how sports are deeply interconnected with wider questions of power and ideology. Rather than seeing sports as "outside" the power relations associated with politics, the economy, the state, and the media, sport, as a social institution, should be understood as a central site of social reproduction and, occasionally, social disruption. It has been argued that sports "have the capacity to be either reproductive or oppositional, repressive or liberating" (Gruneau, 1983/1999, p. 17). As Toby Miller (2009, p. 190) has suggested, "Sport is a key site of pleasure and domination. . . . It involves both the imposition of authority from above and the joy of autonomy from below. It exemplifies the exploitation of the labor process, even as it delivers autotelic pleasures." It is worth noting, however, that some writers, committed to a more orthodox reading of Marx, have argued that the ideas of theorists like Gramsci, discussed earlier, have been misused by sociologists of sport, and others, who have placed too much emphasis on notions of domination by (negotiated) consent rather than by (violent) coercion and have been too eager to find examples of "resistance" in sporting cultures that are focused on non-class identities. Alan Bairner (2007), for example, calls for a return to a more orthodox reading of Gramsci, power, and violence that places more emphasis on political and material class struggles rather than on non-class "cultural" struggles. Bairner states:

> [T]here is a real need for the rehabilitation of Marxism at the level of theory, as well as for Marxist sociologists to stand up and pronounce publicly on the economic injustices of our age. As for Marxist sociologists of sport, the time has surely come for fewer apologies and for a more robust defense of the subtleties of historical materialism as properly understood. If that means retrieving the argument that our identities can best be understood in terms of economics, then so be it. (p. 33)

It is perhaps not necessary to accept the argument that all identities can best be understood, in the last instance, through the prism of economics—which appears to be a reductionist argument that has been challenged by feminists and critical theorists of race for many years now—in order to acknowledge that questions of political economy must remain central to any serious analysis of sports, power, and ideology. The "weight" given to the economic may vary, and even how "the economic" is understood and theorized relative to the state, culture, and civil society will likely remain a matter of debate and argument. But it is clear that figuring out how sports are organized and played has to include taking into considera-tion the issue of "the economic" and that analysis must be historically grounded within the current conjuncture of social forces—cultural, political, and economic.

Such a conjunctural analysis must be sensitive to the ways in which power is inherent in all relationships, is "polymorphous" and found in bureaucracies like the state but also in the "interdependencies" among people (Dunning, 1999). We need to think carefully about what Sallie Westwood (2002) refers to as the differing *modalities* and *sites* of power, in terms of not just class and power, as discussed above, but also the racialized, gendered, and sexualized forms of power. We similarly need to think in terms of *spatial* and *visual* power, topics that are especially important to scholars of sport given the centrality of both embodiment and spectacle to contemporary sports practices.

The challenge for students and scholars of sports interested in the dialectic of cultural struggle through sports will be how to center questions of power in our analyses, avoiding, on the one hand, the pessimistic dismissal of sports as completely ideologically compromised and, on the other, the celebratory and overly optimistic endorsements of sports as positive mechanisms for social change and resistance (Sugden & Tomlinson, 2002). Getting this balance right is important as the current postcolonial period of late capitalism is marked by a remarkable rise in athlete activism, a resurgence of fan-based politics, and a challenging of the accepted ways of organizing sports that requires careful study, theorization, and empir-ical investigation. It is clear that "power from below" (Piven, 2007) remains an ever-present possibility in (re)shaping society and that sports are increasingly playing a key role in the wider processes of social change, political struggle, and ideological contestation.

REFERENCES

Abercrombie, N., & Turner, B. (1978). The dominant ideology thesis. *The British Journal of Sociology, 29*(2), 149–170.

Adorno, T. (2001). *The culture industry: Selected essays on mass culture*. London: Routledge.

Bairner, A. (2007) Back to basics: Class, social theory, and sport. *Sociology of Sport Journal, 24*(1), 20–36.

Birrell, S. (2000). Feminist theories for sport. In J. Coakley & E. Dunning (Eds.), *The hand-book of sports studies* (pp. 61–76). Thousand Oaks: Sage.

Boyle, R., & Haynes, R. (2000). *Power play: Sport, the media and popular culture*. Edinburgh: Edinburgh University Press.

Brohm, J. M. (1976). *Sport: A prison of measured time*. London: Ink Links.

Burdsey, D. (2011). That joke isn't funny anymore. Racial microaggressions, color-blind ide-ology and the mitigation of racism in English men's first-class cricket. *Sociology of Sport Journal, 28*(3), 261–283.

Carrington, B. (2001). Decentering the centre: Cultural studies in Britain and its legacy. In T. Miller (Ed.), *A companion to cultural studies* (pp. 275–297). Oxford: Blackwell.

Carrington, B. (2009). Sport without final guarantees: Cultural studies/Marxism/sport. In B. Carrington & I. McDonald (Eds.), *Marxism, cultural studies and sport* (pp. 1–12). London: Routledge.

Carrington, B. (2010). *Race, sport and politics: The sporting black diaspora*. London: Sage.

Carrington, B. (2012). Introduction: Sport matters. *Ethnic and Racial Studies, 35*(6), 961–970.

Carrington, B., & Andrews, D. L. (2013). Introduction: Sport as escape, struggle and art. In D. Andrews & B. Carrington (Eds.), *A companion to sport* (pp. 1–16). Oxford: Blackwell.

Carrington, B., & McDonald, I. (Eds.). (2009). *Marxism, cultural studies and sport*. London: Routledge.

Clarke, J., & Critcher, C. (1985). *The devil makes work: Leisure in capitalist Britain*. Basingstoke: Macmillan.

Critcher, C. (1986). Radical theories of sport: The state of play. *Sociology of Sport Journal, 3*(4), 333–343.

Delgado, F. (2003). The fusing of sport and politics: Media constructions of U.S. versus Iran at France '98. *Journal of Sport and Social Issues, 27*(3), 293–307.

Dunning, E. (1999). *Sport matters: Sociological studies of sport, violence and civilization*. London: Routledge.

Eagleton, T. (2007). *Ideology: An introduction*. London: Verso.

Foucault, M. (2010). *The birth of biopolitics: Lectures at the Collège de France, 1978 -1979*. London: Picador.

Foy, S., & Ray, R. (2019). Skin in the game: Colorism and the subtle operation of stereotypes in men's college basketball. *American Journal of Sociology, 125*(3), 730–785.

Giddens, A. (1983). Four theses on ideology. *Canadian Journal of Political and Social Theory, 7*(1–2), 18–21.

Goffman, E. (1968). *Asylums: Essays on the social situation of mental patients and other inmates*. New York: Penguin.

Gramsci, A. (2005). *Selections from the prison notebooks*. London: Lawrence and Wishart.

Gruneau, R. (1983/1999). *Class, sports and social development*. Amherst: University of Massachusetts Press.

Gruneau, R. (2017). *Sport and modernity*. Cambridge: Polity Press.

Hall, S. (1981). Notes on deconstructing the "popular." In R. Samuel (Ed.), *People's history and socialist theory* (pp. 227–240). London: Routledge and Kegan Paul.

Hall, S. (1983). The problem of ideology: Marxism without guarantees. In B. Matthews (Ed.), *Marx: A hundred years on* (pp. 57–85). London: Lawrence & Wishart.

Hargreaves, J. A. (Ed.). (1982). *Sport, culture and ideology*. London: Routledge and Kegan Paul.

Hargreaves, J. A. (1989). The promise and problems of women's leisure and sport. In C. Rojek (Ed.), *Leisure for leisure: Critical essays* (pp. 130–149). Basingstoke: Macmillan.

Hargreaves, J. A. (1994). *Sporting females: Critical issues in the history and sociology of women's sport*. London: Routledge.

Hargreaves, J. A., & Vertinsky, P. (Eds.). (2007). *Physical culture, power, and the body*. London: Routledge.

Hargreaves, J. E. (1986). *Sport, power and culture*. Cambridge: Polity Press.

Harrison, A. K. (2013). Black skiing, everyday racism, and the racial spatiality of whiteness. *Journal of Sport and Social Issues, 37*(4), 315–339.

Haslerig, S. J., Vue, R., & Grummert, S. E. (2020). Invincible bodies: American sport media's racialization of Black and white college football players. *International Review for the Sociology of Sport, 55*(3), 272–290.

Hoberman, J. M. (1984). *Sport and political ideology*. Austin: University of Texas Press.

Hoberman, J. M. (1997). *Darwin's athletes: How sport has damaged Black America and preserved the myth of race*. Boston: Mariner Books.

Jackson, S. J. (2015). Assessing the sociology of sport: On media, advertising and the commodification of culture. *International Review for the Sociology of Sport, 50*(4–5), 490–495.

James, C. L. R. (1963). *Beyond a boundary*. Durham, NC: Duke University Press.

Jones, S. G. (1988). *Sport, politics and the working class: Organised labour and sport in inter-war Britain*. Manchester: Manchester University Press.

King, C. R. (2007). Staging the Winter Olympics: Or, why sport matters to white power. *Journal of Sport and Social Issues, 31*(1), 89–94.

Leonard, D. J. (2006). The real color of money: Controlling Black bodies in the NBA. *Journal of Sport and Social Issues, 30*(2), 158–179.

Lorenz, S. L., & Murray, R. (2014). "Goodbye to the gangstas": The NBA dress code, Ray Emery, and the policing of Blackness in basketball and hockey. *Journal of Sport and Social Issues, 38*(1), 23–50.

Lukes, S. (2005). *Power: A radical view*. Basingstoke: Palgrave.

Mann, M. (2013). *The sources of social power: Vol. 4. Globalizations, 1945–2011*. Cambridge: Cambridge University Press.

Marx, K., & Engels, F. (1970). *The German ideology*. New York: International Publishers.

McKay, J., & Rowe, D. (1987). Ideology, the media, and Australian sport. *Sociology of Sport Journal, 4*(3), 258–273.

Messner, M. (1992). *Power at play: Sports and the problem of masculinity*. Boston: Beacon.

Messner, M. (2002). *Taking the field: Women, men, and sports*. Minneapolis: University of Minnesota Press.

Messner, M. (2011). Gender ideologies, youth sports, and the production of soft essentialism. *Sociology of Sport Journal, 28*(2), 151–170.

Mignolo, W., & Walsh, C. (2018). *On decoloniality: Concepts, analytics, praxis*. Durham, NC: Duke University Press.

Miller, T. (2009). Foucault and the critique of sport. In B. Carrington & I. McDonald (Eds.), *Marxism, cultural studies and sport* (pp. 181–194). London: Routledge.

Mills, C. Wright (1956). *The power elite*. Oxford: Oxford University Press.

Montagu, A. (1997). *Man's most dangerous myth: The fallacy of race*. Walnut Creek: AltaMira Press.

Parry, K. D., Cleland, J., & Kavanagh, E. (2020). Racial folklore, Black masculinities and the reproduction of dominant racial ideologies: The case of Israel Folau. *International Review for the Sociology of Sport, 55*(7), 850–867.

Piven, F. F. (2007). Can power from below change the world? *American Sociological Review, 73*(1), 1–14.

Rowe, D. (2015). Assessing the sociology of sport: On media and power. *International Review for the Sociology of Sport, 50*(4–5), 575–579.

Rushin, S. (2013, March 11). The kingdoms of sport. *Sports Illustrated*, 40–51.

Sage, G. H. (1990). *Power and ideology in American sport. A critical perspective*. Champaign: Human Kinetics Publishers.

Said, E. (2003). *Orientalism*. London: Penguin Books.

Schrijnder, S., Amsterdam, N. van, & McLachlan, F. (2021). "These chicks go just as hard as us!" (Un)doing gender in a Dutch CrossFit gym. *International Review for the Sociology of Sport, 56*(3), 382–398. https://doi.org/10.1177/1012690220913524.

Schultz, J. (2005). Reading the catsuit: Serena Williams and the production of Blackness at the 2002 U.S. Open. *Journal of Sport and Social Issues, 29*(3), 338–357.

Scott, J. (1987). *Weapons of the weak: Everyday forms of peasant resistance*. New Haven, CT: Yale University Press.

Smart, B. (2005). *The sport star: Modern sport and the cultural economy of sporting celebrity*. London: Sage.

Sugden, J., & Tomlinson, A. (Eds.). (2002). *Power games: A critical sociology of sport.* London: Routledge.

Washington, M. S., & Economides, M. (2016). "Strong is the new sexy": Women, CrossFit, and the postfeminist deal. *Journal of Sport and Social Issues, 40*(2), 143–161.

Waters, C. (1990). *British socialists and the politics of popular culture 1884–1914.* Stanford, CA: Stanford University Press.

Wenner, L. A. (Ed.) (1989). *Media, sports, and society.* London: Sage.

Wenner, L. A. (Ed.). (1998). *MediaSport.* London: Routledge.

Wenner, L. A. (Ed.). (2013). *Fallen sports heroes, media, and celebrity culture.* Bristol: Peter Lang.

Wenner, L. A., & Billings, A. C. (Eds.). (2017). *Sport, media and mega-events.* London: Routledge.

Westwood, S. (2002). *Power and the social.* London: Routledge.

Whannel, G. (1983). *Blowing the whistle: The politics of sport.* London: Pluto Press.

Whannel, G. (2009). Between culture and economy: Understanding the politics of media sport. In B. Carrington & I. McDonald (Eds.), *Marxism, cultural studies and sport* (pp. 66–88). London: Routledge.

Williams, R. (1977). *Marxism and literature.* Oxford: Oxford University Press.

Willis, P. (1982). Women in sport in ideology. In J. Hargreaves (Ed.), *Sport, culture and ideology* (pp. 117–135). London: Routledge and Kegan Paul.

CHAPTER 4

···

SPORT, POLICY, AND POLITICS

···

MICHAEL P. SAM

THE subject of policy and politics occupies an important place in the study of sport and so-ciety. One reason for this is that policies continually address the delicate balance of values within a society (Lindblom, 1959). A policy, for example, to exempt elite athletes from com-pulsory military service illustrates an enduring dilemma between the need to "treat likes alike" and the need to recognize a diverse population with different needs. Likewise, a code of conduct policy for athletes can reveal the extent to which we value collective interests (to protect commercial/public property) versus individual rights (to protect free speech). Seen in this light, policies reflect the political struggles behind having to rank, balance, or other-wise allocate priority to what we value (Doern & Phidd, 1992; Sam, 2003).

As an empirical research subject, policy is a tangible yet notoriously broad concept since it rarely reflects a singular activity. For example, while a policy may refer to a concrete rule and regulation (such as a policy against sexual harassment), it can also be a commitment to some future action, as when the government promises $X billion to support a major sport event bid. To complicate matters, specific programs or services (e.g., scholarships or athlete cash-award schemes) are also considered policies because they are brought in to induce particular behaviors (e.g., to encourage young athletes to either delay or pursue tertiary education). Generally, then, policies represent public commitments to an issue or problem and provide the impetus for subsequent changes to organizations, budgets, programs, and practices.

This commitment often requires the mobilization of a variety of organizations. A commitment to "active communities" for example, can encompass different areas of policy, including the improvement of recreational facilities, the availability of affordable housing, and access to a range of healthcare services. Likewise, a policy commitment to Olympic success or "talent identification" might necessarily involve the coordination of many agencies and organizations, including schools, businesses, regional/municipal governments, universities, and charities/foundations. Whether these organizations are all equally committed to these goals represents a persistent challenge for policymakers (Sam, 2011). Yet importantly, public authorities often also commit to inaction (a policy decision in its own right). This is evident, for example, in relation to sport and the betting and alcohol industries, where policy links are likely to remain unchanged despite their contradictions.

This chapter begins with a review of the recurring themes and persistent issues in the field. The breadth of recent research testifies to the advances that have taken place since the *International Journal of Sport Policy and Politics* was first devoted to the subject of sport policy and its political climates in 2009. Given the quantity of valuable research and analysis that has focused on this nexus, any review such as the one put forward here is necessarily selective and should not be seen as exhaustive of the issues at play.

ISSUES

With that disclaimer, I will focus on sport as comprising its own stand-alone state-sponsored sector. Following Houlihan (2005), I focus on the roles of government and their effects rather than on the policy activities of international federations or the International Olympic Committee. Unfortunately, this provides limited opportunity to consider important policy issues related to sport, such as physical education policy, the public subsidy of sports stadia, or national broadcasting policies. However, these face many of the same issues in terms of distribution, regulation, and governance which are considered below. The key issues that follow are sufficiently broad in that many of their key elements can be applied in these related contexts.

Elite Sport versus Sport-for-All: The Politics of Priorities

Insofar as policy ascribes political and resource priorities (who gets what, when, and how), it is unsurprising that much of the literature on sport policy focuses on the cleavage between elite and grassroots sport (the latter generally taken to mean "sport-for-all" and/or community/mass participation). Here, the fundamental question surrounds the extent to which authorities (i.e., governments and their agencies, national sport organizations, etc.) prioritize or privilege some concerns over others. This question derives its importance from the ongoing nature of debates among stakeholders and the significant resource distribution decisions that result from them.

At the very broad country or national level, this distributional aspect to the formulation and implementation of sport policy is a useful starting point for analysis. The relative emphasis on elite versus grassroots has become one of the key dependent variables in comparing different sport systems and organizational structures (Green, 2006; Houlihan, 1997; Nicholson, Hoye, & Houlihan, 2010). This kind of analysis points to a level of convergence in state systems and their tendency to devote increasing resources to elite sport (Houlihan & Green, 2008). Yet, despite the apparent convergence in what sport systems look like, there remains considerable variability, with ongoing change and adjustment clearly evident. Even in Australia, one of the first Anglo-Saxon nations to truly commit to a state-sponsored centralized system of elite athlete development (Stewart, Nicholson, Westerbeek, & Smith, 2004), there have been pronounced criticisms levied at the overemphasis on garnering medals (Crawford & Independent Sport Panel, 2009). Whether changes to the balance in emphasis given to elite versus grassroots sports actually materialize (and how) has become important to investigate, not least because such changes can signal transformations in the distributions of authority and resources to various organizations, programs, and budgets (e.g., Houlihan & White 2002).

Distributional issues like this draw in a number of important features of public policy, most notably the power of *organized interests*, including politicians, the business elite, and the emerging (or entrenched) cadre of professional experts that include administrators and sport scientists. Despite being a very small part of any federal/state/provincial budget (compared to health and education), elite sport maintains a particular appeal for elected officials. Indeed, it has been dubbed an "irresistible priority" for states (Houlihan, 2011, p. 367), and the tendency clearly reflects the jingoistic desires for politicians to legitimize and gain support for their government and party ideologies (Allison, 2005). However, in countries where sport has relative autonomy from the state (e.g., Sweden, Norway), such political influence is much more muted, with the sport system itself often operating as a kind of social movement that must wrestle with issues of elitism within its own ranks (Andersen & Ronglan, 2012; Bergsgard, Houlihan, Mangset, Nodland, & Rommetvedt, 2007; Fahlén & Stenling, 2016). Further, in places where sport is developed through a (relatively autonomous) federated network of national, regional, and local organizations, the tension between elite and grassroots sport has given rise to an expanding community of quasi-advocacy organizations that variously attempt to connect both sets of interests (cf. Dowling & Washington, 2017; Sam & Schoenberg, 2020). For instance, both the Canadian Sport for Life (CS4L) group and the Canadian Centre for Ethics in Sport (CCES) support high performance sport, as well as sport-for-all. For CS4L the connection is advanced by promoting physical literacy and lifelong participation, while for the CCES, elite and sport-for-all are linked by its anti-doping program and advocacy of "safe" sport for everyone.

However, within each of these systems and their priorities, other divisions along lines of race, (dis)ability, class, and gender (Comeau, 2013) can readily become flashpoints in the course of framing public policy. That there are such diverse and competing interests at play draws attention to the inherently rhetorical and contested terrains of sport policy. Debates about the values of elite sport versus sport-for-all in fashioning priorities raise fundamental questions about the value of sport in advancing public health, national unity, economic growth, diversity, or community development. By and large, pronouncements about the importance of national unity tend to buttress high performance sport, while sport-for-all is supported for reasons of health promotion (Grix & Carmichael, 2011). These legitimations (Chalip, 1996), ideas (Sam, 2003), or policy paradigms (Sam & Jackson, 2004) are important to identify because they underscore a range of important research questions around the veracity of the claims (Coalter, 2007) and their downstream effects. One claim often made in an attempt to tie grassroots with elite sport, for instance, is the idea of a "demonstration effect"—that watching elite athletes can inspire the public to take up participation (Hogan & Norton, 2000). Yet, even though the evidence supporting this causal connection is weak, the idea that high performance sport leaves behind valuable "legacies" is a powerful rhetorical device often used to justify increased investment in the lead-up to major events (Weed et al., 2015). Notably, criticisms of such causal connections most often fall into the domain of academics because all stakeholders in the elite-grassroots divide need these "convenient fictions" to be upheld (see Donnelly, 2010, p. 85). For instance, Houlihan and White (2002, p. 67) suggest that despite the dubiousness of the demonstration effect, stakeholders found it useful to foster a "strong link between the interests of the national governing bodies, schools and the local authorities" while maintaining the notion of a unified sports development policy.

Regulation: The Politics of Control

A second key area of sport policy focuses on the regulatory measures that are put in place to prevent unwanted elements in sport, such as doping, match-fixing, abuse, and corruption. Whereas the tensions between elite and grassroots sport speak to policy priorities and resourcing issues, the defining feature for regulatory policies is *control* (Majone, 1994). While largely invoked to reduce unwanted individual behaviors, regulatory policies themselves are also increasingly aimed at the systems of organizations that render the behaviors more likely (see Hong, 2016; Hoye, Nicholson, & Houlihan, 2010; Waddington & Møller, 2019).

An important aspect of regulation thus concerns the nature of the "regimes," that is, the collection of institutions and organizations that share responsibility for setting standards, monitoring, and doling out punishments for noncompliance (Gray, 2019; Tak, Sam, & Jackson, 2018b). Scholarly interest in regimes stems from the considerable diversity seen in national/local contexts, sports, and their associated norms. But focus on regimes also necessarily draws attention to the inability of global agencies such as the World Anti-Doping Agency (WADA) to "go it alone" and tends to illuminate the increasing need for regulatory policies to be harmonized across state boundaries (Houlihan & Preece, 2007).

Another distinguishing feature of regulatory policies concerns the particular tools/technologies that may be deployed to control behaviors. These "policy instruments" (Bemelmans-Videc, Vedung, & Rist, 1998) can range from voluntary/noncoercive strategies (e.g., information campaigns, codes of conduct) to more obtrusive/coercive interventions (e.g., sanctions, "whereabouts" schemes for doping regulation). At the heart of these debates are normative questions around the power of the state (in partnership with non-state actors like WADA) to influence the affairs of autonomous organizations and the extent of their authority in suspending individual freedom. With respect to the latter, an important political element in such regulatory measures concerns the consideration of individual rights and civil liberties (Efverström, Ahmadi, Hoff, & Bäckström, 2016; Houlihan, 2004). "Whereabouts" policies, such as those that require athletes to report on their exact location throughout the year for the purposes of doping control, are controversial on the grounds of individual autonomy and rights to self-determination (Hanstad & Loland, 2009). In today's state of affairs, when sporting interests are under increasing scrutiny for a growing number of other integrity issues (e.g. bullying, harassment), the insistence that sport can (and should be left to) self-regulate has become an increasingly tenuous position (e.g., Fahlén, Eliasson, & Wickman, 2015). Although policy may be seen as a symbolic form of commitment, the contentious political issues behind regulation nearly always concern how much intervention is appropriate and/or legitimate (Stone, 1997; Tak, 2018).

As one might expect, much of the research concerning regulatory policies in sport focuses on evaluation and the propensity (or failure) for interventions to shape behaviors (e.g., Houlihan, 2014; Møller & Dimeo, 2014; Tak, 2018; Waddington & Møller, 2019). However, within such assessments, it is also understood that regulatory measures can have effects beyond those that are intended. Over time, regulation can institutionalize the existing roles and responsibilities of the various stakeholders and, by extension, affirm who is to blame for failures and which organization(s) should be responsible for fixing a problem (Tak, Sam, & Jackson, 2018a). This, in turn, raises the possibility that, when faced with a new problem (such as harassment or bullying), authorities might seek to reproduce aspects of an existing regulatory regime, with unanticipated results. Indeed recent proposals for an international surveillance system to prevent abuse and promote athlete welfare (Kerr & Kerr, 2020) are perhaps likely to eventuate for this reason, though with unknown consequences.

Governance: The Politics of Modernization

If governance is the "purposive means of guiding and steering" a community (Kooiman, 1993), it follows that the search for effective governance is a persistent policy concern. The pursuit of effectiveness stems largely from the fact that central authorities seldom operate hierarchically, that is, functioning through an evident and "tidy" command-and-control structure of organizations and activities across national, regional, municipal levels. Sport systems can be remarkably complex. Thus, within any arrangement there exists a range of policies that exist to coordinate activities and programs, to make them more coherent, more responsive, and more competently delivered. That there are such needs for benchmarking exercises, audits, publications of "shared principles," and so on illustrates the embedded structural challenges in translating policy into action (Sam & Schoenberg, 2020).

While the instruments in regulatory policies can be deemed "substantive," the policy instruments in relation to governance can be called "procedural" for the simple reason that they circumscribe how things should be done and by whom (Howlett, 2000; Keat & Sam, 2013). For many scholars, policies aiming to "guide and steer" are tantamount to processes of professionalization and modernization since they can serve to effectively change the (problematic or entrenched) conduct of partner organizations and their decision-making processes. (Stenling & Sam, 2019; Tacon & Walters, 2016). In Canada, "quadrennial planning" (a government-initiated planning exercise intended to make national governing bodies more accountable) was a policy instrument much discussed beginning in the 1980s (Macintosh & Whitson, 1990). More contemporary modernizing policy tools include setting the terms of contracts between state agencies and national sport organizations, performance-based funding, audits, certifications, and benchmarking (Fahlén, 2017; Macintosh & Whitson, 1990; Sam & Macris, 2014).

There are two elements of interest here. The first and most obvious is that national policies, strategies, and white papers can be, in themselves, fundamental steering instruments (Österlind, 2016; Sam, 2005). Typical of the concerns embraced in such documents are prescriptions about the system's organizational architecture and the degree to which it should be aligned, coordinated, or centralized (Phillpots, Grix, & Quarmby, 2011; Sam & Jackson, 2004). Thus, an important subject for scholarly analysis concerns how these policies may (re)define stakeholder roles, responsibilities, and lines of authority, as well as how they advance particular practices or principles. The second core element concerns what is at the heart of the ideas underpinning these efforts. Here, a common theme in Anglo-Saxon states is one of embracing imperatives for accountability and pushing public and nonprofit sector organizations to be more "business-like." In terms of the ideas and discourses (see below) that encourage such sensibilities, these dominant principles have been put forward to make stakeholders self-sufficient (Berry & Manoli, 2018), efficient (Sam, 2009), and equitable (Safai, 2013). As with issues that arise around regulation, the overriding issues concern elements of legitimacy and autonomy. Ultimately, these are foundational questions about who has (or should have) authority in controlling sport. Indeed, a global trend that falls under this broad governance question concerns the mix of public and private organizations, the power relations that result, and how these contribute to the shaping of sport policy strategies (cf. Girginov, 2016; Hu & Henry, 2017).

APPROACHES

Within these broad policy issues, I have touched upon three general analytical dimensions that focus on interests, ideas, and institutions. However, before proceeding, it is important to briefly acknowledge the most basic approach to explain policy development, which is to see it as the product of a rational decision-making process in which:

- a problem or objective is recognized;
- alternative solutions are identified and analyzed;
- a remedy/response is chosen and implemented;
- the remedy is evaluated to correct errors.

This "stage" model of policymaking is an important heuristic in large part because the principles of rational decision-making are highly valued in contemporary organizations. Despite its intuitiveness, the approach rarely (if ever) reflects what occurs. Policymakers will often come up with solutions at the same time as the problems (if not before) with "best practice" often a catch-cry for policy reforms.

Despite these criticisms (and many others), stage models are important because they describe the policy process as a cognitive activity. This in turn sensitizes researchers to important elements in policy, such as the standards of evidence against which decisions are made (Lindsey & Bacon, 2016; Smith & Leech, 2010), as well as the often deliberate search for and design of remedies or solutions (Bloyce & Smith, 2010; Vidar Hanstad & Houlihan, 2015). In more practical terms, the stage model enables researchers to delimit their studies to particular stages of a fluid process, such as policy formulation (Sam, 2005), implementation (Fahlén et al., 2015; Skille, 2008; Stenling, 2014b), and evaluation (Bloyce & Smith, 2010; Lindsey & Bacon, 2016; Stenling, 2014a).

As a broad field, the study of public policy is interdisciplinary and fairly agnostic in its approaches. In sport, early attention to policy arose mainly within the sociology of sport, with Marxist approaches often used to explain the emerging elite sport systems of state agencies (Macintosh & Whitson, 1990; McKay, 1991). Sociology has continued to be a foundational discipline, as evidenced in the school of scholars using figurational sociology to unpack UK sport policy (Bloyce & Smith, 2010), and also with the increasing application of Foucauldian analyses to examine sport policy's disciplining effects (Green & Houlihan, 2006; Piggin, Jackson, & Lewis, 2009b). The subject of policy is also found in sport management, reflecting an eclectic range of perspectives that span positivist and postpositivist outlooks (Funahashi, De Bosscher, & Mano, 2015; Green, 2006). While space limitations preclude consideration of these theories and their nuances, all approaches acknowledge, to varying degrees, the importance of interests, institutions, and ideas. With this in mind, I briefly turn to outlining these as core approaches, along with considering their application and significance in the analysis of sport policy.

Interests

Understanding interest groups is fundamental to all policy analyses. Ontologically, it is an acknowledgment that *power* is at least as important as the *rationality* assumed in the stage model outlined above. The study of interests represents a view of the policy process in which groups or individuals mobilize around specific issues and compete or cooperate to influence decision-making. In this view, policymakers (i.e., governments and their agencies) are not unitary actors; the policies that emerge are the product of complex processes of competition, bargaining, and negotiation among/between groups (Bergsgard et al., 2007; Henry & Nassis, 1999). These groups can variously include political parties, teachers' unions, media consortia, Olympic committees, athlete advocacy groups, and think tanks, as well as diverse state agencies with a range of mandates.

The role of groups and organizations in the policy process is important to analyze for a number of reasons. First, the study of interests is significant because of the inherent concern in politics for democratic input, representation, deliberation, and consultation. While these elements of participatory politics can be cynically viewed, there is evidence in sport of a growing number of quasi-advocacy organizations with increasingly professional lobbying capacity (cf. Comeau & Church, 2010; Dowling & Washington, 2017; Sam, 2011). Thus, as sport matures as an area of public policy, it is possible that this emerging "active advocacy" may ultimately transform the sector in line with its (paid) professionals rather than its traditional volunteer base (Stenling & Sam, 2019). Second, the focus on interests draws attention to the influence of powerful individuals, sometimes called "policy entrepreneurs" (Houlihan, 2005; Houlihan & Lindsey, 2013; Kingdon, 1984), who can shape the agenda by bringing different groups together and/or by shaping the dominant discourses and narratives. While such actors may include politicians and cabinet ministers, this perspective sensitizes us to other actors (such as business elites and private consultants) that, while not having formal authority, exert influence nonetheless. If these interests alert us to the "powerful," the approach is equally attuned to the relative weakness of other interests. For example, it is apparent that one explanation for the continued privileging of elite sport is the absence of "demand groups to represent the interests of the young and the community sports participant" (Houlihan & White 2002, p. 222).

In the end, a focus on interest groups helps to explain policy formation, change, and/or resistance to change. However, essential questions remain regarding the relative influence of agents and, indeed more fundamentally, what enables, incentivizes, or impedes their participation in the policy process. Answers about the underlying dynamics of power ultimately rest in scholars examining why interests have access and how they gain legitimacy at various stages of the policy cycle (cf. Henry & Nassis, 1999; Strittmatter, Stenling, Fahlén, & Skille, 2018). Finding meaningful answers to such complex dynamics necessarily means considering the interplay of institutions and ideas.

Institutions

Institutional approaches are concerned with the constellation of rules, organizational arrangements, conventions, roles, and routines that enable or constrain policymaking (Lowndes & Roberts, 2013; Peters, 2005). The approach is important from the standpoint that while agents matter and may wield considerable influence in policymaking, structures also matter a great deal in shaping the contours of political activity. At the broadest level, institutions can include the basic constitutional design of a government system (e.g., presidential vs. parliamentary), its distribution of powers (e.g., between federal and provincial/state levels) or its governance "style" (e.g., welfarist, neoliberal, corporatist). While these are understood to bring order to politics and policymaking, other meso- and micro-level structures (such as organizational configurations, statutes, and bureaucratic procedures) may also be conceived as institutions.

The importance of the approach is that it pays particular attention to the contexts surrounding policy. Just as the responsibilities and relations between federal and provincial/territorial governments can have enduring effects on sport policy (Comeau, 2013), so too do the ways in which sport is funded, be it via lotteries, taxation, or private sector sponsorship (Bergsgard et al., 2007). Thus, understanding basic institutional arrangements is a key starting point to any analysis of policy. Institutional approaches are evident in studies that focus on particular system types (e.g., Bergsgard & Norberg, 2010), policy regimes (Tak et al., 2018b), and policy communities (Houlihan, 1997). Such analyses point to key determinants of policy implementation, such as the degree to which authority is centralized or dispersed, as well as the possibilities for and hindrances to achieving sectoral coordination. Importantly, studies anchored in these kinds of variant contexts can provide baselines for making comparisons between states, ultimately with a view toward understanding "what works" (or does not work) and under what organizational circumstances. Further, a focus on such institutional arrangements may not only be useful for post hoc explanations of policy processes; they may also help to anticipate the shape and dynamics of future political exchanges (Lowndes & Roberts, 2013).

Yet what institutional approaches have the most to offer analytically lies in what institutions do (Lowndes & Roberts, 2013; Peters, 2005). First, since institutions structure relations, they are an important consideration in explaining interest group influence. For instance, a convention of "evidence-based" policymaking can privilege actors who have the resources to produce evidence, while disempowering those having fewer resources (Piggin, Jackson, & Lewis, 2009a). In such a case, bigger, more established organizations may even have special public relations or advocacy units to commission research studies supporting their policy positions. At the same time, the structure of these interactions can limit who is able to participate in the policy process in the first place. Thus, institutional arrangements have been shown to channel interest group pressures in nationwide consultations surrounding new policy directions (Sam & Jackson, 2006; Stenling & Sam, 2017). In New Zealand, for example, a national task force delineated its consultation hearings according to particular, standardized roles in the sport sector: coaches, administrators, and health advocates. This grouping of (homogeneous) stakeholders resulted in few disagreements and thus shaped the task force's portrayal of problems as technical issues (including organizational reforms) rather than issues of a political nature (such as the setting of priorities) (Sam & Jackson, 2006).

Second, institutions shape political relations by providing "cognitive scripts" and "logics of appropriateness" for actors in the policy process (March & Olsen, 2006). Indeed sport organizations are likely to engage in politics far differently if they are guided by a *market* (an institution characterized by a logic of competition) versus a *network* (characterized by a logic of cooperation) versus a *federation* (characterized by a logic of democratic represen- tation). More concretely, Comeau and Church (2010) identified distinctly different political strategies for women's sport advocacy groups, depending on whether their institutionally defined role was as a co-opted insider (as with the Canadian group) or an external lobbyist (as with the US association). In this view, institutions "influence behavior not simply by specifying what one *should* do but also by specifying what one can *imagine* doing in a given context" (Hall & Taylor, 1996, p. 948). Operating under performance-measurement schemes and medal targets, for instance, national sport organizations have been shown to "rationally" become less responsive to issues around equity, athlete welfare, and maltreat- ment (Sam, 2015; Sam & Dawbin, 2022).

An overriding contribution of this institutional approach lies in its ability to reveal how rules, procedures, routines, and practices can structure policymaking. As one early institutional theorist famously observed, "organization is the mobilization of bias," where "some issues are organized into politics while others are organized out" (Schattschneider, 1961, p. 71). The approach is thus important in showing both how interests are enabled/ constrained in policy debates, as well as how institutions may reinforce particular ideas and logics over time (Österlind, 2016; Stenling, 2014a). Taken together, the utility of this kind of institutional orientation lies in its assessment of how some policies are "ruled in" as appro- priate, while others are "ruled out."

Ideas

If we accept that structures are important in politics, one of the most important elements of structure surrounds the ideas, ideologies, paradigms, and storylines associated with policies (Hall, 1993; Rein & Schön, 1993; Stone, 1989). While it is beyond the scope of this chapter to provide a disambiguation of the various concepts, the main theme that runs throughout this perspective is that ideas (expressed primarily through language) can play an influential role in the policy cycle.

With primacy given to the nature of rhetoric, arguments, and discourses (Kingdon, 1984; Majone, 1989), an ideational approach is implicitly interpretive and critical (Piggin, 2010; Sam, 2003). It draws out alternate meanings to what on the surface may appear as ac- cepted (or "received") wisdom and common sense. Under this analytical lens, for example, are assessments of what has been called the "virtuous cycle," the endless loop of seem- ingly logical forces posited to connect the benefits of elite sport with sport-for-all (Grix & Carmichael, 2011). More broadly, the approach serves to demystify taken-for-granted postures undergirding policy logics; these can be revealed in critical interpretations of "so- cial capital" that often reliably operate as a kind of metaphor or "policy slogan" (Skille, 2014, p. 341).

As with institutions, ideational dimensions provide essential context. Ideologies and values feature frequently as comparative constructs to describe deeply rooted beliefs as well as more "ephemeral ideas" that can impact sport policy (Kristiansen, Parent, & Houlihan, 2016). Indeed this approach is fundamental because broad political ideas, such as *efficiency* (Sam, 2003), *transparency* (Piggin et al., 2009b), and *accountability* (Grix, 2009), take on special significance as they are translated into sport policy. The idea of "continuous improvement" (a feature of modernization agendas), for example, has very real consequences in terms of supporting "ratcheting" targets and the perverse "gaming" that actors sometimes undertake to conform to the idea (Sam & Macris, 2014). Thus, to show participation growth and improvement, sport governing bodies inflate their participation numbers through the use of one-off "clinics" or by extending their seasons, effectively cannibalizing the participation numbers in other sports (see Keat & Sam, 2013).

Equally important to consider is how sport policy issues are framed (Stenling & Sam, 2020), how policy problems are constructed (Österlind, 2016), and how solutions are justified (Sam & Ronglan, 2018). Thus focused, an ideational approach aims to uncover the discursive features underlying the claims that agents and their organizations make in policy debates. For example, in considering the timing, scope, and depth of policy intervention, there is a difference between views of athlete welfare/maltreatment as a "problem" or an "issue" and its representation as an "epidemic" or a "crisis." Likewise, there is an important distinction between claims of doping, match-fixing, or abuse as a case of a few "bad apples" versus the assertion that these are systemic and structural problems that have their origins in previous policies. Invariably, the ideational approach brings to the fore that policy claims are strategic and support particularized interests (Stone, 1997). And, in this way, the focus on frames in the ideational approach helps uncover embedded narratives, tropes, and cognitive shorthands that serve to bind together particular groups of experts, advocates, and/or practitioners.

Finally, whether the sport-specific dominant ideas surround notions of excellence (Kidd, 1988), competitiveness (Sam, 2003; Skille, 2011), or integrity (Gardiner, Parry, & Robinson, 2017), the purpose of this kind of analysis is to challenge the basis of power behind policy discourses and, by doing so, question their legitimacy (e.g., in terms of their fairness, coherence, etc.). The approach thus demands critical attention to the "motherhood and apple pie" ideas often masquerading as straightforward problems and policy solutions.

Debates

In a recent special issue on "theory and methods in sport policy and politics research," the editors of the *International Journal of Sport Policy and Politics* remark that few scholars from political science disciplines engage with sport (Grix, Lindsey, De Bosscher, & Bloyce, 2018). While not a criticism of the current field per se, the observation does highlight the tendency for scholars in this area to either echo received or limited logics or speak past one another. On the first count, Palmer (2013, p. 82), for example, suggests that "sports policy has been restricted in the kinds of theory it adopts," although this claim was based on only a very limited review of sport policy and politics research.

Since policy is what public authorities decide to do (or not do), we should not be surprised that it is analyzed through myriad theories and approaches. Indeed, the ontological and epistemological concerns surrounding sport policy have received considerable attention (Dowling, Brown, Legg, & Beacom, 2018; Henry, Amara, & Al-Tauqi, 2005; Houlihan, 2005). It therefore seems fruitless to lament the insufficient political theory, lack of "social" theory, or even "globalization" theory as they have been applied to the area.

Presently, the field is certainly growing but has not yet become so vast that one cannot draw underlying lessons from the diverse theoretical traditions that have been embraced. For example, whether we call the agents in the process "policy entrepreneurs" or "brokers" or "influential stakeholders" is largely immaterial so long as we remain attuned to the fact that people (within their institutionally derived roles) matter. Likewise, in policy contexts, whether an idea like "sustainable development" is a goal, value, or paradigm is often indistinguishable and only empirically discoverable with respect to how the idea is articulated, by whom, and under what circumstances. Hence, the nuances between discourses, narratives, or frames are chiefly interesting insofar as they share a common concern for language, argument, and the construction of meaning (see Fischer & Forester, 1993).

For this reason, theories of policymaking generally show a broad acknowledgment of the interplay between ideas, interests, and institutions. In particular, Sabatier and Jenkins-Smith's (1993) Advocacy Coalition Framework (ACF) is highly regarded as a means of connecting the different orientations outlined above (Green & Houlihan, 2004). Yet while useful as a comparative, empirical model, the ACF's broad treatment of political context is also its weakness (Hysing & Olsson, 2008), since the answer to the question "What happened?" seems invariably to be "Everything happened," leaving little room for an assessment of what elements mattered most. Indeed, in a recent review of the ACF, the main criticism centers on the need for a more explicit use of its concepts (Pierce, Peterson, & Hicks, 2020), an issue that will invariably require insights from other theoretical approaches (Olsson, 2009).

In this lies one of the recurring challenges endemic to the study of sport policy and politics: whether one's approach should be aimed toward particularity or comparability. The challenge largely plays out as a paradox in which context is highly valued, yet too little or too much of it can be cause for others to ignore the research's relevance. Investigations, for example, establishing the *uniqueness* of the Scandinavian sports model can inadvertently suggest that findings in that context are inapplicable outside of it. For those studying small states (Sam & Jackson, 2017), the need for comparison with other countries is usually a given (and often a condition for publication), while for researchers in larger countries, this is not always the case (e.g., Harris & Houlihan, 2016; Phillpots, Grix, & Quarmby, 2011). Perhaps the different affinities are a reflection of researchers wanting to draw parallels from another country, thereby treading carefully around the criticism that their work should be *more* comparative or, worse, that it is not sufficiently unique. Regardless, if we accept the prevailing logic that sport systems show at least moderate levels of convergence (Bergsgard et al., 2007; Green & Houlihan, 2005), the predominant driver should be to adopt some comparative sensitivity to allow scholars to learn from each and every case. However, for the purposes of advancing the field, it may be unwise to over invest in metaframeworks like the ACF to achieve this lesson-drawing. Since policy is context-specific and takes place across public, private, and commercial boundaries, the continuation of a theoretical agnosticism might be better for identifying and more deeply understanding particularities, such as phenomena like modernization and governance, that cut across belief systems and coalitions.

To that end, some scholars have recently argued for a "decentered" approach to policy, such that the focal point is less on the "state" and its taken-for-granted authority and power (Bevir, 2020). Instead, decentered theorists emphasize agency and "meaning-making" above all else and eschew the use of midlevel theories as explanations (Bevir, 2020). For sport policy scholars, this is perhaps not so much a debate as it is an expansion of the scope of inquiry (Goodwin & Grix, 2011). Indeed, much of this sentiment reflects what Henry and Ko (2014) advance as a critical realist approach in which the key questions are not only about "what works" but are also foundationally anchored in concerns about "for whom does a given policy work" and for whom does it not. Implicitly, this suggests that careful attention be paid to the variety of policies citizens create, how they amend and revise those policies, and how these policies perform (Schlager, 2007, p. 297).

In large part, this realist perspective seems to characterize the chief concerns adopted among scholars in the area. Importantly, it may also explain the sport policy field's on-going *bricolage* with the orientations described above (interests, ideas, and institutions), *sans* the promise of "completeness" offered by frameworks like the ACF. On this count, neo-institutionalists may combine rules with norms/beliefs as "conventions" (Skille & Stenling, 2018) or "chains of legitimating acts" (Strittmatter et al., 2018), while figurational sociologists and network theorists combine interests with institutions as "patterns of inter-action" between actors (Bloyce & Smith, 2010). Such theoretical diversity is welcome, not only for its own sake but ultimately because sport policies seem to share similar "politics." Thus, findings from these diverse research strands can be viewed as "canaries in the coal mines," alerting us to different "localized" policy possibilities as changes unfold elsewhere.

CONCLUSION

Since policy is multifaceted and encompasses elements of planning, strategizing, and de-bate, its analysis offers a particular vantage point. It is, on the one hand, *pragmatic*, in that it generally focuses on the temporary nature of solutions, the limits to rationality, and the imperfections of political bargaining. While this pragmatism and aim for relevance un-derlie the field, it also takes as given the place of values and political contestation. In this view, a sport policy can dictate what an athlete is allowed to ingest, just as it might establish a standard for who is considered "inactive" or "elite." While the former says what we must do, the latter tells us who we are (fit or unfit) and to what we might be entitled (e.g., access to programs, grants, facilities, etc.). If politics is understood as "who gets what, when and how" (Lasswell, 1958), it is clear why policymaking is a fundamental element underpinning virtually all public issues.

Importantly, changes in policy (or the introduction of new policies) invariably entail an attempt to alter the structure or balance of real power within/between organizations. Thus, authority and influence are not only the *means* to achieve desired outcomes; they are also valuable *ends* in themselves for those groups with a vested interest in the shape of future sys-tems. That policy changes often appear as little more than organizational "tinkering" belies the fact that these can profoundly alter the institutional terrain and "rules of engagement" for future political contests. While "good governance" policies, for example, are undoubtedly a positive step toward reducing internal corruption, they are also political instruments that advance the creation of new "rulers" (in the form of auditors), while potentially altering conceptions of trust (see Power, 1997).

For these reasons, policies that address the issues of resource distribution, regulation, and governance are rarely static or complete, but are instead persistently analyzed, evaluated, and debated. Thus, to understand the inherent pragmatics and politics within these policy processes, this chapter has offered three broad, interconnected orientations that together require an understanding of

- the *interests* that demand representation and/or coordination in policy matters (where interests may be drawn along multiple, overlapping lines such as advocates in health, education, parasport, tourism, women's sport, etc.);
- the *institutions* that circumscribe public policy processes, such as the basic machinery and mechanisms that steer government action and central sport authorities, as well as the policy instruments and procedural "rules of engagement" that guide behaviors;
- the *ideas*, paradigms, and discourses that, explicitly or implicitly, underlie prevailing conceptions of public policy problems and how best to address them.

Policy research thus demands that we be aware of the inherent interplay between ideas, interests, and institutions. At a macro level, acknowledging these elements and their accordant perspectives helps to identify the various ways in which sport policies develop over time and across different contexts. At a more micro level, these orientations serve to remind us that, while sport policies can be problematic, the individuals in the process are rarely purposefully ignorant, oppressive, or short-sighted; rather, the ideas they adopt (or inherit) and the institutions in which they operate shape their assessment of what is considered "good" policy.

REFERENCES

Allison, L. (2005). *The global politics of sport: The role of global institutions in sport.* Abingdon, Oxon, U.K.: Routledge.

Andersen, S. S., & Ronglan, L. T. (2012). *Nordic elite sport: Same ambitions, different tracks.* Copenhagen: Copenhagen Business School Press DK.

Bemelmans-Videc, M.-L., Vedung, E., & Rist, R. C. (1998). *Carrots, sticks and sermons: Policy instruments and their evaluation.* New Brunswick, NJ: Transaction Publishers.

Bergsgard, N. A., Houlihan, B., Mangset, P., Nodland, S. I., & Rommetvedt, H. (2007). *Sport policy: A comparative analysis of stability and change.* Oxford: Butterworth-Heinemann.

Bergsgard, N. A., & Norberg, J. R. (2010). Sports policy and politics—the Scandinavian way. *Sport in Society, 13*(4), 567–582.

Berry, R., & Manoli, A. E. (2018). Alternative revenue streams for centrally funded sport governing bodies. *International Journal of Sport Policy and Politics, 10*(3), 429–450.

Bevir, M. (2020, February 26). What is the decentered state? *Public Policy and Administration.* http://dx.doi.org/10.1177/0952076720904993.

Bloyce, D., & Smith, A. (2010). *Sport policy and development: An introduction.* London: Routledge.

Chalip, L. (1996). Critical policy analysis: The illustrative case of New Zealand sport policy development. *Journal of Sport Management, 10*(3), 310–324.

Coalter, F. (2007). *A wider social role for sport: Who's keeping the score?* Abingdon, U.K.: Routledge.

Comeau, G. S. (2013). The evolution of Canadian sport policy. *International Journal of Sport Policy and Politics, 5*(1), 73–93.

Comeau, G. S., & Church, A. G. (2010). A comparative analysis of women's sport advocacy groups in Canada and the United States. *Journal of Sport and Social Issues, 34*(4), 457–474.

Crawford, D., & Independent Sport Panel. (2009). *The future of sport in Australia.* Canberra: Australian Sports Commission.

Doern, G. B., & Phidd, R. W. (1992). *Canadian public policy: Ideas, structure, process* (2nd ed.). Scarborough, Ont.: Nelson Canada.

Donnelly, P. (2010). Rent the podium revisited: Reflections on Vancouver 2010. *Policy Options, 31*(4), 84–86.

Dowling, M., Brown, P., Legg, D., & Beacom, A. (2018). Living with imperfect comparisons: The challenges and limitations of comparative paralympic sport policy research. *Sport Management Review, 21*(2), 101–113.

Dowling, M., & Washington, M. (2017). Epistemic communities and knowledge-based professional networks in sport policy and governance: A case study of the Canadian Sport for Life leadership team. *Journal of Sport Management, 31*(2), 133–147.

Efverström, A., Ahmadi, N., Hoff, D., & Bäckström, Å. (2016). Anti-doping and legitimacy: An international survey of elite athletes'. perceptions. *International Journal of Sport Policy and Politics, 8*(3), 491–514.

Fahlén, J. (2017). The trust-mistrust dynamic in the public governance of sport: Exploring the legitimacy of performance measurement systems through end-users'. perceptions. *International Journal of Sport Policy and Politics, 9*(4), 707–722.

Fahlén, J., Eliasson, I., & Wickman, K. (2015). Resisting self-regulation: An analysis of sport policy programme making and implementation in Sweden. *International Journal of Sport Policy and Politics, 7*(3), 391–406.

Fahlén, J., & Stenling, C. (2016). Sport policy in Sweden. *International Journal of Sport Policy and Politics, 8*(3), 515–531.

Fischer, F., & Forester, J. (1993). *The argumentative turn in policy analysis and planning.* Durham, NC: Duke University Press.

Funahashi, H., De Bosscher, V., & Mano, Y. (2015). Understanding public acceptance of elite sport policy in Japan: A structural equation modelling approach. *European Sport Management Quarterly, 15*(4), 478–504. doi:10.1080/16184742.2015.1056200.

Gardiner, S., Parry, J., & Robinson, S. (2017). Integrity and the corruption debate in sport: Where is the integrity? *European Sport Management Quarterly, 17*(1), 6–23.

Girginov, V. (2016). Russia. In E. Kristiansen, M. Parent, & B. Houlihan (Eds.), *Elite youth sport policy and management: A comparative analysis* (pp. 226–244). Abingdon, U.K.: Routledge.

Goodwin, M., & Grix, J. (2011). Bringing structures back in: The "governance narrative," the "decentred approach" and "asymmetrical network governance" in the education and sport policy communities. *Public Administration, 89*(2), 537–556.

Gray, S. (2019). Achieving compliance with the World Anti-Doping Code: Learning from the implementation of another international agreement. *International Journal of Sport Policy and Politics, 11*(2), 247–260.

Green, M. (2006). From "sport for all" to not about "sport" at all? Interrogating sport policy interventions in the United Kingdom. *European Sport Management Quarterly, 6*(3), 217–238. doi:10.1080/16184740601094936.

Green, M., & Houlihan, B. (2004). Advocacy coalitions and elite sport policy change in Canada and the United Kingdom. *International Review for the Sociology of Sport, 39*(4), 387–403.

Green, M., & Houlihan, B. (2005). *Elite sport development: Policy learning and political priorities.* London: Routledge.

Green, M., & Houlihan, B. (2006). Governmentality, modernization and the "disciplining" of national sport organizations: Athletics in Australia and the United Kingdom. *Sociology of Sport Journal, 23*, 47–71.

Grix, J. (2009). The impact of UK sport policy on the governance of athletics. *International Journal of Sport Policy and Politics, 1*(1), 31–49.

Grix, J., & Carmichael, F. (2011). Why do governments invest in elite sport? A polemic. *International Journal of Sport Policy and Politics, 4*(1), 73–90. doi:10.1080/19406940.2011.627358.

Grix, J., Lindsey, I., De Bosscher, V., & Bloyce, D. (2018). Theory and methods in sport policy and politics research. *International Journal of Sport Policy and Politics, 10*(4), 615–620.

Hall, P. A. (1993). Policy paradigms, social learning, and the state: The case of economic policymaking in Britain. *Comparative Politics, 25*, 275–297.

Hall, P. A., & Taylor, R. C. R. (1996). Political science and the three new institutionalisms. *Political Studies, 44*, 936–957.

Hanstad, D. V., & Loland, S. (2009). Elite athletes' duty to provide information on their whereabouts: Justifiable anti-doping work or an indefensible surveillance regime? *European Journal of Sport Science, 9*(1), 3–10.

Harris, S., & Houlihan, B. (2016). Implementing the community sport legacy: The limits of partnerships, contracts and performance management. *European Sport Management Quarterly, 16*(4), 433–458. doi:10.1080/16184742.2016.1178315.

Henry, I., Amara, M., & Al-Tauqi, M. (2005). A typology of approaches to comparative analysis of sports policy. *Journal of Sport Management, 19*(4), 480–496.

Henry, I., & Ko, L.-M. (2014). Analysing sport policy in a globalising context. In I. Henry & L.-M. Ko (Eds.), *Routledge handbook of sport policy* (pp. 3–10). London: Routledge.

Henry, I. P., & Nassis, P. (1999). Political clientelism and sports policy in Greece. *International Review for the Sociology of Sport, 34*(1), 43–58.

Hogan, K., & Norton, K. (2000). The "price" of Olympic gold. *Journal of Science and Medicine in Sport, 3*(2), 203–218.

Hong, E. (2016). South Korea. In E. Kristiansen, M. Parent, & B. Houlihan (Eds.), *Elite youth sport policy and management: A comparative analysis* (pp. 226–244). Abingdon, U.K.: Routledge.

Houlihan, B. (1997). *Sport, policy, and politics: A comparative analysis.* New York: Routledge.

Houlihan, B. (2004). Civil rights, doping control and the World Anti-Doping Code. *Sport in Society, 7*(3), 420–437.

Houlihan, B. (2005). Public sector sport policy: Developing a framework for analysis. *International Review for the Sociology of Sport, 40*(2), 163–185. doi:10.1177/1012690205057193.

Houlihan, B. (2011). Sports development and elite athletes—Introduction: The irresistible priority. In B. Houlihan & M. Green (Eds.), *Routledge handbook of sports development* (pp. 367–370). Abingdon, U.K.: Routledge.

Houlihan, B. (2014). Achieving compliance in international anti-doping policy: An analysis of the 2009 World Anti-Doping Code. *Sport Management Review, 17*(3), 265–276.

Houlihan, B., & Green, M. (2008). *Comparative elite sport development systems, structures, and public policy* (1st ed.). Amsterdam: Elsevier/Butterworth-Heinemann.

Houlihan, B., & Lindsey, I. (2013). *Sport policy in Britain.* Abingdon, U.K.: Routledge.

Houlihan, B., & Preece, A. (2007). Independence and accountability: The case of the drug free sport directorate, the UK's national anti-doping organisation. *Public Policy and Administration, 22*(4), 381–402. doi:10.1177/0952076707081584.

Houlihan, B., & White, A. (2002). *The politics of sports development: Development of sport or development through sport?* London: Routledge.

Howlett, M. (2000). Managing the "hollow state": Procedural policy instruments and modern governance. *Canadian Public Administration, 43,* 412–431. doi:10.1111/j.1754-7121.2000. tb01152.x.

Hoye, R., Nicholson, M., & Houlihan, B. (2010). *Sport and policy: Issues and analysis.* London: Routledge.

Hu, X., & Henry, I. (2017). Reform and maintenance of Juguo Tizhi: Governmental management discourse of Chinese elite sport. *European Sport Management Quarterly, 17*(4), 531–553.

Hysing, E., & Olsson, J. (2008). Contextualising the Advocacy Coalition Framework: Theorising change in Swedish forest policy. *Environmental Politics, 17*(5), 730–748.

Keat, R. A., & Sam, M. P. (2013). Regional implementation of New Zealand sport policy: New instrument, new challenges. *International Journal of Sport Policy and Politics, 5*(1), 39–54.

Kerr, R., & Kerr, G. (2020). Promoting athlete welfare: A proposal for an international surveillance system. *Sport Management Review, 23*(1), 95–103.

Kidd, B. (1988). The philosophy of excellence: Olympic performances, class power, and the Canadian state. In P. J. Galasso (Ed.), *Philosophy of sport and physical activity: Issues and concepts* (pp. 11–31). Toronto: Canadian Scholar's Press.

KCdon, J. W. (1984). *Agenda, alternatives, and public policies.* Boston: Little, Brown and Company.

Kooiman, J. (1993). *Modern governance: New government-society interactions.* London: Sage.

Kristiansen, E., Parent, M., & Houlihan, B. (2016). *Elite youth sport policy and management: A comparative analysis.* Abingdon, U.K.: Routledge.

Lasswell, H. D. (1958). *Politics: Who gets what, when, how.* New York, World Publishing.

Lindblom, C. E. (1959). The science of muddling through. *Public Administration Review, 19,* 79–88.

Lindsey, I., & Bacon, D. (2016). In pursuit of evidence-based policy and practice: A realist synthesis-inspired examination of youth sport and physical activity initiatives in England (2002–2010). *International Journal of Sport Policy and Politics, 8*(1), 67–90.

Lowndes, V., & Roberts, M. (2013). *Why institutions matter: The new institutionalism in political science.* Basingstoke, U.K.: Palgrave.

Macintosh, D., & Whitson, D. (1990). *The game planners: Transforming Canada's sport system.* Montreal: McGill-Queen's University Press.

Majone, G. (1989). *Evidence, argument and persuasion in the policy process.* New Haven, CT: Yale University Press.

Majone, G. (1994). The rise of the regulatory state in Europe. *West European Politics, 17*(3), 77–101.

March, J. G., & Olsen, J. P. (2006). The logic of appropriateness. In M. Moran, M. Rein, & R. E. Goodin (Eds.), *The Oxford handbook of public policy* (pp. 689–708). Oxford: Oxford University Press.

McKay, J. (1991). *No pain, no gain? Sport and Australian culture.* Sydney: Prentice Hall.

Møller, V., & Dimeo, P. (2014). Anti-doping—the end of sport. *International Journal of Sport Policy and Politics, 6*(2), 259–272.

Nicholson, M., Hoye, R., & Houlihan, B. (2010). *Participation in sport: International policy perspectives.* London: Routledge.

Olsson, J. (2009). The power of the inside activist: Understanding policy change by empowering the Advocacy Coalition Framework (ACF). *Planning Theory & Practice, 10*(2), 167–187. doi:10.1080/14649350902884425.

Österlind, M. (2016). Sport policy evaluation and governing participation in sport: Governmental problematics of democracy and health. *International Journal of Sport Policy and Politics, 8*(3), 347–362.

Palmer, C. (2013). *Global sports policy.* London: Sage.

Peters, B. G. (2005). *Institutional theory in political science: The "new institutionalism"* (2nd ed.). London: Continuum.

Phillpots, L., Grix, J., & Quarmby, T. (2011). Centralized grassroots sport policy and "new governance": A case study of County Sports Partnerships in the UK—unpacking the paradox. *International Review for the Sociology of Sport, 46*(3), 265–281.

Pierce, J. J., Peterson, H. L., & Hicks, K. C. (2020). Policy change: An Advocacy Coalition Framework perspective. *Policy Studies Journal, 48*(1), 64–86.

Piggin, J. (2010). Is resistance futile? The effects of criticising New Zealand sport policy. *International Journal of Sport Policy and Politics, 2*(1), 85–98.

Piggin, J., Jackson, S. J., & Lewis, M. (2009a). Knowledge, power and politics: Contesting "evidenced-based" national sport policy. *International Review for the Sociology of Sport, 44*(1), 87–101.

Piggin, J., Jackson, S. J., & Lewis, M. (2009b). Telling the truth in public policy: An analysis of New Zealand sport policy discourse. *Sociology of Sport Journal, 26,* 462–482.

Power, M. (1997). *The audit society: Rituals of verification.* Oxford: Oxford University Press.

Rein, M., & Schön, D. (1993). Reframing policy discourse. In F. Fischer & J. Forester (Eds.), *The argumentative turn in policy analysis* (pp. 145–185). London: Duke University Press.

Sabatier, P. A., & Jenkins-Smith, H. C. (1993). *Policy change and learning: An advocacy coalition approach.* Boulder, CO: Westview.

Safai, P. (2013). Women in sport policy. In L. Thibault & J. Harvey (Eds.), *Sport policy in Canada* (pp. 317–349). Ottawa: University of Ottawa Press.

Sam, M. P. (2003). What's the big idea? Reading the rhetoric of a national sport policy process. *Sociology of Sport Journal, 20,* 189–213.

Sam, M. P. (2005). The makers of sport policy: A task(force) to be reckoned with. *Sociology of Sport Journal, 21,* 78–99.

Sam, M. P. (2009). The public management of sport: Wicked problems, challenges and dilemmas. *Public Management Review, 11*(4), 499–514.

Sam, M. P. (2011). New Zealand. In M. Nicholson, R. Hoye, & B. Houlihan (Eds.), *Participation in sport: International policy perspectives* (pp. 239–253). New York: Routledge.

Sam, M. P. (2015). "Big brother and caring sister": Performance management and the athlete's entourage. In S. S. Andersen, B. Houlihan, & L. T. Ronglan (Eds.), *Managing elite sport systems: Research and practice* (pp. 16–30). London: Routledge.

Sam, M. P., & Dawbin, T. M. (2022). Policy, modernisation and the politics of sport integrity. In D. Sturm & R. Kerr (Eds.), *Sport in Aotearoa/New Zealand: Contested terrain* (pp. 69–80). Abingdon: Routledge.

Sam, M. P., & Jackson, S. J. (2004). Sport policy development in New Zealand: Paradoxes of an integrative paradigm. *International Review for the Sociology of Sport, 39*(2), 205–222.

Sam, M. P., & Jackson, S. J. (2006). Developing national sport policy through consultation: The rules of engagement. *Journal of Sport Management, 20*(3), 366–386.

Sam, M. P., & Jackson, S. J. (2017). *Sport policy in small states.* Abingdon, U.K.: Routledge.

Sam, M. P., & Macris, L. I. (2014). Performance regimes in sport policy: Exploring consequences, vulnerabilities and politics. *International Journal of Sport Policy and Politics, 6*(3), 513–532.

Sam, M. P., & Ronglan, L. T. (2018). Building sport policy's legitimacy in Norway and New Zealand. *International Review for the Sociology of Sport, 53*(5), 550–571.

Sam, M. P., & Schoenberg, G. (2020). Government sport policy and governance in Australia, New Zealand and Canada. In D. Shilbury & L. Ferkins (Eds.), *Routledge handbook of sport governance* (pp. 65–78). Abingdon, U.K.: Routledge.

Schattschneider, E. E. (1961). *The semisovereign people: A realist's view of democracy in America.* New York: Holt, Rinehart & Winston.

Schlager, E. (2007). A comparison of frameworks, theories, and models of policy processes. In P. Sabatier (Ed.), *Theories of the policy process, 2nd edition* (pp. 293–320). Boulder, C.O.: Westview Press.

Skille, E. Å. (2008). Understanding sport clubs as sport policy implementers: A theoretical framework for the analysis of the implementation of central sport policy through local and voluntary sport organizations. *International Review for the Sociology of Sport, 43*(2), 181–200.

Skille, E. Å. (2011). Sport for all in Scandinavia: Sport policy and participation in Norway, Sweden and Denmark. International Journal of Sport Policy and Politics, 3(3), 327–339.

Skille, E. Å. (2014). Sports policy and social capital. In I. Henry & L.-M. Ko (Eds.), *Routledge handbook of sport policy* (pp. 341–350). London: Routledge.

Skille, E. Å., & Stenling, C. (2018). Inside-out and outside-in: Applying the concept of conventions in the analysis of policy implementation through sport clubs. *International Review for the Sociology of Sport, 53*(7), 837–853.

Smith, A., & Leech, R. (2010). "Evidence. What evidence?" Evidence-based policy making and school sport partnerships in north-west England. *International Journal of Sport Policy and Politics, 2*, 327–345. doi:10.1080/19406940.2010.519341.

Stenling, C. (2014a). The emergence of a new logic? The theorizing of a new practice in the highly institutionalized context of Swedish voluntary sport. *Sport Management Review, 17*(4), 507–519.

Stenling, C. (2014b). Sport programme implementation as translation and organizational identity construction: The implementation of drive-in sport in Swedish sports as an illustration. *International Journal of Sport Policy and Politics, 6*(1), 55–69.

Stenling, C., & Sam, M. (2017). Tensions and contradictions in sport's quest for legitimacy as a political actor: The politics of Swedish public sport policy hearings. *International Journal of Sport Policy and Politics, 9*(4), 691–705.

Stenling, C., & Sam, M. P. (2019). Professionalization and its consequences: How active advocacy may undermine democracy. *European Sport Management Quarterly,* 1–21. doi:https://doi.org/10.1080/16184742.2019.1637915.

Stenling, C., & Sam, M. S. (2020). Sport advocacy: The art of persuasion and its by-products. *Sociology of Sport Journal*, 37(4), 319–327. doi:https://doi.org/10.1123/ssj.2019-0047.

Stewart, B., Nicholson, M., Westerbeek, H., & Smith, A. (2004). *Australian sport—better by design? The evolution of Australian sport policy.* London: Routledge.

Stone, D. A. (1989). Causal stories and the formation of policy agendas. *Political Science Quarterly*, 104(2), 281–300.

Stone, D. A. (1997). *Policy paradox: The art of political decision making.* New York: W. W. Norton.

Strittmatter, A. M., Stenling, C., Fahlén, J., & Skille, E. (2018). Sport policy analysis revisited: The sport policy process as an interlinked chain of legitimating acts. *International Journal of Sport Policy and Politics*, 10(4), 621–635.

Tacon, R., & Walters, G. (2016). Modernisation and governance in UK national governing bodies of sport: How modernisation influences the way board members perceive and enact their roles. International journal of sport policy and politics, 8(3), 363–381.

Tak, M. (2018). Too big to jail: Match-fixing, institutional failure and the shifting of responsibility. *International Review for the Sociology of Sport*, 53(7), 788–806.

Tak, M., Sam, M. P., & Jackson, S. J. (2018a). The politics of countermeasures against match-fixing in sport: A political sociology approach to policy instruments. *International Review for the Sociology of Sport*, 53(1), 30–48.

Tak, M., Sam, M. P., & Jackson, S. J. (2018b). The problems and causes of match-fixing: Are legal sports betting regimes to blame? *Journal of Criminological Research, Policy and Practice*, 4(1), 73–87.

Vidar Hanstad, D., & Houlihan, B. (2015). Strengthening global anti-doping policy through bilateral collaboration: The example of Norway and China. *International Journal of Sport Policy and Politics*, 7(4), 587–604.

Waddington, I., & Møller, V. (2019). WADA at twenty: Old problems and old thinking? *International Journal of Sport Policy and Politics*, 11(2), 219–231.

Weed, M., Coren, E., Fiore, J., Wellard, I., Chatziefstathiou, D., Mansfield, L., & Dowse, S. (2015). The Olympic Games and raising sport participation: A systematic review of evidence and an interrogation of policy for a demonstration effect. *European Sport Management Quarterly*, 15(2), 195–226.

CHAPTER 5

••

SPORT, NATIONALISM, AND NATIONAL IDENTITIES

••

ALAN BAIRNER AND PEIZI HAN

It remains true that "most mainstream commentators on nationalism pay remarkably little attention to sport" (Smith & Porter, 2004, p. 4). By contrast, sport scholars have given the impression of having paid a lot of attention to nationalism. However, there has been a tendency to take for granted such concepts as nation, nation-state, nationality, national identity, and nationalism and to ignore debates about these concepts within mainstream nationalism studies (Bairner, 2008, 2015). In addition, these concepts and the issues to which they relate were for a number of years subsumed within debates about globalization, with the nation being regularly presented as under threat from or, in some instances, resistant to the forces of global homogenization rather than as an object of intrinsic scholarly interest (Bairner, 2001; Giulianotti & Robertson, 2007; Maguire, 1999; Miller, Lawrence, McKay, & Rowe, 2001). As a consequence, the extent to which sport scholarship has contributed to our understanding of the various relationships that exist between these terms has been rather limited. It is frustrating, therefore, that, as early as 1998, the editors of a book (Cronin & Mayall, 1998) that focused on sporting nationalisms argued that to understand the relationship between sport and nationalism, the starting point should be seminal texts by Ernest Gellner (1983), Benedict Anderson (1983), John Breuilly (1993), and Eric Hobsbawm (1992). To what extent have these words been heeded, and why does it matter?

In the first quarter of the 21st century, it is relatively easy to see that nationalism has not gone away. The threat posed by globalization has been averted in two main, often diametrically opposed ways, although globalization concerns have almost certainly played a significant role in the rise of two significant forms of nationalist expression. The return of populist nationalism, last seen, at least in such highly visible ways, in Europe in the 1920s and 1930s, has meant the emergence of political leaders and a form of nationalism that is often racist and xenophobic as well as being generally socially conservative. In the West, although President Donald Trump is the best-known exponent of this brand of nationalism, he has had counterparts in various European countries, including notably Hungary, Poland, and even the United Kingdom, where populist (English) nationalism was at the heart of the decision that the country should leave the European Union. Straddling West and East is President Recep Tayyip Erdoğan of Turkey. Other key figures are Vladimir Putin in Russia, Xi Jinping in the People's Republic of China (PRC), Jair Bolsonaro in Brazil, Narendra Modi in India, and Rodrigo Roa Duterte in the Philippines. These men, and it is surely noteworthy that they are all men, have very different intellectual influences—the Muslim Erdoğan, the Hindu Modi, the Communist Xi—but all of them talk about making their respective countries great and, in so doing, seek to identify and challenge those systems and oppositional forces, real or imagined, that stand in their way. Indeed, nation-state nationalism is alive and well.

The other compelling piece of evidence that nationalism remains a potent force in the world is the emergence and/or persistence of secessionist demands in various parts of the world. The desire for independence in Catalonia and Scotland has grown stronger. Are Irish nationalists completely satisfied with the terms of the Good Friday Agreement, which was heralded as having brought peace to Northern Ireland but may have put in place a potentially formidable obstacle in the way of those who wish to see Northern Ireland leave the United Kingdom and the creation of an independent 32-county Republic of Ireland? How will the Kurdish question be resolved, or that of the Palestinians? In China, both Hong Kong and, to a lesser extent for the time being, Taiwan now find themselves in situations which were previously only filled by Tibet and parts of Xinjiang province in terms of potential demands for independence.

The relationship between sport and these new (or repackaged) forms of nationalism that are now so prominent demand urgent examination by sports studies scholars. But as we shall demonstrate, these are not the only issues that deserve greater attention. For these issues to be fully addressed, however, there must be a secure understanding of the various theories of nationalism that can help us to successfully examine the national significance of sport in different contexts.

Issues

Traditional accounts of nationalism have normally sought to understand the everyday production of the nation through ideologies, institutions, and other large-scale dynamic forces, including sport (Guinness & Besnier, 2016). Indeed, it is sport, arguably more than any other form of social activity in the modern world, that facilitates flag-waving and the playing of national anthems, both formally, at moments such as medal ceremonies, and informally through the activities of fans (Bairner, 2008). The relationship between sport, national identity, and nationalism has involved inextricable connections (Bogdanov, 2011). It has been argued that the manifestation of national identity and nationalism are integral to the enduring popularity of global competitions, events, and contests, revealed not only in the myriad ways in which politicians and politically motivated groups have sought to harness sport to national causes, but also in the very concept of national sports (Bairner, 2009).

Many studies on the relationship between sport and nation have been concerned with how nation-states seek to promote themselves or simply develop their economic and diplomatic activities by harnessing sport as a helpful and highly visible medium (Bairner, 2015). However, Hargreaves (2000, p. 3) claims that much of the scholarly literature in this area has oversimplified the relationship between sport and nationalism by viewing sport as "a mere reflection of politics."

Anderson's (1983) "imagined community" has been referred to by many sport scholars who immediately move on without further scrutiny of the concept, which is now in danger of becoming so overused that it may come to represent nothing more than the suggestion that national identity is all in the mind, with no material basis (Bairner, 2009, 2015). However, Anderson's initial intention was to help us understand the complex nature of national identity formation, weaving together as it does both objective and subjective factors (Bairner, 2009, 2015). With this in mind, examining the relationship between sport, national identity, and nationalism requires far more involvement with mainstream nationalism studies and theories, including primordialism, ethnosymbolism, and modernism.

The emergence of nations and nation-states has been explained through the use of different perspectives. Primordialism and ethnosymbolism, for different reasons, view nations as essential, bounded, and stable, and modernism sees nations as constructed, changeable, and historically contingent (Özkirimli, 2010). Central to the first two is the belief that the nation, as a natural category, is defined by objective criteria, such as language, ethnicity, geography, and religion, and hence predates and shapes modern state formations and nationalist politics (Bairner, 2009; Stokke, 2017). One of the leading critics of modernism, Anthony Smith (1986), emphasizes the relationship between nations and ethnicity and then develops his ethno-symbolists approach, asserting the importance of subjective elements such as common history and memory, symbols and values, as well as mass culture, in national-building. Additionally, he identifies the territorial "homeland" component of nations and suggests that "the landscapes of the nation define and characterize the identity of people" (Smith, 1995, p. 56). In defense of primordialism, Bairner (2009) discusses the relationship between national sports and national landscapes in Britain, Ireland, Spain, and North America, thereby offering insights into the real and material components of nations and sports.

However, the modernist perspective understands nations and nationalism as social constructions that emerge in response to new economic and social challenges (Stokke, 2017). Rooted in modernism, Hobsbawm and Ranger's (1983) "invented tradition" together with Anderson's (1983) "imagined community" are regularly invoked in discussions of the relationship between sport and national identity formation (Blain, Boyle, & O'Donnell, 1993; Giulianotti, 2005; Hrstić & Mustapić, 2015; Silk & Falcous, 2005; Smith & Porter, 2004). Additionally, Billig's (1995) concept of "banal nationalism," which was influenced by the work of constructionists such as Gellner (1983) and Anderson (1983), is central to an influential study of everyday forms of nationhood in terms of the micro-level creation and re-creation of national identity (Hearn, 2007). For example, unlike most nationalism scholars, Edensor (2002, p. 78) devotes a section to sport in his study of national identity and everyday life, concluding:

> Sport is increasingly situated in the mediatised matrix of national life, is institutionalised in schools, widely represented in a host of cultural forms and is an everyday practice for millions of national subjects. These everyday and spectacular contexts provide one of the most popular ways in which national identity is grounded.

Following on from this, and with reference to Billig (1995) and Edensor (2002), Bowes and Bairner (2019) examine the lived experience of sportswomen who have represented England and reveal the importance of national symbols as banal reminders of the nation as well as of the nationalism of everyday life experienced by these women.

Equally important is a key debate over ethnic and civic nationalism (Kohn, 1967). Based on assumptions about primordialism and modernism, Smith (1986) identifies two ideal types of determinants of the nation and national identity: the Western or civic-territorial model, and the Eastern or ethnic model. However, the resultant dichotomy between civic and ethnic nationalism has been consistently criticized in the literature (Bairner, 2001; Brubaker, 1999; Smith, 1986). In reality, as Smith (1995, p. 99) himself observed, pure forms of one or other type of nationalism are not found as "modern nations are simultaneously and necessarily civic and ethnic." According to Kellas's (1991) overlapping social nationalism theory, nationalism can be compartmentalized further into the categories of civic, secessionist, unificatory, and expansionist (see also Bairner, 2001).

Research on sport, national identity, and nationalism has not escaped the type of discussion that has characterized much nationalism and national identity literature more generally, and ranges from considerations of the type of nationalism being displayed to which type is associated with specific nation-states (Kelly, 2007). Based on these different theories of nations and nationalism, sport offers insights into varieties of imperialism, the cultural politics of anti-imperialist struggle, and postcolonial legacies (Bairner, 2008). The global diffusion of British sports such as cricket, rugby union, and soccer undeniably provided cultural support to Britain's expansionist ambitions in the second half of the 19th century (Bairner, 2008). However, although playing the imperial masters' games might well have been considered a sign of cultural inferiority, it also offered colonial peoples some visible opportunities to measure themselves against their present and former rulers (Bairner, 2008). Even China, a semicolonial and semifeudal society in the early 20th century, actively used Western sports as a way of making the "sick man of East Asia" (Xu, 2008, p. 61) healthy and strong again as well as serving the purposes of anti-imperialism (Riordan & Jones, 1999).

To examine the relationship between sport, nation-states, and constitutional nationalism during the Cold War, the experience of the Soviet Union provides considerable evidence of the use of sport in general and especially Olympic sport to advertise a particular brand of communism (Bairner, 2008). In addition, the role of sport in the Cold War was expanded when the United States led a boycott of the 1980 Moscow Olympics and, in return, the Soviet Union and its allies responded in kind when the Games moved to Los Angeles in 1984. In fact, most national leaders in the modern world are highly cognizant of the role that sport can play in boosting confidence and gaining markers of esteem (Bairner, 2008).

Using the PRC as another example, the "two Chinas" issue (between the PRC and the Republic of China, established on the island of Taiwan by the Chinese Nationalist Party [Kuomintang] following defeat at the hands of Mao Zedong's communist army), often centered in the 1950s on the question of who should represent China on the International Olympic Committee (IOC). Furthermore, even when situated outside the IOC, the Chinese Communist Party continued to use sport as a vehicle to advance larger diplomatic and political goals (Xu, 2008). As an example, in 1959, Ping-Pong (table tennis) provided a first World Championship title for the PRC, in Dortmund, Germany (Li & Gao, 2019; Lu & Fan, 2014; Ren, 2010; Xu, 2008). Meanwhile, based on the idea of "Friend First, Competition Second," the PRC used sport and its athletes to serve as ambassadors to Third World countries, facilitating a soft-power approach to diplomacy (Close, Xu, & Askew, 2007). Subsequently, "Ping-Pong diplomacy" even helped to break the ice in Sino-U.S. relations by establishing contact through table tennis players acting as "quasi envoys" (Bairner, 2008, p. 45).

Through such strategies, therefore, sport played a crucial role in the PRC's engagement with the international community in terms of its entry into the United Nations, the normalization of Sino-U.S. diplomatic relations, and, ultimately, its entry onto the world stage as a rising regional and global political-economic player (Close, Xu, & Askew, 2007). Eventually, in 1979, the IOC recognized the Chinese Olympic Committee's right to membership (Ren, 2010). Ever since, sport, not least table tennis, has continued to help construct Chinese national identity in a process aimed at inspiring the patriotism of the people, contributing to foreign relations, and constituting a Chinese collective memory of Chinese people's achievements (Li & Gao, 2019).

However, it is essential not only to be conscious of the state nationalism of globally recognized nation-states whose politicians use sporting success for ideological and propagandist purposes, but also to be aware of its use in cultivating rising support for the political independence of submerged (or stateless) peoples in Europe, Scotland, Catalonia, and the Basque Country (Bairner, 2008; Vaczi, Bairner, & Whigham, 2019; Whigham, Lopez-Gonzalez, and Ramon, 2019). As Bairner (2001, p. 169) observes, "In most nation-states, there exists a hegemonic national identity that is not necessarily inclusive. In such instances, some citizens may well choose to celebrate an alternative national identity, with sport playing an important part in their activities." Indeed, sport offers both fans and athletes opportunities to celebrate a national identity that is different from and, in some cases, opposed to their ascribed nationality (Bairner, 2008).

It is also worth noting which sports have commonly been the most effective tools for cultural resistance by both cultural and political nationalists (Bairner, 2008). With reference to Scotland's constitutional position within the United Kingdom, Bairner (2015, p. 377) describes the oddities that such dynamics can produce: "The anomalous situation . . . allows for the co-existence of nation-state Olympic representation and national governing bodies and teams in a variety of sports, most notably perhaps rugby union and association football."

In Spain's case, Hargreaves (2000) discusses the various relations between sport and nationalism. Importantly, his work explores the differences between nationalist and nonnationalist constructions of sport and offers influential distinctions between the nation-state (Spain) and the historic nation (Catalonia) and between nationality (Spanish) and national identity (Catalan), the latter contributing to many people's support for secession (Bairner, 2015). McFarland (2020) argues that, in Spain, numerous regions have often used sporting endeavors to demonstrate their unique culture, for example, pelota for the Basques and Valencians as well as physical education in Catalonia. Importantly, football has also provided a major focal point for Catalan and Basque national identity (Ball, 2001; Burns, 2000).

In the so-called British Isles, Maguire and Tuck (1998) argue that the rugby union has had the capacity to allow the Celtic nations to challenge an English cultural hegemony that favors a dominant British/English national identity. This can also be found in Harris's (2006) study, which discusses the relationship between Welsh national identity and rugby union. The Irish case is even more complex. For example, Sugden and Bairner (1993) assert that football in Northern Ireland has tended to intensify division rather than forge unity among opposing communities. Moreover, Irish support for national representation, sometimes described as foreign or English, including rugby union, golf, and football, was once considered patriotic rather than nationalistic, and even relatively politically shallow, in the eyes of some followers of the Gaelic games' traditions (Bairner, 2008).

There are several comparative analyses of the relationship between sport and nationalism in Scotland and Catalonia which fill a vacuum that has existed in previous comparative studies of these two submerged nations (Vaczi et al., 2019; Whigham et al., 2019). Here, secessionist ideas can be seen as having emanated from mutually exclusive sets of relationships (Catalan vs. Spanish, Scottish vs. British, and secessionist vs. unionist), while also allowing subjects to pass from one state to another, occupy them nonexclusively, change their minds, or nuance their views (Vaczi et al., 2019). Indeed, Bairner (2008) has argued that these different forms of national identity need not even be mutually exclusive. Indeed, it is possible to support British and Scottish teams or to represent Wales and also the United Kingdom. This can be seen in the Spanish case as well. Although the strength of the relationship between sporting nationalism and political nationalism remains unclear, sports will continue to matter in debates about the political futures of Scotland and Catalonia.

Maguire, Jarvie, Mansfield, and Bradley's (2002, p. 153) discussion of the multilayered and overlapping character of the nationalism and sport nexus suggests that the nationalism associated with sport can be constructed by many different forces and can "be manifested within and between different types of nationalism, be real and imagined, be a creative or reflective force, be both positive and negative, transient and temporary, multifaceted and multilayered and be evolutionary in its format." Furthermore, as mentioned earlier, within the context of globalization, both the relationship between sport and national identity and the future of the nation as well as nation-state have been seriously questioned (Bairner, 2001). To get closer to being able to answer such questions, it is necessary to go beyond the world of sport in the first instance, by engaging with more mainstream nationalism studies and adopting new methods of inquiry.

APPROACHES

Bairner (2015) notes the tendency in the sociology of sport to take for granted such concepts as nation, nation-state, nationality, national identity, and nationalism. Because of this, he has argued that to study the various relationship between sport and these concepts, it is necessary perhaps to adopt a wider range of methodological and theoretical techniques. Bourdieu (1988, p. 153) asserted that "to understand a sport, whatever it may be, one must locate its position in the space of sports." Western societies such as Spain, the United Kingdom, and Ireland have provided particularly fertile soil for sociologists of sport with an interest in nationalism and national identities (Bairner, 2015).

In terms of which sports are most relevant, association football has certainly been most discussed in the literature on sport and nationalism (Brentin & Cooley, 2016). Significantly, Hobsbawm (1992, p. 143) observed that "the imagined community of millions seems more real as a team of eleven named people." According to Sugden and Tomlinson (1998), moreover, football must be regarded as a center for inspiring and expressing national identity and its mobilized political form, nationalism. However, Bairner (2001) argues that although the linkage of sport and nationalism has become a matter of common sense, there is a lack of evidence in terms of which types of nationalism are involved and the precise ways in which they interact with sport.

International sporting competitions, such as the FIFA World Cup and the Olympic Games, have transformed sport into a field in which the nation is directly pitted against the threat of globalization (Brentin & Cooley, 2016). Yet, as Jarvie (2006) argues, it seems that the complicated relationship between nationalism, national identity, and sport is growing, and it certainly shows no signs of dying. Bairner (2001) agrees that, as long as the nation-state continues to be the most common form of political organization, it is hugely important that the members of each nation-state are allowed, if they wish, to feel a sense of belonging to the nation on which that state has been built. Sport helps to provide that, even though Pierre de Coubertin expected that sport, with its internationalist doctrine, could be the sociocultural institution with which to stimulate a unifying and multicultural globalization process, thereby promoting solidarity, peace, and understanding between nations (Bairner, 2008; Brentin & Cooley, 2016; Rowe, 2003). In this respect, Bairner (2001) questions how precisely sport can really help to construct and reproduce the national identity of so many people and asks to what extent the process of globalization can weaken the linkage between sport and national identity.

A discussion of national sports can also be valuable for the study of sport and nationalism since it necessitates some reference to the main debates in nationalism studies. From a primordial perspective, national sports are bound up with the diverse criteria which legitimate historic nationhood, including language, topography, the soil, and blood ties (Bairner, 2008). On the other hand, from a modernist perspective, national sports are simply part of a panoply of elements that serve to legitimize the nation-state (Bairner, 2008). Additionally, Bairner argues that to explore national sports in a specific space can make use of particular concepts of nationalism, such as "imagined community" and "invented tradition," as well as the distinction between ethnic and civic nationalism.

In this respect, case studies are widely adopted to explore the relationship between sport and nations in Europe and North America (Bairner, 2001, 2005, 2009; Sugden & Bairner, 1993; Barrer, 2007; Bartoluci & Doupona, 2019 Bowes & Bairner, 2019; Brentin, 2013; Campos, 2003; Cardoza, 2010; Cronin, 1999; Hargreaves, 1992, 2000; Houlihan, 1997; Jackson, 1994, 1998; Vaczi, 2015, 2016; Vaczi et al., 2019) and increasingly in East Asia (Close, Xu, & Askew, 2007; Jarvie, Hwang, & Brennan, 2008; Lee & Maguire, 2011; Li & Gao, 2019; Lu & Fan, 2014; Ren, 2010; G. Xu, 2008; X. Xu, 2006).

As for specific research approaches, media analysis has long been dominant in national identity studies as a research method and indeed has offered some valuable insights (Lee & Maguire, 2011). According to Madianou (2005), there are two theoretical models to conceptualize the relationship between media and national identity, which can be identified as a top-down model and a bottom-up model. The former regards the mass media as one of the key social institutions that actively construct a sense of national identity among the masses. The latter highlights those robust cultures and identities, which are rooted and manifested in everyday life, and are constructed by normal people's discourses, which are then reflected in the media. In fact, the top-down model has been extensively utilized by both mainstream nationalism scholars and sociologists of sport. For example, Anderson (1983) argues that newspapers can play a significant role in constructing dominant national cultures, meanings, and ideologies, thereby prompting people to become engaged in national discourse. Indeed, there are no other social institutions that can achieve what the media can, especially when covering major sporting events, to make nationalism visible in such dramatic ways and enthusiastically inscribe the existence of an "us" into a cultural collective memory as well as uniting the masses around their shared nation (Tosa, 2015). International mega-events are arguably viewed as a form of ritualized war (Elias, 1996). In this respect, the media project myths of unity and collectivism onto people who then identify representative athletes are embodiments of themselves (Poulton, 2004).

In addition to the mediatization of international sport competitions, Billig (1995, p. 122) identifies sport coverage in daily newspapers as everyday producers of "feeling at home in this world of waved flags," which is associated more closely with the bottom-up model of constructing nationhood. Despite this, scholars have relatively ignored studies of everyday life production carried out by the mass public, even though it seems obvious that daily discourse constantly strengthens people's national identities, sometimes even without their being conscious of its underlying presence (Billig, 1995).

However, due to the rapid changes in communication technologies during recent decades, especially the emergence of social media, the mass media's role in shaping and maintaining national identity has been challenged. The new media have provided additional data sources and increased possibilities for further exploration of the relationship between sport, nationalism, and national identity as lived online. To understand how such new communication technologies can make a difference in sport and national identity studies, it is necessary to be aware of current debates.

On the one hand, the internet and social media contribute to the free flow of information and the promulgation of global consciousness, serving people's individual ties to locality and displacing the hegemonic position of national identity (Lu & Yu, 2019). On the other hand, Castells (1996) observes that national identity is reaffirmed through the internet because of the ways in which the social construction of the internet is constituted as well as designed, organized, owned, used, regulated, and controlled (Lu &Yu, 2019). Additionally, sports fans are marked as manifestations of national character, especially because of the "performances in stadia of fans, their use of music, the clothes they wear and the flags they wave, their responses to sporting action, defeat and victory" (Edensor, 2002, p. 81; see also Brentin & Cooley, 2016). In the virtual world, social media may also actively develop unique and engaging relationships with home teams. It is worth noting that Chinese cyber-nationalism, as a platform and a vehicle, allows nationalist data to reach the mass of the population, gathering people from different classes and regions to organize and express their nationalist sentiments online within and beyond the sports world (Wu, 2010). For example, the remarks of the general manager of the NBA Houston Rockets, Daryl Morey, in support of Hong Kong protests during China's celebration of the 70th National Day of the PRC, seriously hurt the feelings of Chinese NBA fans as well as the wider population and led to a dramatic Chinese online backlash in 2019. Within the context of current tense Sino-U.S. relations, anti-American nationalism united the Chinese fans behind the saying "Chinese Rockets fans are first Chinese. We love Chinese red more than Rockets red" (Wallbank & Cang, 2019). With examples such as this, it is important for more sport and nationalism studies to be conducted within the context of the internet and social media.

Regardless of whether in the context of mass media or social media, the presentation and representation of identities are further activated through ritualized sporting spectacles in global settings by various practices of fandom and spectatorship, which include the everyday consumption of nationally framed sport media and products (Bairner, 2001; Billig,

1995; Edensor, 2002; Fox, 2006; Hobsbawm, 1992). Essentially, no matter whether in a politically charged or a more banal way, mediated sport reminds audiences of the binary of
cultural opposites in terms of distinguishing "us" from "them" and the processes of erasing
the heterogeneous articulations of "us" (Jhally, 1989). Thus, in key ways, as seen through the
lens of sports media, the nation is more real than imagined (Poulton, 2004).

With reference to the priorities underlying much research, Dóczi (2011) observes how
the politicians and media pay more attention to the success of elite athletes, who perform
an identity-constructing function, while amateur sports are comparatively neglected within
public discourse. As national representatives, elite athletes are central to most people's
experiences of sport and national identity and are the symbolic embodiment of imagined
communities within and beyond the sports world (Bowes & Bairner, 2019). Therefore,
some studies have shown that it is important to ask those athletes who play this role about
their identities and sense of belonging (McGee & Bairner, 2011; Tuck, 2003). Despite the
challenges it may present, there is a need for future studies to emphasize the individual
experience of sportsmen and sportswomen (including nonelite athletes) in relation to how
they are constructed by and interact with national and international forces.

More studies of underresearched national contexts in relation to sport are also required.
In addition to engaging with a wider range of methodological and theoretical techniques, it
is necessary to invoke the "intersections between nation and nationalism on the one hand
and [a] range of other categories including social class, race, ethnicity and gender on the
other" (Bairner, 2005, p. 378). It is also worth paraphrasing C. L. R. James's (1963) famous
question and ask: What do they know of sport and national identity if it is only sport and
national identity that they know? As Edensor (2002) argues, national identity is supposed
to be studied at the level of the demotic and the popular. It can also be studied, therefore,
through the lenses of geography, artistic performance, material culture, music, and film.

DEBATES

In addition to having a good understanding of different theories of nationalism and a clearly
thought-out method for studying the relationship between sport, nationalism, and national
identities, it is also important for the generation of new research to be continually looking
out for relatively underexamined examples of how that relationship manifests. For example,
although the relationship between sport, nation, and gender is a growing area of interest, it
has suffered in the past principally because the idea of men as warriors has smoothly elided
into a belief that male athletes are proxy warriors who also fight on behalf of the nation; as
a result, the role of female athletes has tended to be ignored. Yet there are many countries,
China and the United Kingdom included, that owe as much, if not more, to women for their
successes in global competitions and their placings at or near the top of Olympic medal tables. A necessary adjunct to research in this area is further examination of the sport media
and the relative neglect of women's sport and female athletes, even those who have brought
glory to their nation.

As was highlighted in an earlier section, the relationship between sport and what it
means to be Chinese is another issue that demands ever more serious attention, not only
from Chinese scholars but also from those in the West. Although the idea of the modern

nation-state first emerged in Europe and, to some extent, was imposed on other parts of the world as part of the process whereby former empires were dismantled, nationalist ideas emanating from the West exerted a strong influence on those who became central to nation-building projects in Africa and Asia. It is unlikely, for example, if Sun Yat-sen, the architect of the modern Chinese nation, would have developed his ideas about nationalism in the way that he did had he not spent time in exile in Europe, Canada, and even Japan, where Western theories of nationalism were already influential. Similarly, many of the first leaders of newly independent sub-Saharan African states had lived and studied in Western countries: Julius Nyerere (Tanzania) graduated from the University of Edinburgh, Kwame Nkrumah (Ghana) studied at Lincoln University in Pennsylvania, and Jomo Kenyatta (Kenya) attended both University College London and the London School of Economics. Only one step removed from Western experience, Kenneth Kaunda (Zambia) was the son of an ordained Church of Scotland missionary. The challenge for these politicians was to work out to what extent and in what ways Western ideas about the nation could be transplanted to parts of the world in which tribalism remained the foremost mechanism for binding groups of people together. As a result of such tendencies, the relationship between sport and the nation in postcolonial societies deserves rather more attention. Do national sporting achievements help to unite people who belong to different tribes and speak different languages, or does sport simply reflect the near impossibility of establishing uncontested nation-states on such potentially unstable foundations? These questions will be addressed in due course with specific reference to Nigeria and, taking another Asian example, Pakistan. First, however, we consider the issue of athlete naturalization.

There are still strong grounds for believing that the link between nationalism and sports is becoming weaker and that the very existence of international competition is threatened by the twin forces of globalization and consumer capitalism, along with the acceleration of migratory flows (Bairner, 2008). Sports labor migration takes place on three main levels: within nations, between nations on the same continent, and between nations located on different continents and/or in different hemispheres (Maguire, 1999). Although economics plays a vital role in determining the patterns of sports migratory flows, other factors also shape global sport migration in terms of politics, history, geography, and culture (Maguire & Pearton, 2000). Within this process, nationality, more perhaps than national identity, has become increasingly flexible (Maguire & Pearton, 2000). Athletes migrate from one nation-state to another not only to play for different clubs but also, in many instances, to adopt a new sporting nationality. However, the increasing tendency of legally naturalizing athletes leading to nationality changes challenges the "traditional vision of the nation as a group of people belonging to the same culture and having the same ethnic origin" (Poli, 2007, p. 653). In particular, evident unease is generated by athletes playing in international competitions who are deemed by some to be unable to represent the nation "properly." Additionally, these migrating athletes are often regarded as mercenaries and suspected of not being loyal to their adopted country (Chiba, Ebihara, & Morino, 2001). Regardless of the fact that people's attitudes toward these naturalized athletes can be modified by good sporting performances, the essence of both sports fans' attitudes and naturalized athletes' identities are unstable, multifaceted, and fragmented.

From a process-sociological perspective, Maguire (1999; Maguire & Bale, 1994) has provided several valuable thoughts about sport migration, including identifying its character, typology, and pattern as well as its relationship to national identity. For example, in the context of the London 2012 Summer Olympic Games, established-outsider relations were constructed and represented in English media-sport discourse through a series of "I/ we" and "us/them" identity characterizations at a national level and specifically through the using of personal pronouns and references to national traits and symbols (Poulton & Maguire, 2012). In this respect, the English press established a boundary between those "dual nationals" who can be included/embraced as members of "Team GB," and those who were to be excluded/rejected, as "plastic Brits" (Poulton & Maguire, 2012).

In fact, understanding the inclusion of a naturalized athlete as a member of an imagined community can tell us a great deal about the sociocultural and politico-economic climate in a specific country. Nationalism and national identity can also be examined through sport in terms of the social inclusion and exclusion of naturalized athletes not only in their adopted country but also, in some cases, in their country of origin. However, sport naturalization studies are still at the stage of "relative infancy" in terms of conceptual level and empirical inquiry (Maguire, 2004). It is worth noting that in 2019, both Chinese football and winter sports experienced an unprecedented "naturalization fever," with an increase in Winter Olympics medals and FIFA World Cup success as goals. Such tendencies should deservedly attract significantly more academic attention.

As argued earlier, secessionist movements, often using nationalist rhetoric, are globally prominent despite, or perhaps because of, fissures that have opened or reopened in the face of the perceived homogenizing effects of globalization. When a populist leader talks about making the nation great, one immediate response is likely to be to ask the question "What nation?" The cases of Scotland and Catalonia have already been discussed. The fact that they have received considerable attention in the sport studies field reflects not only their contemporary significance but also the dominance of Western scholars and Western case studies in this research area. But what of secessionist politics in other parts of the world?

In much of the developing world, rather than asking "What nation?" there may be a much greater temptation to ask, "Why a nation-state?" and "Why this nation-state?" For example, the marriage between the northern and southern regions in Nigeria has been described as resembling a pair of shears, conjoined so that they cannot be separated but moving in opposite directions. According to Mazi Nnamdi Kanu (2019), the attempt to unite the rich South and the poor North and balance the economies of both regions has simply never worked. This is not surprising in a nation where ethnic pluralism and cultural diversity are often pervaded by a tense and volatile atmosphere emanating from discord and rivalry among different tribes and religions (Adenrele & Olugbenga, 2012). The name of Biafra, located in southeast Nigeria, is best known to the outside world because of the civil war that took place between 1967 and 1970 and resulted in the deaths of countless combatants and of 2 million Biafrans who starved to death in a famine that is now generally agreed to have been the result of a policy of genocide. The war itself was triggered by the predominantly Christian Igbo population of Biafra seeking to secede from the Nigerian state, a demand which has resurfaced in recent years and is not without sporting implications (Ogbah, 2021).

If Biafrans were to get their wish, their football team would likely emerge from the breakup much stronger than that of Nigeria. Ngobua (2019) believes that because athletes from northern Nigeria have never featured prominently in the senior national team, they are nowhere near the level of players from the rest of the nation.

Even though no prominent Biafran sports figure has come out strongly in support of secession, this is perhaps largely due to fear of sanctions and attacks from the government and its agencies. There have been reports in some blogs, however, about moves by former Super Eagles captains Nwankwo Kanu, Mikel Obi, and Augustine (Jay-Jay) Okocha to form a Biafran national team (Opera News, 2020). This is likely an example of Biafran-sponsored propaganda; nevertheless, none of the men has denied the reports. Sport has in the past been the biggest unifying factor in Nigeria. However, as people lose any faith they had in the union, sport may no longer be able to resist calls for national unity.

In a different part of the world, ethnic and sectarian conflicts have been "the common phenomena in Pakistan's politics during the last decades of the twentieth century" (Sudheep, 2016, p. 31). Over time, sport has not only been affected by these divisions but has also helped to exacerbate them. Sindh province made a significant contribution to the development of cricket in Pakistan; however, discrimination based on ethnocentric biases and favoritism has been a major factor in the selection processes in cricket in recent years, leading to the exclusion of Sindhi speakers from national teams. Urdu-speaking migrants and Punjabis have come to dominate the Pakistan Cricket Board and control the selection process (as they do in the bureaucratic and political institutions of the nation-state) (Gul & Bairner, 2021).

In the Sindh Assembly in Karachi in 2013, Provincial Law Minister Ayaz Soomro agreed with Pakistan Muslim League-Functional legislator Nusrat Sehar Abbasi that Sindh was underrepresented on the national team and assured the house that the matter would be taken up with the Pakistan Cricket Board. Despite that assurance, three years later blogger Sahir Palijo (2016) still felt it necessary to pose the question "Why aren't there any Sindhi and Baloch players in our PSL [Pakistan Super League] squads?" In fact, for supporters of Sindh independence, the answer was relatively straightforward inasmuch as the selection of PSL squads was simply a reflection of the discrimination that those from the Sindh province and Balochistan have faced almost from the very formation of Pakistan.

The situation has improved somewhat in recent years. Nevertheless, evidence of discrimination toward young cricketers from Sindh and Balochistan persist. With C. L. R. James's (1963) famous question in mind, the reasons for the dearth of Sindhi cricketers on the Pakistan national team cannot be found in cricket itself. The explanation runs deeper than that and is to be found in the history and political evolution of the country itself. As a Sindhi commentator has argued:

> Problems of national unity in Pakistan stem from the very philosophy of the country—as prophesied by those who wield power. The philosophy and ideology of the state negates the reality, i.e. the existence of nations that together formed Pakistan. The policies and practices based on the philosophy and ideology of the creation of Pakistan have obviously damaged the problems of national unity. (Khan, 1989, cited in Das, 2001, p. 155)

Like Nigeria, the Pakistan state can be regarded as a Western solution to a non-Western problem. Although knowing about cricket in Pakistan is insufficient to permit a full understanding of the tensions that exist within the country, ignoring the country's most popular sport would mean failing to appreciate how these tensions and the reasons for them are recognized in everyday life.

CONCLUSION

More studies of underresearched national contexts in relation to sport are undoubtedly required. In addition, more studies need to shine light on the role of female athletes as national beings and the sociocultural impacts of athlete naturalization. Equally urgent is the need for a wider range of methodological and theoretical techniques. Although print media analysis has tended to dominate the research methods used by sociologists of sport to study national identities and has produced some valuable insights (Lee & Maguire, 2011), the media landscape has changed dramatically, and new digital media articulations, including social media, have become an increasingly significant data source.

In addition, while recognizing the difficulties faced by researchers seeking to access elite performers, much more of the type of data which this can produce is certainly needed, as demonstrated by the work of Tuck (2003), McGee and Bairner (2010), Bowes and Bairner (2019), and Carroll and Bairner (2019), among others. Following on from Steven Jackson's (1994, 1998) pioneering studies, moreover, it would also be beneficial to facilitate more understandings about the intersections between nation and nationalism on the one hand and a range of other categories, including social class, race, ethnicity, and gender, on the other. For example, instead of focusing primarily on how female athletes are represented in their national media, it would be important to learn, from interviews or from their own use of social media, how these women see themselves in relation to the national project.

Nations and nationalism are not about to disappear, and international sport (i.e., sporting competition between nations and/or nation-states) will undoubtedly continue to be the very essence of global sports mega-events unless such events are more permanently put on hold as a result of COVID-19, unavoidable future pandemics, and the threats posed by the climate emergency. Such impacts would open the way to greater emphasis being placed on domestic national competitions, which will, in turn, also raise essential questions about the nation: Who belongs to it? Who doesn't belong? Who wants to make it great? and Who wants to secede from it?

In sum, the first of the key recommendations made in this chapter is that those who wish to understand the relationship between sport, nationalism, and national identities must be fully cognizant of theoretical and conceptual literature in the field of nationalism studies. They must also be prepared to consider new ways of studying sport's relationship with nations and nationalism, for example, by speaking to elite athletes and by moving away from an emphasis on the print media to new social media for the purposes of data. They must endeavor to understand more fully the status of female elite athletes both as national beings and as proxy warriors. Above all, they must be confident that, far from being dead or in the process of dying, nationalism remains a highly significant ideology, as evidenced by the rhetoric and acts of populist world leaders and by the demands of those seeking secession from existing nation-states, both of which have profound implications for sport.

REFERENCES

Adenrele, A., & Olugbenga, O. (2012). Unity in diversity in Nigeria's nationhood: Which way forward? *International Journal of Scientific Research*, 2(8), 482–484.

Anderson, B. (1983). *Imagined communities: Reflections on the origins and spread of nationalism*. Oxford: Verso.

Bairner, A. (2001). *Sport, nationalism, and globalization*. Albany: State University of New York Press.

Bairner, A. (2005). *Sport and the Irish: Histories, identities, issues*. Dublin: University College Dublin Press.

Bairner, A. (2009). National sports and national landscapes: In defence of primordialism. *National Identities, 11*(3), 223–239.

Bairner, A. (2015). Assessing the sociology of sport: On national identity and nationalism. *International Review for the Sociology of Sport, 50*(4–5), 375–377.

Bairner, A. (2008). Sport, nationalism and globalization: Relevance, impact, consequences. *Hitotsubashi Journal of Arts and Sciences, 49*(1), 43–53.

Ball, P. (2001). *Morbo: The story of Spanish football*. London: WSC Books.

Barrer, J. P. B. (2007). "Satan is God!" Re-imagining contemporary Slovak national identity through sport. *Sport in Society, 10*(2), 223–238.

Bartoluci, S., & Doupona, M. (2019). He's ours, not yours! Reinterpreting national identity in a post-socialist context. *International Review for the Sociology of Sport, 55*(4), 490–506.

Billig, M. (1995). *Banal nationalism*. London: Sage Publications.

Blain, N., Boyle, R., & O'Donnell, H. (1993). *Sport and national identity in the European media*. Leicester: Leicester University Press.

Bogdanov, D. (2011). Influence of national sport team identity on national identity. DigiNole. http://purl.flvc.org/fsu/fd/FSU_migr_etd-3624.

Bourdieu, P. (1988). Program for a sociology of sport. *Sociology of Sport Journal, 5*(2), 153–161. https://doi.org/10.1123/ssj.5.2.153.

Bowes, A., & Bairner, A. (2019). Three lions on her shirt: Hot and banal nationalism for England's sportswomen. *Journal of Sport and Social Issues, 43*(6), 531–550. https://doi.org/10.1177/0193723519850878.

Brentin, D. (2013). "A lofty battle for the nation": The social roles of sport in Tudjman's Croatia. *Sport in Society, 16*(8), 993–1008.

Brentin, D., & Cooley, L. (2016). Nationalism and sport: A review of the literature. *Studies on National Movements, 3*. https://snm.nise.eu/index.php/studies/article/view/0306s.

Breuilly, J. 1993. *Nationalism and the state*. Manchester: Manchester University Press.

Brubaker, R. (1999). The Manichean myth: Rethinking the distinction between "civic" and "ethnic" nationalism. In H. Kriesi, K. Armingeon, H. Siegrist, & A. Wimmer (Eds.), *Nation and national identity: The European experience in perspective* (pp. 55–71). Chur, Switzerland: Verlag Rüegger.

Burns, J. (2000). *Barça: A people's passion*. London: Bloomsbury.

Campos, C. (2003). Beating the bounds: The Tour de France and national identity. *International Journal of the History of Sport, 20*(2), 149–174. https://doi.org/10.1080/09523360412331305673.

Cardoza, A. (2010). "Making Italians"? Cycling and national identity in Italy: 1900–1950. *Journal of Modern Italian Studies, 15*(3), 354–377. https://doi.org/10.1080/13545711003768576.

Carroll, G., & Bairner, A. (2019). In from the side: Exile international rugby union players in Britain, blood ties and national identities. *National Identities, 21*(4) 2019, 417–433.

Castells, M. (1996). The net and the self: Working notes for a critical theory of the international society. *Critique of Anthropology, 16*, 9–38.

Chiba, N., Ebihara, O., & Morino, S. (2001). Globalization, naturalization and identity: The case of borderless elite athletes in Japan. *International Review for the Sociology of Sport, 36*(2), 203–221.

Close, P., Xu, X., & Askew, D. (2007). *The Beijing Olympiad*. New York: Routledge.

Cronin, M. (1999). *Sport and nationalism in Ireland*. Dublin: Four Courts Press.

Cronin, M., & Mayall, D. (1998). Sport and ethnicity: Some introductory remarks. In M. Cronin & D. Mayall (Eds.), *Sporting nationalisms: Identity, ethnicity, immigration and assimilation* (pp. 1–13). London: Frank Cass.

Das, S. (2001). *Kashmir and Sindh: Nation-building, ethnicity and regional politics in South Asia*. London: Anthem Press.

Dóczi, T. (2011). Gold fever? Sport and national identity—The Hungarian case. *International Review for the Sociology of Sport, 47*(2), 165–182. https://doi.org/10.1177/1012690210393828.

Edensor, T. (2002). *National identity, popular culture and everyday life*. Oxford: Berg.

Elias, N. (1996). *The Germans: Power struggles and the development of habitus in the nineteenth and twentieth centuries*. Cambridge, U.K.: Polity Press.

Fox, J. (2006). Consuming the nation: Holidays, sports, and the production of collective belonging. *Ethnic and Racial Studies, 29*(2), 217–236. https://doi.org/10.1080/0141987050 0465207.

Gellner, E. (1983). *Nations and nationalism*. Oxford: Blackwell.

Giulianotti, R. (2005). Sport spectators and the social consequences of commodification: Critical perspectives from Scottish football. *Journal of Sport and Social Issues, 29*(4), 386–410.

Giulianotti, R., & Robertson, R. (2007). *Globalization and sport*. Hoboken, NJ: Wiley-Blackwell.

Guinness, D., & Besnier, N. (2016). Nation, nationalism, and sport: Fijian rugby in the local-global nexus. *Anthropological Quarterly, 89*(4), 1109–1141.

Gul, S., & Bairner, A. (2021). Narratives of nationalist politics and sport in Sindh. In M. Vaczi & A. Bairner (Eds.), *Sport and secessionism* (pp. 171–185). London: Routledge.

Hargreaves, J. (1992). Olympism and nationalism: Some preliminary considerations. *International Review for the Sociology of Sport, 27*(2), 119–135. https://doi.org/10.1177/101 269029202700203.

Hargreaves, J. (2000). *Freedom for Catalonia? Catalan nationalism, Spanish identity and the Barcelona Olympic Games*. Cambridge: Cambridge University Press.

Harris, J. (2006). (Re)presenting Wales: National identity and celebrity in the postmodern rugby world. *North American Journal of Welsh Studies, 6*(2): 1–13.

Hearn, J. (2007). National identity: Banal, personal and embedded. *Nations and Nationalism, 13*(4), 657–674.

Hobsbawm, E. J. (1992). *Nations and nationalism since 1780: Programme, myth, reality*. Cambridge: Cambridge University Press.

Hobsbawm, E. J., & Ranger, T. (Eds.). (1983). *The invention of tradition*. Cambridge: Cambridge University Press.

Houlihan, B. (1997). Sport, national identity and public policy. *Nations and Nationalism, 3*(1), 113–137.

Hrstić, I., & Mustapić, M. (2015). Sport and politics in Croatia—Athletes as national icons in history textbooks. *Altre Modernità, 14*, 148–165. https://doi.org/10.13130/2035-7680/6607.

Jackson, S. L. (1994). Gretzky, crisis, and Canadian identity in 1988: Rearticulating the Amercianization of culture debate. *Sociology of Sport Journal, 11*(4), 428–446.

Jackson, S. L. (1998). A twist of race: Ben Johnson and the Canadian crisis of racial and national identity. *Sociology of Sport Journal, 15*, 21–40.

James, C. L. R. (1963). *Beyond a boundary*. London: Stanley Paul and Co.

Jarvie, G. (2006). *Sport, culture and society: An introduction*. London: Routledge.

Jarvie, G., Hwang, D., & Brennan, M. (2008). *Sport, revolution and the Beijing Olympics.* Oxford: Berg.

Jhally, S. (1989). Cultural studies and the sport/media complex. In L. A. Wenner (Ed.), *Media, sports and society* (pp. 70–93). London: Sage.

Kanu, N. (2019, November 6). Soldiers had come to kill me: I would be shot in the head and dumped in a shallow grave. *The Independent.* www.independent.co.uk/news/long_reads/nnamdi-kanu-indigenous-people-of-biafra-conflict 1967-a9169196.html.

Kellas, J. (1991). *The politics of nationalism and ethnicity.* London: Macmillan Education.

Kelly, J. (2007). *Flowers of Scotland? A sociological analysis of national identities, rugby union and association football in Scotland* (Unpublished PhD thesis). Loughborough University.

Khan, D. (1989). A Sindhi view. *Sindhi Quarterly, 17*(4), 11.

Kohn, H. (1967). *The idea of nationalism: A study in its origins and background.* New Brunswick, NJ: Transaction Publishers.

Lee, J., & Maguire, J. (2011). Road to reunification? Unitary Korean nationalism in South Korean media coverage of the 2004 Athens Olympic Games. *Sociology, 45*(5), 848–867. https://doi.org/10.1177/0038038511413429.

Li, G., & Gao, R. (2019). National identity and collective memory: The shaping process and symbolic significance of "national sport" table tennis. *Journal of Shenyang Sport University, 38*(4), 78–85.

Lu, J., & Yu, X. (2019). The internet as a context: Exploring its impacts on national identity in 36 countries. *Social Science Computer Review, 37*(6), 705–722. https://doi.org/10.1177/08944 39318797058.

Lu, Z., &Fan, H (2014). *Sport and nationalism in China.* New York: Routledge.

Madianou, M. (2005). *Meditating the nation: News, audiences and the politics of identity.* London: UCL Press.

Maguire, J. (1999). *Global sport: Identities, societies, civilizations.* Cambridge, U.K.: Polity.

Maguire, J. (2004). Sport labor migration research revisited. *Journal of Sport and Social Issues, 28,* 477–482.

Maguire, J., & Bale, J. (1994). Introduction: Sports labour migration in the global arena. In J. Bale & J. Maguire (Eds.), *The global sports arena: Athletic talent migration in an interdependent world* (pp. 1–21). Portland, OR: Frank Cass.

Maguire, J., Jarvie, G., Mansfield, L., & Bradley, J. (2002). *Sport worlds. A sociological perspective.* Leeds, U.K.: Human Kinetics.

Maguire, J., & Pearton, R. (2000). Global sport and the migration patterns of France '98 World Cup finals players: Some preliminary observations, *Soccer & Society,* 1(1), 175–189. doi:10.1080/14660970008721257.

Maguire, J., & Tuck, J. (1998). Global sports and patriot games: Rugby union and national identity in a united sporting kingdom since 1945. *Immigrants & Minorities, 17*(1), 103–126. https://doi.org/10.1080/02619288.1998.9974931.

McFarland, A. (2020). A team of our own: The role of local and regional identities in Spanish sport. *International Journal of the History of Sport, 37*(1-2), 12–32. https://doi.org/10.1080/09523367.2020.1729133.

McGee, D., & Bairner, A. (2011). Transcending the borders of Irish identity? Narratives of northern nationalist footballers in Northern Ireland. *International Review for the Sociology of Sport, 46*(4), 436–455. https://doi.org/10.1177/1012690210380584.

Miller, T., Lawrence, G., McKay, J., & Rowe, D. (2001). *Globalization and sport: Playing the world.* London: Sage.

Ngobua, D. (2019, April 6). Why northerners don't feature prominently in Super Eagles. *Daily Trust*. https://dailytrust.com/why-northerners-dont-feature-prominently-in-super-eagles. [Accessed March 25, 2020].

Ogbah, J. P. (2021). Sport and secessionism in Biafra. In M. Vaczi & A. Bairner (Eds.), *Sport and secessionism* (pp. 200–218) London: Routledge.

Opera News. (2020). Nigerians react as Kanu Nwankwo set to launch Biafra football team in February. News-af.feednews.com. http://news-af.feednews.com/news/detail/d15d05b41 9067aeb444f2a35b5046220?client=news. [Accessed March 25, 2020].

Özkirimli, U. (2010). *Theories of nationalism: A critical introduction* (2nd ed.). London: Palgrave Macmillan.

Palijo, S. (2016, February 15). Why aren't there any Sindhi or Baloch players in our PSL squads? *The Express Tribune* Blogs. https://blogs.tribune.com.pk/story/32354/why-arent-there-any-sindhi-or-baloch-players-in-our-psl-squads/.

Poli, R. (2007). The denationalization of sport: De-ethnicization of the nation and identity deterritorialization. *Sport in Society*, *10*(4), 646–661. https://doi.org/10.1080/1743043070 1388798.

Poulton, E. (2004). Mediated patriot games. *International Review for the Sociology of Sport*, *39*(4), 437–455. https://doi.org/10.1177/1012690204049072.

Poulton, E., & Maguire, J. (2012) Plastic or fantastic Brits? Identity politics and English media representations of "Team GB" during London 2012. *JOMEC Journal*, *1*(2), 1–30.

Ren, H. (2010). *China and the Olympic movement: University lecture on the Olympics.* Barcelona: Centre d'Estudis Olímpics (UAB), International Chair in Olympism (IOC-UAB). https://library.olympics.com/Default/doc/SYRACUSE/209026/china-and-the-olympic-movement-hai-ren?_lg=en-GB.

Riordan, J., & Jones, R. (1999). *Sport and physical education in China.* London: E. and F. N. Spon.

Rowe, D. (2003). Sport and the repudiation of the global. *International Review for the Sociology of Sport*, *38*(3): 281–294.

Silk, M., & Falcous, M. (2005). One day in September and a week in February: Mobilizing American (sporting) nationalisms. *Sociology of Sport Journal*, *22*(4), 447–471. https://doi.org/10.1123/ssj.22.4.447.

Smith, A. D. (1995). *Nations and nationalism in a global era.* Cambridge, U.K.: Polity.

Smith, A. D. (1986). *The ethnic origins of nations.* Oxford: Blackwell.

Smith, A., & Porter, D. (2004). Introduction. In A. Smith & D, Porter (Eds.), *Sport and national identity in the post-war world* (pp. 1–9). London: Routledge.

Stokke, K. (2017). Nation-state. In D. Richardson (Eds.), *International encyclopedia of geography: People, the earth, environment and technology* (pp. 1–6). John Wiley & Sons. https://doi.org/10.1002/9781118786352.wbieg0736.

Sudheep, M. S. (2016). Re-imagining Nationalism: Ethnic and Religious Movements in Pakistan. *IJPAIR: Indian Journal of Politics and International Relations*, *9*, 31–48.

Sugden, J., & Bairner, A. (1993). *Sport, sectarianism and society in a divided Ireland.* Leicester: Leicester University Press.

Sugden, J., & Tomlinson, A. (1998). Power and resistance in the governance of world football. *Journal of Sport and Social Issues*, *22*(3), 299–316. https://doi.org/10.1177/01937239802 2003005.

Tosa, M. (2015). Sport nationalism in South Korea: An ethnographic study. *SAGE Open*, *5*(4), 1–13.

Tuck, J. (2003). The men in white: Reflections on rugby union, the media and Englishness. *International Review for the Sociology of Sport, 38*(2), 177–199.

Vaczi, M. (2015). "The Spanish fury": A political geography of soccer in Spain. *International Review for the Sociology of Sport, 50*(2), 196–210.

Vaczi, M. (2016). Catalonia's human towers: Nationalism, associational culture and the politics of performance. *American Ethnologist, 43*(2), 353–368.

Vaczi, M., Bairner, A., & Whigham, S. (2019). Where extremes meet: Sport, nationalism, and secessionism in Catalonia and Scotland. *Nations and Nationalism, 26*(4), 943–959. https://doi.org/10.1111/nana.12569.

Wallbank, D., & Cang, A. (2019, October 8). NBA in no-win situation as single tweet sparks China furore. *The Sydney Morning Herald.* https://www.smh.com.au/sport/basketball/nba-in-no-win-situation-as-single-tweet-sparks-china-furore-20191008-p52yih.html.

Whigham, S., Lopez-Gonzalez, H., & Ramon, X. (2019). "Més que un joc?" Sport and contemporary political nationalism in Scotland and Catalonia. *Journal of Sport and Social Issues, 43*(3), 219–244. https://doi.org/10.1177/0193723519836398.

Wu, X. (2010). *Chinese cyber nationalism.* Lanham, MD: Lexington Books.

Xu, G. (2008). *Olympic dreams.* Cambridge, MA: Harvard University Press.

Xu, X. (2006). Modernizing China in the Olympic spotlight: China's national identity and the 2008 Beijing Olympiad. *Sociological Review, 54*(2), 90–107. https://doi.org/10.1111/j.1467-954X.2006.00655.x.

CHAPTER 6

··

SPORT, DIPLOMACY, AND RAPPROCHEMENT

··

STUART MURRAY

RAPPROCHEMENT—THE establishment or resumption of diplomatic relations between estranged or warring nation-states—is a long, arduous process. Professional diplomats negotiate from fixed positions, competition dominates compromise, and progress is often slow, frustrating, or, in many cases, nonexistent. Whether thinking of the strained relationship between Israel and Palestine, the crisis in Yemen (itself a proxy war between Iran and Saudi Arabia), or the 2020 Armenia and Azerbaijan dispute over Nagorno-Karabakh, rapprochement is difficult to achieve, often unsustainable and the prospect of a return to conflict never far away.

To reflect on the role sport plays in such intractable conflicts might seem odd, at first. However, as this chapter argues and demonstrates, sport is a powerful diplomatic device in the relations between adversarial states. Such power is generated by its informal character, its universality, its ability to sublimate conflict by conducting metaphorical battles in the sporting arena, and its rapidly evolving diplomatic role "off the pitch," so to speak. In an anarchical international relations system dominated by sovereign states, power struggles, and "irreducible" security dilemmas, this chapter argues that sports diplomacy can be an effective means of *new* or *informal* conflict resolution (Herz, 1950, p. 159). Sport transcends acrimony in diplomatic relationships, brings alienated leaders together, offers informal pathways beyond staid, formal venues of diplomacy, generates massive public diplomacy opportunities, and unites so-called disparate nations, states, and people via a mutual love of pursuits centered on physical exercise. Moreover, the attraction in using sport as a form of diplomacy is entirely practical. Sports diplomacy is "low-risk, low-cost and high profile" (Keech & Houlihan, 1999, p. 112).

There are many examples of sport leading to political rapprochement. Perhaps the best-known example is the 1971 case of Ping-Pong diplomacy, when the Nixon and Mao governments used a series of very public meetings between their respective sportspeople "as a vehicle to test whether the public of the two countries would be accepting of a more formal diplomatic opening of frozen relations between the two cold war adversaries" (Murray & Pigman, 2014, p. 4). Similarly, the leaders of India and Pakistan often engage in "cricket diplomacy" as a means of diffusing tensions over Kashmir, terrorist attacks, trade disputes, and any number of traditional security issues (Shahid, 2015, p. 51). After 9/11, the U.S. Department of State instigated its SportsUnited initiative as a way to better engage disenfranchised young Muslims across Africa, the Middle East, and South Asia. And, in 2006, after qualifying for the World Cup for the first time in 76 years, Ivory Coast, featuring Didier Drogba and his Muslim and Christian teammates, played a vital role as mediators, messengers, and peacemakers in ending a brutal five-year civil war.

Sport, however, can also be employed to drive people apart, as a vehicle for the promotion and dissemination of antidiplomatic messages. The Munich Massacre, which occurred during the second week of the 1972 Olympic Games, serves as a tragic reminder. The 2004 Asian Cup football tournament, which was held in China, was marred by nationalist vitriol toward Japan by the home nation's fans; everywhere they played, Chinese spectators heckled the Japanese players, sang anti-Japanese songs from the war of liberation, threw bottles at the team bus, and displayed banners reading "Look into history and apologize to the Asian People" and "Return the Diaoyu (Senkaku) Islands!" (Manzenreiter, 2008, p. 423). Sport, it must be remembered, can be employed to heighten tension in international affairs. Writing in 1945 in an article titled "The Sporting Spirit," George Orwell famously noted that international sport "aroused the most combative instincts," regularly produced "orgies of hatred," and was little more than "war minus the shooting" (quoted in Beck, 2013, p. 72).

In short, there are as many examples of sport driving, or keeping, people apart as there are sport leading to conflict mitigation or resolution. This mixed record leads to several nagging questions: If sport has "the power to change the world," as Mandela asserted in 2000, then why hasn't it done so already? How does an observer understand the long, storied, and controversial relationship between sport and politics? And why, in the middle of a civil war, do millions of Ivorians listen to a footballer instead of their president? To answer these questions, and to better understand and promote sport as a tool for rapprochement, a "new" area of grand, abstract theory and practice has recently emerged: sports diplomacy.

Issues

When thinking of the relationship between sport, diplomacy, and rapprochement, the first issue the observer encounters is a well-known phrase: sport and politics do not, or should not, mix. This was a point that Avery Brundage, the "ironfisted" IOC president from 1952 to 1972, often made, insisting that "sports are completely free of politics" (Cashmore, 2010, p. 427). His view echoes sentiments contained within one of the sacred parchments of sport, the Olympic Charter, which stipulates that the Olympic Games "are contests between individuals and teams, and not between countries" (IOC, 2016, p. 21). Rule 50 of the Charter adds that "no kind of demonstration or political, religious or racial propaganda is permitted in any Olympic sites, venues or other areas" (pp. 90–91).

Such views, rules, and codes are, however, anachronistic and politically convenient types of self-assessment, idealized remarks on how sport ought to be, not how it is. Insisting that sport and politics do not mix can be written off as a 20th-century cliché—a phrase or opinion that is overused to the point of being annoyingly incorrect. Indeed, academics such as Hoberman (1984), Houlihan (1994, 2014), Grix and Lee (2013), and Næss (2017) have proven that international sport and the regimes that govern it *are* political. Therefore, whether sport does not or should not mix with politics is a moot point. Such dated, generalized thinking is problematic, for it assumes that all *mixing* is bad, which, in turn, stymies investigation into how sport might be strategically employed as an effective, good tool for rapprochement in conflict settings.

To demonstrate the utility of sport as a diplomatic tool is to first understand why it is effective for rapprochement. Sport is one of the oldest civic institutions created by humans for pleasure, spectacle, and, seen through a diplomatic lens, the sublimation of conflict and the "mediation of estrangement" (Der Derian, 1987, p. 91). Games, play, running, sport, and so on are woven into all human physiognomic systems. Regardless of a person's national identity, sportspeople all over the world practice the same skills: hand-eye coordination, mastery, athleticism, repetition, physical exertion, organization, and discipline, for example. It is these skills that constitute the universal language of sport—a language where no words are spoken—as well as sports' unique ability to transcend political, religious, or cultural differences in international relations by providing an immediate connection between interlocutors. In other words, while humans remain separated by borders, governments, language, religion, and so on, sport is something they all have in common.

The theory informing such diplomatic capacity is well-known. It relates to the psychologist Gordon W. Allport's (1954) famous Contact Hypothesis, or Intergroup Contact Theory, which "states that under appropriate conditions interpersonal contact is one of the most effective ways to reduce prejudice between majority and minority group members" (Schiappa, Gregg, & Hewes, 2005, p. 92). Sport, so the theory goes, is a social institution that increases contact between separated individuals and groups, which, in turn, reduces tension, division, and xenophobia, conditions that can lead to intergroup violence (Allport, 1954). Many others support Allport's Contact Hypothesis. Konrad Lorenz (1966, p. 271), a former Nobel Prize winner, notes that because sport "probably originated from highly ritualized, but still hostile fighting . . . it can be defined as a specifically human form of non-hostile combat, governed by the strictest of culturally developed rules." For Lorenz, sport "contains aggressive motivation," a quality that can be traced back to the "evolution of tribal warfare at the very dawn of culture" (p. 271).

Such views are more than just theory. Writing in 1995, the anthropologist Kendall Blanchard argues that Indigenous peoples have been using sport for conflict resolution for tens of thousands of years. The First People of Australia, for instance, consciously used sport as a tool for rapprochement. Numbering roughly 750,000 in the late 18th century (when the British colonized Terra Australis "Nullis"), the population was divided into 500 clan groups. Separated by natural borders such as rivers or hunting boundaries, each nation had distinct identities, myths, cultures, belief systems, and languages (Hughes, 1988, p. 47). As with any international system, conflict inevitably occurred; however, sport served as an intentional means of rapprochement. *Battendi* (a spear-throwing game), *Marngrook* (a form of football, played with a ball of sewn kangaroo or possum skin), and *Koolche* (a ball-throwing and -hitting game) are good examples of such games played between tribes (Blanchard, 1995).

These games held different purposes for the Indigenous Australians: to "absorb conflict, to increase communication between tribes, to record and celebrate tribal lore," to teach the "young to ultimately become effective tribal providers," and to remind the leaders of the requisite diplomatic skills to manage relations between groups (Salter, 1974, pp. 5–16). Some sports, such as *Prun*, mirrored warfare and were intentional shared means of avoiding actual conflict. Salter describes *Prun* as a sort of mock war used as a means to settle disputes between separate groups of aboriginal communities. Brandishing spears, shields and boomerangs, and wearing elaborate dress and body paints, both the men and the women enter the designated "fighting" and the "sport" begins. (p. 11)

The game is still played to this day. Clan groups continue to "use the event as an opportunity to settle disputes, to entertain themselves, or simply show off their respective skills" (Blanchard, 1995, p. 144).

Throughout antiquity, sport brought strangers closer together and, in the case of the Ancient Olympiad, temporarily halted conflict. Running from 776 to 394 BCE—when the tourney was abolished by the Roman emperor Theodosius I as part of a campaign to eliminate paganism and impose Christianity as a state religion—the Games acted as a symbol of pan-Hellenism among hundreds of separate, different, and (often) warring city-states. The Olympic Truce afforded athletes, spectators, and officials protection while traveling to and from the Games. *Ekecheria*, the Greek word for "a staying of the hand," allowed citizens to travel safely, even while passing through enemy territory. While Sparta, Syracuse, and Athens had their military rivalries and political differences, sport was something they held in common. In other words, the Games transcended politics.

Sport can also be used to reestablish political relationships between adversaries, as was the case with the 1520 meeting between King François I of France and Henry VIII of England. After a century of hostilities, the two kings hosted a summit at the Fields of Cloth of Gold in northern France. For two weeks, François, Henry, and their retinues wrestled, jousted, and competed in archery events as a means of strengthening the bond of friendship after the signing of the Anglo-French Treaty of 1514 (Mattingly, 1938). These brief examples validate Allport's Intergroup Contact Theory. Seen through a diplomatic lens, sport is a common language played by representatives of disparate groups aimed, in some cases, at "minimizing friction in international affairs" (Bull, 1977, p. 166).

However, it is not all fair play when it comes to sports diplomacy. Sport is often co-opted, hijacked, or abused by sovereign states as a nefarious foreign policy tool, which brings into questions its diplomatic efficacy. The 20th century is riddled with such cases. The Fascist Games of 1936 and 1938 (the Football World Cup, which was won by Mussolini's Blackshirts under dubious circumstances) were but preludes to conflicts unequaled since in terms of barbarism, war deaths, and bizarre, Promethean weaponry. As the rubble still smoldered, and the Cold War began, sport continued to be overly politicized. The 1945 Goodwill Tour of the United Kingdom by the football team F.C. Dynamo Moscow "demonstrated the superiority of the Soviet way of life" (Kowalski & Porter, 1997, p. 100) and prompted Orwell to write that famous "war minus the shooting" remark about sports. A few years later, an entire generation of athletes were abused as tools of the state, that is, as "weapons" in an Orwellian context. From the late 1950s until reunification with West Germany in 1990, "more than ten thousand unsuspecting young athletes" were administered roughly "2 million doses of anabolic-androgenic steroids" by the German Democratic Republic (Ungerleider, 2015, p. i). In 1980, the United States of America boycotted the Moscow Olympics, arguing that the Soviet Union had violated the Truce by invading Afghanistan the previous year. Four years later, as sport became a pawn in a much larger political game, the Soviet Union and 13 of its satellite states boycotted the 1984 Los Angeles Olympics due to "chauvinistic sentiments and an anti-Soviet hysteria being whipped up in the United States" (Burns, 1984).

Such incidents showcase the mixed record of sport being used as a type of diplomatic rapprochement. Simply observing that its use is sometimes to the good and sometimes to the bad, however, hardly constitutes good science, deep insight, or heuristic theory and practice. In order to promote and better understand sport as a means of conflict resolution, it is important to review how academics and practitioners currently approach the topic of sports diplomacy.

APPROACHES

The roles that sport may play in rapprochement between various actors in international relations has been approached by a variety of scholars from a wide range of disciplines. As noted, anthropologists such as Blanchard (1995) have examined sport as a means of conflict resolution in First Australian, Native American, and prehistoric African societies. Jarvie (2017) notes the importance of focusing on the sociological and cultural roles that sport plays in binding nations together. Writing in his seminal work, *Sport, Culture and Society*, he argues that "it is impossible to fully understand contemporary society and culture without acknowledging the place of sport" (p. 2). There are many other works that focus on sport and international relations (Budd & Levermore, 2004; Reeves, 2012), sport and war (Mangan, 2004; Blackburn, 2016), and sport for development and peace (Hayhurst, Kay, & Chawansky, 2016).

Far less attention, however, has been paid to the diplomacy behind such cases, that is, the means, process, networks, interests, needs, and fears that inform, motivate, and guide interactions between the broad range of actors that make up the international "sportscape" (Manzenreiter, 2008, p. 38). The theory and practice of sports diplomacy fills these epistemological and ontological gaps, somewhat. For a while, however, sports diplomacy existed on the margins of the field of diplomatic studies. Manuals on diplomatic procedures aimed at novices entering the profession, grandiose memoirs of retiring ambassadors, and forensic accounts of state-qua-state negotiations over arms treaties dominated the canon. Niche areas of diplomatic inquiry, such as sport, culture, and music, all ancient devices for bringing strangers closer together, were written off as silly distractions when compared to the *haute poltique* of classical diplomacy.

As such, the body of literature on sports diplomacy was rather limited and, similarly, was focused on anecdotal, sporadic, and case-study articles on important but familiar narratives: Ping-Pong diplomacy, the role sport played in isolating apartheid South Africa, or the intermittent baseball diplomacy practiced between the United States and Cuba, for instance. Authors such as Goldberg (2000) wrote papers titled "Sporting Diplomacy" but, once more, seemed more interested in retelling common, historical narratives as opposed to building theoretical models and frameworks to better understand why political elites co-opt sport as a foreign policy tool.

A more robust theoretical approach to sports diplomacy began in 2011 with a conference paper at the International Symposium on Cultural Diplomacy in Berlin (Murray, 2011). This "seminal" paper identified the gap in the field of study, reviewed existing definitions, literature, and theories, and ushered in a new era of innovative scholarship on sports diplomacy (Rofe, 2016, p. 214). This era began with a flurry of conference panels on the topic,[1] as well as three special issues of major academic journals: the *Hague Journal of Diplomacy* (2013), *Sport and Society* (2014), and *Diplomacy & Statecraft* (2016). Sports diplomacy also appeared as an independent topic in *The Oxford Handbook of Modern Diplomacy* (2013) as well as *The SAGE Handbook of Diplomacy* (2016). And, further signaling the growing field, a few notable books have recently appeared. Beacom's (2012) *International Diplomacy and the Olympic Movement*, and Dichter and Johns's *Diplomatic Games* (2014), and Kobierecki's *Sports Diplomacy: Sports in the Diplomatic Activities of States and Non-state Actors* (2020) are but a few examples.

Based on this body of scholarship, it is easy to define sports diplomacy. It can be simply understood as a new term that describes an old practice: the power of sport to bring people, nations, and communities closer together via a shared love of physical pursuits. It is a young, dynamic field of study and a growing area of practice for governments the world over. It can be further understood as the strategic use of sport to build investment, study, and trade relationships. The term also relates to the growing trend of governments using sport for diplomacy, specifically a more inclusive method of policy formulation, one featuring governments, nonstate actors, and sports organizations working together for win-win outcomes.

This singular understanding of sports diplomacy quickly became dated, however. The realms it sought to describe—sport, diplomacy, and international relations—proved too complex for one theory to account for. More complex theoretical approaches soon followed, advanced both in my work and that of others. In approaching the challenges here, I noted that when thinking of the scale of sport, or the numbers of different types of sports played, "the observer can suffer temporary mental paralysis when trying to chart, visualize or understand the myriad nodes and networks where sport and diplomacy overlap" (Murray, 2018, p. 6.). In order to alleviate this conceptual confusion, four theoretical categories of sports diplomacy were introduced in *Sports Diplomacy: Origins, Theory and Practice* (Murray, 2018). These, I argued, better accounted for networks, actors, channels, venues, and players where sport and diplomacy converge. Each approach is summarized in Figure 6.1 and, briefly, explained below.

The first category, traditional sports diplomacy, refutes the cliché that sport and politics do not or should not mix. Charting the relationship between sport, politics, and diplomacy from the late 19th century—when truly democratic nations began to emerge—this theoretical lens reveals that sport, politics, and, by extension, diplomacy do mix, all the time, and all over the world. Moreover, they have mixed since time immemorial, regardless of the epoch, the creed of the state, or the civilization. What is true in the past remains true in the present. As Allison (1993, p. 17) notes, capitalists, communists, dictators, and fascists have "all played the game, and believed in it." Seen "through the embassy window," sport is employed by governments to complement, boost, or augment traditional, strategic, and diplomatic goals in an opportunistic, sporadic, and, at times, clumsy fashion (Wilson, 1962, p. 122). In this context, traditional sports diplomacy is simply a "continuation of policy by other means," to borrow from Clausewitz (1997, p. 24).

Governments intentionally co-opt sport as a tool to advance national interests or promote their international brand or as a vehicle to advance specific foreign policy objectives. Of the broad range of sporting vehicles states covet, none is more desirous or effective in terms of public diplomacy than mega-events such as the Summer Olympic Games, football's World Cup, or the Pan American Games. For example, 1.1 billion people watched

Traditional sports diplomacy	Sports diplomacy
The sporadic co-option of sport by states for overtly nationalistic aims. Late 19th century to present. States only.	Mutually reciprocal partnerships between sport, government and the non-state sector in the twenty-first century
Sport-as-diplomacy	Sports anti-diplomacy
The specialised negotiation, communication and representation required to make international sport possible. Also describes the politics of non-state sporting actors. No States.	The abuse of sport for immoral, unethical or intentionally divisive ends.

FIGURE 6.1 The Four Schools of Sports Diplomacy

the opening ceremony of the 2008 Beijing Summer Olympics, a master class in "nation branding" (Berkowitz, Gjermano, Gomez, & Schafer, 2007, p. 164). The audience was treated to an enormous fireworks display (not surprising from the nation that invented fireworks), 14,000 performers played out scenes from Chinese history, and, memorably, 2,008 Fou drummers played in seamless harmony. The message was clear: China is an ancient, proud, and powerful nation that intends to make its presence felt (Xu, 2008). The Games showed the world a "new" China—a cultural, harmonious superpower with great pride in its roots and a confident certainty as to its place and role in both the region and the world (Ho & Bairner, 2012). The Chinese Communist Party strategically employed the 2008 Olympics "to assist the restoration of China's national greatness through the erasing of the memory of a humbled, reduced and subordinate people and its replacement with confident, risen and superordinate people: physical effort twisted into skeins of political action" (Mangan, 2010, p. 2334). Sport, in this traditional, state context, becomes an extension of a government's diplomacy, a means to a means to a foreign policy end.

The second approach to sports diplomacy is characterized by governments teaming up with nonstate sporting actors guided by innovative strategies. This category is often referred to as "new" sports diplomacy or, as this chapter prefers, just plain old sports diplomacy. As noted, this is a far more inclusive, plural, and networked model that embodies the type of state, nonstate, and public partnerships characteristic of 21st-century diplomacy. The purpose of a government, with a ministry of foreign affairs and the diplomats within, is somewhat retrospective: to act as a sporting gatekeeper to facilitate, manage, and evaluate whole-of-nation strategies or policies that enhance a nation's soft-power image, reputation, and partnerships.

By leaving traditional sports diplomacy to the foreign policy mandarins, this newer form focuses on *human*—not traditional—security. Human security is vital in the 21st century because it moves away from "traditional, state-centric conceptions" and "concentrates on the security of individuals, their protection and empowerment" (United Nations, Commission on Human Security, 2009, p. 5). Since the turn of the century, governments, sports organizations, and many other institutions, such as the erstwhile United Nations Office of Sport and Development, have been using sport to address many new, anthropogenic problems: overpopulation, gender inequality, and climate change, to name but a few. If sport cannot "change the world" (and that is a big ask), it can help make human lives better as a diplomatic vehicle promoting, for example, the UN's Sustainable Development Goals.

The third theoretical approach—sports-as-diplomacy—is perhaps the most novel, exciting, and appealing. In this category, the state is entirely disregarded and the observer encouraged to think of sport itself as a form of diplomacy. States are no longer the key referent object in the "international society of sport," a habitus built and inhabited by non-state sporting actors such as the IOC, progressive clubs such as F.C. Barcelona, and sports diplomats such as the American football player Colin Kaepernick. As well as playing, organizing, or administering sport, these institutions and individuals all practice core diplomatic functions: communication, representation, negotiation, intelligence gathering and dissemination, and, most important of all, the minimization of friction (Bull 1977, pp. 163–166).

Their primary focus is sport: playing, organizing, or officiating it. However, in producing and reproducing international sport, they directly contribute to a more peaceful world. This is because international sport requires stability in order to function. Unlike states, non-state sporting actors are not hamstrung by national interests, military budgets, and the stiff, boring "waltz" of traditional diplomacy. Arguably, they are the key to truly realizing the Mandela-esque power of sport "to change the world" and "unite people in a way that little else does" (Mandela, 2000). In the plural, globalized, and "flat" era, when traditional roles are changing, regimes such as FIFA have a far greater role to play than simply organizing football (Friedman, 2007, p. 51). Iconic sportspeople such as the Formula 1 driver Lewis Hamilton, the tennis player Naomi Osaka, and the basketball Colossus that is LeBron James represent the way millions of oppressed people of color feel, and act as powerful emissaries, amplifying the core message behind the Black Lives Matter movement. New sports diplomacy partnerships between cultural and sporting behemoths are blooming. The British Council's flagship initiatives are good examples. Here, Premier Skills, Try Rugby, and International Inspiration have enriched over 25 million young people and 7,600 coaches and created roughly 55 national sports-based policies. Collaboration, innovation, and integration have been vital to these programs. The roles, skills, and responsibilities of sports people, organizations, and business, for example, are rapidly evolving, and not before time. Studying, and harnessing, the unique power of sport-as-diplomacy is vital in the fractious 21st century. Doing so, this school of thought argues, is exactly what Mandela (2000) meant when he said that sport is "more powerful than government."

However, and in order to further understand sports diplomacy as a tool for rapprochement, the dark, Hobbesian elephant in the room also must be addressed. As any observer of sport will insist, sport also has a dark side that can drive people, states, and institutions apart. This fourth and final category—sports antidiplomacy—is defined as "behaviours, actors and attitudes that are distinctly 'un' or anti-diplomatic in their nature" (Murray, 2018, p. 11). The Football Wars are a good, if rare, example. Also known as the 100 Hour War, this was a conflict fought between El Salvador and Honduras in 1969, one that spilled over from a series of controversial, bitterly fought World Cup qualifying matches played out against a collapsing diplomatic relationship.

The poor behavior of international sportspeople can also create the wrong impression a country wishes to foster. In 2016, for instance, five Cuban volleyball players from the national team were convicted of raping a woman while playing in Finland during a game in the Volleyball World League tournament. This incident is downright amoral, illegal, and criminal. The Cuban Volleyball Association, quite rightly, "castigated the athletes' behaviour," saying such actions ran counter to the "discipline and the sense of honor and respect that govern our sport and society" (Bilefsky & Kousa, 2016). Sporting contests can also inflame nationalist sentiments. Returning to the example of cricket diplomacy between India and Pakistan, the Marathi ultranationalist Indian political party Shiv Sena twice dug up the wicket on the eve of a test match, in 1991 and 2000. They were protesting the visit of the Pakistani cricket team, and it worked: both tours were canceled as a result. International sporting competition can thus exaggerate animosity, becoming a prelude to hostility and, in the worst case, violence. None of these incidents endear themselves to the noble practice of diplomacy, the business of peace, and the minimization of friction in international affairs.

"Good" sports diplomacy fosters a sense of international society, while its "bad" opposite undermines the foundations of an international society of sport. When, for example, a president uses sport to increase friction or an Olympic athlete cheats to win gold and rubbishes the notion of Olympism or a terrorist organization deliberately targets an international event because it is a symbol of globalization, their behavior can be described as sports antidiplomacy because it goes *against* the ideal character of both sport *and* diplomacy. To ensure sports diplomacy has a positive future as a tool for rapprochement, a frank appraisal of its limitations, weaknesses, and controversies is vital. Accepting, and amending, the ugly side of international sport is integral to fully potentializing sports diplomacy. Sport is no magic wand or panacea that can simply stop warring parties fighting.

These four schools of sports diplomacy are vital to understanding the complex interplay between sport, diplomacy, and rapprochement. They provide a "map, or frame of reference," that makes the "complex, puzzling" international society of sport more "intelligible" (Kegley & Blanton, 2013, p. 22). The four theories make things a little clearer: "[s]imilar to the way an optometrist uses a phoropter to incrementally overlay lenses of different strengths to produce a clearer image," they sharpen the image and understanding of the role sport has played, plays, and ought to play in international relations (Murray, 2008, p. 36).

DEBATES

Despite the recent gains made in the study of sports diplomacy, several key debates endure when thinking of the relationship between sport, diplomacy, and rapprochement. The first concerns the key referent object (or main player, to use a sporting term) in this discussion so far, sovereign nation-states and, specifically, if they are the best-placed actors to facilitate sports diplomacy exchanges conducive to rapprochement. In short, a more critical perspective would say no. When thinking of states, sport is no different from trade agreements, economic sanctions, or an international summit, for example. It is just another tool in the diplomat and state person's toolbox, the proverbial means to the foreign policy end. In the year before the 2018 PyeongChang Winter Olympics, for example, France, Austria, Germany, and many other nations stated they might not participate in the tournament due to the 2017–2018 North Korea "crisis," a period of heightened tensions sparked by a series of ballistic missile and nuclear tests conducted in July 2017 in the Hermit Kingdom. A brief détente then followed in January 2018, when the North Korean leader Kim Jong Un announced in his New Year's speech, "North Korea's participation in the Winter Games will be a good opportunity to showcase the national pride and we wish the Games will be a success. Officials from the two Koreas may urgently meet to discuss the possibility" (Heekyong & Smith, 2017).

The crisis quickly turned into a thaw in relations as North and South Korean athletes marched together in the Opening Ceremony of the 2018 Winter Olympics, fielded a joint women's ice hockey team, and sent a high-level delegation headed by Kim Yo-jong, the sister of the current General Secretary of the Workers' Party of Korea . More summits and high-profile meetings occurred after the mega-event, but it wasn't long before hard power snuffed out any slight gains made by the soft power of sport. In August 2019, for example, the North conducted a series of short-range missile tests, while the United States of America and South Korea conducted joint military exercises, a "grave provocation," according the North (Reuters, 2018). Subsequent talks held in Stockholm between the North and the United States quickly broke down, the sabers soon started rattling again, and, the following year, North Korean foreign minister Ri Son-gwon concluded that prospects for peace on the peninsula had "faded away into a dark nightmare" (McIntyre, 2020).

In this case, sport was used (or abused) as a foreign policy tool by—particularly—the North. As Lieu (2018) notes, "one doesn't need to be a genius to see that this is what North Korea does: After having created a war-like, crisis atmosphere, [Kim] takes a small step back and there's a collective sigh of relief that there's no war. It does wonders for North Korea's image." Arguably, sovereign nation-states like North Korea have no interest in sport having the "power to change the world" and "unite people in a way that little else does" (Mandela, 2000). In states obsessed with security, survival, and a raison d'état, and operating in a competitive, dangerous, and anarchic international relations system, the limitations of traditional sports diplomacy soon become obvious. Sport, sportspeople, or sporting events are co-opted by governments only if they provide a direct benefit to a state's national interests or help realize a foreign policy goal. In the case of the PyeongChang Games, sport was ultimately "irrelevant to the real sources of power in international affairs. Mere games could play no role in foreign policies that were shaped by hard, tangible national interests such as security and economics" (Keys, 2013, p. 248). For states, "high" hard-power concerns will always override "low" soft-power initiatives. For states, in other words, sport will always come second to war, military, economics, and trade.

A second debate concerns the relationship between sport per se and government. Sport often seems reluctant to work with politics or buy into rapprochement initiatives. Many involved in the world of sport have neither the requisite diplomatic skills nor the compunction to participate in complex, dangerous international relations between sovereign nation-states, kleptocratic criminal regimes, or warring parties of armed rebels. The function of their job is equally clear: to play, organize, administer, or coach sport, to name but a few esoteric roles.

It is not a case of sport and politics not mixing but, rather, that they *should* not mix. Politics infringes on, pollutes, or taints the idealistic image of sport. Images of President Vladimir Putin of Russia sitting in the executive box and hobnobbing with Mohammed bin Salman, the Crown Prince of Saudi Arabia, and Gianni Infantino, the president of FIFA, during the opening game of the 2018 World Cup finals in Russia might appeal to foreign policy mandarins but rarely to sports fans. For many fans, sport has a "spiritual power" and exists in a hallowed realm "above" government (Allison, 1993, p. 5). The appearance of the "suits"—heads of state, for example, who ghost in to toss the coin, declare the games begin—is all too common in high-profile sporting events but, arguably, anathema to the idea that sport should be unencumbered by politics. For critics, a politician's, ambassador's, or diplomat's interest in sport is "nothing more than a sham, a photo-op, or a political gimmick," a bureaucrat feigning a common interest with the public via sport (Murray, 2012, p. 577).

Exploiting elite sporting events for political messaging or talking up sport as a tool for peace or rapprochement can therefore seem disingenuous and, in the hallowed temples of sport, sacrilegious. Sport is not above or below governments. It is beyond them and, arguably, should be left, pure, untapped, and untainted by the corrupt and divisive elements of politics and diplomacy. A third debate concerns the relationship between sports diplomacy and sport for development. The theoretical relationship is best described as confusing, as is the practical realm: states, nonstate actors, sporting regimes, individual sports people, businesses such as Nike, all operate in these realms yet with little interaction, common strategy, or sense of shared mission. Where sports diplomacy ends and sport for development begins is difficult to discern. More recently, and as a result of the fiscal pressures the COVID-19 pandemic has wrought on many governments, aid is being absorbed into diplomacy, a process that has proved unpopular. In June 2020, for example, the British government forced the Department for International Development to merge with the Foreign and Commonwealth Office, a "callous," "outrageous," and "damning" move which left department employees "devastated, demoralized, angry, [and] anxious" (Murphy, 2020). Similar mergers are occurring in the realm of international sport, aid, and development. The U.S. and Australian governments, for example, have folded their sport-for-development activities into their sports diplomacy activities, as illustrated in Australia's much admired Sports Diplomacy 2030 strategy. This strategy is significant because it is represents the first time a sovereign state has developed an esoteric sports diplomacy strategy. Sports Diplomacy 2030 aims to create a better relationship between sports, government, and diplomacy; provides strategic direction (where before there was none); and better harnesses the sporting soft-power assets a sports-mad nation such as Australia possesses in abundance.

The relationship between sport for development and sports diplomacy need not be so confusing, however. A bit of conceptual clarity, as well as both realms spelling out the value proposition to each other, is important and may help bring about a more symbiotic relationship. There is plenty of room, and need, for both fields of study and practice. Indeed, they complement each other. The more established field of sport for development generates social, sporting, and cultural outcomes, whereas sports diplomacy shores up such outcomes by creating the diplomatic and policy architecture required to ensure sustainability between estranged parties. Sports diplomacy is simply an attempt to further evolve the relationship between sport and rapprochement. Conceptually, it is a grand, abstract term; fills a proverbial gap in how, why, and where sport and politics mix (for better or for worse); and seeks to build collaborative and plural coalitions that generate "whole-of-nation" solutions to conflict situations.

The recent growth and appeal of sports diplomacy stems from the argument that sport for development was alone insufficient to build lasting forms of rapprochement (again, because the necessary diplomatic and political will, policy, and structures were often missing). Thus, sport for development efforts can provide "only partial solutions of the problem. If any of them were really decisive it ought either to exclude all of the others or comprehend them in a higher unity" (Huizinga, 2020, p. 2).

Without sounding idealistic, sports diplomacy is an attempt to comprehend the myriad causes, relationships, and actors that overlap around conflict situations. Echoing Allport's famous Contact Hypothesis, which "states that under appropriate conditions interpersonal contact is one of the most effective ways to reduce prejudice between majority and minority group members," the paradigm seeks to unify approaches to conflict resolution, to integrate systems, and to share resources, expertise, and the burdens of using sport in conflict-ridden environments such as Afghanistan, the Horn of Africa, or the Middle East (Schiappa et al. 2005, p. 92).

CONCLUSION

As a social institution, sport increases contact between individuals and groups, reducing tension, division, xenophobia, and the sort of misunderstandings that lead to intergroup violence. As a political institution, diplomacy too has civil and ideal qualities. As the celebrated practitioner-theorist Sir Ernest Satow (1957, p. 1) wrote of one of the oldest human, social, and political institutions, diplomacy is "the best means devised by civilization for preventing international relations from being governed by force alone." Both sport and diplomacy represent historic, higher, civic missions aimed at bringing strangers closer together and transcending a world of walls, borders, and estrangement produced and reproduced by the system of sovereign states.

Sports diplomacy, as both a field of study and a growing area of policy practice for governments, is a grand, abstract theory, as well as an attempt to link sporting outcomes with diplomatic outcomes. Teamwork, plurality, and "whole-of-nation" or "society" approaches characterize this new era, as well as a sense of shared responsibility, resources, and commitment to use sport more effectively to induce conflict resolution conducive to lasting rapprochement. The past decade or so of research and practice has resulted in a robust body of scholarship, as well as new paths and partnerships between governments, academe, and sport. If done correctly, sports diplomacy reduces costs, integrates systems, and provides the hard-power architecture and attitude required to ensure peace that is given a chance. For sports and diplomatic theorists and practitioners who believe in the diplomatic power of sport as a tool for rapprochement, the game has only just begun.

NOTE

1. The 2012 San Diego International Studies Association conference, the 2012 British International Studies Association conference in Edinburgh, and, a year later, a third at the 2013 San Francisco International Studies Association conference.

REFERENCES

Allison, L. (Ed.). (1993). *The changing politics of sport.* Manchester: Manchester University Press.
Allport, G. W. 1954. *The nature of prejudice.* Cambridge, MA: Addison-Wesley.

Beacom, A. 2012. *International diplomacy and the Olympic Movement: The new mediators*. London: Palgrave Macmillan.

Beck, P. J. 2013. "War minus the shooting": George Orwell on international sport and the Olympics. *Sport in History, 33*(1), 72–94.

Berkowitz, P., Gjermano, G., Gomez, L., & Schafer, G. (2007). Brand China: Using the 2008 Olympic Games to enhance China's image. *Place Branding and Public Diplomacy, 3*(2), 164–178.

Bilefsky, D., & Kousa, M.-L. (2016, September 21). 5 Cuban volleyball players convicted of rape in Finland. *New York Times*. www.nytimes.com/2016/09/21/world/europe/finland-rape-cuban-volleyball.html.

Blanchard, K. (1995). *The anthropology of sport*. Westport, CT: Praeger.

Blackburn, K. (2016). *War, sport and the Anzac tradition*. London: Palgrave Macmillan.

Budd, A., & Levermore, R. (2004). *Sport and international relations: An emerging relationship*. Abingdon, Oxon, U.K.: Routledge.

Bull, H. (1977). *The anarchical society: A study of order in world politics*. New York: Columbia University Press.

Burns, J. F. (1984, May 9). Moscow will keep its team from Los Angeles Olympics. *New York Times*. www.nytimes.com/1984/05/09/world/moscow-will-keep-its-team-los-angeles-olympics-tass-cites-peril-us-denies-it.html.

Cashmore, E. (2010). *Making sense of sports*. Abingdon, Oxon, U.K.: Routledge.

Clausewitz, C. von (1997). *On war*. Hertfordshire, U.K.: Wordsworth Editions.

Cooper, A. F., Heine, J., & Thakur, R. (Eds.). (2013). *The Oxford handbook of modern diplomacy*. OUP Oxford.

Constantinou, C. M., Kerr, P., & Sharp, P. (Eds.). (2016). *The SAGE handbook of diplomacy*. Sage.

Der Derian, J. (1987). Meditating estrangement: A theory for diplomacy. *Review of International Studies, 13*(2), 91–110.

Dichter, H. L., & Johns, A. L. (Eds.). (2014). *Diplomatic games: Sport, statecraft, and international relations since 1945*. Lexington, KY: University Press of Kentucky.

Friedman, T. L. (2007). *The world is flat: A brief history of the twenty-first century* (3rd ed.). New York: Picador.

Goldberg, J. (2000). Sporting diplomacy: Boosting the size of the diplomatic corps. *Washington Quarterly, 23*(4), 63–70.

Grix, J., & Lee, D. (2013). Soft power, sports mega-events and emerging states: The lure of the politics of attraction. *Global Society, 27*(4), 521–536.

Hayhurst, L., Kay, T., & Chawansky, M. (2016). *Beyond sport for development and peace: Transnational perspectives on theory, policy and practice*. Abingdon, Oxon, U.K.: Routledge.

Heekyong, Y., & Smith, J. (2017, December 31). North Korea's Kim "open to dialogue" with South Korea, will only use nukes if threatened. *Reuters*. https://www.reuters.com/article/us-northkorea-missiles-kimjongun/north-koreas-kim-open-to-dialogue-with-south-korea-will-only-use-nukes-if-threatened-idUSKBN1EQ0NJ.

Herz, J. H. (1950). Idealist internationalism and the security dilemma. *World Politics: A Quarterly Journal of International Relations, 24*(1), 157–180.

Ho, G., & Bairner, A. (2012). One country, two systems, three flags: Imaging Olympic nationalism in Hong Kong and Macao. *International Review for the Sociology of Sport, 48*(3), 349–365.

Hoberman, J. M. (1984). *Sport and political ideology*. Austin: University of Texas Press.

Houlihan, B. (1994). *Sport and international politics*. New York: Harvester Wheatsheaf.

Houlihan, B. (2014). *The government and politics of sport*. Abingdon, Oxon, U.K.: Routledge.

Hughes, R. (1988). *The fatal shore*. New York: Vintage Books.

Huizinga, J. (2020). *Homo ludens*. Editora Perspectiva SA.

IOC. (2016). *Olympic charter*. Lausanne, Switzerland: International Olympic Committee.

Jarvie, G. (2017). *Sport, culture and society: An introduction* (3rd ed.). Abingdon, Oxon, U.K.: Routledge.

Keech, M., & Houlihan, B. (1999). Sport and the end of apartheid. *The Round Table, 88*(349), 109–121.

Kegley, C. W., & Blanton, S. L. (2013). *World politics: Trend and transformation, 2013–2014* (updated ed.). Boston: Cengage Learning.

Keys, B. (2013). International relations. In S. W. Pope & J. Nauright (Eds.), *The Routledge companion to sports history* (pp. 248–267). Abingdon, Oxon, U.K.: Routledge.

Kobierecki, M. M. (2020). *Sports diplomacy: Sports in the diplomatic activities of states and non-state actors*. Lanham, MD: Lexington Books.

Kowalski, R., & Porter, D. (1997). Political football: Moscow dynamo in Britain, 1945. *International Journal of the History of Sport, 14*(2), 100–121.

Lieu, A. (2018, January 2). North Korea team at Olympics should prompt US boycott, Graham says. *Fox News*. https://www.foxnews.com/world/north-korea-team-at-olympics-should-prompt-us-boycott-graham-says.

Lorenz, K. (1966). *On aggression*. New York: MJF Books.

Mandela, N. (2000). Sport has the power to change the world. Speech presented at 1st Laureus World Sports Awards, Monaco. https://www.laureus.com/news/celebrating-the-legacy-of-a-hero-on-mandela-day.

Mangan, J. A. (Ed.). (2004). *Militarism, sport, Europe: war without weapons (Vol. 5)*. London: Routledge.

Mangan, J. A. (2010). Prologue: "Middle Kingdom" resurgent! Sports dominance as soft power politics on the Pacific Rim—reflections on Rim Realpolitik. *International Journal of the History of Sport, 27*(14–15), 2333–2358.

Manzenreiter, W. (2008). Football diplomacy, post-colonialism and Japan's quest for normal state status. *Sport in Society, 11*(4), 414–428.

Mattingly, G. (1938). An early nonaggression pact. *Journal of Modern History, 10*(1), 1–30.

McIntyre, J. (2020, June 16). Tensions escalate on Korean peninsula as North blows up joint liaison office in provocative message to South. Washington Examiner. https://www.washingtonexaminer.com/policy/defense-national-security/tensions-escalate-on-korean-peninsula-as-north-blows-up-joint-liaison-office-in-provocative-message-to-south.

Murphy, S. (2020, June 21). DfID staff "devastated and demoralised" by Foreign Office merger. The Guardian https://www.theguardian.com/politics/2020/jun/21/dfid-staff-devastated-and-demoralised-by-foreign-office-merger.

Murray, S. (2008). Consolidating the gains made in diplomacy studies: A taxonomy. *International Studies Perspectives, 9*(1), 22–39.

Murray, S. (2011). Sports-Diplomacy: a hybrid of two halves. Discussion Panel-Innovative Forms of Cultural Diplomacy: Influencing Opinion Amongst Citizens in Foreign Countries. International Symposium on Cultural Diplomacy. Berlin, May 11th–15th, Academy of Cultural Diplomacy.

Murray, S. (2012). The two halves of sports-diplomacy. *Diplomacy & Statecraft, 23*(3), 576–592.

Murray, S. (2018). *Sports diplomacy: Origins, theory and practice*. Routledge.

Murray, S., & Pigman, G. A. (2014). Mapping the relationship between international sport and diplomacy. *Sport in Society, 17*(9), 1098–1118.

Næss, H. E. (2017). Sandwiched between sport and politics: Fédération Internationale de l'Automobile, Formula 1, and non-democratic regimes. *International Journal of the History of Sport, 34*(7–8): 1–19.

Reeves, A. S. (2012). Social stratification, gender and sport participation. *Sociological Research Online, 17*(2), 1–17.

Reuters. (2018, August 22). N. Korea says "no interest in denuke talks" as long as South-US military drills in place. Korea Times.http://www.koreatimes.co.kr/www/nation/2019/09/103_274352.html.

Rofe, S. J. (2016). Sport and diplomacy: A global diplomacy framework. *Diplomacy & Statecraft, 27*(2), 212–230.

Salter, M. A. (1974). Play: A medium of cultural stability. In H. Groll (Ed.), *Beitrage zur Geschichte der Leibeserziehung und des sports* (pp. 1–22). Wien: Universitat Wien.

Satow, E. (1957). *A guide to diplomatic practice* (4th ed.). London: Longmans, Green & Co.

Schiappa, E., Gregg, P. B., & Hewes, D. E. (2005). The parasocial contact hypothesis. *Communication Monographs, 72*(1), 92–115.

Shahid, S. A. (2015). India: Pakistan sports as a tool for peace (cricket diplomacy). *International Journal of Coaching Science, 5*(1), 51–63.

Ungerleider, S. (2015). *Faust's gold: Inside the East German doping machine.* New York: Thomas Dunn Books.

United Nations, Commission on Human Security. (2009). Human security in theory and practice. https://www.unocha.org/sites/dms/HSU/Publications%20and%20Products/Human%20Security%20Tools/Human%20Security%20in%20Theory%20and%20Practice%20English.pdf.

Wilson, E. (1962). *Classics and commercials, a literary chronicle of the forties.* Vintage Books.

Xu, G. (2008). *Olympic dreams: China and sports 1895–2008.* Cambridge, MA: Harvard University Press.

CHAPTER 7

SPORT, MILITARISM, AND SIGNIFICATION

MICHAEL L. BUTTERWORTH

To suggest that sport is infused with militarism is hardly a novel claim. From its earliest incarnations, modern sport in the West has embraced the "cult of the warrior" (Burstyn, 1999, p. 42) and presented itself as a symbolic analogue to war. In the United States, this articulation began with early newspaper coverage of college football in the 1890s and 1900s that promoted "stories of valor and heroism and of war as a rite of passage" (Gems, 2000, p. 80). It was further enhanced by the nation's investment in the "national pastime" of baseball, which was seen not only as an affirmation of American identity at home but as a less than subtle vehicle for bolstering U.S. military influence abroad (Elias, 2010). Throughout the 20th century, American football increasingly came to be seen as representative of the nation's character, with the college game serving as a showcase for the "American way of life" (Kemper, 2009) and the National Football League (NFL) perfecting bombastic displays of militant nationalism (Oriard, 2007). The overlap between the ethos of war and the ethos of football was so apparent that, by the time of the Persian Gulf War in 1991, the football-war metaphor became among the most common rhetorical devices for understanding the conflict (Herbeck, 2004; Jansen & Sabo, 1994).

The rhetorical associations between sport and war were commonplace by the end of the 20th century, but the 9/11 terrorist attacks and subsequent "war on terror" amplified their resonance, and sport leagues and organizations eagerly wrapped themselves in the flag and performed conspicuous displays of military resolve. War was no longer merely a clever metaphor to describe the physical demands of athletic competition, and sport was no longer a site to be used only on special occasions to acknowledge and honor the sacrifices made by the nation's Armed Forces. Rather, militarism became fully integrated as a part of sport itself, marking what Howard Bryant (2018, p. 102) calls a "permanent, cultural transformation." That transformation is characterized by a host of both metaphorical and literal military references, including flyovers, sponsorships, on-field enlistment ceremonies, military family reunions, and the participation of military personnel in rituals such as coin tosses, first pitches, and performances of the "Star Spangled Banner" and "God Bless America." Even as the actual conflicts in Iraq and Afghanistan have ended or subsided, "[r]ituals of memorialization and patriotic celebration at sporting events have consistently kept 9/11 and the war on terror in view, with particular attention given to the promotion of the military" (Butterworth, 2019, p. 227).

Militarism in sport is certainly not restricted to experiences in the United States. Indeed, as I have acknowledged in previous work, "the combined forces of globalization, neoliberalism, and militarization have profoundly affected both formal institutions and everyday popular culture in all regions of the planet" (Butterworth, 2017a, p. 3). As important as this point remains, my focus in this chapter will be restricted primarily to the United States (with some exceptions made in comparative cases), both because it is the context which I am best equipped to assess and because it remains the world's most vivid example of sport's deep investment in militarism. While I cannot claim to capture all of the academic conversation on this topic, this chapter will provide an overview of the critical scholarship that interrogates the symbolic relationships between the military and sport. I begin by defining the key issues and terms that characterize this conflation of interests, which will help establish a vocabulary found within much of the literature. I then turn to the primary approaches taken by scholars, with particular interest in sport militarism as an instrument of the state, as a vehicle for league-based propaganda, and as a mythic manifestation of American civil religion. I conclude with a review of debates about sport militarism found both in public and academic commentary.

Issues

Militarism may be understood in both material and symbolic terms. Given the tremendous investment made in military expenditures in the United States, it is appropriate to begin with a focus on militarism's impact on that nation's economy and security. The 2019 defense budget totaled U.S.$732 billion, which accounted for 38% of the world's collective military spending and was nearly the equivalent of the next 10 highest-spending nations combined (Tian, Kuimova, da Silva, Wezeman, & Wezeman, 2020). Although these numbers represent a decline from the peak spending years of the Cold War, the amount of money the United States spends on the military makes it an obvious global outlier. Of course, there are pragmatic reasons given for this imbalance, including the disproportionate role the U.S. plays in maintaining global security and preserving various balances of power. Yet many around the world and within the United States can point to the nation's legacy of military interventions that call into question any defense of the benevolence of the American Empire (e.g., Ferguson, 2004). Indeed, a nation with "the most destructive military capacity in the history of the world" (Jensen, 2004, p. 16) all too often has exercised its might with questionable results, both because of the damage done to those it has targeted and because of the neglect of its own citizens whose needs are underserved in deference to the military's outsized budgetary demands.

This imbalance of material priorities provides the foundation for concerns expressed about the "military-industrial complex." Such a notion finds its origins in the years following World War II, when the United States experienced an economic boom that championed the nuclear family, mass consumption, and suburbanization (Cohen, 2004; Dickinson, 2015). As citizens supported the "American Way of Life" through consumption, government did so through its ideological opposition to godless communists and a commitment to a strong national defense. In 1956, sociologist C. Wright Mills warned in *The Power Elite* of the dangers of conflating economic and military interests. Tracing the ascendance of "military men," Mills predicted, "American militarism, in fully developed form, would mean the triumph in all areas of life of the military metaphysic, and hence the subordination to it of all other ways of life" (p. 223). Only a few years later, President Dwight D. Eisenhower (1961) used his Farewell Address to caution against the excesses of militarism. "In the councils of government," he said, "we must guard against the acquisition of unwarranted influence, whether sought or unsought, by the military-industrial complex. The potential for the disastrous rise of misplaced power exists and will persist" (¶15). Although any endorsement of Eisenhower's wisdom should be measured against his own complicity in facilitating the military's growth in the nuclear age, his parting shot nevertheless has become a permanent rhetorical fixture in the nation's lexicon.

The militarized state expanded in the United States throughout the second half of the 20th century. As the nation squared off against the Soviet Union in a nuclear arms race and fought conventional wars by proxy, it also ended conscription and moved to voluntary enlistment in the armed forces. This transition placed pressure on the Pentagon to recruit these volunteers at the same time that innovations such as the microprocessor, cable, satellite, and the internet dramatically transformed the media and entertainment landscape. Over this time period, the military increasingly became tied to popular culture, the various forms of which often valorized the spectacular and mythic presentation of war. By the turn of the century, the "military-industrial complex" had become an insufficient label. James Der Derian (2001) proposes instead that we identify a "military-industrial-media-entertainment network," or MIME-NET, as a more comprehensive term. As he defines it:

> Unlike the fifties version presaged by President Eisenhower's farewell address, with its computers the size of boxcars, clunky teletype machines, centralized command systems, and glowing vacuum tubes, the new MIME-NET runs on video-game imagery, twenty-four-hour news cycles, multiple nodes of military, corporate, university, and media power, and microchips, embedded in everything but human flesh (so far). (p. 126)

Alongside the development of the MIME-NET, popular sport in the United States similarly grew in scope and influence. Jhally (1984) has called the integration of sport and media the "sports/media complex," a fusing that Wenner (1998) characterizes with the neologism "mediasport." Both of these conceptions recognize the integral nature of military interests as outlined above. Thus, we might think of yet one more "complex," identified by Stempel (2006) as the "televised masculinist sport-militaristic nationalism complex." In his analysis of audience responses to sports programming during the "war on terror," Stempel argues this "complex includes a variety of televised sports that represent, iconize, and naturalize a combination of masculinist and nationalistic ideals and morals and a field of politics where imperialist military projects are imagined and popular support and acquiescence is garnered" (p. 82). In short, drawing on its historic analogous relationship to war and its well-established "masculinist moral capital" (p. 83), sport in the United States serves as arguably the most visible and influential popular culture vehicle for normalizing and promoting military interests.

This evolution from Mills and Eisenhower to Der Derian and Stempel makes clear that militarism is not only a material matter. As important as it is to observe empirically the growth of the U.S. Armed Forces and evaluate its tangible impact, it is equally important to think about militarism's symbolic impact. Indeed, critical studies of militarism typically consider the phenomenon ideologically or discursively. For example, in their study of the "Hollywood war machine," Boggs and Pollard (2007, p. 19) contend, "Militarism appears as a form of *ideology*, a rationality that deeply influences the structures and practices of the general society through storytelling, mythology, media images, political messages, academic discourses, and simple patriotic indoctrination." Similarly, Martin and Steuter (2010, p. 4) define militarism as

> an approach to the world in which global problems are defined primarily as military problems, where the first response of political leadership, and a segment of the population, is the resort to force, and where pride of place in American life is given to the military and to a culture of violence.

The evolution of militarism as a discourse must also be understood in relation to globalization. Much like the relationship between sport and the military, "globalization" is not a new phenomenon. Yet, in the postwar era, globalization can be defined by "the emergence of a global economy, a transnational cosmopolitan culture and a range of international social movements" (Maguire, 1999, p. 3), features that have developed with increasing speed and technological advancement. Especially in terms of sport, scholars have noted the mutual influences between the United States and other Western nations with respect to neoliberal economic practices and popular culture (Miller, Lawrence, McKay, & Rowe, 2001). Much as is the case with militarism, the United States holds disproportionate power to shape the forces of globalization. Between the hegemony of neoliberalism and the assertion of the "Bush Doctrine" during the "war on terror," globalization in the early 21st century is often understood as a project of empire. Thus, Hartnett and Stengrim (2006, p. 10) define globalization as "an ever-expanding form of U.S.-led free trade imperialism, as the global pursuit of economic and political advantage in foreign lands policed by U.S. military power yet not ruled by it in any direct governing manner." Given this dynamic, studies of sport militarism often take into account the discourses manifest in and produced by global culture and politics.

I approach these issues from the perspective of rhetorical studies. Rhetoric's emphasis on persuasive symbol use shares much in common with the discursive focus of critical sociologists and cultural studies scholars. Thus, my attention in this chapter is on practices of signification—that is, the use of symbols, representations, and myths that constitute and, at times, contest political and social life. It is to those practices I now turn.

APPROACHES

The focus on militarism as a discourse or rationality helps to narrow the scope of this chapter. Although the synergies between sport and the military can be examined from various points of view, including applied studies and those that identify similarities between athletes and soldiers, there is a substantial body of critical research that foregrounds processes of signification. In addition to this symbolic emphasis, I also restrict my discussion here primarily to work done in the 21st century. This allows me both to present a manageable overview and to isolate the unique dynamics that are shaped by contemporary technologies and the consequences of the "war on terror." Based on these qualifications, I identify ideological effects that can best be understood by viewing sport militarism as (1) an instrument of the state, (2) a vehicle for league-based propaganda, and (3) a mythic manifestation of American civil religion.

Sport Militarism as an Instrument of the State

The terrorist attacks of 9/11 and the subsequent "Bush Doctrine" and "war on terror" arguably have had more impact on sport militarism than any other moment in U.S. history. This is not to suggest previous moments are unimportant. When the American Legion started its youth baseball program in 1925, for example, it solidified the idea that playing sports could help prepare children to serve the nation and thrive in the military. In 1942, following the bombing of Pearl Harbor, President Franklin Delano Roosevelt issued his famous "Green Light Letter" urging Major League Baseball (MLB) to continue its season for the morale of the nation. The League did so, and also required the "Star Spangled Banner" be performed as a ritual before every game, a precedent subsequently followed by all other sports leagues and organizations. And throughout the 20th century, athletes were called upon to acknowledge the sacrifices of military personnel or support them in appearances with organizations such as the United Service Organizations (USO) (see Butterworth, 2010; Elias, 2010). Despite these and many other examples, nothing quite compares to the comprehensive integration of militarism into sport in the first two decades of the 21st century.

In her analysis of the NFL efforts to support the "war on terror," King (2008, p. 528) suggests the post-9/11 moment can be understood "as a further indication of the militarization of everyday life, and simultaneously, of the 'sportification' of political life" in the United States. She finds evidence of this not only in the linguistic equations of football with war but also in the coordinated efforts between the League and official programs within the U.S. Armed Forces. One such example is the government's investment in Pat Tillman, the former NFL player who gave up his career to join the U.S. Army Rangers and was later killed by fratricide in Afghanistan. As is now well known, initial reports indicated Tillman had been killed by enemy fire, and his death was valorized as a symbol of heroic sacrifice. Demonstrating the synergy between sport, media, and the military, Tillman's funeral was broadcast live on ESPN and he was eulogized by, among others, Vietnam veteran and Arizona senator John McCain. As King concludes, "In focusing on his death rather than on why he died, these dedications constituted sacrifice as the goal rather than asking whether the sacrifice itself made any sense" (p. 534), therefore amplifying the symbolic value of *football player–as–soldier*.

Another example is found in the NFL's "Kickoff Live" programming that launched in 2002. For the 2003 event, the NFL partnered directly with the Pentagon, which had started Operation Tribute to Freedom, a program "for the community to show their appreciation for the troops" (Vinall, 2003, ¶2). In other words, it was a U.S. Department of Defense initiative designed to bolster troop morale under the guise of "community" responses to the "war on terror." The 2003 season opener was in Washington, D.C., so "Kickoff Live" took place on the National Mall, featuring patriotic monuments as a backdrop. Among the 300,000 estimated to be in attendance, 25,000 were members of the military and their families. The

Washington Post reported at the time that "the Pentagon encouraged service people to wear their short-sleeve, open-collar uniforms, to make a good impression on TV" (quoted in King, 2008, p. 536). For King, the "symbolic interpenetration of war and sport" represented by this event made the NFL, in effect, a "Department of Propaganda" (p. 537), with which it promoted the military's interests, including its recruitment efforts.

Similar issues are present in college football. An illustrative case can be found in the annual Armed Forces Bowl, a lower-tier postseason game held in Fort Worth, Texas. Originally named simply the Fort Worth Bowl, the game was rebranded in 2006 with Bell Helicopter–Textron as the naming sponsor (it later became the Lockheed Martin Armed Forces Bowl). The conflation of sport and militarism was strengthened by a partnership with ESPN and additional sponsorship from organizations such as First Command Financial Services. The production had numerous military-themed features, including dedicating each quarter of the game to a different branch of the U.S. Armed Forces, presenting the Great American Patriot award at halftime, inducting new military recruits in an on-field enlistment ceremony, and providing an amusement park–style "fanfest" outside the stadium where fans could interact with armored vehicles, simulation machines, and recruitment booths. All of these elements were amplified by persistent declarations to "support the troops," a theme extended by the Armed Forces Bowl's relationship with America Supports You. Much like Operation Tribute to Freedom, this program has the appearance of a grassroots effort, but it is actually another initiative from the Department of Defense. Thus, "America Supports You presents the illusion that Americans are independently moved to support the military, when, in this case at least, they are given the script by the bureaucracy that depends on the military-industrial complex" (Butterworth & Moskal, 2009, p. 421). Ironically, the troops are largely presented as props, symbolically celebrated within the confines of a college football spectacle but materially expendable within the commitments of the "war on terror."

Part of what makes events such as the Armed Forces Bowl troubling is the ease with which the "support the troops" rhetoric establishes identifications between military personnel and the general public. In many cases, such as the NFL's Salute to Service campaign, this identification works through the athletes, who are aligned with soldiers through "sacrifice, courage, and heroism" (Mangold & Goehring, 2018, p. 513). In other cases, it works by promoting interactivity and approximating the aesthetic virtues of embodying war as sport. Stahl (2010, p. 21) makes this argument in his book *Militainment, Inc.*, an examination of various forms of popular culture that constitute the "virtual citizen-soldier." His treatment of sport focuses on extreme sports, which thrive on images of individual expression, nontraditional forms of competition, and an attitude of rebelliousness. Extreme sports discourse articulates with other physical activities, such as CrossFit (Musselman, 2019) and obstacle races like the Tough Mudder and Spartan Race (Lamb & Hillman, 2015). By linking militaristic attitudes with the rebellious spirit of extreme sports, this discourse "has been put to use as an entry point through which the citizen has been invited to play soldier" (Stahl, 2010, p. 54).

Stahl finds evidence of this kind of "play" in the integration of extreme sports aesthetics in Hollywood films such as *xXx* (2002) and *Behind Enemy Lines* (2001). In *xXx*, protagonist Xander Cage is imagined as a virtual citizen-soldier who sees the battlefield as little more than an extreme sports playground. As he blasts his way through the climax of the film, Cage laments, "I wish I had a camera," modeling the first-person perspectives popularized in extreme sports which help "project the viewer into the endangered body itself" (Stahl,

2010, p. 62). This view is even more pronounced in *Behind Enemy Lines*, the plot of which turns on the adventures of a bored soldier who is frustrated that he sees no action, only to find himself trapped in enemy territory when he recklessly deviates from an assigned mission. The costs of his irresponsible actions—both in lives and in military hardware—are subordinated to the "rush" of navigating the various threats of an enhanced obstacle course. *Behind Enemy Lines* models the extreme sports lifestyle in coordination with the U.S. Navy, which provided consultation and military resources in exchange for oversight on the script. In addition to helping to craft a narrative that feels like a recruitment video, the Navy also produced a recruitment commercial that ran ahead of the film in theaters. As part of the $40 million Accelerate Your Life campaign,

> the ad featured heroic shots on the deck of the aircraft carrier and the glamorization of gadgetry. . . . Rather than appeal to career advancement, job skills, or patriotism, the ad offers the prospect of being shot at, a strange enticement to join any organization. (Stahl, 2010, p. 68)

Stahl acknowledges that glamorizing war is nothing new; however, he details the many ways popular culture hails consumers as virtual participants who see war as little more than a game to be played.

As the Pentagon and U.S. Armed Forces have developed relationships that help integrate sport and sport aesthetics into their promotional efforts, other state organizations have integrated their logics into Americans' daily lives. For example, Schimmel has also used the notion of the "citizen-soldier" as a foundation for understanding how sport militarism has positioned American football fans as protectors of national security. She notes that the Super Bowl, as the single largest sport spectacle in the United States, has been defined as a potential terrorist target, meaning that stadiums are now designed to integrate urban security measures in accordance with the Department of Homeland Security. Beyond this, fans are expected to serve as de facto surveillance officers, reminded that, "If you see something, say something." Even as fans might be on "active duty" in the event of a terrorist attack, the Support Antiterrorism by Fostering Effective Technologies (SAFETY) Act of 2003 prevents them receiving financial compensation should something happen to them. As Schimmel (2012, p. 352) notes, under this form of militarism "it is not the fans who are protected, it is the NFL." Schimmel's (2017, p. 85) work has emphasized how the NFL has coordinated with U.S. officials to create "militarized civic rituals" which "blur the operational and legal separations between citizens and soldiers and war and peace." In short, more than providing opportunities for recruitment and support for military policy, sport militarism also hails citizens as actors within the increasingly militarized spaces in which they live.

Sport Militarism as League-Based Propaganda

If sport leagues and organizations have been eager to partner with military interests, it surely has not been only for altruistic reasons. Indeed, the most obvious displays of sport militarism are also about public relations. For example, NFL Commissioner Pete Rozelle introduced the military flyover for Super Bowl II in 1968 as part of a "conscious effort . . . to bring the element of patriotism into the Super Bowl" (quoted in Oriard, 2007, p. 22). In the aftermath of 9/11, MLB echoed its own precedent of making the national anthem a daily ritual to enhance its patriotic reputation. Commissioner Bud Selig announced at the time, "[E]ach club should ask its fans to sing 'God Bless America' either prior to the game or during the seventh inning stretch" (quoted in Briley, 2017, pp. 117–118). In case the symbolism was unclear, Selig defended his decision from those who felt the performances were excessive, stating, "I honestly don't think that politicizes the issue. After all, we do have troops in Iraq and Afghanistan" (quoted in Butterworth, 2010, p. 31). Moments such as these provide confirmation that sport's leaders value the symbolic capital gained through associations with the military.

American football again provides a relevant context to examine these promotional efforts. Fischer's (2014) study of militarism in the NFL builds on the critiques of the military-industrial complex and MIME-NET that characterize the scholarship discussed thus far. She focuses in particular on the NFL's commemorations on the 10th anniversary of 9/11 and reveals five discursive strategies: (1) emphasizing heroism, (2) conceptualizing a deracialized ethnic nation, (3) valorizing the troops, (4) claiming metaphorical territory, and (5) asserting hegemonic masculinity. Like others (King, 2008; Kusz, 2007), Fischer notes that a player such as Tillman serves as an avatar for the League's uncritical embrace of romantic, heroic sacrifice. Through Tillman's memory, as well as the collage of red, white, and blue imagery, the NFL promotes "hyper-masculine, heavy-hitting, domineering males who make sport their battleground to wage war for freedom and democracy" (Fischer, 2014, p. 216). The symbolic conflation of football with American strength tells us much about militarism's effects in the context of the "war on terror" but also helps explain the accusations that activist athletes such as Colin Kaepernick are disrespectful to the military (Butterworth, 2017a) and that not being able to play football during the coronavirus pandemic would somehow weaken the nation (Zirin, 2020b).

No other league, not even the traditionally conservative National Association of Stock Car Racing (NASCAR), has so thoroughly incorporated the aesthetics of militarism as the NFL. A particularly striking example can be found in the annual Salute to Service campaign, a celebration of the military that lasts throughout the month of November (to overlap with the Veterans Day holiday). Rugg (2016, p. 21) notes that, as opposed to the spectacular displays and rituals that have become commonplace at U.S. sporting events, Salute to Service relies on a "diffused military presence" that "casually incorporates the military into everyday life via the entertainment and branding structures of the league." The initiative launched quietly in 2011, but it became much more visible by 2013, when it added camouflage-themed clothing items worn by coaches and players during the games. Camouflage hats, hoodies, and jerseys are available for fans to purchase, and game-used items are auctioned off to support military charities such as the Pat Tillman Foundation and the Wounded Warriors Project. Similar gear can be purchased by fans of other sports, contributing to the popularization of "military chic" fashion (Achter, 2019) and affirming the public image of teams and leagues.

As illustrative as football is, other sports are also eager to capitalize on military symbolism. Much as the NFL's commemorative practices have affirmed a narrow conception of national identity in the United States, the National Hockey League (NHL) has done the same in Canada. As McDermott and Scherer (2017, p. 129) contend, the CBC's signature sports broadcast, *Hockey Night in Canada*, has been "ideologically encoded to (re)articulate a traditional version of Canadian identity . . . with a broader theme of militarization during an era in which the Canadian political landscape has sharply swung to the right." Here again we see the convergence of league and sports media interests in service of both pro-military rhetoric and the bolstering of the nation's most popular sport. This effort has also been supported by the production of Tickets for Troops, an NHL promotional game that is equal parts military recruitment ad and affirmation of hockey as representative of national identity (Scherer & Koch, 2010). In many ways, sport militarism in Canada has echoed what has happened in the United States, both because of the shared ownership of professional leagues and the pressures Canadian officials felt to support the U.S.-led "war on terror." Regardless of location, however, sports leagues and their media partners have thoroughly normalized militarism as a taken-for-granted component in the production of sporting events and as an integral part of their public relations efforts.

Sport Militarism as a Manifestation of Civil Religion

As I noted earlier, the use of sport militarism as a tool for public relations often overlaps with a mythic conception of national identity. Thus, militaristic rituals in sporting contexts can be understood as an expression of American civil religion. This specific term is not always invoked, but it nevertheless helps capture and summarize an approach that interprets sport militarism as an extension of other unifying discourses. Contemporary scholars most often associate civil religion with sociologist Robert Bellah's (1967) "Civil Religion in America." For Bellah, civil religion is not about spiritual transcendence; rather, it is about the religious logic that allows Americans to identify with one another through shared institutions and civic practices. In the United States, faith in the Constitution, celebrations of holidays such as Independence Day, and remembrances of veterans all serve as sacraments that bind citizens to their nation.

The rituals of civil religion have captured the attention of many scholars interested in nationalism, including notions of the "imagined community" (Anderson, 1991) and "banal nationalism" (Billig, 1995). For most Americans, these practices feel affirmative and benign. Yet, as Marvin and Ingle (1999, p. 32) describe it, "U.S. civil religion does do things. It kills. It commands sacrifice. It transforms infants, non-believers, and converts from other national faiths into Americans." The notion of sacrifice is particularly relevant here, as sport militarism is often framed as an exercise in honoring those who have served in the U.S. Armed Forces. The sacrifices made by veterans—both psychological and physical—provide the foundation for the American imagined community, for it is "the shared memory of blood sacrifice, periodically renewed" (Marvin & Ingle, 1999, p. 4), that constitutes the nation.

Studies of sport memory are an especially useful lens through which to view militarism as an expression of civil religion. Memory scholars typically agree that acts of commemoration and memorialization symbolically invoke the past as means for addressing needs or crises of the present. In the post-9/11 context, sport militarism has tethered the terrorist attacks to other historically significant moments to affirm the virtues of the United States and constitute Americans as a unified public. This process began immediately when sports resumed after a brief hiatus prompted by the tragedy. In subsequent years, sport leagues and organizations produced elaborate ceremonies and rituals designed to "never forget" the lives lost on 9/11, to "support the troops," and to promote "unity and strength" (Butterworth, 2014). While these productions have certainly contributed to efforts to bolster the military-industrial complex and the public relations of sport organizations, they also can be read as enactments of national faith.

A more specific example of this enactment can be found in Fox Sports' cinematic portrayals of the Declaration of Independence that have aired before several Super Bowl broadcasts. In this case, sport media partners with the NFL to leverage the symbolism of football and celebrate a document that is a foundational text in American civil religion (Bellah, 1967). Fox debuted the feature for its coverage of Super Bowl XLII in 2008, and each iteration has incorporated patriotic images, inspirational music, and dramatic readings of the Declaration by former and current NFL players and officials. Whereas some of the images are "neutral" patriotic symbols (such as the flag and notable American landmarks), many of them are explicitly associated with the military. The 2008 production included a segment filmed with star running back LaDainian Tomlinson on a naval carrier and another with Tillman's widow, Marie, standing in front of the statue of her fallen husband located in Freedom Plaza in front of Arizona's University of Phoenix Stadium. Between Marie Tillman and Tomlinson, the narration quotes the Declaration passage "We mutually pledge to each other our lives, our fortunes, and our sacred honor" (quoted in Butterworth, 2008, p. 321). As noted previously, government and League officials conflated Tillman's death with the virtues of heroic service, thus making his inclusion in the Declaration film a confirmation of "the shared memory of blood sacrifice." Any ambiguity about this point was erased by the film's closing frame, which included the text "Fox Sports and the National Football League dedicates this depiction of the Declaration of Independence . . . to all the valiant men and women of our Armed Forces, who have paid the ultimate sacrifice in defense of our freedom and liberty" (quoted in Butterworth, 2008, p. 322), while "Taps" is solemnly played as the score.

In many ways, Fox's Declaration leveraged militarism to present an idealized form of national identity, often understood as "American exceptionalism." This idea—that the United States is a uniquely democratic and free nation chosen by God himself to serve as a model to the rest of the world—is commonly expressed in nationalistic sport narratives. When military personnel are present at sporting events to throw out ceremonial first pitches, hold football-field-size American flags, and perform the "Star Spangled Banner" and "God Bless America," they are presented as exemplars of the nation's indisputable generosity and goodness. Sport is then positioned in alignment with these values, especially at larger, high-profile events such as MLB's World Series (Butterworth, 2017b), the Super Bowl, and the Olympic Games (Silk & Falcous, 2005).

Asserting American exceptionalism through sport militarism relies on uncritical displays of patriotic imagery and platitudes to "support the troops." This leads scholars to interrogate the values taken for granted in these productions. For example, although the military is racially diverse, heroic members of the military are commonly envisioned as white. The Pentagon's 1973 Operation Homecoming, for example, welcomed back POWs from the war in Vietnam in a carefully orchestrated media spectacle. The burden of sacrifice in that war was disproportionately carried by people of color, but the mediation of the soldiers' return "encouraged Americans to remember the war as having been fought by a few hundred white officers who had suffered out of sight for years before, at last, coming home to picture-perfect reunions with doting wives and children" (Darda, 2018, p. 86). Sport militarism has mimicked this ritual, using pregame and halftime programming to stage surprise reunions between military personnel and their families. These moments include both men and women in uniform, and they feature a degree of racial and ethnic diversity; however, given the persistent imagery that promotes the whiteness of the U.S. Armed Forces (Prividera &

Howard, 2006), it is fair to conclude that the representative image remains a young, white soldier coming home to his white (probably blonde) wife.

The privileging of whiteness is also evident in the ways that militarism is protected against challenges to national unity. The ferocity of reactions to athlete activism, most clearly represented by former NFL quarterback Colin Kaepernick, reveals the deep-seated articulations of racial identity with military sacrifice and national virtue. When Kaepernick began kneeling during the national anthem in 2016, he did so in response to a series of incidents in the United States in which members of law enforcement killed unarmed Black men. Those injustices were largely ignored in the subsequent debate that accused him of being unpatriotic and, most important, disrespecting the military (Bryant, 2018; Butterworth, 2020). As Kusz (2017) explains, contemporary militarism has evolved in tandem with the nation's broader cultural shift to the right in the final decades of the 20th century. Echoing the discourses of Christian fundamentalism, the demonization of immigrants and welfare recipients, and the reassertion of masculine authority, "[t]he militarization of American culture has also given rise to a structure of feeling that promotes a fear of others and a suspicion about all those Americans who do not readily affirm the ideas and logics of militaristic nationalism" (Kusz, 2017, p. 234). For Kusz, the definitive symbol of this brand of white nationalism is NFL legend Tom Brady; we might fairly conclude that the inverse is Kaepernick. In short, sport militarism promotes a unified vision of American identity, yet it does so by tacitly reproducing privileges characterized by masculinity and whiteness.

DEBATES

There is a general consensus among critical scholars that sport militarism is unhealthy for democracy. Strong arguments may be made that the relentless articulations of sport with military symbols and the material interests of the U.S. Armed Forces have both dehumanized the troops that are purportedly being honored and anesthetized American citizens to the indulgences of the military-industrial complex. As Ivie (2015, pp. xi–xii) concludes, "The war state is a condition of naturalized militarism. . . . [Militarism] is a totalizing world view." Given this definitive judgment, it is tempting simply to declare no further debate is needed. Yet, Ivie suggests the opposite, noting that understanding the discourses of militarism opens up spaces for resistance, both among scholars and within the communities most directly affected by war and its accompanying symbolism. In other words, scholars should not lose sight of criticism's capacity to engage audiences and facilitate social change.

One area of central importance concerns the symbolic ownership of "the troops." Discourse from government and military officials in the United States has aggressively sought to redefine American cultural attitudes about military personnel. The controversial Vietnam War era cast significant doubt on the virtue of the armed forces, and, for many leaders, public condemnations of the war contributed to an embarrassing defeat. As Stahl (2009, p. 536) details, the pervasive calls to "support the troops" serve to repudiate the "Vietnam Syndrome" and "recuperate public support" for the military. Ostensibly, then, sport militarism is a product of these discursive efforts and its various permutations are designed to affirm and bolster the esteem of military personnel. However, a case can be made that this discourse does a disservice to the troops, for it reifies them as heroic abstractions and deflects the harsh realities of war and the challenges of life after service (Butterworth & Moskal, 2009). Active service members and veterans alike are essentially treated as props, and the symbolic deployment of their images "interpellate viewers as citizens and create the possibility for audiences to cultivate an emotional attachment to the nation-state" (Achter, 2010, p. 63). Although critical scholars are typically careful not to demonize military personnel, the humanity of service members is often diminished in structural critiques of sport militarism.

Another consequence of the totalizing critique that *all* aspects of sport militarism are negative is that scholars may neglect possible positive effects. For example, while acknowledging significant problems with the articulation of higher education with military interests, Andrews, Miller, and Cork (2017) demonstrate that military innovations can result in good things for the larger population. In their evaluation of the "weaponizing" of kinesiology departments, the authors suggest that research on injuries and rehabilitation efforts among military personnel have led to the development of "medical technology and quality of care protocols that have positively impacted the lives of many within the civilian population" (pp. 38–39). In particular, this can be seen in treatments for traumatic brain injuries and innovations in prosthetic limbs. Although it would be preferable that U.S. troops be kept from harm in the first place, few would argue that the development of improved procedures and therapies is an undesirable byproduct.

A final area of debate has less to do with sport militarism discourse itself and more to do with the choices made by scholars. As I noted at the outset of this chapter, sport militarism is neither new nor uniquely American. Nevertheless, and I note this fully aware of my own choices in scholarship and in this chapter, much of the contemporary scholarship on this topic focuses on very recent events and overemphasizes the role of the United States. There is, of course, definitive work about sport militarism in Europe (Magnan, 2003) and recent work on the links between nationalism, militarism, and violence in Asia (Hong & Lu, 2015) and South America (Miller, 2020). Much of this work assists in addressing the issues raised earlier in this chapter with respect to the interdependence of militarism with globalization.

There is also excellent scholarship that evaluates sport militarism in comparative terms. John Kelly, for example, has written extensively about military influences in British sport. Although there are unique features of militarism in the United Kingdom, Kelly also points to effects of the "war on terror" that have been similarly felt in the United States. In particular, he demonstrates how military-themed rituals in association football simultaneously construct British soldiers as heroes and dissenting voices as "others" who threaten the nation's war-time mission (Kelly, 2013). In doing so, he reminds scholars that the logic of sport militarism is shared across different national contexts and is interdependent with globalization. This is even more evident in his assessment of "Western militarism," in which he concludes, "Western countries have increasingly incorporated their citizens by proxy into supporting their military and sport has played one of the most prominent roles in this" (Kelly, 2017, p. 288). By pulling the lens up to view militarism comparatively, Kelly accounts for national ideologies and sporting contests that are less obvious in the review of scholarship that otherwise characterizes this chapter.

For those working within the communication studies and sociology of sport traditions, however, a good case may be made that North America remains the primary continent deserving of focus. Similarly, sport militarism scholars often restrict their analyses to more heavily mediated and commercialized sports such as American football, association football, baseball, and international spectacles such as the Olympic Games. There are reasons for this, as the MIME-NET relies on larger-scale media productions. That said, as evidenced by the discussion of extreme sports earlier in this chapter, smaller and less conventional sporting contexts provide important opportunities for understanding the scope and impact of sport militarism as well.

CONCLUSION

Although sport militarism is not a new phenomenon, this chapter summarizes the contemporary articulations of sport with the military. In the United States, the legacy of the Vietnam Syndrome has coupled with the aftermath of 9/11 to the extent that it has become "functionally impossible to live outside the rhetorical production of war" (Butterworth & Moskal, 2009, p. 413). Even when other areas of popular culture have scaled back the scope and spectacle of "military appreciation" events and "support the troops" platitudes, sport in the United States has only intensified its associations with military symbolism. Critical scholarship on this issue has raised significant concerns about its effects, focusing in particular on the military-industrial complex, the discourses of propaganda, and militarism as an enactment of civil religion. This work has called our investments in militarism into question in the hopes that sport, as well as other forms of popular culture, might help Americans better assess their relationship to the "war state" (Ivie, 2015) and perform more active and varied expressions of democratic citizenship.

As someone who has been writing about this issue for many years, I find it easy to feel that such efforts are all too often ignored. Yet the relentless presentation of military symbolism within sport may be wearing thin on audiences. Beyond academic critics, the handful of critical journalists writing about sport militarism after 9/11 has grown into a much larger chorus of voices. Howard Bryant's (2018) work in *The Heritage* and Dave Zirin's (2020a) consistent efforts are just two examples that suggest there is a growing audience who recognizes the outsized influence of militaristic discourses in sport. Veterans, too, have increasingly expressed concerns. As history professor and retired Air Force Lt. Col. William Astore (2018, ¶29) puts it, "When we blur sports and the military, adding corporate agendas into the mix, we're not just doing a disservice to our troops and our athletes; we're doing a disservice to ourselves. We're weakening the integrity of democracy in America." Ultimately, seeking to preserve that integrity remains the goal for the critical interrogation of sport militarism.

REFERENCES

Achter, P. (2010). Unruly bodies: The rhetorical domestication of twenty-first century veterans of war. *Quarterly Journal of Speech, 96*, 46–68.

Achter, P. (2019). "Military chic" and the rhetorical production of the uniformed body. *Western Journal of Communication, 83*, 265–285.

Anderson, B. (1991). *Imagined communities: Reflections on the origin and spread of nationalism* (Rev. ed.). London: Verso.

Andrews, D. L., Miller, R. H., & Cork, S. (2017). Weaponizing kinesiology: Illuminating the militarization of the sport sciences. In M. L. Butterworth (Ed.), *Sport and militarism: Contemporary global perspectives* (pp. 31–47). London: Routledge.

Astore, W. (2018, August 21). The militarization of sports and the redefinition of patriotism. *Huffington Post.* https://www.huffpost.com/entry/the-militarization-of-sports-and-the-redefinitionof_b_5b7b1319e4b073b95dbc3768?guccounter=1&guce_referrer=aHR0cHM6Ly93d3cuZ29vZ2xlLmNvbS8&guce_referrer_sig=AQAAAB3_6RmeCxIlli8A4ZDYaDlzS_NdR4gwcqr92IGRd7d9ChcGdn4Y5WQfQvmeLQ44mk0_6Gd9gNiiE8vRcIhisoLDHjQjU_tXBauSgg2nVFUde4ZshK64qFHJx49hk8u6pdi5WSzI6lQ4qBQUDDgkXI-mOFCJT5Xbh-SmQEg.

Bellah, R. N. (1967). Civil religion in America. *Daedalus, 96,* 1–21. '

Billig, M. (1995). *Banal nationalism.* London: Sage.

Boggs, C., & Pollard, T. (2007). *The Hollywood war machine: U.S. militarism and popular culture.* Boulder, CO: Paradigm.

Briley, R. (2017). "God Bless America": An anthem for American exceptionalism and empire. In M. L. Butterworth (Ed.), *Sport and militarism: Contemporary global perspectives* (pp. 115–128). London: Routledge.

Bryant, H. (2018). *The heritage: Black athletes, a divided America, and the politics of patriotism.* Boston: Beacon Press.

Burstyn, V. (1999). *The rites of men: Manhood, politics, and the culture of sport.* Toronto: University of Toronto Press.

Butterworth, M. L. (2008). Fox Sports, Super Bowl XLII, and the affirmation of American civil religion. *Journal of Sport and Social Issues, 32,* 318–323.

Butterworth, M. L. (2010). *Baseball and rhetorics of purity: The national pastime and American identity during the war on terror.* Tuscaloosa: University of Alabama Press.

Butterworth, M. L. (2014). Public memorializing in the stadium: Mediated sport, the 10th anniversary of 9/11, and the illusion of democracy. *Communication & Sport, 2,* 203–224.

Butterworth, M. L. (2017a). Sport and militarism: An introduction to a global phenomenon. In M. L. Butterworth (Ed.), *Sport and militarism: Contemporary global perspectives* (pp. 1–13). London: Routledge.

Butterworth, M. L. (2017b). The World Series: Baseball, American exceptionalism, and media ritual. In A. C. Billings & L. A. Wenner (Eds.), *Sport, media and mega-events* (pp. 218–231). London: Routledge.

Butterworth, M. L. (2019). Sport and the post-9/11 American nation. In J. Maguire (Ed.), *The business and culture of sports,* vol. 3 (pp. 225–239). Farmington Hills, MI: Macmillan.

Butterworth, M. L. (2020). Sport and the quest for unity: How the logic of consensus undermines democratic culture. *Communication & Sport, 8,* 452–472.

Butterworth, M. L., & Moskal, S. D. (2009). American football, flags, and "fun": The Bell Helicopter Armed Forces Bowl and the rhetorical production of militarism. *Communication, Culture & Critique, 2,* 411–433.

Cohen, L. (2004). *A consumers' republic: The politics of mass consumption in postwar America.* New York: Alfred A. Knopf.

Darda, J. (2018). Military whiteness. *Critical Inquiry, 45,* 76–96.

Der Derian, J. (2001). *Virtuous war: Mapping the military-industrial-media-entertainment network.* Boulder: Westview Press.

Dickinson, G. (2015). *Suburban dreams: Imagining and building the good life*. Tuscaloosa: University of Alabama Press.

Eisenhower, D. D. (1961, January 17). Farewell address. AmericanRhetoric.com. https://www.americanrhetoric.com/speeches/dwightdeisenhowerfarewell.html.

Elias, R. (2010). *The empire strikes out: How baseball sold U.S. foreign policy and promoted the American way abroad*. New York: New Press.

Ferguson, N. (2004). *Colossus: The price of America's empire*. New York: Penguin Press.

Fischer, M. (2014). Commemorating 9/11 NFL-style: Insights into America's culture of militarism. *Journal of Sport and Social Issues, 38*, 199–221.

Gems, G. R. (2000). *For pride, profit, and patriarchy: Football and the incorporation of American cultural values*. Lanham, MD: Scarecrow Press.

Hartnett, S. J., & Stengrim, L. A. (2006). *Globalization and empire: The U.S. invasion of Iraq, free markets, and the twilight of democracy*. Tuscaloosa: University of Alabama Press.

Herbeck, D. A. (2004). Sports metaphors and public policy: The football theme in Desert Storm discourse. In F. A. Beer & C. de Landtsheer (Eds.), *Metaphorical world politics* (pp. 121–139). East Lansing: Michigan State University Press.

Hong, F., & Lu, Z. (Eds.) (2015). *Sport and nationalism in Asia: Power, politics and identity*. London: Routledge.

Ivie, R. L. (2015). Foreword: Telling the stories of the war state. In E. S. Parcell & L. M. Webb (Eds.), *A communication perspective on the military: Interactions, messages, and discourses* (pp. xi–xiii). New York: Peter Lang.

Jansen, S. C., & Sabo, D. (1994). The sport/war metaphor: Hegemonic masculinity, the Persian Gulf War, and the new world order. *Sociology of Sport Journal, 11*, 1–17.

Jensen, R. (2004). *Citizens of the empire: The struggle to reclaim our humanity*. San Francisco, CA: City Lights Books.

Jhally, S. (1984). The spectacle of accumulation: Material and cultural factors in the evolution of the sports/media complex. *The Insurgent Sociologist, 12*, 41–57.

Kelly, J. (2013). Popular culture, sport and the "hero"-fication of British militarism. *Sociology, 47*, 722–738.

Kelly, J. (2017). Western militarism and the political utility of sport. In A. Bairner, J. Kelly, & J. W. Lee (Eds.), *Routledge handbook of sport and politics* (pp. 277–291). London: Routledge.

Kemper, K. E. (2009). *College football and American culture in the Cold War era*. Urbana: University of Illinois Press.

King, S. (2008). Offensive lines: Sport-state synergy in an era of perpetual war. *Cultural Studies ⇔ Critical Methodologies, 8*, 527–539.

Kusz, K. W. (2007). From NASCAR nation to Pat Tillman: Notes on sport and the politics of white cultural nationalism in post-9/11 America. *Journal of Sport and Social Issues, 31*, 77–88.

Kusz, K. W. (2017). Trumpism, Tom Brady, and the reassertion of white supremacy in militarized post-9/11 America. In M. L. Butterworth (Ed.), *Sport and militarism: Contemporary global perspectives* (pp. 229–244). London: Routledge.

Lamb, M. D., & Hillman, C. (2015). Whiners go home: Tough Mudder, conspicuous consumption, and the rhetorical proof of "fitness." *Communication & Sport, 3*, 81–99.

Magnan, J. A. (Ed.). (2003). *Militarism, sport, Europe: War without weapons*. London: Frank Cass.

Maguire, J. (1999). *Global sport: Identities, societies, civilization*. Cambridge, U.K.: Polity Press.

Mangold, E., & Goehring, C. (2018). Identification by transitive property: Intermediated consubstantiality in the N.F.L.'s Salute to Service campaign. *Critical Studies in Media Communication, 35*, 503–516.

Martin, G., & Steuter, E. (2010). *Pop culture goes to war: Enlisting and resisting militarism in the war on terror*. Lanham, MD: Lexington.

Marvin, C., & Ingle, D. W. (1999). *Blood sacrifice and the nation: Totem rituals and the American flag*. Cambridge: Cambridge University Press.

McDermott, L., & Scherer, J. (2017). War games: The politics of war, torture, and grieving in Canada. In M. L. Butterworth (Ed.), *Sport and militarism: Contemporary global perspectives* (pp. 129–148). London: Routledge.

Miller, T. (2020). *The persistence of violence: Colombian popular culture*. New Brunswick, NJ: Rutgers University Press.

Miller, T., Lawrence, G., McKay, J., & Rowe, D. (2001). *Globalization and sport: Playing the world*. London: Sage.

Mills, C. W. (1956). *The power elite*. New York: Oxford University Press.

Musselman, C. (2019). Training for the "unknown and unknowable": CrossFit and evangelical temporality. *Religions, 10*, 1–19.

Oriard, M. (2007). *Brand NFL: Making and selling America's favorite sport*. Chapel Hill: University of North Carolina Press.

Prividera, L. C., & Howard, J. W. (2006). Masculinity, whiteness, and the warrior hero: Perpetuating the strategic rhetoric of U.S. nationalism and the marginalization of women. *Women & Language, 29*, 29–37.

Rugg, A. (2016). America's game: The NFL's "Salute to Service" campaign, the diffused military presence, and corporate social responsibility. *Popular Communication, 14*, 21–29.

Scherer, J., & Koch, J. (2010). Living with war: Sport, citizenship, and the cultural politics of post-9/11 Canadian identity. *Sociology of Sport Journal, 27*, 1–29.

Schimmel, K. S. (2012). Protecting the NFL/militarizing the homeland: Citizen soldiers and urban resilience in post-9/11 America. *International Review for the Sociology of Sport, 47*, 338–357.

Schimmel, K. S. (2017). Not an "extraordinary event": NFL games and militarized civic ritual. *Sociology of Sport Journal, 34*, 79–89.

Silk, M., & Falcous, M. (2005). One day in September/a week in February: Mobilizing American (sporting) nationalism. *Sociology of Sport Journal, 22*, 447–471.

Stahl, R. (2009). Why we "support the troops": Rhetorical evolutions. *Rhetoric & Public Affairs, 12*, 533–570.

Stahl, R. (2010). *Militainment, Inc.: War, media, and popular culture*. New York: Routledge.

Stempel, C. (2006). Televised sports, masculinist moral capital, and support for the U.S. invasion of Iraq. *Journal of Sport & Social Issues, 30*, 79–106.

Tian, N., Kuimova, A., da Silva, D. L., Wezeman, P. D., & Wezeman, S. T. (2020, April). Trends in world military expenditure, 2019. Stockholm International Peace Research Institute. https://www.sipri.org/sites/default/files/2020-04/fs_2020_04_milex_0.pdf.

Vinall, C. (2003, June 12). Top brass launches Operation Tribute to Freedom to honor troops. U.S. Department of Defense. https://web.archive.org/web/20170930014816/.

Wenner, L. A. (Ed.). (1998). *Mediasport*. London: Routledge.

Zirin, D. (2020a, January 7). Can sports be a site of war resistance? *The Nation*. https://www.thenation.com/article/archive/sports-military-war/.

Zirin, D. (2020b, August 12). Republicans suddenly have a passion for college football. *The Nation*. https://www.thenation.com/article/society/trump-college-football-covid/.

CHAPTER 8

....

SPORT, LAW, AND ETHICS

....

ADAM EPSTEIN

THE purpose of this chapter is to explore how law and ethics intersect in the context of sport. This includes a discussion involving youth, interscholastic, intercollegiate, Olympic-related, and professional sport. Deference is given to U.S. jurisprudence, and the chapter includes topics and examples involving whistleblowing, fraud, misconduct, and concerns related to various forms of abuse by coaches and persons in positions of authority.

Much of the chapter focuses on U.S. college sports, student-athletes, and others in the intercollegiate environment. SafeSport is introduced, a recent U.S. governmental legislative attempt to regulate ethical behavior in the context of sport at the federal level. At the international level, through the hierarchical organization of the International Olympic Committee (IOC) and its international federations, also known generally as the "Olympic Movement," the Olympic Charter's Rule 40 demonstrates the conundrum over the intersection between social media access, private rules, and the balancing of freedom of speech with intellectual property rights. The chapter concludes with examples from student-athletes and others who have attempted to mobilize their efforts to effectuate change.

Before delving into specific sport examples, one might utilize a fundamental definition of ethics as "[t]he discipline dealing with what is good and bad with a moral duty and obligation" (Epstein & Niland, 2011, p. 22). Unfortunately, although many sport organizations, coaches, administrators, and athletes claim they subscribe to the principles of ethics and good sportsmanship, the lines are often blurred between playing by the rules and winning at all costs. For example, in 2010, Jim Calhoun, then the head basketball coach at the University of Connecticut, stated, "We may have broken rules . . . but we did not cheat" (quoted in Epstein & Niland, 2011, p. 22). Can one break rules in sport and yet not cheat? Is cheating in sport a crime? Unfortunately, for those who subscribe to the principle that cheaters never win, sport might not be the best arena to use examples of that mantra. This is especially true after it was revealed that the Houston Astros won the 2017 Major League Baseball (MLB) World Series having stolen opposing teams' coaching signs (Bogage, 2020).

Additionally, the world has changed dramatically in the past few decades. Given the advent of the internet and the rise of smartphones and social media, ethical issues can be discussed and debated around the world in real time by individuals who have never met. Such tools and technology, while amazing and engaging, have also created challenges and ethical dilemmas for sport organizations. Unlike in previous generations, sport participants, regulators, and administrators can instantaneously express and share their opinions with the world in a powerful way as never before with just the click of a button. Such immediate, worldwide access has led to further ethical and legal debates. In some instances, changes in sport might address inequity. Elsewhere, violations of rules, policies, or the spirit of sport might be so outrageous that the law is called upon to react to such misdeeds and transgressions.

Issues

In the study of sport law and its relationship to ethics, there are far too many issues to address in just one chapter. Some issues seem to occur decade after decade, despite attempts to regulate behavior statutorily, contractually, or by enforcing a code of ethics with consequences (Epstein & Osborne, 2018; Epstein & Niland, 2011). The key issues addressed in this chapter include whistleblowing and fraud in its various forms.

Whistleblowing

The definition of "whistleblowing" can vary, but it may be defined as "calling attention to wrongdoing that is occurring within an organization." In the United States, the first law adopted specifically to protect whistleblowers was the 1863 False Claims Act, which tried to combat fraud by suppliers of the U.S. government during the Civil War (Epstein, 2018c).

The False Claims Act exists today with slight modification, and it encourages whistleblowers to reveal violations and wrongdoing against the government by promising a percentage of the money recovered, usually between 10% to 30%. The concept of whistleblowing is most often discussed in the corporate world; examples include the downfall of Enron Corporation and its falsified financial statements and the modern-day Ponzi scheme artist Bernard Madoff's duping investors (Epstein, 2018a, 2018c; Epstein & Niland, 2011).

Whistleblowing and International Sport

In sport, blowing the whistle may include testifying in a legal proceeding or in front of Congress or sharing wrongdoing with the media or other authorities, such as the IOC, an international federation, or a national governing body (NGB) (Epstein, 2018c). The consequences can be devastating to the organization and the whistleblower. Corporations may lose customers or may be fined by the government, and those who blow the whistle suffer greatly personally and professionally, including being retaliated against. The motivation for wrongdoing is to win a championship, to earn a medal, or just to maintain profit over other concerns, such as the environmental or societal impact.

Blowing the whistle on wrongdoing in sport comes in various forms, such as reporting intentional violations of Title IX of the Education Amendments (1972), the U.S. federal law that mandates gender equity in colleges and universities and other federally funded recipients. Investigative reporting has led to the discovery of fraudulent participation by athletes themselves. Insiders have revealed the use of performance-enhancing drugs (PEDs) by competitors, some of whom were former teammates.

For example, Russian Vitaly Stepanov, along with his wife, Yulia Stepanova, revealed the state-sponsored Russian Olympic program in which athletes used (knowingly or unknowingly) PEDs to help them earn medals. The two claimed that 80% of coaches in Russian track used doping to prepare athletes for London's Olympics in 2012. They also alleged that doping was widespread among Russian participants and medalists at the 2014 Sochi Games in Russia itself (Epstein, 2017; Epstein & Osborne, 2018).

Their claims were backed by Grigory Rodchenkov, the director of Russia's antidoping laboratory at the time. In fact, Rodchenkov revealed how Russia's state-run program was able to swap out athletes' urine samples with clean ones to assure that the competitors would not test positive for PEDs. Rodchenkov resides in the United States in a witness protection program for his own safety. An independent report by Canadian Richard McLaren in 2016 revealed that drug testing cheating by Russia was a common, "carefully orchestrated conspiracy" (Epstein, 2017; Epstein & Osborne, 2018).

In response to these allegations, the International Association of Athletics Federations prohibited Russian track-and-field athletes at the 2016 Rio Olympics from competing under the Russian flag. Then, on November 29, 2016, the World Anti-Doping Agency enacted a formal whistleblowing policy, effective in 2017, to formalize the process for protecting and offering assurance of confidentiality to whistleblowers. Despite the outrage over Russia's state-sponsored system, doping in the Olympics is nothing new, nor is it uniquely Russian (Epstein, 2017; Epstein, & Osborne, 2018).

Whistleblowing and College Sport

In U.S. college sport, blowing the whistle on wrongdoing has often centered on claims of academic misconduct. Unfortunately, those who have reported violations have paid a heavy professional, emotional, and reputational price for speaking out. In recent decades, this has led to lawsuits, legal settlements, and job reassignments and terminations within the context of the rules of the National Collegiate Athletic Association (NCAA), the private, nongovernmental, voluntary, member-driven, and nonprofit college sport organization (Epstein, 2013).

One of the first individuals to be characterized as a whistleblower was Jan Kemp, an assistant professor of English, who in the early 1980s exposed preferential treatment of student-athletes at the University of Georgia. She alleged that football players who failed a remedial English class still played in the Sugar Bowl against the University of Pittsburgh in 1982, a violation of the rules. As a result, Kemp was demoted and then fired in 1983, though she was later reinstated. She sued the university, claiming unlawful termination based upon a violation of her freedom of speech. The university claimed that Kemp was dismissed for being a poor professor overall and "did not participate in research, was insubordinate and had difficulty in getting along with her peers and others" (Epstein, 2018c, pp. 72–73).

After a trial, a jury awarded Kemp $2.57 million, though that was later reduced. University of Georgia President Fred C. Davison announced his resignation a month after the verdict. Kemp retired from teaching in 1990 and was named "a hero of the 80s" by *People* magazine.

In 2004, she was the first honoree of the Hutchins Award given by the Drake Group, an organization devoted to academic integrity and ending corruption in college sport (Epstein, 2018c).

In the 1990s, Jan Gangelhoff was involved in a scandal at the University of Minnesota involving its men's basketball team and rules violations over academic dishonesty. Gangelhoff worked in the academic counseling office. Interestingly, it was Gangelhoff who revealed to the press that she in fact was a participant in the misconduct madness. She claimed that she had voluntarily, personally written over 400 papers for 20 Minnesota basketball players from 1994 to 1998. She resigned from the university, and the academic fraud led to resignations of the head coach, the men's athletic director, and a university vice president. The NCAA placed Minnesota's basketball program on four years' probation and reduced the number of athletic scholarships the university could offer student-athletes (Epstein, 2018c).

Mike McQueary, a former quarterback for Pennsylvania State University (PSU) between 1994 and 1997, had his professional life ruined for reporting wrongdoing in 2001 by assistant football coach Jerry Sandusky, who was sexually abusing young boys in the showers. At the time, McQueary served as a full-time assistant coach at PSU, having joined head coach Joe Paterno's staff as a graduate assistant. He reported the Sandusky incidents to Paterno and other high-level administrators and, as a result, was suspended with pay and placed on administrative leave. Sandusky was found guilty of abusing at least ten boys in 2012, but the university terminated McQueary from his job, which he later claimed was retaliation for assisting prosecutors in the case (Epstein, 2018c).

McQueary fought back, filing a $4 million whistleblower lawsuit against PSU for lost wages and claiming "irreparable harm to his ability to earn a living" (Epstein, 2018c, p. 76). McQueary won the case and was awarded $7.3 million, which included compensatory and punitive damages for defamation, on October 27, 2016. In fact, another $5 million was later ordered by a judge for the retaliation against McQueary, pushing his award to $12 million (Boren, 2017; Tribune News Services, 2016).

Given how common cases of whistleblowing have become in intercollegiate athletics, it would be wise to have a written whistleblower policy in place within any organization. In this way, the organization might be able to first address issues internally rather than publicly. Still, in sport, as in business, the choice to report wrongdoing is ultimately an individual decision. No law can protect against retaliation in the short run. As is suggested by these limited examples, blowing the whistle can come with a heavy price, though for many that price is worth the personal cost.

Fraud

Fraud, also known as misrepresentation, involves the intent to deceive another. Fraud is not negligence; rather it is an intentional act. Allegations of fraud may result in criminal prosecution and civil lawsuits to remedy or punish the wrong. But what happens when "everybody is doing it"? Is that fraud? Who is being defrauded then? When it involves those at the highest level of sport, government, or society, fraud is often referred to as corruption, a subject considered elsewhere in this volume.

Indeed, "fraud" is a very general term in any context. The extent to which one person intentionally deceives another is noteworthy and, at times, criminal. Consider, for example, the number of times the international soccer federation FIFA has been involved in accusations of impropriety, and it seems every Olympic year there is some controversy, whether related to doping by competitors or a judging controversy in boxing, figure skating, or gymnastics. Other examples include participation fraud, such as age falsification and impersonation, academic fraud in college sport (and in college admissions), résumé fraud, technology fraud (such as the use of a hidden motor in a bicycle), honest services fraud, in which the FBI investigated payments to college coaches and others as part of the student-athlete recruiting process, and many more infractions (Epstein, 2018a; Epstein & Osborne, 2018; Jaschik, 2019; Schlabach, 2019).

Academic Fraud and College Sport

NCAA member schools have committed egregious violations of NCAA rules, including outrageous examples of academic fraud. Prominent institutions such as the University of North Carolina at Chapel Hill (UNC) found itself mired in such as scandal in which, for 18 years, employees at UNC knowingly steered thousands of students, including 1,500 student-athletes, toward "paper courses." These classes were often independent studies courses that never met, though they did require a research paper (Epstein & Osborne, 2018).

An internal investigation into UNC's Department of African and Afro-American Studies showed that while most of the students enrolled in these courses were not student-athletes, UNC men's basketball players accounted for more than 12% of all student-athletes taking the courses. Many of the suspect classes were taught in the summer by former department chairman Julius Nyang'oro, who subsequently resigned (Epstein & Osborne, 2018). Mary Willingham, a UNC learning specialist who raised concerns over potential academic improprieties at the university and spoke publicly about it, subsequently filed a whistleblower-related lawsuit over the scandal. She claimed she was retaliated against for her outspoken criticism, left her employment with the university, and ultimately agreed to a financial settlement in 2015 (Epstein, 2018c; Epstein & Osborne, 2018).

Interestingly, the NCAA accused UNC of lacking institutional control over athletics, but the university's response was that the NCAA reached beyond the scope of its authority in the first place. UNC declared that this academic concern was not an NCAA matter but rather an internal, institutional-specific academic issue. Shocking to many, the NCAA agreed with UNC's position and took no punitive action. However, UNC instituted various changes in response to the scandal. An independent report authored by Kenneth Wainstein, who conducted an eight-month investigation, led to four employees being fired, five others disciplined, and one former employee having an honorary status removed (Ganim & Sayers, 2014). UNC also enacted over 70 new policies and procedures to prevent academic impropriety in the future (Epstein & Osborne, 2018).

Fraud and Lance Armstrong

Claims made by American cyclist Lance Armstrong that he did not use PEDs resulted in one of the most intriguing cases of fraudulent participation in professional sport history.

Armstrong won the Tour de France seven years in a row, from 1999 to 2005. Though many suspected he found a way to beat the system and use PEDs, the testers could not demonstrate a positive drug test (Epstein, 2013, 2018a; Epstein & Osborne, 2018).

Then, in October 2012, the U.S. Anti-Doping Agency released its report detailing the extent of doping allegations made against Armstrong. This included sworn testimony from 26 people (15 of those being competitors), financial statements, emails, scientific data, and laboratory results—all provided evidence that Armstrong's team, the U.S. Postal Service Pro Cycling Team, operated the most sophisticated doping program in the history of cycling (Epstein, 2018a; Epstein & Osborne, 2018).

As a result, the U.S. Anti-Doping Agency banned Armstrong from competitive cycling for life and stripped him of the titles he had earned since August 1, 1998. Armstrong lost his sponsorships and friends. In fact, in 2010, Floyd Landis, Armstrong's former teammate, filed a complaint against him as a government whistleblower. The Department of Justice joined the case, claiming Armstrong had violated his contract with the U.S. Postal Service. The government's case continued under the False Claims Act. In the end, the case never went to trial and was settled out of court (Epstein, 2018a; Epstein & Osborne, 2018).

Initially Armstrong insisted he was innocent; later, he claimed that the top riders were using PEDs and therefore he needed to as well to compete on a level playing field. Today, contrite, he has admitted his misdeeds and speaks out against the use of PEDs. He is still one of the most well-known athletes in the world, even though his Tour de France wins have been vacated (Epstein, 2018a; Epstein & Osborne, 2018).

APPROACHES

Addressing violations of the rules of sport, law, league polices, or organizational codes of ethics can be regulated by using practical approaches in various ways. For example, a breach of a sponsorship contract for misconduct or disloyalty to the sponsor might not be a violation of the law but could be a justifiable reason to end the contractual relationship. Field-of-play misconduct such as illegal hits or other fouls is usually handled through internal controls such as penalties, fines, and suspensions rather than through a legal proceeding involving the police, a judge, and a jury. Self-regulation of unethical misconduct is most frequently served by private justice, so to speak, by utilizing these internal league controls rather than resorting to the state or federal governmental prosecution (Epstein, 2013).

When it comes to violence in sport, the legal doctrine of implied consent holds that sport participants voluntarily assume certain risks of injury or violence—within reason—during a sports contest even though such contact might be criminal misconduct outside the arena. The implied consent doctrine is one of the strongest defenses to a civil claim or criminal charge during a sports contest. Ultimately, the vital question for sport is where to draw the line between legitimate and illegitimate violence (Epstein, 2013).

Particularly in professional U.S. football and baseball, it is the spectators themselves who are often charged with the crime of hooliganism or disturbing the peace. There are a few examples of criminal charges against players in the sport of ice hockey, but U.S. prosecutors rarely charge athletes for acts committed during a game. In sport law, it is rare for participants to seek the help of the criminal justice system for assistance unless the misconduct is so extreme or outrageous that it falls outside public norms of acceptable behavior in the context of sport itself (Epstein, 2013). The following examples provide various approaches to regulate misconduct in sport.

Contract Clauses

A simple yet effective way to manage conduct in sport is to include special contract clauses that define the relationship between employer and employee (or endorser/endorsee). Contracts define the boundaries, rights, duties, and responsibilities of the parties (Epstein & Lowenstein, 2014). The working relationship can be affected by the contract having specific ethics-based clauses, such as a general termination clause, a morals clause, and a loyalty clause (Epstein, 2011a, 2018a).

In fact, the termination clause in a contract might be the most important clause in any agreement. It allows one party to end the relationship "for cause" or "without cause," depending upon the circumstances. "For cause" means that one party violated the terms of the contract. For example, former Indiana University head basketball coach Kelvin Sampson, who continues to have a successful coaching career, had a clause in his contract allowing the university to terminate him for:

1. "a significant, intentional, repetitive violation of any law, rule (or) regulation" of the NCAA;
2. "failure to maintain an environment in which the coaching staff complies with NCAA . . . regulations";
3. if in Indiana University's "sole judgment" Sampson's conduct "reflect[ed] adversely upon the university and its athletic program." (Epstein, 2011a, pp. 19–20)

Sampson's employment with Indiana University ultimately ended prior to the term of his contract, and this contract language was in play. Still, his contract is not unique, as most coaches today have similar clauses in their agreements. Often, such clauses are intentionally vague or subjective. On other occasions, the contract drafter might decide to be much more specific by listing precise examples for reasons to terminate the relationship (Epstein, 2011a, 2018a).

A more specific example of a termination clause includes a morals clause, also known as "moral turpitude," "morality" clauses, "public image clauses," or "good-conduct clauses." These clauses allow a party to terminate, suspend, or otherwise punish a coach, athlete, or employee for engaging in criminal or reprehensible behavior or conduct that may negatively impact his or her public image and, by association, the public image of the team, league, or company. The rise in ubiquitous social media has made each clause vitally important as tweets, posting, pictures, and so on might give rise to reasons for ending the contractual relationship between the athlete and the team or sponsor. Prominent professional athletes have had their contracts terminated for a variety of moral misdeeds, including use of alcohol or drugs and for committing domestic violence (Epstein, 2011a; Epstein & Osborne, 2018).

A loyalty clause provides the right to terminate a relationship in the event the person fails to wear or use a brand or product when contractually required to do so. A loyalty clause might also be relevant if a player speaks out against a coach, team, referee, league, or organization, thereby demonstrating a lack of loyalty (Epstein, 2011a, 2018a).

These contract clauses remain as important as ever. Recent items that contract drafters employ in athletic agreements today include termination clauses related to sexual abuse and domestic violence (Myerberg, 2018). Even when head coaches, for example, were not the perpetrators, a formal duty is often imposed on them to promptly report to certain authorities—including the police—their knowledge of such misconduct by the coaches, players, and others under their supervision. In the context of federal legislation, this might require the college coach to promptly report to the university's Title IX coordinator any known violations of the college's sexual misconduct policy among the coaching staff and student-athletes; this makes the coach a mandatory reporter having heightened responsibility due to their position of authority (Epstein, 2018d).

Former Ohio State University football coach Urban Meyer's 2018 contract extension required him to "promptly report" any known violations of the school's sexual misconduct policy and to notify the university's Title IX coordinator for athletics about "any known violations" of its sexual misconduct policy—including sexual assault and harassment and "intimate violence"—involving students or staff. His contract stated:

> For purposes of this section 4.1 (e), a "known violation" shall mean a violation or an allegation of a violation of Title IX that Coach is aware of or has reasonable cause to believe is taking place or may have taken place. (Epstein, 2018d, p. 5)

Though these contract clauses are an effective means to privately regulate misconduct, just because the clauses exist does not mean that a party to the contract must terminate the relationship if the clause is violated. However, having the clauses in place provides a legitimate, justifiable contractual means to end the agreement if deemed necessary, for cause. Even for the nonprofessional athlete, such as high school or college athletes involved in interscholastic or intercollegiate sport, violations of league or association policies could warrant suspension or dismissal from sport. This has been particularly troublesome in the era of social media, which has seen nonprofessional athletes suspended for inappropriate tweets and Facebook postings (Epstein, 2018a, 2018d).

Alternative Dispute Resolution

Particularly within the Olympic Movement, litigation is often superseded by alternative dispute resolution (ADR). In professional sports, binding arbitration is often the choice, especially in an environment in which management (owners) and labor (players) are subject to rules governed by a collective bargaining agreement. The most important difference between ADR and litigation is that final decisions are not made by judges or courts. Instead, they are resolved by private arbitrators (or with the help of mediators). Additionally, ADR usually resolves disputes more effectively and efficiently than litigation and is usually less costly. However, arbitration is binding and rarely appealable unless there is evident partiality, fraud, or misconduct on the part of the arbitrator (Epstein, 2012, 2013).

All the major U.S. professional sports use arbitration as a method to resolve grievances. The Olympic Movement uses the Court of Arbitration for Sport to resolve disputes related to the Olympic Games, which might involve rule interpretations, eligibility, and discipline disputes. In 1998, the Ted Stevens Olympic and Amateur Sports Act reemphasized the use of arbitration as the only means to resolve Olympic and amateur sports disputes in the U.S. Olympic and Paralympic Movements. The Act grants the U.S. Olympic Committee (USOC) (now known as the U.S. Olympic & Paralympic Committee since June 2019) the authority "to provide swift resolution of conflicts and disputes involving amateur athlete[s]" (Epstein, 2012, 2013; U.S. Olympic & Paralympic Committee, 2019, para. 1).

Criminal Prosecution and Civil Lawsuits

Certainly, if sport misconduct rises to the level of criminal misconduct, the federal or state government can prosecute the perpetrator in the American legal system. In such a case, the prosecution would have to prove their case using the "beyond a reasonable doubt" standard, a high bar to attain. Similarly, on the civil side, a plaintiff—regardless of the outcome of the criminal case—could bring a civil action seeking monetary damages and the like from the defendant under the lesser standard of proving their case by a "preponderance of the evidence." In either case the judge (or jury) would be the determinant of who wins the dispute (Epstein, 2013).

As mentioned earlier, in 2012 former PSU assistant football coach Jerry Sandusky was found guilty of 45 charges of sexual abuse involving child molestation. The university was fined $2.4 million by the Department of Education for mishandling the case and ignoring its duties under the Clery Act (1990). Mike McQueary, the whistleblower who reported wrongdoing, paid a heavy price personally and professionally, though after a decade of suffering, he prevailed financially after a lawsuit. Then two high-profile administrators, former PSU athletics director Tim Curley and university vice president Gary Schultz, pled guilty to misdemeanor child endangerment. Both were sentenced to serve between 6 and 23 months in prison, pay a $5,000 fine, and perform 200 hours of community service (Couloumbis, 2017; CNN, 2019). Former PSU president Graham Spanier was charged with conspiracy and felony child endangerment, but his conviction was overturned by a judge in 2019 (Associated Press, 2019). Then, in 2020, a court reinstated his conviction and he had to serve two months in a correctional facility followed by two months of house arrest. (Scolforo, 2020).

At Michigan State University (MSU), Larry Nassar, at one time the USA Gymnastics (USAG) national team doctor and an osteopathic physician at MSU, who sexually assaulted hundreds of young women at MSU over more than 20 years, was sentenced in 2018 to 40 to 125 years in prison after pleading guilty to numerous counts of criminal sexual conduct (Levenson, 2018). MSU's president, athletic director, a dean, and many others lost their jobs, became entangled in a legal web, or fell into a jurisprudential abyss by not doing anything to prevent Nassar's continuous misconduct (Gibbons, 2018; Meilhan & Close, 2018).

Many young women suffered both physically and emotionally due to the inaction and lies, some later suffering from posttraumatic stress disorder. Like PSU, MSU was found to have violated the Jeanne Clery Disclosure of Campus Security Policy and Campus Crime Statistics Act (Clery Act). Unlike at PSU, however, Nassar's misconduct was not just campus related; his position as the team physician for USAG affected hundreds of young Olympic-caliber gymnasts. Afterward, hundreds of students from several colleges, including Ohio

State University among others, stepped forward as well to reveal sexual abuse, some of which was discovered many years after the fact (Edmondson, 2018; Roscher, 2019; Smola, 2019).

The Nassar scandal led to complete chaos and criticism regarding the lack of oversight (Armour & Axon, 2018b; Perez, 2018). Along with Nassar, USAG former CEO and president Steve Penny was arrested for tampering with evidence related to the investigation into wrongdoing at the Karolyi Ranch in Walker County, Texas (Armour & Axon, 2018a). Civil lawsuits ensued, and many other NGBs were accused of sexual abuse and misconduct. For example, former U.S. gymnast Sabrina Vega filed suit against Nassar, USAG, the USOC, and the Karolyis, alleging she was sexually abused hundreds of times at the Karolyi Ranch and at competition sites around the world (Associated Press, 2018b). In turn, the Karolyis sued USOC and USAG, saying they should not be held responsible for lawsuits stemming from crimes committed at their training facility, which was immediately shut down after the Nassar scandal broke (Barron, 2018).

As for other NGBs, USA Taekwondo, and the USOC in fact, were accused of sex trafficking by four female athletes who claimed both organizations "sent them to competitions across the world with athletes and coaches thought to be sexual predators" (Young, 2018). Additionally, Ariana Kukors Smith sued USA Swimming, alleging it knew her former coach sexually abused her as a minor and covered it up. She also sued a former U.S. national team coach, saying he failed to report "a reasonable suspicion of child abuse or endangerment" (Associated Press, 2018a, para. 12). Other allegations of sexual abuse included accusations against USA Diving, USA Racquetball, USA Badminton, and USA Volleyball (Alesia, 2018; Reid, 2018; Schrotenboer, 2018).

From the Sandusky and Nassar cases to the cases against various NGBs and accusations on college campuses, acts of sexual impropriety have often dominated discussion and action in recent years. Complaints from student-athletes, U.S. Olympic athletes, and others of sexual abuse and other misconduct have demanded more at all levels of oversight (Hauser & Zraick, 2018).

Legislation: SafeSport

As a direct result of sexual abuse in U.S. Olympic sports, SafeSport was established with the intent to take sexual abuse allegations out of the hands of the 50 or so NGBs that appeared unable to manage or address the issues. For example, the post-Nassar organizational hires at USAG were controversial and ineffective for real change, resulting in frequent turnover (Armour & Axon, 2018a, b; Yan, 2018). The USOC and USAG appeared to be out of control, resulting in resignations and congressional hearings (Connor, 2018; Perez, 2018).

The SafeSport Act, more formally known as the federal Protecting Young Victims from Sexual Abuse and Safe Sport Authorization Act of 2017, was signed into law on February 14, 2018, by President Donald Trump, becoming effective immediately. The Act's stated purpose is "to prevent the sexual abuse of minors and amateur athletes by requiring the prompt reporting of sexual abuse to law enforcement authorities, and for other purposes" (Safe Sport Authorization Act, 2017, Preamble). The Act amended two federal statutes contemporaneously, the Victims of Child Abuse Act (1990) and the Amateur Sports Act (1978), by maintaining the duty to report sexual abuse and requiring certain adults to report within 24 hours (U.S. Center for SafeSport, 2022).

The SafeSport Act provides a limitation of liability provision that protects the sports entity and any officer, employee, agent, or member who reports suspicions of abuse. Failure to comply with the Act allows a claimant to sue in federal district court to recover actual damages or liquidated damages in the amount of $150,000, the costs of the action, reasonable attorney's fees, and the possibility of punitive damages (Safe Sport Authorization Act, 2017; U.S. Center for SafeSport, 2022). NGBs such as U.S. Soccer have begun to require evidence of annual compliance with SafeSport training to serve as a coach under its jurisdiction (Payne, 2018).

Formally acknowledging the misdeeds and charging those who commit violations has sent a strong message to others that such conduct is simply unacceptable. Establishing SafeSport, while not the panacea for the prevention of sexual abuse by coaches and others, is a legislative step sending the message that victims have recourse and are not without a voice anymore. Despite such laws, however, abuse in sport will likely continue.

Olympic Regulation: Ambush Marketing and Rule 40

The IOC is very protective of its brand, and rightfully so, particularly since official Olympic sponsors pay hundreds of millions of U.S. dollars to associate themselves with the Olympic Games. As a result of ambush marketing, in which international companies such as Nike have effectively associated themselves with the Games without paying the requisite official sponsor fees, the IOC established two somewhat effective countermeasures to protect its stakeholders. One requires the host city to make efforts to prevent ambush marketing and force violators to cease such conduct. Nike, for example, is infamous for its cunning ploy to rent billboards throughout the city of Atlanta during the 1996 Olympic Games, giving the impression that Nike was an official Olympic sponsor when it was not. The other measure established a marketing policy known as Rule 40, which essentially bans anyone who participates in the Games (competitors, coaches, trainers, or officials) from using their person, name, picture, or sports performances during the Games for advertising purposes (Epstein, 2017).

Indeed, the IOC has made legitimate attempts to protect its intellectual property through requisite anti–ambush marketing laws during the Games themselves, although the degree to which it has sought to prevent individual athletes from sharing their experiences via social media has been controversial. In fact, the 2016 Olympic Games in Rio de Janeiro represented a well-publicized struggle between individual and virtual free speech and freedom of expression via social media in conflict with Rule 40's requirement that there be no mention of any unofficial sponsor by participants on social media such as Instagram, Facebook, Twitter, and the like nine days before the Games until three days after the Games. The IOC's attempt to monopolize language and prevent certain congratulatory posts, retweeting of results, GIFs, and hashtags (e.g., #Rio2016) a few weeks every two years seemed a bit over the top and hardly enforceable from a legal perspective, especially for today's participants, most of whom grew up with the internet and the capability of voicing and streaming their thoughts and opinions instantly on their smartphones (Epstein, 2017).

No doubt given international criticism and pushback over its Rule 40 social media blackout policy, in 2019 the IOC dramatically rewrote Rule 40. Still recognizing the need to protect its intellectual property from ambush marketing, yet balancing this need with reality, the IOC loosened restrictions under Rule 40 and now enables athletes to thank personal sponsors and receive congratulatory messages from their sponsors via social media and otherwise during the Olympic Games, even if the sponsor is not an official Olympic sponsor, in which case still no Olympic imagery or photos may be used (Anderson, 2019).

DEBATES

The advent of smartphones and social media has given a voice to anyone, anywhere, and at any time. In sport, student-athletes, including Olympic and professional athletes, have utilized these tools to express their concerns and to attempt to effectuate change by instantaneously spreading their message (Epstein, 2014, 2017). This final section addresses how NCAA student-athletes and others have attempted to draw attention to their beliefs.

Student-Athlete Activism

NCAA student-athletes (also referred to as "college athletes") tend to mobilize when they believe their "rights" have been violated or their voices are not being heard by the powers that be. Throughout the years, the most frequent examples relate to race, financial compensation, and gender equity. Most examples include athlete activism involving football players, the driving sport behind the NCAA, its establishment, and its existence in the first place. Student-athlete activism was prominent during the civil rights movement and Vietnam War in the 1960s and 1970s. However, examples of athlete activism occurred much earlier than that.

One of the first examples of student-athlete activism occurred in 1934 at the University of Michigan, when members of its football team did not take kindly to Georgia Tech's demand that Willis Ward, a Black (back then the term "Negro" was used) member of the Michigan squad, not participate in the football game in Ann Arbor. If not heeded, Georgia Tech, an institution based in the "Old South," refused to play and would forfeit the game. Though the Civil War had ended in the previous century, schools in the American South remained largely segregated. Opportunities were not there for Blacks to participate, let alone enroll, in public colleges and universities (Epstein, 2018b; Epstein & Kisska-Schulze, 2017).

As a result, Ward's teammates, among them future U.S. President Gerald Ford, refused to play in the game and threatened to quit the team if Ward had to sit out. Instead, Ward chose to sit out that day, encouraging his teammates to play without him; they did. Still, the fact that the players initiated a protest against the benching of a teammate solely due to his race represented one of the earliest examples of student-athlete mobilization efforts. Michigan won the game 9–2 on October 20, 1934, the team's only victory that season (Epstein, 2018b; Epstein & Kisska-Schulze, 2017).

For decades thereafter, but particularly during the 1960s and 1970s, protests by student-athletes brought about change at various U.S. colleges and universities. For example, on at least three occasions (1927, 1936, and 1968), football players at Howard University, a historically Black institution, refused to play unless they were given better food, training, and living conditions. In fact, the 1968 protest led to the firing of the athletic director as Howard student-athletes demanded "better food, more medical attention, streamlined means of transportation, more equipment, better living conditions and a full-time sports information director" (Epstein & Kisska-Schulze, 2017, p. 85).

In October 1969 at the University of Wyoming, 14 of the football team's African American players wanted to wear armbands in a game scheduled against Brigham Young University (BYU) to protest the racial discrimination at BYU and within the Mormon Church. The players, who referred to themselves as the Black 14, were dismissed from the team the night before the home game. Wyoming won the game 40–7 without the help of those players, who subsequently sued their head coach, Lloyd Eaton, in federal court. Though the Wyoming football players lost their legal claim, it is interesting to note that in 1978 the Mormon Church changed its racially based policy against Blacks, which was the reason the Wyoming players had protested in the first place against BYU (Epstein & Kisska-Schulze, 2017).

Around the same time, San Jose State University, University of California–Berkeley, Michigan State University, and many other schools saw football players displaying acts of solidarity to protest racial disparities in treatment among players and coaches as well. One example, in 1972 at the University of Washington, involved a protest of the Vietnam War itself. The football team refused to take the field for the second half of their homecoming game unless a protest statement was read over the stadium sound system opposing the war, and it worked (Epstein & Kisska-Schulze, 2017).

On November 7, 2015, Anthony Sherrils, a University of Missouri football player, initiated a modern-day student-athlete mobilization related to race relations on his campus and in his region by tweeting:

> The athletes of color on the University of Missouri football team truly believe "Injustice Anywhere is a threat to Justice Everywhere" We will no longer participate in any football related activities until president Tim Wolfe resigns or is removed due to his negligence toward marginalized students' experiences. WE ARE UNITED!!!!!! (quoted in Epstein & Kisska-Schulze, 2017, p. 71)

Within 24 hours, more than 30 members of the football team had joined the protest by boycotting practices and games during the middle of the season. This protest was carried out on social media, and the president of the university resigned a few days later. The success of the boycott demonstrated the impact that student-athletes can have on college campuses. Ironically, the upcoming game after the mobilization was against BYU, the same school that the Black 14 at the University of Wyoming had protested against, and Missouri won this game on November 14, by the score of 20–16 (Epstein & Kisska-Schulze, 2017).

The Missouri football team's 2015 activist effort marked one of the most effective and passionate mobilization campaigns in college sports history. Debate continues today about student-athlete rights, much of it centered on economic injustice in which college coaches earn hundreds of thousands to millions of dollars for their services while the NCAA's position remains steadfast that, as amateurs, student-athletes must not be paid for their services or classified as employees (Epstein & Kisska-Schulze, 2017). Many coaches, such as Clemson University head football coach Dabo Swinney, have been outspoken critics of any attempt to professionalize college sports and its fundamental principle that student-athletes must remain unpaid amateurs, although premier coaching salaries continue to escalate to mythological heights. In 2019 Swinney himself signed a 10-year contract for $93 million (Blackistone, 2019). Nevertheless, in the summer of 2021, after a wave of legislation by individual states which granted more rights for college athletes to earn income, coupled with a separate and unanimous decision by the U.S. Supreme Court which held that the NCAA was in violation of antitrust law by capping education-related benefits, the NCAA altered its policy and now allows student-athletes to earn income for the use of their names, images, and likenesses (NIL) while at the same time holding the line that student-athletes must not be classified as employees by its member colleges and universities (Murphy, 2021).

While great progress has been made in terms of economic rights for student-athletes as evidenced by the NCAA's approval for the acceptance of income based upon the use of name, image, and likeness, student-athletes have yet to succeed in convincing courts that they should be paid for their services as employees. This includes a vigorous attempt by Northwestern University's football team to unionize beginning in 2013, which almost gained approval in the courts until the National Labor Relations Board (NLRB) stepped in and decided in 2015 that it was not yet ready to assert jurisdiction over whether student-athletes should be classified as employees. The NLRB vacated a lower court decision that had ruled in the student-athletes' favor (Epstein & Anderson, 2016; Kisska-Schulze & Epstein, 2014, 2016). Nevertheless, the General Counsel for the NLRB drafted a memorandum on September 29, 2021, offering that in her opinion that not only can certain college athletes be characterized as "employees" under the National Labor Relations Act (NLRA), but that to continue to characterize them as mere "student-athletes" is erroneous. Additionally, she specifically mentioned that players such as those involved in the aforementioned Northwestern University football team indeed have the right to organize, form a union, and be free from retaliation for that effort (NLRB Office of Public Affairs, 2021). Only time will tell how this important yet non-binding opinion plays out in the fast-changing landscape of college sports.

Other Examples of Sport Activism

Activist athletes are not restricted to those in college. Boxer Cassius Clay (who became Muhammad Ali) refused to enlist in the military due to his conscientious objection to the Vietnam War in 1967. At the 1968 Mexico City Summer Olympics, U.S. sprinters John Carlos and Tommie Smith, who won the gold and bronze medals, respectively, in the 200-meter dash, paid dearly for heralding Black Power by raising their fists on the medal podium while the national anthem was being played. Both runners were ejected from the U.S. Olympic team and sent home (Epstein, 2013; Epstein & Kisska-Schulze, 2017).

A few years later, led by iconic U.S. runner Steve Prefontaine, a former NCAA champion from the University of Oregon, outspoken protest of the stringent amateurism rules in track and field that disallowed sponsorships and appearance fees drew attention to the athletes' cause. At that time, the struggle for power in amateur sports between the Amateur Athletic Union and the USOC ultimately led to the enactment of the Amateur Sports Act of 1978, giving a more powerful voice to Olympic athletes than had ever been available before (Epstein, 2013; Epstein & Kisska-Schulze, 2017).

During the mid-1970s, MLB player Curt Flood refused to accept his trade from the St. Louis Cardinals to the Philadelphia Phillies; he filed a lawsuit that went all the way to the U.S. Supreme Court, alleging that professional baseball's reserve clause constituted a form of modern-day slavery. Flood, who vehemently opposed being characterized as a piece of property that could be traded like a slave, ultimately lost his legal battle. However, his public action drew national attention, resulting in MLB's changing its rules regarding the reserve clause in 1975, an action that other major professional sports leagues adopted soon thereafter (Epstein, 2013; Epstein & Kisska-Schulze, 2017).

Today concerns are expressed across all sports at all levels, including the demands of girls and women for equitable treatment and conditions (Lewis, 2018). Hundreds of female athletes have demonstrated how collective mobilization can lead to change, criminal charges, and convictions and even provoke new legislation, such as SafeSport. Prominent public protests by the U.S. women's national soccer and hockey teams have made transparent the pay inequity between them and their male counterparts, as well as their inferior training facilities, travel budgets, flights, meals and other accommodations, despite repeated greater success in athletic competition at the international level.

In their struggle for equal pay, the U.S. women's hockey team in 2017 threatened a boycott of the world championships and got a new deal from USA Hockey. (Svokos, 2019). In 2022, the U.S. women's national soccer team settled their 2019 class action lawsuit against the U.S. Soccer Federation for a total of $24 million after allegations of violations of the Equal Pay Act and Title VII of the Civil Rights Act (Carlisle, 2022).Female cheerleaders have taken their unequal treatment and pay claims, including harassment allegations, to court to be taken seriously by their employer clubs and leagues (Epstein, 2015).

CONCLUSION

The purpose of this chapter has been to demonstrate how sport, law, and ethics interrelate. At all levels, there will be those individuals who violate laws, rules, and policies. In some cases, the criminal law intervenes to seek punishment against the perpetrator of a crime. In other instances, internal controls such as fines and suspensions might better serve to remedy violations within the context of the sport itself which likely do not rise to criminal misconduct. Rather, the internal controls represent private justice.

This chapter necessarily has considered only a handful of examples involving contemporary issues related to whistleblowing and claims of fraud and other misconduct, such as the use of PEDs. Along the way, it has provided an introduction to SafeSport, one legislative attempt to respond to years of sexual and emotional abuse by coaches in the Olympic Movement. Unless rules are enforced through effective penalties, however, there remains no reason to believe that written codes or policies are enough to control abhorrent, unethical behavior or prevent sport participants and others—including coaches—from trying to beat the system.

Contract clauses such as for cause termination and morals and loyalty clauses have been effective means to address violations of these agreements, particularly if there is an ethical rules violation. This includes clauses which address sexual abuse and domestic violence by coaches, players, and others related directly or indirectly to sport. Similarly, alternative forms of dispute resolution such as arbitration are common means to resolve disputes. It might take collective action and mobilization to draw attention to perceived inequity, including economic injustices, to make real change happen. If that is ineffective, the courts might be called in to play.

In the end, the interrelationship between sport, law, and ethics is not a very complex one from any perspective. Simply put, games have rules, and those who break the rules should be punished accordingly. Still, some might say that rules are meant to be broken and that if everyone is cheating, it is not unethical to join them. Those who bend the rules will continue to do so as they have for centuries in sport. On the other hand, technology and social media have aligned individuals who reveal wrongdoing and provide a platform for athletes, for example, to express their voice, especially when an injustice appears to be in play.

Sport administrators and regulators face an epic struggle to keep up with those who commit fraud and misconduct and violate the spirit of sport. Maybe the ultimate force behind change for the better is when public outrage translates into lost profit or revenue for a sport organization, coach, sponsor, or participant. Unfortunately, law is most often reactive rather than proactive; unlike a sport's private rules, the law usually intervenes only in the most egregious of situations. By that time, it might be too late to provide redress for those who have already been wronged, though it could cause a perpetrator to think twice about whether pursuing the spoils of victory is worth the price.

References

Alesia, M. (2018, July 16). "You owe me this": Indianapolis-based USA Diving accused of ignoring alleged sexual abuse of divers. *Indianapolis Star.* https://www.indystar.com/story/news/2018/07/16/usa-diving-sexual-abuse-lawsuit-usa-gymnastics-usa-swimming/787523002/.

Amateur Sports Act. (1978). 36 U.S.C. Sec. 220501 et seq.).

Anderson, J. (2019, October 8). USOPC releases updated Rule 40 allowing athletes more marketing opportunity. *SwimSwam.* https://swimswam.com/usopc-releases-updated-rule-40-allowing-athletes-more-marketing-opportunity/.

Armour, N., & Axon, R. (2018a, October 18). Former USA Gymnastics CEO Steve Penny arrested, indicted for tampering with evidence. *USA Today.* https://www.usatoday.com/story/sports/2018/10/18/former-usa-gymnastics-ceo-accused-removing-files-karolyi-ranch/1680089002/.

Armour, N., & Axon, R. (2018b, September 4). USA Gymnastics CEO forced out after nine months marked by chaos, lack of tangible action. *USA Today.* https://www.usatoday.com/story/sports/olympics/2018/09/04/usa-gymnastics-ceo-kerry-perry-forced-out-following-pressure-usoc/1188567002/.

Associated Press. (2018a, May 21). Ariana Kukors Smith sues USA Swimming, alleges cover-up of former coach's sexual abuse. *ESPN.* http://www.espn.com/olympics/swimming/story/_/id/23563821/ariana-kukors-smith-sues-usa-swimming-alleges-cover-former-coach-sexual-abuse.

Associated Press. (2018b, May 1). World champion gymnast sues Karolyis, groups over Larry Nassar abuse. *Sports Illustrated.* https://www.si.com/olympic-gymnastics/2018/05/01/sabrina-vega-sues-karolyis-groups-larry-nassar-abuse.

Associated Press. (2019, April 30). Ex-PSU president Spanier's conviction overturned. *ESPN.* http://www.espn.com/college-football/story/_/id/26642545/ex-psu-president-spanier-conviction-overturned.

Axon, R., & Armour, N. (2018, January 31). Entire USA Gymnastics board resigns in wake of Larry Nassar scandal, *USA Today.* https://www.usatoday.com/story/sports/olympics/2018/01/31/entire-usa-gymnastics-board-resigns-usoc-larry-nassar-scandal/1082855001/.

Barron, D. (2018, May 1). Karolyis sue USOC, USA Gymnastics. *Houston Chronicle*. https://www.houstonchronicle.com/olympics/article/Karolyis-sue-USOC-USA-Gymnastics-12879736.php.

Blackistone, K. (2019, April 29). Dabo Swinney opposes "professionalizing college athletics." He just signed a $93 million deal. *Washington Post*. https://www.washingtonpost.com/sports/colleges/dabo-swinney-opposes-professionalizing-college-athletics-he-just-signed-a-93-million-deal/2019/04/29/353d576c-6a7e-11e9-be3a-33217240a539_story.html.

Bogage, J. (2020, February 18). What MLB players are saying about the Astros' sign-stealing scandal and apology. *Washington Post*. https://www.washingtonpost.com/sports/2020/02/18/mlb-players-on-astros-cheating-apology/?arc404=true.

Boren, C. (2017, November 7). Mike McQueary ends whistleblower lawsuit against Penn State. *Washington Post*. https://www.washingtonpost.com/news/early-lead/wp/2017/11/07/mike-mcqueary-ends-whistleblower-lawsuit-against-penn-state/?utm_term=.57c81b8dc555.

Carlisle, J. (2022, February 22). USWNT, U.S. Soccer Federation settle equal pay lawsuit for $24 million. *ESPN*. https://www.espn.com/soccer/united-states-usaw/story/4599482/uswntus-soccer-federation-settle-equal-pay-lawsuit-for-$24-million.

Clery Act. (1990). Jeanne Clery Disclosure of Campus Security Policy and Campus Crime Statistics Act, 20 U.S.C. §1092, implemented at 34 C.F.R. §668.46.

CNN. (2019). Penn State scandal fast facts. https://www.cnn.com/2013/10/28/us/penn-state-scandal-fast-facts/index.html.

Connor, T. (2018). Former gymnastics boss takes the fifth at senate hearing on Nassar. *NBC News*. https://www.nbcnews.com/news/us-news/usa-gymnastics-steve-penny-told-staff-keep-quiet-about-nassar-n880056.

Couloumbis, A. (2017, June 2). Former PSU top administrators get jail time. *Pittsburgh Post-Gazette*. https://www.post-gazette.com/news/state/2017/06/02/Former-Penn-State-president-Spanier-gets-jail-time-for-Sandusky-failures/stories/201706020195.

Edmondson, C. (2018, July 20). More than 100 former Ohio State students allege sexual misconduct. *New York Times*. https://www.nytimes.com/2018/07/20/us/politics/sexual-misconduct-ohio-state.html.

Epstein, A. (2011a). An exploration of interesting clauses in sports. *Journal of Legal Aspects of Sport*, 21, 1–41.

Epstein, A. (2011b). Teaching torts with sports. *Journal of Legal Studies Education*, 28, 117–142.

Epstein, A. (2012). Go for the gold by utilizing the Olympics. *Journal of Legal Studies Education*, 29, 313–334.

Epstein, A. (2013). *Sports law*. Mason, OH: Cengage.

Epstein, A. (2014). The Olympics, ambush marketing and Sochi media. *Arizona State University Sports and Entertainment Law Journal*, 3, 110–131.

Epstein, A. (2015). Attack of the cheerleaders! Allegations of violations of the FLSA on an uncertain landscape. *Journal of Law, Business & Ethics*, 21, 23–33.

Epstein, A. (2017). The ambush at Rio. *John Marshall Review of Intellectual Property Law*, 16, 350–381.

Epstein, A. (2018a). Incorporating sport into the ethics segment of the course. *Journal of Business Law & Ethics Pedagogy*, 1, 35–44.

Epstein, A. (2018b). Michigan and sports law. *Journal of Law, Business & Ethics*, 24, 1–50.

Epstein, A. (2018c). The NCAA and whistleblowers: 30–40 years of wrongdoing and college sport and possible solutions. *Southern Law Journal*, 28(1), 65–84.

Epstein, A. (2018d). Ohio State, Urban Meyer and the NCAA Division I manual. *Journal of NCAA Compliance*, 5–6 (July–August), 15.

Epstein, A., & Anderson, P. (2016). The relationship between a collegiate student-athlete and the university: An historical and legal perspective. *Marquette Sports Law Review, 26,* 287–300.

Epstein, A., & Kisska-Schulze, K. (2017). Northwestern University, the University of Missouri and the "student-athlete": Mobilization efforts and the future. *Journal of Legal Aspects of Sport, 26,* 71–105.

Epstein, A., & Lowenstein, H. (2014). Promises to keep? Coaches Tubby Smith, Jimmy Williams and lessons learned in 2012. *Southern Law Journal, 24,* 165–188.

Epstein, A., & Niland, B. (2011). Exploring ethical issues and examples by using sport. *Atlantic Law Journal, 13,* 19–59.

Epstein, A., & Osborne, B. (2018). Teaching ethics with sports: Recent developments. *Marquette Sports Law Review, 28*(2), 301–357.

Ganim, S., & Sayers, D. (2014, October 23). CNN. UNC report finds 18 years of academic fraud to keep athletes playing. https://www.cnn.com/2014/10/22/us/unc-report-academic-fraud/index.html

Gibbons, L. (2018, November 20). Ex-MSU President Lou Anna Simon charged with lying to police amid Nassar investigation. *MLive.* https://www.mlive.com/news/2018/11/ex-msu_president_lou_anna_simo_1.html

Hauser, C., & Zraick, K. (2018, October 22). Larry Nassar sexual abuse scandal: Dozens of officials have been ousted or charged. *New York Times.* https://www.nytimes.com/2018/10/22/sports/larry-nassar-case-scandal.html.

Jaschik, S. (2019, May 5). Donors endowed coaching posts; children subsequently admitted. *Inside Higher Education.* http://www.insidehighered.com/admissions/article/2019/05/13/donors-endowed-coaching-positions-programs-which-children-applied.

Kane, D. (2017). NCAA faces criticism for UNC decision. *News & Observer.* https://www.newsobserver.com/sports/college/acc/unc/article178784981.html.

Kisska-Schulze, K., & Epstein, A. (2014). "Show me the money!" Analyzing the potential state tax implications of paying student-athletes. *Virginia Sports and Entertainment Law Journal, 14,* 13–49.

Kisska-Schulze, K., & Epstein, A. (2016). Northwestern, O'Bannon and the future: Cultivating a new era for taxing qualified scholarships. *Akron Law Review, 49,* 771–812.

Levenson, E. (2018, February 5). Larry Nassar apologizes, gets 40 to 125 years for decades of sexual abuse. *CNN.* https://www.cnn.com/2018/02/05/us/larry-nassar-sentence-eaton/index.html.

Lewis, A. (2018, November 21). Megan Rapinoe: "America needs to confront its issues more honestly." *CNN.* https://www.cnn.com/2018/11/21/football/megan-rapinoe-usa-soccer-equality-colin-kaepernick-spt-intl/index.html.

Meilhan, P., & Close, D. (2018, December 10). USOC, USA Gymnastics officials enabled Nassar's abuse of athletes, investigation reveal. *CNN.* https://www.cnn.com/2018/12/10/us/us-olympic-committee-report-findings-firing/index.html.Murphy, D. (2021, September 1). Everything you need to know about the NCAA's NIL debate. *ESPN.* https://www.espn.com/college-sports/story/_/id/31086019/everything-need-know-ncaa-nil-debate.

Murphy, D. (2021, September 1). Everything you need to know about the NCAA's NIL debate. ESPN. https://www.espn.com/college-sports/story/_/id/31086019/everything-need-know-ncaa-nil-debate

Myerberg, P. (2018, July 23). Ohio State fires wide receivers coach after wife files domestic violence protection order. *USA Today.* https://www.usatoday.com/story/sports/ncaaf/bigten/2018/07/23/ohio-state-fires-wide-receivers-coach-zach-smith-domestic-violence/823752002/.

NLRB Office of Public Affairs. (2021, September 29). NLRB General Counsel Jennifer Abruzzo issues memo on employee status of players at academic institutions. *NLRB*. https://www.nlrb.gov/news-outreach/news-story/nlrb-general-counsel-jennifer-abruzzo-issues-memo-on-employee-status-of

Payne, K. (2018). Letter from CEO Kevin Payne: US Club Soccer to require SafeSport online training. *USClubSoccer.org*. https://www.usclubsoccer.org/news_article/show/975931.

Perez, A. J. (2018, February 28). U.S. Olympic Committee CEO Scott Blackmun resigns. *USA Today*. https://www.usatoday.com/story/sports/olympics/2018/02/28/u-s-olympic-committee-ceo-scott-blackmun-resigns/382569002/.

Reid, S. M. (2018, October 29). USOC audit finds USA Badminton at "high risk" for failing to comply with Safe Sport requirements. *Orange County Register*. https://www.ocregister.com/2018/10/29/usoc-audit-finds-usa-badminton-at-high-risk-for-failing-to-comply-with-safe-sport-requirements/.

Roscher, L. (2019). Ohio State team doctor sexually abused 177 men while school officials failed to act, per report. *Yahoo Sports*. https://sports.yahoo.com/ohio-state-team-doctor-sexually-abused-177-men-while-school-officials-failed-to-act-per-report-162817520.html.

Safe Sport Authorization Act. (2017). Protecting Young Victims from Sexual Abuse and Safe Sport Authorization Act of 2017, 115 P.L. 126.

Schlabach, M. (2019). Three sentenced in Adidas recruiting scandal. *ESPN*. http://www.espn.com/mens-college-basketball/story/_/id/26141993/three-sentenced-adidas-recruiting-scandal.

Schrotenboer, B. (2018, July 25). New Olympic scandal: USA Racquetball fires executive director. *USA Today*. https://www.usatoday.com/story/sports/olympics/2018/07/25/new-olympic-scandal-usa-racquetball-fires-executive-director/831275002/.

Scolforo, M. (2020). Ex-Penn St. president's Sandusky-related conviction restored. *Associated Press*. https://apnews.com/article/college-football-courts-pennsylvania-football-graham-spanier-3e7cdec3685b0f02da3fd450dbf41df3.

Smola, J. (2019, February 1). Ohio State, former students split over mediators in ex-doctor's sexual abuse cases. *Columbus Dispatch*. https://www.dispatch.com/news/20190201/ohio-state-former-students-split-over-mediators-in-ex-doctors-sexual-abuse-cases.

Svokos, A. (2019, May 3). Women's hockey players are protesting playing professionally—but don't call it a boycott. *ABC News*. https://abcnews.go.com/Sports/womens-hockey-players-protesting-playing-professionally-call-boycott/story?id=62802762.

Title IX of the Education Amendments. (1972). 20 U.S.C.A. §1681 et seq.

Tribune News Services. (2016, November 30). Judge adds $5M to Mike McQueary's $7m verdict against Penn State. *Chicago Tribune*. https://www.chicagotribune.com/sports/college/ct-penn-state-abuse-spt-20161130-story.html.

U.S. Center for SafeSport. (2022). SafeSport Code for the U.S. Olympic and Paralympic Movement. *U.S. Center for SafeSport*. https://uscenterforsafesport.org/wp-content/uploads/2022/02/2022-SafeSport-Code.pdf U.S. Olympic & Paralympic Committee. (2019, June 20). U.S. Olympic Committee changes name to U.S. Olympic & Paralympic Committee. *Team USA*. https://www.teamusa.org/News/2019/June/20/US-Olympic-Committee-Changes-Name-To-US-Olympic-Paralympic-Committee.

Victims of Child Abuse Act. (1990). 34 U.S.C. § 20341.

Yan, H. (2018, October 16). USA Gymnastics loses its 2nd president in 2 months. *CNN*. https://www.cnn.com/2018/10/16/us/usa-gymnastics-president-mary-bono-resigns/index.html.

Young, R. (2018). Former athletes file lawsuit against U.S. Olympic Committee, USA Taekwondo for alleged sexual abuse, sex trafficking. *Yahoo Sports*. https://sports.yahoo.com/former-athletes-file-lawsuit-u-s-olympic-committee-usa-taekwondo-alleged-sexual-abuse-sex-trafficking-040923452.html.

CHAPTER 9

....

SPORT, RELIGION, AND BELIEFS

....

ANDREW PARKER AND NICK J. WATSON

DESPITE the fact that there has been a steady growth in the academic literature surrounding sport and religion over the past 30 to 40 years (cf. Novak, 1976; Prebish, 1993; Watson & Parker, 2014), some scholars have expressed concern about the way in which debates about religion have been "marginalized" in sociological analyses of sport during that period (cf. Gibbons, 2017; Gibbons, Watson, & Mierzwinski, 2017; Shilling & Mellor, 2014). In turn, there is general agreement that academics outside of the traditional social science sports studies disciplines (i.e., sociology, history, anthropology, philosophy, and psychology), such as theologians and philosophers of religion, have been slow to recognize the cultural significance of modern-day sports (cf. Watson, 2011b). In this chapter we demonstrate that this trend is slowly changing and that analyses of the sport-religion relationship have begun to emanate from a range of disciplinary fields and subject areas. Focusing particularly on debates surrounding the relationship between sport and the Christian religion, we use some of our previous work to draw attention to the way in which the increasing commercialization of sport has been analyzed by a variety of scholars in this field (cf. Watson, 2007, 2011a, 2011b; Watson & Parker, 2013a, 2013b, 2014, 2015).

Of course, historically speaking, the relationship between the sacred and sport has long been acknowledged from the ritual ball games of primitive times to the athletic spectacles of ancient Greece and the muscular Christian ideals of Victorian Britain (cf. Guttmann, 1978/2004). In turn, a significant body of related scholarly work has emerged that serves to map this relationship across a range of geographical and religious landscapes (cf. Adogame, Watson, & Parker, 2018; Hemmings, Watson, & Parker, 2019; Hoven, Parker, & Watson, 2019; Magdalinski & Chandler, 2002; Parker & Watson, 2017; Parker, Watson, & White, 2016; Twietmeyer, Watson, & Parker, 2018; Watson, Jarvie, & Parker, 2020; Watson & Parker, 2014, 2015). These accounts provide useful insight into the different ways sport (and physical activity) has been appropriated by specific belief systems and the challenges and responses that such practices have encountered both in sporting and religious subcultures.

Given the extent to which notions of spirituality are becoming increasingly prevalent in Western industrialized societies (Graham, 2013) and the way faith-based inference and connotation is routinely evident in and through high-profile sport (Hoffman, 2010;

Krattenmaker, 2010), consideration of the connections between religion and the commercialization of sport is increasingly important. We begin our discussion with a brief overview of the historical literature on the sport-Christianity relationship in order to provide background and context to recent debates. We then explore how this relationship has manifested amid the commercialization of modern-day sport by providing case-study analyses of three particular phenomena: sporting mega-events, celebrity sports stars, and sport and the disabled body. We conclude by suggesting that sport continues to demonstrate vestiges of historical Christian values, but that its increasing commercialization means that these values run the risk of being lost amid a melee of wider popular cultural factors and forces.

ISSUES

A key issue in the academic literature surrounding sport and religion is that of muscular Christianity, an ideology which formed the basis of the innovative role which the English public schools and the Protestant Church in Britain played in the emergence and expansion of formalized sport in the mid-19th century (cf. Neddam, 2004; Parker & Weir, 2012; Watson, Weir, & Friend, 2005). A key player in this transformational process was Thomas Arnold, head teacher at Rugby School (in the English Midlands) between 1828 and 1841, whose desire it was to mold his male students into "good Christian gentlemen" by way of competitive games, an education in the classics, and spiritually grounded notions of discipline, respect, and morality (Mangan, 1988a, 1998b). An educated man, Arnold had attended Winchester School and Oxford University, where he excelled in the classics, his appointment at Rugby being directly linked to criticisms of disorder and unruliness at the school at a time when fears of broader moral breakdown prevailed. He resolved to remedy such evils by introducing new forms of governance and new curricular ventures. Yet the Arnoldian regime amounted to much more than simply playing games; educational pedigree continued to be upheld as the guardian of moral character, and the passing of responsibility to older pupils (prefects) as the gateway to discipline, respect, and Christian manliness (Hargreaves, 1986). News of Arnold's reforms traveled fast both inside and outside of the public schools. One reason for this was the writings of two well-known authors of the time, Charles Kingsley and Thomas Hughes.

During the mid-19th century Charles Kingsley (clergyman, academic, novelist, and poet) and his friend and associate Thomas Hughes (lawyer, politician, and novelist) became key figures in the relationship between sport and religion and, especially, faith-based understandings of sport. Specific aspects of their work stand out as particularly influential in this respect. Perhaps most notable here is Hughes's (1857) classic *Tom Brown's Schooldays*, the story of a boy whose character is shaped during his days at Rugby School in a way that suitably encapsulates these spiritual, moral, and physical standards (Erdozain, 2010; Putney, 2001; Simon & Bradley, 1975). Alongside the work of Kingsley, the sense of high moral value and physical endeavor which *Tom Brown's Schooldays* purveyed collectively formed the basis of what came to be known as "muscular Christianity," a term encapsulating spirituality, physical prowess, moral fortitude, and spiritual excellence. Of course, in reality, muscular Christianity had its roots in a whole range of wider theological, ethical, and moral concerns prevalent in Britain during the 1800s, such as the protection of the weak, the plight of the underprivileged, and the promotion of moral virtue. The incorporation of these (and other) social anxieties into an informal religious framework by Hughes and Kingsley resulted in the foregrounding of a series of core values which, over time, came to underpin and characterize the sport-Christianity relationship: fair play, respect, physical and emotional strength, perseverance, obedience, loyalty, self-control, endurance. Especially significant here was a fervent faith and stoic masculinity which collectively represented an ideal type of "Christian manliness." Similarly important were virtues such as courage, temperance, and *esprit de corps*, all of which became foundational for Baron Pierre de Coubertin in his initiation of the International Olympic Committee and the modern Olympic Games (cf. Lucas, 1964, 1975, 1976).

Coubertin's endorsement of Arnold's work provides but one example of the way these muscular Christian ideals came to shape the development of modern-day sport beyond Britain's shores. Indeed, as Englishness and empire became ever more synonymous with technological advancement, state governance, and civil society, and as the United Kingdom's economic dominance of overseas nations became something of an industry in and of itself, so too sport and games became powerful tools in the battle for hearts and minds around notions of cultural dominance and assimilation. In this sense, the emergence and subsequent development of the muscular Christian ethos was not simply about the widespread diffusion of games, but one of several mechanisms in and through which imperialism was sponsored and propagated on both economic and moral grounds (Mangan, 1988a, 1998b, 2006). Of course, as modern sporting forms evolved and professionalization and commercialization ensued, muscular Christian ideals became less prevalent amid a backdrop of moral and ethical decline (cf. Ladd & Mathisen, 1999; Watson & Parker, 2013a). That said, vestiges of the underlying values of the muscular Christian ethos persist in commercialized sport, where physical prowess and masculine endeavor are often celebrated, glorified, and revered. The "win-at-all-costs" culture of sport has largely been responsible for the promotion and perpetuation of such glorification, and it is to a closer analysis of such processes that we now turn.

APPROACHES

Over the years those exploring the intersections between religion (especially Christianity) and broader spheres of social life have acknowledged the significance of sports as a popular cultural form (cf. Moore, 2003; Price, 2001; Scholes & Sassower, 2013) and have adopted a range of approaches in their analyses of the sport-Christianity interface. One such approach concerns an interrogation of the way historical religious values play out amid the practices of modern-day commercialized sport. By way of illustrating this approach, in this section we present three case studies from our previous work in order to demonstrate how such analyses have been carried out. These cases consider (1) the Olympic and Paralympic Games, (2) the public profiles of celebrity sports stars, and (3) sport and the disabled body.

Approaching the Olympic and Paralympic Games

In their theological analysis of the institutions and governance of sport, Watson and Parker (2013a) present an examination of the institution of modern commercialized sport, outlining the ways in which, for some scholars, the Olympic and Paralympic Games have come to represent a form of cultural idolatry (White, 2008a). Such propositions are based on empirical evidence that self-exaltation, pride, and ruthless competition characterize the modern sporting institution and the ethos of many transnational sports (cf. Hoffman, 2010; Lasch, 1980; McNamee, 2010; Watson & White, 2007). Watson and Parker (2013a) argue that this appears contrary to Coubertin's original conception of the modern Olympic model, which he championed as a "universal humanistic religion," one with the potential to assist in bringing peace to warring nations (Young, 2005).

Amateurism, fair play, strength, and the dualistic Greek philosophy of soundness of body and mind (*mens sana in corpore sano*) were central to Coubertin's vision. Yet historical research demonstrates a range of unhealthy attitudes and social practices that plagued the first five decades of the Olympic institution. Chatziefstathiou (2011) identifies these as elitist exclusionary principles based on "race" and gender, European humanism, and unbridled colonial imperialism. Of course, many now claim that we presently operate in a radically different globalized sporting world where at least some of these issues have begun to be positively addressed (cf. Coakley & Dunning, 2002).

That said, since these early beginnings, a range of new problems have emerged: systematic corruption involving political propaganda (e.g., the so-called Nazi Olympics of 1936), the Olympic movement becoming entwined with the international Cold War during the 1960s and 1970s, overt nationalism, doping scandals, human rights abuses (e.g., the Beijing Games of 2008), and politically motivated terrorism (e.g., the Munich Games of 1972; cf. Lenskyj, 2008). Pointing to the metaphysical root of many of these problems, Higgs (1982, p. 179) argues history has shown that "whether communist, democratic, or fascist, modern governments have one thing in common—a reliance on sports to help define and bolster national pride"—to which might be added national wealth and global status (cf. Kidd, 2010).

Such sentiments have been supported by claims of a "global sporting arms race," which demonstrate a strong correlation between funding arrangements for the development of elite sports programs by the governments of Olympic host nations and national sporting success (cf. De Bosscher, Bingham, Shibli, Van, & de Knap, 2008). In contrast, MacAloon (1997) advocates that global mega-events, such as the Olympics, may provide "favourable conditions . . . for difficult meetings" between "global political elites, including . . . nations at war or [those] having no diplomatic relations with one another" (cited in Keys, 2010, p. 254) and warns social scientists not to polarize the complex sport-politic dyad in the post–Cold War context.

Identifying and combating immoral and inequitable practices within institutions, including those of political origin, is, however, crucial. Steenbergen (2001, p. 48) sees a need here to differentiate between sporting "practices" and "institutions," what he calls the "double character of sport." Drawing upon the work of MacIntyre (2007), Steenbergen's (2001, pp. 48–49) discussion of the "institutional embeddedness of sport" provides a useful starting point for any analysis of the historical evolution of modern sporting institutions:

> Institutions are characteristically concerned with . . . external goods. They are involved in acquiring money and other material goods; they are structured in terms of power and status, and they distribute money and power as rewards. Nor could they do otherwise if they are to sustain not only themselves, but also practices of which they are bearers.

As Steenbergen suggests, there are powerful centrifugal forces that operate in and through the global political economy which, we contend, may well endorse and perpetuate undesirable practices within sport. Indeed, as Higgs and Braswell (2004) (and others) have argued, rather than being regarded as practices and behaviors to avoid, striving for power, status, and reward is, more often than not, seen as a virtue in the microcosm of professional sport. Influenced by these deeply entrenched practices, sport in Western industrialized nations, White (2008b) suggests, has lost its corporate moral compass. Examining in more detail how sport as an institution has evolved within the context of modern social history is, therefore, a fundamental prerequisite if we are to evaluate this cultural phenomenon by way of a Christian worldview.

To understand the evolution and defining characteristics of modern sporting institutions, in this case the modern Olympics, the extensive sociohistorical studies of Guttmann (1978/ 2004, 1994, 2002) and Overman (1997, 2011) are especially helpful (see also Coleman, 1989). Guttmann (1994) elucidates how modern Western sports evolved through the industrial, capitalist, scientific, imperial, and cultural developments of the 19th and 20th centuries. Utilizing the work of Weber (1958), Guttmann cites six defining elements of modern sports: (1) secularization, (2) bureaucratization, (3) specialization, (4) rationalization, (5) quantification, and (6) the obsession with records. Drawing heavily upon Guttmann (and thus Weber, 1958) and others, such as the 19th-century social economist Thomas Veblen (1899/1970), Overman (2011) provides an in-depth analysis of how the formation of Western sports (with a focus on the United States) has been shaped by the related forces of the Protestant work ethic, Puritanism, Calvinism, and aggressive free-market capitalism. In Overman's (1997, p. 350) words, the Victorian Age gave birth to a "phenomenon which dramatically altered the nature of sport and recreation: the fruition of the spirit of capitalism. Sport has more and more to do with making money. . . . The money changers have entered the temple of sport."

Notwithstanding the potential insights which may be drawn from critical analyses of the sporting world, Watson and Parker (2013a) argue that input from systematic and biblical theologians is crucial if we are to understand the complex phenomenon of commercialized sport in the 21st century. The eroding forces of Western secularization on religious thought (Taylor, 2007) and thus sports (Guttmann, 1994) has led to a general disregard for spiritual and religious issues in sports-based research. Reflecting on the London 2012 Games, Watson and White (2012) alternatively suggest that while there are many corrupting influences in the modern Olympic institution that do not sit comfortably with the tenets of the Christian faith and are in need of "redemption," there are, at the same time, many positives that Christians should celebrate and engage with. For example, the display of human excellence and beauty in sporting movement (i.e., aesthetics), the coming together of peoples from diverse backgrounds, and the heavily debated notion of "legacy" (e.g., Gold & Gold, 2009) in relation to the projected social, environmental, health, cultural, and economic benefits that are routinely promised by the Olympic and Paralympic Games.

Approaching the Celebritized Sports Star

In sum, what Watson and Parker (2013a) put forward about the Olympic Games is the argument that, despite the vagaries of modern-day corporate sport, vestiges of historical (muscular) Christian values remain operant. But how, then, might such investigative principles be applied to the public profiles of today's increasingly celebritized sports stars? In their examination of Christian sporting celebrity, Parker and Watson (2015) take these arguments one step further by superimposing their analysis of the corporate onto that of the individual. They do this by utilizing the work of philosophers and social scientists to interrogate the celebrity persona of a notable Christian sporting icon, U.S. football quarterback Tim Tebow. One view that has become prominent in discussions of the sport-religion interface is that sport has become a religion in and of itself and that its rituals and practices help fill a spiritual void in Western culture—where celebrity athletes may be looked upon as figures to be worshiped (cf. Andrews & Jackson, 2001; Rojek, 2001; Smart, 2005; Wenner, 2013).

Historically, the extent to which sport has been seen to occupy the collective consciousness of Western nations has been highlighted by various commentators. For example, a number of "popular" and academic texts (Edge, 1999; Parks, 2002; Percy & Taylor, 1997; Xifra, 2008) have recognized soccer as a new "civil religion," and more recently, Rial (2012) has investigated religiosity in Brazilian professional football within the context of the Neo-Pentecostal diaspora.

Indeed, there are many individual studies that have sought to examine the symbiosis of sport and the Christian faith (and other religions). However, it is the typology of sociologist Harry Edwards (1973) that has been most widely adopted here. In an attempt to demonstrate the structural connections and synergies between religion and the institutions of modern-day sport, Edwards highlights how the latter features (1) a body of formally stated beliefs, accepted on faith by masses of people; (2) "'saints'—those departed souls who in their lives exemplified and made manifest the prescriptions of the dogma of sport"; (3) ruling patriarchs, a prestigious group of coaches, managers, and sportsmen who exercise controlling influence over national sport organizations; and (4) "gods"—star and superstar athletes who, though powerless to alter their own situations, wield great influence and charisma over the masses of fans (pp. 261–262).

A steady stream of studies has examined different elements of Edwards's (1973) work. One element that is particularly pertinent to the present discussion is that of sporting "gods." The way sporting celebrities such as Michael Jordan, Pele, Sachin Tendulkar, David Beckham, Muhammad Ali, and Diego Maradona have been worshiped as "gods" (or "demigods") by their fans has emerged as an interesting area of study (e.g., Archetti, 2002; Nalapat & Parker, 2005). An illustrative example of this "deific projection" (see Williams, 1994) is demonstrated by Michael Jordan's biographer, who, in adopting more than a hint of hyperbole, famously described him as "Jesus in Nikes" (Halberstam, 2001).

At the same time, the "religious" devotion of sports spectators has not gone unnoticed by sports studies scholars and anthropologists who have identified the multiple factors of fandom that are imbued with religious motifs (cf. Crawford, 2004; Mumford, 2011). Some of these are clearly linked to Edwards's (1973) typology, including the zealous devotion and fanaticism of star player identities and the honoring of them as sporting "saints." To this end, Grimshaw (2000) has called for a theological deconstruction of what he interprets to be a post-Christian "pagan mythology" of "fallible gods" through which sports participants and fans may allegedly encounter spiritual experience. Amid the technological advancements and globalized practices of the modern age, the rhetoric surrounding these fallible sports gods has been perpetuated by the mass media via a melding of narratives of religion and sport. It is to the role of media in the identity formation of sporting figures that we now turn.

In their analysis of the self-proclaimed Christian and (former National Football League and later baseball) sporting celebrity Tim Tebow, Parker and Watson (2015, p. 229) argue that commentary around the sport-media-Christianity nexus has intensified in recent years (cf. Hawzen & Newman, 2017; Moore, Keller, & Zemanek, 2011; Newman, 2010; Rial, 2012) and that common among such narratives are criticisms surrounding the extent to which sport is used as "a ready-made billboard for the promotion of Christian values and as a platform for proselytizing sports stars" (see also Krattenmaker, 2010; Parker & Watson, 2017). Taking the career of Tebow as an example of this process of intensification, Parker and Watson (2015, 2017) track the sporting and religious trajectory of this onetime sporting icon in order to depict how modern-day muscular Christianity might manifest amid the commercialized and highly celebritized culture of 21st-century sport. The specific focus of the authors is the extent to which such manifestations have the potential to mesh with political connotation, thereby serving to generate a sense of polarization around ideas concerning the sport-Christianity relationship.

Building on Randolph Feezell's (2013) argument that Tebow represents something of an enigma within the context of U.S. popular culture, Parker and Watson (2015, p. 231) suggest that, over time, Tebow's intentional promotion of Christian values has cast him as both "sportsman and moral custodian, who allows his religious beliefs to be framed as a public spectacle." In his in-depth examination of Tebow's popular cultural profile, Feezell (2013, p. 137) explores the nature and extent of the controversy surrounding what he calls the "Tebow phenomenon" and attempts to unpack the "critical reaction to his public religiosity." Drawing on Krattenmaker's (2010) polemical account of the sport-Christianity relationship in the United States, Feezell goes on to explore the key tenets of the Tebow narrative in order to present a broader analysis of the way the sport-religion relationship plays out in the life of this modern-day muscular Christian. For both Krattenmaker and Feezell, the particularities of the sport-Christianity dyad raise a number of key questions around the intentional infiltration of evangelical Christianity into commercialized sport, the framing (appropriate or otherwise) of the faith-sport relationship, and the proselytization of religious views by high-profile sports personnel via what has been called "platform ministry" (cf. Hoffman, 2010). Utilizing these assertions as a kind of conceptual canvass, Feezell (2013, p. 142) addresses a number of intriguing questions concerning the extent to which (if at all) it is acceptable for high-profile athletes such as Tebow to promote their religious views:

> Tebow's behavior is polarizing because he appears to ignore or at least not acknowledge that the world of religious belief is complicated and diverse. Given the highly public nature of Tebow's conspicuous piety, no wonder that thoughtful people are troubled by either his ignorance or his unconcern with how belief, both private and public, should come to grips with facts about religious diversity.

As far as Feezell is concerned, high-profile Christian athletes have various, and arguably "special," responsibilities in relation to their expressions of faith simply because of their popular cultural currency. Following this line of argument, Feezell suggests that Tebow's expressions of faith are fundamentally flawed on three levels. First, that as a well-informed, privileged, and educated individual Tebow has a responsibility to exhibit a greater sense of awareness of notions of impartiality when it comes to his religious beliefs. Second, that Tebow has a responsibility to adopt a broader sense of reflection, humility, and modesty in relation not only to the expression of his own beliefs but to the existence of others' beliefs. Third, that because of his lifelong affiliation with evangelical Christianity, Tebow demonstrates a spiritual blind spot with respect to his status as a sporting role model insofar as he appears to go beyond the "modeling" of moral and ethical standards, proffering not simply how people should behave but what they should believe.

Approaching Sport and the Disabled Body

Discussion of celebritized sporting personas certainly seems a long way from the work of Thomas Hughes and Charles Kingsley, but what Parker and Watson (2015) highlight is that the foundational tenets of these early debates live on irrespective of time or geographical context. Similarly, the sport-Christianity relationship has emerged amid other contemporary sporting narratives, a further case in point being sport and the disabled body.

Over the past three decades a growing literature has emerged on the theology of both physical and intellectual disability (see Brock & Swinton, 2012; Eiesland, 1994; Watson, Hargaden, & Brock, 2018; Yong, 2007), the origins of which were largely born in the disability (and wider civil) rights movements of the 1970s. On the face of it, such work would appear to contrast sharply with the "win-at-all-costs" mentality of commercialized sport and the celebritized personas it glorifies. Yet as Hauerwas and Vanier (2009), argue, the biblical themes of weakness, vulnerability, mutuality, hospitality, humility, and love are at the heart of the Christian message, and thus a consideration of the disabled body is a necessary part of any values-based assessment of modern-day sport.

The reasons behind the relative lack of theological reflection on disability are many and varied, and a central concern for Reynolds (2008, p. 68) is that theology has been "taken captive by the cult of normalcy"; that is, it has often adopted a starting point rooted in Enlightenment philosophies and ideas such as utilitarianism, rationalism, free-market capitalism, ableism, and intellectualism (see also Creamer, 2009). The prevalence of Platonic-Cartesian dualism in both theology (Wilson, 1989) and sport (Twietmeyer, 2008) has also been a factor in de-emphasizing and devaluing the role of the body (and able-bodied and disabled sport as a whole) in Western culture. Latterly the body has become much talked about in wider social contexts, and this has resulted in robust academic interrogation by the sports studies fraternity (see, for example, Shilling, 2012; Silk, Andrews, & Thorpe, 2017). To varying degrees publications on the theology of disability seek to critique the sociocultural structures and institutions that marginalize, alienate, oppress, and devalue the disabled. Following the seminal work of the Marxist sociologist Michael Oliver (1990) (and advocacy of the social constructionist model of disability), scholars have analyzed how both structural and popular cultural forces have come together historically to impact the status and perceived importance of disability sport (see Howe, 2008; Howe & Parker, 2012; Thomas & Smith, 2009). In turn, a small body of literature has begun to emerge around the connections between sport, theology, and disability, an example of which we now consider.

In their empirical (qualitative) study of sport and embodiment, Howe and Parker (2014) highlight the importance of religious engagement for a group of elite (Paralympic) athletes dealing with issues of impairment. The specific focus of these authors is the extent to which the life stories of their respondents were layered with religious symbolism and inference, and how their spiritual journeys gave them a renewed sense of purpose, meaning, and identity. Howe and Parker illustrate how the transition from life as an able-bodied individual to one with impairment was seen by a number of athletes as a "pilgrimage" through which they found spiritual significance in relation to the changes that had occurred to their bodies and their overall lives. Coming to terms with disability and a reconfigured sense of social status brought with it for many a process of self-reflection which engendered a consideration of "greater purpose" and "religious calling" around notions of advocacy and support for others with disability. Given that such support processes were located within the context of elite sport, crucial to this calling also was a sense of reembodiment. Because of the relationship between the origins of modern-day sport and Christianity (i.e., the benefits of a healthy body and healthy mind) and of the moral and ethical connections between physical activity, embodiment, and the Christian faith, there is a sense in which one might argue that the spiritual journey evident within these reembodiment narratives is somewhat unsurprising. That said, and as Howe and Parker note, not all elite athletes who experience post-accident vulnerability seek to make sense of their "new world" in this way. On the contrary, for some the journey to reembodiment takes place on an entirely secular basis, while others find solace via alternative belief systems. Nevertheless, for a number of the athletes concerned, a holistic "healthy body, healthy mind" ethos was integral to their newfound sense of purpose and calling and, perhaps more important, their understandings of their bodies post-accident. In this way, spiritual and religious reflection allowed these athletes to positively reimagine their "physical selves," which in turn facilitated a renewed sense of hope in relation to their futures and their potential contribution to individuals in similar circumstances as well as to wider society. Indeed, so powerful was this reflective process that some came to see their reembodiment as a process of "transformation" and (metaphorical) "resurrection."

As Howe and Parker (2014) argue, such acts of reembodiment inevitably demand new understandings of personhood around a reconceptualized integration of mind and body (Csordas, 1994; Seymour, 1998). One of the ways they suggest we might make sense of these spiritual journeys is to think of religion as a mechanism for facilitating a reconfiguration of "wholeness" in line with Csordas's (2002) three stages of ritual healing: (1) predisposition, (2) empowerment, and (3) transformation. Utilizing this framework, Howe and Parker (2014) argue that it may well be that elite athletes who have experienced impairment by way of traumatic accident journey through these stages as part of a rite of passage to reembodiment. The first stage (predisposition) requires that the individual believes that a level of rehabilitation is possible, a belief that is devoid of any false sense of hope that they will somehow overcome their impairment and which follows instead an acceptance of and adjustment to their new social reality. The second stage (empowerment) is where the individual realizes that the healing of the body and the mind are linked by some form of spiritual power, where they begin to articulate a faith that is beyond the realities of the social world in which they live, and where a close allegiance to religious doctrine and spiritual experience forms. The final stage, comprising the transformation from "able-bodied nonbeliever" to "impaired believer" follows, it seems, a process of "resurrection." This necessarily requires a wholesale acceptance by the individual of their reconfigured life and the expectations and behaviors which go with it, yet at the same time this acceptance is grounded in a sense of renewed purpose and calling around physical reembodiment, spiritual positivity, and social contribution.

The work of Howe and Parker (2014) suggests that spiritual and religious belief may provide disabled athletes with new understandings not only of embodiment but also of their position in the social world. As a consequence, rather than allowing their lives to be hindered by impairment, these athletes took the symbolism associated with Christ's resurrection as a transformative means by which they could (re)view their journey to reembodiment "as one of fate and destiny; as a road to emancipation; as a blessing in disguise" (p. 21). In this sense, these athletes not only accepted and adjusted to their impaired bodies, but they can be seen as being metaphorically "born again" into a new social existence in and through which they used their newfound religious/spiritual experiences to positively impact their own lives and those of others.

DEBATES

In light of the above discussion, what, we might ask, does the future hold for the scholarly study of the relationship between sport and religion? More specifically, given that the past three decades have witnessed an exponential growth in the number of academic resources around this relationship, and given that the commercialization of sport will foreseeably continue to grow in popularity and cultural significance, how might we more critically address and assess the connections between sport and Christianity?

There are a number of things to consider here. First, we must acknowledge that, however far removed modern-day sport may be from its 19th-century roots, the vestiges of religious and spiritual tradition live on. The public and private lives of the early muscular Christians may not have been subjected to the scrutiny and conjecture of the world's media, but, as we have seen, their influence was significant in shaping public perceptions of the sport-Christianity relationship and the diffusion of related practices. For this reason, critical analyses of modern-day sport are central to our ongoing understanding of the power of sporting institutions and the values imbued therein.

Second, we must acknowledge that the practices and behaviors surrounding 21st-century sport (at both the corporate and the individual level) have not emerged in a social vacuum. On the contrary, part of the reason for the appeal of sporting mega-events and celebrity figures is the synchronicity with which their emergence and development has coincided with the expansion of the sport-media-business nexus in the postwar period. Likewise, disability sport scholars have taken their lead not only from the social justice agendas of bygone days but also from an increasing interest in the body as a cultural phenomenon. Indeed, a continued mapping of the characteristics of sporting institutions within the context of changing social, cultural, political, and economic conditions is critical to our understanding of the way in which their underpinning values are framed and perceived.

Third (and in relation to individual manifestations of these values), we must acknowledge that while the status of sporting personnel (able-bodied or disabled) may initially be confined to a particular context, it is not unusual for them to transcend such boundaries over time (Cashmore & Parker, 2003; Howe & Parker, 2012) becoming not only globally recognized figures but also religious icons in their own right (cf. Nalapat & Parker, 2005). Such a view runs contrary to that of Ward (2011, p. 32), who has pointed out that, while celebrities may, at times, serve as "sources for personal transformation and aspiration," rarely, it seems, do "fans" regard their popular cultural idols as "divine beings" or benchmarks of ethical and/or moral stability. In this sense, the notion of "celebrity worship" has become an accepted part of everyday life. Irrespective, analyses of Christian sporting celebrities should take into account the multiple mechanisms through which their identities are disseminated (i.e., social media) and the impact that this has on their status, influence, and reach.

Finally, we must acknowledge that the public staging of sporting events and personalities is strategically managed and finely honed by marketing and advertising companies whose job it is to continually (re)create and circulate related images in line with consumer demand. The celebrity-media relationship is symbiotic. Indeed, sporting organizations and personalities simply cannot maintain their popular cultural appeal without a marketized media presence, and more broadly there can be no big-time sport without big-time media. In this sense, while at one level the commercialized nature of the modern sporting world might have the potential to militate against its underpinning religious values, global reach creates a level of exposure which necessarily brings these values into public view and, in so doing, serves to showcase (both implicitly and explicitly) their ongoing manifestation.

Conclusion

It has been our intention throughout this chapter to consider the relationship between sport and religion and, in particular, the way in which Christian values might be evident in and through modern-day commercialized sport. Within this context we have explored sporting mega-events, celebrity sport personas, and sport and the disabled body as sites where this relationship might manifest most clearly. In so doing, we have examined the interconnections between historical conceptions of sport and modern-day religious connotation. In turn, we have attempted to demonstrate how sporting institutions past and present have been utilized as a mechanism through which to promote muscular Christian values and, in particular, how the increasing commercialization of sport has created a vehicle through which 21st-century muscular Christianity might be propagated.

Of course, we recognize that there are many additional ways in which such interconnections and attachments might be explored. As we have seen, a number of scholars and empirical researchers have examined sport from different faith and denominational perspectives. These kinds of investigations necessarily stimulate discussion around the nuances of political influence, geographical circumstance, and cultural/economic impact. Opportunities and questions for further academic investigations are, therefore, numerous. Religious scholars may, for example, apply the tools of systematic and biblical theology to examine concepts such as the cult of celebrity and multimedia representations of sport (cf. Ward, 2011).

In seeking to understand sport in postmodern culture, sport scholars have recently implemented "radical orthodoxy," where the task is to view contemporary social phenomena through the lens of orthodox Christian doctrine. Investigations using radical orthodoxy may assist scholars and religious practitioners to further understand and contextualize faith-based values in particular sporting contexts and to undertake theological and cultural analyses in non-Western sporting locales. Additionally, further research into the commercial aspects of sport has the potential to help scholars think more critically about the cultural impact of sport and the influence of sporting individuals and organizations as cites of religious "worship" in and of themselves. In turn, such work has the potential to locate spirituality and religion more firmly as topics of discussion within sport studies as a whole.

References

Adogame, A., Watson, N. J., & Parker, A. (Eds.). (2018). *Global perspectives on sports and Christianity*. London: Routledge.

Andrews, D. L. & Jackson, S. J. (Eds.). (2001). *Sports stars: The cultural politics of sporting celebrity*. London: Routledge.

Archetti, E. P. (2002). The spectacle of a heroic life: The case of Diego Maradona. In D. L. Andrews & S. J. Jackson (Eds.), *Sport stars: The cultural politics of sporting celebrity* (pp. 151–163). London: Routledge.

Brock, B., & Swinton, J. (2012). *Disability in the Christian tradition: A reader*. Grand Rapids, MI: Wm. B. Eerdmans Publishing.

Cashmore, E. E. & Parker, A. (2003). One David Beckham. . . ? Celebrity, masculinity and the Socceratti. *Sociology of Sport Journal, 20*(3), 214–232.

Chatziefstathiou, D. (2011). Paradoxes and contestations of Olympism in the history of the modern Olympic movement. *Sport in Society, 14*(3), 332–344.

Coakley, J., & Dunning, E. (Eds.). (2002). *Handbook of sports studies*. New York: Sage.

Coleman, J. (1989). Sport and contradictions of society. In G. Baum & J. Coleman (Eds.), *Sport* (pp. 21–31). Edinburgh: T. and T. Clark.

Creamer, D. B. (2009). *Disability and Christian theology: Embodied limits and constructive possibilities*. Oxford: Oxford University Press.

De Bosscher, V., Bingham, J., Shibli, S., Van, B. M., & de Knap, P. (2008). *The global sporting arms race: An international comparative study of sports policy factors leading to international sporting success*. Oxford: Meyer and Meyer Sport Ltd.

Crawford, G. (2004). *Consuming sport: Fans, sport and culture*. London: Routledge.

Csordas, T. J. (Ed.) (1994). Embodiment and experience: The existential ground of culture and self. Cambridge: Cambridge University Press.

Csordos, T.J. (2002). Body/meaning/healing. New York: Palgrave Macmillan.

Edge, A. (1999). *Faith of our fathers: Football as religion*. Edinburgh: Mainstream Publishing.

Edwards, H. (1973). *Sociology of sport*. Homewood, IL: Dorsey Press.

Eiesland, N. L. (1994). *The disabled God: Towards a liberation theology of disability*. Nashville, TN: Abingdon Press.

Erdozain, D. (2010). *The problem of pleasure: Sport, recreation and the crisis of Victorian religion*. Suffolk, U.K.: Boydell Press.

Feezell, R. (2013). Sport, religious belief, and religious diversity. *Journal of the Philosophy of Sport, 40*(1), 135–162.

Gibbons, T. (2017). Challenging the secular bias in the sociology of sport: Scratching the surface of Christian approaches to sociology. In A. Adogame, N. J. Watson, & A. Parker (Eds.), *Global perspectives on sports and Christianity* (pp. 13–28). London: Routledge.

Gibbons, T., Watson, N. J., & Mierzwinski, M. (2017). Christianity as public religion: A justification for using a Christian sociological approach for studying the social scientific aspects of sport. *Sport in Society, 22*(2), 209–233.

Graham, E. (2013). *Between a rock and a hard place: Public theology in a post-secular age*. London: SCM Press.

Grimshaw, M. (2000). "I can't believe my eyes": The religious aesthetics of sport as post-modern salvific moments. *Implicit Religion*, 3(2), 87–99.

Gold, J., & Gold, M. (2009). Future indefinite? London 2012, the spectre of retrenchment and the challenge of Olympic sports legacy. *London Journal*, 34(2), 179–196.

Guttmann, A. (1978/2004). *From ritual to record: The nature of modern sports*. New York: Columbia University Press.

Guttmann, A. (1994). *Games and empires: Modern sports and cultural imperialism*. New York: Columbia University Press.

Guttmann, A. (2002). *The Olympics: A history of the modern games*, Champaign, IL: University of Illinois Press.

Halberstam, D. (2001). *Playing for keeps: Michael Jordan and the world he made*. London: Yellow Jersey Press.

Hargreaves, J. (1986). *Sport, power and culture*. London: Routledge.

Hauerwas, S., & Vanier, J. (2009). *Living gently in a violent world: The prophetic witness of weakness*. Downers Grove, IL: Intervarsity Press.

Hawzen, M. G., & Newman, J. I. (2017). The gospel according to Tim Tebow: Sporting celebrity, whiteness, and the cultural politics of Christian fundamentalism in America. *Sociology of Sport Journal*, 34(1), 12–24.

Hemmings, B., Watson, N. J. & Parker, A. (Eds.). (2019). *Sport, psychology and Christianity: Welfare, performance and consultancy*. London: Routledge.

Higgs, R. J. (1982). Sports: A reference guide. London: Greenwood.

Higgs, R. J. & Braswell, M. C. (2004). *An unholy alliance: The sacred and modern sports*. Macon, GA: Mercer University Press.

Hoven, M., Parker, A., & Watson, N. J. (Eds.). (2019). *Sport and Christianity: Practices for the twenty-first century*. London: T&T Clark.

Howe, P. D. (2008). *The cultural politics of the paralympic movement: Through an anthropological lens*. London: Routledge.

Howe, P. D., and Parker, A. (2012). Celebrating imperfection: Sport, disability and celebrity culture. *Celebrity Studies*, 3(3), 270–282.

Howe, P. D., and Parker, A. (2014). Disability as a path to spiritual enlightenment: An ethnographic account of the significance of religion in paralympic sport. *Journal of Disability and Religion*, 18(1), 8–23.

Hoffman, S. J. (2010). *Good game: Christians and the culture of sport*. Waco, TX: Baylor University Press.

Hughes, T. (1857). Tom Brown's school days. London: Macmillan and Co.

Keys, B. (2010). International relations. In S. W. Pope & J. Nauright (Eds.), *Routledge companion to sports history* (pp. 248–267). London: Routledge.

Kidd, B. (2010). Human rights and the Olympic movement after Beijing. *Sport in Society*, 13(5), 901–910.

Krattenmaker, T. (2010). *Onward Christian athletes: Turning ballparks into pulpits and players into preachers*. New York: Rowman and Littlefield.

Ladd, T., & Mathisen, J. A. (1999). *Muscular Christianity: Evangelical Protestants and the development of American sport*. Grand Rapids, MI: Baker Books.

Lasch, N. (1980). *The culture of narcissism: American life in an age of diminished expectations*. London: Abacus.

Lenskyj, H. F. (2008). *Olympic industry resistance: Challenging Olympic power and propaganda*. Albany: State University of New York Press.

Lucas, J. A. (1964). Coubertin's philosophy of pedagogical sport. *Journal of Health, Physical Education, and Recreation, 35*(26–27), 56.

Lucas, J. A. (1975). Victorian "muscular Christianity": Prologue to the Olympic Games philosophy (Part 1). *Olympic Review, 97–98,* 456–460.

Lucas, J. A. (1976). Victorian "muscular Christianity": Prologue to the Olympic Games philosophy (Part 2). *Olympic Review, 99–100,* 49–52.

MacIntyre, A. (2007). *After virtue: A study in moral theory.* Notre Dame, IN: Notre Dame University Press.

Magdalinski. T., & Chandler, T. J. L. (Eds.). (2002). *With God on their side: Sport in the service of religion.* London: Routledge

Mangan, J. A. (Ed.). (1988a). *Pleasure, profit and proselytism: British culture and sport at home and abroad, 1700–1914.* London: Frank Cass.

Mangan, J. A. (1998b). *The games ethic and imperialism: Aspects of the diffusion of an ideal.* London: Frank Cass.

Mangan, J. A. (2006). Christ and the imperial playing fields: Thomas Hughes' ideological heirs in empire. *International Journal of the History of Sport, 23*(5), 777–804.

McNamee, M. (2010). *The ethics of sports: A reader.* London: Routledge.

Moore, M. E., Keller, C., & Zemanek, J. E. (2011). The marketing revolution of Tim Tebow: A celebrity endorsement case study. *Innovative Marketing, 7*(1), 17–25.

Moore, R. L. (2003). *Touchdown Jesus: The mixing of sacred and secular in American history.* Louisville, KY: John Knox Press.

Mumford, S. (2011). *Watching sport: Aesthetics, ethics and emotion for the spectator.* London: Routledge.

Nalapat, A., & Parker, A. (2005). Sport, celebrity and popular culture: Sachin Tendulkar, cricket and Indian nationalisms. *International Review for the Sociology of Sport, 40*(4), 433–446.

Neddam, F. (2004). Constructing masculinities under Thomas Arnold (1828–1842): Gender, educational policy and school life in an early-Victorian public school. *Gender and Education, 16*(3), 303–326.

Newman, J. I. (2010). Full-throttle Jesus: Toward a critical pedagogy of stockcar racing in theocratic America. *Review of Education, Pedagogy, and Cultural Studies, 32,* 263–294.

Novak, M. (1976). *The joy of sports: End zones, bases, baskets, balls, and the consecration of the American spirit.* New York, Basic Books.

Oliver, M. (1990). *The politics of disablement.* Basingstoke, U.K.: Macmillan and St Martin's Press.

Overman, S. J. (1997). *The influence of the Protestant ethic on sport and recreation.* Sydney: Ashgate.

Overman, S. J. (2011). *The Protestant work ethic and the spirit of sport: How Calvinism and capitalism shaped American games.* Macon, GA: Mercer University Press.

Parks, T. (2002). *A season with Verona.* London: Vintage.

Percy, M., & Taylor, R. (1997). "Something for the weekend, sir?" Leisure, ecstasy and identity in football and contemporary religion. *Leisure Studies, 16,* 37–49.

Parker, A., & Watson, N. J. (2015). Sport, celebrity and religion: Christianity, morality and the Tebow phenomenon. *Studies in World Christianity, 21*(3), 223–238.

Parker, A., & Watson, N. J. (2017). Spiritualized and religious bodies. In M. Silk, D. Andrews & H. Thorpe (Eds.), *Routledge handbook of physical cultural studies* (pp. 209–217). London: Routledge.

Parker, A., Watson, N. J., & White, J. B. (2016). *Sports chaplaincy: Trends, issues and debates.* Milton Keynes, U.K.: Ashgate.

Parker, A., & Weir, S. J. (2012). Sport, spirituality and Protestantism: A historical overview. *Theology*, *114*(4), 253–265.

Prebish, C. S. (1993). *Religion and sport: The meeting of sacred and profane.* London: Greenwood Press.

Price, J. L. (Ed.). (2001). *From season to season: Sports as American religion.* Macon, GA: Mercer University Press.

Putney, C. (2001). *Muscular Christianity: Manhood and sports in Protestant America 1880–1920.* Cambridge, MA: Harvard University Press.

Reynolds, T. E. (2008). *Vulnerable communion: A theology of disability and hospitality.* Grand Rapids, MI: Brazos Press.

Rial, C. (2012). Banal religiosity: Brazilian athletes as new missionaries of the neo-Pentecostal diaspora. *Vibrant: Virtual Brazilian Anthropology*, *9*(2), 130–158.

Rojek, C. (2001). *Celebrity.* London: Reaktion Books.

Scholes, J., & Sassower, R. (2013). *Religion and sports in American culture.* New York: Routledge.

Seymour, W. (1998) *Remaking the Body: Rehabilitation and Change.* London: Routledge.

Silk, M., Andrews. D., & Thorpe, H. (Eds.). (2017). *Routledge handbook of physical cultural studies.* London: Routledge.

Shilling, C. (2012). *The body and social theory* (3rd ed.). London: Sage.

Shilling, C., & Mellor, P. A. (2014). Re-conceptualizing sport as a sacred phenomenon. *Sociology of Sport Journal*, *31*, 349–376.

Simon, B., & Bradley, I. (Eds.). (1975). *The Victorian public school: Studies in the development of an educational institution.* Dublin: Gill and Macmillan.

Smart, B. (2005). *The sport star: Modern sport and the cultural economy of sporting celebrity.* London: Sage.

Steenbergen, J. (2001). The double character of sport. In J. Steenbergen., P. De Knop, & A. H. F. Elling (Eds.), *Values and norms in sport: Critical reflections on the position and meanings of sport in society* (pp. 33–56). Oxford: Meyer and Meyer Sport.

Taylor, C. (2007). *A secular age.* Boston: Harvard University Press.

Thomas, N., & Smith, A. (2009). *Disability sport and society: An introduction.* London: Routledge.

Twietmeyer, G. (2008). A theology of inferiority: Is Christianity the source of kinesiology's second-class status in the academy? *Quest*, *60*, 452–466.

Twietmeyer, G., Watson, N. J., & Parker, A. (2018). Sport, Christianity and social justice: Considering a theological foundation. *Quest*, *71*(2), 121–137.

Veblen, T. (1899/1970). *Theory of the leisure class: An economic study of institutions.* London: Allen and Unwin.

Ward, P. (2011). *Gods behaving badly: Media, religion and celebrity culture.* London: SCM Press.

Watson, N. J. (2007). Muscular Christianity in the modern age: "Winning for Christ" or "playing for glory"? In J. Parry, S. Robinson, N. J. Watson, & M. Nesti (Eds.), *Sport and spirituality: An introduction* (pp. 80–93). London: Routledge.

Watson, N. J. (2011a). Identity in sport. A psychological and theological analysis. In J. Parry, M. Nesti, & N. J. Watson (Eds.), *Theology, ethics and transcendence in sport* (pp. 104–147). London: Routledge.

Watson, N. J. (2011b). Introduction. In J. Parry, M. N. Nesti, & N. J. Watson (Eds.), *Theology, ethics and transcendence in sports* (pp. 1–11). London: Routledge.

Watson, N. J., Hargaden, K., & Brock, B. (Eds.). (2018). *Theology, disability and sport: Social justice perspectives.* London: Routledge.

Watson, N. J., Jarvie, G., & Parker, A. (2020). *Sport, physical education, and social justice: Religious, sociological, psychological, and capability perspectives*. London: Routledge.

Watson, N. J., & Parker, A. (2013a). A Christian theological analysis of the institutions and governance of sport: A case study of the modern Olympic Games. *Journal of Religion and Society*, 15, 1–21.

Watson, N. J., & Parker, A. (Eds.). (2013b). *Sports and Christianity: Historical and contemporary perspectives*. New York: Routledge.

Watson, N. J., & Parker, A. (2014). *Sport and the Christian religion: A systematic review of literature*. Newcastle-upon-Tyne, U.K.: Cambridge University Press.

Watson, N. J., & Parker, A. (Eds.). (2015). *Sport, religion and disability*. London: Routledge.

Watson, N. J., Weir, S., & Friend, S. (2005). The development of muscular Christianity in Victorian Britain and beyond. *Journal of Religion and Society*, 7(1), 1–25.

Watson, N. J. & White, J. (2007). "Winning at all costs" in modern sport: Reflections on pride and humility in the writings of C. S. Lewis. In J. Parry, S. Robinson, N. J. Watson, & M. S. Nesti (Eds.), *Sport and spirituality: An introduction* (pp. 61–79). London: Routledge.

Watson, N. J. & White, J. (2012). C. S. Lewis at the 2012 London Olympics: Reflections on pride and humility. *Practical Theology*, 5(2), 153–168.

Weber, M. (1958). *The Protestant ethic and the spirit of capitalism* (Trans. Talcott Parsons). New York: Free Press.

Wenner, L. A. (Ed.). (2013). *Fallen sports heroes, media, and celebrity culture*. New York: Peter Lang.

White, J. B. (2008a). Idols in the stadium: Sport as an "idol factory." In D. Deardorff & J. B. White (Eds.), *The image of God in the human body: Essays on Christianity and sports* (pp. 127–172). Lampeter, Wales: Edwin Mellen Press.

White, J. B. (2008b). The prophet of Copenhagen conversing with competitive sport: Serving God and man in sport: A divided allegiance. In D. Deardorff & J. B. White (Eds.), *The image of God in the human body: Essays on Christianity and sports* (pp. 367–388). Lampeter, Wales: Edwin Mellen Press.

Williams, P. (1994). *The sports immortals: Deifying the American athlete*. Bowling Green, OH: Bowling Green State University Popular Press.

Wilson, M. V. (1989). *Our father Abraham: Jewish roots of the Christian faith*. Grand Rapids, MI: Wm. B. Eerdmans Publishing Company.

Xifra, J. (2008). Soccer, civil religion, and public relations: Devotional-promotional communication and Barcelona Football Club. *Public Relations Review*, 34(2), 192–198.

Yong, A. (2007). *Theology and Down syndrome: Reimaging disability in late modernity*. Waco, TX: Baylor University Press.

Young, D. (2005). From Olympia 776 BC to Athens 2004: The origin and authenticity of the modern Olympic Games. In K. Young & K. B. Wamsley (Eds.), *Global Olympics: Historical and sociological studies of the modern games* (pp. 3–18). Oxford: Elsevier.

PART II

ENTERPRISE AND CAPITAL

CHAPTER 10

···

SPORT, GLOBALIZATION, AND GLOCALIZATION

···

ADAM S. BEISSEL AND DAVID L. ANDREWS

THE scale and scope of contemporary sport culture renders it an illustrative empirical window into the spatially-temporally interdependent conditions and processes of globalization. Twenty-first-century life is characterized by a condition of seemingly ever-increasing and intensifying levels of global interdependency and interconnectivity. Under such circumstances, the major institutions shaping everyday lives—including the focus of this chapter, the elite/professional sport assemblage—act as sites of complex interaction between disparately located peoples, products, spectacles, organizations, governments, and nation-states. When combined with its global popularity, the material, symbolic, and affective reach of sport's transnational architecture is responsible for its being arguably the "most universal aspect of popular culture" (Miller, Lawrence, McKay, & Rowe, 2001, p. 1).

Just in terms of sport's global institutionalization, membership in the United Nations (193 member states) is less than that of FIFA (211 member national federations) or the Olympic Movement (206 national Olympic committee members). Furthermore, in a historical sense, the emergence and global diffusion of sport has long been interwoven with the broader flows of people, technology, media, finance, and ideologies associated with the process of globalization (Appadurai, 1990). The development of national bodies and international sport organizations, the worldwide standardization of rules, the growth of competition between national teams, and the establishment of global competitions such as the modern Olympic Games and FIFA World Cup tournament, are all indicative of the early impacts of sport's globalization. In more recent times, the emergence of a hypercommodified, highly commercialized, and heavily corporatized global sport system is simultaneously a core element of and a vehicle for the quest for market expansion and rationalization so indicative of early 21st-century capitalism's inveterate global actuality.

The globalization of the sport assemblage has been realized through the establishment of multidirectional transnational flows and networks of popular sport practices, products, spectacles, and bodies, which combine to advance sport as an important site of transnational commodity production, cultural consumption, and capital accumulation, some, but not all, of which transcend the national boundaries around which much of the modern sport system is materially structured (Rowe, 2003). Indeed, despite being what could be considered a heightened global age of sport, generative tensions and contradictions—disjunctures and discontinuities, in Appadurai's (1990) terms—unequivocally exist between the global and local forces framing the contemporary sport system. Hence, this chapter represents another attempt to map the "known dimensions" and complexities of the globalization of sport (Maguire, 2015) through recourse to theories, issues, expressions pertaining to glocalization and the sporting glocal: specifically, as they are manifest within the prevailing transnational model of commercialized, corporatized, spectacularized, and celebritized elite/professional sport, which we theorize as *uber-sport* (Andrews, 2019).

ISSUES

In order to grasp sport's complex relation to the processes of contemporaneous globalization, it is first important to position precisely how we are using this pervasive, yet oftentimes vaguely applied term. Our usage of globalization invokes the widening, deepening, and speeding up of worldwide interconnectedness wrought largely by a transforming mode of capitalist production, realized by new technological capacities, and generating an ever-changing array of productive outputs. Within this late capitalist global regime, there has been a palpable intensification of the ways in which "goods, capital, people, knowledge, images, crime, pollutants, drugs, fashions, and beliefs all readily flow across territorial boundaries" (McGrew, 1992, p. 65). As a result, the temporal and spatial barriers that once separated disparate peoples and their cultures have largely—if never wholly—dissipated, leading to new connections, dependencies, and inter/intrarelationships (Harvey, 1989). In this sense, globalization is understood as an empirical condition of the contemporary world characterized by Tomlinson's (1999, p. 2) complex connectivity, or "the rapidly developing and ever-densening networks of global interconnections and interdependencies that characterize modern life." Differently put, globalization has meant that no country, region, city, or individual is completely isolated from the broader processes, practices, and products of the global late capitalist economy.

Over the past half-century, the speed and reach at which intangibles (ideas and information) and tangibles (products and people) circulate the globe has both increased and expanded (Held, McGrew, Goldblatt, & Perraton, 1999) and shows every indication of continuing to do so. As a result, cultures and people that were once so detached are now ever more connected and dependent upon each other, especially through the realms of culture, politics, economics, and technology. In concert with the more questionable widespread entrenchment of (free) market capitalism, contemporary forms of globalization have produced some potentially positive outcomes. These include the newfound ease in global communication for many of the global population, the possibility of breaking down entrenched cultural barriers through increased cultural interchange, and the increased exposure and thus acknowledgment of some of the biggest challenges facing contemporary society (such as the global climate change, financial and economic stability, human rights, international diplomacy, and conflict resolution). Furthermore, the globalization of the concept of civil society, and of global civil society as a system alongside government and business, has opened up possibilities for this "sphere of ideas, values, organizations, networks, and individuals located between the institutional complexes of family, market, and state, and beyond the confines of national societies, polities, and economies" (Anheier, Glasius, & Kaldor, 2001, p. 17). Thus, it should not be overlooked that contemporary globalization intensifies inter- dependent global networks, flows, relations, and present possibilities for making the world *a better place.*

Before we are accused of globalization romanticism, the self-same intensification of global networks and flows and interdependencies/-relationships previously described also presents the possibility of negative outcomes stemming from irresponsible, reckless, and self-interested decisions made without concern for global others. In a more dis- turbing and sobering aspect of globalization, events occurring in one area of the globe can cause worsening environmental, economic, political, and/or social conditions elsewhere, generating intervention(s) or lack thereof during environmental or natural disasters, ec- onomic crisis, political strife, or war and terrorism. In many cases, the problems arising from the international relations of countries are due to established hierarchies of power, entrenched cultural differences, and disparate ideological values. These developments have resulted in worldwide social movements against globalization and the unfettered encroach- ment of (free) market capitalism.

Such antiglobalization/anticorporate capitalist movements oppose the growing influ- ence and unregulated power of multinational corporations, as exercised through trade agreements and deregulated financial markets, and the threats posed to national legislative authority, sovereignty, and multilateralism. At the same time, the discontent with global capitalism and its effects—mainly in the widening income inequality, the breakdown of the welfare state, and the cultural backlash of rising intolerance and xenophobia—have been attributed to the rise of right-wing populism and ethnic nationalism (Bajo-Rubio & Yan, 2019). The Brexit vote in the United Kingdom, the rise of an aggressive nationalism in Europe and around the world, and, of course, the electoral victory of Donald Trump in 2016, can all be understood as expressions of a backlash against globalization. Equally, the global COVID-19 pandemic (the rapid spread of which was facilitated by the complex interconnectedness of the global population) stimulated elements of right-wing populist discourse that unleashed a tsunami of hatred and xenophobia, nationalist absolutism, and antiscience rhetoric. Simultaneously, the pandemic brought the shortcomings of the global capitalist political-economic system into stark relief (specifically those related to the eco- nomic and health policy inadequacies of governmental responses—particularly those of the U.S. government—aimed at protecting the welfare of its citizen constituents). In these ways, rather than a panacea for universal good, globalization is shown to exacerbate societal flaws and create *worsening conditions* for people around the world.

The global prevalence of the corporate sport model (framed by the conjoined processes of commercialization, corporatization, spectacularization, and celebritization) means that sport is an instructive site for examining the processes and effects of globalization. As with other expressions of the global popular (i.e., music, television, film, social media), it is easy to position the cultural impacts or effects of globalization on the contemporary sport system in binary terms. Indeed, there have been numerous attempts to theorize and un- derstand the cultural impacts or effects of globalization on contemporary sport culture, most of which key on the following relations: global-local, universal-particular, sameness- difference, homogeneous-heterogeneous (Giulianotti & Robertson, 2013). From one op- position of these binaries, sport does assert itself as a powerful agent of global cultural standardization. According to this view, globalization is synonymous with homogenization, where everywhere becomes subject to the same *big-box* corporate strategizing, giving rise to a low-level global monoculture—as Buell (1994, p. 1) puts it, a gigantic Walmart with no exit. The effect of globalization, therefore, is the flattening out of cultural difference, leading to global sameness, uniformity, the generic, and homogeneity and resulting in a culture of "nothingness" triumphing over the different, variable, particular, heterogeneous, and "somethingness" (Ritzer, 2004a).

The prevalence of the corporate sport model has resulted in a degree of sporting homogeneity—tantamount to a low-level sporting monoculture—as realized in the relative uniformity of local iterations of the global sport model (manifest in the seemingly routinized instantiation of sport structures, spectacles, spaces, practices, and bodies). Within the sporting context, such globalization is often equated with a form of cultural Americanization (also sometimes referred to as McDonaldization, Coca-Colonization, and/or Disneyfication), wherein cultural products, processes, and lifestyles emanating from some near-mythical American core have come to gain a global presence and influence. Proponents of this view contend that American corporations (i.e., Coca-Cola, McDonald's, Nike, Microsoft, Google, Amazon)—and American culture more generally—are forces of cultural imperialism (Tomlinson, 1999), responsible for imposing highly specific values, tastes, and preferences upon other societies.

Early contributions to the globalization of sport debate by Maguire (1990), advocated a qualified understanding of Americanization as a form of cultural imperialism, as a way of understanding American football's incursion into and resonance within the British sport landscape. According to this line of thought, Americanization was a unidirectional flow of "American cultural forms, products, and meanings . . . imposed on other cultures at the expense of the domestic culture" (Donnelly, 1996, p. 242). The Americanization process entails not only the penetration of U.S. sport practices around the world but also the global diffusion of the ways in which America structures, presents, and delivers sport spectacles and products and "has become the international benchmark for corporate sport" (p. 246). The influence of the American-originated corporatized sport model means that the assemblage of actors (corporations, networks, sponsors, teams, athletes) may change, but the product (media-entertainment spectacle) and purpose (audience and profit maximization) remain unerringly similar around the world.

Although the Americanization and cultural imperialist thesis suggests a resigned submission to a new global corporate monoculture, globalization is anything but a unidirectional and unidimensional phenomenon. Rather than flattening local diversity, many have argued that globalization processes have, in fact, been responsible for the intensification of local difference (Rowe, 2003). According to this viewpoint, local difference has intensified due to nations, cultures, and peoples opposing and rejecting the idea of global uniformity, holding dear to the particularities of their own local cultures. Globalization can therefore be something that "pluralizes the world by recognizing the value of cultural niches and local abilities" (Waters, 1995, p. 136). Globalization's effects on local identities, values, and cultures is not to diminish their particularity; quite the contrary, according to this heterogeneity thesis, local differences have become ever more important within the condition of late capitalist globalization. This is clearly illustrated in the realm of sport, which, unlike other institutions, derives much of its popular resonance and attachments from its ability to appeal to place-bound locality and difference. Sport's oftentimes ingrained attachment to "localized, nationally inflected forms of identity" (Rowe, 2003, pp. 291–292) thus makes it antithetical to the standardizing effects of globalization touted by global homogeniza-tion advocates. The cultural relevance and commercial success of the global sport system is dependent on consumers' affiliations with a particular place-bound identity and/or ex-perience, albeit as they are associated with a town, city, region, or nation. Because of its affective nature, sport plays a considerable role in advancing these forms of collective dif-ferentiation: fans often identifying with place-based teams that reflect a specific locale and its unique cultural signifiers. Sport's entire organizational framework valorizes identity-based competition and attachment to the production of placed-based difference, and thus *repudiates* the enveloping embrace of global homogeneity/standardization within the world system of sport (Rowe, 2003).

Despite advancing important analytical insights, both the homogenization and heterogenization understandings of sporting globalization are responsible for falsely po-larizing "globalization and localization in a manner that implicitly privileges, perhaps even romanticizes, the local" (Andrews & Ritzer, 2007, p. 136). For that matter, from even the most cursory observation it is clear that to singularly categorize any corporate sport structures, processes, and/or outcomes as *either* local *or* global in nature is empirically de-ficient. As Andrews and Ritzer have argued, the global and the local cannot be viewed as in any way discrete or autonomous entities; rather they are multidirectional and mutu-ally reinforcing elements in the globalization process. Indeed, rather than positioning the global and the local as opposites, the contemporary sport landscape provides an opportu-nity for understanding the constitutive interdependence and interrelationship linking the (sporting) global and the (sporting) local (Andrews & Grainger, 2007).

APPROACHES

Leading approaches toward a theoretically based understanding of the relationship between sport and globalization moved the debate beyond the rather crude binary oppositions be-tween "the local" and "the global" to acknowledge the multidirectional and multicausal con-stitutive interrelationships and interdependences of global-local relations (cf. Giulianotti, 1999, 2005; Maguire, 1999, 2005; Miller et al., 2001; Smart, 2007; Van Bottenburg, 2001). Interestingly, Giulianotti's work particularly drew heavily on Robertson's (1992, 1994, 1995, 1997, 2003, 2006, 2012, 2014) pioneering work on the concept of *glocalization*. Instead of positioning the global and local as opposites on the globalization continuum, Robertson's (1992) glocalization theory refers to the global and the local as "complementary and in-terpenetrative," entailing the particularization of universalism and the universalization of particularization (Robertson, 1995, p. 40). According to Robertson (1995), globalization is characterized by a mutually dependent and interpenetrative relationship between change and continuity, sameness and difference, and universality and particularity. In this sense, "the global" does not exist "out there" as somehow separate and distinct from the local. Rather, the global is at once constituted by and constitutive of the local (and vice versa).

According to Robertson's (2013) approach to centering the glocal, globalization does not produce uniformity but rather leads to the fragmentation of existence into glocal realities. Addressing the problematic of global social integration, Giulianotti and Robertson (2007c, 2009, 2012a) suggest that glocalization inevitably involves the twin possibilities and trends of "convergence" and "divergence" by advancing the concept of the "duality of glocality." In this way, there is "an inherent duality in the theory of glocalization, pointing to both sameness and difference, in the continuous interplay of local-global processes" (Giulianotti, 2016, p. 129). At its core, Robertson's interpretation looks upon "globalization as glocalization," in which the two are analytically conflated: glocalization is subsumed under Robertson's conception of globalization (Roudometof, 2016). Or, even more simply, as Ritzer (2007) points out, Robertson's accumulated understanding is that glocalization *is* globalization.

In the context of sport, the notion of glocalization implies that sporting locals exist, but operate in relation to the structures and logics of the global. Through their collaborative work, Giulianotti and Robertson (2004, 2005, 2007a, 2007b, 2007c, 2009, 2012a, 2012b) have used the theory of glocalization to explore the historical, cultural, economic, political, and social dimensions of the complex interrelationships linking globalization and football. As they observe, global sport forms constitute an important site through which "the *universalization of particularism* may take hold, as local or national identities have intensified, as people from different cities and nations commingle and come into routine contact with one another" (Giulianotti & Robertson, 2012a, p. 438, italics added). For example, globally televised sport spectacles—particularly international sport mega-events such as the Olympic Games and World Cup finals in football—provide a global setting for localized communities to express and perform their sense of national identity and belonging in front of international television audiences. In sport, the *particularization of universalism* is also evident, as illustrated in the formal integration of national and regional sport associations into international sport organizations (i.e., IOC, FIFA, World Rugby), the standardization of policies governing sporting practices (i.e., FIFA's Laws of the Game, International Cricket Council rules, antidoping policies), and the organizing of sports into a calendar of world sport events (i.e., the Olympic Games, FIFA Men's and Women's World Cup).

Drawing on Robertson (1995), Andrews and Grainger (2007) developed two understandings of glocalization operating within contemporary sport culture. The first, *organic sporting glocalization*, refers to the process whereby globally significant sport forms, practices, and spectacles are experienced and incorporated into local, regional, and national sporting cultures. In the case of sporting practices, the sport of basketball represents the locally unique aspects of broader American culture—and more specifically the social, cultural, sporting histories of the United States—but has emerged as a globally prominent sport practice that has been glocalized within disparate locations around the world. For example, basketball's style of play in Europe (e.g., slower paced, tactical, team-oriented) differs noticeably from that in the United States (e.g., fast paced, emotional, individualist) given the cultural contexts in which this sporting practice is located.

Whereas organic sporting glocalization is a seemingly authentic and natural process, *strategic sporting glocalization* involves the cultural and commercial forces of transnational capitalism (Andrews & Grainger, 2007). This is a twofold process in which commercially driven sports organizations, league conglomerates, and corporate multinationals differentiate global products and experiences to local markets, rendering a global economy of sporting locals (interiorized glocal strategizing) and local market demands and consumers for global differentiated sport products and experiences, which are then supplied by global sport capital (exteriorized glocal strategizing). Further, considering our earlier example of basketball as glocal sport practice, we can see how the NBA and its members have pursued a commercial growth strategy determined to "capture the Chinese market" by creating differentiated basketball products and viewing experiences, while at the same time engaging a throng of young people in Shanghai as they express their cosmopolitan cultural identity by purchasing a LeBron James jersey featuring his name in Chinese characters. Thus, we can see how, within the context of sport, the glocal represents a continuum that spans seemingly polarized forces, or more precisely, "the interpenetration of the global and the local, resulting in unique outcomes in different geographic areas" (Andrews & Ritzer, 2007, p. 135). Indeed, theorizations of sporting glocalization have provided important frameworks for examining the cultural, economic, and political significance of sport within various national settings (cf. Andersson & Hognestad, 2019; Cho, 2009; Cho, Leary, & Jackson, 2012; Falcous & Maguire, 2006; Falcous & Silk, 2006; Giulianotti & Robertson, 2007a, 2012a, 2012b; Horton, 2011; Khondker & Robertson, 2018; Kobayashi, 2012; Lee, Jackson, & Lee, 2007; Luo, Dai, & Huang, 2015; Tzu-Hsuan, 2012; Weedon, 2012).

Advancing the debate—specifically in response to the glocalization orthodoxy that cultural forms and practices operate in constant tension between the global and the local—Ritzer (2004a, 2004b, 2006) challenges the very possibility that a truly local exists given that virtually no "areas and phenomena throughout the world are unaffected by globalization" (Ritzer, 2004a, p. xiii). Rather than viewing the core tension as existing between the global and the local, Ritzer's contention is that everything we think of as *local* has, unavoidably, been so affected by the *global* that it has become, to all intents and purposes, *glocal* (pp. xiii, xi). In Ritzer's interpretation, glocalization is not a combination of convergence and divergence, but rather a process of heterogenization and divergence, rendering unique outcomes in different geographic areas. Ritzer's (2006, p. 338) conceptual opposite of glocalization is "grobalization," which he defines as the "imperialistic ambitions of nations, corporations, organizations, and the like and their desire, indeed need, to impose themselves on various geographic areas." The grobalization process—evident in the commercial aspects of culture, such as the sale of food and tourist products—aims to overwhelm the local, with the ultimate goal of capital accumulation through unilateral homogenization. Thus, the primary interrelationship shaping contemporary globalizing societies is a binary relationship between the grobal-glocal (as opposed to the global-local) and processes of grobalization-glocalization (versus those of globalization-localization).

Building on Ritzer's (2006) previous work, Andrews and Ritzer (2007) explore grobal-glocal relations in the context of late capitalist sport. In so doing, they provide a counterpoint to the analyses of contemporary sport culture that either falsely polarized the global and the local or, alternatively, relied on a somewhat formulaic understanding of the glocal. Instead, they examine how corporate sport organizations, leagues, and events are simultaneously *grobal* in their scale (through their very corporate structure) and scope (constantly looking to extend market geographies through team and/or broadcast expansion) and *glocal* in their "commercial strategizing for stimulating popular (consumer) consciousness and behaviour at the glocal level" (Andrews & Ritzer, 2007, p. 141). In explicating sport's grobal-glocal relations, they identify four overlapping empirical variants, thereby demonstrating the interpenetrative relationship between the grobal and glocal: (1) the global diffusion of sport practices and formation of the global sport system (indigenous incorporation); (2) the emergence of highly regulated and structured international sport organizations, national governing bodies, and league (corporate reconstitution); (3) the staging and performance of signature global sport events (universal differentiation); and (4) the mobilization of sport practices and symbols as rejections of the local (dichotomous agency). In these ways,

Andrews and Ritzer illustrate the interpenetrative complexities of grobalization and glocalization responsible for the diverse instantiation of grobal-glocal sport.

Two other alternatives to the glocalization approach have also gained traction in recent years. First, the theory of *cosmopolitanism* has emerged as a substantial and insightful commentary on the globalization debate. Although there is not a uniform interpretation of cosmopolitanism in the literature, much of the work draws on Ulrich Beck's (2006) "cosmopolitanisation theory" as a process of internal globalization or globalization within the borders of national societies. Beck (2010, pp. 68–69) defines cosmopolitanism as

> the erosion of clear boundaries separating the markets, states, civilizations, cultures and not least the lifeworlds of different peoples and religions, as well as the resulting worldwide situation of an involuntary confrontation with alien others. The boundaries have of course not disappeared but they have become blurred and porous, letting through streams of information, capital and risk, and even people, though to a lesser extent (tourists can pass, migrants cannot).

In this sense, cities and nations are now inhabited by nationally diverse social groups, many of whom express their cultural identities through what the cultural mainstream considers to be *externally* derived languages, dress, cuisine, food, and music. For Beck, cosmopolitanism can be both a process (cosmopolitanization) and an outcome (the creation of cosmopolitan society). The former is akin to glocalization, whereby glocalization gradually transforms into cosmopolitanization, whereas the latter implies the transformation of a society into a cosmopolitan one that embodies specific value orientations and commitments. Beck further offers the notion of "banal cosmopolitanism" as a means of describing the formation of cosmopolitan cultures and identities that have been incorporated into the cultural mainstream (effectively shorn of any real sense of external provenance) and so rendered as mundane features of everyday life.

With regard to sport, the notion of cosmopolitanism has occasionally informed understandings of sport's relation to the globalization process. Following Beck, Giulianotti and Robertson (2012b, 2013) used "banal cosmopolitanism" to describe how global sport has become an increasingly normalized feature of contemporary *local* life. Followers of elite/professional sport are routinely familiar with sports teams that consist of international athletes hailing from all reaches of the globe (e.g., 14 countries represented in 2020 Barcelona FC's first team, 30% of Major League Baseball players born outside the United States); the normative occurrence of international sport competitions as a regular features in domestic sport media (e.g., Formula 1 on France's Canal+ , English Premier League on the U.S. NBC Sports Network, NBA on China's CCTV-5); and the everyday consumption and display of global sports products and brands (e.g., New Zealand All Blacks jerseys, New York Yankees hats, Nike Air Jordan sneakers). Giulianotti and Robertson (2013, p. 50, italics in original) go on to discuss the sport's *thick* and *thin* varieties of cosmopolitanism in sport:

> [T]hick cosmopolitanism features a full openness toward other cultures, to the extent that individuals and social groups may be willingly and radically transformed through encounters with difference. *Thin cosmopolitanism* features a more pragmatic and utilitarian relationship to other cultures, whereby aspects of the latter are instrumentally utilized in order to sustain or to enhance the host culture.

In this sense, thin sporting cosmopolitanism occurs when features of global sport are used to achieve improved outcomes in local contexts (think of international playing styles adopted by local sports teams), whereas thick sporting cosmopolitanism is a cultural curiosity of local sport followers toward learning new global sport practices and/or consuming sport products (think of New York supporters of London's Chelsea Football Club). Sport scholars have drawn on Beck's theory of cosmopolitanism to explore such topics as the globalization of the modern Olympic Games (Patsantaras, 2015); international football fans' experiences and desires to attend internationally significant sport mega-events (Millward, 2011); how competing national discourses are articulated by and through the media's reporting of football (Skey, 2015; and how Shanghai became one of Asia's major markets for sport consumerism (Lozada, 2006) and sport-based events (Yu, Xue, & Newman, 2018. Collectively, these works have complicated the binary approach of global-local relations and examined cosmopolitan processes and outcomes in their respective locations.

A more recent approach to theorizing globalization has introduced *lobalization* to the globalization lexicon. As a model for explaining how glocalization can occur without the involvement of transnational or multinational corporations, lobalization, sometimes framed as logalization (Lyu & McCarty, 2015), speaks to the direction of global-local interactions that are not global-to-local in a top-down manner but rather local-to-global in a bottom-up fashion. As such, the *lobal* (Chew, 2010) is used to signify the cultural dynamic in which "locally produced and manufactured products are packaged and distributed in a locality under the guise of prestigious imported products . . . a revenge of the local to the global" (Roudometof, 2016, p. 113). Chew (2010) considers the lobal in the Chinese context, by exploring how counterfeit fashion products (e.g., fakes, pass-offs, inspired products) have emerged as commercially successful products displacing global products and properties. Although lobal products are manufactured under highly "McDonaldized" (Ritzer, 2004b) global manufacturing regimes (e.g., mass production, standardization, rationalization, bureaucratization), they are "intentionally inauthentic global products that cater to uninformed local customers, not inauthentic local products that cater to uninformed global consumers" (Chew, 2010, p. 568). In this sense, lobalization illuminates the impact of newly gained production capabilities and market penetration of global capital in local contexts, while at the same time, local capital and citizens generate wealth and status through the creative appropriation of global cultural symbols.

Although there has been little application of lobalization in the sport globalization literature, a useful way of thinking through this approach in the context of sport can be seen in considering the emergent counterfeit sportswear and apparel manufacturing industry that has developed, most particularly in East Asia. Because of their legally questionable status, it is difficult to obtain actual figures on the sales volume and market share of fake and pass-off sportswear and apparel products. However, the local production and consumption of pass-off replica jerseys and merchandise across many sports has emerged as a serious concern for major global sportswear manufacturers such as Nike, Adidas, Puma, and Under Armour (Decker & Lopez, 2019). This includes local production of counterfeit jerseys of major sports franchises (e.g., Manchester United, New York Yankees, Los Angeles Lakers) that are passed off as officially licensed products imported from overseas markets. The immediate positive implications of sportswear lobalization has been for locally produced products to displace global original brands in the domestic context, potentially compromising global market expansion and capital accumulation by the major global sportswear manufacturers. By the same token, lobalization's deception of local consumers is a barrier to the development of local sportswear and apparel industries, raising questions about whether lobalization practices serve to stifle the value of the more "authentically" local in local production economies. It is also important to consider how lobal sports products threaten to disrupt the uneven and asymmetrical power relations of the wider grobal sportswear industry as foreign consumers purchase lobal sports products. Thus, in the case of sportswear manufacturing, particularly related to manufacturing and marketing of counterfeit and "fake" jerseys, there is a multidirectional interrelationship between lobal-grobal and lobalization-grobalization processes.

Although these two recent contributions to the globalization of sport debate are noteworthy, the dominant perspective remains that of glocalization. Despite the recognition of global-local relations and/or theorizations of sporting glocalization becoming an important framework for examining the hybridity of contemporary global sport, substantial variations and differences exist within glocal sport practices, spaces, and bodies. Identifying and acknowledging the sporting glocal does not explain the mechanisms and reasons for why these differences occur and the complicated and multiple ways in which glocalized sport is experienced in different localities around the globe. Thus, complicating the global-local (and grobal-glocal) approach(es) requires a new conceptual framework for explicating and analyzing precisely how sport is experienced in multiple global locals; how it offers differentiated sporting relations, identities, and expressions of locality/globality; and how various local factors inform the broader contemporary sport formations.

DEBATES

One way of thinking through the reasons behind the continuities and discontinuities of glocal sporting difference is with what Andrews (2019) has conceptualized as *uber-sport*. Within the contemporary global sport context, an amalgam of corporate capitalism, consumer culture, neoliberalism, and nationalism frames the constitution and experience of professional sport as a mass entertainment product. If sport in its most generic sense refers to the structure and practice of physically based contests between individuals or collectives, "uber-sport" refers to the currently idealized model of corporatized-commercialized-spectacularized-celebritized sport culture, the hegemonic blueprint for the structure, delivery, and diversified consumptive experience of elite/professional sport. The uber-sport assemblage is a more sophisticated framework for understanding and explaining the varieties of sporting glocals with global locality built into its foundational understandings.

"Uber-sport" is plainly not a term used by either producers or consumers of sports (as they are generally referred to in the American vernacular), even though there is widespread recognition of many of the constituent processes and elements underpinning uber-sport and responsible for its (re)configuration of "professional sports as primarily entertainment businesses" (Szymanski, 2010, p. xii). Of course, uber-sport is nothing more than what Braudel (1982, p. 459) referred to as an explanatory device, involving the strategic "carving up" and representation of reality as a means of privileging a discrete empirical focus (in this case, the complex system of highly rationalized and standardized high-profile, elite, and/or professional team and individual physically based contests) for the purpose of sociohistoric exegesis. The concept of uber-sport thus encompasses the concerted reformation of elite/professional-level physically based contests by the late capitalist processes of replicative *corporatization* (institutional and management reorganization designed to realize profit-driven structures and logics); expansive *commercialization* (sport brand diversification and non-sport-brand promotion across multiple sectors); creative *spectacularization* (entertainment-focused delivery of popular sport spectacles, realized through a combination of structural reformation and cross-platform mass mediation); and *celebritization* (sporting contests constructed around, and a site for the embellishment of, specific public personas) (Andrews, 2019). Uber-sport thus describes a highly rationalized, diversified, yet integrated popular sport phenomenon designed to generate mass audiences/markets, and thereby popularity/profits, across an array of culturally and economically multiplying streams (products, bodies, services, and spaces).

The material and representational instantiation of uber-sport has become a normalized and normalizing agent in the lived experience of spectators, viewers, and consumers alike. The uber-sport form and function transpired first within the United States and is evident across major sport organizations, leagues, and events. Encumbered by this American patina, glocally manifest expressions of uber-sport are perceived, oftentimes pejoratively, as symptomatic of the latest phase in the Americanization of local sport cultures. However, its ubiquity is not restricted to sport within the United States. Uber-sport is also a transnational phenomenon: the spread of culturally oriented late capitalism propelling the global diffusion of the uber-sport model (Andrews & Ritzer, 2007) across national (i.e., Australian National Rugby League, English Premier League, and Indian Premier League) and transnational (i.e., the IOC, FIFA, World Rugby) sport organizations. Through the global circulation, exchange, and surveillance of uber-sport products, information, and expertise, uber-sport has been established as the sport industry standard around the world. While the global diffusion of the uber-sport model brings with it a perceived degree of American-derived homogenization—specifically in terms of institutional objectives and infrastructure—it is far from a universal monolith. In this manner, uber-sport has emerged as a truly transnational phenomenon, existing simultaneously in multiple settings around the globe, yet operating in each of these within the language of the sporting glocal. Uber-sport institutions consciously mobilize the particularities of the glocal sport marketplace (be they metropolitan, regional, or national scales) in looking to engage and animate consumer consciousness and behavior at the glocal level. Although not a word used in common parlance, "uber-sport" thus represents a condition of formulated ubiety: a state of being or existence derived from location in a given time or space, a "whereness." Hence, uber-sport is both grobal and glocal, ubiquitous and ubietous.

The prevalence of the uber-sport form and function is evident across major assemblage relations through glocal sport *bodies, events, spaces, and practices.* Perhaps nowhere is the uber-sport assemblage more evident in the contemporary global sport culture than in the realm of association football. More specifically, the Premier League—the most commercially lucrative and widely viewed sporting league conglomerate—proves a rich empirical site for understanding the globalization process (Ludvigsen, 2020). The Premier League is carried by 80 broadcasters in 212 territories, with a cumulative audience for live programming reaching 1.35 billion (Carp, 2019). The Premier League's meaning and function is dependent on those sub- and supra-, internal and external, assemblage relations which combine to inform its assemblage being and becoming. Thus, we turn to the Premier League as an "object of study" (Saussure, 1959) that renders visible the contextual contingency of contemporary sport formations.

In terms of the ubiety of *glocal sport bodies*, the Premier League's player/athlete assemblage—an important component of the broader uber-sport assemblage—is a product of affective relations between numerous sub- and supra-assemblages, which enable and/or constrain embodied performance and identity. DeLanda (2016) speaks to this scale in relation to the human-rifle-radio assemblage of the modern soldier, whereas Thorpe (2017) highlights the action sporting body–equipment assemblage. Both of these are comparable to the human-boot-ball assemblage of the modern soccer player. In the 1950s, heavy leather boots, soccer balls, cumbersome shin guards, and sweat-retaining cotton shirts (each of them elements of soccer's technological subassemblage), compounded by climate-vulnerable and variable playing surfaces (an aspect of the environmental assemblage), combined to materially affect the physical execution of the game. Compare that scenario with the contemporary professional Premier League footballer, whose ready access to technologically advanced and lightweight boots, soccer balls, shin guards, sweat-removing fabric shirts, more durable and consistent hybrid grass playing surfaces, and scientifically based performance analysis and enhancements combine to produce very different physical and sporting outcomes.

The capacity, performance, and identity of the athlete/player assemblage is also significantly informed by interaction with numerous supra-assemblages, such as coaching, management, biomedicine, psychology, pharmaceuticals, nutrition, corporations, marketing, and media. Crucially, the economic realities and hierarchies of a highly commercialized and corporatized enterprise that pursues profit maximization means these bodies are constantly and at once regulated and disciplined by the external thrusts and impetuses of capital accumulation that perpetuate capital-labor relations in ways that reduce bodies to quantifiable and measurable data points for evaluative analysis. A full international player, like Manchester United's Marcus Rashford, might be expected to play in excess of 55 matches for both club and country in a given year, roughly one game every six days for an entire calendar year. His availability and match fitness will be determined by a series of reducible data points whereby sport scientists determine his chronic and acute training ratio, placing him in various categories related to the perceived risk of future injury. The manager, assuming they subscribe to modern sport scientist orthodoxy, will make lineup considerations based on these data in conjunction with myriad other tangible and intangible factors (opponent, tactics, ability, team dynamics, leadership). Consequently, the Premier League's athlete/player as assemblage is always subject to either internally or externally derived transformation(s): the athlete/player, and the contest/game/event/spectacle to which they contribute, is always in a state of becoming.

With regard to the *glocal sport event*, the Premier League uber-sport serves as an event assemblage through the simultaneous consumerist engagement as a mass-spectated and mass-mediated entertainment spectacle. Although routinely engaged as if it possessed some singular, stable, and essential capacities transcending temporal and spatial differences, the "performance event" (individual game/match/contest) (Martin, 1997, p. 188) is a nonrepeatable and momentary confederation of multiscaled and multisited assemblages (including athletes/players, teams, coaches, medical staff, apparel and footwear technologies, officials, spectators, sponsors, security personnel, stadia, cities, leagues, media broadcast operatives and viewers, to name but a few). Importantly, each of the variously scaled and sited components of the Premier League's *uber-sport* event assemblage possesses its own generative relation, with external assemblages (i.e., the economy, media, fashion, technology, nation, religion, military, and politics, among others) rendering its consumption, as with any assemblage, always open to the potential for externally derived transformative change. As a *mass-spectated entertainment spectacle* for those in physical attendance and viewing broadcasts, the uber-sport performance event is never an unfiltered "interface between performers and public" (Martin, 1997, p. 188). Layers of pregame media positioning, in-game narrativization, and postgame rumination, generated by traditional and social media, mean that any Premier League event is unavoidably subject to preemptive, instantaneous, and retroactive mediated becomings: it is a complex outgrowth of the productive convergence between uber-sport and various media assemblages operating within a given cultural context.

For those consuming/spectating beyond the stadium, consuming the Premier League uber-sport as *a mass mediated entertainment spectacle*, glocalized factors (media, economics, culture, politics) inform the way the performance event is experienced. During a match between the two most popular clubs, Manchester United and Liverpool FC, fans of these clubs all around the globe—from Shanghai to Moscow, New York to Johannesburg—congregate in their official local supporters clubs. Although the global ubiquity of such supporters clubs around the world suggests the ever-growing encroachment of global homogeneity, members of these clubs experience belonging and identity in disparate ways based on their local histories. For example, Liverpool FC's working-class social identity is intertwined with the events, moments, and political histories of Liverpool as city, yet there are shared commonalities and solidarities around working-class identity around the world that appeal to and unite supporters in the formation of Liverpool as football club. Though a steelworker in Buenos Aires and a dock worker in Liverpool have never met, they perhaps both choose to support "working-class Liverpool FC" despite differentiated internalized meanings of what constitutes a "working-class" identity based on their own local histories (local politics, organized labor, industries). When Liverpool won their first ever Premier League title in 2020, local factors and meanings informed the mass-mediated consumption of the trophy-raising celebration for official club supporters groups around the globe, while at the same time, these glocalized experiences became constitutive of Liverpool's glocalized "working-class" assemblage.

The Premier League as uber-sport assemblage is neither an essential, necessary, nor transcendent category. Instead, as an interstitial phenomenon, its form, meanings, properties, and capacities exist and endure within the *glocal sport spaces* created by its multifarious generative elements and relations (both internal and external). As a multiscaled and multisited network of assemblage associations, uber-sport is thus materially and expressively sutured into a situated place, from which it derives its socio-material presence, identity, and influence (DeLanda, 2016; Jacobs, 2006, p. 3). Succinctly capturing this sentiment, Doidge (2018) referred to sport (specifically association football in England) as a "product of a wide range of social actors, relationships and interactions" where the sport's ubiquity and ontological variety mobilize "meanings and identifications" and inscribe them into the popular imagination, emotions, and experience. While always and at once a distinctly British cultural formation, the Premier League cannot be simply reduced or pinned down to one spatial location.

The Premier League incorporates its global spectators/viewers/customers consuming events from multiple spatial locations rendering both its global ubiquity yet simultaneously differentiated localness. The football grounds and stadia themselves are both physical spaces and hyperreal mediations that create a sense of both place and placelessness. Tottenham Hotspur's new U.K.£1 billion, 66,000-seat stadium on High Road in North London was recently opened as a multipurpose facility to serve as the home for not only the local football club but also the NFL's annual International Series. Even as a material place, Tottenham Stadium is an integrative fulcrum of uber-sport, from which ancillary elements are derived. To accommodate the demands of staging multiple games per week, Tottenham Stadium features the world's first retractable football pitch that can instantly transform the stadium from a Premier League ground to an NFL stadium in a matter of moments. While it would be easy to argue the stadium switches instantly from the local to the global, these two cannot be separated. The architecture and facility design required to accommodate the hosting of each sport mean that Tottenham Stadium's locality can never be separated from its globality. There is a multiplicity of connections between homogeneous and heterogeneous component elements, its local and global contextual relations, and the experiences of overseas viewers of the Tottenham Stadium mediated spectacle. Tottenham Stadium, as a space, is thereby constantly (re)made based on locally contextual understandings and meanings of NFL and Premier League stadia around the globe by fans who have, in many cases, never attended a game in North London. What the Spurs' stadium symbolizes to an American NFL football fan, as the physical embodiment of the NFL's globalizing impetus, is both similar to and different from, but equally important to, the construction of space and place for the Spurs supporter. In this state of perpetual becoming, Tottenham Stadium is not only "continually produced by the day-to-day interactions" of its materially and expressive assemblant parts but also through its "multiple relations of exteriority"—points of engagement and influence "with inveterately fluid economic, political, cultural, and technological assemblages" (Delanda, 2016, pp. 19, 73).

Finally, the Premier League uber-sport is prevalent across assemblage relations through *glocal sport practices*. Despite the possibility for ambiguity and incoherence derived from uber-sport's heterogeneous empirical formation, an expressive consistency exhibited across its "nested set of assemblages" frequently provides (codes) uber-sport with a tacit semblance of homogeneity that delineates, or territorializes, its boundaries (DeLanda, 2016, p. 4). That should not imply the erasure of glocalized differences within and between uber-sport assemblages, which are always susceptible to deterritorialization (de-coding of boundaries). For instance, widely referred to in universalizing terms as "the global game," association football is in fact a mobile technology (Ong, 2007): the global sport is an assemblage of nationally localized football, *futebol, fútbol, calcio, sokker, soka*, or soccer assemblages, each of which is potentially (there is no necessary relation) articulated by and becomes an expression of the situated cultural, historic, aesthetic, political, and/or economic regimes of the nation in question.

Although association football in England began as a marginal and unorganized sporting practice in the public school system, it quickly became part of the commercialized leisure industry in the 19th century (Collins, 2018). The English style of play was grounded in a physical, no-nonsense style owing to the factory workers and the industrial class, particularly those located in the northern and West Midland regions of the country. Over time, the league has evolved into a multicultural assemblage comprised of players from all over the world, who each bring their various localized football styles to the league. Thus, despite a rather standard globalization of sporting bodies through the use of highly quantifiable sport science techniques, the sporting practices of local differences can be expressed. All of these sporting practices and national playing styles crystalize Premier League's sport practice assemblage. It is at once locally bound by the dominance of localized British culture and constantly and at once informed and (re)created by the diversity of nationally constructed playing styles and practices of footballers from all over the globe. In this way, the Premier League's playing style possesses no stable empirical center; it is a decentered phenomenon with any perception of an essential or universal playing style being a complete illusion. Rather, the Premier League's playing style is a contingent relationality that is constantly reconstituted based on localized and ever-evolving national playing styles and sport practices around the world, embodied by the players that constitute it, and which work to reframe the playing style of the Premier League as contingent and multiple.

CONCLUSION

If ever there was a need, the events of 2020 have confirmed the contingent relationality of the uber-sport assemblage to even the most resolute skeptic. As an object of study, the Premier League—as a highly rationalized, commercialized, spectacularized, and celebritized model of contemporary sport organization—offers a glimpse into the uber-sport assemblage through the occurrences of two globally circulated phenomena: the COVID-19 pandemic and the Black Lives Matter movement protests/activism. With regard to the former, national culture-specific differences in COVID-19 infection provoked distinct sporting responses in the form of league/competition/event modifications, cancellations, and subsequent reopenings (partial or otherwise). However, the unprecedented disruptions to the structure, delivery, and experience of the uber-sport, precipitated by the pandemic, have "exposed the inner workings of sport as a machine that could be disabled by its own global interdependency" (Rowe, 2020, p. 3). Subject to decades of intensive economic, political, and psychic investments, the various manifestations of uber-sport have created a globally pervasive, if locally manifest and experienced, "consumption habit" (p. 4), whose abrupt cessation prompted widespread experiences of sporting withdrawal among large swaths (if not all) of the global populace.

For the Premier League, the impact of the COVID-19 pandemic on the world's most commodified and commercialized spectacle demonstrates the value of assemblage thinking for examining the grobal-glocal contingencies of uber-sport formations. The Premier League's decision to postpone the 2019–2020 season for 96 days, and ensuing discussions on its potential resumption, garnered enormous media and public discussion, seemingly lending credibility to the seriousness and ubiquitous nature of the pandemic (Rowe, 2020). Indeed, only after the postponement of Premier League (and other sport) fixtures did the seriousness of the pandemic become a material reality for many, as if the Premier League's acknowledgment of the severity of the virus was in some ways a legitimizing force in the wider public health discourse. Soon after, wide-reaching discussions took place among those in the "Football World" (Parnell, Widdop, Bond, & Wilson, 2020)—national and local government authorities, sporting league officials, multinational corporate sponsors, transnational media corporations, journalists and media pundits, team ownership conglomerates, managers and players, and club supporters—facilitating collective activity to hastily attend to the pandemic and address the economic and social impact of the discontinuation of the "global football product." The cooperation of global actants needed to resume the Premier League, after a more than three-month hiatus, exemplifies the globally diffuse economic, political, and social networks and consumption communities (Parnell, Widdop, Bond & Cockayne, 2021).

Yet these debates and decisions engaged/expressed more localized histories and experiences of the COVID-19 pandemic. Both nationwide and local case numbers and positivity rates became key indicators for how the global pandemic was materially and symbolically experienced within/across the United Kingdom. Within England, and specifically in the Northwest, where the pandemic was more widespread, the government's imposition of harsher lockdown policies generated a differentiated experience of COVID-19 than elsewhere. At the same time, the global pandemic's rising/declining rates around the globe, and mitigation strategies and public policies by various governments, informed the prism through which the pandemic was experienced, negotiated, and understood in disparate locations. In this way, the Premier League uber-sports assemblage could not merely be reduced to a single assemblant, but was rather constituted by/of myriad assemblage relations that are themselves contextually specific.

The other element that came to the fore of global consciousness in 2020 was the Black Lives Matter protests/activism, especially the resurgence of antiracist activism following the murder of George Floyd at the hands of the Minneapolis police in May 2020. Floyd's murder reignited the broader Black Lives Matter movement, and specifically the expressions of antiracist activism that had become commonplace, if somewhat neutered, within the U.S. uber-sport context from 2016 to 2020. In the United States, the movement sparked heartfelt pronouncements by prominent athletes but also strategic responses from major professional teams and sport organizations (most notably the WNBA, NBA, and NFL) and sporting footwear and apparel corporations (i.e., Adidas, Nike, and Under Armour) (Montez de Oca, Mason, & Ahn, 2020).

Unlike previous moments in recent sport-related activism, which registered around the world yet prompted negligible response, the protesting aftermath of Floyd's death sparked sport-centered antiracist activism in numerous disparate locales, perhaps pointing to the transnational nature of race-based violence, discrimination, and inequities (Hylton, 2020). This is clearly illustrated in the forms of antiracist protest which became a core element of the English Premier League spectacle in the Project Restart ending to the 2019–2020 season, much of which endured into the subsequent season. The Premier League's solidarity with Black Lives Matter could perhaps be seen as a new awakening to reconcile the League's problematic racial history through such proactive strategies as teams supporting players taking a knee at the start of games; replacing the names of players on shirts with "Black Lives Matter"; and the outspokenness of high-profile players like Raheem Sterling, the Manchester City forward, on the various forms of racism experienced by Black players (Hylton, 2020). The Premier League's strategies and solidarity signify how the Black Lives Matter movement is materially and expressively sutured and situated into place, from which it derives its socio-material presence, identity, and influence. Not limited to the U.S. context from which it emanates, the grobalized-glocalized, ubiquitous-ubietous Black Lives Matter movement engages localized histories and experiences of racism/race-based discrimination as a multiscaled and multisited network of assemblage associations. Thus, the function and meaning of issues of race and racism, and the antiracist and anti-oppressive efforts of the Black Lives Matter movement, are dependent on those sub- and supra-, internal and external, assemblage relations which combine to inform its being and becoming.

The impact of two globally circulated phenomena on the Premier League emphasizes the uber-sport assemblage linking the global and the local in contemporary sport. The uber-sport model offers an alternative to the globalization-localization/grobalization-glocalization approaches to understanding the ways in which contemporary sport culture has become contingently manifest. The rhizomatic contingent relationality of the uber-sport assemblage problematizes the perceived universality, stability, and coherence of these two global phenomena, and how they might not be singularly experienced—they are contextually specific assemblages comprising multiple empirical scales and points of engagement with fluid economic, political, cultural, and technological assemblages. In much the same way, the assemblages of two global phenomena articulate and enmesh with the uber-sport assemblage(s) as a demonstrable part of the "assemblages of assemblages" (Delanda, 2016, p. 14) that comprise the society in which they are situated. Hence, assemblage thinking in examining the grobal-glocal contingencies of uber-sport formations allows for a conceptual possibility for understanding how global-local, glocal-grobal, and ubiquitous-ubietous differentiations are constituted by and constitutive of contemporary globalization. Thus, we put forward uber-sport as a suggestive, and hopefully productive, framing for future research directions and debates within the sport, globalization, and glocalization literature.

ACKNOWLEDGMENTS

Parts of the debate section of this chapter abridge and rework discussions advanced in Andrews (2019). The material is used with the permission of the copyright holder.

REFERENCES

Andersson, T., & Hognestad, H. (2019). Glocal culture, sporting decline? Globalization and football in Scandinavia. *Sport in Society, 22*(4), 704–716.

Andrews, D. L. (2019). *Making sport great again: The uber-sport assemblage, neoliberalism, and the Trump conjuncture.* Cham, Switzerland: Palgrave Pivot.

Andrews, D. L., & Granger, A. D. (2007). Sport and globalization. In G. Ritzer (Ed.), *The Blackwell companion to globalization* (pp. 478–497). Oxford: Blackwell.

Andrews, D. L., & Ritzer, G. (2007). The grobal in the sporting glocal. *Global Networks, 7*(2), 135–153.

Anheier, H., Glasius, M., & Kaldor, M. (2001). Chapter 1: Introducing global civil society. In. H. Anheier, M. Glasius, & M. Kaldor, (Eds.), Global civil society, (pp. 3–22). Oxford: Oxford University Press.

Appadurai, A. (1990). Disjuncture and difference in the global cultural economy. *Theory, Culture & Society, 7*(2–3), 295–310.

Bajo-Rubio, O., & Yan, H. D. (2019). Globalization and populism. In T. Kwan & D. Yu (Eds.), *Contemporary issues in international political economy* (pp. 229–252). Singapore: Palgrave Macmillan.

Beck, U. (2006). *Cosmopolitan vision.* Cambridge, U.K.: Polity.

Beck, U. (2010). *A God of one's own: Religion's capacity for peace and potential for violence.* Oxford: Polity.

Braudel, F. (1982). *The wheels of commerce: Vol. 2. Civilization and capitalism, 15th–18th century.* New York: Harper & Row.

Buell, F. (1994). *National culture and the new global system.* Baltimore, MD: Johns Hopkins University Press, 1994.

Carp, S. (2019, July 17). Premier League global audience climbs to 3.2bn for 2018/19 season. *SportsProMedia.com.* https://www.sportspromedia.com/news/premier-league-audience-figures-global-2018-19-season.

Chew, M. (2010). Delineating the emergent global cultural dynamic of "lobalization": The case of pass-off menswear in China. *Journal of Media & Cultural Studies, 24*(2), 559–571.

Cho, Y. (2009). The glocalization of U.S. sports in South Korea. *Sociology of Sport Journal, 26*(2), 320–334.

Cho, Y., Leary, C., & Jackson, S. J. (2012). Glocalization and sports in Asia. *Sociology of Sport Journal, 29*(4), 421–432.

Collins, T. (2018). *How football began: A global history of how the world's football codes were born.* Oxford: Routledge.

Decker, S., & Lopez, I. (2019, December 4). Nike, 3M seek new weapon in battle against counterfeit goods. *Bloomberg.* https://www.bloomberg.com/news/articles/2019-12-04/nike-3m-seek-new-weapon-in-battle-to-thwart-counterfeit-goods.

DeLanda, M. (2016). *Assemblage theory.* Edinburgh: Edinburgh University Press.

Doidge, K. (2018, July 9). How the World Cup has renewed an emotional sense of belonging in England fans. The British Academy. https://www.thebritishacademy.ac.uk/blog/how-world-cup-2018-has-renewed-emotional-sense-belonging-england-fans/?utm_medium=social&utm_source=twitter&utm_campaign=worldcup2018&utm_content=other&utm_term=blog.

Donnelly, P. (1996). The local and the global: Globalization in the sociology of sport. *Journal of Sport and Social Issues, 20*(3), 239–257.

Falcous, M., & Maguire, J. (2006). Imagining "America": The NBA and local-global mediascapes. *International Review for the Sociology of Sport, 41*(1), 59–78.

Falcous, M., & Silk, M. (2006). Global regimes, local agendas: Sport, resistance and the mediation of dissent. *International Review for the Sociology of Sport, 41*(3–4), 317–338.

Giulianotti, R. (1999). *Football: A sociology of the global game.* Cambridge, U.K.: Polity Press.

Giulianotti, R. (2005). *Sport: A critical sociology.* Cambridge, U.K.: Polity.

Giulianotti, R. (2016). Glocalization and global sport. In R. Robertson & D. Buhari-Gulmez (Eds.), *Global culture: Consciousness and connectivity* (pp. 127–143). Oxford: Routledge.

Giulianotti, R., & Robertson, R. (2004). The globalization of football: A study in the glocalization of the "serious life." *British Journal of Sociology, 55*, 545–568.

Giulianotti, R., & Robertson, R. (2005). Glocalization, globalization and migration: The case of Scottish football supporters in North America. *International Sociology, 21*(2), 171–198.

Giulianotti, R., & Robertson, R. (2007a). *Globalization and sport.* Oxford: Wiley-Blackwell.

Giulianotti, R., & Robertson, R. (2007b). Forms of glocalization: Globalization and the migration strategies of Scottish football fans in North America. *Sociology, 41*(1), 133–152.

Giulianotti, R., & Robertson, R. (2007c). Recovering the social: Globalization, football and transnationalism. *Global Networks, 7*(2), 144–186.

Giulanotti, R., & Robertson, R. (2009). *Globalization and football.* London: Sage Publications.

Giulianotti, R., & Robertson, R. (2012a). Glocalization and sport in Asia: Diverse perspectives and future possibilities. *Sociology of Sport Journal, 29*(4), 433–454.

Giulianotti, R., & Robertson, R. (2012b). Mapping the global football field: A sociological model of transnational forces within the world game. *British Journal of Sociology, 63*(2), 216–240.

Giulianotti, R., & Robertson, R. (2013). Sport and globalization. In D. L. Andrews & B. Carrington (Eds.), *A companion to sport* (pp. 41–60). Oxford: Wiley-Blackwell.

Harvey, D. (1989). *The condition of postmodernity: An enquiry into the origins of cultural change.* Oxford: Blackwell.

Held, D., McGrew, A., Goldblatt, D., & Perraton, J. (1999). *Global transformations: Politics, economics, and culture.* Stanford, CA: Stanford University Press.

Horton, P. (2011). Sport in Asia: Globalization, glocalization, Asianization. In P. Pachura (Ed.), *New knowledge in a new era of globalization* (pp. 119–146). Rijeka, Croatia: Intechopen.

Hylton, K. (2020). Black Lives Matter in sport. . . ? *Equality, Diversity and Inclusion: An International Journal. 40*(1), 41–48.https://doi.org/10.1108/EDI-07-2020-0185.

Jacobs, J. M. (2006). A geography of big things. *Cultural Geographies, 13*, 1–27.

Khondker, H. H., & Robertson, R. (2018). Glocalization, consumption, and cricket: The Indian Premier League. *Journal of Consumer Culture, 18*(2), 279–297.

Kobayashi, K. (2012). Corporate nationalism and glocalization of Nike advertising in "Asia": Production and representation practices of cultural intermediaries. *Sociology of Sport Journal, 29*(1), 42–61.

Lee, N., Jackson, S. J., & Lee, K. (2007). South Korea's "glocal" hero: The Hiddink syndrome and the rearticulation of national citizenship and identity. *Sociology of Sport Journal, 24*, 283–301.

Lozada, Jr., E. P. (2006). Cosmopolitanism and nationalism in Shanghai sports. *City & Society, 18*(2), 207–231.

Ludvigsen, J. A. L. (2020). The Premier League–globalization nexus: Notes on current trends, pressing issues and inter-linked "-ization" processes. *Managing Sport and Leisure, 25*(1–2), 37–51.

Luo, L., Dai, Y., & Huang, F. (2015). Glocalization and the rise of the Chinese basketball market. *International Journal of the History of Sport, 32*(10), 1321–1335.

Lyu, L., & McCarthy, L. (2015). Logalization: Local-global processes and the Shiling leather industrial district in Guangzhou, China. *Asian Geographer, 32*(1), 37–57.

Maguire, J. (1990). More than a sporting "touchdown": The making of American football in Britain 1982 1989. *Sociology of Sport Journal, 7*, 213–237.

Maguire, J. (1999). *Global sport: Identities, societies, civilization.* Cambridge, U.K.: Polity Press.

Maguire, J. (2005). *Power and global sport: Zones of prestige, emulation and resistance.* London: Routledge.

Maguire, J. (2015). Assessing the sociology of sport: On globalization and the diffusion of sport. *International Review for the Sociology of Sport, 50*(4–5), 519–523.

Martin, R. (1997). Staging crisis: Twin takes in moving performance. In P. Phelan & J. Lane (Eds.), *Ends of performance* (pp. 186–196). New York: New York University Press.

McGrew, A. (1992). A global society? In S. Hall, D. Held, & A. McGrew (Eds.), *Modernity and its futures* (pp. 61–116). Cambridge, U.K.: Polity Press.

Miller, T., Lawrence, G., McKay, J., & Rowe, D. (2001). *Globalization and sport: Playing the world*. London: Sage.

Millward, P. (2011). The limits to cosmopolitanism: English football fans at Euro 2008. In D. Burdsey (Ed.), *Race, ethnicity and football: Persisting debates and emergent issues* (pp. 163–173). New York: Routledge.

Montez de Oca, J., Mason, S., & Ahn, S. (2020). Consuming for the greater good: "Woke" commercials in sports media. *Communication & Sport*. https://doi.org/10.1177/2167479520949283.

Ong, A. (2007). Neoliberalism as a mobile technology. *Transactions of the Institute of British Geographers, 32*(1), 3–8.

Parnell, D., Bond, A. J., Widdop, P., & Cockayne, D. (2021). Football worlds: Business and networks during COVID-19. *Soccer & Society, 22*(1–2), 19–26. https://doi.org/10.1080/14660970.2020.1782719.

Parnell, D., Widdop, P., Bond, A., & Wilson, R. (2020). COVID-19, networks and sport. *Managing Sport and Leisure, 27*(1–2), 78–84. https://doi.org/10.1080/23750472.2020.1750100.

Patsantaras, N. (2015). Cosmopolitanism: An alternative way of thinking in the contemporary Olympics. *European Journal for Sport and Society, 12*(2), 215–238.

Ritzer, G. (2004a). *The globalization of nothing*. Thousand Oaks, CA: Pine Forge Press.

Ritzer, G. (2004b). *The McDonaldization of society* (Rev. New Century ed.). London: Sage.

Ritzer, G. (2006). Globalization and McDonaldization: Does it all amount to . . . nothing? In G. Ritzer (Ed.), *McDonaldization: The reader* (2nd ed.) (pp. 335–348). Thousand Oaks, CA: Pine Forge Press.

Ritzer, G. (2007). Introduction. In G. Ritzer (Ed.), *The Blackwell companion to globalization* (pp. 1–14). Oxford: Basil Blackwell.

Robertson, R. (1992). *Globalization: Social theory and global culture*. London: Sage.

Robertson, R. (1994). Globalization or glocalization? *Journal of International Communication. 1*(1), 33–52.

Robertson, R. (1995). Glocalization: Time-space and homogeneity-heterogeneity. In M. Featherstone, S. Lash, & R. Robertson (Eds.), *Global modernities* (pp. 25–44). London: Sage.

Robertson, R. (1997). Comments on the "global triad" and "glocalization." In I. Nobutaka (Ed.), *Globalization and indigenous culture* (pp. 217–255). Tokyo: Institute for Japanese Culture and Classics, Kokugakuin University.

Robertson, R. (2003). The conceptual promise of glocalization: Commonality and diversity. Artefact. http://artefact.mi2.hr/_a04/lang_en/

Robertson, R. (2006). Glocalization. In R. Robertson & J. A. Scholte (Eds.), *Encyclopedia of globalization* (vol. 2) (pp. 545–548). London: Routledge.

Robertson, R. (2012). *European glocalization in global context*. Basingstoke, U.K.: Palgrave.

Robertson, R. (2013). Situating glocalization: A relatively autobiographical intervention. In G. S. Drori, M. A. Hollerer, & P. Walgenbach (Eds.), *Global themes and local variations in organization and management: Perspectives on glocalization* (pp. 25–36). New York: Routledge.

Robertson, R. (2014). Interviews: Roland Robertson. *Globalizations, 11*(4), 447–459.

Roudometof, V. (2016). *Glocalization: A critical introduction*. London: Routledge.

Rowe, D. (2003). Sport and the repudiation of the global, *International Review for the Sociology of Sport, 38*, 281–294.

Rowe, D. (2020). Subjecting pandemic sport to a sociological procedure. *Journal of Sociology, 56*(4), 704–713. https://doi.org/10.1177%2F1440783320941284.

Saussure, F. D. (1959). *Course in general linguistics* (W. Baskin, Trans.). New York: Philosophical Library.

Skey, M. (2015). What nationality he is doesn't matter a damn! International football, mediated identities and conditional cosmopolitanism. *National Identities, 17*(3), 271–287.

Smart, B. (2007). Not playing around: Global capitalism, modern sport, and consumer culture. *Global networks: A Journal of Transnational Affairs, 7*(2), 113–134.

Szymanski, S. (2010). *The comparative economics of sport*. New York: Palgrave Macmillan.

Thorpe, H. (2017). Action sports, social media, and new technologies: Towards a research agenda. *Communication and Sport, 5*(5), 554–578.

Tomlinson, J. (1999). *Globalization and culture*. Cambridge, U.K.: Polity.

Tzu-Hsuan, C. (2012). From the "Taiwan Yankees" to the New York Yankees: The glocal narratives of baseball. *Sociology of Sport Journal, 29*(4), 546–558.

Van Bottenburg, M. (2001). *Global games* (B. Jackson, Trans.). Urbana: University of Illinois Press.

Waters, M. (1995). *Globalization*. London: Routledge.

Weedon, G. (2012). "Glocal boys": Exploring experiences of acculturation amongst migrant youth footballers in Premier League academies. *International Review for the Sociology of Sport, 47*(2), 200–216.

Yu, L., Xue, H., & Newman, J. I. (2018). Sporting Shanghai: Haipai cosmopolitanism, glocal cityness, and urban policy as mega-event. *Sociology of Sport Journal, 35*(4), 301–313.

CHAPTER 11

··

SPORT, SPECTACLE, AND MEGA-EVENTS

··

JOHN HORNE

IN 2020, due to the novel coronavirus, COVID-19, two sports mega-events, the Union of European Football Associations (UEFA) Euro 2020 and the Tokyo Summer Olympic and Paralympic Games 2020, were postponed for the first time outside of wartime. In response, the organizers, the UEFA and Tokyo Organizing Committee of the Olympic Games with the International Olympic Committee (IOC), proactively announced their expectation to put the events on in 2021. In companion, they decided to retain the names Euro 2020 and Tokyo 2020, respectively, to save on rebranding costs as much as anything else. At the time this chapter was initially drawn in September 2020, there was considerable uncertainty about whether these events would actually go ahead. Although some argued for it, few expected the 2020 Olympic Games to be canceled outright. The economic, political, and reputational fallout from taking that course of action would have simply been too great, not just for the organizers and the Olympic movement but also for Japan as a whole. While the 2020 Games had been initially been heralded as a "recovery" or "reconstruction" Games, no one was expecting this theme to take on additional significance courtesy of a global pandemic (Horne & Whannel, 2020, Chapter 1).

In postponing the 2020 Games until 2021, some commentators suggested the possibility for the event to act as a boost to the reputation of each of the main stakeholders involved. At the height of pandemic worries, on Olympic Day, June 23, 2020, IOC President Thomas Bach proclaimed, "The Olympic Flame can be the light at the end of the dark tunnel that we all find ourselves in now" (quoted in Gillen, 2020). Indeed, as this played out, this course of action came at a considerable financial cost. Certainly, at the time there were hopes that a decision to delay and stage the event a year or so later would provide an upturn in the attraction of the global spectacle. As we know now, the 2020 Olympic Games went on in 2021. With competition taking place amidst COVID-19 safety protocols, the usual luster and bluster associated with the Games was truncated, reflecting the many unknowns in a pandemic-stricken world. Even today, as we emerge from the pandemic and much in the elite competitive sports world has returned to something approaching normal, the precise future of sports mega-events remains uncertain. From this standpoint, and drawing largely on the state of research prior to the pandemic, this chapter considers key issues, approaches, and debates in research focused on sports mega-events.

Increasingly we have faced a mega-event "paradox" (Roche, 2017, p. 9) in which there has been both a proliferation of sports mega-events and growing public antipathy toward hosting them. In the past 30 years there has been increasing popularity for cities to stage mega-events, at different scales or tiers, while at the same time there has been increasing resistance by citizens in democratic locations when they have the choice. The disinclination for many potential host cities to bid to stage the Olympics, for example, has led the IOC to make numerous reforms. At the same time, a Transnational Anti-Olympic Network has developed that seeks to challenge the negative impacts of hosting for citizens affected (Robertson, 2020). This development of growth and resistance has a history and involves both a shift in sport and a shift in the attractiveness of sport to urban growth professionals, advertisers working with globalizing corporations, and perhaps especially broadcasters (Horne, 2015b). These issues are considered in the next section.

ISSUES

The study of events in general has taken off in the past 30 years. It is a multidisciplinary field of research. The study of sports mega-events has its origins in tourism and business academics becoming interested in what were called "hallmark events." Recognizing the importance of the topic across a variety of disciplines, researchers in sociology, history, geography, and political science fueled inquiries (Roche, 2000). Today research involves multi- and transdisciplinary approaches, sometimes with multinational teams of researchers.

Gruneau (2017) has outlined how mega-events became an aspect of the staging of modernity in the 19th and 20th centuries. Initially World Expos and industrial exhibitions and then international multisport/Olympic formulas developed as a result (p. 128). Two features of contemporary sports mega-events are, first, that they are deemed to have highly significant social, political, economic, and ideological consequences for the host city, region, or nation in which they occur, and, second, that they will attract considerable media coverage. By this definition, therefore, an unmediated mega-event would be a contradiction in terms, and for this reason the globally mediated sports genre of the mega-event, as a television spectacle, has tended to supplant other forms of "mega," such as World's Fairs or Expos, although these do continue to be enthusiastically hosted and attract substantial numbers of visitors (Roche, 2017).

The Olympic Games could never have attained a global impact without television. The Olympics today are a product of television's power to produce and distribute live global spectacle (Kellner, 2003, Chapter 3). Indeed, it can be argued that the Games are perhaps *better* understood as a television event than as a sporting one. The Olympics do not appear to be popular because of the regular followings of its major sports, either as spectators or as participants. Rather, it is because it has become a spectacularized television show, with the badge of being the "world's best" (although there is another view of the Games as "anti-spectacle"; see the Approaches section). It is the convergence of star, narrative, national identity, "live-ness," and uncertainty that gives the Olympic Games this unique power as a cultural event and why so much effort and expense go into the production of both the Opening and Closing Ceremonies (Horne & Whannel, 2020, Chapter 10; Sugden & Tomlinson, 2012).

At the same time, funding by broadcasters and sponsors has created a double-edged sword. The Olympic business model, for example, which most other mega-events, even at different scales, now follow, is showing signs of the need for change (Horne & Whannel, 2020, pp. 210–213). Sports sponsorship worldwide is currently predicted to fall by U.S.$17 billion in 2020 (Owen, 2020). Critical sports journalists such as Zirin (2014) write about debt, displacement, privatization, and militarization as the main legacies of sports mega-events. Project management experts can point to the massive cost overruns of the Olympics (Flyvbjerg, Stewart, & Budzier, 2016). So what are the key issues involved? The issues that have developed with respect to the study of sports mega-events include defining mega-events, urban development, the politics of rights and labor, legacies and impacts, and resistance to hosting.

Defining Mega-Events

Definitions of mega-events vary across different theoretical understandings and disciplines, for example, economics, geography, political science, urban planning, as well as sociology. Geographer Martin Müller (2015) asked when we know a mega is a mega. Is it size alone or other constituent parts that enable us to say an event is a mega-event? He reviewed other authors' attempts at definition and identified four common features: audience (tourism), mediation (reach), cost, and impact (transformation). Müller thus constructed a consolidated definition: "Mega-events are ambulatory occasions of a fixed duration that attract a large number of visitors, have a large mediated reach, come with large costs and have large impacts on the built environment and the population" (p. 638).

Roche (2000) provided one of the definitions Müller looked at and has not altered his view, even while recognizing that changes have taken place in terms of the scale, reach, and impact of mega-events (Roche, 2017). He approached mega-events sociologically, as phenomena that provide a vivid illustration of the balance between agency and structure in the development of modernity. Roche (2000, p. 1) offered a way to understand the features of mega-events *sociologically* that has been adopted by many others, as "large-scale cultural (including commercial and sporting) events, which have a dramatic character, mass popular appeal and international significance." These characteristics go some way toward explaining the allure or attraction of sports mega-events to potential host cities or nations. For individuals, sports mega-events offer the promise of a festival of sport, with emotional moments, shaping personal (life)time horizons.

Additionally, we need to consider the existence of first, second, and even lower tiers of (sports) mega-events according to their reach and range, cost and size (Black, 2014). Despite Müller's words of caution about discussing different levels of sports mega-events, Roche (2017) identifies tier 1, 2, and 3 "megas." In this chapter, therefore, I will refer to the following as among the most significant sports mega-events: Tier 1, Summer Olympic Games and FIFA Men's World Cup; Tier 2, Winter Olympic Games and UEFA Men's Euro football championship; Tier 3, Commonwealth Games and Pan American Games (see Figure 11.1).

Since 2000 there have been 30 editions of these six sports mega-events, and another 13 are currently scheduled to take place by 2028. Black (2014) argued convincingly that we should

Tier 1	Tier 1	Tier 2	Tier 2	Tier 3	Tier 3
Summer Olympics & Paralympics	FIFA Men's World Cup	Winter Olympics & Paralympics	UEFA Men's EURO	PAN AM Games	Commonwealth Games
2000 Sydney	2002 Japan & South Korea	2002 Salt Lake City	2000 Belgium & Netherlands	2003 Santo Domingo	2002 Manchester
2004 Athens	2006 Germany	2006 Torino	2004 Portugal	2007 Rio de Janeiro	2006 Melbourne
2008 Beijing	2010 South Africa	2010 Vancouver	2008 Austria & Switzerland	2011 Guadalajara	2010 Delhi
2012 London	2014 Brazil	2014 Sochi	2012 Poland & Ukraine	2015 Toronto	2014 Glasgow
2016 Rio de Janeiro	2018 Russia	2018 PyeongChang	2016 France	2019 Lima	2018 Gold Coast
2020 / 2021* Tokyo	2022 Qatar	2022 Beijing-Zhangjiakou	2020 / 2021* 'Pan-Europe': final at Wembley Stadium, London	2023 Santiago	2022 Birmingham
2024 Paris	2026 Canada-Mexico-USA	2026 Milan-Cortina d'Ampezzo	2024 Germany	2027 Barranquilla	2026 Victoria, Australia
2028 Los Angeles					

* In March 2020 due to the impact of the novel coronavirus, COVID-19, it was announced that both mega-events would be postponed until 2021 but would retain the same names, Tokyo Summer Olympic and Paralympic Games 2020 and EURO 2020 respectively.

FIGURE 11.1 Tier 1, Tier 2, and Tier 3 sports mega-events, 2000–2028

look at megas as a means to fund development processes and objectives. In doing so they will inevitably benefit certain vested interests, but not all interests. With respect to "second-order" megas, they are attractive to second-tier locales—for example, large conurbations that are not capital cities and/or that are in small nations—for two main reasons. First, the more "relevance challenged" mega-events can offer the only realistic means of pursuing event-centered development for certain urban areas. Some places can never realistically aspire to host an Olympic Games or the FIFA World Cup finals. Second, lower-order mega-events can act as "springboards" for cities to bid to host first-order mega-events. This was the strategy that the municipality of Rio de Janeiro took, to first host a smaller scale event (the Pan American Games in 2007) and then bid to host the Summer Olympics. Thus, even the process of bidding to host a second- or third-tier sports mega-event can be full of political calculation.

Urban Developments

On the impact of staging the 1992 Olympics on Barcelona, the author Manuel Vázquez Montalbán (1991/2004, p. 34) wrote, "In this city, you were either working for the Olympics, or you were dreading them—there was no middle ground." Horne (2007, pp. 86–91) identified a number of "known unknowns" with respect to the impact of sports mega-events on urban development that have remained part of the political debate: the emphasis on consumption-based development as opposed to social redistribution with respect to the goals of hosting sports mega-events; the "gentrification" of specific areas; the displacement of poor and less powerful communities of people (and subsequent "replacement" of them by wealthier people); and the use of extensive public-sector funds to enhance private corporate-sector gain. For recent investigations of some of these in the context of Brazil and China, see Broudehoux (2017) and de Oliveira (2021).

Undoubtedly local host sites and spaces have benefited from global flows of capital, trade, and finance as well as tourists, but the spatial concentration of the impact of the event and the short-term impacts on employment of hosting sports mega-events have been among the critical points identified when comparing the rhetoric of predicted outcomes with the reality. The impact on tourism flows has never been near what has been predicted by sports mega-event "boosters," mainly because of the displacement of nonsport tourists. While proponents of hosting have to resort to manufacturing consent of local and national publics to get them on their side, opposition coalitions as a result of some or all of these developments have emerged as a result. These "known unknowns"—that is, things that are widely known about sports mega-events but that organizers tended to ignore—were largely derived from academic research (for example, see Lowes, 2002; Urry, 2002).

The Politics of Rights and Labor

Despite the fact that Rule 50.2 in the 2019 version of the Olympic Charter states, "No kind of demonstration or political, religious or racial propaganda is permitted in any Olympic sites, venues or other areas" (International Olympics Committee, 2019a, p. 90), the modern Olympic Movement has had to contend with wars, boycotts, protests, walkouts, and even a terrorist attack (Boykoff, 2016). This rule has been challenged in the wake of the development of athlete activism and protests against inequality and racism by athlete-activists as well as others (Chappelet, 2020).

As Figure 11.1 shows, there is a regularity and rhythm to the production of elite sports mega-events, and all of them are televised with more or less the same production values, even if their estimated reach (and audience size) varies considerably. As the Olympics have become a global televisual event, they have become more available for symbolic political action. Timms (2012) discussed the way that the anti–sweat shop campaign Play Fair used the platform of the Olympics, how it has developed, and the form it took for the London

Olympic Games in 2012. Play Fair brought together a number of labor rights groups to use the hook, unashamedly, of the biggest sporting event in the world. In using the Olympic Games as a platform for its protest, Play Fair provides an example of how activists can mobilize, hijack, or "piggyjack on," for their own purposes, a platform that has already been created (at great cost) by others. As Price (2008, p. 86) pointed out, the Olympic platform had been a "relatively unexplored vehicle for systematic communication" and its value and reach present a very particular opportunity for those able to mobilize it.

In fact, from the late 1960s onward the Olympic Games have been caught up in two main forms of symbolic politics: (1) the *promotional* opportunities offered by the Games to enhance reputations via public diplomacy, "soft power," and/or propaganda by competing, winning medals, and hosting, as well as refusing to participate through different forms of boycott, and (2) the opportunity to *protest* a perceived social injustice by "seizing the platform" that the Games offer (Price, 2008). In addition, the Games have developed amid changes in economic ideologies—from state-led, mixed economies to privatized neoliberal economic orthodoxies (Horne, 2017).

Between 1968 and 1984, the Olympic Games became the site of more highly focused symbolic political contestation in which the boycott became a significant political weapon. Horne and Whannel (2020, Chapter 7) identify four main trends: (1) the emergence of *boycotts* and political theater, particularly from the 1960s to the end of the 1980s; (2) the growth of national and place *promotion* as a form of reputational politics; (3) the growth of the Olympics as an *economic investment opportunity*, as neoliberalism increasingly became the "common sense" of international political economy from the 1980s onward; and (4) since the 2000s the growth of transnational movements *resisting* these developments, and especially the hosting of mega-events.

More generally, the *promotional* opportunities offered by sports mega-events to enhance reputations—by competing with other cities and nations, winning the right to stage them, and actually hosting them—are sometimes referred to as the exercise of "soft power" or public diplomacy, as nations, and increasingly cities, have sought to develop their place in the modern world and establish what has been referred to as "brand identity" (Grix, Brannagan, & Lee, 2019). On the other hand, refusing to participate in a sports mega-event through different forms of boycott can be seen as a form of negative public diplomacy.

The second kind of sports mega-event politics more generally is the opportunity for non-state actors and social movements to *protest* a perceived social injustice. The 1968 Summer Olympics, staged in Mexico City, saw the best example of this in the form of the famous Black Power salute by John Carlos and Tommie Smith in support of the Olympic Project for Human Rights (Hartmann, 2003; Henderson, 2010). Contemporary protests over police violence against Black people, linked to the Black Lives Matter movement, among others, are direct descendants of this action in support of human rights. During the Black Lives Matter protests in June 2020, the Asian Art Museum in San Francisco removed a bust of former IOC President Avery Brundage because of his racist legacy.

Writing for Human Rights Watch, Minky Worden (2015, p. 1) identified five main human rights abuses that have been apparent at sports mega-events:

1. The forced evictions of citizens without due process or compensation.
2. The abuse and exploitation of migrant workers.

3. The silencing of civil society and rights activists.
4. Threats, intimidation and arrest of journalists.
5. Discrimination within nations competing to host or simply competing at the mega-events.

In this context, different international and national actors have sought to impose their frames of reference on the situation. Issues surrounding rights of access to facilities built at public expense or the removal of poor communities from their housing and forced evictions have created struggles over who or what is (made) visible at sports mega-events (Horne, 2018).

Increasingly, the rights of workers involved in sports mega-events—including athletes—have been analyzed (Harvey, Horne, Safai, Darnell, & Courchesne-O'Neill, 2014, Chapter 2). The labor involved in putting on a sports mega-event includes paid and unpaid workers; migrant workers of the global precariat who barely scrape a living wage and those on or earning less than the minimum wage; those who work on the supply chains providing equipment, clothing, and footwear; as well as those selling merchandise associated with events. (On the politics of labor in the buildup to the FIFA Men's World Cup in Qatar scheduled for 2022, see Human Rights Watch, 2020.) In addition to paid workers, volunteers play a major role in the delivery of the events; for example, 70,000 "Games Makers" were trained for the London 2012 Olympics, and the same number of "Field Cast" volunteers were in training ahead of Tokyo 2020. To this mix come a globetrotting elite of professional mega-event management experts and consultants (Cashman & Harris, 2012; Jennings, 2012, p. 3).

Legacies and Impacts

The politics of each and every sports mega-event is conjunctural, meaning that it will be affected by different political circumstances at local, national, regional, and global scales at different times and places. Therefore, in some respects, even the unusual pandemic-ridden case of 2020 is no exception. Nonetheless, since the 1970s there has been growing concern about "gigantism" and "white elephants" in the Olympics—the growth in scale of the events, on one hand, and the potential to build facilities and stadia that will be more costly to use and maintain than they are worth, on the other. Economists and other social scientists have assessed sports mega-events in terms of their costs and benefits (Preuss, 2004; Whitson & Horne, 2006). As we noted earlier, Flyvbjerg and his colleagues (2016) at Oxford University have suggested that the size of cost overruns at the Olympic Games is the largest out of all mega-projects.

Despite this, the question of developing a legacy by hosting an Olympic Games or other sports mega-events had been, until relatively recently, a low-order issue and one that was not seriously entertained until after an event had been concluded. While all bidding cities had a general legacy vision, which was set out in bid books, no detailed operational plans were developed before the Games about how the legacy would be implemented afterward. Legacy plans were not seriously explored until after the Games had been staged, when there was a diminished interest in Olympic matters. The IOC's interest in an Olympic city largely ceased once the Games had been staged, so there was no monitoring or evaluation of post-Games legacy implementation. The legacy concept came of age in the early 2000s as governments recognized more clearly the potential utility of hosting as a tool in achieving a range of sport and nonsport policy objectives (Cashman & Horne, 2013). It also developed as rising concerns were expressed about the costs of staging the events (see Flyvbjerg, Budzier, & Lunn, in press, for analysis).

Legacies established universally to serve everybody might need to be financed by governments, philanthropic organizations, or, exceptionally, private enterprises (Horne 2015a). Prioritizing universal legacies would mean that organizers of sports mega-events would be obligated to deliver them to all without constraints. Rather than just making vague claims regarding legacy, they would have to demonstrate a properly funded legacy management program that continued for some years after the event. For sports mega-events to live up to the promotional claims made for them, the legacies associated with them should follow the principle of universalism; this would require greater control and regulation over FIFA, the IOC, and local Olympic committees by nonmarket actors.

Resistance to Hosting

A final issue, resistance to hosting, melds with recent attempts to recover, re-present, and rewrite the histories of social activism around and within sport and sports mega-events (Hayes & Karamichas, 2012; Harvey, Horne, & Safai, 2009; Harvey et al., 2014). Oliver and Lauermann (2017) and Lauermann and Pauschinger (2019) have identified the ways in which protests against hosting sports mega-events have become widespread. Where they are able to engage in democratic referenda or plebiscites, anti-bid campaigns asking for more transparency and participation have been successful. Between 2014 and 2016, for example, nine bids for the Olympics were blocked, and more have failed since. Proactive resistance strategies before bids have been submitted, rather than reactive ones after the award of an event, seem to have been most effective. Protest early, build alliances (including with academic experts), build a social media presence, seek transparency, monitor for scandals, and question the opportunity costs seem to be the strategies being used today (Horne, 2017; Oliver & Lauermann, 2017, p. 138).

APPROACHES

Three sets of dichotomies can be found when considering academic writing about sports mega-events. Each relates to those broadly positively or negatively disposed toward them: the "boosters" and "skeptics" (see Figure 11.2); those who view the events as "spectacle" or "anti-spectacle"; and those whom Cohen (2013) refers to as the "Olympophiles" and "Olympophobes."

Boosters, those in the left-hand column of Figure 11.2, often work in or with the sport events industry and possibly teach in sport management or business programs. They are largely in support of the organizational status quo while recognizing that some things need improving. Researchers in this column differ in terms of how far the revisions should go, but both revisers and reformers generally enjoy access to the organizing bodies of sports mega-events and may even work with them, as consultants to them, recognizing and boosting their

Boosters/Legitimizers of SMEs	Skeptics/De-Legitimizers of SMEs
Revise the mega-event	*Restructure the mega-event*
Reform the mega-event	*Transform the mega-event*

FIGURE 11.2 Sports mega-event (SMEs) discourses: Main aims and interests

legitimacy. Examples include books that look at theory and practice (Parent & Smith-Swan, 2013) or analyze different aspects of managing these complex projects (Darcy, Frawley, & Adair, 2017; Frawley & Adair, 2013). Occasionally interventions will be made that attempt to adjust the balance of power within sports mega-events, but they also accept the broader organizational framework of mega-events (McGillivray, Edwards, Brittain, Bocarro, & Koenigstorfer, 2019). Boosters often claim a general benefit stems from very particular events and its associated construction projects. In this way they concur with sports administrators adopting the "sport for good" or "Olympism" ideology, including ideas that an event "is good for the health of all," "will increase participation," and so on. From this perspective, a particular interest (corporate or sports) is declared to be a public good as it competes for market (or "field") share with other interests—artistic, creative, literary, or musical. The IOC and its officials and members in particular adopt this view when it is described as an "Olympic family," upholding Olympism and the values of the Olympic Movement. The IOC thus positions itself as the solution to many social problems, not merely sports.

Skeptics, including some journalists, activists, and academic researchers, in the right-hand column of Figure 11.2, are most critical of sports mega-events and argue for the fundamental overhaul of processes and possibly the abandonment of the biggest of the events (Boykoff, 2020; Lenskyj, 2020). Critical research into sports mega-events by academics and journalists that has questioned their legitimacy has given activists who are against the events further information and reasons for campaigning against them (Simson & Jennings, 1992; Zirin, 2014). Skeptics tend to approach sports and sports mega-events as sites of *contestation* and *conflict*. This means that they are more interested in both the politics *of* sport and sports mega-events and politics *in* sport and sports mega-events (Kennelly, 2017; Sykes, 2017). Many start by acknowledging the importance of Marx and subsequent attempts to develop a (neo-)Marxist analysis of sport.

It is the skeptics who tend to describe sports mega-events as a media *spectacle*, whether adopting a Marxist, cultural studies, or critical perspective (Gruneau & Compton, 2017; Kellner, 2003, 2010). Writing before the Los Angeles Summer Olympics in 1984, Whannel (1984, p. 41) argued that "the Olympic Games cannot be both a television spectacle and a people's festival." Others disagree and suggest that the Olympic Games as a cultural practice can embrace aspects of both festival and spectacle (MacAloon, 1984, 2006). Yet Whannel does identify different visions of the Olympic Games, the tensions between them, and the difficulty of holding on to both festival and spectacle in the same globalized event. Writing about the London 2012 Games, Horne and Whannel (2016, p. 213) noted that they "were not confined to stadia, but were viewed in homes, bars, malls and parks, where an atmosphere of festivity and jollity did develop. The Olympic Park became a festive cockpit. There were spontaneous events, informal celebrations, casual merry-making and carnivalesque costumes."

Critical commentary exists within sport management and other sociological and anthropological writing about sports mega-events that draws on Durkheimian influences, and it is here that an alternative view of the Olympics as "anti-spectacle" can be found (Besnier, Brownell, & Carter, 2018; MacAloon, 2006). Hiller (2016) especially suggests that an interactionist approach should remain skeptical of the idea of spectacle. For Hiller (pp. 68–69) the notion of spectacle implies too passive an image of people as social actors. Instead he argues that there are many different forms of response to and participation in the spectacle of an Olympic Games: supportive and critical, enthusiastic and oppositional, empowering and alienating. He argues, "If spectacle stands for elitism, responses that challenge elitism, passivity and social distance can be labelled as anti-spectacle" (p. 68). Similarly, MacAloon (2006) argued that the Olympic torch relay was an example of anti-spectacle. However, this event is also open to capture by economic, political, and nationalist forces (Horne & Whannel, 2010).

As noted earlier, some commentators have suggested that postponing the 2020 Olympic Games until 2021 may boost the reputation of each of the main stakeholders involved. This is certainly the hope of those whom Cohen (2013) calls "Olympophiles," such as the IOC President Thomas Bach, who wrote to Olympic athletes, international sports federations, and, through the Olympic Studies Centre, academics, seeking advice on ways forward in the light of COVID-19 (International Olympics Committee, 2020). At the same time, those whom Cohen calls "Olympophobes" continue to call for a halt to the Olympic spectacle. For example, Lenskyj (2020) sustains the critical approach that she has developed toward what she calls the "Olympic industry" over the past two decades. She looks at Olympic resistance, the Games' links to business, and their impacts on athletes' human rights, among many other topics, in a broad-ranging critique. Developing the ideas of journalist Naomi Klein (2008) about "disaster capitalism," Boykoff (2014) introduced the concept of "celebration capitalism" to describe the "states of exception" that an Olympic Games in particular creates in and brings to the host location (see also Vainer, 2016). Boykoff (2020) also offers more focused insights into the anti-Olympic "NOlympians," partly researched when he visited Japan in 2019. Alongside the "1 year to go" celebrations planned by the Tokyo 2020 Organizing Committee, a coalition of activists from Japan, Korea, Los Angeles, Rio, Paris, and other Olympic host countries and cities met in Tokyo in July 2019. One of the Japanese organizers of this gathering, Hangorin no Kai (Anti-Olympics Group), provided 18 reasons for saying "No!" to the 2020 Games, including displacement, increasing costs to the public, and damage to the local and national environment identified in connection with the construction of the new National Stadium. Together the activists produced a joint statement calling for "NOlympics Anywhere" (Olympics Watch, n.d.). Whether the postponement of Tokyo 2020 to 2021 will lead to fundamental changes to the IOC, the Olympics, or world sport remains one of many unknowns about the current state of the world.

DEBATES

As we have seen, journalists and social scientists alike have raised issues about the opportunities versus the costs, the uneven benefits, and the rhetoric of an Olympic legacy versus the reality. As U.S. journalist Dave Zirin (2014) reiterates, debt, displacement, privatization, and the militarization of public spaces are often the main outcomes of hosting the

Olympics and other sports mega-events. More than a decade ago, Horne and Manzenreiter (2006) identified center-periphery relations in world sport, power relations between nations, the production of ideologies, the relationships between supranational sports associations and sports business, and the media-sport business as the main broad issues needing further inquiry with respect to sports mega-events. These issues are still relevant; in addition, new research priorities can be identified. In the light of the previous discussion, four broad areas of ongoing debate will be briefly highlighted in this section. These are the relationship between sports mega-events and the environment, sports mega-commerce, safety and security, and politics and power.

Environment

The Olympics maintains its environmental credentials are good, yet every Games is also accompanied by stories of displaced people, demolished housing, and environmental damage. Significant air miles are clocked by the 30,000 or more competitors, officials, administrators, consultants, researchers, and journalists who are part of the Olympic traveling circus. And that is before the spectators arrive. In the buildup to an Olympic Games, and over its entire life cycle, thousands of athletes, officials, and administrators will travel to host locations for "trial events," acclimatization, and other purposes. The carbon footprint of the Olympics is often massively underestimated when its "green" credentials are being claimed (Karamichas, 2013).

But there is a climate emergency that will affect all sport in all parts of the world. As Goldblatt (2020, p. 3) notes, "Only a tiny fraction of the world's thousands of sporting bodies, federations, tournaments, leagues and clubs have signed up to the UN Sport for Climate Action Framework, [and] even fewer have actual carbon targets and plans to deliver on these commitments." In October 2019 it was announced, unexpectedly for many in the Tokyo 2020 Organizing Committee, that the IOC would move the marathon and the race-walking events from Tokyo to Sapporo (over 1,000 kilometers north) in Hokkaido because of the sweltering heat and humidity in the Japanese capital. The Winter Olympics in 2022 is likely to rely primarily on artificial snow, and estimates suggest that of 19 prior locations, only 10 will still be reliable winter sports hosts in 2050, and just six in 2080 (Goldblatt, 2020, p. 5).

Commerce and Costs

Television has brought a huge income stream to the Olympic Movement, initially dependent on the USA, but since 1988 sponsorship and television incomes from the rest of the world have become significant too. As such, this income has been shaped by the forces of commodification, globalization, and digitalization; it is increasingly shaped by the convergence of the once distinct technologies of television, computers, and the internet and is having to come to terms with the rise of content streaming via the internet. Since mining the processes of commercialization, the Olympics began to grow more rapidly. From the start of the 1980s, the contradictions have sharpened and the tensions heightened.

Institutions making decisions involving millions of dollars are always likely to engender and encounter a certain amount of corruption. In the case of the Olympics, even with new host venue processes announced by the IOC in June 2019, the final choice of sites, with a great deal at stake, will be taken in a secret ballot by an electorate of around 100 members, who are not answerable to anyone for how they vote. Whole teams of people on bidding committees will still devote much of their time and money considering how best to persuade the future host commissions for the Summer and Winter Games to select them as preferred hosting locations. Judging by the large sums paid by television corporations and sponsoring corporations to obtain the rights, the Olympic "product" remains highly valuable. Yet, this brand is dependent on its image and is hence vulnerable and can be tarnished, not only by corruption but also by potential scandals involving performance-enhancing drugs, gambling and the fixing of results, and overzealous security measures that conflict with the potential festival of sports.

While television (broadcasting revenue) has been the main enabler of sports mega-events such as the Olympics and FIFA Men's World Cup for the past four decades, debates about the actual costs of hosting continue. For example, the operating budget for Tokyo 2020 is U.S.$5.6 billion, covered by "private" funds—that is, from sponsorship, tickets, and marketing. In addition, when awarded the Games in 2013, the Tokyo 2020 bid committee projected the costs of hosting to be U.S.$7.3 billion. After postponement in 2020, the organizers produced a revised estimate for the Games of U.S.$12.6 billion) (see International Olympics Committee, n.d.). However, a report submitted to Japan's National Audit Board in late 2019 suggested an extra U.S.$9.7 billion should be added to the estimate to include other Olympic-related costs (making U.S.$22.3 billion in total). In addition, the Tokyo metropolitan government is spending U.S.$7.4 billion on Olympic-related projects (see "Tokyo 2020 Organizers," 2019). In the same story, academic Bent Flyvbjerg was quoted as saying, "[T]he Olympic Games are the only type of mega-project to always exceed their budget. . . . [A]ll you can do when problems begin . . . is to throw more money at the project." This is especially the case with security.

Security

One of the political controversies since 9/11 (in 2001), and stretching further back to the Munich terrorist attack (in 1972), has been the relationship between the staging of sports mega-events and the growth of the security state (Lyon, 2003). Societies have seen a continuing transformation of surveillance capabilities as the supposed threat of terrorist attacks has grown. Sports mega-events have offered opportunities for new security equipment and procedures and surveillance operations to be trialed. The very success of the Olympics as a global spectacle has required ever-greater investment in security, to the extent that the Games have become, for the security industry, an invaluable exercise in research and development paid for by the public purse. Other technologies and businesses also seek to use the Games as an opportunity to showcase their innovations; hence Tokyo 2020 was being heralded as an opportunity to demonstrate technological solutions to future demographic trends, city living, and environmental change. As it shifts to being staged a year later it will likely be heralded as an example of the power of sport in dealing with disease and even global pandemics.

Politics and Power

Zimbalist (2015, p. 122) suggests, "Hosting sports mega-events . . . tends to reinforce the existing power structure and patterns of inequality." Sports mega-events also tend to impact negatively on poor people—through pre-event construction and the post-event "gentrification" of locations and the crowding out of spending on welfare and the general redirection of scarce resources toward the priority of delivering a mega-event. As a result, the contestation of sports mega-events continues. For example, in 2010 I was invited to contribute to an open workshop in São Paolo, Brazil, for activists struggling over developments in their cities resulting from the hosting of the FIFA Men's World Cup in 2014 (Horne, 2010). Also in 2010, the FIFA Men's World Cup in South Africa presented several examples where the trade-off between housing projects for people in need and the building of a stadium went in favor of the latter. In the desire to host a sport mega-event, profit and event delivery often come before democracy and social justice, leading to a variety of responses and resistances (Desai, 2016; Farred, 2016). One of the unintended legacies of hosting a World Cup is that it can lead to social mobilization—and sometimes confrontations, as was witnessed in Brazil in 2013 and 2014 (Broudehoux, 2016; Omena, 2020; Vainer, 2016). Some organizers have attempted to integrate and incorporate NGOs and protest groups into the planning of events. But the mobilization of people and communities affected remains one of the most unstable and unpredictable of the social legacies of hosting sports mega-events.

CONCLUSION

What does all this amount to? What key questions remain regarding sports mega-events, and what direction will research take? Here we identify four sets of questions, each relating to the debates discussed.

Health and Public Safety

What are the consequences of COVID-19 for the future of sports mega-events? What are the public health consequences of sports mega-events as mass gatherings? The first of these will remain as possibly the central question, at least in the short term. The unprecedented impact of the novel coronavirus on human life in general and sport and sports mega-events in particular is still not fully appreciated. Needless to say, in future public health will increasingly feature in research into sports mega-events, although it has not been prominent to date. Yet it is simply too soon to speculate about the precise impact COVID-19 will have on future intentions to bid and campaigns to do so.

Climate Change

What are the environmental consequences and future of sports mega-events? Can they ever be truly sustainable? The report "Playing against the Clock: Global Sport, Climate Emergency and the Case for Rapid Change" (Goldblatt, 2020) places a huge responsibility on sports organizations, and especially those responsible for sports mega-events, to act urgently to mitigate negative effects on the environment. Whether they do so or not will be one of the key questions to be investigated in the future.

Sport in a Crisis of Capitalism

Some commentators have already begun to ask about the activities of "sporting disaster capitalists" who might be looking to seize an opportunity in the midst of the corona virus crisis (Liew, 2020). What is the future of sport without spectators or with much smaller live audiences? Can there be spectacles without spectators? The importance of live spectators and fans for sport as spectacle has often been stressed, yet already competitive matches in such sports as football (soccer), baseball, and sumo have been played in empty stadiums and arenas (Begley, 2020; CBS News, 2020; Morita, 2020).

If the result is that TV audiences grow, will this mean even greater power ceded to broadcasting corporations? Additionally, will a combination of traditional sport and eSports become the new future in light of COVID-19?

Power

Anticipating Zimbalist (2015), academic David Runciman (2010) noted, "In reality, sports tournaments rarely do much to transform the fortunes of the countries that host them—at least not for the better—let alone change the fate of whole continents. But they can tell us a lot about where power really lies." This is likely to remain the case with respect to sports mega-events. Western/advanced capitalist hegemony remains stubbornly operant in the IOC. Some have argued that holding the Olympics at a single site or set of appropriate fixed locations might help to reduce building and waste. Could such plans alter the "roving colonialism" of sports mega-events (Sykes, 2017)?

In *NOlympians*, rather than outright abolition of the Olympics, Boykoff (2020) suggests changes consistent with other proposals about major reforms to sports mega-events (Horne & Manzenreiter, 2006), including the establishment of an independent bid review and accountability board to analyze candidates for hosting and a broadening of IOC membership and making voting preferences public (as FIFA has done in the wake of the 2015 scandal). In addition, Boykoff suggests that the bidding process should be more transparent and public referenda should be mandatory for all bids; an attempt should be made to ensure real sustainability, not greenwashing, and genuine environmental oversight should be introduced; finally, Olympic Villages should be made available after the event as affordable housing for marginalized populations.

No single output of academic research is responsible for bringing about social change, but its collective and combined influence is apparent in such developments as Agenda 2020, approved by the IOC (Horne & Whannel, 2020, Chapter 9). In the wake of the FIFA scandal in 2015 the IOC, as well as FIFA, has sought to present itself as self-reforming in its processes and procedures. Agenda 2020 sought to respond to several of the criticisms found in research, the writings of investigative journalists, and the struggles of activists. Currently the IOC is interested in reframing the political agenda by describing changes in the process of hosting as "the evolution of the revolution" (International Olympics Committee, 2019b).

Additionally, by inviting the IOC Athletes Commission to consider modifying Rule 50 in light of athlete-activists' demands (Shefferd, 2020), the IOC appears to be listening to its critics. How far this reassertion of the autonomy of sports governing bodies to put their own houses in order may be acceptable to critics and skeptics, and how sufficient to bring about real reform to its processes, are important questions to be investigated in the future.

REFERENCES

Begley, E. (2020, May 8). Crowd noise played over loudspeakers as football returns to South Korea. *BBC*. https://www.bbc.com/sport/live/football/52581366.

Besnier, N., Brownell, S., & Carter, T. (2018). *The anthropology of sport: Bodies, borders, biopolitics*. Oakland: University of California Press.

Black, D. (2014). Megas for strivers: The politics of second-order events. In J. Grix (Ed.), *Leveraging legacies from sports mega-events* (pp. 13–23). Basingstoke, U.K.: Palgrave Macmillan.

Boykoff, J. (2014). *Activism and the Olympics: Dissent at the Games in Vancouver and London*. New Brunswick, NJ: Rutgers University Press.

Boykoff, J. (2016). *Power games. A political history of the Olympics*. London: Verso.

Boykoff, J. (2020). *NOlympians: Inside the fight against capitalist mega-sports in Los Angeles, Tokyo and beyond*. Halifax, Canada: Fernwood Publishing.

Broudehoux, A.-M. (2016). Mega-events, urban image construction, and the politics of exclusion. In R. Gruneau & J. Horne (Eds.), *Mega-events and globalization: Capital and spectacle in a changing world order* (pp. 113–130). London: Routledge.

Broudehoux, A.-M. (2017). *Mega-events and urban image construction: Beijing and Rio de Janeiro*. London: Routledge.

Cashman, R., & Harris, R. (2012). *The Australian Olympic Caravan from 2000 to 2012: A unique Olympic events industry*. Petersham, Australia: Walla Walla Press.

Cashman, R., & Horne, J. (2013). Managing legacy. In S. Frawley & D. Adair (Eds.), *Managing the Olympics* (pp. 50–65). London: Palgrave Macmillan.

CBS News. (2020, May 6). South Korean baseball returns—in empty stadiums with fake fans. https://www.cbsnews.com/news/kbo-baseball-south-empty-stadiums-fake-fans-coronavirus/.

Chappelet, J. L. (2020). The unstoppable rise of athlete power in the Olympic system. *Sport in Society*, 23(5), 795–809.

Cohen, P. (2013). *On the wrong side of the track? East London and the post Olympics*. London: Lawrence & Wishart.

Darcy, S., Frawley, S., & Adair, D. (Eds.). (2017). *Managing the Paralympics*. London: Palgrave Macmillan.

de Oliveira, N. G. (2021). *Mega-events, city, and power*. London: Routledge.

Desai, A. (2016). Beyond Madiba magic and spectacular capitalism: The FIFA World Cup in South Africa. In R. Gruneau & J. Horne (Eds.), *Mega-events and globalization: Capital and spectacle in a changing world order* (pp. 81–94). London: Routledge.

Farred, G. (2016). The World Cup, the security state and the colonized other: Reflections on Brazil, Russia, South Africa and Qatar. In R. Gruneau & J. Horne (Eds.), *Mega-events and globalization: Capital and spectacle in a changing world order* (pp. 149–164). London: Routledge.

Flyvbjerg, B., Budzier, A., & Lunn, D. (in press). Regression to the tail: Why the Olympics blow up. *Environment and Planning A: Economy and Space.*

Flyvbjerg, B. Stewart, A., & Budzier, A. (2016). *The Oxford Olympics study 2016: Cost and cost overrun at the games.* Oxford: Oxford University.

Frawley, S., & Adair, D. (Eds.). (2013). *Managing the Olympics.* London: Palgrave Macmillan.

Gillen, N. (2020, June 23). Bach records video message to celebrate "very different" Olympic Day. *Inside the Games.* https://www.insidethegames.biz/articles/1095597/bach-records-video-for-olympic-day.

Goldblatt, D. (2020, June 20). Playing against the clock: Global sport, climate emergency and the case for rapid change. *Rapid Transition Alliance.* https://www.rapidtransition.org/resources/playing-against-the-clock/.

Grix, J., Brannagan, P. M., & Lee, D. (2019). *Entering the global arena: Soft power strategies and sports mega-events.* London: Palgrave Pivot.

Gruneau, R. (2017). *Sport and modernity.* Cambridge, U.K.: Polity Press.

Gruneau, R., & Compton, J. (2017). Media events, mega-events and social theory: From Durkheim to Marx. In L. A. Wenner & A. C. Billings (Eds.), *Sport, media and mega-events* (pp. 33–47). London: Routledge.

Hartmann, D. (2003). *Race, culture, and the revolt of the Black athlete: The 1968 Olympic protests and their aftermath.* Chicago: University of Chicago Press.

Harvey, J., Horne, J., & Safai, P. (2009). Alterglobalization, global social movements, and the possibility of political transformation through sport. *Sociology of Sport Journal, 26*(3) 383–403.

Harvey, J., Horne, J., Safai, P., Darnell, S., & Courchesne-O'Neill, S. (2014). *Sport and social movements: From the local to the* global. London: Bloomsbury Academic.

Hayes, G., & Karamichas, J. (Eds.). (2012). *Olympic games, mega-events and civil societies: Globalisation, environment and resistance.* London: Palgrave MacMillan.

Henderson, S. (2010). "Nasty demonstrations by Negroes": The place of the Smith-Carlos podium salute in the civil rights movement. In K. Brewster (Ed.), *Reflections on Mexico '68* (pp. 78–92). London: Routledge.

Hiller, H. (2016). *Host cities and the Olympics: An interactionist approach.* London: Routledge.

Horne, J. (2007). The four "knowns" of sports mega-events. *Leisure Studies, 26*(1), 81–96.

Horne, J. (2010, November 8). Seven thoughts about (sports) mega-events. Unpublished talk, Impactos Urbanos e Violacoes de Direitos Humanos Nos Megaeventos Esportivos (Urban Impacts and Human Rights Violations of Sports Mega-Events) International Seminar, University of São Paolo, Brazil.

Horne, J. (2015a). Managing World Cup legacy. In S. Frawley & D. Adair (Eds.), *Managing the World Cup* (pp. 7–25). London: Palgrave.

Horne, J. (2015b). On sports mega-events and capitalist modernity. *International Review for the Sociology of Sport, 50*(4 5), 466 471.

Horne, J. (2017). Sports mega-events, media and symbolic contestation. In L. A. Wenner & A. C. Billings (Eds.), *Sport, mega-events, and media* (pp. 19–32). London: Routledge.

Horne, J. (2018). Understanding the denial of abuses of human rights connected to sports mega-events. *Leisure Studies, 37*(1), 11–21.

Horne, J., & Manzenreiter, W. (2004). Accounting for mega-events: Forecast and actual impacts of the 2002 football World Cup finals on the host countries Japan/Korea. *International Review for the Sociology of Sport, 39*(2), 187–203.

Horne, J., & Manzenreiter, W. (2006). An introduction to the sociology of sports mega-events. In J. Horne & W. Manzenreiter (Eds.), *Sports mega-events: Social scientific analyses of a global phenomenon* (pp. 1–32). Oxford: Blackwell/Sociological Review Monograph.

Horne, J., & Whannel, G. (2010). The "caged torch procession": Celebrities, protestors and the 2008 Olympic torch relay in London, Paris and San Francisco. *Sport in Society*, *13*(5), 760–770.

Horne, J., & Whannel, G. (2016). *Understanding the Olympics* (2nd ed.). London: Routledge.

Horne, J., & Whannel, G. (2020). *Understanding the Olympics* (3rd ed.). London: Routledge.

Human Rights Watch. (2020). *"How can we work without wages?" Salary abuses facing migrant workers ahead of Qatar's FIFA World Cup 2022*. New York: Human Rights Watch.

International Olympics Committee. (n.d.). Tokyo 2020. https://tokyo2020.org/en/organising-committee/budgets/.

International Olympics Committee. (2019a). Olympic Charter. https://stillmed.olympic.org/media/Document%20Library/OlympicOrg/General/EN-Olympic-Charter.pdf.

International Olympics Committee. (2019b). Press release. https://www.olympic.org/news/evolution-of-the-revolution-ioc-transforms-future-olympic-games-elections.

International Olympics Committee. (2020, April 29). IOC president Bach writes to Olympic Movement: Olympism and Corona. https://www.olympic.org/news/ioc-president-bach-writes-to-olympic-movement-olympism-and-corona.

Jennings, W. (2012). *Olympic risks*. Basingstoke, U.K.: Palgrave Macmillan.

Karamichas, J. (2013). *The Olympic Games and the environment*. Basingstoke, U.K.: Palgrave Macmillan.

Kellner, D. (2003). *Media spectacle*. London: Routledge.

Kellner, D. (2010). Media spectacle and media events: Some critical reflections. In N. Couldry, A. Hepp, & F. Krotz (Eds.), *Media events in a global age* (pp. 76–92). London: Routledge.

Kennelly, J. (2017). *Olympic exclusions: Youth, poverty and social legacies*. London: Routledge.

Klein, N. (2008). *The shock doctrine: The rise of disaster capitalism*. New York: Picador USA.

Lauermann, J., & Pauschinger, D. (2019). Protest and the games. Play the Game. https://www.playthegame.org/news/news-articles/2018/0529_protests-and-the-games-article-series/.

Lenskyj, H. J. (2020). *The Olympic Games: A critical approach*. Bingley, U.K.: Emerald.

Liew, J. (2020, March 16). Beware sporting disaster capitalist not letting this crisis go to waste. *The Guardian*. https://www.theguardian.com/sport/blog/2020/mar/16/beware-sporting-disaster-capitalists-crisis-go-to-waste).

Lowes, M. (2002). *Indy dreams and urban nightmares. Speed merchants, spectacle, and the struggle over public space in the world-class city*. Toronto: Toronto University Press.

Lyon, D. (2003). *Surveillance after September 11*. Cambridge, U.K.: Polity.

MacAloon, J. (1984). *Rite, drama, festival, spectacle: Rehearsals towards a theory of cultural performance*. Philadelphia, PA: Institute for the Study of Human Issues.

MacAloon, J. (2006). The theory of spectacle: Reviewing Olympic ethnography. In A. Tomlinson & C. Young (Eds.) *National identity and global sports events* (pp. 15–39). Albany: State University of New York Press.

McGillivray, D., Edwards, M., Brittain, I., Bocarro, J., & Koenigstorfer, J. (2019). A conceptual model and research agenda for bidding, planning and delivering major sport events that lever human rights. *Leisure Studies*, *38*(2), 175–190.

Montalbán, M. V. (1991/2004). *An Olympic death*. London: Serpent's Tail.

Morita, H. (2020, March 25). Spring tourney roundup: Sumo wrestlers rock empty stadium. *NHK World Japan*. https://www3.nhk.or.jp/nhkworld/en/news/backstories/987/.

Müller, M. (2015). What makes an event a mega-event? Definitions and sizes. *Leisure Studies*, *34*(6), 627–642.

Oliver, R., & Lauermann, J. (2017). *Failed Olympic bids and the transformation of urban space.* Basingstoke, U.K.: Palgrave Macmillan.

Olympics Watch. (n.d.). Tokyo 2020. https://olympicswatch.org/tokyo-2020/.

Omena de Melo, E. (2020). Just because of 20 cents? For a genealogy of the Brazilian "demonstrations cup." *International Journal of Urban Sustainable Development, 12*(1), 103–118.

Owen, D. (2020, May 18). Sports sponsorship predicted to fall by $17 billion in 2020. *Inside the Games.* https://www.insidethegames.biz/articles/1094389/sports-sponsorship-fall-prediction.

Parent, M., & Smith-Swan, S. (2013). *Managing major sports events.* London: Routledge.

Preuss, H. (2004). *The economics of staging the Olympics: A comparison of the Games 1972–2008.* Cheltenham, U.K.: Edward Elgar.

Price, M. (2008). On seizing the Olympic platform. In M. E. Price & D. Dayan (Eds.), *Owning the Olympics: Narratives of the new China* (pp. 86–114). Ann Arbor: University of Michigan Press.

Robertson, C. (2020, June 17). Organizing a transnational anti-Olympics summit: An oral history, part 1. *Olympics Watch.* https://olympicswatch.org/2020/06/17/organizing-a-transnational-anti-olympics-oral-history-part-1/.

Roche, M. (2000). *Mega-events and modernity.* London: Routledge.

Roche, M. (2017). *Mega-events and social change: Spectacle, legacy and public culture.* Manchester, U.K.: Manchester University Press.

Runciman, D. (2010, May 22). Football's goldmine. *The Guardian.*

Shefferd, N. (2020, June 14). Global athlete call on IOC and IPC to "immediately abolish." *Rule 50. Inside the Games.* https://www.insidethegames.biz/articles/1095305/global-athlete-rule-abolition.

Simson, V., & Jennings, A. (1992). *The lords of the rings: Power, money and drugs in the modern Olympics.* London: Simon & Schuster.

Sugden, J., & Tomlinson, A. (Eds.). (2012). *Watching the Olympics: Politics, power and representation.* London: Routledge.

Sykes, H. (2017). *The sexual and gender politics of sport mega-events.* London: Routledge.

Timms, J. (2012). The Olympics as a platform for protest: A case study of the London 2012 "ethical" games and the Play Fair campaign for workers' rights. *Leisure Studies, 31*(3), 355–372.

Tokyo 2020 organizers put price tag at ¥1.35 trillion. (2019, December 22). *Japan Times on Sunday.*

Tomlinson, A., & Whannel, G. (Eds.). (1984). *Five ring circus: Money, power and politics at the Olympic Games.* London: Pluto Press.

Urry, J. (2002). *The tourist gaze* (2nd ed.). London: SAGE.

Vainer, C. (2016). Mega events and the city of exception. Theoretical explorations of the Brazilian experience. In R. Gruneau & J. Horne (Eds.), *Mega-events and globalization: Capital and spectacle in a changing world order* (pp. 97–112). London: Routledge.

Whannel, G. (1984). The television spectacular. In A. Tomlinson & G. Whannel (Eds.), *Five ring circus: Money, power and politics at the Olympic Games* (pp. 30–43). London: Pluto.

Whitson, D., & Horne, J. (2006). Underestimated costs and overestimated benefits? Comparing the impact of sports mega-events in Canada and Japan. In J. Horne & W. Manzenreiter (Eds.), *Sports mega-events: Social scientific analyses of a global phenomenon* (pp. 73–89). Oxford: Blackwell/Sociological Review Monograph.

Worden, M. (2015). Raising the bar: Mega-sporting events and human rights. *Human Rights Watch World Report 2015.* http://www.hrw.org/world-report/2015/essays/raising-bar.

Zimbalist, A. (2015). *Circus maximus: The economic gamble behind hosting the Olympics and the World Cup.* Washington, D.C.: Brookings Institution Press.

Zirin, D. (2014). *Brazil's dance with the devil: The World Cup, the Olympics, and the fight for democracy.* Chicago: Haymarket Books.

....

CHAPTER 12

SPORT, OLYMPIC IDEALS, AND REALITIES

....

ALAN TOMLINSON

I never thought of Samaranch as particularly reflective, as opposed to tactical. In the tactical sense, he was brilliant and he had certain strategic strengths as well. What I never found was a philosophical commitment to any basic principles. (Pound, 2004, p. 264)

JUAN Antonio Samaranch was president of the International Olympic Committee from 1980 to 2001, a Spanish sports administrator under the Franco regime, and despite the damning judgmental statement that opens this chapter, Dick Pound, a former IOC vice president and the first president of the World Anti-Doping Agency, could also write that "on balance" Samaranch's presidency was "by far the most important of any" in the history of an IOC dating from 1894. But no "philosophical commitment to any basic principles"? How could this be true of someone holding the most powerful custodial position in the Olympic "Movement," a movement priding itself on its commitment to a long-established set of principles and ideals? Pound's judgment highlights how fragile Olympic ideals are when faced with the pragmatics of everyday realities.

The modern Olympics lays claim to being the world's most successful multisport, globally inclusive, and high-profile sporting competition. Since 1896, when the IOC and its founder, Baron Pierre de Coubertin, launched the inaugural modern Olympics in Athens, the only canceled Summer Olympics were those planned for the war years of 1916, 1940, and 1944. Tokyo 2020, a victim of the COVID-19 pandemic, and seeking to stage Tokyo 2020 in 2021, potentially created a new category of postponed Olympic events, disrupting the historical four-year cycles of the Games, known in IOC-speak as the Olympiad, climaxing with the Games event itself in the fourth year of the cycle.

Where a country failed to deliver on its commitment, an enthusiastic substitute stepped adeptly into the breach. London did this to land the 1908 Summer Olympics. Rome, chosen over Berlin at the fourth session of the IOC in London in 1904 (*Revue Olympique*, 1904, p. 72), was to have staged the 1908 event, but "a fragile national economy, competing city factions across the country, and lack of support from the national Italian government in

1906 caused de Coubertin to doubt the strength of the commitment" (Tomlinson, 2012, p. 2). Great Britain stepped in and first-choice Rome was abandoned, with the tragic eruption of Mount Vesuvius in April 1906 providing a rationale for the withdrawal of the Italian host city.

The London 1908 Games were secured with a combination of agile organization, lobbying, and arrogance. In 1905, a central organization for national sport—the British Olympic Association, essential for IOC-defined eligibility as a host city—had been formed in a meeting at the House of Commons, and Lord Desborough was appointed president. The following year Desborough, an Oxford University fencer, athlete, and rower, competed at the Athenian Games, doubling as King Edward VII's "British representative" and letting it be known that London/England could take on the 1908 Games. For a man who swam across the dangerous base of the Niagara Falls twice, lived life with the "tranquil consciousness of an effortless superiority" (Matthew, 2004) nurtured by his time at Balliol College Oxford, and was said to have been at one point in his busy life sitting on 115 committees of various kinds (Baker, 2008), a mission to persuade Coubertin's IOC coterie that England was the best bet to salvage and then secure the IOC's reputation was mere child's play. Desborough could also neatly slot the Games into and around the schedule of the planned Franco-British Exhibition. The latter event's "organisers . . . were powerful advocates of the Olympic Movement and intended to make the Games the centrepiece of the festival" (Miller, 2008, p. 58).

Small events piggybacking on larger projects gave the Olympic story a historical pedigree. This was evident early, with the 1904 Games in St. Louis, Missouri, when the small-scale Games was shoehorned into the 1904 World's Fair and spread over four and a half months. The early Games were modest in scale and high in ideals. The history of their survival provides an overarching narrative of expansion in which the balance between ideal and reality has been accommodated, lost, and retrieved time and time again. It is vital to any adequate understanding of this process to recognize the ways in which Olympic rhetoric and discourse intertwine with particular cultural, political, and economic forces. In the following section, recurrent issues that have threatened Olympic ideals at selected points in Olympic history are the focus of discussion.

ISSUES

The Olympic Games is the highest-profile multidiscipline sport event in human history. Its contemporary manifestation as a global media event has attracted the largest viewing figures for any sporting event. The London 2012 Olympic Games reportedly generated 3.6 billion viewers worldwide, with Beijing's 2008 Summer Olympics coming a close second with 3.5 billion viewers (Sponsorship Intelligence, 2012, p. 4). Only the FIFA Men's World Cup has rivaled these figures. Yet this successful and high-profile mega-event (see Horne, this volume) has been haunted by recurrent and broad issues that underlie the many crises and challenges faced by the IOC and the Olympics in a changing, volatile, and globalizing world. Such issues are bound up with fundamental questions about what the Olympics actually stand for and what the term "Olympism" itself conveys to respective audiences and constituencies.

The committee established by Coubertin in Paris in 1894—the International Committee of the Olympic Games—first met on June 19, three days after a swish Congress banquet. The meeting was presided over by Demetrias Bikélas, a prominent Greek resident of Paris and active member of La Société de Panhellénique de Gymnastique. Thirteen individuals were listed in the account of the meeting published in the inaugural edition of the *Bulletin of the International Committee of the Olympic Games*, as the committee described itself. The members were from France, Greece, Russia, Bohemia, Sweden, Italy, Hungary, Great Britain (England), New Zealand, the USA, and Argentina—essentially representing Western and Central Europe, as well as some of the loud and energetic voices of the New World. Coubertin recruited university professors, a general, a lord, a count, and a doctor. Steeped in his own aristocratic background, he was particularly adept at recruiting privileged individuals with grand-sounding titles, resources to hand, and a surfeit of free time. In this way, the 25-year-old English aristocrat Lord Ampthill found himself nominated by the Congress as a member of the committee. Ampthill certainly had a sporting pedigree, having "captained the boats" at his school, Eton College, and excelled in rowing when at New College, Oxford (Prior, 2008). He was president of the Oxford University Boat Club and of its debating society, the Oxford Union. His prowess in rowing and speaking left little time, it seems, for serious study, and he graduated with a third-class honors in modern history, a modest achievement at best but no barrier to a privileged career in colonial administration in India. His contribution to Olympic history was not a prolonged one, and along with two other members comprising the inaugural committee, his involvement with the fledgling IOC did not outlast the 1890s. Lord Ampthill's "mandate" is reported as lasting from 1894 to 1898, just two years after Athens staged the inaugural modern (Summer) Olympics (Miller, 2008, p. 416). Coubertin's "job was done; the committee had served its publicity function, and the Games were up and running" (Allison & Tomlinson, 2017, p. 61). Essentially, the IOC was created as a nonrepresentative, nonaccountable body of white males from privileged and elite backgrounds. When looking closely at the genesis of the ideals and sometimes idealism of the IOC and its Olympic product, these historical antecedents are of more than passing interest or minor relevance.

Coubertin's vision of the value of athletics infused his ongoing definitions and formulations of Olympism and the Olympic Games. From the very start, he argued that by drawing on the example of ancient Greece the importance of the body could be once again recognized for its own qualities rather than treated as inferior to and dependent upon the mind. This was the theme of his address to the closing banquet of the Paris Congress of 1894:

> Gentlemen, man is not made up of two parts. The body and the mind. There are three: body, mind, and character. Character is not formed by the mind, it is formed above all by the body. That is what the ancients knew, and that is what we are relearning, painfully. (Coubertin, 2000, p. 532)

Taking an idealized model of the nature of Olympism in ancient Greece, he sought, in his own words, and champagne glass in hand, to carry his listeners to

> lofty heights. . . . I raise my glass to the Olympic idea, which has crossed the mists of time like a ray from the all-powerful sun and is returning to shine on the gateway to the twentieth century with the gleam of joyful hope. (p. 532)

Coubertin's evolving model of Olympic ideals included adherence to a model of sportsmanship comprised of fair play and the spirit of chivalry, recognition of a community of all athletic disciplines, commitment to both internationalism and nationalism, and the idea of equality of chances alongside the existence of an elite (p. 528).

In the Olympic Charter of 2020 these formative values appear alive and well as articulated in seven "fundamental principles of Olympism." Summarized, these principles constitute a formulation of the core ideals of the IOC and the Olympic Movement (International Olympic Committee, 2020, p. 11). First, Olympism is a philosophy of life balancing the qualities of body, will, and mind by blending culture and education in a way of life anchored in joyful effort, good educational examples, and a universal respect for fundamental ethical principles. Second, Olympism seeks to support humankind's harmonious development, aiming to promote a peaceful society ensuring the preservation of human dignity. Third, the Olympic Movement embodies the actions of all participants, under the supreme authority of the IOC, and covers five continents, bringing together top, "great" athletes at its "great sports festival," and is symbolized by five interlocking rings. Fourth, in recognition of the practice of sport as a human right, all must have the possibility to participate in an Olympic spirit, with no discrimination, and in the spirit of fair play, friendship, and solidarity. Fifth—in the wordiest principle of the seven—sport must be recognized, by sports organizations, as a sphere of political neutrality, and such organizations, free of outside interference, must ensure the application of principles of good governance. Sixth, no form of discrimination must be exercised. Seventh, to belong to the Olympic Movement one must comply with the Olympic Charter and be recognized by the IOC.

It is obvious that these seven fundamental principles are regularly and predictably threatened by the everyday practices of states, governments, corporations, sport federations, and athletes. Nonetheless, for 17 days every four years, the IOC mantra can be presented to the world as a rationale for the Summer and the Winter Olympics. We know that these "high bar" principles are more than vulnerable, that their rhetoric borders on the risible, that everyday life is not (however much many might like it to be) shaped by fair play, friendship, and solidarity. But, to take the echoing phrase of outgoing IOC president Avery Brundage following the Palestinian terrorist assassination of the Israeli Olympic delegation in Munich in 1972, "The Games must go on" (quoted in Guttmann, 1984, p. ix), whatever the situation. The shattering of a fundamental principle of Olympism (friendship, solidarity) by an attack that turned the Olympic Village into a war zone could nevertheless be used in a form of rhetorical wordplay as a rejustification of the principle. Countless such examples of "principle adaptation" can be found in any Olympic Games throughout the history of their modern form.

Irishman Lord Killanin inherited the presidency of the IOC in 1972 and needed all his journalistic experience and diplomatic skills to keep the Olympic project on the rails after the deaths of the Israeli athletes at the Munich Games. It was a nightmarish moment at which to assume the presidency, with challenges aplenty, running the gamut from the money problems stemming from the Munich Games to some 65 countries boycotting the 1980 Moscow Games. Killanin (1983) himself recalled that had the U.S.-led boycott of the Moscow Games fully succeeded, it would have broken the Olympic Movement. His assertion cannot of course be tested, and the tit-for-tat boycott by the USSR (and all its communist allies except Romania) in Los Angeles in 1984 also failed to undermine the Games. In the end, the lesson from the two boycotts was that a sports event could be used to great effect as a means of political promotion. And as the Games limped forward from 1984, it was the Cold War that could be seen, ironically, as their savior. The success of the Los Angeles entrepreneurial model guaranteed the further growth of the event in future Olympic cycles, with biennial Games (Summer and Winter) from 1992 and 1994 onward giving the worldwide sponsors a more evenly spread exposure for their goods and brands. But throughout these growth years two major issues—doping and gigantism—were to test the robustness of the Olympic ideals.

Doping

In the years after his retirement from the IOC presidency in 1980, Lord Killanin (1983, p. 155) wrote that the "most obnoxious aspect of sport, and specifically that of international competition, is the use of drugs to aid performance." He saw the problem as a practice that was on the rise and which had become "more and more subtle" in its adoption and application. From his vantage point, it not only threatens the welfare of the individual but also "jeopardises the whole future spirit of sport. It is more insidious than even the greatest commercial and political exploitation. . . . Unfair practices undermine the whole concept of competition" (p. 155). Unless attitudes toward doping were changed, Killanin believed, competition "as we know it" would be destroyed by unsavory practices to unlevel the Olympic playing fields.

Doping came to light as a problem in the 1950s and 1960s, mainly in cycling, and the death of a Danish cyclist at the Rome Olympics stimulated the IOC's creation of a Medical Commission, though initially little action was taken until the young IOC member from Belgium, Prince Alexandre de Mérode, took the chair of the commission (Chappelet & Kübler-Mabbott, 2008, p. 133). He instituted the first antidoping controls in 1968 at both the Winter Olympics in Grenoble and Mexico City's Summer Games. Several countries had also begun studying the problem at the time, and a Council of Europe resolution against doping was adopted in 1966. Further, in 1976 the Council included a clause in the European Charter on Sport for All "denouncing the use of medication for the purpose of improving performance" (Chappelet & Kübler-Mabbott, 2008, p. 133). Still, it was another 12 years until the positive drug test for Canadian sprinter Ben Johnson brought the topic into worldwide headlines at the 1988 Seoul Olympic Games. The following year saw the Council of Europe convert its charter into a convention aimed at promoting antidoping policies at the level of national states as a way to facilitate harmonization of such policies at the international level. Governments became more widely involved in their commitments to seek out and eliminate doping, and the IOC itself stimulated the formation of the World Anti-Doping Agency in 1999. Yet the world of sport continues to generate controversial cases in which forms of doping have persisted, whether in the hypocritical and lying practices of shamed U.S. cyclist Lance Armstrong (McNamee, 2012) or the swapping of Russian test samples implemented by state-linked Russian bodies at the 2014 Sochi Winter Games (Allison & Tomlinson, 2017, p. 137).

The notion of "doping" has been expanded (see Dimeo & Henning, this volume) beyond the spheres of pharmaceutical interventions and laboratory experimentation, and the power of money and technology has been further recognized in the notions of "financial doping" and "technological doping." This extension of the concept to embrace economic and technical means of gaining an advantage has amplified the need to question the ethical basis of purportedly inclusive Olympic competition (Muniz-Pardos et al., 2021).

Gigantism

A recurrent issue concerning the Olympics has been the sheer scale of the event and the escalating ambitions of host cities, which in return for flattering the Olympics and its "movement" in the bidding process looked to do a better, bigger, and more spectacular job in staging the event itself than had any previous Games. The leader of Atlanta's triumphant bid for the 1996 Games, Billy Payne, recalled the team's response on returning home in September 1990: "We came back euphoric, but knowing nothing whatsoever about what we would do next" (quoted in Tomlinson, 2000, p. 176). They would become fast learners of course, supported by teams of planners, investors, and creative event-managers, ensuring that the most southerly city in the Northern Hemisphere to have hosted the Olympics (a point of distinctiveness claimed by the rather desperate-sounding bidding team) would not lack stories and narratives to fill its opening and closing ceremonies in 1996. Not least, the Opening Ceremony featured a wooden-looking Muhammad Ali trembling toward the cauldron to light the Olympic flame for a city proud to claim, in the words of the British TV commentator, "that the Games were taking place for the first time in a city where most of the people are black" (quoted in Tomlinson, 2000, p. 167). And this cultural emphasis was foregrounded by the high-profile of rhythm and blues and soul music featured in the popular-musical elements of the opening and closing ceremonies.

Gigantism has been a direct consequence of the combined influence of global broadcasting and the development of an Olympic sponsorship program creating exclusive "worldwide" partners. What Jean-Loup Chappelet and Brenda Kübler-Mabbott (2008, p. 80) have called the fifth period in the history of the Olympics, from 1996 to 2008, saw "the Games reach a size that renders their logistical organization extremely perilous, and makes government involvement absolutely essential." Presciently, Chappelet and Kübler-Mabbott proposed that the Games be held in less wealthy cities such as Rio de Janeiro, the eventually successful candidate for the 2016 Summer Games. In effect, they called for a form of downscaling of the Games in an overall review of the format of the event and its sports program. To do this, Chappelet and Kübler-Mabbott proposed that the established format based on principles of time, place, and action should be reevaluated (pp. 96–99). They argued that a longer Games beyond the 17-day period would relieve logistical problems. In posing this, they recognized that the Games operate across regions within nations rather than (for the most part) within host cities and that spreading things out, in terms of both the timeline and the locale, would achieve more efficient use of facilities without threatening the spirit of the Games. Further, they noted that the content of the Games could be reduced by removing particularly expensive events.

In the end, Chappelet and Kübler-Mabbott (2008, p. 105) argued that, regardless of however gigantism is tackled, the best way to pass on Olympic values would be "by means of the emotions aroused among the genuine participants in the widest sense (athletes, support staff, spectators, the media, young people etc.)"; thereby "the Games will preserve their unique value as a cultural heritage for humanity," something which sets them apart from other major sports events. Their posing of the notion of "genuine participants," though, downplays the significance of the global media and consumer audience which, in whatever combination of modes of communication and consumption takes place, keeps the broadcasters and the sponsors happy and ensures that the "never-ending global competition" (Gold & Gold, 2013) rolls on, and that one Olympics after another, at least economically, "blows up" (Flyvbjerg, Budzier, & Lunn, 2020), mired in the effects of predictable cost overruns to giant budgets and associated costs, with potentially dire consequences for local communities and regions.

APPROACHES

Many theoretical and interpretive models and frameworks have been used to account for the survival of the Olympic phenomenon and its claimed ideals. It is not the task of this chapter to provide a comprehensive synthesis of the thousands of studies that have been produced on almost every imaginable aspect of Olympic history, culture, sociology, and politics. The narrower focus of the chapter is on the claimed ideals, the values sustained by Olympic sympathizers, apologists, and followers that have allowed the Olympics to ride crisis after crisis and reemerge as a global cultural phenomenon claiming to speak for the interests of peoples and populations across the world. Nevertheless, particular theoretical frameworks carry with them their own forms of interpretive baggage, and in this section selected writings on the Olympics are signposted and evaluated.

Work from within the Olympic Movement itself constitutes a particular mode of research and writing, one that seeks to illuminate the history of the Olympics from its ancient setting in Greece through to the form taken by the so-called revival of the Games in their modern form by Coubertin. The IOC's International Olympic Academy, for instance, has the aim

> to create an international cultural centre in Olympia, to preserve and spread the Olympic Spirit, study and implement the educational and social principles of Olympism and consolidate the scientific basis of the Olympic Ideal, in conformity with the principles laid down by the ancient Greeks and the revivers of the contemporary Olympic movement, through Baron de Coubertin's initiative. (quoted in Chatziefstathiou & Henry, 2012, p. 5)

Of course, there is a remarkable level of naïveté in this institutional aim, and the contributors to such a research mission are clearly converts to the Olympic cause. Not surprisingly, this kind of research tends to feature examples that might act as an interpretive glue between the practices of ancient Greeks and the activities framing the Olympic Games of the modern, Coubertin-inspired models. In a sense, such efforts embrace what may be seen as a quasi-religious mission, one which doubles as a heritage project and is dismissive of, or even blind to, more critical work locating the Olympics as part of a particular political economy or cultural formation anchored in a highly specific set of values and ideals.

Serious and open-minded research on the Olympics, very different from that of apologists of the kind discussed above, has produced extremely valuable work by historical sociologists, political scientists, and institution/management scholars. John J. MacAloon's (1981) groundbreaking study of the origins of the modern Games located Coubertin within a political-cum-cultural moment that allowed, as one may say in French, an *épanouissement*, a blossoming of a new cultural formation that transcended the specific nationalism of a single country or era. Here, Coubertin is recognized as a *rénovateur*, skillfully weaving his way across pedagogic and political networks in pursuit of his ambition to profile, propose, and inaugurate his Olympic vision (MacAloon, 1981).

In a similar vein, political scientist Christopher Hill (1992, pp. 31, 241) confirmed the "primacy of politics" in Olympic matters in the simple observation that "since those far-off days of 1896 almost every celebration of the Olympics has been fraught with politics," and noting further that the theme of "gigantism" has preoccupied Olympic debate "for many years, since long before the number of athletes, journalists, officials and hangers-on reached its present grotesque size." A careful and rigorous institutional analysis of Olympism's history, organization, and actors is provided by Chappelet and Kübler-Mabbott (2008), although they tend to tiptoe lightly across the themes of corruption and criminality that have plagued the modern history of the IOC and its Games.

More explicitly critical approaches have been provided by investigative journalists and campaigning academics. Symson and Jennings (1992) paved the way in such critical interrogation with a study that exposed the dubious leadership claims and ruthless opportunism of selected Olympic figures by tracing the financial trails and networks of interests that could allow the purported ideals of Olympism to be so widely abused. Particularly thoughtful critical work on such networks has been produced by scholars such as Lenskyj (2000) and Boykoff (2014a, 2014b, 2016). Boykoff (2016, p. 12) sees in the thoughts and beliefs of Coubertin and "other true believers" a "religious fervour" that could be added to "flag-waving nationalism" and unproblematically stirred "into a potent brew of Olympism." Still, Boykoff (2014b, p. 100) recognizes that such a potent brew has no patent for the IOC and its flag-wavers and can be reshaped and remixed by the forces of global political and cultural influences: "The Olympics, as an ambitious, massive, political-economic project with indispensable socio-cultural components, is the quintessential illustration of celebration capitalism." In celebration capitalism, everyday rules and norms are temporarily suspended; public-private partnerships draw heavily on the public sector; festive commercialism legitimates the torch relay and the corporately sponsored Cultural Olympiad; a security industry booms as a protective framework for all; and finally, a language or rhetoric of sustainability and environmental concern add a conscience-cleansing process to the procedures. What can easily be seen in Boykoff's scathing critical analysis of the contemporary realities of "Olympism" are the processes through which the core Olympic values and ideals and practices and events such as the Olympic Games can be appropriated and exploited for political and financial gain in ways that are profitable to the privileged and the powerful and merely marginally—if at all—beneficial to the poor and the powerless. This is not to say, on the basis of such a critical contextualization of the Olympics, that the Games and Olympism are beyond repair. Toward that possibility, Boykoff (2014a, p. 174) provides an interventionist call to engagement in the conclusion to his study of activism at the Olympics: "To dismiss sports is to needlessly forfeit the common ground vital to meaningful political engagement. Nay-saying in the name of the kneejerk."

A neglected approach to understanding the nature of the Olympics and its cultural, political, and economic significance is found in the field of design studies and the history of design. In adopting this lens, Jilly Traganou (2016) has provided a fascinating and richly informed study of the design dimensions of the Olympics, the culmination of a personal and professional odyssey of a dozen years. Fieldwork visits to European venues—Athens, Barcelona, Rome, and Sarajevo—and to Sapporo and Tokyo in Japan, were interspersed with archival and newspaper research on selected Olympic events. She also conducted illuminating interviews with key informants, giving her core case studies on the Athens 2004 Summer Olympics and the Summer Games of London 2012 an insider feel to the reportage of the making of the event, in contrast with the organizational or emblematic representations of the event. The book constitutes a bold, scholarly, and highly original contribution, though Traganou explicitly states that she "does not focus on sport or spectacle" (p. 6), a wise decision given the breadth of research and writing on the history, politics, and sociology of the Olympic Games. Design history, Traganou proposes, holds "the promise of contributing to the field of Olympic history a polyphony that it currently lacks" (p. 20). Voices, actor networks, a mingling actor world with stakeholders populating Olympic landscapes "across a wide social spectrum" (p. 19) embraced by the Olympic design milieu; this is the polyphony that Traganou identifies.

Critical theory and cultural analysis have combined in interrogative work on the meaning and significance of "Olympism." Some have argued, from a post-modern sociological perspective rejected by Graham McFee (2010, pp.115-116), that claims about the 1936 Olympic Games, for instance, are not knowable, as no "truth" is possible for there is no single account available of such an event that can be considered to constitute *the* truth. In this vein, no single Olympic Games represents an ideal model of the Olympic ideals or principles. It is inescapable that every Olympic Games represent much more than the parroted rhetoric of the *rénovateur* Coubertin. To stage an effective Olympic Games, it has become inevitable that a hosting city, in collaboration with its country, must perform a "necessary arrogation" (Tomlinson, 1999) of the Olympic ideal, shifting or selecting from the fundamental principles or ideals, and working up a universal, yet unique, model for its own Games (Tomlinson, 2013). As expressed in Olympic opening ceremonies, such a model must embrace four elements. First, it needs to be solipsistic, referencing the history and heritage—in however an imagined or stereotyped fashion—of the host city itself and of selected dimensions of and narratives from the country's history. Second, it must represent and respect the supranationalist idealism of the IOC and its Movement. Third, it must exhibit a respect for national pride, in the slot at the front of the Parade of the Athletes as well as in the solipsistic telling of the story of the nation. Fourth, and this has become increasingly essential, it will provide a form of regional boosterism, taking care not to offend the city's near neighbors. Essentially, the framing ceremonies of an Olympic Games provide a formula that has become critical to the symbolic and rhetorical dimensions of the event. They are flexible rituals that allow Olympic partners to fit the gloves onto the hands of whoever is waving the magic wand, or carrying the torch for, Olympism. Even Coubertin (2000, p. 580) acknowledged that the various ceremonies were not easy to embed in the Olympic program, and it took decades before the wider Olympic "family" accepted them as central to the staging of the event. In a speech in 1935 preceding the following year's Summer Olympics in Berlin, the 72-year-old Coubertin reaffirmed his belief that the Olympics had endured due to the implantation of a religious sentiment into the internationalism and democracies of the modern world (p. 580), and that ceremonies were fundamental to this process. And Coubertin recognized that this was an incremental and long-term process, noting, "I had to impose these ceremonies one after another on a public that was opposed to them for a long time, seeing them merely as theatrical displays, useless spectacles" (p. 580). Imposed or not, ceremonies have become central to the symbolic profile of the Olympics and to the globalized context of respective Games (Tomlinson, 1996).

Debates

A Tarnished Product

If the expressed ideals of Olympism can be so easily exposed as little more than malleable elements of an other-worldly mantra or formulaic slogans of advertising partners and commerce-oriented sponsors, how is it that the *argot* of Olympic enthusiasts survives its countless encounters and collisions with reality? How is it that the lofty ideals of the Olympic moment, so many times debunked in the post-Games assessments about the value of hosting the event and its promised legacies to the community, are so easily revived in the ambitious bids and futuristic plans that are put forward for future Games? As far back as 1976, Jack Ludwig easily saw through the feel-good Olympian claims made by Montreal about the benefits of hosting the games. Writing about what was, without the rose-colored glasses, an infamously costly event that presented the city with a U.S.$1.5 billion debt that it took 30 years to pay off, he dismissed what he saw in the staged bonhomie in the Closing Ceremony, a sense that "this was indeed the end. Tomorrow there was—nothing" (Ludwig, 1976, p. 164). At this point in the Olympic story, morale was at a serious low following the 1972 Munich Games, at which the 11-strong Israeli national Olympic team was killed by the Palestinian terrorist group Black September. Not surprisingly, over the following years, cities were not queueing their candidacies to win a bid to host the event, and the widespread boycott of the Moscow Summer Games had consolidated a deepening disillusion with the Olympic project. How could the benefits of hosting a sports event justify human, financial, and political crises on the scale of the Munich deaths, Montreal's debts, and Moscow's celebration of its Cold War stand-off with the USA and 64 other boycotting nations? Answers to such questions are inevitably varied and complex, and necessarily always contingent upon particularized temporal and spatial contexts.

For example, the 1980 boycott was not a sporting problem or issue for Moscow itself: the USSR's haul was 80 gold, 69 silver, and 46 bronze medals; runner-up in the medals table was close ally East Germany, with 47, 37, and 42 medals, respectively. This amounted to 321 of the 631 medals won, 50.87% of those available. Bulgaria, with its wrestling and weightlifting steroid-enhanced competitors, gained 41 medals and clinched third place. Indeed, tiny Cuba was fourth in the table, with 20 medals. Hungary, Romania, and Poland made up the other socialist state success stories, although there was much evidence and conjecture linking this "success" to widespread doping that flew under the radar. By the mid-1990s, the IOC had begun to take action to deal with the problem, though the positive interventions to reduce doping were not a sufficient moral reboot that "saved" the reputation and profile—perhaps the latter more than the former—of the IOC and the Olympic Games. Rather, plain and simply put, it was money. Indeed, if there is one moment that embodies the globalization and commodification of the sporting product it is the Summer Olympics of 1984, the Los Angeles Olympics. Writing on the eve of the event, Richard Gruneau (1984, p. 2) noted, "Los Angeles in 1984 is already known as the 'Corporate Games.' More cynical critics call it 'the Hamburger Olympics'—an Olympics where the race for private sponsorship has assumed greater importance than the eventual race for the finish line." Gruneau did not argue that this represented an economic transformation as such; rather, it was a, perhaps inexorable, advanced expression of the ways in which sport and sporting activities were becoming incorporated into a relentlessly expanding international capitalist marketplace. On this count, it has also been argued (Tomlinson, 2017) that Los Angeles '84, in its intensification of the commodification of the Olympic brand and the Olympic media product, established the template for all 10 host cities from that pivotal year on through to Tokyo 2020. To put the Los Angeles bid in context, only Tehran had been in the running for 1984, and Los Angeles became the sole candidate after Tehran withdrew its bid before the 1978 decision-making process got under way (Mackay, 2015). The key point of this episode in Olympic history is that market-fueled U.S.-based financial clout could bail out a crisis-ridden IOC on two conditions: first, some core Olympic principles could be jettisoned, and second, virtually nothing could be excluded from the reach of sponsorship and branding.

Legacy: Lofty Goals and Broken Promises

Many derivative contemporary debates abound stemming from the "bloating" that resulted from the blatant commodification that undergirded the logic of the model used in Los Angeles; these include concerns related to citizenship, participation, and the future and legacies of the Olympic Games. The now near universality of this model has been challenged and questioned by critical scholars and analysts, and citizens and communities, in the face of the realities of its overexpansion (gigantism), excessive costs, vulnerability to corruption, and ethical myopia—and never more so than throughout the global COVID-19 pandemic of 2020 and beyond. Olympic values, as emphasized throughout this chapter, have long lent themselves to adaptation, and a prominent emphasis in IOC discourse since the beginning of the 21st century is on the notion of "legacy." In a trawl of IOC minutes, the first use of the term "legacy" appears to have been at an IOC meeting, July 25–26, 1984, on the eve of the L.A. Summer Games. Frank King, chair of the Calgary 1988 Winter Games Organizing Committee, described Calgary's financial plan as geared toward the primary objective of providing "the greatest possible participation to athletes, officials and spectators and to leave a legacy of Olympic facilities fully paid for" (Tomlinson, 2014a, p. 138). For successive Olympic events over the following third of a century it has not been difficult to find social, cultural, and economic examples of events failing to match King's bold optimism. Post-Olympic venues lying neglected after the Athens 2004 Summer Games may be the most graphic single case of the white-elephant syndrome in Olympic history, though other, less tangible legacies than economic and infrastructural ones should not be neglected. It has been argued that Athens 2004 "succeeded in re-baptising the worn-out Olympic values in a new and traditional ethical narrative" (Panagiotopoulou, 2014, p. 186) and that cultural programming at London 2012 and in the planning for the Rio 2016 games (Garcia, 2013) laid the foundation for a more sustained set of cultural legacies embedded in the Cultural Olympiad. It remains beyond dispute, nevertheless, that the broken promises of Olympic planners and boosters have animated anti-Olympic values in increasing cases of citizen opposition and protest.

Citizenship and Participation

Highly effective protesters in Berlin in the early 1990s, opposing a bid for the 2000 Games, created an Anti-Olympic Committee, employed anti-slogans ("Sports for the People Instead of Olympics" and "N'Olympia in Berlin"), created a counter-mascot of a grinning bear, and replaced and defaced bid posters. Berlin crashed out of the race in the first round of IOC voting in September 1993, securing only 9 of 88 votes (Colomb, 2012). This remains a relatively neglected campaign that established a hugely effective model for testing the claims of pro-Olympic bidders and boosters. On the theme of "participation," though, Traganou (2016) brings out the full range of actors and voices that contribute to the Olympic event, from bid to conception, through implementation and aftermath. Traganou shows that London 2012—with its adaptable and pictorially placeless emblem, a jagged, ragged, and adaptable image of the year/date of the event, with the venue, London, and the Olympic rings printed unassertively within separate digits of the emblem—created an innovative brand that framed the event as "everyone's." She also argues that dissent can be articulated in "designerly" ways, noting that in Vancouver a Poverty Torch Relay, part of the Third Poverty Olympics held a week before the Winter Games, "exemplified a conscious act of assembling with a clear, designerly conception of disobedience" (p. 275). "End Poverty: It's Not a Game" was the slogan used by the Vancouver urban protest group. Traganou sees potential in the Olympic mega-event to "activate a tipping point that allows for the imagining of change" (p. 286). This is also seen as a process in which authorship of design meanings shifts from the individual designer to the collective and facilitates citizen designers (following examples of citizen journalists) becoming part of the cast in an expanding theater of actors in the design milieu. Thus, "the participatory nature of the projects renders obsolete the former distinction between designers and users" (p. 287). Traganou also issues (following Bruno Latour) a call to arms to critics and designers to merge, to unite in counterbalancing and demystifying the "power of the powerful" (p. 334), drawing on the capacity of the designer to construct conditions that can foster "designerly engagements" (p. 335).

Modest Scaling Back of Gigantism and Traditionalism

In August 2016 the IOC announced that sport climbing would be included in the 2020 Olympic program and confirmed in June the following year that 3X3 basketball—an established event at the Youth Olympic Games—would also be included in the Tokyo schedule. Skateboarding and surfing were to make their debut in Tokyo as well. In December 2020 IOC president Thomas Bach announced that Paris 2024 would include breakdancing, a further unconventional activity in terms of conventional Olympic sensibilities, to be staged at one of the city's most prominent gathering places, Place de la Concorde. To make way for the newer sports, the IOC decided that the number of boxing and weightlifting categories would be reduced, and requests for other new sports, such as coastal rowing and mixed-relay cross-country athletics, were turned down (Ingle, 2020). Overall, the number of athletes who would be competing in Paris was projected at a 10,500 maximum, certainly a lot of athletes but nevertheless a small symbolic reduction from the number projected to participate in the eventually postponed Tokyo 2020 games. Bach (2020) justified the changes in efforts to grow the appeal of the Olympic Games to youth, claiming that changes of these kinds make the Games "more gender balanced, more youthful and more urban."

Reimagining Olympic Values

Whatever glossy take can be superimposed on the IOC and its actions, it has not been difficult to build a case damning the organization as "elitist, domineering and crassly

commercial at its core" (Boykoff & Tomlinson, 2012, p. 19). Indeed, any long-term observer of the Olympics has rich material to hand to call for a reimagining of the Games
(Abrahamson, 2020). Such a reimagining would seem to necessarily entail questioning
the predictable mantra and the rhetoric of the IOC and its movement. Still, in doing so,
even friendly critics such as Abrahamson wear conflicting emotions on their sleeves.
Abrahamson writes, "I care deeply about the Olympic movement and its possibility to effect
change in our broken and fragile world, [it is impossible to deny that the IOC] is at an inflection point in its, and our, collective history." For Abrahamson, observer of and reporter
on 10 editions of the Olympics since the Salt Lake City corruption scandal broke in 1998, a
bold reimagining would involve a review of the whole Olympic system, including the IOC
itself, its myriad dormant or nominal regional/continental Olympic committees, national
Olympic committees, and the program of sport itself. This last matter seems particularly
prescient at a time when the sports order of the day for the youth of the world (at least in
relatively strong economies) has emerged in the form of eSports, attracting hundreds of
millions of participants. Yet, constructive as he wishes to be, Abrahamson has no template
for reform, advising the IOC to find a few spare hundred million dollars to bring in a consultancy to "re-imagine the IOC itself and the Olympic movement." Thus, even as there is
little debate over the needs for reform, the debates about what needs to be done continue
and have eluded prioritization.

Toward the end of 2020, eight months or so into the global pandemic, Bach selected appropriate snippets from the IOC's mantra manual for an opinion piece in *The Guardian*.
Here Bach fell back on "old saws," saying that the "athletes personify the values of excellence, solidarity and peace" and that they are "a reaffirmation of our shared humanity and
contribute to unity in all our diversity" (Bach, 2020). Citing his lifelong experience as an
Olympian, he urged that such "magic" unfolded by the Olympic Games and uniting "the
entire world in peace is something worth fighting for every day." Certainly, this remains
a noble goal, and has been exploited by Japan's prime minister proposing that the Tokyo
event offers the opportunity for diplomatic encounters with North Korea (Pavett, 2020). Yet
the show must go on, and the treadmill keeps moving, giving little pause for reflection and
reform. Inertia is a powerful force, and speaking for the IOC, Bach and his colleagues continue to disperse several billion of the IOC's monies in an ongoing fight to protect the 17-day
bonanza of a Summer Olympic Games that has become entrenched for both good and ill. In
advancing his case in his *Guardian* pitch, Bach continues to emphasize the increasingly my-
opic claim that political neutrality is central to the Olympic model. From his veteran career
as Olympian, Bach can no longer see—if he ever did—that Olympic ideals themselves are
a cultural political construct and that the mounting of Games themselves has increasingly
become an exercise of archetypal political praxis.

Conclusion

In many ways, Coubertin's project has succeeded, and the "Olympic logic" has been
naturalized in political waters and in many people's sensibilities. As a case in point, U.K.
Prime Minister Tony Blair promised the IOC decision-makers a "magical and memorable"
Games for London in 2012, an event that would "do justice to the great Olympic ideals"
(Lee, 2006, p. xiv). In doing so, he didn't really have to spout the ideals, merely smile for
the audience. Of course, there are limits to the realities of what an Olympic Games may

yield, even as they are framed amid a finite set of Olympic ideals. The latter will always appear more formed than the diverse experiences that make up the Olympic realities for the billions of people across all continents, something vividly seen in the over 306 billion items shared on the internet across the 17 days of the London 2012 Games, a phenomenon that caused some to dub the event the "Socialympics" (Tomlinson, 2014b; Arnoldi, 2012, p. 1).

To conclude, the Olympic "magic," so beloved by Bach, can help overcome (and mask) the problem of consistently missing its legacy goals (Tomlinson, 2014a). The Games and their rhetoric can be sustained because Olympic realities are so diverse, so dispersed and disparate, that the notion of Olympic ideals or fundamental principles can be, time after time, pulled out of the air and waved as a beacon of hope in a tempestuous world. Yet we all know, of course, that magicians depend upon sleight of hand and planned deception, and there is more than an element of the magical in how the most successful IOC leaders and apologists have called up, revived, and sustained the "magic" of Olympism.

From a more sociologically informed vantage point, contemporary 21st-century Olympism and the IOC's Games can be adequately understood only as an ideological formation offering—as one among a number of sporting bodies and their mega-events—temporary escape from the mundanities of everyday life, one that fills the coffers of the IOC via outlandish levels of corporate buy-in and broadcasting rights. Such sporting spectacle can—in the stadium, in the city square, in the local pub, and even alone in your living-room—provide captivating moments of athletic beauty, in which all aware of the performer or performance can share and recall a state of what Hans Ulrich Gumbrecht (2008) has called "focused intensity." Very likely all sports fans and participants have felt this kind of empathetic immersion in the sporting moment or have buzzed with the anticipation of experiencing such a moment. Yet it is clear that such experiences are not dependent upon an unthinking commitment to the Seven Commandments of Olympism.

Max Weber, adapting Goethe's concept of elective affinities, showed how the spirit of capitalism lay alongside the Calvinist Protestant ethic, with no causal relationship between them but deep and connecting affinities of time and place (Tomlinson, 2008, p. 68). The modern Olympics arose in just such a way, and the quasi-religious rhetoric of its representatives has proved simultaneously flexible and enduring through time and across space. As the apologists for Olympism have advanced reification in their preacherly way, those most interested in the actualities of the Olympic pact (Cohen, 2016), those focused on its inherent economic gamble (Zimbalist, 2015), those most concerned over the increasingly "integrated world of global spectacle" (Compton, 2016) have poked gaping holes in the Olympic logic. Yet, even with compelling evidence that the Olympic model is riddled with contradictions and flaws, there is relatively little contestation or predilection to dismiss the relevance of the seven sacrosanct Olympic ideals. As John MacAloon (2006, p. 32) astutely observed, Olympic officials have long been used to signing sponsorship contracts with partners while simultaneously battling "those sponsors in defense of the values of the Olympic movement." There is little evidence—or reason—to believe that such contradictions and ongoing structural flaws will not continue to be evident as the Games in Paris 2024 and Los Angeles 2028 are mounted and play out, and the Queenslanders on Australia's Gold Coast plan a Summer Olympics 2032 jamboree.

Alongside this, Olympic boosters can continue to attribute great possibilities to the very malleable values of Olympism. They can work to turn the "inconvenience" of a global pandemic into an opportunity to reshape the Games to fit a post-corona world (AIPS Media,

2020a) and offer the Games as a source of "light at the end of the dark tunnel following this incredibly difficult period for humanity," as veteran Olympian John Coates, the IOC's Coordination Commission chair, put it in Tokyo in November 2020 (AIPS Media, 2020b). It is hard not to see such opportunistic moves as part of what has been a very successful bag of magician's tricks. And while there remains a nimbleness here on the part of the IOC, citizen engagement, seen in the advance of the "Socialympics," will surely advance transparency in ways never imagined before. Within this digital dynamic, more and more citizen protest will continue to articulate and gain force in making demands for serious reform of the Olympic behemoth, raising questions about the credibility of the IOC and its sacred values as never before.

Acknowledgments

I am grateful to Lawrence Wenner for his excellent editorial response to the initial version of this chapter. His assiduous editing combined insightful suggestions for inserts and for the strengthening of the arguments, all delivered with an uncommon courtesy.

References

Abrahamson, A. (2020, October 25). This year of living dangerously, and surely the Olympics can and should be reimagined. *Wire Sports*. https://www.3wiresports.com/articles/2020/10/25/this-year-of-living-dangerously-and-surely-the-olympics-can-and-should-be-reimagined.

AIPS Media. (2020a, September 25). IOC and Tokyo 2020 agree on measures to deliver a Games fit for a post-corona world. *AIPS Media: Official Publication of the International Sports Press Association.* https://www.olympic.org/news/ioc-and-tokyo-2020-agree-on-measures-to-deliver-games-fit-for-a-post-corona-world.

AIPS Media. (2020b, November 18). IOC back in Tokyo as world prepares for next year's Games. *AIPS Media: Official Publication of the International Sports Press Association.* https://www.olympic.org/news/ioc-back-in-tokyo-as-world-prepares-for-next-year-s-games.

Allison, L., & Tomlinson, A. (2017). *Understanding international sport organisations: Principles, power and possibilities.* London. Routledge.

Arnoldi, Janice. (2012, October 1). Socialympics: How sports organizations and athletes used social media at London 2012. *Sport Law.* https://www.sportlaw.ca/wp-content/uploads/2013/01/Social-Media-and-the-Games.pdf.

Bach, T. (2020, October 24). The Olympics are about diversity and unity, not politics and profit: Boycotts don't work. *The Guardian.* https://www.theguardian.com/sport/2020/oct/24/the-olympics-are-about-diversity-and-unity-not-politics-and-profit-boycotts-dont-work-thomas-bach.

Baker, K. (2008). *The 1908 Olympics.* Cheltenham, U.K.: SportsBooks.

Boykoff, J. (2014a). *Activism and the Olympics: Dissent at the games in Vancouver and London.* New Brunswick, NJ: Rutgers University Press.

Boykoff, J. (2014b). *Celebration capitalism and the Olympic Games.* London: Routledge.

Boykoff, J. (2016). *Power games: A political history of the Olympics*. London: Verso.

Boykoff, J., & Tomlinson, A. (2012, July 5). Olympian arrogance. *New York Times*, Section A, p. 19.

Chatziefstathiou, D., & Henry, I. P. (2012). *Discourses of Olympism: From the Sorbonne 1894 to London 2012*. Basingstoke, U.K.: Palgrave Macmillan.

Chappelet, J.-L., & Kübler-Mabbott, B. (2008). *The International Olympic Committee and the Olympic system: The governance of world sport*. London: Routledge.

Cohen, P. 2016. The Olympic compact: Legacies of gift, debt and unequal exchange. In G. Poynter, V. Viehoff, & Y. Li (Eds.), *The London Olympics and urban development: The mega-event city* (pp. 48–69). London: Routledge.

Colomb, C. (2012). *Staging the new Berlin: Place marketing and the politics of urban reinvention post-1989*. London: Routledge.

Compton, J. (2016). Mega-events, media, and the integrated world of global spectacle. In R. Gruneau & J. Horne (Eds.), *Mega-events and globalization: Capital and spectacle in a changing world order* (pp. 48–64). London: Routledge.

Coubertin, P. de (2000). *Pierre de Coubertin 1863–1937: Olympism—selected writings* (Norbert Müller, Ed.). Lausanne: International Olympic Committee.

Flyvbjerg, B., Budzier, A., & Lunn, D. (2020). Regression to the tail: Why the Olympics blow up. *Environment and Planning A: Economy and Space*. Advance online publication. https://ssrn.com/abstract=3686009.

Garcia, B. (2013). The London 2012 cultural Olympiad and torch relay. In V. Girginov (Ed.), *Handbook of the London 2012 Olympic and Paralympic Games: Vol. 1. Making the games* (pp. 199–214). London: Routledge.

Gold, J. R., & Gold, M. M. (2013). Beijing-London–Rio de Janeiro: A never-ending global competition. In V. Girginov (Ed.), *Handbook of the London 2012 Olympic and Paralympic Games: Vol. 1. Making the games* (pp. 291–303). London: Routledge.

Gruneau, R. (1984). Commercialism and the modern Olympics. In A. Tomlinson & G. Whannel (Eds.), *Five-ring circus. Money, power and politics at the Olympic Games* (pp. 1–15). London: Pluto Press.

Gumbrecht, H. U. (2006). *In praise of athletic beauty*. Cambridge, MA: Harvard University Press/Belknap.

Guttmann, A. (1984). *The games must go on: Avery Brundage and the Olympic Movement*. New York: Columbia University Press.

Hill, C. R. (1992). *Olympic politics*. Manchester, U.K.: Manchester University Press.

Ingle, S. (2020, December 7). "More urban": Competitive breakdancing added to Paris 2024 Olympics. *The Guardian*. https://www.theguardian.com/sport/2020/dec/07/breakdancing-paris-2024-olympic-games-ioc.

International Olympic Committee. (2020). Olympic Charter. https://stillmed.olympic.org/media/Document%20Library/OlympicOrg/General/EN-Olympic-Charter.pdf.

Killanin, L. (1983). *My Olympic years*. New York: William Morrow and Company.

Lee, M. (2006). *The race for the 2012 Olympics: The inside story of how London won the bid*. London: Virgin Books.

Lenskyj, H. J. (2000). *Inside the Olympic industry: Power, politics and activism*. New York: SUNY Press.

Ludwig, J. (1976). *Five ring circus: The Montreal Olympics*. New York: Doubleday.

MacAloon, J. J. (1981). *This great symbol: Pierre de Coubertin and the origins of the modern Olympic Games*. Chicago: Chicago University Press.

MacAloon, J. J. (2006). Reviewing Olympic ethnography. In A. Tomlinson & C. Young (Eds.), *National identity and global sports events: Culture, politics and spectacle in the football World Cup and the Olympic Games* (pp. 13–29). Albany: State University of New York Press.

Mackay, D. (2015, November 7). Los Angeles were the only bid for the 1984 Summer Olympics following the withdrawal of Tehran before the final selection in 1978. *Inside the Games.* https://www.insidethegames.biz/articles/1031466/los-angeles-were-the-only-bid-for-the-1984-summer-olympics-following-the-withdrawal-of-tehran-before-the-final-selection-in-1978.

Matthew, H. C. G. (2004, September 23). Asquith, Herbert Henry, first Earl of Oxford and Asquith (1852–1928). In *Oxford dictionary of national biography.* http://www.oxforddnb.com/view/article/30483.

McFee, G. (2010). *Ethics, knowledge and truth in sports research: An epistemology of sport.* London: Routledge.

McNamee, M. (2012). Lance Armstrong, anti-doping policy, and the need for ethical commentary by philosophers of sport. *Sport, Ethics and Philosophy, 6*(3), 305–307.

Miller, D. (2008). *The official history of the Olympic Games and the IOC: Athens to Beijing, 1894–2008.* Edinburgh: Mainstream Publishing.

Muniz-Pardos, B., Sutehall, S., Angeloudis, K., Guppy, F., Bosch, A., & Pitsiladis, Y. (2021, January 13). Recent improvements in marathon run times are likely technological, not physiological. *Sports Medicine.* https://link.springer.com/article/10.1007%2Fs40279-020-01420-7.

Panagiotopoulou, R. (2014). The legacies of the Athens 2004 Olympic Games: A bitter-sweet burden. *Contemporary Social Science, 9*(2), 173–195.

Pavett, M. (2020, November 7). Japanese prime minister suggests Tokyo 2020 would be an "opportunity" for potential N. Korea meeting. *Inside the Games.* https://www.insidethegames.biz/articles/1100457/suga-north-korea-tokyo-2020-meeting.

Pound, R. W. (2004). *Inside the Olympics: A behind-the-scenes look at the politics, the scandals, and the glory of the Games.* Toronto: John Wiley.

Prior, K. (2008). Russell, (Arthur) Oliver Villiers, second Baron Ampthill (1869–1935). In *Oxford dictionary of national biography.* https://doi.org/10.1093/ref:odnb/35874.

Revue Olympique. (1904). Paris: International Committee for the Olympic Games.

Sponsorship Intelligence. (2012, December). London 2012 Olympic Games: Global broadcast report. https://stillmed.olympic.org/Documents/IOC_Marketing/Broadcasting/London_2012_Global_%20Broadcast_Report.pdf.

Symson, V., & Jennings, A. (1992). *The lords of the rings: Power, money and drugs in the modern Olympics.* London: Simon & Schuster.

Tomlinson, A. (1996). Olympic spectacle: Opening ceremonies and some paradoxes of globalization. *Media, Culture & Society, 18*(4), 583–602.

Tomlinson, A. (1999). *The game's up: Essays in sport, leisure and popular culture.* Aldershot, U.K.: Ashgate/Arena.

Tomlinson, A. (2000). Carrying the torch for whom? Symbolic power and the Olympic ceremony. In K. Schaffer & S. Smith (Eds.), *The Olympics at the millennium: Power, politics and the games* (pp. 167–181). New Brunswick, NJ: Rutgers University Press.

Tomlinson, A. (2008). Olympic values, Beijing's Olympic Games, and the universal market. In M. E. Price & D. Dayan (Eds.), *Owning the Olympics: Narratives of the new China* (pp. 67–85). Ann Arbor: University of Michigan Press.

Tomlinson, A. (2012). Lording it: London and the getting of the Games. In J. Sugden & A. Tomlinson (Eds.), *Watching the Olympics: Politics, power and representation* (pp. 1–17). London: Routledge.

Tomlinson, A. (2013). The best Olympics never. In M. Perryman (Ed.), *London 2012: How was it for us?* (pp. 47–61). London: Lawrence and Wishart.

Tomlinson, A. (2014a). Olympic legacies: Recurrent rhetoric and harsh realities. *Contemporary Social Science, 9*(2), 137–158.

Tomlinson, A. (2014b). Seizing the Olympic platform: 6.6 million and counting. In V. Girginov (Ed.), *Handbook of the London 2012 Olympic and Paralympic Games: Vol. 2. Celebrating the Games* (pp. 239–251). London: Routledge.

Tomlinson, A. (2017). Twenty-eight Olympic summers: Historical and methodological reflections on understanding the Olympic mega-event. In L. A. Wenner & A. C. Billings (Eds.), *Sport, media and mega-events* (pp. 51–68). London: Routledge.

Traganou, J. (2016). *Designing the Olympics. Representation, participation, contestation.* London: Routledge.

Zimbalist, A. (2015). *Circus maximus: The economic gamble behind hosting the Olympics and the World Cup.* Washington, D.C.: Brookings Institution Press.

CHAPTER 13

··

SPORT, CORRUPTION, AND FRAUD

··

LISA A. KIHL AND CATHERINE ORDWAY

THE purpose of this chapter is to present key issues identified through the persistent presentation of corrupt behaviors within the sport industry. It is well recognized there are enormous amounts of money washing through and generated by the sport industry. The International Criminal Police Organization (n.d.), better known as Interpol, has observed, "With large profits to be made and a limited risk of detection, competition manipulation has become attractive to criminals." Market analysts estimate that, prior to the COVID-19 shutdowns, the "global sports market" (as variously defined) generated somewhere between U.S.$500 billion (Business Research Company, 2019) and U.S.$756 billion (Sports Value, 2020) annually, with a "compound annual growth rate of 4.3% since 2014" (Business Research Company, 2019). This expansion is based on television and digital broadcasting, fitness centers and gymnasium operators, ticketing, betting, advertising, sponsorship, and merchandise. The revenue is roughly equally divided between the participatory and spectator segments of the industry. In 2020, in response to the pandemic, we have seen community sport and participation in the fitness industry halted around the world, and Sports Value (2020, p. 5) anticipated "global professional sport will lose more than US$15 billion from the impacts of COVID-19." The COVID-19 responses not only create new integrity challenges but severely hamper the ability for sport organizations and law enforcement agencies to combat existing threats to sport integrity.

Despite scholarship and concerted global and national efforts to limit corruption risks and activities, corruption in sport competitions and management practices is a persistent feature of the sport industry. This chapter addresses the conceptualization of the manipulation of sports competitions (which is defined to include match-fixing and doping) and corruption and fraud from elite to community levels, including systematic corruption in international sport federations (IFs). These forms of corruption in sport are influenced by transnational organized crime (TOC) groups and have been impacted recently by responses to COVID-19. In this treatment, we are not placing a normative value on the chosen sport corruption issues discussed in this chapter as the only, or necessarily the most important, in the sport corruption space. Rather, our aim is to consider an assortment of corrupt activities that continue to occur in a range of sporting contexts. In framing the intricacies inherent in these issues, we challenge readers to think prudently about how certain types of corruption evolve and how corruption routinely occurs in particular settings with, it seems, little focus on genuine reform. Last, given the evolving nature and persistence of corruption, we call on the sport industry and scholars to think more boldly, both theoretically and practically, in seeking meaningful reform.

Issues

In order to understand *how* to combat corruption in sport, we need to first understand *what* we mean by defining the terms being used throughout, before examining *why* these forms of corruption are occurring and *who* the various actors are. The forms of corruption we have chosen to highlight in this chapter are (1) manipulation of sporting competitions, (2) fraud in community sport organizations (CSOs), and (3) international federation systematic corruption. The actor we have focused on as having an increasing and nefarious influence, particularly in relation to the manipulation of sporting competitions and international federation systematic corruption, is TOC groups. First, we define our terms.

Manipulation of Sporting Competitions

Simplistically, past considerations of corruption in sport have been limited to an analysis of "cheating to win" (doping) and/or "cheating to lose" (match-fixing) (Ordway & Opie, 2017, p. 54). During the past decade, the nature and methodology used to manipulate on-field sporting competitions has evolved. The form, type, and increased scale of manipulation—as well as the kinds of actors and their motivations, strategies, collaborators, and resultant associated corrupt practices—suggested the manipulation terrain has advanced well beyond the historically simple understandings of match-fixing and doping. The Council of Europe has recognized this evolution, as well as the need to gain consistency in terminology to develop necessary regulations and laws. In drafting the Macolin Convention (Council of Europe, 2014) and in subsequent meetings, the Council of Europe (2020) sought conceptual clarity regarding manipulation of sport competitions. Article 3(4) of the Macolin Convention defines manipulation of sports competitions as:

> intentional arrangement, act or omission aimed at an improper alteration of the result or the course of a sports competition in order to remove all or part of the unpredictable nature of the aforementioned sports competition with a view to obtaining an undue advantage for oneself or for others. (Council of Europe, 2014)

The definition highlights that such acts or arrangements must be intentional. This creates some confusion where doping is also intended to come within this Convention, but as defined by the World Anti-Doping Code (World Anti-Doping Agency, 2022), antidoping rule violations may be unintentional. This inconsistency goes beyond the scope of this chapter, and we will therefore not be addressing doping as a form of corruption in this context.

The "acts or omissions" referred to in Article 3(4) are those aimed at altering the result or aspects of the competition, removing the unpredictability element, and are implemented to seek advantage. The Macolin Convention "restricts the use of match-fixing purely to the on-venue action where the manipulation is implemented" (Council of Europe, 2018, p. 2; Council of Europe, Directorate General of Democracy, Directorate of Anti-Discrimination, Children's Rights and Sport Values Department, Sport Conventions Division, 2018, p. 11). This definition clarifies that match-fixing is a particularized variant of "manipulation of a sporting competition," and thus the terms should no longer be used synonymously.

The term "match-fixing" itself has generated disagreements and debates about its meaning. Spapens and Olfers (2015, p. 355) noted in earlier research that "there was no accepted definition of match fixing." The lack of definitional agreement has stemmed from the difficulty in discerning and measuring the methodology used in the fix (Nowy & Breuer, 2017). During the past two decades, scholars and practitioners have paid considerable attention to the examination of the meaning and categorization of match-fixing (e.g., Hill, 2008; Preston & Szymanski, 2003). Match-fixing has generally meant influence over or prior knowledge of a competition outcome (win, lose, draw, and/or score margins) or a specific event within the competition (i.e., spot-fixing—a double fault served in tennis or a no ball bowled in cricket). Key variants may be separated into two categories: non-gambling- and gambling-motivated fixes. Spapens and Olfers (2015) have further delineated the categories of non-gambling and gambling corruption by whether the fix was achieved through bribery and/or coercion.

Non-gambling fixes refer to manipulating the outcome of a competition for sporting reasons. This may include improving a team's league standing, avoiding relegation, competing against a weaker team in the next round of a competition, or improving a team's draft position. This form of non-gambling fix may also involve bribing the opponent in order to secure the win. The fix is typically agreed upon between the opponents prior to the start of the game or by individual team members. Evidence of fixes of this kind in boxing and wrestling have been unearthed from as early as 388 BCE (Griffith, 2014).

With the increased commercialization of sport and rapid development of sports gambling (particularly online gambling), the notion of match-fixing has extended to include financially motivated fixes through gambling. Here individuals gamble through illegal, underregulated, or legal betting operators on the final results of a competition and/or a specific event within the competition, taking advantage of predetermined sporting outcomes. These outcomes may be achieved through coercion or bribery of different actors (match officials, players, coaches, and/or administrators). The betting monitoring company Sportradar suggested, "The global annual criminal proceeds from betting-related match-fixing are estimated at €120 million" (European Union Agency for Law Enforcement Cooperation, 2020, p. 1).

Based on the Council of Europe's (2019) definition of manipulation of sports competitions, an associated typological framework (Council of Europe, Directorate of Anti-Discrimination, Sport Conventions Division, 2020) was created to assist in the practical application and diagnoses of diverse sporting manipulations found across the globe.

Manipulated practices have considerably advanced to include, among other practices, engaging in fraudulent "ghost games" (discussed below), using sports clubs as shell companies, practicing poor governance, influencing player agents, using insider information, and overlooking conflicts of interest. Manipulation of sport competitions is generally carried out to gain an advantage, usually financial.

The typology is an important tool that assists in understanding the nature of manipulations by categorizing (a) the type of manipulation, (b) who engages in the manipulation, and (c) their motivations. Three types of sports competition manipulations are recognized: (1) the direct interference of the natural course of a sport competition, (2) the alteration of an athlete's identity and/or personal information to interfere with the natural course of a competition, and (3) alteration that is contrary to sport rules and criminal laws. Each of these is further classified by the context in which the manipulation occurs, the assessment of whether manipulation involves the perversion of governance practices or exploitation of power, and by whether it involves external influences and/or was a planned or opportunistic action. While the working definitions and typologies here may not be perfect, they do begin to provide a common language and clarity for measuring, analyzing, investigating, and creating relevant regulations and programs to respond to sport competition manipulation. In this chapter, we will focus on match-fixing.

Fraud in Community Sport Organizations

Fraud in CSOs, also known as occupational fraud, is a persistent problem and has become a widespread global concern. Wells (2005, p. 44) defines occupational fraud as "the use of one's occupation for personal enrichment through the deliberate misuse or misapplication of the employing organisation's resources or assets." CSOs are vulnerable to fraud as they are mostly managed by volunteers who trust one another. They often operate in a club system that is vulnerable because they lack internal controls and resources (e.g., Doherty, Misener, & Cuskelly, 2014) that are critical for discovering and preventing fraud (Greenlee, Fischer, Gordon, & Keating, 2007). Worldwide, different cases of fraud have been reported in a range of sports clubs (e.g., baseball, cricket, American football, ice hockey, netball, football [soccer], softball) involving individuals who have stolen significant amounts of money (Kihl, Misener, Cuskelly, & Wicker, 2021). Recent examples include the following:

United States: A former treasurer for both a football (soccer) club and a youth lacrosse organization embezzled U.S.$758,001 over a six-year period to pay his mortgage and credit card debt (Dornblaser, 2018). This volunteer treasurer used his knowledge and expertise as a financial advisor to exploit the lack of internal oversight mechanisms by writing checks to himself and withdrawing money from the club accounts. The court found him guilty, sentenced him to 20 years on probation, and ordered him to pay retribution and fines.

United Kingdom: A netball club treasurer was given a 20-month jail sentence for stealing U.K.£50,000 of club funds over five years ("Shropshire Netball Official," 2016).

The treasurer was a licensed accountant and had full control over the club's bank accounts. She stole cash while collecting club fees and paying their bills. The media reports stated that she needed the "money to pay her tax bill and had intended to pay the money back," and that she had "both gambling and alcohol addictions" (paras. 11, 12).

Australia: A Junior Rugby League Club had over AUD$33,000 stolen over a seven-month period by their treasurer (Frost, 2016, para. 13). The individual exploited the club's oversight policies by writing and cashing/depositing checks as well as stealing cash from the club's registrations and fundraising. The media reported that the treasurer acted suspiciously at meetings, being "very vague about expenditures" (para. 13). She pled guilty and was given a suspended two-and-a-half-year jail sentence and was required to pay restitution.

Documented cases of fraud in CSOs, such as these examples, show that volunteers serving in treasurer, president, and board member roles can abuse their positions and defraud organizations of irreplaceable funds (Kihl et al., 2021). Kihl and colleagues found that fraud in CSOs was typically carried out through different forms of embezzlement (e.g., writing forged and blank checks, siphoning funds into personal accounts, creating phony supplier accounts, and opening personal credit cards). Unfortunately, fraud in CSOs receives scant attention in the literature, and there is little evidence that it is understood as a concern for communities. This is disappointing because the impact of fraud on participants and local communities can be substantial. The biggest impacts are the actual financial losses, which by necessity limit the opportunities that can be offered for participants. Such fraudulent "hits" create stress for club administrators and members and serve to undermine the long-term sustainability of clubs. Fraud also undermines the community's trust in CSOs, which in turn negatively impacts fundraising and goodwill.

International Federation Systematic Corruption

Corruption within umbrella sporting organizations at the regional and international levels is not a new phenomenon. In the past decade, going beyond the individualistic nature of fraud in CSOs, cases of systematic corruption involving bribery, fraud, money laundering, conflicts of interest, nepotism, and cronyism have been exposed in several IFs, including FIFA (Jennings, 2006, 2016), World Athletics (Krieger, 2018), and the International Volleyball Federation (Fabian, 2020). We will examine the most recent cases involving the International Boxing Association (AIBA) and the International Weightlifting Federation (IWF) to outline corruption indicators and gaps.

As their sports are on the Summer Olympic Games program, the organizations representing boxing and weightlifting have participated in high-level meetings since 2012 to develop agreed Key Governance Principles and Basic Indicators (Association of Summer Olympic International Federations, 2016). The members of the Association of Summer Olympic International Federations (ASOIF), including AIBA and the IWF, supported the five principles, namely:

1. Transparency
2. Integrity
3. Democracy
4. Sports development and solidarity
5. Control mechanisms

It was agreed these principles "be immediately embraced by all IFs in all their respective activities, decisions, processes and regulations" (Association of Summer Olympic International Federations, 2016, p. 6). However, the ASOIF Governance Task Force also makes it clear in this document that the degree to which each IF should implement these principles will differ on a case-by-case basis, and that "[e]ach IF owns its evaluation and monitoring system" (p. 3). This emphasis on self-regulation at the international level highlights the key weakness in the anticorruption framework. Research into IF governance demonstrates that faith in the IF's autonomy in decision-making is misplaced, and that instead it often manifests in systematic corrupt practices by federation executives (Forster, 2016; Geeraert, 2019). The two recent cases—concerning the AIBA and the IWF—illustrate how national member federations are incapable of addressing corruption and holding IF executives to account.

Boxing: The AIBA and Poor Governance Practices

After an extensive series of inquiries, in June 2019 the International Olympic Committee (IOC) suspended its recognition of the International Boxing Association (IBA - formerly the AIBA) (International Olympic Committee, 2019). The IOC's decision reflected ongoing concerns with AIBA's governance, ethics, fiscal management, and refereeing and judging (International Olympic Committee, 2020). Nenad Lalovic, chair of the IOC Inquiry Committee, declared AIBA had created "very serious reputational, legal and financial risks" for the IOC (Dunbar, 2019).

While AIBA has had a history of corruption issues, in 2017 the IOC Executive Board publicly expressed concerns about AIBA's level of debt and poor governance practices. The IOC demanded AIBA provide a progress report detailing (1) the results of an independent financial audit, (2) the results of ASOIF Governance Task Force review of AIBA's governance,[1] and (3) proof that AIBA would continue to address refereeing and judging changes based on the post-Rio 2016 Olympic Games review. A report from AIBA summarizing these activities was delivered to the IOC on January 31, 2018 (International Olympic Committee Inquiry Committee, 2019, p. 2).

The IOC provided AIBA with three opportunities (April 2018, July 2018, and October 2018) to document how they were addressing their governance, doping, and financial shortcomings. However, the IOC Executive Board was not satisfied with the AIBA's progress on these matters. It appears from the IOC Inquiry Committee report that the AIBA's poor adherence to good governance practices and regular breaches of the IOC ethical code arose through systematic mismanagement and insufficient oversight. Specifically cited were concerns that AIBA lacked clear governance processes, that its conflict-of-interest rules did not adhere to the IOC's code of ethics, and that the organization failed to carry out basic third-party due diligence and background checks (International Olympic Committee Inquiry Committee, 2019).

One of many examples relates to the lack of scrutiny surrounding the merry-go-round of appointments to the AIBA presidency role. Following the decision of the AIBA Disciplinary Commission on October 9, 2017, to suspend the AIBA president Ching-kuo Wu for alleged violations of various provisions of the AIBA Statutes and Codes (International Boxing Association, 2017), AIBA Vice President Franco Falcinelli was appointed via mail vote as acting interim president on October 15 (Latvian Boxing Federation, 2017). After only four months, however, Falcinelli (2018, para. 3) resigned at the AIBA Congress, claiming a need to "dedicate more time to [his] family." As the most senior vice president, Gafur Rahimov (Rakhimov) was immediately appointed to replace Falcinelli, despite having been denied entry to the Sydney 2000 Olympic Games by the Australian government on the grounds of "the safety and security of the Australian community" (International Boxing Association Executive Committee, 2018; Wilson, 2000, para. 6). The AIBA Executive Committee would also have been aware that in 2012 and 2013, the U.S. government identified Rahimov as a key member of a TOC, the Brothers' Circle, which is alleged to have specialized in the production and trafficking of heroin internationally (U.S. Department of the Treasury, 2012, 2013). This decision was updated by the U.S. Office of Foreign Assets Control (2017, para 5) in 2017 to indicate that Rahimov was believed to be a supporter of another TOC, Thieves-in-Law.[2] When Falcinelli wrote to the AIBA Executive Committee opposing Rahimov's presidential candidacy on these grounds (Morgan, 2018), the Executive Committee provisionally suspended Falcinelli (only to lift the suspension two months later) (International Boxing Association, 2018).

The AIBA also had extraordinary debt and liquidity issues. Poor financial practices and bad investments led to the organization being nearly bankrupt, with debts of about CHF17 million. Furthermore, AIBA owed creditors approximately CHF29 million by the end of June 2021, and it was not clear how it was going to pay its debts (International Olympic Committee Inquiry Committee, 2019). There is no suggestion by the IOC Inquiry Committee that Rahimov's alleged links with TOC groups, which he denies, and his membership on the AIBA Executive Committee since 1998 (Rahimov, 2018) are directly linked; rather, as noted by the IOC Inquiry Committee (2019, p. 6):

> According to US law, US persons are prohibited from dealing with sanctioned persons or entities, directly or indirectly, controlled by sanctioned persons. As a consequence, this designation may have an impact on the relationship between AIBA and the US boxing entities, or more generally US companies or companies with significant presence in the US, as well as US sponsors of AIBA. . . , This includes many US and non-US banks, including the bank of the IOC, which refuses to make any payments to AIBA at the moment.

Adding to these challenges, AIBA has struggled with the reform efforts to ensure sustainable fair management practices of their judges and referees. Despite a new scoring system from 2013 (International Olympic Committee Inquiry Committee, 2019), several athletes vehemently criticized the fairness of the judging. For example, Irish boxer Michael Conlan accused AIBA of corruption after he lost a controversial decision to his Russian competitor. The AIBA suspended all 36 referees and judges involved in the Rio 2016 Olympic tournament while an investigation was held to examine corruption allegations ("AIBA Sidelines," 2016). The investigation described the AIBA's internal culture as "driven by power, fear and lack of transparency" (International Olympic Committee Inquiry Committee, 2019, p. 7). In the end, no match results were changed, but the flawed referees and judges selection process was replaced with an independent Swiss Timing electronic draw system from 2017 (International Boxing Association, 2016). One of the candidates in the 2020 presidential election, Ramie Al-Masri, chair of the German Boxing Association Referees' Commission, sought to address the continued allegations. A computer scientist, Al-Masri was employed by the company contracted by the AIBA to develop the AIBA database (Mackay, 2020).

The Inquiry Committee report concluded it remains to be seen how "the AIBA will fulfil its roles and responsibilities according to the IOC charter" (International Olympic Committee Inquiry Committee, 2019, p. 10). The corruption and poor governance within AIBA not only impacts the reputation of boxing and the Olympic movement; it also dramatically impacts the central stakeholders of the sport: the athletes. The persistent corruption in this case highlights the need for external accountability and greater athlete involvement in sport governance.

Weightlifting: The IWF and the Corrupt Authoritarian President

On January 5, 2020, the German television network ARD aired a documentary film, *Der Herr der Heber* (The Lord of the Lifters) that made serious accusations of corruption within the IWF (The Dark Side of Sport, 2020). The film alleged the IWF Executive Board, including its president, Tamás Aján, directed and participated in extensive corrupt activities, some over several decades, including "financial irregularities, property investment, doping control testing and sample manipulation combined with doping fine payment irregularities" (McLaren, 2020, p. 6). After initially denying the allegations (International Weightlifting Federation, 2020d), the Executive Board appointed Richard McLaren, the Canadian lawyer who had conducted the investigations into the state-sponsored doping in Russian sport following the Sochi 2018 Olympic Winter Games, and his investigative team to conduct an independent investigation into the ARD allegations. McLaren then liaised with the Executive Board via the newly established IWF Oversight and Integrity Commission.

Instead of being suspended for the period of the investigation, Aján continued to operate on a "business as usual" basis: "For the 90-day period, and consistent with the practice of good governance, IWF President Tamas Ajan has delegated a range of operational responsibilities to IWF Vice President Ursula Papandrea, who will temporarily serve alongside Ajan in an Acting President role" (International Weightlifting Federation, 2020b, paras. 2, 4). Aján continued to manage the IWF office, organized Executive Board meetings, and met with financial advisors and the auditors. He effectively "blocked" Papandrea from carrying out her assigned presidential duties that had been "granted to her by the Terms of Reference, which authorised her management and supervision of the activities of the IWF and of the Secretariat" (McLaren, 2020, p. 15). Furthermore, Aján did not provide Papandrea signatory authority to financial accounts and failed to fully disclose to her all the various IWF bank accounts. Several members of the Executive Board were in violation of the terms of reference to fully cooperate, and "[s]ome Members actively attempted to deceive and frustrate the investigation process" (McLaren 2020, p. 13).

McLaren's overriding observation was that for over almost half a century, Aján had used an "autocratic authoritarian" leadership style to control every aspect of the administration and governance of the IWF. The IWF bylaws provided the president with exclusive authority over the secretariat, the Congress, and the Executive Board. The president had the power to staff and oversee the secretariat, which allowed Aján to appoint his son-in-law as director-general (CEO), and to control the IWF's financial accounts and activities. Aján exploited poor governance practices to deceive the Executive Board and to hide his corrupt management practices. For example, he was the sole signatory on the deposits and receipts of cash payments into the Federation's bank accounts. He directly collected doping fines, competition and membership fees, and event sponsorships in cash. Aján withdrew substantial amounts of cash from the accounts without approval or financial oversight.

The report noted the financial accounting was incomplete, the documentation of expenses and revenue was in utter disarray, and approximately U.S.$10.4 million was unaccounted for (McLaren, 2020). Aján also used cash to buy votes for himself and his handpicked Executive Board to shore up support for his almost 45-year reign. The last two IWF electoral congresses featured widespread vote-buying for the presidential and senior-level positions of the Executive Board, matters which were in clear violation of the organizational bylaws and ethical guidelines (McLaren, 2020). Beyond this, individuals who had earlier raised concerns about Aján's corrupt practices were bullied and punished (p. 18). The findings confirmed the Executive Board did not fully understand the "overall affairs of the IWF" and consequently failed in their role as overseers of the organization (McLaren, 2020, p. 4). The sport of weightlifting also has a considerable history and culture of doping, and the report claimed Aján interfered with the IWF Anti-Doping Commission and that there were some 40 positive doping tests of gold and silver medalists that were hidden from IWF records (McLaren, 2020). This last claim has been investigated by the International Testing Agency (2021). Concerns about the effectiveness of the oversight role of the World Anti-Doping Agency (WADA) continue to be addressed (International Testing Agency, 2022).

The McLaren report has triggered investigations by law enforcement authorities, WADA, and the IOC to investigate further corruption and the breach of financial laws and antidoping rules (Hartmann & Butler, 2020a). Since the report was published, loyal Executive Board members have continued to bully IWF staff and met secretly on October 13, 2020, to revoke Papandrea's authority as interim president (USA Weightlifting, 2020). The IOC, USA Weightlifting, and British Weightlifting condemned the Executive Board's decision (Baldwin, 2020; International Olympic Committee, 2020). Papandrea referred to the "old guard" as "a bunch of cowards who were too scared to stand up to Aján themselves" (Oliver, 2020b; Ostrowicz, 2020). Reminiscent of the AIBA experience outlined earlier, the Executive Board initially replaced Papandrea with Maj. Gen. Intarat Yodbangtoey of Thailand, who was referred to in the McLaren (2020, p. 87) report as the "vote broker distributing the $5,000 USD cash bribe[s] from a bag." Additionally, concerning for the IOC, WADA, and IWF member federations is the claim that

> Thailand is one of the three nations banned from the Tokyo 2020 Olympic Games because of its doping record. Seven of 19 members on the Board are from countries that are banned from Tokyo or can send only a reduced number of athletes because of multiple doping violations. (Oliver, 2020a, paras. 6–7)

This indicates that integrity may not be high on the list of priorities for those federations. After a backlash, Yodbangtoey was replaced the next day by Great Britain's representative, Michael Irani, as IWF interim president (International Weightlifting Federation, 2020a). In his new role, Irani, who has been on the Executive Board since 1992, has also been criticized for introducing a comprehensive Confidentiality Agreement, which it is suggested is intended to further stymie transparency (Hartmann & Butler, 2020b). This culture of poor governance can be expected to persist unless the IOC introduces a rule, similar to that enjoyed by FIFA (2020, art. 8(2), p. 13), whereby noncompliant IF boards can be replaced by a "normalisation committee." The lack of oversight and emphasis on self-regulation will also continue to allow systemic corruption to thrive.

Approaches

Influence of Transnational Organized Crime on Sport

For the past decade, scholars (e.g., Carpenter, 2012; Hill, 2010) and international sport leaders (e.g., IOC President Thomas Bach) have warned the sport community about global threats to sport integrity, which include corruption. An emerging narrative to these integrity concerns pointed to organized crime groups being involved in various criminal activities, such as drug trafficking, match manipulations, bribery, money laundering, and illegal betting. In 2014, the Director-General David Howman of WADA declared, "The biggest threat to sport is organised crime . . . and we should not 'compartmentalise it into match-fixing or bribery, it's organised crime. . . . I think, now, organised crime controls at least 25 percent of world sport in one way or another'" (quoted in Shine, 2014).

Globalization has served to expand the nature of criminal pursuits and provides greater ease for organized criminals to upgrade into TOC. The physical opening of borders, the electronic financial markets, online gambling, and digital broadcasting have given TOC groups unprecedented numbers of open doors to move through. Match-fixing expert Declan Hill has repeatedly warned nations of the pending "[t]sunami of corruption" as TOC groups have infiltrated countries such as Australia, Canada, New Zealand, and the USA (e.g., "Declan Hill Warns," 2014; Lewis, 2018). As a result, every region and country across the globe has experienced an increase in international criminal activity in sport. A TOC group is defined as

> a structured group of three or more persons, existing for a period of time and acting in concert with the aim of committing one or more serious crimes or offences across national borders . . . in order to obtain, directly or indirectly, a financial or other material benefit. (United Nations Office on Drugs and Crime, 2004, p. 5)

TOC both involves an activity and is an entity (Lin, 2010). Regardless of the size, structure, and type of criminal organization, TOC syndicates engage in poly-criminal activities, including betting fixes (Caneppele, Langlois, & Verschuuren, 2020; European Union Agency for Law Enforcement Cooperation, 2020), money laundering, drug trafficking, extortion, and firearm trafficking. The poly-criminal activities create "a shadow socioeconomic system" (Lin, 2010, p. 9) that supplies illicit services and demands (e.g., monitoring online betting, facilitating match-fixing through approaches and bribery, and finances to support bribes). As sport corruption, as with most forms of corruption, operates in the shadows, it is difficult to get an accurate picture of where TOC groups currently thrive. Globalization has also enabled the range of TOC activities in sport to diversify, further challenging detection and disruption.

Globalization conceptually helps explain the nature of TOC. Three main aspects of globalization have accelerated the facilitation of TOC group involvement in match manipulations: "Globalisation of the economy, international movement of people, commodities and capital, and progress in telecommunications and information technology" (Lin, 2010, p. 12). As an economic force, globalization has opened the global market for sport and sport betting. For example, identified Southeast Asian and Chinese criminal networks have been purchasing financially troubled smaller football clubs for the purposes of match-fixing and money laundering (European Union Agency for Law Enforcement Cooperation, 2020). We have also seen examples of Asian TOC groups financially backing match-fixing operations in several European countries where localized criminal groups orchestrated the corrupt activities. The Asian groups move money across international borders to cover costs (Yusof, 2014).

The second concept, a TOC as an entity, focuses on how criminal groups manage their diverse operations based on business models that safeguard racketeering (Lin, 2010). The opening of borders has changed the structure of criminal activities, from a previous reliance on hierarchically organized crime units to working in more sophisticated networks that reflect entrepreneurial-spirited partnerships (European Union Agency for Law Enforcement Cooperation, 2020). Such TOC group partnerships are market driven and malleable, allowing for the effective facilitation of competition manipulation and other crimes by local criminal groups financed or co-financed by foreign match-fixing operations. TOC groups engaging in the commercial enterprise of sports corruption have mostly emerged from European member states, Asian countries, and the former Soviet bloc, including Russia and Armenia. TOC groups form networks composed of a number of criminal groups from different countries, forming often intricate webs to facilitate a range of crimes, including sport corruption (European Union Agency for Law Enforcement Cooperation, 2020; Heron & Jiang, 2010). This understanding has been reflected in the 2017 Resolution 7/8 on Corruption in Sport to the United Nations Convention against Corruption (United Nations Office on Drugs and Crime, n.d.).

The ever-changing structures of TOC groups and networks makes detection and deterrence more difficult for governments and law enforcement. Hence, the increased importance for cooperation among national governments, local and international law enforcement, sport data companies, sports betting operators, and sport governing bodies to share information and educate the sport industry and the public about the nature of corruption in sport and strategies to deter it. These cooperation efforts are mandated by the Macolin Convention (Council of Europe, 2014, 2019) and reflected in partnerships between Interpol and the European Union Agency for Law Enforcement Cooperation and governing bodies (e.g., IOC), between sport leagues and sport governing bodies (e.g., Union of European Football Associations, National Basketball League, Tennis Integrity Unit) and commercial operators, including Sportradar.

TOC Groups and the Manipulation of Sporting Competitions: Focus on Match-Fixing

The sporting world has increasingly been infiltrated by TOC groups who are approaching players, coaches, and match officials to persuade them (often with financial and other forms of bribes) into fixing either the outcome or specific aspects of a competition. Research has documented a variety of competition-fixing schemes, primarily focused on match-fixing, in Greece (e.g., Manoli & Antonopoulos, 2015), Malta (e.g., Aquilina & Chetcuti, 2014), Italy (Boeri & Severgnini, 2013), the Netherlands (Spapens, & Olfers, 2015), Taiwan (Lee, 2017), and elsewhere. Cases of match-fixing and money laundering have been found in tennis, football, basketball, badminton, cricket, rugby, darts, and snooker, particularly at the lower levels, demonstrating that all sports should be vigilant to threats of TOC (IGaming Business, 2020). The European Union Agency for Law Enforcement Cooperation (2020) estimated the global sports betting market was worth €1.69 trillion per year and annual betting-related match-fixing earnings for global criminal organizations was €120 million. This considerable size of the betting market, in addition to gaps in national sport corruption legislation and international legislation frameworks, technological innovation, and poor sport governance, has served to make sport corruption an attractive enterprise for TOC groups (Caneppele et al., 2020).

Innovative digital media strategies have allowed crime groups to use social media to approach individuals to commit manipulations and to communicate the details on the fix with their fellow corrupt actors. The International Cricket Council (2018, art. 4) has attempted to combat this trend by banning players' mobile phones on match day since the early 2000s. As a further precaution, members of the Australian cricket teams "have been instructed to screen shot suspicious online approaches from unfamiliar accounts" (Le Grand, 2017), and companies like Sportradar can now unveil pseudonyms used by corrupt actors on social media (IGaming Business, 2020).

Additionally, the emergence of online betting (both legal and illegal) and new betting products and services (e.g., betting apps, live betting, proposition bets) has provided many opportunities for criminal groups to decrease their risk of detection. Weak, or "gray," regulation of betting markets is exploited by engaging different betting strategies to utilize these weaknesses (Rebeggiani, 2015). Here, TOC groups layer or spread their bets by using a number of "mules" (individuals) to place small bets so as to not raise betting alerts and to diversify their bets (Caneppele et al., 2020). Detection is also avoided by using proxy accounts, using multiple betting accounts, or using diverse platforms.

The European Union Agency for Law Enforcement Cooperation (2020) has identified TOC groups most frequently target football and tennis matches because of their worldwide popularity and ease of spot-fixing (e.g., red cards or own goals in football or foot faults in tennis) and use robust methodology to abuse online technology and infiltrate lower-level competitions, as illustrated in the following cases:

Football: One of the most notable TOC cases was uncovered by the European Union Agency for Law Enforcement Cooperation's "Operation Veto" in 2013. For over 10 years, a Singaporean criminal organization led by Tan Seet Eng (a.k.a. Dan Tan) organized a global match-fixing syndicate that aimed to influence over 380 international football matches in Africa, Asia, Latin America, and Europe (European Union Agency for Law Enforcement Cooperation, 2013). Matches were manipulated for betting purposes in professional leagues, the World Cup, and European championship qualifiers, as well as two Champions League games. Lower-division semiprofessional matches were also manipulated (Borden, 2013). The Singaporean crime syndicate worked closely with European, Latin American, and Russian criminal groups that helped facilitate the corrupt activities. Tan sent money across borders to organized crime groups and used violence to enforce the "rules" (Hill, 2013, p. 260). These TOC groups used their respective networks to assist in approaching and bribing players, coaches, match officials, and others. To avoid detection from sports data monitoring organizations (e.g., Genius Sports, Sportradar), large quantities of smaller bets on lower-level sports were placed in worldwide online betting operations. In this process, Tan used U.S.$3 million to bribe individuals to manipulate matches and earned over U.S.$11 million in betting profits.

Tennis: In 2018, members of an Armenian-Belgian criminal organization were arrested in Spain and imprisoned in Belgium after being found guilty of bribing tennis professionals to fix matches from 2014 to 2019. The fixed matches for betting purposes were on lower-level tournaments on the Challenger and Future tours. The criminal group bribed a professional tennis player "who acted as the link between the gang and the rest of the criminal group" (European Union Agency for Law Enforcement Cooperation, 2019, para. 2). The TOC group members were found guilty of corruption, money laundering, forgery, and belonging to a criminal gang (EU-Crime and Security in Europe, 2018).

TOC groups' diversification of activities regarding sports match-fixing has been quite easy as they have taken advantage of the liquidity of betting markets, lax regulations, and the low risk of being caught. Since the 2012 mapping of the match-fixing legislation throughout 27 European countries (KEA, 2013) and globally (International Olympic Committee & United Nations Office on Drugs and Crime, 2013), there have been significant regulatory developments across a range of jurisdictions (e.g., Australia [Opie & Lim, 2017; Australian Government, 2020], Zimbabwe [Chingwere, 2020], and Sri Lanka [Fidel Fernando, 2019]). The International Cricket Council has been critical of India's failure to introduce match-fixing legislation (Chakraborty, 2020). The former international cricketer, and when Pakistan's prime minister, Imran Khan, who is also the patron-in-chief of the Pakistan Cricket Board, gave approval for match-fixing to become a criminal offense (Press Trust of India, 2020). Meanwhile, sports betting regulation has undergone major reform in several countries, including Brazil (Seckelmann, 2020) and the USA (Balsam, 2019), without the corresponding sport corruption legislation.

In the cases cited above, the lack of oversight and accountability, the ease of coordinating the match-fixing, and the availability of online betting made their efforts a low-risk crime and high-profit endeavor, showcasing the growing opportunities for TOC groups. As globalization progresses and online betting expands, it seems likely that TOC groups will increasingly seek to enter different global sporting contexts as well as develop new strategies to exploit weak sport regulation and lower-level competitions to expand their corrupt practices, including during times of global crisis.

Debates

There has been much debate about how to address sport governing bodies' inability to reduce the risk of corruption in sport in both national and international contexts. A range of good governance frameworks have been proposed, particularly for IFs, as outlined earlier (e.g., Chappelet & Mrkonjic, 2013; Geeraert, Scheerder, & Bruyninckx, 2013). Geeraert, Alm, and Groll (2014) and Henry and Lee (2014) have argued for IFs to comply with widely embraced and necessary standards such as accountability, democracy, social responsibility, and transparency to curb corruption. Still, adhering to good governance places an emphasis on self-regulation, with all its inherent pitfalls. Indeed, two influential guiding documents—the *Basic Universal Principles of Good Governance of the Olympic and Sports Movement* and *Key Governance Principles and Basic Indicators*—are nonbinding, and the IOC has limited authority to hold IFs accountable (Geeraert, 2019).

On this point, Chappelet (2018) has argued addressing corruption requires going beyond self-regulation and adherence to governance guidelines and should include an international legal framework to enforce compliance. Chappelet suggested using Pérez's (2003) corporate governance model to safeguard sport integrity. Pérez's hierarchical model integrates management and governance systems into five levels. Chappelet applied Pérez's model to the IOC, illustrating how Level 1 in the IOC's management represents its administration; Level 2 in the IOC's governance represents the IOC's sessions and executive board; Level 3 in the management of IOC's governance and regulations represents their audits, ethics, and election commissions; Level 4 in IOC governance represents their courts such as the Court of Arbitration for Sport; and Level 5 in the mega-governance of the IOC represents Swiss laws, European law, and international legal instruments. IFs have too often demonstrated they are incapable of self-regulation, and thus external regulation clearly seems warranted. Chappelet's analysis provides strong arguments for oversight models that support abiding by existing laws and encourage working with governments when new laws are needed, with the goal of achieving transparent democratic managerial practices that feature independent accountability authorities, structures, and practices.

We have also seen various integrity policies (match-fixing and antidoping policies) and/or government units (e.g., Sport Integrity Australia, Finnish Center for Integrity in Sport) that address specific types of corruption. Rather than implementing an overarching system that supports integrity more broadly and includes both noncorrupt but unethical (e.g., conflict of interest) and corrupt (e.g., match-fixing, financial improprieties) practices in sport, we have generally observed a movement away from anticorruption and toward the adoption of more athlete-welfare-focused integrity policies (e.g., SafeSport) to prevent specific kinds of integrity breaches (e.g., sexual assault, doping, and match-fixing). Chappelet (2018) argued effective reform of corrupt governing bodies requires moving beyond good governance principles. Certainly, efforts to maintain integrity in sport need holistic rather than piecemeal reform (Pope, 1996, p. 5). This requires the conceptualization and development of an overarching sport integrity system that limits integrity risks and addresses breaches.

Huberts and Six (2012) defined an integrity system as a process whereby individuals, institutions, policies, practices, and agencies contribute to safeguarding the integrity of organizations. Sport integrity systems are responsible for specifying the required elements and conditions that lead to effectively monitoring, preventing, and penalizing integrity violations in ways that minimize integrity risks in governance and sports competitions. Kihl (2019) suggested a sport integrity system is comprised of three main components: (1) sport actors, (2) internal environment, and (3) external environment. Actors serve as generators and guardians of integrity (Huberts & Six, 2012); these can include internal stakeholders (e.g., an integrity officer or team, governing board members, administrators, coaches, athletes), as well as those external to the organization (e.g., watchdog groups, sports data intelligence agencies, government, media). The internal environment takes stock of organizational characteristics (structure and culture) and ethical management practices (compliance system and values-based programs). Last, assessments of the external environment need be made of those external guardians who are peripheral to national or international sport governing bodies; these include evaluations of independent regulatory environments (i.e., laws, regulations, and external regulatory oversight agencies) as well as broader social environments (i.e., media and community members) and their functioning as external checks and balances. Effective checks and balances are essential mechanisms for guardianship and accountability in that they can ensure that sport governing boards operate within legal and social boundaries. Kihl (2019) argued it is important for the various components of the sport integrity system to work with sufficient coherence to ensure integrity risk containment, including ways to proactively encourage the appropriate (and penalize the inappropriate) exercise of power throughout sport systems. Enabling this would require that international governing bodies work collaboratively to support and coordinate with their counterparts in territorial/regional sport governing bodies. Likewise, to mount an effective sport integrity system, national governing bodies must work with state/provincial governing bodies, which would in turn coordinate with local clubs to adopt and implement specific measures, policies, and practices essential to ensuring integrity within their domains of governance. In short, sport integrity requires a systematic approach to effectively deal with the complexities of protecting sport governance and sporting competitions. Focusing on such an approach is ripe for future research. Such research is essential in mapping the state of integrity systems and ultimately holds the key to providing functional knowledge about how to enhance processes and strategies that build trust about integrity in sport.

Fraud Diamond

Fraud in both CSOs and IFs can be explained and better understood by using Wolfe and Hermanson's (2004) fraud diamond. The fraud diamond is theorized to require a combination of four factors: incentive, opportunity, capability, and rationalization. Using the examples of CSO and IF fraud outlined earlier, consider the four fraud diamond factors as follows:

1. Individuals possess an *incentive* to commit fraud (i.e., motivation to commit fraud).
2. Individuals must have the *opportunity* to commit fraud (i.e., ineffective control or governance system that permits an individual to carry out fraud).
3. Individuals must have the *capability* to commit fraud (i.e., having the character and skill to commit fraud).
4. Actions must be *rationalized* as morally acceptable (i.e., reasoning that the fraud is not criminal but, rather, is acceptable behavior.

Kihl et al. (2021) extended Wolfe and Hermanson's (2004) fraud diamond model to create the CSO fraud indicators. These take stock of the incentives, opportunities, capabilities, and rationalizations in fraud calculations. Incentives to commit fraud relate to personal financial stresses (e.g., supporting lavish lifestyles and addictions, having mental health issues). Opportunities that volunteers exploit to commit fraud include having access to an organization's bank accounts, insufficient financial oversight mechanisms (checks and balances), perceived trustworthiness of individuals in leadership positions, and vacancies in key positions (e.g., treasurer). The capabilities of fraudsters can be evaluated by assessing their level of education, their level of professional expertise (e.g., being trained in accounting), and their level of specialized knowledge of particular sporting endeavors. Finally, fraudsters must rationalize their activities by denying responsibility, often arguing that they had good intentions for using the funds, and may engage in self-justification-facilitating beliefs that they "deserved" the money.

To help detect and prevent fraud in sport organizations it is important to adopt specific internal control mechanisms. In particular, CSOs and IFs not only need to implement and follow financial controls, but also must be in full compliance with laws and regulations (Zack, 2003). This requires the allocation of organizational resources to prevent fraud and to demonstrate that preventing fraud is an organizational priority. Finally, sport organizations must engage in internal and sport community education to advance awareness and broad oversight transparently. It has become increasingly important that athletes and organization members require that their administrators follow ethically driven financial guidelines and not rely on wishful *laissez-faire* faith and trust that individuals will not prey on their vulnerabilities.

COVID-19 Responses Inspiring the Reemergence of Ghost Games

Due to responses to the COVID-19 pandemic, sporting leagues' abilities to play and stage competitions worldwide has been significantly disrupted, and with this has come lessened opportunities for sports betting. The pandemic has led criminal organizations to seek alternative opportunities to generate revenue by manipulating sporting events in two main ways. First has been the reemergence of ghost games.[3] A "ghost game" is

> a match which simply does not take place as stated, and is falsely advertised to bookmakers, punters and the public, in order to achieve profit from the betting markets, with the perpetrators having advance knowledge of the final score, which they have decided. (Brodkin, 2020, p. 3)

More difficult to organize than match-fixing, this scenario entails criminal syndicates recruiting a bookmaker to post the odds, which, in turn, generally leads to other bookmakers posting odds (Holden, 2018). The "game" is then promoted on social media or a fake game website, and assuming the games are not flagged as suspicious, the ghost game proceeds. Data scouts share fictional in-play game information (penalties, corner kicks, score updates, and final result) with the betting companies in real time. Crime syndicates generally target low-profile league games to avoid undue attention. For example, a ghost game tournament in Ukraine was promoted in April 2020. In the scam, a "three-day 'ghost tournament' of club friendlies" between four Ukrainian football clubs, FC Berdyansk, Metropolskata Chereshnya, Tavriya Skif Rozdol, and FC Lozovatka, was advertised on social media (Kerr, 2020). The low-profile clubs had minimal international recognition, which allowed match manipulators to generate interest and frame opportunity for bettors. Their game promotions were sufficiently believable that a sports data company provided odds on the games.

In a second example, TOC syndicates continued their corrupt activities during the pandemic disruptions by targeting entry-level professional tennis competitions. During COVID-19, professional tennis largely came to a halt. However, a number of privately organized tournaments were mounted for, mostly, lower ranked players. While the privately organized events largely went unscrutinized as they were not technically subject to the sports anticorruption rules, registered players and officials were nonetheless warned by the Tennis Integrity Unit (2020b) that they were expected to uphold those rules. Between January and March 2020, the Tennis Integrity Unit received a total of 38 match alerts from betting companies, almost doubling the 21 alerts for the same period in 2019 (Tennis Integrity Unit, 2020a). Between April and June 2020 24 suspicious match alerts were reported (Tennis Integrity Unit, 2020b). The mounting of unsanctioned events and the increase in match alerts does not definitively prove that match-fixing increased due to the COVID-19 pandemic. Nonetheless, the Tennis Integrity Unit was sufficiently concerned by this evidence that they launched an education and awareness campaign that highlighted the susceptibility of lower-circuit tennis players to corruption (Deloit, 2020). It is well-documented that lower-circuit players do not (and really cannot) earn sufficient revenue to support their careers and thus are extremely vulnerable to criminals seeking to manipulate matches (Lewis, Wilkinson, & Henzelin, 2018). The "red flags" seen in the rise of match alerts during the pandemic demonstrates how motivated TOC groups are to create opportunity out of adversity.

CONCLUSION

In this chapter, we have illustrated how vulnerable sport organizations are to diverse forms of corruption and malfeasance along a number of fronts. CSOs are vulnerable to fraud when volunteer administrators, motivated by financial difficulties, exploit opportunities through a lack of internal control mechanisms, rationalize their behaviors as acceptable, and use their professional capabilities to commit fraud. IFs are vulnerable due to their reliance on self-regulation (Geeraert, 2019) and lack of democratic representation, in particular limited athlete representation in decision-making. Self-regulation in sport is an oxymoronic state of affairs that allows organizations to function without meaningful external oversight and accountability. The cases of the IWF and AIBA involve classic examples of historic, systematic corruption and illustrate the inability of the IOC and international government bodies to provide effective oversight.

The relative ease of infiltration of TOC groups into different sports across the globe remains of increasing concern. TOC groups have become robust and sophisticated enterprises that form partner networks to exploit the globalization of sport, online betting, limited regulatory frameworks, and the lack of coordination between local and global law enforcement, government, betting industries, and sport governing bodies. The cases outlined throughout reinforce that, especially during an international and/or national crisis, it is important that sport governing bodies, law enforcement, and betting companies are more vigilant in their prevention activities to counter expected concomitant rises in match-manipulation attempts.

In conclusion, there is no easy answer to the web of challenges related to curbing corruption in sport. It is clear that the COVID pandemic is the worst possible time to reduce resources for integrity and education staff and programs. As we have argued, the most promising pathway forward entails building an international sport integrity system that could serve as a mechanism to minimize integrity risks and counteract integrity violations. Such a system requires multiple actors, multiple levels, and the cohesive coordination of diverse stakeholders at local, national, regional, and international levels. At the international level, an overarching anticorruption oversight body, independently funded and governed, must be an integral part of that system. Putting such a system in place is essential to address the quickly evolving nature and robust persistence of corruption in contemporary sport.

NOTES

1. The ASOIF Governance Task Force was unable to assess the AIBA for its third report "due to major organisational changes in process during the period of the assessment" (Association of Summer Olympic International Federations, 2020, pp. 13, 14, 46).
2. Rahimov challenged the Office of Foreign Assets Control decision in the U.S. District Court (*Gafur-Arslanbek Akhemdovich Rakhimov, Plaintiff, v. Andrea M. Gacki, et al., Defendants*, Civil Action No. 19-2554 (JEB) 04-20-2020). Rahimov also successfully argued that he had been defamed by the *Sydney Morning Herald* newspaper, author Andrew Jennings, and the Australian publisher for claims made in the book *The Great Olympic Swindle* (AP News, 2002).
3. As early as 2009, there were reports of ghost games of international team friendlies and in lower league games.

REFERENCES

AIBA sidelines all Olympic judges and referees. (2016, October 6). *Irish Times*. https://www.iri shtimes.com/sport/other-sports/aiba-sidelines-all-olympic-judges-and-referees-1.2819141.

AP News. (2002, February 2). Uzbek Olympic official wins case. https://apnews.com/article/7adc173506e1b0e66263e503a83aaacb.

Aquilina, D., & Chetcuti, A. (2014). Match-fixing: The case of Malta. *International Journal of Sport Policy and Politics, 6*(1), 107–128.

Association of Summer Olympic International Federations. (2016). ASOIF Governance Task Force (GTF) report approved by ASOIF general assembly. https://www.asoif.com/sites/defa ult/files/download/asoif_governance_task_force_report.pdf.

Association of Summer Olympic International Federations. (2020, June). Third review of International Federation Governance. https://www.asoif.com/sites/default/files/download/asoif_third_review_of_if_governance_fv-0616.pdf.

Associated Press. (2017, December 19). 11 arrested in Croatia, Slovenia in sports corruption case. https://apnews.com/1ab1b52ef4a244e6a264c66d8d976b62.

Australian Government. (2020, August 10). Sport Integrity Australia Act 2020, No. 6, 2006. https://www.legislation.gov.au/Details/C2020C00258.

Baldwin, A. (2020, October 15). Weightlifting: USA, Britain slam ousting of IWF interim president. *Reuters*. https://www.reuters.com/article/us-weightlifting-usa-idUSKBN2701G5.

Balsam, J. (2019, September 6). Legislating for game integrity as U.S. states legalize sports betting. *Law in Sport*. https://www.lawinsport.com/topics/item/legislating-for-game-integrity-as-u-s-states-legalize-sports-betting.

Boeri, T., & Severgnini, B. (2013). Match rigging in Italian professional soccer: The economic determinants of corruption. In M. Haberfeld & D. Sheehan (Eds.), *Match-fixing in international sports* (pp. 101–112). Springer.

Borden, S. (2013, February 4). Police call match-fixing widespread in soccer. *New York Times*. https://www.nytimes.com/2013/02/05/sports/soccer/investigation-finds-suspected-fixing-in-680-soccer-matches.html.

Brodkin, O. (2020, April 6). Ghost games: An explanation. Sportradar White Paper. https://www.sportradar.com/integrity/ghost-games-an-explanation/.

Business Research Company. (2019, May). Sports market: By type (participatory sports, spectator sports, sports team and clubs, racing and individual sports and spectator sports), by competitive landscape, and by region, opportunities and strategies—Global forecast to 2022. https://www.thebusinessresearchcompany.com/report/sports-market.

Caneppele, S., Langlois, F., & Verschuuren, P. (2020). Those who counter match-fixing fraudsters: Voices from a multistakeholder ecosystem. *Crime, Law and Social Change, 74*, 13–26.

Carpenter, K. (2012). Match-fixing—the biggest threat to sport in the 21st century? *International Sports Law Review, 2*(1), 13–24.

Chakraborty, S. (2020, June 25). India should amend match-fixing as "criminal offence": ICC. *Cricket Addictor*. https://cricketaddictor.com/cricket/india-amend-match-fixing-criminal-icc/.

Chappelet, J. L. (2018). Beyond governance: The need to improve the regulation of international sport. *Sport in Society, 21*(5), 724–734.

Chappelet, J. L., & Mrkonjic, M. (2013). Basic indicators for better governance in international sport (BIBGIS): An assessment tool for international sport governing bodies (No. 1/2013). IDHEAP.

Chingwere, M. (2020, August 27). Sport integrity bill approved. *The Herald*. https://www.herald.co.zw/sport-integrity-bill-approved/.

Council of Europe. (2014, September 18). Council of Europe Convention on the Manipulation of Sports Competitions. https://rm.coe.int/CoERMPublicCommonSearchServices/DisplayDCTMContent?documentId=09000016801cdd7e.

Council of Europe. (2018, November 8). Convention on the Manipulation of Sports Competitions—The Macolin Convention (CETS n° 215): Updated concept of manipulations of the sports competitions. https://rm.coe.int/t-mc-2018-87rev-e-concept-of-sports-manipulations final/16808ccb6a.

Council of Europe. (2019). Details of Treaty No. 215: Convention on the Manipulation of Sports Competition. https://www.coe.int/en/web/conventions/full-list/-/conventions/treaty/215.

Council of Europe. (2020). Convention on the manipulation of sports competitions: The Macolin Convention. https://rm.coe.int/CoERMPublicCommonSearchServices/DisplayDCTMContent?documentId=09000016801cdd7e.

Council of Europe. Directorate General of Democracy, Directorate of Anti-Discrimination, Children's Rights and Sport Values Department, Sport Conventions Division. (2018, October 23). Convention on the Manipulation of Sports Competitions—Macolin Convention (CETS n° 215). https://rm.coe.int/09000016809004c2.

Council of Europe, Directorate of Anti-Discrimination, Sport Conventions Division. (2020, June 16). Convention on the Manipulation of Sports Competitions—Macolin Convention (CETS No. 215): Typology of sports manipulations—resource guide. https://rm.coe.int/t-mc-2020-17-goc-typology-resource-guide-final-version-june-2020/16809eb850.

The Dark Side of Sport. (2020, January 15). Geheimsache doping: *Der herr der heber* (The lord of the lifters. YouTube. https://www.youtube.com/watch?v=FLYzWqP1UF4.

Declan Hill warns Australian sporting bodies of match-fixing threat. (2014, May 14). *ABC*. https://www.abc.net.au/news/2014-05-13/sporting-bodies-told-to-brace-for-27tsunami-of-corruption27/5450660.

Deloit, S. (2020, April 11). TIU report: Tennis lower circuits targeted by corruptors. *Gambling News*. https://www.gamblingnews.com/news/tiu-report-tennis-lower-circuits-targeted-by-corruptors/.

Doherty, A., Misener, K., & Cuskelly, G. (2014). Toward a multidimensional framework of capacity in community sport clubs. *Nonprofit and Voluntary Sector Quarterly, 43*(2S), 124S–142S.

Dornblaser, C. (2018, July 7). Hanover sports treasurer to pay back $750K from embezzlement. *York Dispatch*. https://www.yorkdispatch.com/story/news/crime/2018/07/10/hanover-sports-treasurer-pay-back-750-k-embezzlement/771362002/.

Dunbar, G. (2019, June 26). IOC strips Olympic status from troubled boxing body AIBA. *Associated Press*. https://apnews.com/e0bc25202d484c9ba07ce5d3fbca2412.

EU-Crime and Security in Europe. (2018, June 8). Mob watch: Belgian-Armenian tennis fixing gang targeted by raids. https://eu-ocs.com/belgian-armenian-tennis-fixing-gang-targeted-by-raids/.

European Union Agency for Law Enforcement Cooperation. (2013, February 6). Update: Results from the largest football match-fixing investigation in Europe. https://www.europol.europa.eu/newsroom/news/update-results-largest-football-match-fixing-investigation-in-europe.

European Union Agency for Law Enforcement Cooperation. (2019, January 10). Fraud on the tennis court: Criminal network gain missions fixing professional matches. https://www.europol.europa.eu/newsroom/news/fraud-tennis-court-criminal-network-gained-millions-fixing-professional-matches.

European Union Agency for Law Enforcement Cooperation. (2020, August 5). The involvement of organised crime groups in sports corruption. https://www.europol.europa.eu/publications-documents/involvement-of-organised-crime-groups-in-sports-corruption.

Fabian, T. (2020). Volleygate: A history of scandal in the largest international sport federation. *Sport History Review, 51*(1), 84–101.

Falcinelli, F. (2018, January 7). Resignation speech. https://www.iba.sport/wp-content/uploads/2018/01/7_January-2018-Dubai-Exco-Resignation-Speech-by-Franco-Falcinelli.pdf.

Fidel Fernando, A. (2019, November 11). Sri Lanka passes bill criminalising match-fixing. *ESPN Cricinfo*. https://www.espncricinfo.com/story/_/id/28057905/sri-lanka-passes-bill-criminalising-match-fixing.

FIFA. (2020, September). FIFA statutes. https://resources.fifa.com/image/upload/fifa-statutes-2020.pdf?cloudid=viz2gmyb5xopd24qrhrx.

Forster, J. (2016). Global sports governance and corruption. *Palgrave Communications, 2*(1), 1–4.

Frost, P. (2016, June 10). Update: Former Brothers' treasurer stole $30K from the club. *Courier Mail*. https://www.sunshinecoastdaily.com.au/news/former-brothers-treasurer-stole-30000-club/3042866/.

Geeraert, A. (2019). The limits and opportunities of self-regulation: Achieving international sport federations' compliance with good governance standards. *European Sport Management Quarterly, 19*(4), 520–538.

Geeraert, A., Alm, J., & Groll, M. (2014). Good governance in international sport organizations: An analysis of the 35 Olympic sport governing bodies. *International Journal of Sport Policy and Politics, 6*(3), 281–306.

Geeraert, A., Scheerder, J., & Bruyninckx, H. (2013). The governance network of European football: Introducing new governance approaches to steer football at the EU level. *International Journal of Sport Policy and Politics, 5*(1), 113–132.

Greenlee, J., Fischer, M., Gordon, T., & Keating, E. (2007). An investigation of fraud in nonprofit organizations: Occurrences and deterrents. *Nonprofit and Voluntary Sector Quarterly, 36*, 676–694.

Griffith, S. (2014, April 18). Match-fixing isn't anything new! 1,700-year-old Greek contract reveals terms for foul play during a wrestling match. *Daily Mail.* www.dailymail.co.uk/sciencetech/article-2606950/First-proof-match-fixing-Ancient-contract-describes-terms-delibarately-throwing-Greek-wrestling-match.html.

Hartmann, G., & Butler, N. (2020a, November 12). FBI and Swiss police dig into weightlifting scandal, while IOC is undecided. *Play the Game.* https://www.playthegame.org/news/news-articles/2020/0652_fbi-and-swiss-police-dig-into-weightlifting-scandal-while-ioc-is-undecided/.

Hartmann, G., & Butler, N. (2020b, November 12). Weightlifting: When cleaners come with dirty hands. *Play the Game.* https://www.playthegame.org/news/news-articles/2020/0651_weightlifting-when-cleaners-come-with-dirty-hands/.

Henry, I., & Lee, P. C. (2004). Governance and ethics in sport. In S. Chadwick & J. Beech (Eds.), *The business of sport management* (pp. 25–42). Pearson Education.

Heron, M., & Jiang, C. (2010). The gathering storm: Organised crime and sports corruption. *Australian and New Zealand Sports Law Journal, 5*(1), 99.

Hill, D. (2008). *The fix: Soccer and organized crime.* McClelland & Stewart.

Hill, D. (2010). A critical mass of corruption: Why some football leagues have more match-fixing than others. *International Journal of Sports Marketing & Sponsorship, 11*(3), 38–52.

Hill, D. (2013). *The insider's guide to match-fixing in football.* Toronto: Anne McDermid & Associates.

Holden, J. T. (2018). Ghosts in the machines: How corrupters manipulate games that never happened. *Gaming Law Review, 22*(10), 630–634.

Huberts, L. W., & Six, F. E. (2012). Local integrity systems: Toward a framework for comparative analysis and assessment. *Public Integrity, 14*(2), 151–172.

IGaming Business. (2020, October 12). Managing betting integrity risks using data, tech and intelligence. *YouTube.* https://www.youtube.com/watch?v=dIIvOTGZIjCI.

International Boxing Association. (2016, December 17). AIBA Executive Committee ratifies AOB rule changes following successful first implementation at Youth World Championships. https://www.aiba.org/blog/aiba-executive-committee-ratifies-aob-rule-changes-following-successful-first-implementation-youth-world-champi onships/.

International Boxing Association. (2017, October 10). AIBA President Ching-Kuo Wu has been immediately suspended by the chair of AIBA Disciplinary Commission. https://www.aiba.org/blog/aiba-president-ching-kuo-wu-immediately-suspended-aiba-disciplinary-commission/.

International Boxing Association. (2018, November 26). AIBA Executive Committee lifts provisional suspension of Vice President Mr. Franco Falcinelli. https://www.aiba.org/blog/aiba-executive-committee-lifts-provisional-suspension-vice-president-mr-franco-falcinelli/.

International Boxing Association, Executive Committee. (2018, January 11). Text new interim president. https://d21c25674tgiqk.cloudfront.net/2018/01/11_January-2018-Dubai-ExCo-Announcement-of-EC-Decision-by-AIBA-Lawyer.pdf.

International Cricket Council. (2018, October 18). ICC's minimum standards for players' and match officials' areas at international matches. https://icc-static-files.s3.amazonaws.com/ICC/document/2018/12/16/f3b76dad-9668-4a64-aeb8-0e8684d8e28b/-FV-Effective-from-1-December-2018-PMOA-Minimum-Standards-CEC-approved-.pdf.

International Criminal Police Organization. (n.d.) Corruption in sport. https://www.interpol.int/en/Crimes/Corruption/Corruption-in-sport.

International Olympic Committee. (2019, June 26). IOC wraps up final day of the 134th session. https://www.olympic.org/news/ioc-wraps-up-final-day-of-the-134th-session.

International Olympic Committee. (2020, October 14). Statement by the IOC regarding the situation of the IWF. https://www.olympic.org/news/statement-by-the-ioc-regarding-the-situation-of-the-iwf-1?fbclid=IwAR28h5AGMUPXHRu_J8KkuFhYnZ5pt2uDj_ZrPYM-5ZoWdnkgp60aAYDeIzo.

International Olympic Committee, Inquiry Committee. (2019, May 21). IOC Inquiry Committee on AIBA situation: Report to the IOC Executive Board. https://stillmed.olympic.org/media/Document%20Library/OlympicOrg/News/2019/05/IOC-IC-Report.pdf.

International Olympic Committee & United Nations Office on Drugs and Crime. (2013, July). Criminalization approaches to combat match-fixing and illegal/irregular betting: A global perspective. https://www.unodc.org/documents/corruption/Publications/2013/Criminalization_approaches_to_combat_match-fixing.pdf.

International Testing Agency. (2021, June 24). FINAL REPORT: Anti-Doping Rule Violations and related allegations of misconduct from 2009 to 2019. https://ita.sport/uploads/2021/06/ITA-Final-Report-on-IWF.pdf

International Testing Agency. (2022, March 2). The ITA asserts, ADRVs and prosecutes weightlifters based on WADA I&I investigations, McLaren report and LIMS data. https://ita.sport/news/the-ita-asserts-adrvs-and-prosecutes-weightlifters-based-on-wada-ii-investigations-mclaren-report-and-lims-data/

International Weightlifting Federation. (2020a, October 15, 2020). Dr Michael Irani, IWF interim president. https://www.iwf.net/2020/10/15/dr-michael-irani-iwf-interim-president/.

International Weightlifting Federation. (2020b, January 22). IWF acts decisively to restore reputation. https://www.iwf.net/2020/01/23/iwf-acts-decisively-restore-reputation/.

International Weightlifting Federation. (2020c, April 15). IWF executive board accepts resignation of IWF president Tamas Ajan. https://www.iwf.net/2020/04/15/iwf-executive-board-accepts-resignation-iwf-president-tamas-ajan/.

International Weightlifting Federation. (2020d, January 6). IWF rejects ARD allegations. https://www.iwf.net/2020/01/06/iwf-rejects-ard-allegations/.

Jennings, A. (2006). Foul! The secret world of FIFA: Bribes, vote rigging and ticket scandals. HarperSport.

Jennings, A. (2016). The dirty game: Uncovering the scandal at FIFA. Random House.

KEA European Affairs. (2013, July 25). Match-fixing in sport: A mapping of criminal law provisions in EU 27—March 2012. https://op.europa.eu/en/publication-detail/-/publication/c2c73b46-f1b4-436e-be55-a1488afd3ea0.

Kerr, J. (2020, April 2). Match-fixers accused of running "ghost tournament" during COVID-19 crisis. *SBS*. https://theworldgame.sbs.com.au/match-fixers-accused-of-running-ghost-tournament-during-covid-19-crisis.

Kihl, L. A. (2019). Sport integrity system: A proposed framework. In D. Shilbury & L. Ferkins (Eds.), *Routledge handbook of sport governance* (pp. 395–409). Routledge.

Kihl, L. A., Misener, K. E., Cuskelly, G., & Wicker, P. (2021, March 29). Tip of the iceberg? An international investigation of fraud in community sport. *Sport Management Review*. https://doi.org/10.1016/j.smr.2020.06.001.

Krieger, J. (2018). Manipulation in athletics: Historical and contemporary ties between on- and off-field corruption in the International Association of Athletics Federations (IAAF). *International Journal of the History of Sport, 35*(2–3), 231–246.

Latvian Boxing Federation. (2017, October 15). Franco Falcinelli appointed new AIBA interim president. https://www.facebook.com/195938683779534/photos/franco-falcinelli-appointed-new-aiba-interim-presidentreference-in-made-to-the-a/1855598894480163/.

Lee, P. C. (2017). Understanding the match-fixing scandals of professional baseball in Taiwan: An exploratory study of a Confucianism-oriented society. *European Sport Management Quarterly, 17*(1), 45–66.

Le Grand, C. (2017, September 4). Cricketers to oust match-fixing approaches on social media. *The Weekend Australian*. https://www.theaustralian.com.au/news/cricketers-to-oust-matchfixing-approaches-on-social-media/news-story/f65a9a7bfb3399c3eaa6ce018d868558.

Lewis, A., Wilkinson, B., & Henzelin, M. (2018, December 19). Independent review of integrity in tennis: Final report. *International Tennis Integrity Agency*. https://www.tennisintegrityunit.com/storage/app/media/Independent%20Reviews/Final%20Report_191218.pdf.

Lewis, M., (2018, September 11). Declan Hill predicts rise in sports corruption. *The Charger Bulletin*. https://chargerbulletin.com/declan-hill-predicts-rise-in-sports-corruption/.

Lin, L. S. (2010). Conceptualizing transnational organized crime in East Asia in the era of globalization: Taiwan's perspective. Research paper #146. Research Institute for European and American Studies. Athens, Greece.

Mackay, D. (2020, November 3). German referee announces he is standing for AIBA president. *Inside the Games*. https://www.insidethegames.biz/articles/1100298/german-ref-to-stand-for-aiba-president.

Manoli, A. E., & Antonopoulos, G. A. (2015). "The only game in town"? Football match-fixing in Greece. *Trends in Organized Crime, 18*(3), 196–211.

McLaren, R. H. (2020, June 6). Independent investigator report to the Oversight and Integrity Commission of the International Weightlifting Federation. *McLaren Global Sport Solutions*. Updated. https://www.iwf.net/wp-content/uploads/downloads/2020/08/CORRECTED-300720-FULL-REPORT-MASTER-FINAL-FOR-PUBLICATION-v2.pdf.

Morgan, L. (2018, September 21). Exclusive: Falcinelli calls on Executive Committee to support Konakbayev over Rakhimov for AIBA president. *Inside the Games*. https://www.insidethegames.biz/articles/1070212/exclusive-falcinelli-calls-on-executive-committee-to-support-konakbayev-over-rakhimov-for-aiba-president.

Nowy, T., & Breuer, C. (2017). Match-fixing in European grassroots football. *European Sport Management Quarterly, 17*(1), 24–44.

Office of Foreign Assets Control. (2017, December 28). Notice of OFAC sanctions actions. FR Doc. 2017-28030. U.S. Federal Register. https://www.federalregister.gov/documents/2017/12/28/2017-28030/notice-of-ofac-sanctions-actions.

Oliver, B. (2020a, October 13). IWF Board ousts Papandrea and appoints Thailand's Intarat new Interim president. *Inside the Games*. https://www.insidethegames.biz/articles/1099553/iwf-new-interim-president.

Oliver, B. (2020b, October 31). Ousted leader Papandrea claims IWF's "old guard" are as big a problem to weightlifting as Aján was. *Inside the Games*. https://www.insidethegames.biz/index.php/articles/1100208/iwf-old-guard-as-bad-as-ajan-papandrea.

Opie, H., & Lim, G. (2017). The Australian legal framework for countering match-fixing. In S. Steele & H. Opie (Eds.), *Match-fixing in sport* (pp. 59–74). London: Routledge.

Ordway, C., & Opie, H. (2017). Integrity and corruption in sport. In N. Schulenkorf & S. Frawley (Eds.), *Critical issues in global sport management* (pp. 38–63). Routledge.

Ostrowicz, S. (2020, November 2). Ursula Papandrea: A corrupt federation. Weightlifting House. YouTube. https://www.youtube.com/watch?v=OtvvtoUGuU4.

Pope, J. (1996). (Ed.) *The TI source book*. Transparency International.

Press Trust of India. (2020, June 17). PM Imran Khan has approved draft to make match-fixing a criminal offence: Pakistan Cricket Board. *Scroll.in*. https://scroll.in/field/964960/pm-imran-khan-has-approved-draft-to-make-match-fixing-a-criminal-offence-pakistan-cricket-board.

Preston, I., & Szymanski, S. (2003). Cheating in contests. *Oxford Review of Economic Policy*, 19(4), 612–624.

Rahimov, G. (2018). About Gafur Rahimov. AIBA. https://boxingfuture.org/.

Rakhimov v. Gacki (2020, April 4). *Casetext*. https://casetext.com/case/rakhimov-v-gacki.

Rebeggiani, L. (2015). Use and misuse of regulation in fighting betting related corruption in sport—The German example. United Nations Office on Drugs and Crime. https://mpra.ub.uni-muenchen.de/68610/.

Seckelmann, U. (2020, February 28). Hedging your bets: How to regulate Brazil's multi-billion-dollar sports betting market. *Lawinsport*. https://www.lawinsport.com/topics/regulation-a-governance/item/hedging-your-bets-how-to-regulate-brazil-s-multi-billion-dollar-sports-betting-market?category_id=164.

Shine, O. (2014, October 7). Crime controls 25 percent of world sport, anti-doping chief says. Reuters. http://www.reuters.com/article/sportcorruptionidINKCN0HW10020141007.

Shropshire netball official jailed for taking £50,000 of club funds during five years of fraud. (2016, October 22). *Telford News*. https://www.shropshirestar.com/news/crime/2016/10/22/shropshire-netball-official-jailed-for-taking-50000-of-club-funds-during-five-years-of-fraud/.

Spapens, T., & Olfers, M. (2015). Match-fixing: The current discussion in Europe and the case of the Netherlands. *European Journal of Crime, Criminal Law and Criminal Justice*, 23(4), 333–358.

Sports Value. (2020, March). COVID-19 economic impact on sports industry: Report. https://www.sportsvalue.com.br/wp-content/uploads/2020/04/COVID-19-Economic-impact-Sports-Value-Mar-2020.pdf.

Tennis Integrity Unit. (2020a). Tennis integrity briefing note: January–March 2020. https://www.tennisintegrityunit.com/media-releases/tennis-integrity-unit-briefing-note-january-march-2020.

Tennis Integrity Unit. (2020b). Tennis integrity briefing note: April–June 2020. https://www.tennisintegrityunit.com/media-releases/tiu-briefing-note-april-june-2020.

United Nations Office on Drugs and Crime. (n.d.). Corruption and sports. https://www.unodc.org/unodc/en/corruption/sports.html.

United Nations Office on Drugs and Crime. (2004). United Nations Convention against Transnational Organized Crime and the Protocols Thereto. https://www.unodc.org/documents/middleeastandnorthafrica/organised-crime/UNITED_NATIONS_CONVENTION_AGAINST_TRANSNATIONAL_ORGANIZED_CRIME_AND_THE_PROTOCOLS_THERETO.pdf.

USA Weightlifting. (2020, October 13). Statement on IWF Executive Board Action. Team USA. https://www.teamusa.org/USA-Weightlifting/Features/2020/October/13/Statement-on-IWF-Executive-Board-Action.

U.S. Department of the Treasury. (2012, February 23). Treasury imposes sanctions on key members of the Yakuza and Brothers' Circle criminal organizations. https://www.treasury.gov/press-center/press-releases/Pages/tg1430.aspx.

U.S. Department of the Treasury. (2013, October 30). Treasury designates associates of key Brothers' Circle members. https://www.treasury.gov/press-center/press-releases/Pages/jl2196.aspx.

Wells, J. T. (2005). *Principles of fraud examination*. Wiley.

Wilson, S. (2000, September 10). Australia denies Olympic officials. AP News. https://apnews.com/article/ae419ef60784f216e59b1f89b93b93f8.

Wolfe, D. T., & Hermanson, D. R. (2004). The fraud diamond: Considering the four elements of fraud. *The CPA Journal, 74*(12), 38–42.

World Anti-Doping Agency. (2022) . World anti-doping agency resources. https://www.wada-ama.org/en/resources

Yusof, Z. M. (2014). *Foul! The inside story of Singapore match fixers*. Straits Times Press.

Zack, G. M. (2003). *Fraud and abuse in nonprofit organizations: A guide to prevention and detection*. Wiley.

CHAPTER 14

··

SPORT, CITIES, AND COMMUNITIES

··

DANIEL S. MASON

HOSTING sports teams and events has been a highly contested topic for cities throughout the world, and in particular for North American cities of all sizes. The process through which local interests have sought events and teams is not new; it has occurred frequently since the late 19th century with the emergence of modern, organized sport. Since that time, public and private interests have worked to develop infrastructure to accommodate teams and games, often following logics of economic and tourism development, and to increase quality of life, civic pride, and status. This chapter reviews the issues that underpin the process through which cities have actively sought to host professional sports teams and one-off and recurring sporting events and have been complicit in facilitating the drivers of what has become an ongoing saga of the public funding of private enterprise. In addition, the chapter will review the different approaches to understanding this process that have emerged, and the consensus (or lack thereof) that has been reached. The focus will be on the North American context, as the closed-system structure of professional sports is very different from that found in many other parts of the world, and this has facilitated a zero-sum game for cities competing in the "stadium game."

Prior to getting into some of the issues, approaches, and debates in this area, a short overview of the conditions that have led to this point is required. Much of the discourse surrounding the public financing of sports facilities has been bound up in notions of boost-erism and intercity competition (Johnson, 1983), where city planners have viewed hosting sports franchises and events as a means to promote city image (Herstein & Berger, 2013) and redevelop/reinvent the urban landscape. However, the costs for doing so vary widely depending on the size of the event and the infrastructure required (Gotham, 2011). Where events and team facilities are part of broader urban (re)vitalization projects, cities have also developed comprehensive and integrated marketing strategies to attempt to embed events and teams in broader city marketing initiatives (Kavaratzis, 2007) to capitalize on possible changes to the ways people view the city itself. However, many of these plans are being undertaken with a heightened sense of urgency and concerns over the state of cities and their downtowns, particularly in U.S. Rust Belt cities that have witnessed middle-class suburban flight since the 1950s and feature increasingly underserviced and impoverished urban cores (Hackworth & Nowakowski, 2015).

Further, declining financial support from higher levels of government has led city leaders to scramble to create new ways to generate revenues while remaining attractive places to live, work, and visit. The result has been an increasing influence of private interests in civic affairs. As Collins (2008, p. 1184) has noted:

> In response to increased fiscal autonomy, local governments were forced to become more en-
> trepreneurial, and public-private cooperatives emerged as a template for urban governance.
> In declining city centers, developers and city officials formed coalitions with the common
> goal of revitalizing downtowns.

With many larger urban centers suffering from deindustrialization, a new focus on experiential amenities and a service-based economy emerged (Hannigan, 1998). As a result, the desire to host events and teams became more critical to the plans of civic leaders desperate to reinvent their cities and revitalize moribund downtowns using arts, cultural, and sports venues. This process has been described as "creative placemaking" (Loh, 2019) and represents a desire to tap into the uniqueness of the local urban context while (re)using land and creating growth in communities. Thus, cities have pursued many large-scale development projects in cities, and the development of sports venues to host events and teams both fits a movement toward an experiential economy and aligns with the broader interests of local land-based growth coalitions (Albrechts, 2004; Logan & Molotch, 2007). However, as will be described later in this chapter, there have been many issues associated with these types of projects, including stadiums and arenas. As Flyvbjerg (2007) explains, large-scale urban projects are risky due to their complexity, involve conflicting interests, can change in scope over time, are difficult to budget for due to unforeseen circumstances, and can feature misinformation regarding benefits, costs, and risk. "The results are cost overruns and/ or benefit shortfalls for the majority of projects" (p. 579).

The benefits that these projects can confer can be divided into two broad categories: tangible and intangible. Proponents of event hosting and construction often rely on economic impact studies that forecast increased jobs and visitors. However, decades of independent academic study have debunked many of these claims, finding that the presence of a team or the hosting of an event typically has little to no impact on a local economy due to its relatively small size compared to the broader economy. In fact, events and teams are more likely to change the patterns of economic activity within cities rather than grow the economy itself (Coates, 2007). In addition, claims of increased attendance from new facilities are overstated due to the novelty effect of new facilities which wears off over time (Soebbing, Mason, & Humphreys, 2016). However, research has shown that economic impacts are still misunderstood by local residents. For example, Santo (2007, p. 464) surveyed residents in Portland, Oregon, regarding the possibility of hosting a Major League Baseball team and found that the "most common reason that respondents provided for [financially supporting a team] was a belief that an MLB team and stadium would improve the local economy. . . . This indicates the persistence of misconceptions regarding the economic benefits of sports development strategies."

Notwithstanding these issues, research on the intangible benefits of sport events and teams has found substantial positive benefits for communities. In a study of housing prices and proximity to sports facilities, Feng and Humphreys (2018, pp. 207–208) reported:

> [O]ur results suggest that cities continue to subsidize the construction of professional sports facilities, despite the lack of evidence that these facilities generate important tangible economic benefits because the facilities generate important intangible economic benefits. The presence of a professional sports facility and team will generate substantial intangible benefits that are capitalized into housing values and enjoyed by the residents of the community.

Intangible benefits are linked to quality of life, where teams and events are positioned as important amenities in local communities. Thus, benefits sought from hosting teams and events are articulated in terms of psychic income, enhanced community image, and/or visibility (Crompton, 2004). In a comprehensive overview of intangible benefits, Orlowski and Wicker (2019) examined the various ways in which scholars have measured the intangible benefits of sport and sporting success and the manner through which facilities can contribute to downtown development. Despite the presence of intangible benefits, there are some underlying issues that complicate the public funding of sport events and franchises in North American cities.

ISSUES

For cities seeking franchises and events, a chief concern relates to who benefits and who is responsible for paying for them. Expectations from both public and private sectors have changed over the decades, as have the benefits that are purported. However, prior to providing an overview of benefits and costs, it is important to understand the conditions surrounding the negotiations that occur. Perhaps the fundamental issue is the bargaining leverage that leagues and event holders have held over cities. For sports teams, this is ensured by the closed system that major professional sports leagues operate under in the North American context. Many leagues in other countries operate under an open system, where teams will advance in a hierarchy of leagues based on their competitive performance. Thus, competition is organized such that individual clubs can rise to the highest-level league in a given sport. This is facilitated by the practices of promoting the best teams to stronger leagues and relegating weaker teams to less competitive leagues. The distinct advantage of this is that, over time, teams will typically end up playing at a level commensurate with the amount of financial and fan support the team receives. In this kind of system, teams rarely relocate, as the clubs are embedded within their local communities and more lucrative or larger markets often already have multiple clubs operating within them. In contrast, leagues in North America restrict the number of available franchises and assign geographic territories to franchises that reduce economic competition among league clubs. In addition, leagues will often leave a small number of viable markets vacant, which then can be used by existing clubs to exact more subsidies from their current markets because the cities fear losing their local team to relocation. Alternatively, teams can persuade vacant markets to provide substantial subsidies in order to lure existing franchises to move. Such leverage also allows leagues to charge significant expansion fees to add new franchises to the league.

This bargaining imbalance has been further skewed by increasing pressures on cities to compete with other cities on a global scale. As discussed earlier, as higher levels of government have reduced spending, cities have been forced to become more entrepreneurial in order to attract and retain talented workers and investment. This has not been lost on teams and event rights holders, who argue that having a prominent professional sports franchise or major sporting events can become a point of differentiation between cities with similar size and amenities. However, more recently, communities have become more leery of investing in such projects, as more pressing civic concerns increasingly take precedent. Thus, the appetite to bid to host major events in major North American cities has waned, as evidenced by cities such as Boston and Calgary opting not to enter formal bids to host the Summer and Winter Olympic Games, respectively. Despite this trend, several major concerns remain that relate to the manner through which events and teams are sought by various interests in communities. As Gotham (2011, p. 198) writes:

> Scholars have noted several sources of resistance to mega events, including the considerable secrecy, lack of accountability and transparency and undemocratic nature of organizations that run mega events; the propensity of growth coalitions to underestimate the costs, misjudge the negative environmental impacts and overstate the potential economic and social benefits of mega events; and the recognition that developers and sponsors typically engage in self-serving rhetoric and deceit to mislead governments and the public sector in order to get projects approved.

The remainder of this section will elaborate on these issues. First, a significant concern is the overestimation of benefits, typically by event/facility proponents. These overestimations can be related to economic and additional ancillary developments, or even the legacies actually left behind following events. Phillips and Barnes (2015, p. 550) suggest that "legacies often fall short of their expectations for a number of reasons including measurement challenges, flawed goals and the temporary nature of the 'special authority' responsible for the legacy plan." Further, costs can be greatly underestimated, which can skew the expectations local residents have for the financial burden they are undertaking. In a study of megaprojects of all types, Flyvbjerg (2007) found costs overruns of 44.8% for urban rail projects, 33.8% for bridges and tunnels, and 20.4% for roads, with 9 out of every 10 projects experiencing this issue.

Flyvbjerg (2007) provides a comprehensive overview of issues associated with megaprojects, such as stadiums and arenas. He noted that planners and project proponents will overestimate benefits and underestimate costs due to "delusional optimism" about the projects, something seemingly linked to the desire to see the facilities built. In addition, he contends that proponents may deliberately inflate benefits and downplay costs in order to ensure their approval. However, Flyvbjerg argues that the latter explanation for underestimations and overruns is more likely, given that projections are made by established planners and estimates are vetted extensively by experts. He surmises that ongoing problems would likely be rooted out with experience rather than continue to occur, a pattern evident across many countries and time periods: "Therefore, on the basis of our data, we are led to reject optimism bias as a primary cause of cost underestimation and benefit overestimation" (p. 585). A more likely explanation is the political behavior of stakeholders who stand to benefit from such projects.

In addition to concerns of cost overruns and overestimated benefits and legacies, another issue surrounding facility construction for sport events and teams relates to a lack of transparency and involvement of other stakeholders, where local governments engage in "stadium financing in an unlawful and undemocratic manner, by ostracizing the community from taking part in the decision-making process" (Lee, 2002, p. 863). Blanco (2015, p. 129) asserts that large-scale development projects, such as facilities built to host franchises and events, "have been less permeable to citizen engagement than social policies." Further, budgets can be obscured by complex financial models. For example, Olympic events typically finance their operations through event revenues, while the infrastructure itself is funded by other sources, such as public financing. This can make events seem to be profitable on the operations side, but conceal the total costs of event hosting from taxpayers (Lauermann, 2016).

Another issue that arises with facility construction relates to the siting of the facilities themselves. In postindustrial cities, brownfield areas are usually present at or near downtown cores, which are targeted as facility locations. However, while this may involve new use of otherwise underutilized land, the areas near where the brownfields are located are also home to underprivileged groups who are displaced by the construction, either by direct eviction or by being priced out of the market with rising property values and gentrification, as is seen when building the facility stimulates surrounding real estate development. In many cases, proponents see the acquisition of land in these areas as a path of least expense/resistance, one that disrupts the fewest lives of local residents who wield political clout (Panton & Walters, 2018). Further, the kinds of events that are held and amenities that are built in surrounding districts are not designed for consumption by these same residents. This obviously creates value-laden questions about which local citizens' interests are being met and valued (McCann, 2002). Such tendencies often illuminate that ways that cities may ignore local residents' interests in the pursuit of mobile and wealthy consumers for the amenities that are being built (Eisinger, 2000; Gillen, 2009) and may be trying to use entrepreneurial market forces to solve difficult land use issues (vacant, derelict land) that have been created by those very same market forces (Hackworth & Nowakowski, 2015).

However, in recent decades the hosting of sport and cultural events has become more contested with the increased mobilization of local interest groups. In a study of the New Orleans World's Fair, Gotham (2011, pp. 209–210) found:

> Unlike the past, where opposition to mega events was often muted or exceptional, today we witness the proliferation of a variety of mobilisations and sustained protests led by opposition coalitions dedicated to drawing global attention to the inequities and antidemocratic nature of spectacles.

This would suggest that some of the long-standing issues associated with event hosting and facility construction may be easing with an increase in awareness of planning issues; meanwhile, stakeholder groups are becoming more sophisticated and engaged in their efforts to have a say in the process. From a planning perspective, Flyvbjerg (2007) suggests other ways megaprojects can be scrutinized in order to reduce overestimations and overruns. First, he identified reference-class forecasting as a means to improve project accuracy: "The reference class forecasting method is beneficial for non-routine projects such as stadiums, museums, exhibit centers, and other local one-off projects" (p. 588). This method involves forecasting on the basis of comparison to a class of similar projects elsewhere. As Flyvbjerg has put it, "use of the outside view does not involve trying to forecast the specific uncertain events that will affect the particular project, but instead involves placing the project in a statistical distribution of outcomes from this class of reference projects" (p. 591). In doing so, forecasting avoids the optimism and political biases that local planners may have.

Approaches

The previous section discussed some of the issues associated with event hosting and sports facility construction in cities; this section will review some of the research perspectives that scholars have adopted to explain and understand this phenomenon. Due to space limitations, select approaches will be considered. However, it is important to acknowledge other approaches to studying these dynamics, including stakeholder theory (Friedman & Mason 2004, 2005; Friedman, Parent, & Mason, 2004; Parent, 2008; Parent & Deephouse, 2007) and contingent valuation method (Humphreys, Johnson, Mason, & Whitehead, 2018; Johnson, Groothuis, & Whitehead, 2001; Johnson, Whitehead, Mason, & Walker, 2012; Wicker, Whitehead, Mason, & Johnson, 2017).

Framing

As discussed earlier, issues related to the funding of sports infrastructure to host sport events or teams have included a lack of transparency and consistent tendencies to overestimate benefits and underestimate costs. As Flyvbjerg (2007) found, this can be attributed to, in part, the deliberate misrepresentation of financial costs by development proponents. If proponents are able to *sell* the idea of the project to taxpayers and, at times, voters, they are even more likely to be successful. The question remains: How do proponents convey their messages regarding benefits and costs to local residents/taxpayers? To address this, scholars have used media framing as a way to understand the strategies and means through which facility proponents craft arguments and convince audiences of the benefits of such projects.

For example, Sapotichne (2012) focused on rhetorical strategies in local media coverage to frame the construction of a sports facility in Seattle, Washington, and Sant and Mason (2015) examined the media frames employed to generate support for hosting the 2010 Olympic Winter Games in Vancouver. Sant, Mason, and Chen (2019) examined how arena proponents framed the negative self-image of the Canadian city of Edmonton in an attempt to justify the public funding of a facility there. Further, Sant and Mason (2019) looked at rhetorical strategies used to support sports arenas in smaller Canadian communities. As explained by Russo and Scarnato (2018, p. 458), "the discursive power of the media should be central to political economy approaches to urban studies." Thus, researchers have attempted to examine the kinds of arguments that are crafted and legitimated, and who is responsible for their creation. In a discussion of entrepreneurial cities, Gillen (2009) identified the importance of local narratives (such as that found in media coverage of a project) in establishing discursive arguments for the efficacy of urban entrepreneurship and the projects that support them.

The importance of media coverage in shaping opinion is particularly critical when it comes to publicly financing sport facilities:

> Despite independent scholarly research clearly showing that the intangible benefits of sports teams and facilities do not justify the amounts of public subsidies, taxpayers continue to vote in favor of using public funds to support the construction of sports facilities for major league sports teams in North America. Our results indicate that this is due, in part, to the way in which stadium proponents frame the issue in the local newspaper. (Buist & Mason, 2010, pp. 1506–1507)

Collins and Grineski (2007) argue that, at the planning stages, pledges of universal benefits for residents in funding stadiums ultimately reward wealthy interest groups with little evidence of local residents benefiting. This suggests that how benefits are framed, and who in the end receives such benefits, remains an important dynamic.

Status

Civic status and the ability of a new facility or the hosting of an event to improve a city's status can figure prominently in the discourse used to build arguments to publicly fund events and facilities. In fact, recent research suggests that proponents are moving away from traditional economic development arguments and toward intangible benefits such as status (Buist & Mason, 2010; Sant, Mason, et al., 2019; Sapotichne, 2012). These arguments fit within broader discussions of cities, globalization, and competition, where civic leaders are increasingly aware of a global hierarchy of cities and their own city's place in it (Zhang & Zhao, 2009).

Here, traditional city comparators related to income and productivity have often recently been replaced by rankings of livability and quality of life, which are viewed as keys to location decisions by businesses and residents (Blomquist, Berger, & Hoehn, 1988; Rogerson, 1999). Hosting sporting events and franchises that garner widespread media exposure can signal that a city has reached a certain level within this status hierarchy. Edensor and Millington (2008, p. 178) point out that "sporting clubs are able to advertise place in a way that place marketers can only dream about." This can apply to large-scale sporting events as well as events and facilities in smaller communities (Mason, Buist, Edwards, & Duquette, 2007). In fact, some have argued that status is a "fundamental driver of sport-related growth initiatives, in cities of all sizes" (Duquette & Mason, 2008, p. 233).

Research has also made clear that sport events and franchises are deemed more critical to civic status in some cities than others (Chen & Mason, 2016; Mason, Washington, & Buist, 2015). For example, in North America there are limits put on the number of available major league franchises. This means only a finite number of cities can host a team and lay claim to being "major league." However, for smaller cities within this select group, hosting a team and competing against larger, more prominent cities provides an exchange affiliation with higher status cities, such as when Cleveland, Ohio, plays against a team from New York City. Conversely, New York City does not benefit in the same way as Cleveland does within such an exchange. This may help to explain why smaller urban areas that are on the edge of being considered major league may deem hosting an event or attracting or retaining a major league sports franchise a much more critical policy decision than larger centers.

Unfortunately, this may make them more vulnerable to acceding to the demands of teams for subsidies.

In addition to city size, the degree to which the city has faced urban decline or is emerging as a growing center may also influence how civic leaders value sport events and teams as a means to improve status. In a discussion of larger Canadian cities, Hiller (2007, p. 56) wrote:

> While the urban hierarchy is still skewed in favour of "Toronto, Vancouver, and Montreal" and their urban regions, the two Alberta cities demonstrate characteristics not typical of other Canadian urban areas—which make them arriviste or upstart cities in some way. Our conception of an arriviste city is one that has recently obtained more power and influence, but often lacks general acceptance and respect.

Some local stakeholders see hosting a major league team or large sporting event as a way to gain such acceptance and respect. In the U.S. context, Sarmiento (2018) found that the arrival of the Thunder of the National Basketball Association coincided with broader urban development that redefined Oklahoma City for those both inside and outside the city. These arguments and logics are not limited to larger cities: "Local political actors in smaller communities become caught up in the rhetoric over the competitiveness of their city/regions and the pursuit of mobile capital" (Soebbing et al., 2016, p. 1676), where communities also benchmark themselves against larger cities that also have franchises in the leagues their teams play in.

Branding

A city's status is important because it can allow the city to market itself as an ideal place to live, work, and visit. As explained by Kavaratzis (2007), cities are evaluated by people much in the same way that they assess brands in other product or service categories. In fact, "the marketing of places has been one of the defining features of the entrepreneurial modes of urban governance that have come to prominence since the 1970s" (Kavaratzis, 2004, p. 59). Cities thus compete with one another much in the same way that other commercial products do (Zhang & Zhao, 2009). A key to city branding is identifying distinctive characteristics that can differentiate it from others and encompass matters such as history, governance, culture, existing perceptions of the city, and entertainment and sporting attractions. However, a key challenge is ensuring that these elements fit with the broader brand of the city (Zhang & Zhao, 2009). Here, hosting events and franchises can sometimes be seen as a shortcut that will bring attention to the brand. Yet such strategies can backfire when media coverage focuses more on issues associated with the team or event rather than the messages the city wants to convey through its foundational marketing and branding strategies (Carey & Mason, 2016).

Urban Regime Theory

The final approach considered here is urban regime theory (Stone, 1989), recognizing that "urban politics research in the United States over the past two decades has overwhelmingly been shaped by urban regime theory" (Pierre, 2014, p. 865). The focus of the theory is to explain how cities develop the capacity to govern. This is accomplished through the align-ment of the interests of political and business elites in cities, who are driven by broader institutional aims to create this common ground. This allows stakeholders who may be weaker politically to work to achieve their goals by serving a broader identifying agenda that also furthers the interests of those in power (Stone, 1993). When these alliances are sus-tained over a period of time in the pursuit of an agenda, a regime emerges.

The "Games-hosting literature has embraced regime politics as a plausible explanation for determining why municipalities bid to host these large-scale events" (Phillips & Barnes, 2015, p. 554), and there have been several studies of event and event hosting strategies using regime theory. For example, Andranovich, Burbank, and Heying (2001) reviewed strategies to host the Olympic Games, and Henry and Paramio-Salcines (1999) examined strategies used by the U.K. city of Sheffield. In addition, Sack and Johnson (1996) explored dynamics underlying the Volvo International tennis tournament in New Haven, Connecticut, and Misener and Mason (2008, 2009, 2010) assessed comprehensive event hosting strategies in Edmonton, Manchester in the United Kingdom, and Melbourne. The latter research found that all three cities had characteristics of symbolic regimes, which used sport events as a means to reposition the city's image.

One critique of urban regime theory has been that it focuses too much on local affairs and does not take into account broader global forces and the influence of higher levels of government. However, Lauermann (2016, p. 314) noted that event planning "mobilizes ex-pertise for both local and translocal audiences," and Blanco (2015, p. 280) has argued that examining the local context still has value: "Urban regime analysis . . . can enrich network governance theory by providing it with analytical tools to understand how the 'local' filters the 'global,' conditioning both the intensity and the direction of governance shifts." This would suggest that urban regime theory remains an important, perhaps ideal, way to ex-amine how and why cities choose to allocate public funds to host sport events and build infrastructure to house local sports franchises.

DEBATES

Although it is clear today that events and facilities do not confer the kinds of economic benefits that proponents suggest they do, there is still considerable disagreement regarding whether these projects should still be undertaken. This can be broken down into two fun-damental camps. The first position is bound up in a broader critique of neoliberalism and the commodification of cities. Seen this way, discussion of the public funding of projects is symptomatic of a broader concern over neoliberal, transnational logics, and where the need to expend resources to "compete" is the root of the problem.

Neoliberal Critiques

Some scholars argue that the pursuit of growth and mobile forms of capital by political and business elites is not an inevitable outcome of the emergence of the entrepreneurial city, but rather a neoliberal discourse that allows business elites to influence capital infrastructure projects in a way that allows them unprecedented opportunities to profit (Blanco, 2015). Thus, while "there is considerable convergence of opinion in the literature that the fundamental context in which cities are currently acting is the heightened mobility of capital" (Rogerson, 1999, p. 970), there is less consensus about how civic governance should occur in such an environment and whose interests it should serve. Gotham (2011) found that mega-events serve as sites of contestation due to their ability to initiate debate over how cities are represented. Further, he argues that the rhetoric of growth and development can be employed to obscure the narrow interests of powerful stakeholders in cities. Similarly, in a study of downtown Phoenix, Arizona, Collins and Grineski (2007, p. 32) revealed many of the promised benefits of a new stadium were not realized, other than "concentrating increasing revenues in the hands of fewer and larger business operators."

In addition to disproportionately benefiting wealthy and powerful interests in cities, another critique of the entrepreneurial city is in the commodification of the community. Commodification processes are in evidence when cities lose common identifiers, spaces, and institutions to corporate names and when civic landmarks become property that can be traded, marketed, and valued in terms of their consumption value. For the purposes of discussion, it is fruitful to focus on naming rights agreements for stadiums and events. Dynamics underlying naming rights agreements are reliant on a process that involves "a collaboration between the state and capital in order to take something that had previously been unpriced and unsold and render it into something alienable and capable of generating revenue" (Madden, 2019, p. 889). From this perspective, neoliberal austerity has forced municipal governments to seek out new revenue sources—such as corporate names for sports and leisure facilities—that were previously not known for their market value. At the same time, local residents begin to view their primary role as consumers. And while sports facilities provided the initial space for this process to occur, it has spread to other urban landmarks and infrastructure (Rose-Redwood, Vuolteenaho, Young, & Light, 2019). "[A]s tech capitalists, real estate developers, sports team owners, and other elites seek to cement their place as the new ruling class, they will continue to appropriate, rename, and reinscribe urban space" (Madden, 2019, p. 891). Although naming rights provide only one example of the concerns expressed over neoliberal ideologies and their effects, they showcase a microcosm of concerns about the impacts of neoliberalism and entrepreneurialism in contemporary North American cities:

> As a form of public-private partnership, naming rights sponsorships are a political technology of neoliberal governance that have played a significant role in the commodification of urban place identities. The process of toponymic commodification—that is, the use of place names, or toponyms, as commodities—is radically transforming the identities of public places into marketized assets, the value of which is increasingly being framed solely in terms of a name's rent-generating capacity. (Rose-Redwood et al., 2019, p. 748)

As more civic names become marketized, place identities become more murky, especially where agreements expire and new naming agreements are renegotiated.

Critiques of neoliberalism also manifest in arguments over the role of private interests in any local government affairs. Supporters of this view argue that there are virtually no cases where public money should be used to support or subsidize the private sector. As a result, there are no conditions where building sports facilities or hosting events using public funds would be in the public interest. A less extreme view considers the possibility of public-private partnerships but is leery of how private interests are privileged in these relationships. As explained by Erie, Kogan, & MacKenzie (2010, p. 645):

> Public–private partnerships . . . purportedly improve the efficiency and effectiveness of re-development programs by harnessing market forces and tapping private capital for public projects. In doing so, however, they create the possibility that public resources—for example, tax revenues, land-use authority—will be made to serve private objectives.

Erie et al. identify three ways this can occur: (1) poor contract design and information asymmetry between the two sides, (2) failure to implement agreements and/or opportunistic renegotiation, and (3) a lack of monitoring on the part of public officials. Further, Erie et al. found that cities tend to enter into public-private arrangements when they are vulnerable (i.e., they do not have the resources to undertake the projects themselves) and do not necessarily have the capacity to manage them.

The two examples provided, naming rights agreements and public-private partnerships, illustrate how neoliberal governance can put local communities and their residents in vulnerable positions when they accede to the demands of private interests. However, in adopting this critical posture, other scholars have argued that the conditions of governance within entrepreneurial cities leave room for contestation and negotiation. For example, in a study of Cincinnati, Ohio, Gillen (2009) advances a case about how addressing the needs and concerns of a diverse population actually serves the broader interests of an entrepreneurial city attempting to position itself as a safe, diverse community. Further, Gillen argues that

> while it is important to recognize a social fabric within the neoliberal agenda of the entre-preneurial model of urban governance, citizens and their interests in an entrepreneurial state are neither passive nor do they function as a purely economic unit for urban govern-ance. (p. 108)

This suggests that critiques of urban governance may entail taking stock of more nuanced processes and need to go beyond explanations reliant on merely representing interest groups as lying in the path of powerful stakeholders in the city.

Franchises, Events, and Broader Development

While much of the research and debate surrounding sports events and teams have focused on discrete events and facilities, more recent scholarly work and urban development strategies have viewed sports infrastructure as part of a much larger development that has the potential to benefit more than political and business elites and a focus on downtown development (Judd, 1995; Mason, 2016). In this context, redevelopment decisions can be constructed in a manner that represents the interests of the city as a whole and avoids pitfalls that privilege certain interests over others. This shift changes the understanding of entrepreneurial cities from sites of domination with "powerful actors . . . demonstrating their ability to impose meaning on pliable matter and docile subjects" (Sarmiento, 2018, p. 330) to opportunities to redevelop and redefine cities while providing amenities than can be enjoyed by others besides wealthy consumers.

A key to acknowledging this vantage point has been recognizing the importance of sport to the quality of life in cities by focusing on how the interests of local residents and those who seek to market and promote cities might fruitfully align in order to attract and retain capital. As explained by Blomquist et al. (1988, p. 89), "People are interested in comparing the bundle of amenities available at one location to bundles elsewhere." Here, attempts to make a city more livable to appeal to potential residents and businesses also make the communities better for those already living there. This process can be seen in the emergence of quality-of-life rankings as part of place-promotion strategies; such classifications "have been added to other measures of locational advantage to aid the process of attracting inward investment of global activities" (Rogerson, 1999, p. 972). In this context, quality of life would be linked to residents' overall well-being or utility, and an index to measure it in cities would include "traditional economic goods such as food and drink, shelter, clothing, transportation, and entertainment" (Blomquist, 2006, p. 483).

With an increasing focus on quality of life as a measure of a city and a means of comparison with other cities, the importance of flagship development projects—which may include a sports and entertainment facility as an anchor—increases in value as a means to signal the broader amenities that a city can offer to residents and visitors alike (Kavaratzis, 2007). However, a key to this is the manner in which the sports facility development is embedded into the surrounding community and combined with other planning initiatives in the city (Davies, 2006; Mason, 2016; Rosentraub, 2014). Scholars such as Rosentraub (2003, 2014), a previous critic of stadium development projects for their lack of returns for city investment, began to examine sports facility development in the context of broader urban development. Revealed in these examinations was the potential for cities to leverage the need for one amenity—in this case a sports facility built for a team or a major sporting event—into part of a comprehensive urban (re)development project. Other scholars have examined this phenomenon and the different ways in which cities have integrated projects, including the creation of "sport zones" that cluster facilities to give projects coherence and designate areas for different types of activities" (Smith, 2010). This allows communities the opportunity to use sport to brand parts of their cities, or even the city as a whole (such as Melbourne) as a sport city (Smith, 2005). This has occurred in the North American context too, where Indianapolis and other cities have clustered sports amenities in the downtown core to create an attractive zone for both visitors and residents (Rosentraub, 2003).

This strategy is not confined to larger cities. Carey and Mason (2013) assessed how the city of Kamloops in British Columbia developed infrastructure to position itself as the "Tournament Capital of Canada." Decisions by smaller cities can be critical, as they often lack the resources to develop multiple amenities:

> While larger cities might have many amenities to choose from, such as sports facilities, aquariums, convention centers, and/or theatres, the decision to publicly fund an arena in a smaller Canadian city may be at the expense of other development opportunities. In other words, the decision to build an arena is at the expense of building another amenity, rather than adding to a menu of existing ones. (Mason et al., 2007, p. 104)

Because these projects can be defining for local communities, an increasing effort has been made to ensure that unique characteristics of the cities are incorporated into the development. For example, iconic architecture, or the preservation/integration of existing architecture, can make developments distinct from those in other cities. This serves to differentiate the development from a branding perspective but can also tap into the existing identity of the local community. Ahlfeldt and Manning (2010, p. 630) have argued that

> architecture contributes to more than the business economy. When a structure generates positive spillovers for the local community or neighborhood, the use of public funds to cover the additional costs that arise from adopting an unconventional stadium architecture may be justifiable in economic terms.

They conclude that proximity to the downtown is often essential to the success of such strategies.

However, it is important to note that the success of these projects will typically depend on other characteristics of the city (Sarmiento, 2018; Vinodrai, 2010). In a study of Portland, Maine, Lees (2006) found that there were historical and geographically contingent reasons that helped to explain why that city had been successful in leveraging local sport and cultural amenities. Still, it is important to realize that with more cities pursuing sport-anchored development projects, it becomes less likely that any competitive advantages will be realized by sport-anchored strategies designed for economic development purposes (Fleming, Ghilardi, & Napier, 2006). If anything, this further emphasizes both caution and the need to integrate local characteristics to make these developments unique:

> [T]his is not to suggest that all viewers experience sports or architecture in the same way, but rather that these realms have been intentionally woven together, and that to whatever extent these realms are powerful in their capacity to shape urbanites' experiences of redevelopment, their power comes in part from their mutual imbrication. (Sarmiento, 2018, p. 339)

If amenities can be developed in a way to provide opportunities to improve the quality of life of residents over and above the discrete enjoyment of those who might attend a sporting event at a new facility, there is a much greater likelihood that public investment may be justifiable.

CONCLUSION

Sport is an important part of local communities. As the considerations in this chapter have shown, public funding of sport teams and events can be a polarizing and contentious subject for civic stakeholders and scholars alike. An overriding key issue here is the manner in which debates over event hosting or building publicly funded facilities take place. Done right, they can create opportunities for meaningful dialogue to occur around broader issues facing cities. In other words, regardless of one's position on who should pay, who benefits, and what those benefits might be from sport-anchored development, healthy and transparent public dialogue can be a desirable outcome in itself, as it facilitates conversations between various stakeholders about what cities are, whom civic leaders serve, and how land-use decisions can be transformative:

> Hence, rather than viewing mega events and other spectacles as instruments of hegemonic power, I advance a conception of mega events as destabilising events that display inequalities and social problems, provoke intense conflict and engender collective struggles over the

allocation of material and cultural resources. In this conception, it is useful to view mega events as contested cultural terrains that express a variety of disparate representations and effects. Rather than starting with an assumption that mega events reflect and reinforce dominant ideologies, we can view mega events as discursive fields of contestation and struggle where a variety of contending groups and organisations battle to legitimate their conceptions of a city as valid and authoritative and delegitimate rival interpretations and meanings. (Gotham, 2011, p. 201)

In closing, this chapter has reviewed the relationship between sport and cities, with a focus on the North American context. In doing so, it has revealed the need to examine the complexities of individual cities and their relationships between sport, sport events, and teams. Largely, research has examined two ends of a spectrum: how elites have developed the capacity to benefit from events and teams and the ways disenfranchised groups have been burdened by them. In the future, more nuanced approaches must examine how events and teams can provide a means of contestation between the competing interests at play and how they can be designed and negotiated to benefit different groups in the city. Hopefully, the research agenda and concerns raised in this chapter advance this. The assessments of scholars can help cities understand when it may be reasonable to justify providing public funds for sport-anchored development.

REFERENCES

Ahlfeldt, G., & Maennig, W. (2010). Stadium architecture and urban development from the perspective of urban economics. *International Journal of Urban and Regional Research, 34,* 629–646.

Albrechts, L. (2004). Strategic (spatial) planning reexamined. *Environment and Planning B: Planning and Design, 31*(5), 743–758.

Andranovich, G., Burbank, M. J., & Heying, C. H. (2001). Olympic cities: Lessons learned from mega-event politics. *Journal of Urban Affairs, 23*(2), 113–131.

Ashworth, G., & Kavaratzis, M. (2009). Beyond the logo: Brand management for cities. *Journal of Brand Management, 16*(8), 520–531.

Blanco, I. (2015). Between democratic network governance and neoliberalism: A regime-theoretical analysis of collaboration in Barcelona. *Cities, 44,* 123–130.

Blomquist, G. C. (2006). Measuring quality of life. In R. J. Arnott & D. P. McMillen (Eds.), *A companion to urban economics* (pp. 483–501). Hoboken, NJ: Blackwell Publishing.

Blomquist, G. C., Berger, M. C., & Hoehn, J. P. (1988). New estimates of quality of life in urban areas. *American Economic Review, 78,* 89–107.

Bryson, J. M., & Roering, W. D. (1987). Applying private-sector strategic planning in the public sector. *Journal of the American Planning Association, 53*(1), 9–22.

Buist, E. A., & Mason, D. S. (2010). Newspaper framing and stadium subsidization. *American Behavioral Scientist, 53*(10), 1492–1510.

Carey, K. M., & Mason, D. S. (2013). Comprehensive sporting event strategies and smaller cities: A case study of Kamloops, British Columbia. In T. Mihalic & W. Gartner (Eds.), *Tourism: Developments, issues and challenges* (pp. 285–230). Hauppage, NY: Nova Publishers.

Carey, K. M., & Mason, D. S. (2016). Damage control: Media framing of sport event crises and the response strategies of organizers. *Event Management, 20,* 119–133.

Chen, C., & Mason, D. S. (2016). Professional sports franchises and city status: Los Angeles and the National Football League. In V. Fletcher (Ed.), *Urban and rural developments: Perspectives, strategies and challenges* (pp. 133–150). Hauppage, NY: Nova Science Publishers.

Coates, D. (2007). Stadiums and arenas: Economic development or economic redistribution? *Contemporary Economic Policy, 25*(4), 565–577.

Collins, T. W. (2008). Unevenness in urban governance: Stadium building and downtown redevelopment in Phoenix, Arizona. *Environment and Planning C: Government and Policy, 26*(6), 1177–1196.

Collins, T. W., & Grineski, S. E. (2007). Unequal impacts of downtown redevelopment: The case of stadium building in Phoenix, Arizona. *Journal of Poverty, 11*(1), 23–54.

Crompton, J. (2004). Beyond economic impact: An alternative rationale for the public subsidy of major league sports facilities. *Journal of Sport Management, 18*(1), 40–58.

Davies, L. E. (2006). Sporting a new role? Stadia and the real estate market. *Managing Leisure, 11*(4), 231–244.

Duquette, G. H., & Mason, D. S. (2008). Urban regimes and sport in North American cities: Seeking status through franchises, events and facilities. *International Journal of Sport Management and Marketing, 3*(3), 221–241.

Edensor, T., & Millington, S. (2008). "This is our city": Branding football and local embeddedness. *Global Networks, 8*(2), 172–193.

Eisinger, P. (2000). The politics of bread and circuses: Building the city for the visitor class. *Urban Affairs Review, 35*(3), 316–333.

Erie, S. P., Kogan, V., & MacKenzie, S. A. (2010). Redevelopment, San Diego style: The limits of public-private partnerships. *Urban Affairs Review, 45*(5), 644–678.

Feng, X., & Humphreys, B. (2018). Assessing the economic impact of sports facilities on residential property values: A spatial hedonic approach. *Journal of Sports Economics, 19*(2), 188–210.

Fleming, T., Ghilardi, L., & Napier, N. K. (2006). Rethinking small places—urban and cultural creativity. In D. Bell & M. Jayne (Eds.), *Small cities: Urban experience beyond the metropolis* (pp. 185–201). New York: Routledge.

Flyvbjerg, B. (2007). Policy and planning for large-infrastructure projects: Problems, causes, cures. *Environment and Planning B: Planning and Design, 34*(4), 578–597.

Friedman, M. T., & Mason, D. S. (2004). A stakeholder approach to understanding economic development decision making: Public subsidies for professional sport facilities. *Economic Development Quarterly, 18*(3), 236–254.

Friedman, M. T., & Mason, D. S. (2005). Stakeholder management and the public subsidization of Nashville's Coliseum. *Journal of Urban Affairs, 27*(1), 93–118.

Friedman, M. T., Parent, M. M., & Mason, D. S. (2004). Building a framework for issues management in sport through stakeholder theory. *European Sport Management Quarterly, 4*(3), 170–190.

Gillen, J. (2009). The co-production of narrative in an entrepreneurial city: An analysis of Cincinnati, Ohio, in turmoil. *Geografiska Annaler: Series B, Human Geography, 91*(2), 107–122.

Gotham, K. F. (2011). Resisting urban spectacle: The 1984 Louisiana World Exposition and the contradictions of mega events. *Urban Studies, 48*(1), 197–214.

Hackworth, J., & Nowakowski, K. (2015). Using market-based policies to address market collapse in the American Rust Belt: The case of land abandonment in Toledo, Ohio. *Urban Geography, 36*(4), 528–549.

Hannigan, J. 1998. *Fantasy city: Pleasure and profit in the post-modern metropolis.* New York: Routledge.

Henry, I. P., & Paramio-Salcines, J. L. (1999). Sport and the analysis of symbolic regimes: A case study of the city of Sheffield. *Urban Affairs Review, 34*(5), 641–666.

Herstein, R., & Berger, R. (2013). Much more than sports: Sports events as stimuli for city re-branding. *Journal of Business Strategy, 34*(2), 38–44.

Hiller, H. H. (2007). Gateway cities and arriviste cities: Alberta's recent urban growth in Canadian context. *Prairie Forum, 32*(1), 47–66.

Humphreys, B. R., Johnson, B. K., Mason, D. S., & Whitehead, J. C. (2018). Estimating the value of medal success in the Olympic Games. *Journal of Sports Economics, 19*(3), 398–416.

Johnson, A. T. (1983). Municipal administration and the sports franchise relocation issue. *Public Administration Review, 43*(6), 519–528.

Johnson, B. K., Groothuis, P. A., & Whitehead, J. C. (2001). The value of public goods generated by a major league sports team: The CVM approach. *Journal of Sports Economics, 2*(1), 6–21.

Johnson, B. K., Whitehead, J. C., Mason, D. S., & Walker, G. J. (2012). Willingness to pay for downtown public goods generated by large, sports-anchored development projects: The CVM approach. *City, Culture and Society, 3*(3), 201–208.

Judd, D. R. (1995). Promoting tourism in US cities. *Tourism Management, 16*(3), 175–187.

Kavaratzis, M. (2004). From city marketing to city branding: Towards a theoretical framework for developing city brands. *Place Branding, 1*(1), 58–73.

Kavaratzis, M. (2007). City marketing: The past, the present and some unresolved issues. *Geography Compass, 1*(3), 695–712.

Lauermann, J. (2016). Boston's Olympic bid and the evolving urban politics of event-led development. *Urban Geography, 37*(2), 313–321.

Lee, P. (2002). The economic and social justification for publicly financed stadia: The case of Vancouver's BC Place Stadium. *European Planning Studies, 10*(7), 861–873.

Lees, L. (2006). Gentrifying down the urban hierarchy: "The cascade effect" in Portland, Maine. In D. Bell & M. Jayne (Eds.), *Small cities: Urban experience beyond the metropolis* (pp. 91–104). New York: Routledge.

Logan, J. R., & Molotch, H. L. (2007). *Urban fortunes: The political economy of place.* Berkeley: University of California Press.

Loh, C. G. (2019). Placemaking and implementation: Revisiting the performance principle. *Land Use Policy, 81*, 68–75.

Madden, D. J. (2019). The names of urban dispossession: A concluding commentary. *Urban Geography, 40*(6), 888–892.

Mason, D. S. (2016). Sports facilities, urban infrastructure, and quality of life: Rationalizing arena-anchored development in North American cities. *Sport and Entertainment Review, 2*, 63–69.

Mason, D. S., Buist, E. A., Edwards, J. R., & Duquette, G. H. (2007). The stadium game in Canadian Hockey League communities. *International Journal of Sport Finance, 2*(2), 94–107.

Mason, D. S., Washington, M., & Buist, E. A. (2015). Signaling status through stadiums: The discourses of comparison within a hierarchy. *Journal of Sport Management, 29*(5), 539–554.

McCann, E. J. (2002). The cultural politics of local economic development: Meaning-making, place-making, and the urban policy process. *Geoforum, 33*(3), 385–398.

Misener, L., & Mason, D. S. (2008). Urban regimes and the sporting events agenda: A cross-national comparison of civic development strategies. *Journal of Sport Management, 22*, 603–627.

Misener, L., & Mason, D. S. (2009). Fostering community development through sporting events strategies: An examination of urban regime perceptions. *Journal of Sport Management, 23,* 770–794.

Misener, L., & Mason, D. S. (2010). Towards a community centred approach to corporate community involvement in the sporting events agenda. *Journal of Management and Organization, 16,* 494–513.

Orlowski, J., & Wicker, P. (2019). Monetary valuation of non-market goods and services: A review of conceptual approaches and empirical applications in sports. *European Sport Management Quarterly, 19*(4), 456–480.

Panton, M., & Walters, G. (2018). "It's just a Trojan horse for gentrification": Austerity and stadium-led regeneration. *International Journal of Sport Policy and Politics, 10*(1), 163–183.

Parent, M. M. (2008). Evolution and issue patterns for major-sport-event organizing committees and their stakeholders. *Journal of Sport Management, 22*(2), 135–164.

Parent, M. M., & Deephouse, D. L. (2007). A case study of stakeholder identification and prioritization by managers. *Journal of Business Ethics, 75*(1), 1–23.

Phillips, C., & Barnes, M. (2015). Whose legacy is it, anyway? A tale of conflicting agendas in the building of the Hamilton Pan Am Soccer Stadium. *Annals of Leisure Research, 18*(4), 549–568.

Pierre, J. (2014). Can urban regimes travel in time and space? Urban regime theory, urban governance theory, and comparative urban politics. *Urban Affairs Review, 50*(6), 864–889.

Rogerson, R. J. (1999). Quality of life and city competitiveness. *Urban Studies, 36*(5–6), 969–985.

Rosentraub, M. (2003). Indianapolis, a sports strategy and the redefinition of downtown redevelopment. In D. Judd (Ed.), *The infrastructure of play* (pp. 104–124). New York: M. E. Sharpe.

Rosentraub, M. S. (2014). *Reversing urban decline: Why and how sports, entertainment, and culture turn cities into major league winners.* New York: CRC Press.

Rose-Redwood, R., Vuolteenaho, J., Young, C., & Light, D. (2019). Naming rights, place branding, and the tumultuous cultural landscapes of neoliberal urbanism. *Urban Geography, 40,* 747–761.

Russo, A. P., & Scarnato, A. (2018). "Barcelona in common": A new urban regime for the 21st-century tourist city? *Journal of Urban Affairs, 40*(4), 455–474.

Sack, A. L., & Johnson, A. T. (1996). Politics, Economic Development, and the Volvo International Tennis Tournament. *Journal of Sport Management, 10*(1), 1–14.

Sant, S. L., & Mason, D. S. (2015). Framing event legacy in a prospective host city: Managing Vancouver's Olympic bid. *Journal of Sport Management, 29*(1), 42–56.

Sant, S. L., & Mason, D. S. (2019). Rhetorical legitimation strategies and sport and entertainment facilities in smaller Canadian cities. *European Sport Management Quarterly, 19*(2), 160–177.

Sant, S. L., Mason, D. S., & Chen, C. (2019). "Second-tier outpost"? Negative civic image and urban infrastructure development. *Cities, 87,* 238–246.

Santo, C. A. (2007). Beyond the economic catalyst debate: Can public consumption benefits justify a municipal stadium investment? *Journal of Urban Affairs, 29*(5), 455–479.

Sapotichne, J. (2012). Rhetorical strategy in stadium development politics. *City, Culture and Society, 3*(3), 169–180.

Sarmiento, E. (2018). The affirming effects of entrepreneurial redevelopment: Architecture, sport, and local food in Oklahoma City. *Environment and Planning A: Economy and Space*, *50*(2), 327–349.

Smith, A. (2005). Reimaging the city: The value of sport initiatives. *Annals of Tourism Research*, *32*(1), 229–248.

Smith, A. (2010). The development of "sports-city" zones and their potential value as tourism resources for urban areas. *European Planning Studies*, *18*(3), 385–410.

Soebbing, B. P., Mason, D. S., & Humphreys, B. R. (2016). Novelty effects and sports facilities in smaller cities: Evidence from Canadian hockey arenas. *Urban Studies*, *53*(8), 1674–1690.

Stone, C. N. (1989). *Regime politics: Governing Atlanta, 1946–1988*. Lawrence: University Press of Kansas.

Stone, C. N. (1993). Urban regimes and the capacity to govern: A political economy approach. *Journal of urban affairs*, *15*(1), 1–28.

Vinodrai, T. (2010). The dynamics of economic change in Canadian cities: Innovation, culture, and the emergence of a knowledge-based economy. In T. Bunting, P. Filion, & R. Walker (Eds.), *Canadian cities in transition: New directions in the twenty-first century* (pp. 87–109). Toronto: Oxford University Press.

Vuolteenaho, J., Wolny, M., & Puzey, G. (2019). "This venue is brought to you by . . .": The diffusion of sports and entertainment facility name sponsorship in urban Europe. *Urban Geography*, *40*(6), 762–783.

Wicker, P., Whitehead, J. C., Mason, D. S., & Johnson, B. K. (2017). Public support for hosting the Olympic Summer Games in Germany: The CVM approach. *Urban Studies*, *54*(15), 3597–3614.

Zhang, L., & Zhao, S. X. (2009). City branding and the Olympic effect: A case study of Beijing. *Cities*, *26*(5), 245–254.

CHAPTER 15

....

SPORT, THE ENVIRONMENT, AND GEOPOLITICS

....

TOBY MILLER

CLIMATE change imperils the very Earth itself. Past and present industrial processes have exposed the planet to potentially irrevocable harm as we enter what the scientific community announced in 2016 as the Anthropocene—an epoch characterized by major geological and ecological transformations brought about by human activity (Anthropocene Working Group, Subcommission on Quaternary Stratigraphy, 2019).

In the late 1960s and early 1970s, the word "pollution" was in vogue to explain environmental hazards. Both a ubiquitous and a local sign, pollution was increasingly seen to be everywhere yet often viewed as isolable: particular waterways, neighborhoods, or fields suffered negative externalities from mining, farming, and manufacturing. A central concern was how to restore these places to their prior state: pristine, unspoiled, enduring. Pollution was about corporate malfeasance, governmental neglect, and public ignorance. Responses to it focused on how to remedy malign impacts. The common view was that pollution could be cleaned up if governments compelled companies to do so, and would soon be over once those involved understood the problem.

But when greenhouse gases, environmental racism, global warming, and occupational health appeared on the agenda, pollution reached beyond national boundaries and became ontological, threatening life itself, in demographically unequal ways. In Latour's (2018, pp. 15–16) words, "[I]t is as though a significant segment of the ruling classes . . . had concluded that the earth no longer had room for them and for everyone else."

Sports lay powerful claims to incarnating nature: the fastest woman on earth (khushiss69, 2010), the longest leap (Olympics, 2015), the quickest racehorse (Deubet, 2013). But these achievements are not only about muscularity, skill, dedication, and coordination. They rely on training, technique, technology, travel, and the transformation of space to create events that showcase athletic prowess and records. Achievement in sport relies on a host of environmental transformations: everything from human kinesiology to animal enslavement, vitamin supplements to equipment, stadia to horse floats, telecommunications infrastructure to medical facilities, school coaches to betting addicts, and tax arrangements to corporate contracts. Far from being instantiations of natural ability, these interventions exemplify the sporting domain's seemingly inexorable will and entitlement to control and change nature and its imbrication with national and international public and private agents.

Despite that anthropomorphic will to power, sports never transcend their tie to the environment, from traditional golf links to Formula 1 venues. They produce massive carbon footprints via construction, repairs, maintenance, transport, energy, sanitation, water use, and media coverage, through which they endeavor to promote themselves as good environmental citizens (Warren, 2020). Sports are part of our anthropocentric conjuncture, from risks to playing fields, from industrial pollution to the damage done when flyboys and -girls of international competitions trample their way across time zones in search of glory. The impact is mutual. Skiing, hockey, cricket, tennis, and many other sports are affecting global warming, which in turn affects them (Bonnemains, 2014; Kay, 2019; Martin, 2019; Miller, 2018).

And this starts from the ground up in the spaces dedicated to sports. Estimates of sports' environmental impact often exclude construction, and concrete is the world's largest emitter of carbon after the United States and China, at 8% of the global total (Lehne & Preston, 2018; Watts, 2019). In 1965, fewer "than 12 materials were in wide use: wood, brick, iron, copper, gold, silver, and a few plastics" (Graedel, Harper, Nassar, & Reck, 2015, p. 6296). Today there is a comprehensive "materials basis to modern society": the computer chip that enabled me to type this chapter contains more than 60 of them (Graedel et al., 2015). Unearthing these things is a drain on natural resources. We have a finite supply of the basic ingredients of modern material life, and potential substitutes rarely deliver equivalent quality. It is no surprise to learn that the 126 pro sports teams of the United States and Canada need monumental amounts of energy to power their stadia, which have been built and are run via this unsustainable extravaganza. Fewer than a third of those buildings deploy renewable energy; the National Hockey League luxuriates in using 321 million gallons of water a year, and the Dallas Cowboys draw on 750 megawatts of electricity on game day—almost four times the total power available to Liberia's 4 million people (McHale, 2019).

Sports lustfully seek and gleefully accept sponsorship from the extractive industries, imbuing them with positive images derived from its pleasurable connotations. An unwarranted clean and green image often associates polluting corporations with a "moderate" pseudo-environmentalism that "no longer represents a hindrance to the economy" (Beck, 2009, p. 103). Big polluters make particular use of this service as part of their search for a "social license to operate," an invidious concept developed two decades ago by the United Nations Commission on Sustainable Development (1998) that calls on capitalists seeking to exploit territory to regard local communities as "stakeholders" (Wilburn & Wilburn, 2011).

That multiple oxymoron "corporate social responsibility" (CSR) greenwashes a multitude of social harms, ecology notable among them (Fifka & Jaeger, 2020). Hundreds of public, private, and mixed projects of international development utilize sports to bolster their image, frequently via "Astroturf organizations" that disingenuously mimic grassroots social movements while actually being corporate shills (Trendafilova, Babiak, & Heinze, 2013). They establish a structural and indexical homology between the extractive and sporting industries, exploiting the brief and fragile life of the star athlete *contra* the lengthy and powerful impact of environmental despoliation (Levermore, 2010; Silk, Andrews, & Cole, 2005). This is in keeping with the "selective disclosure" of policies concerning carbon footprints that have now become a norm among capitalists. Here, corporate "spin" aims to share positive information about its masters' environmental records while concealing negative aspects (Marquis, Toffel, & Zhou, 2016). As an analysis in the *Economist* puts it, "The human face that CSR applies to capitalism goes on each morning, gets increasingly smeared by day and washes off at night" (Crook, 2005, p. 4).

Sports are hence complicit, both directly and indirectly, with what Robert Nixon (2011, p. 2) calls the "slow violence" of ecological destruction:

> [a] violence that occurs gradually and out of sight, a violence of delayed destruction that is dispersed across time and space, an attritional violence that is typically not viewed as violence at all . . . neither spectacular nor instantaneous, but rather incremental and accretive, its calamitous repercussions playing out across a range of temporal scales.

Issues

Having adumbrated how the prevailing political economy is complicit with our environmental crisis, I'll now examine some key issues: the Summer and Winter Olympics, association football, health, and activism.

Olympics

The Summer and Winter Games regularly promote themselves by bloviating about efficiency and technology allied to beauty and ancestry. That rhetoric underpins "an international bacchanal of physical perfection and triumphant will swaddled in human rights abuses and environmental catastrophe" (West, 2016). Ironically and tragically, medal tables often correlate with sizable populations, subvention, and wealth (Forrest, McHale, Sanz, & Tena, 2017).

Such self-promotion has showcased industrial development in an unproblematic, celebratory fashion. The 1964 Tokyo Summer Olympics were a calling card from Japan to the world, announcing a fabulous new modernity that had emerged from its own ideological disgrace of fascism and the Allies' appalling firebombing of Tokyo and nuclear ruination of Hiroshima and Nagasaki (Tagsold, 2010). Pictorial commemorations half a century later highlighted "Tokyo Reborn" and "Made in Japan" ("1964: Memories," 2014). But this transformation of "a war-ravaged city into a major international capital, seemingly overnight," concealed "a dark side . . . environmental destruction and human misery" (Whiting, 2014). The tramway system was virtually destroyed in favor of freeways. Hundreds of thousands of homeless cats and dogs were killed. A high-speed rail link between Tokyo and Osaka inundated waterways with concrete and landfill and destroyed a centuries-old seaweed field. Rivers stagnated, sludge proliferated, sea life perished, and estuaries became cesspools. Such factors were barely noticed in the bright lights of a newly lit and seemingly eternal day that blasted wartime horrors into the past (Jorgenson & Clark, 2016).

Such unwarranted triumphalism has been the signal message of other Olympiads, evident well beyond attempts to symbolize moving beyond a war-torn Japan. The 1992 Winter Games in France took place in areas already devastated by tourism. Resorts had destroyed flora, irrigation, and drainage, diverted hydrological systems, and extracted water to manufacture snow. The Olympics extended freeways, widened roads, built new viaducts and tunnels, electrified rail, and doubled airport capacity, thereby disrupting animal habitats and migration, ruining forests, diminishing riparian diversity, and generating additional sewage (May, 1995, pp. 271–272).

As part of greenwashing, today's dominant Olympian discourse dutifully embraces ecological responsibility—at a discursive level. The International Olympic Committee's (2018, p. 11) Carbon Footprint Methodology promises "effective carbon reduction strategies.". But its commercial partners have included such major polluters as McDonald's, Coca-Cola, Visa, Dow, Toyota, and General Electric. Throughout planning and implementation, the IOC, sponsors, and local organizers seek social licenses to operate to legitimize their environmental impact (Samuel & Stubbs, 2013). They most typically claim a high moralism while often dodging essential environmental standards as the IOC "issues no hard-and-fast requirement for Games hosts" (Müller, 2015, p. 197). The evidence here is considerable:

> Athens was a particularly disingenuous and disastrous games, environmentally speaking. Judged by its own claims, environmental NGOs found almost every single target had been abandoned or missed. Beijing remains one of the most polluted places on earth. Rio, which intended to use the games as a way of turbocharging investment in the city's woefully inadequate sewage systems, abandoned the project altogether. (Goldblatt, 2016, p. 606; see also Huijuan, Fujii, & Managi, 2013)

The 2012 London Olympic Authority boasted of the "greenest ever" Games. Its pay-to-play charade awarded BP, BMW, BT, Cisco, EDF Energy, and General Electric the status of "sustainability partners" (Boykoff & Mascarenhas, 2016). The city required 40 venues covering 500 hectares, with huge implications for construction, maintenance, transport, post-Games utilization, gentrification, consumption, pollution, noise, light, water, and sewage (Pitts & Liao, 2013). Over 3.5 million tons of carbon dioxide were emitted (Short, 2015), compared to Britain's annual average of 550 million tons (Davis, 2009; Samuel & Stubbs, 2013). Sochi's 2014 Games were won and promoted via a putative commitment to carbon neutrality, one that was quickly "scaled back to offsetting the additional emissions during the Games," with the promised zero-waste bid "downgraded to 'reducing waste.'" Waterways were polluted and forests devastated (Müller, 2015, p. 202). The ecological promises made in Sochi's bid were left unfulfilled (Azzali, 2017). The eventual costs of this celebration of ecological vandalism—the price of public expenditure on the event, not its environmental impact— was U.S.$51 billion to U.S.$55 billion, the most expensive games of all time (Müller, 2014; Ramaswamy, 2015). Much of the snow used came from water extracted from streams and lakes; it was supercooled, then blasted from a cannon onto competition surfaces (Short, 2015). And the ski resort used in the Games was owned by oligarch Vladimir Potanin's holding company. It became a core part of his mining subsidiary's search for a social license to operate, and this was used to impress state officials (Farchy, 2016).

Beyond those infrastructural questions, consider the astonishing levels of carbon emitted by flying thousands of athletes, horses, bureaucrats, journalists, and objects to and from the Games (International Civil Aviation Organization, 2016). Tourism apparatchiks, boosters, travel writers, corporate shills, and their scholarly chorines seem chronically unaware of Olympic travel's environmental implications. As a result, their response is often symbolic and reformist at best (Jiménez-García, Ruiz-Chico, Peña-Sánchez, & López-Sánchez, 2020).

Football

Association football (soccer) has an appalling environmental record throughout the world. Clubs and bureaucrats engage in, and brazenly publicize, recycling and waste management, but those activities do not require the capital outlays needed to install vital environmental technology (Walters & Tacon, 2011) of the kind used in the construction of Juventus's Torino home (GA^e Engineering, n.d.). As of 2018, just one pro team in the world, Forest Green Rovers, an English League One club, was certified carbon-neutral by the UN ("Doing the Right," 2018). And its boast of being "the world's first vegan football club" (Forest Green, n.d.) has been greeted by opposition fans chanting "You dirty vegan bastard" (quoted in Gallan, 2019). A study of the English Premier League for the 2016–2017 season disclosed that teams' domestic travel alone generated approximately 1,134 tons of CO_2 equivalent (Tóffano Pereira, Filimonau, & Mattos Ribeiro, 2019). In the shameful case of Arsenal Football Club, such luxury meant taking a 14-minute executive-jet flight to nearby Norwich (de Menezes, 2015). And consider the impact of spectators' transport, food, and waste at the 2004 FA Cup Final, held in Cardiff. Most attendees came from London and Manchester by car, traversing 43 million kilometers. That multiplied the match's carbon footprint by a factor of 8. Once at the ground, visitors drank and ate highly processed commodities, which required large amounts of energy to prepare and dispatch (Collins & Flynn, 2008). Subsequent studies confirm that such issues also apply to regular home and away games (Dosumu, Colbeck, & Bragg, 2017).

The efforts of activists and environmentally responsible academics to uncover football's ecological crimes come to naught when state and capital priorities influence decisions otherwise. Norwegian and South African scientists studying the probable environmental impact of the 2010 Men's World Cup Finals issued stern warnings prior to the event (McCarthy, 2009; Republic of South Africa, Department of Environmental Affairs and Tourism, Norwegian Agency for Development Cooperation, & Norwegian Embassy in South Africa, 2009). *Contra* such materially based knowledge, South Africa's (2004) Accelerated and Shared Growth Initiative argued for the growth and equity that would supposedly derive from staging the Finals. President Thabo Mbeki proclaimed a "development World Cup" as part of an "African renaissance" (quoted in Levermore, 2011, p. 887). His administration used traditional economistic arguments and enunciated anthropocentric shibboleths about alchemically combining such desires with being green (Hyde-Clarke, Ottosen, & Miller, 2014). Government tender documents invited competition to offset aviation footprints, but no contracts were issued. This was hardly surprising, coming as it did from a state that has largely neglected potential alternative energy sources and statutes mandating the environmental assessment of projects (Ahmed & Pretorius, 2010). South Africa lacked adequate stadia and high-speed rail and sought to rectify that (Estrada, 2010). Improvements were made to mass transit, but freeways received more investment. Excluding construction, the development World Cup had the largest carbon footprint of any commercial event in world history at 1.65 million tons—twice the 2008 Beijing Olympics and nine times the 2006 Finals in Germany (Crabb, 2018; Levermore, 2012; Sturrock, 2018).

Offset programs designed to minimize the footprint of the 2014 World Cup Finals in Brazil failed—2.72 million tons of carbon were emitted (Crabb, 2018; Sturrock, 2018). Even FIFA's (2019, p. 68) self-serving report acknowledges that the 2018 event in Russia generated well over 2.1 million tons. Beyond that, FIFA's current associates "include Gazprom, the largest supplier of natural gas to Europe and the first company to start digging for oil in the Arctic Circle, airline Qatar Airways, car manufacturer Hyundai and China's second-largest dairy company, Mengniu" (Tweedale, 2018).

Looking ahead, FIFA awarded the 2022 Finals to Qatar, despite its problematic campaigning, grotesque labor abuses, notorious contempt for human rights—and wholesale unsustainability as a venue, given the region's limited natural resources, vast importation of workers to construct venues, and abundant use of air-conditioning in stadia (Abusin, Lari, Khaled, & Al Emadi, 2020). The 2026 World Cup event will be shared across Canada, Mexico, and the United States, which make up 14% of the world's landmass (Taylor, 2019). Travel will therefore be a major issue. Transporting three and a half million people accounted for 84% of the 2010 Finals' emissions, mostly via international flights (Spanne & *The Daily Climate*, 2014).

On other fronts, fan, club, media, and bureaucratic travel to Europe's 2019 Champions League and Europa League Finals generated 35,000 tons of carbon dioxide, while the Euro 2020 Finals could almost have been designed to create maximal ecological chaos; they were scheduled for Germany, Hungary, Scotland, England, Azerbaijan, Holland, Italy, Denmark, Russia, Ireland, and Spain (McKie, Savage, & Cornwall, 2019). The tournament's postponement because of the COVID-19 syndemic did not produce a more ecologically rational itinerary based in one country (UEFA, 2020).

Television coverage of football is another contributor to environmental irresponsibility. The United Kingdom's National Grid ESO notes the electricity demand created by audience activity during halftime in the World Cup, when people head for the kitchen and bathroom. As a consequence, football viewers are the Grid's biggest drains on power (Carbon Trust, n.d., 2016; Miller, 2018; National Grid, 2014a). Power use surges by as much as 10% in what is known as the "TV pick-up" or "half-time kettle effect" (Selectra, 2020). The Grid has correlated viewership and energy during England's tragicomic departure from the 1990 World Cup: "A whopping 2800MW at the end of the penalty shoot-out!" (National Grid, 2010, 2020). During Brazil's matches in the 2014 competition, U.K. surges totaled 4,348 megawatts, the equivalent of a million and a half kettles being turned on simultaneously (National Grid, 2014b). And watching football via mobile telephone multiplies spectators' carbon footprint 10-fold in comparison with television or WiFi (Carbon Trust, n.d., 2016; TePoel, 2017).

Health

Professional and amateur sports increasingly face disruption and illness because of climate change (Bernard et al., 2020; Wallace, Widenman, & McDermott, 2019). Cricket is transmogrifying due to radical shifts in patterns of rain, heat, pestilence, soil, drought, pollution, and light. Players show the impacts on cognitive failure, skin disorders, hyperthermia, cramp, and exhaustion from sun, heat, and exertion (Stay et al., 2018; University of Leeds, British Association for Sustainable Sport, & University of Portsmouth, 2019). Similar issues apply to tennis (Australian Conservation Foundation & Monash Climate Change Communication Research Hub, 2020; Périard et al., 2014). Presumptively winter sports such as football have become other sites for such risks, not only when competitions occur in equatorial zones but during international contests perversely held in the heat of summer (Nybo, Flouris, Racinais, & Mohr, 2020). We may have reached the point at which the very notion of a Summer Olympics will increasingly imperil the health of participants (Smith et al., 2014).

Much scholarly work remains to be done on the impact of pollution on athletes' performance and long-term well-being (Rundell, 2012). The available research suggests that many health problems confront retirees as they engage in recreational physical activity undertaken in places with high environmental despoliation that can damage lungs, heart, and skin and dampen cerebration (Bos, De Boever, Int Panis, & Meeusen, 2014; Cooper, Batt, & Palmer, 2020; Giles & Koehle, 2014). A new international system for establishing the epidemiology of sports injuries and illnesses accounts for climate change, but is so recent that its effectiveness in propelling environmental rationality into policymaking is untested (Bahr et al., 2020).

Activism

Notable athletes sometimes engage in activism to draw attention to environmental issues. Former Arsenal footballer Héctor Bellerín promised to pay for 3,000 trees to be planted for every game his side won in June 2020 ("Hector Bellerin," n.d.). But while such cute acts of individual philanthropy attract media coverage, the public doesn't show great interest in its idols' environmental messages (Becker, 2013; Thrall et al., 2008; Till, Stanley, & Priluck, 2008).

More organically, there are signs of significant popular activism. Denver citizens voted against hosting the 1976 Winter Olympics due to the rapacious ski industry's environmental destructiveness; progressives successfully opposed Amsterdam's bidding for the 1992 Summer Games; and the people of Hamburg and Boston both rejected their city governments' campaigns to gain the 2024 Olympiad ("Colorado Rejects," 1972; Ramaswamy, 2015; Vaccaro, 2015). Most recently, a spirited green youth movement refuses the craven politics of world leaders who are beholden to barons of industry and finance, fossil-fuel giants, and technology moguls (Wearden & Carrington, 2019). Tens of thousands of Western European school pupils went on strike in 2019 with the slogans #FridaysForFuture and "There's no Planet B" ("Children's Climate," 2019). Women decided to "birth strike" because they felt unable to guarantee climate security to future generations (Doherty, 2019). Both groups have participated in Extinction Rebellion (n.d.). Some football supporters reject wholesale corporate control and call for greener boot prints (Davies, 2019; Football Supporters Association, n.d.; Keoghan, 2014). And Protect Our Winters (n.d.) has 130,000 members dedicated to converting "passionate outdoor people into effective climate advocates." But much work remains to convince sports fans to recognize that their adored pastimes imperil the globe.

Regulation

Prelates of ecological modernization and their chorines in sports studies and the state apparatus often imagine economic growth and environmentalism modifying one another in a postpolitical cornucopia of sustainability. But that hasn't happened (Johnson & Ali,

2018; Kim & Chung, 2018). Instead, "environmental degradation and resource exhaustion are being diagnosed as management problems rather than as a crisis or breakdown; this management exercise then becomes a new source of dynamism for capitalism" (Goldman & Schurman, 2000, p. 567). Meanwhile, CSR generates new markets, massages labor, delivers positive public relations, and heightens brand recognition (Klein, 2012; Thomson & Boutilier, 2011). Following the CSR pathway, capital not only obtains free rides from host nations but cultivates the image of itself as a responsible international subject whose exemplary liberal self-governance means it does not require regulation.

In the realm of sport, plutocracy often prevails over democratic control, as exemplified in awarding environmental ratings for stadia (Bullock, 2017) or the United Nations Climate Change (2018) Conference's Sports for Climate Action Framework. Such developments are all about capitalist businesses eluding critical expressions of the public interest by insisting they know what it is and how to serve it (Barrett, Bunds, Casper, & Edwards, 2019). This accords with the fashion for "governance," which in itself has become a euphemistic term deployed by politicians and bureaucrats to block serious bodies of law that could protect the environment from sports and its "governing" mandarins (Baram, 2009; Warren, 2020). Indeed, much evidence suggests that avoidance of democracy has become a core principle. It can be no surprise that it took a court order for FIFA to introduce hydration breaks during the heat of the 2014 Finals (Earls, 2019). We can only imagine future attempts in sports to bend the unborn to the tastes of the present, to intervene genetically so that athletes of the future have fast-twitch muscle fibers, chauvinistic fantasies, or blue eyes (Habermas, 2003).

It has become exceedingly clear that we need to think decades ahead when pondering the costs, benefits, causes, and effects of how environmental lifeworlds are altered by sports. Consideration of this longer shadow is in stark contrast to the duration of sports events, even those that necessitate years of planning, construction, and competition (Ahmed & Pretorius, 2010). National boundaries and interests are brought into question by the border-crossing impact of environmental despoliation (Dean, 2001). Private and public sporting policies need to be predicated on environmental justice, holding polluters accountable for their ecological crimes, whether tennis-ball manufacturers or football oligarchs (Lynch, Long, Barrett, & Stretesky, 2013; Mullenbach & Baker, 2020; Rigolon, Fernandez, Harris, & Stewart, 2019; Schlosberg, 2007).

Several sporting agencies and bodies, such as the International Association of Athletics Federations (n.d.) and the World Anti-Doping Agency (n.d.), transcend physical and legislative frontiers. In this vein, we need a global environmental regulator of sports in partnership with fans, unions, scientists, governments, and international associations. A Court of Arbitration for Sports and the Environment should match the border-crossing Court of Arbitration for Sport (n.d.). Along the lines of the World Intellectual Property Organization (n.d.), there must be a World Environmental Organization, an entity whose plausible implementation would require both national accreditation and the credible use of expertise in the face of untethered capital interests.

Finally, we need a cohort of investigative journalists to unveil the truth to sports fans. There are predictably few examples beyond the fine work of Roberto Fuentes Vivar (2019), Jean-Luc Ferré (2020), Sergi López-Egea (2019), and Dave Zirin (2020), who rightly blew the whistle on Australian Open tennis as "the tip of a melting iceberg." Such writing can have decided impact, as could the work of sports scholars if they made climate change a centerpiece of their teaching and research. Indeed, this could be advanced if the authors of textbooks and syllabi highlighted these issues as important as established norms. But for that to happen, both groups would need to depart from their identities as salaried fans and take their professional responsibilities more seriously (Mahiri & Van Rheenen, 2010; Reed, 2018).

APPROACHES

Having outlined sports' galling complicity with global warming and what might be done about it, the remaining task is to explore theoretical options for comprehending this problem. Philosophy and environmental materialism have been used both to legitimize and to demystify the environmental postures prevalent in contemporary sporting culture. Such approaches can help explain the disastrous consequences of "naturalized" decisions about sports and their environmental impacts and divert sports and sports studies from their current de facto embrace of environmental criminality, on the one hand, and malign neglect, on the other (Carmichael, 2020; Gibbs, Gore, McGarrell, & Rivers, 2010). While philosophy offers a conceptual backdrop to the current conjuncture, environmental materialism poses *Cui bono?* questions of public and private investments in sports, examining the operation and malfeasance of states' and capital's ecological impact.

Reconsidering Philosophical Tendencies

A complex heritage underpins worldviews that focus on the interests of human beings (anthropocentrism) versus the planet as a whole (ecocentrism). The anthropomorphic arrogance underpinning the slow violence explained earlier by Nixon (2011) derives from a heritage that has informed imperialism, colonialism, industrialization, and the commodification of sports. Of course, such "big picture" insights are rarely discussed by the exuberant fanboys of sports journalism's "toy store" and the fallen and failed jocks who overpopulate sports studies, most particularly those engaged in the cheerleading field of sport management (McEnnis, 2020). However unconsciously, they are legatees of a powerful tradition that represents and legitimizes the excesses of the Enlightenment and modernity.

The complex originary contradictions of development included a heartfelt desire for transformation of enslaved nations, whether for religious or liberal reasons. Consider the cultural policies of Spain's *conquista de América*, Portugal's *missão civilizadora*, and France's *mission civilisatrice*. That legacy was predicated on notions of supremacy and victory through environmental destructiveness. Hobbes (1998, pp. 105–106) argued that as part of "the war of all against all," it was right for people to domesticate or destroy nature. Descartes (2007, p. 1) maintained that "reason or good sense . . . distinguishes us from the lower animals." For Kant (2011), humans' capacity to transcend our "spontaneity and natural constitution" elevated us above other creatures, legitimizing the destructive use of power via what Hegel (1954, pp. 242–243, 248–250; 1988, pp. 50, 154, 161) called "the right of absolute proprietorship." That point of view justifies clearing land and building stadia, courts, and fields wherever we wish and traveling to events as we choose.

On this reading, the core of human consciousness is a struggle for freedom from risk and want. William James (1909) proclaimed that "nature is but a name for excess" that must be tamed and transcended. Nature's "tedious chronicle," where there is "nothing new under the sun," is rightly and righteously disrespected and disobeyed (Hegel, 1988). From this standpoint, we can climb rocky peaks, having flown over many more to get there, to symbolize our putative rights and responsibilities of conquest.

This anthropocentric discourse embodies two baleful, problematic certitudes: human sovereignty over the world and a paradoxical implication that its exercise will not fundamentally challenge the basis of life. That discourse has legitimized the suzerainty of the Global North through imperialism and capitalism. Sports have expressed superiority over other peoples and dominion over nature, both through the colonial spread of football, cricket, tennis, golf, athletics, and so on, and their latter-day commodification. Little wonder that cultural studies theorist Stuart Hall (2011, p. 723) described the neoliberal subject, always ready for adventure, as a "self-sufficient urban traveller—mobile, gym-trim, cycling gear, helmet, water bottle and other survival kit at the ready, unencumbered by 'commitments,' untethered, roaming free."

But the vulnerability of sporting bodies also exemplifies a confronting existential reality. Plato (1972) referred approvingly to the power of natural disasters to unmake "crafty devices"; when these "tools were destroyed," new inventions and a pacific society, based on restraint rather than excess, could emerge. For all his privileging of consciousness, Kant (2011) gave an impassioned account of the natural world as equally beautiful *and* sublime, aesthetic *and* awesome. That paradoxical amalgam forced him to confront a space beyond both nature and human semiosis—a terrifying place where "the shadows of the boundless void into the abyss before me." This raised a horrifying specter, an apocalyptic vision that one day we may realize there is nothing left, nothing else, nothing beyond. Such anxieties obliged him to recognize that the objects of natural science had a history and hence, perhaps, a limited future. Kant remained anthropocentric, convinced that "the human being . . . deserves to be called *knowledge of the world*, even though he constitutes only one part of the creatures on earth," but his terror in the face of that abyss helped animate this chapter. Hume (1739/1896, 1955) questioned the dominant anthropocentric perspective. He maintained that animals, like people, "learn many things from experience," developing "knowledge of the nature of fire, water, earth, stones, heights, depths, etc." in addition to processing instructions as part of their domestication. Rather than being merely sensate, some of our fellow creatures apply logic through inference—what he called "the reason of animals." More simplistically, albeit empathetically, Bentham (1970) said of our duty of care to animals that "the question is not, Can they *reason?* nor, Can they *talk?* but, Can they *suffer?*" And even Kant acknowledged animals' capacity for reflection.

It took Engels (1946, p. 9) to recognize the fundamental truth of environmentalism: "[N]ature does not just *exist*, but *comes into being and passes away.*" Our environment has a history, a present, and a future—it is not a given that simply endures. He noted anthropocentrism's peculiar faith in "the *absolute immutability of nature*," that however "nature itself might have come into being, once present it remained as it was as long as it continued to exist." In that context, Luxemburg (1970) criticized attempts to "seek refuge and repose in nature" that ignored the fact that nature was reshaped and its lifespan shortened by industrial capital. Heidegger (1977, pp. 288, 296, 299) argued against "the unreasonable demand" that nature "supply energy which can be extracted and stored," bending seasonal rhythms to year-round demands of work, growth, and competition (also see Swanton, 2010). Latour (2015, p. 221) avows that "while we emancipated ourselves, each day we also more tightly entangled ourselves in the fabric of nature." One need only consider flying across the world and against one's own climate to ensure that cricket has 12 months of television rights to sell, or convening the Olympics during early spring to suit U.S. television network targets, to see how this has played out in contemporary reality.

The anthropomorphic tendencies of this legacy are further animated today by methodological nationalism and self-interest. In the environmental sphere, they are incarnate in the "Human Exceptionalism Paradigm" and ecological modernization (Catton & Dunlap, 1978; Spaargaren & Mol, 1992). Such "administrative research" supports technological innovation, buoyant demand, mendacious marketing, and property relations (Lazarsfeld, 1941) in the name of capitalist efficiency and governmental normativity. It focuses on climate change as a consequence of the supposed absence of pure market forces (Ostrom, 2000), arguing that once prices are placed on such negative externalities as pollution, everything can be put to rights (Hardin, 1968).

Environmental Materialism

There are glimmers of hope amid the largely problematic received logics of dominant philosophy, thanks to environmental materialism (Fisk, 1980; Foster, 1999; Miller, 2019). Environmental materialism is a tendentious syntagm, for it brings together concepts from science and Marxism. That combination was far from unusual in the first 50 years of the 20th century. It fell victim both to Cold War ideology, which saw many scientists suffer Redbaiting, and state-socialist human-rights violations, which forced progressives to reevaluate the Second World. Today it attracts opprobrium from essentialist ideologues who wish to associate environmental hazards with a putative human nature rather than actually existing social systems.

Nevertheless, renewed interest in environmental materialism is emerging across the human sciences. Both an activist logic and a scholarly method, environmental materialism opposes "any political system that sees nature only through the lens of demands for unlimited economic growth" (Light, 1998, pp. 345, 348). It focuses on labor and the environment, not supply and demand (Barber et al., 2018; Bertrand, 2019; Davis, 2017). Environmental materialism measures ecological survival separately from monetary exchange, prioritizes sustainability over profit, and seeks democratic control of business. For while early modernity was dedicated to producing and distributing goods in a struggle for the most effective and efficient forms of industrialization, with devil take the hindmost and no thought for the environment, today's risk society necessitates enumerating, euphemizing, and managing those dangers. In recognition of that reality, over the past two decades environmental Marxism has emerged, connecting nature to capital and labor as constitutive variables of analysis and favoring regulation of business and work to ensure they comply with ecological principles (Benton, 1996; Brevini & Lewis, 2018; Goldman & Schurman, 2000; Martínez-Alier, 2012; Maxwell, Raundalen, & Vestberg, 2015; O'Connor, 1998). Such approaches can be blended with the science of climate change to address sporting events, health, activism, and regulation.

DEBATES

Scholarly work on sport and the environment has tentatively embraced environmental materialism from diverse disciplinary vantage points, but has a long way to go. The academic literature on the topic in the languages I can read is sparse, and is richest in medical and other fields outside the sociology of sport and its close relatives. This is in keeping with the implicit and explicit fandom animating much of our field of play in sport studies. By contrast with obsessions over student scholars' educational achievements versus their sporting ones, how to make people jump higher or run faster, or celebrations of Olympic mythology, environmental studies has largely been neglected. It is therefore difficult to provide a section on debates in the way that can be done with other important areas, such as race, gender, sexuality, and the place of political economy in sports studies.

Most of the helpful contributions I have found in my research into these topics come from journals specializing in environmental science, health, the law, and tourism. *Nature* and the *British Medical Journal*, two of the world's most important scientific scholarly publications, were inspired by #FridaysForFuture (Fisher, 2019; Stott, Smith, Williams, & Godlee, 2019). Sport studies must learn from the example of their editors, for our principal journals—from sports medicine to kinesiology, history, communications, economics, management, and sociology—have barely contributed to the environmental struggle, and there are few relevant books or substantive treatments (Bunds & Casper, 2018; Casper & Pfahl, 2015; Hayes & Karamichas, 2012; Karamichas, 2013; Mallen, Stevens, & Adam, 2011; McCullough & Kellison, 2017; Millington & Wilson, 2016 Scheu, Preuß, & Könecke, 2019; Stoddart, 2012; see also *Journal of Sport & Social Issues*, 33(2) of 2009 and *Sociology of Sport Journal*, 35(1) of 2018).

If we were to have serious debates in sports textbooks and journals, in contexts where the environment was both crucial and ordinary—crucial in that it has to do with planetary survival, ordinary in that it should be a conventional part of any course, article, or book about sports—what would those debates cover? The main one is this: whether national and international sporting contests that cannot be conducted via renewable energy simply shouldn't exist—no NBA, no World Cup, no Olympics, no Indian Premier League as we know them.

Until flight becomes less destructive, it shouldn't be used. The immense costs of airports and planes in the United States and their fuel use could be turned into a national rail network, expanding the Acela beyond the northeastern corridor as per plans that date back six decades. This would mean reducing transcontinental travel for major U.S. pro and college sports unless they embark on a serious rail initiative, which in the interim might mean purchasing high-quality trains for their players and affiliated staff, in the long term contributing to the cost of laying down freight infrastructure. It would mean that the billionaires' subsidies for new stadia from gullible governments should come with guaranteed use of renewable materials in construction and clean-energy power. Right now one can travel via fast trains from northern London to southern Spain. If the Olympics can be postponed for reasons of health, why not to help secure our environment?

Contributing to such debates implies the need for new kinds of collaboration and autodidacticism within sports studies: a need to read beyond orthodox epistemological fancies, newspaper puff pieces, governmental niceties, and conventional industry research.

We must study, *inter alia*, the science of climate change, lifecycle assessment, and the physics, chemistry, and epidemiology associated with the production, use, and disposal of sporting technologies, from stadium materials to media coverage. Most important, we must acknowledge the urgent nature of our ecological crisis and our complicity in creating and sustaining it.

CONCLUSION

Conventional political-economic space and time have to be transcended in order to advance a globally sustainable ecology that can counter the elemental risks created by capitalist growth. Such changes can be accommodated by even conservative philosophers: Edmund Burke (1986, pp. 192–195), no radical he, acknowledged each generation as "temporary possessors and life-renters" of the natural and social world. People must maintain "chain and continuity" rather than acting ephemerally, as if they were "flies of a summer." Burke called for "a partnership not only between those who are living, but between those who are living, those who are dead, and those who are to be born" to sustain "the great primeval contract of eternal society." Such intergenerational care has long been a centerpiece of African American and indigenous environmental thought (Escobar, 1995; Smith, 2007; Vickery & Hunter, 2014). It should be our lodestar as we revise what constitutes relevance for sports studies, basing that transformation in our material world that is so direly threatened by ecological disaster.

The lesson of sporting despoliation is clear. Nature's duality—that it is self-generating and sustaining, yet its survival is contingent on human rhetoric and conduct—makes it vulnerable. The Earth's reaction to our interference will strike back, sooner or later, in mutually assured destruction. Changes to the material world threaten the survival of the planet's most skillful and willful, productive and destructive inhabitant. Only by rejecting anthropomorphic sporting narcissism and parthenogenesis in favor of environmental materialism can sports and its scholars transcend their record of ignorance and irresponsibility, whether those failings be conscious or otherwise.

REFERENCES

Abusin, S., Lari, N., Khaled, S., & Al Emadi, N. (2020). Effective policies to mitigate food waste in Qatar. *African Journal of Agricultural Research, 15*(3), 343–350.

Ahmed, F., & Pretorius, L. (2010). Mega-events and environmental impacts: The 2010 FIFA World Cup in South Africa. *Alternation, 17*(2), 274–296.

Anthropocene Working Group, Subcommission on Quaternary Stratigraphy. (2019, May 21). Results of binding vote by AWG: What is the "Anthropocene"? Current definition and status. http://quaternary.stratigraphy.org/workinggroups/anthropocene/.

Australian Conservation Foundation & Monash Climate Change Communication Research Hub. (2020). Love 40 degrees? Climate change, extreme heat and the Australian Open. https://d3n8a8pro7vhmx.cloudfront.net/auscon/pages/16968/attachments/original/157 9232498/Love_40_degrees_climate_report_Jan2020.pdf?1579232498.

Azzali, S. (2017). The legacies of Sochi 2014 Winter Olympics: An evaluation of the Adler Olympic Park. *Urban Research & Practice 10*(3), 329–349.

Bahr, R., Clarsen, B., Derman, W., Dvorak, J., Emery, C. A., Finch, . . . Chamari, K. (2020). International Olympic Committee consensus statement: Methods for recording and reporting of epidemiological data on injury and illness in sport 2020 (including STROBE Extension for Sport Injury and Illness Surveillance (STROBE-SIIS)). *British Journal of Sports Medicine, 54*(7), 372–389.

Baram, M. (2009). Globalization and workplace hazards in developing nations. *Safety Science, 47*(6), 756–766.

Barber, D. A., Stickells, L., Ryan, D. J., Koehler, M., Leach, A., van der Plaat, D., Keys, C., Karim, F., & Taylor, W. M. (2018). Architecture, environment, history: Questions and consequences. *Architectural History Review, 22*(2), 249–286.

Barrett, M., Bunds, K. S., Casper, J. M., & Edwards, M. B. (2019). A descriptive analysis of corporate environmental responsibility in major league professional sport. *Journal of Applied Sport Management, 11*(3), 35–46.

Beck, U. (2009). *World at risk.* (C. Cronin, Trans). Cambridge, U.K.: Polity.

Becker, A. B. (2013). Star power? Advocacy, receptivity, and viewpoints on celebrity involvement in issue politics. *Atlantic Journal of Communication, 21*(10), 1–16.

Bentham, J. (1970). *The principles of morals and legislation.* Darien, CT: Hafner.

Benton, T. (Ed.). (1996). *The greening of Marxism.* New York: Guilford.

Bernard, P., Chevance, G., Kingsbury, C., Baillot, A., Romain, A. J., Molinier, V., Gadais, T., & Dancause, K. N. (2020). Climate change, physical activity and sport: A systematic review. *Sports Medicine, 51*(5), 1041–1059.

Bertrand, A. (2019). A rupture between human beings and earth: A philosophical critical approach to coviability. In O. Barrière, M. Behnassi, G. David, V. Douzal, M. Fargette, T. Libourel, . . . S. Morand (Eds.), *Coviability of social and ecological systems: Reconnecting mankind to the biosphere in an era of global change. Vol. 1: The foundations of a new paradigm* (pp. 269–284). Cham, Switzerland: Springer.

Bonnemains, A. (2014). Quelle capacité d'adaptation pour les stations de sports d'hiver de haute altitude des Alpes du Nord? Mise en regard de la vulnérabilitié territorial et du plan énergie climat territorial Tarentaise Vanoise. *Sud-Ouest Européen, 37*, 29–39.

Bos, I., De Boever, P., Int Panis, L., & Meeusen, R. (2014). Physical activity, air pollution and the brain. *Sports Medicine, 44*(11), 1505–1518.

Boykoff, J., & Mascarenhas, G. (2016). The Olympics, sustainability, and greenwashing: The Rio 2016 Summer Games. *Capitalism Nature Socialism, 27*(2), 1–11.

Brevini, B., & Lewis, J. (Eds.). (2018). *Climate change and the media.* New York: Peter Lang.

Bullock, G. (2017). *Green grades: Can information save the earth?* Cambridge, MA: MIT Press.

Bunds, K., & Casper, J. (2018). Sport, physical culture and the environment: An introduction. *Sociology of Sport Journal, 35*(1), 1–7.

Burke, E. (1986). *Reflections on the revolution in France and on the proceedings in certain societies in London relative to that event* (C. C. O'Brien, Ed). Harmondsworth, U.K.: Penguin.

Carbon Trust. (n.d.). Carbon bootprint of the FA Community Shield. https://www.carbontrust.com/media/360767/carbon-bootprint-infographic.pdf.

Carbon Trust. (2016). The "carbon bootprint" of Euro 2016: Which nation's fans have the lowest carbon footprint when watching games. https://www.carbontrust.com/news/2016/06/the-carbon-bootprint-of-euro-2016-which-nations-fans-have-the-lowest-carbon-footprint-when-watching-games/.

Carmichael, A. (2020). Time for practice: Sport and the environment. *Managing Sport and Leisure*, doi:10.1080/23750472.2020.1757493.

Casper, J. M., & Pfahl, M. E. (Eds.). (2015). *Sport management and the natural environment*. Abingdon, U.K.: Routledge.

Catton, W. R., Jr., & Dunlap, R. E. (1978). Environmental sociology: A new paradigm. *American Sociologist*, 13(1), 41–49.

Children's climate rallies gain momentum in Europe. (2019, January 25). BBC News. https://www.bbc.co.uk/news/world-europe-46999381.

Collins, A., & Flynn, D. (2008). Measuring the environmental sustainability of a major sporting event: A case study of the FA Cup Final. *Tourism Economics*, 14(4), 751–768.

Colorado rejects Olympics. (1972, November 8). *Ludington Daily News*, 5.

Cooper, D., Batt, M., & Palmer, D. (2020). Epidemiology of injury and retirement from sport among former international athletes. *British Journal of Sports Medicine*, 54(Suppl. 1), A88–A89.

Court of Arbitration for Sport. (n.d.). https://www.tas-cas.org/en/index.html.

Crabb, L. A. H. (2018). Debating the success of carbon-offsetting projects at sports mega-events: A case from the 2014 FIFA World Cup. *Journal of Sustainable Forestry*, 37(2), 178–196.

Crook, C. (2005, January 22). The good company. *Economist*, Survey 3–4.

Davies, G. H. (2019, February 5). Which football club tops the green league? *GHDavies*, blog. http://www.garethhuwdavies.com/environment/environment_blog/which-football-club-top-the-green-league/.

Davis, T. H. (2009, July 26). A mixed record so far on environmental issues. *Financial Times*. https://www.ft.com/content/31503024-77eb-11de-9713-00144feabdco.

Davis, W. (2017). Visuality and vision: Questions for a post-culturalist art history. *Estetika: The Central European Journal of Aesthetics*, 54(2), 238–257.

Dean, H. (2001). Green citizenship. *Social Policy & Administration*, 35(5), 490–505.

de Menezes, J. (2015, November 28). Arsenal criticized for taking "ridiculous, ludicrous and farcical" 14-minute plane flight to Norwich. *Independent*. https://www.independent.co.uk/sport/football/premier-league/arsenal-criticised-for-taking-ridiculous-14-minute-plane-flight-to-norwich-a6752486.html.

Descartes, R. (2007). *Discourse on the method of rightly conducting one's reason and seeking truth in the sciences. Early Modern Texts*. http://www.earlymoderntexts.com/assets/pdfs/descartes1637.pdf.

Deubet, T. (2013, September 8). 10 greatest race horses. *YouTube*. https://www.youtube.com/watch?v=h5-p4wl2Qfs.

Doherty, S. (2019, March 13). The activists going on "birth strike" to protest climate change. *Vice*. https://www.vice.com/en_ca/article/wjmkmz/the-activists-going-on-birth-strike-to-protest-climate-change.

Doing the right thing: Forest Green Rovers are world's first UN-certified carbon neutral club. (2018, August 1). *Inside World Football*. http://www.insideworldfootball.com/2018/08/01/right-thing-forest-green-rovers-worlds-first-un-certified-carbon-neutral-club/.

Dosumu, A., Colbeck, I., & Bragg, R. (2017). Greenhouse gas emissions as a result of spectators travelling to football in England. *Nature*, 7, 6986.

Earls, M. (2019, July 2). As the world heats up, soccer must adapt. *Scientific American*. https://www.scientificamerican.com/article/as-the-world-heats-up-soccer-must-adapt/.

Engels, F. (1946). *The dialectics of nature* (C. P. Dutt, Trans). London: Lawrence and Wishart.

Escobar, A. (1995). *Encountering development: The making and unmaking of the third world.* Princeton, NJ: Princeton University Press.

Estrada, D. (2010, June 3). World Cup 2010: Climate change fouls and goals. *Guardian.* http://www.theguardian.com/environment/2010/jun/03/climate-change-world-cup.

Extinction Rebellion. (n.d.). https://rebellion.earth.

Farchy, J. (2016, May 16). Norilsk Nickel buys palladium to lower market volatility. *Financial Times* https://next.ft.com/content/4e9d314e-1b4b-11e6-a7bc-ee846770ec15.

Ferré, J.-L. (2020, January 16). Les contraintes climatiques obligent le monde du sport à se repenser. *La Croix.* https://www.la-croix.com/Sport/contraintes-climatiques-obligent-monde-sport-repenser-2020-01-16-1201072242.

FIFA. (2019). 2018 FIFA World Cup Russia™ sustainability report. https://img.fifa.com/image/upload/ya7pgcyslxpzlqmjkykg.pdf.

Fifka, M. S., & Jaeger, J. (2020). CSR in professional European football: An integrative framework. *Soccer & Society, 21*(1), 61–78.

Fisher, D. R. (2019). The broader importance of #FridaysForFuture. *Nature Climate Change, 9,* 430–431.

Fisk, M. (1980). Materialism and dialectic. *Critique: Journal of Socialist Theory, 12*(1), 97–116.

Football Supporters Association. (n.d.). https://thefsa.org.

Forest Green. (n.d.). The world's first vegan football club. https://www.fgr.co.uk/our-ethos/100-vegan.

Forrest, D., McHale, I. G., Sanz, I., & Tena, J. D. (2017). An analysis of country medal shares in individual sports at the Olympics. *European Sport Management Quarterly, 17*(2), 117–131.

Foster, J. B. (1999). Marx's theory of metabolic rift: Classical foundations for environmental sociology. *American Journal of Sociology, 105*(2), 366–405.

GAᵉ Engineering. (n.d.). Juventus stadium. https://www.gae-engineering.com/project/juventus-stadium/.

Gallan, D. (2019, December 11). Mocked by some, but "green" soccer club wants to save the world. CNN. https://edition.cnn.com/2019/12/11/football/forest-green-rovers-spt-intl/index.html.

Gibbs, C., Gore, M. L., McGarrell, E. F., & Rivers, III, L. (2010). Introducing conservation criminology: Towards interdisciplinary scholarship on environmental crimes and risks. *British Journal of Criminology, 50*(1), 124–144.

Giles, L. V., & Koehle, M. S. (2014). The health effects of exercising in air pollution. *Sports Medicine, 44,* 223–249.

Goldblatt, D. (2016). *The Games: A global history of the Olympics.* New York: W. W. Norton.

Goldman, M., & Schurman, R. A. (2000). Closing the "great divide": New social theory on society and nature. *Annual Review of Sociology, 26,* 563–584.

Graedel, T. E., Harper, E. M., Nassar, N. T., & Reck, B. K. (2015). On the materials basis of modern society. *Proceedings of the National Academy of Sciences of the United States of America, 112*(20), 6295–6300.

Habermas, J. (2003). *The future of human nature* (W. Rehg, M. Pensky, & H. Besiter, Trans.). Cambridge, U.K.: Polity Press.

Hall, S. (2011). The neo-liberal revolution. *Cultural Studies, 25*(6), 705–728.

Hardin, G. (1968). The tragedy of the commons. *Science, 162*(3859), 1243–1248.

Hayes, G., & Karamichas, J. (Eds.). (2012). *Olympic Games, mega-events and civil societies: Globalization, environment, resistance.* New York: Palgrave Macmillan.

Hector Bellerin plants trees. (n.d.). OneTreePlanted. https://bellerintrees.raisely.com/.

Hegel, G. W. F. (1954). *The philosophy of Hegel* (C. J. Friedrich, Ed., C. J. Friedrich, P. W. Friedrich, W. H. Johnston, L. G. Struthers, B. Bosanquet, W. M. Bryant, & J. B. Baillie, Trans.). New York: Modern Library.

Hegel, G. W. F. (1988). *Lectures on the philosophy of world history. Introduction: Reason in history* (H. B. Nisbet, Trans.). Cambridge: Cambridge University Press.

Heidegger, M. (1977). *Basic writings from Being and Time (1927) to The Task of Thinking (1964)* (D. F. Krell, Ed., J. Stambaugh, J. G. Gray, D. F. Krell, J. Sallis, F. A. Capuzzi, A. Hofstadter, W. B. Barton, Jr., V. Deutsch, W. Lovitt, & F. D. Wieck, Trans.). New York: Harper & Row.

Hobbes, T. (1998). *On the citizen* (R. Tuck & M. Silverthorne, Trans. and Eds.). Cambridge: Cambridge University Press.

Huijuan, C., Fujii, H., & Managi, S. (2013). Environmental impact of the 2008 Beijing Olympic Games. Economics Discussion Paper, 2013-30, Kiel Institute for the World Economy. http://www.economics-ejournal.org/economics/discussionpapers/2013-30.

Hume, D. (1739/1896). *A treatise of human nature* (L. A. Selby-Bigge, Ed.). http://michaeljohnsonphilosophy.com/wp-content/uploads/2012/01/5010_Hume_Treatise_Human_Nature.pdf.

Hume, D. (1955). *An inquiry concerning human understanding with a supplement: An abstract of a treatise of human nature.* (C. W. Hendel, Ed.). Indianapolis, IN: Bobbs-Merrill.

Hyde-Clarke, N., Ottosen, R., & Miller, T. (2014). Nation-building and the FIFA World Cup, South Africa 2010. In T. Chari & N. A. Mhiripiri (Eds.), *African football, identity politics and global media narratives: The legacy of the FIFA 2010 World Cup* (pp. 15–28). London: Palgrave Macmillan.

International Association of Athletics Federations. (n.d.). https://www.worldathletics.org/home.

International Civil Aviation Organization. (2016). ICAO carbon emissions calculator. https://www.icao.int/environmental-protection/CarbonOffset/Pages/default.aspx.

International Olympic Committee. (2018). Carbon footprint methodology for the Olympic Games. https://library.olympic.org/Default/doc/SYRACUSE/184686/carbon-footprint-methodology-for-the-olympic-games-international-olympic-committee?_lg=fr-FR.

James, W. (1909). *A pluralistic universe: Hibbert lectures at Manchester College on the present situation in philosophy.* http://hudsoncress.net/hudsoncress.org/html/library/western-philosophy/James,%20William%20-%20A%20Pluralistic%20Universe.pdf.

Jiménez-García, M., Ruiz-Chico, J., Peña-Sánchez, A. R., & López-Sánchez, J. A. (2020). A bibliometric analysis of sports tourism and sustainability (2002–2019). *Sustainability, 12*(7), 2840–2858.

Johnson, J., & Ali, A. E. 2018. Ecological modernization and the 2014 NHL sustainability report. *Sociology of Sport Journal, 35*(1), 49–57.

Jorgenson, A. K., & Clark, B. (2016). The temporal stability and developmental differences in the environmental impacts of militarism: The treadmill of destruction and consumption-based carbon emissions. *Sustainability Science, 26*(11), 505–514.

Kant, I. (2011). *Observations on the feeling of the beautiful and sublime and other writings* (P. Frierson & P. Guyer, Eds.). Cambridge: Cambridge University Press.

Karamichas, J. (2013). *The Olympic Games and the environment.* New York: Palgrave Macmillan.

Kay, S. (2019, April 22). Winter is going: How climate change is imperiling outdoor sporting heritage. *Sports Illustrated.* https://www.si.com/nhl/2019/04/22/climate-change-canada-winter-sports-hockey-backyard-rinks.

Keoghan, J. (2014). *Punk football: The rise of fan ownership in English football.* Worthing, U.K.: Pitch Publishing.

khushiss69. The fastest woman on the track on this earth. (2010, September 10). YouTube. https://www.youtube.com/watch?v=cxMlBKif59Q.

Kim, K.-Y., & Chung, H. 2018. Eco-modernist environmental politics and counter-activism around the 2018 PyeongChang Winter Games. *Sociology of Sport Journal, 35*(1), 17–28.

Klein, P. (2012, December 28). Three ways to secure your social license to operate in 2013. *Forbes.* http://www.forbes.com/sites/csr/2012/12/28/three-ways-to-secure-your-social-lice nse-to-operate-in-2013/.

Latour, B. (2015). Fifty shades of green. *Environmental Humanities, 7*(1), 219–225.

Latour, B. (2018). *Down to earth: Politics in the new climatic regime* (C. Porter, Trans.). Cambridge, U.K.: Polity.

Lazarsfeld, P. F. (1941). Remarks on administrative and critical communications research. *Studies in Philosophy and Social Science, 9*(1), 2–16.

Lehne, J., & Preston, F. (2018). Making concrete change: Innovation in low-carbon cement and concrete. Chatham House. https://www.chathamhouse.org/sites/default/files/publications/ 2018-06-13-making-concrete-change-cement-lehne-preston-final.pdf.

Levermore, R. (2010). CSR for development through sport: Examining its potential and limitations. *Third World Quarterly, 31*(2), 223–241.

Levermore, R. (2011). Sport-for-development and the 2010 Football World Cup. *Geography Compass, 5*(12), 886–897.

Levermore, R. (2012). The paucity of, and dilemma in, evaluating corporate social responsibility for development through sport. *Third World Quarterly, 32*(3), 551–569.

Light, A. (1998). Reconsidering Bookchin and Marcuse as environmental materialists: Toward an evolving social ecology. In A. Light (Ed.), *Social ecology after Bookchin* (pp. 343–384). New York: Guilford Press.

López-Egea, S. (2019, December 13). El reto climático en los grandes deportes. *elPeriódico.* https://www.elperiodico.com/es/deportes/20191213/deporte-alerta-cambio-climatico-7773643.

Luxemburg, R. (1970). *Rosa Luxemburg speaks* (M.-A. Waters, Ed.). New York: Pathfinder Press.

Lynch, M. J., Long, M. A., Barrett, K. L., & Stretesky, P. B. (2013). Is it a crime to produce ecological disorganization? Why green criminology and political economy matter in the analysis of global ecological harms. *British Journal of Criminology, 53*(6), 997–1016.

Mahiri, J., & Van Rheenen, D. (2010). *Out of bounds: When scholarship athletes become academic scholars.* New York: Peter Lang.

Mallen, C. A., Stevens, J., & Adam, L. J. (2011). A content analysis of environmental sustainability research in a sport-related journal sample. *Journal of Sport Management, 25*(3), 240–256.

Marquis, C., Toffel, M. W., & Zhou, Y. (2016). Scrutiny, norms, and selective disclosure: A global study of greenwashing. *Organization Science, 27*(2), 483–504.

Martin, L. (2019, February 6). Climate change set to disrupt Australia's summer sports calendar. *Guardian.* https://www.theguardian.com/environment/2019/feb/06/climate-cha nge-set-to-disrupt-australias-summer-sports-calendar.

Martínez-Alier, J. (2012). Environmental justice and economic degrowth: An alliance between two movements. *Capitalism Nature Socialism, 23*(1), 51–73.

Maxwell, R., Raundalen, J., & Vestberg, N. L. (Eds.). (2015). *Media and the ecological crisis.* New York: Routledge.

May, V. (1995). Environmental implications of the 1992 Winter Olympic Games. *Tourism Management, 16*(4), 269–275.

McCarthy, M. (2009, December 8). Football's carbon footprint comes under fire. *Independent*. https://www.independent.co.uk/environment/climate-change/footballs-carbon-footprint-comes-under-fire-1836035.html.

McCullough, B., & Kellison, T. B. (Eds.). (2017). *Handbook on sport, sustainability, and the environment*. New York: Routledge.

McEnnis, S. (2020). Toy department within the toy department? Online sports journalists and professional legitimacy. *Journalism, 21*(10), 1415–1431.

McHale, K. (2019). Give the fans what they really want: How professional sports stadiums across the world can positively impact the environment. *Texas Environmental Law Journal, 49*(1), 127–158.

McKie, R., Savage, M., & Cornwall, P. (2019, May 11). As English fans get set to cross Europe, anger rises at football's carbon bootprint. *Guardian*. https://www.theguardian.com/environment/2019/may/11/anger-carbon-bootprint-english-football-finals-champions-league-europa-league.

Miller, T. (2018). *Greenwashing sport*. London: Routledge.

Miller, T. (2019). La crisis ambiental: El Marxismo contra el antropocentrismo filosófico. In P. Aroch Fugellie, E. G. Gallegos, M. M. S. Madureira, & F. Victoriano (Eds.), *Das Kapital: Marx, actualidad y crítica* (pp. 200–214). Mexico City: Siglo Veintinuo/Universidad Autónoma Metropolitana, Unidad Cuajimalpa.

Millington, B., & Wilson, B. (2016). *The greening of golf: Sport, globalization and the environment*. New York: Oxford University Press.

Mullenbach, L. E., & Baker, B. L. (2020). Environmental justice, gentrification, and leisure: A systematic review and opportunities for the future. *Leisure Sciences: An Interdisciplinary Journal, 42*(5–6), 430–447.

Müller, M. (2014). After Sochi 2014: Costs and impacts of Russia's Olympic Games. *Eurasian Geography and Economics, 55*(6), 628–655.

Müller, M. (2015). (Im-)mobile policies: Why sustainability went wrong in the 2014 Olympics in Sochi. *European Urban and Regional Studies, 22*(2), 191–209.

National Grid. (2010). National Grid powers up for World Cup 2010. http://www.nationalgrid.com/uk/Media+Centre/WorldCup2010.

National Grid. (2014a, May 30). National Grid up for the World Cup. www2.nationalgrid.com/mediacentral/uk-press-releases/2014/national-grid-up-for-the-world-cup/.

National Grid. (2014b, July 11). World Cup fans switched on to Brazil. http://media.nationalgrid.com/press-releases/archive/world-cup-fans-switched-on-to-brazil/.

National Grid. (2020, April 6). The "lockdown effect" on TV viewing habits and the electricity grid. https://www.nationalgrideso.com/news/lockdown-effect-tv-viewing-habits-and-electricity-grid.

1964: Memories of the Tokyo Olympics. (2014). *Japan News*. http://tokyo-olympics.the-japan-news.com/#titlePage.

Nixon, R. (2011). *Slow violence and the environmentalism of the poor*. Cambridge, MA: Harvard University Press.

Nybo, L., Flouris, A. D., Racinais, S., & Mohr, M. (2020). Football facing a future with global warming: Perspectives for players health and performance. *British Journal of Sports Medicine, 55*(6), 1–2.

O'Connor, J. (1998). *Natural causes: Essays in ecological Marxism*. New York: Guilford.

Olympics. (2015, December 8). Bob Beamon's long jump Olympic record. *YouTube*. https://www.youtube.com/watch?v=KYb_6tH44gk.

Ostrom, E. (2000). Reformulating the commons. *Swiss Political Science Review*, 6(1), 29–52.

Périard, J. D., Racinais, S., Knez, W. L., Herrera, C. P., Christian, R. J., & Girard, O. (2014). Thermal, physiological and perceptual strain mediate alterations in match-play tennis under heat stress. *British Journal of Sports Medicine*, 48(Suppl. 1), i32–i38.

Pitts, A., & Liao, H. (2013). An assessment technique for the evaluation and promotion of sustainable Olympic design and urban development. *Building Research and Information*, 41(6), 722–734.

Plato. (1972). *The laws* (T. J. Saunders, Trans.). Harmondsworth, U.K.: Penguin.

Protect Our Winters. (n.d.). About POW. https://protectourwinters.org/our-work/about-pow/.

Ramaswamy, C. (2015, November 30). Hosting the Olympics: The competition noone wants to win. *Guardian* https://www.theguardian.com/sport/shortcuts/2015/nov/30/hosting-olympics-hamburg-drop-out-2024-games.

Reed, S. (2018). "I'm not a fan. I'm a journalist": Measuring American sports journalists' sports enthusiasm. *Journal of Sports Media*, (13)1, 27–47.

Republic of South Africa. (2004). Accelerated and shared growth initiative. https://www.daff.gov.za/docs/GenPub/asgisa.pdf.

Republic of South Africa, Department of Environmental Affairs and Tourism, Norwegian Agency for Development Cooperation, & Norwegian Embassy in South Africa. (2009). Feasibility study for a carbon neutral 2010 FIFA World Cup in South Africa. http://www.norway.org.za/NR/rdonlyres/3E6BB1B1FD2743E58F5B0BEFBAE7D958/114457/FeasibilityStudyforaCarbonNeutral2010FIFAWorldCup.pdf.

Rigolon, A., Fernandez, M., Harris, B., & Stewart, W. (2019). An ecological model of environmental justice for recreation. *Leisure Sciences: An Interdisciplinary Journal*, doi:10.1080/01490400.2019.1655686.

Rundell, K. W. (2012). Effect of air pollution on athlete health and performance. *British Journal of Sports Medicine*, 46(6), 407–412.

Samuel, S., & Stubbs, W. (2013). Green Olympics, green legacies? An exploration of the environmental legacies of the Olympic Games. *International Review for the Sociology of Sport*, 48(4), 485–504.

Scheu, A., Preuß, H., & Könecke, T. (2019). The legacy of the Olympic Games: A review. *Journal of Global Sport Management*, 6(3), 212–233.

Schlosberg, D. (2007). *Defining environmental justice: Theories, movements, and nature.* Oxford: Oxford University Press.

Selectra. (2020, January 22). What happens when everyone in the UK watches the World Cup at the same time? https://selectra.co.uk/energy/news/world/world-cup-2018-electricity-surges.

Short, J. R. (2015, August 3). The green and the gold: Can we soften the environmental impact of the Olympics? *The Conversation*. https://theconversation.com/the-green-and-the-gold-can-we-soften-the-environmental-impact-of-the-olympics-45530.

Silk, M., Andrews, D. L, & Cole, C. L. (Eds.). (2005). *Sport and corporate nationalisms.* Oxford: Berg.

Smith, K. K. (2007). *African American environmental thought: Foundations.* Lawrence: University of Kansas Press.

Smith, K. R., Woodward, A., Lemke, B., Otto, M., Chang, C. J., Mance, A. A., Balmes, J., & Kjellstrom, T. (2014). The last Summer Olympics? Climate change, health, and work outdoors. *The Lancet, 388*(10045), P642–644.

Spaargaren, G., & Mol, A. P. J. (1992). Sociology, environment, and modernity: Ecological modernization as a theory of social change. *Society and Natural Resources, 5*(4), 323–344.

Spanne, A., & *The Daily Climate*. (2014, June 19). Brazil World Cup fails to score environmental goals. *Scientific American*. http://www.scientificamerican.com/article/brazil-world-cup-fails-to-score-environmental-goals/?WT.mc_id=send-to-friend.

Stay, S., Cort, M., Ward, D., Kountouris, A., Orchard, J., Holland, J., & Saw, A. (2018). Core temperature responses in elite cricket players during Australian summer conditions. *Sports, 6*(4), 164–172.

Stoddart, M. C. J. (2012). *Making meaning out of mountains: The political ecology of skiing*. Vancouver: UBC Press.

Stott, R., Smith, R., Williams, R., & Godlee, F. (2019). Schoolchildren's activism is a lesson for health professionals. *British Medical Journal, 365*, 1–2.

Sturrock, L. (2018, July 12). The environmental impact of the World Cup—Are FIFA scoring sustainability goals? The Great Projects. https://www.thegreatprojects.com/blog/environmental-impact-of-the-world-cup.

Swanton, C. (2010). Heideggerian environmental virtue ethics. *Journal of Agricultural and Environmental Ethics, 23*(1–2), 145–166.

Tagsold, C. (2010). Modernity, space, and national representation at the Tokyo Olympics 1964. *Urban History, 37*(2), 289–300.

Taylor, L. (2019, September 9). Football appears too self-important to bother itself about climate emergency. *Guardian*. https://www.theguardian.com/football/blog/2019/sep/09/football-too-self-important-bother-about-climate-emergency.

TePoel, D. (2017). Digital sport history, with costs: An ecocentric critique. *Journal of Sport History, 44*(2), 350–366.

Thomson, I., & Boutilier, R. G. (2011). Social license to operate. In P. Darling (Ed.), *SME mining engineering handbook* (pp. 1779–1796). Littleton, CO: Society for Mining, Metallurgy and Exploration.

Thrall, A. T., Lollio-Fahkreddine, J., Berent, J., Donnelly, J., Herrin, W., Paquette, Z., Wenglinski, R., & Wyatt, A. (2008). Star power: Celebrity advocacy and the evolution of the public sphere. *International Journal of Press/Politics, 13*(4), 362–385.

Till, B. D., Stanley, S. M., & Priluck, R. (2008). Classical conditioning and celebrity endorsers: An examination of belongingness and resistance to extinction. *Psychology & Marketing, 25*(2), 179–196.

Tóffano Pereira, R. P., Filimonau, V., & Mattos Ribeiro, G. (2019). Score a goal for climate: Assessing the carbon footprint of travel patterns of the English Premier League clubs. *Journal of Cleaner Production, 227*, 167–177.

Trendafilova, S., Babiak, K., & Heinze, K. (2013). Corporate social responsibility and environmental sustainability: Why professional sport is greening the playing field. *Sport Management Review, 16*(3), 298–313.

Tweedale, A. (2018, November 21). FIFA talks a good game but its drive for sustainability highlights football's hypocrisy. *Telegraph*. https://www.telegraph.co.uk/football/2018/11/21/fifa-talks-good-game-drive-sustainability-highlights-footballs/.

UEFA. (2020). Venues confirmed for EURO 2020. https://www.uefa.com/uefaeuro-2020/news/025e-0fac6d3ee9e4-85b1a76389ea-1000/.

United Nations Climate Change. (2018). Sports for climate action framework. https://unf ccc.int/sites/default/files/resource/Sports_for_Climate_Action_Declaration_and_Framew ork.pdf.

United Nations Commission on Sustainable Development. (1998). Chapeau for business and industry. *Background Paper No. 1.* http://www.un.org/documents/ecosoc/cn17/1998/bac kground/ecn171998-bp1.htm.

University of Leeds, British Association for Sustainable Sport, & University of Portsmouth. (2019). Hit for six: The impact of climate change of cricket. https://basis.org.uk/hit-for-six.

Vaccaro, A. (2015, April 2). They just don't want the Olympics. *Boston.com.* http://www.bos ton.com/news/local-news/2015/04/02/they-just-dont-want-the-olympics.

Vickery, J., & Hunter, L. M. (2014). Native Americans: Where in environmental justice theory and research? Institute of Behavioral Science Population Program, University of Colorado, Boulder. Working Paper 4. http://www.colorado.edu/ibs/pubs/pop/pop2014-0004.pdf.

Vivar, R. F. (2019, September 24). Deporte y cambio climático. *Milenio.* https://www.milenio. com/opinion/roberto-fuentes-vivar/las-otras-competencias/deporte-y-cambio-climatico.

Wallace, J. P., Widenman, E., & McDermott, R. J. (2019). Physical activity and climate change: Clear and present danger? *Health Behavior and Policy Review, 6*(5), 534–545.

Walters, G., & Tacon, R. (2011). Corporate social responsibility in European football: A report funded by the UEFA research grant programme. http://www.sportbusinesscentre.com/wp-content/uploads/2012/08/CSR2.pdf.

Warren, G. (2020). Mega sports events have mega environmental and social consequences. *Missouri Law Review, 85*(2).

Watts, J. (2019, February 25). Concrete: The most destructive material on earth. *Guardian.* https://www.theguardian.com/cities/2019/feb/25/concrete-the-most-destructive-mater ial-on-earth.

Wearden, G., & Carrington, D. (2019, January 24). Teenage activist takes school strikes 4 climate action to Davos. *Guardian.* https://www.theguardian.com/environment/2019/jan/24/school-strikes-over-climate-change-continue-to-snowball.

West, L. (2016, August 10). How to talk about female Olympians without being a regressive creep—A handy guide. *Guardian.* https://www.theguardian.com/commentisfree/2016/aug/09/female-olympians-guide-gaffes-athletes-sports-makeup-shorts-marital-sta tus-lindy-west.

Whiting, R. (2014, October 24). Negative impact of 1964 Olympics profound. *Japan Times.* http://www.japantimes.co.jp/sports/2014/10/24/olympics/negative-impact-1964-olympics-profound/.

Wilburn, K. M., & Wilburn, R. (2011). Achieving social license to operate using stakeholder theory. *Journal of International Business Ethics, 4*(2), 3–16.

World Anti Doping Agency. (n.d.). https://www.wada-ama.org/.

World Intellectual Property Organization. (n.d.). https://www.wipo.int/portal/en/index.html.

Zirin, D. (2020, January 17). The Australian Open is the tip of a melting iceberg. *The Nation.* https://www.thenation.com/article/environment/australian-open-fires-climate-change/.

CHAPTER 16

··

SPORT, LEADERSHIP, AND SOCIAL RESPONSIBILITY

··

EMILY S. SPARVERO AND LAURENCE CHALIP

THERE is a consensus among sport industry professionals, sport media, and sport management researchers that sport organizations face increasing pressure to demonstrate social responsibility. Sport organizations have responded to that pressure, with many manufacturers, teams, leagues, and events publicizing their commitment to social responsibility. Against this backdrop, leaders attempt to balance the demands of meeting their business objectives (e.g., profitability, on-the-field success) with their responsibility to society and their communities.

Sport organizations can adopt corporate social responsibility (CSR) programs to address a nearly endless array of societal ills. Companies typically report these as part of their public relations (e.g., Bloomberg, 2020; Visa, 2020). If a social purpose can be claimed, it can be included. Examples are charitable giving, addressing climate change, engaging in fair trade, enabling volunteer programs, and many more.

Historically, sport organizations have chosen CSR activities that are unlikely to alienate their fan base, with an emphasis on youth, health, and education charities. When CSR targets seem uncontroversial, there is unlikely to be a conflict between engagement with a social issue and positive public relations benefits for the organization. So nearly all North American teams in the major leagues have private charitable foundations (Sparvero & Kent, 2014); sporting goods (e.g., Dick's Sporting Goods, 2019) and apparel (e.g., Columbia Sportswear Company, 2019) manufacturers proclaim their CSR bona fides on the Web, in annual reports, and through community impact statements.

In recent years, sport organizations have become involved in more divisive social justice issues, which has complicated the task facing industry leaders. In 2020, the world faced a global pandemic that forced most sport leagues to cancel or substantially modify their seasons. At the same time, many sport organizations in the United States decided to make public displays in support of the Black Lives Matter (BLM) protest movement. The NBA lettered "Black Lives Matter" on its courts and allowed players to wear customized jerseys with approved social justice messages and to kneel during the national anthem. According to a September 2020 Harris Poll, 39% of fans reported watching fewer NBA games, and 38% of those fans attributed their decline in viewership to their feeling that "the league has become too political" (Badenhausen, 2020). However, NBA Commissioner Adam Silver denied that the league's promotion of BLM had caused viewers to tune out; instead he pointed to core fans who had become more engaged with and supportive of the NBA because of its social activism (Jones, 2020). In an interview with ESPN (2020) during the NBA Finals, Silver said that he expected "a sort of return to normalcy, those [BLM] messages will largely be left to be delivered off the floor." Silver's response raises the following question: If the league's engagement with BLM helped to create more engaged fans while simultaneously promoting a social "good," why—as a leader—would Silver choose to discontinue that advocacy?

The actions of the NBA reflect a larger trend in sports. In its 2020 year-end survey, the *Sports Business Journal* asked what role the sports industry should play in social causes ("Where Do You Stand," 2020). Forty-six percent of sport industry executives replied that the industry should play a larger role, and 37% replied that the industry should maintain its current level of involvement. When asked whether they would align with a player or brand that was outspoken on social justice issues, only 11.4% replied that they would be less likely to align with a player or brand that was outspoken on social justice issues, and there was a widespread belief that the industry would benefit in the long term from having a more active voice in social causes. At the same time, 58% of respondents stated that, in their experience, fans do not want events and games to have social messaging. The results of this survey highlight a tension that must be negotiated by leaders in the sport industry.

Although the recent *Sports Business Journal* poll suggests that leaders of sport organizations would be well served by increasing attention to social issues, a historical examination provides evidence that the opposite is actually the case. For example, American sprinters Tommie Smith and John Carlos were condemned at the 1968 Olympics and later for their display of the Black Power salute, which was widely considered "disgraceful, insulting, and embarrassing" (Hartmann, 2003, p. 11). As that case amply illustrates, there are ongoing and vital tensions between sport and social engagement. Two stand out: first, sport leaders must typically prioritize development of their sport or sporting organization over social engagements (Houlihan & White, 2003); second, if any social engagement risks alienating patrons or other stakeholders, it may seem a risk not worth taking (Hartmann & Kwauk, 2011; O'Brien, Ginesta, & Holden, 2020). Matters like these can provoke tensions, making it difficult for sport organizations to work effectively with social service agencies (Hayhurst & Frisby, 2010). As a result, business priorities can cause the public relations purposes of CSR to overwhelm or even dictate social engagements. Ethical conundrums may be engendered. These matters are considered in greater detail in the following two sections.

ISSUES

While the leaders of an organization direct its CSR involvement, the intentions and actions of leaders have rarely been explicitly examined in the treatment of sport and CSR. In the *Routledge Handbook of Sport and Corporate Social Responsibility* (2013), "leadership" is most frequently included in reference to facilities certified as promoting Leadership in Energy and Environmental Design (LEED), and there is little consideration of how the practice of leadership influences managerial decisions related to CSR. In the sport management literature, "leadership" typically references anyone whose decisions, choices, or actions might influence the sport organization or sport outcomes (cf. O'Boyle, Murray, & Cummins, 2015). Thus characterized, this can include managers, coaches, and even athletes. More typically, "leadership" is used as a synonym for team ownership or management (cf. Heinze, Soderstrom, & Zdroik, 2014). Regardless of framing and parameters, it is clear that little thought has been given to what we know from leadership theory and how that might inform the overall design and implementation of CSR programs.

This oversight is not unique to sport management. Waldman and Siegel's (2008) letters on the topic of the socially responsible leader note the absence of leadership in much of the CSR research. They worry that CSR research which ignores the role of leadership "may yield imprecise conclusions regarding the antecedents and consequences of these activities" (p. 118). Waldman and Siegel's concerns were specified as a response to the growing popularity of CSR as a business activity supported particularly by Porter and Kramer's (2006) CSR taxonomy. That taxonomy divides CSR into four dimensions: (1) moral obligations, (2) sustainability, (3) license to operate, and (4) reputation. The taxonomy holds that moral obligations are grounded in the corporation's willingness to make ethical decisions and to act as a good citizen. Sustainability results from choices that treat workers, communities, and environments fairly and with respect. License to operate represents the corporation's right to undertake social activities. As a consequence of these three elements, the corporation's reputation is enhanced, which is key because that can enhance the brand, consumer response, and share price.

Within the field of sport management, Walker and Parent (2010) worry that justifications for CSR, particularly as represented by Porter and Kramer's (2006) framework, fail to provide sufficient guidance to leaders regarding choices and decisions they might make about CSR. Yet, in the face of the relative lack of explicit exploration into the dynamic relationship and tensions between leadership and CSR, much of the extant research has focused on mapping the field, with an emphasis on motivation and outcomes. Here, many researchers have asked basic questions: Why do leaders of sport organizations pursue socially responsible behaviors (e.g., Babiak & Kihl, 2018; Cobourn & Frawley, 2017)? How do they do so (e.g., François, Bayle, & Gond, 2019; Rowe, Karg, & Sherry, 2019)? And to what end (e.g., Mamo, Agyemang, & Andrew, 2021; Trendafilova, Ziakas, & Sparvero, 2017)?

Organizations across nearly all industries face increasing calls to demonstrate CSR, and sport organizations may be particularly well-positioned to respond to such calls. Babiak and Wolfe (2009) suggest four ways in which sport organizations are distinct from organizations in other industries that pursue CSR programs. First, the passion that fans feel for their team and favorite athletes may make fans particularly receptive to prosocial messaging. Second, the same fundamental economics that provide North American sport leagues with antitrust protection and public subsidies can create a *quid pro quo* in which sport properties face increased pressure to engage in socially responsible behaviors. Third, the very public nature of both a sport team's business operations and its athletes' actions may cause the team to engage in CSR as a hedge against negative impacts associated with poor performance and/or player misdeeds. And fourth, sport organizations must manage a complex set of stakeholder relationships, and CSR activities affect and are affected by this network.

In a complementary assessment, Smith and Westerbeek (2007) also identified features that may make sport particularly well suited to serve as a vehicle for CSR: mass media distribution and power, youth appeal, positive health impacts, social interaction, sustainability awareness, cultural understanding/integration, and immediate gratification benefits.

It has therefore been suggested that sport's distinctive character makes it useful for event organizers and sport governing bodies to make use of CSR in their governance and policy activities (François, Bayle, & Mutter, 2019). Whether the features claimed to make sport uniquely appropriate or effective for CSR actually make a difference has not been studied because the requisite comparative studies have not been systematically undertaken. A rigorous comparison of the value CSR contributes to sport organizations versus the value CSR contributes to non-sport found that CSR imparts less value in the sport setting than outside it (Rayne, Leckie, & McDonald, 2020). Contrary to dominant assertions about sport's utility for CSR, it is possible that sport identifications and the popular social positioning of sport undermine its efficacy as a vehicle for CSR. More comparative work is needed to tease out the comparative efficacy of CSR in sport contexts versus non-sport contexts and to identify what may undergird key differences that are revealed.

Given sport's claimed potential as a context for CSR activity, it is not surprising that we have seen its implementation in a variety of forms. In their review of professional sport team organizations, Walzel, Robertson, and Anagnostopoulos (2018) found that the majority (58%) of CSR research has focused on ways that sport organizations have supported local organizations and local social initiatives, with the second highest focus (10%) being on giving to charities and foundations. While these types of programs have received the most attention, CSR applies across the organization, including its environmental sustainability, its supply chain, and its people.

In 1979, Carroll proposed a model of corporate social performance in which a four-part taxonomy of CSR was embedded: economic, legal, ethical, and discretionary. In 1991, Carroll recast his taxonomy as a pyramid, thereby suggesting that the types of CSR are hierarchically structured. Accordingly, profitability (i.e., economic responsibility) and obeying laws and regulations (i.e., legal responsibility) are those responsibilities required by society. At the next levels are the organization's ethical responsibility to do what is just and fair—something that is both expected and valued by society. At the top of the pyramid is the philanthropic responsibility to be a good corporate citizen—to do something which is desired by society. Whether structuring the taxonomy in terms of this hierarchy accurately describes the CSR of sport organizations was examined by Sheth and Babiak (2010). Their research found that team owners and community relations directors ranked ethical and philanthropic responsibilities as the most important, while legal and economic responsibilities were ranked third and fourth, respectively. Findings suggest that sport organizations may prioritize some CSR activities over others, but perhaps not precisely as described by Carroll. Whether owners' claims about priorities mirror their behaviors and choices was not assessed.

More recent work has used institutional theory (e.g., McCullough, Pfahl, & Nguyen, 2016; Trendafilova, Babiak, & Heinze, 2013) to understand CSR activity. Institutional theory suggests that organizations engage in CSR because of isomorphic pressures. These institutional pressures are thought to result from organizations seeking strategic advantage and/or attempting to avoid increased regulation. In their study of the pro-environmental practices of North American professional sport teams, Babiak and Trendafilova (2011) found that motives for pro-environmental practices included the desire to conform to institutional pressures and what they termed "strategic motives," including image enhancement, partnership development, and financial opportunities. Barrett, Bunds, Casper, and Edwards (2019) extended that work by exploring how sport leaders could leverage environmental

CSR through cause-related marketing campaigns. Their work is more prescriptive than evaluative, as it asserts that cause-related marketing can be advantageous, but it doesn't test that assertion. Thus, in keeping with the common approach to CSR research, this research effort on sport CSR has remained largely descriptive. Nevertheless, there is some limited evidence that CSR programs might have small indirect effects on sport brand affiliation (Baena, 2018) and/or consumer sport choice (Yu, 2021).

The distance between an organization's motives for pursuing CSR activities and its success in accomplishing its goals through such programs is bridged through both the contribution of resources to the programs and the quality of engagement with the CSR activities. For example, in their study of a local CSR program associated with Major League Baseball, Babiak and Kihl (2018. p. 129) found that community stakeholders expected the pro sport team to "engage in meaningful CSR initiatives, that is, programs addressing specific community needs, identifying sound objectives, and delivering programs that [meet] those objectives." Of course, individuals who were attracted to the program were already moderately or highly identified with the affiliated team, which may have contributed to positive feelings about the program.

This concern is consistent with Levermore's (2010, p. 236) finding that in CSR programs intended for use in sport for development, the CSR initiatives can be "distant and disengaged." He noted that CSR provided public relations "cover," particularly for industries that might otherwise generate negative PR related to their primary activities (e.g., oil and gas, pharmaceuticals, clothing manufacturing). Levermore's concerns over what often drives CSR efforts comes from consistent evidence that CSR has become a strategic element in the overall marketing communications mix. In such contexts, it is worrisome that marketing objectives can supersede or even displace social objectives that are claimed, thereby compromising what is purportedly the chief concern of CSR efforts.

Organizations may engage in CSR either because they hope to benefit financially, or because they believe they are having a positive societal impact through their actions, or some combination of both. Evidence about outcomes associated with CSR activity is mixed. Indeed, outcomes stemming from CSR efforts for businesses may not always be positive. For example, Inoue, Kent, and Lee (2011) found that CSR had a negative effect on operating margins for professional franchises in American baseball and football, and negative effects on future margins for professional franchises in American baseball, football, basketball, and ice hockey. Sheth and Babiak (2010) found no significant relationship between CSR activity and winning, revenues, or team value; however, they did observe that teams with lower winning percentages were more likely to indicate that their top priorities were related to their ethical and philanthropic responsibilities, suggesting that CSR activities may be used to stimulate support in lieu of support garnered by winning. More recent work in the broader context of service industries suggests that failure to attend to external partnerships, as well as the capacities and capabilities of the organization seeking to undertake CSR, could render poor or negative outcomes from CSR programs (Sinthupundaja, Chiadamrong, & Kohda, 2019). Thus, the effects of CSR on the financial performance of sport organizations may depend on the strategic implementation of CSR rather than on CSR per se.

There is some evidence that CSR might support some desired business outcomes in sport contexts. Walker and Kent (2009) found that CSR had a significant effect on corporate reputation, word of mouth, and merchandise purchases. Those effects were moderated by the individual's identification with the team such that CSR was more influential for those who had lower team identification. Giannoulakis and Drayer (2009) present evidence that the NBA Cares program improved fans' perceptions of the players. Further, Lacey and Kennett-Hensel (2010) found that perceptions of a team's CSR were positively associated with trust in and commitment to the team, which could enhance purchase intention and consumption behaviors. Subsequent work has shown that community-oriented CSR programs can buoy stakeholder support for the sport organization (Babiak & Kihl, 2018) because stakeholders expect sport organizations to add palpable value to the community. Nevertheless, the effect of CSR on consumer behavior depends on consumer awareness of the programs, and may be less effective for sport organizations than non-sport organizations even if consumers are aware of the programs (Rayne et al., 2020). That may result from social constructions of sport that treat it as special and separate from its broader social, economic, and political contexts (Chalip, Schwab, & Dustin, 2010). It may also result from other facets of sport-based CSR, as reviewed earlier. The benefits from sport-based CSR programs are indirect and small and require strategic integration with the organization's overall marketing communications campaign.

Although CSR is often touted as a moral imperative, evidence suggests that across the business world such efforts are typically undertaken as a strategic tool for business development (Hamza & Jarboui, 2020). That claim is consistent with the sport-centered research we have reviewed so far, as well as with other CSR applications that have been put forward in sport. For example, the city of Arlington (2005), Texas, provided U.S.$325 million in public funding for the Dallas Cowboys stadium. As a part of the stadium deal, Jerry Jones, the owner of the Dallas Cowboys, agreed to make a U.S.$500,000 donation each year to local organizations to provide programs for youth sport, recreation, and education purposes. The Orlando Magic built the NBA's first LEED-certified arena. The certification caused the cost of construction to be 10% higher than a non-LEED arena, but it was mandated in the Magic's agreement with the city. The increased construction costs were offset by the the city of Orlando's consequent willingness to cover the land and infrastructure costs for the arena (Kellison & Mondello, 2012). Examples such as these suggest that CSR activities, which can magnify good intent by professional teams, can actually be undermarket "paybacks" for public subsidies to private enterprise.

Our understanding of CSR in sport has developed alongside research on the ethical demands of leadership. In an update of his foundational work on CSR, Carroll (1991) introduces the concept of the immoral, amoral, and moral manager and the relation of each to CSR. He describes the amoral manager as neither moral nor immoral, but rather as someone unaware of possible negative impacts of their decisions. Moral managers are presented as the ideal; they "not only conform to accepted and high levels of professional conduct, they also commonly exemplify leadership on ethical issues" (p. 45). The concept of the moral manager has gained a small foothold in the sport management literature. The *Journal of Intercollegiate Sport* published a special issue on ethical leadership in 2014, which accelerated adoption of the term within sport management. Burton and Welty Peachy (2014) applied the concept of a moral manager to college athletic directors and viewed it as an attribute of an ethical leader. In other words, the best sport leaders are assumed to be those whose behaviors can be deemed to be ethical on the basis of an established ethical model, such as the one proposed by Carroll. As a component of ethical leadership, CSR is thereby deemed to be an indicator of good leadership. Ethics, leadership, and CSR become conflated, relegating leadership to an ascription of character that obscures contingencies and the consequently significant differences context can compel (cf. Rahman, 2016).

Recently, there have been fledgling attempts to tie ethical leadership and moral management to social responsibility (and CSR) in particular sport contexts. Sport leaders are often described as "servant leaders" responsible for providing "other-centered service" (e.g., Burton, Welty Peachey, & Wells, 2017). Thus, in their review, Robertson, Walzel, and Shilbury (2019) argue that social responsibility has become a prevailing norm in sport governance, with the concomitant implication that sport leaders should support socially responsible initiatives through their organizations. The complexities here can often be challenging. For example, Lamont and Kennelly (2019) argue that sports with extreme physical challenges can be unhealthy, and they challenge the ethical propriety of leadership that provides and profits from such sports. They suggest that support for such sports, including CSR efforts that aim to garner that support, can be socially irresponsible. Still, as Painter, Sahm, and Schattschneider (2021) recognize, ethics and social responsibility are socially constructed, and consequently CSR initiatives are necessarily viewed variously in different contexts. They found, for example, that media tend to report CSR activities by professional women's soccer organizations less frequently and less favorably than in reports of CSR programs for male soccer organizations. As these examples suggest, the notion that sport leaders should embrace CSR is widely touted, but context, social expectations, and social constructions may mediate and/or moderate the link between sport leadership and CSR, as well as their interpretation by media and consequently the public. In other words, CSR is not a moral imperative for sport leaders; rather, it is a consequence of the ways that sport leaders frame it with reference to the contexts within which they work and the choices they have available to them (cf. Djaballah, 2017).

In the broader academic literature, there have been more intentional efforts to understand CSR in the context of leadership theory. CSR has been linked to ethical leadership, authentic leadership, and transformational leadership, all of which are of course framed as desirable attributes for leaders. For example, a study of an Australian bank found that explicit CSR (i.e., strategic CSR activity associated with business goals) was associated with autocratic leadership and public relations, and implicit CSR (i.e., CSR that is embedded in an organization's framework) was linked to authentic or emergent leadership (Angus-Leppan, Metcalf, & Benn, 2010). Other work finds that employee perceptions of CSR and their associated behaviors depend, at least in part, on the degree to which they see the organizational leadership to be ethical (Choi, Ullah, & Kwak, 2015; De Roeck & Farooq, 2018; Hansen, Dunford, Alge, & Jackson, 2016). A review of factors facilitating and fostering CSR finds that adoption and implementation of CSR depend on the personal values of organizational leaders and on the availability of necessary resources to formulate and implement CSR programs (Saha, Cerchione, Singh, & Dahiya, 2020). Further research to determine the degree to which findings such as these generalize to sport contexts needs to be undertaken. This is especially true given the common claim that sport is somehow a uniquely suitable vehicle for CSR (e.g., Babiak & Wolfe, 2009; François, Bayle, & Gond, 2019; Smith & Westerbeek, 2007). The following section considers that matter in greater detail.

APPROACHES

Research on CSR and associated leadership has incorporated micro-theories having to do with organizational behavior, consumer behavior, stakeholder management, and leadership.

As reviewed earlier, studies have made use of convenient or popular theories that may justify the foci or measures used. Theories have been lenses and/or justifications; too often they have not been effectively tested or further elaborated (cf. Colquitt & Zapata-Phelan, 2007; Niederman & March 2019). Given the complexities to be examined, multiple micro-theories are sometimes referenced in an attempt to formulate a model to justify measures and findings in a particular study. In some instances, the focus has been specifically on the phenomena associated with CSR leadership, but too often with thin or specious connections to theory. Those matters are elaborated in this section.

Beyond sport, there have been efforts to formulate theories for CSR leadership (e.g., Fernando & Lawrence, 2014) or to apply popular micro-theories (e.g., Mitnick, 1995) or social macro-theory (e.g., Scherer, 2018). Those theoretical efforts have not yet informed sport CSR research, although Levermore and Moore (2015) argue that this is fundamental to advance meaningful understandings in the sport context. Instead, two theoretical frameworks have remained popular: stakeholder theory (e.g., Babiak & Kihl, 2018; Walters & Tacon, 2010) and Carroll's ethical theory (e.g., Kim, Overton, Hull, & Choi, 2018; Sheth & Babiak, 2010). Stakeholder theory is often applied in an attempt to explain which individuals, groups, and/or organizations CSR programs set in sport can or should seek to serve or placate, how CSR might do so, and why. Carroll's theory is often incorporated to evoke the importance of engaging an ethical imperative and to specify the multiple levels at which CSR can and should work. Thus, stakeholder theory considers the panoply of persons and organizations needing and/or affected by CSR, while ethical models presuppose the moral necessity of CSR and the levels at which it might be implemented. While these theories provide service as models and explanations, they have been little tested, elaborated upon, or critiqued in sport leadership research.

The sport-based research has primarily made use of self-report instruments, interviews, and case studies. Consequently, it is overwhelmingly descriptive. It is evident that the work could do a good deal more to build theory from those efforts, and it seems apparent that much more could be done to test relevant theories in CSR leadership contexts. However, such rigor may be overlooked in light of the considerable culturally grounded, but for the most part little tested, positive reception for CSR activities (Elving, Golob, Podnar, Ellerup-Nielsen, & Thomson, 2015) and endorsement of their importance by organizational leaders (Meindl, Ehrlich, & Dukerich, 1985). Consequently, clarion calls and justifications for CSR and post-hoc supportive attributions of leadership prevail.

The descriptive nature of the work on CSR leadership and its reliance on justificatory micro-theoretical frameworks has obscured its significant macro-theoretical contexts. Consequently, the larger macro-theoretical considerations remain too often presupposed rather than examined with scrutiny. Businesses function in a sociopolitical setting which is itself founded on fundamental economic postulates. These assert that in order to be sustainable, an organization will act in its own self-interest. The foundation for this idea—and for free markets more broadly—is expressed in Adam Smith's (1776/1990) seminal argument for capitalism, *An Inquiry into the Nature and Causes of the Wealth of Nations*. In that book, Smith recognizes the interconnectedness of actors in the economy. He writes:

> Man has almost constant occasion for the help of his brethren, and it is in vain for him to expect it from their benevolence only. . . . Give me that which I want, and you shall have this which you want, is the meaning of every such offer; and it is in this manner that we obtain from one another the far greater part of those good offices which we stand in need of. (pp. 7–8)

Smith posits that man is "led by an invisible hand to promote an end which was no part of his intention. . . . [B]y pursuing his own interest he frequently promotes that of the society more effectually than when he really intends to promote it" (p. 217). Interestingly, Smith's macro-theoretical economic framework has not been tested or even noted in CSR leadership research, although it has been argued that his consequent views on ethics might be pertinent (Brown & Forster, 2013).

In general, economically apprised theories having to do with social choice and behavior have not informed CSR research. Consequently, beyond CSR's apparent value for public relations, it is not clear how or why CSR matters in a market economy. If they are normal goods, then social programs should be suitably provided in the marketplace (cf. Reed, 2013). This is well-illustrated by professional sport teams that adopt environmentally friendly practices because there are financial and PR payoffs for their operations. In cases like this, corporate investment in CSR reflects leader/manager preferences in pursuit of profitability rather than social need.

On the other hand, if there are programs that are naturally not rivals in supply, nonexcludable when consumed, or that create effects not captured in normal pricing mechanisms, then some external engagement and coordination may be necessary to redress the consequent market failure (Salanié, 2000; Winston, 2006). In other words, if the social program is unlikely to have any competitors, or if users don't preclude further users, or if there are broad social benefits from a program, then normal market pricing mechanisms aren't optimally engaged. In such instances, correctives are needed to address the particular source of market failure. It seems reasonable to expect that social engagements might help to redress market failures—but not just any social engagement. What would need to be done, how it would be implemented, and the nature of its targets would depend on the nature of supply, consumption, and/or flow-on effects requiring remediation. It is worth investigating whether a sport organization is in the best position to address any market failure. Sport organizations excel at sports, and often at marketing, promotion, fan development, and talent identification. Sport teams are not structured to provide the social programs that communities may most need or want. To date, research has not contextualized sport-based CSR within its socioeconomic context. Consequently, there are not yet CSR analyses addressing marketplace supply, conditions of demand, or the complexity of program effects. There need to be, and the public relations value of CSR needs to be considered with reference to those. We are not suggesting that detailed economic models are required (although those might be useful); rather, we are suggesting that CSR research, including research into its leadership, should examine the political economy of CSR, including its manifestations in and through sport.

Milton Friedman (1970)—a neoclassical economist and adherent of Smith's (1776/1990) view of markets—makes several key observations related to understanding the nexus of leadership and social responsibility. First, Friedman poses that businesses themselves cannot have responsibilities; only *individuals* can have responsibilities. Therefore, executives who make the decisions about CSR are the agents of the owners of the corporation, and it is to these owners that executives are ultimately responsible. Further, individual executives as persons may perceive a social responsibility, but not in their capacity as an employee. With regard to this responsibility, individuals—who act as the principal rather than as agents of owners—can make decisions about how to spend their time and money in accordance with their own preferences and understanding of the individual's social responsibility. If CSR activities increase an organization's expenses, there is a financial profit forgone by the company's owners. Likewise, if CSR activities decrease an organization's revenues, profit is forgone. Thus, a basic question arises: Under what conditions is an individual acting as the owner's agent empowered to make decisions that may affect profits or a financial surplus?

As applied to social responsibility, the views espoused by Smith and Friedman suggest that the best outcomes will result when corporations (or teams) engage in CSR in order to achieve their business objectives. As presented in the literature, this view is often reduced to the idea that businesses have only a fiduciary responsibility to shareholders (Friedman, Parent, & Mason, 2004; Godfrey, 2009; Sheth & Babiak, 2010). This view can miss the bigger picture, which is that a successful and profitable business enables agents (i.e., executives, owners, shareholders) to use their returns. Agents who maximize their organization's profits are then free to support whichever social causes or charities they find most compelling.

Further, this view can obscure the difference between CSR as a cost versus CSR as an investment. If short-term costs are eventually recouped and profits are enhanced as a consequence of social action, then account systems should treat CSR as an investment pursuant to a future stream of benefits rather than as an expense. Indeed, there is evidence from the construction industry that CSR can have a financially detrimental short-term effect, but a financially beneficial effect in the long term (Lu, Ye, Chau, & Flanagan, 2018). Thus, the timelines for evaluative CSR studies may need to be lengthened, and the accounting practices of organizations engaging in CSR may need to be reconsidered.

Classical economic theory posits that the direct donation of private returns not only allows agents to select a beneficiary that shares the agents' values but likely will have a greater impact by allowing experts to put the funds to their best use. For example, which would better serve the cause of children's literacy: a sports team investing the organization's time, money, and personnel to develop its own curriculum or the owner of a financially successful team donating money to a local school to fund a reading specialist or librarian? Economic theory clearly suggests the latter would be a better choice. Yet, although agency is a core theoretical element, alternative choices and implementations for agency are rarely examined systematically or tested when considering leadership in CSR contexts. And in the sporting context as well as others, they need to be.

In fact, the outcomes and consequences of CSR programs implemented by sport organizations are rarely subjected to rigorous outcome evaluation (Pava & Krausz, 1997; Salazar, Husted, & Biehl, 2012). Rather, research has focused on methods, processes, and rationale and, as we suggested earlier, has not tackled fundamental economic presuppositions that are the context for CSR choices and activities. CSR efforts have become a fad, not because evaluations persuasively demonstrate their value because they feel like good things to do. Too often, this sense, rather than considered evidence, has fueled both researchers and stakeholders in their advocacy for CSR programs. Consequently, opportunities to explore fundamental business underpinnings, to determine whether both adopted strategies and tactics are better than alternatives, and to assess how contextual variations might inform those strategies and tactics have been missed. Those are opportunities worth grasping.

DEBATES

Given the seemingly universal and hegemonic popularity of CSR, there has been very little debate about it. The vast majority of research assumes that CSR can be a good thing, so too often these received blinders position inquiry to finds ways to validate CSR or to suggest considerations for its implementation. Levermore (2010, 2011) has been one of the most critical voices, arguing that CSR through sport is poorly linked to business objectives, fails to consider context adequately, and may be compromised by problematic public perceptions about sport. Criticisms like these have much more to do with fundamental questions about the utility of sport for CSR and the quality of their CSR interventions than with CSR per se or the economic value of CSR.

A core concern here has to do with the actual purposes of CSR. Are sport organizations really endeavoring to be purposefully socially responsible, or are CSR programs much more public relations initiatives intended to serve the bottom line? Multiple case studies suggest that the targets for CSR are dictated more by trends and shifts in the popularity of social issues than by any ongoing social purpose or objective (Heath & Waymer, 2019). Other research suggests that the public relations claims for sport CSR benefits may on occasion actually mask a much darker reality. For example, research by Millington, Giles, van Luijk, and Hayhurst (2021) strongly suggests that claims about environmental sustainability through sport-based CSR are in fact public relations tools to enable practices that actually undermine sustainability. In other words, CSR through sport can provide a veil of legitimation for practices that are antithetical to the claims made about the social value provided. There are grounds, then, for consumer skepticism about CSR (Rim & Kim, 2016).

If CSR is fundamentally a public relations exercise, there is an incentive for organizations to find ways to take credit rather than to assign the task to partner organizations that might arguably be better placed to execute the program. Optimal agency may sometimes conflict with optimal public relations. Consider, for example, the National Football League's Play 60 program (NFL Enterprises, 2021). The NFL launched the program in 2007 to promote physical activity for youth; it has its own website and has provided television ads, all of which are heavily branded as NFL products. The program's media states that it has "committed more than $352 million to youth health and fitness" by offering "programming, grants, and awareness campaign." The program is simultaneously a CSR activity and a public relations effort under NFL control. What is not mentioned in any NFL media is that prior to this program's launch the NFL had partnered with the National Recreation and Park Association to promote active recreation. From the standpoint of program delivery, that partnership provided access to parks and recreation programs throughout the United States. It did not, however, enable the kind of NFL branding that Play 60 enables. So now the NFL executes its program independently and has relegated public parks and recreation to recipients of grants that the NFL Foundation Grassroots chooses to award (e.g., Smith, 2016). The ways that public relations concerns might affect or even compromise corporate delivery of social programs require historically and theoretically informed examination.

Agency is not simply a matter of either/or. There is substantial work in management demonstrating the value of partnerships and alliances, especially for purposes of social engagement, which can clearly apply to sport organizations (Babiak & Yang, 2020). There is also work suggesting that it can be advantageous for sport organizations to co-brand with non-sport organizations (Cousens & Bradish, 2018). Accordingly, two or more organizations jointly brand a product or service. If appropriately implemented, co-branding might be a means to enable sport organizations to transfer delivery of social engagements while retaining or possibly enhancing the public relations advantage (Singh, 2016). Sparvero and Warner (2018) found that the American Heart Association effectively contributed its public health expertise to Play 60's school-based program and conferred legitimacy on a program that helps the NFL achieve its marketing and fan development objectives, but that may actually work against anti-obesity objectives. The work on co-branding and on partnerships as mechanisms to enhance delivery of social programs has barely informed work on CSR. Yet it should.

Mainstream business writing is increasingly explicit about the commercial utility of CSR. For example, corporate insider Moyo (2021) argues that CSR is essential to assure positive branding and sustainable profitability. Building on that argument with examples from her service on numerous corporate boards, she contends that ethical acumen should be probed along with financial acumen when corporate leaders are hired. So doing, she suggests, can assure that CSR will be woven into the fabric of the organization's operations.

The internal and external public relations contexts of CSR through sport is salient to sport insiders. Speaking as commissioner of the NBA, Adam Silver commented on the racial unrest in the United States: "We were not in a position, given that we were attempting to return to play in the middle of social unrest, to avoid being a part of the conversation . . . given that some of the most high profile Black people in the world play in the NBA" (quoted in Mannix, 2020, para. 19). Speaking for Nike, its CEO Phil Knight said:

> It's not enough to do good things. You have to let people know what you're doing. . . . When it comes to product, America gets its opinions from advertising. When it comes to Nike as a whole, America gets its opinions from the press. . . . We can't make rules that keep drug dealers from wearing our stuff, and we can't solve the problems of the inner city, but we sponsor a lot of sports clinics for youth. (quoted in Willigan, 1992, p. 101)

The matter of agency comes into play as well. There has been substantial growth of organizations purporting to focus on the positive outcomes that can result from sport for development (Svensson & Woods, 2017). But with the exception of some of these efforts aimed at remediating social inequality and even facilitating peace, sport organizations exist to provide sport; they are not social service agencies. This highlights the matter of agency. Sport organizations have very different missions and needs than the agencies through which they might seek to partner when executing a social program, which can render interaction dysfunctional (Anagnostopoulos & Shilbury, 2013; Svensson, 2017). The challenges are made more acute when the sport organization and one or more of its partners operate in different economic or cultural sectors because operational objectives, outputs, evaluation criteria, contingencies, and outlook depend, in part, on sector (Green, 2020).

When one considers such matters, the vital role of contingencies becomes salient. Different contexts render different rewards, different potential sanctions, and consequently different considerations and challenges. Financial performance is among the most salient contingencies, which is a key reason that social salience and consumer response matter so deeply when planning, implementing, and evaluating CSR programs. Of course, there is nothing new to the insight that contingencies play a pivotal role in driving the behavior of individuals and organizations. Indeed, contingencies may be the best predictors we have of organizational (Davis & Luthans, 1980) and individual (Ledoux, 2017) behavior. People respond to the rewards, sanctions, and consequent incentives with which they are familiar. They and their organizations evaluate, decide, and make choices driven by such contingencies, even when they themselves may justify those evaluations, decisions, and choices with reference to more socially acceptable criteria. In fact, the human tendency to rationalize and/or self-deceive has long been observed and studied (Jacobson, 1993; Taylor, 1923). Self-justification and rationalization of actions are not mere deceptions; they can be psychologically adaptive and can confer social status (Chance & Norton, 2015). So situational rewards, sanctions, and incentive play a vital role in leader behaviors, even when the individuals and their organizations themselves neither recognize nor acknowledge them.

It is surprising, therefore, that the expected and experienced incentives, rewards, and sanctions associated with CSR, as well as leader interpretations of those, have been so little studied. When the pronouncements of interviewees and official documents are reified—as in the interview, document, and case studies that typify CSR and leadership research—underlying dynamics of organization behavior are obscured (Argyris, 2004). For that reason, treating CSR moralistically, which is how the vast majority of research treats it, is very problematic. The study of CSR and the managerial behaviors that drive it need to do much more to examine the nature, variations, and effects of contingencies in order to serve both theory development and effective practice with discernable outcomes. Structural analyses of organizations, their operations, their contexts, and consequent contingencies are needed (e.g., Davis & Luthans, 1980).

This need extends most particularly into the examination of leadership in the adoption of and design of CSR efforts. Too often leadership is invoked as an ex-post explanation for CSR choices and strategies. Such explanations are often attractive because the notion of leadership has become de facto aligned with behaviors and/or outcomes that are popular. Obviously, such thinking is reliant on cloudy circular reasoning and wishful tautological thinking. Indeed, bookstore shelves are filled with books purporting to explain leadership in ways that are responsive to what will be seen, most particularly in the future, as popular and forward-looking, that is, to get ahead of the curve for competitive advantage. Yet, whether one or more individuals may actually lead effectively depends on the contingencies within which they work, how they manage those contingencies (Ayman & Lauritsen, 2018), and the learning that informs and results from their management of contingencies (Sims & Lorenzi, 1992). Accordingly, leadership that is effective, and ultimately morally grounded, can be invoked with reference to CSR only when contingencies have been identified and probed for effects that can be demonstrable. Leadership is neither a cause nor an explanation for CSR; rather, effective leadership must be seen as an integral element of process—one that is best studied longitudinally.

CONCLUSION

Socially responsible leadership in sporting contexts has become an increasingly attractive topic for study. The research to date has predominantly been descriptive and couched within the framework of CSR. There is a substantial literature on the topic of sport and CSR, with numerous examples of what researchers have deemed successful programs, why sport organizations do or should choose to develop and implement such programs, and the marketing, financial, and fan development outcomes sought by selected programs. Micro-theories have been applied to the work largely as heuristic conveniences. While leadership and CSR have been examined and reexamined separately in the sport management literature, there has been little effort to apply understandings of either topic to the other. Thus, we have two bodies of work that exist in separate academic silos. This should not be surprising, as the CSR literature largely ignores the agency of individuals within an organization to make decisions related to the organization's CSR engagement. Instead, the organization itself is treated as the decision-making entity. When the role of the individual leader(s) of an organization is missing from analysis, it is not surprising that there has been little effort to synthesize models of leadership and social responsibility.

There are substantial and attractive opportunities to use and build better theory through that effort. Structural analyses incorporating psychological, social, and economic insights will be particularly useful as they can enable exploration of contextual effects and boundary conditions. The structure and impacts of key variables, such as contingencies and agency, can be highlighted. Leadership behaviors in the context of social responsibility might then be better understood.

Fundamental economic theories having to do with market efficiency and failure could thereby also be explored. Since CSR is a business function in the context of market economies, it is essential to explore its rationale and effects in that context. Incorporating economic questions and insights can enable better modeling and application. It may also help to inform fundamental examination of market dynamics.

Structural analyses and evaluations informed by economic theory impose preexisting theoretical frameworks. As useful as those may be, they can also exclude other insights (Greenwald, Pratkanis, Leippe, & Baumgardner, 1986). The application of multiple micro-theories can consequently prove useful, particularly if those are synthesized to better explain CSR and leadership phenomena across different contexts (cf. Cairney & Weible, 2017; Hwang, 2015).

If contingencies, market dynamics, and agency are as fundamental as social, behavioral, and economic models assert, then their contributions to context matter. When, if ever, is sport similar to or different from other contexts for social engagements and leadership? How do differences in sector and/or culture affect those (Green, 2020)? How, when, and why do different sport subcultures or governance structures matter? Relevant theory requires comparisons that address these matters (Clarke, 2003; Strauss, 1995).

When CSR is accepted unquestioningly as a noble and desirable pursuit of sport organizations, as it typically is, there is little incentive for researchers or industry professionals to consider the contexts in which such programs reside. Future research will benefit by undertaking a more considered approach to theory building and theory testing, differentiating public relations from social purpose, paying attention to context and contingencies, and incorporating macro-theoretical concerns having to do with the socioeconomics of firm behavior. Doing so will enable a more rapid advance of the field while contributing to fundamental understandings of sport organization behavior.

References

Anagnostopoulos, C., & Shilbury, D. (2013). Implementing corporate social responsibility in English football: Towards multi-theoretical integration. *Sport, Business and Management, 3*(4), 268–284.

Angus-Leppan, T., Metcalf, L., & Benn, S. (2010). Leadership styles and CSR practice: An examination of sensemaking, institutional drivers, and CSR leadership. *Journal of Business Ethics, 93*(2), 189–213.

Argyris, C. (2004). *Reasons and rationalizations: The limits to organizational knowledge.* Oxford: Oxford University Press.

Ayman, R., & Lauritsen, M. (2018). Contingencies, context, situation, and leadership. In J. Antonakis & D. V. Day (Eds.), *The nature of leadership* (pp. 138–166). Newbury Park, CA: Sage.

Babiak, K., & Kihl, L. A. (2018). A case study of stakeholder dialogue in professional sport: An example of CSR engagement. *Business and Society Review, 123*(1), 119–149.

Babiak, K., & Trendafilova, S. (2011). CSR and environmental responsibility: Motives and pressures to adopt green management practices. *Corporate Social Responsibility and Environmental Management, 18*(1), 11–24.

Babiak, K., & Wolfe, R. (2009). Determinants of corporate social responsibility in professional sport: Internal and external factors. *Journal of Sport Management, 23*(6), 717–742.

Babiak, K., & Yang, D. (2020). Toward developing strategic partnerships between SDP and corporate organizations: Elements of effective partnership interactions. In J. Welty Peachey, B. C. Green, & L. Chalip (Eds.), *Partnerships and alliances in sport for development and peace: Considerations, tensions, and strategies* (pp. 189–215). Champaign, IL: Sagamore-Venture.

Badenhausen, K. (2020, September 2). NBA playoff ratings slip as fans grumble that league has become "too political." *Forbes.* https://www.forbes.com/sites/kurtbadenhausen/2020/09/02/poll-38-of-sports-fans-say-nba-is-too-political-for-reason-why-they-are-watching-less/?sh=6ca27af87aac.

Baena, V. (2018). The importance of CSR practices carried out by sport teams and its influence on brand love: The Real Madrid Foundation, *Social Responsibility Journal, 14*(1), 61–79.

Barrett, M., Bunds, K. S., Casper, J. M., & Edwards, M. B. (2019). A descriptive analysis of corporate environmental responsibility in major league professional sport. *Journal of Applied Sport Management, 11*(3), 35–46. https://trace.tennessee.edu/jasm/vol11/iss3/8.

Bloomberg. (2020). Bloomberg impact report 2020. https://assets.bbhub.io/company/sites/56/2021/04/Impact_Report_2020.pdf.

Brown, J. A., & Forster, W. R. (2013). CSR and stakeholder theory: A tale of Adam Smith. *Journal of Business Ethics, 112*(2), 301–312.

Burton, L., & Welty Peachey, J. (2014). Ethical leadership in intercollegiate sport: Challenges, opportunities, and future directions. *Journal of Intercollegiate Sport, 7*(1), 1–10.

Burton, L., Welty Peachey, J., & Wells, J. (2017). The role of servant leadership in developing an ethical climate in sport organizations. *Journal of Sport Management, 31*(3), 229–240.

Cairney, P., & Weible, C. M. (2017). The new policy sciences: Combining the cognitive science of choice, multiple theories of context, and basic and applied analysis. *Policy Sciences, 50*(4), 619–627.

Carroll, A. B. (1979). A three dimensional conceptual model of corporate social performance. *Academy of Management Review, 4*(4), 497–505.

Carroll, A. B. (1991). The pyramid of corporate social responsibility: Toward the moral management of stakeholders. *Business Horizons, 34*(4), 39–48.

Chalip, L., Schwab, K., & Dustin, D. (2010). Bridging the sport and recreation divide. *Schole: A Journal of Leisure Studies and Recreation Education, 25*(1), 1–10.

Chance, Z., & Norton, M. I. (2015). The what and why of self-deception. *Current Opinion in Psychology, 6*, 104–107.

Choi, S. B., Ullah, S. M., & Kwak, W. J. (2015). Ethical leadership and followers' attitudes toward corporate social responsibility: The role of perceived ethical work climate. *Social Behavior and Personality, 43*(3), 353–365.

City of Arlington. (2005). Charitable contribution and pledge agreement. https://arlingto ntx.gov/UserFiles/Servers/Server_14481062/File/City%20Hall/Depts/City%20Secret ary/ATT_Stadium_Legal_Documents/Exhibit-E-Charitable-Contribution-and-Pledge-Agreement.pdf.

Clarke, A. E. (2003). Situational analyses: Grounded theory mapping after the postmodern turn. *Symbolic Interaction, 26*(4), 553–576.

Cobourn, S., & Frawley, S. (2017). CSR in professional sport: An examination of community models. *Managing Sport and Leisure, 22*(2), 113–126.

Colquitt, J. A., & Zapata-Phelan, C. P. (2007). Trends in theory building and theory testing: A five-decade study of the Academy of Management Journal. *Academy of Management Journal, 50*(6), 1281–1303.

Columbia Sportswear Company. (2019). Sustainability accounting standards board index. https://cscworkday.blob.core.windows.net/hrforms/Recruiting/Career_Site/CR_Reports/2019_CSC_SASB_Index.pdf.

Cousens, L., & Bradish, C. L. (2018). Sport and corporate partnerships. In D. Hassan (Ed.), *Managing sport business* (pp. 421–439). London: Taylor & Francis.

Davis, T. R., & Luthans, F. (1980). A social learning approach to organizational behavior. *Academy of Management Review, 5*(2), 281–290.

De Roeck, K., & Farooq, O. (2018). Corporate social responsibility and ethical leadership: Investigating their interactive effect on employees' socially responsible behaviors. *Journal of Business Ethics, 151*(4), 923–939.

Dick's Sporting Goods. (2019). Purpose playbook. https://s27.q4cdn.com/812551136/files/doc_downloads/2019PurposePlaybook.pdf.

Djaballah, M. (2017). Giving sense to corporate social responsibility in sporting events: A case study of the Quiksilver Pro France. In J. J. Zhang & B. G. Pitts (Eds.), *Contemporary sport marketing: Global perspectives* (pp. 55–71). Milton Park, U.K.: Taylor & Francis.

Elving, W. J. L., Golob, U., Podnar, K., Ellerup-Nielsen, A., & Thomson, C. (2015). The bad, the ugly, and the good: New challenges for CSR communication. *Corporate Communications, 20*(2), 118–127.

ESPN. (2020, October 4). Adam Silver talks NBA bubble, when next season could start [Video]. YouTube. https://www.youtube.com/watch?v=R4PbOVFw4l8.

Fernando, S., & Lawrence, S. (2014). A theoretical framework for CSR practices: Integrating legitimacy theory, stakeholder theory and institutional theory. *Journal of Theoretical Accounting Research, 10*(1), 149–178.

François, A., Bayle, E., & Gond, J. P. (2019). A multilevel analysis of implicit and explicit CSR in French and UK professional sport. *European Sport Management Quarterly, 19*(1), 15–37.

François, A., Bayle, E., & Mutter, O. (2019). CSR and sports-event organizers: State of play, controversies and perspectives. In M. Desbordes, P. Aymar, & C. Hautbois (Eds.), *The global sport economy: Contemporary issues* (pp. 89–115). Abingdon, U.K.: Routledge.

Friedman, M. (1970, September 13). The social responsibility of business is to increase profits. *New York Times Magazine,* pp. 121–126.

Friedman, M. T., Parent, M. M., & Mason, D. S. (2004). Building a framework for issues management in sport through stakeholder theory. *European Sport Management Quarterly, 4*(3), 170–190.

Giannoulakis, C., & Drayer, J. (2009). "Thugs" versus "good guys": The impact of NBA cares on player image. *European Sport Management Quarterly, 9*(4), 453–468.

Godfrey, P. C. (2009). Corporate social responsibility in sport: An overview and key issues. *Journal of Sport Management, 23*(6), 698–716.

Green, B. C. (2020). On the consequences of context and perspective: Sector, governance, and cultural considerations in SDP partnerships. In J. Weltey Peachey, B. C. Green, & L. Chalip (Eds.), *Partnerships and alliances in sport for development and peace: Considerations, tensions, and strategies* (pp. 75–85). Champaign, IL: Sagamore-Venture.

Greenwald, A. G., Pratkanis, A. R., Leippe, M. R., & Baumgardner, M. H. (1986). Under what conditions does theory obstruct research progress? *Psychological Review, 93*(2), 216–229.

Hamza, S., & Jarboui, A. (2020). CSR: A moral obligation or a strategic behavior? In B. Orlando (Ed.), Corporate social responsibility (pp. 1–15). London: InTech Open. https://www.intechopen.com/chapters/73912.

Hansen, S. D., Dunford, B. B., Alge, B. J., & Jackson, C. L. (2016). Corporate social responsibility, ethical leadership, and trust propensity: A multi-experience model of perceived ethical climate. *Journal of Business Ethics, 137*(4), 649–662.

Hartmann, D. (2003). *Race, culture, and the revolt of the Black athlete: The 1968 Olympic protests and their aftermath.* Chicago: University of Chicago Press.

Hartmann, D., & Kwauk, C. (2011). Sport and development: An overview, critique, and reconstruction. *Journal of Sport and Social Issues, 35*(3), 284–305.

Hayhurst, L. M. C., & Frisby, W. (2010). Sport for development NGO perspectives on partnerships with high performance sport. *European Sport Management Quarterly, 10*(1), 75–96.

Heath, R. L., & Waymer, D. (2019). Elite status talks, but how loudly and why? Exploring elite CSR micro-politics. *Corporate Communications, 24*(2), 232–247.

Heinze, K. L., Soderstrom, S., & Zdroik, J. (2014). Toward strategic and authentic corporate social responsibility in professional sport: A case study of the Detroit Lions. *Journal of Sport Management, 28*(6), 672–686.

Houlihan, B., & White, A. (2003). *The politics of sport development: Development of sport or development through sport?* London: Routledge.

Hwang, K. K. (2015). Culture-inclusive theories of self and social interaction: The approach of multiple philosophical paradigms. *Journal for the Theory of Social Behaviour, 45*(1), 40–63.

Inoue, Y., Kent, A., & Lee, S. (2011). CSR and the bottom line: Analyzing the link between CSR and financial performance for professional teams. *Journal of Sport Management, 25*(6), 531–549.

Jacobson, A. J. (1993). A problem for causal theories of reasons and rationalizations. *Southern Journal of Philosophy, 31*(3), 307–321.

Jones, B. (2020, November 3). Adam Silver goes deep on the wildest year in NBA history. *Gentlemen's Quarterly.* https://www.gq.com/story/adam-silver-nba-bubble-moty-interview.

Kellison, T. B., & Mondello, M. J. (2012). Organisational perception management in sport: The use of corporate pro-environmental behaviour for desired facility referenda outcomes. *Sport Management Review, 15*(4), 500–512.

Kim, J. K., Overton, H., Hull, K., & Choi, M. (2018). Examining public perceptions of CSR in sport. *Corporate Communications, 23*(4), 629–647.

Lacey, R., & Kennett-Hensel, P.A. (2010). Longitudinal effects of corporate social responsibility on customer relationships. *Journal of Business Ethics, 97*(4), 581–597.

Lamont, M., & Kennelly, M. (2019). Sporting hyperchallenges: Health, social, and fiscal implications. *Sport Management Review, 22*(1), 68–79.

Ledoux, S. F. (2017). *What causes human behavior: Stars, selves, or contingencies?* Ottawa: BehaveTech Publishing.

Levermore, R. (2010). CSR for development through sport: Examining its potential and limitations. *Third World Quarterly, 31*(2), 223–241.

Levermore, R. (2011). The paucity of, and dilemma in, evaluating corporate social responsibility for development through sport. *Third World Quarterly, 32*(3), 551–569.

Levermore, R., & Moore, N. (2015). The need to apply new theories to "Sport CSR." *Corporate Governance, 15*(2), 249–253.

Lu, W., Ye, M., Chau, K. W., & Flanagan, R. (2018). The paradoxical nexus between corporate social responsibility and sustainable financial performance: Evidence from the international construction business. *Corporate Social Responsibility and Environmental Management, 25*(5), 844–852.

Mamo, Y., Agyemang, K. J., & Andrew, D. P. (2021). Types of CSR initiatives and fans' social outcomes: The case of professional sport organizations. *Sport Marketing Quarterly, 30*(2), 146–160.

Mannix, C. (2020, August 13). Adam Silver opens up about the NBA bubble: "It's better than what we envisioned." *Sports Illustrated.* https://www.si.com/nba/2020/08/13/adam-silver-nba-bubble-coronavirus-social-justice-future.

McCullough, B. P., Pfahl, M. E., & Nguyen, S. N. (2016). The green waves of environmental sustainability in sport. *Sport in Society, 19*(7), 1040–1065.

Meindl, J. R., Ehrlich, S. B., & Dukerich, J. M. (1985). The romance of leadership. *Administrative Science Quarterly, 30*(1), 78–102.

Millington, R., Giles, A. R., van Luijk, N., & Hayhurst, L. M. (2021). Sport for sustainability? The extractives industry, sport, and sustainable development. *Journal of Sport and Social Issues.* https://doi.org/10.1177/0193723521991413.

Mitnick, B. M. (1995). Systematics and CSR: The theory and processes of normative referencing. *Business & Society, 34*(1), 5–33.

Moyo, D. (2021). *How boards work and how they can work better in a chaotic world.* New York: Basic Books.

NFL Enterprises. (2021). Play 60. https://www.nfl.com/causes/play60/.

Niederman, F., & March, S. (2019). The "theoretical lens" concept: We all know what it means, but do we all know the same thing? *Communications of the Association for Information Systems, 44*, 1–33. https://doi.org/10.17705/1CAIS.04401.

O'Boyle, I., Murray, D., & Cummins, P. (Eds.). (2015). *Leadership in sport.* Abingdon, U.K.: Routledge.

O'Brien, J., Ginesta, X., & Holden, R. (2020). Sport and power relations in the twenty-first century. In J. O'Brien, R. Holden, & X. Ginesta (Eds.), *Sport, globalisation and identity: New perspectives on regions and nations* (pp. 218–221). London: Routledge.

Painter, D. L., Sahm, B., & Schattschneider, P. (2022). Framing sports' corporate social responsibility: US women's vs men's soccer leagues. *Corporate Communications: An International Journal, 27*, 1–14. https://doi.org/10.1108/CCIJ-03-2021-0035.

Paramio-Salcines, J. L., Babiak, K., & Walters, G. (Eds.). (2013). *Routledge handbook of sport and corporate social responsibility.* London: Routledge.

Pava, M. L., & Krausz, J. (1997). Criteria for evaluating the legitimacy of corporate social responsibility. *Journal of Business Ethics, 16*(3), 337–347.

Porter, M., & Kramer, M. (2006, December). Strategy and society: The link between competitive advantage and corporate social responsibility. *Harvard Business Review, 84*(12), pp. 1–14.

Rahman, M. M. (2016). *Leadership: Analysis of trait, behaviour, and contingency theories.* Norderstedt, Germany: GRIN Verlag.

Rayne, D., Leckie, C., & McDonald, H. (2020). Productive partnerships? Driving consumer awareness to action in CSR partnerships. *Journal of Business Research, 118*(1), 49–57.

Reed, C. (2013). *The efficient market hypothesists: Bachelier, Samuelson, Fama, Ross, Tobin and Shiller.* London: Palgrave.

Rim, H., & Kim, S. (2016). Dimensions of corporate social responsibility (CSR) skepticism and their impacts on public evaluations toward CSR. *Journal of Public Relations Research, 28*(5–6), 248–267.

Robertson, J., Walzel, S., & Shilbury, D. (2019). Intersections of governance and social responsibility in sport. In M. Winand & C. Anagnostopoulos (Eds.), *Research handbook on sport governance* (pp. 118–132). Cheltenham, U.K.: Edward Elgar Publishing.

Rowe, K., Karg, A., & Sherry, E. (2019). Community-oriented practice: Examining corporate social responsibility and development activities in professional sport. *Sport Management Review, 22*(3), 363–378.

Saha, R., Cerchione, R., Singh, R., & Dahiya, R. (2020). Effect of ethical leadership and corporate social responsibility on firm performance: A systematic review. *Corporate Social Responsibility and Environmental Management, 27*(2), 409–429.

Salanié, B. (2000). *Microeconomics of market failures.* Cambridge, MA: MIT Press.

Salazar, J., Husted, B. W., & Biehl, M. (2012). Thoughts on the evaluation of corporate social performance through projects. *Journal of Business Ethics, 105*(2), 175–186.

Scherer, A. G. (2018). Theory assessment and agenda setting in political CSR: A critical theory perspective. *International Journal of Management Reviews, 20*(2), 387–410.

Sheth, H., & Babiak, K. M. (2010). Beyond the game: Perceptions and practices of corporate social responsibility in the professional sport industry. *Journal of Business Ethics, 91*(3), 433–450.

Sims, H. P., Jr., & Lorenzi, P. (1992). *The new leadership paradigm: Social learning and cognition in organizations.* Newbury Park, CA: Sage.

Singh, J. (2016). The influence of CSR and ethical self-identity in consumer evaluation of cobrands. *Journal of Business Ethics, 138*(2), 311–326.

Sinthupundaja, J., Chiadamrong, N., & Kohda, Y. (2019). Internal capabilities, external cooperation and proactive CSR on financial performance. *Service Industries Journal, 39*(15–16), 1099–1122.

Smith, A. (1776/1990). *An inquiry into the nature and causes of the wealth of nations.* Chicago: Encyclopaedia Britannica.

Smith, A. C. T., & Westerbeek, H. M. (2007). Sport as a vehicle for deploying corporate social responsibility. *Journal of Corporate Citizenship, 25*(1), 43–54.

Smith, B. (2016, April 1). Making ends meet: It takes a village of funders to re-make a park. *Parks and Recreation.* https://www.nrpa.org/parks-recreation-magazine/2016/april/making-ends-meet-it-takes-a-village-of-funders-to-re-make-a-park/.

Sparvero, E. S., & Kent, A. (2014). Sport team nonprofit organizations: Are sports doing well at "doing good"? *Journal of Applied Sport Management, 6*(4), 98–116.

Sparvero, E. S., & Warner, S. (2018). NFL Play 60: Managing the intersection of professional sport and obesity. *Sport Management Review, 22*(1), 153–166.

Strauss, A. (1995). Notes on the nature and development of general theories. *Qualitative Inquiry, 1*(1), 7–18.

Svensson, P. G. (2017). Organizational hybridity: A conceptualization of how sport for development and peace organizations respond to divergent institutional demands. *Sport Management Review, 20*(5), 443–454.

Svensson, P. G., & Woods, H. (2017). A systematic review of sport for development and peace organisations. *Journal of Sport for Development, 5*(9), 36–48.

Taylor, W. S. (1923). Rationalization and its social significance. *Journal of Abnormal Psychology and Social Psychology, 17*(4), 410–418.

Trendafilova, S., Babiak, K., & Heinze, K. (2013). Corporate social responsibility and environmental sustainability: Why professional sport is greening the playing field. *Sport Management Review, 16*(3), 298–313.

Trendafilova, S., Ziakas, V., & Sparvero, E. (2017). Linking corporate social responsibility in sport with community development: An added source of community value. *Sport in Society, 20*(7), 938–956.

Visa. (2020). Environmental, social and governance report. https://usa.visa.com/content/dam/VCOM/global/about-visa/documents/visa-2020-esg-report.pdf.

Waldman, D. A., & Siegel, D. (2008). Defining the socially responsible leader. *Leadership Quarterly, 19*(1), 117–131.

Walker, M., & Kent, A. (2009). Do fans care? Assessing the influence of corporate social responsibility on consumer attitudes in the sport industry. *Journal of Sport Management, 23*(6), 743–769.

Walker, M., & Parent, M. M. (2010). Toward an integrated framework of corporate social responsibility, responsiveness, and citizenship in sport. *Sport Management Review, 13*(3), 198–213.

Walters, G., & Tacon, R. (2010). Corporate social responsibility in sport: Stakeholder management in the UK football industry. *Journal of Management & Organization, 16*(4), 566–586.

Walzel, S., Robertson, J., & Anagnostopoulos, C. (2018). Corporate social responsibility in professional team sports organizations: An integrative review. *Journal of Sport Management, 32*(6), 511–530.

Where do you stand on social issues in sports? (2020, November 23). *Sports Business Journal.* https://sportsbusinessjournal.com/Journal/Issues/2020/11/23/Reader-Survey/social-political.aspx.

Willigan, G. E. (1992). High-performance marketing: An interview with Nike's Phil Knight. *Harvard Business Review, 70*(4), 90–101.

Winston, C. (2006). *Government failure versus market failure: Microeconomics policy research and government performance.* Washington, D.C.: ABI-Brookings.

Yu, C.-L. (2021). The role of CSR in sport consumption decision-making, *Marketing Intelligence & Planning, 39*(1), 17–32.

CHAPTER 17

SPORT, ECONOMICS,
AND FINANCE

BILL GERRARD

Sport is big business. It is estimated that the global sports industry was worth U.S.$756 billion in 2018 (Somoggi, 2020). The sports industry covers both participatory sport and spectator sport. Participatory sport is by far the biggest component of the global sports industry, accounting for most of the U.S.$270 billion of the sport retail business in 2018 as well as the U.S.$115 billion expenditure worldwide on club and gym fees (Somoggi, 2020). The focus of this chapter is on professional (spectator) sports, particularly professional team sports which, although accounting for only U.S.$170 billion (22.5%) of the revenues in the global sports industry (Somoggi, 2020), has a massive public profile and social media presence and dominates the discussions of the sports business. For example, the English Premier League (EPL) is the biggest domestic soccer league in the world, with 20 teams generating total revenues in excess of €5.4 billion in season 2017–2018, implying average annual revenue per team that season of over €270 million (Sports Business Group, 2019).

The objective of this chapter is to analyze professional team sports from the perspective of economics and finance. The chapter is structured as follows. In the Issues section the basic business model of a professional sports team is outlined, followed by a discussion of professional sports leagues as both self-regulated sporting structures and business entities. Two key interrelated issues are identified: (1) the financial viability of professional sports teams and (2) the sporting viability of professional sports leagues. The Approaches section sets out four different theoretical lenses for framing the sports business: (1) allocative (mainstream) economics, (2) corporate finance, (3) strategic management, and (4) radical political economy. A key point throughout the chapter is that the allocative economics, corporate finance, and strategic management approaches tend to be dominated by a focus on individual agents. It is the radical political economy approach that gives more emphasis to the social, cultural, and historical contexts of economic and financial behavior. The Debates section considers three issues in sports economics and finance as applied to professional team sports: (1) the impact of team ownership objectives on professional sports leagues, (2) the need for professional sports leagues to adopt an activist self-regulatory role to maintain the financial viability of teams and the sporting viability of leagues, and (3) the danger that excessive league regulation could undermine the incentives for teams to innovate.

ISSUES

Professional team sports comprise two basic entities: teams and leagues. Teams compete in tournaments, which are regulated by the leagues. Both teams and leagues are business entities in the sense of generating revenues from the sale of the rights to view the sporting contests between the teams and the sale of images associated with the sporting contests. We will consider the business models of both teams and leagues in turn and identify key concerns about the sporting and financial viability of these business models.

The Pro Sports Team Business Model

Pro sports teams sell two types of sporting product: (1) sporting contests as spectator events and (2) images associated with the team and its players. The sale of these sporting products generates four basic types of revenue streams, as illustrated in Figure 17.1. Traditionally the principal source of team revenues was gate revenues. Professional team sports emerged in the latter half of the 19th century as industrialization and urbanization created a working class concentrated in cities and towns, with disposable income to spend on leisure-time pursuits (see, for example, Ford, 1977). Professional sports teams offered elite-level sporting competition as a spectator event. The basic business model was cost-driven. Elite players, especially those from the working class, needed to be employed and paid, which, in turn, required team owners to generate revenues from the sporting contests. This involved the first "enclosure movement" in professional sports as sporting contests were moved from the open-to-all public spaces (the village green) to an enclosed private space (the sport stadium) where spectators faced a pay-to-view barrier (the turnstile), with gate receipts as the principal revenue source for teams. However, the development of radio and television created a new opportunity to follow sporting contests without attending the contest in the stadium. Gradually a new revenue source developed for teams as they sold media companies the rights to broadcast games on radio and television. The value of media rights for games was limited initially by broadcasting over free-to-air channels via public-service providers or commercial advertising-financed broadcasters. Eventually, as satellite, cable, and internet technology developed, the possibilities of a second enclosure movement emerged via

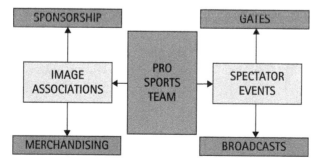

FIGURE 17.1 The revenue streams of a pro sports team

pay-to-view platforms (the electronic turnstile), either by charging subscriptions to access dedicated sports channels or charging fees to access broadcasts of specific sporting events.

The second type of sporting product sold by pro sports teams is image associations. Broadly speaking, there are two main image-based revenue streams: merchandising sold to fans and sponsorship sold to other businesses who want to use sport to market their own goods and services to targeted customer groups, both those attending games at sports stadia and those viewing games on television and online. Alcohol and tobacco companies were initially the major sponsors of sport, but with the increasing restrictions on advertising these products motivated by public-health concerns, sport sponsorship now tends to be dominated by financial services, cars, sportswear, and sports gaming, although there are growing ethical and public-health concerns about sport being used to glamorize and promote gambling (McDaniel, Mason, & Kinney, 2004).

The economic size of a pro sports team, measured by its ability to generate revenues, depends ultimately on the size of its fan base and the size of the league in which it competes. A team's fan base is a product of history and geography. Fans typically form their initial affiliations to teams either based on locality—residency and/or family connections—or sporting success. Big-market teams tend to be in large metropolitan areas and have a history of sporting success. The economic size of the team is also dependent on the economic size of the league in which it competes since the economic size of the league is critical for a team's ability to generate media revenues.

Table 17.1 provides a summary of the team revenues for the Big Five domestic European soccer leagues in season 2017–2018. The Big Five are the top-tier leagues in England, France, Germany, Italy, and Spain which generate the five highest total team revenues of all domestic soccer leagues worldwide. The EPL dominates, with total revenues of €5.4

Table 17.1 Team Revenues, Big Five European Domestic Soccer Leagues, 2017–2018

	England (EPL)	France (Ligue 1)	Germany (Bundesliga)	Italy (Serie A)	Spain (La Liga)
Revenues (€m)					
Matchday	757	191	538	257	510
Media	3,210	791	1,248	1,294	1,609
Commercial	1,473	710	1,382	666	954
Total	5,440	1,692	3,168	2,217	3,073
Revenues (%)					
Matchday	13.92	11.29	16.98	11.59	16.60
Media	59.01	46.75	39.39	58.37	52.36
Commercial	27.08	41.96	43.62	30.04	31.04
Total	100.00	100.00	100.00	100.00	100.00
Other KPIs					
Average League Gate	38,495	22,575	43,879	23,848	26,771
Local Spend (€)	2,896	1,996	2,431	1,935	2,734

Source: Sports Business Group (2019); author's calculations.

billion, more than €2 billion ahead of the next two biggest leagues financially, the German Bundesliga and the Spanish La Liga, each with total revenues just over €3 billion. Although the German Bundesliga has the highest average attendance at league games, this does not translate into the highest match-day receipts. It is the EPL that generates the highest match-day revenues, which includes not only ticket sales but also corporate hospitality and other food and beverage sales in the stadium as well as car parking. However, most of the revenue gap between the EPL and the rest of the Big Five is due to media revenues, with EPL teams cumulatively earning €3.2 billion from the sale of their media rights in 2017–2018, which exceeds the total revenues from all sources of the German Bundesliga teams and is more than double the value of the media rights of the Spanish La Liga, which ranks second in media revenues. The EPL teams also lead in commercial revenues (i.e., merchandising and sponsorship), although the advantage over the German Bundesliga is relatively small (i.e., under €100 million).

Two key performance indicators (KPIs) for the revenues of pro sports teams are (1) Media%, measuring the financial dependency of teams on the value of their media rights, and (2) Local Spend, measuring the nonmedia revenues relative to the fan base (using average league gate as a proxy for the team's active fan base). These two KPIs highlight the high dependency of the EPL and the Italian Serie A on media revenues, but whereas EPL teams have partly mitigated the risk of volatility in the media rights market by also having the highest Local Spend, the dependency of Italian Serie A teams on media revenues is exacerbated by having the lowest Local Spend.

The importance of the revenue-generating potential of a pro sports team is that ultimately the economic size of a team drives its ability to attract the best players. Higher revenues allow teams to spend more on playing talent, so the big-market teams will be able to afford the best players and create a "virtuous circle" where higher revenues lead to better sporting performance via higher expenditures on playing talent and, in turn, better sporting performance will lead to higher revenues to the extent that a component of team revenues is "win-elastic." For example, winning teams are likely to attract more fans to their games, generating higher match-day revenues and higher merchandising sales. In addition, sponsorship contracts typically have performance-related clauses, and the distribution mechanisms for media revenues usually tend to reward more successful teams either because their games are broadcast more frequently or media revenues are treated partly as prize money, with higher shares awarded to teams finishing higher in the league (see, for example, the discussion later in the chapter of the distribution mechanism used by the EPL for media revenues).

The player wage budget is the key financial decision by a pro sports team and depends crucially on the objectives of the team ownership, as will be discussed in detail in the Debates section. Increased wage costs to increase the playing quality of the team's squad of players would be expected to produce greater sporting success and, consequently, increased revenues. But the overall impact of financial performance (i.e., profitability) will depend on whether the increased revenues exceed the increased wage costs. This is where the objectives of the team ownership play a decisive role in determining the extent to which the ownership is prepared to sacrifice short-term financial performance in pursuit of sporting glory.

The overall level of player wages in pro team sports is essentially determined by two sets of factors: demand-pull factors and cost-push factors. Demand-pull factors focus on the revenue-generating capabilities of teams and leagues. Ultimately the economic value of playing talent (as with all types of labor services) depends on the incremental revenues generated, what economists call marginal revenue product (MRP). Thus, the economic value of Player X at Team A in League 1 depends on Player X's expected win contribution to Team A (i.e., the expected improvement to the team's sporting performance) and the economic size of both Team A and League 1, which together determine the team's ability to generate increased revenues from Player X's win contribution. In addition, Player X's economic value will also depend on the expected impact on team revenues of the image contribution of Player X and the nonfinancial returns of Player X's win contribution to the extent that the team ownership values sporting performance in its own right and not merely as a means to generate revenues. Overall, it follows that, as the revenues of teams and leagues increase, the economic value of playing talent as measured by MRP will increase, so we should expect player wage costs to track revenues over time.

The cost-push (or supply-side) factors affecting player wages mainly reflect the structure of the players' labor market, specifically the extent to which there is an open competitive market (known as free agency) or the market is regulated with restrictions on the ability of players to bargain with more than one team and often reserving bargaining rights to the player's current team only (known as a player reservation system). The rationale for league regulation of the players' labor market will be discussed in the Debates section. For the moment, suffice it to say that the greater the degree of free agency in the players' market, the greater the share of their economic value that players are able to achieve.

The wage costs of the Big Five leagues in European soccer are summarized in Table 17.2. Pro soccer teams in Europe are typically constituted as independent limited companies with publicly available audited accounts. Hence there is very reliable financial data on pro soccer teams in Europe, but unfortunately there is no accounting requirement to separately disclose player wage costs. Hence the financial analysis of European soccer has had to rely on data on total wage costs. Following the precedent set by Szymanski and Smith (1997), it has generally been agreed that total wage costs act as a reliable proxy for player wage costs,

Table 17.2 Wage Costs, Big Five European Domestic Soccer Leagues, 2016–2017 and 2017–2018

	England (EPL)	France (Ligue 1)	Germany (Bundesliga)	Italy (Serie A)	Spain (La Liga)
Wage Costs (€m)					
2016–2017	2,894	1,078	1,478	1,401	1,691
2017–2018	3,217	1,262	1,674	1,472	2,033
Revenues (€m)					
2016–2017	5,301	1,643	2,793	2,062	2,865
2017–2018	5,440	1,692	3,168	2,217	3,073
Wage-Turnover Ratio (%)					
2016–2017	54.59	65.61	52.92	67.94	59.02
2017–2018	59.14	74.59	52.84	66.40	66.16

Source: Sports Business Group (2019); author's calculations.

given that by far the largest proportion of wage costs of all pro sports teams is accounted for by player wage costs. Given the revenue dominance of the EPL, it is no surprise that it has the highest wage costs in the Big Five. Similarly, it is no surprise that wage costs are lowest in the French Ligue 1, which has the lowest revenues within the Big Five. However, what may be surprising is that the German Bundesliga lags behind the Spanish La Liga in wage costs (especially in 2017–2018) and is only just ahead of the Italian Serie A despite the German Bundesliga's having the second highest revenues in the Big Five. This reflects differences in cost-push factors, particularly the much tighter financial regulation of soccer teams in the Bundesliga. These cost-push differences are highlighted by the wage-turnover ratio (also known as the wage-revenue ratio), a crucial KPI for pro sports teams and, indeed, for any talent-based business where wage costs are the dominant cost item and, as a consequence, profitability depends critically on the gap between wage costs and revenues. The wage-turnover ratio can help identify changes in cost-push factors by controlling for revenue-induced growth in player wages since, effectively, demand-pull factors imply a constant wage-turnover ratio with wages and revenues growing at equal rates. The standout feature of Table 17.2 is the low and stable wage-turnover ratio in the Bundesliga in 2016–2017 and 2017–2018 because of their financial regulatory regime and is indicative of a financially sustainable business model. The other Big Five leagues have significantly higher wage-turnover ratios, and, with the exception of the Italian Serie A, their wage-turnover ratios increased significantly in 2017–2018 compared to the previous year. A high and increasing wage-turnover ratio is indicative of potential issues for the financial sustainability of a team's business model.

The Pro Sports League Business Model

Pro sports leagues have a dual nature. They are, first and foremost, a self-administered sporting structure which determines the structure of the sporting tournament for its member teams, sets the rules and regulations for the tournament, and is responsible for ensuring that the rules and regulations are enforced and the agreed sanctions on players and teams for any breaches of the league rules and regulations are implemented. These rules and regulations include the rules of the sport itself governing the individual sporting contests between teams and enforced by referees and other match officials. But league rules and regulations also govern the overall structure of the league tournament as well as player eligibility to participate in matches and the operation of players' labor market, including player movement between teams. But leagues are typically also business entities in their own right, actively involved in generating revenues, which necessitates a distribution mechanism to determine how centrally generated revenues are shared among the member teams.

As regards the sporting structure of leagues, there are two key structural dimensions: the tournament structure and the tournament entry mechanism. There are two basic tournament structures: round-robin (or league) tournaments, in which all teams play each other, with teams ranked at the end of the season based on the overall record in all of their matches, and elimination (or cup or knockout) tournaments, in which teams are paired and the winner of the match (or a series of matches) proceeds to the next round. European domestic soccer leagues traditionally have been organized as round-robin tournaments with all teams playing each other home and away, and often with a separate elimination tournament organized by the national governing body of the sport rather than the league. Indeed in English professional soccer there are three domestic tournaments every season: the league, the league cup (an elimination tournament organized by the league), and the FA Cup, organized by the Football Association, the governing body for all soccer played in England. In the North American major leagues there is a single tournament that combines elements of both a round-robin tournament and an elimination tournament, with teams playing a round-robin regular season in order to qualify for the end-of-season playoffs, an elimination tournament to determine the league champions. End-of-season playoffs can generate a significant uplift in revenues not only by adding lucrative end-of-season playoff games to the schedule but also by increasing interest in regular-season games as teams compete for playoff places. In recent years European team sports have emulated the North American major leagues, a process that Hoehn and Szymanski (1999) have termed "the Americanization of European football," including the introduction of end-of-season playoffs to determine some of the league outcomes, promotion and relegation, and qualification for pan-European tournaments.

The second key structural dimension of the sporting structure of leagues is whether leagues are closed or merit hierarchies. A closed league is one in which membership is fixed from season to season, with teams entering or exiting the league only in exceptional circumstances, such as a decision by the league to expand by admitting new teams to its membership or a member team's leaving the league either because of bankruptcy or to join a rival league. In a closed league such as the North American major leagues there is no promotion or relegation. By contrast, a merit hierarchy is a league organized as a set of divisions in a hierarchical structure with promotion and relegation of teams at the end of each season based on their sporting performance (although occasionally relegation may be imposed on teams for serious breaches of league rules). For example, English soccer has a full pyramid structure consisting officially of 11 levels with the 20-team EPL at the apex of the pyramid, followed by the Football League with three 24-team divisions (Levels 2–4), which constitutes the full-time professional levels of the sport. Below the top four levels, teams are mostly semiprofessional, although the pyramid does extend via promotion and relegation into the amateur levels. It has been estimated that the full pyramid structure comprises 20 levels in some localities encompassing over 140 leagues and more than 7,000 teams. Closed-league structures tend to be adopted by leagues organized as a franchise system, whereas merit hierarchies are more common in leagues operating as members' associations. Neale (1964), adopting a North American perspective on sports economics, considers one of the peculiarities of the pro team sports industry that distinguishes it from other industries is that each major league is more akin to a single multidivisional organization rather than a group of independent competing firms.

As business entities, leagues differ to the extent to which there is centralized selling of merchandise, sponsorship, and media rights. Centralized revenue generation implies the need for a distribution mechanism to allocate these league revenues to the member teams. This distribution mechanism is inevitably a potential source of tension between teams, with big-market teams arguing that they deserve larger shares since they attract more fans to the league, as discussed below in the context of the EPL. The distribution mechanism for media revenues in the EPL provides a good example of the tensions involved and the different allocative principles to be considered. The EPL media rights distribution formula differentiates between the revenues from domestic rights and those generated by the sale of overseas rights. The domestic rights revenues are distributed on the basis of 50% equally divided between the teams (including "parachute" payments for relegated teams for two years), 25% merit payments based on final league position (with the bottom team receiving a 1/210 share, and each place above that receiving an additional 1/210 share so that the league champions receive a 20/210 share of the merit payments), and 25% facility fee based on how often a team's home games have been televised. The overseas rights revenues were distributed equally until 2019, when, under pressure from the bigger teams with the biggest numbers of overseas fans, the EPL voted to implement the "grandfather rule" such that teams would be guaranteed at least the same amount as in the previous overseas media deal, but any uplift would be distributed on the basis of league position (i.e., as merit payments), with the proviso that the ratio of the highest and lowest payments would be capped at 1.8. Hence the EPL media distribution mechanism attempts to reconcile equity, performance incentives, and recognition that the bigger teams create more value for the league. The result is a complex compromise that, at least for the moment, has the majority support of the teams.

The two key issues facing all pro sports leagues are the interconnected issues of maintaining their sporting and financial viability. Financial viability requires that the teams can survive as business entities given the financial objectives of their owners. As will be discussed in the Debates section, team ownership objectives form a spectrum ranging from those who run their teams as conventional businesses with the objective of earning profits and an acceptable rate of return, to owners who put a priority on sporting success and are prepared to deficit-finance their teams by debt and/or equity to cover operating losses. The operating profitability of teams is largely dependent on the wage-turnover ratio. Teams can get trapped in an "arms race" of spiraling player wage costs as they compete in auction-type players' labor markets. This risk of unsustainable player wage costs is particularly acute in merit hierarchies, with risks increased by the threat of relegation as well as the desire to gain promotion to more financially lucrative higher divisions.

"Sporting viability" refers to the necessity to maintain competitive sporting tournaments to attract fans. It is known as the uncertainty-of-outcome hypothesis, first formulated by Rottenberg (1956). From this perspective, sport is unscripted drama with no requirement that the audience suspend belief that the outcome has been predetermined (unlike in the theater). Uncertainty of outcome requires competitive balance, defined as the degree to which teams have an equal opportunity of sporting success. A key research theme in sport economics has been the development of measures of competitive balance and empirically investigating the extent to which competitive balance impacts gate attendances and TV viewing audiences. Kringstad and Gerrard (2007) identify three types of ex post facto measures of competitive balance based on league outcomes: (1) win dispersion, measuring the distribution of the league outcomes in a single season; (2) performance persistence, measuring the degree to which league outcomes are replicated across seasons; and (3) prize concentration, a specific type of performance persistence, measuring the distribution of championship winners (and other "tail outcomes") across seasons.

The problem facing leagues is that any long-term trend toward a loss of competitive balance will reduce the uncertainty of outcome, thereby undermining sporting viability. This, in turn, can impact negatively on team/league revenues and thereby undermine financial viability. In the Debates section we will consider the degree to which leagues should intervene to maintain the financial and sporting viability of member teams, and what types of intervention are likely to be most effective. This will lead to a further debate about the danger that excessive regulation by leagues may undermine the ultracompetitive nature of the pro sports industry and reduce the incentives for teams to innovate, raising questions about the long-term viability of pro sports leagues.

APPROACHES

Marshall (1922, p. 1) defined economics as the "study of mankind in the ordinary business of life." But this traditional general, all-encompassing, and application-focused definition of economics concerned with wealth and welfare has been supplanted by a much more restricted definition of economics. This alternative conception that Fraser (1937) labels "Type B" economics, in contrast to the "Type A" economics of Marshall, emerged initially in the marginalist revolution in economics in the late 19th century, led by Walras, Menger, and Jevons. Robbins (1984) formalized this approach in his definition of economics as a theoretical and positive science concerned with the study of the allocation of scarce resources. As a consequence of the dominance of "allocative economics" (i.e., Type B economics), the Marshallian study of the ordinary business of life has become somewhat Balkanized into separate disciplines. Hence, in approaching the formal study of one particular domain of the ordinary business of life, namely pro sport, it is useful to separate out four alternative approaches that provide different lenses to frame and interpret the ordinary business of life. A brief characterization of each follows.

Allocative Economics

The choice-theoretic and market-theoretic approach to the study of economic behavior as optimizing allocative behavior is concerned with trading in markets. This embraces Robbins's (1984) restrictive definition of economics, in which the theoretical focus is on rational economic agents, with economic behavior modeled as constrained optimization. The economic system is viewed as a set of interdependent markets in which utility-maximizing households sell labor services and purchase goods and services, while profit-maximizing firms buy labor services to produce goods and services to be sold. The myriad individual economic decisions of firms and households are coordinated by the price mechanism, which acts as an "invisible hand." The basic theorem of allocative economics is that if markets are perfectly competitive, then the price mechanism will ensure a socially optimal, market-clearing general equilibrium in which the quantities demanded and supplied in every market are equal. Perfect competition (more appropriately termed "perfect resource allocation") requires that markets be atomistic in structure, with no individual trader possessing sufficient market power to influence the market price. Perfect competition also requires that the informational structure of markets be such that all traders are fully informed on the price and quality of all goods or services being traded. This informational requirement has been formalized as the efficient market hypothesis in asset markets. The principal corollary of the invisible hand theorem is that suboptimal market outcomes are due to imperfections in market and/or informational structures. For example, from the allocative-economics perspective, unemployment is conceptualized as excess supply of labor services, which occurs if the "price" of labor (i.e., the wage rate) is above its market-clearing level. It follows that unemployment will be automatically remedied if the wage rate falls to the market-clearing level unless market imperfections are causing wage rigidity and preventing wage rates from falling.

Corporate Finance

This includes the financial performance analysis of businesses using accounting data, business asset valuation, both the valuation of the business as a whole (known as corporate valuation) as well as the valuation of its constituent assets, and the investment decision on the acquisition of additional business assets. The underpinning logic of both financial performance analysis and corporate valuation is the business-finance model, as summarized in Figure 17.2. Here, financing capital in the form of equity and debt is invested in business assets comprising tangible assets, intangible assets, and current assets. These business assets are operated to produce goods and services that are sold to generate revenues that are used to cover operating costs (including wage costs) and pay taxes. The residual net income (i.e., profit after tax) is either paid out as returns to the providers of financing capital—dividend payments to equity providers and interest payments to debt providers—or retained and reinvested in the business, which represents an increase in equity capital. The data for the business-finance model is provided by the company accounts: the income statement (showing the relationship between revenue and net income), the balance sheet (showing the company's assets and liabilities), and the cash flow statement (showing the company's operating, investment, and financing cash flows received and paid out). Financial performance analysis focuses on the rates of return generated by the financing capital invested in the company. Asset valuation involves estimating the current market value of business assets. There are two approaches to asset valuation. Comparative valuation involves using the market values of similar assets (or businesses) that have been recently traded and therefore have a known market value. Fundamental valuation involves projecting the expected cash flows to be generated by a business asset (or a business as a whole), which

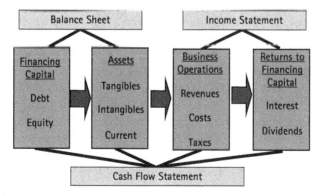

FIGURE 17.2 The business finance model

involves evaluating the expected future rates of return based on current performance and an assessment of the future prospects of the business.

Strategic Management

This track represents a move away from the structuralist approach of allocative economics in which the behavior of firms is largely seen as determined by market structure (i.e., external factors), as summarized, for example, in the Structure-Conduct-Performance paradigm that acted as an organizing principle in the economic study of industrial organization (Sawyer, 1981). Strategic management as it emerged in the work of Porter (1980) provides a more dynamic view of the competitive process focused more on the internal strategic decision-making of firms. The core research question in strategic management is to explain the sources of sustainable competitive advantage that underpins the market dominance of large firms and is not bid away by the competitive process, at least in the short to medium term. Two complementary approaches have emerged: the resource-based view (Barney, 1991) and the dynamic capabilities approach (Teece, 2007). The basic proposition of the resource-based view is that sustainable competitive advantage is derived from resources that are unique to a firm and only imperfectly imitable by rivals. Attention has focused on tacit knowledge (Polanyi, 1966) as a unique resource that is difficult for rival firms to imitate. Tacit knowledge is just that, tacit and never fully explicitly codified, but is largely acquired directly through on-the-job training within the firm. Tacit knowledge is what Becker (1962) defined as specific human capital that has value only within the firm in which it is acquired. Dynamic capabilities theory (Teece, 2007, p. 1319) essentially provides a more dynamic perspective on the importance of a firm's unique resources, emphasizing the need to "continuously create, extend, upgrade, protect and keep relevant the enterprise's unique asset base." The resource-based view and dynamic capabilities approach have both highlighted the role of asset orchestration as a key attribute of effective management in being able to "identify resource gaps and fill them in response to new opportunities, repeatedly" (Chatterji & Patro, 2014, p. 396).

Radical Political Economy

Outside the mainstream neoclassical paradigm of allocative economics there are a number of very diverse schools of thought that agree on the imperative to situate the analysis of human behavior in its social, cultural, and historical contexts, in contrast to the mainstream emphasis on the decontextualized rational economic agent. However, beyond this broad agreement there is often little in the way of common ground. Two of the most prominent schools of thought are the Marxist and the radical (or post-)Keynesian schools. The key themes in the Marxist analysis of the capitalist mode of production include the labor theory of value, surplus value as the source of profit derived from the exploitation and alienation of workers, the tendency toward a declining rate of profit, and the internal contradictions of the capitalist system that will ultimately lead to its collapse. The radical Keynesian school rejects the mainstream conception of the economic system as an exchange economy regulated by the price mechanism, emphasizing instead the circular flow of income, the importance of multiplier effects for output and employment levels consequent on changes in aggregate demand, and the all-pervasive effect of uncertainty, with particular emphasis on the effects on private investment, which Keynes (1936) identified as the principal source of volatility in the macro economy. Radical political economy offers a much more contextualized account of economic and financial processes that recognizes the historical specificity of the ordinary business of life. However, as the discussion in the Debates section will show, this perspective has had relatively little influence in the economic and financial analysis of pro sport.

Debates

Debate 1: The Objectives of Team Owners

A basic assumption in mainstream economics is that the objective of firms is profit maximization. However, the recognition of the separation of ownership and control in large firms creating scope for managerial discretion over the objectives of firms led to the profit-maximization assumption being increasingly questioned. Consequently, the managerial theories of the firm began to emerge in the 1960s, postulating that firms are trying to maximize sales, growth, or managerial utility rather than profit. This debate was replicated in sports economics. Sloane (1971) argued that soccer teams should be treated as utility maximizers and suggested that the team owner utility function should include playing success, average gate attendance, the health of the league, and profits. Quirk and El-Hodiri (1974) distilled the debate over team owner objectives to whether sporting success enters their objective function directly, creating the sportsman-owner effect (i.e., utility maximization), or only indirectly as a means to generating profit (i.e., profit maximization). If team owners pursue sporting success in its own right as a merit good, then these teams will invest in playing talent beyond the level consistent with profit maximization, trading off lower financial performance in return for higher sporting performance. The performance trade-off is illustrated in Figure 17.3. The performance frontier represents the locus of full-efficiency optimal combinations of financial and sporting success given the economic size of a team. Optimizing teams will seek to operate on the performance frontier at or above the level of sporting performance consistent with profit maximization.

Gerrard (2005) tested empirically for the existence of such a performance trade-off in the EPL by comparing teams listed on the stock market with nonlisted teams and found that listed teams had higher levels of profitability after controlling for differences in economic size. But the improved profitability was not achieved at the expense of poorer sporting performance. Gerrard explained this finding as due to efficiency improvements as a consequence of being listed on the stock market, which mitigated the performance trade-off in the short term.

From the corporate finance perspective, the debate over ownership objectives is crucial in determining the valuation of pro sports teams. The enterprise value of a conventional business as reflected in the combined market value of its equity and debt (i.e., financing capital) should represent the current discounted value of the expected future free cash flows (i.e., operating cash flows net of investment and tax cash flows). The price-earnings valuation ratio provides a standardized measure of the market value of the equity component

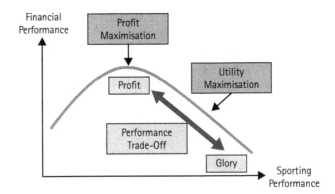

FIGURE 17.3 The performance trade-off

of the enterprise value as a multiple of current net income. Pro sports teams are typically very anomalous, with excessively high enterprise values and valuation multiples given their current and expected future profitability. The explanation of the excessively high enterprise values of pro sports teams beyond that justified by conventional business criteria is that the excess value lies in the expected future sell-on values of pro sports teams as a "trophy asset" (Turney, 2017) to potential buyers who value the nonfinancial returns from sporting success.

A radical political economy perspective on ownership has also been evident in the debate over team ownership, particularly in regard to questioning the legitimacy of a market for the ownership of pro sports teams. This debate has been especially relevant in European team sports, where teams tend to be constituted as clubs. Morrow (2003) considers whether soccer teams should be considered businesses or social institutions. Some soccer leagues in Europe have been active in regulating the ownership structure of teams. For example, the Bundesliga has the "50+1" rule, which requires that teams must retain over 50% of their voting rights in order to be members of the Bundesliga and thereby preventing external investors taking a controlling stake in any team. The EPL and the Football League in English soccer both have a "fit and proper person" rule for individuals appointed to a team's board of directors. There have been various campaigns for fans to be represented on a team's board of directors or even to take control of their teams; such moves are particularly prominent when teams are in severe financial distress. In England there is a government-backed initiative, Supporters Direct, to increase fan ownership and representation (Morrow, 2003). The leading Spanish soccer team, Barcelona, with an elected president is often held up as a democratic model for fan involvement in team governance (Hamil, Michie, & Oughton, 1999).

Debate 2: League Regulation

As discussed in the Issues section, a foundational proposition of sports economics is that the sporting and financial viability of pro sports leagues depends on the uncertainty of outcome. So the conventional wisdom is that competitively balanced leagues will thrive and competitively dominated leagues will struggle. The degree of competitive balance depends ultimately on the economic size distribution of teams and the extent to which differences in the economic size in teams are replicated in the distribution of playing talent between teams. Pro sports leagues have developed several regulatory mechanisms to influence the distribution of playing talent. These regulatory mechanisms can be broadly categorized into three groups: (1) revenue redistribution, (2) player allocation systems, and (3) player wage expenditure controls.

Revenue-redistribution mechanisms can attempt to equalize the distribution of playing talent by equalizing team revenues, the fundamental driver of team expenditure on playing talent. Historically the principal mechanism for revenue redistribution was shared gate receipts. In recent years revenue redistribution has occurred indirectly through the collective selling of media and other image rights by the league, with a significant proportion of these revenues being distributed among teams on an equal-shares basis.

Player allocation systems attempt to directly control the distribution of playing talent by replacing an open-market allocation of playing talent (i.e., free agency) with an administered allocation. There are two main forms of player allocation systems: player reservation systems and player draft systems. Player reservation systems reserve the rights in the first instance to teams to offer new playing contracts to their current players. Under player reservation systems, players are allowed to bargain with other teams only if their current team waives the right to retain them, often in return for monetary compensation, such as the payment of transfer fees in soccer, or nonfinancial forms of compensation, such as player exchanges and draft picks. Player draft systems are an administered allocation of new players (i.e., rookies) entering the league where teams select from a centralized list. The sequence in which teams select players is usually based on a reverse-order principle, with poorer performing teams in the league getting earlier picks in each round of the draft (Kahane, 2006).

Rather than directly controlling the allocation of players between teams, some leagues have attempted to do this indirectly by controlling player wage expenditure. One such intervention historically was to set a maximum wage, as in the case of English professional soccer, where the league set maximum weekly wage rates for all players. This practice was abandoned only after the threat of strike action in 1961. Such practices are unlikely to be sustainable in law nowadays and in most legal systems are likely to be deemed a restraint of trade. Hence, for leagues seeking to equalize the distribution of playing talent by equalizing player wage expenditures, the focus has been on total player wage expenditures by teams and setting a maximum either in the form of a salary cap that cannot be exceeded or, alternatively, a maximum above which teams incur a luxury tax, which is then redistributed to other teams.

From the perspective of allocative economics, the debate over league regulation has been dominated by Rottenberg (1956), who argued that the distribution of playing talent would be unaffected by whether or not leagues imposed a player reservation system or allowed free agency. This argument is now known as the "Rottenberg invariance proposition." It is an application of the Coase (1960) theorem that the allocation of property rights determines the distribution of income but leaves the allocation of real resources unaffected. In the case of the distribution of playing talent, if both team owners and players are wealth-maximizers, it follows that players will move to the teams where their economic value is maximized irrespective of whether there is a player reservation system or free agency. The best players will move to the biggest teams whatever the regulatory regime. The type of regulatory regime determines who can instigate player movements between teams and the distribution of the economic value of playing between team owners and players, but not the distribution of playing talent across teams. Player reservation systems assign team owners the rights to instigate player trades, and economic theory predicts that owners will be able to exploit their bargaining power to gain a larger share of the economic value generated by players. In contrast, free agency allows players greater freedom to bargain with any team at the end of their current contract, allowing players to gain a higher share of their economic value.

The Rottenberg invariance proposition remains highly contentious, particularly with respect to its key prediction that the labor market regime will not affect the distribution of playing talent. El-Hodiri and Quirk (1971, p. 1319) essentially agreed with the Rottenberg invariance proposition, arguing that the equalization of the distribution of playing talent in the long run requiring "rules to prohibit the sale of player contracts among teams guarantees convergence over time to equal playing strengths," although they did recognize that the sportsman-owner effect would undermine the long-term tendency to equal playing strength. However, Daly and Moore (1981, pp. 93, 94) disagreed; they suggested that the reserve clause in Major League Baseball had meant that "the 1965–76 period involved a greater degree of competitive equality and a lower correlation between city size and winning percentage," while "the effective termination of the reserve clause for veteran players in 1976 has been followed by a series of free agent transactions which have on balance clearly strengthened big city teams."

Although the impact of the labor market regime on the distribution of playing talent remains unsettled, it is generally agreed that a move to free agency will result in a greater share of economic value of playing talent accruing to the players. Scully (1974) estimated that under the reserve clause baseball players earned only 15% to 20% of their MRP in the late 1960s. Zimbalist (1992) found that, with the advent of free agency, rookie players continued to earn only a fraction of their economic value. However, Zimbalist also found that players who became free agents after six years in the MLB earned more than their MRPs, thereby compensating for the restrictions earlier in their careers. Further evidence of the impact on player wages from the introduction of free agency can be seen in Figure 17.4, which shows the wage-revenue ratio in the EPL. Free agency was introduced in European soccer in 1996 following the *Bosman* ruling by the European Court of Justice in September 1995, which deemed that the transfer system, particularly the payment of transfer fees for out-of-contract players, was in breach of the principle of free mobility of labor within the European Union (Késenne, 2006). Initially Bosman free agency applied only to players moving between teams in different member-states, but it was very quickly adopted for both domestic and international player transfers. As can be seen in Figure 17.4, it led to a dramatic realignment of player wages in the EPL, with the wage-revenue ratio rising in the space of four years from a pre-Bosman level of 47.1% in 1996 to 60.9% in 2000.

Salary caps are generally accepted to be the most effective means of influencing the sporting and financial viability of leagues. But salary caps vary in their objectives and design. A "hard" cap that sets the same absolute maximum on player wage expenditure for all teams is the most effective type to equalize the distribution of playing talent,

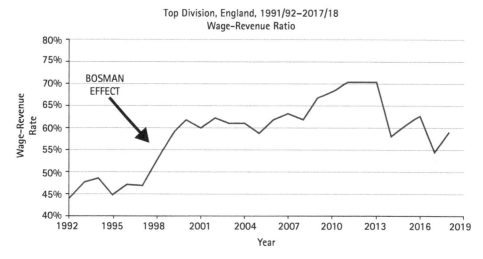

FIGURE 17.4 Wage-revenue ratio, EPL, 1991–1992 to 2017–2018

Source: Sports Business Group (2019); author's calculations.

whereas setting a maximum on player wage expenditure as a proportion of designated revenues is a "softer" cap that is more appropriate when ensuring the financial
viability of teams takes precedence over competitive balance. An alternative approach
to ensuring financial viability is to set a break-even requirement overall for teams and
then leave it to their discretion to determine the level of player wage expenditures compatible with break-even. This is essentially the approach adopted by UEFA, the governing body for European soccer, in its Financial Fair Play approach to regulating teams
participating in the pan-European tournaments, the UEFA Champions League, and the
UEFA Europa League; several domestic soccer leagues, such as the EPL, have adopted
a version of Financial Fair Play (Peeters & Szymanski, 2014). UEFA was motivated
by the dual concerns of ensuring the financial solvency of the teams competing in its
tournaments and trying to limit the competitive advantage of debt-financed teams (Drut
& Raballand, 2012). UEFA's regulatory regime owes less to allocative sports economics
and more to the political economy of managing its tournaments that involve teams from
55 member national associations of very different economic status while facing the pe-
riodic threat from the biggest teams to form a breakaway European super league (Drut
& Raballand, 2012).

Another form of softer salary cap involves exemptions to foster the long-term viability
of leagues. For example, the salary cap adopted by English Premiership rugby union teams
involves additional allowances for players developed within the team's own academy system
to incentivize teams to continue to invest in youth development. Another type of exemp-
tion is for iconic players seen as crucial to developing the fan base of the league, particularly
when a league is trying to compete with well-established leagues in other team sports, as in
the case of the Australian soccer league and Major League Soccer in the USA and Canada.
For example, the L.A. Galaxy in Major League Soccer was able to sign David Beckham
under the Designated Player Rule and able to pay him more than twice the team's total
salary cap (Badenhausen, 2012).

Debate 3: Innovation and the Moneyball Story

Fetter (2003, p. 384) warns of the dangers of league regulation in undermining the incentives to innovate, pointing out that

> there was much to be said for baseball's traditional ways, for the scope it gave to innovation and initiative by individual franchises' unwillingness to submit to the levelling down process implicit in the quest for competitive balance, a quest that . . . could easily lead to cooperative mediocrity.

Fetter provides a detailed account of the history of innovation in baseball as small-market and/or emerging teams innovated to be able to compete with the larger, more established teams. Such innovations include the separation of the roles of the general manager and field coach; the farm systems for developing young players; franchise relocation, particularly the postwar movement of franchises to the cities in the boom states of western USA; and stadium construction and redevelopment. Indeed publication of Fetter's book coincided with the publication of *Moneyball* by Michael Lewis (2003), which told the story of how Billy Beane, the general manager of the Oakland Athletics, developed the use of data analytics as an innovative competitive strategy.

From the perspective of allocative economics and corporate finance, Moneyball is an application of the efficient market hypothesis. Traditionally baseball teams valued batters using the two conventional batting statistics: batting average and slugging average. However, analysis of baseball data (known as sabermetrics) had shown that these metrics are not the best predictors of team win percentages. Rather, sabermetricians such as Bill James (Gray, 2006) had long argued that on-base percentage (OBP), defined as the proportion of at-bats that a batter reaches base, is a better predictor since it includes all the ways that a batter gets to base. In particular, OBP takes account of walks, which traditionally had been treated as a pitcher error rather than an indicator of the batter's skill in selecting which pitches to leave and which to attempt to hit. As a consequence, walks represented what economists call a "free lunch," a valuable commodity that is undervalued in the market. Oakland took advantage of the informational inefficiency of other teams to gain a competitive advantage. Hakes and Sauer (2006) tested the Moneyball hypothesis and found that (1) OBP was the best predictor of team winning percentage in the period 1999–2003; (2) OBP had no significant impact on batter salaries between 2000 and 2003; but (3) OBP became the most significant determinant of batter salaries in 2004 after the publication of *Moneyball*, just as predicted by the efficient market hypothesis when other traders are alerted to an informational inefficiency.

From the perspective of strategic management, Oakland used data analytics as a "David" strategy to compete effectively with resource-richer "Goliath" rivals by innovating to make efficiency gains. Gerrard (2007) estimates that in the first nine years of Beane's tenure as general manager, 1998–2007, Oakland achieved efficiency gains of 59.3% above the league average. Other baseball teams have also adopted data analytics, and indeed *Moneyball* has sparked innovation in the use of data analytics throughout team sports and individual sports worldwide. Rather than realizing Fetter's fear that league regulation is likely to produce competitive mediocrity, salary caps and other league interventions have provided a further stimulus to teams to innovate to find ways to be more competitive. Unfortunately, these innovations have sometimes involved breaching the rules.

CONCLUSION

The importance of sport as a political tool has long been recognized. Back in Ancient Rome, Juvenal reputedly summed up the public policy of Roman emperors as *panem et circenses* (bread and circuses)—that is, feed and entertain the masses. Elite sports, especially professional team sports, are the modern circus for the masses. Yet the economic study of sport is still in its relative infancy as a subdiscipline, dating back only to the publication of Rottenberg's paper in 1956. The practicalities of ensuring the sporting and financial viability of pro team sports both in the short/medium term and in the longer term remain work in progress. Key issues concerning the motivation of team owners, the impact of league regulations, and the need to maintain incentives for teams to innovate require further research. Leagues must also remain alert to the challenges of detecting unethical behavior by teams with an "only-winning-matters" attitude to sporting competition. And this concern with the ethical dimension reinforces a theme throughout this chapter: that there is a pressing need for sports economics to develop a more holistic understanding of sport by situating the economic and financial analysis of sport in its social, cultural, and historical contexts.

REFERENCES

Badenhausen, K. (2012, November 30). David Beckham departs MLS after earning $255 million. *Forbes.* https://www.forbes.com/sites/kurtbadenhausen/2012/11/30/david-beckham-departs-mls-after-earning-255-million/#544c09124da5.

Barney, J. B. (1991). Firm resources and sustained competitive advantage. *Journal of Management, 17,* 99–120.

Becker, G. S. (1962). Investment in human capital: A theoretical analysis. *Journal of Political Economy, 70,* 9–49.

Chatterji, A., & Patro, A. (2014). Dynamic capabilities and managing human capital. *Academy of Management Perspectives, 28,* 395–408.

Coase, R. H. (1960). The problem of social cost. *Journal of Law and Economics, 3,* 1–44.

Daly, G., & Moore, W. J. (1981). Externalities, property rights and the allocation of resources in Major League Baseball. *Economic Inquiry, 19,* 77–95.

Drut, B., & Raballand, G. (2012). Why does financial regulation matter for European professional football clubs? *International Journal of Sport Management and Marketing, 1,* 73–88.

El-Hodiri, M., & Quirk, J. (1971). An economic model of a professional sports league. *Journal of Political Economy, 79,* 1302–1319.

Fetter, H. D. (2003). *Taking on the Yankees: Winning and losing in the business of baseball.* New York: W. W. Norton.

Ford, J. (1977). *This sporting land.* London: New English Library.

Fraser, L. M. (1937). *Economic thought and language: A critique of some fundamental economic concepts.* London: A. & C. Black.

Gerrard, B. (2005). A resource-utilization model of organizational efficiency in professional sports teams. *Journal of Sport Management, 17,* 143–169.

Gerrard, B. (2007). Is the Moneyball approach transferable to complex invasion team sports? *International Journal of Sport Finance, 2,* 214–230.

Gray, S. (2006). *The mind of Bill James: How a complete outsider changed baseball.* New York: Doubleday.

Hakes, J. K., & Sauer, R. D. (2006). An economic evaluation of the Moneyball hypothesis. *Journal of Economic Perspectives, 20,* 173–185.

Hamil, S., Michie, J., & Oughton, C. (Eds.). (1999). *A game of two halves? The business of football.* Edinburgh: Mainstream.

Hoehn, T., & Szymanski, S. (1999). The Americanization of European football. *Economic Policy, 28,* 205–233.

Kahane, L H. (2006). The reverse-order-of-finish draft in sports. In W. Andreff & S. Szymanski (Eds.), *Handbook on the economics of sport* (pp. 643–645). Cheltenham, U.K.: Edward Elgar.

Késenne, S. (2006). The Bosman case and European football. In W. Andreff & S. Szymanski (Eds.), *Handbook on the economics of sport* (pp. 636–642). Cheltenham, U.K.: Edward Elgar.

Keynes, J. M. (1936). *The general theory of employment, interest and money.* London: Macmillan.

Kringstad, M., & Gerrard, B. (2007). Beyond competitive balance. In M. M. Parent & T. Slack (Eds.), *International perspectives on the management of sport* (pp. 149–172). London: Elsevier.

Lewis, M. (2003). *Moneyball: The art of winning an unfair game.* New York: W. W. Norton.

Marshall, A. (1922). *Principles of economics: An introductory volume* (8th ed.). London: Macmillan.

McDaniel, S. R., Mason, D. S., & Kinney, L. (2004). Spectator sport's strange bedfellows: The commercial sponsorship of sporting events to promote tobacco, alcohol and lotteries. In T. Slack (Ed.), *The commercialisation of sport* (pp. 287–306). London: Routledge.

Morrow, S. (2003). *The people's game? Football, finance and society.* Basingstoke, U.K.: Palgrave Macmillan.

Neale, W. C. (1964). The peculiar economics of professional sports: A contribution to the theory of the firm in sporting competition and in market competition. *Quarterly Journal of Economics, 78,* 1–14.

Peeters, T., & Szymanski, S. (2014). Financial fair play in European football. *Economic Policy, 29,* 343–390.

Polanyi, M. (1966). *The tacit dimension.* London: Routledge & Kegan Paul.

Porter, M. E. (1980). *Competitive strategy: Techniques for analyzing industries and competitors.* New York: Free Press.

Robbins, L. (1984). *An essay on the nature and significance of economic science* (3rd ed.). London: Macmillan.

Quirk, J., & El-Hodiri, M. (1974). The economic theory of a professional sports league. In R. E. Noll (Ed.), *Government and the sports business* (pp. 33–80). Washington, D.C.: Brookings Institution.

Rottenberg, S. (1956). The baseball players' labor market. *Journal of Political Economy, 64,* 242–258.

Sawyer, M. C. (1981). *The economics of industries and firms* (2nd ed.). London: Croom Helm.

Scully, G. W. (1974). Pay and performance in Major League Baseball. *American Economic Review, 64,* 915–930.

Sloane, P. J. (1971). The economics of professional football: The football club as a utility maximiser. *Scottish Journal of Political Economy, 18*, 121–146.

Somoggi, A. (2020, March 18). Coronavirus's economic impact on the sports industry. *Sports Value, blog.* https://www.sportsvalue.com.br/en/coronaviruss-economic-impact-on-the-sports-industry/.

Sports Business Group. (2019). *World in motion: Annual review of football finance.* Manchester, U.K.: Deloitte.

Szymanski, S., & Smith, R. (1997). The English football industry: Profit, performance and industrial structure. *International Review of Applied Economics, 11*, 135–153.

Teece, D. J. (2007). Explicating dynamic capabilities: The nature and microfoundations of (sustainable) enterprise performance. *Strategic Management Journal, 28*, 1319–1350.

Turney, D. (2017). Professional sports franchise valuation. *Toptal.* https://www.toptal.com/finance/mergers-and-acquisitions/sports-franchise-valuation.

Zimbalist, A. (1992). Salaries and performance: Beyond the Scully model. In P. M. Sommers (Ed.), *Diamonds are forever: The business of baseball* (pp. 109–133). Washington, D.C.: Brookings Institution.

CHAPTER 18

....

SPORT, MARKETING, AND CONSUMER CULTURE

....

T. BETTINA CORNWELL

In sport, marketing takes two major forms: the marketing *of* sports and marketing *via* sports. While some might refer to both activities under the umbrella term "sport marketing," they are decidedly different, and to reduce confusion and advance insights about the dynamics at play, each should be considered unique activities.

Sports marketing is the marketing of sport, much like services marketing is the marketing of services and wine marketing is the marketing of wine. Some see a host of unique characteristics in sport (for discussion, see the special issue in the *Journal of Global Sport Management* on this topic, introduced by Andrew, Grady, & Kim, 2019) that makes the marketing of it special, but such arguments have counterexamples. Sport has followers who are often passionate, true, but music has followers who are often equally passionate. Sport is an amalgamation of industries, but tourism is also an amalgamation. Sport is seen as both collaborative and competitive, but the auto industry, airlines, and higher education are also highly competitive and collaborative. My point is that sport is a complex industry and decidedly interesting (at least to those who follow it), but not so special in its nature and its attributes that it cannot be viewed through constructs that pertain to other industries. As defined by the American Marketing Association, "Marketing is the activity, set of institutions, and processes for creating, communicating, delivering, and exchanging offerings that have value for customers, clients, partners, and society at large" (Gundlach & Wilkie, 2009, p. 260). Simply put, sport marketing is an application of marketing to sport.

Sport marketing is an activity undertaken by a sport organization or its representative. Sponsorship solicitation and implementation is also an activity undertaken by sports organizations, but it is possible only in conjunction with another entity. Sponsoring is more akin to a strategic alliance (Urriolagoitia & Planellas, 2007) where two (or more) entities come together for a contractually agreed upon period of time. Sponsorship-linked marketing should be seen as the orchestration and implementation of marketing activities with the goal of building and communicating an association between partners based on this starting contractual commitment (Cornwell, 2008). The parameters of sponsorship-linked marketing have been expanded to fuel synergies through partnership to engage audiences (Cornwell, 2019). Early discussions in business regarding the purposes of sponsoring emanated from the sponsor's perspective (Cornwell, Weeks, & Roy, 2005; Meenaghan, 1991). However, more recent work considers the value of communication and engagement for both the sponsor (brand/company) and the sponsored (property rights holder) (Cornwell, 2020; Cornwell & Kwon, 2020). Such nuances in definition and strategy are important because they influence the ways in which theory, methods, and conceptual distinctions evolve and are applied in research. Sponsorship-linked marketing is a particular type of marketing.

To consider the intersection of sport, marketing, and consumer culture, some essential understandings about consumer culture frame considerations. Featherstone (1990) identified three perspectives on consumer culture. First, it can be viewed as resulting from capitalism's supporting unabated accumulations of consumer goods, proliferation of consumption contexts, and pervasive salience of leisure and consumption activities. Second, consumer culture can be perceived from a sociological view, where the satisfaction from goods depends on displaying and sustaining differences in society. Third, consumer culture can be viewed from an emotional or image-based perspective, where consumer cultural imagery and sites of consumption generate excitement and aesthetic pleasures. Featherstone concludes that "consumer culture uses images, signs and symbolic goods which summon up dreams, desires and fantasies which suggest romantic authenticity and emotional fulfilment in narcissistically pleasing oneself, instead of others" (p. 19). Consumer culture theory, in turn, considers consumption not as economic rationalism but as cultural meaning that is created, sustained, and transformed by myths, narratives, and ideologies (Hannerz, 1992, p. 16).

With this brief characterization of its component parts, we are now ready to ask the question: Are sport and marketing implicated in the development, sustenance, and ongoing transformation of consumer culture? The answer is yes, and some of the reasons for this are seen in the key issues considered in the following section.

Issues

Sport supports emotional well-being (Donaldson & Ronan, 2006), exercise reduces anxiety (Long & Stavel, 1995), and identifying with a team is associated with development of a positive social and self-concept (Branscombe & Wann, 1991). How is it that sport, and its next of kin fitness, once the antidote to what ails you, have become naturalized as part and parcel of consumer culture? Two processes are key: commercialization and globalization. These are intertwined with a plethora of issues. Further, issues of sustainability, cost, and representation, as they are directly related to the forces of commercialization and globalization, will also be considered.

Commercialization

The commercialization of sport as mass media entertainment has been seen as a movement from a focus on appreciating the technical aspects of competition to a focus on titillating action, scoring, and winning outcomes (cf. Hughes & Coakley, 1984). Commercialization, the management of something for profit, is made possible by the entertainment aspects of sport as a product. As mass media developed, entertainment for the masses was its life-blood, and here sport has played an essential role in the development and vibrancy of both legacy and new media.

Even as we are enmeshed in an advanced era of the globalization of sport and consumer culture, research finds sport audiences are still able to discern, and are sensitive to, the advancing reaches of commercialization. For example, Woisetschläger, Backhaus, and Cornwell (2017) examined the extent to which sponsorship deal characteristics (i.e., contract length, regional proximity of the sponsor to the sport, sponsorship fee, and sponsorship type) influence the sport consumer's perceptions of sponsor motives to engage in a partnership. Using a sample of nearly 3,000 individuals in Germany, and considering 44 top professional soccer sponsorships, they found that regionally proximate and long-term sponsors are associated with positive inferences that fans make about such partnerships. In contrast, high fees and distant sponsors and stadium-naming rights deals were associated with fans' perceptions that calculative motives were driving sponsors' strategies.

Importantly, this latter finding was qualified by a second study, showing that high sponsorship fees, when supporting a low-tier sport, could be seen positively by fans as supporting a sport in need. One of the important points of this work is that deal characteristics, not marketing or advertising directed to fans or consumers of sport, were influential in driving perceptions of consumers. The other point worth noting is that the sponsoring of sport by companies known in the region is most often viewed as motivated by the sponsor's liking for the team or for the sport or as motivated by the feeling that, as a member of the community, they should be a sponsor. Much evidence supports the notion that sport audiences reward companies with positive attitudes and patronage when they are seen as sponsoring sport entities because they like or care for the team or because it is what they "should be doing" as part of their responsibilities to a regional community.

Globalization

There are many definitions of globalization. The World Health Organization (n.d.) has one of the most general and encompassing:

> Globalization, or the increased interconnectedness and interdependence of peoples and countries, is generally understood to include two inter-related elements: the opening of international borders to increasingly fast flows of goods, services, finance, people and ideas; and the changes in institutions and policies at national and international levels that facilitate or promote such flows.

This characterization accepts that globalization has the potential for both positive and negative outcomes. At times, the positive outcomes for sport can be difficult to discern.

Considering how these dynamics may play out in sport, Giulianotti and Numerato (2018) adapt Robertson's (1992) multiphase model of globalization to describe three phases in the globalization of sport and consumer culture. Phase 1 (late 19th century to the mid-1940s) emphasized global sport professionalization and the assent of mass consumer culture with links to sport. Phase 2 (late 1940s to late 1980s) is viewed as an expansion period, when sport linked to more commercialized youth sports and to popular culture; brands, media, and consumer identities in sport flourished. Phase 3 (early 1990s to now) is a transnational hypercommodification period with greater globalization of factors worldwide. What exactly does greater globalization look like in sport?

Lucie Thibault (2009), upon receiving the Earle F. Zeigler Award for meritorious research, titled her address to the North American Society for Sport Management "Globalization of Sport: An Inconvenient Truth." Thibault considered four issues that affect the field of sport management and pertain to marketing and sponsorship concerns as well. First, she considered the use of workforces in developing countries by transnational corporations in the production of sportswear and sport equipment. On this topic she recognized the low wages and poor conditions for workers making products for multinational companies. Second, she considered the influence of increased migration by athletes in pursuit of more lucrative employment in affluent countries. Third, she considered changes in the global sport media complex that have forced sport to adapt to the needs of global media and which have taken control of important sport properties through acquisition. Fourth, she considered the significant impact of sport on the natural environment. Thibault's clear-minded and well-supported concerns for sport in 2009 are concerns that persist.

Without doubt, the globalization of sport and consumer culture could not have been possible without relentless advancements in technology. From broadcast media to social media and the variant streaming possibilities now available to consume, produce, reproduce, and share sport, contemporary engagement with sport is evolving moment by moment. Not surprisingly, the myriad possibilities for engagement have fueled the possibility of hyperconsumption. For example, in a study of Spanish football fans, Llopis-Goig (2012, p. 396) characterizes how foundational consumption has become in fan engagement:

> The interviews with fans, journalists and sport managers show that consumption has become a core dimension in relations between fans and football clubs, which has produced a profound transformation in the behavioural repertoire of the typical fan. In general terms, this has produced a broadening and intensification of the consumption of football. . . . [T]he behavioural repertoire of the fan is not limited to attending the league game that his or her team plays in its own stadium once every fifteen days, or to watching games broadcast free of charge on television every week, regardless of which teams are playing. These would be two of the most typical behaviours from what we could define as the previous era, but in the age of hyper-consumption, others have arisen and intensified.

Many of those "other" fan behaviors that are now integral in supporting hyperconsumption could not have been fully imagined a decade ago. In today's environment, one can snap a photo via an app with your team's mascot virtually superimposed and then post this to social media, where one can accumulate "likes," and then go on to share similar posts with others, all within five minutes. Fueled by the addition of social media as a profound catalyst in the reaction of fans to sport, we now have naturalized a consumption process that scholars (such as Giulianotti & Numerato, 2018) characterize as "transnational hypercommodification."

Yet even as the excesses of a globalized consumer culture concern many, a more nuanced and balanced view provokes asking: Are there any positive aspects of technology that are part and parcel of hyperconsumption? Across nine contexts, including sport, research has shown that generating content (via social media during an activity such as attending team sport) increases enjoyment with the experience and accelerates the perception of the time passing during the event (Tonietto & Barasch, 2020). Time flies when you are having fun.

Here, researchers argue that enjoyment is increased through feelings of engagement and presence. Indeed, many fans across the globe enjoy many aspects of hyperconsumption.

Commercialization and its globalization, obviously interrelated and complementary processes, have sped transnational hypercommodification. These twin forces as manifest in sport have fueled many other changes in the relationship of sport to consumer culture. Addressed in the next subsections are three key issues: sustainability, cost, and representation.

Sustainability

When thinking of the most pressing issues surrounding sport that are fueled by marketing and consumer culture, environmental sustainability might not make the list, but it should. The U.S. National Environmental Policy Act of 1969 committed that country to sustainability by declaring it national policy "to create and maintain conditions under which humans and nature can exist in productive harmony, that permit fulfilling the social, economic and other requirements of present and future generations" (U.S. Environmental Protection Agency, 2020). The 1987 United Nations definition is not very different, describing sustainable development as "meeting the needs of the present without compromising the ability of future generations to meet their own needs." How is sustainability an issue in marketing, sport, and consumer culture?

Let's consider one indicator of the sport-environment link. The U.S. Travel Association (2019) reports that in 2018, travel to attend or participate in sports constituted 8% of U.S. domestic travel, or approximately 190 million trips. In the same year, 37% of incoming international travelers indicated their interest in attending a professional sporting event (U.S. Travel Association, 2019). Naturally, outgoing international travel is also related to attending and participating in sporting events.

A review of research in 2013 found very little research that had considered marketing and environmental sustainability in the sport sector (Chard, Mallen, & Bradish, 2013). By 2018, this was beginning to change. Trendafilova and McCullough (2018) found 84 peer-reviewed articles dealing with management of sport, spectators, and facilities. Further, these authors found that the research studies could be grouped into seven categories: performance/evaluation of environmental performance, marketing/communication about sustainability, fan engagement/behaviors relative to sport sustainability, procurement policies, facility management, managerial decision-making, and social sustainability through community engagement. While marketing considerations were notably featured in these research strains, they were most often focused on marketing communications about sustainability issues. Given that marketing communications facilitate sports being consumed and valued (Wenner, 2013), one could be concerned that communications regarding sustainability might be perceived as "greenwashing," where one appeals to consumers' environmental concerns, but more is said than done. Toward understanding the dynamics at play, researchers have considered the environmentally friendly behaviors of fans, as well as the attitudes of those fans toward organizations. For example, in referencing intercollegiate sport, findings show that "spectators expected the athletic department to have an environmental action plan and engage in sustainable initiatives" (Trendafilova & McCullough, 2018, p. 15; also see Casper, Pfahl, & McCullough, 2017).

Research on communication has found that sports entities have varied greatly in the extent to which they have communicated effectively about their sustainability initiatives (e.g., Ciletti, Lanasa, Ramos, Luchs, & Lou, 2010; Francis, Norris, & Brinkmann, 2017). One is left with the impression that sport organizations are in the process of being sensitized to the important potential roles they may play in sustainability and that so much more could, and hopefully will, be accomplished. Importantly, there is intriguing evidence that many fans may be willing to help pay for their team's environmentally sustainable initiatives (Greenhalgh & Drayer, 2020).

Cost

Being a sports fan comes with a price, sometimes quite considerable. The cost per game of being a fan of a U.S. National Football League team ranges from approximately U.S.$100 to $200 for the combination of ticket, parking, and ubiquitous beer and hotdog (Berkeley School of Information, 2018). Similar cost profiles are found in other major league sports, according to research conducted at the University of Southern California's Price Center for Social Innovation (Perreault, 2020). For example, with an average income for a family of four in Los Angeles of U.S.$78,673, after essential costs the typical family has about U.S.$284 per month remaining for discretionary spending. Considering the 11 professional teams that play in the greater Los Angeles metro area, only one team could offer a family of four a sporting game for $100 (Perreault, 2020). The conclusion was that most professional sports teams are pricing out middle-class fans from attending their games.

The ever-increasing costs associated with being a fan need to be put into perspective. While we know that skyrocketing player salaries can seem shocking to some fans, it is important to remember that professional team owners often benefit similarly, although their profits are not as commonly reported. The average annual player salary for the 2019–2020 season was U.S.$8.32 million in the National Basketball Association, U.S.$5.3 million in the India Premier League, U.S.$4.03 million for Major League Baseball, U.S.$3.26 million for the English Premier League, and U.S.$3.26 million in the National Football League (Gough, 2020). In comparison, the median wage in the United States in 2019 was approximately U.S.$40,000. Therefore, an NBA player earns on average about 208 times what the median worker earns. As a point of comparison, in 2015 the average CEO earned U.S.$13.8 million per year, or 204 times what his or her median worker earned (Chamberlain, 2015). While research has shown that compensation is more strongly linked to performance for sport professionals than in corporate finance (Garner, Humphrey & Simkins, 2016), the disparity between these athletes and average workers is similarly disturbing. Research considering the compensation of CEOs and senior management in sport finds that star athletes and star managers are compensated similarly but that managers often receive additional compensation in stock options (Kaplan & O'Reilly, 2008). In business, when CEO-to-worker pay ratios are excessive, it has been found that consumers are less likely to purchase products and less likely to want a job with the company (Benedetti & Chen, 2018), but this type of research has not been undertaken in sport.

Needless to say, the costs associated with being a fan of sport, which link to athlete and coach pay, team owner compensation, and many other factors, differ significantly for men's and women's sports. As costs are often associated with perceived value for consumers, this has worked against women's sports being equally valued and undergirds pay disparities between male and female athletes and coaches, despite good philosophical (and even legal) grounds for equal pay for equal work (Archer & Prange, 2019). As a result, the average salary in the NBA for the 2018–2019 season was U.S.$6.4 million, whereas the average salary in the WNBA was U.S.$71,653, and the average ticket price was U.S.$89 in the NBA and U.S.$17.42 in the WNBA (WSN, 2019).

Representation

Women historically have had less access to sport, but even with increased access, women and girls are underrepresented in media coverage (Cooky, Messner, & Musto, 2015; Petty & Pope, 2019). When women in sport are portrayed in media, they are often hypersexualized (Fink, 2012), taking the focus away from their athletic abilities. Further, women remain chronically underrepresented in the upper echelons of sport organizations due to stereotypes, discrimination, and gendered organizational culture (Burton, 2015; Sartore & Cunningham, 2007). These entrenched tendencies come in the face of compelling research suggesting that disproportionately low media representation of women in sport is not anchored in giving people what they want to see (Cooky, Messner, & Hextrum, 2013). Rather, much of the disparity that results in women's sports being disadvantaged in the marketplace is traceable to male decision-makers being overrepresented at all levels of sport. This managerial fact has contributed to a logic to build the sport enterprise in favorable ways to represent men's athletic prowess and to reward male athletes more lucratively. History is repeating itself with discrimination and exclusion of LGBTQ+ people in sport (Denison, Bevan & Jeanes 2021). In this issue of representation and inclusion, sports marketing and sponsorship are necessarily implicated.

APPROACHES

Theory

Sport marketing is largely a theory borrower. This should not be surprising and is not meant to be a value judgment. After all, studies of how sports marketing works or how sport-anchored sponsorships can yield favorable outcomes are really just inquiries into human behavior and effective communication. Thus, theoretical influences abound from across the social sciences. For example, to understand sport spectator loyalty, inquiry about essential constructs such as consumer satisfaction have been borrowed from market research and identity theory from social psychology (Trail, Anderson, & Fink, 2005). Similarly, research on sponsorship often borrows from cognitive psychology to understand memory and recall of sponsor brands (Cornwell, Humphreys, Maguire, Weeks, & Tellegen, 2006; Weeks, Humphreys, & Cornwell, 2018). Sponsorship research may readily adopt marketing, psychology, and communication-based theories to understand attitudes and purchase intentions to make experiences, products, and services more appealing to sports fans and consumers (Henderson, Mazodier & Sundar, 2019).

Although there is no one distinctive body of theory used to study the intersection of sport, marketing, and consumer culture, in 2018 the *Journal of Consumer Culture* published a special issue, "Global Sport and Consumer Culture" (Giulianotti & Numerato, 2018). The special issue poses a plethora of theoretical approaches to study social structures and divisions as they relate to sport marketplace consumption, the attractiveness and dynamics of sport-centered celebrity culture, the making of sport consumers, and the effective framing of "glocal" (i.e., the tailoring of local sensibilities to globalized) aspects of global consumer sport (Giulianotti & Numerato, 2018). The special issue showcased diverse theoretical tactics in studying topics such as "glocalization" in cricket (Khondker & Robertson, 2018) and the branding and consumption of global celebrity sportswomen on the social media platform Instagram (Toffoletti & Thorpe, 2018).

While theoretical approaches to the study of sports marketing and sponsorship have been diverse, some select innovative theoretical strains are worth mention as promising. For example, sport marketing research aimed at understanding user-generated content, such as social media posts, has often utilized a Uses and Gratifications Theory lens (Katz, 1987) that assumes audience members make active conscious choices about the media with which they interact based on their goals and motivations and the degree to which they are satisfied by their attainment. For example, Clavio and Kian (2010) found that female and male followers of a female athlete on Twitter differed in their uses and gratifications: women were likely to follow due to affinity for the athlete and males were likely to follow because the athlete was physically attractive. In contrast, Yan, Steller, Watanabe, and Popp (2018) have advanced a structurational theory of public attention (Webster, 2011) which argues that macro-constructs, such as program availability, the technology available and adopted by users, and controls exerted by institutions, all interact with consumers' motives and satisfactions. Such a position poses that fan behavior is not based entirely on individual free will and interest goals, but rather is bounded by macro-structures about which the individual may or may not be aware. Key research findings by Yan et al. (2018), conducted in the context of U.S. collegiate football, suggest that user-generated content on social media platforms does depend a good deal on the macro-level structures that are in place. The takeaway here, especially with the increasing availability of big data sets that capture individual behaviors on social media, is that more nuanced understandings of the roles that macro-structures play in the sport marketplace will be helpful in understanding sport-centric communication and consumer behavior.

Similarly, studies of sport sponsorship have featured innovative theoretical approaches. For example, research by Pappu and Cornwell (2014) utilizing Structure Mapping Theory, originally developed by Gentner (1983) to understand consumer response to brands such as KFC or Subway sponsoring charities such as the Red Cross or the Leukemia Foundation, shows much promise. Pappu and Cornwell proposed that fit, defined as "the 'sense' or 'logic' of a particular brand sponsoring a particular object" (Olson & Thjømøe, 2011, p. 57), such as a team or event, can be attenuated when suspicion regarding the nature and goodness of fit of the relationship is aroused. According to Gentner, similarity is an outcome of the cognitive comparison of objects (here, sponsor and sport property). Importantly, the similarity between objects depends not only on their commonality but also on their aligned differences (Spiggle, Nguyen, & Caravella, 2012). For example, one's structure of understanding finds an aligned difference when a brand such as the worldwide restaurant chain McDonald's sponsors a sport event such as the Olympics. Both McDonald's and the

Olympics are related to health, but the former often is associated with unhealthy foods and the latter with healthy athletes. This is an aligned difference that leads to perceptions of similarity. In their research, Pappu and Cornwell present theoretical arguments and empirical findings suggesting that fit and similarity interact when influencing the nonprofit's brand clarity and resulting attitudes. For example, a low-fit sponsor for the Red Cross charity such as KFC damages the brand clarity of the nonprofit more than the higher-fit sponsorship with Subway. Sadly, when nonprofits take sponsorship support from poor-fitting sponsors, it is their brand clarity that is damaged, not that of the sponsor. Broadly taken, this line of research offers many lessons and warnings for brands looking to build their reputation through sponsorship in sport.

Method

Again, not surprisingly, methodological approaches to studying sport, marketing, and sponsorship in the context of consumer culture have been diverse. Exploring this, a special issue of the journal *Measurement in Physical Education and Exercise Science* sought to consider the state of methodological and statistical tactics being used in sport management research (Byon & Zhang, 2019), including those used to study marketing and sponsorship strategies and effectiveness. This collection of studies converges on the fact that while sport management research has been growing considerably in sophistication, it has been slow to adopt approaches utilized in parent disciplines of marketing and management. For example, Cunningham and Ahn (2019) found that while research on the sports marketplace often depends heavily on analysis-of-variance techniques, they have frequently been employed incorrectly in analysis, leading to specious findings. Analysis-of-variance techniques are widely employed in experimental research in sport marketing and sponsorship. This trajectory showcases a learning curve that is not so different from that seen in marketing research only a few decades ago, when the then fledgling discipline borrowed from management, psychology, and sociology and struggled with validity issues in its quest to be more scientific in approaching inquiry and reporting findings. On a more positive note, the trend lines in the evolution of sport management research methods, as well as their applicability to sports marketing and sponsorship, are encouraging.

Research using qualitative approaches have also faced a learning curve in approaching the dynamics of sport marketing and sponsorship. Here, there has been a continued reliance on traditional approaches, such as case studies and interviews, which can bring considerable richness and depth of insight at the cost of more limited generalizability. Toward expanding qualitative tactics, Hoeber and Shaw (2017), in a special issue in *Sport Management Review*, showcase some promising alternative methodological strategies. Throughout the special issue, strong cases are made for the value of community-based research, indigenous methodologies, participatory action research, autoethnographies, and narratives in advancing inquiry about sport marketing and sponsorship. While such approaches cannot replace the broader generalizability found in large-sample empirical studies, all are more sensitive to the "voice" and underlying concerns of consumers, matters that may often be given lesser priority or lost in client-driven surveys and questionnaires.

Measurement

The quest for stable measurement and the development of valid standardized scales is challenging for any disciplinary area, and here the research on sport marketing and sponsorship is no different. Still, in terms of many issues of measurement, and in particular the development of scales, there has been considerable progress. Sport marketing research has benefited from the development of specific measures in a number of areas. For example, understanding the psychological dynamics of the sports fan is an essential consideration to both marketing and sponsorship effectiveness. Here, measures of sports fans' *basking in reflected glory* (BIRGing) and *cutting off reflected failure* (CORFing) (Wann & Branscombe, 1990) are quintessential and have been utilized in a broad range of studies that pertain to marketing and sponsorship strategies (see Spinda, 2011 for self-report measures).

In another area, measurement guidance has been fueled by the development of an *athlete coping strategies* scale (Gaudreau & Blondin, 2002) in exercise science. From services marketing, standardized measures of the *personality in sports teams* have been developed, which include dimensions of competitiveness, prestige, morality, authenticity, and credibility; these have been valuable in sport marketing and sponsorship research (Tsiotsou, 2012). In examining the success of branding strategies, the *athlete brand image scale*, with dimensions of athletic expertise, attractive appearance, and marketable lifestyle, has shown particular promise (Arai, Ko, & Kaplanidou, 2013). Valuable as well have been scales to measure *sport consumer motivation*, which includes nuanced assessments of the dimensions of autonomy and control (Funk, Beaton & Alexandris, 2012).

As we can see, in measurement as well borrowing is common, the rule rather than the exception. Compilation also guides measurement strategies. For example, a measure of *sponsorship-linked purchase* intent was developed based on meshing several extant marketing measures (Cornwell & Coote, 2005). Hybrid measurement strategies are common elsewhere in sponsorship research. A promising measure of *authenticity in horizontal marketing partnerships* was developed based on diverse research on consumer behavior (Charlton & Cornwell, 2019), and a stable measure of congruence between sponsor and sponsored (sport, team, product) has been developed to guide decision-making (Fleck & Quester, 2007).

DEBATES

Three interconnected debates are at the center of sport, marketing, and consumer culture. First is whether corporate social responsibility is a beacon for goodness in the tension between sport and commercialization. The second regards the role corporations might take, beyond corporate social responsibility (CSR), in brand activism. An essential question here is whether consumers of sport can trust the move from mutually beneficial CSR strategies to one of brands taking stands on social issues without being seen as co-opting those issues for their own gain. Last, with or without brands as partners in change, what roles can consumers of sport take to change the trajectory of sport, marketing, and consumer culture?

Corporate Social Responsibility

Any thoughtful discussion of sport, marketing and consumer culture has to address responsibility. The posture of companies and brands, including sport organizations, toward public responsibility should stem transparently and seamlessly from their mission statements and policies. In other words, CSR should ideally not be "tacked on" (to make an organization look good) but something that actually exists at the core of organizational identity. Whether or not this is the case, it is clear that conceptualizations of corporate social responsibility differ significantly around the world. There are many definitions of CSR (Dahlsrud, 2008), and the ambit of activities included and the nature of responsibility have evolved over time. Nonetheless, an overview of CSR and some consideration of the debates about how it may best manifest in the organizational contexts of sport are in order.

The European Commission describes CSR as the process whereby enterprises integrate social, environmental, and ethical human rights concerns into their core (European Commission Communication, 2011). Alternatively, CSR has been defined as a company commitment to minimizing or eliminating any harmful effects on society and maximizing its long-term beneficial impacts (Mohr, Webb, & Harris, 2001).

To put the evolution of CSR in perspective, Frederick (2008, p. 523) outlined the following stages of its development:

> 1950–1960s: [C]orporate managers act voluntarily and philanthropically as public trustees and social stewards.
>
> 1960–1970s: [L]egally-required corporate responses were emphasized to address social issues.
>
> 1980–1990s: [B]usinesses develop ethical corporate cultures to support stakeholders and communities through social contracts.
>
> 1990–2000s: [C]orporations become global citizens and correct negative impacts on human societies and the natural environment.

While many corporations may still operate as if CSR is optional, meta-analytic research across 42 studies has shown that effective organizational implementation of CSR policies enhances the financial performance of corporations (Wang, Dou, & Jia, 2016). Still, many corporations and organizations may need further encouragement, policy nudges, or pressure to do better.

At the intersection of sports, marketing, and corporate social responsibilities there are at least three common CSR configurations: (1) sport initiating a CSR program with which sponsors may or may not align, (2) sport in and of itself being considered a CSR initiative for sponsors, and (3) sponsors fashioning a CSR program that is integrated with their sport sponsorship. In the first area of interest are CSR programs within sport organizations such as the Right to Play program associated with the Olympics (see Bradish & Cronin, 2009 for additional examples). A review of the literature found that the majority of studies focused on this type of CSR investigated community-based programs (Walzel, Robertson, & Anagnostopoulos, 2018). Another main way in which sport, marketing, and CSR align is when sport is sponsored. Many companies and brands have found that sponsorship of a deserving sport, and most particularly the sponsorship of sporting events and activities aimed at advancing development and peace, has served to effectively showcase their CSR commitments and contribute to both needs and the common good (see Levermore, 2010; Smith & Westerbeek, 2007). Evidence suggests that even the sponsoring of a professional team in and of itself can stimulate sport consumers in holding positive CSR perceptions about organizations and encourage related positive behavioral intentions toward sponsoring brands (Demirel, 2020).

Some corporate initiatives seek out and sponsor sports with particular characteristics to both reach and serve various publics. For example, Toyota's 2016 sponsorship of the Special Olympics allowed the company to speak not only to sports fans and consumers but also to its employees and vendors about their commitment to inclusiveness (Cornwell, Howard-Grenville, & Hampel, 2018). Still, a considerable critique of CSR is that corporate spending is comparatively small while publicity about such efforts is large, raising questions about veracity and authenticity in CSR efforts. Interestingly, consumers notice and prefer brands that contribute more of their profits to a cause in relative versus absolute terms (Keenan, Wilson & John 2022). It is fair to say that CSR activities in conjunction with sport can be both more vibrant and impactful. At the same time, it is clear that there is more that companies and their brands should and can be doing to support societal issues of concern, and that such efforts can both help with the bottom line and provide meaningful social benefits.

Bad Guy–Good Guy Debates

Over the years, there has been much public concern regarding the labor practices of athletic footwear and apparel manufacturers, a sensitivity that has only risen with the ubiquity of "athleisure" in mainstream fashion. Here there has been much finger-pointing about "sweatshops," and obviously there are considerable public relations dangers for brands thought to be engaging in impropriety in labor practices. This has garnered a good deal of research attention. For example, Kozinets and Handelman (2004) documented the anti-Nike activism of the 1980s and 1990s that served to stimulate the company to change its policies regarding sweatshop labor in production of its products. Perhaps because Nike was a brand leader in the athletic footwear and apparel space, it drew criticism in other areas as well. In this same period, despite movement toward a progressive pro-woman stance, Nike was still found to promote dominant norms, including celebrity feminism (Cole & Hribar, 1995). Nike admitted to past mistakes in a video from their founder, Philip Knight (sz9, 2014), and vowed to do better with a strategy that went beyond the usual tropes of damage control.

Many campaigns and YouTube posts later, the 2018 Nike "Just Do It" campaign launched. An extension of the original 1988 campaign, the new "Just Do It" campaign was inspired by the 2016 moment when NFL quarterback Colin Kaepernick knelt during the U.S. national anthem to protest the treatment of minorities by police. This Nike corporate social advocacy campaign has been analyzed for its motives, which were varied and complex (Kim, Overton, Bhalla, & Li, 2020), and for the resulting attitudes among Blacks, which were predominantly positive (Intravia, Piquero, Leeper Piquero, & Byers, 2020). Similarly, Nike's "Dream Crazy" campaign, featuring Kaepernick, has sparked thoughtful analysis. It is seen as a corporate political advocacy strategy that supports social issues of concern but deliberately alienates some stakeholders (Hoffmann, Nyborg, Averhoff, & Olesen, 2020), a result that obviously has considerable risks. What can be agreed upon is that Nike has not stood in the shadows. The company has taken up social issues with a clear-minded understanding that doing so will result in the loss of a large segment of consumers and investors. The use of their powerful platform has spurred inquiry into the role that corporations play in consumer culture specifically and in society overall.

The advent of "brand activism" is often greeted with skepticism as "woke washing" (Vredenburg, Kapitan, Spry, & Kemper, 2020). It is understandable that consumers might be wary. One need only look with hindsight at sport sponsorships to see that they may be riddled with complexities. One particularly profound sponsorship example involved Virginia Slims, a cigarette brand, sponsoring the women's professional tennis tour as a way to target women (Toll & Ling, 2005). In this gambit, "Virginia Slims co-opted women's liberation slogans to build a modern female image from 1968 through to the 1980s, and its market share grew from 0.24% to 3.16% during that time period" (p. 172). However, years later and with the benefit of hindsight, the offset between elite female athleticism and the health risks associated with cigarette smoking remain stark.

Some companies have a good deal of "brand latitude" (Charlton & Cornwell, 2020). This can stem from having been good corporate citizens and historic advocacy and support for social issues, which increases their being able to support an array of new initiatives. An example here is Patagonia, a sportswear company known for its environmentally friendly founder and policies. As the 2020 U.S. presidential election approached, concern over climate change was overshadowed by the urgencies of a global pandemic. In response to this shift of focus, Patagonia sewed a tag into some of its shorts that read "Vote the assholes out" (Evans, 2020) to remind consumers of the importance of aligning their votes with environmentally sensitive policies, but also as a reminder that Patagonia represents the "good guys." As we can see from this example, some brands in the sport marketplace are going beyond CSR to brand activism. However, the question remains: Are companies and brands trustworthy partners for fans and consumers who want to change the consumer culture of sport?

Consumer Power

Are fans consumers? To characterize fans as consumers seems at first to yield to the omnipresence of commercialization that a good many find distasteful. Yet this may be unavoidable. On this point, Crawford (2004, p. 4) has concluded that so much in sport relates "directly or indirectly to acts of consumption" that "being a fan is primarily a consumer act and hence fans can be seen first and foremost as consumers." This inescapable fact is made more palatable by considering Holbrook's (1987, p. 128) definition of consumer research:

> (1) consumer research studies consumer behavior; (2) consumer behavior entails consumption; (3) consumption involves the acquisition, usage, and disposition of products; (4) products are goods, services, ideas, events, or any other entities that can be acquired, used, or disposed of in ways that potentially provide value; (5) value is a type of experience that occurs for some living organism when a goal is achieved, a need is fulfilled, or a want is satisfied; (6) such an achievement, fulfillment, or satisfaction attains consummation; conversely, a failure to achieve goals, fulfill needs, or satisfy wants thwarts consummation; (7) the process of consummation (including its possible breakdowns) is therefore the fundamental subject for consumer research.

Holbrook's writing and that of his contemporaries (e.g., Stern, 1993; Van Raaij, 1993) broadened thinking about consumer behavior in light of postmodern critiques of marketing. Indeed, for many scholars, the pendulum of change swung, and the concerns of consumer behavior research rightly expanded so that it would no longer be only the handmaiden of marketing. For sport, in summary, fans are consumers that acquire valued experiences from events; these experiences may be satisfying, or they may be disappointing, and both outcomes should be of interest. When fans are disappointed not by the score of the game but by the commercialized experience, what then?

There is an overwhelming desire by many critics (see the discussion of Zygmunt Bauman's postmodern critique in Blackshaw, 2002 and the edited book on the commercialization of sport by Slack, 2004) to cast brands, business, and marketing as the villain when it comes to the development of a consumer-centric culture in sport and elsewhere. While there are grains of truth in these kinds of assessment, there are inherent fallacies as well about the "hypodermic needle" powers of marketing communication. When one adopts this kind of seemingly comfortable critical position, one sees individuals as victims and denies the power of consumers as well as their responsibilities in creating consumer culture.

It is perhaps easier to see the power that consumers hold in the sport marketplace by looking at a different context for a moment. What if consumers exerted their power to change consumer culture by refusing to eat white bread that is low in fiber, high in sugar, and generally less healthy than brown bread? Would piles of white bread be left on the shelves, and if so, would this be noticed? Would marketers continue to produce it? What if consumers refused to drink sugar-sweetened beverages like soda? Would marketers continue to produce, advertise, and promote them?

Considering the soda example in more depth, over the past few decades the consumption of sugar-sweetened beverages, and in particular soda, has been associated with tooth decay (Bernabé, Vehkalahti, Sheiham, Aromaa, & Suominen, 2014), obesity (Olsen & Heitmann, 2009), and cancer (Hodge, Bassett, Milne, English, & Giles, 2018), to name only a few areas of worry. As a result, consumers around the world have become concerned about the role of sugar-sweetened beverages in their health and reduced their consumption; in some countries, laws were instituted with the goal of reducing sales. In fact, the trend line of per capita soft drink consumption over 15 years (Holodny, 2016) tracks across a graph like a downhill skier from mountaintop to lodge. Admittedly, some consumption of soda has moved to alternatives such as tea and energy drinks that may also be sugar-sweetened, but consumption of soda has declined, not because brands decided not to sell as much but because consumers decided not to drink as much.

Let me return to sport and to the power of consumers in sport consumption. What if sports fans refused the single-use throw-way containers in the typical sport day experience and rewarded with their patronage only those teams and stadia that were environmentally friendly? What if fans began to reduce their consumption of "big-time" professional sport and began following, attending, and supporting more grassroots sports? What if individuals increased their support of women in sport and the brands that sponsor women's teams? Moreover, what if sports fans told expensive, male-dominated, and environmentally unfriendly sports organizations of their decision? Is it hypocritical to complain about commercialization, short-sightedness, and injustice in sport, and to lay all the blame on marketing, greed, and consumption-oriented culture, while at the same time continuing to consume those very products? If there is one thing that the Covid-19 pandemic taught the world, it is that sport is not the same without fans. Fans as consumers can change the production, dissemination, and consumption of sport.

CONCLUSION

Sport marketing, as the marketing *of* sport, and sponsorship, as marketing *via* sport, are recursive factors in sport consumer culture. Commercialization and globalization have stimulated many of the issues that now confront sports, such as the rising cost of sport attendance and participation, the environmentally unsustainable aspects of sport, and the lack of fair representation and compensation in sport. Indeed, these and many other issues stand at an inflection point. Sports marketing and sponsorship research are addressing many of these issues by borrowing both theory and method from parent disciplines such as marketing, management, and consumer studies, but also from psychology, sociology, and gender studies. While there is no sport-specific body of theory or unique research paradigms, sport marketing and sponsorship research have been developing their own set of priorities and approaches.

Sport and marketing sit at an uneasy juncture with consumer culture. Fans as consumers are at once satisfied with much of what they have known sport to be, but as many are priced out of sport spectatorship and made uneasy with sport that degrades the natural environment in the face of climate change and fails to represent and compensate all its participants fairly, some fans and consumers are ready for change. Importantly, it is clear that fans have potential partners in the sport marketplace to help redress social issues as brand activism takes root.

The ability of the public to scrutinize corporations and organizations, to learn their values from what they have put in writing (e.g., mission statements, financial declarations) and through their deeds and practices has never been more readily available. If, as Crawford (2004) outlined, a cultural product such as sport involves production, texts, and audiences, and if audiences do not just consume but also produce this cultural product, and if, as argued here, they have more power than they realize, then sport consumers can alter sport consumer culture. And marketing will follow.

REFERENCES

Andrew, D. P., Grady, J., & Kim, S. (2019). Is there anything unique about sport management? An introduction to the JGSM special issue on "the uniqueness of the sport context." *Journal of Global Sport Management, 6*(1), 1–6. doi:10.1080/24704067.2019.1641831.

Arai, A., Ko, Y. J., & Kaplanidou, K. (2013). Athlete brand image: Scale development and model test. *European Sport Management Quarterly, 13*(4), 383–403.

Archer, A., & Prange, M. (2019). "Equal play, equal pay": Moral grounds for equal pay in football. *Journal of the Philosophy of Sport, 46*(3), 416–436.

Berkeley School of Information. (2018). Cost of being a sports fan, https://ischoolonline.berke ley.edu/analysis-cost-of-being-sports-fan/.

Benedetti, A. H., & Chen, S. (2018). High CEO-to-worker pay ratios negatively impact consumer and employee perceptions of companies. *Journal of Experimental Social Psychology*, 79, 378–393.

Bernabé, E., Vehkalahti, M. M., Sheiham, A., Aromaa, A., & Suominen, A. L. (2014). Sugar-sweetened beverages and dental caries in adults: A 4-year prospective study. *Journal of Dentistry*, 42(8), 952–958.

Blackshaw, T. (2002). The sociology of sport reassessed in light of the phenomenon of Zygmunt Bauman. *International Review for the Sociology of Sport*, 37(2), 199–217.

Bradish, C., & Cronin, J. J. (2009). Corporate social responsibility in sport. *Journal of Sport Management*, 23(6), 691–669.

Branscombe, N. R., & Wann, D. L. (1991). The positive social and self-concept consequences of sports team identification. *Journal of Sport and Social Issues*, 15(2), 115–127.

Burton, L. J. (2015). Underrepresentation of women in sport leadership: A review of research. *Sport Management Review*, 18(2), 155–165.

Byon, K. K., & Zhang, J. J. (2019). Critical statistical and methodological issues in sport management research. *Measurement in Physical Education and Exercise Science*, 23(4), 291–300.

Casper, J., Pfahl, M., & McCullough, B. P. (2017). Is *going green* worth it? Assessing fan engagement and perceptions of athletic department environmental efforts. *Journal of Applied Sport Management*, 9(1), 106–134.

Chamberlain, A. (2015, August 25). CEO to worker pay ratios: Average CEO earns 204 times median worker pay. *Glassdoor Economic Research Blog*. https://www.glassdoor.com/research/ceo-pay-ratio/.

Chard, C., Mallen, C., & Bradish, C. (2013). Marketing and environmental sustainability in the sport sector: Developing a research agenda for action. *Journal of Management and Sustainability*, 3, 45–62.

Charlton, A. B., & Cornwell, T. B. (2019). Authenticity in horizontal marketing partnerships: A better measure of brand compatibility. *Journal of Business Research*, 100, 279–298.

Charlton, A. B., & Cornwell, T. B. (2020). Brand latitude. Working Paper. Illinois State University.

Ciletti, D., Lanasa, J., Ramos, D., Luchs, R., & Lou, J. (2010). Sustainability communication in North American professional sports leagues: Insights from web-site self-presentations. *International Journal of Sport Communication*, 3(1), 64–91.

Clavio, G., & Kian, T. M. (2010). Uses and gratifications of a retired female athlete's Twitter followers. *International Journal of Sport Communication*, 3(4), 485–500.

Cole, C. L., & Hribar, A. (1995). Celebrity feminism: Nike style post-Fordism, transcendence, and consumer power. *Sociology of Sport Journal*, 12(4), 347–369.

Cooky, C., Messner, M. A., & Hextrum, R. H. (2013). Women play sport, but not on TV: A longitudinal study of televised news media. *Communication & Sport*, 1(3), 203–230.

Cooky, C., Messner, M. A., & Musto, M. (2015). "It's dude time!" A quarter century of excluding women's sports in televised news and highlight shows. *Communication & Sport*, 3(3), 261–287.

Cornwell, T. B. (2008). State of art and science in sponsorship-linked marketing. *Journal of Advertising*, 37(3), 41–55.

Cornwell, T. B. (2019). Less "sponsorship as advertising" and more sponsorship-linked marketing as authentic engagement. *Journal of Advertising*, 48(1), 49–60.

Cornwell, T. B. (2020). *Sponsorship in marketing: Effective partnerships in sports, arts and events*. London: Routledge.

Cornwell, T. B., & Coote, L. V. (2005). Corporate sponsorship of a cause: The role of identification in purchase intent. *Journal of Business Research, 58*(3), 268–276.

Cornwell, T. B., Howard-Grenville, J., & Hampel, C. E. (2018). The company you keep: How an organization's horizontal partnerships affect employee organizational identification. *Academy of Management Review, 43*(4), 772–791.

Cornwell, T. B., Humphreys, M. S., Maguire, A. M., Weeks, C. S., & Tellegen, C. L. (2006). Sponsorship-linked marketing: The role of articulation in memory. *Journal of Consumer Research, 33*(3), 312–321.

Cornwell, T. B., & Kwon, Y. (2020). Sponsorship-linked marketing: Research surpluses and shortages. *Journal of the Academy of Marketing Science, 48,* 607–629.

Cornwell, T. B., Weeks, C. S., & Roy, D. P. (2005). Sponsorship-linked marketing: Opening the black box. *Journal of Advertising, 34*(2), 21–42.

Crawford, G. (2004). *Consuming sport: Fans, sport and culture.* London: Routledge.

Cunningham, G. B., & Ahn, N. Y. (2019). Moderation in sport management research: Room for growth. *Measurement in Physical Education and Exercise Science, 23*(4), 301–313.

Dahlsrud, A. (2008). How corporate social responsibility is defined: An analysis of 37 definitions. *Corporate Social Responsibility and Environmental Management, 15*(1), 1–13.

Demirel, A. (2020). CSR in sport sponsorship consumer's perceptions of a sponsoring brand's CSR. *International Journal of Sports Marketing and Sponsorship, 21*(2), 371–388.

Denison, E., Bevan, N., & Jeanes, R. (2021). Reviewing evidence of LGBTQ+ discrimination and exclusion in sport. *Sport Management Review, 24*(3), 389–409.

Donaldson, S. J., & Ronan, K. R. (2006). The effects of sports participation on young adolescents' emotional well-being. *Adolescence, 41*(162), 369–389.

European Commission Communication. (2011). Sustainable development goals. https://ec.eur opa.eu/info/sites/info/files/recommendations-subgroup-corporate-social-responsibility_ en.pdf.

Evans, J. (2020, September 19). The full story behind Patagonia's "vote the assholes out" tag. *Esquire.* https://www.esquire.com/style/mens-fashion/a34078539/patagonia-vote-the-assholes-out-shorts-tag-meaning/.

Featherstone, M. (1990). Perspectives on consumer culture. *Sociology, 24*(1), 5–22.

Francis, T., Norris, J., & Brinkmann, R. (2017). Sustainability initiatives in professional soccer. *Soccer & Society, 18*(2–3), 396–406.

Fink, J. S. (2012). Homophobia and the marketing of female athletes and women's sport. In G. B. Cunningham (Ed.), *Sexual orientation and gender identity in sport: Essays from activists, coaches, and scholars* (pp. 49–60). College Station, TX: Center for Sport Management Research and Education.

Fleck, N. D., & Quester, P. (2007). Birds of a feather flock together . . . definition, role and measure of congruence: An application to sponsorship. *Psychology & Marketing, 24*(11), 975–1000.

Frederick, W. C. (2008). Corporate social responsibility: Deep roots, flourishing growth, promising future. In A. Crane, A. Williams, D. Matten, J. Moon, & D. S. Siegel (Eds.), *The Oxford handbook of corporate social responsibility* (pp. 522–531). New York: Oxford University Press.

Funk, D. C., Beaton, A., & Alexandris, K. (2012). Sport consumer motivation: Autonomy and control orientations that regulate fan behaviours. *Sport Management Review, 15*(3), 355–367.

Garner, J., Humphrey, P. R., & Simkins, B. (2016). The business of sport and the sport of business: A review of the compensation literature in finance and sports. *International Review of Financial Analysis, 47*, 197–204.

Gaudreau, P., & Blondin, J. P. (2002). Development of a questionnaire for the assessment of coping strategies employed by athletes in competitive sport settings. *Psychology of Sport and Exercise, 3*(1), 1–34.

Gentner, D. (1983). Structure-mapping: A theoretical framework for analogy. *Cognitive Science, 7*(2), 155–170.

Giulianotti, R., & Numerato, D. (2018). Global sport and consumer culture: An introduction. *Journal of Consumer Culture, 18*(2), 229–240.

Gough, C. (2020, March 8). Average annual player salary in the sports industry in 2019/2020, by league. Statista. https://www.statista.com/statistics/675120/average-sports-salaries-by-league/.

Greenhalgh, G., & Drayer, J. (2020). An assessment of fans' willingness to pay for team's environmental sustainability initiatives. *Sport Marketing Quarterly, 29*(2) 121–133.

Gundlach, G. T., & Wilkie, W. L. (2009). The American Marketing Association's new definition of marketing: Perspective and commentary on the 2007 revision. *Journal of Public Policy & Marketing, 28*(2), 259–264.

Hannerz, U. (1992). *Cultural complexity*. New York: Columbia University Press.

Henderson, C. M., Mazodier, M., & Sundar, A. (2019). The color of support: The effect of sponsor–team visual congruence on sponsorship performance. *Journal of Marketing, 83*(3), 50–71.

Hodge, A. M., Bassett, J. K., Milne, R. L., English, D. R., & Giles, G. G. (2018). Consumption of sugar-sweetened and artificially sweetened soft drinks and risk of obesity-related cancers. *Public Health Nutrition, 21*(9), 1618–1626.

Hoeber, L., & Shaw, S. (2017). Contemporary qualitative research methods in sport management. *Sport Management Review, 20*(1), 4–7.

Hoffmann, J., Nyborg, K., Averhoff, C., & Olesen, S. (2020). The contingency of corporate political advocacy: Nike's "dream crazy" campaign with Colin Kaepernick. *Public Relations Inquiry, 9*(2), 155–175.

Holbrook, M. B. (1987). What is consumer research? *Journal of Consumer Research, 14*(1), 128–132.

Holodny, E. (2016). The epic collapse of American soda consumption in one chart. https://www.businessinsider.com/americans-are-drinking-less-soda-2016-3.

Hughes, R., & Coakley, J. (1984). Mass society and the commercialization of sport. *Sociology of Sport Journal, 1*(1), 57–63.

Intravia, J., Piquero, A. R., Leeper Piquero, N., & Byers, B. (2020). Just do it? An examination of race on attitudes associated with Nike's advertisement featuring Colin Kaepernick. *Deviant Behavior, 41*(10), 1221–1231.

Kaplan, A., & O'Reilly, N. J. (2008). The CEO–"star athlete" analogy: The role of variable compensation in professional sport. *International Journal of Sport Management and Marketing, 3*(4), 358–373.

Katz, E. (1987). Communication research since Lazarsfeld. *Public Opinion Quarterly, 51*, S25–S45.

Keenan, E. A., Wilson, A. V., & John, L. K. (2022). When less is more: Consumers prefer brands that donate more in relative versus absolute terms. *Marketing Letters, 33*, 1–13.

Khondker, H. H., & Robertson, R. (2018). Glocalization, consumption, and cricket: The Indian Premier League. *Journal of Consumer Culture, 18*(2), 279–297.

Kim, J. K., Overton, H., Bhalla, N., & Li, J. Y. (2020). Nike, Colin Kaepernick, and the politicization of sports: Examining perceived organizational motives and public responses. *Public Relations Review, 46*(2), 1–10

Kozinets, R. V., & Handelman, J. M. (2004). Adversaries of consumption: Consumer movements, activism, and ideology. *Journal of Consumer Research, 31*(3), 691–704.

Levermore, R. (2010). CSR for development through sport: Examining its potential and limitations. *Third World Quarterly, 31*(2), 223–241.

Llopis-Goig, R. (2012). From "socios" to "hyper-consumers": An empirical examination of the impact of commodification on Spanish football fans. *Soccer & Society, 13*(3), 392–408.

Long, B. C., & Stavel, R. V. (1995). Effects of exercise training on anxiety: A meta-analysis. *Journal of Applied Sport Psychology, 7*(2), 167–189.

Meenaghan, T. (1991). The role of sponsorship in the marketing communications mix. *International Journal of Advertising, 10*(1), 35–47.

Mohr, L. A., Webb, D. J., & Harris, K. E. (2001). Do consumers expect companies to be socially responsible? The impact of corporate social responsibility on buying behavior. *Journal of Consumer Affairs, 35*(1), 45–72.

Olsen, N. J., & Heitmann, B. L. (2009). Intake of calorically sweetened beverages and obesity. *Obesity Reviews, 10*(1), 68–75.

Olson, E. L., & Thjømøe, H. M. (2011). Explaining and articulating the fit construct. *Journal of Advertising, 40*(1), 57–70.

Pappu, R., & Cornwell, T. B. (2014). Corporate sponsorship as an image platform: Understanding the roles of relationship fit and sponsor-sponsee similarity. *Journal of the Academy of Marketing Science, 42*(5), 490–510.

Perreault, O. (2020, January 9). Professional sports are pricing out the middle-class fans. *Ticket News.* https://www.ticketnews.com/2020/01/pro-sports-pricing-out-fans/.

Petty, K., & Pope, S. (2019). A new age for media coverage of women's sport? An analysis of English media coverage of the 2015 FIFA Women's World Cup. *Sociology, 53*(3), 486–502.

Robertson R. (1992). *Globalization: Social theory and global culture.* London: Sage.

Sartore, M. L., & Cunningham, G. B. (2007). Explaining the under-representation of women in leadership positions of sport organizations: A symbolic interactionist perspective. *Quest, 59*(2), 244–265.

Slack, T. (Ed.). (2004). *The commercialisation of sport.* London: Routledge.

Smith, A. C., & Westerbeek, H. M. (2007). Sport as a vehicle for deploying corporate social responsibility. *Journal of Corporate Citizenship, 25*, 43–54.

Spiggle, S., Nguyen, H. T., & Caravella, M. (2012). More than fit: Brand extension authenticity. *Journal of Marketing Research, 49*(6), 967–983.

Spinda, J. S. (2011). The development of basking in reflected glory (BIRGing) and cutting off reflected failure (CORFing) measures. *Journal of Sport Behavior, 34*(4), 392–420.

Stern, B. B. (1993). Feminist literary criticism and the deconstruction of ads: A postmodern view of advertising and consumer responses. *Journal of Consumer Research, 19*(4), 556–566.

sz9. (2014, January 12). Nike better world history featuring Phil Knight. *YouTube.* https://www.youtube.com/watch?v=XaWhAhwWwio.

Thibault, L. (2009). Globalization of Sport: An Inconvenient Truth1. *Journal of Sport Management, 23*, 1–20.

Toffoletti, K., & Thorpe, H. (2018). The athletic labour of femininity: The branding and consumption of global celebrity sportswomen on Instagram. *Journal of Consumer Culture*, 18(2), 298–316.

Toll, B. A., & Ling, P. M. (2005). The Virginia Slims identity crisis: An inside look at tobacco industry marketing to women. *Tobacco Control*, 14(3), 172–180.

Tonietto, G. N., & Barasch, A. (2020). Generating content increases enjoyment by immersing consumers and accelerating perceived time. *Journal of Marketing*, 85(6), 83–100. doi:0022242920944388.

Trail, G. T., Anderson, D. F., & Fink, J. S. (2005). Consumer satisfaction and identity theory: A model of sport spectator conative loyalty. *Sport Marketing Quarterly*, 14(2), 98–111.

Trendafilova, S., & McCullough, B. P. (2018). Environmental sustainability scholarship and the efforts of the sport sector: A rapid review of literature. *Cogent Social Sciences*, 4(1), 1–15.

Tsiotsou, R. (2012). Developing a scale for measuring the personality of sport teams. *Journal of Services Marketing*, 26(4), 238–252.

U.S. Environmental Protection Agency of the United States. (2020). Learn about sustainability. https://www.epa.gov/sustainability/learn-about-sustainability#what.

U.S. Travel Association. (2019). The impact of sports on the travel industry. https://www.ustravel.org/system/files/media_root/document/2019_Sports-Travel_07.11.19.pdf.

United Nations Sustainability. (1987). Sustainability. https://www.un.org/en/academic-impact/sustainability.

Urriolagoitia, L., & Planellas, M. (2007). Sponsorship relationships as strategic alliances: A life cycle model approach. *Business Horizons*, 50(2), 157–166.

Van Raaij, W. F. (1993). Postmodern consumption. *Journal of Economic Psychology*, 14(3), 541–563.

Vredenburg, J., Kapitan, S., Spry, A., & Kemper, J. A. (2020). Brands taking a stand: Authentic brand activism or woke washing? *Journal of Public Policy & Marketing*, 39(4), 444–460.

Walzel, S., Robertson, J., & Anagnostopoulos, C. (2018). Corporate social responsibility in professional team sports organizations: An integrative review. *Journal of Sport Management*, 32(6), 511–530.

Wang, Q., Dou, J., & Jia, S. (2016). A meta-analytic review of corporate social responsibility and corporate financial performance: The moderating effect of contextual factors. *Business & Society*, 55(8), 1083–1121.

Wann, D. L., & Branscombe, N. R. (1990). Die-hard and fair-weather fans: Effects of identification on BIRGing and CORFing tendencies. *Journal of Sport and Social Issues*, 14(2), 103–117.

Webster, J. G. (2011). The duality of media: A structurational theory of public attention. *Communication Theory*, 21(1), 43–66.

Weeks, C. S., Humphreys, M. S., & Cornwell, T. B. (2018). Why consumers misattribute sponsorships to non-sponsor brands: Differential roles of item and relational communications. *Journal of Experimental Psychology: Applied*, 24(2), 125–144.

Wenner, L. A. (2013). Media, sport, and consumer culture. In P. M. Pedersen (Ed.), *Routledge handbook of sport communication* (pp. 410–420). London: Routledge.

Woisetschläger, D. M., Backhaus, C., & Cornwell, T. B. (2017). Inferring corporate motives: How deal characteristics shape sponsorship perceptions. *Journal of Marketing*, 81(5), 121–141.

World Health Organization. (n.d.). Globalization. https://www.who.int/topics/globalization/en/.

WSN. (2019). NBA vs WNBA: Revenue, salaries, viewership, attendance and ratings. https://www.wsn.com/nba/nba-vs-wnba/.

Yan, G., Steller, D., Watanabe, N. M., & Popp, N. (2018). What determines user-generated content creation of college football? A big-data analysis of structural influences. *International Journal of Sport Communication, 11*(2), 219–240.

CHAPTER 19

···

SPORT, TOURISM, AND SOCIAL IMPACTS

···

HEATHER J. GIBSON AND SHERANNE FAIRLEY

As tourism became increasingly specialized in the 1990s, there was a growing recognition about travel associated with sport. Initially, when a group of scholars began to focus on sport tourism as an area of study, there was much debate around the definition of "sport tourism" (e.g., Gibson, 1998b; Higham & Hinch, 2002; Weed & Bull, 2004). Through the years we have reached somewhat of a consensus that sport tourism breaks down into three main types: (1) travel to actively participate in sport, (2) travel to spectate at a sport event, and (3) travel related to nostalgia. The third form of sport tourism has always received less attention and has also been the most contested (e.g., Ramshaw & Gammon, 2005). Yet a quick review of the literature shows that there is an active group of scholars who have coalesced around this nostalgia/heritage sport tourism focus (e.g., Cho, Ramshaw, & Norman, 2014; Fairley, 2003; Ramshaw, 2020; Ramshaw & Gammon, 2005).

The first decade of sport tourism–related scholarship gave rise to two issues which are relevant to this chapter. The first was a focus on economic impact, primarily of sport tourism events (e.g., Daniels & Norman, 2003; Turco, 1998). This focus was not surprising, as communities were starting to use sport tourism as an economic development tool in the late 1990s, and many of these studies were commissioned by tourism agencies and emerging sports commissions. The second issue was a critique about the overly descriptive, atheoretical nature of early work (e.g., Gibson, 2004; Weed, 2006). However, the focus on description at this stage was not unexpected since the state of knowledge necessitated delimiting the area of study and conceptualizing and describing what comprised sport tourism. However, if, as sport tourism scholars, we were to move forward in developing this emerging area of study located at the intersection of sport management, tourism management, and leisure studies (this was the home to some of the early publications and themed conferences; cf. Gammon & Kurtzman, 2002), we needed to move into the next phase of knowledge development: understanding *the how* and *the why* (Gibson, 2004).

At this stage we had not actively incorporated event management scholarship into this intersection. While Getz (1998) had written a paper on sport tourism in the event management context, event management had not penetrated sport and tourism management to the extent it has today. In fact, as we noted earlier, while our spectator sport tourists were called "event sport tourists" (Gibson, 1998b) in our early work, and while we were often researching sport tourism in event-related contexts (e.g., Higham & Hinch, 2002, 2001; Ryan & Lockyer, 2002), the event was not the main focus. Today we have seen a definite shift in the prominence of the event context. This shift has been so extensive that the focus on sport tourism has been somewhat subsumed by the focus on sport events (Gibson, 2017). Indeed, some may question the viability of this area of study going forward. Yet, at the same time, we can point to a resurgence of interest from practitioners and the industry, particularly in niche areas of sport tourism such as youth sports. Also evident is a growing interest among academics throughout Asia, particularly in China and Japan (Dong, 2020; Hinch & Ito, 2018). As authors of this chapter, in reflecting back as well as projecting into the future, we are provided with an opportunity to examine some of the most significant developments in sport tourism research which helped to counter the early critiques of being atheoretical.

Issues

Responses to the critiques about lack of theory and being overly descriptive, as well as the focus on economic impacts, led us in two directions. First was the identification of appropriate concepts and theories that might enhance the explanatory power of sport tourism–related work to help us build a body of work that was sequential and could push our understanding forward. Weed (2006), drawing upon Forscher's (1963) classic treatise on "chaos in the brickyard," challenged us to move beyond the individual case study approach to work toward building a cohesive body of knowledge about sport tourism. Gibson's (2006) edited book, *Sport Tourism Concepts and Theories,* provided a compendium of potential theories that might be used to frame our work. Certainly, in the research on the active sport tourist there is evidence that scholars did heed the call to frame their work in appropriate theories. For example, Kaplanidou and Vogt (2007) used the Theory of Planned Behavior to understand participants in a cycling event. The concepts of involvement and enduring involvement, which have a long history in leisure studies, were applied to understand participation in Master's Games (Ryan & Lockyer, 2002) and travel to take part in running events (McGehee, Yoon, & Cardenas, 2003), and were combined with a benefits-sought framework to investigate cycle tourists (Gibson & Chang, 2012). A constraints framework, again from leisure studies, has been a popular approach to understanding participation patterns in snow sports (Hudson, 2000; Williams & Fidgeon, 2000) and surfing tourism among women (Fendt & Wilson, 2012), as has using serious leisure (Stebbins, 1982) to examine commitment and experiences in active sport tourism contexts (e.g., Shipway & Jones, 2007). Lamont, Kennelly, and Wilson (2012) added the idea that active sport tourists not only negotiate but prioritize constraints on their participation; they examined this within the event travel career framework proposed by Getz (2008). Getz combined serious leisure (Stebbins, 1982), Pearce's (1998) travel career, and Unruh's (1979) social worlds to develop the event travel career framework, which has spawned a series of studies on running (Getz & Anderson, 2010) and mountain biking (Getz & McConnell, 2011). Buning and Gibson (2015) proposed some further developments to what they called the active sport event travel career in their study of cycling within a U.S. context by providing more detail on career development and how this intersected with the events in which these cyclists chose to participate. Recently, Aicher, Buning, and Newland (2020) put more focus on the social worlds aspect of the active sport event travel career among runners and found that degree of immersion in the running social world shapes not only event participation but also related tourism behaviors.

These are only some of the conceptual approaches that have been used by researchers on active sport tourism; the application of these various frameworks has provided some unique insights into how and why active sport tourists participate in their various sports. More important, we have seen a shift in focus to understand the meanings and benefits that such participation has for these individuals, notably with a recent focus on the well-being associated with participation in active sport tourism (Mirehie & Gibson, 2020). However, some notable gaps remain, particularly in that much of the focus on active sport tourism has not interrogated the sociostructural issues associated with participation, such as gender, race, and class (Gibson & Mirehie, 2018). Active sport tourism is still mainly experienced by white, middle-class, and predominantly male participants, as was evident over 20 years ago, when some of the first papers were written (Bordelon & Ferreira, 2019; Gibson, 1998a). Another issue of importance is that there are few current researchers focusing on active sport tourism. This was evident in editing a special issue of the *Journal of Sport & Tourism,* where it took several rounds of the call for papers to attract a sufficient number of submissions (Gibson, Lamont, Kennelly, & Buning, 2018). Of course, some of this can be attributed to researchers being pushed to publish in higher-impact journals, but the sister special issue "Sport Tourism and Sustainable Destinations" (Hinch, Higham, & Moyle, 2016), for example, attracted enough papers for two issues. In delving more deeply into this topic, it is evident from the recent literature that there are an increasing number of studies on sport participation and also a growing focus on understanding the whys and hows of participation and links to health and well-being (e.g., Mirehie & Gibson, 2020). However, more troubling for sport tourism, is that many of these projects have ignored the touristic aspects of participation (e.g., Raggiotto & Scarpi, 2020), when we know that the very act of traveling not only contributes to well-being (e.g., Smith & Diekmann, 2017) but is part of the reason people take part in these events. So perhaps one pressing issue is that participation in event contexts may not be conceptualized and understood to its full extent without a focus on the touristic components of the experience.

As we reflect back on the original event sport tourism category, where the focus was on the hosting of events and spectators traveling to them, we can see that much research about the Sydney 2000 Olympic Games acted as a catalyst for the expansion of different disciplinary approaches to study sport tourism and events. The work of the Cooperative Research Center for Sustainable Tourism's Sydney Olympics Tourism Impacts Study is a source of much of the work that we see today on leveraging and flow-on tourism (see Faulkner et al., 2001). The application of concepts from marketing and the call to reconceptualize our thinking away from impact to leveraging (Chalip, 2004; Faulkner et al., 2001) were significant shifts in the way we think about events, and will be explored in more depth below. Additionally, in a project funded by the Australian Research Council, Green (2001) applied concepts from anthropology and proposed a sociocultural approach to understanding volunteering associated with Sydney 2000, at a time when much of the existing work was focused on volunteer motivation (e.g., Farrell, Johnston, & Twynam, 1998). Following the long tradition of focusing on resident responses to tourism, Waitt's (2003) study on the sociological and social-psychological impacts of hosting the Olympics on Sydney residents reflected not only the growing focus on the social impacts of event hosting that were beginning to emerge at the time but also growing concerns from sociologists and others about the legacy of hosting these sport mega-events (e.g., Cashman, 2003; Preuss, 2007).

Within research on nostalgia sport tourism, the big issue has always been the legitimacy of this form of sport tourism (Ramshaw & Gammon, 2005; Weed & Bull, 2004). The original conception of nostalgia sport tourism emanated out of Redmond's (1991) work and was used to describe sport-related travel associated with visiting museums, sport halls of fame, stadium tours, and other sport-themed tourism (Gibson, 1998b). Fairley (2003) broadened this definition and noted that the nostalgia around sport tourism could be based on social experience rather than event or sport memory. Ramshaw and Gammon (2005) have suggested that nostalgia sport tourism is a form of heritage tourism and should be conceptualized as such. While this debate is not settled, scholars continue to work in this area and produce theoretically informed work pushing the boundaries of our knowledge on nostalgia. One such trend is to move beyond a focus on nostalgia relating to famous stadia or sports halls of fame to consider intangible forms of nostalgia such as the social experiences among longtime fans of a particular team or memories of significant sporting triumphs or losses as social nostalgia (Fairley, 2003; Fairley, Gibson, & Lamont, 2018). Several key papers explore the idea that nostalgia is multidimensional, and we can see that, for the participants of these studies, nostalgia is linked to multiple attachments, such as family and identity (Cho et al., 2014; Fairley et al., 2018). Indeed, as nostalgia gained prominence in the COVID-19 era, Gammon and Ramshaw (2020) suggested that nostalgia might be a coping mechanism people use to deal with changes in everyday life, such as stay-at-home orders enacted by many countries during spring 2020. Closer still to sport tourism, Weed (2020) mentions nostalgia as one of the key concepts in understanding the effects on and potentially the reshaping of sport and tourism in response to the COVID-19 pandemic.

Approaches

With much of the contemporary focus on sport tourism residing largely within event contexts, we will devote this part of our chapter to a more in-depth focus on the conceptual approaches that have predominated in the sport-event tourism domain: (1) legacy versus leverage, (2) social impacts and social legacies, and (3) small-scale sport tourism events.

Legacy or Leverage?

Events are believed to provide benefits to destinations; however, research has suggested that these benefits do not occur as a matter of course (Brown, Chalip, Jago, & Mules, 2002; Chalip, 2004, 2006; Chalip & Leyns, 2002; O'Brien & Chalip, 2007). Economic impact studies provide mixed results (Gratton, Dobson, & Shibli, 2000; Mules, 1998). Given the significant public investment in events like the Olympic Games, and rising questions about whether such events actually produce the touted benefits (Maennig, 2007), scholars turned to event legacy. Event legacy focuses on long-term impacts from events (Preuss, 2007). Specifically, Preuss defined legacy as "all planned and unplanned, positive and negative, tangible and intangible structures created for and by a sport event that remain longer than the event itself" (p. 211). Many potential types of legacies have been identified, including infrastructure, knowledge, policy, networks, sport, social capital, and environmental impacts (Dickson, Benson, & Blackman, 2011; Preuss, 2015; Swart & Bob, 2012). Legacy assessments have been mixed; for example, Swart and Bob listed 33 positive and 39 negative legacies.

The International Olympic Committee included legacy in its charter in 2003, and since then potential host cities must detail a legacy plan in their bid documents (Leopkey & Parent, 2012). Leopkey and Parent noted that while the first mention of legacy was found in the bid documents for the 1956 Melbourne Olympic Games, the 2000s saw a significant increased focus on legacy effects among candidate cities. However, as Chalip and Heere (2013) suggest, host governments and event owners often use a narrative of legacy to legitimate significant public expenditures on sport events with little attention given to measurement and accountability. Indeed, basic questions arise about how and when one should assess whether a legacy has occurred. Further, many questions about who should be held accountable for legacy benefits remain unanswered. Most typically, public funds are spent before and during the event. Most committees formed to host events disband at their conclusion, and the stakeholders in the community responsible for making claims about the impacts and legacies of the events have often moved on to different roles by the time legacy is discussed and examined. As a consequence, legacy is often criticized as being mere rhetoric (Tomlinson, 2014). In contrast, Chalip (2004) advocates for the use of an ex ante approach known as event leveraging, rather than the ex post approach that is legacy. Event leveraging focuses on strategic planning, views the event as the "seed capital," and asks what a destination can do with an event to generate desired benefits (O'Brien & Chalip, 2007). Chalip (2017, p. 29) makes a good case that leveraging is of more use than legacy "because it focuses on strategic processes, rather than categories of outcome, and can thereby be applied across disparate contexts."

Chalip's (2004) original event leveraging model suggests that destination stakeholders can capitalize on the hosting of an event by strategically planning to capitalize immediate benefits from event visitors and trade, to entice visitor spending, lengthen visitor stays, and enhance business relationships. Further, destinations can use the opportunity to generate long-term benefits by utilizing the event-related media to showcase the destination and enhance its image. The leveraging framework includes identifying a leverageable resource, identifying the opportunities, creating strategic objectives from the opportunity, and developing means to achieve the objectives (Chalip, 2004). Research on event leveraging has highlighted the need to consider culture, attitudes and beliefs, and systems and structures (Chalip, Green, Taks, & Misener, 2017). Constraints and barriers to destinations leveraging events should also be considered; for example, host city contracts that involve commitments to global suppliers may prevent local businesses and tourism organizations from maximizing the value of the event to the local population (Kelly, Fairley, & O'Brien, 2019).

Alternatively, an event portfolio approach, which is itself a leveraging strategy, changes the focus from singular events to a holistic and synergistic view of events at a destination (Chalip, 2004; Getz, 2008; Ziakas, 2010). Specifically, event portfolios are based on "a series of interrelated events in terms of resources, theming, and markets which are strategically patterned on the basis of their operation and thematic readiness" (Ziakas, 2014, p. 329). The event portfolio facilitates the sharing of resources, collaborations, and cross-leveraging opportunities to achieve tourism outcomes (Ziakas & Costa, 2011), while often considering the diversity of events, seasonality, and timing in selecting events (Clark & Misener, 2015; Kelly & Fairley, 2018a). The portfolio approach provides a balanced approach and opportunities for smaller events that may otherwise be overlooked (Getz, 2008). Some destinations, however, may be dominated by one genre of event, such as sport events, as is the case of the Sunshine Coast, Australia. Benefits from event portfolios are maximized only when strategic leveraging takes place (Kelly & Fairley, 2018a). The Sunshine Coast has one of the most recognized examples of this approach. As part of their strategic approach to leveraging their event portfolio, the Sunshine Coast has an established Events Board (with tourism, events, and government organizations represented) and an event strategy that outlines clear strategic goals. Guided by their event strategy, the Events Board provides advice to tourism and government organizations that direct funding for events. Additionally, long-term funding contracts and the provision of human resources to manage each transaction are used to establish long-term relationships between events and the destination.

Social Impacts and Social Legacies

Questions about legacies from sport mega-events generated a related line of research with a focus on social legacies. Chalip's (2006) treatise on social leveraging and Misener and Mason's (2006) work on building community networks and social capital were part of a "turning of the tide" from a focus on economic impact to more intangible outcomes from hosting events. The timing on this change of focus occurred when London had been awarded the 2012 Olympic Games and South Africa was getting ready to host the 2010 FIFA World Cup, and conversations were on legacy (for London 2012) and nation-building for South Africa. In the tourism journals, following the resident-impact line of inquiry, a body of knowledge about social impacts had emerged (Fredline, 2005). For example, Gursoy and Kendall (2006) found that hosting mega-events, in this case the 2002 Salt Lake City Winter Olympics, resulted in positive social outcomes such as increased pride, self-esteem, and community spirit. Enhanced pride and community spirit were again identified in South Korea's hosting of the 2002 FIFA World Cup (Kim, Gursoy, & Lee, 2006). Similarly, Ohmann, Jones and Wilkes (2006) found that Germany's hosting of the 2006 FIFA World Cup instilled a sense of unity and national pride among its citizenry. Burgan and Mules (1992) had already invoked the concept of "psychic income" to describe this enhanced sense of pride, patriotism, and excitement, as expressed by residents of Brisbane in their hosting of the 1982 Commonwealth Games. Psychic income appeared to explain, at least during the event, why many of the negative impacts associated with hosting were forgotten as residents got caught up in the excitement and euphoria induced by the sporting competition. Similarly, as South Africa was getting ready for FIFA 2010, scholars reflected back on the 1995 Rugby World Cup and how President Nelson Mandela, as depicted in the movie *Invictus*, tried to establish a sense of collective spirit in the Rainbow Nation through rugby and advanced several treatises on nation-building through the hosting of such mega-events in the South African context (e.g., Labuschagne, 2008; Van Der Merwe, 2007). However, criticism associated with the 1995 Rugby World Cup pointed out that the collective spirit boost soon faded as the memory of winning the Cup diminished and the long history of challenges in that multiethnic nation was too complex to be solved by a sport event (Van Der Merwe, 2007). Nonetheless, with the impetus shifting to a focus on legacy, in particular among politicians and event owners such as the IOC and FIFA, some scholars shifted their attention to the intangible outcomes of hosting under the umbrella term of "social impacts" or "social legacy" (e.g., Fredline, 2005; Minnaert, 2012; Prayag, Hosany, Nunkoo, & Alders, 2013; Schulenkorf, 2009).

This shift away from economic impacts, a focus often described as "disappointing" by residents (e.g., Kim, Gursoy, & Lee, 2006), pointed to needs for research to be sensitive to the more complex social and political micro-contexts of many hosting countries. Since the 1990s, sociologists, in particular, had been writing about the breakdown of community and social networks (Putnam, 1995). There were also growing concerns about the increasing sociostructural divide and resulting increases in social inequality and the breakdown of social capital (e.g., Gould & Hijzen, 2016). Perhaps it is not surprising that governments started conceptualizing their mega-event hosting strategies in terms of building or rebuilding social cohesion. Waitt (2003) noted this with respect to the Sydney 2000 Olympic Games, and Cornelissen, Bob, and Swart (2011) focused attention on South Africa's nation-building goals in hosting the 2010 FIFA World Cup. As stated earlier, the idea of building social capital through sport and events had already been raised (e.g., Misener & Mason, 2006). Several empirical studies emerged, evaluating the degree to which event hosting was linked to psychic income as the immediate emotional response but also to longer-term outcomes such as social capital (e.g., Gibson et al., 2014), building national identity among peoples with different ethnic identities (Heere et al., 2014), happiness (Hallman, Breuer, & Kuhnreich, 2013), and national well-being (Kavetsos & Szymanski, 2010). While the research showed that the psychological response associated with hosting (psychic income) was indeed present, the longer-term goals of building social unity were often not met (e.g., Gibson et al., 2014). The missing part of these initiatives appeared to stem from the relative lack of social leveraging that was associated with the pursuit of these longer-term goals (Chalip, 2006).

So while research on the social benefits of event hosting has grown and moved into the realm of sport for development (e.g., Schulenkorf, Thomson, & Schlenker, 2011) or has been used to examine volunteer legacies (e.g., Downward & Ralston, 2006), critiques over hosting these sport mega-events have escalated, so much so that the pool of potential host cities has considerably declined (Sidhant, 2020). Critique levied at these sport mega-events is nothing new; in the sociology of sport, such a skeptical posture has a long tradition (e.g., Whitson & McIntosh, 1993). However, in the work in sport tourism in the late 1990s, some of these concerns became more central to inquiry in the emerging area of study focused on how tourism was associated with hosting these events. Higham (1999), in a commentary paper, used this tradition of critiquing these mega-events as a point of departure to suggest focusing on another avenue of study in sport tourism events, that of small-scale event tourism.

Small-Scale Sport Tourism Events

As we said, in the late 1990s and early 2000s, as communities began to invest in sport as a tourism development strategy, many of the early studies on these small-scale events were focused on economics (Daniels & Norman, 2003; Turco, 1998). The tourism-event funding model at local levels is often based on investing public monies (tourist taxes generated from commercial lodging) into tourist ventures (e.g., hosting small-scale sport events) that generate economic activity for the community (i.e., return on investment). It is common for these event organizers to track hotel room nights and expenditure data from local businesses to demonstrate that these public monies have been used effectively. However, when leveraging strategies use grants to entice event managers to adopt a strategy designed to generate tourism, it may result in "mission drift" by shifting the event managers' attention from their core purpose of staging the event (Kelly & Fairley, 2018b). When the focus of event managers shifts to tourism, they spend less time on the staging of their own event, leading to a product of lesser quality.

At the level of small-scale events in those early days, sports commissions, convention and visitors bureaus, as well as parks and recreation departments were encouraged to host sport events that would attract visitor spending from outside the community while making use of existing facilities and leveraging existing sport events (Daniels & Norman, 2003; Higham, 1999). In the United States, calls were made to recognize the tourism value of college sports (Gibson, Willming, & Holdnak, 2003); in New Zealand, Super 12 rugby was positioned as a way of counteracting seasonality in tourism (Higham & Hinch, 2002); and motor sports were used to diversify tourism on the Gold Coast in Australia (e.g., Fredline & Faulkner, 1998). While each of these initiatives focused upon economic impacts, they also measured social impacts, such as the effects of event hosting on local communities (Fredline, 2005) and understanding how sport tourists might be encouraged to engage in non-sport-related activities while visiting a destination, known as flow-on tourism (Gibson et al., 2003).

By about 2010, hosting small-scale sport events for many communities had become a major part of their tourism strategies. Indeed, Gibson, Kaplanidou, and Kang (2012) argued that, for communities with sport facilities and a sport-centric culture, small-scale event sport tourism was a form of sustainable tourism development. We also saw a shift at this time in how event sport tourism was being conceptualized. Contrary to the earlier focus on spectators, the growth in travel for participatory sport events was a noticeable development (Kaplanidou & Gibson, 2010). As we noted earlier, this gave rise to a line of research on sport-event participation experiences (e.g., Lamont et al., 2012; Shipway & Jones, 2007). Another development occurred at the community level as more communities recognized the economic potential associated with hosting small-scale sport events, particularly those featuring youth sport.

In 2019, it is estimated that sport tourists spent US $45.1 billion, including expenditures by venues and event organizers (Sports ETA, 2019). Also in 2019, Wintergreen Research, Inc. reported that youth sport travel spending alone was estimated at U.S.$15 billion per year. In the meantime, some communities had invested heavily in new facilities to host these sport events, using both public monies as well as commercial investment. This resulted in a proliferation of "mega-complexes," where sports facilities are combined with hotels and other guest services that specifically target traveling youth sport families (Drape, 2018). While the youth sport industry understands the economic significance of this form of small-scale sport tourism and the local sports commissions and other agencies involved in hosting recognize that tourism is economically beneficial to their communities (a fact that was made abundantly clear when the COVID-19 pandemic interrupted these contests [Drape & Chen, 2020]), there has been little interest from academics on examining the tourism associated with youth sport for these families (Garst, Gagnon, & Stone, 2019; Mirehie, Gibson, Kang, & Bell, 2019; Scott & Turco, 2007). Taks, Chalip, Green, Kesenne, and Martyn (2009) examined the flow-on tourism behaviors that take place as a result of some of the bigger youth sport tournaments. Still, the majority of research on youth sport participation has largely omitted consideration of tourism impacts. Indeed, costs associated with mandated travel have increased the time, money, and resources needed to participate in youth sport, disproportionally affecting those who lack the finances to participate (e.g., Knight & Holt, 2013).

Despite some of the growing concerns over the "big money" in youth sport, we still suggest that small-scale sport events have more positive potential for both communities and participants. As Higham (1999) suggested over 20 years ago, such events can bypass many of the negatives associated with hosting sport mega-events. Not surprisingly, research on sport-event participation has grown in tandem with more communities finding benefits in hosting participatory sport events. However, as noted, when considering active sport tourism, the focus on participation has come with reduced focus on understanding the touristic nature of small-scale sport events (e.g., Raggiotto & Scarpi, 2020). Further, returning to our earlier discussion on leveraging, Kennelly (2017) finds few event organizers understand how to effectively leverage their events to maximize both tourism benefits and participation experience. Much remains for future inquiry into this dynamic.

DEBATES

Our narrative shows that, over 20 years after study on the topic began, there is a body of theoretically informed work on various aspects of sport tourism, some of which has been accomplished in partnership with relevant agencies. However, the biggest debate today appears to be over the continued relevance of sport tourism in Western academic communities, particularly in light of the ascendance of event management in relation to both tourism management and sport management. Where is the focus on tourism in much of the contemporary research on events in general, and sport events in particular? We even have diverging opinions on this ourselves. It may be that our assessments stem from our different geographical contexts. While Australia is a more strategic leader in cohesive planning of sport events and event tourism, in the United States the importance of tourism in events varies widely depending on whom you are talking to, and event management and planning is largely dispersed among small independent agencies. In Australia, tourism and events often sit together within one organization; for example, Tourism and Events Queensland is a state statutory body in charge of events and tourism in Queensland.

One notable development since the mid- to late 1990s, when we saw the first coalescence around sport tourism, has been the rising prominence of events, both as an industry sector and an academic area of study. As a field, events and event management is claimed by hospitality, tourism, sport management, recreation, and event management in and of itself. The discipline housing degree programs or the events sector you work in will shape how you view tourism's role in events. Not surprisingly, tourism academics tend to think of events as "just tourism." Often they cannot understand why, over the past 10 years in university settings, students have been gravitating to event management degrees in such numbers that concerns have grown over the decrease in student enrollment in tourism programs. In fact, many of these event management students have no interest in tourism, as they do not see it as relevant to their future jobs as event planners.

In sport management degree programs, where there has been an appreciation of sport tourism for over 20 years, we have also seen a move away from the tourism aspects of sport events. Thus, while sport event management has grown in emphasis, both as an academic degree component and an area of research, we risk losing tourism, and by extension sport tourism, as an area of academic focus in parts of the world that were first associated with this area of study. A significant exception is continued growing interest in sport tourism from governments and scholars in the East, most notably in Asia. However, while it is encouraging to see scholars from a broader range of countries focusing on sport tourism, some of the earlier critiques about overly descriptive and atheoretical work remain. We hope, as was the case with our work in the late 1990s, that this turn of interest will fuel a new phase of research. There is promise for new ideas and approaches that can push the boundaries of our understanding about sport tourism in these countries, rather than emulating studies published in Western contexts over the past 20 years. Of course, we hope that this emergent stimulus of interest will be helpful in reframing and bringing culture-specific considerations more forward on the research agenda.

Another resilient area of debate surrounds the notion of leveraging, and the extent to which both academics and practitioners understand what it entails. As Kennelly (2017) found in her study of participatory events in the United Kingdom, few event organizers understood the need to leverage their events. This mirrors Chalip and Leyns's (2002) conclusion almost 20 years ago in their studies about leveraging sport events on the Gold Coast in Australia. As journal reviewers and editors, we know that it is not uncommon to see manuscripts that claim to have a focus on leveraging, but in reality the focus remains on questions of impact rather than on how event-related actors devise and implement strategies to leverage outcomes from an event.

A new twist in discussions of sport mega-events that lead us to the legacy and leveraging debate is concern over the costs and resources devoted to hosting these events. In particular, there is growing concern that countries from the developing world are bidding for and hosting large-scale events; some observers suggest that it is irresponsible to burden such countries (or any country) with unnecessary debts given unrealistic expectations of benefits (Dowse & Fletcher, 2018). Indeed, these bids are often motivated by unproven claims about economic benefits (Whitson & Horne, 2006), with limited mention that the major beneficiaries of such events are most typically the elites, while everyday taxpayers are left with sometimes considerable burdens (e.g., Tomlinson, 2014).

The COVID-19 pandemic has had a considerable impact on sport, tourism, and sport tourism. The Tokyo 2020 Olympic Games have been postponed, and many other international and domestic sport events have been postponed or canceled. Just how sport tourism will recover remains unknown. Some professional sports have received special dispensation from governments to continue play despite state and national restrictions on social distancing and travel. For example, the National Rugby League and the Australian Football League have resumed playing in Australia, with some teams being forced to relocate to another state in order to continue playing, and strict protocols around social contact with others. Likewise, in the United States, the National Basketball Association has created a "bubble" at the ESPN Disney Wide World of Sports to finish a season that was interrupted by the sudden stay-at-home orders in spring 2020.

In tourism, the economic fallout from the pandemic has been particularly acute, as many countries have created tourism-centric economies since the previous global disruptions on tourism flows in the early to mid-2000s. Since 2014, international tourism had resumed exponential growth each year and in some parts of the world had reached a crisis point of too many visitors, a condition referred to as "overtourism" (Weber, 2017). The almost complete shutdown of international tourism in April and May 2020 showed residents of these tourism-receiving communities what local life is like without hordes of visitors (Haywood, 2020). Some have suggested that tourism in these communities could be reenvisioned (Haywood, 2020), although the economic realities of having little to no tourism have also become apparent. Will the economic imperatives win out?

Similar discussions have been occurring in the youth sport world, led by the Aspen Institute's (2015) Project Play (Farrey, 2020). Without organized sport, physical activity during the early days of the pandemic-related lockdowns increased in outdoor venues such as parks and empty streets, and people of all ages rediscovered cycling and walking (Ding, del Pozo Cruz, & Green, 2020; Venter, Barton, Gundersen, Figari, & Nowell, 2020). The number of youth in organized sport has been declining over the past decade (e.g., Aspen Institute, 2015); will the pandemic exacerbate this downward trend? Many U.S. youth sport tournaments were held despite public health concerns (Allentuck, 2020).

Conclusion

In bringing this chapter to a close, it is time to think about the future of inquiry of sport tourism by reflecting on our dual critiques of early work in sport tourism for being too focused on economics and for being too often atheoretical. First, we should make clear that we still believe there is a role for economic-focused work. In the post-COVID-19 era, using a cost-benefit analysis to examine the economic returns from sport tourism initiatives for communities will be imperative (Mules & Dwyer, 2005). For associated industries and communities, accurate estimates of economic impact will be needed to guide policy and engender support from government and residents alike. However, one lesson from research on sport events over the past 20 years is that economic benefit cannot be assumed. This is most particularly the case for the larger events involving major infrastructure development and the multilevel disruption of life for host communities.

As our discussion in this chapter has shown, there has been a two-pronged approach, centered on legacy and leveraging, to event-related research. While our knowledge had advanced in these two areas, Chalip and Fairley (2019) argued in the introduction to their special issue of the *Journal of Sport & Tourism* that there is still a need for a strategic approach to leveraging. Understanding the principles of leveraging and building partnerships remains limited as event organizers are understandably preoccupied with planning and executing the event itself. Thus, going forward, we suggest that there is still much work to be done in untangling the principles of leveraging and how best to apply them in sport tourism and event management. If we are to continue to stage sport mega-events in the face of increased opposition from potential host cities, a shift from legacy to leveraging is warranted. Citizens deserve accountability and return on investment from their backing of these events. The need to revisit the ethics of hosting is in line with the growing call for attention to sustaina-bility in sport and tourism generally, and in event hosting in particular.

This returns us to a discussion about the size and scale of events for communities. Proponents of small-scale events have demonstrated that while they are not perfect, their strategic use offers the prospect of a balanced event portfolio (Ziakas, 2014), whereby communities can host events that complement their image as a destination (Chalip & Leyns, 2002) and use existing facilities and infrastructure (Gibson et al., 2012). Such strategies may offer the best way forward for many communities.

In the midst of the COVID-19 pandemic, some of the first events communities returned to were for youth. Because of this, the larger events industry has come to recognize that the pandemic has opened the door to the need to think differently about events and how they might be staged. For example, eSports, one of the new genres in the sport industry before the pandemic, held in-person competitions with live audiences. During the pandemic, the integration of new technologies into people's lives during spring/summer 2020 has raised questions about the changing expectations of hosting and attending events. For example, does the next eSports event need to be held in person at a convention center, or can it be held virtually?

On another technology-driven front, the integration of AI generally in tourism has gathered speed during the pandemic. While we are not suggesting that in-person partici-pation in sports (for spectators and athletes) or traveling will disappear, accepted ways of doing things changed drastically in January 2020. As in the work of Project Play (Farrey, 2020) and in youth sport after COVID-19, the wider tourism and events industries have also been reenvisioning the future (e.g., UN World Tourism Organization, 2020).

While we do not envision that people will stop traveling, attending sport events, and participating in sport tourism in person, we have seen glimpses of new ways of participa-tion, such as virtual marathons. However, we have also seen more people cycling and (re) discovering participating in physical activities outside (Venter et al., 2020). To what extent will this continue and reshape the sport tourism opportunities that are offered? Over the past few years, the IOC has sanctioned the inclusion of skateboarding, sport climbing, and surfing in the Olympic Games as a way of reaching the younger generations, some of whom have turned away from traditional (Olympic) sports (Farrey, 2020). At the recreational level, the growing popularity of ultramarathons, adventure racing, and mud runs and the rise in interest in cycling and running may continue to reshape sport tourism offerings as more people seek to compete and socialize with other participants in greater numbers. It is pos-sible that as some of those individuals who became engaged in physical activity during the pandemic enter higher levels of commitment, they may be encouraged to seek participation in sport tourism opportunities (e.g., Buning & Gibson, 2015; Getz & McConnell, 2011).

We think there has definitely been some progress in the theoretical development of work in sport tourism, both deductively and inductively. Here, new theoretical suppositions have been proposed, such as the event travel career (Getz, 2008), and there has been some re-finement advanced through grounded theory applications, such as the active sport event travel career (Buning & Gibson, 2015). Further, we have seen promising refined approaches to leveraging in small-scale sport settings (Kelly & Fairley, 2018b; Kelly et al., 2019) and explorations of the multidimensional nature of nostalgia (Cho et al., 2014) in sport tourism. However, as Chalip and Fairley (2019, p. 157) note about the tendency for a focus on sport events beginning to dominate the sport tourism knowledge base, "Although we have learned a great deal in recent years about ways to enhance the policy utility of sport events, the field remains undertheorized and overly general." We concur, but we also revert to an essential question we raised earlier: Will research on sport events continue to subsume sport tourism, or will sport event researchers rediscover the integral role that tourism plays in these events, both on the demand and supply sides of event experiences?

REFERENCES

Aicher, T., Buning, R., & Newland, B. (2021). Running through travel career progression: Social worlds and active sport tourism. *Journal of Sport Management, 27*(1), 32–44 https://doi.org/10.1177/1356766720948249.

Allentuck, D. (2020, May 12). A big youth baseball tournament was played in Missouri. *Was it too soon?* New York Times. https://www.nytimes.com/2020/05/12/sports/baseball/coronavirus-youth-baseball-tournament-missouri.html.

Aspen Institute. (2015). Project Play: Facts: Sports activity and children. http://www.aspenprojectplay.org/the-facts.

Bordelon, L., & Ferreira, S. (2019). Mountain biking is for (white, wealthy, middle-aged) men: The Cape Epic mountain bike race. *Journal of Sport & Tourism, 23*, 41–59.

Brown, G., Chalip, L., Jago, L., & Mules, T. (2002). The Sydney Olympics and Brand Australia. In N. Morgan, A. Pritchard, & R. Pride (Eds.), *Destination branding: Creating the unique destination proposition* (pp. 163–185). Oxford: Butterworth-Heinemann.

Buning, R., & Gibson, H. (2015). The evolution of active sport event travel careers. *Journal of Sport Management, 29*, 555–564.

Burgan, B., & Mules, T. (1992). Economic impact of sporting events. *Annals of Tourism Research, 19*, 700–710.

Cashman, R. (2003). What is "Olympic legacy"? In M. Moragas, C. Kennett, & N. Puig (Eds.), *The legacy of the Olympic Games 1984–2000: International Symposium Lausanne, 14th, 15th and 16th November 2002* (pp. 31–42). Lausanne: International Olympic Committee.

Chalip, L. (2004). Beyond economic impact: A general model for sport event leverage. In B. Ritchie & D. Adair (Eds.), *Sport tourism: Interrelationships, impacts and issues* (pp. 226–252). Clevedon, U.K.: Channel View Publications.

Chalip, L. (2006). Towards social leverage of sport events. *Journal of Sport & Tourism, 11*(2), 109–127.

Chalip, L., & Fairley, S. (2019). Thinking strategically about sport events. *Journal of Sport & Tourism, 23*(4), 155–158.

Chalip, L., & Green, B. C. (2001). *Leveraging large sports events for tourism: Lessons learned from the Sydney Olympics.* Supplemental proceedings of the Travel and Tourism Research Association 32nd Annual Conference, Fort Myers, FL, June 10–13.

Chalip, L., Green, B. C., Taks, M., & Misener, L. (2017). Creating sport participation from sport events: Making it happen. *International Journal of Sport Policy and Politics, 9*(2), 257–276.

Chalip, L., & Heere, B. (2013). Leveraging sport events: Fundamentals and application to bids. In I. Henry, & L.-M. Ko (Eds.), *Routledge handbook of sport policy* (pp. 209–220). London: Routledge.

Chalip, L., & Leyns, A. (2002). Local business leveraging of a sport event: Managing an event for economic benefit. *Journal of Sport Management, 16*, 132–158.

Cho, H., Ramshaw, G., & Norman, W. (2014). A conceptual model of nostalgia in the context of sport tourism: Reclassifying the sporting past. *Journal of Sport & Tourism, 19*(2), 145–168.

Clark, R., & Misener, L. (2015). Understanding urban development through a sport events portfolio: A case study of London, Ontario. *Journal of Sport Management, 29*, 11–26.

Cornelissen, S., Bob, U., & Swart, K. (2011). Sport mega-events and their legacies: The 2010 FIFA World Cup. *Development Southern Africa, 28*(3), 305–306.

Daniels, M., & Norman, W. (2003). Estimating the economic impacts of seven regular sport tourism events. *Journal of Sport Tourism, 8*(4), 214–222.

Dickson, T. J., Benson, A. M., & Blackman, D. A. (2011). Developing a framework for evaluating Olympic and Paralympic legacies. *Journal of Sport & Tourism, 16*, 285–302.

Ding, D., del Pozo Cruz, B., & Green, M. (2020). Is the Covid-19 lockdown nudging people to be more active: Big data analysis. *British Medical Journal Sports Med.* Advance online publication. doi:10.1136/bjsports-2020-102575.

Dong, E. (Ed.). (2020). *Sport tourism development: Foundation and cases.* Beijing: China Science Publishing.

Downward, P., & Ralston, R. (2006). The sports development potential of sports event volunteering: Insights from the XVII Manchester Commonwealth Games. *European Sport Management Quarterly, 6*, 333–351.

Dowse, S., & Fletcher, T. (2018). Sport mega-events, the "non-West" and the ethics of event hosting. *Sport and Society, 21*(5), 745–761.

Drape, J. (2018, September 12). The youth sports megacomplex comes to town, hoping teams will follow. *New York Times.* https://www.nytimes.com/2018/09/12/sports/youth-sports-costs.html.

Drape, J., & Chen, D. (2020, March 16). Tears and disbelief as coronavirus cancels youth sports. New York Times. https://www.nytimes.com/2020/03/16/sports/coronavirus-cance led-youth-sports.html.

Fairley, S. (2003). In search of relived social experience: Group-based nostalgia sport tourism. *Journal of Sport Management, 17*, 284–304.

Fairley, S., Gibson, H., & Lamont, M. (2018). Temporal manifestations of nostalgia: Le Tour de France. *Annals of Tourism Research, 70*, 120–130.

Farrell, J., Johnston, M., & Twynam, D. (1998). Volunteer motivation, satisfaction and management at elite sporting competition. *Journal of Sport Management, 12*, 288–300.

Farrey, T. (2020, June 1). How can sports help build America? Aspen Institute. https://www.aspeninstitute.org/blog-posts/how-sports-can-help-rebuild-america/.

Faulkner, B. Chalip, L., Brown, G., Jago, L., March, R., & Woodside, A. (2001). Monitoring the tourism impacts of the Sydney 2000 Olympics. *Event Management, 6*, 231–246.

Fendt, L., & Wilson, E. (2012). "I just push through the barriers because I live for surfing": How women negotiate their constraints to surf tourism. *Annals of Leisure Research, 15*(1), 4–18.

Forscher, B. (1963). Chaos in the brickyard. *Science, 142* (3590), 339.

Fredline, E. (2005). Host and guest relations and sport tourism. *Sport in Society, 8*(2), 263–279.

Fredline, E., & Faulkner, B. (1998). Resident reactions to a major tourist event: The Gold Coast Indy Car Race. *Festival Management and Event Tourism, 5*, 185–205.

Gammon, S., & Kurtzman, J. (Eds.). (2002). *Sport tourism: Principles and practice.* Eastbourne, U.K.: LSA Publications.

Gammon, S., & Ramshaw, G. (2020). Distancing from the present nostalgia and leisure in lockdown. *Leisure Sciences, 43*(1–2), 131–137. doi: 10.1080/01490400.2020.1773993

Garst, B., Gagnon, R., & Stone, G. (2019). "The credit card or the taxi": A qualitative investigation of parent involvement in indoor competition climbing. *Leisure Sciences, 42*(5–6), 589–608. https://doi.org/10.1080/01490400.2019.1646172.

Getz, D. (1998). Trends, strategies and issues in sport-event tourism. *Sport Marketing Quarterly, 7*, 8–13.

Getz, D. (2008). Event tourism: Definition, evolution, and research. *Tourism Management, 29*, 403–428.

Getz, D., & Anderson, T. D. (2010). The event-tourist career trajectory: A study of high-involvement amateur distance runners. *Scandinavian Journal of Hospitality and Tourism, 10*(4), 468–491.

Getz, D., & McConnell, A. (2011). Serious sport tourism and event travel careers. *Journal of Sport Management, 25*, 326–338.

Gibson, H. (1998a). Active sport tourism: Who participates? *Leisure Studies, 17*(2), 155–170.

Gibson, H. (1998b). Sport tourism: A critical analysis of research. *Sport Management Review, 1*, 45–76.

Gibson, H. (2004). Moving beyond the "what is and who" of sport tourism and understanding "why." *Journal of Sport Tourism, 9*(3), 247–265.

Gibson, H. (Ed.). (2006). *Sport tourism: Concepts and theories.* London: Routledge.

Gibson, H. (2017). Commentary: Sport tourism and theory and some other developments: Some reflections. *Journal of Sport & Tourism, 21*(2), 153–158.

Gibson, H., & Chang, S., (2012). Cycling in mid and later life: Involvement and benefits sought from a bicycle tour. *Journal of Leisure Research, 44*(1), 23–49.

Gibson, H., Kaplanidou, K., & Kang, S. J., (2012). Small-scale event sport tourism: A case study in sustainable tourism. *Sport Management Review, 15*, 160–170.

Gibson, H., Lamont, M., Kennelly, M., & Buning, R. (2018). Introduction to the special issue Active Sport Tourism. *Journal of Sport & Tourism, 22*(2), 83–91.

Gibson, H., & Mirehie, M. (2018). Sport tourism and feminism. In L. Mansfield, J. Caudwell, B. Wheaton, & R. Watson (Eds.), *The Palgrave handbook of feminisms in sport, leisure and physical education* (pp. 681–697). London: Palgrave Macmillan.

Gibson, H., Walker, M., Thapa, B., Kaplanidou, K., Geldenhuys, S., & Coetzee, W. (2014). Psychic income and social capital among host nation residents: A pre-post analysis of the 2010 FIFA World Cup in South Africa. *Tourism Management, 44*, 113–122.

Gibson, H., Willming, C., & Holdnak, A. (2003). Small-scale event sport tourism: Fans as tourists. *Tourism Management, 24*, 181–190.

Gould, D., & Hijzen, A. (2016, August 16). Growing apart, losing trust? The impact of inequality on social capital. IMF Working Papers. https://www.imf.org/en/Publications/WP/Issues/2016/12/31/Growing-Apart-Losing-Trust-The-Impact-of-Inequality-on-Social-Capital-44197.

Gratton, C., Dobson, N., & Shibli, S. (2000). The economic importance of major sports events: A case study of six events. *Managing Leisure, 5*, 17–28.

Green, B. C. (2001). Leveraging subculture and identity to promote sport events. *Sport Management Review, 4*, 1–19.

Gursoy, D., & Kendall, K. (2006). Hosting mega events: Modeling locals' support. *Annals of Tourism Research, 33*, 603–623.

Hallman, K., Breuer, C., & Kuhnreich, B. (2013). Happiness, pride and elite sporting success: What population segments gain most from national athletic achievements? *Sport Management Review, 16*, 226–235.

Haywood, K. M. (2020). A post COVID-19 future—tourism re-imagined and re-enabled. *Tourism Geographies, 22*, 599–609.

Heere, B., Walker, M., Gibson, H., Thapa, B., Geldenhuys, S., & Coetzee, W. (2014). Questioning the validity of race as a social construct: An examination of race and ethnicity in the "Rainbow Nation." *African Social Science Review, 7*(1), 24–43.

Higham, J. (1999). Commentary: Sport as an avenue of tourism development: An analysis of the positive and negative impacts of sport tourism. *Current Issues in Tourism, 2*, 82–90.

Higham, J., & Hinch, T. (2002). Tourism, sport and seasons: The challenges and potential of overcoming seasonality in the sport and tourism sectors. *Tourism Management, 23*, 175–185.

Hinch, T., & Higham, J. (2001). Sport tourism: A framework for research. *International Journal of Tourism Research, 3*, 45–58.

Hinch, T., Higham, J., & Moyle, B. (2016). Sport tourism and sustainable destinations: Foundations and pathways. *Journal of Sport & Tourism, 20*(3–4) 163–173.

Hinch, T., & Ito, E. (2018). Sustainable sport tourism in Japan. *Tourism Planning & Development, 15*, 96–101.

Hudson, S. (2000). The segmentation of potential tourists: Constraint differences between men and women. *Journal of Travel Research, 38*, 363–368.

Kaplanidou, K., & Gibson, H. (2010). Predicting behavioral intentions of active event sport tourists: The case of a small-scale recurring sports event. *Journal of Sport & Tourism, 15*, 163–179.

Kaplanidou, K., & Vogt, C. (2007). The interrelationship between sport event and destination image and sport tourists' behaviors. *Journal of Sport & Tourism, 12*(3–4), 183–206.

Kavetsos, G., & Szymanski, S. (2010). National well-being and international sports events. *Journal of Economic Psychology, 31*(2), 158–171.

Kelly, D., & Fairley, S. (2018a). The utility of relationships in the creation and maintenance of an event portfolio. *Marketing Intelligence & Planning, 36*(2), 260–275.

Kelly, D., & Fairley, S. (2018b). What about the event? How do tourism leveraging strategies affect small-scale events? *Tourism Management, 64*, 335–345.

Kelly, D., Fairley, S., & O'Brien, D. (2019). It was never ours: Formalised event hosting rights and leverage. *Tourism Management, 73*, 123–133.

Kennelly, M. (2017). "We've never measured it, but it brings in a lot of business": Participatory sport events and tourism. *International Journal of Contemporary Hospitality Management, 29*, 883–899.

Kim, H., Gursoy, D., & Lee, S. (2006). The impact of the 2002 World Cup on South Korea: Comparisons of pre and post games. *Tourism Management, 27*, 86–96.

Knight, C. J., & Holt, N. L. (2013). Strategies used and assistance required to facilitate children's involvement in tennis: Parents' perspectives. *Sport Psychologist, 27*, 281–291.

Labuschagne, P. (2008). The impact of sport on nation building: A critical analysis of South Africa and the 2010 FIFA World Cup. *Africa Insight, 38*(3), 3–14

Lamont, M., Kennelly, M., & Wilson, E. (2012). Competing priorities in constraints in event travel careers. *Tourism Management, 33*, 1068–1079.

Leopkey, B., & Parent, M. M. (2012). Olympic Games legacy: From general benefits to sustainable long-term legacy. *International Journal of the History of Sport, 29*, 924–943.

Maennig, W. (2007). One year later: A reappraisal of the economics of the 2006 Soccer World Cup. *Hamburg Contemporary Economic Discussions, 10*, 1–18. https://papers.ssrn.com/sol3/papers.cfm?abstract_id=1520530

McGehee, N., Yoon, Y., & Cardenas, D., (2003). Involvement and travel for recreational runners in North Carolina. *Journal of Sport Management, 17*, 305–324.

Minnaert, L. (2012). An Olympic legacy for all? The non-infrastructural outcomes of the Olympic Games for socially excluded groups (Atlanta 1996–Beijing 2008). *Tourism Management, 33*, 361–370.

Mirehie, M., & Gibson, H. (2020). The relationship between female snow-sport tourists' travel behaviors and well-being. *Tourism Management Perspectives, 33*(1), 1000613.

Mirehie, M., Gibson, H., Kang, S. J., & Bell, H. (2019). Parental insights from three elite-level youth sports: Implications for family life. *World Leisure Journal, 61*(2), 98–112.

Misener, L., & Mason, D. (2006). Creating community networks: Can sporting events offer meaningful sources of social capital? *Managing Leisure, 11*, 39–56.

Mules, T. (1998). Taxpayer subsidies for major sport events. *Sport Management Review, 1*(1), 25–43.

Mules, T., & Dwyer, L. (2005). Public sector support for sport tourism events: The role of cost-benefit analysis. *Sport in Society, 8*, 338–355.

O'Brien, D., & Chalip, L. (2007). 19 sport events and strategic leveraging: Pushing towards the triple bottom line. In A. G. Woodside & D. Martin (Eds.), *Tourism management: Analysis, behaviour, and strategy* (pp. 318–338). Wallingford, U.K.: CAB International.

Ohmann, S., Jones, I., & Wilkes, K. (2006). The perceived social impacts of the 2006 football World Cup on Munich residents. *Journal of Sport & Tourism, 11*(2), 129–152.

Pearce, P. L. (1988). *The Ulysses factor: Evaluating visitors in tourist settings.* New York: Springer-Verlag.

Prayag, G., Hosany, S., Nunkoo, R., & Alders, T. (2013). London residents' support for the 2012 Olympic Games: The mediating effect of overall attitude. *Tourism Management, 36*, 629–640.

Preuss, H. (2007). The conceptualization and measurement of mega sport event legacies. *Journal of Sport & Tourism, 12*(3–4), 207–228.

Preuss, H. (2015). A framework for identifying the legacies of a mega sport event. *Leisure Studies, 34*(6), 643–664.

Putnam, R. (1995). Bowling alone: America's declining social capital. *Journal of Democracy, 6*, 65–78.

Raggiotto, F., & Scarpi, D. (2020). Living on the edge: Psychological drivers of athletes' intention to re-patronage extreme sporting events. *Sport Management Review, 23*, 229–241.

Ramshaw, G. (2020). *Heritage and sport: An introduction.* Summit, PA: Channel View Publications.

Ramshaw, G., & Gammon, S. (2005). More than just nostalgia? Exploring the heritage/sport tourism nexus. *Journal of Sport Tourism, 10*(4), 229–241.

Redmond, G. (1991). Changing styles of sports tourism: Industry/consumer interactions in Canada, the USA and Europe. In M. Sinclair & M. Stabler (Eds.), *The tourism industry: An international analysis* (pp. 107–120). Wallingford, U.K.: CAB International.

Ryan, C., & Lockyer, T. (2002). Masters' games involvement—the nature of competitors' involvement and requirements. *Event Management, 7*, 259–270.

Schulenkorf, N. (2009). An ex ante framework for the strategic study of social utility of sport events. *Tourism and Hospitality Research, 9*, 120–131.

Schulenkorf, N., Thomson, A., & Schlenker, K. (2011). Intercommunity sport events: Vehicles and catalysts for social capital in divided societies. *Event Management, 15*, 105–119.

Schumacher, D. G. (2015). National Association of Sports Commission's report on the sports travel industry. https://www.sportscommissions.org/Portals/sportscommissions/Documents/About/NASC%20Sport%20Tourism%20Industry%20Report.pdf

Scott, A. K., & Turco, D. (2007). VFRs as a segment of the sport event tourist market. *Journal of Sport Tourism, 12*(1), 41–52.

Shipway, R., & Jones, I. (2007). Running away from home: Understanding visitor experiences and behaviour at sport tourism events. *International Journal of Tourism Research, 9*, 373–383.

Sidhant, W. (2020). Exorbitant costs and minimal benefits: The impacts of hosting the Olympics. *Chicago Policy Review.* https://chicagopolicyreview.org/2020/05/06/exorbitant-costs-and-minimal-benefits-the-impact-of-hosting-the-olympics/.

Smith, M., & Diekmann, A. (2017). Tourism and wellbeing. *Annals of Tourism Research, 66*, 1–13.

Sports ETA. (2019). Sports tourism: State of the industry report (2019). https://www.sportseta.org/research/state-of-the-industry-report

Stebbins, R. (1982). Serious leisure: A conceptual statement. *Pacific Sociological Review, 25*(2), 251–272.

Swart, K., & Bob, U. (2012). Mega sport event legacies and the 2010 FIFA World Cup. *African Journal for Physical Health Education, Recreation and Dance, 18*(Suppl. 2), 1–11.

Taks, M., Chalip, C., Green, C., Kesenne, S., & Martyn, S. (2009). Factors affecting repeat visitation and flow-on tourism as sources of event strategy sustainability. *Journal of Sport & Tourism, 14*(2–3), 121–142.

Tomlinson, A. (2014). Olympic legacies: Recurrent rhetoric and harsh realities. *Contemporary Social Science, 9*, 137–158,

Turco, D. (1998). Travelling and turnovers measuring the economic impacts of a street basketball tournament, *Journal of Sport Tourism, 5*(1), 7–14.

Unruh, D. R. (1979). Characteristics and types of participation in social worlds. *Symbolic Interaction, 2*(2), 115–130.

UN World Tourism Organization. (2020, May 28). Global guidelines to restart tourism. https://www.unwto.org/news/unwto-launches-global-guidelines-to-restart-tourism.

Van Der Merwe, J. (2007). Political analysis of South Africa's hosting of the Rugby and Cricket World Cups: Lessons for the 2010 Football World Cup and beyond? *Politikon, 34*, 67–81.

Venter, Z., Barton, D., Gundersen, V., Figari, H., & Nowell, M. (2020). Urban nature in a time of crisis: Recreational use of green space increases during the Covid-19 outbreak in Oslo, Norway. *Environmental Research Letter.* https://doi.org/10.1088/1748-9326/abb396.

Waitt, G. (2003). Social impacts of the Sydney Olympics. *Annals of Tourism Research, 30*, 194–215.

Whitson, D., & Horne, J. (2006). The Glocal Politics of Sports Mega-Events: Underestimated costs and overestimated benefits? Comparing the outcomes of sports mega-events in Canada and Japan. *The Sociological Review, 54*, 71–89.

Weber, F. (2017). *Tourism destinations under pressure: Challenges and innovative solutions.* Lucerne: Lucerne University of Applied Sciences and Arts.

Weed, M. (2006). Sports tourism research 2000–2004: A systematic review of knowledge and a meta-evaluation of methods. *Journal of Sport & Tourism, 11*(1), 5–30.

Weed, M. (2020). The role of the interface of sport and tourism in the response to the COVID-19 pandemic. *Journal of Sport & Tourism.* doi:10.1080/14775085.2020.1794351.

Weed, M. E., & Bull, C. J. (2004). *Sports tourism: Participants, policy and providers.* Oxford: Elsevier.

Whitson, D., & McIntosh, D. (1993). Becoming a world-class city: Hallmark events and sport franchises. *Sociology of Sport Journal, 10*, 221–240.

Williams, P., & Fidgeon, P. R. (2000). Addressing participation constraint: A case study of potential skiers. *Tourism Management, 21*, 379–393.

Wintergreen Research, Inc. (2019). Youth team, league, and tournament sports: Market shares, strategies, and forecasts, worldwide, 2019 to 2026. https://www.wintergreenresearch.com/.

Ziakas, V. (2010). Understanding an event portfolio: The uncovering of interrelationships, synergies, and leveraging opportunities. *Journal of Policy Research in Tourism, Leisure & Events, 2*(2), 144–164.

Ziakas, V. (2014). Planning and leveraging event portfolios: Towards a holistic theory. *Journal of Hospitality Marketing & Management, 23*(3), 327–356.

Ziakas, V., & Costa, C. (2011). Event portfolios and multi-purpose development: Establishing the conceptual grounds. *Sport Management Review, 14*, 409–423.

PART III

PARTICIPATION AND CULTURES

CHAPTER 20

....

SPORT, HEALTH, AND
WELL-BEING

....

PARISSA SAFAI

AT the risk of stating a cliché, the world is currently in the midst of the most unprecedented public health, social, political, economic, and human rights crisis in human history. According to data from Johns Hopkins University's COVID-19 Dashboard, and at the
time of reviewing this chapter proof (mid-April 2022), over 504 million cases and nearly
6.2 million deaths have occurred around the world as a consequence of COVID-19. These
figures are widely recognized as underestimates of the actual number of cases and deaths
as effective, reliable, and sustained testing in countries around the world has been virtually
absent, at best variable, and highly dependent on trust and cooperation (or lack thereof)
between governments, the medico-scientific community, and the public at large (e.g., see
Balmford, Annan, Hargreaves, Altoè, & Bateman, 2020).

There have been other global pandemics over the course of human history (e.g., the 1918
influenza [H1N1] pandemic). Yet the complexities and complications of the COVID-19 pandemic have proven to be much more pronounced due to a range of factors. For example, the
ease and speed of transmission of SARS-CoV-2 (the virus that causes COVID-19) within
and across regions as well as within and among particular groups of individuals (e.g., the
elderly, Black and Indigenous people of color, those in poverty) has rendered COVID-19
particularly virulent. Another confounding issue is the host of still relatively unknown
factors that shape the epidemiological patterns and clinical presentations of those infected
and suffering with COVID-19. Simply put, despite huge advances in our scientific understanding of the virus and the disease in a relatively short span of time, we still do not know
why some infected individuals are asymptomatic, why some are viral super-spreaders, and
why some are long-haulers and suffer extraordinarily long aftereffects of the disease. And
unlike other pandemics, the impact of COVID-19 has been unmatched given the near complete disruption of heightened and more intensive interdependencies that exist between
populations, cultures, and economies in our contemporary globalized world.

There is no avoiding the metaphoric "elephant in the room" with this chapter—exploring
the relationships between sport, health, and well-being during this time of a global pandemic is, simply put, weird. On one hand, at a time when so many people are sick or dying,
and even more are trying to simply survive lockdowns and isolation, staggering job losses

and economic instability, social unrest and political protest, increased food insecurity, interrupted education, and exponential increases in anxiety, depression, and stress, unpacking the common belief that sport is good for you feels like an exercise (no pun intended) in futility. And yet, on the other hand, there may be no more opportune time to do so, as the profound disruption of our daily lives as a consequence of COVID-19 demands of us to take fuller and more critical stock of the real or imagined sport-health dyad. In so doing, we may open and shift thought and praxis to re-create our beliefs, associations, and practices about sport and health. We may, in fact, take up Arundhati Roy's (2020) call to conceptualize the pandemic as "a portal, a gateway between one world and the next" and as providing the impetus to "break with the past and imagine [our] world anew."

This chapter explores the central questions: Is sport healthy, and can it contribute to well-being? Organized in three parts, the chapter will first examine key conceptual challenges associated with answering this question. For example, what do we mean when we refer to the concepts of sport, health, and well-being? The second section will explore the challenges faced by critical social scientists in disrupting the commonplace notion of sport as good for one's health, and the third section will highlight the wicked questions: Can contemporary sport be good for one's health, and if so, how?

ISSUES

Famous quotes about the healthfulness of sport are plentiful. The ancient Greek physician Hippocrates is credited with saying that "sport is the preserver of health," while American essayist Ralph Waldo Emerson (1883, p. 204) once wrote, "Sport is the bloom and glow of a perfect health." It should be no surprise that famous athletes and sport leaders have oft made a causal link between sport and health. For example, Indian cricketer Kapil Dev enthused, "Apart from education, you need good health, and for that, you need to play sports," and English decathlete Daley Thompson declared, "Sport and health are so important to our nation that they deserve to be right at the front of people's minds" (quoted in Bryant, 2008). And one could be forgiven for thinking that sport is the magical cure for all of humanity's problems when the president of the International Olympic Committee Juan Antonio Samaranch, in his address during the Opening Ceremony of the 1996 Olympic Games, espoused, "Sport is friendship, sport is health, sport is education, sport is life, sport brings the world together."

Such quotes can be easily dismissed as just fodder for motivational posters or inspirational greeting cards. What is of much greater concern, however, is the way such rhetoric is routinely woven into the policies and resource-distributing decisions of national and international governments and public-, private- and third-sector organizations (see the 2016 special issue of the *International Journal of Sport Policy and Politics* on "sport, physical activity and public health" (Mansfield & Piggin, 2016) for a range of national and international examples). Certainly, the website for sportanddev.org (2020), an online platform dedicated to resources and communications on sport and development, is rife with sport-health associations, including such definitive statements as the following:

There is an overwhelming amount of scientific evidence on the positive effects of sport and physical activity as part of a healthy lifestyle. The positive, direct effects of engaging in regular physical activity are particularly apparent in the prevention of several chronic diseases, including: cardiovascular disease, diabetes, cancer, hypertension, obesity, depression and osteoporosis. (para. 1)

And:

Sport and physical activity can make a substantial contribution to the well-being of people in developing countries. Exercise, physical activity and sport have long been used in the treatment and rehabilitation of communicable and non-communicable diseases. Physical activity for individuals is a strong means for the prevention of diseases and for nations is a cost-effective method to improve public health across populations. (para. 5)

In 2003, the United Nations adopted Resolution 58/5, Sport as a Means to Promote Education, Health, Development and Peace, "[noting] that sport and physical education are a major tool not only for health and physical development but also for acquiring values necessary for social cohesion and intercultural dialogue" (para. 8). More recently, and right in the midst of the pandemic, the World Health Organization (2020, para. 1) formalized its partnership with the IOC, signing "an agreement to work to promote health through sport and physical activity." The press release for the partnership hails the WHO-IOC collaboration as especially relevant for the following reason:

The current COVID-19 pandemic is particularly affecting people with noncommunicable diseases (NCDs). The agreement has a special focus on preventing NCDs through sport. Physical activity helps lower blood pressure and reduce the risk of hypertension, coronary heart disease, stroke, diabetes, and various types of cancer (including breast cancer and colon cancer). (para. 3)

Where Dr. Tedros Adhanom Ghebreyesus, WHO's director-general, states that "physical activity is one of the keys to good health and well-being" (World Health Organization, 2020, para. 2), IOC President Thomas Bach notes, "Over the last few months in the current crisis, we have all seen how important sport and physical activity are for physical and mental health. Sport can save lives" (para. 6). He goes further to state, "The IOC calls on the governments of the world to include sport in their post-crisis support programmes because of the important role of sport in the prevention of NCDs, but also of communicable diseases" (para. 6).

Although it is premature to know if or how governments will "include sport in their post-crisis support programmes," current national legislation and sport policies give us insight into existing understandings of the sport-health relationship and suggest the possible (perhaps even likely) directions in which sport systems in pandemic/postpandemic times may head (cf. Misener & Misener, 2016). For example, in Canada, the very first statement in the preamble to the Physical Activity and Sport Act states, "[T]he Government of Canada recognizes that physical activity and sport are integral parts of Canadian culture and society and produce benefits in terms of health, social cohesion, linguistic duality, economic activity, cultural diversity and quality of life" (Government of Canada, 2003, para. 5). The 2012 Canadian Sport Policy (CSP), which operationalizes the Act and was endorsed by federal and provincial-territorial ministers of sport until 2022, frames "improved health and wellness" as a societal outcome of participation in sport: "Canadians participate in sport activities in a manner that strengthens their personal development, provides enjoyment and relaxation, reduces stress, improves physical and mental health, physical fitness and general well-being, and enables them to live more productive and rewarding lives" (Sport Information Resource Center, 2012, p. 4). In addition, and of particular note for this chapter, as will be discussed below, the CSP also draws linkages between sport, personal health, and the economy. "Increased economic development and prosperity" is identified as another societal outcome of sport participation among Canadians, "where sport delivers benefits, for increasing numbers, to individual health and well-being, and contributes to socio-economic outcomes" (p. 5). In sum, the CSP aims to advance a vision of sport whereby "Canadians improve their standard of living and economic well-being through sport; communities benefit from healthier citizens and the reduction of health care costs; and the sport and tourism sectors benefit from legacies of hosting of local, regional, national and international sport events" (p. 4).

For critical sport scholars, red flags with these statements, legislative acts, and policies abound—not just with the loftiness and presumptuousness of these suggested connections between sport and health, but also with the discursive slipperiness embedded in these texts and the implications of such fuzzy definitions for the ways in which material resources are distributed (cf. Piggin, 2020). It has been well recognized by sport scholars that sport is routinely yoked together and used interchangeably with such terms as physical activity, physical literacy, physical education, exercise, fitness, tourism, and play (for example, and not an exhaustive list, Bloyce & Smith, 2009; Coalter, 2007; Green, 2004; Grix & Carmichael, 2012; Malcolm, 2016; Mansfield & Malcolm, 2014; Oliver, Hanson, Lindsey, & Dodd-Reynolds, 2016; Waddington, 2000; Weed, 2016). The challenge in collapsing these terms together is captured well by Safai and Malcolm (2016, p. 159):

> Sport is a physical activity; sport is often used in physical education curricula; it incorporates exercise; and may even involve an element of play. However, this does not mean that sport is the same as physical education, exercise or play. The conflation of sport with physical education, exercise and play obscures its differences in intensity, frequency and duration of participation from other forms of physical activity. We must be cognisant of these differences since the institutionalised, competitive, rigorous and complex nature of sport has markedly different consequences for health than physical education, exercise or play.

To be clear, critical sport scholars do not suggest that organized and competitive sport is completely incapable of being healthful for individuals, groups, or communities. Rather, concerns have been and are being raised about the seemingly wholescale promotion of such *definitive* sport = health statements (i.e., sport is healthful for all, as is implicit in many national "sport for all" programs) that poorly distinguish between and yet still blend together sport, physical activity, physical literacy, physical education, exercise, fitness, tourism, and play in the service of health.

Similar conceptual concerns arise with the terms "health" and "well-being" or "wellness," which are routinely used synonymously and interchangeably in public consciousness and in public or social policy- and program-making circles (alongside "healthcare" and "medicine," which are also often used as though identical to one another) (see Dodge, Daly, Huyton, & Sanders, 2012). There are numerous examples of the tautological quality in definitions of "health" and "well-being." For example, in efforts to move away from the more narrow biomedical understanding of health (as the absence of disease), the World Health Organization's (1948) canonized definition of health situates it as a state of well-being (specifically, "a state of complete physical, mental and social wellbeing and not merely the absence of disease or infirmity"). In the *Oxford English Dictionary*, health is defined in part as "[w]ell-being, welfare, safety; deliverance" ("Health," 2020), and well-being is defined as "the state of being healthy, happy, or prosperous; physical, psychological, or moral welfare" ("Well-being," 2020). It is important to note that even the term "welfare" poses similar challenges as it too is often employed synonymously with health and well-being. In the following, we can see Melanie Lang, editor of the 2021 Routledge Handbook of Athlete Welfare fall back on using these concepts to define each other even though she is attempting to disentangle them from one another (personal communication, March 2018):

> Well-being is a quality or emotional state of being comfortable, healthy, or happy and is linked to being satisfied with a particular thing/aspect of life. Welfare is a broader term that comprises health, safety, happiness, prosperity etc. and that relates to the overall quality of life and concerns about this. As such, well-being is a component of the broader concept of welfare, with well-being being a contributing factor in an individual's overall welfare.

There are not enough pages in this chapter to be able to properly, or perhaps even adequately discuss the attempts to define health and well-being. Scholars from a multitude of disciplinary areas across the range of humanities and natural, medical, and social sciences have dedicated tomes to different interpretations of what is and is not health and well-being (e.g., see Godlee, 2011; Huber et al., 2011; La Placa, McNaught, & Knight, 2013; Larson, 1999; Wiseman & Brasher, 2008). With tongue in cheek, Smith (2008) captures his dissatisfaction with the WHO's unrealistic definition of health as a state of "complete" well-being when he writes, "It's a ludicrous definition that would leave most of us unhealthy most of the time." The key takeaway from this discussion on this confusing state of affairs is that such discursive slipperiness "may set the limits to what it is possible to think, and thus the understandings of the choices that can be made' (Newman, 2005, p. 128) and leaves wide open the opportunity for governing bodies (whether governments, health agencies, sport organizations, or corporations) to manipulate such fuzzy language to suit specific agendas at specific times (Grix & Carmichael, 2012).

The good news for critical sport and health scholars is that more nuanced characterizations of health and well-being are multidimensional (i.e., from the health of our cells to the health of our planet) in conceptualization and much more sensitive to the wider and intersectional determinants of health and the material conditions of social life that constrain or facilitate health and well-being for individuals and groups (cf. Marmot & Wilkinson, 1999; Naci & Ioannidis, 2015; Raphael, Bryant, & Rioux, 2010). For example, the Canadian Index of Wellbeing (2020) defines well-being thus:

> The presence of the highest possible quality of life in its full breadth of expression focused on but not necessarily exclusive to: good living standards, robust health, a sustainable environment, vital communities, an educated populace, balanced time use, high levels of democratic participation, and access to and participation in leisure and culture.

In this example, we can see—via the association to standards of living, the environment, education, and engaged citizenship—well-being (and health) situated as a collective and political issue. These attempts to understand health and well-being as one's capacity to cope, adapt, and manage life (cf. Huber et al., 2011), as helped or hindered by broader social structures and processes, challenge the more individualistic and inward-looking focus of extant definitions as well as the over-/medicalization of social life, which some suggest is stimulated by the pathologization of "incomplete" states of well-being (see Godlee, 2011). In this vein, health and well-being are not limited to lifestyle choices, or the consequences of biological advantage conferred upon someone by their good genes, or even access to good healthcare services. Rather health and well-being are political because they are resources of power that possess dimensions of quality and quantity, they can be shaped by political institutions and interventions (or their lack), they are linked to social relations such that some enjoy more health and well-being than others, and they are elements of our human rights (cf. Bambra, Fox, & Scott-Samuel, 2005). The bad news, however, is that these more diverse, interconnected, multidimensional, and power-sensitive understandings of health and well-being do not necessarily translate into the ways health and well-being—and even sport—are being promoted and lived in the day-to-day. The following section expands on these points.

APPROACHES

Despite the availability of fresher and more refined notions of health and well-being—ones that connect the personal to the communal and to the political—mainstream approaches to the operationalization or enacting of health and well-being (and even sport, as will be discussed below) in our daily lives remain quite entrenched in individualistic ideologies of good health as personal responsibility and as evidence of good moral conduct. This approach is commonly referred to as "healthism" (Crawford, 1980), whereby health is wholly conceived as a product of individual choice and practice, and where such "concepts as willpower, self-discipline and lifestyle operate to define health as a personal trouble rather than public issue" (Safai, Johnson, & Bryans, 2016, p. 271). Poor health is not understood as a result of or even a symptom of systemic or structural disadvantage and inequity between individuals and/or groups, but rather as a product of an individual's inability to be disciplined, hard-working, in control, or to "do the right thing" (Crawford, 1977; Greenhalgh & Wessely, 2004; Howell & Ingham, 2001).

Healthism flourishes within neoliberalism, which is defined in this chapter in the broadest terms possible—from a concretized political economic approach to governance in many nation-states to a governing rationality and "an everyday experience" (Hamann, 2009, p. 39) that cuts across social and cultural dimensions of life. Both healthism and neoliberalism encourage individuals to think and act solely about and through themselves (particularly through their wallets and bank accounts) and encourage the hollowing out of public government and the public sector in the name of fiscal responsibility and/or the need to stimulate and protect business and industry above all (Ingham, 1985). In so doing, healthism (as situated within and buttressing neoliberalism) minimizes a government's capacity to equitably foster and be responsible for the health and well-being of its citizens and, perhaps more profoundly, undermines the belief that the determinants of health and well-being are connected to and derive from social relations and the ways in which power and material resources are distributed (or not) among individuals and/or groups in our communities (Armstrong, Armstrong & Coburn, 2001; Skrabanek, 1994). In a healthist approach to health, it doesn't matter if you vote for or against racist and fascist political regimes in national elections; it matters only that you purchase and use a membership to the fitness club without question (Wiest, Andrews, & Giardina, 2015). And it doesn't matter whether the fitness club and its instructors encourage patrons to ask critical questions about access, privilege, and health inequalities; it matters only that muscles are kept toned and that fat is controlled (see Markula & Chikinda, 2016).

Within the logics of these neoliberal times, well-being is similarly influenced by healthism and its ideology of personal responsibility. Conservative estimates of the global wellness movement suggest it is a multitrillion-dollar industry annually, with devotees paying for such things as detoxifications, juice cleanses, coffee enemas, specialized fitness classes, biometric technologies, silent meditative spa retreats, controlled diets, life coaching, beauty regimes, chakra healing, customized tonics and skin oils, healing crystals, and the list goes on (Global Wellness Institute, 2018). Critics of the modern wellness movement offer scathing assessments of the ways in which false and at times outright dangerous misinformation is peddled to people, especially women, in the pursuit of "health, happiness, and prosperity." Gunter (2018) routinely attacks the wellness-industrial complex for "grifting off desperate women" looking for health information, care, or even just validation of their health concerns, by reproducing long-ingrained patriarchal beliefs that women's bodies are impure, flawed, and in need of help from outside experts (Wiseman, 2019, para. 15). In an editorial that is as much about the rise of anti-intellectualism as it is about the dangers of the cult of wellness, McCartney (2019) similarly notes:

> Of course, the ultimate irony of the wellness industry is that it is aimed at the people least likely to benefit from it. It is not the well-off people with gym memberships, fitness trackers and a regular Whole Foods habit who are most likely to die young. It is the people whose social disadvantage make it more likely that they will smoke, to suffer more of the adverse consequences of alcohol, who have less access to green spaces to exercise, have jobs with less control and often more stress. It is citizens who are most wealthy, and healthy, who are invited to spend their money on accumulating interventions that don't work. Yet they can paradoxically be harmed and easily become anxious patients as they accumulate the side effects of too much medicine. Marketing and advertising can make people into patients unnecessarily, while people who really could benefit from becoming a patient are left with less resource to do so. This paradox makes everyone sicker.

The cult of wellness implies that people can make their own "health, happiness, and prosperity" if only they believe enough and buy enough—an approach that seamlessly dovetails with consumer capitalism and neoliberalism. Healthism deflects attention away from the health-compromising determinants of social life that are often beyond the control of the average individual to focus only on seeing the world through rose-tinted glasses or a "pull yourself up by the bootstraps" mentality (Tirado, 2015). In her exploration of the dangers of relentlessly pushing people to think, feel, and act optimism and happiness, Ehrenreich (2009, p. 8) writes:

> [P]ositive thinking has made itself useful as an apology for the crueler aspects of the market economy. If optimism is the key to material success, and if you can achieve an optimistic outlook through the discipline of positive thinking, then there is no excuse for failure. The flip

side of positivity is thus a harsh insistence on personal responsibility: if your business fails or your job is eliminated, it must be because you didn't try hard enough, didn't believe firmly enough in the inevitability of your success.

For example, the rise of precarious labor markets and the gig economy results in many workers not being able to enjoy health and dental benefits that accompany stable, permanent, and full-time jobs—let alone enough disposable income or free time to pursue sport or any form of physical activity. This holds dangerous consequences in the event of illness or injury for many individuals and communities, and yet there is seemingly little critical or sustained attention paid to this issue in the public sector as governments shift toward new public management and the embrace of an entrepreneurial ethos (Connell, Fawcett & Meagher, 2009; Diefenbach, 2009; McSweeney & Safai, 2020; Vosko, 2006). In other words, the answer to addressing the precarity of the contemporary job market is not in enacting and enforcing labor policies and workplace legislation that ensures material and health stability for workers but, rather, encouraging workers to work harder and to persevere. As Bambra, Smith, Garthwaite, Joyce, and Hunter (2011, p. 403) note, however, such approaches and such policies "attempt to tackle health inequalities by trying to 'empower' people or encouraging them to feel happier, more confident or more responsible, without necessarily addressing the key, underlying issue."

Sport is implicated in the promotion of this ideology of personal responsibility as it is most typically posed as a lifestyle choice that morally good people should adopt. In large part, the weaving of sport in healthist doctrine is facilitated by the easy conflation of physical activity, physical literacy, physical education, exercise, fitness, tourism, and such with sport. As noted earlier, the blurring of sport with any and all forms of physical culture renders sport, as one specific form of physical culture and as one area of social or public policy, amenable to manipulation by those who want to fit it into their agendas—including those who are trying to advance or reinforce neoliberal, healthist agendas. Mansfield (2016, p. 714) makes this point clear when she states, "Sport can also be thought of as a relatively cheap and malleable policy tool which helps to explain its continued appeal as a simple solution to complex, deeper-seated social problems like health inequalities." Yet, just as it is problematic to equate sport to physical activity, play, exercise, and so on, it is bizarre to suggest that sports participation will adequately address or redress serious personal and/ or social health issues. If we set aside COVID-19 for a moment, the top causes of death globally are chronic conditions (e.g., diabetes, cancers, malnutrition, heart disease) that are multifactorial in causation and treatment (Roser & Ritchie, 2016). Proponents of the social determinants of health (SDOH) paradigm know that there is no way that playing rugby can solve such conditions. Rather, critical sport and health scholars urge attention to the cleanliness of the air in which the rugby pitch is located, to the aesthetic appeal to and safety of green spaces for local citizens, to the accessibility of public transit to get a player to and from practice, and to the stability and sensitivity of the job market so that people can eat regularly, live in a safe home, and have time to play football.

Furthermore, as many critical sport sociologists note, conflating physical activity, physical education, exercise, fitness, and so on with sport results in everything getting operationalized as sport, with its heightened focus on performance and competition (e.g., Green, 2007; Kirk, 2010; Murphy & Bauman, 2007; Ressler, Richards, & Wright, 2016). Critical sport scholars have long known that the performance principle and the culture of risk (i.e., a culture that produces and reproduces the tolerance of health-compromising beliefs, behaviors, and practices) that underpin organized, competitive sport often endanger good health (see the chapter in this volume by Dominic Malcolm and Emma Pullen for a fuller discussion). The potential public health benefits that may be seen from getting individuals and communities engaged at some level of active living or physical activity more broadly (i.e., not in just organized, competitive sport) get taken up in extraordinarily functionalist ways. There is no shortage of dose-response studies that attempt to ascertain how many minutes of physical activity at what level of intensity and frequency are needed for some beneficial physiological effect on the body. Indeed, in the Canadian context, guidelines from the Canadian Society for Exercise Physiology (n.d.) on movement, sleep, and screen time dominate public health messaging. Parents are repeatedly told that their children should be getting at least 60 minutes of moderate to vigorous physical activity each day and that they themselves should be logging at least 150 minutes of moderate to vigorous physical activity each week!

My intent is not to suggest that these guidelines are inappropriate or lacking in scientific rigor or credibility, or even that sport cannot be healthful for individuals and communities. Rather, I want to draw attention to how unquestioningly sport, organized in the narrow terms of performance and competition, gets taken up as healthful for all, as well as how broader physical activity guidelines are reductive and disconnected from well-established and long-standing insights on the impact of the material conditions of life on health (Kay, 2016). In the guidelines from the Canadian Society for Exercise Physiology, which seem to have a remarkably sticky and enduring quality given how long and how well they have been taken up by all levels of Canadian government and in the public sector more broadly (cf. Bercovitz, 2000), it is the number of minutes one sleeps, watches a screen, and moves that seem to matter the most. Absent in these guidelines is the fact that the minutes in our days are contained and structured by broader social, cultural, political, and economic institutions, forces, and processes that operate to the advantage of some more than others. More critical relational analyses that foreground power between individuals and groups need to be layered into these prescriptive guidelines, and to this end, there must be more engagement with and input from critical sport and health scholars who advance an SDOH approach to the study and operationalization of sport, health, and well-being in the service of public/population health. Kay (2016, p. 555) states:

> Social scientists within the academic sport science community can help bridge this chasm, by contributing social scientific theories, methodologies and knowledge to this area. Such offers must be constructive: to dismiss health behaviourists as not addressing "context" is not adequate, when their theoretical frameworks do; to argue that they do not address it "properly" is not sufficient without elucidation and to elucidate by only offering grand theory is not only unhelpful but actively counterproductive, reinforcing the notion that "social influences" exist only as some abstraction that is beyond translation into practice. Tangible specifics are required to demonstrate how social science knowledge can enhance understanding of health behaviour and efforts to enhance it.

Kay's words are prescient, but calling on just the "academic sport science community" to mobilize is limiting. Advancing the critical sociocultural study of sport, health, and well-being so as to make a difference in public-sector guidelines, policies, and programs is about advancing a "relevant and engaged" public sociology of sport that can contribute to "the terms of the debate," not just by adding to the body of knowledge, but also by having researchers who specifically draw the connections between their work and the larger debates and problems, and by seeking ways to engage various publics when disseminating that research. (Donnelly, 2015, p. 422; see also Bairner, 2009; Cooky, 2017; Ingham & Donnelly, 1990)

This represents a prime, albeit challenging opportunity for critical sport and health scholars. It is one, however, that is certainly not supported by the functionalist, positivist, and managerial paradigms of the moving body and classic and healthist health promotion prescriptions that dominate the research and teaching agendas of many (if not most) kinesiology departments in higher education—departments where more critical social, cultural, and historical interrogations of sport, health, and well-being are increasingly being pushed to the wayside (Safai, 2016; see Andrews, Silk, Francombe, & Bush, 2013).

DEBATES

This section will explore the questions: Can sport be good for one's health, and if so, how? Such questions "exhibit the characteristics of 'wicked problems,' in that they are difficult to define/interpret, are based in competing/uncertain causes, and generate further issues when solutions are applied" (Sam, 2009, p. 499). It is important to note that any attempts I offer here to answer these questions must begin with my own admission that I like sport, as do most (if not all) sport sociologists, even those who engage a critical standpoint. I think it is safe for me to suggest, on behalf of the wider sociology of the sport community, that we are not "anti-sport" as much as we are uncomfortable with and resistant to the current ways in which the sport system—from grassroots to the highest levels of national and international competition—is predominantly structured, organized, and delivered. We are extraordinarily concerned by how the mainstream sport agenda is set in ways that do not adequately attend to remediating the conditions that make sport inaccessible or unhealthy for some individuals and groups, or that do not legitimately develop or sustain humane and healthy sport for all.

In some cases, it is blatantly clear why the "sport is healthful for all people all the time" message is misleadingly and inappropriately trotted out by individuals and groups. When former FIFA president Sepp Blatter is the first author of a peer-reviewed paper in the *Scandinavian Journal of Medicine & Science in Sports* titled "Football for Health—Science Proves That Playing Football on a Regular Basis Contributes to the Improvement of Public Health" (Blatter & Dvorak, 2014), we know that the unspoken yet obvious agenda of the piece is to promote FIFA and its version of football, not public health. For critical sport and health scholars, it is not that football holds no potential to contribute to the improvement of public health but that corrupt sport leaders such as Blatter, and the sport governing bodies and governments that have been shown to be in cahoots with these criminals, fail to safeguard the health and lives of people around the world (Jennings, 2011; Masters, 2015). The deaths of numerous migrant construction workers involved in the building of venues for the Qatar FIFA World Cup scheduled for 2022—the exact number of which still remains shrouded in mystery to this day, but ranging anywhere from 34 to over 1,200 depending on the source (Gibson & Pattison, 2014; Ingraham, 2015; Pattison, 2020)—negate any "proof" of football's ability to contribute to public health as public health is far more dependent upon sound and enforced labor laws, occupational health regulations, workplace safety standards, and labor reform when needed than on playing a game of football or hosting a sporting mega-event.

The Blatter example is admittedly sensational, but questioning how sport-health agendas get set is vital for our better understanding of if and how sport can be good for one's health. As noted earlier, functionalist, positivist, and managerial approaches dominate much of government and public-sector discourse on sport and health. Such approaches endure not because of nefarious backroom wheeling and dealing between, for example, exercise physiologists and policymakers, but because of such factors as the capacity for individuals and groups to define key issues and put forth persuasive "evidence" that supports their definitions in ways that capture and hold the attention and support of key government actors; the presence and strength of advocacy coalitions and their successful (or not) lobbying of government decision-makers; the opening of "policy windows" amid welcoming political environments; or even just the heightened capacity of some individuals and groups to take advantage of circumstantial geopolitical or economic opportunities to advance their vision of the "ways things should be" (Bundon & Hurd-Clarke, 2015; Green, 2004, 2007; Green & Houlihan, 2004; Milton & Grix, 2015; Mansfield, 2017; Misener & Misener, 2016; Weiss, 1989).

A prime example of the way such factors play out in the setting of sport-health agendas is close to home for me, as colleagues from my own academic department were recruited by a coalition of the Canadian Off-Highway Vehicle Distributors Council, the All Terrain Quad Council of Canada, the Motorcyclists Confederation of Canada, and the Government of Nova Scotia to determine if riding all-terrain vehicles (ATVs) and off-road machines (ORMs) offered fitness and health benefits to participants. The research team found that "off-road riding was found to impose a true physiological demand that would be expected to have beneficial effects on health and fitness according to current [physical activity] recommendations" and that the "metabolic demand of off-road riding is at an intensity level associated with health and fitness benefits in accord with the guidelines of both Health Canada and the [American College of Sports Medicine]" (Burr, Jamnik, Shaw, & Gledhill, 2010, pp. 1350, 1353). The authors conclude:

> [O]ff-road vehicle riding is similar in aerobic demand to many other recreational, self-paced, sporting activities such as golf, rock climbing, and alpine skiing. This examination of off-road vehicle riding is valuable for understanding the physical demands of this alternative mode of recreational [physical activity] in the context of potential health-related fitness outcomes. (p. 1353)

And in yet another publication, the authors suggest that ATV and off-road riding may even positively influence one's sense of well-being:

> [I]t is possible that the higher levels of vitality, general happiness and [quality of life] of recreational off-road vehicle riders is a consequence of participation in the sport and thus further research is warranted to determine if this type of alternative activity should be recognized as a means to increase the health and [quality of life] of Canadians. (Burr, Jamnik, & Gledhill, 2010, p. 10)

Not surprisingly, these findings have also been challenged (see Bissix, MacCormick, & Milburn, 2013), but, also not surprisingly, these types of findings have been welcomed and robustly taken up by proponents of ATV and ORM riding as *the evidence* that such activities boost health and as *the evidence* that such activities should be supported more by government through, at minimum, the establishment of more trails for ATV and ORM use. However, more critical sociocultural readings of the setting of the pro-ATV/ORM agenda highlight a range of issues that rub against the supposed fitness and health benefits, including the exclusionary nature of off-road riding (in general, riders tend to be middle- to upper-class men), injury concerns arising from off-road riding accidents and traumas (especially among youth riders), and risks to the environment (e.g., see Muller, 2016).

This example highlights the point that we must acknowledge, *a priori*: that the question "Can sport be good for one's health and, if so, how?" can be answered only when we have a clear understanding of who is posing the question and what agenda they hope to advance. In his exploration of the Kieran Pathways Society, a human-powered active transportation (i.e., walking, cycling, skiing, canoeing, using a wheelchair, etc.) group in Nova Scotia struggling to advance the development of trails/corridors that exclude motorized vehicles and to push back against their provincial government's collaborations with off-highway vehicle groups, Pitter (2009, p. 347, emphasis added) states:

> The dynamics surrounding the production and consumption of space in this case study illustrate how the state, civil society, and commercial institutions play various roles in the creation of recreational sport spaces. The commercial manufacturers and distributors of [off-highway vehicles] have played a significant role through corporate funding/sponsorship. Their influence appears to have been greatest through their collective actions via the Canadian Off-Highway Vehicle Distributors Council that works to legitimize the sport through various public relation initiatives *and research*.

The movement (if we can call it that) promoting ATV riding for health highlights the breadth and depth of the lobbying and persuasive efforts of specific stakeholders—who tap into and call upon particular forms of sport science and scientific evidence that favor their interests—on governments that, in the context of public roadways and community trails, "have an implicit duty of care to manage risks prudently to reduce harm, and to mitigate financial and reputational impairment to its corporate body" (Bissix, 2015, p. 346). The wicked problem permeating the question "Can sport be good for one's health, and if so, how?" arises, in part, from how such concepts as sport, health, well-being, risk, and harm get defined and whose definition gets understood as most legitimate; these are problems of power and social relations. As such, and continuing in the context of leisure and recreation, Tink, Peers, Nykiforuk, and Mayan's (2019, pp. 454–455) observations are particularly poignant:

> Paying attention to the ways expert discourses of science, medicine, and public health have supported, and continue to support, various forms of institutionalized governance, conversations between philosophers and practitioners of leisure and recreation could begin by interrogating the relationship between the governors and the governed. That is, philosophers and practitioners of leisure and recreation could interrogate how particular knowledge(s) and power relations have resulted in recreation spaces being oriented toward certain bodies or subjects.

For many critical sociologists, sport, health, and well-being are issues of equity, related more to access and opportunity than to measures of performance, biological processes, or lifestyle choice. In this line of argument, sport can be healthy for individuals and communities only if the social, cultural, political, and economic conditions necessary for personal and community health have been met. As such, any sport program that is disconnected from the social and material conditions of life and one's political right to health has limited potential to positively influence health and well-being (cf. Safai, Johnson, & Bryans, 2016). Take for example, one of Sport Canada's recent initiatives to increase sport participation among girls and women, LGBTQ2+ identifying individuals and groups, persons with disabilities, and newcomers to Canada: the Sport Support Program—Innovation Initiative (SSP-II). Fully embracing an entrepreneurial ethos, the SSP-II provides financial support to individuals or organizations for the development and testing of "innovative quality sport approaches in order to develop evidence-based solutions to improve sport participation" (Government of Canada, 2019, para. 5). This attempt to improve sport participation for these commonly underrepresented groups is commendable, but as McSweeney and Safai (2020, p. 12) note, the federal government's turn to public entrepreneurship (PE) and new public management (NPM) to advance accessibility in sport is problematic for Canadians:

> NPM and PE, as embedded in and reproductive of neoliberalism, assume that all individuals are equally motivated and have equal opportunity and means with which to navigate through and be successful in society while, at the same time, hollowing out the very public supports and services that ensure some degree of safety for those who struggle to survive or thrive in neoliberal regimes.

The SSP-II's focus on girls and women is particularly worrisome given that it attempts to employ tactics that are informed by neoliberal and market-centric modes of thinking in efforts to address the consequences of problems very much created by a neoliberal and market-centric political economy:

> The SSP-II may encourage initiatives to boost girls' and women's participation in sport, but it does [so] in a political economic system that continues to depend upon the unpaid labour of girls and women outside of the formal economy, and the inequitable social relations that arise from this arrangement. (McSweeney & Safai, 2020, p. 14)

Just knowing and stating that these paradoxes exist is insufficient for critical sport and health scholars. In this vein, let us heed Kay's (2016) call to better translate and communicate our perspectives and our evidence to the relevant decision-making bodies and to the public at large. In so doing, we move forward our research and advocacy for accessible, equitable, humane, and healthy sport for all outside of "a Phantom Zone of irrelevance," "divorced from everyday public policy activity, media discourse and public awareness" (Raphael, 2009, p. 193).

CONCLUSION

In this chapter, I have endeavored to unsettle the commonplace notion that sport is good for one's health and well-being all the time by examining key conceptual challenges embedded in the associations made between sport and health, by exploring the challenges faced by critical social scientists in disrupting this widely held belief, and by questioning whether contemporary sport can be good for one's health and, if so, how? I prefaced this work, however, by acknowledging the surreal feel of writing about sport and health amid the unprecedented and most consequential global health crisis of our times. This concluding section returns to the issue of COVID-19 as there can be no doubt that the pandemic will impact and set the sport and health research agenda for years to come. In fact, it takes but a fraction of a second on any good search engine to see that it already has. Special issues in top-tier journals are in the process of being crafted, edited book collections are being proposed, virtual colloquia are being dedicated to the topic, and calls on what should be the focus for critical sport sociologists are already being offered (e.g., Evans et al., 2020).

In the critical sociocultural study of sport scholarship, researchers from all over the world are already actively interrogating the ways in which people, communities, organizations, and government have been impacted by and are responding to COVID-19 in sport, specifically, and in social life more broadly. Researchers are making plain both (1) the ways in which the pandemic and the response to the pandemic contribute to the continued (if not amplified or accelerated) marginalization and disempowerment of already vulnerable groups and communities that, de facto, disproportionately suffer higher levels of illness and death (e.g., Malcolm & Velija, 2020) and (2) the ways in which people—especially athletes—are mobilizing together against irresponsible governing bodies that value their own vested interests over human lives. In describing the ways in which Canadian Olympic athletes banded together in the early months of the pandemic to push back against the IOC's indecision about postponing the Tokyo Olympic Games, Donnelly (2020, p. 39) states, "We all hope that the pandemic is creating the possibility of new alternatives for societies, for a new social contract. And we hope that athletes' voices have now been released from the culture of control to continue their demands for fairness, equity, and human and labour rights" (see also Mann, Clift, Boykoff, & Bekker, 2020).

COVID-19 has forced many people to step out of their taken-for-granted routines and to critically examine—from a "social distance"—those sport norms, behaviors, and practices that were commonly accepted without question. Rowe (2020, p. 7) explains:

> [I]t is in the general interest for sport to resume service. But that does not mean repeating its mistakes—as in other areas of social life, the pandemic provided an opportunity for reflection. If sport is, as so many have loudly proclaimed, a vital part of social life, then it must bend to the will of the social, not override it.

Sport and health scholars play a vital role here. "Creating the possibility of new alternatives for societies" requires information, advocacy, and action from vocal and engaged critical sport and health scholars committed to offering and insisting upon conceptual clarity; advancing health paradigms sensitive to the wider social, political, and economic determinants of health; recognizing health as a political right of all people; and working with and through government and public sector policy circles. Rowe (2020, p. 7) writes, "It is unlikely that sport after the pandemic will be transformed, but it will certainly be changed." At the risk of stating the obvious, we must do all that we can to ensure that it will change for the better of all.

References

Andrews, D. L., Silk, M., Francombe, J., & Bush, A. (2013). McKinesiology. *Review of Education, Pedagogy, and Cultural Studies, 35*(5), 335–356.

Armstrong, P., Armstrong, H., & Coburn, D. (Eds.). (2001). *Unhealthy times: Political economy perspectives on health and care in Canada.* Toronto: Oxford University Press.

Bairner, A. (2009). Sport, intellectuals and public sociology: Obstacles and opportunities. *International Review for the Sociology of Sport, 44*(2–3), 115–130.

Balmford, B., Annan, J. D., Hargreaves, J. C., Altoè, M., & Bateman, I. J. (2020). Cross-country comparisons of Covid-19: Policy, politics and the price of life. *Environmental and Resource Economics, 76*(4), 525–551.

Bambra, C., Fox, D., & Scott-Samuel, A. (2005). Towards a politics of health. *Health Promotion International, 20*(2), 187–193.

Bambra, C., Smith, K. E., Garthwaite, K., Joyce, K. E., & Hunter, D. J. (2011). A labour of Sisyphus? Public policy and health inequalities research from the Black and Acheson Reports to the Marmot Review. *Journal of Epidemiology & Community Health, 65*(5), 399–406.

Bercovitz, K. L. (2000). A critical analysis of Canada's "Active Living": Science or politics? *Critical Public Health, 10*(1), 19–39.

Bissix, G. (2015). A multidimensional framework for assessing the acceptability of recreational all-terrain vehicle access on community trails and local public highways. *Leisure/Loisir, 39*(3–4), 345–359.

Bissix, G., MacCormick, K., & Milburn, C. (2013). Is this the new smoking? An expert panel review of the York University OHV health benefits study. *Journal of Health Promotion International, 28*(1), 133–143. doi:10.1093/heapro/dar099.

Blatter, J. S., & Dvorak, J. (2014). Football for health—science proves that playing football on a regular basis contributes to the improvement of public health. *Scandinavian Journal of Medicine & Science in Sports, 24*(Suppl. 1), 2–3. https://doi.org/10.1111/sms.12270.

Bloyce, D., & Smith, A. (2009). *Sport policy and development: An introduction.* London: Routledge.

Bryant, T. (2008, July 14). Daley Thomson interview: The full transcript. *The Guardian.* https://www.theguardian.com/sport/2008/jul/14/olympicgames2008.athletics7.

Bundon, A., & Hurd Clarke, L. (2015). Honey or vinegar? Athletes with disabilities discuss strategies for advocacy within the Paralympic movement. *Journal of Sport and Social Issues, 39*(5), 351–370.

Burr, J. F., Jamnik, V. K., & Gledhill, N. (2010). Health related quality of life of off-road vehicle riders. *Health & Fitness Journal of Canada, 3*(1), 4–11. https://doi.org/10.14288/hfjc.v3l1.50.

Burr, J. F., Jamnik, V. K., Shaw, J. A., & Gledhill, N. (2010). Physiological demands of off-road vehicle riding. *Medicine & Science in Sports & Exercise, 42*(7), 1345–1354.

Canadian Index of Wellbeing. (2020). What is wellbeing? https://uwaterloo.ca/canadian-index-wellbeing/what-wellbeing.

Canadian Society for Exercise Physiology. (n.d.). 24-hour movement guidelines. https://cseguidelines.ca/.

Coalter, F. (2007). London Olympics 2012: The catalyst that inspires people to lead more active lives? *Perspectives in Public Health, 127*(3), 109–110.

Connell, R., Fawcett, B., & Meagher, G. (2009). Neoliberalism, new public management and the human service professions: Introduction to the special issue. *Journal of Sociology, 45*(4), 331–338.

Cooky, C. (2017). "We cannot stand idly by": A necessary call for a public sociology of sport. *Sociology of Sport Journal, 34*(1), 1–11.

Crawford, R. (1977). You are dangerous to your health: The ideology and politics of victim blaming. *International Journal of Health Services, 7*(4), 663–680.

Crawford, R. (1980). Healthism and the medicalization of everyday life. *International Journal of Health Services, 10*(3), 365–388.

Diefenbach, T. (2009). New public management in public sector organizations: The dark sides of managerialistic "enlightenment." *Public Administration, 87*(4), 892–909.

Dodge, R., Daly, A., Huyton, J., & Sanders, L. (2012). The challenge of defining wellbeing. *International Journal of Wellbeing, 2*(3), 222–235.

Donnelly, P. (2015). Assessing the sociology of sport: On public sociology of sport and research that makes a difference. *International Review for the Sociology of Sport, 50*(4–5), 419–423.

Donnelly, P. (2020). We are the games: The COVID-19 pandemic and athletes' voices. *Sociología del Deporte, 1*(1), 35–40. https://doi.org/10.46661/socioldeporte.5011.

Ehrenreich, B. (2009). *Bright-sided: How positive thinking is undermining America.* New York: Metropolitan Books.

Emerson, R. W. (1883). *Essays: First series.* Boston: Houghton, Mifflin.

Evans, A. B., Blackwell, J., Dolan, P., Fahlén, J., Hoekman, R., Lenneis, V., McNarry, G., Smith, M., & Wilcock, L. (2020). Sport in the face of the COVID-19 pandemic: Towards an agenda for research in the sociology of sport. *European Journal for Sport and Society, 17*(2), 85–95. doi:10.1080/16138171.2020.1765100.

Gibson, O., & Pattison, P. (2014, December 23). Death toll among Qatar's 2022 World Cup workers revealed. *The Guardian.* https://www.theguardian.com/world/2014/dec/23/qatar-nepal-workers-world-cup-2022-death-toll-doha.

Global Wellness Institute. (2018). Wellness now a $4.2 trillion global industry—with 12.8% growth from 2015–2017. https://globalwellnessinstitute.org/press-room/press-releases/wellness-now-a-4-2-trillion-global-industry/.

Godlee, F. (2011). What is health? *British Medical Journal, 343,* d4817. doi:10.1136/bmj.d4817.

Government of Canada. (2019). Sport Support Program. https://www.canada.ca/en/canadian-heritage/services/funding/sport-support.html.

Government of Canada. (2003). Physical Activity and Sport Act. Bill C-12: An act to promote physical activity and sport, S.C., c. 2. https://laws-lois.justice.gc.ca/PDF/2003_2.pdf.

Green, M. (2004). Changing policy priorities for sport in England: The emergence of elite sport development as a key policy concern. *Leisure Studies, 23*(4), 365–385.

Green, M. (2007). Olympic glory or grassroots development? Sport policy priorities in Australia, Canada and the United Kingdom, 1960–2006. *International Journal of the History of Sport, 24*(7), 921–953.

Green, M., & Houlihan, B. (2004). Advocacy coalitions and elite sport policy change in Canada and the United Kingdom. *International Review for the Sociology of Sport, 39*(4), 387–403.

Greenhalgh, T., & Wessely, S. (2004). "Health for me": A sociocultural analysis of healthism in the middle classes. *British Medical Bulletin, 69,* 197–213.

Grix, J., & Carmichael, F. (2012). Why do governments invest in elite sport? A polemic. *International Journal of Sport Policy and Politics, 4*(1), 73–90.

Gunter, J. (2018, August 1). Worshipping the false idols of wellness. *New York Times*. https://www.nytimes.com/2018/08/01/style/wellness-industrial-complex.html.

Hamann, T. H. (2009). Neoliberalism, governmentality, and ethics. *Foucault Studies*, 6(1), 37–59.

Health. (2020). *Oxford English Dictionary*. https://www-oed-com.ezproxy.library.yorku.ca/view/Entry/85020?rskey=tUfgDI&result=1&isAdvanced=false#eid.

Howell, J., & Ingham, A. (2001). From social problem to personal issue: The language of lifestyle. *Cultural Studies*, 15(4), 326–351.

Huber, M., Knottnerus, J. A., Green, L., van der Horst, H., Jadad, A. R., Kromhout, D., . . . Smid, H. (2011). How should we define health?. *BMJ (Clinical Research)*, 343, d4163. https://doi.org/10.1136/bmj.d4163.

Ingham, A. (1985). From public issue to personal trouble: Well-being and the fiscal crisis of the state. *Sociology of Sport Journal*, 2(1), 43–55.

Ingham, A. G., & Donnelly, P. (1990). Whose knowledge counts? The production of knowledge and issues of application in the sociology of sport. *Sociology of Sport Journal*, 7(1), 58–65.

Ingraham, C. (2015, May 27). The toll of human casualties in Qatar. *Washington Post*. https://www.washingtonpost.com/news/wonk/wp/2015/05/27/a-body-count-in-qatar-illustrates-the-consequences-of-fifa-corruption/?arc404=true.

Jennings, A. (2011). Investigating corruption in corporate sport: The IOC and FIFA. *International Review for the Sociology of Sport*, 46(4), 387–398.

Johns Hopkins University. (2020). Coronavirus disease dashboard. https://gisanddata.maps.arcgis.com/apps/opsdashboard/index.html#/bda7594740fd40299423467b48e9ecf6.

Kay, T. (2016). Bodies of knowledge: Connecting the evidence bases on physical activity and health inequalities. *International Journal of Sport Policy and Politics*, 8(4), 539–557.

Kirk, D. (2010). *Physical education futures*. London: Routledge.

La Placa, V., McNaught, A., & Knight, A. (2013). Discourse on wellbeing in research and practice. *International Journal of Wellbeing*, 3(1), 116–125.

Lang, M. (Ed.) (2021). *Routledge Handbook of Athlete Welfare*. Oxon: Routledge.

Larson, J. S. (1999). The conceptualization of health. *Medical Care Research and Review*, 56(2), 123–136.

Malcolm, D. (2016). *Sport, medicine and health: The medicalization of sport?* London: Routledge.

Malcolm, D., & Velija, P. (2020). COVID-19, exercise and bodily self-control. *Sociología del Deporte*, 1(1), 29–34. https://doi.org/10.46661/socioldeporte.5011.

Mann, R. H., Clift, B. C., Boykoff, J., & Bekker, S. (2020). Athletes as community; athletes in community: Covid-19, sporting mega-events and athlete health protection. *British Journal of Sports Medicine*, 54(18), 1071–1072.

Mansfield, L. (2016). Resourcefulness, reciprocity and reflexivity: The three Rs of partnership in sport for public health research. *International Journal of Sport Policy and Politics*, 8(4), 713–729.

Mansfield, L. (2017). The imperative of physical activity in public health policy and practice. In J. Piggin, L. Mansfield, & M. Weed (Eds.), *Routledge handbook of physical activity policy and practice* (pp. 79–91). London: Routledge.

Mansfield, L., & Malcolm, D. (2014). The Olympic movement, sport and health. In J. Baker, P. Safai, & J. Fraser-Thomas (Eds.), *Health and elite sport: Is high performance sport a healthy pursuit?* (pp. 187–203). London: Routledge.

Mansfield, L., & Piggin, J. (Eds.). (2016). Sport, physical activity and public health. *International Journal of Sport Policy and Politics*, 8(4), 533–748.

Markula, P., & Chikinda, J. (2016). Group fitness instructors as local level health promoters: A Foucauldian analysis of the politics of health/fitness dynamic. *International Journal of Sport Policy and Politics, 8*(4), 625–646.

Marmot, M., & Wilkinson, R. G. (1999). *Social determinants of health.* Oxford: Oxford University Press.

Masters, A. (2015). Corruption in sport: From the playing field to the field of policy. *Policy and Society, 34*(2), 111–123.

McCartney, M. (2019, January 4). Don't fall prey to the cult of wellness. *The Globe and Mail.* https://www.theglobeandmail.com/opinion/article-dont-fall-prey-to-the-cult-of-wellness/.

McSweeney, M., & Safai, P. (2020). Innovating Canadian sport policy: Towards new public management and public entrepreneurship? *International Journal of Sport Policy and Politics.* https://doi.org/10.1080/19406940.2020.1775678.

Milton, K., & Grix, J. (2015). Public health policy and walking in England—analysis of the 2008 "policy window." *BMC Public Health, 15*(1), 1–9. https://doi.org/10.1186/s12 889-015-1915-y.

Misener, L., & Misener, K. E. (2016). Examining the integration of sport and health promotion: Partnership or paradox? *International Journal of Sport Policy and Politics, 8*(4), 695–712.

Muller, B. (2016). Mending man's ways: Wickedness, complexity and off-road travel. *Landscape and Urban Planning, 154,* 93–101.

Murphy, N. M., & Bauman, A. (2007). Mass sporting and physical activity events: Are they bread and circuses or public health interventions to increase population levels of physical activity? *Journal of Physical Activity and Health, 4*(2), 193–202.

Naci, H., & Ioannidis, J. P. A. (2015). Evaluation of wellness determinants and interventions by citizen scientists. *Journal of the American Medical Association, 314*(2), 121–122.

Newman, J. (2005). Participative governance and the remaking of the public sphere. In J. Newman (Ed.), *Remaking governance: Peoples, politics and the public sphere* (pp. 119–138). Bristol, U.K.: Policy Press.

Oliver, E. J., Hanson, C. L., Lindsey, I. A., & Dodd-Reynolds, C. J. (2016). Exercise on referral: Evidence and complexity at the nexus of public health and sport policy. *International Journal of Sport Policy and Politics, 8*(4), 731–736.

Pattison, P. (2020, March 16). Qatar World Cup: Report reveals 34 stadium worker deaths in six years. *The Guardian.* https://www.theguardian.com/global-development/2020/mar/16/qatar-world-cup-report-reveals-34-stadium-worker-deaths-in-six-years.

Piggin, J. (2020). What is physical activity? A holistic definition for teachers, researchers and policy makers. *Frontiers in Sports and Active Living, 2*(72), 1–7. doi:10.3389/fspor.2020.00072.

Pitter, R. (2009). Finding the Kieran way: Recreational sport, health, and environmental policy in Nova Scotia. *Journal of Sport and Social Issues, 33*(3), 331–351.

Raphael, D. (2009). Escaping from the phantom zone: Social determinants of health, public health units and public policy in Canada. *Health Promotion International, 24*(2), 193–198.

Raphael, D., Bryant, T., & Rioux, M. (Eds.). (2010). *Staying alive: Critical perspectives on health, illness, and health care* (2nd ed.). Toronto: Canadian Scholars' Press.

Ressler, J. D., Richards, K. A. R., & Wright, P. M. (2016). The sociopolitics of sport, physical education, and school health in the United States. *International Journal of Sport Policy and Politics, 8*(4), 745–748.

Roser, M., & Ritchie, H. (2016). Burden of disease. Our World in Data. https://ourworldind
ata.org/burden-of-disease.

Rowe, D. (2020). Subjecting pandemic sport to a sociological procedure. *Journal of Sociology.* https://doi.org/10.1177/1440783320941284.

Roy, A. (2020, April 3). The pandemic is a portal. *Financial Times.* https://www.ft.com/cont
ent/10d8f5e8-74eb-11ea-95fe-fcd274e920ca.

Safai, P. (2016). Sociology of sport: Canada. In K. Young (Ed.), *Sociology of sport: A global subdiscipline in review* (pp. 323–342). London: Emerald Press.

Safai, P., Johnson, J., & Bryans, J. (2016). The absence of resistance training? Exploring the politics of health in high performance youth triathlon. *Sociology of Sport Journal, 33*(4), 269–281.

Safai, P., & Malcolm, D. (2016). Sport, health and medicine. In B. Houlihan (Ed.), *Sport and society: A student introduction* (3rd ed.) (pp. 157–179). London: Sage.

Sam, M. P. (2009). The public management of sport: Wicked problems, challenges and dilemmas. *Public Management Review, 11*(4), 499–514.

Skrabanek, P. (1994). *The death of humane medicine: And the rise of coercive healthism.* Suffolk, U.K.: Social Affairs Unit.

Smith, R. (2008, July 8). The end of disease and the beginning of health. *The BMJ Opinion,* blog. http://blogs.bmj.com/bmj/2008/07/08/richard-smith-the-end-of-disease-and-the-beginning-of-health/.

sportanddev.org. (2020). The health benefits of sport and physical activity. Retrieved from https://www.sportanddev.org/en/learn-more/health/health-benefits-sport-and-physical-activity.

Sport Information Resource Center. (2012). Canadian Sport Policy. Sport Canada: Canadian Heritage. https://sirc.ca/wp-content/uploads/files/content/docs/Document/csp2012_en.pdf.

Tink, L. N., Peers, D., Nykiforuk, C. I. J., & Mayan, M. (2019). Rereading the history of recreation in Canada: Moving beyond the politics of health, *Leisure/Loisir, 43*(4), 445–457. doi:10.1080/14927713.2019.1697350.

Tirado, L. (2015). *Hand to mouth: Living in bootstrap America.* New York: Penguin.

United Nations. (2003, November 17). General Assembly Resolution 58.5, Sport as a means to promote education, health, development and peace, A/Res/58/5. https://documents-dds-ny.un.org/doc/UNDOC/GEN/N03/453/21/pdf/N0345321.pdf?OpenElement.

Vosko, L. F. (Ed.). (2006). *Precarious employment: Towards an improved understanding of labour market insecurity.* Montreal: McGill-Queen's University Press.

Waddington, I. (2000). *Sport, health and drugs: A critical sociological perspective.* London: E and FN Spon.

Weed, M. (2016). Should we privilege sport for health? The comparative effectiveness of UK government investment in sport as a public health intervention. *International Journal of Sport Policy and Politics, 8*(4), 559–576.

Weiss, J. (1989). The powers of problem definition: The case of government paperwork. *Policy Science, 22*, 97–121.

Well-being. (2020). Oxford English Dictionary. https://www-oed-com.ezproxy.library.yorku.ca/view/Entry/227050?redirectedFrom=wellbeing#eid.

Wiest, A. L., Andrews, D. L., & Giardina, M. D. (2015). Training the body for healthism: Reifying vitality in and through the clinical gaze of the neoliberal fitness club. *Review of Education, Pedagogy, and Cultural Studies, 37*(1), 21–40.

Wiseman, E. (2019, September 8). Jennifer Gunter: "Women are being told lies about their bodies." *The Guardian*. https://www.theguardian.com/lifeandstyle/2019/sep/08/jennifer-gunter-gynaecologist-womens-health-bodies-myths-and-medicine.

Wiseman, J., & Brasher, K. (2008). Community wellbeing in an unwell world: Trends, challenges, and possibilities. *Journal of Public Health Policy*, 29(3), 353–366.

World Health Organization. (1948). Preamble to the Constitution of WHO as adopted by the International Health Conference, New York, 19 June–22 July 1946; signed on 22 July 1946 by the representatives of 61 states (Official Records of WHO, no. 2, p. 100) and entered into force on 7 April 1948. http://apps.who.int/iris/bitstream/handle/10665/44192/9789241650472_eng.pdf;jsessionid=6447223ACB1FD217E4E2ABB2F153EF48?sequence=1

World Health Organization. (2018). *Global action plan on physical activity 2018–2030: More active people for a healthier world*. Geneva: World Health Organization. https://apps.who.int/iris/bitstream/handle/10665/272722/9789241514187-eng.pdf

World Health Organization. (2020, May 16). WHO and International Olympic Committee team up to improve health through sport. https://www.who.int/news/item/16-05-2020-who-and-international-olympic-committee-team-up-to-improve-health-through-sport

CHAPTER 21

....

SPORT, AGGRESSIVE PLAY, AND VIOLENCE

....

KEVIN YOUNG

WHILE human aggression and violence have always fascinated scholars, even a hasty review of the existing research on aggression and violence *in sport* will immediately reveal three things. First, despite its pervasive, diverse, and enduring presence in human communities, the subject matter has traditionally been approached in limited ways. With the notable exception of crowd violence, and specifically soccer "hooliganism" (see Williams, in this volume), "sports violence" has typically been conceived of as an on-field entity, as something that involves the practices and attitudes of (usually male) athletes *in situ*. This approach tends to exclude other forms sports violence might take, such as violence away from the field of play as well as the involvement of females. Second, and again with the notable exception of research on soccer hooliganism, sports violence research seems to appeal to researchers far less today than in the past, although this might reflect a reluctance to use the term "sports violence" rather than a reluctance to study its various manifestations. And third, aggression and violence in sport have been consistently ignored by mainstream sociology, including criminology, and studied almost entirely by practitioners in the subdisciplines of the sociology of sport and the psychology of sport. The aggregate outcome of these factors is a field of study that is often surprisingly narrow and less sociologically sophisticated than it might be. As so many chapters in this volume demonstrate, "sports aggression" and "sports violence" might—I would argue *should*—mean many things and include many behaviors. However, so far at least, the research has not met its potential.

After identifying some key definitional issues with respect to how to think about aggression and violence, this chapter revisits perhaps the most enduring of player violence typologies in the sociology of sport field and explores the relatively recent expansion in risk-pain-injury research. The key role of gender in sports aggression and violence is also acknowledged, as are the main interpretive perspectives sociologists of sport have implemented to date in this area. The chapter proposes an alternative—specifically, a broader—way of thinking about aggression and violence in sport that arguably brings the subject matter back to the social processes and structures that give rise to it in the first place, and in so doing underlines the true diversity and pervasiveness of aggression and violence in sport.

ISSUES

One of the immediate problems that any scholar wanting to study aggression and violence in sport faces is the bewildering constellation of terms used to define the subject matter, many of which have been deployed interchangeably and often carelessly. Put simply, and as Cashmore (2000, p. 436) has observed fairly, sports aggression and violence are "difficult to pin down." The sociology of sport literature contains references to a very long list of terms, most of which, confusingly, bear relevance to the dynamics at play and which, to be fair, also (and perhaps necessarily) appear in this chapter. As Coakley and Donnelly (2009, p. 187) note, this list includes, but is not limited to, terms such as "physical, assertive, tough, rough, competitive, intense, intimidating, risky, aggressive, destructive, and violent." It is understandable that these signifiers appear in the aggression and violence research—indeed, it would be difficult to imagine such research without them. All of them are relevant, but they do not necessarily imply or invoke the same thing.

The two most salient terms are, of course, "aggression" and "violence." To this end, Coakley and Donnelly (2009, pp. 187–188), who have been as succinct on these matters as anyone, define *aggression* as "verbal or physical actions grounded in an intent to dominate, control, or do harm to another person," while *violence* is understood by them to refer to "the use of excessive physical force, which causes or has the potential to cause harm or destruction." As with all such attempts, these definitions are not completely satisfactory and inevitably contain ambiguities. But Coakley and Donnelly are correct to suggest that aggression is normally regarded as a broader and more generic concept, while violence is typically used to refer to physical forms of aggression, and especially excessive and injurious forms. The adoption of these terms in this chapter is similarly based upon such a distinction.

From Aggressive Play to Athlete Crime: A Sliding Scale

Several typologies of player aggression/violence exist, but none more enduring than the approach developed by the late Canadian sociologist Michael Smith (1983), who classified problematic player behavior into four basic categories, the first two being "relatively legitimate" and the last two "relatively illegitimate" in the eyes of both sports officials and the law. While the typology has been summarized many times in the literature, it remains a useful tool for understanding how player violence is treated by the courts and is worth briefly revisiting here.

- *Brutal body contact* includes what Smith called the "meat and potatoes" of our most popular sports, such as tackles, blocks, body checks, collisions, hits, and jabs. Depending on the sport under scrutiny, these are all acts that can be found within the official rules of a given sport, and to which most would agree that consent is expressly given or, at the very least, implied.
- *Borderline violence* involves acts prohibited by the official rules of a given sport but that occur routinely and are more or less accepted by many people connected with the game. Examples might include the fist fight in ice hockey; the late hit and personal foul

in North American football; the "wandering" elbow in basketball, soccer, and road racing; the high tackle and scrum punch in rugby; and the "beanball" (a pitch aimed deliberately at a batsman's head) in baseball. Importantly, all of these actions carry potential for causing injury as well as prompting further conflict between players, such as the bench-clearing brawl in ice hockey, players charging the mound in baseball, or retaliatory fighting in any of these other sports. Historically speaking, sanctions imposed by sports leagues and administrators for borderline violence have been notoriously light, and the clubs themselves have done all they can to protect their players, especially their key players.

- *Quasi-criminal violence* violates the formal rules of a given sport, the law, and, to a significant degree, the informal norms of players. This type of violence usually results in serious injury, which, in turn, precipitates considerable official and public attention. Quasi-criminal violence in ice hockey may include "cheap shots," "sucker punches," or dangerous high-stick work, all of which can cause severe injury and which often elicit in-house suspensions and fines, as well as occasionally prompting civil law action.

- *Criminal violence* includes behaviors so seriously and obviously outside of the boundaries of acceptability of both the sport and the wider community that they are addressed and sanctioned formally by the criminal justice system from the outset. Excessive and injurious on-field acts of violence and player hostilities that flow over into the community and away from the arena are cases in point.

Smith's typology addresses what criminologists (e.g., Ball-Rokeach, 1971, 1980) have long called the question of the "legitimacy of violence," that is, the legitimation/de-legitimation process with regard to what is perceived as acceptable violence and what is not. This typology is useful, but it has one obvious limitation: keeping up with the times. Since the late 1960s and the early 1970s there has been a shift in what may be categorized as "legitimate" and "illegitimate" player violence, no doubt prompted by shifting scales of civil and legal tolerance when it comes to forms of interpersonal violence in general. Using Smith's categories, incidents previously considered *quasi-criminal violence, borderline violence,* or even *brutal body contact* are being more closely scrutinized today and, where litigated, may be dealt with under criminal rather than tort law. In this respect, there has been some collapsing of Smith's categories, and the typology requires updating to fit a dynamic sociolegal climate.

It thus becomes possible to conceive of aggression and violence among athletes, including at times, and confusingly, behavior prized and protected within the subculture of the sport, as sports *crime.* In-depth assessments of how player violence and sports injury cases are adjudicated by the courts and the sorts of legal defenses available to prosecuted athletes have been advanced in a number of countries (e.g., USA—Horrow, 1980; UK—Gardiner, Felix, James, Welch, & O'Leary, 1998; Canada—Dennie & Young, 2019). Importantly, this legal literature demonstrates, among other things, that it is not only sport scholars who have struggled to adequately and consistently classify the subject matter since what constitutes wanted and unwanted (Atkinson & Young, 2008) player aggression is very much dependent on the vagaries of changing legal settings and climates. Simply put, the forms of player aggression and violence that legal jurisdictions are willing to tolerate varies massively.

The Outcomes of Athlete Aggression/Violence: Risk-Pain-Injury Research

To state the obvious, the outcomes of aggressive play and violence in sport include physical pain and injury. Indeed, injury in sport is so ubiquitous that it has long been viewed as an "unthwarted epidemic" (Vinger & Hoerner, 1981). But how have scholars responded? To consider the place of risk, pain, and injury (RPI) in sport in relation to broader questions about athlete aggression and violence might, again, seem like an obvious thing to do, but the fact of the matter is that the sociological study of RPI is relatively new. An explanation may be found in the fact that scholarly attention to RPI has traditionally been subsumed under the umbrella classification of *sports violence* rather than viewed as an area of study unto itself. In Canada, initial sociological inquiry was pioneered in the 1980s and early 1990s by Smith (1983, 1987, 1991), who posed preliminary questions about the social, physical, and legal dimensions of risk. While recognizing the scholarly significance of injury research and laying the foundation for future sociological work, Smith mainly approached injury as a downside to sport played aggressively rather than as an autonomous field of research per se.

Beginning in the 1980s, and in step with a broader turn to "body" studies in the parent discipline (cf. Featherstone, Hepworth, & Turner, 1991; Frank, 1991; Shilling, 1993), a number of sociologists of sport (mainly based in Britain and North America) examined RPI more closely. Since then, the literature has expanded rapidly, itself splintering off in various directions to consider, for instance, the role of medical practitioners such as physical therapists and clinicians and, most recently, concussion, suicide, and mental health. Aspects of injury which have been rigorously examined so far by sociologists include contextual factors such as how RPI is affected by specific sport cultures, gender influences, explanations of how injury is directly *lived* and reflected upon by athletes themselves, and the implications of injury for health and social policy. As the following list demonstrates, the sociological literature on RPI is already impressively diverse. Each element has obvious overlaps with questions of aggression and violence: Nixon (1992, 1993, 1994a, 1994b, 1996) placed pain and injury in the context of *cultures of risk* that characterize sport, as well as the socially stratified *sportsnets* (or networks of social relationships) that athletes belong to; Sabo (1986, 1994) examined the gendered underpinnings of sports injury and the philosophical codes many athletes adopt to approach pain; Hughes and Coakley (1991) drew from deviancy theory to explain violence and injury in sport as outcomes of overconformity to a *sport ethic* that pervades sport and prioritizes risk over well-being; Curry (1993), Donnelly and Young (1988), and Holmes and Frey (1990) showed how athletes who shy away from pain are seldom attributed status as "real athletes"; Roderick and colleagues (Roderick, 1998, 2006a, 2006b; Roderick, Waddington, & Parker, 2000), Safai (2004), Howe (2001), Walk (1997), and Malcolm (2017) explored the complicity of the medical industry and other organizations in sports injury; Theberge (1997), Pike (2000), and Charlesworth (2004) were among the first sociologists examining the experience of pain and injury in the lives of female athletes. This work continues (Theberge, 2015; Wiebe, 2014); Malcolm (2009, 2018) and Liston (Liston, McDowell, Malcolm, Scott, & Waddington, 2016) are among those leading the sociological charge examining concussion and brain injury. And finally, accompanied by colleagues and singly, I have investigated (1) how RPI has social, subcultural, and occupational dimensions (Young, 1993); (2) how sports injury comes with obvious economic costs to both individuals and communities (Young & White, 2000); (3) the various sense-making strategies male and female athletes use to play through pain that allow them to return to play even when at risk of further injury (Young, 1997; Young & White, 1995; Young, White, & McTeer, 1994); (4) how consent and liability issues are interpreted by the justice system when sports injury is litigated (Dennie & Young, 2019; Young, 1993; Young & Wamsley, 1996); as well as (5) how the media might take advantage of sports-related pain (Young, 2019a).

Clearly, the sociological study of RPI has mushroomed impressively—so impressively, in fact, that, taken as a whole, RPI work likely represents the second largest corpus of inquiry related to sports aggression and violence after hooliganism research in the entire sport violence field (Young, 2019b). Crucially, it also clearly underlines how research on sports aggression and its outcomes cannot be divorced from gender dynamics. As Sparkes and Smith (2008, p. 689) remark:

> Sporting men and boys, particularly in contact sports like rugby with a high risk of injury, are socialized to mask, hide and disregard pain, as well as to objectify and dissociate from their bodies and the bodies of others in order that they might both take and inflict pain. Thus, pain is normalized in specific sporting subcultures and certain ways of coping . . . and functioning . . . are valorized and legitimated as part of the social construction of gender identity.

However, since an expanding literature on females and injury is showing that girls and women also prize risk and willingly subject themselves to pain and injury on a regular basis using normalizing strategies similar to those of men (Theberge, 2015; Wiebe, 2014; Young, 1997; Young & White, 1995), socialization into sport per se and the notion of the sport ethic (Coakley, 2015) seem at least as important as gender in explaining why both male and female athletes accept risk and live through and return from pain and injury in sport.

Existing at both the cause *and* effect ends of the sport-safety continuum, the partnership of risk, pain, and injury represents a menacing alliance with real consequences for individuals, communities, and nations. Where the study of the constituent elements of this alliance is concerned, sociologists of sport have made encouraging advances, despite coming to the area relatively late. These advances have taken us beyond the uncritical borders of the early epidemiological work on the subject, but more work and knowledge are needed, on all fronts, especially as the risks associated with certain sports become clearer. At the time of writing, North American sports bodies, and ice hockey and football regulators in particular, seem to be taking head injuries and concussions more seriously than ever before, and extensive studies and initiatives are underway. Concussion protocols are expanding, and new legislation has been introduced in many jurisdictions.

Understandably, much of the concussion research is taking place in the traditional medical sciences (Hardes, 2017; Harrison, 2014; Kuhn, Yengo-Kahn, Kerr, & Zuckerman, 2017; Malcolm, 2017), but social scientific and sociological work is underway, posing questions that range from the values that give rise to head injury acceptance (Anderson, 2012; Liston et al., 2016) to the complex relationship that exists between clinicians and athletes (Malcolm, 2009, 2017) to ethical issues surrounding concussion and player safety (Caron & Bloom, 2015; McNamee, Partridge, & Anderson, 2015). Research on sport and concussion is also underway in many countries. So far, I have homed in on Britain and North America, but studies are investigating concussion in, for example, Italian football (Broglio et al., 2010), Irish rugby (Fraas, Coughlan, Hart, & McCarthy, 2013), as well as in other multination studies (Cusimano et al., 2017). What remains unclear is how ready the world of sport is to listen, and react responsibly, to head injury science in the concussion-related "battle for truth" (Fainaru-Wada & Fainaru, 2013).

It is clear from what we know so far that sport can lead to injurious outcomes not only because of the inherent nature of athletic activity per se or the equipment needed to play it but also because of the way that sport activity is perceived, planned, practiced, and policed (Young, 2019b). Obviously, these multiple elements point to the importance of considering the contributory roles of parents, coaches, clinicians, administrators, leagues, media, sponsors, and peer subcultures, as well as players. As our understanding of both the intrinsic dangers of sport and the socially constructed ways of perceiving, planning, practicing, and policing sport grows, and as public concern mounts regarding participant (and especially child) safety throughout the sports world, it seems likely that sport organizations and the public will find themselves better prepared to face, if not thwart, any injury "epidemic" that endures.

APPROACHES

Disagreements about what constitutes aggressive play and sports violence, as well as the root causes of RPI in sport, are clearly visible in the theoretical approaches which have been applied to the subject matter. Eller (2006, p. 31) correctly summarizes the main camps of this literature:

> The two most general perspectives are the "internal" and the "external"—that is, whether the cause or source of violence is "inside" the violent individual (in his head or her "mind" or personality or genes) or "outside" the violent individual (in the social situations, values, or structures in which he or she acts). These two overarching perspectives correspond roughly to biology and psychology on the one hand and sociology and anthropology on the other.

While the external perspective is, of course, preferred by sociologists, it should be noted that a host of psychological and biological perspectives have been adopted in the sports aggression/violence literature over time, especially early on, but which remain popular in some quarters, certainly sport psychology, for instance. Instinct theory (Berczeller, 1967; Lorenz, 1966; Morris, 1967), the so-called frustration-aggression hypothesis (Berkowitz, 1978; Dollard, Doob, Miller, Mower, & Sears, 1939; Pirks, 2010; Russell & Drewry, 1976), the hostile and instrumental aggression approach (Berkowitz, 1993; Marasescu, 2014; Mintah, Huddleston, & Doody, 1999), catharsis theory (Arms, Russell, & Sandilands, 1979; Atyeo, 1979; Beisser, 1967; Brill, 1929, p. 434; Goldstein & Arms, 1971; Marsh, Rosser, & Harré, 1978; Sipes, 1973), and, most recently, the reversal theory of John Kerr (Apter, 1989; Kerr, 2004; Kerr & de Kock, 2002; Shepherd, Lee, & Kerr, 2006) have all been applied at various times and in various contexts to sports aggression and violence. A perhaps unsurprising thread in critical responses from scholars who prioritize social and cultural dynamics is that such approaches overlook matters such as how forms of social stratification and power relations—not innate biological characteristics—are key drivers of aggression and violence in sport. Needless to say, approaches emphasizing the fundamentally social and cultural bases of aggression and violence have always had more appeal to sociologists.

Theoretical Influences

Social Learning

Albert Bandura's (1973, 1977) widely influential social learning theory (SLT) rejects the centrality of biological drives in behaving aggressively and shifts the focus to how punishment and reward play important roles in the modeling of behavior. Bandura argues that aggression and violence, like any other behaviors, are learned through observation and imitation and depend upon the degree to which one "emulates the behaviour of a role model" (Sellers, Cochcan, & Branch, 2005, p. 381). While accepting the Skinnerian view that we learn through direct reinforcement of our responses to stimuli, Bandura adds that we also learn to aggress by observing the consequences of other people's actions. His theory suggests that people imitate aggressors who are similar to themselves, who are rewarded for their actions, and who hold cultural prestige. Simply put, if aggression is defined as pleasurable, meaningful, or rewarding, it will continue. Scholars of violence in Canadian ice hockey (e.g., Robidoux, 2001) have contended that fist fighting and vicious forms of body checking are learned via the social psychological dynamic that Bandura outlined. Applied to other settings, Kreager (2007) has used SLT to explain how violence in American school sports develops from forms of gender learning (notably dangerous notions of masculinity), and Muir and Seitz (2004) have applied it in showing how misogynistic rituals are learned and reproduced in collegiate rugby. While human behavior is clearly the outcome of both imitation and complex forms of social learning at the hands of influential role models, critics of SLT have argued that this approach underestimates people's choice-making abilities and have pointed to the essential fact that "watching is not the same thing as doing." In other words, not all people who are raised around smokers smoke, and not all athletes who see others cheat do in fact cheat. Seen this way, social roles and statuses can be rejected and "cycles of violence"—including those that occur in sport—can be modified or "broken." Put simply, learning is a fundamental part of the social process, but learned behavior can also be "unlearned."

Techniques of Neutralization

Growing directly out of the foundational Chicago school of the early part of the 20th century, the techniques of neutralization (TN) approach (Sykes & Matza, 1957, 1989) focuses less on the social causes of behavior and more on the ways in which structural conditions are translated into action by individuals, thus allowing them to perform certain tasks. As with all interactionist approaches, the TN approach focuses on micro-level relations, especially between the actor and those who seek justifications for the act (such as the authorities). In this way, and building on C. Wright Mills's (1940) earlier notion of "vocabularies of motive," Sykes and Matza (1957) offer a way of explaining behaviors such as delinquency or violence by outlining five possible strategies (or "techniques") of "neutralizing" harm inflicted by the behavior: (1) denying responsibility, (2) denying injury, (3) denying victimization,

(4) "condemning the condemners," and (5) "appealing to higher loyalties." The TN approach has been widely used in the deviancy and criminological research, particularly in attempts to explain the behavior of young offenders, but it has also found a home in research on deviance and violence in sport. For instance, with colleagues, I have found this approach helpful in explaining justificatory strategies used by injured athletes that allow them to accept pain and return to play (Young et al., 1994) and by those involved in abusive practices in animal sports (Atkinson & Young, 2005b). Critics of the TN approach have correctly observed that it is more a modest framework for making sense of certain episodes of, for instance, delinquent, deviant, or violent behavior than it is a fully fledged theory per se. However, as classic differential association theorists (e.g., Sutherland, 1947, 1973) have indicated, doing crime and deviance is as much about the *sense-making* of the act (i.e., the motivations and rationalizations that allow it to take place) as it is about the techniques of *doing* the act itself. Since athletes and other individuals behaving deviantly, aggressively, or violently have to constantly rationalize their actions (both to themselves and to others), the TN approach contains real potential for explaining aspects of sports behavior.

Violent Subcultures

Also directly influenced by the Chicago school, and not entirely distinct from the TN approach (as techniques of neutralization are frequently used by members of subcultural groups to justify pro-violence norms), the violent subcultures approach has been used to explain high rates of violence in certain socially definable groups, such as youth gangs and collectivities. As Smith (1983) observed, this two-pronged body of research tends to be splintered into assessments of a "violent societal subculture hypothesis." For example, one prong is seen in early U.S. ethnographic work that showed how youth gangs operationalize situation-specific behaviors, such as physical intimidation and fighting, that do not pervade all aspects of participants' lives (cf. Wolfgang & Ferracuti, 1967), while another prong engaged a "violent occupational subculture hypothesis," which confirmed that those occupying work settings develop unique value systems that guide their behaviors inside that setting. While both approaches have been used in the sociology of sport, and while the research on sport subcultures is now considerable (Atkinson & Young, 2008), it is the latter approach that has been most relevant for sports violence research thus far. In particular, a vibrant literature examining the pro-violence occupational culture of North American ice hockey now spans half a century (e.g., Atkinson & Young, 2008; Faulkner, 1973, 1974; Robidoux, 2001; Vaz, 1982). This subcultural research may be criticized for suggesting that the behaviors and values that characterize recreational or work settings are evident only in those settings. It is quite clear that pro-aggression and pro-violence attitudes which are cultivated and revered in the world of sport neither develop solely from within those settings nor are restricted to them in their manifestation.

Figurational Sociology

Based centrally upon the extensive writing of Norbert Elias (1994), figurational, or "process" sociology, sets out to explain the "complex chain of interdependencies and power relationships" that exist in and across human communities (Layder, 1986, p. 370). At the core of this approach is a rejection of the traditional dichotomy of understanding individuals and society existing independently of one another. Instead, figurationalists attempt to bridge the micro-macro divide and view human behavior as sets of actions in broad interconnected webs of relationships between actors (Layder, 1986; Mouzelis, 1993) that are underpinned by power differentials between the actors (Layder, 1986). A central theme in Elias's (1994, 1996) research on long-term civilizing processes is that Western societies have become relatively "unexciting" social environments. With the general pacification of cultures over time, including greater restraint exercised by individuals over habitual acts of aggression, a collective need to devise and organize cultural activities that strike a balance between personal pleasure and restraint occurs. As outward displays of emotion, including aggression, become less socially acceptable (Elias, 1994), individuals pursue a range of activities that elicit exciting significance in highly controlled contexts of interaction.

Where sport is concerned, Elias and Dunning (1986) and Dunning (1999) have examined the role of aggression in arousing "exciting significance" for spectators. They argue that sports involving a moderate degree of aggression (even rule-violating forms) are seen as generally tolerable, and this allows individuals to participate (as either competitors or spectators) in practices that are taboo in other social spheres. In the language of figurational sociology, sports contests represent interactive scenarios that legitimate a "controlled decontrolling" of emotions (Elias & Dunning, 1986). Sport is considered "mimetic" because it resembles war-like competition; that is, it is socially and emotionally significant to individuals because it promotes excitement through controlled violence in a contest that is not as harmful as actual war (Goodger & Goodger, 1989; Sheard, 1999). Using this approach, Atkinson (2002) examines spectator enjoyment of relatively tolerable violence in North American professional wrestling.

Victimology

An obvious departure from conventional thinking about violence in sport, victimology was introduced by criminologists concerned that, in the offender-victim dyad, the direct experiences of the victim were being overlooked (Karmen, 2004, p. 8). Thus, victimological perspectives began to focus on those who are harmed in situations of conflict or abuse (Elias, 1986, pp. 3–4). Originally applied to studying offenses like sexual assault and street crimes like mugging, it is also possible to conceive of aspects of the offender-victim relationship in sport. In this connection, victimology may be understood as an approach rooted in the idea that people who participate in potentially dangerous institutional settings, such as sport, have inherent rights to safety, respect, and key information (Young, 1993; Young & Reasons, 1989). Moreover, athletes who are paid to participate in sport and, as such, are members of complex economic organizations, should be viewed as workers and thus deserve formal and legal protections for the risks they endure. Early victimological research in the sociology of sport (Young, 1993) displayed Marxist and cultural studies leanings, addressing the multiple ways athletes, or other sports participants, are systematically victimized (e.g., physically, socially, economically, psychologically) by exploitative and corporatized sports structures. In brief, victimologists shift attention from the causes of violence per se to the sources of suffering and its treatment in social institutions. Victimological studies of sports violence (e.g., Young, 1993; Young & Reasons, 1989) challenge labor officials and courts to view the exploitation of athletes as a type of white-collar crime. Practices such as pressuring athletes to play while injured or informally threatening their job security if they refuse to play in pain should be considered exploitative and a violation of athletes' basic right to personal safety.

The victimological approach is not heavily, or explicitly, utilized in the sociology of sport, but psychologists and sociologists of sport do study groups of abused athletes from quasi-victimological perspectives. For example, studies of the sexual victimization of athletes by coaches have been conducted using feminist approaches (e.g., Brackenridge, 1996, 2001). Similarly, in describing how he dropped out of professional soccer due to "overt and covert institutionalized racism" Moran (2000, p. 190) examines racism in English sport from a victim's perspective. In a further example of the victimological approach, David (2005, p. 12) refers to the lack of scholarly attention to sexual and physical abuse of children in sport (he refers to this absence as a "black hole"). David argues that the abuse of children in local and global sports cultures has been ignored and that sports personnel in highly competitive athletic circles rarely question whether things such as intensive training, indoctrination into winning-at-all-costs attitudes, isolation from nonathletes, emotional manipulation, and dietary control should be seen as reasonable or, in fact, *victimizing* elements of the sports process.

Symbolic Interaction

Rooted in the symbolic interactionist tradition (e.g., Goffman, 1974), Hughes and Coakley (1991) have described how athletes in aggressive sports settings use "interpretive frames" to gauge commitment to the group and sport. They describe how, from an early age, athletes are taught to strive for distinction, accept no limits as players, make sacrifices for their sport, and play through pain and injury as part of an overarching "sport ethic." While not all athletes in sport are socialized quite so completely or assess all athletic performances in relation to this ethic, this maxim is so pervasive that most athletes encounter it, and must reconcile themselves against it, at some point in their sport careers. As Coakley and Donnelly (2004, p. 91) put it, it "becomes a means to prove self-worth and to reaffirm membership in the subcultural in-group of the select few who play the game at a high level."

Hughes and Coakley (1991) suggest that the bulk of athlete behavior during competition or training exists in accordance with the requisites of the sport ethic. They illustrate athlete behavior on a statistical "normal curve," locating everyday athlete behavior at the heart of the curve and behavior that deviates from the sport ethic at either tail of the curve. On the one tail, they place a category of behaviors they call "positive" deviance. These are athlete behaviors that pursue the principles of the sport ethic to an unhealthy extent. An example of positive deviance is dangerous weight reduction (for instance, through dehydration strategies) in order to make a weight category in boxing or wrestling or in order to please judges in so-called appearance sports such as gymnastics or figure skating. On the other tail, Hughes and Coakley describe "negative" deviance, which involves athlete behaviors that reject the importance of the sport ethic. Disobeying a coach's instructions to work hard in training or to play in a certain kind of way are examples of negative deviance.

Similar to the subculture of violence perspective described earlier, the main conceptual contribution of Hughes and Coakley's (1991) typology is the idea that sports insiders decipher rule violation using group-specific codes, categories, and discourses. In sport settings, aggressive behavior is defined and controlled by *situated* actors who understand the unique principles of their own sport ethic. The sport ethic "tool" thus allows us to understand how decisions about positive and negative deviance are *negotiated* and how athletes are taught to rationalize rule-breaking or excessive behavior as a normal and acceptable part of sports culture through a set of "neutralizing techniques" (Sykes & Matza, 1957). However, Hughes and Coakley's typology seems far better suited to explain the behaviors and values of committed high-performance athletes and less suited to explain those at the recreational or amateur levels. Moreover, its ability to explain violent acts by nonathletes that occur in the context of sport (such as coaching abuse) or player violence that occurs away from the game (such as partner abuse) is unclear.

Certainly, theories of aggression and violence in sport are numerous and diverse and represent several academic disciplines. The preceding review is neither exhaustive nor covers all of the explanatory perspectives that have been used to make sense of aggressive and violent behavior in the sporting context. The volume of empirical research on violence in sport is also impressive, but again, sociologists of sport have usually limited their inquiries, as suggested at the outset, to two principal dimensions of the subject matter: violence among athletes, or player violence, and violence among fans, or crowd violence. Most monographs and textbooks reflect this convention, especially with respect to crowd violence interpreted as an example of collective behavior (e.g., Leonard, 1998; Lewis, 2007; McPherson, Curtis, & Loy, 1989; Russell, 2008; Smith, 1983; Snyder & Spreitzer, 1989; Wann, Melnick, Russell, & Pease, 2001).

Methodological Quandaries

Just as there have been varied theoretical influences in the study of sports-related aggression and violence, methodological approaches have also varied. Part of the complexity of explaining aggression and violence is that it is not easy to study. Since so much of the subject matter is deviant, harmful, illegal, or criminal or could lead to embarrassment, loss of reputation, or discipline, aggression and violence in sport are often cloaked in secrecy. As any scholar of crime or deviance would attest, this throws up complicated methodological quandaries that are tough to overcome (Sugden, 2012). In my own work on the various dimensions of the phenomenon, I have found that while, for example, coaxing athletes and others to speak about RPI in sport is relatively uncomplicated, all the fieldwork savvy in the world still leaves so many other parts of the sports aggression/violence puzzle tough to access and decipher. Let me use my own investigative forays into the field for illustration:

- Where North American crowd violence is concerned, I have found that professional teams often minimize violence or security problems that their own security personnel acknowledge. In fact, the only way I came to be aware of fan disorder at certain clubs was through security personnel violating club policy and risking their jobs by leaking their records to me after strict assurances of confidentiality had been elicited (Fong, 2015; Kern, 2015; Young, 1988, 2002).
- In both the United Kingdom and Canada, I have discovered a clear shift over time in athlete willingness to talk openly about aggressive practices such as hazing. In the

1980s in Canada (Young, 1983), it was relatively easy to encourage athletes to open up about how they initiated rookies. However, by the time of the much more tightly policed 1990s and the current period (Bryshun & Young, 1999, 2007), young athletes concerned not only about the possible implications of being singled out for their own involvement but also for incriminating their coaches had become far more wary, and many teams had "closed shop" under coach- or player-imposed "gag orders." In many settings, hazing is now fully subterranean and athletes refuse to engage outsiders or betray insider trust.

- If coaxing male or female athletes to speak openly about RPI in sport is relatively uncomplicated, getting them to speak about such matters as coaching style, intimidation, coercion, bullying, and pressure is not, and I have found that many male and female athletes become noticeably (and understandably) guarded around these issues (e.g., Young, 1997; Young & Atkinson, 2013; Young et al., 1994; Young & White, 1995).

- In my work on animal abuse with Michael Atkinson, we have jointly found that researching the world of training, kenneling, and racing dogs comes with access, deception, and trust issues (Atkinson & Young, 2005b). My research on rodeo practices, where horses and other animals are used for public entertainment, has revealed similar fieldwork imbroglios that even extend to respected veterinarians and animal welfare activists defeatedly offering access-denying apologies—"I can't talk about that, sorry" (Gerber & Young, 2013; Young, 2017; Young & Gerber, 2014).

- Despite the apparent candor and transparency of views offered by journalists on player violence, even the most staunch supporter of old-fashioned "rock 'em, sock 'em" ice hockey tempers his or her views in the presence of a prying social scientist asking tricky questions (Young, 1990, 1991; Young & Atkinson, 2013).

Of course, the sociology of sport literature is replete with admirable examples of challenging research on important, but delicate, sports violence topics which would never be possible without the methodological acumen of the researchers themselves. In this connection, the respective ethnographic ventures of colleagues Michael Atkinson (in Canada) and John Sugden (in the United Kingdom) stand out as exemplars of savvy fieldwork producing knowledge on tough-to-access and -research sports-related violence topics. Relevant work by Atkinson includes studies of abuse in animal sports, such as hunting pastimes (Atkinson, 2014; Atkinson & Young, 2005b), oppositional uses of the environment (Atkinson, 2009), violence against the self (Atkinson, 2007, 2008, 2011, 2015), the link between dangerous masculinities and risky urban practices (Atkinson, 2009), and criminal activity in the world of ticket scalping (Atkinson, 2000). Relevant work by Sugden includes exposés of corruption in the world's most powerful soccer body (Sugden & Tomlinson, 2003), studies of innovative underground economies connected to soccer hooligan culture (Sugden, 2002), and explorations of how sport can be used to mitigate ethnic conflict and xenophobic traditions (Sugden, 2010; Sugden & Tomlinson, 2017; Sugden & Wallis, 2007). Without these sorts of research undertakings, which come with obvious risks for the researchers themselves (ranging from status and identity risks to personal safety risks), we would understand aggressive sports behavior less and be far less well-prepared to deal with it from a practical point of view.

DEBATES

As the amalgam of theoretical approaches, methods, and definitions thus far strongly suggests, the customary parameters of what is considered *sports violence* could be broadened to include aggressive, threatening, harmful, or otherwise unjust practices enacted within the context of sport. Indeed, that sports violence may be far more expansive and varied than commonly assumed is the tip of the iceberg in defining this area and its priorities. A case may be made that it is sociologically useful—indeed sociologically *necessary*—to approach a much broader range of actions as "sports-related violence" (SRV) rather than "sports violence" per se. Expanding conceptualizations in this manner supports the need to move beyond the decontextualizing inclination of existing research. This means moving beyond the embedded tendency to view types of sports violence as separate episodes of social action, unrelated to other types or to broader social structures and processes, as well as highlighting the links and associations that underpin many, if not all, forms of SRV.

In moving toward a more expansive definition of SRV, and in addition to definitions and theories woven through the existing body of research on violence in sport, my own work is primarily influenced by two existing definitions of aggression and violence. The first comes from a likely source. Jay Coakley (1998, p. 199) defines aggression in the following way:

> Aggression originates in some combination of (1) frustration coupled with anger, opportunities, stimulus cues, and social support; (2) strategies used by athletes and encouraged by peers, parents, coaches, spectators, and sponsors; and (3) definitions of masculinity emphasizing violence as a basis for becoming a man and superior to a woman.

This definition is careful and thorough. It is sufficient on its own to sustain ongoing empirical and theoretical work. But, in addition to overlooking the many and complex ways that females also contribute to aggression and violence in sport, it lacks the victimological, social justice, and community health dimensions that are arguably essential in seriously engaging with the manifestation and outcomes of aggression and violence. In this respect, a second definitional influence is useful. The World Health Organization (2002, p. 4) defines violence thus:

> [T]he intentional use of physical force or power, threatened or actual, against oneself, another person, or against a group or community, that either results in or has a high likelihood of resulting in injury, death, psychological harm, maldevelopment, or deprivation.

Here, then, the focus shifts from how processes of aggression take place to the damages and harms they may cause for individuals and communities and, as such, also opens the door to consider questions of social justice.

Sensitive to the concerns underpinning both of these definitions, SRV, which encompasses notions of aggression *and* violence, may be defined in a twofold fashion:

1. Direct acts of physical violence contained within or outside the rules of the game that result in injury to persons, animals or property.
2. Harmful or potentially harmful acts conducted in the context of sport that threaten or produce injury or that violate human justices and civil liberties.

Following this definition, the varied manifestations of SRV may be far more expansive than previously thought. Elsewhere (Young, 2019a), I have made a case for what I call an "SRV matrix"—a way of conceiving of SRV behaviors in terms of a number of "cells," each one representing a specific *formation* of the phenomenon. Specifically, formations of SRV have included not only episodes of collective disorder by sports crowds and the aggressive practices of athletes who incur pain and impose injury on opponents, but also a far broader landscape of harmful and even abusive behaviors. Again, examples include athletes involved in violence away from the playing field; athlete hazing/initiation; forms of stalking, harassment, and threat; offenses by coaches, administrators, or medical staff; parental abuse; abuse of animals; political violence; offenses against workers and the public; and offenses against the environment. Practices such as these are not normally thought of as "aggression" or "violence" in sport, but one might reasonably ask "Why not?" After all, they clearly represent concrete and potentially harmful acts that cannot be separated from sporting processes. Their framing as aggression or violence begins to make sense when the socially embedded character of sport is more closely scrutinized. Crucially, none of these examples suggests that aggression and violence occur naturally, as the aforementioned psychological theories contend. Rather, all of the acts suggest that these practices are caused and manifested *socially*.

On a scale of social legitimacy, and echoing Smith's (1983, p. 9) earlier typology, some of the behaviors (e.g., certain aspects of player violence, athlete hazing, the use of certain animals in certain ways in sport) represent behaviors that, over time, have been viewed as *relatively* legitimate. While considered deviant in the eyes of some observers, such behaviors occur frequently and may be widely accepted within the culture of sport. On the other hand, other behaviors (e.g., sexual harassment or assault of athletes by coaches, other forms of explicit animal cruelty in sport) represent behaviors that are entirely less acceptable on a number of levels, including the official rules of a given sport, the informal norms and values of players or of the general public, as well as the law of the land. Needless to say, in both cases, what is considered legitimate and illegitimate depends on *who* is doing the defining, as well as *when* one is doing the defining. And it is on this exact matter—the matter of how we understand violence in sport and what we propose to do about it—that people and groups disagree and where violence in sport intersects with questions of culture, tradition, power, and ideology (Coakley & Donnelly, 2009; Donnelly & Young, 2004). As with sport more generally, what is considered sports violence is certainly "contested terrain" (Donnelly & Young, 1985, p. 20) and means different things to different groups of people (Bourdieu, 1978, p. 826).

Some behaviors are deeply grounded in culture, tradition, and ritual and, despite facing robust opposition, show no signs of disappearing any time soon. Boxing, bullfighting, fox hunting, dog and horse racing, ice hockey, and golf are all sports and pastimes which have encountered resistance to their "violent" outcomes—whether the injured parties are human, animal, or environmental. Fox hunting in Britain represents an exceptional case of a "blood" sport that has been both prohibited at the level of government and marginalized at the level of popular image, though such is the strength of its place in British society that it persists despite an outright ban. Further, other types of SRV, though hardly new, have taken on entirely more sinister trappings in a changed and changing global community, as Atkinson and Young (2005a) demonstrate in their study of political violence and terrorism at the Olympic Games. In this particular case, the threat of political violence has now significantly altered the way sport is played, funded, policed, and insured. The ripple effects on what a "secure" Olympic Games both costs and "looks like" are enormous (Atkinson & Young, 2012). But many sports at many levels are affected. That Manchester United felt it necessary to appoint the Premier League's first antiterror expert in 2017 is telling (Austin, 2017).

Each of the behaviors represented by the respective SRV cells has received a certain amount of scholarly attention. Some (fan violence, and soccer hooliganism in particular, is again an obvious example) have been far more comprehensively examined than others, and some have been curiously understudied (such as cruelty in animal sports, parental abuse, political violence related to sport, and environmental offenses). Taken individually, the cells have certainly been approached as forms of aggression, violence, or abuse that may threaten, hurt, or victimize, but scholars have fallen short of interpreting them as dimensions of "sports violence" per se. Very little is known about the links they may share. In this sense, a sociological assessment is important because it acknowledges differences at the same time as underscoring common threads and overlaps.

A number of points can be made in this regard. First, and perhaps most important, the proposed SRV cells all feature one common critical attribute: they all unite violent, harmful, or victimizing practices *through* sport. In other words, *sport* (rather than, for instance, other social institutions such as the workplace, the family, the church, or education) is the context of and common denominator for these activities. In order both to understand SRV phenomena and to react responsibly to them, acknowledging that they are centrally connected to the sports process is critical. Second, all of the SRV cells represent the attempt by a group or individual to exert *control* over others. In this respect, all dimensions of SRV may be understood in terms of themes of power, dominance, and control, or what Donnelly and Young (2004) (borrowing from sociologist David Garland) call "cultures of control." Third, in terms of who "does" the behavior, who supports and funds the behavior, and who consumes and watches it, most, if not all, of the cells display strongly *gendered* underpinnings. Unsurprisingly, given the male preserve that sport has traditionally represented, men and masculinity feature centrally, and rarely flatteringly. However, as the preceding review shows, the involvement of females is certainly increasing as opportunities for female involvement in sport have opened up. This raises important questions as to whether SRV behavior is best understood as part of socialization into *gendered* roles and identities in sport, or socialization into sport per se.

CONCLUSION

Although largely ignored by mainstream sociology, aggression and violence in sport are complex and multidimensional phenomena that have generated a substantial corpus of research in the sociology of sport subdiscipline. Much of this research is high in quality and helpful with respect to developing our knowledge and understanding. But it is also the case that this literature, viewed overall, is limited in both scope and potential. As far as scope is concerned, the research is unquestionably lopsided. Other than admittedly robust literatures on soccer hooliganism and what I have called here RPI (the study of risk, pain, and injury in sport), very little is known about the other forms "sports violence" might take, violence away from the field of play, or the involvement of females. As far as potential is concerned, the research has arguably been hampered by the limited way the subject matter has been conceived of and defined.

The principal goal of this chapter is to offer an alternative perspective on how we think about the social behaviors, processes, and values involved in sports-related violence. So far, almost all of the research has zoned in on single and unitary dimensions of the subject matter. This approach is both understandable and necessary, and the field in general remains in need of further concrete investigations into *all* of the varied manifestations of SRV. However, a single-subject approach to SRV is problematic. It tends to disassociate, or decontextualize, the topic under scrutiny from what I have called the broader landscape of SRV and, in so doing, creates the impression that the various elements of SRV are "stand-alone" entities, unconnected to other elements of the sports violence process. This is not true, and any sociological study of even the most narrowly defined aspect of SRV must explain how, in cause, expression, and outcome, the subject matter does not operate in isolation from other aspects of this process or, in fact, from larger sociological matters. As Elias (1986, p. 26) has argued, "[Studies] of sport which are not studies of society are studies out of context." As such, in addition to reviewing the field and approaches within it, this chapter has endeavored to show that SRV inevitably involves larger sociological factors such as social control, social stratification, and social change. Rather than viewing athlete aggression and violence in isolation, the chapter considers these issues through the lens of existing debates to place the subject matter in broader and more expansive sociological context.

REFERENCES

Anderson, E. (2012, October). Masculinity and sport-induced head trauma. *Psychology Today.* http://www.psychologytoday.com/blog/masculinity-today/201210/masculinity-and-sport-induced-head-trauma-1.

Apter, M. (1989). *Reversal theory: Motivation, emotion and personality.* London: Routledge.

Arms, R. L., Russell, G. W., & Sandilands, M. L. (1979). Effects on the hostility of spectators of viewing aggressive sports. *Review of Sport and Leisure, 4,* 115–127.

Atkinson, M. (2000). Brother, can you spare a seat: Developing recipes of knowledge in the ticket scalping subculture. *Sociology of Sport Journal, 17*(2), 151–170.

Atkinson, M. (2002). Fifty million viewers can't be wrong: Professional wrestling, sports-entertainment and mimesis. *Sociology of Sport Journal, 19,* 47–66.

Atkinson, M. (2007). Playing with fire: Masculinity and exercise supplements. *Sociology of Sport Journal, 24*(2), 165–186.

Atkinson, M. (2008). Triathlon, suffering and exciting significance. *Leisure Studies, 27*(2), 165–180.

Atkinson, M. (2009). Parkour, anarcho-environmentalism and poiesis. *Journal of Sport and Social Issues, 33*(2), 169–194.

Atkinson, M. (2011). Male athletes and the culture of thinness in sport. *Deviant Behavior, 32*(3), 224–256.

Atkinson, M. (2014). The terrier [men]. *Sociology of Sport Journal, 31*(4), 420–437.

Atkinson, M. (2015). The loneliness of the fell runner: An ethnographic foray. In G. Molnar & L. Purdy (Eds.), *Ethnographies in sport and exercise research* (pp. 96–110). London: Routledge.

Atkinson, M., & Young, K. (2005a). Political violence, terrorism and security at the Olympic games. In K. Young & K. Wamsley (Eds.), *Global Olympics: Historical and sociological studies of the modern games* (pp. 269–294). Oxford: Elsevier Press.

Atkinson, M., & Young, K. (2005b). Reservoir dogs: Greyhound racing, mimesis and sports-related violence. *International Review for the Sociology of Sport, 40*(1), 335–356.

Atkinson, M., & Young, K. (2008). *Deviance and social control in sport.* Champaign, IL: Human Kinetics.

Atkinson, M., & Young, K. (2012). Shadowed by the corpse of war: Sport spectacles and the spirit of terrorism. *International Review for the Sociology of Sport, 47*(3), 286–307.

Atyeo, D. (1979). *Violence in sports.* Toronto: Van Nostrand Reinhold.

Austin, J. (2017). Manchester United appoint anti-terror expert in a Premier League first. *The Independent.* https://www.independent.co.uk/sport/football/premier-league/manchester-united-appoint-anti-terror-expert-in-premier-league-first-a7533366.html.

Ball-Rokeach, S. (1971). The legitimation of violence. In J. F. Short & M. E. Wolfgang (Eds.), *Collective violence* (pp. 100–111). Chicago: Aldine.

Ball-Rokeach, S. (1980). Normative and deviant violence from a conflict perspective. *Social Problems, 28,* 45–62.

Bandura, A. (1973). *Aggression: A social learning analysis.* Englewood Cliffs, NJ: Prentice-Hall.

Bandura, A. (1977). *Social learning theory.* Englewood Cliffs, NJ: Prentice-Hall.

Beisser, A. R. (1967). *The madness in sports.* New York: Appleton Century Crofts.

Berczeller, E. (1967). The aesthetic feelings and Aristotle's catharsis theory. *Journal of Psychology, 65,* 261–267.

Berkowitz, L. (1978). Whatever happened to the frustration-aggression hypothesis? *American Behavioural Scientist, 21*(5), 691–709.

Berkowitz, L. (1993). The problem of aggression. In L. Berkowitz (Ed.), *Aggression: Its causes, consequences and control* (pp. 1–24). New York: McGraw Hill.

Bourdieu, P. (1978). Sport and social class. *Social Science Information, 17*(6), 819–840.

Brackenridge, C. (1996). *Child protection in sport: Politics, procedures and systems. Report on a Sport Council seminar for national governing bodies.* Cheltenham, U.K.: C and GCHE.

Brackenridge, C. (2001). *Spoilsports: Understanding and preventing sexual exploitation in sport.* London: Routledge.

Brill, A. A. (1929). The way of the fan. *North American Review, 226,* 400–434.

Broglio, S., Vagnozzi, R., Sabin, M., Signoretti, S., Tavazzi, B., & Lazzarino, G. (2010). Concussion occurrence and knowledge in Italian football (soccer). *Journal of Sports Science and Medicine, 9,* 418–430.

Bryshun, J., & Young, K. (1999). Sport-related hazing: An inquiry into male and female involvement. In P. White & K. Young (Eds.), *Sport and gender in Canada* (pp. 269–292). Toronto: Oxford University Press.

Bryshun, J., & Young, K. (2007). Hazing as a form of sport and gender socialization. In K. Young & P. White (Eds.), *Sport and gender in Canada* (2nd ed.) (pp. 302–327). Don Mills, Canada: Oxford University Press.

Caron, J. G., & Bloom, G. A. (2015). Ethical issues surrounding concussions and player safety in professional ice hockey. *Neuroethics, 8,* 5–13.

Cashmore, E. (2000). *Sports culture: An A–Z guide.* New York: Routledge.

Charlesworth, H. (2004). *Sports-related injury, risk and pain: The experiences of English female university athletes* (Unpublished doctoral dissertation). Loughborough University, U.K.

Coakley, J. (1998). *Sports in society: Issues and controversies* (6th ed.). New York: McGraw Hill.

Coakley, J. (2015). *Sports in society: Issues and controversies* (11th ed.). New York: McGraw Hill.

Coakley, J., & Donnelly, P. (2004). *Sports in society: Issues and controversies* (1st Canadian ed.). Toronto: McGraw-Hill Ryerson.

Coakley, J. & Donnelly, P. (2009). *Sports in society: Issues and controversies* (2nd Canadian ed.). Toronto: McGraw-Hill Ryerson.

Curry, T. (1993). A little pain never hurt anyone: Athletic career socialization and the normalization of sports injury. *Symbolic Interaction, 16*(3), 273–290.

Cusimano, M., Casey, J., Jing, R., Mishra, A., Solarski, M., Techar, K., & Zhang, S. (2017). Assessment of head collision events during the 2014 FIFA World Cup tournament. *Journal of the American Medical Association, 317*, 2548–2549.

David, P. (2005). *Human rights in youth sport.* London: Routledge.

Dennie, M., & Young, K. (2019). Complexities in Canadian legal approaches to sports injury. In K. Young (Ed.), *The suffering body in sport: Shifting thresholds of risk, pain and injury* (pp. 141–161). Bingley, U.K.: Emerald Press.

Dollard, J., Doob, L., Miller, N., Mower, O., & Sears, R. (1939). *Frustration and aggression.* New Haven, CT: Yale University Press.

Donnelly, P., & Young, K. (1985). Reproduction and transformation of cultural forms in sport: A contextual analysis of rugby. *International Review for the Sociology of Sport, 20*(1–2), 19–39.

Donnelly, P., & Young, K. (1988). The construction and confirmation of identity in sport subcultures. *Sociology of Sport Journal, 5*(3), 223–240.

Donnelly, P., & Young, K. (2004). "Sports-related violence" as an outcome of cultures of control in sport. Paper presented at the Pre-Olympic Scientific Congress, Thessaloniki, Greece, August 6–10.

Dunning, E. (1999). *Sport matters: Sociological studies of sport, violence and civilization.* London: Routledge.

Elias, N. (1994). *The civilizing process.* Oxford: Basil Blackwell.

Elias, N. (1996). *The Germans: Studies of power struggles and the development of habitus in the nineteenth and twentieth centuries.* Oxford: Polity Press.

Elias, N., & Dunning, E. (Eds.). (1986). *Quest for excitement: Sport and leisure in the civilizing process.* Oxford: Basil Blackwell.

Elias, R. (1986). The hidden dimensions of victimization: Victims, victimology, and human rights. In R. Elias (Ed.), *The politics of victimization: Victims, victimology and human rights* (pp. 3–8). New York: Oxford University Press.

Eller, J. D. (2006). *Violence and culture: A cross cultural and interdisciplinary perspective.* Toronto: Thomson Wadsworth.

Fainaru-Wada, M., & Fainaru, S. (2013). *League of denial.* New York: Crown Business.

Faulkner, R. (1973). On respect and retribution: Toward an ethnography of violence. *Sociological Symposium, 9*, 17–36.

Faulkner, R. (1974). Making violence by doing work: Selves, situations, and the world of professional hockey. *Sociology of Work and Occupations, 1*, 288–312.

Featherstone, M., Hepworth, M., & Turner, B. S. (Eds.). (1991). *The body: Social processes and cultural theory.* London: Sage.

Fong, B. (2015). *The manifestations and media perceptions of violent sport crowds: A figurational analysis of the North American context.* (Unpublished honors thesis). University of Calgary.

Fraas, M., Coughlan, G., Hart, E., & McCarthy, C. (2013). Concussion history and reporting rates in elite Irish rugby union players. *Physical Therapy in Sport, 15*, 136–142.

Frank, A. W. (1991). For a sociology of the body: An analytic review. In M. Featherstone, M. Hepworth, & B. S. Turner (Eds.), *The body: Social processes and cultural theory* (pp. 36–110). London: Sage.

Gardiner, S., Felix, A., James, M., Welch, R., & O'Leary, J. (1998). *Sports law*. London: Cavendish.

Gerber, B., & Young, K. (2013). Horse play in the Canadian west: The emergence of the Calgary Stampede as contested terrain. *Society & Animals, 21*(6), 523–545.

Goffman, E. (1974). *Frame analysis*. Cambridge, MA: Harvard University Press.

Goldstein, J. H., & Arms, R. L. (1971). Effects of observing athletic contests on hostility. *Sociometry, 34*(1), 83–90.

Goodger, J., & Goodger, B. (1989). Excitement and representation: Toward a sociological explanation of the significance of sport in modern society. *Quest, 41*, 257–272.

Hardes, J. (2017). Governing sporting brains: Concussion, neuroscience, and the biopolitical regulation of sport. *Sport, Ethics & Philosophy, 11*, 281–293.

Harrison, E. (2014). The first concussion crisis: Head injury and evidence in early American football, *American Journal of Public Health, 104*, 822–833.

Holmes, D., & Frey, J. (1990, February). The kind of people who skydive. *Parachutist*, 28–32.

Horrow, R. (1980). *Sports violence: The interaction between private lawmaking and the criminal law*. Arlington, VA: Carrollton Press.

Howe, P. D. (2001). An ethnography of pain and injury in professional rugby union: The case of Pontypridd RFC. *International Review for the Sociology of Sport, 36*(3), 289–303.

Hughes, R., & J. Coakley (1991). Positive deviance among athletes: The implications of overconformity to the sport ethic. *Sociology of Sport Journal, 8*(4), 307–325.

Karmen, A. (2004). The rediscovery of crime victims and the rise of victimology. In A. Karmen (Ed.), *Crime victims: An introduction to victimology* (pp. 1–41). Toronto: Thomson/Wadsworth.

Kern, N. (2015). *The role of surveillance in the control of North American sport crowd violence—Understood in figurationalist terms: From 2000 to present day* (Unpublished honors thesis). University of Calgary.

Kerr, J. H. (2004). *Rethinking violence and aggression in sport*. London: Routledge.

Kerr, J. H., & de Kock, H. (2002). Aggression, violence and the death of a Dutch soccer hooligan: A reversal theory explanation. *Aggressive Behaviour, 28*, 1–10.

Kreager, D. A. (2007). Unnecessary roughness? School sports, peer networks and male adolescent violence. *American Sociological Review, 72*(5), 705–772.

Kuhn, A., Yengo-Kahn, A., Kerr, Z., & Zuckerman, S. (2017). Sports concussion research, chronic traumatic encephalopathy and the media: Repairing the disconnect. *British Journal of Sports Medicine, 51*, 1732–1733.

Layder, D. (1986). Social reality as figuration: A critique of Elias's conception of sociological analysis. *Sociology, 20*, 367–386.

Leonard, W. (1998). *A sociological perspective of sport* (5th ed.). Boston: Allyn and Bacon.

Lewis, J. (2007). *Sports fan violence in North America*. Lanham, MD: Rowman and Littlefield.

Liston, K., McDowell, M., Malcolm, D., Scott, A., & Waddington, I. (2016). On being "head strong": The pain zone and concussion in non-elite rugby union. *International Review for the Sociology of Sport, 53*(6), 668–685.

Lorenz, K. (1966). *On aggression*. London: Routledge.

Malcolm, D. (2009). Medical uncertainty and clinician-athlete relations: The management of concussion injuries in rugby union. *Sociology of Sport Journal, 26*, 191–210.

Malcolm, D. (2017). *Sport, medicine and health: The medicalization of sport?* London: Routledge.

Malcolm, D. (2018). Concussion in sport: Public, professional and critical sociologies. *Sociology of Sport Journal, 35*(2), 141–148.

Marasescu, M. R. (2014). The role of hostile and instrumental aggression in sport. *Linguistic and Philosophical Investigations, 13*, 170–175.

Marsh, P., Rosser, E., & Harré, R. (1978). *The rules of disorder*. London: Routledge and Kegan Paul.

McNamee, M., Partridge, B., & Anderson, L. (2015). Concussion in sport: Conceptual and ethical issues. *Kinesiology Review, 4*, 190–202.

McPherson, B., Curtis, J., & Loy, J. (Eds.). (1989). *The social significance of sport: An introduction to the sociology of sport*. Champaign, IL: Human Kinetics.

Mills, C. Wright. (1940). Situated actions and vocabularies of motive. *American Sociological Review, 5*, 904–913.

Mintah, J., Huddleston, S., & Doody, S. G. (1999). Justification of aggressive behaviors in contact and semi-contact sports. *Journal of Applied Psychology, 29*, 597–605.

Moran, R. (2000). Racism in football: A victim's perspective. *Soccer and Society, 1*(1), 190–200.

Morris, D. (1967). *The naked ape*. New York: McGraw Hill.

Mouzelis, N. (1993). On figurational sociology. *Theory and Culture Society, 10*, 239–253.

Muir, K. B., & Seitz, T. (2004). Machismo, misogyny, and homophobia in a male athletic subculture: A participant-observation study of deviant rituals in collegiate rugby. *Deviant Behaviour, 25*, 303–327.

Nixon, H. L., II. (1992). A social network analysis of influences on athletes to play with pain and injury. *Journal of Sport and Social Issues, 16*(2), 127–135.

Nixon, H. L., II. (1993). Accepting the risks of pain and injury in sport: Mediated cultural influences on playing hurt. *Sociology of Sport Journal, 10*(2), 183–196.

Nixon, H. L., II. (1994a). Coaches' views of risk, pain, and injury in sport with special reference to gender differences. *Sociology of Sport Journal, 11*(1), 79–87.

Nixon, H. L., II. (1994b). Social pressure, social support, and help seeking for pain and injuries in college sports networks. *Journal of Sport and Social Issues, 18*(4), 340–355.

Nixon, H. L., II. (1996). The relationship of friendship networks, sports experiences, and gender to expressed pain thresholds. *Sociology of Sport Journal, 13*(1), 78–87.

Pike, E. (2000). *Illness, injury and sporting identity: A case study of women's rowing* (Unpublished doctoral dissertation). Loughborough University, U.K.

Pirks, M. (2010). Does frustration lead to violence? Evidence from the Swedish hooligan scene. *Kyklos, 63*(4), 450–460.

Robidoux, M. (2001). *Men at play: A working understanding of professional hockey*. Montreal: McGill-Queen's University Press.

Roderick, M. (1998). The sociology of risk, pain and injury: A comment on the work of Howard Nixon II. *Sociology of Sport Journal, 15*, 64–79.

Roderick, M. (2006a). Adding insult to injury: Workplace injury in English professional football. *Sociology of Health and Illness, 28*(1), 76–97.

Roderick, M. (2006b). *The work of professional football: A labour of love?* London: Routledge.

Roderick, M., Waddington, I., & Parker, G. (2000). Playing hurt: Managing injuries in English professional football. *International Review for the Sociology of Sport, 35*(2), 165–180.

Russell, G. (2008). *Aggression in the sports world: A social psychological perspective*. Toronto: Oxford University Press.

Russell, G. W., & Drewry, B. R. (1976). Crowd size and competitive aspects of aggression in ice hockey: An archival study. *Human Relations, 29*(8), 723–735.

Sabo, D. (1986). Pigskin, patriarchy and pain. *Changing Men: Issues in Gender, Sex, and Politics,* 16(Summer), 24–25.

Sabo, D. (1994, November 6). The body politics of sports injury: Culture, power and the pain principle. Paper presented at the National Athletic Trainers Association, Dallas, TX.

Safai, P. (2004). Negotiating with risk: Exploring the role of the sports medicine clinician. In K. Young (Ed.), *Sporting bodies, damaged selves: Sociological studies of sports-related injury* (pp. 269–286). Oxford: Elsevier Press.

Sellers, C. S., Cochcan, J. K., & Branch, K. A. (2005). Social learning theory and partner violence: A research note. *Deviant Behaviour, 26,* 379–395.

Sheard, K. (1999). A stitch in time saves nine: Birdwatching, sport, and civilizing processes. *Sociology of Sport Journal, 16,* 181–205.

Shepherd, D. J., Lee, B., & Kerr, J. H. (2006). Reversal theory: A suggested way forward for an improved understanding of interpersonal relationship in sport. *Psychology of Sport and Exercise, 7,* 143–157.

Shilling, C. (1993). *The body and social theory.* London: Sage.

Sipes, R. G. (1973). War, sports and aggression: An empirical test of the two rival theories. *American Anthropologist, 75,* 64–86.

Smith, M. D. (1983). *Violence and sport.* Toronto: Butterworths.

Smith, M. D. (1987). Violence in Canadian amateur sport: A review of literature. Report for the Commission for Fair Play. Ottawa: Government of Canada.

Smith, M. D. (1991). Violence and injuries in ice hockey. *Clinical Journal of Sports Medicine, 1,* 104–109.

Snyder, E., & Spreitzer, E. (1989). *Social aspects of sport* (3rd ed.). Englewood Cliffs, NJ: Prentice Hall.

Sparkes, A. C., & Smith, B. (2008). Men, spinal cord injury, memories and the narrative performance of pain. *Disability and Society, 23*(7), 679–690.

Sugden, J. (2002). *Scum airways: Inside football's underground economy.* London: Mainstream Press.

Sugden, J. (2010). Critical left realism and sport interventions in divided societies. *International Review for the Sociology of Sport, 45*(3), 258–272.

Sugden, J. (2012). Truth or dare: Examining the perils, pains and pitfalls of investigative methodologies in the sociology of sport. In K. Young & M. Atkinson (Eds.), *Qualitative research on sport and physical culture* (pp. 233–252). Bingley, U.K.: Emerald.

Sugden, J., & Tomlinson, A. (2003). *Badfellas: FIFA family at war.* London: Mainstream Press.

Sugden, J., & Tomlinson, A. (2017). *Sport and peace building in divided societies: Playing with enemies.* London: Routledge.

Sugden, J., & Wallis, J. (Eds.). (2007). *Football for peace? The challenges of using sport for coexistence in Israel.* Aachen: Meyer.

Sutherland, E. (1947). *The professional thief.* Chicago: University of Chicago Press.

Sutherland, E. (1973). *Principles of criminology.* Chicago: University of Chicago Press.

Sykes, G., & Matza, D. (1957). Techniques of neutralization: A theory of delinquency. *American Sociological Review, 22,* 664–670.

Sykes, G., & Matza, D. (1989). Techniques of neutralization: A theory of delinquency. In D. H. Kelly (Ed.), *Deviant behaviour: A text-reader in the sociology of deviance* (pp. 232–250). New York: St. Martin's Press.

Theberge, N. (1997). "It's part of the game": Physicality and the production of gender in women's hockey. *Gender and Society, 11*(1), 69–87.

Theberge, N. (2015). Social sources of research interest in women's sport related injuries: A case study of ACL injuries. *Sociology of Sport Journal, 32*(3), 229–247.

Vaz, E. (1982). *The professionalization of young hockey players.* Lincoln: University of Nebraska Press.

Vinger, P. F., & Hoerner, E. F. (1981). *Sports injuries: The unthwarted epidemic.* Littleton, MA: PSG Publishing Company.

Walk, S. (1997). Peers in pain: The experiences of student athlete trainers. *Sociology of Sport Journal, 14*(1), 22–56.

Wann, D. L., Melnick, M., Russell, G., & Pease, D. (2001). *Sport fans: The psychology and social impact of spectators.* London: Routledge.

Wiebe, E. (2014). *Battered bodies, pink nails: The next generation of elite Canadian female wrestlers and their experiences at the crossroads of femininity and sport* (Unpublished honor's thesis). University of Calgary.

Wolfgang, M. E., & Ferracuti, F. (1967). *The subculture of violence: Toward an integrated theory in criminology.* London: Tavistock.

World Health Organization. (2002). World report on violence and health. https://www.who.int/violence_injury_prevention/violence/world_report/en/summary_en.pdf.

Young, K. (1983). *The subculture of rugby players: A form of resistance and incorporation* (Unpublished MA thesis). Canada: McMaster University.

Young, K. (1988). *Sports crowd disorder, mass media and ideology* (Unpublished doctoral dissertation). Canada: McMaster University.

Young, K. (1990). *Treatment of sports violence by the Canadian mass media. Report to Sport Canada's Applied Sport Research Program.* Ottawa: Government of Canada.

Young, K. (1991, November 6–9). Writers, rimmers, and slotters: Privileging violence in the construction of the sports page. Paper presented at the North American Society for the Sociology of Sport. Wisconsin: Milwaukee.

Young, K. (1993). Violence, risk, and liability in male sports culture. *Sociology of Sport Journal, 10*(4), 373–396.

Young, K. (1997). Women, sport, and physicality: Preliminary findings from a Canadian study. *International Review for the Sociology of Sport, 32*(3), 297–305.

Young, K. (2002). Standard deviations: An update on North American sports crowd disorder. *Sociology of Sport Journal, 19*(3), 237–275.

Young, K. (2014). Toward a less speciesist sociology of sport. *Sociology of Sport Journal, 31*(4), 387–401.

Young, K. (2017). Animal racing: Shifting codes of Canadian social tolerance. In J. Maher, P. Beirne, & H. Pierpoint (Eds.), *The Palgrave international handbook of animal abuse studies* (pp. 271–288). London: Palgrave MacMillan.

Young, K. (2019a). *Sport, violence and society* (2nd ed.). New York: Routledge.

Young, K. (2019b). *The suffering body in sport: Shifting thresholds of risk, pain and injury.* Bingley, U.K.: Emerald Press.

Young, K., & M. Atkinson, M. (2013). Sporting violence and deviant bodies. In D. L. Andrews & B. Carrington (Eds.), *A companion to sport* (pp. 327–340). Malden, MA: Wiley Blackwell.

Young, K., & Gerber, B. (2014). Necropsian nights: Animal sport, civility and the Calgary Stampede. In J. Gillett & M. Gilbert (Eds.), *Sport, society and animals* (pp. 154–169). London: Routledge.

Young, K., & Reasons, C. (1989). Victimology and organizational crime: Workplace violence and the professional athlete. *Sociological Viewpoints, 5*, 24–34.

Young, K., & Wamsley, K. (1996). State complicity in sports assault and the gender order in twentieth century Canada: Preliminary observations. *Avante, 2*(2), 51–69.

Young, K., & White, P. (1995). Sport, physical danger, and injury: The experiences of elite women athletes. *Journal of Sport and Social Issues, 19*(1), 45–61.

Young, K., & White, P. (2000). Researching sports injury: Reconstructing dangerous masculinities. In J. McKay, M. Messner, & D. Sabo (Eds.), *Masculinities, gender relations and sport* (pp. 108–126). Los Angeles: Sage.

Young, K., White, P., & McTeer, W. (1994). Body talk: Male athletes reflect on sport, injury, and pain. *Sociology of Sport Journal, 11*(2), 175–195.

CHAPTER 22

···

SPORT, INJURY, AND MEDICAL INTERVENTION

···

DOMINIC MALCOLM AND EMMA PULLEN

INJURIES are incredibly common in sport. Among a U.K. population approaching 70 million, there are an estimated 30 million sport injuries per year. Typically, 25% of those who apply to run a major city marathon will never make the starting line. In the course of an Olympic Games, around 20% of participants will pick up a *new* injury or illness (figures exclude existing conditions). Better-resourced national Olympic committees will typically have a medical staff-to-athlete ratio of 1:6. According to U.K. government figures, injuries within professional football (soccer) are 2,000 times more frequent than in the *average* occupation (Malcolm, 2017).

These striking statistics are very much in contrast to socially prevalent understandings of sport as inherently healthy, what Waddington (2000) first called the sport-health ideology. Indeed, it is perhaps the very routine nature of injury in sport which contributed to its neglect among sociologists of sport prior to the early 1990s. Most early studies of sports injury were incorporated within studies of violence in sport rather than health and medicine. The early 1990s, however, saw a rapid expansion of this field, a development attributed to both the commercialization of sport and the associated economic "cost" of injuries (Loland, Skirstad, & Waddington, 2006), as well as the rising impact of more embodied sociological approaches to the study of sport (Young, 2004). As the field has grown, we have seen the overt medicalization of sport with (1) healthcare increasingly positioned as fundamental to the enterprise of sport performance and (2) physical activity/exercise/sport identified as "medicine," a "miracle cure," and an inherent part of being a responsible citizen in contemporary, neoliberal societies (Malcolm, 2017). Social concerns about sports injuries have increasingly moved beyond the musculoskeletal to the neurological (Ventresca & McDonald, 2019) and mental (Young, 2019) suffering. Sport injury and medicine is an exciting and dynamic field propelled by social processes both within and beyond sport.

ISSUES

···

In the sociology of sport, research on injury and medicine has tended to coalesce around three key issues. Broadly, these can be categorized in research foci exploring (1) the contextually specific definition of injury used by sport participants, (2) the propensity of participants to disregard restrictions to their physical abilities, and (3) the relative availability of suitably trained medical professionals.

Early sociological work on sport injury was particularly focused on sporting cultures and socialization processes that led to culturally specific perceptions of sport injury. Following Kotarba's (1983) work, *Chronic Pain*, which highlighted the extent pain and injury are given meaning and definition through social interactions, studies began to explore the multiple *ways* sporting cultures influenced injury definition. This was initially explored through the experiences of sport injury in elite, semi-elite, and professional sporting populations (Curry, 1993; Nixon, 1993, 1994; Roderick, Waddington, & Parker, 2000; Young, 1993, 2004), driven by indicative evidence that suggested a significant incidence rate within these populations. Research demonstrated how perceptions of injury were deeply connected with the particular kinds of cultural practices that characterized different sports (Howe, 2001; Krane, Greenleaf, & Snow, 1997), the influence of social networks (Nixon, 1992, 1994), gender and athletic status (Messner, 1992; Young & White, 1993; Young, White, & McTeer, 1994), athlete attitudes toward risk (Young & White, 1995), and the precarity of sport as an occupation (Roderick, 2006). The insights from this work have demonstrated the sociocultural aspects of sport injury experience and how this, in turn, has shaped pain and injury attitudes and experiences in sport.

A range of cultural factors relating to the structure of sport and elite sports ideologies was identified. The popular "win at all costs" mentality, commercial incentives, and the hierarchical structure of sport teams (with coaches, managers, medical staff, and athletes) were all viewed as contributing to the rationalization of risk, experiences whereby pain and injury were managed as part and parcel of sporting practice. This was particularly the case in popular contact sports such as the various football codes that were seen to (re)produce dominant cultural sporting masculinities (Sabo, 1989).

Gender has also received significant scholarly attention as a stand-alone issue, consistently identified as a factor in how injury is contextually defined by sports participants. Various studies were in concert in recognizing the extent to which gender identities have come to impact both attitudes and definitions of injury (Dashper, 2013; Messner, 1992; Nixon, 1996; Pike, 2005; Spencer, 2012, 2013; Young & White, 1994; Young et al., 1994). While males were found to be more likely to experience injury through their participation in contact sports (Nixon, 1996), the performance of a successful sporting masculinity was linked to the very embodiment of pain and injury and the making of the idealized sporting masculine body (Spencer, 2012, 2013). On the other hand, physical injury of the female body was often seen as a digression from sporting femininity, with injury experienced as particularly disruptive to female identity (Dashper, 2013).

Although work exploring the issue of contextually specific definitions of injury has often focused on different (yet interconnected) sociocultural factors, it has largely demonstrated the extent sporting environments engender "cultures of risk" (Frey, 1991) or, specifically, a normalization of pain and injury and the continued participation by sportspeople despite injury. Indeed, the propensity of participants to disregard restrictions to their physical abilities and "play hurt" has been a second important issue within the field. As a consequence, traditional biomedical definitions of injury (relating to a breakdown in the structure of the body) rarely apply in the context of sport. A more culturally appropriate definition of (sports) injury would be a bodily condition which fundamentally restricts an individual's ability to perform at their desired sporting level. Simply stated, an athlete who plays sport after bandaging a broken finger and medicating for pain is not "injured" in any meaningful, social sense. This functional classification of injury is both prevalent and highly significant in sport subcultures.

Extending our understanding of the "culture of risk," scholarly attention has also focused on the embodied or lived experiences of athletes as they manage injury through continued participation. Research on this issue is expansive and has explored the self-management of injury by athletes across a variety of different sports, from elite through to amateur sporting populations (see Allen-Collinson, 2005; Andreasson & Johansson, 2019; Atkinson, 2007; Charlesworth & Yong, 2006; Dashper, 2013; Howe, 2001; Markula, 2015; Matthews, 2019, 2020; Roderick, 2006; Roderick et al., 2000; Sparkes, 1996; Theberge, 2006). Through the use of ethnographic methodologies and narrative inquiry (see Methodological Strategies section below), studies have demonstrated the link between embodied and culturally located sporting knowledges in the propensity of participants to disregard restrictions to their physical abilities and "play hurt" (Dashper, 2013; Matthews, 2019; Sparkes, 1996). The stories frequently demonstrated how involvement in sport came with an acceptance of certain risks and the potential of severe injury (especially in the case of more extreme sports) and a certain degree of embodied knowledge that allows participants to differentiate between different forms of pain and injury, that is, between those "real" injuries that prevent play compared with "niggles" that were able to be self-managed (Malcolm & Pullen, 2019; Pullen & Malcolm, 2018). This area of research has been influential in demonstrating the importance of a "sporting identity" in nonelite sporting populations (Allen-Collinson, 2005; Sparkes, 1996). More recent studies have demonstrated how perceptions of "sporting identity" among more recreationally focused participants are illustrative of the pervasiveness of neoliberal health governance that conflates sport and exercise consumption with self-care as it relates to body image and idealized notions of "health" (Pullen & Malcolm, 2018). Indeed, this later work has been particularly influential in demonstrating the role of the sport-health ideology in shaping our understandings about why lay sports participants also tend to disregard restrictions to their physical abilities and incur often chronic forms of injury (see also Hanold, 2010). The dynamics at play with elite athletes, it should be noted, considerably contrast with the very different contexts and social relational demands of recreational sport.

The third key issue addressed is the relative availability of suitably trained medical professionals. Indeed, this is an issue that has developed in significance over time and has done much to influence the current debates within the field. Early research by Roderick, Waddington, and Parker (2000), Waddington and Roderick (2002), and Waddington, Roderick, and Naik, (2001) examined the role of healthcare professionals in professional football. These researchers identified the complex network of social relations between club doctors, physiotherapists, managers, coaches, and players and the occurrence of often unethical medical practices. This included, for example, the ability of managers and coaches to influence clinical outcomes—despite having limited medical knowledge—and the informal relationships between actors that place clinical staff in a weak position to resist threats to their clinical autonomy (Waddington et al., 2001). These findings raised key questions about the ethical conduct of sports medicine professionals and "accepted" practices, and exposed the multifaceted relationship between sport and medicine, the relative informality of the field, and the "medicalization" of elite sport (Malcolm & Safai, 2012).

Scholarly attention given to this key issue has largely focused on elite and professional sport (Malcolm & Scott, 2011; Malcolm & Sheard, 2002; Theberge, 2008). This is perhaps unsurprising given the documented culture of injury tolerance and the inclusion of sport medicine professionals within the networks and structures of elite sport. Yet, reflective narratives about injury experiences in amateur or lay sporting populations have stimulated some exploration about the use of healthcare services, public health knowledge(s), and alternative medicines within such groups (Malcolm & Pullen, 2019; Pike, 2005; Pullen, Malcolm, & Wheeler, 2018; Pullen & Malcolm, 2018). Pike's was perhaps the first study in amateur sporting populations to detail the relative lack (or unavailability) of suitably trained medical professionals within public healthcare. Drawing on the ethnographic study of a group of rowers, Pike highlighted the perceived incompetence of general practitioners (or family physicians) to diagnose sport-related injuries, leading to accounts of an overreliance on prescription drugs and use of complementary or alternative medicine. Subsequently Pullen et al. (2017), Pullen and Malcolm (2018), and Malcolm and Pullen (2019) explored the use of public healthcare and specific healthcare services in lay or public populations that engage in a range of sporting, exercising, and leisure practices. Drawing on neoliberal health governance frameworks to contextualize participants' injury experiences (Pullen & Malcolm, 2018), these studies provided unique insight into the efficacy of the recent integration of sport and exercise medicine services within the United Kingdom's National Healthcare Service. This body of work further demonstrates the reliance that has been granted to normative and accepted health knowledge(s) of injury rehabilitation and/or prevention through sporting networks and, increasingly, online and digital media (Malcolm & Pullen 2019; see also Kimmerle, Gerbing, Cress, & Thiel, 2012)

APPROACHES

In identifying the widespread acceptance of pain and injury among athletes and the way that athletes "normalize," rationalize, and provide legitimating ideologies for their tolerance of this behavior, a relatively high degree of consensus among researchers emerged. There are few if any studies which have challenged the main thrust of these observations. However, there are some distinct differences in approach and explanatory emphasis, and we explore these here in three main sections: foundational principles, theoretical applications, and methodological strategies.

Foundational Principles

The foundational principles focus on three specific areas: the distinct culture of sport, sport's relationship to broader notions of masculinity, and the organizational dynamics specific to sport.

Two concepts were initially introduced to understand the distinct culture of sport. First, Frey (1991) argued that evident within sport was a set of subcultural norms that effectively enabled coaches and managers to transfer their own risk of failure to athletes. The reification of this cultural dynamic insulated coaches from potentially threatening questions about the legitimacy of their training routines and playing tactics and provided management with (moral if not legal) exoneration from responsibilities associated with the potentially harmful effects of their "working practices." Frey termed this "the culture of risk."

On the heels of Frey's work, in an article published a few months later, Hughes and Coakley (1991) developed the idea of the sports ethic. This ethic contained four key components:

1. Dedication, exhibited through unwavering commitment and self-sacrifice
2. Distinction, where victory is both the key marker of success and the motivation to continuously improve performance
3. Deferral of risk, prioritizing immediate performance concerns over longer-term or extrinsic outcomes
4. Refusal to accept or modify behavior in light of potential obstacles.

Hughes and Coakley argued that while these norms were not unique to sport, they were particularly marked, and variously perpetuated, in sport cultures (e.g., in coaches' interactions with players and media commentary). Conformity to the sport ethic was central to enabling individuals to see themselves, and to be recognized by others, as legitimate members of sporting subcultures. The implications of the sport ethic could be seen in a range of health-harming activities, including tolerance of injury (hence fueling a culture of risk).

Alongside these ideas, scholars highlighted the importance of the sport-masculinity nexus in fostering attitudes towards the tolerance of injury. Here, Sabo (1989) had already written about the pain principle, or the patriarchy-based belief that pain is both an inevitable experience and valued as character building (for men). Messner (1990) subsequently developed these ideas both through a broader conceptual analysis of masculinity and violence (specifically pointing toward the socialization experiences of boys as they learn that "real" men can both personally tolerate and are able to inflict pain on others) and in detailed empirical work with males about their pain and injury experiences in sport (Messner, 1992). Young's (1993) research extended these analyses, initially by examining how this gendered ordering of workplace practices was institutionally supported (e.g., through the legal system) and latterly through interview-based research which first explicitly tied male experiences of sport injury to the sociology of the body, and then sought an empirical comparison with the injury experiences of female athletes.

Third, strategies for the analysis of the specific organizational dynamics of sport were developed by Nixon (1992). Nixon expanded ideas about the culture of risk in sport through his notion of the "risk-pain-injury paradox" (where athletes' desperate attempts to achieve sporting success lead them to play while injured, which actually reduces their chances to perform well and makes success less likely). He sought to explain this by drawing on social network analysis to inform his concept of "sportsnets." Sportsnets are the "webs" of interaction between coaches, managers, medical staff, and athletes, as well as spectators, administrators, and investors in sports clubs. Because the sportsnet is primarily oriented toward producing winning teams (in the short term), the quality of medical care (if judged by longer-term health outcomes) is necessarily compromised. Because the more powerful actors in the sportsnet (administrators, coaches) want to maximize the probability of success, they "transfer" their risk of failure by encouraging and cajoling athletes to play through pain and injury. Most distinctively, perhaps, Nixon identified seven features of sportsnets which were likely to reinforce an athlete's propensity to endure pain and injury;

specific characteristic of sportsnets were that they were large, dense, more centralized, hier-archical, closed, homogeneous, and stable.

The logic of Nixon's concept of sportsnets was that a fuller understanding of the injury-related behavior of athletes lay in the study of the attendant healthcare professionals. Walk (1997) specifically referred to this logic in his study of student athletic trainers in U.S. college sport and found that his original hypothesis about the unconventional, incompetent, and unethical practice of medicine in sport had largely been confirmed. Various studies have shown how a process of negotiation, exchange, and trust building is the central character-istic of the interaction between clinicians and athletes (and coaches). The degree to which clinicians comply with the broader culture of risk in sport varies according to a number of workplace contingencies—context, clients, and co-workers in Malcolm's (2017) terms. But an important conceptual development in this regard was Safai's (2003) description of a "cul-ture of precaution" that, to a greater or lesser extent, may be invoked by medical personnel to resist some of the more extreme elements of the culture of risk in sport. This once sideline research concern has now become sufficiently developed to constitute a separate and dis-tinct approach to sport and injury, one focused on the social organization of sport medicine (Malcolm & Safai, 2012).

Theoretical Applications

A variety of theoretical perspectives has been deployed in this area. The number and range of theories applied in studies of sport injury are too extensive for a comprehensive account to be provided, but four distinct theoretical approaches are most evident, with the concep-tual work of Goffman, Bourdieu, Elias, and Foucault particularly prominent.

The strongest theoretical influence on early research on sport and injury came via micro-sociological perspectives, with their emphasis on how the way individuals make sense of their everyday interactions creates particular subcultural norms. Kotarba's (1983) aforemen-tioned *Chronic Pain* set the scene. Drawing on symbolic interactionism, phenomenology, and existential sociology, Kotarba compared and contrasted the injury behavior of athletes and manual laborers and provided various theoretical interpretations of their interactions with healthcare providers. Attention then turned more specifically to the work of Goffman (1959, 1963). Pike (2005) noted that previous work on injury had essentially depicted sport in terms that Goffman would have described as a monolithic institution. Drawing on Goffman's (1959) dramaturgical perspective of impression management, Pike argued that female rowers particularly valued complementary and alternative medicines (relative to "mainstream" medicine) because these interactions tended to enable rather than constrain the athlete's sense of self by facilitating rather than restricting sports participation. Similarly, Roderick (2006) and Allen-Collinson and Hockey (2007) drew on Goffman's notion of stigma and spoiled identities to explain how interpretative social interactions shaped the in-jury experiences of English professional footballers and serious leisure runners, respectively.

The work of Bourdieu (1984, 1990), and particularly the concept of habitus, was ini-tially deployed by Howe (2001) in his ethnographic study of a professional rugby club. Tied closely to the rapid commercialization of the sport at that time, Howe argued that members of the club became socialized into a distinct pattern of social conduct (what Howe called a "club habitus"), such that the management of players' pain and injury became more directly connected to financial concerns and the desire to get playing productivity and value for money out of contracted players. Turner and Wainwright (2003) similarly considered the notion of institutional habitus but related it also to the individual habitus of professional ballet dancers. While perhaps not necessarily a study of sport, the importance of performance and the normalization of injury among dancers and athletes are very similar. For Turner and Wainwright, the dancers' injury experiences needed to be understood in the context of the occupational demands of early age socialization, increasingly demanding schedules/more athletic performances, and interactions within the ballet company community. Attitudes to pain and injury are thus contextually specific but always part of habitus; indeed, they are the physical embodiment of social relations.

The theoretical concepts developed by Elias (1939/2000) similarly lend themselves to the study of sport and injury, and Eliasian or figurational sociologists had been prominent in the studies of violence in sport that formed the antecedents to the development of this field. Indeed, one of the first explicitly theoretical analyses of sport and injury (Roderick, 1998) critiqued Nixon's social network analysis–informed research from this perspective, advocating an approach that was more explicitly developmental, examined changes in injury experiences over time, used the concept of figuration to encapsulate the interchange between structures (sportsnets) and agency, and replaced Nixon's implicitly unidirectional notion of power with a broader recognition of interdependence and power balances. Subsequent studies of injury in professional rugby have used Elias's concept of figuration (Malcolm, 2006; Malcolm & Sheard, 2002), and Elias's sociology of knowledge has been deployed to understand the interaction of athletes and clinicians in relation to injury (Malcolm, 2011). These scholars argued that interactions are structured according to mutually coexisting but contrasting bodies of knowledge, which are shaped by and make sense within distinct social contexts. Malcolm (2011) points to the specific career insecurities and conceptualizations of time which drive athletes to exhibit more involved (and less detached and less rational) forms of thinking. He identifies the significance of the lack of autonomy of sports medicine (characteristic of applied as opposed to "pure" scientific domains) and the "outsider" position occupied by those delivering healthcare in sport. Finally, Atkinson (2007), in considering the pain and suffering experienced by triathletes, has argued that participants create "pain communities" through a shared habitus in which pain and suffering are actively sought. He understands this as the product of what Elias and Dunning (1986) referred to as the quest for excitement, which itself is characteristic of a particular juncture in what has been described as Elias's central theory, the theory of civilizing processes (see Gibson & Malcolm, 2019 for an overview).

A final influential body of theory is grounded in the work of Foucault (1979). Initially Pringle and Markula (2005) drew on Foucault to highlight the competing notions of masculinity experienced by male rugby players. While not fundamentally challenging dominant notions which link pain, injury, and sport with being male, the discourses they found were neither consistent nor unambiguous. This, they argued, challenged much of the previous gender-oriented work, which largely depicted forms of hegemonic masculinity as stable. Hanold (2010) similarly invoked Foucault's notions about the power-knowledge nexus to explore how discourses of the running body, feminine ideals, and pain "create" female ultrarunners' bodies. Hanold argued that technologies of dominance and the self combined to produce normative and docile bodies which were simultaneously subjective, individualized, and personal. Seen this way, ultrarunning was revealed as a site of pleasure and domination and embracing neoliberal notions of self-management and responsible citizenship that were shaped through pain and suffering.

Methodological Strategies

Sociological research on sport and injury is almost entirely underpinned by a constructionist ontology and an interpretivist epistemology; that is to say, injury in sport is seen to be a phenomenon that has distinct personal meaning and needs to be understood using immersive qualitative techniques. While aligned to the sociology of sport more broadly, this orientation might in part stem from the desire to produce accounts which are distinct from the historically dominant medical paradigm used to understand pain and injury. Indeed, epidemiological studies of injury, such as those drawn on in the introduction to this chapter, are relatively plentiful, and sociologists of sport have variously drawn on these to contextualize their work and, at times, provide a syntheses of quantitative data (Malcolm, 2017; White, 2004). Equally, however, it should be noted that the research methods primarily employed in this field are entirely in keeping with the theoretical orientations described earlier.

In line with these principles, a notable aspect of this field is the overwhelming dependence on semistructured interviews. This has been the mainstay of research into sports entailing a variety of risks, from running to rugby. Deviations from this approach are relatively few and far between. While initially Curry and Strauss (1994) drew on visual methods to construct a "photo essay" on the normalization of sport injuries, and Nixon (1993) analyzed mediated cultural influences (an approach much revived by the more recent focus on brain injury in sport; see, e.g., Cassilo & Sanderson, 2018; Ventresca, 2019), these merit mention as the exceptions that prove the rule. More of a critical mass has emerged around ethnographic studies of injury (e.g., Atkinson, 2007; Howe, 2001; Pike, 2005), which have explored sports as diverse as triathlon, rugby, and rowing. Additionally, there is a corpus of autoethnographic work (Hockey & Allen-Collinson, 2007; Sparkes, 1996) describing experiences of musculoskeletal injuries, the impact of facial injury incurred when horse riding (Dashper, 2013), and the qualitatively distinct phenomenology of acquiring brain injury through sport (Dean, 2019). Finally, mention should be made of Thiel et al.'s distinctive mixed-methods approach, combining qualitative interview data with an extensive set of quantitative data derived from elite sport performers in Germany (Mayer & Thiel, 2018; Thiel et al., 2011.

DEBATES

There are, perhaps, three main ongoing debates in this field. They focus on the role of gender in mediating injury and medical treatment, the degree of voluntarism/coercion experienced by participants, and the balance between healthcare professionals' promotion of health and performance. It is perhaps easiest to understand these debates if we address them in reverse order.

Investigations of the healthcare provision in sport opened a window to a range of examples which have contrasted with the idealized yet often claimed representations of medical practice. Enmeshed within the confines of the sportsnet (Nixon, 1992) and constrained as an applied rather than purely scientific discipline (Malcolm, 2011), healthcare professionals revealed considerable personal discomfort in their interview accounts of working in sports medicine. The troubling aspects of this work ranged from concerns about the scientific uncertainty of some of the conditions to which they were required to attend (i.e., concussion; see below) to the desires of both athletes and coaches to act against medical advice and, ultimately, to the outright rejection of core medical ethical principles such as respecting patient autonomy and confidentiality and the overarching core requirement to "first do no harm" (Malcolm, 2016). The common issue underlying all of these concerns was the "right" balance that needed to be struck between the pursuit of health and performance.

This clash of goals strikes at the heart of the sport-medicine interface. As we have seen, the sport ethic and culture of risk effectively prioritize performance over other considerations. These goals are so antithetical to the principles of medicine that, from a philosophical perspective, Edwards and McNamee (2006) have cogently argued that sports medicine cannot (logically) be defined as a branch of medicine. Sociologically, interest has focused on the way these tensions are "lived" in the context of sport. Walk's (1997) study of student athletic trainers in the United States and Waddington and Roderick's (2002) research on professional football in England demonstrated how significant the subcultural concerns of sport were relative to the principles of medical practice. Safai's (2003) work raised an important caveat to this, illustrating limits to the compliance of clinicians, the areas that were beyond compromise, and how clinicians promoted an ethos of precaution as a countervailing force to the subcultural emphasis on performance. Malcolm and Sheard (2002) added further nuance to our understanding, arguing that the commercialization of sport (rugby) had increased the economic value of players and had thus, relatively speaking, heightened the significance of longer-term player health implications for the powerful sportsnet actors.

Two factors mediate this ongoing debate: context and personnel. The variance between studies could be accounted for by the different contexts in which they are set. Commitment to the sports ethic and culture of risk may be ever-present in sport but will differ by degree within professional, elite college, and more leisure-based sport forms. The balance of power between administrators, coaches, and participants will also vary. Isolated practitioners will act differently from those who work on a healthcare team. The seven key features of sportsnets identified by Nixon (1992) have important explanatory power in this debate too. But equally, the research suggests that healthcare providers from different disciplinary backgrounds are more or less flexible in their commitment to the principles of medical good practice. This is evident in the work of both Waddington (2000) and Theberge (2008, 2009), who identified important differences between medical doctors and allied professions such as physiotherapy and sport training. Scott and Malcolm (2015) argued that the combination of medical and nonmedical skills and techniques routinely deployed by sports physiotherapists enabled them to become central actors on multidisciplinary healthcare teams, posing a challenge to traditional professional hierarchies through an evolving sense of practical, flexible, and diverse "usefulness" to athletes and coaches. Physiotherapists and athletic therapists found it easier, literally, to be part of the team.

This context leads us to the second debate: the degree of voluntarism/coercion experienced by participants. The clash between dominant sporting practices and medical principles has been at the core of scholarly discussions and debates in the treatment of sport injury and the practice of sport medicine (Malcolm, 2016; Safai, 2003; Scott & Malcolm, 2015). The debate is typically positioned around ethical and cultural questions of paternalism (on behalf of the athletes' welfare [McNamee, 2014]), physicians' knowledge/background (Safai, 2003; Testoni et al., 2013, and athletes' prerogatives (Anderson, 2007).

Questions of paternalism are often contextualized through discussions of power relations that sit at the heart of decisions concerning treatment options, duration of rehabilitation, athlete welfare, and return to play (McNamee, 2014). An examination of power relations and established networks within professional sports clubs (Malcolm, 2006, 2017; Malcolm & Sheard, 2002; Roderick & Waddington, 2000; Waddington et al., 2001) has demonstrated the degree to which physicians' decisions about appropriate treatment are based on principles external to the athletes' welfare and thus act in a way that deprives the athlete of genuine and effective choice. Indeed, this presents a form of subtle or implicit coercion as it limits the autonomy of athletes by often presenting "choice" in a way that positions the decision to return to play as an expected but ultimately false obligation (Anderson, 2007). While this is not to deny that the welfare of the athlete is underrepresented in decision-making processes, something that McNamee sees as essential to a process of "harm minimization," the locus of power sits predominantly with the established network and vested interests of club coaches, managers, and physicians. Decisions, therefore, are often taken on behalf of the athlete and are based on a culturally specific set of values and practices not necessarily in the best interests of the long-term health and welfare of the athlete.

Indeed, how decisions are presented to athletes—and how subtle or implicit coercion may be applied—is partly influenced by the physician treating the athlete. Professional sport doctors and physicians will negotiate the "culture of risk" when deciding on the course of action for an injured athlete. This is influenced by medical professional knowledge as well as more personal, tacit, and contextually produced knowledge physicians may have experienced in their role across different sporting practices (Channon, Matthews, & Hillier, 2020). Safai's (2003) contribution is particularly relevant here, for interviews with sport medicine physicians highlighted that the "idiosyncratic nature" of treatment guidelines as athlete treatment is partly informed by the physicians' own motivations drawn from a wealth of personal and professional experience. It is important to recognize, however, that coercion does not exist without a degree of voluntarism. Rather, the interactions that take place between the physician and the athlete entail degrees of both cooperation and conflict. Indeed, as mentioned earlier, the locus of power is partly reinforced by the contextually specific motivations of the athlete.

This brings us to the third question in the debate on the degree of voluntarism/coercion experienced by participants: athlete's prerogative (see Anderson, 2007; Thomas, 1991). Arguably, while the athlete-physician relationship is marked by uneven power relations, research has demonstrated the degree to which athletes acknowledge risk, understand the short-term and precarious nature of their career, and consent to treatment practices and quick return to play despite impacts on their longer-term health. Indeed, there is a voluntary acceptance of the "gray" area of medical practice within the sports culture. This is demonstrated by McNamee, Coveney, Faulkner, and Gabe's (2018) account of platelet-rich plasma treatment in sport medicine, a "novel" treatment that lacks a substantial medical evidence base. McNamee et al. are careful to note that the treatment has to be authorized by players, be consistent with their conception of their own best interests (as opposed to, say, the clinician's or their agent's), and be arrived at based on reasonable comprehension of the intervention and all alternatives (including nonintervention). Athlete agency and prerogative thereby influence some of the demands placed on physicians in treatments, often most particularly in treatments that lack a robust medical base. Arguably, the culture of risk (including player perceptions of personal health risk), degrees of "fully" informed consent, and the position of the player within the precarious and unequal economy of sport will exert influence on how athletes conceive "their own best interest" (McNamee et al., 2018). However, it is important to recognize the significant degree of athlete voluntarism in sport medicine cultures.

The final debate—the role of gender in mediating injury and medical treatment—stems from the recognition that sport is a gendered domain structured by masculine ideologies. This has encouraged scholarship to focus on the degree to which this impacts how sport injury is experienced and treated, as well as the degree to which injury perpetuates the female frailty myth (Dashper, 2013; Messner, 1992; Nixon, 1996; Pike & Maguire, 2003; Spencer, 2012; Theberge, 2006; Young & White, 1993; Young et al., 1994). As the dates of these references suggest, this has been less a topic of debate in recent years, but it is likely to reemerge as a salient issue in a cultural moment defined by the increasing commercialization of women's sport. As women's sport continues to move toward the dictates of a commercial sporting economy, it is expected that this topic will present itself, once again, as a compelling issue for study in the field of sport injury and medicine.

Similarly, and reflective of a scholarly "turn" in sport injury research more widely, recent research has been directed toward how males and females are affected by concussion (see Ventresca & McDonald, 2019). Given the degree to which female bodies have long been "medicalized" and aspects of "femaleness" presented as a problem for sport, gendered experiences of concussion in sport will need to chart a difficult path between the importance of a medical science that recognizes population diversity and the reproduction of traditional narratives of female frailty and ideological justifications of restrictions to female sports participation.

CONCLUSION

Sociological research on sport, injury, and medical intervention has developed considerably since the early 1990s. Despite some theoretical and methodological diversity, a significant degree of consensus has developed over the importance of the sport ethic, the culture of risk, and the role of masculinity in creating a distinct set of sporting practices. Because such practices are closely associated with athletic identity, and because they are enabled rather than constrained by institutional actors and ideologies, they are particularly resistant to change. We now have a relatively detailed understanding of these phenomena across a range of sports, different competitive levels, and cultural contexts (though further work is required in this respect). There are, however, two key areas that promise to stimulate this field and enable its productive development.

First, concerns around concussion, brain injury, and chronic traumatic encephalopathy have given this area of study a new sense of social significance. While Safai (2003) briefly touched on head injuries (more specifically, brain injury), the first sustained analysis was

Malcolm's (2009) account of how clinicians sought to manage players with these conditions in a context of increasing regulation, widespread scientific uncertainty, and limited treatment options. In many respects the sociology of sport has been slow to react to what has become a major social issue. Furthermore, the dominance of research based on media representations of this issue (e.g., Cassilo & Sanderson, 2018), compared to the lived experience of the condition (e.g., Dean, 2019), is a considerable contrast to earlier research on pain and injury. However, fueled by allegations that the U.S. National Football League had failed to address the short- and long-term significance of brain injuries, concerns about concussion have spread across sports and across the globe and now constitute a cultural crisis (Malcolm, 2020). Uniquely among sport injuries, concussion is specifically and extensively regulated within the rules of many team and contact sports. This "new reality" speaks to each of the three main issues identified in the Debates section.

Social debates about the need to mitigate the harms of concussion have effectively raised awareness of the culture of risk in sport and brought bodies of public opinion into line with those sociologists of sport who have called for cultural change. Media analysis provides contradictory evidence about whether brain injury concerns are enabling a paradigmatic shift in the celebration of traditional forms of masculinity or whether the cultural backlash represents an entrenchment of this position (although both are logically possible). Concerns stemming from research which has identified higher reported rates of concussion and longer recovery periods for female athletes has served to question the degree to which masculinity fuels the normalization of injury in sport and/or the degree to which the gendering of sports injury perpetuates the female frailty myth. Debates about the regulation of brain injury necessarily evoke questions of coercion through cultural norms and the freedom (of athletes) to participate in activities that are relatively dangerous. There is considerable work to be done to help us understand why it is that athletes remain autonomous in decisions about playing with all *other* injuries, the speed with which they return from injury, and the tests they must undergo before being allowed back into training and competition. Consequently, while a pathway out of the current concussion crisis is not particularly clear, the value of sociological input is compelling.

The quest for answers to these sociological questions leads us to the second key stimulus for this area of study, namely the influence of concepts from the related field of the sociology of health and illness. Sociologists of sport have drawn on ideas such as illness narratives (Smith & Sparkes, 2005) and biographical disruption (Malcolm & Pullen, 2019) to understand the behavior of injured athletes, as well as ideas about medical uncertainty (Malcolm, 2009), professional relations (Malcolm & Scott, 2011; Theberge, 2008) and the influence of everyday work settings on clinical practice (Waddington, 2000). As we further investigate brain injury in sport we will undoubtedly need to understand more about the way medical knowledge about particular conditions is constructed, the promise and pitfalls of neurology in particular, and the way dementia has developed into a dominant social issue in the 21st century.

REFERENCES

Allen-Collinson, J. (2005). Emotions, interaction and the injured sporting body. *International Review for the Sociology of Sport, 40*(2), 221–240.

Allen-Collinson, J., & Hockey, J. (2007). "Working out" identity: Distance runners and the management of disrupted identity. *Leisure Studies, 26*(4), 381–398.

Anderson, L. (2007) Doctoring risk: Responding to risk-taking in athletes. *Sports, Ethics and Philosophy, 1*(2), 119–134.

Andreasson, J., & Johansson, T. (2019). Triathlon bodies in motion: Reconceptualizing feelings of pain, nausea and disgust in the Ironman Triathlon. *Body and Society, 25*(2), 119–145.

Atkinson, M. F. (2007). Playing with fire: Masculinity and exercise supplements. *Sociology of Sport Journal, 24,* 165–186.

Bourdieu, P. (1984). *Distinction: A social critique of the judgement of taste* (R. Nice, Trans.). Cambridge, MA: Harvard University Press.

Bourdieu, P. (1990). *The logic of practice* (R. Nice, Trans.). Stanford, CA: Stanford University Press.

Cassilo, D., & Sanderson, J. (2018). "I don't think it's worth the risk": Media framing of the Chris Borland retirement in digital and print media. *Communication and Sport, 6*(1), 86–110.

Charlesworth, H., & Yong, K. (2006). Injured female athlete experiential accounts from England and Canada. In S. Loland, B. Skirstad, & I. Waddington (Eds.), *Pain and injury in sport: Social and ethical analysis* (pp. 89–107). London: Routledge.

Channon, A., Matthews, C. R., & Hillier, M. (2020). Medical care in unlicensed combat sports: A need for standardised regulatory frameworks. *Journal of Science and Medicine in Sport, 23,* 237–240.

Curry, T. J. (1993). "A little pain never hurt anyone": Athletic career socialization and the normalization of sports injury. *Symbolic Interaction, 16,* 273–290.

Curry, T. J., & Strauss, R. (1994). A little pain never hurt anybody: A photo-essay on the normalization of sport injuries. *Sociology of Sport Journal, 11,* 195–208.

Dashper, K. (2013). Getting better: An autoethnographic tale of recovery from sporting injury. *Sociology of Sport Journal, 30*(3), 323–339.

Dean, N. (2019) "Just act normal": Concussion and the (re)negotiation of athletic identity. *Sociology of Sport Journal, 36,* 22–31.

Edwards, S., & McNamee, M. (2006). Why sports medicine is not medicine. *Health Care Analysis, 14*(2), 103–109.

Elias, N. (1939/2000). *The civilising process: Sociogenetic and psychogenetic investigations.* Oxford: Blackwell.

Elias, N., & Dunning, E. (1986). *Quest for excitement: Sport and leisure in the civilising process.* Oxford: Blackwell.

Foucault, M. (1979). *Discipline and punish: The birth of the prison.* New York: Vintage Books.

Frey, J. H. (1991). Social risk and the meaning of sport. *Sociology of Sport Journal, 8,* 136–145.

Gibson, K., & Malcolm, D. (2019). Theorizing physical activity health promotion: Towards an Eliasian framework for the analysis of health and medicine. *Social Theory and Health, 18,* 66–85.

Goffman, E. (1959). *The presentation of self in everyday life.* New York: Doubleday Anchor Books.

Goffman, E. (1963). *Stigma: Notes on the management of spoiled identity.* Englewood Cliffs, NJ: Prentice-Hall.

Hanold, M. (2010). Beyond the marathon: (De)construction of female ultrarunning bodies. *Sociology of Sport Journal, 27,* 160–177.

Howe, P. D. (2001). An ethnography of pain and injury in professional rugby union: The case of Pontypridd RFC. *International Review for the Sociology of Sport, 35*(3), 289–303.

Hockey, J., & Collinson, J. A. (2007). Grasping the phenomenology of sporting bodies. *International Review for the Sociology of Sport, 42*, 115–131.

Hughes, R., & Coakley, J. (1991). Positive deviance among athletes: The implications of overconformity to the sport ethic. *Sociology of Sport Journal, 8*, 307–325.

Kimmerle, J., Gerbing, K., Cress, U., & Thiel, A. (2012). Exchange of complementary and alternative medical knowledge in sport-related internet fora. *Sociology of Sport Journal, 29*(3), 348–364.

Kotarba, J. (1983). *Chronic pain: Its social dimensions*. London: Sage.

Krane, V., Greenleaf, C. A., & Snow, J. (1997). Reaching for gold and the price of glory: A motivational case study of an elite gymnast. *Sport Psychologist, 11*, 53–71.

Loland, S., Skirstad, B., & Waddington, I. (2006). *Pain and injury in sport: Social and ethical analysis*. London: Routledge.

Malcolm, D. (2006). Unprofessional practice? The status and power of sports physicians. *Sociology of Sport Journal, 23*(4), 376–395.

Malcolm, D. (2009). Medical uncertainty and clinician-athlete relations: The management of concussion injuries in rugby union. *Sociology of Sport Journal, 26*(2), 191–210.

Malcolm, D. (2011). Sports medicine, injured athletes and Norbert Elias's sociology of knowledge. *Sociology of Sport Journal, 28*, 284–302.

Malcolm, D. (2016). Confidentiality in sports medicine. *Clinics in Sports Medicine, 35*, 205–215.

Malcolm, D. (2017). *Sport, medicine and health: The medicalization of sport?* London: Routledge.

Malcolm, D. (2020). *The concussion crisis in sport*. London: Routledge.

Malcolm, D., & Pullen, E. (2019). "Everything I enjoy doing I just couldn't do": Sport-related injury and biographical disruption. *Health: An Interdisciplinary Journal for the Social Study of Health, Illness and Medicine*. Advance online publication. doi.org/10.1177/1363459318800142.

Malcolm, D., & Safai, P. (2012). *The social organization of sports medicine: Critical socio-cultural perspectives*. New York: Routledge.

Malcolm, D., & Scott, A. (2011). Professional relations in elite sport healthcare: Workplace responses to organisational change. *Social Science and Medicine, 72*(4), 513–520.

Malcolm, D., & Sheard, K. (2002). Pain in the assets: The effects of commercialization and professionalization on the management of injury in English rugby union. *Sociology of Sport Journal, 19*(2), 149–169.

Markula, P. (2015). (Im)Mobile bodies: Contemporary semi-professional dancers' experiences with injuries. *International Review for the Sociology of Sport, 50*(7), 840–864.

Matthews, C. R. (2019). On (not) becoming: Involved-detachment and sports violence. In D. Malcolm & P. Velija (Eds.), *Figurational research in sport, leisure and health* (pp. 70–85). London: Routledge.

Matthews, C R. (2020). "The fog soon clears": Bodily negotiations, embodied understandings, competent body action and "brain injuries" in boxing. *International Review for the Sociology of Sport*. Advance online publication. doi.org/10.1177/1012690220907026.

Mayer, J., & Thiel, A. (2018). Presenteeism in the elite sports workplace: The willingness to compete hurt among German elite handball and track and field athletes. *International Review for the Sociology of Sport, 53*(1), 49–68.

McNamee, M. (2014). *Sport, medicine, ethics*. London: Routledge

McNamee, M. J., Coveney, C. M., Faulkner, A., & Gabe, J. (2018). Ethics, evidence based sports medicine, and the use of platelet rich plasma in the English Premier League. *Health Care Analytics, 26*, 344–361.

Messner, M. (1990). Where bodies are weapons: Masculinity and violence in sport. *International Review for the Sociology of Sport, 25*(3), 203–220.

Messner, M. (1992). *Power at play: Sport and the problems of masculinity.* Boston: Beacon Press.

Nixon, H. L. (1992). A social network analysis of influences on athletes to play with pain and injuries. *Journal of Sport and Social Issues, 16,* 127–135.

Nixon, H. L. (1993). Accepting the risks of pain and injury in sport: Mediated cultural influences on playing hurt. *Sociology of Sport Journal, 10,* 183–196.

Nixon, H. L. (1994). Coaches' views of risk, pain and injury in sport, with special reference to gender differences. *Sociology of Sport Journal, 11,* 79–87.

Nixon, H. L. (1996). Explaining pain and injury attitudes and experiences in sport in terms of gender, race, and sports status factors. *Journal of Sport and Social Issues, 20, 33–44.*

Pike, E. (2005). Doctors just say "rest and take ibuprofen": A critical examination of the role of "non-orthodox" health care in women's sport. *International Review for the Sociology of Sport, 40,* 201–219.

Pike, E. C., & Maguire, J. A. (2003). Injury in women's sport: Classifying key elements of "risk encounters." *Sociology of Sport Journal, 20,* 232–251.

Pringle, R., & Markula, P. (2005). No pain is sane after all: A Foucauldian analysis of masculinities and men's rugby experiences. *Sociology of Sport Journal, 22,* 472–497.

Pullen, E., & Malcolm, D. (2018). Assessing the side-effects of the "Exercise Pill": The paradox of physical activity health promotion. *Qualitative Research in Sport, Exercise and Health, 10*(4), 493–504.

Pullen, E., Malcolm, D., & Wheeler, P. (2018). How effective is the integration of sport and exercise medicine in the English national health service for sport related injury treatment and health management? *Journal of Sports Medicine and Physical Fitness.* Advance online publication. doi:10.23736/S0022-4707.18.08389-5.

Roderick, M. (1998). The sociology of risk, pain and injury: A comment on the work of Howard L. Nixon II. *Sociology of Sport Journal, 15,* 64–79.

Roderick, M. (2006). *The work of professional football.* London: Routledge.

Roderick, M., Waddington, I., & Parker, G. (2000). Playing hurt: Managing injuries in English professional football. *International Review for the Sociology of Sport, 35,* 165–180.

Sabo, D. (1989). Pigskin, patriarchy and pain. In D. Sabo and M. Messner (Eds.), *Sex, violence, and power in sports: Rethinking masculinity* (pp. 82–88). Freedom, CA: Crossing Press.

Safai, P. (2003). Healing the body in the "culture of risk": Examining the negotiations of treatment between sport medicine clinicians and injured athletes in Canadian intercollegiate sport. *Sociology of Sport Journal, 20,* 127–146.

Scott, A., & Malcolm, D. (2015) "Involved in every step": How working practices shape the influence of physiotherapists in elite sport. *Qualitative Research in Sport, Exercise and Health, 7*(4–5), 539–557.

Smith, B., & Sparkes, A. (2005). Men, sport, spinal cord injury, and narratives of hope. *Social Science and Medicine, 61*(5), 1095–1105.

Sparkes, A. (1996). The fatal flaw: A narrative of the fragile body-self. *Qualitative Inquiry, 2*(4), 463–494.

Spencer, D. C. (2012). Narratives of despair and loss: Pain, injury and masculinity in the sport of mixed martial arts. *Qualitative Research in Sport, Exercise and Health, 4*(1), 117–137.

Spencer, D. C. (2013). *Ultimate fighting and embodiment: Violence, gender and mixed martial arts.* London: Routledge.

Testoni, D., Hornik, C. P., Smith, P. B., Benjamin, D. K., & McKinney, R. E. (2013). Sports medicine and ethics. *American Journal of Bioethics, 13*(10), 4–12.

Theberge, N. (2006). The gendering of sports injury: A look at "progress" in women's sport through a case study of the biomedical discourse on the injured athletic body. *Sport in Society, 9*(4), 634–648.

Theberge, N. (2008). The integration of chiropractors into healthcare teams: A case study from sports medicine. *Sociology of Health and Illness, 30,* 19–34.

Theberge, N. (2009). "We have all the bases covered": Constructions of professional boundaries in sport medicine. *International Review for the Sociology of Sport, 44,* 265–282.

Thiel, A., Diehl, K., Giel, K. E., Schnell, A., Schubring, A., Mayer, J., Zipfel, S. and Schneider, S. (2011). The German young Olympic athletes' lifestyle and health management Study (GOAL Study): Design of a mixed-method study. *BMC Public Health, 11*(410).

Thomas, C. E. (1991). Locus of authority, coercion, and critical distance in the decision to play an injured player. *Quest, 43*(3), 352–362.

Turner, B., & Wainwright, S. (2003). Corps de ballet: The case of the injured ballet dancer. *Sociology of Health and Illness, 25*(4), 269–288.

Ventresca, M. (2019). The curious case of CTE: Mediating materialities of traumatic brain injury. *Communication and Sport, 7*(2), 135–156.

Ventresca, M., & McDonald, M. (2019). *Sociocultural examinations of sports concussions.* New York: Routledge.

Waddington, I. (2000) *Sport, health and drugs: A critical sociological investigation.* London: E and FN Spon.

Waddington, I., & Roderick, M. (2002). The management of medical confidentiality in English professional football clubs: Some ethical problems and issues. *British Journal of Sports Medicine, 36*(2), 118–123.

Waddington, I., Roderick, M., & Naik, R. (2001). Methods of appointment and qualifications of club doctors and physiotherapists in English professional football: Some problems and issues. *British Journal of Sports Medicine, 35,* 48–53.

Walk, S. (1997). Peer in pain: The experiences of student athletic trainers. *Sociology of Sport Journal, 14*(1), 22–56.

White, P. (2004). The costs of injury from sport, exercise and physical activity: A review of the evidence. In K. Young (Ed.), *Sporting bodies, damaged selves* (pp. 309–332). Oxford: Elsevier.

Young, K. (1993). Violence, risk and liability in male sports culture. *Sociology of Sport Journal, 10*(4), 373–396.

Young, K. (Ed.). (2004). *Sporting bodies, damaged selves: Sociological studies of sports-related injury.* Oxford: Elsevier Press

Young, K. (2019). *The suffering body in sport: Shifting thresholds of risk, pain and injury.* Bingley, U.K.: Emerald Publishing

Young, K., & White, P. (1995). Sport, physical danger and injury: The experiences of elite women athletes. *Journal of Sport and Social Issues, 19,* 45–61.

Young, K., White, P., & McTeer, W. (1994). Body talk: Male athletes reflect on sport, injury and pain. *Sociology of Sport Journal, 11,* 175–194.

CHAPTER 23

··

SPORT, SCIENCE, AND TECHNOLOGY

··

MARY G. MCDONALD AND JENNIFER J. STERLING

SPORT, science, and technology are intrinsically intertwined. One only need explore the rise of Western sport between the 1880s and the 1920s to understand this phenomenon. That is, what is now largely recognized as sport—organized, competitive, rule-bounded, and physical—emerged as an effect of various technoscientific developments that also produced urbanization, mass transportation, and burgeoning mass communication networks. Fast-forward to contemporary times and one can observe a variety of ways in which technoscience—as an array of cultural and material practices—conjoins with bodies and systems to constitute sport, physical activity, and fitness and health regimes.

Sport studies scholars have long used a variety of theoretical, methodological, and conceptual tools to detail these relationships. As sport studies represents an interdisciplinary knowledge project, these social theories, methods, and concepts have largely been drawn from the humanities and social sciences. Increasingly, scholars within the interdisciplinary field of science and technology studies (STS) have also turned their attention to analyzing the ever-expanding technoscientific sporting landscape and sport studies scholars have increasingly utilized existing and emerging STS frameworks (Sterling & McDonald, 2020).

This research has included methodologies that investigate the ways in which human actors are central in applying technoscience to enhance sporting experiences for athletes and fans alike. These manifestations of technoscience include modifications that have been made over the years to sporting bodies, equipment, playing surfaces, and event security, as well as the movement to digital media platforms through which fans may interact, to mention but a few examples. Critical analysis further investigates the ways power circulates through these processes. More recent theorizing has brought posthumanist analyses to this subject matter to reveal that technologies, in and of themselves, can be thought of as actors that engage with humans in ways that also shape sport. This sensibility has necessitated a shift away from long-standing premises about the ascendency of humans, traceable to the Enlightenment, which have led to important reorientations that recognize the interconnectedness of humans and nonhumans.

In this chapter we draw upon critical perspectives from sport studies and STS in considering key issues, approaches, and debates related to science, technology, and sport. We first discuss some important themes that have been examined by scholars. The brief and partial survey of existing research in the Issues section reveals that the mobilization of science and technology is often implicated in inequalities and binaries constructed via relations between race and gender, and natural and artificial—which in turn serve to organize and regulate, or rule, bodies.

In the Approaches section we more directly interrogate the assumptions about technoscience, humans, and broader social worlds upon which this scholarship is based. Here we also point to the productive work of feminist perspectives which move beyond binary assumptions to reveal that bodies are not simply surveilled and controlled to instead suggest that bodies are unruly and too complex to simply fall in line. We then discuss both actor network theory and new materialisms to demonstrate how more-than-human technoscientific objects can interact with human bodies—often in unpredictable ways. Importantly, the Approaches section connects to the recent "ontological turn" that highlights the increasing focus on the character and makeup of being across many academic disciplines. Illustrative examples make clear differences in the ontological assumptions that distinguish between human and more-than-human approaches. These discussions further explicate dominant shifts in how and why these assumptions are brought to bear on the study of technoscience and sport.

Our consideration moves on to the Debates section, where we home in on a particular case study: the controversies inherent within the movement to create "Big Data." In particular this section explores the "quantified self" movement, the term used to characterize the increasing use of self-tracking devices in sport, fitness, and physical activity as well as the attendant data and worldviews these devices help to coproduce. This example further illustrates the related debates, contributions, and limitations of both human-centered and more-than-human approaches as applied to the study of sport, physical activity, health, and technoscience. Our concluding section offers suggestions for further research.

ISSUES

Explorations of technoscientific relationships with, approaches to, and effects on sport have evolved alongside sport's increasing engagement with the "inseparable interweaving of science and technology" (Fouché, 2017, p. 2). Providing early critiques of the role of sport in producing both gendered and racialized scientific understandings of the body, sport studies scholars have explored "medically justified" restrictions on girls' and women's sports participation, as a (dis)proving ground for scientific racism, and more direct interrogations of the role of sports science and its laboratories. Historical and ethical explorations of performance enhancements have also proliferated in the field, alongside conceptualizations of athletes as cyborgs and post- or transhuman others. Joined by digital and data-driven amalgams, explorations of ongoing technoscientific innovation have further opened the door to broader influences, including from STS, that acknowledge nonhuman actants as important foci. This revisiting of selected scholarship reveals that technoscience is too often used in sport in the service of ruling, regulating, and (re)defining bodies. While far from an exhaustive survey, in this section we discuss these major issues and themes as an introduction to sport, science, and technology intersections and invite their continued examination.

Technoscientific Constructions

Critical work on the ways in which science, technology, medicine, and increasingly biomedicine (Clark, Mamo, Fishman, Shim, & Fosket, 2003) shape our understandings of moving bodies is an ongoing consideration and concern in the critical study of sport. Beyond the positivist or performance-focused application of the sports sciences, critical perspectives suggest that technoscience frequently helps to co-construct broader cultural understandings and perpetuate inequalities. As Fouché (2017, p. 13) so eloquently argues, "science and technology have been used as fulcrums to boost deleterious racial, social, cultural, gendered, and genetic agendas." Feminist and critical race scholars, in particular, have drawn compelling linkages between sport, medicine, science, sexism and racism.

These efforts have illuminated, for example, the late 19th- and early 20th-century myths of female physical malady, which structurally served to relegate many women to less physical leisure pursuits. Vertinsky's (1994) extensive examination of 19th-century medical ideologies and women's physical activity offers a key analysis of these histories and their ongoing legacies. In examining the notion of the "eternally wounded woman," Vertinsky demonstrates how the prevalent scientific and medical opinions of the time influenced, and were influenced by, popular beliefs about women's biological and social roles. Thus, dominant understandings of the "nature of women" often resulted in restricted sporting opportunities and, importantly, "the assumed entitlement to medical management of the female body" (p. 1). As such, key biomedical thinking around "biology as destiny" continues to shape the degree to which girls and women—as well as those who identify as transgender, gender fluid, or nonbinary—are able to participate in sport or advance alternate understandings of their own active bodies.

This assumed or dominant "advantage thesis" as discussed by Sullivan (2011, p. 402)—"that all males (born or 'made') have a physical advantage over all females (born or 'made')"—is often coupled with "fair play" discourse in attempts to scientifically and medically define sex in women's sports. Research on the historical and ongoing practice of gender verification also known as sex testing—discussed more fully in the Approaches section and elsewhere in this anthology—is a clear illustration of continuing techno-medico-scientific concerns. Reflecting feminist scholarship on science more broadly (see, for example, Birke, 1999; Harding, 1986; McNeil, 2007; Murphy, 2012), concerns about the scientific construction and medical oversight of women's active bodies continue to be advanced in work such as Thorpe's (2016) research on biomedical technologies and amenorrhea and Jette's (2018) examination of the governance of pregnant women's (in)activity.

Critical race scholarship has similarly interrogated how notions of race have been molded by mutually reinforcing cultural and technoscientific understandings, particularly along Black-white racial binaries and particularly in the United States. For example, Wiggins's (1989) historical unpacking of myths and assumptions around alleged Black athletic superiority as partially produced by scientific racism points to the longtime social and scientific obsession with the physicality of Black bodies. Pointing to athletes such as cyclist Marshall "Major" Taylor and track star Jesse Owens, Wiggins uncovers the various, evolving, and competing racial theories used to explain Black athletic performance throughout the 20th century. This includes physical anthropologist W. Montague Cobb's more legitimate alternative that "proper training and incentive [rather than race] were the key factors in the making of a champion" (Cobb as cited in Wiggins, 1989, p. 161). Schultz (2019, p. 327) offers an additional and more specific examination of these historical white supremacist myths, and their ongoing legacies, in her scholarship on "racialized osteology" and "Black" bones in the context of collision and aquatic sports, where a racialized "imaginary" is created "that at once dehumanizes those of African descent as it holds them up as superhuman beings."

Sport as an enduring platform for persistent and evolving forms of technoscientific racism in an "age of biology" (St Louis, 2004) is reflected in research such as Oates and Durham's (2004) exploration of the gendered and racialized quantification of Black male bodies in the NFL Draft. Carter and Dyson's (2015) actor network theory–guided examination of racism and sickle cell trait screening in U.S. collegiate athletics and Barnes's (2021) analysis of sleep culture in the NBA, where even the Black athletic body at rest is intensely monitored, regulated, and enmeshed in scientific racism and medical discrimination, offer additional recent analyses. Studies of racial science more generally point to a need for continued research on the confluence of race (and its intersections) with science, medicine, and technology. Key writings in this area include Harding's (1993) wide-ranging collection of essays in The "Racial" Economy of Science: Toward a Democratic Future, Pollock's (2012) tracing of racialized medical technologies in Medicating Race: Heart Disease and Durable Preoccupations with Difference, and Benjamin's (2019a, 2019b) exploration of the "New Jim Code" in Race after Technology: Abolitionist Tools for the New Jim Code, as well as her edited anthology on carceral technoscience.

Finally, scholars have interrogated the ways in which sporting scientific knowledge is itself constructed, accepted, challenged, and revised. The laboratory spaces of sports and exercise science are important sites for this process, as elaborated upon by Johnson's (2013a) reimagining of athletes as "model organisms," complicit in the generation and application of generalizable findings, and Gibson's (2019) ethnographic findings around the de- and rehumanization processes at work in the production of exercise physiology knowledge. Pronger's (1995) integration of Foucault's (1979, p. 429) "anatomo-politics of the body" situates how explicit and implicit lessons of the gross anatomy lab render the body a mechanical object, docile and "tamed to be useful to the needs of society." These and additional analyses document the "epistemic inequities" found within medical, technoscientific, and performance-oriented understandings of sporting bodies, all of which serve to privilege positivist, quantitative, and predictive ways of knowing (Andrews, 2008, p. 46). From inscription to integration, mechanistic understandings of the body as "an analyzable and endlessly improvable [and repairable] piece of equipment" (Fouché, 2017, p. 13) additionally drive the production of natural/unnatural binaries and inform their scholarly exploration.

Un/natural Bodies

Scholars have undertaken examinations of the cultural, ethical, and economic pressures which contribute to the use of performance-enhancing mechanisms in sport. A predominant approach to enhancing athletic performance has been to appeal to sport's often paradoxical commitment to fair play, or meritocracy (Fouché, 2017). Such quests for advancements in achievement at once seemingly both invite and eschew disruptions to "natural," "authentic," and "organic" human bodies and performances thanks to perceived "unnatural," "artificial," or "inorganic" nonhuman modifications produced by such entities as pharmaceuticals, equipment, prosthetics, and the built environment.

Research examining the often controversial bodies of athletes modified by internal means has been plentiful and has focused primarily on the impacts of various ingestible or injectable forms of sporting enhancement. This includes Dimeo and Møller's (2018) ongoing critique of antidoping systems and policies, Carter's (2014) contextualization of performance-enhancing drugs within a broader history of sports medicine and antidoping discourses, (especially in British contexts), and Tolleneer, Sterckx, and Bonte's (2013) wide-ranging edited collection on the ethics and morality of doping-related technologies. *Genetically Modified Athletes* by Miah (2004) offers additional insights, extending research into a now-present future. Henne (2015), as well, provides a further interrogation in *Testing for Athlete Citizenship* through her examination of the institutionalization, legalization, and gendered comingling of doping and sex regulations in sport.

Magdalinski's (2009) and Fouché's (2017) investigation of both internal and external modifications serve to explicate the unstable and uneven processes by which technoscience is differentially negotiated in sport. Applied or integrated, "unnatural" designations can range from enabling and therefore presumably neutral, to enhancing and thus often characterized in popular discourses as "thoroughly inappropriate" (Magdalinski, 2009, p. 7) and going "too far" (Fouché, 2017, p. 7). Questioning the taken-for-granted "nature" of sport, the body, performance, and health, Magdalinski highlights the contradictions of "cultural resistance" to mechanical and chemical interventions and the fluidity of binary positions that posit "athletic purity against technological intrusion" (p. 13). Fouché's research compares modes of surveillance, such as the athlete biological passport, with technoscientific "artifacts" such as Speedo's LZR swimsuit to examine the ways in which technoscience is deployed to justify the inclusion and exclusion of particular bodies and to initially embrace, and later disallow, material innovations. Both authors also adopt a wider focus—beyond notions of "fair play" entrenched in antidoping discourse—to acknowledge the broader social and cultural implications of technoscience on understandings of gender, nation, and ability.

A subset of research on the un/natural has explored human-technology interactions in sport as ethically and ontologically confounding statuses, seen in characterizations of the athletic body as cyborgs, posthumans, transhumans, and bio-others. Henne's (2020) excellent overview of feminist technoscience contributions to studies of sport provides a useful guide and productive critique of this literature, particularly in regard to Haraway's (1991) conceptualization of the cyborg as a boundary-blurring, nature-culture, material-semiotic entity. Haraway's cyborg framing suggests that bodies are never simply "natural" but rather always already imbued with technoscientific enhancements, from nutritious food to eyeglasses and pacemakers. Assessing scholarship engaging with Haraway's enduring cyborg trope—including research on bodily enhancement (e.g., Butryn, 2003; Miah, 2003) and disability (e.g. Howe, 2011; Norman and Moola, 2011)—Henne (2020, p. 150) concludes that many studies "focus on how the cyborg problematizes the presumed binary division between human and machine" and the concomitant pleasure or anxiety they provoke. Still, Henne argues that some of Haraway's most crucial insights are infrequently taken up, as cyborgian analyses most often center the (individual) sporting body as imbued with technologies and sometimes fail to meaningfully critique broader historical and cultural forces at work.

More recent collisions with the technoscience in sport include a turn to digital "flesh-technology-information" amalgams (Haggerty & Ericson as cited in Millington, 2014, p. 496) or "corporealgorithmic" couplings (Williamson, 2015, p. 146) seen across a range of queries around sport 2.0's engagement with social media and eSports (e.g., Miah, 2017; Witkowski, 2012), fandom and fantasy sports (e.g., Evans, 2008; Ruihley & Hardin, 2013), the data-driven quantification of self and sporting bodies (e.g., Baerg, 2017; Lupton, 2016), and sport's automation (e.g., Finn, 2016). While Guttman's (1978) oft-cited claims mark quantification as a hallmark of modern sport, Millington and Millington (2015, p. 141) point to the increased scale and speed of human measurement—its volume, velocity, and variety—as it is "emboldened in new ways, and to an entirely new extent" in the "Age of Big Data."

Speaking to a morphing of the aforementioned "body as machine" metaphor—from engine to information system—Lupton (2013, p. 27) repositions the body as an interlinked "smart machine," or "digital cyborg," where "devices not only become prosthetics of the body but extend the body into a network with other bodies and with objects." "Smart" technologies are additionally recognized by Shelby, Barnes, Parvin, and McDonald (2020, p. 318) for their "abilities to create and circulate a veneer of technological progress and innovation" while maintaining the inequitable dis/advantages in the context of "smart" cities, as seen in their hosting of and surveillance activities during mega-events. This is particularly evident in the heightened pursuit of "securitization" ushered in the through post-9/11-era legislation, wherein antiterrorism technologies flowing to and from sporting mega-events are part of a system of now ordinary and increasingly naturalized militarized civic rituals (Schimmel, 2017).

The rapid increase, engagement, and integration of nonhuman technologies, as well as ongoing technoscientific constructions and regulation of sporting bodies, has elicited further responses from scholars of sport. Such approaches, outlined in the sections that follow, acknowledge mixed-reality futures and also merge physical-digital dualities (Miah, 2017), which together can "encompass multiplicity and provide ways to grapple with the potentially far-reaching effects that technology can produce" (Kerr, 2016, p. 12).

APPROACHES

STS scholar John Law (2017) argues that technoscientific practices are methods that shape the world. This status allows scholars to move away from problematic legacies of positivism grounded in the scientific method and the discovery of "natural" laws or truths of science. As illustrated by the themes examined in the previous section, critical sport scholars argue against such naturalization processes to instead investigate the cultural forces influencing sport as well as technoscience itself.

In what follows, we revisit one theme mentioned in the Issues section in greater depth: gender verification in sport. This case helps to better illuminate the observations of feminist critics who posit that despite technoscientific binary policing strategies, bodies are too complex to be fully governed and do not simply fall in line. The section then turns to defining and considering actor network theory (ANT) and new materialism, thus further elaborating upon the complex human-nonhuman interactions that constitute sport technoscientific assemblages. In sum, the following discussion of gender verification, in contrast to ANT and new materialist perspectives, is purposeful in teasing out the different ontological assumptions associated with human-centered versus more-than-human approaches in regard to science, technology, and sport intersections.

Thinking through the Body and Disrupting Binaries

As alluded to in the Issues section, technoscience remains powerful in helping to buttress the gender binary in sport and the broader culture. Anne Fausto-Sterling's work has been particularly illuminating and shows how technoscientific sexism continues to bolster problematic ontological assumptions about the dualistic nature of the human body as articulated via the seemingly natural categories of men and women. In one illustrative case, Fausto-Sterling (2000) discusses elite sport's role in this process by narrating Spanish hurdler Maria José Patiño's (now Martínez-Patiño) failure to "pass" a chromosomal test then necessary to compete in women's track events at the 1988 Olympic Games. Triggered by a perceived threat to "fair play" and Cold War fears regarding the alleged excessive musculature of women from communist nations, sex-testing technologies were mobilized in the 1960s to ensure that men—and their perceived biologically superior bodies—were not masquerading as women in international sport competitions.

Patiño subsequently discovered that her body possessed "atypical" chromosomes, and thanks to her own activism, she was reinstated to the sport years later. Still, Patiño's disqualification is part of a long list of technological, medical, and scientific "regulatory interventions designed to police intersex, hormonal, and chromosomal variation among women athletes" (Pape, 2019, p. 6). The recent testing of some elite women's track competitors for "excessive" testosterone is similarly embedded in problematic dualistic assumptions which deny significant overlap within and between gendered categories which then serve to construct and promote the alleged inferiority of "female" bodies. In embracing such logics, sport administrators reaffirm the myth of biological, categorical gender differences and hierarchies.

Furthermore, these hormonal interrogations have largely focused on athletes from the Global South such as India's Dutee Chand and South Africa's Caster Semenya. Although Chand and Semenya have challenged these testosterone-based eligibility regulations, these policies reproduce a long history whereby medical experts position the bodies of women of color as both "sexually ambiguous and in the service of the co-production of whiteness and femininity" (Pape, 2019, p. 19).

Against this dominant cultural common sense, feminist analysis reveals that the world is not so neatly cordoned off into binaries and that determining sex and who counts as a woman are not simply Northern scientific exercises but social decisions influenced by broader assumptions about gender, race, class, and nation (Fausto-Sterling, 2000; Mahomed & Dhai, 2019; Pape, 2019). Relatedly, such dominant assumptions also influence the type of knowledge about bodies that most scientists and technologists produce. Still gender verification "cannot do the work the IOC wants it to do. A body's sex is simply too complex. There is no either/or. Rather there are shades of difference" (Fausto-Sterling, 2000, p. 3).

These examples demonstrate that technoscience has played a powerful role in reshaping broader ideologies that promote bodily hierarchies—both within sport and beyond. Yet feminist critics, activists, and scientists have been at the forefront in creating alternative accounts, including those that posit the messy, unruly character of sporting bodies and of technoscience. As Pape's (2019) scholarship suggests, the aim of these counternarratives is not to reject science in total. Rather, feminists challenge the technoscientific practices that police and render bodies passive to a medicalized gaze. Instead they often create "alternative ways of conceptualizing the sexed body as complex, dynamic and indeterminate" (p. 18). In doing so, these critics point to the limitations of an influential social institution, sport, which is still largely organized around the presumption of a neat and discrete gender binary.

This sensibility further suggests that "nature" or "biology," much like technoscience itself, are not separate from but intertwined with culture. Such a material-semiotic standpoint promotes an ontological sensibility that critiques the nature/culture and natural/unnatural binaries which too frequently operate within sport and within scholarship about sport. One only need return to the topics that we discussed in the Issues section to see these binaries operating in sport—including those featured in dominant discussions about performance-enhancing drugs, the use of prosthetics as aids to athletic prowess, and the interpretations of Haraway's (1991) cyborg allegory in existing sport scholarship.

Moving past such dualistic thinking allows for a further reimagining of related normative Western/Northern ontologies, thoughts, and actions within and beyond sport. This rethinking involves the recognition of the always already collapsed character of such binaries as masculine/feminine, active/passive, and human/nonhuman. Such boundary-blurring awareness is further elaborated upon via such approaches as ANT and new materialism (McDonald & Sterling, 2020). As examined more fully in the next subsection, the result is a realization of the liveliness of bodies and of their interconnectedness. This also highlights the need to deploy alternative frameworks to capture existing and emerging interrelationships in order to imagine not just sport but broader social worlds differently (Law, 2017).

Beyond Human-Centeredness: Actor Network Theory and New Materialisms

Just as feminist analyses disrupt binary thinking about bodies and cultures, so too have other scholars moved beyond human-centered analyses to recognize the influential role of nonhuman actors interacting with their human counterparts. A good deal of groundwork has been laid to acknowledge the agency of technology via ANT. At first glance, ANT seemingly serves only as a method, but it is also grounded in important ontological concerns consistent with those posthumanist perspectives that grant agency to things. Tenets of ANT can be traced to the ideas of STS scholars Bruno Latour and Michel Callon, as well as sociologist John Law (2017). Early work around this topic documented scientists working in their laboratories and thus directly engaging the complicated webs of practices and relationships that constitute the social construction of technoscience. This ANT-inspired scholarship complements the ethnographies of laboratories discussed in our Issues section.

In particular, ANT "represents technoscience as the creation of larger and stronger networks" (Sismondo, 2010, p. 81). These networks encompass the materiality of humans, objects, and things. This is an important point, for as Sismondo explains, science and technology often "work" by "translating material actions and forces from one form to another"

(p. 83). Further, this framing "views the world as a ceaseless struggle between actants (human and non-human) to achieve stable networks, some of which become relatively permanent, others of which are fleeting or evanescent" (Carter & Dyson, 2015, p. 66). It is additionally important to note that nonhuman objects and things clearly acquire meaning as they interact with humans, once again revealing the material-semiotic character of these networks in action.

Kerr's (2016) *Sport and Technology: An Actor-Network Theory Perspective* is representative of the sporting corpus that applies ANT to trace, often ethnographically, the dynamic actions of particular sporting networks and assemblages. In Kerr's estimation:

> ANT encapsulates the notion that the "whole is greater than the sum of its parts" through arguing that combining humans and non-humans can create assemblages that have vastly different qualities and capacities from singular parts. This is easily understood in the case of sport where athletes can be understood as possessing particular and often impressive qualities owing to the athlete-assemblage, consisting of a human plus a variety of technologies, and training that transforms the human into something surpassing human ability. (p. 25)

Kerr illustrates this process by offering an example of a particular cycling network enrolled with human riders and technoscientific objects, including bicycles, helmets, aerodynamic uniforms, and roads. The synchronous movement of these elements thus demonstrates that humans are a part of complex assemblages that act together with various consequences—effects that are in turn dependent on the scale, shape, and scope of a given network. This conceptualization additionally reveals that agency is not simply the province of intentional actions committed by human actors, as sociologists largely believe; rather, ANT suggests that agency is the product of diverse interactions between webs of human and nonhuman interactions (Kerr, 2016).

ANT has much in common with "new" materialisms in promoting the vitality of nonhumans, including the inanimate technoscientific objects as we have just discussed, but also in relationship to affect, animals, and natural elements such as plants, grass, and trees. The adjective "new" suggests a distinction between Marxist analyses of materialism as grounded in human conscious action, both in creating and in challenging capitalist bodily exploitation. The plural form of materialism signifies the term is often applied in heterogeneous ways (Truman, 2019). We have additionally placed the "new" in quotation marks here to suggest that more recent iterations of the concept are not so new. This is evident in Ahmed's (2008) historical tracing of longtime feminist STS contributions as well as in the oeuvre of such theorists as Gilles Deleuze and Félix Guattari, whose writings continue to inspire diverse new materialist engagements (Pringle, 2020).

Broadly speaking, new materialisms recognize the formative power of matter "otherwise understood as things, objects, bodies, spaces, and places" (Lupton, 2019, p. 1999) that exist outside of conscious human intentionality while signifying a specific "impetus and trajectory" (Frost, 2011, p. 69). But such an understanding, including regarding the dynamic character of the human body, should not be equated with privileging matter over narrative. Rather, new materialists promote a nondualistic ontology in that "biology is culturally mediated as much as culture is materialistically constructed" (Ferrando, 2013, p. 31). In this way matter is not fixed and waiting to be molded by social forces but is always already within a process "which is dynamic, shifting, inherently entangled, diffractional, and performative" (p. 31).

This standpoint equally highlights the insight that what is researched cannot stand apart from the way it is researched. The term "onto-epistemology" captures this enmeshment for

> practices of knowing and being are not isolable; they are mutually implicated. We don't obtain knowledge by standing outside the world; we know because we are of the world. We are part of the world in its differential becoming. The separation of epistemology from ontology is a reverberation of metaphysics that assumes an inherent difference from human and non-human, subject and object, mind and body; matter and discourse. (Barad, 2007, p. 185)

Such new materialist–inspired onto-epistemological perspectives continue to emerge in the study of sport, leisure, and fitness regimes (see, for example, Fullagar, 2017; King & Weedon, 2021; Markula, 2019; Newman, Thorpe, & Andrews, 2020; Pringle, 2020). This includes analyses that engage the natural sciences, but without "a return to positivism, empiricism, or foundationalism" (Markula, 2019, p. 1). These analyses are additionally important, as Markula suggests, as they "account for multiple forms of forces that impact on the formation of assemblages and the affects within them" (p. 5). Ventresca's (2019) scholarship helps to illustrate these points while demonstrating the complex liveliness of human brains when subjected to sports-related traumatic brain injuries (TBIs), as frequently experienced in such collision sports as American gridiron football. Building upon recent developments in the medical humanities and neuroscience, Ventresca shows that the dynamism of brains cannot be fully captured and tamed via modern medicine's technoscientific advances, nor via popular discourses.

Rather, the etiology of chronic traumatic encephalopathy (CTE) as a disease is ambiguous, defying simple cause-and-effect medical models that cannot account for multiple confounding bodily variation, for example, in genetics and cardiovascular health. Nor do simple cause-and-effect scientific understandings and medical diagnoses fully recognize the plasticity and adaptability of brains. Ventresca's (2019, p. 149) analysis thus underscores "the inherent complexity of brain matter and its refusal to be fully predictable." Still, recognizing the ontology of the brain's materiality and unpredictability is not enough to address sport TBIs—but it does suggest the inadequacy of medicalized searches for "one size fits all" pharmaceutical cures and technoscientific solutions such as new helmet designs to combat CTE. Ventresca instead suggests that the "only way to definitively reduce CTE risk is to eliminate head impacts with which the condition is linked" via "drastic forms of organizational and cultural transformation" within the "violent traditions of collision sports" (p. 149).

A similar sensitivity, this time in regard to the liveliness of matter, is readily apparent in King and Weedon's (2020) posthuman scholarship on whey protein. The dairy industry has repurposed this nitrogen-rich, but also environmentally toxic, waste byproduct of cow's milk and cheese from its original unruly and ecologically destructive character into a variety of foodstuffs. These technoscientific products—protein shakes, nutritional supplements, and bodybuilding enhancements—are consumed by diverse groups, including athletes, fitness enthusiasts, malnourished patients, as well as the general public. While many might think these consumables exist only as inanimate objects within a U.S.\$7.9 billion protein powder industry, King and Weedon demonstrate otherwise, revealing the substance's transubstantiations and travels through bodies and the environment. Once ingested, whey protein is absorbed by the body, thus revealing "the shared, relational subjectivity—*and embodiment*—of the eater and eaten" (p. 93). This digestive metabolizing process sees the substance converted into many forms, including the energy necessary to construct muscle.

Typically, excessive nitrogen is then excreted as urine, which once again metamorphizes differently—but in ways that maintain its recalcitrant toxicity, thus polluting wastewater systems. While acknowledging the substance's commodified multispecies entanglement with animals, ecologies, humans, and technologies, this analysis further reveals whey effluent's agentic capacities and the dynamism of matter. This framework further suggests that animate bodies and inanimate technoscientific artifacts "intra-act" in an ongoing practice of becoming (Barad, 2007).

DEBATES

As demonstrated in the previous section, posthumanist onto-epistemological reorientations are important interventions in the largely human-centered, anthropocentric analyses that constitute critical sport studies (Millington & Wilson, 2017). However, these and related shifts are not without their own complexities. The "statistical turn," "Age of Big Data," and "datafication of sport" (Millington & Millington, 2015), as these trends have been variously characterized, have at their core many of the debates and tensions that are inherent in framing the issues and operationalizing the approaches we have discussed. As the growth and integration of "digital data"—via statistical features and analyses aimed at enhancing fan experiences and athlete performance—have exponentially surged in sport, so has research on its countless relationships and impacts. This rapidly expanding area highlights ongoing struggles for scholars to choose or to strike a balance between human-centered and non- or more-than-human-centered onto-epistemologies while navigating myriad intertwined issues that require nuanced understandings and varying degrees of technoscientific expertise.

In this section, we illustrate key tensions and debates engendered by human-centered and more-than-human standpoints that are raised via research on the quantified self, or self-tracking. We offer a brief summary of this research as understandings of the quantified self have been varied—and fraught with many of the aforementioned struggles faced by scholars pursuing research on technoscientific phenomena. Focusing on self-tracking as applied to sport and health settings also reveals important ethical concerns, particularly around privacy and data ownership and usage, that are currently largely unresolved. To capture this state of affairs, we first very briefly discuss related research to expose tensions within the human-centered study of self-tracking by outlining the possibilities and limitations of tracking devices and their production of bodily data. We then revisit and further map additional tensions via a discussion of more-than-human approaches. Most notably, these tensions focus on the ways in which agency and thus power are attributed to human and nonhuman actants.

The Quantified Self

The quantified self is an especially important site of analysis since digital technological advances have allowed for the increasing use of devices and software which help individuals use numerical representations to monitor (often biometrically), among many things, bodily processes and activities, including heart rate recovery and the number of miles run. While athletes and many in the general public have long paid attention to their bodies, for example monitoring the effects of particular diet or exercise regimes via pen and paper, a new expansive digital market has emerged (Lupton, 2016). This includes a variety of "wearables" such as "wristbands fitted with motion sensors" that "use algorithms to track and trace one's physical responses and everyday activities, such as walking or sleeping" (Rich & Miah, 2017, p. 84).

Fitness enthusiasts and athletes have been particularly drawn to these technologies, typically as modes to enhance health and performance, as well as to access the informational means to design alternative practices to reduce injuries. It is unsurprising then, that commercially driven North American professional sports teams such as those in the NFL, NHL, NBA, and WNBA routinely use wearable sensors and devices to generate athletes' bodily information, which is then wirelessly uploaded to the Cloud or sent to computers and mobile devices for further scrutiny by coaches and analysts (Karkazis & Fishman, 2017). Presumably this biometric data then provides fodder for "statistical analyses of physical and physiological characteristics" to assess "performance and recovery," thus offering an evidentiary basis from which to craft needed interventions and more efficacious athlete training routines (p. 46). It is additionally important to note that self-tracking appears to play into existing sport training as a significant scientific practice "because computer devices, platforms, and algorithms are viewed, like the numbers they generate, as neutral, apolitical, unbiased, and more accurate than human perceptions and judgments" (Lupton, 2013, p. 27).

Numerous scholars have investigated the complicated effects and tensions that accompany a society increasingly reliant on the knowledge produced via these and similar digital technologies. Chief among them is Deborah Lupton (2013, 2016, 2019), who has written about both the productive effects of self-tracking as well as its limits. According to Lupton (2013, p. 29), advocates of self-tracking, including for health and performance purposes, envision a world where self-tracking exists as an important life skill, which

> can provide a means of establishing control over the vast amounts of data that are produced about oneself. The discourse of control in quantified self discussions, therefore, is not only about controlling one's body and one's self using data, but exerting control over data themselves.

Read from the view of Foucauldian-inspired analyses, these practices also allow for athletic bodies to be rendered knowable and for individuals to learn more about their bodies, health, and athletic prowess through "self-tracking and quantification" (Rich & Miah, 2017, p. 87).

However, such technologies may not simply provide information for users, but depending on content and context, may serve to control behavior and shape what counts as health, athletic prowess, physical fitness, and well-being (Lupton, 2016). This is certainly the case with the FitnessGram, a web-based fitness tool used in many U.S. physical education classes that relies upon measuring devices and hidden statistical calculations to normalize narrow notions of health and fitness (Jette, Esmonde, Andrews, & Pluim, 2020).

The increasing tendency by sports organizations and coaches to collect biometric data raises related ethical concerns, especially since, as performance measures, athletes' biometric information is typically not governed by health laws and policies designed to protect patient confidentiality and privacy. That is, organizations "measure [and collect] variables such as heart rate, respiration, motion, blood oxygenation, brain activity, muscle function, body temperature, and changes in blood pressure" (Karkazis & Fishman, 2017, p. 46) without sufficient attention to myriad concerning practices. Karkazis and Fishman provide a list of such problems: questions about the actual veracity and validity of the data and the various ways in which it might be interpreted, increased surveillance and threats to athlete privacy, potential problems with confidentiality and security of the collected data, conflicts and questions as to who owns the information, and the misuse of data to coerce and intimidate athletes in such settings as contract negotiations.

Additionally, a wholesale focus on biometric data drawn from self-monitoring devices serves to hide the social determinants of health and human performance (Lupton, 2013). In this particular cultural moment, such an emphasis further reproduces dominant neoliberal ideologies which posit that individual citizens and citizen-athletes are personally responsible for their own health, well-being, and athletic prowess (Lupton, 2013). It is important to recognize that such framing of the numerical data generated via tracking devices is far from neutral and also obscures the ways in which sexism, racism, and classism continue to shape bodies and access to sport and training opportunities. Taken together, all of these insights detail a complex social process of benefits and risks, which further highlights that there is far more at stake in using digital tracking technologies than advocates might initially realize or make clear to users.

In contrast to sociological standpoints that conceive of digital technologies as intelligent tools at the disposal of humans are more-than-human studies of digital technologies that are riddled with persistent controversial issues and concerns. Scholars working with ANT and new materialist assessments have reimagined the human body as but one node in a complex assemblage of networked processes. These processes embrace mobile apps with device sensors, wireless connections articulating to the Internet of Things and analytical algorithms—the sum of which has served to transform bodily measures into quantified flows of data related to sports performance (Rich & Miah, 2017). Feminist new materialisms are particularly well equipped to examine the political dimensions of sport-body-digital technology relationships given their commitments to explicate the complex ways in which agency operates within particular social-justice-oriented concerns and contexts. In doing so they move beyond Foucauldian-inspired applications of neoliberal disciplining to highlight "the potential vital forces of more-than human assemblages" (Lupton, 2019, p. 1999).

Consistent with the theorizing of such scholars as Donna Haraway, Karen Barad, Rosi Braidotti, and Jane Bennett, and as suggested previously, feminist new materialist perspectives strive to capture the "the vitalities, perversities, and vibrancies that emerge with and through human-nonhuman assemblages" (Lupton, 2019, p. 1999). This relational onto-epistemological approach moves beyond commonsense assumptions that posit technologies as simply instrumental or as governing devices. One illustrative example is Esmonde's (2019) analysis of the "digital materiality" that highlights runners' embodied sense of self and of place. Esmonde concludes that these human and more-than-human tracking entanglements collectively combine to produce more than just health-defining data, but also shape and enable runners' (re)gendered perceptions of their bodies, pleasures, and experiences of the environment.

Despite these insights, there is a good measure of controversy regarding the uncritical use of ANT as well as certain renditions of new materialist-informed analyses—as they apply to the quantified self and otherwise. While countering Enlightenment mythologies that abstract complex relationships in ways that promote human action as of central importance, there are compelling critiques to be made of these shifts in approach. Critics suggest that too often these viewpoints flatten out divergent contributions that exist between human and nonhuman actants. Instead, critics argue, ANT and new materialisms, including feminist new materialisms, can often grant symmetrical agency to each actor's role in a given network. In doing so, these outlooks downplay the "response-ability" of humans in leading the formation of these technoscientific forces at work (Haraway, 2016).

Furthermore, as a good deal of feminist new materialist-oriented research reveals, nothing prohibits different theorizing to explore how specific political instantiations around racism, sexism, and classism have become part of broader techno-human assemblages. And yet, too often human-created social forces are downplayed within versions of ANT and some forms of new materialist theorizing. Writing about a context beyond digital technologies but with transferrable insights, Carter and Dyson (2015) make exactly this claim in regard to sickle cell trait screening practices and NCAA college athletics. They note the simultaneously powerful role of assembled networks, which often takes attention away from the commodified racialized contexts of college sport, as well as the "double cost" of some versions of ANT: "a view of agency that does not distinguish sufficiently between its human and non-human forms and, a corollary of this view of agency, an insubstantial view of social structure" (p. 75).

Similar tensions are at play within discussions about the quantified self in relationship to the vital confluence of animate and inanimate actors seeking stable networks. Here, broader criticisms make clear the limitations of many ANT- and new materialist–informed perspectives in failing to fully explicate powerful contextual and political forces, matters which help reveal why some networks emerge and others do not (Carter & Dyson, 2015). For critics, this once again suggests both the need to recognize the materiality of nonhuman actors, such as heart rate monitors and other wearable tracking devices as well as the activity of bodily traits themselves, and to acknowledge the response-abilities of hierarchically positioned human actors within particular social, political, and economic contexts (Carter & Dyson, 2015; King & Weedon, 2021; Sterling & McDonald, 2020).

CONCLUSION

In this chapter we have offered a brief look at the relationships between technoscience and sport, while including illustrative cases within broader physical activity and health settings. This admittedly partial and introductory overview has highlighted the strong (and ongoing) histories of critical work about the body in technoscientific physical cultures. We have also mapped out recent ontological shifts that have ushered in new ways to study and think about complex human-technoscientific entanglements. As such, this chapter has also briefly captured emerging more-than-human analyses that are important in disrupting the long-standing anthropocentrism characteristic of dominant sport studies perspectives. This movement to disrupt anthropocentrism is aligned with those posthumanist approaches that reject "humanist assumptions of an independent, disembodied and autonomous subject . . . thus refocusing attention to embodiment, connectivity, and co-evolution" (Roelvink & Zolkos, 2015, p. 215).

In revisiting existing scholarship, we were struck by how few studies exist (at least in English-language outlets) that are written from non-Western and/or Indigenous viewpoints. This is in contrast to the growth of postcolonial and Indigenous STS, as well as postcolonial and Indigenous feminist STS frameworks more broadly. It is important to note that long before the rise of ANT and new materialism, Indigenous and non-Western perspectives argued against Western suggestions that human activity should be cordoned off from non-human actors as all exist in relation to each other in constituting the material world.

There is considerable work that needs to be done to adopt Indigenous and postcolonial lenses to explicate technoscience and sport (Henne & Pape, 2018; Thorpe, Brice, & Rolleston, 2020). Collectively this scholarship reveals, much as with sport itself, that technoscientific "playing fields" are far from level materially, ideologically, and politically, matters increasingly recognized given the history of Western imperialism and colonization. Illustrative of this standpoint is Johnson's (2013b) ethnographic research on the dominant Western/Northern norms that position Global South exercise physiology labs as substandard and merely "developing." In contrast, Johnson's thick description of a Cape Town exercise physiology laboratory's practices exposes that local scientists view their place much differently: they see their laboratory experiments as innovative and thus resistant to the "perceived Euro-American center of knowledge production," in this case in regard to their ability to more fully map out the bodily processes that help produce athletes' fatigue (p. 293).

Work exploring human and nonhuman technoscientific interactions will undoubtedly continue to evolve. It is our hope that such investigations will increasingly also center concerns around race, gender, class, and ability, as well as consider their intersections. Indeed, as previously noted, too often these relations of power disappear when analyses focus on nonhumans' agentic qualities. King and Weedon's (2021) recent exegesis advises sports scholars to investigate the complex intertwined historical, contextual, political, and technoscientific forces that coproduce sporting bodies—as ensconced within and intraacting with—material environments. This shift to contemplate "ecological embodiment" is not simply an academic exercise but is particularly necessary in this period of massive climate change (King & Weedon, 2021).

In a similar way, there needs to be more intersectional work, detailing the convergences of historically specific constructions of racism, sexism, classism, and ableism in regard to sporting technosciences' impact on human bodies. This is particularly important given, for instance, that the bulk of investigations into new manifestations of scientific racism prioritizes men athletes—although, as previously mentioned, the scholarship on gender verification's intersectional collusion with scientific racism and colonialism is a notable and important exception (Mahomed & Dhai, 2019; Pape, 2019). It is additionally important to point out that there are still many issues which deserve added scholarly scrutiny. For example, the contextual experiences of transgender athletes with technoscientific and medical interventions merit broader analytic attention (however, see Teetzel, 2017).

Furthermore, more recent events will certainly compel scholars to investigate the biopolitics of the COVID-19 pandemic in sporting settings. The U.S. case is a particularly telling site for analysis with bodily politics at play, and this is especially so given the debilitating, disproportionate impact of the virus on communities of color. Sport organizations have had divergent responses to the global pandemic's deadly effects. For example, in 2020 both the WNBA and NBA cordoned themselves off from coronavirus exposure in protective isolating "bubbles" in an effort to safely play to ensure profitability, all the while consuming scarce testing resources. These leagues' use of high-tech tracking devices, such as titanium rings designed for players to wear to allegedly detect COVID-19 exposures based upon pulse, breathing rates, and bodily temperature (Previte, 2020), further suggest new opportunities for scholars to investigate complex human-technology interactions.

COVID-19 analyses are additionally important given that sporting enterprises from U.S. youth sport leagues and NCAA college sport to the MLB have, to various degrees, ignored the scientific consensus on the necessity of radically modifying and/or suspending play as infections rise. At the time we are writing this chapter, such practices further participate in dominant narratives used by President Donald J. Trump's administration in playing politics while downplaying the devastating impact of the disease. In the midst of widespread infections, hospitalizations, and deaths, such denials recreate preexisting Trumpian discourses, touting the existence of fake news and disputing settled scientific knowledge. In this alleged "post-fact" era, as critical voices advocate the need to move away from positivism's limitations, this particular entanglement with its tensions between evidence and opinion, as well as between science and myth, suggests that it is absolutely necessary to engage the types of arguments this chapter has helped to illuminate.

REFERENCES

Ahmed, S. (2008). Some preliminary remarks on the founding gestures of "new" materialism. *European Journal of Women's Studies, 15*(1), 23–39.

Andrews, D. L. (2008). Kinesiology's inconvenient truth: The physical cultural studies imperative. *Quest, 60*(1), 45–62.

Baerg, A. (2017). Big data, sport, and the digital divide: Theorizing how athletes might respond to big data monitoring. *Journal of Sport and Social Issues, 41*(1), 3–20.

Barad, K. (2007). *Meeting the universe halfway: Quantum physics and the entanglement of matter and meaning.* Durham, NC: Duke University Press.

Barnes, S. (2021). "The best recovery you could possibly get": Sleep, rest, and the National Basketball Association. *Sociology of Sport Journal, 38*(1), 16–25. doi:10.1123/ssj.2019-0111.

Benjamin, R. (Ed.). (2019a). *Captivating technologies: Race, carceral technoscience, and liberatory imagination in everyday life.* Durham, NC: Duke University Press.

Benjamin, R. (2019b). *Race after technology: Abolitionist tools for the new Jim Code.* New York: Polity Press.

Birke, L. (1999). *Feminism and the biological body.* Edinburgh: Edinburgh University Press.

Butryn, T. M. (2003). Posthuman podiums: Cyborg narratives of elite track and field athletes. *Sociology of Sport Journal, 20*(1), 17–39.

Carter, B., & Dyson, S. M. (2015). Actor network theory, agency and racism: The case of sickle cell trait and US athletics. *Social Theory & Health, 13*(1), 62–77.

Carter, N. (2014). *Medicine, sport and the body: A historical perspective.* London: Bloomsbury.

Clarke, A. E., Mamo, L., Fishman, J. R., Shim, J. K., & Fosket, J. R. (2003). Biomedicalization: Technoscientific transformations of health, illness, and U.S. biomedicine. *American Sociological Review, 68*(2), 161–194.

Dimeo, P., & Møller, V. (2018). *The anti-doping crisis in sport: Causes, consequences, and solutions*. London: Routledge.

Esmonde, K. (2019). Training, tracking and traversing: digital materiality and the production of bodies and/in space in runners' tracking practices. *Leisure Studies*, 38(6), 804–817.

Evans, S. B. (2008). Whose stats are they anyway? Analyzing the battle between Major League Baseball and fantasy game sites. *Texas Review of Entertainment & Sports Law*, 9(2), 335–351.

Fausto-Sterling, A. (2000). *Sexing the body: Gender politics and the construction of sexuality*. New York: Basic Books.

Ferrando, F. (2013). Posthumanism, transhumanism, antihumanism, metahumanism, and new materialism. *Existenz: An International Journal in Philosophy, Religion, Politics and the Arts*, 8(2), 26–32.

Finn, J. (2016). Timing and imaging evidence in sport: Objectivity, intervention, and the limits of technology. *Journal of Sport and Social Issues*, 40(6), 459–476.

Foucault, M. (1979). *Discipline and punish: The birth of the prison* (A. Sheridan, Trans.). New York: Vintage.

Fouché, R. (2017). *Game changer: The technoscientific revolution in sports*. Baltimore, MD: Johns Hopkins University Press.

Frost, S. (2011). The implications of new materialism for feminist epistemology. In H. E. Grasswich (Ed.), *Feminist epistemology and philosophy of science: Power in knowledge* (pp. 69–83). New York: Springer.

Fullagar, S. (2017). Post-qualitative inquiry and the new materialist turn: Implications for sport, health and physical culture research. *Qualitative Research in Sport, Leisure, Exercise and Health*, 9(2), 247–257.

Gibson, K. (2019). Laboratory production of health and performance: An ethnographic investigation of an exercise physiology laboratory. *Sport in Society*, 22(9), 1604–1622.

Guttmann, A. (1978). *From ritual to record: The nature of modern sport*. New York: Columbia University Press.

Haraway, D. (1991). *Simians, cyborgs and women: The reinvention of nature*. New York: Routledge.

Haraway, D. (2016). *Staying with the trouble: Making kin in Chthulucene*. Durham, NC: Duke University Press.

Harding, S. (1986). *The science question in feminism*. Ithaca, NY: Cornell University Press.

Harding, S. (Ed.). (1993). *The "racial" economy of science*. Bloomington: Indiana University Press.

Henne, K. E. (2015). *Testing for athlete citizenship: Regulating doping and sex in sport*. New Brunswick, NJ: Rutgers University Press.

Henne, K. (2020). Possibilities of feminist technoscience studies of sport: Beyond cyborg bodies. In J. Sterling & M. G. McDonald (Eds.), *Sport, society, and technology: Bodies, practices and knowledge production* (pp. 147–174). New York: Palgrave.

Henne, K., & Pape, M. (2018). Dilemmas of gender and global sports governance: An invitation to Southern theory. *Sociology of Sport Journal*, 35, 216–225.

Howe, P. D. (2011). Cyborg and supercrip: The Paralympics technology and the (dis)empowerment of disabled athletes. *Sociology*, 45(5), 868–882.

Jette, S. (2018). Sport for all, or fit for two? Governing the (in)active pregnancy. In R. Dionigi & M. Gard (Eds.), *Critical perspectives on sport and physical activity across the lifespan* (pp. 211–216). London: Palgrave Macmillan.

Jette, S., Esmonde, K., Andrews, D. L., & Pluim, C. (2020). Big bodies, big data: Unpacking the Fitness Gram black box. In J. Newman, H. Thorpe, & D. Andrews (Eds.), *Sport, physical culture and the moving body: Materialisms, technologies, ecologies* (pp. 131–150). New Brunswick, NJ: Rutgers University Press.

Johnson, A. (2013a). The athlete as model organism: The everyday practice of the science of human performance. *Social Studies of Science, 43*(6), 878–904.

Johnson, A. (2013b). Measuring fatigue: The politics of innovation and standardization in a South African lab. *Biosocieties, 8*(3), 289–310.

Karkazis, K., & Fishman, J. R. (2017). Tracking US professional athletes: The ethics of biometric technologies. *American Journal of Bioethics, 17*(1), 45–60.

Kerr, R. (2016). *Sport and technology: An actor-network theory perspective.* Manchester, U.K.: Manchester University Press.

King, S., & Weedon, G. (2020). Embodiment is ecological: The metabolic lives of whey protein powder. *Body & Society, 26*(1), 82–106.

King, S., & Weedon, G. (2021). On the nature of the body in sport and physical culture: From bodies and environments to ecological embodiment. *Sociology of Sport Journal, 38*(2), 131–139. doi:10.1123/ssj.2020-0038.

Law, J. (2017). STS as method. In U. Felt, R. Fouche, C. A. Miller, & L. Smith-Doerr (Eds.), *The handbook of science and technology studies* (pp. 31–57). Cambridge, MA: MIT Press.

Lupton, D. (2013). Understanding the human machine. *IEEE Technology and Society Magazine, Winter,* 25–30.

Lupton, D. (2016). *The quantified self: A sociology of self-tracking.* Cambridge, U.K.: Polity Press.

Lupton, D. (2019). Toward a more-than-human analysis of digital health: Inspirations from feminist new materialism. *Qualitative Health Research, 29*(4), 1998–2009.

Magdalinski, T. (2009). *Sport, technology and the body: The nature of performance.* London: Routledge.

Mahomed, S., & Dhai, A. (2019). Global injustice in sport: The Caster Semenya ordeal—prejudice, discrimination and racial bias. *SAMJ South Africa Medical Journal, 109*(8), 548–551, http://dx.doi.org/10.7196/samj.2019.v109i8.14152.

Markula, P. (2019). What is new about new materialism for sport sociology? Reflections on body, movement and culture. *Sociology of Sport Journal, 36*(1), 1–11.

McDonald, M. G., & Sterling, J. (2020). The troubling waters of the 2016 Rio de Janeiro Olympic Games. In J. Newman, H. Thorpe & D. Andrews (Eds.), *Sport, physical culture and the moving body: Materialisms, technologies, ecologies* (pp. 197–207). New Brunswick, NJ: Rutgers University Press.

McNeil, M. (Ed.). (2007). *Feminist cultural studies of science and technology.* New York: Routledge.

Miah, A. (2003). Be afraid, very afraid: Cyborg athletes, transhuman ideals, and posthumanity. *Journal of Evolution & Technology, 13*(2). https://www.jetpress.org/volume13/miah.html.

Miah, A. (2004). *Genetically modified athletes: Biomedical ethics, gene doping and sport.* London: Routledge.

Miah, A. (2017). *Sport 2.0: Transforming sports for a digital world.* Cambridge, MA: MIT Press.

Millington, B. (2014). Amusing ourselves to life: Fitness consumerism and the birth of biogames. *Journal of Sport and Social Issues, 38*(6), 491–508.

Millington, B., & Millington, R. (2015). "The datafication of everything": Toward a sociology of sport and big data. *Sociology of Sport Journal, 32*(2), 140–160.

Millington, B., & Wilson, B. (2017). Contested terrain and terrain that contests: Donald Trump, golf's environmental politics, and a challenge to anthropocentrism in physical cultural studies. *International Review for the Sociology of Sport, 52*(8), 910–923.

Murphy, M. (2012). *Seizing the means of reproduction: Entanglements of feminism, health, and technoscience.* Durham, NC: Duke University Press.

Newman, J., Thorpe, H., & Andrews, D. (Eds.). (2020). *Sport, physical culture and the moving body: Materialisms, technologies, ecologies.* New Brunswick, NJ: Rutgers University Press.

Norman, M. E., & Moola, F. (2011). "Bladerunner or boundary runner"? Oscar Pistorius, cyborg transgressions and strategies of containment. *Sport in Society, 14*(9), 1265–1279.

Oates, T. P., & Durham, M. G. (2004). The mismeasure of masculinity: The male body, "race" and power in the enumerative discourses of the NFL draft. *Patterns of Prejudice, 38*(3), 301–320.

Pape, M. (2019). Expertise and non-binary bodies: Sex, gender and the case of Dutee Chand. *Bodies & Society, 25*(4), 3–28.

Pollock, A. (2012). *Medicating race: Heart disease and durable preoccupations with difference.* Durham, NC: Duke University Press.

Previte, S. (2020, June 19). NBA to use "smart rings," big data to fight coronavirus in Disney bubble. *New York Post.* https://nypost.com/2020/06/19/nba-to-use-smart-rings-to-detect-coronavirus-within-bubble/.

Pringle, R. (2020). What can new materialism do for the critical study of sport and physical culture? (Who does this book think it is?). In J. Newman, H. Thorpe, & D. Andrews (Eds.), *Sport, physical culture and the moving body: Materialisms, technologies, ecologies* (pp. 321–334). New Brunswick, NJ: Rutgers University Press.

Pronger, B. (1995). Rendering the body: The implicit lessons of gross anatomy. *Quest, 47*(4), 427–446.

Rich, E., & Miah, A. (2017). Mobile, wearable and ingestible health technologies: Towards a critical research agenda. *Health Sociology Review, 26*(1), 84–97.

Roelvink, G., & Zolkos, M. (2015). Affective ontologies: Post-humanist perspectives on the self, feeling and intersubjectivity. *Emotion, Space and Society, 14*, 47–49.

Ruihley B. J., & Hardin, R. (2013). Meeting the informational needs of the fantasy sport user. *Journal of Sports Media, 8*(2), 53–80.

Schimmel, K. (2017). Not an "extraordinary event": NFL games and militarized civic ritual. *Sociology of Sport Journal, 34*(1), 79–89.

Schultz, J. (2019). Racialized osteology and athletic aptitude, or "black" bones as red herrings. *Journal of Sport History, 46*(3), 325–346.

Shelby, R., Barnes, S., Parvin, N., & McDonald, M. G. (2020). The conjoined spectacles of the "smart Super Bowl." *Engaging Science, Technology, and Society, 6*, 312–319.

Sismondo, S. (2010). *An introduction to science and technology studies.* Cambridge, MA: MIT Press.

Sterling, J., & McDonald, M. G. (Eds.). (2020). *Sports, society, and technology: Bodies, practices and knowledge production.* New York: Palgrave.

St Louis, B. (2004). Sport and common-sense racial science. *Leisure Studies, 23*(1), 31–46.

Sullivan, C. F. (2011). Gender verification and gender policies in elite sport: Eligibility and "fair play." *Journal of Sport and Social Issues, 35*(4), 400–419.

Teetzel, S. (2017). Athletes' perceptions of transgender eligibility policies applied in high-performance sport in Canada. In E. Anderson & A. Travers (Eds.), *Transgender athletes in competitive sport* (pp. 68–79). London: Routledge.

Thorpe, H. (2016). Athletic women's experiences of amenorrhea: Biomedical technologies, somatic ethics and embodied subjectivities. *Sociology of Sport Journal, 33*(1), 1–33.

Thorpe, H., Brice, J., & Rolleston, A. (2020). Decolonizing sport science: High performance sport, Indigenous cultures, and women's rugby. *Sociology of Sport Journal, 37*(2), 73–84.

Tolleneer, J., Sterckx, S., & Bonte, P. (Eds.). (2013). *Athletic enhancement, human nature and ethics: Threats and opportunities of doping technologies.* New York: Springer.

Truman, S. E. (2019). Feminist new materialisms. In P. A. Atkinson, S. Delmont, M. A. Hardy, & M. Williams (Eds.), *The Sage encyclopedia of research methods.* London: Sage. https://dx.doi.org/9781529746808.

Ventresca, M. (2019). The curious case of CTE: Mediating materialities of brain injury. *Communication & Sport, 7*(2), 135–156.

Vertinsky, P. (1994). *The eternally wounded woman: Women, doctors, and exercise in the late nineteenth century.* Urbana: University of Illinois Press.

Wiggins, D. K. (1989). "Great speed but little stamina": The historical debate over Black athletic superiority. *Journal of Sport History, 16*(2), 158–185.

Williamson, B. (2015). Algorithmic skin: Health-tracking technologies, personal analytics and the biopedagogies of digitized health and physical education. *Sport, Education and Society, 20*(1), 133–151.

Witkowski, E. (2012). On the digital playing field: How we "do sport" with networked computer games. *Games and Culture, 7*(5), 349–374.

....

CHAPTER 24

SPORT, DRUGS, AND DOPING

....

PAUL DIMEO AND APRIL HENNING

DOPING in sport is an issue that continues to provoke concerns related to the corruption of sport. Examples of wide-scale and organized doping, usually known as systematic doping, are covered extensively by global media and attract significant attention. They are "newsworthy." A salient example is that of the Russian systematic doping scandal (McLaren, 2016), which has been widely covered in global media as well as being the basis for an award-winning documentary (Fogel, 2017). Another example is the Lance Armstrong story, which has also continued to receive attention through three detailed documentaries, a movie, books, and interviews (including the *Oprah Winfrey Show*) since evidence was revealed about his doping in 2012 (U.S. Anti-Doping Agency, 2012; Zenovich, 2020).

This chapter focuses on how the cultural narratives around the excessive and obvious incidences of doping serve to hide, and to justify, a stark imbalance of power between the organizations implementing antidoping and those who are subject to that authority: primarily athletes, but also athlete support personnel, including parents.

This power imbalance will be explored by focusing on five main issues: (1) the production of the World Anti-Doping Code, (2) Code compliance, (3) strict liability, (4) the appeals and arbitration processes, and (5) antidoping culture. We then explore the range of academic research approaches and discuss the extent to which some of these implicitly accept, ignore, or challenge the more critical issues of power imbalances. Finally, we consider the ongoing debates about the future of antidoping, specifically whether there should be changes made to the Code that would allow for some collective bargaining of athletes' rights, as well as greater consideration of the main issues outlined above.

ISSUES

....

The organization that coordinates antidoping globally, or what they refer to as the "collaborative worldwide movement for doping-free sport" (World Anti-Doping Agency, n.d.), is the World Anti-Doping Agency (WADA). It sets out the rules and procedures for antidoping in the World Anti-Doping Code (WADC), which is implemented by national antidoping organizations and other signatories, including sports federations and event organizers. The

WADC was first written in 2003, and then revised for 2009, 2015, and 2021. How this policy was developed and the approach it adopted is the first key issue around antidoping.

Policy Development

The WADC is a very powerful policy document. It sets out many core features of antidoping: who can be tested, how they are tested, responsibilities of athletes and organizations, which substances and methods are prohibited, the range of antidoping rule violations (ADRVs), and the processes available following an ADRV. This underpins a testing system that has grown over the past two decades to the point where over 300,000 antidoping tests are conducted every year.

The first version of the WADC was written in the period between WADA's formation in 1999–2000 and 2003. It was the first global policy for antidoping and built on the approach previously taken by the International Olympic Committee. The IOC has provided 50% of WADA's funding and many key personnel, including the first WADA president, Canadian lawyer and IOC vice president Dick Pound. The WADC was initially written by a handful of people who focused on strongly responding to the doping scandals of the 1990s (Ritchie, 2013). The emphasis was, and remains, on forcing athletes to take responsibility for knowing the rules and for any substances found in their sample, as well as being available every day for testing. It does not differentiate between types of sport, age, levels of education or competition, or the functional impact of any detected substance on performance in specific events. It aims for drug-free sport in a universal sense, using a one-size-fits-all model. Substances can be prohibited before any research-based evidence demonstrates their effect on health or performance. Sanctions focus on individuals, leading to confusion about what happens when ADRVs occur in team sport situations. The initial standard ban for a first violation was two years, a sanction that was later increased to four years. This increase was made with no consideration of how a banned athlete might be able to handle the repercussions of a sanction, including resulting mental health challenges or replacing income from sport for that period (Dimeo & Møller, 2018; Hong, Henning, & Dimeo, 2020).

Subsequent versions of the WADC were revised after consultation with stakeholders. However, these consultations are only advisory comments, and there is no requirement that WADA take any specific contributions into account. There is no auditing system or direct accountability to any other organization. The final decisions about the WADC rest with WADA's executive and foundation boards. In the course of the three revisions so far, the core strategies have been augmented, including the increase of the standard ban for the categories of substances most associated with performance enhancement to four years. There has been increased authority to sanction athletes for innocuous violations, including cases in which cocaine use or a single missed test has led to four-year bans (although the 2021 WADC will have shorter bans for cocaine, heroin, ecstasy, or cannabis if used for reasons not associated with competitions or performance enhancement). Athletes have some, if limited, involvement in decision-making processes about the WADC, through the 12-member Athlete Committee (World Anti-Doping Agency, n.d.). It is unclear the extent to which WADA has responded to the concerns of academic researchers on key matters such as excessive surveillance, invasion of privacy, the disproportionate length of sanctions, appeals processes, and other issues (Dimeo & Møller, 2018).

Code Compliance

The second key issue is compliance with the WADC. After the Code was published in 2003, WADA's leadership proceeded to increase the number of compliant stakeholders with the support of a UNESCO convention. Thus, by 2008 over 90 countries had ratified the convention (Czarnota, 2012, p. 48). Stakeholders include national governments, sports federations, event organizations, and other relevant groups. Some federations were reluctant to sign the Code, including those representing football, cycling, cricket, and Australian Rules Football (Czarnota, 2012). It is important to note that the main four U.S. team sports leagues are not signatories. Instead, those leagues worked with athlete unions to collectively bargain antidoping rules that are specific to those sports. The U.S. National Collegiate Athletic Association is also not a signatory, choosing to carry out its own antidoping program. Some international sports federations were also initially reluctant to join, such as those representing football and cycling. However, there were consequences for noncompliance, including that those not in compliance would be ineligible to compete at the Olympic Games. There was also a level of public expectation that all sports organizations should be explicitly supportive of the campaign against doping (Engelberg, Moston, & Skinner, 2012; Houlihan, Downward, Yamamoto, Rasciute, & Takasu, 2020).

Once a sports federation has become a signatory, all clubs and athletes associated with that sport become subject to the WADC. As such, most athletes do not have a choice regarding participation in the antidoping system. Of course, athletes do have an alternative: they can choose to give up their competitive sporting careers. Lack of initial awareness about the strictures of the Code has implications for groups such as youth athletes. Indeed, a considerable number of young athletes will become subject to the Code before they fully understand what that means, before their parents understand it, and before they have had any formal antidoping education. The scope of jurisdiction is also unclear. This is how the WADC defines an athlete:

> Any Person who competes in sport at the international level (as defined by each International Federation) or the national level (as defined by each National Anti-Doping Organization). An Anti-Doping Organization has discretion to apply anti-doping rules to an Athlete who is neither an International-Level Athlete nor a National-Level Athlete, and thus to bring them within the definition of "Athlete." In relation to Athletes who are neither International-Level nor National-Level Athletes, an Anti-Doping Organization may elect to: conduct limited Testing or no Testing at all; analyze Samples for less than the full menu of Prohibited Substances; require limited or no whereabouts information; or not require advance TUEs (therapeutic use exemptions). However, if an Article 2.1, 2.3 or 2.5 anti-doping rule violation is committed by any Athlete over whom an Anti-Doping Organization has authority who competes below the international or national level, then the Consequences set forth in the Code must be applied. For purposes of Article 2.8 and Article 2.9 and for purposes of antidoping information and education, any Person who participates in sport under the authority of any Signatory, government, or other sports organization accepting the Code is an Athlete. (World Anti-Doping Agency, 2021, p. 165–166)

It is therefore possible for testing to include a much wider range of individuals than just elite or professional athletes who have the benefit of education and support provided by their sports organizations' specialist advisors. Athletes below national-level standing can also be included. The Comment section World Anti-Doping Agency, 2021, p. 166) goes on to say that noncompeting fitness athletes and masters (older age) athletes can still be tested and sanctioned. There have been numerous cases of nonelite athletes being sanctioned for deliberate and inadvertent doping (see Dimeo & Møller, 2018).

Given the vague and wide definition of an athlete who can be tested, the reach of the WADC becomes a more significant issue when considering Article 5.2, "The Scope of Testing." Article 5.2 begins, "Any Athlete may be required to provide a Sample at any time and at any place by any Anti-Doping Organization with Testing authority over him or her' (WADC, 2015, p. 37). It is well known that elite athletes selected for the Registered Testing Pool are required to give one hour per day of whereabouts information, and that all athletes are subject to random out-of-competition and in-competition testing. However, there has been much less discussion about the need for any athlete, regardless of age, ability, or level of competition, to allow testers to demand a sample "at any time and in any place" (see Dimeo & Møller, 2018).

An overarching issue that requires further analysis is the invasion of privacy, and a second related issue is the potential formal and informal (i.e., social stigma) consequences of not following the rules. A positive test has wide ramifications, including not being able to "associate" with other athletes or attend sports events or club activities during the period of a ban. Thereafter, the label of "doper" is hard to shake off and can overshadow athletes' (nonsport) professional career status and undermine opportunities for career progression. This all seems out of balance with the nature of many "violations."

Athlete support personnel are also subject to the WADC. This is reasonable if these personnel are limited to coaches or team doctors, as their use or supply of banned substances could increase the risk of athletes using banned substances. However, the extension of such sanctions to include parents is troubling. Article 21.2.6 says, "Athlete Support Personnel shall not Use or Possess any Prohibited Substance or Prohibited Method without valid justification" (WADC, 2015, p. 116). It is possible, then, for a parent, guardian, or potentially any family member to violate the Code if they use or possess a prohibited substance, including such banned medical products as ephedrine. There appears to be no systematic attempt to communicate the extent of this reach with parents and guardians, and thus there remains a potentially serious vagueness about these rules and who may be subject to them.

Strict Liability

A third key issue is that of strict liability. Prior to the establishment of WADA and the consistent use of this principle, a number of athletes appealed their doping bans by claiming they did not intend to consume the substance. Even Canadian sprinter Ben Johnson had initially responded to the stripping of his 1988 Olympic gold medal by insisting that his drink must have been spiked by a stranger who came into the athletes' dressing room. Despite evidence in the 1994 case involving English runner Diane Modahl (McArdle, 1999), who was found to be innocent after her sample came back positive for testosterone (it had degraded in high temperatures), the authors of the first WADC took the position that any positive test should lead to a sanction. The exact words in Article 2:

It is each Athlete's personal duty to ensure that no Prohibited Substance enters his or her body. Athletes are responsible for any Prohibited Substance or its Metabolites or Markers found to be present in their Samples. Accordingly, it is not necessary that intent, Fault, negligence or knowing Use on the Athlete's part be demonstrated in order to establish an antidoping rule violation under Article 2.1. (WADC, 2015, p. 18)

Therefore, intent has been removed from the sanctioning process. In the subsequent article on attempted use, the WADC is even stronger:

The success or failure of the Use or Attempted Use of a Prohibited Substance or Prohibited Method is not material. It is sufficient that the Prohibited Substance or Prohibited Method was Used or Attempted to be Used for an anti-doping rule violation to be committed. (p. 20)

The potential to violate the rules is further expanded in Article 2. Evading testers or refusing or failing to submit a sample can lead to a sanction, as can three whereabouts failures in a 12-month period. Tampering or attempted tampering with the antidoping process can lead to an ADRV. Simply possessing a banned substance is also seen as an ADRV. Trafficking, attempted trafficking, administration or attempted administration, complicity, and associating with an individual serving a doping ban can also be ADRVs.

It remains the athlete's responsibility to ensure they do not break any of these rules. Athletes can appeal a sanction based on lack of intent, lack of fault, or lack of awareness. Some of the most controversial appeals focus on the last appeal, wherein contamination has occurred through various means including meat, water, in the manufacturing process of nutritional supplements, or even cocaine ingested through kissing (Dimeo & Møller, 2018). However, strict liability is based on some key assumptions that are questionable: that athletes are of a mature age, are fully aware and educated about the WADC, and are not pressured into taking a substance by their coach, team doctor, or even parents. In such complex waters, athletes realistically put much trust in their support team for assistance and oversight. Still, there have been many cases when either that trust has been abused or mistakes have been made in the provision of medicine (Amos, 2007; Anderson, 2010). Yet the WADC places full responsibility on the athlete even when there might be very legitimate situations in which they have not doped deliberately. This simplistic notion of conscious performance-enhancing substance use being the essence of doping does not take into account the range of ADRVs and the range of potential unintentional violations covered under the strict liability principle in the WADC.

Appeals and Arbitration

After a positive test or other evidence leading to an ADRV, the athlete (or support person) is provisionally charged and suspended. An athlete can take their case to the Court of Arbitration for Sport; however, Court arbitrators are required to ensure only that the WADC rules have been followed. They cannot challenge the nature of the rules or decide on proportionality. If an athlete appeals a sanction, the burden of proof lies with them—a type of "guilty until proven innocent" approach. As such, appeals can be very expensive and time consuming and still result in a ban. If contamination came from a nutritional supplement, for example, the scientific analysis can cost thousands of dollars, and even then it might not identify the source of the substance in question. Even when the source is identified and accepted, athletes may still be sanctioned on the basis that they have been negligent.

Antidoping Culture

The power of the WADC and its antidoping discourse has permeated sport. Antidoping can function as a kind of soft power, playing on perceived norms, morality, and a sport ethic that works to convince athletes and stakeholders that doping-free sport is both the ideal and the only acceptable outcome. Even sports that are not signatories to the WADC have developed their own antidoping or drug-testing programs, partly in response to views of doping as morally wrong that have been advanced by antidoping advocates. These messages and harsh antidoping policies like the WADC have led to a sport culture that is, on the surface at least, intolerant of doping.

While part of WADA's strategy is deterring use through testing and tough sanctioning, there is a stigmatizing component to this strategy. Athletes who test positive under any circumstances are labeled "dopers," even when the athletes are found to be at little or no fault and receive reduced sanctions. Sanctioned athletes are often alienated from their sport and fellow athletes, making the path back from a doping violation difficult (Hong et al., 2020). This label can follow athletes throughout their careers and extend beyond their competitive years to sometimes long-lasting repercussions in their nonsport lives. Amateur athletes who fall afoul of the system may have their names attached to their doping violation for years afterward, as announcements of sanctions often appear high in results in internet searches of athletes' names (Henning & Dimeo, 2018a).

Antidoping culture in sport can also prevent athletes from speaking out about the flaws in the system or calling for reform. Athletes who question antidoping or its processes may face a backlash from fellow athletes, sponsors, and fans. There is a broad view that athletes are generally supportive of antidoping, but surveys using indirect questioning methods on doping have found that large portions—in some studies even a majority—of athletes admit to doping (de Hon, Kuipers, & van Bottenburg 2015; Elbe & Pitsch, 2018; Ulrich et al., 2018). This gap between what athletes say publicly and do privately indicates that the powers that be in sport culture have become intolerant of critiques or challenges to the antidoping system. To protect their own careers and reputations, athletes may choose to say nothing about their concerns or negative experiences with antidoping for fear of being labeled a doper themselves.

Taken together, our five key issues show that athletes have been systematically disempowered by the WADC and antidoping more generally. They have not been consulted and do not have sufficient protections. Athletes can easily slip up and receive a ban that is difficult to appeal. We will now review the various social science research approaches to the topic that have emerged over the past two decades.

APPROACHES

Social science research on antidoping has considered a wide range of issues. In this section, we offer an overview of paradigmatic approaches, though this is not fully comprehensive due to the scale of research in this area. Most notably, we will not be reviewing the body of work that critically describes the historical development of drug use and antidoping policy, as this is too extensive to assess in a single chapter.

Promotion of Antidoping

One approach that researchers have taken broadly supports the assumptions and ethos of antidoping initiatives. This approach to research seeks to understand athletes and sport in ways that can be used to promote clean sport aims and programs. Additionally, this approach may develop interventions to bolster components of the system, including those related to knowledge, education, testing, and understanding the most optimal methods and timings for interventions (Mazanov, Huybers, & Connor, 2011). WADA and the IOC have offered considerable research funding to projects that promote antidoping policy and doping prevention, either through interventions or evaluations leading to improvements.

Several projects have focused on the provision of antidoping education, not just to athletes but to coaches, doctors, and parents (Patterson, Backhouse, & Duffy, 2016). This type of research supports the development and dissemination of "high-level" messaging about clean sport, cultural values around fair play and competitions, and specific detailed educational programs delivered either online or in face-to-face workshops. A more recent type of project that supports antidoping focuses on how to promote intelligence gathering about doping by encouraging whistleblowing. The research conducted by Erickson, Patterson, and Backhouse (2019) has been directly influential in new programs being developed by antidoping agencies, particularly in the United States.

Social-psychological studies have been developed to assess and predict athletes' likelihood of doping and to help design prevention interventions. Key theoretical concepts, including rational choice theory and moral disengagement, have been applied based on the assumption that doping is a deliberate, conscious, and voluntary act that relies on some form of moral deficiency. These approaches implicitly assume doping to be "wrong" or "deviant," while antidoping is morally correct. Researchers have explored the association of doping with negative traits, including Machiavellianism, psychopathy, and narcissism (Nicholls, Madigan, Backhouse, & Levy, 2017), although only the first two were positively linked to doping attitudes. A recent study associated athletes' attitudes to doping with narcissism and controlling behaviors by coaches (Matosic, Ntoumanis, & Boardley, 2020). Other studies looking at athletes and risk have highlighted factors such as perceptions of others' use, return from injury, or career transition points, and several inquiries have focused on the use of nutritional supplements as a precursor to use of banned substances, and therefore a potential "gateway" predictor (Hurst, Kavussanu, Boardley, & Ring, 2019). There is now a well-developed survey tool for trying to understand and predict risk of doping by athletes on the basis on their attitudes toward cheating, drugs, and moral factors: the Performance Enhancement Attitude Scale (Petróczi & Aidman, 2009). Overall, such studies aim to understand the stages through which an athlete might go in order to reach the point of deciding to dope, and to develop ways to inform potential interventions to prevent this occurring.

There have been numerous studies on the ethics of doping and antidoping. These have diverged remarkably. However, a number of sports philosophers have come to the conclusion that sport should be drug-free in order to promote the fairness of competition. In particular, the various research projects conducted separately by McNamee (2012) and Loland and Hoeppeler (2012) have served to outline the basic tenets of this position.

Outside of the social sciences, and therefore beyond the scope of this chapter, some biomedical and biochemistry studies have supported the development of antidoping testing procedures, including finding new analytical methods for detecting banned substances. Another disciplinary area that tends to focus on improving implementation is sports law, where researchers discuss the application of the WADC in appeals and arbitration cases. These tend to be complex analyses about how rules are interpreted and applied rather than broad discursive explorations of the policy systems. As such, it is difficult to classify them as either supportive, accepting, or critical. Still, we can argue that if their focus is on the detail, application, and operational aspects of antidoping, then, at a basic level, they accept the principles and practices of antidoping and seek to promote and improve them by ensuring more effective and consistent legal processes.

Acceptance of Antidoping

This second approach is often characterized by research that seeks to understand and help inform antidoping rather than promote or critique it. This approach to research takes antidoping as a component part of sport to be examined and understood. However, the indirect use of apparently "neutral" evidence could be for either purpose.

One example of this approach is seen in the work employing social science prevalence surveys to explore the true extent of doping. These are usually meant to be in contrast to the 1.5% to 2% of adverse analytical findings that result from the over 300,000 antidoping tests conducted globally every year (Dimeo & Taylor, 2013). Several surveys have used the randomized response technique, which assures the respondent of anonymity by not asking for any personal details, and then adds a layer of assurance by asking a random question (like month of birth) and indicating the respondent should answer truthfully only if they meet a criterion—for example, only answer truthfully if they were born in a month that begins with "J." Estimated prevalence is then drawn from probability models based on the responses. This aims to reduce social desirability bias and increase honest responses. There have been several randomized response technique surveys conducted since 2010, most of which find a higher prevalence than WADA's official testing results show, with some studies showing up to 44% of doping in the previous year (Pitsch & Emrich, 2012; Ulrich et al., 2018). The extensive empirical and methodological issues associated with these surveys are outside the scope of this chapter. It is sufficient to say that these researchers have highlighted, with a critical eye, that antidoping testing systems are inefficient and ineffective, that prevalence varies according to sport and country, and that detailed prevalence information can support an intelligence-led targeted testing approach. This research is often used in support of the principle of testing and aims to improve it.

Other groups of researchers have criticized the implementation of specific components of antidoping without criticizing the overall system. Discussions of the problems facing athletes who test positive inadvertently, for example through using a contaminated supplement, tend to focus on how to reduce the likelihood of this happening through increasing awareness among athletes, coaches, and doctors (Martínez-Sanz et al., 2017). Similarly, studies that explore mistakes made by laboratories that lead to innocent athletes being sanctioned have concluded that, rather than a radical overhaul of the system, the laboratories need greater scrutiny and athletes should have access to relevant information

(Pielke & Boye, 2019). With regard to athlete experiences of antidoping, Elbe and Overbye's (2014) survey led to suggestions for improving the processes in which urine samples are collected. Other surveys have questioned how athletes perceive antidoping policy systems and their level of trust or the system's "perceived legitimacy" (Efverström, Ahmadi, Hoff, & Bäckström, 2016; Henning & Dimeo, 2018b; Overbye & Wagner, 2014). Overall, such studies explore aspects within the current policy, but rather than take a broader view on whether the policy itself should be reconsidered, although some of them indeed do so, they tend to highlight the problems noted earlier in this chapter associated with athlete disempowerment and the monopoly of power held by WADA in the determination and implementation of policies and procedures.

Several studies have questioned aspects of the WADC and global implementation. Surveys on incomplete harmonization have highlighted that some countries and sports are more advanced than others in their approach to antidoping (Hanstad, Skille, & Loland, 2010). Meanwhile, the small number of studies exploring the challenges facing authorities in controlling doping supply routes tend to highlight weaknesses in order to improve control mechanisms and thus support the notion of clean sport and the ambitions of antidoping agencies (Paoli & Donati, 2014). An exception to this is a study by Fincoeur, van de Ven, and Mulrooney (2015), who demonstrated that excessive control and the shift toward criminalization have had damaging impacts, leading them to call for a "rethink" of global policies toward drug use in sport. A brief contrast of these approaches shows that, within the research field of antidoping, studies can be used to make different arguments, some of which help advance more credible challenges to flaws in existing policies and practices.

Challenging Antidoping

This third approach to antidoping research includes the work of critical researchers who question the fundamental rationale of antidoping and those who investigate alternative systems for addressing doping in sport.

When the WADC was first produced, leading scholars criticized the civil rights abuses inherent in processes endorsed in the Code and, more specifically, questioned the implementation of a "whereabouts" system in which athletes have to tell the authorities their locations for living, training, and competing, and those in the Registered Testing Pool are mandated to provide details of where they can be located if required for testing for one hour per day. Waddington (2010) argued that athlete surveillance had become so intense that the only other group in society facing the same types of surveillance methods were convicted sex offenders. Møller (2011) compared the whereabouts system to a form of house arrest.

Some scholars also criticized the extension of the Prohibited List to include social drugs like cannabis and cocaine, arguing that these should be left to the state's police procedures (Waddington, Christiansen, & Gleaves, 2013). While these analyses did not lead directly to calls for overhauling antidoping, they directed attention to potential reforms, including less surveillance, more respect for athletes' privacy, and removal of social drugs from the WADC. These have ultimately not been accepted by WADA, as evidenced by the continued inclusion of these substances in subsequent versions of the Code, although, as noted earlier, the 2021 Code will standardize and reduce the sanctions to be applied (World Anti-Doping Agency, 2021). However, sports that did not accept the WADC—especially those in North America with powerful athlete unions—developed antidoping systems that were adapted to protect athletes and give more reasonable sanctions (i.e., treatment for recreational drug use) for doping offenses.

Other scholars have argued in favor of a greatly reduced Prohibited List, or even its complete removal. In different ways, researchers, including Savulescu, Foddy, and Clayton (2004), have argued in favor of complete liberalization or practices that would allow athletes to use old and new technologies, many of which are available to the wider public. Again, these ideas have not been accepted by antidoping authorities. But there have been some sports, such as bodybuilding, that have made it clear to competitors that a selection of events will have testing and a selection of events will not have testing. The natural body-building movement emerged as a consequence of widespread doping in the sport, around the same time that Olympic sports were beginning to take antidoping seriously.

There have been calls for a harm-reduction approach to doping, such as that proposed by Kayser and Tolleneer (2017). This kind of approach can build on several strategies, in-cluding reducing the Prohibited List, using health (not fair play) as the only criterion for banning a substance, allowing doping under medical supervision, or moving to a system in which athletes are comprehensively tested for overall health (including effects of drugs) rather than testing only for evidence of drug use. Related to this, some researchers argue that athletes' health would be better protected by their having access to doping information, relatively safe products, hygienic conditions for doping, and peer support (Kayser, Mauron, & Miah, 2007; Smith & Stewart, 2015). These views reflect a similar shift around social drug use, away from the "war on drugs" model toward "safe spaces" and other forms of accept-ance and support.

The world of sport has not moved away from the "war on drugs" model. However, there was a period during the late 1990s and early 2000s when the sport of cycling controlled ex-cessive Erythropoietin (EPO) use by monitoring hematocrit levels, as there was no test that identified exogenous EPO in athletes' urine or blood samples. EPO stimulates the produc-tion of red blood cells and can aid endurance. Riders could monitor their blood levels and use EPO up to the point of remaining consistently just under the 50% limit. This threshold approach could be used for other substances to allow a sanctioned level of use that would pose fewer risks than unregulated illicit use.

DEBATES

There are several ongoing debates around doping and drug use in sport among both academics and policymakers. Here, we focus on four that center on questions of athlete rights and welfare: (1) athletes' voice in policymaking, (2) protection for minors or others forced to dope, (3) recreational drug use, and (4) post-sanction support for returning to sport.

Athletes' Voice

The WADC is a document that directly impacts athletes and can have severe consequences for those who violate it. As noted, the WADC was produced in response to doping scandals by a group of sport officials determined to "clean up" sport. Athletes were, and continue to be, largely left out of discussion and debates around regulations, including questions of testing and sanctions. Athletes are currently represented within WADA by an Athlete Commission that was established in 2005—two years after the first WADC became effective. It is comprised of athletes who are drawn from representatives to national Olympic committees, national antidoping committees, or the IOC. However, the Athlete Commission does not have voting rights in WADA's Executive Committee, which is the Agency's policymaking body. As such, this governance structure leaves out the central stakeholder group in the organization's mission. Thus far, WADA has not taken steps to include athletes, leaving the composition of the Executive Committee at 50% members from the Olympic Movement and 50% from national public authorities.

Athletes and athlete groups have called for better representation and voting power within antidoping. Global Athlete, for example, is an independent athlete group seeking better athlete representation in sport, especially in antidoping. This effort mirrors, in some ways, the athletes' unions in U.S. professional sports that have successfully collectively bargained their respective league's drug and antidoping policies. However, WADA has so far resisted including more athletes on their committees, and it is far from clear how unified the "athletes' voice" would be and what sort of policy changes they would individually or collectively try to propose and support. Of additional concern would be amateur or nonelite athletes who are increasingly subject to the WADC but are not protected by education, medical support, or unionization and are unlikely to be able to afford legal representation, but for whom any sanction holds real risks of damaging their reputation and career outside of sport (Henning & Dimeo 2018a).

Protection for Minors and Other Vulnerable Athletes

The definition of an athlete is widely construed in the WADC, as noted. The Code lays out the responsibilities of athletes but is less clear on the responsibilities that WADA has toward athletes. Young athletes competing at a high level, for example, can be brought into the system before they have received antidoping education or are empowered or able to make choices about their training, nutrition, medications, and so on. These athletes are vulnerable to abuse by unethical coaches or parents. Further, they can be subjected to the invasive sample-collection process, presenting ethical debates about consent. Minor athletes who violate doping rules can receive the same sanctions as adults, raising questions about the proportionality of punishment to the responsibility that can actually be attributed to athletes whose cognitive and emotional development has not yet advanced to adulthood. Similarly, some athletes may be pressured or even forced to dope by coaches, sports organizations, or national bodies. The clearest examples are East German athletes who were unwittingly required to do so (Ungerleider & Bradley, 2001). In such cases athletes may be given drugs without their consent or be coerced into use. Under the strict liability principle in the WADC, athletes are responsible for whatever is found in their samples.

In both of these latter examples, vulnerable athletes may be sanctioned. Cases involving minors or other athletes coerced into doping have called attention to this issue, although little has been done to address their harms at the policy level. Researchers have also noted a range of problems with strict liability (Boye, Skotland, Østerud, & Nissen-Meyer, 2017; Geeraets, 2018; Henning & Dimeo, 2018a), but as the whole system hangs on preventing athletes from explaining away any use of prohibited substances—zero tolerance—athletes may end up with punishments for offenses they may not have intended to commit.

Recreational Drugs

The inclusion of recreational drugs on the Prohibited List is fodder for a long-standing debate. Athletes who test positive for recreational drugs—including those that may have no performance-enhancing effects, such as cannabis—have been subject to the same sanctions as athletes who intentionally use known enhancers. While outside sport there has been a turn to treatment for recreational drug use, sport has been slower to change. The 2021 WADC allows for a reduced sanction for recreational drug use, although there would still be a ban from sport and potentially a requirement for rehabilitation.

Post-Sanction Support and Returning to Sport

Antidoping attempts to deter doping and, failing that, to detect and punish it. Part of its deterrence strategy is linking doping with cheating. Athletes who test positive are dopers, and dopers are posited to be bad no matter the situation and always deserving of punishment. The WADC sets out the standard sanction of four years. While this is a long time in many athletic careers, the protocol does offer the chance of returning to sport following a competition ban. However, the power of antidoping messaging is such that athletes who test positive are often stigmatized both in and out of sport—they are forever labeled "dopers." This can make returning to sport and recovering sponsorships or other support extremely difficult. While some stakeholders have been vocal that athletes should be banned for life for a first offense (see Sumner, 2017; Tucker, 2012), others have argued that there needs to be allowance for athletes to resume their careers following serving a ban (Hong et al., 2020).

Athletes who test positive are not provided with post-sanction support. Though they may face loss of income, isolation from their sport, and loss of social support and may be at risk for mental health problems, they are generally left to deal with the fallout from a positive test on their own (Hong et al., 2020).

CONCLUSION

This chapter has sought to review the debates and research on doping behaviors and antidoping policies. The Russian doping crisis has brought the issue into public life through continued media coverage, which has led to increased calls for more action to prevent doping. The retesting of samples from the 2008 and 2012 Olympic Games shows that the problem of doping has not gone away, despite 20 years of WADA's promotion of global policies around education, testing, and sanctions.

Academic research on doping and antidoping has blossomed in that time. Studies range from highly detailed contemporary histories to ethical and philosophical discussions and works of sociological, psychological, and criminological empirical and theoretical developments. There have been many attempts to use research for pragmatic purposes in support of antidoping's broader themes and principles. By contrast, there have been numerous critical analyses which explore the fundamental aims and strategies created and implemented by WADA.

It seems clear that global policymaking is now much more highly structured than the fragmented nature of policy from the 1960s to the 1990s, or even in the early years of WADA. This global structure limits open debate on liberalization and harm reduction, while prioritizing funding opportunities for researchers seeking "social impact" from their applied research supportive of received policies. The global consensus around the benefits of antidoping, as well as its broad institutional support, serve to gloss over the significant intrusions into athletes' lives and privacy, risks of accidental doping leading to career sanctions and stigmatization, the lack of opportunity for returning from a doping ban, and the broadening of critical issues to nonelite and youth sections of the athlete community. The future of antidoping appears to be a slowly changing landscape monopolized by WADA and its stakeholders that has gradually shifted more and more toward empowering WADA. In such a landscape, athletes struggle to be heard and critical academic research is increasingly sublimated by studies aiming to find helpful solutions and interventions to reduce doping behaviors.

Moreover, in the rush to use applied research to propose tweaks or radical changes to policy, there is a risk that both overseers and spectators become detached from deeper, embedded engagement with participants. Several scholars have aimed to develop a stronger understanding of cultural and practical aspects of doping and related forms of performance enhancement (Henning & Andreasson, 2021; Matthews & Jordan, 2020; Monaghan, 1999; see also van de Ven, Mulrooney, & McVeigh, 2019). These studies are important because athletes, especially in nonelite contexts where there is less WADA surveillance and more self-determination, are developing networks and making decisions about their own health and bodies in the pursuit of performance, lifestyle, or body image ambitions.

One of the main contributions social science can make to the study of doping and antidoping is through more objective, nonjudgmental explorations of values, ideas, and day-to-day practices in which risk is negotiated and drug use either resisted or normalized. Indeed, there may be situations in which risk is actually reduced through self-protective networks of information and support or enabling environments (Henning, McLean, Andreasson, & Dimeo, 2020). Only by developing a more nuanced, less ideologically presumptive, and less policy-oriented approach can we improve understanding and appreciation of antidoping as a sociological intervention that overlaps and interacts with other value systems and practices. This would empower athletes by recognizing their agency and accepting their choices rather than seeing them through the lens of antidoping policymakers as passive, docile recipients of a policy they have no choice but to accept and comply with.

References

Amos, A. (2007). Inadvertent doping and the WADA Code. *Bond Law Review, 19*(1), 1–25.
Anderson, J. (2010). *Modern sport law: A textbook.* Oxford: Hart.

Boye, E., Skotland, T., Østerud, B., & Nissen-Meyer, J. (2017). Doping and drug testing: Anti-doping work must be transparent and adhere to good scientific practices to ensure public trust. *EMBO Reports, 18*(3), 351–354.

Czarnota, P. A. (2012). The World Anti-Doping Code: The athlete's duty of "utmost caution" and the elimination of cheating. *Marquette Sports Law Review, 23*(1), 45–74.

De Hon, O., Kuipers, H., & van Bottenburg, M. (2015). Prevalence of doping use in elite sports: A review of numbers and methods. *Sports Medicine, 45*(1), 57–69.

Dimeo, P., & Møller, V. (2018). *The anti-doping crisis in sport: Causes, consequences, solutions.* London: Routledge.

Dimeo, P., & Taylor, J. (2013). Monitoring drug use in sport: The contrast between official statistics and other evidence. *Drugs: Education, Prevention, Policy, 20*(1), 40–47.

Efverström, A., Ahmadi, N., Hoff, D., & Bäckström, Å. (2016). Anti-doping and legitimacy: An international survey of elite athletes' perceptions. *International Journal of Sport Policy and Politics, 8*(3), 491–514.

Elbe, A., & Overbye, M. (2014). Urine doping controls: The athletes' perspective. *International Journal of Sport Policy and Politics, 6*(2), 227–240.

Elbe, A. M., & Pitsch, W. (2018). Doping prevalence among Danish elite athletes. *Performance Enhancement & Health, 6*(1), 28–32.

Engelberg, T., Moston, S., & Skinner, J. (2012). Public perception of sport anti-doping policy in Australia. *Drugs: Education, Prevention and Policy, 19*(1), 84–87.

Erickson, K., Patterson, L., & Backhouse, S. (2019). "The process isn't a case of report it and stop": Athletes' lived experience of whistleblowing on doping in sport. *Sport Management Review, 22*(5), 724–735.

Fincoeur, B., van de Ven, K., & Mulrooney, K. (2015). The symbiotic evolution of anti-doping and supply chains of doping substances: How criminal networks may benefit from anti-doping policy. *Trends in Organized Crime, 18*, 229–25.

Fogel, B. (Director). (2017). *Icarus.* USA: Netflix.

Geeraets, V. (2018). Ideology, doping and the spirit of sport. *Sport, Ethics and Philosophy, 12*(3), 255–271.

Hanstad, D. V., Skille, E., & Loland, S. (2010). Harmonization of anti-doping work: Myth or reality? *Sport in Society, 13*(3), 418–430.

Henning, A., & Andreasson, J. (2021). "Yay, another lady starting a log!" Women's fitness doping and the gendered space of an online doping forum. *Communication & Sport, 9*(6), 988–1007. https://doi.org/10.1177/2167479519896326.

Henning, A., & Dimeo, P. (2018a). The new front in the war on doping: Amateur athletes. *International Journal of Drug Policy, 51*, 128–136.

Henning, A., & Dimeo, P. (2018b). *Perceptions of legitimacy, attitudes and buy-in among athlete groups: A cross-national qualitative investigation providing practical solutions.* Montreal: World Anti-Doping Agency.

Henning, A., McLean, K., Andreasson, J., & Dimeo, P. (2020). Risk and enabling environments in sport: Systematic doping as harm reduction. *International Journal of Drug Policy, 91*, 102897. https://doi.org/10.1016/j.drugpo.2020.102897.

Hong, H. J, Henning, A., & Dimeo, P. (2020). Life after doping: A cross-country analysis of organisational support for sanctioned athletes. *Performance Enhancement and Health, 8*(1), 100161. https://doi.org/10.1016/j.peh.2020.100161.

Houlihan, B., Downward, P., Yamamoto, M. Y., Rasciute, S., & Takasu, K. (2020). Public opinion in Japan and the UK on issues of fairness and integrity in sport: Implications for anti-doping policy. *International Journal of Sport Policy and Politics*, 12(1), 1–24.

Hurst, P., Kavussanu, M., Boardley, I., & Ring, C. (2019). Sport supplement use predicts doping attitudes and likelihood via sport supplement beliefs. *Journal of Sports Sciences*, 37(15), 1734–1740.

Kayser, B., Mauron, A., & Miah, A. (2007). Current anti-doping policy: A critical appraisal. *BMC Medical Ethics*, 8(1), 1–10.

Kayser, B., & Tolleneer, J. (2017). Ethics of a relaxed anti-doping rule accompanied by harm-reduction measures. *Journal of Medical Ethics*, 43, 282–286.

Loland, S., & Hoppeler, H. (2012). Justifying anti-doping: The fair opportunity principle and the biology of performance enhancement. *European Journal of Sport Science*, 12(4), 347–353.

Martínez-Sanz, J., Sospedra, I., Ortiz, C., Baladía, E., Gil-Izquierdo, A., & Ortiz-Moncada, R. (2017). Intended or unintended doping? A review of the presence of doping substances in dietary supplements used in sports. *Nutrients*, 9(10), 1093. https://doi.org/10.3390/nu9101093.

Matthews, C., & Jordan, M. (2020). Drugs and supplements in amateur boxing: Pugilistic amateurism and ideologies of performance. *Qualitative Research in Sport, Exercise and Health*, 12(5), 631–646. https://doi.org/10.1080/2159676X.2019.1664623.

Matosic, D., Ntoumanis, N., & Boardley, I. (2020). Linking narcissism, motivation, and doping attitudes in sport: A multilevel investigation involving coaches and athletes. *Journal and Sport and Exercise Psychology*, 38(6), 556–566.

Mazanov, J., Huyber, T., & Connor, J. (2011). Qualitative evidence of a primary intervention point for elite athlete doping. *Journal of Science and Medicine in Sport*, 14(12), 106–110.

McArdle, D. (1999). Elite athletes' perceptions of the use and regulation of performance enhancing drugs in the United Kingdom. *Journal of Legal Aspects of Sport*, 9(1), 43–54.

McLaren, R. (2016). *The independent person: 2nd report*. Montreal: World Anti-Doping Agency.

McNamee, M. J. (2012). The spirit of sport and the medicalisation of anti-doping: Empirical and normative ethics. *Asian Bioethics Review*, 4(4), 374–392.

Møller, V. (2011). One step too far—about WADA's whereabouts rule. *International Journal of Sport Policy and Politics*, 3(2), 177–190.

Monaghan, L. (1999). Challenging medicine? Bodybuilding, drugs and risk. *Sociology of Health and Illness*, 21(6), 707–734.

Nicholls, A., Madigan, D., Backhouse, S., & Levy, A. (2017). Personality traits and performance enhancing drugs: The dark triad and doping attitudes among competitive athletes. *Personality and Individual Differences*, 112, 113–116.

Overbye, M., & Wagner, U. (2014). Experiences, attitudes and trust: An inquiry into elite athletes' perception of the whereabouts reporting system. *International Journal of Sport Policy and Politics*, 6(3), 407–428.

Paoli, L., & Donari, A. (2014). *The sports doping market: Understanding supply and demand, and the challenges of their control*. New York: Springer-Verlag.

Patterson, L., Backhouse, S., & Duffy, P. (2016). Anti-doping education for coaches: Qualitative insights from national and international sporting and anti-doping organisations. *Sport Management Review*, 19(1), 35–47.

Petróczi, A., & Aidman, E. (2009). Measuring explicit attitude toward doping: Review of the psychometric properties of the Performance Enhancement Attitude Scale. *Psychology of Sport and Exercise, 10*(3), 390–396.

Pielke, R., & Boye, E. (2019). Scientific integrity and anti-doping regulation. *International Journal of Sport Policy and Politics, 11*(2), 295–313.

Pitsch, W., & Emrich, E. (2012). The frequency of doping in elite sport: Results of a replication study. *International Review for the Sociology of Sport, 47*(5), 559–580.

Ritchie, I. (2013). The construction of a policy: The World Anti-Doping Code's "spirit of sport" clause. *Performance Enhancement and Health, 2*(4), 194–200.

Savulescu J., Foddy B., & Clayton M. (2004). Why we should allow performance enhancing drugs in sport. *British Journal of Sports Medicine, 38*, 666–670.

Smith, A. C., & Stewart, B. (2015). Why the war on drugs in sport will never be won. *Harm Reduction Journal, 12*(1), 1–6.

Sumner, C. (2017). The spirit of sport: The case for criminalisation of doping in the UK. *International Sports Law Journal, 16*(3–4), 217–227.

Tucker, R. (2012, 1 May). Lifetime ban for sport: A debate continued. *The Guardian.* https://www.theguardian.com/sport/blog/2012/may/01/guardian-sport-network-lifetime-ban-doping#:~:text=So%20as%20expected%2C%20CAS%20on,ban%20longer%20than%20six%20months.

Ulrich, R., Pope, H., Cléret, L., Petróczi, A., Nepusz, T., Schaffer, J., Kanayama, G., Comstock, D., & Perikles, S. (2018). Doping in two elite athletics competitions assessed by randomized-response surveys. *Sports Medicine, 48*, 211–219.

Ungerleider, S., & Bradley, B. (2001). *Faust's gold: Inside the East German doping machine.* New York: Macmillan.

U.S. Anti-Doping Agency. (2012, August 24). Reasoned decision of the United States antidoping agency on disqualification and ineligibility. http://cyclinginvestigation.usada.org/.

van de Ven, K., Mulrooney, K., & McVeigh, J. (Eds.). (2019). *Human enhancement drugs.* London: Routledge.

Waddington, I. (2010). Surveillance and control in sport: A sociologist looks at the WADA whereabouts system. *International Journal of Sport Policy and Politics, 2*(3), 255–274.

Waddington, I., Christiansen, A. V., & Gleaves, J. (2013). Recreational drug use and sport: Time for a WADA rethink? *Performance Enhancement and Health, 2*(2), 41–47.

World Anti-Doping Agency. (n.d.). Who we are. https://www.wada-ama.org/en/who-we-are#:~:text=The%20World%20Anti%2DDoping%20Agency's,movement%20for%20doping%2Dfree%20sport.&text=The%20World%20Anti%2DDoping%20Agency,and%20gove rnments%20of%20the%20world.

World Anti-Doping Agency. (2021). *World Anti-Doping Code.* Montreal World Anti-Doping Agency.

Zenovich, M. (Director). (2020). *Lance.* Bristol, CT: ESPN.

....

CHAPTER 25

SPORT, ALCOHOL, AND RITUAL

....

CATHERINE PALMER

In many sporting contexts, alcohol is used as a form of sociality, bonding, and a rite of passage across team celebrations, initiations, and similar events. Drinking is central to a range of forms of socialization and transitions in sport. It is a membership norm of many amateur and professional sports and is often a social convention after practices and games and at other club- or league-related events (Clayton, 2012; Collins & Vamplew, 2002). Drinking rituals in sport have a long cultural lineage and are situated in broader understandings of the role of alcohol in society. This is the starting point for this chapter, which traces the key issues and debates that emerge from the relationship between sport, alcohol, and ritual. In particular, analysis examines where, how, and by whom sporting rituals are typically performed, and the social meanings attached to them. Here, the importance of "drinking talk" in memorializing sports-based rituals is a point of focus, along with a discussion of risk and ritual in sport. This sets up a consideration of the tensions implicit in both the pleasures and problems that emerge from sport, alcohol, and ritual, along with a discussion of who performs rituals and to what ends. This builds on the typical focus of men, sport, and alcohol-based rituals and examines the rituals of alcohol among women, older athletes, and athletes with disability.

Building from this range of issues, debates, and concerns with sport, ritual, and alcohol, the chapter continues an ongoing research agenda that asks sociologists to extend our conceptual, theoretical, and empirical frameworks for thinking about sports-associated drinking, that is, to chart the "attendant rituals, customs and paraphernalia within the social and cultural contexts" in sport (Hunt & Barker, 2001, p. 171). The chapter is thus concerned to unravel how and why sport-related drinking practices can be understood as ritual in different contexts and among different social groups (Nichter, Quintero, Nichter, Mock, & Shakib, 2004; Rhodes, 1995, 2009).

ISSUES

....

Most Western countries have a long history of drinking. The late anthropologist Mary Douglas (1987) noted that the modern use of alcohol has its cultural origins in rituals and religious belief systems, while early Mass Observation surveys in the United Kingdom suggest that drinking in public houses was an important form of social connection in the 19th and early 20th centuries (Collins & Vamplew, 2002; Dimeo, 2013), observations that continue to hold true to this day (Markham & Bosworth, 2016; Thompson, Milton, Egan, & Lock, 2018). Indeed, the perception of the "value of alcohol for promoting relaxation and sociability is one of the most significant generalisations to emerge from cross-cultural studies of drinking" (Heath, 1995, p. 334).

The term "ritual" is often used to refer to the social, ceremonial, and performative aspects of both sport and alcohol consumption. I return to the predominantly anthropological approaches to the study of ritual later in the chapter, for they usefully guide our wider theoretical and methodological understandings and approaches. For the moment, I use the term "ritual" to refer to a prescribed set of activities that are shared and widely understood within a community and that occur within a particular place and according to a set sequence. Rituals involve actions, rules, and symbolism that are mutually understood by those performing and attending the ritual practice. Rituals involving alcohol can include both the mundane and the memorable. Indeed, consuming alcohol is now synonymous with markers of both memorable and mundane, with births, weddings, deaths, and other life occasions being among the more memorable life events to be celebrated or remembered through the consumption of alcohol. Drinking rituals are also used to define far less momentous passages, such as the daily or weekly transitions from work to leisure/home, or even the beginning and completion of a specific task, when alcohol often "cues" the transition from work time to play time.

Sports-based rituals fit with this idea of the mundane and the memorable. They may include the ritual wearing of "lucky socks" before a game, the ritual spraying of champagne (or taking a "shoey," where champagne is drunk from the winner's shoe) from the victory podium or, as I return to later, more worrying shared cultural practices such as hazing. But sports-based rituals are more than just mundane and memorable. Drinking rituals in sport can be a source of enormous enjoyment and social connection among drinking peers, yet they can also bring into sharp relief debates about the health risks and consequences of alcohol consumption, and they intersect with key sociological concerns and broader social debates about risk, individual choice, gender, age, urban space, and the nighttime economy. These issues frame this section, beginning with hegemonic masculinity and ritual.

Hegemonic Masculinity and Ritual

Much of the discourse and scholarship on sport and alcohol has characterized the relationship as a "holy trinity," wherein the relationship between sport, drinking—particularly heavy drinking—and masculinity remains a popular orthodoxy (Clayton & Harris, 2008; Jackson, 2014; Wenner & Jackson, 2008). The relationship between men, sport, and alcohol, and the cultural power relations within this relationship, has often been framed through a lens of "hegemonic masculinity." The concept owes its intellectual legacy to the Australian sociologist Raewyn Connell (1987, 1995) and can be understood as a representation of what men should be and do (Connell & Messerschmidt, 2005). Hegemonic masculinity provides a theory for the "pattern of practices that legitimize the patriarchal system in society" (Martinez-Garcia & Rodriguez-Mendez, 2019, p. 2). Essentially a culturally idealized form of "being a man," hegemonic masculinity is a way of identifying and understanding those attitudes and practices among men that involve men's domination over women and the power of some men over other (often minority groups of) men. Hegemonic masculinity manifests in particular attitudes and behaviors, in this case the rituals of sports-based drinking.

In these rituals of sports-based drinking, hegemonic masculinity is enacted in situations such as Mad Monday celebrations, when footballers in Australia dress as superheroes, nuns, or nurses at end-of-season celebrations, pub crawls, and "booze cruises" that invariably involve men "cutting loose," "letting go," and being "off the leash" (Palmer, 2014). Many of these—and other—accounts of having fun and losing control have been "condoned and encouraged within the strictures of hegemonic masculinity" (Thurnell–Read, 2011, p. 978; see also Peralta, 2007).

Hazing as Ritual

To provide a more extended example, among the more problematic associations between masculinity, sport, and alcohol is the practice of hazing. While many sporting teams use alcohol as part of a ritual to initiate new team members (drinking games, boat races, and "skulling" competitions, for example), such practices can be construed as hazing when participation in these initiation rituals involves undue risk of physical or psychological harm imposed by veteran members of a group and are presented as a requirement for full membership status, regardless of one's willingness to participate (Crow & Macintosh, 2009; McGinley, Rospenda, Lui, & Richman, 2016). Most typically, hazing initiation ceremonies involve forcing new team members to drink a large volume of alcohol in a very short period of time (Clayton, 2012). Irrespective of the ritual, hazing is explicitly designed to embarrass and humiliate the neophyte initiates.

While hazing rituals are also found in other masculine settings such as military and paramilitary organizations (De Albuquerque & Paes-Machado, 2004; Johnson, 2011), hazing in sport is often a feature of high school, college, and university sports rather than veteran or community team settings, suggestive of an early and widespread breeding ground for hegemonic masculinity. The scale of hazing among college, school, and university sport is of note. Allan and Madden (2008), for example, surveyed more than 11,000 undergraduate students in North America and found that hazing almost always involved the dangerous consumption of alcohol, humiliation, sleep deprivation, and the performance of various sexual acts. The analytical point here is that the rituals of hazing, in sport or elsewhere, embed and embody a set of gender-based power relations with serious social and psychological risks and consequences.

However, and to return somewhat to my anthropological interests in cross-cultural drinking, the idea of ritual shaming and drunkenness as aspects of hegemonic masculinity in "laddish" cultures, for example, would be "strongly opposed by the men of rural Spain in the late 1970s," where "intoxication was ugly and socially disapproved of" (Clayton & Harris, 2008, p. 313). It is the tensions and contradictions inherent in studies of drinking, sport-related or otherwise, that underpin this chapter.

Stories of Drinking Rituals

Recounting stories about consuming alcohol is common in many Western societies. In the aftermath of drinking events—the morning after the night before—tales of debauchery, excess, transgression, and misbehavior are frequently shared by and among those doing the drinking. Tutenges and Sandberg (2013) describe the stories of sex, risk, and harm and bodily fluids shared by young Danish holiday makers at a Bulgarian resort when recalling their overconsumption of alcohol. Fjær (2012) observed in a study of Norwegian youth that drinking stories serve to demarcate group membership, obtain retrospective information about intoxicated moments that they fail to remember, and transform distressing events into positive memories. Griffin, Bengry-Howell, Hackley, Mistral, and Szmigin (2009, p. 470) recount stories of overconsumption or "annihilation" shared by young people in Britain, the authors suggesting that stories are "told (and retold) for the entertainment of the friendship group, and serve to bind the group together."

In their study of narratives of drinking among French climbers and older Australian athletes, Palmer, Le Hénaff, Bonnet, and Féliu (2020) note that drinking talk in sport is similarly an important means of sharing and shaping identity that speaks to the ritual functions of sociality and celebration. Writing about talking about drinking, Palmer et al. note that "drinking talk" is an important source of membership and belonging among these two contrasting sporting communities—French climbers and older Australian athletes—where "having a story to tell is an opportunity to display and sustain their sense of identity both as friends and as followers of a particular sporting team" (p. 20). More critically, they note that the shared humor and sociality of drinking—conveyed through the narratives and stories of drinking—emerged as being unexpectedly significant for the research corpus on alcohol and sport.

The ritual function of talking about drinking (and sport) is the capacity of the story to "tell us much about the individuals who share them as well as the society, culture and social network in which they are embedded" (Sandberg, Tutenges, & Pedersen, 2019, p. 407). As Workman (2001, p. 431) notes, "performance stories, when assembled collectively, tell their own story about the un-questioned functions and meanings beneath established drinking practices." That is, talking about drinking and, for researchers, *listening* to talk about drinking provide an inherently social context within which to garner critical information about health behaviors, cultural values, and leisure and lifestyle practices.

For a ritual to "work," its cultural properties must be shared and understood by those in attendance. This extends to talking about drinking rituals. A key part of the shared cultural currency of a drinking story is that its content and narrative structure are familiar to others in the storytelling group. In their analysis of drinking stories among young Norwegian drinkers, Sandberg et al. (2019, p. 406) outline five classic themes that feature in most drinking stories: "sex, bodily harm, bodily fluids, lawbreaking and pranks." In his study of drinking narratives among U.S. college students, Workman (2001) outlines five storylines: (1) the adventure story, which describes drinking and risk taking; (2) the stupid story, which is told for entertainment; (3) the naked and puking story, which is self-explanatory; (4) the regretted sex story; and (5) the college story, which provides context to the drinking behaviors.

Palmer et al. (2020), in their analysis of drinking narratives by climbers and older athletes, posit that there is a similar thematic framework for drinking stories in sport. While their analysis is preliminary, the authors suggest that this thematic framework might include (1) conferring accomplishment of a physical task (such as climbing) and/or (2) demarcating belonging to a membership group. When analyzed together, these themes, the authors suggest, "offer insights into the meanings ascribed to the social exchanges in drinking and offer important reminders of the consequences for drinking behaviours in sport" (p. 1).

To return to the earlier concept of hegemonic masculinity, the gendered nature of storytelling about drunken ritual performances has been acknowledged in terms of who is telling the stories and what the stories are about. Sandberg et al. (2019) recognize that women are increasingly sharing stories of their intoxication, yet their own analysis of drinking stories by young men has been criticized for failing to engage with the hegemony of the drinking stories their participants describe, which often feature the sexual humiliation of women (Tutenges & Sandberg, 2013). As Radcliffe and Measham (2014, p. 348) note, "the gendered organisation of these drinking practices extends beyond the stories and context of their telling." This is certainly a cautionary note for stories of sports-based drinking rituals.

Risk and Ritual

Earlier in the chapter, I noted that hazing was a practice that involved a high degree of risk to social and psychological welfare. This is part of a broader concern with risk and ritual in sport. Along with smoking, using recreational drugs, and practicing unsafe sex, drinking continues to command considerable attention as one of the behaviors practiced by young people, in particular, that are perceived to put their health at risk. In terms of health risks and drinking rituals, several studies have looked at drinking games, where many (often high-alcohol-content) drinks are consumed rapidly, resulting in injuries and in some cases fatalities. Jayne, Holloway, and Valentine (2010), for example, have examined the phenomenon among groups of backpackers, and as noted earlier, there are a number of initiations into sporting clubs that involve drinking games of one sort or another (Clayton, 2012; Lake, 2012; McDonald & Sylvester, 2014; Palmer, 2009).

Beccaria and Sande (2003, p. 101) argue—fairly dramatically—that drinking games inside peer groups are a form of practice that involve playing with the limits between intoxication and death. Yet among those who take part in the activity, this is rarely front of mind, where the objective risk of taking part in an activity has effectively been stripped from the subjective experience of those who engage in it. Dobson, Brudalen, and Tobiasson (2006, p. 50), for example, followed a group of Norwegian youth who pursued a number of activities that were considered "normless and regarded as a necessary part of being a so-called *russ* [a final-year high school student]." While many of the *russ* activities were clearly dangerous (e.g., sleeping on a roadway traffic island), the behaviors of participants were considered to be courting risk only by those who were outside of the activities. For those taking part, however, the activities were seen as necessary rites of passage marking the end of high school and the transition into the adult world. This conflicting discourse is a point to which I'll return, for understanding and balancing the tensions between the "fun" of collective drinking—in sport or elsewhere—with the real (and potential) costs and consequences to individual or public health is a major challenge for policymakers (Jayne et al., 2006).

These rites of passage, as a component of a ritual, have resonance with sports-based rituals and their inherent emphasis on drinking to excess. While social anthropology and related disciplines have long had an interest in the social aspects of drinking, there has been a more recent shift from looking at the sociality of drinking to getting "legless and pissy-arse falling down drunk" (Young, 1995, p. 48). That is, studies of *drunkenness* are now a key way through which we can think about notions of becoming, belonging, and the other dimensions of sociality that we find in sport. Indeed, studies of ritual drunkenness—variously defined as "heroic drinking," "extreme drinking" (Glassman, Dodd, Sheu, Rienzo, & Wagenaar, 2010), and "coma drinking" in German-speaking countries—are in many ways emblematic descriptors of sports-based drinking rituals, for it is widely assumed and theorized that heavy, problematic drinking is an integral part of sporting identities, cultures, and practices. Certainly the material presented so far would suggest this is the case. Moreover, the risks of ritual, along with issues of masculinity and drinking talk, highlight the tensions between the problem and the pleasure of sports-based drinking. This shapes sports-based drinking rituals in unique ways that various disciplinary approaches have tried to account for.

APPROACHES

Studies of sport-related drinking rituals bring together many interests across disciplinary paradigms in the social and health sciences and the concerns of public policy. In this section, I begin with an overview of the "classic" disciplinary approaches to ritual in social anthropology, including the examples of communitas, liminality, and rites of passage. I then examine some of the positions to emerge from within the health and medical sciences. In contrast to anthropological approaches to ritual—and ritual drinking—these approaches tend to frame sports-based drinking rituals as problematic public policy concerns rather than as pleasurable, symbolically redolent social acts. These are not meant to be viewed as opposing standpoints, rather as ones that offer complementary, if at times contradictory, perspectives on alcohol, sport, and society more broadly. The analysis then considers other theoretical approaches to sociality that account for ritual in the context of a changing sporting demographic.

Anthropology and Ritual

Ritual has long been a cornerstone of anthropological thought, yet curiously, sport-related drinking rituals have hovered on the margins of interest from social anthropology, with ethnographic studies of sport-related drinking tending to focus instead on the "carnivalesque" nature of major sporting events, in which drinking is seen as an adjunct to the event more broadly rather than the central focus of the study being on drinking as an everyday social practice (Giulianotti, 1995; Millward, 2009). In Donnelly's (2013) account of drinking with the "derby girls," drinking was a persistent backdrop to her ethnographic work with a group of roller derby players rather than the explicit focus of her wider analysis of roller derby as a particular social formation in late modernity.

But many of the ideas from anthropological theory are especially useful for theorizing sports-based drinking rituals. Here, I look at the ideas of communitas, liminality, and rites of passage. Traditional anthropological studies argue that rituals are comprised of a series of set sequences of events that are mutually understood. A ritual needs to unfold in a particular order for it to make sense, socially and symbolically. These socially ordered events include rites of passage and, within, or as well as the ideas of communitas and liminality.

Rites of Passage

To take each in turn, as first termed by the French anthropologist Arnold van Gennep (1960), a rite of passage involves three phases that an individual or society moves through: separation, liminality, and incorporation. In the first stage, an individual or group of people withdraw or separate from their current status and prepare to move from one social state or status to another. A group of students gathering backstage before their university graduation is an example here. For van Gennep, this stage of separation involves "symbolic behaviour signifying the detachment of the individual or group . . . from an earlier fixed point in the social structure" (p. 6). The transition (or liminal) phase is the period between stages, in which the individual or group has left one state or status but has not yet entered or joined the next. Continuing the example of graduation, this stage would be symbolically represented by the graduands gathering to be conferred. They have left the state of "student" but have not yet reached the state of "graduate." The state of liminality is also referred to as being "betwixt and between." In the third phase of reaggregation or incorporation, the "passage is consummated [by] the ritual subject. Having completed the rite and assumed their 'new' identity, one re-enters society with one's new status" (p. 8). Our students have become graduates, recognized by symbols and celebrations such as testamurs and the throwing of caps in the air.

Ritualized drinking rites of passage in sport include hazing and "booze cruises." The middle phase of liminality is often regarded as the stage in which the person, usually a man, is off the leash and out of control in extreme drinking rituals, after which the drinker is reincorporated into society or a community as a differently constituted person. The neophyte has survived hazing and is accepted into the team; the storyteller now has a story to share with the rest of the group; and so on. In other words, the social meanings that are shared and carried through rites of passage in sport are symbolic vehicles for identifying and constructing cultural values, for shaping social interactions and relationships, and for defining behavioral norms and expectations in sport.

The final part of these anthropological understandings of ritual and rites of passage is the notion of "communitas." Attributed to the late anthropologist Victor Turner (1969, p. 11), communitas refers to "a relational quality of full, unmediated communication, even communion, between people of definite and determinate identity, which arises spontaneously in all kinds of groups, situations, and circumstances." Communitas, then, characterizes groups that share a sense of oneness, sameness, and being in common. Importantly, communitas develops among persons who experience liminality as a group. In sports-based drinking rituals, communitas could refer to dedicated football fan or follower groups, such as seen in Palmer's work on "the Grog Squad" (Palmer, 2009, Palmer & Thompson, 2007), where community is squarely built around drinking identities. Importantly, however, the intense social bonds that form among drinking peers also highlight exclusions in sport, that is, those who sit outside of the group. As Douglas (cited in Wilson, 2005, p. 13) argues, "drinking acts to mark the boundaries of personal and group identities, making it a practice of inclusion and exclusion."

A Note on Health and Medicine

Research in the health and medical sciences has long focused on the etiology of alcohol consumption and its effects on and consequences for individual and population health; alcohol is widely considered to be a leading cause of preventable death, disease, injury and disability, contributing to 3.2% of deaths and 4% of disability-adjusted life years globally (Casey, Harvey, Eime, & Payne, 2012). Research globally suggests that hazardous drinking is a serious social and public health problem (Connor, Kydd, Shield, & Rehm, 2013; World Health Organization, 2011).

The problem of drinking as a health issue and as a subject for health and medical science saw an increasing characterization of alcohol and drug dependency as a disease or a pathological behavior (Agar, 2003). It was soon realized, however, that while a person may suffer the individual effects of alcohol misuse in terms of its physical effects on them, society as a whole suffers from the many consequences of alcohol abuse and dependence. Solutions to alcohol misuse became located within a public health model (Gilbert, 1993). Here, the endogenous, biological, and "agentic" aspects of alcohol and other drug use were emphasized when searching for treatment and solutions. Accordingly, ways of framing and attempting to understand alcohol use moved beyond a focus on the individual to a social or a population-level focus on the consequences of alcohol and other drug use (Seddon, 2010). This returns us to sociality.

In other words, while the "problem" of drinking, particularly drinking to excess, remains a key concern for health professionals, my interest here is less with the health-damaging behavior and the consequences of drinking and more with the social dimensions and understandings that underpin it. Borrowing from Wilson (2005), I suggest that researchers should be able to discuss and conduct research into alcohol consumption from the perspective that it is not always a problem, that in some cases it is both normal and normative and a rich source of pleasure, enjoyment, and sociality.

Moving Forward, New Perspectives

While traditional anthropological understandings of ritual are still widely applicable to sports-based rituals, the shift toward interdisciplinarity, along with an increasingly diverse demographic in sport, calls for greater theoretical diversity in our approaches to understanding ritual. Here, I examine the need for new theoretical, conceptual, and analytical frameworks that have emerged from research on women's relationship to alcohol in sport, and the relationship between sport, alcohol, and ritual relative to a growing emphasis on cultural and gender diversity in sport.

These new perspectives do intersect with some of the debates dealt with in the next section. As such, I introduce the approach here and return to the debate that such approaches generate in the following section.

The increased focus on women as fans or consumers of sport (Toffoletti, 2018) presents the opportunity to rethink the "sport-alcohol nexus" (Palmer, 2011) and the rituals it entails through alternative theoretical frameworks to hegemonic masculinity. To develop this line of thought, the analysis here suggests the need for a feminist framework for the sport-alcohol nexus that considers women's experiences of drinking relative to contemporary formations of postfeminist femininity. This entails paying critical attention to the social conditions whereby drinking is made fun and appealing to women, and the various ways women negotiate changing expectations of contemporary femininity in sport-related drinking contexts. Such an approach takes up the agenda of sport feminisms by attending to shifting dynamics of gender power relations that inform how gender identities are constructed, experienced, and performed, as well as attending to the embodied practices and politics of sports participation for subjects located differently in the gender order and within particular sociocultural contexts.

In term of sports-based drinking rituals, this may entail documenting women's rites of passage through sport. Where are gender politics embedded and embodied in rituals by women? To what extent do issues of power manifest in ways that may either reinforce or challenge negative ritual practices such as hazing? That is, we need to also consider whether such practices can be seen as legitimate cultural spaces through which women's identities as sporting actors are played out. Here, there is a need to acknowledge that sport-related drinking for women is as pleasurable and problematic as it is for men. My research on women's drinking in Australian Rules football suggests that this is certainly the case (Palmer, 2013). In other words, rethinking drinking and sporting rituals to include women's experiences and understandings, and to account for the contexts that shape gendered agency and desires, opens up the space for feminist analyses of sport-related drinking that recognize the changing nature of participation in and consumption of sporting rituals.

Emerging Methods for Analyzing Ritual

In considering our (old and new) disciplinary approaches to understanding sport, alcohol, and ritual, it is also necessary to consider the methodological approaches adopted. Here, I underscore the importance of new and emerging qualitative methods in particular to tease out some of the more nuanced understandings of the relationships between sports consumers and alcohol. As I have suggested elsewhere, the "very different ways through which people produce, consume and communicate the images that construct the holy trinity of alcohol, sport and gender raise a series of questions usefully explored through ethnography, visual methods, focus groups, interviews and surveys" (Palmer, 2011, p. 173). To this I would now add digitally informed methods such as photovoice and the scroll-back method along with interviews and ethnography. While photovoice (or photo interview) is in use as a method in the sociology of sport more broadly, bringing it to the context of sport, alcohol, and ritual will inevitably raise ethical issues that researchers will need to be attentive to.

The scroll-back method is a more recent advance that is beginning to be used to document people's experiences, using the timeline on Facebook, Instagram, or similar social media as visual aides-memoires to particular memorable and/or mundane events (Ørmen & Thorhauge, 2015). Here participants walk the interviewer through how they have used social media to record the importance (or not) of particular events they have kept in their social media account (Robards & Lincoln, 2017). Notwithstanding the earlier comments about sensitivity to ethics, the scroll-back method, it may be seen, can have great utility for capturing people's experiences of sport, alcohol, and ritual over time. They would be a useful adjunct to the research on "drinking talk," especially, in situations such as those noted by Fjær (2012), where talking about drinking can provide retrospective information about intoxicated moments that participants fail to remember and help transform distressing events into positive memories.

What is important here is that adopting new methods or approaches to make sense of ritual, sport, and alcohol is not an ambit academic exercise. It can also lead to fruitful change. Understanding the normal and normative dimensions of alcohol consumption may, in turn, influence behavioral change, as well as tactics used in public health or policy interventions. Writing about drinking and young people in Europe, Eisenbach-Stangl and Thom (2009, p. 1) note that in order

> to understand youthful binge drinking and associated behaviours, and to find ways of intervening to prevent or reduce harm, it is necessary to understand the prevailing concept(s) of acceptable and unacceptable forms of intoxication and intoxicated behaviours and its/their wider social and cultural determinants.

DEBATES

The key debates in studies of sports-based drinking rituals revolve around (1) a tension between the pleasure and the problem of drinking and (2) issues of inclusion and representation in terms of who is typically involved in sporting rituals. That is, there is an imperative to shift the focus beyond hegemonic masculinity, both theoretically and empirically, in order to include a range of issues, people, and sports that scholars haven't typically considered, so as to develop a fuller understanding of the who, how, and why of sport-related drinking

The Problem of Pleasure

An ongoing debate in studies of sport-related drinking is the tension between the pleasure and the problem of drinking—that is, how to write about enjoyment without valorizing it, how to recognize that drinking can be fun and problematic at one and the same time. While the "problem" of drinking, particularly drinking to excess, remains a key concern for health professionals, the place for sociology, and the social sciences more generally, is less with the health-damaging behavior and the consequences of drinking and more with the social dimensions and understandings that underpin it. Borrowing from Wilson (2005), I suggest that alcohol consumption in some cases is both normal and normative and a rich source of pleasure, enjoyment, and sociality. Studies of ritual underscore the importance of this.

The pleasure of intoxication, its absence in critical discourse, and the challenges it presents for policy formulation are by no means new debates in studies of *illicit* drug and alcohol use, particularly by young people (Coveney & Bunton, 2003; Duff, 2008; Dwyer, 2008; Järvinen & Østergaard, 2011; Measham, Aldridge, & Parker, 2001; Moore, 2008; Zajdow, 2010). To return to the earlier theme of risk and rituals, scholars have drawn attention to the "preoccupation of earlier research with risk awareness and (especially) risk-unawareness among young people and for ignoring the positive expectations and experiences youths have in relation to drugs" (Järvinen & Østergaard, 2011, p. 334).

Drinking-based rituals, such as hazing, that are infused with gender and cultural power, however, warrant attention here. These rituals, which lack the communitas of shared, enjoyed drinking, skirt the idea that the fun of drinking is widespread but can only be partially enjoyed by those doing the hazing. In other words, while the issues of pleasure and enjoyment of much of sports-associated drinking can be central to understanding its ritual function, consideration of pleasure can be problematic for other policy research areas (such as gambling or tobacco) that are informed by discourses of health promotion, moderation, and harm reduction.

New Sites and Subjects

Other debates include how to move beyond the implicit assumption that sport-related drinking is wholly and universally bound to a particular kind of masculinity. How to reconcile behaviors traditionally conceived as hegemonic masculinity with groups who don't, on the face of it, fit this profile? This raises a series of questions as to how best to understand the social meanings ascribed to drinking in a context where women's participation—in both sport and drinking cultures—is becoming accepted rather than viewed as an act of "transgressive femininity," and where older and disabled athletes (among others) are engaging more fully with both sport and alcohol consumption. These new sites and subjects may prove fruitful for further investigation into sport, alcohol, and ritual.

In my work on women, sport, and alcohol, for example, I have been arguing for the concept of hegemonic *drinking* instead of hegemonic masculinity (Palmer, 2013; Palmer & Toffoletti, 2019). By "hegemonic drinking," I refer to the cultural privileging of forms and practices of drinking where drinking to excess is valorized and carries social and discursive weight for women as well as for men. Many of the rituals of drinking involve hegemonic drinking, by men and women alike. For example, my research with female followers of Australian Rules football suggests that practices of drinking to excess, which share the characteristics of ritual and rite of passage outlined earlier, are seen as legitimate ways in which women's identities as sporting fans and supporters are expressed.

Older Athletes, Alcohol, and Sports-Based Rituals

What about older athletes? In my research on the ways in which older athletes incorporate drinking practices into their social and sporting identities (Palmer, 2020), I argue that their drinking can share the same symbolic and ritual structure as it does among other sporting populations. Drinking among participants at the Australian Masters Games, for example, was an important source of sociality and celebration—a site of ritual—yet these markers of membership and belonging have not been fully considered in research on either sport and alcohol or alcohol and older populations.

For older athletes, a consideration of the wider social dimensions of their sporting lives has long been missing. My analysis of drinking practices and the Australian Masters Games suggests that alcohol plays an important role in setting up for, settling in, and then winding down from the event's activities (Palmer, 2020). An expanded sociological perspective on sport-related drinking that engages with cultural practices, social meanings, and lived experiences by sports people at various stages of life is key to developing a more fulsome understanding of the interconnections between sport, alcohol, and sociality. In addressing this underdeveloped opportunity for a broader research agenda on sport and alcohol, a recalibration and widening of popular understandings of sport, aging, and alcohol (both as separate and as interrelated concerns) may provide opportunities for examining new kinds of aging and new entanglements between sport, alcohol, and society.

To return to an earlier observation, writing about ritual, sport, and alcohol among older athletes is not an ambit academic exercise. It can also lead to change. We know from research on drinking more broadly that alcohol use among older people is a growing concern for professionals. Including older sportspeople in research that can help us understand the social contexts and meanings of drinking may contribute in important ways to the growing evidence base here.

Alcohol and Athletes with Disability

The issues raised in relation to older sportspeople are applicable to considering the relationships between drinking and sportspeople with disability. As is the case with older athletes, drinking has not, to date, been a focus of our studies on sport and disability. Yet there is equally an opportunity for a focused research agenda that can include the pleasurable as well as potentially problematic relationships to alcohol that may exist for sportspeople with disability, as we find with able-bodied, particularly male athletes worldwide.

While the empirical data is lacking, a consideration of how the nexus of sport, alcohol, and ritual understandings are shared among athletes and/or fans with disability potentially allows engagement with some of the debates in disability research about agency and opportunity (Smith & Sparkes, 2005). Moreover, including former athletes whose lives involved drinking, who now may perceive a denial of social opportunity, would extend discussions about sport and disability beyond issues of access and participation to consider this unique social context of sporting consumption as fans or followers, as well as sportspeople.

In much the same way that examining alcohol use among older athletes can contribute to a broader research agenda on sport and alcohol, a widening of popular understandings of sport, disability, and alcohol (both as separate and as interrelated concerns) may provide opportunities for examining disability and new interactions between sport, alcohol, and society.

Rituals beyond Drinking

While drinking, and drinking to excess, carries considerable normative currency in sport, it would be disingenuous to suggest that this is always the case. Nondrinkers are becoming more and more conspicuous in sport, with religious beliefs and notions of care of the self and physical austerity by athletes being key factors here. This raises a number of issues and debates for sports-based rituals: How do nondrinking players celebrate? Are they excluded from team sociality? Are other cultural practices introduced instead? Writing about a county cricket club in the north of England, Fletcher and Spracklen (2013, p. 1) note the ways in which drinking acts as a practice of exclusion among British Pakistani Muslim cricketers, pointing out that "ritualized drinking is not and cannot, be enjoyed by all. British Muslims (the majority of whom are of South Asian descent) for instance, are restricted from drinking alcohol due to the demands of Islam."

Researchers have focused minimal attention on nondrinkers and how they coexist with drinkers in the particular social setting of sport, yet the demographic profile of many sports has changed due to migration, ethnic diversity, and shifting relationships to religion and faith, which has led to increasing numbers of sportsmen (and women) choosing not to consume alcohol as a marker of their religion. Of interest here is Burdsey's (2010) research on the experiences of British Muslims in first-class cricket, particularly the ways in which the role and significance of Islam in their sporting lives shape their participation in sport, their relationship to alcohol, and the ways in which this intersects with their experiences of participation in or belonging to a sporting team. In particular, it is the degree to which dominant subcultural and off-field aspects of professional cricket—such as drinking alcohol—are perceived to run counter to observing the obligations of Islam that is of interest here. More specifically, interactions between Muslim and non-Muslim cricketers around alcohol consumption can highlight some of the politics of exclusion that can accompany sport-related drinking.

This emphasis on the rituals among older, disabled, and nondrinking sportspeople highlights something of a blind spot in how we approach analyses of sport-related drinking. The relationship between sport, alcohol, and ritual has been fairly limited in theoretical, conceptual, and methodological terms, and moving past this blind spot opens up new agendas for studies of sport and alcohol. The relative absence of discussion of drinking by female fans or sportswomen, the emergence of nondrinking sportsmen and women, and the growing visibility of older athletes and athletes with disability, among other things, have all created a new set of research questions and problems for critical interrogation through sustained, theoretically informed, empirical social research.

CONCLUSION

The treatment in this chapter has outlined the relationship between sport, alcohol, and ritual. It has continued an ongoing research agenda that asks sociologists to extend our conceptual, theoretical, and empirical frameworks for thinking about sports-associated drinking, in this case that which is embodied and enacted through ritual practices. The changing nature of sport—the inclusion of new sites, subjects, and empirical settings—opens new research agendas for social sciences as well as underscoring the continuing importance of long-standing conceptual frameworks such as ritual for understanding the sport-alcohol nexus.

A key theme that runs through the consideration of examples such as hazing, drinking talk, and risky rituals, as well as the discussion about new sites and subjects, such as women, older athletes, nondrinkers, and sportspeople with disability, is that sports-associated drinking, like other forms of drinking, does not take place just anywhere. It is an inherently social act that is subject to a variety of rules and norms regarding who may drink what, when, where, why, how, and with whom.

This socially prescribed and sequenced set of rules around drinking return us to the fundamental properties and function of rituals. Rituals highlight the distinctive structural or cultural environments that both frame and situate sport-related drinking and the diverse cultural practices that underpin and sustain it (Agar, 2003; Durant & Thakker, 2003). Rituals highlight the social aspects of drinking, the contexts in which it takes place, and the backgrounds and milieus that inform it. Rituals describe the "social meanings that participants attach to their [alcohol use and misuse], and the social processes by which such meanings are created, reinforced and reproduced" (Neale, Allen, & Coombes, 2005, p. 1584).

From the starting point of social anthropological uses of ritual, the chapter widened the theoretical and methodological approaches to consider new feminisms and digitally informed methods to engage with new sites and subjects of sport, alcohol, and ritual. Reimagining the sport-alcohol nexus to include new approaches, methods, sites, and subjects that can shed light on wider articulations of the pleasurable and problematic relationships between sport, alcohol, and social identity is not an ambit academic exercise. The analysis in this chapter also highlighted the capacity for social and policy change in widening our understandings about people's alcohol consumption beyond that which is more customarily understood or socially sanctioned. While it is easy to dismiss drinking rituals in sport as trivial, the shared communitas—through drinking talk and experiences—serves an important social function. It provides a useful barometer for understanding how people behave while drinking that has broader implications for social scientists and health professionals, among others. By expanding the scope for analysis, considerations in this chapter point to many opportunities for more broadly addressing the diverse social concerns over the sport-alcohol nexus.

REFERENCES

Agar, M. (2003). Towards a qualitative epidemiology. *Qualitative Health Research*, 13(7), 974–986.

Allan, E. J., & Madden, M. (2008). Hazing in view: College students at risk: Initial findings from the national study of student hazing. Report. University of Maine.

Beccaria, F., & Sande, A. (2003). Drinking games and rite of life projects: A social comparison of the meaning and functions of young people's use of alcohol during the rite of passage to adulthood in Italy and Norway. *Young*, 11(2), 99–119.

Burdsey, D. (2010). British Muslim experiences in English first-class cricket. *International Review for the Sociology of Sport, 45*(3), 315–334.

Casey, M., Harvey, J., Eime, R., & Payne, W. (2012). Examining changes in the organisational capacity and sport-related health promotion policies. *Annals of Leisure Research, 15*(3), 261–276.

Clayton, B. (2012). Initiate: Constructing the "reality" of male team sport initiation rituals. *International Review for the Sociology of Sport, 41*(3–4), 295–316.

Clayton, B., & Harris, J. (2008). Our friend Jack: Alcohol, friendship and masculinity in university football. *Annals of Leisure Research, 11*(3–4), 311–330.

Collins, T., & Vamplew, W. (2002). *Mud, sweat and beers: A cultural history of sport and alcohol.* Oxford: Berg.

Connell, R. (1987). *Gender and power: Society, the person and sexual politics.* Cambridge, U.K.: Polity Press.

Connell, R. W. (1995). *Masculinities.* Berkeley: University of California Press.

Connell, R. W., & Messerchmidt. J. W. (2005). Hegemonic masculinity: Rethinking the concept. *Gender & Society, 19*(6), 829–859.

Connor, J., Kydd, R., Shield, K., & Rehm, J. (2013). Alcohol-attributable burden of disease and injury in New Zealand: 2004 and 2007. Research report commissioned by the Health Promotion Agency. Wellington: Health Promotion Agency.

Coveney, J., & Bunton, R. (2003). In pursuit of the study of pleasure: Implications for health research and practice. *Health: An Interdisciplinary Journal for the Social Study of Health, Illness and Medicine, 7*(2), 161–179.

Crow, R., & Macintosh, E. (2009). Conceptualizing a meaningful definition of hazing in sport. *European Sport Management Quarterly, 9*(4), 433–451.

De Albuquerque, C. L., & Paes-Machado, E. (2004). The hazing machine: The shaping of Brazilian military police recruits. *Policing and Society, 14*(2), 175–192.

Dimeo, P. (2013). *Drugs, alcohol and sport: A critical history.* London: Routledge.

Dobson, S., Brudalen, R., & Tobiasson H. (2006). Courting risk—The attempt to understand youth cultures. *Young: Nordic Journal of Youth Studies, 1*, 49–58.

Donnelly, M. (2013). Drinking with the derby girls: Exploring the hidden ethnography in research of women's flat track roller derby. *International Review for the Sociology of Sport, 49*(3–4), 464–484.

Douglas, M. (Ed.). (1987). *Constructive drinking: Perspectives on drink from anthropology.* Cambridge: Cambridge University Press.

Duff, C. (2008). The pleasure in context. *International Journal of Drug Policy, 19*(5), 384–392.

Durant, R., & Thakker, J. (2003). *Substance use and abuse: Cultural and historical Perspectives.* London: Sage.

Dwyer, R. (2008). Privileging pleasures: Temazepam injection in a heroin marketplace. *International Journal of Drug Policy, 19*(5), 367–374.

Eisenbach-Stangl, I., & Thom, B. (2009, February). Intoxication and intoxicated behaviour in contemporary European cultures: Myths, realities and the implications for policy, (prevention) practice and research. Policy Brief. Vienna: European Centre for Welfare Policy and Research.

Fjær, E. G. (2012). The day after drinking: Interaction during hangovers among young Norwegian adults. *Journal of Youth Studies, 15*(8), 995–1010.

Fletcher, T., & Spracklen, K. (2013). Cricket, drinking and exclusion of British Pakistani Muslims. *Ethnic and Racial Studies, 37*(8), 1–19.

Gilbert, M. J. (1993). Anthropology in a multidisciplinary field: Substance abuse. *Social Science and Medicine, 37*(1), 1–3.

Giulianotti, R. (1995). Football and the politics of carnival: An ethnographic study of Scottish football fans in Sweden. *International Review for the Sociology of Sport, 30*, 191–217.

Glassman, T. J., Dodd, V. J., Sheu, J. J., Rienzo, B. A., & Wagenaar, A. C. (2010). Extreme ritualistic alcohol consumption among college students on game day. *Journal of American College Health, 58*(5), 413–423.

Griffin, C., Bengry-Howell, A., Hackley C., Mistral, W., & Szmigin, I. (2009). "Every time I do it I absolutely annihilate myself": Loss of (self-)consciousness and loss of memory in young people's drinking narratives. *Sociology, 43*(3), 457–476.

Heath, D. B. (Ed.). (1995). *International handbook on alcohol and culture*. Westport, CT: Greenwood Press.

Hunt, G., & Barker, J. C. (2001). Socio-cultural anthropology and alcohol and drug research: Towards a unified theory. *Social Science & Medicine, 53*, 165–188.

Jackson, S. (2014). Globalization, corporate nationalism and masculinity in Canada: Sport, Molson beer advertising and consumer citizenship. *Sport in Society, 17*(7), 901–916.

Järvinen, M., & Østergaard, J. (2011). Dangers and pleasures: Drug attitudes and experiences among young people. *Acta Sociolgoica, 54*(4), 333–350.

Jayne, M., Holloway, S. L., & Valentine, G. (2006). Drunk and disorderly: Alcohol, urban life and public space. *Progress in Human Geography, 30*(4), 451–468.

Jayne, M., Valentine, G., & Holloway, S. L. (2010). Emotional, embodied and affective geographies of alcohol, drinking and drunkenness. *Transactions of the Institute of British Geographers, 35*, 540–544.

Johnson, J. (2011). Across the threshold: A comparative analysis of communitas and rites of passage in sport hazing and initiations. *Canadian Journal of Sociology, 36*(3), 199–226.

Lake, R. (2012). "They treat me like I'm scum": Social exclusion and established-outsider relations in a British tennis club. *International Review for the Sociology of Sport, 48*(1), 112–128.

Markham, C., & Bosworth, G. (2016). The village pub in the twenty-first century: Embeddedness and the "local." In I. Cabras, D. Higgins, & D. Preece (Eds.), *Brewing, beer and pubs: A global perspective* (pp. 266–281). London: Palgrave Macmillan.

Martinez-Garcia, M.-L., & Rodriguez-Mendez, C. (2019). "I can try it": Negotiating masculinity through football in the playground. *Sport, Education and Society, 25*(2), 199–212.

McDonald, B., & Sylvester, K. (2014). Learning to get drunk: The importance of drinking in Japanese university sports clubs. *International Review for the Sociology of Sport, 49*(3–4), 331–345.

McGinley, M., Rospenda, K. M., Lui, L., & Richman, J. A. (2016). It isn't all just fun and games: Collegiate participation in extracurricular activities and risk for generalized and sexual harassment, psychological distress, and alcohol use. *Journal of Adolescence, 53*, 152–163.

Measham. F., Aldridge, J., & Parker, H. (2001). *Dancing on drugs: Risk, health and hedonism in the British club scene*. London: Free Association Books.

Moore, D. (2008). Erasing pleasure from public discourse on illicit drugs: On the creation and reproduction of an absence. *International Journal of Drug Policy, 19*(5), 353–358.

Millward, P. (2009). Glasgow Rangers supporters in the city of Manchester: The degeneration of a "fan party" into a "hooligan riot." *International Review for the Sociology of Sport, 44*(4), 381–398.

Neale, J., Allen, D., & Coombes, L. (2005). Qualitative research methods within the addictions. *Addiction, 100*, 1593–1684.

Nicheter, M., Quintero, C. Nichter, M., Mock, J., & Shakib, S. (2004). Qualitative research: Contributions to the study of drug use, drug abuse and drug user-related interventions. *Substance Use & Misuse, 39*(10–12), 1907–1969.

Ørmen, J., & Thorhauge, A. M. (2015). Smartphone log data in a qualitative perspective. *Mobile Media & Communication, 3*(3), 335–350.

Palmer, C. (2009). "The Grog Squad": An ethnography of beer consumption at Australian Rules football matches. In L. A. Wenner & S. J. Jackson (Eds.), *Sport, beer and gender: Promotional culture and contemporary social life* (pp. 225–241). New York: Peter Lang.

Palmer, C. (2011). Key themes and research agendas in the sport-alcohol nexus. *Journal of Sport & Social Issues, 35*(2), 168–185.

Palmer, C. (2013). Drinking like a guy: Women and sport-related drinking. *Journal of Gender Studies, 1*, 483–495.

Palmer, C. (2014). Sport and alcohol—who's missing? New directions for a sociology of sport-related drinking. *International Review for the Sociology of Sport, 49*, 263–277.

Palmer, C. (2020). Sport, alcohol and older athletes. In S. Gee (Ed.), *Sport, alcohol and social inquiry: A global cocktail* (pp. 83–97). Bingley: Emerald Press.

Palmer, C., Le Hénaff, Y., Bonnet, C., & Féliu, F. (2020). Drinking talk among climbers and Masters athletes. *International Journal of the Sociology of Leisure, 4*, 7–21.

Palmer, C., & Thompson, K. (2007). The paradoxes of football spectatorship: On field and on line expressions of social capital among the "Grog Squad." *Sociology of Sport Journal, 24*, 187–205.

Palmer, C., & Toffoletti, K. (2019). Sport, alcohol and women: An emerging research agenda. *Journal of Australian Studies, 43*(1), 103–117. doi.org/10.1080/14443058.2019.1574862.

Peralta, R. (2007). College alcohol use and the embodiment of hegemonic masculinity among European American men. *Sex Roles, 56*, 741–756.

Radcliffe, P., & Measham, F. (2014). Repositioning the cultural: Intoxicating stories in social context. *International Journal of Drug Policy, 25*(3), 346–347.

Rhodes, T. (1995). Researching and theorizing "risk": Notes on the social relations of risk in heroin users' lifestyles. In P. Aggleton, G. Hart, & P. Davies (Eds.), *AIDS: Sexuality, safety and risk* (pp. 125–143). London: Taylor & Francis.

Rhodes, T. (2009). Risk environments and drug harms: A social science for harm reduction approach. *International Journal of Drug Policy, 20*, 193–201.

Robards, B., & Lincoln, S. (2017). Uncovering longitudinal life narratives: Scrolling back on Facebook. *Qualitative Research, 17*(6), 715–730.

Sandberg, S., Tutenges, S., & Pedersen, W. (2019). Drinking stories as a narrative genre: The five classic themes. *Acta Sociologica, 62*(4), 406–419.

Seddon, T. (2010). *A history of drugs: Drugs and freedom in the liberal age.* Abingdon: Routledge.

Smith, B., & Sparkes, A. (2005). Men, sport, and spinal cord injury and narratives of hope. *Social Science and Medicine, 61*(5), 1095–1105.

Thompson, C., Milton, S., Egan, M., & Lock, K. (2018). Down the local: A qualitative case study of daytime drinking spaces in the London borough of Islington. *International Journal of Drug Policy, 52*, 1–8.

Thurnell-Read, T. (2011). Off the leash and out of control: Masculinities and embodiment in Eastern European stag tourism. *Sociology, 45*(6), 977–991.

Toffoletti, K. (2018). *Women sport fans: Identification, participation, representation*: New York: Routledge.

Turner, V. (1969). *The ritual process: Structure and anti-structure*. New York: Aladine de Gruyer.

Tutenges, S., & Sandberg, S. (2013). Intoxicating stories: The characteristics, contexts and implications of drinking stories among Danish youth. *International Journal of Drug Policy*, 24(6), 538–544.

van Gennep, A. (1960). *The rites of passage*. Chicago: University of Chicago Press.

Wenner, L. A., & Jackson, S. J. (Eds.). (2008). *Sport, beer and gender: Promotional culture and contemporary social life*. New York: Peter Lang.

Wilson, T. M. (2005). Drinking cultures: Sites and practices in the production and expression of identity. In T. M. Wilson (Ed.), *Drinking cultures: Alcohol and identity* (pp. 1–24). Oxford: Berg.

Workman, T. A. (2001). Finding the meanings of college drinking: An analysis of fraternity drinking stories. *Health Communication, 13*, 427–447.

World Health Organization. (2011). *Global health risks: Mortality and burden of disease attributable to selected major risks*. Geneva: WHO.

Young, M. (1995). Getting legless, falling down pissy arsed drunk: Policing men's leisure. *Journal of Gender Studies, 4*(1), 47–62.

Zajdow, G. (2010). "It blasted me into space": Intoxication and an ethics of pleasure. *Health Sociology Review, 19*(2), 218–229.

CHAPTER 26

··

SPORT, COACHING, AND PERFORMANCE

··

JIM DENISON AND ZOË AVNER

CENTRAL to the act of coaching is planning. That is, for any coach, a daily concern is always: What should I have the athletes I coach do in practice today to achieve our performance objectives? While seemingly straightforward, what can make this question difficult for coaches to answer is the entangled multiplicity of forces and "knowledges" that shape coaches' decision-making (Konoval, Denison, & Mills, 2019). As a result, what coaches have their athletes do in practice can more accurately be described as "a series of discontinuous segments whose tactical function is neither uniform or stable . . . but can come into play in various strategies" (Foucault, 1978, p. 100). It is in this way that the "truth of planning" contains "multiple possibilities for action and negotiation" (Foucault, 2000, p. 85).

For many coaches, any degree of ambiguity surrounding the design and implementation of their practice plans can raise the following concern: How will I ever know how to act with certainty? And it is the web of issues, approaches, and debates that surround this concern that we intend to focus upon in this chapter. More specifically, as Foucauldian-informed coach developers, we consider in what follows four key works that challenge a number of coaching norms by pointing out the varied and often unintended consequences associated with these norms. In doing this, we hope to illustrate the importance of coaches becoming more comfortable with uncertainty, ambiguity, and difference when planning their approach to training athletes, given that we know that knowledge and practice are never innocent or neutral but always inherently political and context bound.

ISSUES

··

In Denison's work with coaches as a coach developer, he often begins by asking coaches the following question: Can you name some factors related to performance enhancement in your sport that you were previously unaware of and as a result had no impact on your day-to-day decision-making?

Not surprisingly, the range of responses to this query is quite broad. Coaches make mention of everything from diet to technique, sleep, gene expressions, and a variety of concerns over motivation and mental states. Probing further, the coach developer queries, "Knowing so much more is good, right?" To this, most coaches respond, "Yes." Yes, they say, because compared to even just 10 years ago, coaches believe they understand and know so much more about human performance that can enable them to program their athletes' development more reliably and systematically. Few coaches, very few, respond, "No," while some, perhaps hedging a bit, say, "It depends." Interestingly, those who respond "No" and "It depends" offer the same reason for their answers as the coaches who respond "Yes," but with a revealing twist. They suspect that their increased monitoring and the controlling tactics used to advance their athletes' development can be problematic if they serve to limit or restrict their athletes' autonomy and decision-making.

With this simple question, therefore, we believe a central paradox or contradiction, causing fundamental tensions about what it means to be an effective coach, reveals itself. Put clearly, while advances in knowledge about effective training have given coaches more to pay attention to and digest, this information has also brought an exponential increase in the number of variables that a coach has to monitor and control. At the same time, this broadened and increased control can undermine coaches' attempts to approach coaching in more holistic, athlete-centered, and empowering ways (Avner, Denison, Jones, Boocock & Hall, 2021). And the demands for coaches to maintain control over a widened set of often interlocking variables can compromise their efforts to develop more resilient, responsible, mindful, aware, and thinking athletes—qualities that practically all coaches say they want to foster. This is especially true in light of systematic evidence about the strong relationship between athlete engagement and performance success (Kidman & Lombardo, 2010; Miller & Kerr, 2002). Thus, in the practice of coaching, we have a systemic control-empowerment paradox that can leave many coaches wondering: How do I organize my practices to get done what I want to get done while at the same time providing the athletes I coach the space and time to discover, explore, and learn for themselves?

What is most important to recognize about this paradox is that it is not necessarily new. Discussions and debates surrounding authoritative coaching versus cooperative coaching versus humanistic coaching, for example, have been ongoing for decades. For example, humanistic coaching and teaching approaches such as Teaching Games for Understanding (Bunker & Thorpe, 1982) and variants, such as Game Sense (den Duyn, 1997), have steadily grown in popularity over the past 40 years. All of these were framed as alternatives to more traditional, technique-focused, controlling, and authoritative coaching and teaching approaches. In contrast to more controlling normative tactics, these humanistic coaching approaches foreground pedagogies based on guided discovery and the use of game-like scenarios to support the development of athletes' critical thinking, problem-solving, and decision-making skills (Harvey, Pill, & Almond, 2018). Because of their game-centeredness, these pedagogies have been most widely embraced in team sports and are commonly seen, for example, in soccer (Hubbal & Robertson, 2004) and rugby union (Light & Evans, 2013). Despite not being new, the divide between "coach-control" or "coach-led" and "athlete-empowerment" or "athlete-centered" frameworks continue to engender impassioned, yet unfortunately mainly polarized, debates across a variety of research, education, and performance settings. In fact, one could argue that this chasm has, at least as voiced in rhetoric, never been wider than it is today, nor more difficult for coaches to navigate (Denison, Mills, & Konoval, 2017).

In other words, in light of the complexities and tensions inherent here, to suggest to coaches that they merely go down either the control or empowerment pathway with respect to how they interact with athletes and incorporate the latest sport science into their training plans makes little sense. By way of example, it would seem foolish for a coach to ignore the benefits that could come from tracking an athlete's sleep because it might somehow be construed as disempowering. But equally, it would seem foolish to ignore the disempowering consequences and side effects that could result from heavy-handed tracking of an athlete's sleep efficacy. As a result, coaches need to open their eyes to all that their practices do and be willing to accept that achieving any type of firm certainty in their decision-making is likely unattainable. This point was made well by Jones and Hemmestad (2021, p. 16), who argued for a greater recognition of coaching as an intellectual activity involving "situationally prudent judgements" rather than the rote application of a range of sport science techniques, however well tested they may seem. Similarly, Bjorndal and Ronglan (2021) pointed to the many reasons behind the need for coaches to abandon the idea of being able to definitively solve problems and instead recognize and come to appreciate that effective coaching constitutes a never-ending balancing act.

Despite these efforts by coaching scholars and coach educators to challenge coaches to become more comfortable with not always knowing what to do, there is no denying that the dominant story circulating within sport today remains the same: coaches need to adopt a science-driven, technology-rich, measurement-oriented perspective—far more on the control side of the control-empowerment paradox—to be effective. We believe, however, that it is important to continue to challenge this "best practice" narrative, just as Mills, Denison, and Gearity (2020) did in their Foucauldian discourse analysis of what coaching the "right" way means. In this powerful representation of Mills's failed efforts to reach his potential as a middle-distance runner, a number of paradoxes in his training were revealed. That is, although he was doing everything his coach said he should be doing (and more), this study showed how the belief in absolutes as a coach can undermine an athlete's performances. As such, it is critical that coaches are able to question what might be considered right or correct when it comes to planning their athletes' training. Thus, in what follows, we discuss how a Foucauldian approach can support coaches in this endeavor.

APPROACHES

On Foucauldian Analysis

Michel Foucault (1926–1984) was a highly influential French theorist and political activist. His extensive pluri-disciplinary body of work centered on theorizing modern processes of power—how power circulates through discourses or "ways of knowing which are perpetuated through our everyday practices" (Markula & Silk, 2011, p. 48) and how subjectivities are constituted within and through specific relations of power-knowledge. As such, Foucault fundamentally challenged a dominant hierarchical and repressive understanding of power, arguing instead for an understanding of power as productive, relational, diffuse, omnipresent, and inextricably tied to the production, negotiation, alteration, and circulation of discourses (Markula & Silk, 2011).

The principal aim of Foucault's body of work was to help individuals liberate themselves from what he articulated as the double-bind of individualizing knowledges and power relations. To that end, he carried out forms of historical investigations, or "genealogies," which sought to (1) historicize modern social practices and (2) challenge the dominant narrative of scientific progress, which positions modern practices as more humane, rational, and progressive than their premodern counterparts. For instance, in one of his most thought-provoking genealogical analyses, *Discipline and Punish: The Birth of the Prison* (1995), Foucault traced how disciplinary techniques and instruments used both in monasteries and in the army gradually spread in the 18th and 19th centuries to other social institutions (e.g., schools, prisons, hospitals, factories), where they were adopted as "blueprints" to maximize order and productivity. What Foucault aimed to show through these historical mappings was that, although the substitution of premodern sovereign power and its associated public spectacles of violence for modern disciplinary power might appear progressive, such blithe efforts at porting science to practice were, in fact, anything but benign.

In particular, Foucault was very concerned with the increasingly widespread application of disciplinary techniques and instruments and the way in which they were used to control individuals. In this sense, much of his work centered on (1) identifying how disciplinary power operates to discipline and normalize individual subjects through specific spatial, temporal, organizational, and evaluative practices (matters which we detail in the next subsection of this chapter) and (2) showing how these techniques and instruments have come to be accepted as "normal," "true," and "correct" through the complex interplay of relations of power-knowledge and various historical contingencies. In doing so, he aimed to destabilize modern relations of power-knowledge and their associated truth regimes (Foucault, 1978). As well, his approach aims to draw attention to all that modern disciplinary power (overtly and covertly) does—including its unintended and problematic effects, such as those that accompany the scientized production of overly compliant, docile bodies. Ultimately, Foucault (1984) sought to open up space for individuals to "think themselves otherwise" and devise new, less problematic, and more ethical social practices and modes of being.

Because of Foucault's (1995) elaborate theorization of modern disciplinary power and his insights regarding the historical formation of knowledge, we find that his conceptual toolkit is exceptionally, and perhaps uniquely, well positioned to help support coaches in navigating the complexities of the control-empowerment paradox central to considerations in this chapter. As well, Foucault's insights can aid coaches in developing more "dexterity" in their understanding and application of modern coaching "truths" and "best practices." To illustrate the value of a Foucauldian approach, in the next sections we review four key studies which have used his toolkit to effectively challenge some long-standing norms of coaching practice. As we will show, these norms and practices, although they might be highly useful and productive in many regards, can also be problematic in other, arguably more important ways. The studies in the review that follows were chosen because they provide insightful examples of how to apply Foucault's different disciplinary techniques and instruments to problematize various coaching norms, to understand all that they really may do, and to pose options to coaches for alternative fruitful pathways to their goals while more fully engaging athletes under their tutelage.

Spatial Practices

The first study we consider showed how a range of everyday *spatial practices* used within the context of women's gymnastics created a particular paradox that can be problematic for athlete development (Barker-Ruchti & Tinning, 2010). By "spatial practices" we mean practices used by a coach that repeatedly assign specific things to happen in specific spaces, such as practices that regularly rank individuals by their abilities. In this study, the authors conducted a year-long ethnography of an Australian high-performance women's gymnastics club comprised of seven gymnasts and two coaches. Their ethnographic tactics included researcher observations, participant observations, and long-form interviews aimed at understanding the gymnasts' specific training experiences. In addition, the researchers wanted to understand how various coaching knowledges and practices emerged and why they were prioritized by the coaches at the expense of other knowledges and practices. In doing so, Barker-Ruchti and Tinning sought to draw attention to the creation of overt and covert meanings, including perceptions about their effects, including those that may have been unintended, that these privileged and entrenched coaching knowledges and practices produced.

Among the many intriguing findings that Barker-Ruchti and Tinning reported as significant was the surprising degree to which spatial arrangements at the club, with its highly structured, enclosed, and partitioned space, made the gymnasts' experiences of their training highly monotonous. At the same time, this monotony restricted the gymnasts' ability to explore a variety of solutions to the "movement problems" their coaches had set for them because, paradoxically, the precise distribution of individuals in a space featuring confining, enclosed, and highly partitioned spaces served to create a training culture centered around coach control and dependency.

Still, of course, it is well recognized that spatial arrangements in sport can have productive effects. For example, in Barker-Ruchti and Tinning's (2010) study, it was clear that locating the gymnasts in specific places allowed the coaches to know where the gymnasts were and thus coach with greater intensity and efficiency. While this did accelerate the gymnasts' learning, given that it made it easier for the coaches to detect and correct mistakes, such a strong concentration of authority and surveillance left the gymnasts with virtually no opportunities to exercise any independence or take any responsibility for their growth and development as gymnasts. Rather, the rigid apportionment of space contributed to athletes being made into highly compliant bodies. This importantly shed light on another operant paradoxical tension, between activity and passivity. In short, while the gymnasts were active in terms of their bodily movements and could execute very complex skills, the manner in which they were trained by their coaches to become active left them extremely passive in terms of being able to make decisions, create their own routines, and reflect upon both their sport and their lives.

In total, and as a result of this passivity, Barker-Ruchti and Tinning concluded that the coaches' meticulous control over their gymnasts' bodies led the gymnasts to develop an identity that was overwhelmingly marked by diligence, submission, and perfectionism, matters that left them feeling anything but empowered. Indeed, instead of building confidence and autonomy, the gymnasts reported that they became resentful of their coaches and dissatisfied with their sport, which, as the study's results confirmed, led many of them to become frustrated and disappointed with their inability to shape and control their realities. And over time, gymnastics, a sport they once loved, began to lose its appeal to such a degree that, in the end, half of the gymnasts in the study reported being burned out, quitting gymnastics, or retiring early.

Importantly, as Barker-Ruchti and Tinning's (2010) findings also illuminated, the spatial arrangements at the gymnastics club being studied were by no means natural or occurring by accident. Rather, these arrangements were formulated by engaging a whole host of social, political, and subjective factors (e.g., national sporting codes, the endorsement of traditional masculine and militaristic training cultures and regimens to offset "a relaxed Australian way of life," capitalist economic drivers, the coaches' previous athletic experiences, as well as their beliefs and preferences). These were put in place in order to secure and sanction a number of desired behaviors, many of which had little to do with enhancing performance. All of which begs a fundamental question: Why do common received spatial practices and the problematic effects they can have so often go unquestioned?

Temporal Practices

The second study we focus on showed how a range of everyday *temporal practices* used within the context of a university cross-country running program created a particular paradox that can be problematic to athlete development (Denison, 2007). By "temporal practices," we mean those practices used by a coach that constantly divide time into ever smaller units and consistently break any action, movement, or activity down into more precise and demarcated elements. This study entailed a retrospective case study within which the author revisited how, as a coach, he had made sense of one of his university cross-country runner's underperformance while competing at the conference championships. As the focus of his analysis, the author-coach began to interrogate how many of the normal and taken-for-granted practices that he had regularly implemented had centered on the control and measurement of time, and how these prioritized practices might explain the runner's underperformance.

As a distance-running coach, Denison (2007) had always believed that discipline as a runner was a good thing and underpinned being able to develop essential abilities to stay on task and execute skills correctly without being distracted. And to some considerable degree this is true. Athletes need to be dedicated, focused, and consistent with what, how, and when they do things. Such skills help athletes in being able to execute any number of skills efficiently and automatically. Accordingly, the author-coach had no qualms when he was coaching this runner (pseudonymized as "Brian") in specifying the time of day he should run as well as the duration and intensity of each run. Associated with this was the amount of time the author-coach allowed Brian for recovery from his workouts, the interval that was allowed between the repetitions he did on the track, and the number of easy days prescribed between his hardest days of training. In other words, the author-coach was more or less endeavoring to have full control over the details of shaping and directing Brian's running rhythms and cycles.

There is little doubt that the high degree of coach control recounted in this study did in fact make Brian very fit. But as the author-coach also began to realize, the more he controlled the temporal aspects of Brian's running, the further he removed Brian from the process or act of being a runner. And it was the result of recognizing this unintended consequence that the author-coach began to consider what he might have contributed to Brian's underperformance rather than Brian "psyching out," as he had originally thought.

Thus, what presents itself here is a paradox that stems from using a stopwatch to impose order and control on an athlete. While such a practice can be extremely useful in producing a fully prepared athlete, it can also have unintended effects that can begin to limit the field of possible actions that athletes' believe they can follow. As such, it is important for coaches to regularly evaluate any unintended motivational and psychological effects their reliance on a number of temporal practices might be having on their athletes in order to prevent them from losing a sense of ownership of their performance.

Organizational Practices

The third study we highlight showed how a range of everyday *organizational practices* used within the context of university strength and conditioning coaching created a paradox that can be problematic for athlete development (Gearity & Mills, 2013). By "organizational practices," we mean practices used by a coach that ensure that each stage, series, or segment of development "makes sense" by systematically combining a range of smaller units into a more comprehensive plan. In this study, Gearity had been a university strength and conditioning coach for eight years. And as his empirical material, he reflected on how he began to rethink, with the help of Foucault (1995), a number of his normal organizational practices. Gearity noted a principal concern over whether his tried and true strength regimens were inadvertently producing at the same time athletic and docile bodies, creating a paradox he found to be extremely problematic. Briefly, as defined by Foucault, a docile body is one that is extremely passive and obedient. A key concern was that fueling docility works against athletes' abilities to learn or think for themselves.

For example, Gearity became aware of how his training plans were always meticulous in their details. His training protocols were hierarchically organized by increasing complexity, followed by careful examination. Foremost, his approach to training aimed at ensuring the efficiency of these processes and making sure that his athletes were able to pass the exams or benchmarks that dominated his thinking as a coach. What's wrong with this, one might ask? Indeed, these strategies did enable the coach's athletes in this study to progress through their training regimen in a timely manner and develop some important athletic skills. Yet, at the same time, as Gearity noted in his narrative reflection on his practices, physical testing throughout the year, a so-called objective measure of improvement, had become such a strong focus for the athletes that he coached that their sense of progress and preparedness became completely oriented around a fixed and stable point—reaching the next benchmark—as opposed to thinking about what they needed to be able to do to succeed in competition. Again, we are not arguing that it is bad for a coach to have a plan. Rather, what we find interesting and worthwhile to point out, based on the findings in this study, is how this coach, despite his success, started to become troubled by all that his training programs were doing, both intentionally and inadvertently. That is, Gearity began to realize what other things, besides making his athletes stronger, could be happening to the athletes he was coaching because of how he had implemented a variety of widely endorsed and received organizational coaching practices. In Gearity's reflections, there was rising cognizance of additional training side effects, leaving residue that might be less desirable to both athletic and personal development, matters that consequently deleteriously affected essential affinities of athletic engagement often overlooked.

As a final word about this study, there is little doubt that a docile body can be, in some sense, successful and win. In fact, some coaches, given the choice, might prefer to keep athletes they are coaching docile. It certainly is an easier way to coach and to maintain firm control. But when one takes a broader view of what excellence means in the context of human experience, coaching in such mechanistically organized ways in pursuit of exquisite performances comes with risks. Blithely relying on received organizational practices and ignoring individual differences inherently only exacerbates a fundamental athletic-docile bodies paradox. Consequently, taking such a tack can be both highly ineffective in advancing holistic athletic development and call into question the ethical propriety of a coach's well-intentioned but rigid methods.

Evaluation Practices

The fourth study we feature showed how a range of everyday *evaluation practices* used within the context of professional rugby created a particular paradox that can be problematic for athlete development (Williams & Manley, 2016). By "evaluation practices," we mean practices used by a coach that continually seek greater means and methods of observation and surveillance, as well as practices that routinely establish and reinforce specific norms or best practices. In this study, Williams and Manley considered the unintended consequences associated with rugby coaches' use of video analysis technologies. They were concerned with how surveillance technologies used by coaches might serve to undermine athlete learning, erode coach-athlete trust, and make athletes into mere functionaries. To investigate these concerns, the researchers situated themselves within a premier British rugby club for five months and conducted a series of interviews with both coaches and athletes pertaining to the club's use of video analysis.

Central to the authors' analysis was the idea that, with the development of a new approach to coaching such as video analysis, concerns can emerge about who is in control of its implementation and interpretation. The results of this study showed that, with the coaches' quest for increased efficiency, numerical monitoring, and so-called evidence-based decision-making through the use of video analysis, there came rising risks of making the rugby players at this particular club into machines and the coaches into technocrats.

To be clear, Williams and Manley (2016) did see some positive artifacts resulting from the use of video analysis, such as the opportunity to provide players with specific feedback about various essential skills such as passing and tackling. Still, their primary takeaway from considering the dynamics of constant evaluation was that there could be considerable problematic consequences to athlete engagement if the increased use of surveillance tactics in sport training techniques for rugby continued without a corresponding critical dialogue. In Williams and Manley's stocktaking, these consequences were fourfold: (1) a dampening of players' natural enthusiasm for playing sport as the human aspect becomes increasingly redundant, (2) a detrimental influence on athletes' health and well-being, (3) a decline in performance as natural highs are stripped away through an unremitting emphasis on data, and (4) the risk of athletes becoming bioengineered and socially empty beings due to a decline in social interaction. These consequences raise the question: How much of a good thing is the growing trend within sport to observe, and attempt to measure, all that goes into a performance?

DEBATES

Having considered these four illustrations of how a Foucauldian approach can be fruitfully applied to identify critical coaching issues resulting from the use of disciplinary techniques and instruments—issues which, as these studies clearly illustrate, more often than not go unnoticed and unaddressed or are misunderstood and misaddressed—we turn our attention to some enduring debates and wider challenges about the prospects for change in the coaching profession.

In many respects, the approach we have taken in this chapter points strongly to what is an ongoing debate within the field of coach education. Namely, what coaching "knowledges" count? As we signaled earlier, despite the efforts of many coaching scholars to challenge coaches to become more comfortable with not always knowing what to do, the central and overriding message to coaches, for the most part, remains the same: to be effective you need to adopt a science-driven, technology-rich, measurement-oriented, command-and-control coaching style. And strengthening this message is how the specter of performance, as a visible and clear outcome attached to every sport contest, looms large over the perceived value and merit of any coaching scholar's work.

In other words, given that the central meaning or substance of sport revolves around performance, and ideally facilitating a winning performance, any type of nuanced perspective on performance, such as is likely to come from a Foucauldian point of view, typically receives resistance, being questioned or disregarded as too abstract or theoretical to matter. In this sense, the challenge that faces Foucauldian coaching scholars in establishing the legitimacy, value, and merit of this type of work lies in its perceived *indirect* connection to performance enhancement—indirect, that is, from the point of view of most coaches who believe that a *direct* line to performance enhancement exists from research conducted in the so-called harder sport sciences, such as exercise physiology and biomechanics.

Our use of the terms "direct" and "indirect," of course, points to very specific meanings with respect to knowledge production and any debate over what knowledges should count. Positivism, and the idea that a researcher's findings are useful only if they resulted from direct observation in a laboratory setting, has served to marginalize other types of sport-related research for decades. And by "other types" of research, we are of course referring to qualitative social science research that has as the basis of its findings the use of such indirect measures as interviews, narratives, and fieldwork—methods employed in the studies considered earlier.

The marginalization of qualitative social science research with respect to the practice of coaching, however, is increasingly being questioned. Mills, Denison, and Gearity (2017), for example, exposed a fundamental paradox with sport scientists studying sport performance in a laboratory. They wrote, "[W]hile 'natural' sport scientists typically pursue the *truth* by working in controlled or artificial settings, it is in the *nuanced*, ambiguous and ever-changing *real-world* that athletes perform" (p. 26, emphasis added). In other words, they continued,

> if a finding is true in a laboratory or some other strictly controlled environment, but not in the real-world of sport, then it follows that that finding by definition is not true; or at least its "trueness" is only specific to the lab or the uniquely controlled context in which it was "discovered." (p. 27)

Thus, we contend that what is necessary for sport-related research conducted through a qualitative Foucauldian lens, such as the four studies we discussed, to be taken seriously in the world of applied sport is a shift in thinking with respect to how research is judged and evaluated by coaches as useful for them to meet the performance-enhancement demands they so clearly face. This, of course, raises the question: How can such a shift in thinking occur? As Foucauldian-informed coaching researchers, we believe the most effective way to bring about this shift in thinking is to reassure coaches that "thinking with Foucault" as a coach does not mean retreating to a relativist abyss absent of reasoned analysis (Eisner, 1983). Put differently, with a Foucauldian-informed coaching approach it is still possible as a coach to make decisions and act with the aim of enhancing performance. In fact, as previously argued, we believe that thinking with Foucault uniquely positions coaches to understand and effectively address many of their athletes' performance-related challenges. And in what follows we discuss two misconceptions that are often attributed to more nuanced or conceptually oriented sport-related research regarding coaches' authority and the expertise necessary to lead and direct the athletes they coach.

All Opinions Are Equal

In many coaching circles the idea that the coach has absolute authority and power over their athletes remains strong. This view has sustained itself because of a number of long-standing conceptions of effective coaching, such as the "coach as expert" discourse. This discourse has led to the belief that coaches who subscribe to a less hierarchical and more relational understanding of power, as suggested by Foucauldian coaching researchers, are in effect saying that their athletes' opinions are equal to, if not superior to, theirs. This has raised the troubling concern for many coaches that their authority, experience, and expertise will be forever questioned, if not undermined. Such an absolute understanding of knowledge and expertise, however, misrepresents Foucault's take on power. Foucault absolutely appreciated and recognized the importance of experience and expertise. What concerned him was not the need to equalize power among individuals within groups or institutions, such as teams, but how those with greater degrees of power within groups or institutions, such as coaches relative to athletes, can use their power ethically to minimize dominance.

In this respect, on many occasions the more ethical course of action for a coach to take might be to exert their authority and expertise in a very direct manner. For example, it makes complete sense from a Foucauldian point of view that a coach would prescribe strict guidelines for their athletes to follow when introducing a new skill that, if completed incorrectly, could lead to injury. What makes this example ethical from a Foucauldian perspective is that the coach's exertion of control in this situation is not being used to dominate their athletes, as is so often the case with coaches' uncritical use of various disciplinary techniques, but to support and facilitate the athletes' healthy growth and development.

As another example of how a coach's knowledge and expertise certainly do matter, consider a youth academy soccer coach. More often than not this coach's knowledge of tactics will be superior to the players'. What becomes important from a Foucauldian point of view, therefore, is how this coach can convey their superior knowledge of tactics in a way that does not make the players docile. This requires coaching in a way that considers the multiple approaches coaches can take, as opposed to just one, to enable their players to discover and explore for themselves how to become competent tacticians in a variety of competitive situations. Such an approach recognizes how athlete learning is endless and emergent and can follow many paths, as opposed to being entirely directed and dictated by a coach (Orth, van der Kamp, & Button, 2019). In this respect, a coach's performance-enhancing intentions can clearly be strengthened with a more nuanced appreciation of pedagogy and skill acquisition.

No Practice Can Ever Be the Right Practice

For many coaches the idea that their training plans need to be more flexible and responsive to a complex array of evolving demands and sources of information, as sport-related research from a Foucauldian perspective would suggest, could be understood to mean that no workout, drill, or exercise is better than any other. As a result, coaching can become seen as a "hand's off" practice where really anything goes. However, when thinking with Foucault as a coach, one actually needs to be more "hand's on" for the precise reason that there will be fewer certainties and guidelines to follow. For example, a coach who appreciates difference and diversity and the important role these can play in performance will have to be smarter and more creative and work harder to design effective training practices that refute simplistic, "one size fits all" approaches to athlete development. In other words, we believe the move to an interactionist and contextual perspective on coaching, which can come with a Foucauldian take on knowledge and practice, will enable coaches to appreciate their athletes as individuals, as opposed to machines, who each possess unique adaptive qualities.

In this respect, a coach is likely to be more effective if they avoid using instructional metaphors that reduce their athletes' bodies into parts by recognizing instead the holistic and entirely human makeup of those bodies. This subtle shift in language might seem trivial to someone who sees little beyond the surface level of an instruction or piece of feedback, but referring to an athlete's joint as a gear or their lungs as an engine can have a profound influence; it can lead, for example, to coaches establishing time scales for learning that fail to acknowledge how any number of personal and environmental factors can impact an athlete set with a particular skill development task or movement problem to solve. In this sense, an athlete never arrives at practice as an empty vessel ready to be filled with a coach's knowledge and wisdom. Rather, athletes need to be seen by coaches as collaborators in their daily training environment who play an integral part in any performance-enhancement agenda or system.

The point we are making here about athletes' bodies and skill development as open and fluid, as opposed to linear and predictable, should not be taken to mean that athletes are not limited by certain genetic, mechanical, or cognitive factors, or that some workouts or drills can be plain wrong. Flexion around the joints and gravity's effect on posture, after all, are not matters up for debate. But when a mechanical conception of the body begins to dominate a coach's pedagogy to the extent that they believe that a direct path to performance enhancement can be found if only they keep working hard enough, it becomes easy to lose sight of the fact that one's athletes are not robots to be programmed but instead bring with them to every practice their own particular energy. And the fact of the matter is that this energy does things a coach most likely knows, but it also may do things that a coach cannot know or even anticipate. In other words, a coach is never coaching an inert object who will respond to commands and prompts in a presubscribed way, but an individual human being, with all manner of intentions and unique dynamics, who will react in myriad ways to what is happening to and around them. The challenge this presents to a coach is how to utilize this energy to maximize an athlete's performance capacities and capabilities. And we would argue that it is a challenge that no coach should take lightly if they want to see their athletes or teams succeed.

Summary

As we have tried to illustrate by presenting these two misconceptions that are often attributed to so-called indirect sport-related research, a coach who thinks with a Foucauldian-informed mindset can still be focused on advancing their athletes' performance gains forward. What changes is the manner in which they will do so. For example, as opposed to thinking about practices as fixed and true, a coach might begin to describe them as discursive and political. Again, and as we have tried to illustrate throughout this Debates section, this distinction might seem trivial or too abstract to address given a coach's performance pressures. But speaking differently is central to reimaging the present and practicing in new or more progressive ways. Or as Foucault (1972) might put it, innovation and performance enhancement is as contingent on knowing what to say and do from situation to situation as it is on knowing how to problematize the specific conditions that generated the understanding of what one should or is supposed to say and do from situation to situation. Accordingly, and as we will discuss in our conclusion, becoming an effective coach can no longer be seen as a stage of development or a point to reach after a set period of time or following a number of specific experiences. It is instead a never-ending process of learning, discovery, and self-transformation.

Conclusion

From our extensive line of research working with a variety of coaches, as well as our combined 20-plus years of teaching coaching courses at the undergraduate and graduate level with a focus on helping coaches think critically about what has become normal, we have come to appreciate that many coaches feel uneasy about the status quo. These coaches have expressed to us an interest in thinking differently because of their underlying sense that "not everything is quite right" with many of their relied-upon strategies and the so-called best practices of the profession. Knowing where to turn to address those concerns, however, they often feel to be outside their scope of practice. Thus, too often coaches tend to carry on as usual and try to solve a whole host of problems when the "true cause" is not clearly understood and consequently often goes unaddressed (Denison & Avner, 2011).

Compounding this situation is the fact that actually implementing practices that are truly different, and which may require relinquishing some level of control, can be difficult and challenging for many coaches. To upend one's long-term assumptions, to challenge one's highly esteemed mentors, or to set aside cherished memories and buck tradition is never easy. These actions can seriously threaten a coach's sense of self or lead others to question their competence. Moreover, the privileging of reductionist received understandings of coaching expertise (de Haan & Knoppers, 2020), the considerable prevalence of job insecurity, and the precarity and distrust that is pervasive in many high-performance and elite coaching contexts, (Potrac, Jones, Gilbourne, & Nelson, 2012) all serve to make change difficult. And when these are brought together, their cumulative weight tends to reaffirm the status quo. As a result, and what has become one of the ultimate paradoxes of coaching, coaches are often being undermined by many of their own practices without even knowing it.

Accordingly, a state of affairs within coaching continues to exist whereby the critical examination of assumptions and practices are seldom emphasized in coach education courses, especially given their tendency to privilege technocratic knowledge over critical thinking (Avner, Markula, & Denison, 2017; Cushion, 2013). In response to this entrenched tendency, we believe that an emergent line of critical coaching research (both by ourselves and by other scholars) is showing that learning to question what appears to be "right" or "correct" is an essential skill for coaches to develop if they are to truly coach in different ways that are both more ethical and effective. Entailed in making this a reality, coaches will have to move beyond surface rhetoric, such as simply making claims to be athlete-centered, and examine all that their practices might be doing along the control-empowerment spectrum, and the tensions between their poles. This includes, most importantly, addressing the numerous disciplinary and controlling effects of received, normalized, taken-for-granted "best" coaching practices (Avner, Denison, & Markula, 2019; Denison, Mills, & Konoval, 2017).

In closing, we would like to return to an earlier section of this chapter, where we indicated how Denison might engage a coach he is working with. During this initial engagement period, here is something else that he often puts forward. He asks coaches to think back to why they became interested in coaching in the first place. Almost all respond that what most fueled their interest were experiences that had to do with the freedom, expression, and creativity of sport. Central here were matters that spoke to the fun and enjoyment that sport offered in a world that was otherwise seen as rigid, fixed, overly mechanistic, and technocratic. Given that such overriding concerns really undergird being drawn to sport in foundational ways, it seems irresponsible not to ask, or even require, that coaches consider all of the ways to approach coaching in pursuit of the increased likelihood of helping athletes under their guidance become embodied and engaged thinking beings. Through systematic work in rethinking some foundational assumptions embedded in coaching education and by prioritizing more egalitarian approaches central to the ethos of coaching that grants creativity and autonomy to athletes, coaches may come to embrace a markedly redrawn received logic, one that will offer room for coaches and athletes to work together rather than being stifled by the powers of conventional wisdom and an unthinking endorsement of numerous problematic norms.

References

Avner, Z., Denison, J., Jones, L., Boocock, E., & Hall, E. T. (2021). Beat the game: A Foucauldian exploration of coaching differently in an elite rugby academy. *Sport, Education and Society, 26,* 676–691.

Avner, Z., Denison, J., & Markula, P. (2019). "Good athletes have fun": A Foucauldian reading of university coaches' uses of fun. *Sports Coaching Review, 8,* 43–61.

Avner, Z., Markula, P., & Denison, J. (2017). Understanding effective coaching: A Foucauldian reading of current coach education frameworks. *International Sport Coaching Journal, 4,* 101–109.

Barker-Ruchti, N., & Tinning, R. (2010). Foucault in leotards: Corporeal discipline in women's artistic gymnastics. *Sociology of Sport Journal, 27,* 229–250.

Bjorndal, C. T., & Ronglan, L. T. (2021). Engaging with uncertainty in athlete development: Orchestrating talent development through incremental leadership. *Sport, Education and Society, 26,* 104–116.

Bunker, D., & Thorpe, R. (1982). A model for the teaching of games in secondary schools. *Bulletin of Physical Education, 18,* 5–8.

Cushion, C. (2013). Applying game centered approaches in coaching: A critical analysis of the dilemmas of practice impacting change. *Sports Coaching Review, 2,* 61–76.

de Haan, D., & Knoppers, A. (2020). Gendered discourses in high-performance sport. *International Review for the Sociology of Sport, 55,* 631–646.

den Duyn, N. (1997). *Game sense: Developing thinking players workbook.* Canberra: Australian Sports Commission.

Denison, J. (2007). Social theory for coaches: A Foucauldian reading of one athlete's poor performance. *International Journal of Sports Science & Coaching, 2,* 369–383.

Denison, J. (2010). Planning, practice and performance: The discursive construction of coaches' knowledge. *Sport, Education & Society, 15,* 461–478.

Denison, J., & Avner, Z. (2011). Positive coaching: Ethical practices for athlete development. *Quest, 63,* 209–227.

Denison, J., Mills, J. P., & Konoval, T. (2017). Sports' disciplinary legacy and the challenge of "coaching differently." *Sport, Education and Society, 22,* 772–783.

Eisner, E. W. (1983). The art and craft of teaching. *Educational Leadership, 40,* 4–13.

Foucault, M. (1972). *The archaeology of knowledge and discourse on language.* New York: Pantheon Books.

Foucault, M. (1978). *The history of sexuality: Vol. 1. An introduction.* London: Penguin.

Foucault, M. (1984). *The history of sexuality: Vol. 3. The care of the self.* New York: Vintage Books.

Foucault, M. (1995). *Discipline and punish: The birth of the prison.* New York: Vintage.

Foucault, M. (2000). Polemics, politics, and problematizations: An interview with Michel Foucault. In P. Rabinow (Ed.) & L. Davis (Trans.), *Ethics: Subjectivity and truth* (pp. 80–110). London: Penguin.

Gearity, B. T., & Mills, J. P. (2013). Discipline and punish in the weight room. *Sports Coaching Review, 1,* 124–134.

Harvey, S., Pill, S., & Almond, L. (2018). Old wine in new bottles: A response to claims that teaching games for understanding was not developed as a theoretically based pedagogical framework. *Physical Education and Sport Pedagogy, 23,* 166–180.

Hubball, H., & Robertson, S. (2004). Using problem-based learning to enhance team and player development in youth soccer. *Journal of Physical Education, Recreation & Dance, 75,* 38–43.

Jones, R. L., & Hemmestad, L. B. (2021). Reclaiming the "competent" practitioner: Furthering the case for the practically wise coach. *Sports Coaching Review, 10*, 1–19.

Kidman, L., & Lombardo, B. (2010). *Athlete-centered coaching: Developing decision makers* (2nd ed.). Worcester, U.K.: Innovative Print Communications.

Konoval, T., Denison, M., & Mills, J. P. (2019). The cyclical relationship between physiology and discipline: One endurance running coach's experiences problematizing disciplinary practices. *Sports Coaching Review, 8*, 124–148.

Light, R. L., & Evans, J. R. (2013). Dispositions of elite-level Australian rugby coaches towards game sense: Characteristics of their coaching habitus. *Sport, Education and Society, 18*, 407–423.

Markula, P., & Silk, M. (2011). *Qualitative research for physical culture.* Basingstoke, U.K.: Palgrave.

Miller, P. S., & Kerr, G. A. (2002). Conceptualizing excellence: Past, present, and future. *Journal of Applied Sport Psychology, 14*, 140–153.

Mills, J. P., Denison, J., & Gearity, B. (2017, Summer). "Social" science as sport science. *Sport and Exercise Scientist, 52*, 26–27.

Mills, J. P., Denison, J., & Gearity, B. (2020). Breaking coaching's rules: Transforming the body, sport, and performance. *Journal of Sport and Social Issues, 44*, 244–260.

Orth, D., van der Kamp, J., & Button, C. (2019). Learning to be adaptive as a distributed process across the coach-athlete system: Situating the coach in the constraints-led approach. *Physical Education and Sport Pedagogy, 24*, 146–161.

Potrac, P., Jones, R. L., Gilbourne, D., & Nelson, L. (2012). "Handshakes, BBQs, and bullets": Self-interest, shame and regret in football coaching. *Sports Coaching Review, 1*, 79–92.

Williams, S., & Manley, A. (2016). Elite coaching and the technocratic engineer: Thanking the boys at Microsoft! *Sport, Education and Society, 21*, 828–850.

CHAPTER 27

··

SPORT, EMOTION, AND ENGAGEMENT

··

PAUL A. POTRAC, BRIAN T. GEARITY,
ADAM J. NICHOL, AND EDWARD T. HALL

[E]motions are not trivial. They are a pervasive and fundamental part of our daily lives. They give colour and meaning to virtually all of our experiences—from the most mundane to the most extraordinary situations. Although they are often portrayed as less interesting and important than thinking and acting, emotions are intricately connected to our daily thoughts and behaviours. They sustain or threaten our most valued relationships and identities. (Harris, 2015, p. 3)

As highlighted by Harris and many others (e.g., Barbalet, 1998, 2001, 2002; Denzin, 1984; Jacobsen, 2019; Turner & Stets, 2006), emotions are an essential aspect of our everyday lives. Indeed, they feature in all social phenomena, be it the macro, micro, organizational, political, economic, cultural, personal, or the religious (Bericat, 2016; Denzin, 1984; Turner & Stets, 2006; Zietsma, Toubiana, Voronov, & Roberts, 2019). In recent decades, emotions have been the subject of sustained inquiry in mainstream sociology (Bericat, 2016; Stets & Turner, 2014). Here, scholars (e.g., Bloch, 2012; Burkitt, 2014; Fineman, 2005, 2008; Harris, 2015; Hochschild, 1983; Thoits, 1999, 2011; von Scheve, 2013; Zembylas, 2006) have utilized a variety of theoretical frameworks to not only examine how emotions (e.g., guilt, joy, anger, and pride, among others) are enacted, embodied, and produced in relations with others, but also to consider the consequences of emotional experience for individual and group life.

Despite the foundational (e.g., Dunning, 1986; Elias & Dunning, 1986; Ferguson, 1981; Maguire, 1991, 1992, 2001; Snyder, 1990; Snyder & Ammons, 1993; Zurcher, 1982) and more recent (e.g., Collinson, 2005; Cottingham, 2012; Gearity & Henderson Metzger, 2017; Hayton, 2017; Ives, Gale, Potrac, & Nelson, 2021; Maguire, 2011; Nelson, Potrac, Gilbourne, Allanson, Gale, & Marshall, 2014; Ortiz, 2010; Potrac, Mallett, Greenough, & Nelson, 2017; Lee-Sinden, 2013; Smith, 2008; van Ingen, 2011) contributions of sociology of sport scholars, emotion remains a largely underresearched and undertheorized topic within the subdiscipline's literature. Arguably, this limited coverage of emotions leaves us open to the accusation of producing strangely inhuman accounts of the relations, interactions, rituals, practices, and inequalities that comprise sporting structures, institutions, and organizations (Potrac, Smith, & Nelson, 2017; Roderick, Smith, & Potrac, 2017). Rather than being the outcome of a purposeful effort to relegate emotions to the "ontological basement" of scholarly inquiry (Liston & Garrison, 2003), however, this situation arguably reflects the history and size of our subdiscipline.

Fortunately, there is a diverse range of generative theoretical frameworks (e.g., Burkitt, 2014; Stets & Turner, 2014; Ten-Houten, 2007; Turner and Stets, 2006; von Scheve, 2013, among others) and methods (e.g., Bellocchi, 2015; Flam & Keres, 2015; Godbold, 2015; Holmes, 2015) that may be utilized to systematically examine emotions in sport and, indeed, integrate emotion into the study of other dynamics, issues, and priorities (e.g., sport, ideology, and power; sport, labor and migration; sport, social exclusion, and discrimination; and sport, leadership, and social responsibility, among others). Importantly, the utilization of these intellectual resources would allow for the generation of more detailed insights into, as well as explanations of, important social phenomena in sport (Bericat, 2016; Peterson, 2014). Equally, while we can use theories of emotion to enrich the sociology of sport, it is also important to recognize how research in our subdiscipline may contribute to wider sociological developments regarding emotion. That is, sport can provide a valuable arena for developing, testing, and refining theory in the sociology of emotion (Maguire, 2011; Peterson, 2014). Arguably, the latter could also constructively support our efforts to address issues that have drawn scorn from some sociologists (Bourdieu, 1988; Peterson, 2014).

Reflecting the arguments made above, this chapter considers some of the ways in which we might productively engage with emotions in the sporting milieu. In order to achieve this aim, the chapter is divided into three interconnected parts. The Issues section addresses foundational information regarding the sociological study of emotion. The Approaches section provides an overview of several theoretical perspectives that have been utilized to advance our understandings of emotion (i.e., symbolic interactionist, dramaturgical, relational, structural, and poststructural). The Debates section considers some of the ways in which such theorizing could be utilized to frame and enrich emotions research in the sociology of sport subdiscipline. Finally, the conclusion briefly summarizes the key issues explored across the chapter.

Issues

Like many concepts in the social sciences (e.g., culture, identity, power), there is no one accepted definition of emotion (Bericat, 2016; Harris, 2015). Harris noted that more than 20 different definitions of emotion were articulated by scholars in the 1980s and 1990s alone. Denzin (1984, p. 6), for example, conceptualized emotion as

> a lived, believed-in, situated, temporally embodied experience that radiates through a person's stream of consciousness, is felt in and runs through his [sic] body, and, in the process of being lived, plunges the person and his [sic] associates into a wholly new and transformed reality—the reality of a world that is being constituted by the emotional experience.

Kemper (1987, p. 267) defined emotions as "a complex, organised response disposition to engage in certain classes of biologically adaptive behaviours . . . characterised by a distinctive state of physiological arousal, a distinctive feeling, or affective state, a distinctive state of receptivity, and a distinctive pattern of expressive reactions." Meanwhile, Thoits (1990) proposed that emotions consist of a number of interrelated parts: situational cues, physiological changes, emotion labels, and expressive gestures. More recently, Burkitt (2014) suggested that emotions are best understood as complex, embodied, and relational phenomena that allow our body-minds to register socially meaningful relationships and interactions. Indeed, he argued that "without the body-mind, we could not feel our situations and patterns of relationships, yet without the social meaning of these relations, our feelings and emotions would be random and meaningless" (p. 15).

Despite these definitional differences, researchers in the sociology of emotion generally agree that "emotions constitute the bodily manifestation of the importance that an event in the natural or social world has for" individuals (Bericat, 2016, p. 493) and that they consist of these core elements:

1. The biological activation of key body systems.
2. Socially constructed constraints on what emotions should be experienced and expressed in a situation.
3. The application of linguistic labels provided by culture to internal sensations.
4. The overt expression of emotions through facial, voice, and other paralinguistic moves.
5. Perceptions and appraisals of situations or events. (Turner & Stets, 2005, p. 9)

Alongside recognizing the "positive" and "negative" valences of emotions (i.e., they can make an individual feel good or bad), sociologists also distinguish between different levels of emotion (i.e., primary and secondary) and types of emotional experience (e.g., anticipatory, consequent, global, reflex, reflexive, situational, specific, structural) (Bericat, 2016; Turner, 2009). Primary emotions are generally considered to be universal, related to evolution, and biologically innate and to include emotions such as fear, anger, depression, and happiness (satisfaction) (Bericat, 2016; Turner, 2009). In contrast, secondary emotions are understood as those that can be formed through the combination of primary emotions and are capable of being transmitted socially and culturally (Bericat, 2016; Turner & Stets, 2005). These emotions include, but are not limited to, love, shame, resentment, guilt, nostalgia, and disappointment (Bericat, 2016; Turner, 2009). Both primary and secondary emotions can also vary in the intensity with which they are experienced (i.e., they can be experienced in strong, moderate, or weak ways) (Bericat, 2016; Turner, 2009). Global emotions, meanwhile, are conceptualized as "generic responses to the outcome of interaction, which are involuntary and not conditioned by interpretation or cognitive attribution" (Bericat, 2016, p. 492). For example, an individual may experience a generalized feeling of pleasure or displeasure (e.g., feeling up/good or down/bad). In contrast, specific emotions are defined by the interpretive effort of an individual and are assigned to specific events, interactions, and objects (Bericat, 2016; Lawler, 2001). Here, an individual may feel pride if they attribute their pleasurable feelings to their own choices, actions, and achievements, or gratitude if they consider their positive feelings to result from the actions or choices of another person or group (Lawler, Thye, & Yoon, 2008).

For Kemper (2006, p. 97), structural emotions are those which "result from a relatively stable power-status-relationship." This includes, for example, those between workers and their supervisors or between parents and young children (Kemper, 2006). Anticipatory emotions are those which are generated through our contemplation of the possible outcomes of future interactions and social encounters. For example, a worker preparing for an appraisal meeting with their supervisor may take into account interactions of a similar nature in the past and, importantly, their outcomes (Kemper, 2006). Indeed, it is this consideration of possible outcomes that will generate an anticipatory emotion (e.g., hope, anxiety) for that individual (Kemper, 1978a, 1978b, 2006). In contrast, consequent emotions are those that result from a particular event, interaction, or encounter (e.g., the pride a worker experiences after receiving a positive appraisal from a supervisor). According to Kemper (1978a, 1978b, 2006), these emotions "constitute the surface flux of social life, because they are often short term and most susceptible to change and variation within the ongoing flow of interaction" (Kemper, 2006, p. 97).

Jasper (2011, pp. 2–3) defined reflex emotions (e.g., anger, joy, surprise, and disgust) as those that accompany "our reactions to our immediate physical and social environments." These emotions generally appear and subside quickly and are accompanied by various facial and bodily expressions (e.g., a smile or a grimace) (Jasper, 2011). In comparison, reflexive emotions are relatively stable and long term in nature. For Jasper, reflexive emotions comprise affective loyalties and moral emotions. Affective loyalties refer to our cognitive appraisals of others, especially our attachments to them; they are primarily concerned with love, liking, trust, and admiration, along with their negative counterparts (Jasper, 2011). Moral emotions are connected to "feelings of approval and disapproval based on moral intuitions and principles" (p. 3). These can include feeling compassion for those who are more unfortunate than us, and indignation over injustice.

Despite the conceptual and empirical progress made, it is important to recognize that the sociology of emotions has a relatively short academic history in comparison to other fields of inquiry. While emotions are considered "essential for forming and perpetuating human societies" (Clark, 2002, p. 155), it has only been during the course of the past 40 to 50 years that the sociological analysis of emotion has been accepted as a bona fide area of research (Bericat, 2016; Turner, 2009). This state of affairs has been attributed to two principal reasons. The first relates to the historical development of sociology, especially its traditional emphasis on macro-level issues, which subsequently led to emotion being positioned as an implicit, secondary concern (Barbalet, 2001, 2002; Turner, 2009). While Durkheim, Mead, Marx, Simmel, and Weber all alluded to emotions, arguably only Cooley and Goffman paid significant theoretical attention to them (Barbalet, 2001; Turner, 2009). For the former, this included how pride and shame were connected to people's evaluations of the self. For the latter, it was showing how embarrassment was a sustaining social mechanism in organizations (Barbalet, 2001; Turner, 2009). Turner argued that subsequent generations of sociologists exacerbated the limited attention paid to emotion through their conservative approach to inquiry. He noted that they were "highly self-conscious of [sociology's] classical founders (indeed, to the point of being obsessive)" (p. 340). Ultimately, then, reason and emotion came to be regarded as opposite ends of a continuum, with emotion and irrationality at one end, and cognition and rationality at the other (Turner & Stets, 2005).

The second factor that constrained the sociological consideration of emotions is the ontological positioning of emotion in many Western nations. Specifically, emotions were considered solely physiological and psychological phenomena; they were the product of the inner working of individuals and directly related to personality and brain function (Turner & Stets, 2006; Zembylas, 2005). Consequently, they were primarily regarded as the investigative preserve of biologists and psychologists (both cognitive and social) (Turner & Stets, 2006; Zembylas, 2005). This situation significantly improved in the 1970s, when a small group of sociology scholars (e.g., Collins, 1975; Heise, 1979, Hochschild, 1975, 1979; Kemper, 1978a, 1978b; Scheff, 1979; Schott, 1979) "began to conceptualize emotions more explicitly and to develop theories and research programs for their study" (Turner, 2009, p. 340). This crucial, foundational scholarship was expanded upon in future decades to the point where the sociological study of emotion came to be "considered the cutting edge of micro-sociology and, to a lesser extent, some macro sociologies" (p. 340).

Like all fields of inquiry, the sociology of emotions is not without its own share of limitations, inconsistencies, contradictions, and debates (Bericat, 2016; Turner, 2009). Turner suggested these unresolved issues include (1) the multifaceted nature of emotions and their subsequent definition; (2) tensions between the sociocultural and biological dimensions of emotional experience, especially the degree to which emotion is activated and constrained by sociocultural influences (e.g., vocational vocabularies, feeling and display rules, and feeling ideologies) or, instead, by the body's biological systems; (3) the limited number of emotions explored; (4) a paucity of inquiry addressing the interconnections of, and relationships between, different emotions; and (5) the positioning of cognitive appraisal ahead of emotional activation. In terms of the last element, for example, Turner believes that sociologists have traditionally tended to subscribe to the view that cognitive appraisal precedes emotional activation rather than considering how emotions, cognitions, social structures, and cultures may interact in more nuanced and complex ways. Turner suggested that emotional arousal may precede cognitive appraisal and that

> once emotions are aroused and attended to cognitively, the flow of emotions may change as individuals become aware of others' reactions to their actions, as they bring to bear relevant social structural conditions, or as they invoke cultural vocabularies and normative codes. (p. 342)

In a similar vein, Bericat (2016) contends that inquiry within the sociology of emotions has tended to (1) produce static and one-dimensional analyses of humans' emotional lives that suggest emotions are experienced in an independent and isolated manner and (2) prioritize the micro-interactions of emotional experience at the expense of a consideration of macro-social emotions. Despite these issues, there is much we can learn from and contribute to the sociology of emotions as we better "incorporate affective structures and emotional dynamics" (Bericat, 2016, p. 505) into the scholarship of our subdiscipline (Jones, Potrac, Cushion, & Ronglan, 2011; Peterson, 2014; Potrac, Mallett, Greenough, & Nelson, 2017; Roderick et al., 2017).

APPROACHES

While sociologists recognize that emotions operate at different levels of reality (e.g., the biological and the neurological), their scholarly efforts have naturally focused on explaining emotional experience from a broadly social-relational perspective (Bericat, 2016; Cantó-Milà, 2016; Turner, 2009). That is, rather than being "hermetically sealed" (Bericat, 2016,

p. 492) away from our social and physical environments, emotions are considered to be inextricably entwined with our efforts to navigate relationships and achieve goals with other people and things, as well as the ways we experience the disruptions and uncertainties that social life can present (Turner, 2009).

To date, a diverse range of scholarship addressing the socially constructed, enacted, and embodied aspects of emotional experience has collectively illustrated a rich "emotion culture of ideologies, norms, logics, vocabularies, and other symbolic elements that specify what individuals are to feel in particular types of situations and how they are to express emotions" (Turner, 2009, p. 341; von Scheve & Ismer, 2013; Zembylas, 2007). Indeed, Stets and Turner (2014, p. 1) noted that, despite being "late in recognising how important emotions are in understanding the social world," sociology has made substantial progress in its exploration of human emotion at the micro, meso, and macro levels of social life. In this section, we provide a brief overview of some of the principal approaches utilized. These are (1) symbolic interactionist, (2) dramaturgical, (3) ritual, (4) structural, (5) relational, and (6) poststructural theories. Importantly, this list should not be considered definitive in terms of capturing the full range of sociological thinking on emotions. Equally, we do not have the space to do more than provide an initial sketch of underpinning tenets of these selected approaches. As such, we encourage readers to also engage with specialist texts and collections within the sociology of emotion literature (e.g., Barbalet, 2001, 2008; Denzin, 1984; Hopkins, Flam, Kuzmics & Kleres, 2009; Turner & Stets, 2006; von Scheve & Salmela, 2014, among others).

Symbolic Interactionist Theorizing of Emotion

Inspired by the work of Mead (1934) and Cooley (1964), symbolic interactionist theorizing conceptualizes emotional experience as being interwoven with matters of socialization, identity, and the self (Bericat, 2016; Turner, 2009). Indeed, emotions are considered to be the mediating force between Gestalt and cybernetic ideas about the self that feature in symbolic interactionist thought (Turner, 2009). Here, the former refers to individuals seeking consistency and congruence both in their cognitions of the self and in their cognitions about others' responses to the self (Turner, 2009). The cybernetic addresses the ways in which individuals emit gestures that are consistent with the self, engage in role taking and actively interpret others' responses to these gestures, and make adjustments to their behavior when the responses and feedback of others are inconsistent with their conceptions of the self (Stets & Trettevik, 2014; Turner, 2009).

Emotions such as pride, shame, anger, and distress are, then, tied to an individual's efforts to confirm and sustain the image they have of themselves (e.g., self-concept) and the specific identities they occupy in their interactions with others (e.g., role identity) (Bericat, 2016; Stets & Turner, 2014; Turner, 2009; Turner & Stets, 2005). For example, Schott's (1979) theorizing contends that guilt, shame, and embarrassment are activated when individuals believe their actions deviate from accepted norms, leading them to feel obliged to engage in corrective behaviors.

In a related vein, McCall and Simmons (1978) and Stryker (1980, 2004) have suggested that, while identity verification can lead to positive emotions (e.g., pride and joy) and increased salience of a role identity, consistent nonverification can have the opposite effect.

This can include negative emotional experiences (e.g., guilt and shame) and the relegation of a particular role identity in an individual's overarching hierarchy of identity salience (or prominence). Burke (1991, 1996) also highlighted how individuals can experience distress when there is incongruence between their behaviors and the actual (i.e., direct feedback from others) and reflected (i.e., an individual's perception of how others view them) appraisals of others. In generating psychoanalytic variants of symbolic interactionist theorizing, Scheff (1988) and Turner (1999, 2002, 2007) build on Cooley's "view that pride and shame are the gyroscopes of human action" (Turner, 2009, p. 345). Finally, and more recently, the affect control model of emotion (see Lively & Heise, 2014; MacKinnon & Heise, 2010) considers how "emotions emerge from automatic and unconscious comparisons of the impression of the self that has been created by recent events with the kind of person that is supposed to be in the situation" (Lively & Heise, 2014, p. 51).

Dramaturgical Theorizing of Emotion

Dramaturgical theorizations of emotion are built on the foundational scholarship of Goffman (1959, 1967) and Hochschild (1979, 1983). For Goffman, shame and embarrassment are the products of unsuccessful or inappropriate presentation of the self to an audience. In order to avoid such occurrences, he argued that individuals and groups strategically utilize cultural scripts (e.g., ideologies, norms, and values), staging props (e.g., material objects and scenery), and dramaturgical techniques (e.g., circumspection, discipline, and loyalty) to purposely manipulate and navigate their face-to-face encounters with others (Scott, 2015; Turner, 2009).

In building upon Goffman's dramaturgical insights, Hochschild (1979, 1983) developed the concept of an emotion culture. This is composed of emotional ideologies (i.e., what are considered to be appropriate attitudes, feelings, and emotional responses) and the three ways in which these ideologies are manifested or made concrete in social life. The latter consists of framing rules (i.e., what interpretations and meanings are to be found in a social situation), feeling rules (i.e., what emotions are to be felt, to what intensity, and their valence on a continuum of positive to negative), and display rules (i.e., which emotions are to be overtly expressed in a social situation or encounter) (Charmaz, Harris, & Irvine, 2019; Turner, 2009). Her theorizing also illuminated the disjuncture between emotional cultures and the actual emotions that employees in service-driven occupations experience. Indeed, she coined the term "emotion work" to conceptualize the ways employees use impression management techniques (i.e., deep and surface acting) to manage their emotional demeanor (Charmaz et al., 2019; Hochschild, 1983; Turner, 2009).

These significant insights were further developed by Thoits (1990) and Clark (1990). Specifically, Thoits examined the discrepancy between actual feelings and feeling rules, the various emotional strategies utilized by individuals, and the circumstances that can contribute to the failure of an individual's efforts to manage their emotions in line with social, cultural, and organizational norms. Clark examined the micro-economies and micro-politics of emotion work. The former is concerned with the strategic exchange of emotions for psychic gain or profit, while the latter refers to how individuals seek to enhance their position and status in relation to others. Here, she illustrated how sympathy (and other emotions) could be purposively utilized to advance individual interests (e.g., as a culturally acceptable means to "put down" another person, to highlight another's weaknesses or vulnerabilities, or to get into the good graces of a superordinate) in specific social encounters and, indeed, the larger unit or organization in which that encounter was embedded.

Ritual Theorizing of Emotion

Primarily inspired by the scholarship of Durkheim (1912/1965) and Collins (1975, 2004, 2008), the ritual theorizing of emotion focuses on social gatherings and collective interactions (Bericat, 2016; Summers-Effler, 2006). Here, rituals are considered to comprise co-presence, shared emotional moods, common values, and a mutual focus of attention (Turner, 2009). Participation in rituals can generate collective effervescence (i.e., they intensify our feelings of social experience) and a high level of group consciousness (i.e., they promote shared beliefs, ideas, and moral attitudes) (Bericat, 2016; Turner, 2009). For example, Collins's (1981, 2004) theorizing describes both the positive and often unifying emotions directed toward the group itself and the emotional energy (i.e., trust and positive emotions) that an individual can experience through their participation in rituals. For Collins, emotional energy is the main motivating force in social life, incorporates both lows (e.g., apathy and depression) and highs (e.g., enthusiasm and joy), and is essential to the formation "of social bonds, group solidarity, interpersonal relationships, class cultures, networks of creativity, intellectual communities and, ultimately, macrostructures" (Boyns & Luery, 2015, p. 150). Insightfully, Collins's work highlighted how individuals often have expectations regarding the emotional energy gains to be realized through their participation in certain rituals. As such, individuals are inclined to gravitate toward those that transcend their expectations and produce increases in their emotional energy, while limiting their participation in those that are underwhelming and lead to a subsequent decrease in emotional energy (Boyns & Luery, 2015).

While Collins's (2004, 2008) theorizing largely concentrated on the positive dimensions of emotional energy, others (e.g., Boyns & Luery, 2015; Summers-Effler, 2002) have sought to conceptualize the negative dimensions of emotional energy. For example, Summers-Effler highlighted that when individuals believe they are both powerless and trapped in an interaction ritual, they may experience emotions such as fear, guilt, shame, and anxiety. In these circumstances, individuals may also utilize strategies to help minimize the loss of emotional energy rather than maximize their levels of positive emotional energy (Summers-Effler, 2002; Turner, 2009). Summers-Effler (2004a, 2004b) also adopted a perspective on the self different from the one favored by Collins. Specifically, rather than viewing the self as solely a situationally flexible and strategic front that is presented to others, she emphasized its stable and coherent aspects. Here, she illustrated how the affirmation of the self can enhance positive emotional energy and make an individual more willing to commit to group symbols, while the converse can lead to less emotional energy and a reduced likelihood of feeling solidarity with and commitment to group symbols (Summers-Effler, 2004a, 2004b; Turner, 2009).

Structuralist Theorizing of Emotion

Structural theories of emotion address the distribution of emotional energy across social classes (Turner, 2009). Indeed, theorists adopting this position (e.g., Barbalet, 1998, 2001;

Collins, 1975, 1990; Turner, 2010) "argue that valued resources like money, power, prestige, or anything of value are always distributed unequally, thus creating social classes or
subpopulations who share a given level of resources, including types and levels of emotional energy" (Turner, 2009, p. 350). For example, Collins highlighted how people's access
to and control of various resources can impact micro-level encounters and interactions.
He suggested that those who comprise the upper echelons of society are more likely to experience positive emotions (e.g., pride, confidence) toward the self than those in the lower
classes. In a similar vein, Barbalet (2001) highlighted how emotions such as fear, confidence, shame, vengefulness, and resentment can be distributed differently across social
classes. Central to his theorizing are the processes of social comparison and attribution,
where individuals assess and interpret their share of resources in relation to those of others.
Such comparisons can generate feelings of resentment when members of a particular social
class perceive another group to have gained resources in a manner that violates normative
beliefs about social justice and fairness.

   Equally, there is evidence that fear can arise when a social group finds they lack the power
to pursue their interests. This fear can be subsequently transmuted into alienation when a
social group determines that their limited access to resources is of their own making or, indeed, anger, aggression, and vengefulness if another subpopulation is believed to be responsible for their situation. Barbalet (2001) suggested that confidence is often generated when
individuals consider their futures to be both controllable and predictable, a circumstance
that is often disproportionately distributed to members of the more powerful and affluent
classes in a society. More recently, Turner (2010) highlighted how the uneven distribution
of resources brought about by structural arrangements leads those in the lower classes to
experience more negative emotions. These emotions can include shame and humiliation
when individuals blame themselves for not being able to secure necessary resources, and
also intense anger toward institutional entities (e.g., corporations, schools, political systems) that they consider to be responsible for their situation (Turner, 2010).

Relational Theorizing of Emotion

In recent years, emotions have been examined by scholars subscribing to the relational turn
in sociological inquiry (e.g., Burkitt, 2014; Crossley, 2010). At the heart of this evolving line
of theorizing is the assertion that emotions cannot be turned on or off in our interactions
and relationships with others. Instead, they are "a permanent dimension of our being in the
world and being towards others" (Crossley, 2010, p. 62). From this perspective, emotions are
considered to be generated in, and through, our networked relations with others (Crossley,
2010). Indeed, it is our relational positioning to others that informs the meanings we give
to their behaviors and choices and the ways that they affect us. We cannot love or hate, for
example, "without that relational sense," as "when we love or hate someone it is usually to
do with the way that they have affected us or the way they have behaved in a certain situation" (Burkitt, 2014, p. 15).

   Burkitt (1997, 1999, 2002, 2014) also described how everyday emotional experience is
connected to wider cultural norms and practices (e.g., gender, social class, and ethnicity
relations). Here, networks of relations overlap and intersect, so that there is no separation
of "the macro—the relations between classes, groups, and factions—from the micro—the
face-to-face interactions of particular situations" (Burkitt, 2014, pp. 20–21). However, rather
than influencing emotions in a deterministic manner, he argued that emotional experience

is informed by the emotional scripts that individuals bring to their encounters with others and, indeed, the emotional dispositions (i.e., a tendency to feel certain emotions) that an individual has developed through their biography (Burkitt, 2014). As such, while relations of power can influence emotional experience, social relations retain elements of dynamism and unpredictability and are, ultimately, co-created (Burkitt, 1997, 1999, 2002, 2014). In drawing upon the insights of Bourdieu (1979/1984), Dewey (1983), and Elias (1978), Burkitt's theorizing recognizes that emotions have corporeal and embodied aspects. In particular, he described how individuals appropriate "certain forms of bodily carriage and movement" as well as "ways of handling objects and manipulating them, which are culture specific" (Burkitt, 1999, p. 116). That is, "the body is essential in making (rather than simply) experiencing meaning" (Burkitt, 2014, p. 116).

Poststructuralist Theorizing of Emotion

Poststructuralism is associated with the theorizing of scholars such as Deleuze, Derrida, and Foucault (Ritzer & Stepnisky, 2017). Although Foucault did not construct a theory of emotion per se, scholars have primarily drawn upon his theoretical approach to understand the discursive construction of emotion (e.g., Dadich & Olson, 2017; Zembylas, 2002, 2003, 2014). In particular, sociologists adopting a poststructural perspective have addressed the role of ideology, culture, and power in creating emotion discourses, as well as the ways people may resist or adopt them (Zembylas, 2011, 2014). They do this by (1) focusing on what emotions do and their effects, (2) situating emotional experience within a historical analysis of relations of power-knowledge, and (3) considering how these relations have contributed to our enactment of or resistance to particular emotions (Zembylas, 2011, 2014).

Poststructural theorists frequently place the body (i.e., its cognitions, emotions, and behaviors) at the heart of their analyses. One of Foucault's (1977, p. 136) central concepts is that of the docile body, which he defined as a body "that may be subjected, used, transformed and improved." He argued that in capitalist societies organizational practices in schools, workplaces, and hospitals (among other settings) are purposefully utilized to produce docile bodies (Bialostok & Aronson, 2016; Leung & Caspersz, 2019). These organizational practices, also known as technologies of discipline, primarily relate to the strict control of time, space, and flow in many institutions. Other docile producing practices include what Foucault labeled the means of correct training. These consist of hierarchical observation, normalizing judgment, the examination, and the panopticon (Ball, 2019; Kelly, 2016).

Rather than positioning emotions as biologically determined or psychological traits, Foucauldian-inspired scholarship seeks to illustrate how dominant discourses and the disciplinary practices described above produce an individual's emotions and their effects (Zembylas, 2011, 2014). Here, Abu-Lughod and Lutz (1990, p. 14) noted that

> power relations determine what can, cannot, or must be said about self and emotion, what is taken to be true or false about them, and what some individuals can say about them. . . . Emotion discourses establish, assert, challenge, or reinforce power or status differences.

Relatedly, poststructuralists also raise important questions regarding who benefits from these relations of power-knowledge and their effects (i.e., who would want to evoke a particular emotional response within an institution, and why). Here the technologies of discipline provide useful theoretical concepts to understand the "normalisation of emotion" (Lee-Sinden, 2013, p. 613). For example, the reinforcement of certain emotions (e.g., guilt and shame) for not working hard all the time subtly coerces people to work harder. Indeed, if an individual accepts and normalizes these emotions, they may never critique or problematize the relations of power-knowledge that gave rise to them.

Similarly, positive emotions (e.g., happiness or tranquility) can also shape people's outlook on social life and could result in the production of a docile body. Building on Foucault's concept of the technologies of the self, Zembylas (2011, 2014) suggested that we should practice increased emotional reflexivity in our everyday lives; that is, we should problematize emotional experience as it is connected to the relations of power and social discourses that shape them. Ultimately, it is only through this questioning of taken-for-granted assumptions that we can change social structures and develop new, and hopefully better, ways of living (Zembylas, 2011, 2014).

DEBATES

In this section, we outline some ways in which we might (1) enhance our understanding of emotions in the social relations, institutions, and structures that comprise sport and (2) contribute to the wider sociological analysis of emotions through sport (Peterson, 2014). It is, of course, important to recognize that the topics and issues we explore here do not exhaust the ways we might fruitfully consider emotion. Indeed, there are numerous theoretical approaches (e.g., attribution, power-status, cultural, exchange, and evolutionary theories; see Bericat, 2016; Stets & Turner, 2014; Turner & Stets, 2005) and issues (see Jacobsen, 2019; Potrac, Smith, et al., 2017; Roderick et al., 2017) that we were unable to address in this chapter. Equally, the issues we focus on should not be assumed to represent the most important topics to explore. Rather, they reflect our orientations, baggage, and interests as researchers. Taking our lead from Peterson (2014), we do, however, hope that they might stimulate inquiry and debate and contribute to an emotionally rich(er) sociology of sport.

The concept of identity has been, and remains, at the heart of much inquiry within the sociology of sport subdiscipline (e.g., Dean, 2019; Hickey & Roderick, 2017; Ives et al., 2021; Joncheray, Level, & Richard, 2016; Jones, 2006; Thorpe & Olive, 2016, among many others). Researchers have provided rich and nuanced insights into the various ways in which identities are "created, maintained, communicated, presented, negotiated, challenged, reproduced, reinvented, and narrated" in sport (Scott, 2015, p. 21). Despite the progress made, there has been little consideration of the ways in which emotions can act as markers of adequacy in identity performance, that is, how emotions might tell individuals that their role performances are adequate or, indeed, inadequate (Serpe & Stryker, 2011). Potential avenues for developing such scholarship, as well as contributing to the wider examination of emotions through sport, include critically exploring the connections between emotion and (1) negative/stigmatized identities, (2) multiple identities, as well as (3) within and across social encounters (Stets & Trettevik, 2014). In terms of the first, future research could systematically address the emotions that are produced when a negative/stigmatized identity is activated in sport. For example, a stigmatized identity such as being a gay male footballer, coach, or match official in men's professional soccer may generate a mixture of positive and negative emotions. These could include positive emotions that emanate from others' viewing the player, coach, or official in the same ways that the individual views themselves. Equally, an individual may experience negative emotions through such identity verification. Indeed, Stets and Trettevik (2014, p. 46) suggested that, in such circumstances, the individual holding this identity "may feel negative emotions because they activate the third-order belief system that society devalues this identity." That is, the negative emotions result from the individual's understanding of wider sociocultural norms and beliefs rather than the identity verification process itself. Arguably, such insights would help to move our understandings beyond the view that successful identity verification always results in positive emotions (e.g., joy, pride, happiness) and raised self-esteem and, conversely, that only nonverification generates negative emotions (e.g., distress, anxiety, shame) and lowered self-esteem (Stets & Trettevik, 2014).

Much existing research addressing identity in sport has tended to focus on the experience and performance of one identity at a time (e.g., being a player, manager, coach, or fan). There has, in comparison, been a paucity of work that has explicitly addressed the emotional experiences associated with the multiple (and perhaps conflicting) identities that individuals hold, as well as the ways in which their salience is hierarchically organized (Hickey & Roderick, 2017; Ives et al., 2021; Stamp, Nelson, & Potrac, 2021; Stets & Trettevik, 2014). Here, it may be argued that social life may present situations where more than one important identity is activated for an individual (Stets & Trettevik, 2014). This could include a coach being fired for the unsuccessful playing record of a team. In this case, the coach might experience anger and frustration at their employer's decision to terminate their employment, guilt for letting other people down (e.g., players, fans, and boosters), shame at not being able to perform the role in a successful manner, fear, guilt, and sadness at not being able to provide for their family (as a spouse or parent), and the embarrassment that might come from revealing this status change to family members, friends, and colleagues. In such cases, the nonverification (i.e., the perceived failure to perform roles to the required identity standard) of two or more identities (e.g., being a coach, a parent/guardian, a spouse, a son or daughter, among others) may lead to more negative emotions being experienced than if only one identity (e.g., being a coach) was not verified. Similarly, successful performance and the awarding of a new contract may generate not only positive emotions that come from the individual's coaching identity being verified (i.e., performing a role in line with or exceeding normative identity standards) but also the emotions tied to their being seen to perform other important roles successfully (e.g., being a "good" spouse or partner, parent/guardian, and son or daughter, among others) (Ives et al., 2021; Stets & Trettevik, 2014). Indeed, the verification of multiple identities might generate an emotional experience (e.g., types and intensity of emotion) different from that when only one identity is verified by others (Ives et al., 2021; Stets & Trettevik, 2014).

To date, research addressing the emotional dimensions of identity verification has tended to focus on emotional experience at one point in time (Stets & Trettevik, 2014). In contrast, there has been limited inquiry addressing the temporal and emergent nature of emotions (i.e., how emotions carry over from and, indeed, inform future situations) (Magill, Nelson, Jones, & Potrac, 2017; Thompson, Potrac, & Jones, 2015). As such, researchers in the sociology of sport may wish to consider how the emotions that an individual brings to a situation may influence those that are experienced in that situation and, importantly, connect to identity verification (or nonverification) (Stets & Trettevik, 2014). For example, following a run of poor competition results, a head coach meeting with administrators and boosters/sponsors may enter the encounter feeling frustrated and anxious. In this case, these emotions may predispose the coach to interpret the comments, reactions, and feedback of others in a manner that disconfirms their identity (i.e., that others disapprove of the individual's role performance as a coach). Similarly, the opposite may apply for a head coach, who having enjoyed a series of good competition results, enters this situation feeling happy and confident (Stets & Trettevik, 2014). In both cases, prior emotions may influence current feelings, including felt identity verification. Relatedly, researchers might also consider how identity verification (or nonverification) in an earlier encounter might influence emotional experience in a later encounter with the same group or individual or, indeed, others (Stets & Trettevik, 2014).

Alongside exploring issues pertaining to emotions and identity verification, scholars may wish to further develop our critical understanding of the emotional demands and strategies that feature in the doing of sports work (Potrac, Mallett, et al., 2017; Roderick et al., 2017). While researchers (e.g., Hayton, 2017; Magill et al., 2017; Nelson et al., 2014; Potrac, Mallett, et al., 2017; Potrac, Smith, et al., 2017) have generated initial insights about the emotion management and emotional labor that sporting volunteers, coaches, managers, and athletes might engage in, there is considerable opportunity for furthering our empirical and conceptual insights of this topic. One way of working toward this goal is to utilize Clark's (1990) micro-political typology of emotional strategies that individuals use in social encounters (especially contested ones) to navigate hierarchy and advance their place or standing in a particular social network (e.g., within a sporting organization). These are (1) expressing negative-other emotions, (2) expressing positive-other emotions indicating one's own inferiority or equality, (3) controlling the balance of emotional energy, (4) eliciting obligation, and (5) expressing positive-other emotions indicating one's own superiority. From our perspective, this framework also provides a productive avenue for building on our existing understanding of the micro-political interactions that feature in the everyday doing of sports work for a variety of stakeholders (Potrac & Jones, 2009; Potrac, Jones, Gilbourne, & Nelson, 2013; Potrac, Mallett, et al., 2017; Potrac, Smith, et al. 2017; Toner, Nelson, Potrac, Gilbourne, & Marshall, 2012).

Another avenue of potential research involves utilizing Bolton's (2005) expansion of Hochschild's (1983) groundbreaking theorizing. Like Hochschild, Bolton argued that emotional labor entails more than capitalist organizations cajoling and coercing employees into displaying prescribed emotions and managing proscribed emotions in exchange for a wage. Indeed, rather than being passive, compliant, or "crippled actors" within organizations (p. 48), she positions employees as active and reflexive agents, who are, within constraints, capable of "making their own histories" (p. 39). That is, they are able to "navigate, negotiate, and [sometimes] overcome [organizational] feeling rules that have the capacity to constrain employees" (Addison, 2017, p. 12). Based on the assumptions outlined above, Bolton developed her own typology of emotion management, which consists of the pecuniary, the prescriptive, the presentational, and the philanthropic.

Pecuniary emotion management is that which relates to commercial values (e.g., profit seeking, cynical performances, and instrumental motivation), while prescriptive emotion management is based on organizational and/or professional rules of conduct (e.g., an altruistic and sincere desire to provide a high-quality experience or service). Both pecuniary and prescriptive emotion management are primarily tied to the role and obligations an individual has within an organization. In contrast, presentational and philanthropic emotion management are seen to operate outside of organizationally created feeling rules and are associated with our social literacy (i.e., our understanding and application of the wider social rules of interaction). Presentational emotion management occurs when a social actor purposely seeks to maintain the "interaction order" and support "a sense of stability and ontological security to participants" (Bolton, 2005, p. 97). This could include, for example, an athlete showing a teammate a smile because they said or did something kind or using humor to defuse a tense or difficult situation.

Philanthropic emotion management is that which is undertaken as a gift from one social actor to another (e.g., a coach showing kindness to an upset athlete or anxious parent). It is, of course, important to recognize that this framework is not without its criticisms. However, we believe that there is much to be gained from our engagement with Bolton's ideas, and those of her critics (e.g., Addison, 2017), if we are to better understand the ways in which sports work can entail managing our own emotions, influencing others' emotions, and be variously demanding, exciting, boring, exhausting, tedious, arduous, joyful, and stressful (Charmaz et al., 2019). Indeed, Bolton's (2005) and Clark's (1990) respective theorizing could prove useful in future efforts to recognize how emotion management in sports work is both an interpersonal as well as an intrapersonal phenomenon. Indeed, there has, to date, been little direct consideration of (1) the ways in which sports workers "simultaneously manage their own emotions as they manage others" (Charmaz et al., 2019) and (2) how such emotion work is experienced and undertaken in hierarchical, collaborative, and/or adversarial relationships (Charmaz et al., 2019).

Exciting possibilities also exist to advance our understanding of emotion and social relations by using poststructural approaches. For many years, scholars have drawn upon Foucault's (1977) work to show the problems associated with sport's reliance on disciplinary practices within a neoliberal society (e.g., Denison, 2007; Gearity & Mills, 2012). While illustrating the discursive construction of coaches and athletes as docile bodies, this work has unfortunately tended to ignore the emotions that inherently feature in these social processes and interactions.

This situation arguably stems from researchers centering on Foucault's original emphasis on uncovering the logic and rationalities that underpin and guide cultural practices in sporting organizations. That is, scholars have tended to address questions related to the discursive construction of knowledge, where knowledge is synonymous with reason, not emotion. As such, there remains considerable promise in critically examining emotions as they are connected to the transactions "between larger social forces and the internal psychic terrain of the individual" (Zembylas, 2011, p. 33).

To address the limited poststructural consideration of emotion in sport, Crocket (2017, p. 22) recently called for a greater examination of how "affect, emotions, and embodiment" relate to the discursive construction of identities. Following Zembylas's (2003, 2014) inquiry in education, researchers could examine how affect, emotions, and embodiment create sport workers' identities and, in turn, how sport workers may problematize certain identities. The findings of such work could be utilized to inform the preparation and ongoing development of sports workers, especially in terms of helping them to critically interrogate their beliefs and values (Denison, 2019) and to recognize the "ways in which emotions colour their decisions and practices" (Zembylas, 2011, p. 39). Importantly, feminist scholars and scholars of color have been doing this work for some time (Ahmed, 2014; Butler, 1990; Collins, 2002; Gilligan, 1982; Noddings, 1984) and often in response to the patriarchy, sexism, racism, and misogyny produced by societies' dominant rationalities.

Drawing upon the work of Ahmed (2004, 2014) and Bishop (2002), we could extend the sociology of sport by examining the emotions involved in relations of othering and, indeed, allyship (Bishop, 2002). Such work could, for example, examine the emotions exhibited toward National Football League player Colin Kaepernick following his taking a knee during the playing of the U.S. national anthem (Ahmed, 2004). Here the emphasis would be on connecting emotions to the profound aversion that some individuals and groups have toward others based on skin color, as well as the emotions experienced by those who are against racism and oppression (Ahmed, 2004, 2014).

Scholars might also probe further into the emotions of othering and allyship involved in ageism, sexism, racism, and forms of discrimination related to religion, sexual orientation, and disability in sport. Furthermore, while it is generally accepted that microaggressions result in emotional harm to the receiver of these identity-based insults and attacks, the emotions of the perpetrator are understudied within sport (Gearity & Henderson Metzger, 2017). Again, following Ahmed (2004, 2014), sociologists of sport could research why, for example, a white, nondisabled, heterosexual coach, administrator, or owner may feel that it is acceptable to look at those belonging to other (intersectional) communities with disgust and thus feel compelled to microaggress, discipline, and treat them as something lesser or inferior.

Notably absent in Côté and Gilbert's (2009) oft-cited definition of coaching effectiveness and expertise is any mention of emotion. Clearly, emotions feature intrapersonally and interpersonally in coaches' working lives, but their impact on the self and others, as well as how coaches learn what emotions do, is not well understood (Potrac, Mallett, et al., 2017). Here, Zembylas's (2002, 2011, 2014) work addressing the intrapersonal, interpersonal, and sociopolitical dimensions of emotion could help to develop new insights in the sociology of sport, especially in terms of understanding the ways in which certain emotions may be allowed or disallowed and, relatedly, their connection to the complex webs of power relations in which coaches, athletes, and other sports workers (e.g., match officials) are enmeshed. Finally, Matias and Zembylas's (2014) approach to understanding the complex intersection of racism, emotion (e.g., disgust, care), allyship, whiteness, and white teacher education could be combined with the literature addressing care in sport (Cronin & Armour, 2018) to support interventions and research concerning the development of anti-oppressive practices and policies in sport.

CONCLUSION

In this chapter, we considered the sociological dimensions of individual and collective emotional experience. We also outlined a number of ways sport sociologists might incorporate emotions into the study of sporting institutions, relations, and interactions. These ideas not only represent ways of enriching our understanding of emotion in sport, but they may also represent a means of contributing to a wider investigation of emotion through sport (Bericat, 2016; Peterson, 2014; Turner, 2009). Ultimately, we believe it is important that our accounts of the interactions (including the everyday, the mundane, and the dramatic) and relations that comprise the social worlds of sport recognize how emotion and cognition are inextricably intertwined (Harris, 2015; Potrac, Smith, et al., 2017). Indeed, rather than being solely the innate and private property of individuals, emotions are also socially constructed, negotiated, and regulated phenomena (Peterson, 2014; Stets & Turner, 2014). Importantly, they are capable of enabling and constraining personal and collective experiences, actions, and opportunities. As such, emotions warrant further and detailed consideration in our scholarship (Charmaz et al., 2019; Harris, 2015).

References

Abu-Lughod, L., & Lutz, C. (1990). *Language and the politics of emotion*. Cambridge: Cambridge University Press.

Addison, M. (2017). Overcoming Arlie Hochschild's concepts of the "real" and "false" self by drawing on Pierre Bourdieu's concept of habitus. *Emotion, Space and Society, 23*, 9–15.

Ahmed, S. (2004). *The cultural politics of emotion* (1st ed.). Edinburgh: Edinburgh University Press.

Ahmed, S. (2014). *The cultural politics of emotion* (2nd ed.). Edinburgh: Edinburgh University Press.

Ball, S. (2019). A horizon of freedom: Using Foucault to think differently about education and learning. *Power and Education, 11*(2), 132–144.

Barbalet, J. (1998). *Emotion, social theory, and social structure: A macrosociological approach*. Cambridge: Cambridge University Press.

Barbalet, J. (2001). *Emotion, social theory, and social structure: A macrosociological approach*. Cambridge: Cambridge University Press.

Barbalet, J. (2002). *Emotions and sociology*. Oxford: Wiley.

Barbalet, J. (2008). Emotion in social life and social theory. In M. Greco & P. Stenner (Eds.), *Emotions: A social science reader* (pp. 106–111). London: Routledge.

Bellocchi, A. (2015). Methods for sociological inquiry on emotion in educational settings. *Emotion Review, 7*(2), 151–156.

Bericat, E. (2016). The sociology of emotions: Four decades of progress. *Current Sociology, 64*(3), 491–513.

Bialostok, S. M., & Aronson, M. (2016). Making emotional connections in the age of neoliberalism. *Ethos, 44*(2), 96–117.

Bishop, A. (2002). *Becoming an ally: Breaking the cycle of oppression in people* (2nd ed.). Nova Scotia: Fernwood Publishing.

Bloch, C. (2012). *Passion and paranoia: Emotions and the culture of emotions in academia*. Farnham: Ashgate.

Bolton, S. (2005). *Emotion management in the workplace*. London: Palgrave Macmillan.

Bourdieu, P. (1979/1984). *Distinction: A social critique of the judgement of taste*. Cambridge: Harvard University Press, Routledge.

Bourdieu, P. (1988). Program for a sociology of sport. *Sociology of Sport Journal, 5*(2), 153–161.

Boyns, D., & Luery, S. (2015). Negative emotional energy: A theory of the "dark-side" of interaction ritual chains. *Social Sciences, 4*(1), 148–170.

Burke, P. (1991). Identity processes and social stress. *American Sociological Review, 56*, 836–849.

Burke, P. (1996). Social identities and psychosocial stress. In H. Kaplan (Ed.), *Psychological stress: Perspectives on structure, theory, life course, and methods* (pp. 141–174). Orlando: Academic Press.

Burkitt, I. (1997). Social relationships and emotions. *Sociology, 31*(1), 37–55.

Burkitt, I. (1999). *Bodies of thought: Embodiment, identity and modernity*. London: Sage.

Burkitt, I. (2002). Complex emotions: Relations, feelings and images in emotional experience. *Sociological Review, 50*(2), 151–167.

Burkitt, I. (2014). *Emotions and social relations*. London: Sage.

Butler, J. (1990). *Gender trouble: Feminism and the subversion of identity*. London: Routledge.

Cantó-Milà, N. (2016). Linking emotions: Emotions as the invisible threads that bind people together. *Sociological Research Online, 21*(1), 132–135.

Charmaz, K., Harris, S. R., & Irvine, L. (2019). *The social self and everyday life: Understanding the world through symbolic interactionism*. Oxford: Wiley-Blackwell.

Clark, C. (1990). Emotions and micropolitics in everyday life: Some patterns and paradoxes of place. In T. Kemper (Ed.), *Research agendas in the sociology of emotions* (pp. 305–333). Albany: State University of New York Press.

Clark, C. (2002). Taming the brute being: Reckons with emotionality. In J. Kotarba & J. Johnson (Eds.), *Postmodern existential sociology* (pp. 155–182). Lanham: Alta Mira.

Collins, P. H. (2002). *Black feminist thought: Knowledge, consciousness, and the politics of empowerment*. London: Routledge.

Collins, R. (1975). *Conflict sociology: Toward an explanatory science*. Cambridge: Academic Press.

Collins, R. (1981). The role of emotions in social structure. In K. Scherer & P. Ekman (Eds.), Approaches to emotion (pp. 385–396). London: Routledge.

Collins, R. (1990). Stratification, emotional energy, and the transient emotions. In T. Kemper (Ed.), *Research agendas in the sociology of emotions* (pp. 27–57). Albany: State University of New York Press.

Collins, R. (2004). *Interaction ritual chains*. Princeton: Princeton University Press.

Collins, R. (2008). *Violence: A micro-sociological theory*. Princeton: Princeton University Press.

Collinson, J. A. (2005). Emotions, interaction and the injured sporting body. *International Review for the Sociology of Sport, 40*(2), 221–240.

Cooley, C. (1964). *Human nature and social order*. New York: Schocken Books.

Côté, J., & Gilbert, W. (2009). An integrative definition of coaching effectiveness and expertise. *International Journal of Sports Science & Coaching, 4*(3), 307–323.

Cottingham, M. D. (2012). Interaction ritual theory and sports fans: Emotion, symbols, and solidarity. *Sociology of Sport Journal, 29*(2), 168–185.

Crockct, H. (2017). Problematizing Foucauldian ethics: A review of technologies of the self in sociology of sport since 2003. *Journal of Sport and Social Issues, 41*(1), 21–41.

Cronin, C., & Armour, K. (Eds.). (2018). *Care in sport coaching: Pedagogical cases*. London: Routledge.

Crossley, N. (2010). *Towards relational sociology*. London: Routledge.

Dadich, A., & Olson, R. (2017). How and why emotions matter in interprofessional healthcare. *International Journal of Work Organisation and Emotion, 8*(1), 59–79.

Dean, N. (2019). "Just act normal": Concussion and the (re)negotiation of athletic identity. *Sociology of Sport Journal, 36*(1), 22–31.

Denison, J. (2007). Social theory for sport coaches: A Foucauldian reading of one athlete's poor performance. *International Journal of Sports Science & Coaching, 2*(4), 369–383.

Denison, J. (2019). What it really means to "think outside the box": Why Foucault matters for coach development. *International Sport Coaching Journal, 6*(3), 354–358.

Denzin, N. (1984). *On understanding emotion.* San Francisco: Jossey-Bass.

Dewey, J. (1983). Human nature and conduct. In J. A. Boydston (Ed.), *John Dewey: The middle works, 1899–1924,* vol. 14 (pp. 1–227). Carbondale: Southern Illinois University Press.

Dunning, E. (1986). Sport as a male preserve: Notes on the social sources of masculine identity and its transformations. *Theory, Culture and Society, 3*(1), 79–90.

Durkheim, E. (1912/1965). *The elementary forms of the religious life.* New York: Free Press.

Elias, N. (1978). *What is sociology?* London: Hutchinson.

Elias, N., & Dunning, E. (1986). *The quest for excitement: Sport and leisure in the civilising process.* Oxford: Blackwell.

Ferguson, J. D. (1981). Emotions in sport sociology. *International Review of Sport Sociology, 16*(4), 15–25.

Fineman, S. (2005). Appreciating emotion at work: Paradigm tensions. *International Journal of Work Organisation and Emotion, 1*(1), 4–19.

Fineman, S. (2008). *The emotional organization: Passions and power.* Oxford: Blackwell.

Flam, H., & Kleres, J. (2015). *Methods of exploring emotions.* London: Routledge.

Foucault, M. (1977). *Discipline and punish: The birth of the prison* (A. Sheridan, Trans.). New York: Random House.

Gearity, B. T., & Henderson Metzger, L. (2017). Intersectionality, microaggressions, and microaffirmations: Towards a cultural praxis of sport coaching. *Sociology of Sport Journal, 34,* 160–175.

Gearity, B. T., & Mills, J. P. (2012). Discipline and punish in the weight room. *Sports Coaching Review, 1*(2), 124–134.

Gilligan, C. (1982). *In a different voice.* Cambridge: Harvard University Press.

Godbold, N. (2015). Researching emotions in interactions: Seeing and analysing live processes. *Emotion Review, 7*(2), 163–168.

Goffman, E. (1959). *The presentation of self in everyday life.* New York: Doubleday.

Goffman, E. (1967). *Interaction ritual: Essays on face-to-face behaviour.* New York: Anchor Books.

Harris, S. (2015). *An invitation to the sociology of emotions.* London: Routledge.

Hayton, J. W. (2017). "They need to learn to take it on the chin": Exploring the emotional labour of student volunteers in a sports-based outreach project in the North East of England. *Sociology of Sport Journal, 34*(2), 136–147.

Heise, D. (1979) *Understanding events: Affect and the construction of social action.* Cambridge: Cambridge University Press.

Hickey, C., & Roderick, M. (2017). The presentation of possible selves in everyday life: The management of identity among transitioning professional athletes. *Sociology of Sport Journal, 34*(3), 270–280.

Hochschild, A. (1975). The sociology of feeling and emotion: Selected possibilities. In M. Millman & R. Kanter (Eds.), *Another voice* (pp. 280–307). New York: Anchor.

Hochschild, A. (1979). Emotion work, feeling rules, and social structure. *American Journal of Sociology, 85*(3): 551–575.

Hochschild, A. (1983). *The managed heart: The commercialization of human feeling.* Berkeley: University of California Press.

Holmes, M. (2015). Researching emotional reflexivity. *Emotion Review, 7*(1), 61–66.

Hopkins, D., Kleres, J., Flam, H., & Kuzmics, H. (2009). *Theorizing emotions: Sociological explorations and applications.* Frankfurt: Campus Verlag.

Ives, B., Gale, L., Potrac, P., & Nelson, L. (2021). Uncertainty, shame and consumption: Negotiating occupational and non-work identities in community sport coaching. *Sport, Education and Society, 26*(1), 87–103.

Jacobsen, M. (2019). *Emotions, everyday life and sociology.* London: Routledge.

Jasper, J. M. (2011). Emotions and social movements: Twenty years of theory and research. *Annual Review of Sociology, 37,* 285–303.

Joncheray, H., Level, M., & Richard, R. (2016). Identity socialization and construction within the French national rugby union women's team. *International Review for the Sociology of Sport, 51*(2), 162–177.

Jones, R. (2006). Dilemmas, maintaining "face," and paranoia: An average coaching life. *Qualitative Inquiry, 12*(5), 1012–1021.

Jones, R., Potrac, P., Cushion, C., & Ronglan, L. T. (2011). *The sociology of sports coaching.* London: Routledge.

Kelly, P. (2016). *The self as enterprise: Foucault and the spirit of 21st century capitalism.* London: Routledge.

Kemper, T. (1978a). *A social interactional theory of emotions.* London: Wiley.

Kemper, T. (1978b). Toward a sociology of emotions: Some problems and some solutions. *American Sociologist, 13,* 30–41.

Kemper, T. (1987). How many emotions are there? *American Journal of Sociology, 93,* 263–289.

Kemper, T. (2006). Power and status and the power status theory of emotions. In J. Stets & J. Turner (Eds.), *Handbook of the sociology of emotions* (pp. 87–113). New York: Springer.

Lawler, E. (2001). An affect theory of social exchange. *American Journal of Sociology, 107,* 321–352.

Lawler, E., Thye, S., & Yoon, J. (2008). Social exchange and micro social order. *American Sociological Review 73*(4), 519–542.

Lee-Sinden, J. (2013). The sociology of emotion in elite sport: Examining the role of normalization and technologies. *International Review for the Sociology of Sport, 48*(5), 613–628.

Leung, E., & Caspersz, D. (2019). Chinese workers' history: Passive minds docile bodies. *Journal of Management History, 25*(3), 304–322.

Liston, D., & Garrison, J. (2003). *Teaching, learning and loving: Reclaiming passion in educational practice.* London: Routledge.

Lively, K., & Heise, D. (2014). Emotions in affect control theory. In J. Stets & J. Turner (Eds.), *Handbook of the sociology of emotions,* vol. 2 (pp. 51–76). New York: Springer.

MacKinnon, N., & Heise, D. (2010). *Self, identity and social institutions.* London: Palgrave.

Magill, S., Nelson, L., Jones, R., & Potrac, P. (2017). Emotions, identity, and power in video-based feedback sessions. Tales from women's professional football. *Sports Coaching Review, 6*(2), 216–232.

Maguire, J. (1991). Towards a sociological theory of sport and the emotions: A figurational perspective. *International Review for the Sociology of Sport, 26*(1), 25–35.

Maguire, J. (1992). Towards a sociological theory of sport and the emotions: A process-sociological perspective. In E. Dunning & C. Rojeck (Eds.), *Sport and leisure in the civilizing process* (pp. 96–120). London: Palgrave.

Maguire, J. (2001). Fit and flexible: The fitness industry, personal trainers and emotional service labour. *Sociology of Sport Journal, 18*(4), 379–402.

Maguire, J. A. (2011). Welcome to the pleasure dome? Emotions, leisure, and society. *Sport in Society, 14,* 913–926.

Matias, C. E., & Zembylas, M. (2014). "When saying you care is not really caring": Emotions of disgust, whiteness ideology, and teacher education. *Critical Studies in Education, 55*(3), 319–337.

McCall, G. J., & Simmons, J. L. (1978). *Identities and interactions.* New York: Free Press.

Mead, G. H. (1934). *Mind, self, and society.* Chicago: University of Chicago Press.

Nelson, L., Potrac, P., Gilbourne, D., Allanson, A., Gale, L., & Marshall, P. (2014). Thinking, feeling, acting: The case of a semi-professional soccer coach. *Sociology of Sport Journal, 19*(1), 19–40.

Noddings, N. (1984). *Caring: A feminine approach to ethical and moral education.* Berkeley: University of California Press.

Ortiz, S. (2010). Competing with her mother-in-law: The intersection of control management and emotion management in sport families. *Studies in Symbolic Interaction, 35,* 319–344.

Peterson, G. (2014). Sports and emotions. In J. Stets & J. Tuner (Eds.), *Handbook of the sociology of emotions,* vol. 2 (pp. 495–510). New York: Springer.

Potrac, P., & Jones, R. (2009). Power, conflict and cooperation: Towards a micro-politics of coaching. *Quest, 61*(2), 223–236.

Potrac, P., Jones, R., Gilbourne, D., & Nelson, L. (2013). Handshakes, BBQs, and bullets: A tale of self-interest and regret in football coaching. *Sports Coaching Review, 1*(2), 79–92.

Potrac, P., Mallett, C., Greenough, K., & Nelson, L. (2017). Passion and paranoia: An embodied tale of emotion, identity, and pathos in sports coaching. *Sports Coaching Review, 6*(2), 142–161.

Potrac, P., Smith, A., & Nelson, L. (2017). Emotion in sport coaching: An introductory essay. *Sports Coaching Review, 6*(2), 129–141.

Ritzer, G., & Stepnisky, J. (2017). *Sociological theory* (10th ed.). London: Sage.

Roderick, M., Smith, A., & Potrac, P. (2017). The sociology of sports work, emotions and mental health: Scoping the field and future directions. *Sociology of Sport Journal, 34*(2), 99–107.

Scheff, T. J. (1979). *Catharsis in healing, ritual, and drama.* Berkeley: University of California Press.

Scheff, T. J. (1988). Shame and conformity: The deference-emotion system. *American Sociological Review, 53,* 395–406.

Schott, S. (1979). Emotion and social life: A symbolic interactionist analysis. *American Journal of Sociology, 84,* 1317–1334.

Scott, S. (2015). *Negotiating identity: Symbolic interactionist approaches to social identity.* Cambridge: Polity Press.

Serpe, R., & Stryker, S. (2011). The symbolic interactionist perspective and identity theory. In E. Schwartz, K. Luyckz, & V. Vignoles (Eds.), *Handbook of identity theory and research* (pp. 225–248). New York: Springer.

Smith, T. (2008). Passion work: The joint production of emotional labour in professional wrestling. *Social Psychology Quarterly, 71,* 157–176.

Snyder, E. E. (1990). Emotion and sport: A case study of collegiate women gymnasts. *Sociology of Sport Journal, 7,* 254–270.

Snyder, E. E., & Ammons, R. (1993). Baseball's emotion work: Getting psyched to play. *Qualitative Sociology, 16,* 111–132.

Stamp, D., Nelson, L., & Potrac, P. (2021). More than just a "pro": A relational analysis of transition in professional football. *Sport, Education and Society, 26*(1), 72–86.

Stets, J., & Trettevik, R. (2014). Emotions in identity theory. In J. Stets & J. Turner (Eds.), *Handbook of the sociology of emotions,* vol. 2 (pp. 33–49). New York: Springer.

Stets, J., & Turner, J. H. (Eds.). (2014). *Handbook of the sociology of emotions.* Vol. 2. New York: Springer.

Stryker, S. (1980). *Symbolic interactionism: A social structural version.* San Francisco: Benjamin Cummings.

Stryker, S. (2004). Integrating emotion into identity theory. *Advances in Group Processes, 21*(1), 1–23.

Summers-Effler, E. (2002). The micro potential for social change: Emotion, consciousness, and social movement formation. *Sociological Theory, 20*(1), 41–60.

Summers-Effler, E. (2004a). Defensive strategies: The formation and social implications of patterned self-destructive behaviour. *Advances in Group Process, 21,* 309–325.

Summers-Effler, E. (2004b). Little girls in women's bodies: Social interaction and the strategizing of early breast development. *Sex Roles, 51*(1–2), 29–44.

Summers-Effler, E. (2006). Ritual theory. In J. Stets & J. Turner (Eds.), *Handbook of the sociology of emotions* (pp. 135–154). New York: Springer.

Ten-Houten, W. (2007). *A general theory of emotions and social life.* London: Routledge.

Thoits, P. A. (1990). Emotional deviance: Research agendas. In T. D. Kemper (Ed.), *Research agendas in the sociology of emotions* (pp. 180–203). Albany: State University of New York Press.

Thoits, P. A. (1999). Self, identity, stress, and mental health. In C. Aneshensel, C. Phelan, & A. Bierman (Eds.), *Handbook of the sociology of mental health* (pp. 345–368). New York: Springer.

Thoits, P. A. (2011). Mechanisms linking social ties and support to physical and mental health. *Journal of Health and Social Behaviour, 52*(2), 145–161.

Thompson, A., Potrac, P., & Jones, R. (2015). "I found out the hard way": Micro-political workings in professional football. *Sport, Education, & Society, 20*(8), 976–994.

Thorpe, H., & Olive, R. (2016). *Women in action sport cultures: Identity, politics and experience.* New York: Springer.

Toner, J., Nelson, L., Potrac, P., Gilbourne, D., & Marshall, P. (2012). From "blame" to "shame" in a coach-athlete relationship in golf: A tale of shared critical reflection and the re-storying of narrative experience. *Sports Coaching Review, 1*(1), 67–78.

Turner, J. H. (1999). Toward a general sociological theory of emotions. *Journal for the Theory of Social Behavior, 29,* 132–162.

Turner, J. H. (2002). *Face-to-face: Towards a sociological theory of inter-personal behaviour.* Stanford: Stanford University Press.

Turner, J. H. (2007). *Human emotions: A sociological theory.* London: Routledge.

Turner, J. H. (2009). The sociology of emotions: Basic theoretical arguments. *Emotion Review, 1*(4), 340–354.

Turner, J. H. (2010). The stratification of emotions: Some preliminary generalizations. *Sociological Inquiry, 80*(2), 168–199.

Turner, J., & Stets, J. (2005). *The sociology of emotions.* Cambridge: Cambridge University Press.

Turner, J., & Stets, J. (2006). Sociological theories of human emotions. *Annual Review of Sociology, 32,* 25–52.

Van Ingen, C. (2011). Spatialities of anger: Emotional geographies in a boxing program for survivors of violence. *Sociology of Sport Journal, 28*(2), 171–188.

von Scheve, C. (2013). *Emotion and social structures: The affective foundations of social order.* London: Routledge.

von Scheve, C., & Ismer, S. (2013). Towards a theory of collective emotions. *Emotion Review, 5*(4), 406–413.

von Scheve, C., & Salmela, M. (2014). *Collective emotions.* Oxford: Oxford University Press.

Zembylas, M. (2002). Constructing genealogies of teachers' emotions in science teaching. *Journal of Research in Science Teaching, 39*(1), 79–103.

Zembylas, M. (2003). Emotions and teacher identity: A poststructural perspective. *Teachers and Teaching, 9*(3), 213–238.

Zembylas, M. (2005). Discursive practices, genealogies, and emotional rules: A poststructuralist view on emotion and identity in teaching. *Teaching and Teacher Education, 21*(8), 935–948.

Zembylas, M. (2006). *Teaching with emotion: A postmodern enactment.* Charlotte: Information Age Publishing.

Zembylas, M. (2007). Theory and methodology in researching emotions in education. *International Journal of Research and Method in Education, 30*(1), 57–72.

Zembylas, M. (2011). Teaching and teacher emotions: A post-structural perspective. In C. Day & J. Lee (Eds.), *New understandings of teachers' work: Emotions and educational change* (pp. 31–43). New York: Springer.

Zembylas, M. (2014). The place of emotion in teacher reflection: Elias, Foucault and "critical emotional reflexivity." *Power and Education, 6*(2), 210–222.

Zietsma, C., Toubiana, M., Voronov, M., & Roberts, A. (2019). *Emotions in organisation theory.* Cambridge: Cambridge University Press.

Zurcher, L. (1982). The staging of emotion: A dramaturgical analysis. *Symbolic Interaction, 5*(1), 1–22.

CHAPTER 28

··

SPORT, CHILD MALTREATMENT, AND SEXUAL VIOLENCE

··

MICHAEL J. HARTILL

GIVEN the chapter title, there are some issues to address before proceeding. First, child maltreatment is clearly not confined to sexual violence (or child sexual abuse), and sexual violence is clearly not an experience limited to those who are designated "children." Indeed, the reduction of child maltreatment to its *sexual* form is itself an issue of concern in a field where an overwhelming focus on one form of abuse can leave other practices and behaviors unproblematized and research underresourced. However, since the earliest research into the sexual exploitation of athletes, researchers have been acutely aware that the problem of sexual violence was closely related to nonsexual violence toward athletes. Equally, the focus on children and child abuse within research and the media has led to a parallel focus within policy at the expense of violence experienced by adults in sport. Nevertheless, the public outrage that often follows media attention on *sexual* crimes against children has undoubtedly, if unevenly, paved the way for the introduction of initiatives and policies aimed at preventing *all* forms of abuse in sport, across the age spectrum. Therefore, the 2007 International Olympic Committee's *Consensus Statement on Sexual Harassment and Abuse in Sport* was updated in 2016 to include a wider range of "non-accidental violence" (Mountjoy et al., 2016). Still, the issue remains that this headline-monopolizing problem, often centered on "pedophiles" and lone "predators," has surely drawn attention and resources away from abuses that are equally, if not more insidiously, embedded within the norms of athleticism. It must also be recalled, however, that the initial drive to highlight concerns around *sexual* violence was based, at least in part, on the resounding silence about sexual harassment, exploitation, and abuse in sport that existed prior to the late 1990s and which has continued well beyond that point. This chapter, then, is focused on sexual violence toward children in sport, but not to the exclusion of other forms of violence, nor indeed to sexual violence perpetrated against athletes who are above the age of 17.

I won't dwell on definitions, but it is important to note that all those concerned about abuse, maltreatment, and sexual violence in sport have a stake in understanding what behaviors and practices fall under these terms. The recent IOC Consensus Statement

(Mountjoy et al., 2016) offers broad definitions and many examples of the range of abuses and "non-accidental" violence that are known to occur in sport. The statement also makes it clear that violence must be conceptualized not only at the individual level but also at the organizational and structural levels. Definitions of child maltreatment refer to acts of *commission* (where harm is inflicted) or *omission* (where there is a failure to prevent harm). Definitions of *sexual* violence make it clear that both *contact* and *non*contact behaviors fall under this category.

ISSUES

Historical Context: Minimization, Denial, and Cover-up

The work on child abuse in sport in the United Kingdom grew out of the women's movement. The establishment of the Women's Sport Foundation (U.K.) in 1984 is arguably a key moment, especially as Celia Brackenridge took on an early leadership role. It is important, then, to recognize the climate of the period in which this research and advocacy developed. In a 1985 *Guardian* newspaper article citing Brackenridge, Peter Lawson, then general secretary of the Central Council for Physical Recreation, stated:

> Women's influence in the school sports system has wrecked it. . . . Women are basically anti-competition and achievement in school sports. . . . Women shy away from taking responsibility. It's nothing to [do] with the system: it's to do with their make-up. (quoted in Cunningham, 1985, p. 21)

Just a year later, Brackenridge brought the issue of child sexual abuse in sport directly to the heart of the male preserve in British sport, delivering a paper entitled " 'Problem, What Problem?' Thoughts on a Professional Code of Practice for Coaches" (Brackenridge & Lyons, 1986) at the Annual Conference of the British Association of National Coaches. They argued that "it is only a matter of time before cases of negligence or abuse are brought to the wider public view" (cf. Brackenridge, 2017, p. 6). Prior to 1986 there is no evidence of any child protection measures being implemented within any sport, in the United Kingdom or elsewhere. Indeed, there is no evidence that the sexual abuse of children in sport had been raised prior to this date. The early focus of researchers and campaigners, then, was on the sexual abuse and exploitation of athletes, with a predominant focus on sexual violence perpetrated by men and boys toward women and girls (e.g., Crosset, 1986; Lenskyj, 1992; cf. Hartill, 2005).

Despite Brackenridge's campaigning and emerging research evidence, in the United Kingdom it was only when Olympic swimming coach Paul Hickson received a 17-year sentence on September 27, 1995, that the political and policy landscape began to shift. According to Summers (2000, p. 155), who conducted her PhD investigation during the period that the Hickson case came to light, one governing body informant told her that abuse was "an issue that many coaches regarded as irrelevant, and feared created an atmosphere of hysteria in which they could be falsely accused." Thus, Brackenridge (1998a, p. 4) observed:

> Just as some individuals in particular sport organizations have taken a lead in pressing for child protection . . . others have contributed to denial or inertia. Amongst the latter group are

representatives at all levels of British sport, from ministers at the top, down to volunteer club officials at the bottom.

Similarly, in Canada, Peter Donnelly (1999, p. 108) observed that "sports organizations have, until recently, acted as if such things could not possibly occur in the pristine world of sport." Thus, denial, minimization, and resistance emerged as central themes in the early response to abuse in sport. To illustrate, in 1993, when the British Amateur Swimming Association was setting up its first safeguarding policy and procedures (Hickson had been arrested in 1992), the then executive director of the American Swimming Coaches Association (ASCA) was happy to appear in a BBC television documentary asserting that ASCA would not permit any suspicions of sexual abuse against a coach to be officially reported by parents or athletes *unless* the accusation had been assessed by another coach who also agreed there were grounds for an official report. ASCA's rationale was explicit: "I would absolutely guarantee you that if we were to allow [parents or swimmers to report] we would have many more spurious accusations than we'd have factual cases" (BBC, 1993). Unsurprisingly, in recent years, U.S. Swimming has received many allegations of sexual abuse by coaches. Therefore, a clear picture emerges of a deeply reluctant sport sector gradually being forced into establishing processes, policies, and systems for prevention. The impetus for this change has largely been generated by public outrage following public disclosures by victims.

"Tip of the Iceberg?" Measuring Abuse in Sport

"Is this just the tip of the iceberg?" is undoubtedly the most common question asked by the (English-speaking) media when a high-profile case comes to light. It is also the question that those in charge of sport are most likely to be unable to answer. The deep and widespread reluctance to accept that abuse is a serious problem *in* sport no doubt goes some way to explaining why there have been so few studies into the prevalence of abuse in sport. This also highlights why such studies are so important. Seemingly, then, sport agencies have not wanted to know the extent to which their communities have been subjected to (sexual) abuse, harassment, exploitation, and violence while participating in sport.

Yet those countries that are able to demonstrate progress in the twin quantitative pillars of *prevalence* and *incidence* will find themselves in a far stronger position to develop a meaningful prevention strategy. Unfortunately, this fairly obvious point seems to have eluded the vast majority of those responsible for sports governance at national and international levels. Nevertheless, in the past few years there have been some important exceptions and research has generated crucial quantitative data about the scale and character of sexual violence and child maltreatment in sport. I will touch on some of this work to illustrate the current state of knowledge in this area.

Prevalence

Early studies on *sexual harassment* tended to focus on female populations. Fasting, Brackenridge, and Sundgot-Borgen (2000) reported that 28% of Norwegian elite female athletes had experienced *sexual harassment* from someone within sport. Fasting and Knorre (2005) found that 45% of female athletes and exercisers in the Czech Republic reported experiencing some form of sexual harassment. Similarly, Fasting, Chroni, Hervik, and Knorre (2011) uncovered important differences in national contexts, revealing Norwegian female students report experiencing significantly less sexual harassment in sport (24%) compared to Czech (42%) and Greek (44%) female students. The most common experiences from someone within sport were "repeated unwanted sexual glances, etc." (22%), "ridicule" (19%), and "unwanted physical contact" (16%). In a recent study of female and male Zambian athletes, Fasting, Huffman and Svela Sand (2015) found no statistically significant differences between female and male athletes across a range of harassment and abuse experiences; indeed, the male sample reported more sexual harassment than did the female.

From a representative sample of Quebec youth ages 14 to 17, Parent, Lavoie, Thibodeau, Hébert, and Blais (2016) found 0.5% were sexually abused by a coach during their lifetime; within the group of athletes, the prevalence was 0.8%, similar to rates found in other studies (Alexander, Stafford, & Lewis, 2011; Nielsen, 2001). However, this study included only *contact* sexual abuse. Including *noncontact* sexual abuse, Leahy, Pretty, and Tenenbaum (2002) found a prevalence of 10% among Australian community and elite athletes. In the United Kingdom, Alexander et al. (2011) included a wider range of harm, surveying a self-selecting (rather than random) sample of 6,060 students (75% of whom were female). Around 75% of respondents said they had experienced "emotional harm," 24% "physical harm," 29% "sexual harassment," and 3% said they had experienced "sexual harm." In relation to sexual abuse by a coach or other adults in sport, the rate drops to 0.3%.

However, Parent et al., (2016, p. 2667) argue that rates in many studies of sport "remain questionable as they are based on nonrepresentative samples." They also note the underrepresentation of boys and men, low response rates (especially for boys), and other factors that make comparison unsafe, such as different research designs and different definitions of sexual abuse. Using a retrospective, self-report, Web survey, Vertommen, Schipper-van Veldhoven, et al. (2016) assessed the prevalence of "interpersonal violence" in organized youth sport in Flanders and the Netherlands; 4,043 adults answered questions on their experiences in youth sport. Applying the UN's inclusive definition of violence,[1] this study found:

> 38% of all respondents reported experiences with psychological violence, 11% with physical violence, and 14% with sexual violence. Higher prevalence rates were found within particular groups, namely minority ethnic, lesbian/gay/bisexual (LGB), and disabled athletes, and those competing at the international level report significantly more experiences of interpersonal violence in sport. (p. 223)

Adapting protocol from Vertommen et al. (2016) to study sexual violence in elite German athletes, Ohlert, Seidler, Rau, Rulofs, and Allroggen (2017) found, from 1,529 respondents (16 years and above), that 38% had experienced at least one sexual violence situation (contact and noncontact behaviors) in sport, and 11% reported a severe form. Fasting et al. (2015) asked 410 Zambian athletes (54% male) if someone in sport had "tried to have sex with you against your will" or if they had experienced "forced sexual behaviour." This generated a prevalence of 37% for sexual abuse, with a significant difference between the oldest female athletes (47%) and the oldest males (25%). Interestingly, this study found that significantly more men experienced sexual abuse at the community level (39%) compared to the national/international level (24%). They also found that athletes in team sports (43%) had experienced significantly more sexual abuse than athletes in individual sports (20%), especially among men (45% compared with 18%). Overall, prevalence for sexual harassment was 69%.

Most attempts to quantify *child* sexual abuse rely on retrospective surveys of adults' experiences as children. However, in the only known study of its kind to date, Parent et al. (2016) conducted a prevalence study with a representative sample of 6,450 14- to 17-year-olds in Quebec. For those in the sample considered to be "athletes" (i.e., affiliated with a sports club), the prevalence rate of sexual abuse was 8.8%, which, while alarmingly high, is somewhat lower than the rate of 10.2% for the general population (Parent et al., 2016). This may suggest that sports participation might actually be a protective factor against sexual abuse. Furthermore, whereas early studies consistently reported that the risk of sexual violence within sport was higher for females, this study found no significant gender differences.

Official Reports

As important as such data are, they tell us little about the extent to which the abuse of children in sport is being reported, the nature of such reports, or official responses to them. As Jud, Fegert, and Finkelhor (2016, p. 17) note, "far less attention has been paid to analysing *reported* incidents of alleged child maltreatment." Official statistics on child abuse have long been understood to be unreliable indicators of the prevalence of abuse due to low reporting rates. However, analyses of reports made to authorities provide important insights into reporting (and recording) behavior—patterns and variations within and between communities or sectors—and the cultural context within which reporting systems and structures exist. Such data are a necessary complement to prevalence studies and inform strategic approaches to policymaking and prevention efforts. Governments have their own systems for recording reports/cases of child abuse; however, these systems generally do not extend to collating data on the specific setting or context in which it occurs. Generally speaking, then, we currently have very little idea of the volume or characteristics of official reports that are made in relation to sport contexts (for exceptions, see Hartill & Lang, 2018; Rhind, McDermott, Lambert, & Koleva, 2015).

"Uncontrolled Experiments": Safeguarding Policy Implementation

The gradual recognition that children's participation in sport can also be a path to exploitation and abuse has resulted in significant changes to the policy landscape of sport over the past 10 to 15 years. Currently, the pace of change internationally is perhaps more rapid than at any previous point (again, due to high-profile media coverage of sexual abuse). However, the vast majority of policy interventions have been implemented without an associated program of (independent) evaluation. As a consequence, many important opportunities to develop a greater understanding of "what works" within the sport context have been, and continue to be, missed. Thus, opportunities to disseminate such knowledge to wider audiences may have also been missed. So while organizational compliance is perhaps monitored and measured in some national contexts (possibly coupled with the threat of a reduction in funding for noncompliance), robust, systematic evaluation of safeguarding and child protection in sport programs is not evident.

One exception is the research commissioned by the English Football Association to evaluate its policy on child welfare (Brackenridge, Pitchford, Russell, & Nutt, 2007). Findings pointed toward positive changes in attitude, knowledge, and practice across the range of stakeholders in football. However, this project was curtailed after less than three years of what was intended to be a five-year study due to shifting priorities. Nevertheless, in scale, scope, and depth, this study exceeds by far any similar studies. Other evaluation research efforts are few and far between (e.g., Hartill & Prescott, 2007; Rulofs, 2007; Stirling, Kerr, & Cruz, 2012; Vertommen, Stoeckel, Vandevivere, Van Den Eede & De Martelaer, 2016). Therefore, it must be noted that even among those governing bodies of sport that have committed resources to safeguarding, independent evaluation of their initiatives and programs has not been incorporated.

Kerr, Stirling, and MacPherson (2014, p. 752) examined seven national "athlete protection initiatives" from four countries, finding "that the content of the various initiatives is loosely associated with scholarly work in the area" and "none of the initiatives has been evaluated empirically." This study included the Child Protection in Sport Unit (England). Therefore, while a great deal of activity has taken place in British sport in relation to safeguarding children (and vulnerable adults), we know very little about that activity. As the U.K. system is often held up as an international model of best practice, this is an important point. In this context, MacDonald and Roberts's (1995) finding that the vast majority of prevention programs in the United Kingdom "had not been evaluated prior to introduction, and to all intents and purposes had the status of uncontrolled experiments" (Tomison, 2000, p. 4) seems highly relevant. In the context of international sport and safeguarding, it seems there are now many simultaneous uncontrolled experiments, with little thought to the wider learning that could emerge if research was embedded within the policy development process.

Child protection initiatives in sport have most often developed in environments characterized by a heightened public awareness of child *sexual* abuse in sport, often prompted, or at least accompanied, by media reports of "sex beasts" and suchlike "preying" on children within sports contexts. In such circumstances, the political objective of "taking action" (and being seen to do so) may supersede all other concerns, perhaps especially those around monitoring and evaluation (Coalter, 2007). As Weiss (1997) puts it, "[A] considerable amount of ineffectiveness may be tolerated if a programme fits well with prevailing values, if it satisfies voters, or if it pays off political debts" (quoted in Coalter, 2007, p. 42). Regardless of the sociopolitical environment within which *child protection, safeguarding, or athlete welfare* emerges, governing agencies must establish clear, measurable outcomes by which their interventions can be evaluated. In their absence, the concern is that powerful organizations may feel able to operate unchecked, trumpeting their own perceived successes without any demonstrable evidence of efficacy.

APPROACHES

In this section I focus on theory development. This is necessarily highly selective and not intended to be a comprehensive review. The recognition of sexual violence against women and children within sport has been underpinned, indeed driven by feminist criticism, theory, and advocacy from the start. Drawing on feminist movements and arguments from the 1960s and 1970s (e.g., Griffin, 1971), feminist and pro-feminist scholars explored and exposed gender relations extant within the patriarchal organization of sport (e.g., Hall, 1985). Coupled with the gradual recognition of child sexual abuse as a widespread social problem (e.g., Cook & Howells, 1981; Rush, 1980) in the 1980s, research began to illustrate the range of exploitative practices and abuses that occur within sport (e.g., Brackenridge, 1994; Curry, 1998; Donnelly, 1997; Jones, Glintmeyer, & McKenzie, 2005; Kane & Disch, 1993; Messner & Sabo, 1994). Kirby, Greaves, and Hankivsky (2000, p. 46) found "athletes describe what appears to be a thriving sexist environment in high performance sports" which provided the backdrop for sexual violence.

Within sport research, Brackenridge and colleagues (e.g., Brackenridge, 1994, 1997, 1998b, 2001; Brackenridge & Kirby, 1997; Cense & Brackenridge, 2001) led the way in both empirical and theoretical work on sexual violence in sport. Brackenridge approached the problem from a feminist standpoint, combining both psychological and sociological perspectives and drawing on a vast array of literature from within and especially beyond the study of sport. A great deal of theorizing has framed sexual crime in pathological terms, yet for Brackenridge (2001, p. 126) "pathologising sexual abuse distracts from other much more useful areas of risk analysis and management to do with individual agency and the athlete, and perhaps, most importantly, the gender culture of sport." Thus, Cense and Brackenridge (2001, p. 68) state, "[I]n a sports culture that thrives on authoritarian leadership, the climate is ripe for individual exploitation." However, for Brackenridge (2001, p. 135) "all instances of sexual exploitation arise from expressions of agency within structural limits and cultural contexts . . . [therefore] sport researchers [must] link their analyses of structure, culture and agency to case-studies and ethnographies of real-world settings" (see also Brackenridge & Fasting, 2005).

A number of researchers have taken up this call, adding significant texture and insight. For example, Barker-Ruchti and Tinning (2010) build on a substantive body of Foucauldian theorizing within the sociology of sport, utilizing an ethnographic approach to explore and elucidate "disciplinary technologies" within women's artistic gymnastics. Jenny McMahon (McMahon & DinanThompson, 2011) offers an autoethnography of her own elite swimming career to illustrate disciplinary regimes, and their harmful effects, within high-performance swimming. Others have investigated the value systems, normative practices, and dominant discourses within sports coaching (e.g., Fasting, Sand, & Sisjord, 2018; Lang, 2015; Nielsen, 2001; Stirling & Kerr, 2009). Focusing specifically on sexual abuse, Owton and Sparkes (2017) undertook a "collaborative autoethnography" to explore one individual's experiences of "grooming" and sexual abuse in sport (see also Bisgaard & Toftegaard Støckel, 2019). Their paper illustrates well how qualitative approaches can provide a valuable vehicle not only for enhancing understanding of a concealed and exploitative practice but also as an ethical means for "survivors" to tell their story and to make their own meaningful contribution. Similarly, a collaborative project between a number of European researchers provided space and time for those with a personal experience of sexual violence in sport to tell their stories and also enabled a platform for them to tell those stories directly to policymakers (Hartill et al., 2020; Rulofs et al., 2020). I return to this issue below.

Focusing on emotional abuse, Stirling and Kerr (2014) usefully draw on ecological approaches to child maltreatment (e.g., Belsky, 1980), where "child abuse is understood to be a product of the characteristics of the environments in which it occurs rather than simply being the result of the actions of certain individuals" (Jack, 2001, p. 185). Applying this stratified, systems approach to the coach-athlete relationship at each level (ontological, micro-, exo-, macro-) Stirling and Kerr then use this framework to suggest and organize solutions or prevention strategies. As opposed to policies aimed at preventing sexual abuse that focus on keeping perpetrators out of sport, they propose that normalized, emotionally abusive coaching practices are best prevented through the "education of coaches on ethical coaching conduct and alternative, nonabusive philosophies and strategies for athlete development" (Stirling & Kerr, 2014, p. 130).

In relation to sexual violence in sport, Brackenridge's (2001) seminal text *Spoilsports* remains the most complete theoretical offering. Brackenridge introduces a "contingency model of sexual exploitation in sport" (p. 140) in order to capture "three-dimensionally the multi-dimensional complexities of sexual exploitation in sport" (p. 145). In this model, levels of *risk* for and *resistance* to sexual exploitation are contingent upon three interacting dimensions: (1) coach inclination, (2) sport opportunity, and (3) athlete vulnerability. This model represents a "work-in-progress towards finding a comprehensive theory of sexual exploitation in sport" (p. 145). Brackenridge lays out the key debates that critical sport researchers must engage with, identifying key differences and weaknesses between psychology-based and sociology-based conceptualizations of sexual exploitation: "Both disciplines . . . tend to over-emphasise aspects of sexual exploitation that can most easily be accommodated and explained within their particular parameters and to ignore those that cannot" (p. 107). This remains a challenge; currently there is no agreed theoretical or conceptual framework within the field of sexual violence or sex offending.

While recent theorizing from psychology insists that social and cultural influences must be included in any universal theory of child sex offending (e.g., Ward, 2014; Ward & Beech, 2006), they fail to offer theoretical or methodological tools through which the sociocultural might be appropriately interrogated and incorporated into theories of "causation." Of course, introducing sociocultural structures into such theories adds complexity to an already complex area. Brackenridge (2001, p. 107) recognized this explicitly, making it clear that theorists must "account for the complexities of gender-power relations." Yet she also notes that "socio-cultural analyses of power often lack the specificity of understanding that can come from looking at individual perpetrator and victim experiences . . . within specific sporting circumstances" (p. 127). She concludes that "any theoretical resolution will have to incorporate both the organizational sexuality of sport and its interpersonal sex-gender relations in ways which expose the problem of men" (p. 241).

In an attempt to build on Brackenridge's theoretical work, I have suggested that Pierre Bourdieu offers an epistemological framework for the development of empirical studies that may allow for the individual *and* sociocultural to be more cohesively and robustly accounted for (Hartill, 2017). Bourdieu's perspective connects the individual with the wider social universe in a manner that addresses both the individual and structural antecedents of social action. Simultaneously, his conceptual framework—the heart of which is the triad *habitus*, *field*, and *capital*—provides analytical tools through which social practice can be explored and interrogated (see also Bisgaard & Toftegaard Støckel, 2019). In this conceptualization, the social agent is one with the capacity for choice, but whose thought and action are intimately connected to the sociocultural universe or *field* within which they act. This seems necessary for an accurate representation of the historically persistent practice of childhood sexual abuse, the cultural conditions for which we persistently reproduce.

Therefore, building on the many research studies and victim testimonies in this area of inquiry, sport appears to be a *field* that structures a perception of children's bodies as objects, instruments, or tools to be recruited and exploited in the pursuit of adult ends. It is recognized as a sector underpinned by *patriarchal* interests that prioritize *the masculine* and a masculinity that is principally demonstrated by bodily conquest and domination—the exemplar being sexual conquest. Further, it is a *homosocial* field thoroughly immersed in sexualized symbolism, yet denying any relation to sexuality or sexual/erotic practices (at least those beyond the heteronormative). This occurs amid a symbolic *economy* wherein hierarchy and rank are central and the relation between adult and child/athlete is frequently akin to one of master-servant, where the servant's body may be idolized and fetishized, but where their voice has little or no currency. All of this culminates in a *social practice* where the adult role is consecrated by the scientification and professionalization of the athletic field ("coaching pedagogy") and the infantilization and disempowerment of the (child-) athlete. And finally, such practices occur within a social *universe* that works hard to keep itself separate from wider political structures, reveling in its idiosyncrasies and mythologies and aggressively guarding its autonomy and exclusiveness, encouraging membership while delineating clear separation between members and nonmembers, where everyone is welcome but only the initiated have access to its privileges and secrets. Thus, for the child-athlete (if not also their mature self) to speak out about the violation is an act that risks revealing the true nature of the *field* that has structured their cognitive structures (or *habitus*). Such a revelation places the individual at odds with the athleticist *capital* they have come to embody through persistent sport labor. Such an act, for the young athlete enchanted by *the game*, is virtually unthinkable, and so they labor, endure, and remain silent.

The sexual victimization of children occurs across social institutions (or *fields*), but not outside of them. Therefore, theoretical accounts that fail to authentically evaluate and incorporate social structures allow institutions to escape the necessary interrogation and elucidation of "rape-supportive" cultures (Sanday, 2007). Applying such an analysis enables the mechanisms of domination within social institutions such as *sport* to be more fully illuminated. If this risks a disenchanting view of our much treasured institutions and practices, not least the beloved world of *sport*, the volume of revelations about child (sexual) abuse in those institutions over the past two decades or so should perhaps indicate that such an approach is vital.

It seems that the field is now entering an important new phase in its development. The past five years or so have seen a marked acceleration in the publication of empirical research on maltreatment and abuse in sport. This is surely leading to more sophisticated theoretical positions on the various issues at stake as well as a clearer, perhaps more forceful demarcation of theoretical and conceptual territory.

DEBATES

In this section I focus on three areas of relative failure in relation to the international sport community and sector: (1) a failure to report and to ensure that abuse and sexual violence is reported, (2) a failure to investigate through appropriately resourced independent inquiries, and (3) a failure to provide an environment where victims/survivors feel valued and included.

Failure to Report: Mandatory Reporting Laws

It is well established by self-report studies and analysis of official statistics that the substantial majority of child maltreatment is not reported to official agencies. Consequently, most child abuse goes undetected and unpunished. Therefore, reporting legislation is extremely important. Reporting laws vary by nation, and there are significant differences in the degree to which an individual or organization is required to make a formal report when they suspect abuse. The obligation to report suspicions has steadily been introduced in sport policy since the start of the 21st century. However, "mandatory reporting" (MR) laws include the potential for criminal prosecution for *failing* to report suspected abuse. Therefore, in 2017 three senior administrators at Pennsylvania State University were convicted for failing to report their knowledge of Jerry Sandusky's sexual abuse during his employment as a football coach at the university.

However, where MR laws are in place, they vary significantly in *form* and *consequence*. For example, MR laws can differ in the types of abuse included within the duty to report and also by which groups are mandated reporters and which are not. Consequences for noncompliance also vary. For example, in Ireland, where MR was introduced in 2017 for a range of professionals, including those in organized sport, failures to report are dealt with through internal disciplinary procedures with "no legal consequences of not reporting" (Independent Inquiry into Child Sexual Abuse, 2018, p. 11). However, in France in 2016 "there were 88 convictions for failing to report 'mistreatments, deprivations, sexual assaults or abuse committed against a minor' " (p. 12).

Other countries stipulate reporting of abuse only in *policy* rather than in *law*. For example, in England every sport governing body publishes a policy stating that any suspicions of abuse *must* be reported to the governing body and/or an appropriate agency. However, as the pressure group Mandate Now has vociferously pointed out over the past decade, in England and Wales there is no *legal* obligation for adults in sport (and other similar, "regulated" activities, where those with responsibility for children are subject to criminal background checks) to report child abuse. That is, there are no legal sanctions for *not* reporting. To explore MR, the Independent Inquiry into Child Sexual Abuse held two seminars and heard a range of views. A representative for the Council of Europe's Convention on the Protection of Children against Sexual Exploitation and Sexual Abuse (Lanzarote Convention) told the inquiry that "the Lanzarote Convention had found that when there was mandatory reporting a larger number of cases are reported" (Independent Inquiry into Child Sexual Abuse, 2018, p. 10). It also heard from Professor Ben Mathews, who investigated the impact of MR in a specific jurisdiction (State of Western Australia). Focusing on a seven-year period, before (2006–2008) and after (2009–2012) the introduction of a mandatory reporting duty for child sexual abuse, Mathews, Ju Lee, and Norman (2016, p. 62) found "the number of substantiated investigations doubled, from an annual mean of 160 in the pre-law period to 327 in the post-law period, indicating twice as many sexually abused children were being identified."

There has been little discussion of MR within sport. Under German law, the "guarantor position" means that if someone with responsibility for a child comes to know about an incident of sexual violence against that child and they do not take preventative action, they can be liable to prosecution. This is called the "guarantor obligation." In 2013, the national agency for youth sport in Germany published guidelines making it clear that members of sport organizations occupy a "guarantor position" to protect young people from harm.[2] More recently, the U.S. Safe Sport Authorization Act 2017 (U.S. Congress, 2017) extended existing mandatory reporting requirements to any adult authorized to interact with minor or amateur athletes. Such individuals must immediately report *suspicions* of abuse to the U.S. Center for Safe Sport and the appropriate law enforcement agencies. The Act also introduced a requirement for "prevention training" (as opposed to the more common focus on "indicators of abuse"). The Commonwealth of Australia's (2017b, 2017c) Royal Commission into Institutional Responses to Child Sexual Abuse recommended the introduction of both a *failure to report* offense and a *failure to protect* offense and that sport and recreation institutions would fall within their scope. In the former, "the offence would be committed if the person fails to report to police in circumstances where they *know, suspect*, or *should have suspected* . . . that an adult associated with the institution was sexually abusing or had sexually abused a child" (2017c, pp. 100–101; emphasis added). Significantly, they note:

> We appreciate that including *should have suspected* imposes criminal liability for a failure to report a suspicion that the person did not form. However, we are satisfied that this is a necessary step to take, particularly in light of the evidence we have heard from a number of senior representatives of institutions effectively denying that they had any knowledge or had formed any belief or suspicion of abuse being committed in circumstances where their denials are very difficult to accept. (Commonwealth of Australia, 2017a, p. 2)

This returns us to the point made at the start of this chapter. There is now an abundance of evidence to indicate widespread failings within the international sport sector. High-profile cases across the past three decades illustrate this clearly, and central to this failure has been a failure to report suspected abuse. The organizational ramifications of inadequate (and illegal) responses to reports can be significant, if and when they are revealed. Therefore, while national legislation on child protection sits outside the remit of the sport sector, this is clearly an issue that the sector has a stake in and would be wise to consider at significantly greater depth than it seemingly has to date. Advocates of MR refer to increased reporting of child abuse, higher quality of reports, higher rates of reporting by *non*mandated groups, and far stronger legal support for mandated reporters than that currently enjoyed by "whistleblowers." These are all features that would be very welcome within sport.

Failure to Inquire: Independent Inquiries into Abuse in Sport

A common practice in relation to child abuse, especially where it results in "serious harm" or death, is to establish an independent inquiry to investigate what went wrong and what lessons can be learned to inform future strategy. Therefore, it is significant that the Dutch government established a commission to examine *sexual* child abuse across sport in the Netherlands between 1970 and 2017 (Stevens & Vertommen, 2020). This inquiry found that one out of eight children experienced at least one form of unwanted sexual behavior from trainers or teammates during their sports career (DeVries, Ross-Van Dorp, & Myjer, 2016). However, given the 30-year history of this field, it is perhaps surprising that more democratic national governments and their departments or units responsible for sport have not deemed it appropriate to establish independent inquiries into this issue.

To date, aside from the Dutch inquiry, it is perhaps the Royal Commission into Institutional Responses to Child Sexual Abuse (established in 2013 by the Australian government) that leads the way by requiring a select group of national sport governing bodies to appear before it and submit evidence in relation to their response to child abuse (Commonwealth of Australia, 2017b). The German Independent Commission into Child Sexual Abuse, running from 2016 to 2023, has made an explicit call for victims from sport contexts to come forward and tell their story. In the United Kingdom, the Independent Inquiry into Child Sexual Abuse in institutions in England and Wales, established in 2015, invited victims to provide confidential accounts to its Truth Project and reported specifically on accounts given by victims of sexual abuse in sport (Darling, Pope, Mooney, King, & Ablett, 2020). However, to date, it has chosen not to inquire into the extent or efficacy of prevention measures within sport, unlike other institutions, such as organized religion, politics, and social care. This is despite the fact that the National Police Chiefs Council reported that of the 3,960 different institutions featured in the Operation Hydrant[3] database, 10% relate to sport (9% to children's and young people's associations and clubs, 11% relate to religion, 17% to children's homes, and 40% to education; interestingly, 69% of victims in this database are male). In something of a (weak) proxy for a public inquiry, in 2015, at the invitation of the U.K. minister for sport, the Paralympian Baroness Tanni Grey-Thompson (2017, p. 4) "look[ed] into issues surrounding the so-called 'Duty of Care' that sports have towards their participants." Her report states:

> [P]eople did not want to be seen to be causing trouble or jeopardise their sporting career, and felt they had little power to bring about change. Many reported that bullying behaviour could at least sometimes be the "norm" in sport, and that they felt that they just had to "get on with it." (pp. 20–21)

Such experiences have been reported many times within research studies and victim testimony. The failure to establish independent inquiries with full investigative powers, into abuse *specifically* within sport, has at least two overarching consequences. First, those with responsibility for sport governance (individuals who often occupy the same role for many years) and the institutions they represent have not been subjected to appropriate scrutiny on the issue of child and athlete welfare. Therefore, those who have presided over—or been directly involved in—the concealment of abuse remain in post and impede essential reform. Second, inquiries that *have* included sport have been limited to *sexual* violence against *children*. This is despite the fact that (1) research data clearly indicate that children and athletes in sport are subject to physical and psychological maltreatment at levels beyond that of sexual abuse and (2) abuse and sexual violence within sport does not stop at the boundary of childhood.

Recently, high-profile allegations of abuse or wider concerns about unethical conduct within elite sport in the United Kingdom have triggered a number of "independent reviews" into specific sports. Indeed, since 2016 seven independent reviews have been established in football (Sheldon, 2021), canoeing (Sport Resolutions, 2017), cycling (Phelps, Kelly, Lancaster, Mehrzad, Panter, 2017), equestrian (Sport Resolutions, 2018), tennis (Sport Resolutions, 2019), athletics (Sport Resolutions, 2020), and gymnastics (established August 2020). This process has been supported by Sport Resolutions, an independent, not-for-profit national body for arbitration in sport. This is a promising development that will provide ground for sharing of practice (good and bad) within the sector as well as for metareviews. However, it does rely on a piecemeal, reactive approach when it is clear that a holistic, proactive approach is sorely needed.

It seems reasonable to conclude that governments and sport leaders have not considered the problem of abuse in sport to be of sufficient scale or severity to warrant the investment such inquiries would demand. However, given the many independent inquiries into child abuse since the 1980s, it is surprising that sport has been largely excluded from such scrutiny. It would appear that for the majority of the world this scrutiny has been avoided entirely. Regrettably, then, there are currently no appropriately resourced, appropriately broad inquiries of national systems in this field. Anecdotally, it seems evident that "laissez-faire" would be an appropriate description of the international approach of governments to the implementation, monitoring, and regulation of abuse prevention or "safeguarding" in sport systems.

Failure to Include: "Survivors," Athlete Activism, and Participation

Over the past few decades the call to "listen" to children's voices has become commonplace. Thus, various child safeguarding standards and criteria, such as the Australian Catholic University's (2017) Safeguarding Children Capability Framework, emphasize the importance of "children and young people's engagement in child-centred participatory processes." This principle is certainly not in dispute, and while progress has been made, it is also clear that more efforts are required in this area (e.g., Everley, 2020). However, there had been no parallel move within the sport sector to emphasize the importance of including "survivor" voices within, say, prevention or training initiatives or in the development of safeguarding strategies, policies, and procedures. It seems asymmetric, at best, to persistently argue for the elevation of children's voices, yet remain silent on the importance of including those who were abused *as* children. Therefore, while there have been some small but significant pockets of activity, there is currently no evidence base concerning the participation of individuals with a personal experience of abuse within the safeguarding in sport terrain, either in advocacy or policy development.

The VOICE Project (Rulofs et al., 2020, p. 77) was conceived as a direct response to the absence of "survivor" voices within the (international) sport community. The testimony of 72 individuals personally affected by sexual violence in sport provided many examples of minimization, denial, and concealment when victims reported their experiences at the local and national levels. According to Colin Harris, who was abused by a coach connected to Chelsea Football Club in the United Kingdom in the 1970s:

> During the period after I disclosed, I spoke to many organizations. Initially I felt optimistic and that I was being taken seriously. For a brief period I had the impression . . . I could be

> part of th[e] change process. However . . . there was no follow up and no engagement—just a painful and demeaning silence. I felt that my voice was being lost, buried. (quoted in Rulofs et al., 2020, p. 77)

This might be considered further abuse or "symbolic violence" (Bourdieu et al., 1999), whereby victims of abuse may occasionally be invited to serve a specific purpose (for example, to heighten public awareness of a campaign or initiative) but are ultimately excluded from meaningful activity, such as training or policy development and research. Harris notes, "I have sensed an expectation, amongst *some*, that survivors . . . should be limited to recalling their past experience and that policy-making should be left to the 'professionals'" (Harris & Hartill, 2021, p.284). Similarly, in relation to the mental health sector, Rose (2017, p. 780) argues that Fricker's (2007) notions of "epistemic injustice" and "epistemic violence" are

> widespread in the mental health arena. That is to disqualify us as knowers just because we are positioned as irrational, unreasonable, incoherent, lacking insight and so on. Bluntly put, the mad cannot do "science" because that space of ultimate rationality is, by definition, closed to irrational beings.

The emergence of critical approaches such as mad studies and survivor studies since the mid-1990s has fundamentally challenged the exclusion of "service users," "survivors," "lived experience," and "experts by experience" from both research and policy development. Faulkner (2017, p. 512) highlights core elements of this movement:

> As mental health service users, we take each other's stories seriously where often the professionals do not. Telling our stories and listening to each other's stories is the cornerstone of peer support, empowerment and recovery. But it is also a political act and begins the process of creating and building our experiential knowledge.

Clearly, such sentiment chimes strongly with methodological developments within qualitative research referred to above. While it may be premature to refer to a "survivor community" in relation to sport, individuals with a personal experience of abuse in sport certainly now have a presence within the sports landscape, and this is increasingly organized. There are some prominent examples. The longest-running survivor-led organization operating in sports (to my knowledge) is the Respect Group, cofounded in 2004 by former ice-hockey player Sheldon Kennedy. In the USA, former England swimmer Katherine Starr established the not-for-profit Safe 4 Athletes in 2011. In the United Kingdom, the Offside Trust was born out of the "football abuse scandal" in 2016, led by former professional footballers Steve Walters and Chris Unsworth. In Spain, the former Olympic gymnast Gloria Viseras established the not-for-profit Oro Plata y Bronce (Gold, Silver and Bronze) in 2017 (and was recently recruited to FIFA). The voluntary group VOICES Belgium emerged from the VOICE Project in 2019. While systematic analysis is needed, anecdotally it seems evident that these organizations are founded on the notion of listening to and taking seriously the stories that individuals tell and that this goes beyond peer support and sits squarely in the realm of political and cultural change. This was never more evident than at the opening of the VOICE Project conference in 2018 (in Cologne), when a number of individuals briefly stood and told the audience of key stakeholders of their experience of abuse and their desire for change. They were accompanied by opening statements from "survivor-advocates"

Gloria Viseras, Karen Leach, and Colin Harris, sexual abuse "survivors" from gymnastics, swimming, and football, respectively.

According to Rose (2017, p. 781), "survivor movements" resemble earlier movements based on identity, such as those challenging discrimination on the basis of gender, ethnicity, disability, and sexuality, where "silenced and despised groups re-valued their experience and engaged in a cultural politics of affirmation" responding to their oppression by forging new identities. Yet in the development of the "safeguarding in sport" field, over the past two decades Faulkner's (2017, p. 503) observation that "experiential knowledge remains at the bottom of the hierarchy, marginalising the voices of lived experience," rings true. Beresford's (2007, p. 330) observation regarding the benefits of service user involvement in health and social care policy, well over a decade ago, may be apposite for the current climate within sport, where (optimistically) it might be suggested that "interest in such involvement has greatly increased, [but] there is little evidence of its value or efficacy." Thus, while I would suggest that the inclusion of individuals with personal experience of abuse should be something all national sport bodies should be open to, much more research is required regarding the experiences of individuals recruited to such activity. As Brackenridge (2004, p. 20) argued in relation to children, "consultation, on the rare occasions when it happens, is used as a mask for continuing paternalism by those for whom radical change would threaten their power base." Certainly, such experiences have been reported as sport bodies *and* researchers have begun to include "survivors" in more substantive ways.

CONCLUSION

More than 20 years ago, Celia Brackenridge (2001) began *Spoilsports* by noting that the proverbial "cat"—sexual exploitation in sport—was "out of the bag." In the intervening years the pace of change, across the global sport sector, has often felt glacial. However, following unprecedented international media coverage of sexual abuse in sport over the past several years, based on the fortitude of individuals making public disclosures, it may be that the sector has moved beyond the point of no return. That is, any sport body of significance that doesn't at least take account of the potential for child sexual abuse will find itself increasingly out of step with the wider sports world. Nevertheless, the preference *not* to look continues to dominate, and it is perhaps the case that the development of "safeguarding in sport" has also provided governing authorities with a convenient reason not to inquire into past abuses. The familiar narratives "We have changed," "Things are different now," and "Let's look forward" have left many victims feeling as though their experiences don't count and don't matter. This ostrich-like stance, with heads in the sand, has served sports agencies well, right up to the point that past abuse becomes headline news, at which point their deliberate and persistent disposition *not to look* is rightly bundled together with, if not considered an antecedent to, the abuse itself.

Sport enjoys a privileged place within the global imagination, often promoting itself with notions of respect, honor, and equality. Yet the abuse, and concealment of abuse, within sport provide clear markers of the distance between marketing slogans and reality. The notion of "safe sport"—"an athletic environment that is respectful, equitable and free from all forms of non-accidental violence to athletes" (Mountjoy et al., 2016)—provides a benchmark against which the sector, especially its "safeguarding" initiatives and interventions, must be tested empirically. Yet as Coalter (2007, p. 117) warns, "limited project funding is concentrated on provision rather than evaluation." If child and athlete welfare is to improve, the sector must address its historical underspending in this area, while recognizing the crucial role of research for a holistic, proactive, and strategic approach to safeguarding and athlete welfare.

Finally, the philosophy of defining success by volume of medals, and funding sports on that basis, is an approach diametrically opposed to the values underpinning *safe sport*. While international and national sports federations may have lately come to position themselves alongside "safeguarding values," they are simultaneously the architects and guardians of a system that treats children and young people as commodities. Within such a system, where athletes are means to ends, exploitation and abuse will continue to blight the lives of many who endeavor within the fields of athleticism.

NOTES

1. "[A]ll forms of physical or mental violence, injury and abuse, neglect or negligent treatment, maltreatment or exploitation, including sexual abuse while in the care of parent(s), legal guardian(s) or any other person who has the care of the child."
2. With thanks to Bettina Rulofs (Wuppertal University) for providing this information.
3. The police operation established in 2017 to investigate non-recent child sexual abuse involving an institution, organization, or person of public prominence.

REFERENCES

Alexander, K., Stafford, A., & Lewis, R. (2011). *The experiences of children participating in organized sport in the UK*. Edinburgh: University of Edinburgh, National Society for the Prevention of Cruelty to Children.

Australian Catholic University. (2017). Safeguarding children capability framework. https://safeguardingchildren.acu.edu.au/research-and-resources/acu-safeguarding-children-capability-framework.

Barker-Ruchti, N., & Tinning, R. (2010). Foucault in leotards: Corporeal discipline in women's artistic gymnastics. *Sociology of Sport Journal, 27,* 229–250.

BBC. (1993, August 25). On the line: Secrets of the coach.

Belsky, J. (1980). Child maltreatment: An ecological integration. *American Psychologist, 35*(4), 320–335.

Beresford, P. (2007). The role of service user research in generating knowledge-based health and social care: from conflict to contribution. *Evidence & Policy, 3*(3), 329–341.

Bisgaard, K., & Toftegaard Støckel, J. (2019). Athlete narratives of sexual harassment and abuse in the field of sport. *Journal of Clinical Sport Psychology, 13,* 226–242.

Bourdieu, P., Accardo, A., Balazs, G., Beaud, S., Bonvin, F., Bourdieu, E., . . . Wacquant, L. J. D. (1999). *The weight of the world: social suffering in contemporary society*. Cambridge: Polity.

Brackenridge, C. H. (1994). Fair play or fair game: Child sexual abuse in sport organisations. *International Review for the Sociology of Sport, 29*(3), 287–299.

Brackenridge, C. H. (1997). "He owned me basically": Women's experience of sexual abuse in sport. *International Review for the Sociology of Sport, 32*(2), 115–130.

Brackenridge, C. H. (1998a, January). Child protection in British sport: A position statement. Cheltenham: Cheltenham & Gloucester College of Higher Education.

Brackenridge, C. H. (1998b). Healthy sport for healthy girls? The role of parents in preventing sexual abuse in sport. *Sport, Education and Society*, 3(2), 59–78.

Brackenridge, C. H. (2001). *Spoilsports: Understanding and preventing sexual exploitation in sport*. London: Routledge.

Brackenridge, C. H. (2004). Silent voices: Consulting children in sport. Brunel University *Research Archive*. http://bura.brunel.ac.uk/handle/2438/626.

Brackenridge, C. H. (2017). *Abuse in sport: A selection of writings by Celia Brackenridge*. e-book. Brunel University.

Brackenridge, C. H., & Fasting, K. (2005). The grooming process in sport: Narratives of sexual harassment and abuse. *Auto/Biography*, 13, 33–52.

Brackenridge, C. H., & Kirby, S. (1997). Playing safe? Assessing the risk of sexual abuse to young elite athletes. *International Review for the Sociology of Sport*, 32(4), 407–418.

Brackenridge, C. H., & Lyons, K. (1986, December). "Problem, what problem?" Thoughts on a professional code of practice for coaches. Paper presented to the Annual Conference of the British Association of National Coaches, Bristol, England.

Brackenridge, C. H., Pitchford, A., Russell, K., & Nutt, G. (2007). *Child welfare in football: An exploration of children's welfare in the modern game*. London: Routledge.

Cense, M., & Brackenridge, C. H. (2001). Temporal and developmental risk factors for sexual harassment and abuse in sport. *European Physical Education Review*, 7(1), 61–79.

Coalter, F. (2007). *A wider social role for sport: Who's keeping the score?* London: Routledge.

Commonwealth of Australia. (2017a). Factsheet: Criminal justice report: Failure to report offence. Royal Commission into Institutional Responses to Child Sexual Abuse. https://www.childabuseroyalcommission.gov.au/criminal-justice.

Commonwealth of Australia. (2017b). Final report: Recommendations. Royal Commission into Institutional Responses to Child Sexual Abuse. https://www.childabuseroyalcommission.gov.au/final-report.

Commonwealth of Australia. (2017c). Final report: Volume 14—Sport, recreation, arts, culture, community and hobby groups. Royal Commission into Institutional Responses to Child Sexual Abuse. https://www.childabuseroyalcommission.gov.au/final-report.

Cook, M., & Howells, K. (Eds.). (1981). *Sexual interest in children*. London: Academic Press.

Crosset, T. (1986, November). Male coach–female athlete relationships. Paper presented at the First Interdisciplinary Conference for Sport Sciences, Sole, Norway.

Cunningham, J. (1985, June 24). When the sprint for fair play turned into an obstacle race: Prejudice against women in sport. *The Guardian*, p. 21.

Curry, T. J. (1998). Beyond the locker room: Campus bars and college athletes. *Sociology of Sport Journal*, 15, 205–215.

Darling, A., Pope, L., Mooney, J.-L., King, S., & Ablett, G. (2020). Truth Project thematic report: Child sexual abuse in sports. Independent Inquiry into Child Sexual Abuse. https://www.iicsa.org.uk/document/truth-project-thematic-report-child-sexual-abuse-sports-executive-summary.

DeVries, K., Ross-Van Dorp, C., & Myjer, E. (2016). *Rapport van de Onderzoekscommissie Seksuel Intimidatie en Misbruik in de Sport*. Nieuwegein, Netherlands: Arko Sports Media.

Donnelly, P. (1997). Child labour, sport labour. *International Review for the Sociology of Sport*, 32, 389–406.

Donnelly, P. (1999). "Who's fair game?" Sport, sexual harassment, and abuse. In P. White & K. Young (Eds.), *Sport and gender in Canada* (pp. 107–128). Ontario: Oxford University Press.

Everley, S. (2020). The child protection in sport unit—Supporting national governing bodies in hearing the voices of children: An evaluation of current practice. *Child Abuse Review*, 29(2), 114–129.

Fasting, K., Brackenridge, C.H., & Sundgot-Borgen, J. (2000). The Norwegian women project: Females, elite sports and sexual harassment. Norwegian Olympic Committee & Confederation of Sports. https://library.olympic.org/Default/doc/SYRACUSE/76806/females-elite-sports-and-sexual-harassment-the-norwegian-women-project-2000-kari-fasting-celia-brack?_lg=en-GB.

Fasting, K., Chroni, S., Hervik, S. E., & Knorre, N. (2011). Sexual harassment in sport toward females in three European countries. *International Review for the Sociology of Sport*, 46(1), 76–89.

Fasting, K., Huffman, D., & Svela Sand, T. (2015). *Gender-based violence in Zambian sport: Prevalence and prevention.* Oslo: Norwegian Olympic and Paralympic Committee and Confederation of Sports.

Fasting, K., & Knorre, N. (2005). *Women in sport in the Czech Republic: The experience of female athletes.* Oslo: Norwegian School of Sport Sciences & Czech Olympic Committee.

Fasting, K., Sand, T. S., & Sisjord, M. K. (2018). Coach-athlete sexual relationships: Coaches' opinions. *International Journal of Sports Science & Coaching*, 13(4), 463–470.

Faulkner, A. (2017). Survivor research and mad studies: The role and value of experiential knowledge in mental health research. *Disability and Society*, 32(4), 500–520.

Fricker, M. (2007). Epistemic Injustice: Power and the Ethics of Knowing. Oxford: Oxford University Press.

Grey-Thompson, T. (2017). Duty of care in sport: Independent report to government. U.K. Department for Digital, Culture, Media and Sport. https://www.gov.uk/government/publications/duty-of-care-in-sport-review.

Griffin, S. (1971, September). Rape: The all-American crime. *Ramparts*, 26–35.

Hall, M. A. (1985). How should we theorise sport in a capitalist patriarchy? *International Review for the Sociology of Sport*, 21, 109–113.

Hartill, M. (2005). Sport and the sexually abused male child. *Sport, Education and Society*, 10(3), 287–304.

Hartill, M. (2017). *Sexual abuse in youth sport: A sociocultural analysis.* London: Routledge.

Hartill, M., & Lang, M. (2018). Reports of child protection and safeguarding concerns in sport and leisure settings: An analysis of English Local Authority data between 2010 and 2015. *Leisure Studies*, 37(5), 479–499.

Hartill, M., Murphy, K., Taylor, S., Schroer, M., Axmann, G., Viseras, G., Leach, K., Harris, C., & Rulofs, B. (2020). *Good practice guide: Supporting individuals affected by sexual violence in sport—a guide for sport organizations based on the results and experiences of the project VOICE. Voices for truth and dignity: Combatting sexual violence in European sport through the voices of those affected.* Cologne: German Sport University.

Hartill, M., & Prescott, P. (2007). Serious business or "any other business"? Safeguarding and child protection policy in British rugby league. *Child Abuse Review*, 16, 237–251.

Harris, C., & Hartill, M. (2021). Sexual abuse "survivor" research in sport. In M. Lang (Ed.), *Routledge handbook of athlete welfare* (pp. 277–288). London: Routledge.

Independent Inquiry into Child Sexual Abuse (England & Wales). (2018). Mandatory reporting seminar 1—existing obligations to report child sexual abuse: A summary report. https://www.iicsa.org.uk/research-seminars/mandatory-reporting-child-sexual-abuse.

International Olympic Committee. (2007). *Consensus statement on sexual harassment and abuse in sport.* Lausanne: IOC.

Jack, G. (2001). An ecological perspective on child abuse. In P. Foley, J. Roche, & S. Tucker (Eds.), *Children in society: Contemporary theory, policy and practice* (pp. 185–194). Basingstoke, U.K.: Palgrave & the Open University.

Jones, R. L., Glintmeyer, N., & McKenzie, A. (2005). Slim bodies, eating disorders and the coach-athlete relationship: A tale of identity creation and disruption. *International Review for the Sociology of Sport, 40,* 377–391.

Jud, A., Fegert, J. M., & Finkelhor, D. (2016). On the incidence and prevalence of child maltreatment: A research agenda. *Child and Adolescent Psychiatry and Mental Health, 10*(1), 1–5. https://doi.org/10.1186/s13034-016-0105-8.

Kane, M. J., & Disch, L. J. (1993). Sexual violence and the reproduction of male power in the locker room: The Lisa Olson incident. *Sociology of Sport Journal, 10,* 331–352.

Kerr, G., Stirling A., & MacPherson, E. (2014). A critical examination of child protection initiatives in sport contexts. *Social Sciences, 3*(4), 742–757.

Kirby, S., Greaves, L., & Hankivsky, O. (2000). *The dome of silence: Sexual harassment and abuse in sport.* London: Zed Books.

Lang, M. (2015). Touchy subject: A Foucauldian analysis of coaches' perceptions of adult-child touch in youth swimming. *Sociology of Sport Journal, 32*(1), 4–21.

Leahy, T., Pretty, G., & Tenenbaum, G. (2002). Prevalence of sexual abuse in organised competitive sport in Australia. *Journal of Sexual Aggression, 8,* 16–36.

Lenskyj, H. J. (1992). *Sexual harassment: Female athletes' experiences and coaches' responsibilities.* Ottawa: Coaching Association of Canada. https://books.google.co.uk/books/about/Sexual_Harassment.html?id=2MbewQEACAAJ&redir_esc=y.

MacDonald, G., & Roberts, H. (1995). *What works in the early years? Effective interventions for children and their families in health, social welfare, education and child protection.* Essex, U.K.: Barnardos.

Mathews, B., Ju Lee, X., & Norman, R. E. (2016). Impact of a new mandatory reporting law on reporting and identification of child sexual abuse: A seven-year time trend analysis. *Child Abuse & Neglect, 56,* 62–79.

McMahon, J., & DinanThompson, M. (2011). "Body work—regulation of a swimmer body": An autoethnography from an Australian elite swimmer. *Sport, Education and Society, 16*(1), 35–50.

Messner, M. A., & Sabo, D. (1994). *Sex, violence and power in sports: Rethinking masculinity.* Trumansburg, NY: Crossing Press.

Mountjoy, M., Brackenridge C., Arrington, M. E., Blauwet, C., Carska-Sheppard, A., Fasting, K., . . . Budgett, R. (2016). International Olympic Committee consensus statement: Harassment and abuse (non accidental violence) in sport. *British Journal of Sports Medicine, 50,* 1019–1029.

Nielsen, J. T. (2001). The forbidden zone: Intimacy, sexual relations and misconduct in the relationship between coaches and athletes. *International Review for the Sociology of Sport, 36*(2), 165–182.

Ohlert, J., Seidler, C., Rau, T., Rulofs, B., & Allroggen, M. (2017). Sexual violence in organized sport in Germany. *German Journal of Exercise and Sport Research, 48*(1), 59–68.

Owton, H., & Sparkes, A.C. (2017). Sexual abuse and the grooming process in sport: Learning from Bella's story. *Sport, Education and Society, 22*(6), 732–743.

Parent, S., Lavoie, F., Thibodeau, M.-È., Hébert, M., & Blais, M. (2016). Sexual violence expe-rienced in the sport context by a representative sample of Quebec adolescents. *Journal of Interpersonal Violence, 31*(16), 2666–2686.

Phelps, A., Kelly, J., Lancaster, S., Mehrzad, J., & Panter, A. (2017). Report of the independent review panel into the climate and culture of the world class programme in British cycling. British Cycling and UK Sport. https://www.britishcycling.org.uk/about/article/20170614-about-bc-news-British-Cycling-publishes-the-cycling-independent-review-0.

Rhind, D., McDermott, J., Lambert, E., & Koleva, I. (2015). A review of safeguarding cases in sport. *Child Abuse Review, 24*, 418–426.

Rose, D. (2017). Service user/survivor-led research in mental health: epistemological possibilities. *Disability & Society, 32*(6), 773–789.

Rulofs, B. (2007). Prevention of sexualized violence in sport—An analysis of the prelimi-nary measures in North Rhine-Westphalia. In B. Rulofs (Ed.), *Silence protects the wrong people: Sexualized violence in sport—Situation analysis and opportunities for action* (pp. 19–30). Duesseldorf: Ministry of North Rhine-Westphalia.

Rulofs, B., Doupona Topič, M., Diketmüller, R., Martin Horcajo, M., Vertommen, T., Toftegaard Støckel, J., & Hartill, M. (2020). *Final report: Voices for truth and dignity—Combatting sexual violence in European Sport through the voices of those affected.* Cologne: German Sport University.

Rush, F. (1980). *The best kept secret: Sexual abuse of children.* New York: McGraw-Hill.

Sanday, P. R. (2007). *Fraternity gang rape: Sex, brotherhood, and privilege on campus.* New York: New York University Press.

Sheldon, C. (2021). Independent Review into Child Sexual Abuse in Football 1970-2005. The Football Association. https://www.thefa.com/news/2021/mar/17/clive-sheldon-qc-independent-commission-report-released-20210317

Sport Resolutions. (2017). British Canoeing independent investigation: Key findings and recommendations.https://www.sportresolutions.com/services/investigations-and-reviews/canoeing-independent-investigation.

Sport Resolutions. (2018). British Equestrian Federation independent review. https://www.sportresolutions.co.uk/services/investigations-and-reviews/british-equestrian-federation-independent-review.

Sport Resolutions. (2019). Lawn Tennis Association independent review: Report of the review panel.https://www.lta.org.uk/globalassets/about-lta/safeguarding/independent-review-report.pdf.

Sport Resolutions. (2020). Independent Review of UK Athletics safeguarding: Executive summary and recommendations. https://www.sportresolutions.com/services/investigations-and-reviews/uk-athletics-independent-review.

Stevens, V., & Vertommen, T. (2020). Bringing network governance into the field of violence and integrity in sports. *Journal of Public Administration and Governance, 10*(2), 93–107.

Summers, D. (2000). *Child protection in voluntary sector sport organisations* (Unpublished doctoral dissertation). University of Bristol.

Stirling, A. E., & Kerr, G. A. (2009). Abused athletes' perceptions of the coach-athlete relation-ship. *Sport in Society, 12*(2), 227–239.

Stirling, A. E., & Kerr, G. A. (2014). Initiating and sustaining emotional abuse in the coach-athlete relationship: An ecological transactional model of vulnerability. *Journal of Aggression, Maltreatment & Cauma, 232*, 116–135.

Stirling, A. E., Kerr, G. A., & Cruz, L. C. (2012). An evaluation of Canada's National Coaching Certification Programme's "make ethical decisions" coach education module. *International Journal of Coaching Science, 6*, 4560.

Tomison, A. M. (2000). Evaluating child abuse prevention programs. *Issues in Child Abuse Prevention, 12*, 1–20. National Child Protection Clearinghouse, Australian Institute of Family Studies.http://citeseerx.ist.psu.edu/viewdoc/download?doi=10.1.1.629.6446&rep=rep1&type=pdf.

Vertommen, T., Schipper-van Veldhoven, N.,Wouters, K., Kampen, J. K., Brackenridge, C. H., Rhind, D. J. A., Neels, K., & Van Den Eede, F. (2016). Interpersonal violence against children in sport in the Netherlands and Belgium. *Child Abuse & Neglect, 51*, 223–236.

Vertommen, T., Stoeckel, J. T., Vandevivere, L., Van Den Eede, F., & De Martelaer, K. (2016). A green flag for the flag system? Towards a child protection policy in Flemish sport. *International Journal of Sport Policy and Politics, 8*(1), 15–31.

Ward, T. (2014). The explanation of sexual offending: From single factor theories to integrative pluralism. *Journal of Sexual Aggression, 20*(2), 130–141.

Ward, T., & Beech, A. R. (2006). An integrated theory of sexual offending. *Aggression and Violent Behaviour, 11*(11), 44–63.

Weiss, C. H. (1997). How can theory-based evaluation make greater headway? *Education Review, 21*, 501–524.

CHAPTER 29

··

SPORT, SCANDAL, AND SOCIAL MORALITY

··

DAVID ROWE AND CATHERINE PALMER

THERE is a deep and enduring relationship between sport and scandal. On occasion, sport consumes enormous quantities of media space, often out of all proportion to the serious-ness of the transgression that prompted the scandal (Rowe, 2011, Chapter 6). In contrast, a transgression related to sport may receive much less attention than its gravity would, on most objective criteria, deserve. To understand the social dynamics of the phenomenon of the sport scandal, it is necessary to analyze the specific characteristics of sport as a cultural form, the place of the institution of sport in society, and, crucially, its deep interdepend-ence with the institution of the media. Deploying sociological and anthropological theories, concepts, and methods, this chapter explores why sport is so susceptible to scandal and why such scandals resonate widely across the socioscape and, crucially, traverse the me-diascape that provides professional sport with such extraordinary visibility and influence. It questions, in the tradition of labeling theory (Cohen, 2002), whether there is an une-quivocal relationship between transgression and scandal, arguing instead that scandals are produced out of a range of structural, agentic, and contingent factors that determine their profile, duration, and consequences.

Sport scandals are enormously variable, involving moral and ethical conduct deemed to be dubious, and range from relatively mundane transgressions of folkways and mores—essentially, matters of *etiquette*, manners or convention—to serious breaches of social norms involving the civil and criminal law. Crucial to such assessments are the elevated status of the social institution of sport and the widespread prescription that sportspeople are not merely high-functioning technicians of celebrated forms of physical culture but "role models" whose privileged, prominent position means that they are expected to set an example to wider society, especially to the young. This ethical positioning of sport and sportspeople in society entails the constant prospect that a sport scandal will erupt (Palmer, 2015). This transpiration—and it will be argued that there are no fixed criteria by which a dispute, controversy, or act acquires the status of a scandal, let alone one in which sport is unequivocally responsible for what has occurred—is produced by factors that are both endogenous and exogenous to sport, often blurring boundaries between media dis-course, sport governance, and political intervention. The sociological task is to understand the relationships involved and to separate cause and effect in the making, trajectory, and consequences of the sport scandal.

ISSUES

A scandal is a phenomenon that is deceptively self-evident. Most people would intuitively feel that they know a scandal when they see one, but what precisely constitutes scandal, and its separation from a common or garden-variety breach of rules, is quite difficult to ascertain. The reason is that there is a variable correspondence between a transgressive act, attitudes to that transgression, and the response once it is detected. Conventional definitions of scandal, such as "Scandal serves as a term to delineate a breach in moral conduct and authority" (Lull & Hinerman, 1997, p. 3) or that "the term refers to actions or events involving certain kinds of transgression which become known to others and are sufficiently serious to elicit a public response" (Thompson, 2000, p. 13), open up rather than resolve a series of other questions. These include: Is there moral and ethical consensus about inappropriate conduct? Who determines that a breach has occurred? Who has the authority to penalize a transgression? The difficulty of answering such questions in a categorical manner has led prominent analysts of scandal to describe it as a "theoretically messy area" (Tiffen, 1999, pp. 13, 157) in which the outcomes of such "developing dramas" are uncertain.

Matters of scandal, especially those regarding elite professional sport, are complicated further by the development of the institution of the media in modernity. It is difficult to imagine a transgression becoming a scandal without being widely reported by the news media. But as sociologists, political scientists, and communication and media scholars have long argued, the media do not merely act as neutral conveyors of information but are actively involved in shaping interpretations of the infinitesimally small percentage of daily events in the world that they choose to cover (Couldry & Hepp, 2016). Indeed, there is a strong line of argument that the news media not only "mediate" reality for their audiences but are deeply implicated in the shaping of the society on which they report. This theory of "mediatization" as it relates to sport (Frandsen, 2019), and the more general acknowledgment of the media as vectors of scandal (Bisbort, 2008), help to explain why it is de rigueur for scandals and media to be regarded as inextricable, and why media sport scandals are important objects of critical sociological investigation.

The central role of the media explains why influential collections on scandal, such as those by Lull and Hinerman (1997) and Tumber and Waisbord (2019), address, respectively, "media scandals" and "media and scandal." In the specific case of the sport scandal, this role of the media is especially important given the convergence of the institutions of sport and media (Wenner, 1998). The media, which largely (directly and indirectly) fund professional sport and are responsible for its cultural reach, receive enormous value because of sport's prime position within the "attention economy" (Hutchins & Rowe, 2012). But this intimate relationship between sport and media is problematic: must, say, sport governance or conduct be central to a transgression being regarded as a sport scandal? Or can there be only a tenuous link with sport as long as the media can draw a connection between, for example, a sport celebrity with enormous profile and any questionable conduct irrespective of its specific relationship to sport? Sport is especially susceptible to scandal for three principal reasons: that (1) especially through its modern Olympic tradition, it is infused with the romantic myth of noble competition that demands unimpeachable behavior by athletes; (2) the rule-based competitive structure that created modern sport out of folk physical play is subject to multiple potential transgressions deemed to be "foul play" and "cheating"; and (3) its high visibility via the media and creation of stars and even full-blown celebrities (Andrews & Jackson, 2001) draws intense interest to the conduct of sportspeople, including that of a partisan kind by sport fans of opposing clubs and countries (Rowe, 2004).

There is a deep irony concerning the moral weight that contemporary sport is expected to carry in the light of the historical transition since the 19th century from the predominantly leisure-based practice of amateur physical culture (Hargreaves, 1986) to a highly stratified institution in which, at its apex, values of ruthless capital accumulation predominate (Clarke & Critcher, 1985). The irony is compounded by the fact that the major source of funding for contemporary sport—the commercial media complex—is also the primary promoter of sporting scandals, especially when they involve celebrities (see Smart, this volume). So, for example, if sport celebrities such as golfer Tiger Woods or footballer David Beckham are alleged or confirmed to be engaged in marital infidelity (the former, seemingly, compulsively), then the media who made them extraordinarily *famous* are also instrumental in making them, at least in this respect, *infamous* (Rowe, 2011). That is not, though, to suggest that all the elements of the media are engaged in such exposure and saturation coverage. Those who have studied sports journalism (Boyle, 2006, 2019) as a "beat" within wider news and entertainment media have noted the frequent reluctance of sports journalists to compromise their working relationships with their regular sources in sport by engaging in the kind of critically investigative journalism that produces scandals ranging from the petty to the criminal. Here, the interpenetration of elements of the sport and media industries is highlighted as a contributory factor in how transgressions may be ignored, suppressed, or illuminated in a blaze of publicity (see Rowe & Boyle, this volume). It is a matter that requires attention to the ways in which different types of sport scandal are produced and handled.

Social Implications of Sport Scandals

Sport scandals take many forms and can be classified using a range of criteria, from degrees of gravity to principal themes and subjects. As noted earlier, there is no fixed relationship between transgression and response, but it is appropriate to develop the analysis by focusing first on the most serious acts, the criminal, and the gravest of crimes, murder. In such cases, there can be little debate that something truly scandalous has occurred, but there are still many uncertainties about the level of responsibility of the social institution of sport for the tragic outcome when a sportsperson kills another human being. Lamentably, murders are carried out both by sportspeople and others, and not all are given equal media attention. A murder trial involving a celebrity sportsperson, like those in which film stars, musicians, and even politicians take part, inevitably attracts the publicity that is the essential prerequisite of a scandal defined as the mutually reinforcing relationship between a transgressive act and its societally mediated response. One of the most notorious involves the U.S. footballer, commentator, and actor O. J. Simpson (Hunt, 1999), who was tried and found not guilty of the 1994 stabbing murder of his wife Nicole Brown Simpson and her friend Ron Goldman in a criminal court in 1995 on grounds of there being insufficient proof "beyond reasonable doubt," while later being found guilty in a "wrongful death" civil trial according to its lower burden of proof, the "balance of probabilities," in 1997 (Toobin, 2016). The scandal was enormous in terms of both coverage and duration, running from the televised pursuit of Simpson by police cars and media helicopters along the freeways of Los Angeles through to the live coverage of the criminal trial to the ensuing books, television documentaries, and films (including *OJ: Trial of the Century*; see Ferner, 2014). It was a sport scandal of epic proportions not because any sport organization was directly implicated in it but because Simpson's celebrity sport and entertainment status turned two of the 23,730 homicides in the USA in 1994 (Associated Press, 1995) into a global media event.

Similarly, the 2014 trial and conviction of Olympic and Paralympic runner Oscar Pistorius (nicknamed "The Bladerunner" on account of his prosthetic legs) for the murder of his girlfriend Reeva Steenkamp was a globally prominent sport scandal of the most serious kind that was also deemed to be "the trial of the century" (Geertsema-Sligh & Worthington, 2020). That it did not receive quite the attention of the Simpson trial around the world, despite Pistorius being found criminally responsible for murder, probably reflects the global geography of scandal in that it took place in South Africa rather than at the center of the Anglo-American media sphere. But there is another key reason Simpson's trial garnered so much interest: much of the focus was on the possibility that an African American man could be justly tried in the United States in a case involving the murder of a white woman and man. Sport scandals necessarily resonate with major social issues that extend well beyond sport. In this instance it is, first, regarding Simpson, a matter of "race" (Baker & Boyd, 1997)—the issue that a quarter of a century later would coalesce around the Black Lives Matter movement. Second, with respect both to Simpson and Pistorius, it concerns sport-related gendered violence (Rowe, 2014, 2019a). "Race" and gender matters are, of course, by no means restricted to the domain of sport, but neither can sport claim to be exempt from them. Sport scandals generate discomfiting questions about the degree to which the institution itself might be in some way implicated in the incidence of racism and sexism and, in turn, reproduce these and other forms of social inequality, including class prejudice, homophobia, ageism, and ableism.

The intersections between sport and scandal therefore bring into play a host of wider social issues. Many involve accounts of sportsmen behaving badly (Fordyce, 2015), with explanations—or mitigating pleas—of behavior being altered or encouraged by alcohol (see Palmer, this volume) or recreational drugs. Palmer (2014) has noted that accounts of drinking and drunken misadventures often feature in narratives surrounding sporting celebrities framed as "falls from grace," tending to paint the athlete as the "fool or villain" (Lines, 2001). This is the theme of a book that provides multiple instances of the dramatic decline through public scandals of individual and team sports celebrities, coaches, and commentators (Wenner, 2013). Yet the scandal can often reveal a sportsperson's deeper struggle with drugs and alcohol (Palmer, 2015). Their difficulties often come to light following an off-field misdemeanor, the coverage of which "focuses on deviant behaviour when drunk, such as driving under the influence, marital infidelity, violence, and breaking team rules" (Jones, 2014, p. 485). The complexities and contexts of sport scandals, and the centrality of media to their circulation (Rowe, 2019b), point us to how sociological and anthropological theories, concepts, and methods can be usefully deployed to explain the ongoing fascination with scandals in and beyond sport.

APPROACHES

The various approaches to making sense of scandals are both theoretical and methodological in nature. They involve interpreting the significance of scandal at both a "nuts and bolts" practical level, whereby the scandal is subject to analysis through particular methodological frameworks, and at a conceptual level, whereby scandals receive wider theoretical attention that can explain their ongoing cultural traction. This section begins with an overview of some of the methodological approaches to analyzing sport, scandal, and social morality, including the ecology of scandal frameworks (Lull & Hinerman, 1997) constructed as mediated sports scandals. The section then examines some of the main theoretical approaches that have been developed to explain how and why scandals develop, circulate, are consumed, and are even reconfigured. Here, concepts such as redemption narratives, moral panics, consumptive deviance, and social drama are introduced to underscore the utility of sociological and anthropological approaches to understanding sport, scandal, and social morality.

Methodological Approaches

Despite the media storm that often surrounds a sport scandal and suggestions of an unprecedented "loss of innocence" (Rapp, 2011), these scandals tend to follow fairly predictable patterns. Once the scandal has erupted or hit the headlines, it then unfolds in the manner that Lull and Hinerman (1997, p. 17) refer to as the "ecology of scandal." This framework is comprised of four components: (1) *scandal susceptibility*: some people and institutions are more vulnerable to scandal than others; (2) *polysemia*: audiences interpret scandals in multiple ways; (3) *intertextuality*: scandals are interleaved both vertically and horizontally with one another as well as with other narratives; and (4) *scandal hierarchy*: the tendency of both the media and audiences to rank scandals according to their degree of moral turpitude.

Palmer (2015) has applied the ecology of scandal framework to her analysis of Australian sport's "darkest day" (originally called the "blackest day"): a 12-month investigation into the involvement of organized crime in sport by the Australian Crime Commission. The Commission's report found that the integrity of professional sport in Australia was under threat from match-fixing, the manipulation of sports betting markets, and the illegal sale and distribution of performance-enhancing drugs (Australian Crime Commission, 2013, p. 1). It was launched dramatically at a joint media conference by Home Affairs and Justice Minister Jason Clare and Minister for Sport Kate Lundy, with the heads of Australia's five largest sports standing behind them (Gordon, 2013). In a context where doping and match-fixing are seen by many to be inevitable aspects of sport in advanced capitalist, late modern societies (see Dimeo & Henning, this volume; Tak, this volume), the former head of the Australian Sports Anti-Doping Authority, Richard Ings, declared, "This is not a black day in Australian sport, this is the blackest day" (quoted in Gordon, 2013). This event, now more commonly referred to as "the darkest day in Australian sport" (for example, Doherty, 2013), provides an instructive site for advancing understandings of scandals and their relevance to the sociology of sport. For Palmer (2015, p. 518), scandal susceptibility occurred through the institution of sport being "highly vulnerable to organised crime infiltration." Sports fans, officials, the general public, and the Australian Crime Commission all responded to the scandal differently, pointing to the polysemic nature of scandal interpretation. Intertextuality was evident in the interweaving of subscandals of the manipulation of sports betting markets and the illegal sale and distribution of performance-enhancing drugs. The *scandal hierarchy* was suggested through the counterposition that corruption, doping, and match-fixing (see Kihl & Ordway, this volume) were relatively low-order scandals compared to, say, sexual abuse in sport (see Hartill, this volume). The ecology of scandal framework is, then, a useful approach to tracing how a scandal unfolds and the social responses to it. The reactions of the sportspeople implicated in a specific scandal also follow a certain narrative logic.

The "ecological" approach promoted by Lull and Hinerman (1997) suggests that, once a scandal breaks, the response of the athlete involved usually takes one of five forms. First, there can be a full and swift public admission of fault and a plea for forgiveness; witness the weeping, contrite public apologies of the former captain and vice captains of the Australian men's cricket team following the so-called Sandpapergate (discussed below) in the 2018 tour of South Africa (Knaus, 2018). As Agyemang (2011) and Brown (2014) have argued, a public apology is the principal way to prevent brand damage to an athlete and their sponsors. Performative contrition is enacted in similar ways when women athletes transgress (a rarer phenomenon, discussed later). For example, Allison, Pegoraro, Frederick, and Thompson (2019) describe the "image repair strategies" of U.S. soccer player Abby Wambach's arrest for driving under the influence and tennis player Maria Sharapova's admission of a failed drug test. Wambach presented a posture of mortification in garnering sympathy, although Sharapova's evasive techniques of denial provoked a range of reactions, from sympathetic to hostile.

The second tactic, according to Lull and Hinerman (1997), is to denigrate the person who is the victim or complainant in the scandal. Criticizing the motives and/or moral character of the accuser shifts the focus from the accused to the accuser. This discursive play is common in scandals involving allegations of sexual assault of women by men via gender-laden commentary, accusing the woman of being drunk, a homewrecker, a "groupie," a sexual extortionist, a "gold digger," or "asking for it" being among the more common tactics. Reports of the case of former men's Australian National Rugby League (NRL—the women's league is the NRLW) player Jarryd Hayne, who was found guilty of sexual assault (before a judge-ordered re-trial), describe the prosecution casting doubt over the complainant's evidence that she did not anticipate Hayne's intentions of sex, given that he had left a taxi meter running (Australian Associated Press, 2021).

Third is the vilification of the so-called scandalmonger, the intention being to take the heat off the alleged perpetrator by "blaming the messenger." One of the most prominent examples of this tactic was the aggressive campaign waged for many years by cyclist Lance Armstrong against fellow cyclists, support staff, and, especially, the journalist David Walsh (2015), who alleged that Armstrong was involved in the systematic, clandestine use of performance-enhancing drugs. Armstrong, who persistently attacked his accusers as liars with grievances and publicity seekers, finally admitted guilt in 2013 in a highly publicized television interview with Oprah Winfrey.

Fourth, scandals ascend, following Stanley Cohen's (2002) renowned framework in *Folk Devils and Moral Panics* (which is addressed in greater detail later), into a "media scandal amplification spiral," whereby commentary on the scandal escalates unless and until there is an ensuing process of "de-amplification." This is the fifth and, from the perspective of the people and organizations held responsible for the scandal, the most desired possibility in what might be called the genealogy of scandal—apart, of course, from one not being detected in the first place. It means that interest in the story lapses due to "scandal fatigue" on the part of media and audiences alike as part of the well-worn "natural history" of scandal. As will be discussed below, though, especially in the "digital age" (Mandell & Chen, 2016) scandals remain permanently available for excavation, exposure, and recirculation through, in yet another related concept, the archaeology of scandal. That is, of course, provided that the scandal does not come to define permanently the transgressor's reputation and to obliterate any other aspects of their sport career and personal history (as discussed below regarding the redemption narrative).

These frameworks for interpreting scandals, sporting or otherwise, are useful for mapping the potential ways in which a scandal may unfold. They provide critical approaches for tracing the progress of a scandal across the socioscape and, crucially, the mediascape that provides professional sport with such extraordinary visibility. Deeper theoretical engagement with many of the practices deemed to be scandalous is required in shaping these methods of inquiry.

Theoretical Approaches

Theories explaining how scandals develop and circulate, and how we respond to them, span the social sciences. Sociological and anthropological theories are especially well equipped for dealing with the function of scandals as moral barometers of social life in late modernity. They take a view of sport scandals that requires maintaining some distance from the "tabloid frenzy" and the interventions of "moral entrepreneurs" (Cohen, 2002) in order to understand how narratives are fashioned within the mediated public sphere (see Rowe & Boyle, this volume). This is the domain where popular understandings of—and sometimes official reactions to—controversies are manifest that may scandalize some and leave others largely indifferent or even hostile to those identified as victims. Scandals are not static phenomena, and sport scandals, like physical culture itself, are characterized by movement. Of particular appeal in sport culture is the narrative of a "journey" from hero to villain to, in some instances, the redeemed.

Narratives of Redemption

In theorizing sport scandals, in a domain where "heroization" is a familiar process (Parry, 2020), an approach that emphasizes narratives of redemption is common. It follows a "rise, fall and redemption" hermeneutic structure (Whannel, 1999, 2002). Here, the achievements of the athlete are first celebrated and lauded. Then comes the scandal or fall from grace. In some cases, the scandal is so deplorable that redemption is virtually possible—for example, regarding former USA Gymnastics national team doctor Larry Nassar, who was sentenced to several life terms for multiple sexual offenses against young female gymnasts (Kerr, Battaglia, & Stirling, 2019). The suicide of a transgressor sometimes brings a different kind of narrative closure, such as that of former U.S. Gymnastics coach John Geddert, an associate of Nassar, who took his own life after being charged with human trafficking and sexual assault (White & Nichols, 2021). However, a different scandal dynamic may be evident if related to organizational and institutional structures rather than personalities. The reputation of the governing body, USA Gymnastics, is less easily captured and assessed than that of a "rogue individual," an analytical obstacle in addressing scandal narratives involving large, complex bodies like the International Olympic Committee (Jennings & Sambrook, 2000) or FIFA (Mersiades, 2018). As is discussed below, scandal redress for organizations is more closely associated with governance and policy reform.

But in many other cases in sport, especially if the scandal was a relatively low-order affair in the scandal hierarchy, the male athlete (the majority of transgressors) might be redeemed by means of the "bad boy makes good" trope. Whannel's (2002, pp. 145, 146) work on the former footballing greats Paul Gascoigne and George Best traces a cycle of "celebration, punishment, redemption and self-discipline," whereby the movement of both men from positions of footballing preeminence to those of a "dislocated star" is used to describe the scandalous behavior of many sportsmen since. Harrington and Schimmel (2013) apply this redemption narrative arc to the career of former tennis player Andre Agassi, who "bounced back" from rampant cocaine addiction to marry the leading German tennis player Steffi Graff. We see similar redemption stories in golf. Tiger Woods's well-reported (Starn, 2011) fall from grace (exposed as a serial adulterer in 2009 and arrested for driving under the influence of alcohol or drugs in 2017) and redemption (winning the U.S. Masters in 2019) now has a new plotline: whether the golfer can recover physically and reputationally from a serious car accident in 2021 caused by his driving at excessive speed (Mark, 2021). In tennis, Nick Kyrgios, the sport's self-anointed "bad boy," seemingly won over the Australian public by fundraising for the bushfires which ravaged the country in the summer of 2020 (Jackson, 2020), as well as by calling fellow tennis player Novak Djokovic a "tool" for Djokovic's lax attitude toward COVID-19 (Williams, 2021). Each such example illustrates the ease with which sporting careers can map onto particular discursive patterns. The rise, fall, rise, and possible multiple repetitions of the cycle (Wenner, 2013) echo mythologies that are of an almost biblical nature, constantly connecting the distant, insulated world of professional sport to social practices and values that touch everyday lives across whole societies. Although some of the attention given to celebrity sportspeople may be voyeuristic, it is also entangled with social debates about ethical conduct and the proto-apocalyptic anxieties regarding social disintegration loudly expressed in mediated moral panics (Rowe, 2009).

Moral Panics

Alongside narratives of redemption, Cohen's (2002) aforementioned theorizing of "moral panics" offers a widely used (and, for Tiffen, 2019, often abused) approach to explaining the ways in which scandals develop and circulate and how various audiences and social constituencies respond to them. The concept captures the emotional, collective, and disproportionate reactions to a perceived threat to social order by a scandalous breach producing a "contagion" effect. Moral panics, Cohen argues, create "folk devils," social deviants who are often marginal yet visible individuals or groups who become scapegoats for social problems. This is the labeling approach that places greater emphasis on the social actor than the act (Becker, 1963). In sport and entertainment, though, the folk devil in a moral panic may well be a celebrity, such as Lance Armstrong with regard to doping or former boxer Mike Tyson and the late basketballer Kobe Bryant in the context of rape cases. Regarding Tyson, the "tide of condemnation from anti–domestic violence advocates" led the Nevada State Athletic Commission to deny him a boxing license (Wynn, 2003, p. 99). For Bryant, the racial politics of a Black man accused of assaulting a woman was juxtaposed against the narrative of the respectable family man (Markovitz, 2006). In these latter instances, the mediascape—Tyson was found guilty, but the charges against Bryant were dropped—positioned both men as folk devils who represented threats to the social order through their "hypersexual" masculinity, upon which racially coded descriptions were then overlaid (see Andrews & Silk, 2010; Leonard & King, 2011).

Here, it is clear that successful, affluent African American sportsmen—irrespective of their guilt or innocence—are not immune to social prejudice. Such stories often have many twists and turns. To return to the redemption narrative, after the criminal case against Bryant was dropped when his accuser declined to testify—although a separate civil suit was settled out of court, and he made a nonincriminating apology to her—he went on to sign multiyear, multimillion-dollar contracts with his sponsors. When Bryant tragically died with his daughter and others in a helicopter accident in 2020, there was a reluctance to raise the issue of his alleged culpability as a sex offender and, in direct contrast, to erase instead the incident from history and the career of a sportsmen who was to be posthumously admitted to the Basketball Hall of Fame. For this reason, media commentary often deemed Bryant's legacy "complicated," especially for survivors of sexual assault (Newberry & La Ganga, 2020) and feminists (Dionne, 2020).

Moral panic discourse, though, is not amenable to complexity, as it relies on an "inventory" involving "exaggeration and distortion" (Cohen, 2002) and simplified theories of causation. It focuses on the posited threat of folk devils to social order and urgent calls for heightened control of them through the state (the legislature, executive, judiciary, and police) from campaigning news media. The racial tone introduced into many such debates insinuates that Black sportsmen will somehow degrade the moral fiber of the institution of sport and the society at large (Carrington, 2010). Sport scandals are, then, highly efficient vehicles for conveying the urgency of such "crises." However, celebrities like Bryant and Woods are, as the word implies, widely *celebrated* and have access to the expensive scandal-management resources mobilized to counter the moral panic and their incipient folk devil status. They can also be redeemed and rehabilitated by subsequent sporting success and charitable work (notably through their own foundations) that mitigate the opprobrium of scandal. Finally, larger social and political developments may work to suppress the moral panic in favor of victims who are widely blamed. For example, the rise of the Black Lives Matter (BLM) movement (Evans, Agergaard, Campbell, Hylton, & Lenneis, 2020), which gained greater impetus after the May 2020 police killing of George Floyd in Minneapolis (which occurred only four months after the death of Bryant), was a major impediment to the racialized "deviancy" amplification of sport scandals as moral panics. BLM, it can be proposed, helped to de-amplify the moral panic framing the racialized "deviance" of the Black athlete and of other African Americans. However, much less serious issues involving forms of conduct of limited social significance can be construed as deviant, leading some to theorize responses to negative sport-related headlines in terms of consuming salacious media content.

Consumptive Deviance

The notion of consumptive deviance has its origins in Blackshaw and Crabbe's (2004) poststructuralist-inspired approach to understanding how societies respond to or consume sport deviance. They attempt to "find a method for articulating the worlds of deviance in sport in which the very concept of deviance itself had been substantially undermined by societal change and concomitant advances in social theory" (p. 76). Blackshaw and Crabbe argue that, while acts of deviance can be met with moral judgments by authority—as witnessed in how a moral panic builds—they can equally be seen through a lens of popular culture. That is, deviance—interpreted as the conduct embedded in the sport scandal—has become something to consume as entertainment.

Central to the consumptive deviance approach is the idea that consumers of scandal voyeuristically enjoy the transgressive behavior involved, without themselves incurring the risks to character or livelihood faced by the celebrity at the center of the transgression either through their actions or from speculation and gossip about them. Consumptive deviance— and the scandals that sit within it—is deviance by proxy. Drawing on representations of English Premiership League football as soap opera or social drama, Blackshaw and Crabbe (2004) describe the allegations of sexual (consensual), drug- and alcohol-related deviance among players. They suggest that such scandals excite and titillate readers and viewers, who consume them in a manner that is treated (no doubt hypocritically in many instances) as remote from their own intimate relationships or social encounters. The authors propose that "deviance has become a scripted performance, one of the many commodified experiences within late modern societies" (p. 76). There are limits to this theory of consumptive deviance, in that serious crimes like murder and rape perpetrated by sportspeople can hardly be classified as mere tabloid fodder for audiences seeking salacious celebrity gossip. Nonetheless, even the most apparently trivial and "hyped up" transgression-turned-scandal can be a rich resource for sociological inquiry in tracing the contours of what was, is, and will be socially normative.

Social Drama

The reference to English Premiership League football as soap opera is not misplaced in the theorization of scandals that considers them as social drama, wherein the function of a scandal is to propose—or even impose—a particular moral order on society and on the ways in which people live. Tomlinson (1997, p. 67) describes scandals as providing "contexts for 'communal' moral reflection and debate at a time when traditional sources of authority—religion, the state, and education—are in decline." From this perspective, each sport scandal, irrespective of its depth, is instructive for the sociological and anthropological analysis of sociocultural structure and agency. For example, in their work on Finnish "elite scandals," Kantola and Vesa (2013, p. 296) use social anthropologist Victor Turner's work on social drama and liminality to suggest that "scandals in the media provide liminal-like places of modernity where the normal order of society is abolished temporarily as societal moralities become a matter of public negotiation." Here they draw attention to the inherently performative nature of scandals, which are enactments of behavior subject to scrutiny as the members of societies negotiate and recalibrate the moral and ethical order.

Of particular utility for analyses of sporting scandals is Kantola and Vesa's (2013) interest in how moralities shift over time. This recognition of the place of social history in the contemporary understanding of transgression clearly resonates with studies of sport scandals. It invites questions about how the nature of scandals, and public responses to them, change across epochs. For example, in the heyday of amateur sport in the 19th and early 20th centuries, to be paid to play sport was in most cases scandalous (Hargreaves, 1986). Today it is scandalous to underpay or economically exploit professional sportspeople. Paying for play is no longer the foundation of a reliable "morality play" in sport, and it is not always clear which acts continue to count as controversial and which no longer provoke public outrage. Critical sociological theories and methods seek to counter approaches to sport scandals that offer decontextualized description over explanation, inflate their sociohistorical significance, or dismiss them as frivolous. Various permutations of the heroic rise, fall, and redemption narrative in sport scandals, appropriately analyzed, provide lessons about how society's "moral contours" (Wenner, 2013, p. x) and boundaries are drawn and redrawn. They reveal that, for transgressors to be judged incorrigible or granted a second chance, a combination of factors comes into play involving the nature of the infraction, the reactions of state and civil society, and, crucially, representation in the mediated public sphere. Sport scandals therefore are perpetually subject to evolving social, cultural, and political debates about sport as a social institution and the ethical responsibilities of those associated with it.

Debates

Sport scandals generate two principal modes of debate. The first revolves around the transgression and the degree of complicity of the institution of sport in it, alongside judgments of the roles and responsibilities of perpetrators and, if applicable, victims. The second concerns the scandal and the extent to which it is warranted, overexposed, or underplayed. Both debates are sociologically significant because they probe the structures of power in society, interrogating the ways in which the sport field, as the sociologist Pierre Bourdieu (1984/2010) conceives it, operates to distribute various forms of capital—social, cultural, economic, symbolic, and physical. Sport scandals entail a meeting of fields, with the media field crucial in influencing what is known about the world of sport and its wider social relations, and what remains relatively hidden (see Rowe & Boyle, this volume). As debates unfold, the construction and trajectory of sport scandals are shown to be highly variable in their propensity to resonate outside a sport field populated by formal organizations, businesses, sports workers, sport media agents, and fans.

Proportionality and Visibility

Sport, as argued, is scandal-prone because at its apex it is characterized by rigid rules, noble myths, commercial appeal, high media visibility, and passionate, partisan fandom. The high-pitched cultural tenor of "sportainment" is constantly reinforced by intense surveillance, some of it in real-time mediated contests, of sporting performance in a competitive context designed to produce winners and losers. Broadcast sports commentators and journalists have a vested interest in treating quite routine failings as scandalous because, in producing "noise," they project consequence onto the relatively inconsequential, and thereby generate attention that can be monetized. In contact sport contests, for example, a player may impede others by breaking the rules, such as by shirt-tugging or tripping in association football, or they may try to fool match officials by diving (so-called simulation), in pretending that they have been impeded. Those offended by such behavior—live-broadcast commentators or fans of the opposing team—often express *outrage*, a response that is a key building block of scandal. Globally there are millions of such moments every week when sport administrators, commentators, journalists, coaches, players, and fans perform as if something truly scandalous (defined, as noted, as a transgression of major societal importance) has occurred, but in most cases concern over such infractions will soon subside and be largely forgotten.

However, a small number of sporting transgressions witnessed live on television will be durable and extensive enough to take on the proportions of scandal. Usually, again in contact sport, these events will involve violence (the unsanctioned or excessive use of physical force; see Young, this volume), injury, or even death (Rowe, 2019a). The reaction to a sporting fatality, like that of the Australian cricketer Phillip Hughes, killed by a blow to the neck by a ball in 2014 (English, 2017), does not focus entirely on the athlete involved. It may concentrate more on the rules that allow or encourage intimidation, or on the dimensions of sporting culture that demand the ruthless pursuit of success. Sporting fatalities such as Hughes's require a literal postmortem and a coronial determination of the cause of death. They also put into perspective what might be regarded potentially as a legitimate scandal—placing sportspeople in jeopardy in pursuit of profit and popular pleasure—as opposed to a confected scandal stimulated by the need to generate viewers, readers, and "clicks."

But some occurrences with much less dire effects do produce scandals with some features characteristic of a moral panic. For example, the case of Sandpapergate, mentioned earlier, during a South Africa men's cricket match against Australia in Cape Town, the Australia captain, vice captain, and a junior player were involved in an act of illicit ball tampering that deployed a small sheet of sandpaper secreted in the trousers of the junior player that was detected by the umpires and cameras. Worldwide headlines resulted (although sometimes, as in the case of Davies, Leclere, & Moore, 2018, the initial details were inaccurate), even in countries with little interest in cricket, and the Australian prime minister said angrily that he was "shocked and bitterly disappointed" by the transgression (quoted in Rowe, 2019b, p. 329). This moral affront to playing sport honorably, especially in a game that has carefully cultivated its increasingly outmoded though much mythologized "gentlemanliness," created the perfect conditions for a sport scandal. Sandpapergate, in acquiring the suffix that inevitably likens the transgression to the scandal that led to the fall of U.S. President Richard Nixon, Watergate, is a measure of seriousness, albeit a much overused one (Hinkle, 2010). The idea of a sport scandal becoming a "-gate" has the essential element of conspiracy and cover-up, but it is a journalistic trope rather than a reliable indicator of the magnitude of the transgression. It may be, as here, exposed in plain sight but conceived beyond the public gaze.

Of particular importance to debates surrounding such scandals is the extent to which they can be limited to the sport field or spill over into wider social domains. One way in which sport organizations can seek to deflect criticism is to contend that the errant conduct, while lamentable, can also be found across whole societies. This argument is routinely made with regard to recreational drug use by sportspeople, which, while generally illegal and certainly proscribed by sport governing bodies, is in measures of scandalous conduct at the lower end of offenses, despite the banner headlines it provokes when discovered and punished. But the stakes are higher when involving, for example, racism, homophobia, or gendered violence (Rowe, 2019a). Most such offenses are not, like foul play on the field, able to be easily witnessed by large numbers of people. Instead, they must be detected, perhaps through the use of professional lip readers interpreting on-screen utterances (hence the now common covering of the mouth by abusive sportspeople), formal inquiries, camera phones or police reports. Often they do not occur in a sporting context, but in the street, hotel, or private home, and in such cases it may be asked whether they constitute sport scandals simply because they involve perpetrators connected to sport. For example, violence involving intimate partners or casual acquaintances is a much more serious matter than cheating in sport via performance-enhancing drugs, but it does not determine the outcomes of sport contests, and the victims' only connection to sport may be via the violent offender. Perversely, then, criminal acts by sportspeople may be treated as less scandalous (that is, receive less media coverage and condemnation of the assailant) than those that are principally offenses against sport itself. For this reason, critical debates surrounding sport scandals require closer attention to questions of proportionality regarding the actual offense rather than privileging the visibility arising from media coverage and the clamor produced by affective fandom.

Questions of proportionality also raise the issue of whether sport scandals matter. They can be salacious and messy affairs that point to individual failings on the part of the transgressor. Most are ephemeral (although permanently on the record) and quickly replaced in the news cycle by the next series of emergent scandals. In some cases, however, the effects of a scandal are more extensive and longer lasting. Where institutions of sport (rather than individuals) are implicated, and systemic patterns of transgressive social practices traced and evidenced, a different scandal dynamic can contribute to important social action and policy change. Indeed, policy shifts within and by federal governments, nongovernment organizations, national sport governing bodies, and supranational organizations such as the International Olympic Committee or Union Cycliste Internationale, all evidence how a chain of events—from successive scandals triggering a call to action through to changes in policy and governance—can lead to longer-term systemic and structural change in sport and society.

Scandals and Policy Change

Houlihan (2005) notes that policy often emerges out of "crisis." At a national level, sport and social policies have been developed by governments and sport governing organizations in response to scandals of institutionalized misconduct, including sexual abuse, doping, and racial vilification. At an international level, global governing bodies have implemented whole-of-sport policies in response to instances of doping, athlete maltreatment, and abuse in sport when they have entered the mediated public sphere as scandals. Antidoping policy development is one area in which significant policy change has been prompted by successive crises. The death of the Danish cyclist Knud Jensen at the Rome Olympic Games in 1960 led the IOC to address athlete welfare by establishing a Medical Commission (Dimeo, 2007).

The death of Tom Simpson in the 1967 Tour de France was the catalyst for the Council of Europe to enter the antidoping policy arena (Houlihan, 2011), and the positive drug test of Canadian sprinter Ben Johnson at the Seoul Summer Olympics in 1988 resulted in a major policy change toward doping by the Canadian government and by the IOC (Dubin, 1990), where doping was cast as a moral and ethical as well as a health problem (Hunt, 2011). These scandals, all of which garnered enormous media coverage, were followed by the Festina Affair at the 1998 Tour de France, when the entire Festina cycling squad was expelled from the race after a team car was stopped, searched, and found to contain large supplies of performance-enhancing drugs. This event triggered multiple police investigations, arrests, and convictions (Smith, 2017). The admission by the team's director of sport, Bruno Roussel, to French police that doping was a systematic practice within the team, led to a formal inquiry and police action that then changed policy and practice in the sport. The introduction of athlete biological passports in cycling followed in monitoring long-term changes in the bodily markers of drug use (Smith, 2017). Although these individual doping scandals mark out telling cultural patterns in sport (here, cycling), Plassard, Ohl, and Schoch (2020) also note that, cumulatively, they can highlight the challenges for institutional redemption as sports attempt to rebuild credibility in the face of widespread public mistrust and condemnation.

The wider governance of sport can also change following a scandal and ensuing public debate. The Australian Crime Commission's claims of the involvement of organized crime and the call for greater institutional accountability following the "darkest day in Australian sport," for example, was instrumental in the establishment of the Integrity in Sport Commission in Australia (Coughlan, 2020). The IOC has similarly been compelled to adopt new modes of governance and organizational accountability following scandals relating to athlete abuse. Many cases of maltreatment have been reported (Kerr, Wilson, & Stirling, 2019) where athletes at different levels (e.g., children, adolescents, adults, and elite) and across sporting contexts (including gymnastics, swimming, athletics, and football) have been subjected to multiple forms of abuse (e.g., emotional, sexual, and physical) (Lang, 2020). These scandals have resulted in federal investigations and subsequent convictions (see Hartill, this volume) and provided the impetus for the IOC's Consensus Statement on harassment and abuse (Mountjoy et al., 2016), which calls for structural and cultural change to prevent the ill treatment of athletes. The notorious arrests for corruption at the 2015 FIFA Congress in Zurich also led to governance change and pressured the newly reelected FIFA president, Sepp Blatter, to resign (Rowe, 2017). At such moments, scandals can precipitate major reforms across the whole sport field.

Scandals and Institutional Change

In Australia, a range of policies has been developed in response to scandals relating to sexual misconduct and racism. A series of scandals involving sexual assault led to the creation of the Australian Football League's ([AFL] 2005) Respect and Responsibility Policy. The National Vilification and Discrimination policy framework (Australian Football League, 2013) was then formulated in an attempt to counter incidents of racial, sexual, and other forms of vilification or discrimination in the AFL. As with the development of antidoping policy in Europe, the formulation of policies relating both to racism and sexual misconduct in the

AFL was prompted by the amplification of crises of sporting organizations and forceful public demands for victims and complainants to have appropriate avenues of redress.

Policy agenda are set by both endogenous and exogenous events. Changes to governance following allegations of systemic racism within the Collingwood AFL football club provides an example here. Collingwood is one of the 18 teams that make up the men's AFL. Following complaints from former player Héritier Lumumba (2020) that the club had a racist culture, in 2020 the club's board commissioned an independent investigation into racism and cultural safety. A key finding of the "Do Better" Report was that Collingwood had a culture of "structural racism" and that the board needed "to drive structural change within the organisation" (Holmes, 2021). Such change might have begun with little fanfare or media glare, but the club's president, Eddie McGuire, held a media conference (with Collingwood CEO Mark Anderson and club Integrity Committee members Jodie Sizer and Peter Murphy), where he declared the release of the report to be a "historic and proud day" for Collingwood. McGuire—a divisive and omnipresent figure in Australian public culture, with a record of insensitive comments about Indigenous footballers (Heenan & Dunstan, 2013)—found himself again at the center of a media scandal. Following mounting condemnation of McGuire's language at the press conference and calls for him to step down (Estcourt, 2021), he tendered his resignation eight days later.

The Collingwood case highlights the fast-moving nature of scandal amplification. Lamentably, racism at the club was not in itself the scandal, because there was little surprising evidence in the report. Yet it quickly escalated to scandal status through the media and public response to McGuire's ill-judged media conference image management (Wilson, 2021). The scandal did, however, accelerate progressive organizational change. The appointment of an antiracism expert group, comprising leaders drawn from Indigenous and culturally and linguistically diverse communities, presented a new model for leadership for the AFL and for sports governance in general (Gould, 2021). Indeed, far from being frivolous dramas of transgression and misdemeanor, scandals of this kind can serve important functions by calling organizations and individuals to account and in bringing about significant cultural and policy change.

CONCLUSION

This chapter has assessed various ways in which sport scandals are sociologically relevant. As mediated public events, they are particularly useful for interrogating wider social logics and provide an intense focus for analyzing contemporary sociocultural politics in contexts ranging from the hyperlocal to the global. As we have demonstrated, some sport scandals have material effects by building momentum for change in the policies and practices of governments, commercial corporations, and sport organizations, and affect wider social attitudes, values, and behavior. So they always have some capacity to resonate well beyond transgressions that vested interests routinely try first to cover up, and then to marginalize and underplay. Often an organization will claim that a problem, even if it exists, has been exaggerated, is rare and individualized or, contrastingly, so common that it is society at large that is to blame. An important, developing role of critical sociologists of sport is to counter such strategies by "joining the dots" and highlighting the historical continuities and institutional connections that create the conditions for scandal and to provide clear indications of ways in which damaging social transgressions in and around sport can be exposed, challenged, managed, discouraged, and even eradicated.

Two key issues around which sport scandals revolve are "race" and gender, sometimes in combination. A scandal may involve direct (such as racial vilification or sexual assault) or indirect (like sport and media organizations blaming and stigmatizing victims) racism and sexism. Therefore, the complexity of sport scandals needs to be recognized and their analysis should avoid replicating the tabloid media headlines that offer simple, decontextualized narratives, explanations, and solutions. With regard to gender, there is no doubt that the majority of sport scandals involve transgressions by men. As sport, like governments, major businesses, and other social institutions and organizations, is traditionally male-dominated, men have long been in a position to abuse their power. Sport and other such loci of male power are under increasing pressure to relinquish masculine control in pursuit of gender equity. As women's sport grows in popularity and influence worldwide, and women athletes become well-known public faces recognized in nightclubs and on streets, it is quite possible that more women will be implicated as perpetrators in sport scandals. This is not, of course, to propose that sportswomen will simply replicate the bad behavior of some sportsmen, but that the opportunities to transgress in some way and to be "caught" will necessarily increase with visibility and celebrity. An example is the charging of NRLW player Nita Maynard after she allegedly assaulted two security guards outside a Sydney pub (Keoghan, 2021). New research opportunities, then, are likely to emerge concerning the gendering of sport scandals in considering whether and how women athletes transgress, both on and off the field, in ways that resemble and differ from men. Research of this kind would offer important new knowledge about the dynamic gender order of sport and wider society, looking past scandal hyperbole to highlight the centrality of social structural issues and relations of power.

Finally, in reflecting on the sport scandal and the rise-fall-rise narrative arc, there is a need for more work on the limits of redemption within the ecology of scandal. Under what circumstances can perpetrators be "forgiven," and when are they "irredeemable"? Some transgressions may breach, in traditional anthropological and sociological terms, a taboo. The abuse of minors by coaches or spousal homicide by athletes, for example, would be expected to constitute transgressions that would be beyond redemption, but what others in changing societies with lively social media networks now qualify as taboo? Future research and scholarship on sport scandals should therefore always address the nature of the transgression, the reaction, the relationship between them, and the outcome.

References

Agyemang, K. (2011). Athlete brand revitalisation after a transgression. *Journal of Sponsorship*, 4(2), 137–144.

Allison, R., Pegoraro, A., Frederick, E., & Thompson, A. (2019). When women athletes transgress: An exploratory study of image repair and social media response. *Sport in Society*, 23(3), 1–23.

Andrews, D., & Jackson, S. (2001). *Sport stars: The cultural politics of sporting celebrity*. London: Routledge.

Andrews, D., & Silk. M. (2010). Basketball's ghettocentric logic. *American Behavioral Scientist,* *53*, 1626–1664.

Associated Press. (1995, October 24). Murder rate fell in 1994 for 3rd consecutive year, agency says. *New York Times*, p. 19.

Australian Associated Press. (2021, March 10). Jarryd Hayne trial: Woman denies she thought they would have sex when he came over. *The Guardian*. https://www. theguardian.com/sport/2021/mar/10/jarryd-hayne-trial-woman-denies-she-thou ght-they-would-have-sex-when-he-came-over.

Australian Crime Commission. (2013). Threats to the integrity of professional sport in Australia. Crime Profile Series, Organised Crime in Professional Sport. http://www.crim ecommission.gov.au/sites/default/files/files/Professional_sports_Factsheet_251111.pdf.

Australian Football League. (2013). National vilification and discrimination policy. https:// www.afl.com.au/clubhelp/policies/member-protection-and-integrity/national-vilification-and-discrimination-policy.

Australian Football League. (2005). Respect and responsibility policy. https://s.afl.com.au/sta ticfile/AFL%20Tenant/AFL/Files/AFL-Respect-and-Responsibility-Policy.pdf.

Baker, A., & Boyd, T. (Eds.). (1997). *Out of bounds: Sports, media, and the politics of identity.* Bloomington: Indiana University Press.

Becker, H. S. (1963). *Outsiders: Studies in the sociology of deviance*. New York: Free Press.

Bisbort, A. (2008). *Media scandals*. Westport, CT: Greenwood.

Blackshaw, T., & Crabbe, T. (2004). *New perspectives on sport and "deviance": Consumption, performativity, and social control*. London: Routledge.

Bourdieu, P. (1984/2010). *Distinction: A social critique of the judgement of taste.* London: Routledge.

Boyle, R. (2006). *Sports journalism: Contexts and issues*. London: Sage.

Boyle, R. (2019). *Changing sports journalism practice in the age of digital media.* London: Routledge.

Brown, K. A. (2014). Is apology the best policy? An experimental examination of the effectiveness of image repair strategies during criminal and noncriminal athlete transgressions. *Communication & Sport, 4*(1), 23–42.

Carrington, B. (2010). *Race, sport and politics: The sporting Black diaspora*. London: Sage.

Clarke, J., & Critcher, C. (1985). *The devil makes work: Leisure in capitalist Britain.* London: Macmillan.

Cohen, S. (2002). *Folk devils and moral panics: The creation of the mods and rockers* (3rd ed.). London: Routledge.

Coughlan, M. (2020, February 25). Sport Integrity Australia to tackle doping. *Canberra Times*. https://www.canberratimes.com.au/story/6647035/sport-integrity-australia-to-tackle-doping.

Couldry, N., & Hepp, A. (2016). *The mediated construction of reality*. Oxford: Polity.

Davies, G., Leclere, M., & Moore, C. (2018, March 25). Is this the moment Australia cheated against England in the ASHES? Player at the centre of scandal caught on camera appearing to pour sugar into his pocket "to tamper with the ball." *The Daily Mail/Mail Online*. http:// www.dailymail.co.uk/news/article-5541529/Is-moment-Australia-cheated-against-Engl and-ASHES.html.

Dimeo, P. (2007). *A history of drug use in sport, 1876–1976: Beyond good and evil.* London: Routledge.

Dionne, E. (2020, January 28). We can only process Kobe Bryant's death by being honest about his life. *Time.* https://time.com/5773151/kobe-bryant-rape-case-complicated-legacy/.

Doherty, L. (2013, February 8). Did Australian sport's darkest day come too soon? *The Roar.* https://www.theroar.com.au/2013/02/09/did-australian-sports-darkest-day-come-too-soon/.

Dubin, C. L. (1990). *Commission of inquiry into the use of drugs and banned practices intended to increase athletic performance.* Ottawa: Canadian Government Publishing Centre.

English, P. (2017). The death of Phillip Hughes: Commemorative journalism and the cricket community, *Communication & Sport, 5*(1), 95–109.

Estcourt, D. (2021, February 9). "Unacceptable and insulting": Open letter calls on McGuire to quit. *The Age.* https://www.theage.com.au/national/victoria/unacceptable-and-insulting-open-letter-calls-on-mcguire-to-quit-20210208-p570on.html.

Evans, A. B., Agergaard, S., Campbell, P. I., Hylton, K., & Lenneis, V. (2020). "Black Lives Matter": Sport, race and ethnicity in challenging times. *European Journal for Sport and Society, 17*(4), 289–300.

Ferner, A. (Producer). (2014). *OJ: Trial of the century* [film]. Every Hill Films/RAW.

Fordyce, T. (2015, June 15). Sports stars behaving badly: Have they lost touch with reality? *BBC Sport.* https://www.bbc.com/sport/33098940.

Frandsen, K. (2019). *Sport and mediatization.* London: Routledge.

Geertsema-Sligh, M., & Worthington, N. (2020). News constructions of South Africa's trial of the century: Identity discourse in the Steenkamp shooting and Pistorius trial. *Journalism Studies, 21*(15), 2196–2213.

Gordon, M. (2013, February 8). Blackest day in Australian sport. *Sydney Morning Herald.* https://www.smh.com.au/sport/blackest-day-in-australian-sport-20130207-2e1mb.html.

Gould, R. (2021, February 17). Collingwood has set up an expert "anti-racism" group in response to a bombshell report about the club's racist past. *The Australian.* https://www.theaustralian.com.au/sport/afl/collingwood-has-set-up-an-expert-antiracism-group-in-response-to-a-bombshell-report-about-the-clubs-racist-past/news-story/09300d71049986fb227e5a5562bc2e74.

Hargreaves, J. (1986). *Sport, power and culture: A social and historical analysis of popular sports in Britain.* Cambridge, U.K.: Polity.

Harrington, C. L., & Schimmel, K. (2013). Andre Agassi and the tides of tennis celebrity: Image, reconstruction and confession. In L. A. Wenner (Ed.), *Fallen sports heroes: Media and celebrity culture* (pp. 63–76). New York: Peter Lang.

Heenan, T., & Dunstan. D. (2013, May 31). Eddie McGuire, Adam Goodes and "apes": A landmark moment in Australian race relations. *The Conversation.* https://theconversation.com/eddie-mcguire-adam-goodes-and-apes-a-landmark-moment-in-australian-race-relations-14840.

Hinkle, B. (2010, November 25). Prefix-gate: Sports history's most notable crimes and scandals. *Bleacher Report.* https://bleacherreport.com/articles/527039-suffixgate-notable-crime-and-scandal-in-sports-history.

Holmes, T. (2021, February 1). Collingwood football club is guilty of systemic racism, review finds. Australian Broadcasting Corporation. https://www.abc.net.au/news/2021-02-01/collingwood-is-guilty-of-systemic-racism-review-finds/13055816.

Houlihan. B. (2005). Public sector sport policy: Developing a framework for analysis. *International Review for the Sociology of Sport, 40*(2), 163–187.

Houlihan, B. (2011). Doping and the Olympics: Rights, responsibilities and accountabilities (watching the athletes). In. J. Sugden & A. Tomlinson (Eds.), *Watching the Olympics: Politics, power and representation* (pp. 94–104). London: Routledge.

Hunt, D. M. (1999). *O. J. Simpson facts and fictions: News rituals in the construction of reality.* Cambridge: Cambridge University Press.

Hunt, T. M. (2011). *Drugs games: The International Olympic Committee and the politics of doping, 1960–2008.* Austin: University of Texas Press.

Hutchins, B., & Rowe, D. (2012). *Sport beyond television: The internet, digital media and the rise of networked media sport.* New York: Routledge.

Jackson, R. (2020, January 16). Nick Kyrgios: How tennis's loudest talent became a hero to the quiet Australians. *The Guardian.* https://www.theguardian.com/sport/2020/jan/16/nick-kyrgios-how-tenniss-loudest-talent-became-a-hero-to-the-quiet-australians.

Jennings, A., & Sambrook, C. (2000). *The great Olympic swindle: When the world wanted its Games back.* London: Simon and Schuster.

Jones, C. (2014). Alcoholism and recovery: A case study of a former professional footballer. *International Review for the Sociology of Sport, 49*(3–4), 485–505.

Kantola, A., & Vesa, J. (2013). Mediated scandals as social dramas: Transforming the moral order in Finland. *Acta Sociologica, 56*(4), 295–308.

Keoghan, S. (2021, April 4). She is shattered: NRLW player charged after allegedly assaulting Northies bouncers. *Sydney Morning Herald.* https://www.smh.com.au/sport/nrl/she-is-shattered-nrlw-player-charged-after-allegedly-assaulting-northies-bouncers-20210404-p57gdf.html.

Kerr, G., Battaglia, A., & Stirling, A. (2019). Maltreatment in youth sport: A systemic issue. *Kinesiology Review, 8*(3), 237–243.

Kerr, G., Willson E., & Stirling, A. (2019). *Prevalence of maltreatment among current and former national team athletes.* Toronto: University of Toronto/AthletesCAN.

Knaus, C. (2018, March 31). Whose idea what is? Who took the sandpaper? The questions David Warner didn't answer. *The Guardian.* https://www.theguardian.com/sport/2018/mar/31/whose-idea-was-it-who-took-the-sandpaper-the-questions-david-warner-didnt-answer.

Lang, M. (Ed.). (2020). *The Routledge handbook of athlete welfare.* London: Routledge.

Leonard, D. J., & King, C. R. (2011). Lack of Black opps: Kobe Bryant and the difficult path of redemption. *Journal of Sport and Social Issues, 35*(2), 209–223.

Lines, G. (2001). Villains, fools or heroes? Sports stars as role models for young people. *Leisure Studies, 20*(4), 285–303.

Lull, J., & Hinerman, S. (1997). The search for scandal. In J. Lull & S. Hinerman (Eds.), *Media scandals: Morality and desire in the popular culture marketplace* (pp. 1–33). Cambridge, U.K.: Polity, Columbia University Press.

Lumumba, H. (2020, June 25). I found racism runs through the AFL—it has failed to uphold the rights and safety of Black players. *The Guardian.* https://www.theguardian.com/sport/2020/jun/25/i-foundracism-runs-through-the-afl-it-has-failed-to-uphold-the-rights-and-safety-of-black-players.

Mandell, H., & Chen, G. M. (Eds.). (2016). *Scandal in a digital age.* New York: Palgrave Macmillan.

Mark, D. (2021, February 25). Tiger Woods took the golfing world by storm—his highs and lows have made headlines ever since. ABC News. https://www.abc.net.au/news/2021-02-25/how-tiger-woods-became-golfs-biggest-star/13187832.

Markovitz, J. (2006). Anatomy of a spectacle: Race, gender, and memory in the Kobe Bryant rape case. *Sociology of Sport Journal, 23*(4), 396–418.

Mersiades, B. (2018). *Whatever it takes: The inside story of the FIFA way.* Cheyenne, WY: Powderhouse Press.

Mountjoy, M., Brackenridge, C., Arrington, M., Blauwet, C., Carska-Sheppard, A., Fasting, K., . . . Budgett, R. (2016). International Olympic Committee consensus statement: Harassment and abuse (non-accidental violence) in sport. *British Journal of Sports Medicine, 50*, 1019–1029. doi:10.1136/bjsports-2016-096121.

Newberry, L., & La Ganga, M. L. (2020, February 4). For survivors of sexual assault, Kobe Bryant's legacy is complicated. *Los Angeles Times.* https://www.latimes.com/california/story/2020-02-04/kobe-bryant-sexual-assault-survivors-legacy.

Palmer, C. (2014). Drinking, downfall and redemption: Biographies and athlete addicts. *Celebrity Studies, 7*(2), 169–182.

Palmer, C. (2015). On controversies and scandals. *International Review for the Sociology of Sport, 50*(4–5), 558–562.

Parry, K. D. (2020). The formation of heroes and the myth of national identity. *Sport in Society.* https://doi.org/10.1080/17430437.2020.1733531.

Plassard, F., Ohl, F., & Schoch, L. (2020). Cycling alone: Team Sky's difficult quest for credibility during the 2015 Tour de France. *International Review for the Sociology of Sport, 56*(2), 212–232.

Rapp, T. (2011, October 29). What will be the next big sports scandal? *Bleacher Report.* https://bleacherreport.com/articles/914888-what-will-be-the-next-big-sports-scandal.

Rowe, D. (2004). *Sport, culture and the media: The unruly trinity* (2nd ed.). Maidenhead, U.K.: Open University Press, McGraw-Hill Education.

Rowe, D. (2009). The concept of the moral panic: An historico-sociological positioning. In D. Lemmings & C. Walker (Eds.), *Moral panics, the press and the law in early modern England* (pp. 22–40). New York: Palgrave Macmillan.

Rowe, D. (2011). *Global media sport: Flows, forms and futures.* London: Bloomsbury Academic.

Rowe, D. (2014). Gender, media and the sport scandal. In J. Hargreaves & E. Anderson (Eds.), *Handbook of sport, gender, and sexuality* (pp. 470–479). London: Routledge.

Rowe, D. (2017). Sports journalism and the FIFA scandal: Personalization, co-optation, investigation. *Communication & Sport, 5*(5), 515–533.

Rowe, D. (2019a). Gendered violence in, of and by sport news. In C. Carter, L. Steiner, & S. Allan (Eds.), *Journalism, gender and power* (pp. 128–143). London: Routledge.

Rowe, D. (2019b). Scandals and sport. In H. Tumber & S. Waisbord (Eds.), *Routledge companion to media and scandal* (pp. 324–332). London: Routledge.

Smith, C. (2017). Tour du dopage: Confessions of doping professional cyclists in a modern work environment. *International Review for the Sociology of Sport, 52*(1), 97–111.

Starn, O. (2011). *The passion of Tiger Woods.* Durham, NC: Duke University Press.

Thompson, J. B. (2000). *Political scandal: Power and visibility in the media age.* Cambridge, U.K.: Polity.

Tiffen, R. (1999). *Scandals: Media, politics and corruption in contemporary Australia.* Sydney: University of New South Wales Press.

Tiffen, R. (2019). Moral panics. In H. Tumber & S. Waisbord (Eds.), *Routledge companion to media and scandal* (pp. 46–54). London: Routledge.

Tomlinson, J. (1997). "And besides, the wench is dead": Media scandals and the globalization of communication. In J. Lull & S. Hinerman (Eds), *Media scandals: Morality and desire in the popular culture marketplace* (pp. 65–84). Cambridge, U.K.: Polity: Columbia University Press.

Toobin, J. (2016). *The People vs. O. J. Simpson: The run of his life.* London: Arrow.

Tumber, H., & Waisbord, S. (Eds.). (2019). *Routledge companion to media and scandal.* London: Routledge.

Walsh, D. (2015). *Seven deadly sins: My pursuit of Lance Armstrong.* New York: Atria.

Wenner, L. A. (Ed.). (1998). *MediaSport.* London: Routledge.

Wenner, L. A. (Ed.). (2013). *Fallen sports heroes, media and celebrity culture.* New York: Peter Lang.

Whannel, G. (1999). Sports stars, narrativization and masculinities. *Leisure Studies, 18*(3), 249–265.

Whannel, G. (2002). *Media sport stars: Masculinities and moralities.* London: Routledge.

White, E., & Nichols, A. (2021, February 26). Ex-US Olympics gymnastics coach charged with human trafficking dies. *Sydney Morning Herald.* https://www.smh.com.au/sport/force-fraud-and-coercion-ex-us-olympics-gymnastics-coach-charged-with-human-trafficking-20210226-p5760g.html.

Williams, C. (2021, February 10). Nick Kyrgios calls Djokovic a "tool" after tennis quarantine demands, takes shot at Bernard Tomic's girlfriend. *Huffington Post.* https://www.huffingtonpost.com.au/entry/nick-kyrgios-calls-djokovic-a-tool-australian-open_au_6006215fc5b697df1a083b6b.

Wilson, C. (2021, April 13). Ed, it should never have ended like this. *The Age.* https://www.theage.com.au/sport/afl/ed-it-should-never-have-ended-like-this-20210209-p570zg.html.

Wynn, N. (2003). Deconstructing Tyson: The Black boxer as American icon. *International Journal for the History of Sport, 20*(3), 9–114.

CHAPTER 30

··

SPORT, SOCIAL MOVEMENTS, AND ATHLETE ACTIVISM

··

DOUGLAS HARTMANN

SINCE its inception, modern sport has celebrated itself as an arena of social progress and change—a positive force for unity and solidarity, peace, and cross-cultural understanding, as well as in its contributing to struggles against racism and social injustices and, more recently, supporting movements for human rights, gender equity, and social development. However, progressive social change *in* sport, as well as social change in society *through* sport, has rarely been automatic or inevitable. To the contrary, sport-based social progress has almost always required self-conscious criticism, organized mobilization, and strategic resistance, and has typically brought along with it tension, conflict, counterresistance, and outright backlash, responses often fostered by sports leaders and the athletic establishment itself. The dynamics of progress and change in and through sport are further complicated by sport's complicity with profit and power, as well as by sport's own aversion to politics. Indeed, for many, there is a belief that sport and politics "shouldn't mix." In spite of (or because of) all this, movements and activism have been an essential part of sport's history and its complicated relationship to progressive ideals and broader societal change (Coakley, 2015; Kilcline, 2017; Nauright & Wiggins, 2017; Zirin, 2008).

Sport-based activism and athlete protest typically emerge in relationship to broader struggles for justice, equity, and inclusion outside of sport. And much like social movements themselves, sociological scholarship on sport activism and broader social movements ebbs and flows over time. With the emergence of a new and unprecedented wave of athletic activism in the past decade (Agyemang, Singer, & Weems, 2020; Cooky & Antunovic, 2020; Hartmann, 2019; Lawrence, 2020; Valiente, 2019; see also Wikipedia, 2020), sport studies have witnessed a veritable explosion of new research and theory on the topic. One of the most basic insights of this emerging body of work is that sport is a powerful platform for calling attention to all manner of social issues and injustices (Kaufman & Wolfe, 2010). Another is that athletes, especially athletes from various marginalized and disadvantaged backgrounds, are the drivers of the most powerful moments and significant movements in and around sport (Cunningham et al., 2019). Nevertheless, assessing the impact and effectiveness of sport-based activism remains a challenge.

Many other basic and underlying questions remain as well: What drives sport-based activism and movements, and what constrains them? How can athletic movements be most effective or impactful? And why is activism in and through sport so controversial and challenging in the first place? This chapter examines how sport scholars conceptualize these issues, the new and established empirical research on sport-based movements and activism they have conducted, and new developments in the field. It is an exploration that reveals a great deal about the cultural power of sport as well as the difficulty of making concrete, material change both in and through the athletic arena.

Issues

There is a large and well-established body of work on collective action and social movements in mainstream, disciplinary sociology (cf. Della Porta & Diani, 2020; Marx & McAdam, 1994). Typically seen as a branch of political sociology, this literature is based upon an understanding of the power of activism, protest, and resistance for bringing attention to social injustices and public problems and advocating for needed social change.

Among its contributions, social movements scholarship has highlighted the crucial role of organizations and resources in movement organizing (classic "resource mobilization" theory), established the importance of framing (Benford & Snow, 2000), categorized tactics and protest repertoires (McAdam, 1983), and, more recently, theorized the dynamics of opposition and backlash (Earl, 2003; Hess & Martin, 2006) and documented how culture, identity, and emotions drive and determine both activism and boundary-making within activism (Wang, Piazza, & Soule, 2018), especially in so-called new social movements. While sport scholars tend not to engage with the mainstream sociological literature on collective action and social movements directly (for an important exception, see Davis-Delano & Crossett, 2008, this broader body of research informs the bulk of sport-based research and theory on these topics.

Terms and Concepts

As with the general movements literature, sport scholars use many different concepts and terms to identify, conceptualize, and analyze sport-based organizing and activism: protest, advocacy, resistance, struggle, opposition, mobilization; social movements, social movement organizations, and resource mobilization; collective behavior and/or collective action; revolution, transformation, and social change. What unifies and undergirds most of these terms, and indeed the subfield itself, is the attention to actors, initiatives, and groups organized by athletes and others in and around the sporting establishment that speak on social problems and matters of social inequality and/or push for change of some sort. Because they are set in contrast to established institutional and/or governmental processes and conventional electoral politics, social movements and activism are sometimes referred to as extra-institutional or contentious politics, politics by other means, or, as in Scott's (1985) well-known formulation "weapons of the weak."

Of all the terms in the social movements lexicon, "social change" is perhaps the most complicated and least theorized. One reason is that social change in the modern world is ubiquitous and unrelenting; capitalism, for example, is a dynamic social system predicated on the need for constant productivity, innovation, and economic growth. This means that movements are not just a matter of pushing for change in the face of stasis; rather, they require a critical sense of what is problematic or unjust about existing social arrangements as well as some strategy for how to move in new directions or operate on new terms. Here, it should be noted that while sport-based movements often proceed from clear critiques and causes, they sometimes lack viable, strategic goals and understandings of the resources and skills necessary to effectively combat the entrenched power and privilege of the established order. *Making* social change, in other words, is much harder than just calling for something different, and it often requires working within or through existing institutions rather than just standing in opposition to them, as well as a willingness to embrace and endure conflict.

Topics

Here, it is important to note that sport scholars who study movements—as is the case for movement scholars in general (cf. Blee & Creasap, 2010)—have a strong tendency to associate activism with actors, initiatives, and events in service of conventionally liberal and progressive causes, to the relative neglect of more conservative or even reactionary agendas. In international circles, in fact, some traditionalists go so far as to hold up the Olympic Movement as the source of the true spirit and high ideals of sport, fighting an ongoing battle against the Olympic "industry," which includes all of the nefarious exploitative, unethical, and even destructive elements bound up with promoting and staging the Games as a global corporate endeavor (cf. Kidd, 2013; MacAloon, 2016).

Struggles against racism, anti-Blackness, white supremacy, and racial inequality are at the center of a great deal of athletic organizing and activism, especially in the United States (cf. Bryant, 2018; Zirin, 2005), and as such tend to dominate the research and theory of sport scholars. This pattern was exemplified in the summer of 2020, which witnessed a global explosion of athletically based social awareness, advocacy, and activism on behalf of the Black Lives Matter movement in the wake of the killing of George Floyd in Minneapolis, Minnesota. Given the visibility and excellence of athletes of color in many of the most popular and profitable sports in the global sports world, as well as sport's historic claims for being an avenue of opportunity, equality, and mobility, this emphasis is probably not surprising.

The focus on race-based activism is also associated with (and a driver of) the tendency for sport-based social movements to prioritize greater access, opportunity, and inclusion across the athletic landscape and in social life. However, the preeminence of race can make it easy to overlook activism and movements based on other social problems and dimensions of inequality and injustice—sexism and patriarchy, homophobia, ability bias, exploitative labor practices and skyrocketing economic inequalities, globalization, climate change and environmental degradation, antifascism, and the like. The almost singular emphasis on race, furthermore, makes it difficult to recognize and theorize the more multifaceted, intersectional approach—where issues of racism are intertwined, for instance, with problems of sexism and homophobia or the excesses of global capitalism—that many contemporary activists now bring to their advocacy and protest. Diverse and encompassing as this list may be, it also signals that the political orientation for athletic activism is on a continuum that stretches essentially from reformist to radical.

Unique Characteristics

For all of the parallels with mainstream movement research, activism and protest in, around, and through sport presents its own unique set of analytic challenges. Some of these stem from sport's own cultural prominence in the social world. Indeed, the cultural centrality of and mass media attention that is placed on sport are integral to the resulting visibility of athlete activism. When it comes to cultural prominence, there is, literally, no comparable institution or set of practices in the world like sport. Fundamental as well are the many ways in which sport is dependent upon and complicit with power and profit in the modern world—relationships facilitated by its structural nexus with nationalism, militarism, and the state, transnational corporations and global capitalism, sexism and patriarchy, heteronormativity, gentrification, urban development, and environmental exploitation. Such tendencies are amplified by the social and political conservativism of leaders in the sporting establishment as well as that of many sports fans themselves. In fact, when these conservative, and even reactionary elements are set against sport's positive, progressive ideals, good arguments may be made for theorizing sport as a "contested social terrain" (Birrell & Theberge, 1994; Carrington, 2010; Messner, 1988)—as an arena that is not singular or unified but rather a complicated, even contradictory multidimensional field marked by a large number of prominent organizations and events with an incredible array of political orientations, ideologies, and forces (see also Gruneau, 1988; Hall, 1994).

Perhaps the most tricky and idiosyncratic dimensions of both activism and analysis in the contested terrain of sport involve sport's complicated relationship to politics—or, more precisely, the combination of deeply rooted ideals about sport, cultural beliefs about politics, and long-standing taboos about the need to keep these two unique socio-institutional fields separate and distinct (Green & Hartmann, 2014).

Sport, Protest, and Politics

On the one hand, sport is often idealized as a kind of pure, safe, and special place, an almost sacred sociocultural sphere that transcends the conflicts and complexities of regular social life. Politics, on the other hand, is assumed to be the opposite: complicated, contested, and inherently bound up with power, conflict, and social struggle. At least by Western cultural conventions, then, sport and politics are set in opposition to each other, and, more specifically, it is often believed that sport needs to be protected from the intrusion or contamination of the political realm. Protest, in this schema, is rendered as just a more extreme or amplified version of politics—used by people in society who lack traditional power and resources to foment division, push for social change, or even just make their voices heard.

These cultural norms are, of course, constructed and aspirational. Sport is always bound up with the complexities of social life, whether it is realized and acknowledged or not. Calls for unity always imply—indeed are built upon—other social differences and distinctions. The use of anthems and flags or military tributes in sport ceremonies may be organic or inspiring for some, but not necessarily for those who are marginalized by dominant conceptions of the nation or left out of them altogether (McDonald, 2020). And again, and perhaps most directly to the point, concrete change in and through sport, for instance in terms of increased access or inclusion, has almost always provoked a good deal of conflict and opposition—or, put differently, has been the product of the agency of activist critique and collective resistance.

Nevertheless, these cultural convictions, or "myths" as Coakley (2015) might call them, run deep. And, connected as they are with sport's own self-satisfied ideology about being an arena of meritocracy, fairness, advancement for the disempowered and all of the better things in life (Serazio, 2019), they make activism in sport difficult because such activism almost immediately and by logical definition calls into question the accuracy and universalizability of sport's own founding ideologies. "If sport is automatically and inevitably progressive," the received wisdom goes, "then protest, activism, and conflict shouldn't be necessary." In other words, these ideals enable advocacy and change in certain arenas and on certain topics, but they also constitute the outer limits of all sport-based activism and change (see Henderson, 2009 with respect to the limitations for civil right protest). Suffice it to say, these cultural constructions and social forces not only present challenges to mobilization in and through sport, but they also help to focus and frame the approaches sport scholars take to analyzing athletically oriented activism.

APPROACHES

There are two features that distinguish the scholarly literature on sport-centered activism and social change. One is that, at least until very recently, most knowledge and theory have derived from research on a fairly limited number of cases—case studies, more specifically, of high-profile incidents and protests, often with elite celebrity athletes at the center (cf. Boykoff, 2017; Hartmann, 2019; Schmidt, Frederick, Pegoraro, & Spencer, 2019). The antiapartheid boycott of South African sport would be one prominent, historical case in point (Booth, 1998). The other is the previously mentioned emphasis on race-based athletic activism and organizing; this especially has been the case in recent years and in the North American context.

There is no better example of how these two defining characteristics combine and thus inform research and theory than the 1968 Black Olympic activism in the United States— the movement inspired by Muhammad Ali that is most famously associated with Tommie Smith and John Carlos's iconic clenched first salute on the victory stand in Mexico City. Ever since Harry Edwards's (1969/2020) initial account, *The Revolt of the Black Athlete*, a virtual cottage industry of scholarly studies and popular treatments has been produced (Bass, 2004; Harris, 1995; Hartmann, 2003a; Spivey, 1984; Carlos & Zirin, 2011), and these studies have both shaped and reflected theories of sport, politics, and protest to a remarkable degree ever since (Polite & Hawkins, 2012; see also Bryant, 2018; Hartmann, 2009)—not to mention the entire field of sport sociology (Leonard & King, 2009a) and sports-based activists and organizers themselves (Brooks & Althouse, 2009; Leonard & King, 2009b; O'Bonsawin, 2015; Ratchford, 2012; Ruffin, 2014).

Overarching Contributions and Limitations

The preponderance of attention to the activism of 1968 captures both the contributions and the limitations of dominant approaches to athletically oriented protest and social movements. Among its strengths, the scholarship on the Olympic champions Smith and Carlos and their dramatic victory stand gesture has put a premium on studying activism at the highest levels of competition, contributed to the fascination with symbolic statements and gestures, most particularly at sport's spectacularized mega-events, and highlights the primacy of mass media and public opinion as focal domains of contestation, action, and analysis.

Less productively, however, these emphases have sometimes served to diminish the attention given to other, key dimensions of athletic organizing and protest. For example, there is a tendency to minimize or ignore all of the backstage labor and organizational support contributed by Edwards and the Olympic Project for Human Rights in building awareness and a whole series of protest actions in the year leading up to the Mexico City Games. Relatedly, the focus on the elite, medal-winning male athletes misses all of the other, more localized mobilizations and actions that emerged all across the country; it also ignores the role that women of color played—or tried to play—in the movement, and connections to broader, global struggles against apartheid and for human rights. More broadly, the emphasis on the dramatic actions of the most prominent male athletes creates blinders with respect to the subsequent ways in which more institutional actors used the pressure of Olympic activism to challenge egregious racism within the world of sport. It can also fail to attend to all of the other activism and meaningful institutional reforms that grew out of these actions: the athletes rights movement, the push for athletic representation and unionization by elite and collegiate athletes, the ongoing struggles for gender equity, equitable opportunity of disability sport, and, more broadly, for alternative visions of sport (see Hartmann, 2003a, Chapters 6 & 7).

These points of analytic emphasis—or the relative lack thereof—are not just abstract, academic concerns. They shape and reflect how scholars understand current forms of athletic activism and future waves of sport-based mobilization. To wit: what makes the current, 21st-century wave of athletic activism unprecedented is not just the elite male athletes who have played leading roles (LeBron James, Colin Kaepernick, or Michael Bennett) or key actions (the University of Missouri Tigers football team or football [soccer] players in Europe). Rather, it is the broad-based activism that has emerged all across the sporting landscape, in an incredible array of sports, and at all levels of sport, including grassroots, scholastic, and community-based athletics. It is the leading role that female athletes such as U.S. soccer star Megan Rapinoe, WNBA player Maya Moore, and tennis greats Serena Williams and Naomi Osaka have played. It is the involvement of white allies and advocates—coaches, owners, establishment leaders, and support staff. It is in how sustained this movement has been, its connections with local causes and initiatives, and the increasing public support it has received.

An awareness of the insights and blind spots of previous case studies can help us begin to recognize and theorize all of this and situate it within the vast, global network of activists and movement organizations in and around sport that have emerged in international and Olympic circles in recent decades, and the broad range of issues that drive them (Boykoff, 2014; Kilcline, 2017; Zheng & Garcia, 2017): climate change and environmentalism, democracy and anti-authoritarianism, urban development, housing, and gentrification, corporate profit and exploitative labor practices, gender equity, queer and trans sport, peace and human rights (Kidd & Donnelly, 2000. Such an orientation can also help us realize where and to what extent the pockets of organizing, transformation, and change have taken hold within the sporting establishment itself. Some notable examples here include disability and Paralympic sport (Howe, 2008), the antiglobalization/–sweat shop movement from a few years back (Sage, 1999), and the network of organizations and initiatives that coalesce under the "sport for development" umbrella (Kidd, 2008; see also Coalter, 2013; Welty-Peachy, 2020).

Movements in Context

One of the first steps and core insights of any proper sociological approach is to set sport-based activism, protest, and social movements in relation to resistance and mobilization in the broader sociopolitical landscape. In other words, movement scholars frame sport-based activism in dynamic, iterative relationships with other activism, protests, and social movements in society. From its critique and protest strategies to its connections with other activists and polarized public reception, the Black activism of the late 1960s, for example, was closely connected to the broader civil rights movement and the shift toward Black Power. Today a similar dynamic remains true, as seen in activism that has been inspired by and is in dialogue with the Black Lives Matter movement and its attention to anti-Black racism, white supremacy, police brutality, and broader struggles for justice on a variety of fronts (Coombs & Cassilo, 2017; Modiano, 2017). And social contextualization is important not just for understanding race-based movements: it is no accident that the push for gender equity in sport has coincided with the onset of the Me Too movement, or that protests against corporatization, global capitalism, and extreme economic inequalities in and around sport came to the fore with the rise of the Occupy movement protests against worldwide corporate greed.

Not only is sport-based activism more likely to emerge when conducted in the context of broader movements and mobilization; it also appears more likely to be sustained and impactful when this is the case. That said, one of the major challenges for analysts of sport-based activism is to understand whether sport-based movements merely reflect broader social forces and movements or actively, independently drive and shape them.

Motivations, Resources, and Constraints

Because acts of athletic defiance were so individualistic, isolated, and sporadic for so many years (from the 1970s through at least the early 2000s), it wasn't long ago that the main questions for scholars of athletic activism and sport-based movements involved questions about barriers and constraints (cf. Khan, 2012). The previous section itemized a number of the broader institutional characteristics and social forces that make athletically oriented activism and change difficult: the conservatism of both establishment elites and sports fans in general, the sport-media industry's reliance upon and complicity with institutions of power and profit, and long-standing cultural norms about sport and its problematic relationship to politics. Here, we should add the ongoing surveillance of and attempts to suppress athletic discontent via private security forces or in concert with state agencies, as documented most consistently by scholars of Olympic activism (Boykoff & Fussey, 2014).

In addition, scholars have identified a range of individual-level costs, consequences, and disincentives to activism (Kaufman, 2008). The loss of income from commercial endorsements has received a good deal of attention (Cunningham & Regan, 2011; Niven, 2019), stimulated, among other things, by Michael Jordan's now (in)famous statement "Republicans buy shoes too" when he was pushed to endorse a Democratic political candidate in the 1990s. Threats of organizational retaliation and ostracism are also quite familiar (Lapchick, 1995). On this latter point, it is important to recall that Colin Kaepernick still hasn't played in the NFL since he spoke out against Black oppression and led the "take a knee" protests in 2016 and 2017. Legal and contractual barriers can also stand in the way (Brown & Brison, 2017).

There used to be a lot of hand-wringing about athletes lacking the self-consciousness and collective commitment needed for activism (Agyemang & Singer, 2011; Bryant, 2018). Some of this extended from traditional understandings of athlete identities and expectations for athletes. Basically, athletes were seen as being so dedicated to training and performance that they had little time for political and social issues; deeply held stereotypes of athletes as "dumb jocks" were also at play. The activism of recent years has exposed the limitations of these assumptions, however, and revealed that many athletes—especially those from various poor, marginalized, and disempowered communities and backgrounds (Agyemang, Singer, & Delorme, 2010)—are not only aware of social issues and injustices but deeply committed to finding ways to fight against them (Leonard & King, 2009b). On this point, Cunningham and colleagues (2019) insist that the involvement of athletes themselves is crucial in terms of authenticating and legitimating all activism in the sport context.

With the recent rise and unprecedented levels of resistance in and around sport, scholars have turned to explaining what motivates protest and drives activism for individual athletes. One of the unique contributions of sociologists on this front is to highlight the importance of peer groups, social networks, and collective identities (Houghteling & Dantzler, 2019). Another point of sociological insight involves exposure to and connections with other activists, thought leaders, and movement organizations; such connections contribute to the fortitude, actual knowledge, and concrete material resources required for individuals to initiate sport-based social action and remain committed to it.

Activists and movement organizations outside the athletic arena can be especially important resources for elite athletes who compete for teams or in cities and even countries far removed from their own previous experiences. Labor unions in professional sports provide social and organizational support for athlete activists as well, though, frankly, there is less research and writing on this topic than is ideal (perhaps because athletic unions themselves are so underdeveloped, at least in the U.S. context). A sustained network of sport-based activists and social movement organizations that promote athletic activism does exist in some international sport settings, and is particularly vibrant in anti-Olympic circles (Boykoff, 2011, 2014). The pro-democracy organizing of football fans in Europe, especially in the South and East, have given rise to the concept of "supporter activism" (Hodges & Brentin, 2018; Zheng & Garcia, 2017). However, it should be noted that much contemporary sport-based activism, in both the United States and around the globe (and as with other movements of the moment), is decentralized and diffused—or, more positively, bottom-up, locally focused, and network-driven, and more likely to be, as they say, leader-full rather than leader-less (cf. Valiente, 2019).

Media expertise and technology are other essential resources for recruiting activist athletes as well as for movement mobilization more generally and in the framing of social problems for public audiences. Indeed, as in other social domains, social media platforms have become increasingly powerful tools for both mobilization and cooperation, as well as for public engagement (Galily, 2020; Sanderson, Frederick, & Stocz, 2016; Schmittel & Sanderson, 2015; Yan, Pegoraro, & Watanabe, 2018). That said, both traditional journalism and new social media platforms can be double-edged swords, matters that are given more consideration below.

Goals and Tactics

Another key, classically sociological aspect of movement analysis involves classifying (or categorizing) activist actors and movement organizations. Some of this work involves identifying different characteristics (or dimensions) of resistance or generating formal theoretical typologies or historical periodizations (cf. Edwards, 2016). Movement goals and protest strategies are often at the center of such conceptual exercises.

Several analytic distinctions are helpful when approaching the study of any given activist, protest action, or movement initiative in the domain of sport. One is the distinction between protests against injustices, inequities, or social problems *within* sport versus activism which is undertaken *through* sports to use the athletic arena as a platform or vehicle for calling attention and contributing to larger movements for justice and change in broader society (Birrell & Therberge, 1994). In the former, sport is the *target* of activism and protest; in the latter, sport is the *tool*, the platform, or the vehicle. Another useful analytic distinction is between activism designed to call attention to social problems and injustices in contrast to activism pushing for actual, concrete changes, social transformations, or institutional reforms. This is what might be described as the difference between "consciousness-raising" and "demand making" (Hartmann, 2009). Other dimensions by which scholars differentiate athletic activism include the degree of activist self-consciousness, levels of engagement and types of protest, and how extensive, reformist, or transformational demands may be (Cooper, Macaulay, & Rodriguez, 2019).

The lines between various dimensions of activism, as well as the relationships between them, can be blurry in both sociological analysis and actual social practice. Recent qualitative studies suggest that athletes who are concerned about social issues consider a broad array of activities, ranging from social justice actions and public acts of rebellion to mentorship and intervention-oriented sports programming, to "count" as activism and mobilization (Kluch, 2020). Relatedly, the demands for equal compensation for professional women soccer players are concrete calls for change within the world of sport, but at the same time they have powerful symbolic implications for the broader Me Too movement. Indeed, the push for gender equity in sport through legal means such as Title IX advocacy in the United States is one of the most widely referenced examples of sport-based resistance having broader societal consequences (cf. Brake, 2012; Sharrow, 2017).

An incredible array of statements, demonstrations, and protest actions have been employed by activists and organizations in recent years. This repertoire has included symbolic gestures during ceremonies and the use of emblems, patches, and statements on uniforms and warmup suits, as well as formal statements, extended interview commentaries during press conferences, boycotts, and strikes (Lawrence, 2020; Wikipedia, 2020). These diverse and creative tactics remain to be fully itemized and catalogued as well as assessed in terms of their efficacy in meeting various demands or goals. That said, demonstrations embedded within the existing sporting practices are most controversial (and unsettling for the establishment), especially when they impinge upon the integrity of actual competition or on long-established symbology and ceremonies, as in the case of Olympic ritual (MacAloon, 2019).

General social movement theory would suggest that symbolic gestures are most impactful for dramatizing social concerns and building support, while boycotts and strikes would be more appropriate when targeted to concrete demands for change and specific institutional actors. However, actual strikes and boycotts in sport are fairly rare (for exceptions, see Booth, 2003; Yan et al., 2018). Strategies for more sustained institutional change in and through sport remain fairly undeveloped, and it is not clear that athletic activists connect tactics and goals closely in the first place. More positively, all actions have a greater likelihood of meeting their goals if undertaken in solidarity with others and can draw resources from nonsport movements and organizations. Outcomes aside, there is a delicate balancing act that all athletic activism must attend to as well. This stems from entrenched sport/politics norms noted earlier; for instance, if athlete activists lean too far toward protest on causes that lack societal legitimacy, they risk alienating athletes, fans, and others in the sporting establishment who are their most immediate audience and likely supporters.

Backlash and Opposition

If there is one unspoken truism about athletically based protest, it is that any meaningful contestation or change in, around, or through sport will provoke opposition of its own—pushback, criticism, counterprotest, and even backlash. Power and privilege, after all, don't give up without a fight. Of course, this is the case for all activism and social movements. Nevertheless, backlash and opposition to sport-based activism are only beginning to be systematically analyzed by scholars.

One promising avenue of work on this topic is in the sport literature on media and communication, which has been tracking public reactions to sport-based protest and activism, both in terms of traditional public opinion surveys and (increasingly) in terms of social media reaction and response (Chaplin & Montez de Oca, 2019; Cunningham & Gill, 2016; Johnson, Reinke, Noble, & Camarillo, 2020). Among other findings, these analyses suggest that athletic activism is as likely to reflect or even intensify preexisting individual beliefs about phenomena such as nationalism (Smith & Tryce, 2019), patriotism (Montez de Oca & Suh, 2020), or racial attitudes (Intravia, Piquero, & Leeper Piquero, 2018) as it is to change anyone's mind. If the dynamics that have been demonstrated in public opinion research from mainstream political science are a guide (cf. Abrajano & Hajnal, 2017 Tesler, 2013), then the social divisions and polarizations of the broader social world are often reproduced and all too often intensified and/or exacerbated as a result of sport-seated protest. As a result, some scholars have used research on activism response and opposition to reveal the workings of power and privilege in maintaining the social status quo in sport and through it (cf. Dickerson & Hodler, 2020).

Another related avenue of research on opposition involves the increasingly overt use of the sporting arena by conservative actors, activists, and leaders to promote their own particular ideologies and political agendas. On the forefront here has been the divisive U.S. presidency of Donald Trump. While studies of the political and movement mobilization of sport under Trump and other right-wing leaders are only now beginning to be written (cf. Andrews, 2019; Siegel, 2019), it seems clear that Trump's actions have been historically unprecedented among U.S. presidents, Republican or Democrat. In his explicit and deliberate politicization of sport, most particularly for the purposes of fomenting social division and by often using Black athletes as a target, Trump's posture and inflammatory tweeting is aimed at pushing back on the legitimacy of athletes' social-cultural concerns and their right to engage in free speech. Still, while his stance has served as an argument for the explicit separation of politics from sport, it has also stimulated the continued rise in the overt political deployment of sport, catalyzing new waves of activism and counterprotest to his intervention (Trimbur, 2019).

Attention to the opposition and backlash to athletic activism, as well as to the emergence of more overt political conservativism in and around sport, presents the opportunity to frame the study of sport-based activism and change more broadly as dynamic, interactive, and uncertain processes or systems. In doing so, scholars need to recognize that social movements are as likely to provoke backlash as to find support, and thus view activism in and through sport as a complicated dance of resistance and counterresistance with a range of potential outcomes, not all of which are progressive or predictable. Nepstad and Kenney's (2018) analytic framing of sport-based activism in terms of legitimation battles, backfire dynamics, and tactical innovations is one step in this more expansive, interactive direction. Another area where the back-and-forth dynamics between activism and security, surveillance, and suppression are vividly evident is in studies of policy and power in the infrastructure behind the Olympic Games (Boykoff & Fussey, 2014).

DEBATES

With all the sport-based organizing and athlete activism of recent years, new scholarship has started to reexamine old assumptions, analyze new developments in the arena, and pave the way for future research. Among the most important developments in the field is recognition of the vital role played by women athletes in the sport activist arena.

Female and Feminist Athletic Activism

Historically, but especially in recent years, female athletes are far more active than is often recognized, not only by other activists and in the media but all too often by sport scholars themselves (Cooky, 2017b). This is unfortunate because women of all levels and abilities, and especially queer and trans women and women of color (McDonald, 2008), have been on the leading edge of advocacy, activism, and protest in the sports arena. Larger proportions of female (compared to male) athletes seem more aware of social injustices and more committed to social action. Their protests tend to be respectfully voiced, but with notable creativity and tactical innovation. Here the interaction between scholarship and action seems particularly robust. Women in sport have been inspired by and have drawn on a prolific body of feminist sport scholarship, where issues of inequitable access and inclusion have long been prioritized, along with reimagined ways to envision alternatives to dominant forms of athletic participation and their engagement with the sport-media-cultural complex (Birrell & Theberge, 1994). This applies to fans of women's sports as well as female athletes (Antunovic & Hardin, 2012).

As with other areas of analysis, the recognition of female and/or feminist athletic activism is not just a matter of giving credit where credit is due. For example, while the NBA has been noted for its attention to police brutality and anti-Black racism in recent years, it is the WNBA that has led the way in bringing public attention to these issues, regularly offering frank talk at press conferences and developing novel strategies to advance representation and resistance. Moreover, female athlete activists often bring an inclusive, intersectional vision to both their critiques of social life and their visions of social change (Lavelle, 2019; see also Carrington, 1998). All these points were on display in the #SayHerName campaign (and to a lesser extent #BlackTransLivesMatter) deployed in the summer of 2020 that borrowed thematically from strategies used by U.S. voting rights activists such as Stacey Abrams and the critical legal scholar Kimberlé Williams Crenshaw (Ziller & Prada, 2017).

Just as significant, women activists in the athletic arena have modeled how to shift from protest to concrete actions and sustainable institutional reforms, often on very specific causes at the local, community level. Elite WNBA player Maya Moore's decision to take a leave of absence from basketball at the height of her career to help overturn wrongful convictions in the criminal justice arena is perhaps the most widely published example of a phenomenon that is actually less about publicity than about concrete legal-political challenges and social changes that impact the lives of regular, everyday people.

Social Media, Digital Technologies, and Traditional Sports Journalism

As alluded to previously, one area of emerging power and innovation in sport-based activism is social media and other new communication technologies. Communication and media studies scholars have led the way in documenting and analyzing social media as a tool for sport-based organizing, protest, and public outreach. In addition, media scholars have been studying the changing role of sports journalism in an era of activism and social movements. Indeed, among the biggest trends in the sports world in recent years is that sports reporters increasingly see it as their business and obligation to report on social issues—including politics—in and around the athletic arena (Broussard, 2020; Schmidt, 2018). Given the extent to which athletic activism centers public opinion, issue awareness, and consciousness-raising, the significance of media communication as both a site of and tool for mobilization cannot be overemphasized.

These scholars are also well aware that communication in any medium or technological format can be a flashpoint for opposition and counterresistance to sport-based activism. In the age of digital and social media, the social dynamics of activist communication have become even more multifaceted and tenuous (for an important, nonsport treatment, see Tufekci, 2017). And with the emergence of more socially sensitive and politically engaged ownership-operated media and public relations teams, and all that is at stake financially in these politics, the athletic establishment has begun to take an active role in curating the public statements and images of players, clients, and teams (Mirer & Grubic, 2020). With this nascent development, media can be not only a site of activism and counteractivism; it can also be a source that challenges and changes the tenor of establishment control by both co-opting and transforming the meaning of its standing.

The Corporatization of Activism

The increasingly complicated, multifaceted dynamics of mobilization, communication, and control of messaging call attention to another, fairly new development in the sport/ activism landscape: the corporatization of activism and protest (Hayhurst & Szto, 2016). An even more aggressive variation on corporate social responsibility through sport (Godfrey, 2009) and part of a larger societal trend toward the professionalization of movements, sometimes called "astroturfing" (Stewart & Hartmann, 2020), has seen strategic companies and media outlets marketing activist athletes as a way to promote their brands as progressive societal forces. There are a multitude of reasons to be suspicious about the intent and implications of this "woke" capitalism (Montez de Oca, Mason, & Ahn, 2020). Perhaps the most famous suspect example here is Nike's commercialization of Kaepernick and his messages of protest (Boykoff & Carrington, 2020), but leagues and teams that have come late to social justice causes are targets of criticism as well.

It is also useful to put the corporate embrace of activism in the context of long-standing concerns by those in the athletic establishment who are wary of the potential financial costs of protest and athletic organizing. For example, one recent economic study found that the NFL's television ratings decreased by almost 10% during the protest-inflected 2016 season, and then again in the season following, after it was further associated with protests (Brown & Sheridan, 2020). However, the reported impacts of this ongoing visibility of protests by athletes were mixed. While indeed some viewers said that they tuned out due to protests, others said they were frustrated with Kaepernick's exclusion. And, at the bottom line, evidence in this study (Brown & Sheridan, 2020) also suggested that the overall magnitude of economic effects resulting from the Kaepernick-fueled protests were "relatively muted." Clearly, market disruption—even just the threat of market disruption—can also be a reason for owners and leadership to work with athletes to shape or soften activism (Watanabe, Yan, & Soebbing, 2019), as well as to devise pathways to garner profit from it.

Outcomes and Assessment

Perhaps the single biggest opportunity and need for future research is in the realm of outcomes, impacts, and assessment. Aside from case studies of a few exceptional and exceptionally successful actions—the South African anti-apartheid movement of the 1960s and 1970s (Booth, 2003) and the threatened 2015 boycott by the University of Missouri Tigers football team which led to the departure of the school's leader (Yan et al., 2018)—little empirical work exists. The relative absence of assessment of institutional accomplishments or outcomes is a long-standing weakness of the entire social movements field, an area that has tended to focus on organizational dynamics, protest tactics, and dramatic events (Giugni, 1998). Basic analytic challenges on this front center around the difficulties inherent in operationalizing success, especially given that many movements never really advance beyond generic critique to clearly articulating specific goals or collecting data to measure and evaluate accomplishments.

The previously cited research on public opinion responses to sport-based activism is an exception and pivotal starting point. This literature offers data and concrete criteria for evaluation on two of the topics on which analysts and activists are most convinced of the efficacy of sport-based activism: issue awareness and consciousness-raising, what Wasow (2020) has called "agenda seeding." Findings here too are somewhat mixed. Some recent studies have shown that athletic activism can contribute to advancing progressive social attitudes and may even motivate certain forms of political participation among like-minded citizens (cf. Towler, Crawford, & Bennett, 2020). However, responses to athletic activism in this study and others show that it can be just as likely to reproduce existing beliefs for those who are prepositioned in opposition. Furthermore, some general movement research (Giugni, McAdam, & Tilly, 1999) suggests that protest on one topic or in a specific venue—as well as how these acts are framed in the media—can have unintended consequences or produce backlash. It seems safe to say that the dynamics of resistance and movement-building, opposition and counterresistance, and their impacts on public opinion are more complicated and uncertain than many traditional, straightforward instrumentalist theories might predict.

While generalization about outcomes is difficult given the paucity of research, several speculative propositions can be derived from the myriad other research and findings already cited. For example, available case studies provide some sense of the characteristics and conditions under which protest can be effective. Athlete boycotts and strikes, for example, can be most impactful when they are targeted to egregious injustices, well-timed, and well-resourced and when significant revenues are at stake for sports organizations and elite stakeholders (Watanabe et al., 2019). In addition, although strikes and boycotts may be rare in sport, the *threat* of withholding participation (or athletic labor) is a powerful communicative tactic for heightening attention to social issues and pressuring leaders to enact reforms (Hartmann, 2009). In this vein, it seems that sport is a powerful arena for issue awareness and perhaps even consciousness-raising.

If contemporary sports activism is largely motivated by societal issues and institutions outside of the athletic establishment proper, it also appears that the most tangible accomplishments come within the institutions of sport itself. In a familiar social movement/institutional transformation pattern (cf. Rojas, 2006), these gains are achieved in collaboration with conventional establishment actors who work to reform existing programs, policies, and initiatives. There are good reasons for activists and their allies to be cautious or even critical about how co-optation and compromise between activists and establishment actors can modify and minimize change, processes that Thorpe and Wheaton (2011 p. 834) have described as "the politics of incorporation." Still, it is also important not to be too cynical about these processes. From a more institutional point of view, radical protests and trans-formative initiatives (even failed ones) often create pressure and make space for changes that can yield meaningful, if not fully satisfactory, improvements to real people's lives in both sport and society. This is one dimension of what has been called a "radical flank" effect (Haines, 2013). Indeed, the effects here are considerable. They may be seen not only from pressures toward gender equity (advanced in concert with Title IX in the United States) and unionization that emerged in response to the athletes' rights movement, but from advocacy for green sport, equity in the Paralympics, and realigned goals for sport for development programs across the globe. These various initiatives have exerted broader impacts at more localized community-based levels, as well as influencing policy and practices in national and global institutions.

One final note of caution on outcomes and accomplishments: because of the visibility of athletes (and sports itself) in the mass media and public imagination, it can be easy to overstate the independent causal role of athletic activism and protest in bringing about concrete social change, especially outside the world of sport. In the wake of Black Lives Matter activism in recent years, for instance, athletic activists have sometimes been credited with the banning of Confederate monuments and symbols in the U.S. South (Wikipedia, 2020), when these outcomes were actually decades in the making, based upon the work of numerous, nonsport organizations and activists. Such attributions not only overstate the significance of athletic activism, but they obscure the importance of long-term orga-nization and the sustained institutional commitments required for any meaningful social transformation.

Public Engagement

One final development in the field of sport-based social movements research that has consequences for future scholarship involves the role of analysts themselves. With the emergence of public sociology in the mainstream of the discipline (Burawoy, 2005), there has been increasing pressure from a younger generation of scholars for research that is more directly engaged in advocacy and support of social movements and change within and through sport (Boykoff, 2018; Carter-Francique, Gill, & Hart, 2017; Cooky, 2017a). Among other factors, the emergence of social media has allowed scholars to reach audiences be-yond the classroom. Not only does the call for more activist, engaged scholarship encourage scholars to orient their work in more public and concretely impactful directions; it also raises timeless social scientific questions about the relationship between traditional em-piricist approaches to the study of sport and more critically oriented research and theory.

CONCLUSION

Research on athletic activism and sport-based social movements reveals, among other things, both the power of sport as a venue for calling attention to social issues and for ad-vocacy for social change inside and outside of sport. It reveals, as well, the challenges of making actual and meaningful social change in and through the athletic arena. On the progressive, social change side of the ledger, it seems that activism in and through sport is particularly effective in communicative and dramaturgical ways—bringing difficult social issues to public attention and framing them in new and impactful ways, as well as helping to clear a path for certain institutional reforms within the athletic arena itself. In terms of limitations, we see that it can be difficult to move from protest to actual social change, and that the most radical forms of protest are resisted and often shunted aside in favor of more limited, symbolic reforms. In addition, broader, more societal visions of change often run up against the collectivity of conservative actors, practices, and forces endemic to the sporting establishment, as well as deeply entrenched liberal democratic beliefs about sport as an inherently progressive yet apolitical social force.

None of this is to minimize the import and broader theoretical significance of studying sport-based activism, protest, and movements for social change. Quite the contrary, understanding the power and complexity of sport-based activism can contribute to a broader, more nuanced understanding of the complicated cultural status and social force of sport in countries throughout the world. In terms of the general sociological study of social movements, the study of sport-based activism highlights the value of studying both popular culture as well as the more symbolic, ideological, and expressive dimensions of all activism and change. Indeed, if there is one area in which the study of sport-based activism, protest, and social movements has genuine contributions to make to mainstream sociological work on social movements and collective action, this is it (see again Hall, 1994). Here, it also worth noting that theories of sport as "contested social terrain" refer not only to the multifaceted and cross-cutting forces at play within the world of sport but also to sport's own unique prominence and visibility in local, national, and, increasingly, globalized communities and cultures. The cultural prominence of sport dictates that the contests, divisions, and movement dynamics that play out in sport have broader meaning and symbolic significance, and their impacts thus extend well "beyond the boundaries" of sport itself (James, 1963/2013).

Returning to the field of sport studies, it is also important to continue to pay attention to new and emerging developments within sport-based activism and mobilizing and to ask essential questions about whether (or to what extent) they challenge the very culture of sport itself. Does the emergence of a diverse, new generation of self-conscious and highly committed athlete activists threaten long-established beliefs about the neutral, apolitical nature of sport? Does the fact that conservative actors appear increasingly assertive and explicit about their own politics in the sporting arena mean that traditional convictions about the necessary separation of sport and politics, not to mention the unifying power of sport, are in the process of being renegotiated? Are the politics of the sports world itself shifting or breaking into new, multifaceted, and even stratified directions? Perhaps. Certainly such trends need to be carefully tracked by scholars in coming years. However, it may also be the case that we find out that these emergent trends are still largely contained within traditional cultural conventions and that contemporary protests merely serve to reinscribe them, albeit in new cultural forms.

To illustrate this possibility, let me refer to a historical example that goes back to 1960s-era Black activism in sport. In 1973, sport sociologist and anti-apartheid activist Richard Lapchick conducted a survey asking white and Black Americans whether they agreed or not with Smith and Carlos's Olympic victory stand demonstration. On the one hand, Lapchick (1975) found polarized opinions: Black Americans supported Smith and Carlos by an almost two-thirds majority, while white Americans displayed the exact inverse attitudes (two-thirds were against the display). On the other hand, Lapchick discovered that there was a key point on which white and Black respondents agreed: that politics had no place in sport. Thus, the difference in attitudes toward Smith and Carlos was not so much the result of different ideals about sport, but rather stemmed from the fact that white and Black Americans had very different understandings about what was political. For Black Americans, the victory stand demonstration was not a political act but a moral statement, one that was completely in line with the high ideals of the civil rights movement and sport's historic claim to being an avenue for racial advancement, social equality, and justice. White Americans, in stark contrast, dismissed the gesture precisely because they did not agree with Smith and Carlos's racial views and thus perceived the gesture as a form of protest politics that had no place in sport.

A similar dynamic may be unfolding in the contemporary race-based athletic activist arena. What we may be witnessing with the rise of support for athletic activism on behalf of Black Lives Matter may not be a reworking of traditional sport/politics taboos so much as a demonstration of shifts in public opinion regarding anti-Black racism, police brutality, and the need for social change (Parker, Horowitz, & Anderson, 2020; see also Knoester, Ridpath, & Allison, 2020). Moreover, this combination of shifting public opinion, which seems to line up with many of the tenets of contemporary athletic activism, might actually serve to reproduce traditional cultural conventions about sport, politics, and protest rather than undermining or reorganizing them (see also Montez de Oca & Suh, 2020 on patriotism).

Such complex dynamics and possibilities point to a crucial point about the limitations of all sport-based activism: that it is all, and always will be, bound up, in both productive and constraining ways, with bigger, broader forces in society itself, forces that may be seen in but exist largely outside of the purview of sport. This begs the old chicken-or-egg quandary about sport and its relation to social life. In the contemporary moment, then, it may not be sport-based activism that is driving and determining support for Black Lives Matter, but rather public support for Black Lives Matter that is driving how we think about the morality and legitimacy of this athletic activism itself.

Some of these musings—written in the turbulent summer of 2020, when sport-based Black Lives Matter activism was at a fever pitch—about the workings of sport-seated protests and their relation to larger sociocultural dynamics risk going too deep or getting too abstract or analytical. Do regular citizens and sports fans, after all, really think about any of this? A good deal of sport scholarship would indeed suggest they do not. In fact, there is a school of thought that insists the broad significance and social force of sport in society stem from the passionate yet deeply uncritical and un-self-conscious, ways in which athletes, sports fans, and others in the sports world engage with it (Gusfield, 1987; Hartmann, 2003b). And in many ways, this is precisely the point. In a variation of the anthropologist Clifford Geertz's (1973) classic "deep play" concept, many actors in the athletic arena participate passionately yet disavow the import and broader social significance of their engagement, seeing sport as a set of activities that at the end of the day is not to be taken too seriously. And the effect of this cultural orientation may be that sport is less likely to be seen as or valued as a place to impact society and social change and more likely viewed as a place where the social status quo can be reproduced without opposition or pushback.

This suggests one final dimension about sport's unique, and perhaps ultimately conservative functioning, with respect to activism, protest, and social change. On the one hand, the cultural prominence of sport gives athletic activists the ability to bring attention to and promote numerous social causes. On the other hand, sport's paradoxical relation to play can mean that such activism is either ignored or dismissed as illegitimate. How this dynamic is recognized, and how it is engaged, will determine how far athletic activism can go in realizing sport's potential to advance meaningful social change in the 21st century.

REFERENCES

Abrajano, M., & Hajnal, Z. L. (2017). *White backlash: Immigration, race, and American politics.* Princeton: Princeton University Press.

Agyemang, K., & Singer, J. N. (2011). Toward a framework for unverstanding Black male athlete social responsibility (BMASR) in big-time American sports. *International Journal of Sport Management and Marketing, 10,* 46–60.

Agyemang, K., Singer, J. N., & Delorme, J. (2010). An exploratory study of Black male college athletes' perceptions on race and athlete activism. *International Review for the Sociology of Sport, 45,* 419–435.

Agyemang, K., Singer, J. N., & Weems, A. J. (2020). "Agitate! agitate! agitate!" Sport as a site for political activism and social change. *Organization.* https://doi.org/10.1177/135050842 0928519.

Andrews, D. L. (2019). *Making sport great again: The Uber-sport assemblage, neoliberalism, and the Trump conjuncture.* New York: Springer.

Antunovic, D., & Hardin, M. (2012). Activism in women's sports blogs: Fandom and feminist potential. *International Journal of Sport Communication, 5*(3), 305–322.

Bass, A. (2004). *Not the triumph but the struggle: The 1968 Olympics and the making of the Black athlete.* Minneapolis: University of Minnesota Press.

Benford, R. D., & Snow, D. A. (2000). Framing processes and social movements: An overview and assessment. *Annual Review of Sociology, 26,* 611–639.

Birrell, S., & Theberge, N. (1994). Ideological control of women in sport and feminist resistance and transformation for sport. In M. Costa & S. R. Guthrie (Eds.), *Women and sport: Interdisciplinary perspectives* (pp. 323–376). Champaign: Human Kinetics.

Brake, D. L. (2012). *Getting in the game: Title IX and the women's sports revolution.* New York: NYU Press.

Blee, K. M., & Creasap, K. C. (2010). Conservative and right-wing movements. *Annual Review of Sociology, 36,* 269–386.

Booth, D. (1998). *The race game: Sport and politics in South Africa* (Vol. 4). Psychology Press.

Booth, D. (2003). Hitting apartheid for six? The politics of the South African sports boycott. *Journal of Contemporary History, 38*(3), 477–493.

Boykoff, J. (2011). The anti-Olympics. *New Left Review, 67,* 41–59.

Boykoff, J. (2014). *Activism and the Olympics: Dissent at the games in Vancouver and London.* New Brunswick: Rutgers University Press.

Boykoff, J. (2017). Protest, activism, and the Olympic games: An overview of key issues and iconic moments. *International Journal of the History of Sport, 34,* 162–183.

Boykoff, J. (2018). Riding the lines: Academia, public intellectual work, and scholar-activism. *Sociology of Sport Journal, 35,* 81–88.

Boykoff, J., & Carrington, B. (2020). Sporting dissent: Colin Kaepernick, NFL activism, and media framing contests. *International Review for the Sociology of Sport, 55*(7), 829–849.

Boykoff, J., & Fussey, P. (2014). London's shadow legacies: Security and activism at the 2012 Olympics. *Contemporary Social Science, 9,* 253–270.

Branch, J. (2017, September 7). The awakening of Colin Kaepernick. *New York Times.* https://www.nytimes.com/2017/09/07/sports/colin-kaepernick-nfl-protests.html.

Brooks, D., & Althouse, R. (2009). Revolt of the Black athlete: From global arena to the college campus. *Journal for the Study of Sports and Athletes in Education, 3,* 195–214.

Broussard, R. (2020). "Stick to sports" is gone: A field theory analysis of sports journalists' coverage of socio-political issues. *Journalism Studies, 21*(12), 1627–1643.

Brown, J., & Sheridan, B. J. (2020). The impact of national anthem protests on National Football League television ratings. *Journal of Sports Economics, 21*(8), 829–847.

Brown, S., & Brison, N. (2017). More than an athlete: Constitutional and contractual analysis of activism in professional sports. *Arizona State University Sports & Entertainment Law Journal, 7,* 249–290.

Bryant, H. (2018). *The heritage: Black athletes, a divided America, and the politics of patriotism.* Boston: Beacon Press.

Burawoy, M. (2005). For public sociology. *American Sociological Review, 70*(1), 4–28.

Carlos, J., & Zirin, D. (2011). *The John Carlos story: The sports moment that changed the world.* Haymarket Books.

Carrington, B. (1998). Sport, masculinity, and Black cultural resistance. *Journal of Sport and Social Issues, 22,* 275–298.

Carrington, B. (2010). *Race, sport and politics: The sporting black diaspora.* Sage.

Carter-Francique, A. R., Gill, E., & Hart, A. (2017). Converging interests: Black scholar-advocacy and the Black college athlete. In B. J. Hawkwins, A. R. Carter-Francique, & J. N. Cooper (Eds.), *Critical race theory: Black athletic sporting experiences in the United States* (pp. 85–119). New York: Palgrave Macmillan.

Chaplin, K. S., & Montez de Oca, J. (2019). Avoiding the issue: University students' responses to NFL players' national anthem protests. *Sociology of Sport Journal, 36*(1), 12–21.

Coakley, J. (2015). Assessing the sociology of sport: On cultural sensibilities and the great sport myth. *International Review for the Sociology of Sport, 50,* 402–406.

Coalter, F. (2013). *Sport for development: What game are we playing?* Routledge.

Cooky, C. (2017a). "We cannot sit idly by": A necessary call for a public sociology of sport. *Sociology of Sport Journal, 34,* 1–32.

Cooky, C. (2017b). Women, sports, and activism. In H. McCammon, V. Taylor, J. Reger, & R. Einwohner (Eds.), *The Oxford handbook of US women's social movement activism* (pp. 602–622). New York: Oxford University Press.

Cooky, C., & Antunovic, D. (2020). This isn't just about us: Articulations of feminism in media narratives of athlete activism. *Communication and Sport, 8,* 692–711.

Coombs, D., & Cassilo, D. (2017). Athletes and/or activists: LeBron James and Black Lives Matter. *Journal of Sport and Social Issues, 41,* 425–444.

Cooper, J. N., Macaulay, C., & Rodriguez, S. H. (2019). Race and resistance: A typology of African American sport activism. *International Review for the Sociology of Sport, 54,* 151–181.

Cunningham, G. B., Dixon, M. A., Singer, J. N., Oshiro, K. F., Ahn, N. Y., & Weems, A. (2019). A site to resist and persist: Diversity, social justice, and the unique nature of sport. *Journal of Global Sport Management, 6,* 30–48. doi:10.1080/24704067.2019.1578623.

Cunningham, G. B., & Gill, Jr., E. J. (2016). "Hands up, don't shoot" or shut up and play ball? Fan-generated media views of the Ferguson Five. *Journal of Human Behavior in the Social Environment, 26*(3–4), 400–412.

Cunningham, G. B., & Regan, M. R. (2011). Political activism, racial identity and the commercial endorsement of athletes. *International Review for the Sociology of Sport, 47*, 657–669.

Davis-Delano, L. R., & Crosset, T. (2008). Using social movement theory to study outcomes in sport-related social movements. *International Review for the Sociology of Sport, 43*(2), 115–134.

Della Porta, D., & Diani, M. (2020). *Social movements: An introduction.* John Wiley & Sons.

Dickerson, N., & Hodler, M. (2020). "Real men stand for our nation": Constructions of an American nation and anti-Kaepernick memes. *Journal of Sport and Social Issues, 45*, 329–357. doi:0193723520950537.

Earl, J. (2003). Tanks, tear gas, and taxes: Toward a theory of movement repression. *Sociological Theory, 21*(1), 44–68.

Edwards, H. (1969/2020). *The revolt of the Black athlete.* New York: Free Press.

Edwards, H. (2016, November). The fourth wave: Black athlete protests in the second decade of the 21st century. Invited keynote address at annual meeting of North American Society for the Sociology of Sport. Tampa, FL.

Galily, Y. (2020). "Shut up and dribble!"? Athletes activism in the age of Twittersphere: The case of LeBron James. *Technology in Society, 58*, 101–109.

Geertz, C. (1973). Deep play: Notes on the Balinese cockfight. In C. Geertz, *The interpretation of cultures* (pp. 412–454). New York: Basic Books.

Giugni, M. G. (1998). Was it worth the effort? The outcomes and consequences of social movements. *Annual Review of Sociology, 98*, 371–393.

Giugni, M., McAdam, D., & Tilly, C. (Eds.). (1999). *How social movements matter* (Vol. 10). Minneapolis: University of Minnesota Press.

Godfrey, P. C. (2009). Corporate social responsibility in sport: An overview and key issues. *Journal of Sport Management, 23*, 698–716.

Green, K., & Hartmann, D. (2014). Politics and sports: Strange and secret bedfellows. In D. Hartmann & C. Uggen (Eds.), *The social side of politics* (pp. 87–102). New York: W. W. Norton.

Gruneau, R. (Ed.) (1988). *Popular cultures and political practices.* Toronto: Garamond Press.

Gusfield, J. (1987). Sports as story: Form and content in agonistic games. In S. Kang (Ed.), *The Olympics and cultural exchange* (pp. 207–237). Seoul: Hanyang University Institute for Ethnological Studies.

Haines, H. H. (2013). Radical flank effects. In D. A. Snow, D. della Porta, B. Klandermans, & D. McAdam (Eds.), *The Wiley-Blackwell encyclopedia of social and political movements* (Volume 3, pp. 1048–1050). New York: Wiley-Blackwell.

Hall, S. (1994). Deconstructing the popular. In R. Samuel (Ed.), *People's history and socialist theory* (pp. 227–239). London: Routledge.

Harris, O. (1995). Muhammad Ali and the revolt of the Black athlete. In E. J. Gorn (Ed.), *Muhammad Ali: The people's champ* (pp. 54–69). Urbana: University of Illinois Press.

Hartmann, D. (2003a). *Race, culture, and the revolt of the Black athlete: The 1968 Olympic protests and their aftermath.* Chicago: University of Chicago Press.

Hartmann, D. (2003b). What can we learn from sport if we take sport seriously as a racial force? Lessons from C. L. R. James's *Beyond a Boundary. Ethnic and Racial Studies, 26*(3), 451–483.

Hartmann, D. (2009). Activism, organizing, and the symbolic power of sport: Reassessing Harry Edwards's contributions to the 1968 Olympic protest movement. *Journal for the Study of Sports and Athletics in Education, 3*, 181–195.

Hartmann, D. (2019). The Olympic "revolt" of 1968 and its lessons for contemporary African American athletic activism. *European Journal of American Studies, 14* (1). https://journals.openedition.org/ejas/14335.

Hayhurst, L. M., & Szto, C. (2016). Corporatizing activism through sport-focused social justice? Investigating Nike's corporate responsibility initiatives in sport for development and peace. *Journal of Sport and Social Issues, 40,* 522–544.

Henderson, S. (2009). Crossing the line: Sport and the limits of civil rights protest. *International Journal of the History of Sport, 26,* 101–121.

Hess, D., & Martin, B. (2006). Repression, backfire, and the theory of transformative events. *Mobilization International Quarterly, 11*(2), 249–267.

Hodges, A., & Brentin, D. (2018). Fan protest and activism: Football from below in South-Eastern Europe. *Soccer & Society, 19*(3), 329–336.

Houghteling, C., & Dantzler, P. A. (2019). Taking a knee, taking a stand: Social networks and identity salience in the 2017 NFL protests. *Sociology of Race and Ethnicity, 6*(3), 396–415.

Howe, D. (2008). *The cultural politics of the Paralympic movement: Through an anthropological lens.* London: Routledge.

Intravia, J., Piquero, A. R., & Piquero, N. L. (2018). The racial divide surrounding United States of America national anthem protests in the National Football League. *Deviant Behavior, 39*(8), 1058–1068.

James, C. L. R. (1963/2013). *Beyond a boundary.* Durham: Duke University Press.

Johnson, T., Reinke, L., Noble, G., & Camarillo, T. (2020). Shut up and dribble? How popularity, activism, and real-world events shape attitudes towards LeBron James and race. *Social Science Journal.* https://doi.org/10.1080/03623319.2020.1768484.

Kaufman, P. (2008). Boos, bans, and other backlash: The consequences of being an activist athlete. *Humanity and Society, 32,* 215–239.

Kaufman, P., & Wolff, E. A. (2010). Playing and protesting: Sport as a vehicle for social change. *Journal of Sport and Social Issues, 34,* 154–175.

Khan, A. I. (2012). *Curt Flood in the media: Baseball, race, and the demise of the activist athlete.* Jackson: University Press of Mississippi.

Kidd, B. (2008). A new social movement: Sport for development and peace. *Sport in Society, 11,* 370–380.

Kidd, B. (2013). The Olympic Movement and the sports-media complex. *Sport in Society, 16,* 439–448.

Kidd, B., & Donnelly, P. (2000). Human rights in sports. *International Review for the Sociology of Sport, 35,* 131–148.

Kilcline, C. (2017). Sport and protest: Global perspectives. *International Journal of the History of Sport, 34,* 157–161.

Kluch, Y. (2020). "My story is my activism!" (Re-)definitions of social justice activism among collegiate athlete activists. *Communication & Sport.* doi:2167479519897288.

Knoester, C., Ridpath, B. D., & Allison, R. (2020, September). Should athletes be allowed to protest during the national anthem? An analysis of public opinions among US adults. *SocArXiv Papers.* doi:0.31235/osf.io/phyf2.

Lapchick, R. E. (1975). *The politics of race and international sport: The case of South Africa.* Westport: Greenwood Press.

Lapchick, R. E. (1995). Race and college sport: A long way to go. *Race & Class, 36,* 87–94.

Lavelle, K. L. (2019). "Change starts with us": Intersectionality and citizenship in the 2016 WNBA. In D. A. Grano & M. L Buttersworth (Eds.), *Sport, rhetoric, and political struggle* (pp. 39–54). New York: Peter Lang.

Lawrence, A. (2020, August 29). Athletes have only scratched the surface of their power to bring change. *The Guardian.* https://www.theguardian.com/sport/2020/aug/29/athletes-have-only-scratched-the-surface-of-their-power-to-bring-change?CMP=Share_iOSApp_Other.

Leonard, D. J., & King, C. R. (2009a). The legacies of Harry Edwards for sport sociology. *Journal for the Study of Sports and Athletes in Education, 3,* 133–252.

Leonard, D. J., & King, C. R. (2009b). Revolting Black athletes: Sport, new racism, and the politics of dis-identification. *Journal for the Study of Sports and Athletes in Education, 3,* 215–232.

MacAloon, J. J. (2016). Agenda 2020 and the Olympic movement. *Sport in Society, 19*(6), 767–785.

MacAloon, J. J. (2019). Hyperstructure, hierarchy, and humanitas in Olympic ritual. *Anthropology Today, 35*(3), 7–10.

Marx, G. T., & McAdam, D. (1994). *Collective behavior and social movements: Process and structure.* Englewood Cliffs: Prentice Hall.

McAdam, D. (1983). Tactical innovation and the pace of insurgency. *American Sociological Review, 48,* 735–754.

McDonald, M. G. (2008). Rethinking resistance: The queer play of the Women's National Basketball Association, visibility politics and late capitalism. *Leisure Studies, 27,* 77–93.

McDonald, M. G. (2020). Once more, with feeling: Sport, national anthems, and the collective power of affect. *Sociology of Sport Journal, 37,* 1–11.

Messner, M. (1988). Sports and male domination: The female athlete as contested ideological terrain. *Sociology of Sport Journal, 5,* 197–211.

Mirer, M., & Grubic, A. (2020). Promotional space or public forum: Protest coverage and reader response in team-operated media. *Communication & Sport, 8*(4–5), 489–506.

Modiano, C. (2017). The NFl, activism, and #BlackLivesMatter. In D. J. Leonard, K. George, & W. Davis (Eds.), *Football, culture and power* (pp. 228–253). London: Routledge.

Montez de Oca, J. M., Mason, S., & Ahn, S. (2020). Consuming for the greater good: "Woke" commercials in sports media. *Communication & Sport.* doi:2167479520949283.

Montez de Oca, J., & Suh, S. C. (2020). Ethics of patriotism: NFL players' protests against police violence. *International Review for the Sociology of Sport, 55*(5), 563–587.

Nauright, J., & Wiggins, D. K. (Eds.). (2017). *Sport and revolutionaries: Reclaiming the historical role of sport in social and political activism.* London: Routledge.

Nepstad, S. E., & Kenney, A. M. (2018). Legitimation battles, backfire dynamics, and tactical persistence in the NFL anthem protests, 2016–2017. *Mobilization: An International Quarterly, 23,* 469–483.

Niven, D. (2019). The effect of economic vulnerability on protest participation in National Football League. *Social Science Quarterly, 100,* 997–1008.

O'Bonsawin, C. (2015). From Black power to Indigenous activism: The Olympic movement and the marginalization of oppressed peoples, 1968–2012. *Journal of Sport History, 42,* 200–219.

Parker, K., Horowitz, J. M., & Anderson, M. (2020). Amid protests, majorities across racial and ethnic express support for Black Lives Matter movement. *Pew Research Center, Social and Demographic Trends.* https://www.pewsocialtrends.org/2020/06/12/amid-protests-majorities-across-racial-and-ethnic-groups-express-support-for-the-black-lives-matter-movement/.

Polite, F. G., & Hawkins, B. (2012). *Sport, race, activism, and social change: The impact of Dr. Harry Edwards' scholarship and service.* San Diego: Cognella.

Ratchford, J. (2012). Black fists and fool's gold: The 1960s Black athletic revolt reconsidered: The LeBron James decision and self-determination in post-racial America. *Black Scholar, 42,* 49–59.

Rojas, F. (2006). Social movement tactics, organizational change and the spread of African-American studies. *Social Forces, 84,* 2147–2166.

Ruffin, H. G. II. (2014). Doing the right thing for the sake of doing the right thing: The revolt of the Black athlete and the modern student-athletic movement, 1956–2014. *Western Journal of Black Studies, 38*, 260–278.

Sage, G. H. (1999). Justice do it! The Nike transnational advocacy network: Organization, collective actions, and outcomes. *Sociology of Sport Journal, 16*, 206–235.

Sanderson, J., Frederick, E., & Stocz, M. 2016. When athlete activism clashes with group values: Social identity threat management via social media. *Mass Communication and Society, 19*, 301–322.

Schmidt, H. C. (2018). Sport reporting in an era of activism: Examining the intersection of sport media and social activism. *International Journal of Sport Communication, 11*, 2–17.

Schmidt, S. H., Frederick, E. L., Pegoraro, A., & Spencer, T. C. (2019). An analysis of Colin Kaepernick, Megan Rapinoe, and the national anthem protests. *Communication & Sport, 7*(5), 653–677.

Schmittel, A., & Sanderson, J. (2015). Talking about Trayvon in 140 characters: Exploring NFL players' tweets about the George Zimmerman verdict. *Journal of Sport and Social Issues, 39*, 332–345.

Scott, J. C. (1985). *Weapons of the weak: Everyday forms of peasant resistance.* New Haven: Yale University Press.

Serazio, M. (2019). Fair game: The invisible ideologies of "apolitical" escapism. In *The power of sports: Media and spectacle in American culture* (pp. 223–281). New York: New York University Press.

Sharrow, E. A. (2017). "Female athlete" politic: Title IX and the naturalization of sex difference in public policy. *Politics, Groups, and Identities, 5*, 46–66.

Siegel, B. (2019). "True champions and incredible patriots": The transformation of the ceremonial White House visit under President Trump. *Journal of Emerging Sport Studies, 2*, 1–35.

Smith, B., & Tryce, S. A. (2019). Understanding emerging adults' national attachments and their reactions to athlete activism. *Journal of Sport and Social Issues, 43*, 167–194.

Spivey, D. (1984). Black consciousness and Olympic protest movement. In D. Spivey (Ed.), *Sport in America: New historical perspectives* (pp. 239–272). Westport: Greenwood Press.

Stewart, E., & Hartmann, D. (2020). The new structural transformation of the public sphere. *Sociological Theory.* doi:0735275120926205.

Tesler, M. (2013). The return of old-fashioned racism to white Americans' partisan preferences in the early Obama era. *Journal of Politics, 75*(1), 110–123.

Thorpe, H., & Wheaton, B. (2011). "Generation X Games," action sports and the Olympic movement: Understanding the cultural politics of incorporation. *Sociology, 45*, 830–847.

Towler, C. C., Crawford, N. N., & Bennett, R. A. (2020). Shut up and play: Black athletes, protest politics, and Black political action. *Perspectives on Politics, 18*(1), 111–127.

Trimbur, L. (2019). Taking a knee, making a stand: Social justice, Trump America, and the politics of sport. *Quest, 71*(2), 252–265.

Tufekci, Z. (2017). *Twitter and tear gas: The power and fragility of networked protest.* New Haven: Yale University Press.

Valiente, C. (2019). Football fandom, protest and democracy: Supporter activism in Turkey: by Dağhan Irak. London: Routledge.

Wang, D., Piazza, A., & Soule, S. A. (2018). Boundary-spanning in social movements: Antecedents and outcomes. *Annual Review of Sociology, 44*, 167–187.

Wasow, O. (2020). Agenda seeding: How 1960s Black protests moved elites, public opinion and voting. *American Political Science Review, 114*(3), 638–659.

Watanabe, N., Yan, G., & Soebbing, B. P. (2019). Market disruption as a regime for athlete activism: An economic analysis of college football player protests. *Sport Management Review*, 22, 600–612.

Welty-Peachy, J. (Ed.). (2020). *Partnerships and alliances in sport for development and peace: Considerations, tensions, and strategies.* Sagamore Press.

Wikipedia. (2020). U.S. national anthem protests (2016–present). https://en.wikipedia.org/wiki/U.S._national_anthem_protests_(2016–present).

Yan, G., Pegoraro, A., & Watanabe, N. M. (2018). Student-athletes' organization of activism at the University of Missouri: Resource mobilization on Twitter. *Journal of Sport Management*, 32, 24–37.

Zheng, J., & Garcia, B. (2017). Conclusions: The rising importance of supporter activism in European football. In B. Garcia & J. Zheng (Eds.), *Football and supporter activism in Europe* (pp. 277–285). Palgrave Macmillan.

Ziller, T., & Prada M. (2017). The WNBA has been at the forefront of protesting racial injustice. *SBNation.* https://www.sbnation.com/2017/9/24//16357206/national-anthem-protest-wnba-history-donald-trump.

Zirin, D. (2005). *What's my name, fool? Sports and resistance in the United States.* Chicago: Haymarket Books.

Zirin, D. (2008). *A people's history of sports in the United States: 250 years of politics, protest, people and play.* New York: The New Press.

CHAPTER 31

···

SPORT, ANIMALS,
AND HUMANS

···

MICHAEL ATKINSON AND KASS GIBSON

DESPITE 30 years of spotty, and now more patterned, human-animal research in sport and leisure, the study of animal intersections with sports cultures remains a peripheral but nonetheless fascinating field of inquiry in the parent discipline. Once the terrain of almost exclusively evangelical animal companion enthusiasts or morally outraged animal rights advocates, the study of how animals are included in human sport and leisure pursuits attests to how animals are both subjects and objects of human concern across diverse fields of play (Gibson, 2020). As Young (2017) articulates, there is indeed an expansive "animal-sport complex" in the West worthy of sustained critical inspection. Fascinating, in such an animal-sport complex, is how animals are socially constructed as meaningful through human sport and leisure (Danby, 2018), how animal struggles in sport now align with broader cultural turns to social justice and inclusion for marginalized beings (Carter & Charles, 2013), and how addressing core sociological concepts through animal studies (such as agency, emotion, sociality, and community) has the potential to decenter the human as the exclusive subject of sociological inquiry (Atkinson, 2014).

Notwithstanding this ostensible diversity in human-animal research, Gibson (2020) justifiably underlines how studies in the area patently emphasize the former set of actors over the latter. Human-animal research in sport predominantly attests to the meaning of animal companionship for *humans*; how the abuse of animals in sport underlines morally bankrupt or speciesist cultures of real or symbolic violence which need rehabilitation for the common human good; and how the overuse, neglect, or denial of the presence of animals in sport is buttressed by, and an outcome of, oppressive capitalistic and commodity-fetishized social environments that treat animals as unlimited natural resources for consumption. Yet to emerge, however, is a sociology *of* "sporting" animals that is *for* animals as a genuinely emancipatory, social justice–based field. If sociology proper, and the sociology of sport and physical culture more specifically, now resolutely positions itself as an interventionist field of praxis committed to improving the lives of the marginalized (Cooky, 2017), surely sociologists of sport can no longer apolitically sit on the zoological sidelines. Stated differently, who among active sport researchers in the field is taking a proverbial knee for animals through critical research and politically oriented public sociological work?

Part of the ambiguity of what, precisely, a sociology of human-animal relationships in sport advocates for is rooted in deep conceptual tensions related to the position of "different" actors involved in the very organization of sport. Sport, like leisure, is a human construct and as such is conceptually, symbolically, and intersubjectively meaningful only to humans. On these grounds alone, a sociology of human-animal or multispecies sport/leisure is not only an ontological misnomer; it overtly implies multispecies consent and equality in sports practice (see Young, 2017). Animal-based sports such as show jumping, rodeo, canicross, diverse forms of animal racing, polo, pit fighting, fishing, dog agility trials, and a host of others scarcely resemble anything nondomesticated and untrained animals self-organize and do together on their own with agency or as collective expressions of their own physical cultures. Paintings of dogs playing poker on crushed-velvet canvases are as equally absurd depictions of animal physical cultures as the concept of dogs finding meaning by running in tandem across the frozen tundra of Alaska for a "personal best time." Further, while it may be morally comforting to consider dogs who walk with their owners through parks or on trails (Fletcher & Platt, 2018), horses venturing out on vacation with their caretakers (Buchmann, 2017), or dolphins enjoying tourists swimming alongside them (Warkentin, 2011) as pleasurable leisure, these activities are generally organized almost exclusively for human purposes and ends. "Leisure time" for most animals rarely involves anything resembling time-based running, fetching, travel, or intense physical exertion; quite to the contrary, it generally involves relaxation, casual interaction with other animals, and copious amounts of sleep. Ironically, animal sport and recreation pastimes are often designed by their animal owners to provide opportunities for movement and expression denied to animals daily *because* of their passive commodity position as domesticated companion species (i.e., my dog needs to go for a run because she's locked in the house all day, or my horse travels with me on vacation because he's been raised by humans, alienated from other horses, and thus is lonely without me). Even more complicated, and beyond the score of this chapter, is the analysis of how many supposed animal traits and drives (e.g., hunting, retrieving, running, etc.) have been partially altered through human intervention via selective breeding and training over time.

A more reality-congruent and evocative line of possibility, we feel, would be the development of an *interspecies physical cultural studies* (ISPCS). Here, an ISPCS shifts the focus away from human-centered animal sports cultures by acknowledging the plurality of physical cultures (if we first adopt the notion that cultures are established as problem-solving sets of practices) in the natural world, and that different species practice physicality/embodiment in a range of radically contextual ways. Nonhuman animals, in their natural habitats, engage in organized, patterned, expressive physical activities such as acquiring food, building shelters, defending themselves, being social members of groups, displaying emotions, and even playing together on their own terms that may or may not align with human desires. As such, it is not an extraordinary conceptual leap to suggest animal species share unique physical cultures that do not map perfectly onto human physical cultures even at the most unreflexive (i.e., nonsymbolic) and rudimentary levels. In their research on humans and fish sharing the "dance of angling," Markuksela and Valtonen (2019, pp. 355–356) find, "Fish in a body of water swim their routes below the surface and propel their sensing bodies through the water. Fish also have their own bodily routines and rhythmicity (e.g., eating, sleeping, mating) that form underwater patterns, constituting the secrets of the world of the fish."

An ISPCS attends, then, to how "the secret [physical cultural] worlds" of nonhuman animal physical cultures scrape up against and are encroached upon by human physical cultures (and vice versa) as a matter of complicated micrological and macrological social tectonics inside and outside of sport. ISPCS further examines how animals-humans are directly mixed together in the practice of human-oriented sports and leisure pastimes and how dominant relations of material (human) power and inequality between species are reproduced through sports and leisure cultures. Space is also included in ISPCS for the purposes of examining the practice of physical cultures from the positions and perspectives of animals and for exploring the possibilities of interspecies relationships in human sport and leisure becoming more equitable and needs-sensitive to nonhumans. Finally, an ISPCS must challenge the field of animal studies to be less anthropocentric and include a wider range of animals as subjects of inquiry. Curious is how even the most ardent animal enthusiast in sport ignores the critical study of beetles or frogs as being affected by human sport and leisure cultures. Indeed, it seems, even among marginalized participants in sport and leisure, there is a clear hierarchy of privileged animals, with horses and dogs at the very top (Gibson, 2020).

In the remainder of this chapter, we review dominant currents and slowly emerging eddies in a (potential) *interspecies physical cultural studies*. We present the case that there are preferred subjects, theories, and methods in human-animal studies in the sociology of sport, and that even recent innovative movements, including new materialist musings, perhaps offer little other than an insertion of animals into human studies. Toward the end of the chapter, we suggest an ISPCS necessitates a truly interdisciplinary focus that not only breaks free from sociologically dominant theorizing of animals in sport and leisure but also presses physical cultural studies to expand the conceptualization of physical culture to beyond human studies alone.

ISSUES

As we have documented elsewhere (Atkinson, 2014; Gibson, 2020), the study of animals in/as/and sport began in order to better understand sociological problems, most notably social order and social change. For example, Elias (1986/2008) argues changes to fox hunting can be understood only as part of broader social, cultural, and psychological changes in Western societies. Even accepting criticisms that Elias's study of the pacification of early sporting forms, including fox hunting, was empirically weaker than necessary (Green, Liston, Smith, & Bloyce, 2005), Elias theorizes changes in social organization, social control of, and attitudes toward violence, and emotional restraint more broadly (see Malcolm, 2005, 2019). Similarly, Clifford Geertz (1972)—an anthropologist trained by sociologist Talcott Parsons—uses cockfighting in order to better understand Balinese social order. With that said, anthropologists had given more consideration to the cultural importance of animals (Douglas, 1966; Evans-Pritchard, 1956; Levi-Strauss, 1966) than most sociologists (and truly, most sociologists of sport). Nonetheless, Geertz (1972, p. 17) provides intimate details of the structure and organization of pre-match preparation and care of cocks and the role, performance, and effects of in-match gambling to trace the migration of Balinese cultural norms—including, for example, gendered practices and status hierarchies—to their embodiment in and through the cockfight as "a simulation of the social matrix."

Of course, these examples do not mark the emergence of an identifiable field of human-animal sport research. Increased focus on human-animal sport to the extent that clearly articulated and concatenated research programs—and an associated body of literature—centering animals in analyses of sport mark a zoological focus developed as scholars worked to address critiques of sociologists (of sport and leisure) ignoring "the permeating social influence of animals in our larger cultural fabric and our more idiosyncratic individual modes of interaction and relationships" (Bryant, 1979, p. 400). Initially, and including the aforementioned studies by Elias and Geertz, zoological perspectives on sport addressed animal blood sports. Indeed, violence in human-animal sport has been studied extensively (e.g., Evans & Forsyth, 1997; Hawley, 1989; Kalof & Taylor, 2007; Wade, 1990; Windeatt, 1982; Worden & Darden, 1992). The appeal of blood sport forms to researchers is the obvious possibility for and importance of sociological explanations of how collective (abusive) actions and social and cultural norms explain abuse as opposed to commonsense accounts of individual (pathological) personalities and behaviors. Furthermore, as Young (2017) documents, animal blood sports, especially fighting and baiting, have long histories across the globe, including, but not limited to, ancient Rome, Persia, China, India, and Japan. This historical and cultural ubiquity of blood sports—and the sportization of fishing and hunting (e.g., Markuksela & Valtonen, 2019; von Essen & Tickle, 2020)—means the primary issues of concern for scholarly interest have included how the practice and economies of blood sports continue despite running contrary to general public values and legality (Atkinson & Young, 2005, 2008), subcultural rationalization and justification of violence and abuse (Atkinson, 2014; Gibson, 2014), and broader philosophical and political rhetoric regarding the ethical and moral treatment of animals.

Understanding the permeating social influence of animals as articulated by Clifton Bryant, however, requires researchers to study the (mostly) accepted, quotidian human-animal sports, a task taken to with alacrity in human-canine and human-equine relationships (e.g., Carr, 2014; Dashper, 2017; Fletcher & Platt, 2018; Sanders, 1999). For example, scholars have addressed dog agility and canicross as examples of emotional attachment, assignment of meaning to activities, and negotiation of action between humans and dogs (Baldwin & Norris, 1999; Gillespie, Leffler, & Lerner, 2002; Hultsman, 2012; Merchant, 2020; Nottle & Young, 2019). Similarly, studies of the "equiscape"—the multifaceted cultural and geographical field of human and equine leisure practices—chart processes of emotional connection, negotiated participation, and identity markers in human-equine encounters (Dashper, 2017; Dashper, Abbott, & Wallace, 2019; Gilbert & Gillett, 2012; Wipper, 2000). Such research is largely referred to as "multispecies sport," and its growing interest has led some to argue for yet another turn in the social sciences, the so-called animal turn (see Danby, Dashper, & Finkel, 2019).

Researchers have argued that a shift in attention to uncontested and seemingly unproblematic activities as part of the animal turn is necessary because such activities have been largely overlooked by researchers and also because it serves as an example of rising interest among social scientists to include nonhuman actors in their research (Dashper, 2019). In the first instance, then, the animal turn in the sociology of sport and leisure reflects increasing interest in moving beyond exclusively human (social) actions and concerns. In effect, researchers began to explicitly acknowledge and address nonhuman actors beyond how they affect human outcomes (Catlin, Hughes, Jones, Jones, & Campbell, 2013; Danby et al., 2019). Multispecies sport researchers have responded to Donna Haraway's (2003) call to focus on being with nonhuman animals through a range of practices in which, purposefully or otherwise, humans and animals coevolve and co-inhabit space (see also Lynch, 2019).

So-called multispecies sport research focuses largely on the formation of intimate and mutually constitutive relationships of humans and animals in human leisure activities. Such work largely becomes the study of animals as companion species. Conceptualizing animals as companion species is driven by fundamental questioning of the ways in which nonhuman animals experience suffering and pleasure. Haraway (2003, 2008) reignited in-depth exploration of what these pleasures, pains, cognitions, and agencies mean for human relationships with animals in our homes, on the streets, on the farm, and in medical laboratories (see Arluke & Sanders, 1996). In the context of multispecies sport, this results in researching human-animal relationships *in* and *through* human sporting and leisure activities involving animals. Dashper (2017, p. 12) succinctly summarizes the general approach of companionship perspectives in her own research in the equiscape, which she characterizes as being designed to "understand how horses and humans come into contact with each other, become entangled and engaged with each other, shape each other, through various different sport and leisure-related practices." The animal turn has shifted focus from core questions of social order, social action, and social change to social interaction and the mutual constituting nature of human-animal relationships. For us, however, the paradox of violence is nonetheless the defining issue of the field.

First, human-animal sport originally landed on the radar of sociologists through concerns over animal blood sports, where, as argued above, violence is central to all analyses. Second, multispecies sport and leisure scholarship is defined by its supposed opposition to violence. As such, violence is central to the sociological problem (see Campbell, 2019) of human-animal/multispecies sport and leisure. Yet, by downplaying the implications of this, multispecies sport researchers have ignored trying to understand

> what it is about modern society that makes it possible for people to shower animals with affection and to maltreat or kill them, to regard them as sentient creatures and also as utilitarian objects. How is it that people seem able to balance such significantly conflicting values and live comfortably with such contradiction? (Arluke & Sanders, 1996, p. 5)

This returns us to Young's (2017, p. 81) identification of an animal-sport complex requiring further study:

> [R]eplete as it is with all of its disturbing—and sometimes illegal—characteristics and practices, [it] is only a "complex" because of the involvement of humans. In and of itself, this renders the animal-sport relation a fundamentally social one and underlines the necessity of bringing a sociological imagination to this relationship.

In this context, Young rather understates the involvement of humans. Humans are not simply involved in human-animal/multispecies sport. The basis, purpose, meaning, structure, organization, and performance of sport are conducted on human terms and primarily for human benefit.

We see violence not only as a fundamental issue in human-animal/multispecies sport but also as a challenge of postmodernity. In the same way that Jean Baudrillard (1975) came to understand Marxism as substantiating capitalist mentalities and values, multispecies sport scholars unintentionally vindicate animal subservience. Baudrillard criticizes Marx's theory of species being for rooting human potential in production. Both what and how we produce something provides a mirror for us to see human nature. Put simply, species being holds that true consciousness and fulfillment is to be found in intimate connection and involvement in the production process. Baudrillard identifies that from such a perspective Marx is reducing humanity to economic producers in the same way that capitalism does, thereby actually legitimating capitalist schemes of production. In response, Baudrillard argues that "in order to find a realm beyond economic value (which is in fact the only revolutionary perspective), then *the mirror of production* in which all Western metaphysics is reflected, must be broken" (p. 47, emphasis in original).

Proponents of multispecies sport, such as Dashper (2019, p. 135), who focus on aspects of human-animal interaction in terms of agency, communication, and co-constitution, are correct in their observation that insufficient attention has been given to determining the answer to the question "[W]hose leisure are we talking about?" However, by foregrounding agency and identity as central issues, downplaying violence, and accepting that "nonhuman animals should not be excluded from ideas of leisure on the grounds of inability to exercise some degree of agency" (p. 134), how are we to assess the expressions of agency that do not fit within our expectations of animal behavior and communication? Acknowledging sport as more-than-human is clearly insufficient to break this mirror (Giraud, 2019). Clearly, multispecies sport scholars are yet to navigate anthropologist Tim Ingold's (1994, p. 1) baseline observation that "just as humans have a history of their relations with animals, so also animals have a history of their relations with humans. Only humans, however, construct narratives of this history."

APPROACHES

Theoretical readings of animals in the sociology of sport and leisure literature are a complex but somewhat predictable pastiche of thought. The earliest theoretical trends are rooted in Chicago-style symbolic interactionism and Leicester school figurational sociology. Studies in the former theoretical vein (predominantly nestled in the sociology of deviance) attend to, largely, how illegal animal hunting and fighting cultures in the southern United States (and elsewhere) are discursively constructed by subcultural insiders as morally justifiable (Hawley, 1989; Worden & Darden, 1992). Taking culturally relativistic stances, insiders to poaching and pit fighting subcultures symbolically construct the use of animals for blood sports to be rational, long-term, localized cultural traditions. The latter, while sharing focal affinities with symbolic interactionist work, scrutinized the historical emergence, sociogenesis, and sportization of animal sports such as fox hunting, birding, and coursing in England as evidence of civilizing processes (Atkinson & Young, 2008; Dunning, 1999). Here, the substitution of animals in violent sports as replacements for human beings roughly represents a psychogenic cultural shift toward self-restraint codes and practices. Both theoretical traditions position animals as secondary or even tertiary subjects of interest in favor of conceptual dissections of how animal sports reveal tensions between social classes, rural versus urban cultures, and the tensions between historical codes of masculinity and emerging social ethics condemning violence against animals.

Over the past two decades, feminist (Kheel, 1999), cyborg (Haraway, 2008), environmentalist (Wilson & Millington, 2020), and ethics-oriented (Morris, 2014) readings of animal sports displaced blood sport–based research and associated theoretical preferences. Across these theoretical strands a consistent focus on considering sport and leisure as a mélange of more-than-human involvement is evident. Questions of animal agency, the phenomenology of experience between species in natural environments, the ethics of human domination of animals, and the coproduction of sport and leisure through multispecies mingling are raised. Thematically, the field turned toward studying less violent, dominance-oriented, and mastery-based encounters between humans and animals to illustrate how animals might benefit from "meaningful" sport and leisure with humans and how animal rights issues intersect with vulnerable other social actors. While we have argued in this chapter that such projects might collectively fail in their attempts to radically shift thinking about animals in sport and leisure, they coalesce to produce a different sensibility regarding how human-animal relationships, and their consequences, unfold in practice. Particularly noteworthy are how different human-animal interactions are considered in human sport and leisure worlds, such as Markwell's (2019) account of humans and lizards.

Most recently, the rhizomatic actor network and neo-materialist fetish in the sociologies of sport and leisure have ushered in (somewhat) new thinking about animal significance in sport, leisure, and tourism. Taking the lead from actor network theory and the general argument that humans and animals are symmetrical actants in complex networks of material and symbolic action, the general theoretical oeuvre is to consider how humans, animals, environments, and built structures must be analyzed concomitantly (Wilson & Millington, 2020). King and Weedon's (2020) analysis of animal-derived whey protein supplements is equally informed by actor network and new materialist interests in nonhuman "things" as actants with agency. Unfortunately, however, these sorts of analyses tend to bring animal research full circle in the process of displacing the animal as a worthy subject of inspection *alone* amid a dizzying array of (largely human) material/environmental concerns. Animals become, once more, punctuated as central but yet peripheral actants in human-animal networks. In the rush to illustrate how humans are more than socially discursive constructions and enmeshed within dense material, symbiotic networks of existence, animal subjectivities, communities, and physical cultures are negated. Curiously absent in this emerging tradition are potentially more holistic and informative theoretical innovations focused on the interdependence of humans and animals, and the moral value of animals themselves apart from human meaning or use. Especially untapped are postcolonial theories which challenge sociologists of sport and leisure to see themselves and others as human colonists of animal physical cultures—regardless of their intentions. Similarly, Indigenous or First Nations spiritual constructions of animals as sacred members of the web of all life remain extensively overlooked or given only hand-wave references to being relevant.

Substantively, as we have noted throughout this chapter, there is a Malthusian overabundance of studies on dogs and horses. As such, understanding human-animal engagements and co-constitution in sport is often predicated on privileging certain animals and their associated concepts of animal insertion in sport. Said differently, different forms of animal integration are relatively overlooked and understudied when dogs and horses (i.e., the closest of animal companions in developed Western societies) are afforded the opportunity to form emotional bonds with (or therapy for) humans generally and are then foregrounded in research specifically. Despite the claims of proponents of multispecies sport scholarship (e.g., Danby et al., 2019), multispecies research focuses narrowly on particular, privileged non-human animals. Even in blood sports, as with the paradox of violence outlined above being routinely overlooked, dogs are still prioritized (Atkinson, 2014). Across approaches, then, other subordinate, less privileged roles animals occupy in (multispecies) sport and leisure events are still largely ignored (Gillett & Gilbert, 2014).

Understanding human-animal sport as examples of human-animal companionship and co-constitution has been developed most successfully through ethnographic and autoethnographic work. A thoroughgoing explanation of ethnographic research is certainly beyond the scope of this chapter; interested readers should consult Arluke and Sanders (1996, pp. 18–40), who, although not using the term "multispecies," identify and explore core methodological and theoretical challenges for the field. Of particular importance here is the articulation of inside and incursive ethnographies with animals. Classically, insider ethnography involves researchers studying situations where their personal relationships and investments predate the research project. Incursive ethnography, then, involves researchers entering new situations and environments. Following the animal turn in sport and leisure, insider ethnography is a hallmark of multispecies and more-than-human work (Atkinson, 2014; Atkinson & Gibson, 2014; Atkinson & Young, 2005). This is attributable to practical considerations of ease of entrée, for example. Epistemologically, the ability to reproduce "a complete and emotionally informed account, not just of the human perspective, but also that of the animal" (Arluke & Sanders, 1996, p. 29) is a defining feature of insider, multispecies ethnography. For example, Dashper (2019, p. 136) notes that "research in the field of human-horse relationships stresses the importance of working together across species boundaries, employing the language of partnership over that of force and coercion" which is best—or indeed only—developed through insider status.

In their reflection on the field's ongoing development and promise, Danby et al. (2019, p. 291) have encouraged researchers to consider how:

> The emerging multidisciplinary field of human-animal studies encourages researchers to move beyond a narrow focus on human-centric practices and ways of being in the world, and to recognise that human and nonhuman beings are positioned within shared ecological, social, cultural and political spaces. Wider social debates related to ethics and welfare, environmental concerns and climate change, and human rights and responsibilities to the wider world, are not detached from the field of leisure studies which is both influenced by and can influence wider discourses. The broader field of human-animal studies has tended to focus on topics such as care, welfare and work, or specific human-animal encounters, such as those between people and companion animals or pets . . . and leisure has received much less focus to date. . . . [R]esearchers [need to] to think beyond our taken-for-granted humanist frameworks and to consider explicitly the ways in which leisure spaces and practices are co-produced, shaped and experienced by human and nonhuman animals, and what those multispecies encounters add to understandings of leisure as integral to our well-being and happiness in contemporary societies.

However, the received projection of "our well-being" too often leads to the individual, insider researcher's (ethnographic or autoethnographic) moral sentiments also being projected as a sociological process and an unintended defining feature of multispecies sport ethnography. Even when attempts are made to promote nonhuman animals as significant, such positionings ultimately relate back to human-centered politics, problems, networks, and sport/leisure. Recognizing animals as actors in networks makes analytic sense, but as Cudworth (2016, p. 243) reminds us, "simply including non-human animals as a sociological subject does not a critical [and, we would add, inclusive or progressive] sociology make."

Even when efforts are made to decenter the human, as noted previously, only a small proportion of animals are afforded the opportunity to express agency or be worthy of consideration. Although there is not ultimate consensus among zoologists, estimates suggest there are in excess of 8.7 million species of plants and animals on planet Earth; of the 8.7 million, nearly 2 million are animals. Yet the number of animals studied in the sociology of sport and leisure accounts for about two dozen of them. Prouse's (2019) pioneering account of the relationship between mosquitoes, the Zika virus, the 2016 Olympic Games in Rio de Janeiro, population health, and urban political ecologies underpinned by power relations stands out as a landmark analysis of how something as small as an insect matters socially and, by extension, sociologically. Prouse (2019) deftly articulates how seemingly insignificant beings, and their capacity for agency, simply must be taken into account. But the analysis eventually progresses to where most animal studies eventually land; a focus on the effect on the unbuilt or natural environment (and their inhabitants) from human pursuits such as sports mega-events. While Prouse's study is groundbreaking for its attention to a different nonhuman in sport studies, sociologists of sport and leisure tend to focus on domesticated or working animals, in part because they have been objects of human use for millennia and because autoethnographies of one's own personal animal fascination(s) may make light sociological work.

DEBATES

While many of the debates and tensions in animal sport and leisure have been documented in this chapter so far, four are worth specific consideration. First, an argument can be made that across the swath of research efforts in the sociology of animal sport and leisure, a general tendency abounds to reproduce the diffuse ideology that nonhumans hold inferior moral and subjective statuses to humans. While the first era of animal research in sport underscored the abusive treatment of nonhumans as morally reprehensible (but culturally justifiable), the second era generally questions and presents what more moral, ethical, and coproductive sports and leisure practices might look like and evoke. Still, the latter line of research replicates a conceptualization of animals as moral patients requiring human stewardship to live their "best lives" and the need for animal/leisure sport enthusiasts to wield a morally guided, Foucauldian-like governmental biopower over nonhumans. Yet for animal rights advocates, decades-old questions about animals as being subjects of their own lives are too often essentially sidestepped, as are questions regarding animal self-determination and cultural autonomy free from human sport and leisure interests.

In Atkinson's (2014) analysis of "terrier work" in rural England, he questioned what it would be like to perceive fox hunting from the imagined perspectives of the dogs and foxes involved as part of his discussion of what animal standpoint theory might offer to the sociology of animals in sport. Farmers and the owners of the terriers used to flush out and kill foxes from dens situated on farmland (because foxes prey on small farm animals used for human consumption) share constructions of the foxes as unwanted pests and/or objects of a hunting game. To this end, the terrier men who supply culling services construct their efforts as morally righteous because they are (temporarily) saving the lives of chickens, rabbits, and other small animals while protecting the entire rural ecosystem from fox over-population. Humans, as the dominant narrative script goes, are self-positioned as the moral and biological regulators of multispecies landscapes. Yet if we adopt a different perspective and view the countryside as the home of animals like foxes who have adapted their phys-ical (hunting) cultures in response to human encroachment, the practice becomes morally gray. Such moral ambiguity is further darkened by a consideration of how terriers are bred, kept, and trained by hunters to engage in close, violent encounters with foxes (a species with whom they would rarely come into close contact). In the entire zoological network manipulated through "terrier work," foxes, dogs, chickens, lambs, and other animals are scarcely considered as moral patients worthy of protection or as subjects of their own lives.

Second, and in relation to the above, our worry is that the burgeoning new materialist and actor network theoretical wave in the sociology of sport may stagnate critical thinking regarding the actual material conditions of animal lives inside and outside of sport and leisure zones. Quite simply, and as rudimentary sociology instructs, markedly imbalanced power relationships rarely produce equitable grounds of empathetic social interaction. Animals are neither equal nor powerful in the context of human sport and leisure, or in sport and leisure research. Embedding them, through a theoretical sleight of hand, as actors with definitive agency in human-defined networks obfuscates the core power differential existing between humans and nonhumans. Take, for example, the sorts of animals we reg-ularly study, as noted throughout the chapter. Sociologists prefer to swim with dolphins, not sharks. We love to ride horses, but rarely bulls. We run with dogs but not jaguars, and we lounge musing about the world with small cats but not large lions. Our preferences for seeing bonding, therapy, co-constitution, and mutually beneficial play potential for ani-mals tend to begin at the same point where their domestication has been achieved. Here, we would also add that Western sports and leisure practices, and Western preferred an-imal companion species (for white middle-class and working-class people) are gener-ally the subjects of interest. The sociology of animal sports holds little interest outside of North America and Western Europe. In Wacquant's (2005) terms, and perhaps save for the hunting literature, there is not a wild, untamed, carnal sociology of animals in sport and lei-sure. Further still, ignoring that animals possess physical cultures that exist independently of human thought, need, or intervention is common. Our seeming inability to consider how animals might play a role in human sporting pastimes, or to use them constructively to theorize about the complexity of human life, demonstrates perfectly that this has been largely a relationship of indifference. Animals can be willing participants in sport, leisure, and tourism processes, but certainly not on their terms alone.

While sociological and societal concerns about concussion and head trauma are well documented within the massive pain and injury literature in sport, a rare few sociologically dissect the pain, injury, and trauma experienced by animal "athletes" or participants in sport and leisure pursuits. In Atkinson and Young's (2005) study of the greyhound racing figuration they documented a veritable laundry list of physical, emotional, and psycholog-ical suffering that animals endure in both the front and back regions of the racing industry. Animals are temporarily injured or permanently maimed (and as a result, often euthanized and unceremoniously discarded) in a full spate of animal sports like bullfighting, dog sledding, equestrian events, fishing, hunting, racing, polo, and others. The denial of animal pain and injury (ironically, in an academic subdiscipline overflowing with case studies of human injury through sport) underlines the widely shared speciesist perspective that animals feel neither pain nor injury akin to humans (Young & Gerber, 2014). The negation of their lived material conditions of pain and suffering, we argue, illustrates how thinking about the agency of animals in more-than-human sport is a premature and sociological distraction from core problems related to the biopower humans continue to wield over animals across sport and leisure contexts.

Third, and once more related to recent theorizing, citing the vulnerability of animal lives to draw awareness to the vulnerability of human life illustrates a prima facie conflation that the immediate concerns for animals are always similar to the (social) problems of humans. Clearly, and perhaps an uncomfortable and unpopular take, while patriarchal cultures around the world have historically subjugated women and animals with brutal and inhumane consequences, animal rights issues are not inherently a feminist issue. While we have clearly intimated that intersectional analysis might be apropos in the study of animals (in that there are clear hierarchies of intersectional oppression in which animals are mistreated in sport and how), co-opting animal subjectivities and lived experiences as perfect parallels to the marginalization of women and feminist politics overreaches at times—especially given how many feminist scholars and other critical/identity politics researchers of animal sport and leisure forget about the pervasive subjugation of animals as they get dressed each morning or when they sit down every evening at the dinner table to exercise their human (bio)power over animals. Stated differently, comparative parallels in oppression make sense as long as those being drawn in such comparisons do not lose their unique identities, needs, and focal concerns in the process.

Kerr, Stirling, and Wilson (2020), similar to other social scientists of high-performance sport, document how vulnerable young, predominantly female athletes routinely fall prey to sexual predators in sport. While the extensive sexual exploitation of young athletes is only now, more to the pity, receiving the critical interrogation it warrants as evidence of cultures of insidious patriarchal power in sport, sociologists of sport are generally unaware of and unconcerned with how animal sexuality is oppressively surveilled, controlled, and regulated by both men and women in sports and leisure cultures. The predatory and exploitative breeding of animals, regardless of their biological sex, through either forced or selective insemination, spaying or neutering, and penning up to prevent them from engaging in sensual encounters with other animals, are all standard practices in animal sport and leisure cultures. It is interesting that, in a field which sanctifies Foucault, no critical scholar of animal sports has produced a genealogical or archaeological reading of the power-imbalanced animal sexual histories in sport. The takeaway from this must be that even "woke" critical scholarship ostensibly sees nonhuman animals as unimportant, even from a posture which resolutely extols how sexual agency, choice, and consent (especially for the intersectionally vulnerable and marginalized) are fundamental to upholding universal "my body, my choice" cultural values, ethics, and laws. What rights to sexual agency, reproduction, and desire do sporting animals have, then? The lack of theoretical engagement with sexuality and desire within the study of animal physical cultures is somewhat astonishing to us because critical scholars of multispecies sport have addressed the capacity for animals to share meaningful bonds, emotions, relationships, and indeed the capacity to touch each other in sensual ways. As such, researchers are clearly sensitive to the affective lives of nonhuman beings. But the concept of a fleshy, desiring, carnal, animal sexuality is entirely absent in the field because human cultures predominantly view animal sexuality as something to be managed as a matter of rational commodity production or as entirely unrelated to the existential needs of "my" companion, sport, or therapy animal/pet. Even when scholars such as Palmer (2001) have extended critical/feminist Foucauldian thinking to studies of human-animal power relationships, animal desire and sexuality are sociological nonstarters.

Finally, we see great opportunities missed in the (non)creation of collaborative research efforts involving researchers from sociology, psychology, history, human geography, zoology, and the biosciences to study unique animal physical cultures (not sport, not leisure) and how embodiment is practiced in enduring, meaningful ways among animal groups. Researchers could be engaged less in trying to understand how humans are material in creating ties to "others" or in how humans and animals may learn to accomplish things together and put more effort into understanding how the physical cultural of embodiment of nonhumans teaches us something uniquely profound about its social and phenomenological aspects across unique species. Important in such efforts could be the resultant production of much more nuanced understandings of how contextually embodied movement and physical expression cut across human-animal cultures, and how such expression is not, in most instances, mutually oriented or reconcilable with a common cooperative purpose. Understanding sites of multispecies collision and more equitable interspecies physical cultural mosaics of existence could come to the fore. Sociologists of sport should, and we would argue must, learn to lean on other academics in such collaborations as they possess expertise far beyond the disciplinary knowledge we hold. This is why we prefer the term *interspecies physical cultural studies*, as it explicitly challenges researchers to extend their minds far beyond the sociology of animals in sport and leisure in both theory and substantive research.

Attending to the complicated physical cultures that animals share requires innovation both methodologically and theoretically. Van Dooren, Kirksey, and Münster (2016, p. 6) suggest that researchers genuinely interested in animal studies would benefit from a range of "passionate immersion" methodologies in the fields where animals live. Describing immersive methodologies as ethnography, ethno-ethnology, anthropology of life, anthropology beyond humanity, and more-than-human geographies, Van Dooren et al. call for interdisciplinary methods of animal study which privilege the animal and inspect how animal cultural logics unfold in context. Their description of the need to immerse oneself in the "liveliness of existence" (p. 8) in order to understand and theorize animal realities beyond the human (and their associated physical cultures), like Locke's (2013) account of ethnoelephantology, illustrates not only how researchers in other spaces are already engaged in complex multidisciplinary work, but also how far the sociology of (animal) sport and physical culture lags behind. Kuhl's (2019) work on field encounters with wolves draws similar attention to the methodological benefits of watching, participating with, learning from, and respecting animals in their own environments on (mostly) their own terms. Finally, Wright, Suchet-Pearson, Lloyd, Burarrwanga, and Burarrwanga's (2009, p. 509) work on wilderness tourism documents the importance of Indigenous ways of seeing, approaching, and teaching about the "intercultural zones" that humans and animals share as part of a densely interconnected web of life (see also Todd, 2014). Individually and collectively, each of these studies challenges dominant and emerging ontologies and epistemologies in the sociology of animal sport, leisure, and physical culture.

Conclusion

Upon final reflection, and after separate and joint research efforts on animals in and around sports cultures, we maintain that nonhumans remain tacitly separate and unequal in sociological thinking. We find this rather curious given the field's decisive pivot in the past decade toward unapologetic political intervention and public academic work. A broad discipline committed to social justice, equity, and inclusion appears to have made a collective decision regarding the status of animals; they are diffuse actants in networks but are mainly seen as unworthy of conceptualization as vulnerable *citizens* with subjectivities and lives/ physical cultures of their own. As long as the sociology of animals in sport and leisure leans toward reaffirming nonhumans as decentered subjects through expressive human play, or as subjects of research to further probe the complexity of the human lived/material experience, few theoretical and methodological breakthroughs will occur. Studies of multispecies companionship and sensual explorations of the (sporting) world teach us a great deal of how animals are integrated into human lives for exciting and significant bonding. Further still, the environmental and neo-materialist turn, one could argue, may actually lessen the moral status of animals as focus is shifted away from them as subjects with emplaced, embodied, and situated existence and toward their lives as components in intricately interlaced biosystems.

We lobby, then, for the exploration and inspection of an interspecies physical cultural studies that strives to do more than merely add animals into the mix, replicate human exceptionalism, conceptualize how humans are co-constituted with nonhumans, utilize animal studies to promulgate avant-garde sociological theory about human experience, or fetishize human sport cultures as the only physical cultures worth attention. An ISPCS seeks not to argue how animals are more like "us" or, in contrast, how we are more like "them" in poignant phenomenological or network research. Instead, an ISPCS, a necessarily interdisciplinary field of inquiry, must struggle to consider how animals share their own unique physical cultures, how such cultures intersect and are interfered with by humans and other animals alike. It unwaveringly accounts for how animals with power (read *humans*) co-opt and exploit the physical cultural capabilities of other animals for sport and leisure interests.

An ISPCS lays bare the historical and ongoing human cultural constructions of animals that position them as objects of human use (including self-actualization) in a vast spectrum of contexts. Rather than automatically aligning the plight of nonhuman animals with feminist, racial, queer, or environmental standpoints on marginalization and its dehumanizing impacts, an ISPCS begins with, at times, the standpoint of animals (and their radically contextual sentience) (Atkinson, 2014). Whereas all marginalized actors may share suffering experiences, animal experiences are different from humans' along important ontological lines, and as such must not become symbolic prostheses for others' politics. Animal lives are worthy of their own unique theorization that may not align with critical theoretical streams in human sociology. The ISPCS, more than anything else, requires those committed to interspecies cultural studies to expand their minds, theories, methods, collaborations, and personal comfort zones to learn from animals rather than simply writing traditional sociological stories about them.

REFERENCES

Arluke, A., & Sanders, C. R. (1996). *Regarding animals.* Philadelphia: Temple University Press.

Atkinson, M. (2014). The terrier [men]. *Sociology of Sport Journal, 31*(4), 420–437.

Atkinson, M., & Gibson, K. (2014). Communion without collision: Animals, sport and interspecies co-presence. In J. Gillett & M. Gilbert (Eds.), *Sport, animals and society* (pp. 268–290). New York: Routledge.

Atkinson, M., & Young, K. (2005). Reservoir dogs: Greyhound racing as sports-related violence. *International Review of the Sociology of Sport, 40*(3), 335–356.

Atkinson, M., & Young, K. (2008). *Deviance and social control in sport.* Champaign: Human Kinetics.

Baldwin, C. K., & Norris, P. A. (1999). Exploring the dimensions of serious leisure: "Love me—Love my dog!" *Journal of Leisure Research, 31*(1), 1–17.

Baudrillard, J. (1975). *Mirror of production.* St. Louis: Telos Press.

Bryant, C. (1979). The zoological connection: Animal related human behavior. *Social Forces, 58,* 399–421.

Buchmann, A. (2017). Insights into domestic horse tourism: The case study of Lake Macquarie, NSW, Australia. *Current Issues in Tourism, 20*(3), 261–277.

Campbell, C. (2019). *Has sociology progressed?* Gewerbestrasse, Switzerland: Palgrave Pivot.

Carr, N. (2014). *Dogs in the leisure experience.* London: CABI.

Carter, B., & Charles, N. (2013). Animals, agency and resistance. *Journal for the Theory of Social Behaviour, 43*(3), 322–340.

Catlin, J., Hughes, M., Jones, T., Jones, R., & Campbell, R. (2013). Valuing individual animals through tourism: Science or speculation? *Biological Conservation, 157*(1), 93–98.

Cooky, C. (2017). We cannot stand idly by: A necessary call for a public sociology of sport. *Sociology of Sport Journal, 34*(1), 1–11.

Cudworth, E. (2016). A sociology for other animals: Analysis, advocacy, intervention. *International Journal of Sociology and Social Policy, 36*(3–4), 242–257.

Danby, P. (2018). Post-humanistic insight into human-equine interactions and wellbeing within leisure and tourism. In J. Young & N. Carr (Eds.), *Domestic animals, humans, and leisure* (pp. 58–176). Abingdon, U.K.: Routledge.

Danby, P., Dashper, K., & Finkel, R. (2019). Multispecies leisure: Human-animal interactions in leisure landscapes. *Leisure Studies, 38*(3), 291–302.

Dashper, K. (2017). *Human-animal relationships in equestrian sport and leisure.* Abingdon, U.K.: Routledge.

Dashper, K. (2019). Moving beyond anthropocentrism in leisure research: Multispecies perspectives. *Annals of Leisure Research, 22*(2), 133–139.

Dashper, K., Abbott, J., & Wallace, C. (2019). "Do horses cause divorces?" Autoethnographic insights on family, relationships and resource intensive leisure. *Annals of Leisure Research, 23*(3), 1–18.

Douglas, M. (1966). *Purity and danger: An analysis of concepts of pollution and taboo.* London: Routledge and Kegan Paul.

Dunning, E. (1999). *Sport matters: Sociological studies of sport, violence and civilization.* London: Routledge.

Elias, N. (1986/2008). An essay on sport and violence. In N. Elias & E. Dunning (Eds.), *Quest for excitement: Sport and leisure in the civilising process* (revised ed.) (pp. 150–173). Dublin: University College Dublin Press.

Evans, R., & Forsyth, C. (1997). Entertainment to outrage: A social historical view of dogfighting. *International Review of Modern Sociology, 27*(2), 59–71.

Evans-Pritchard, E. (1956). *Nuer religion.* Oxford: Clarendon Press.

Fletcher, T., & Platt, L. (2018). (Just) a walk with the dog? Animal geographies and negotiating walking spaces. *Social & Cultural Geography, 19*(2), 211–229.

Geertz, C. (1972). Deep play: Notes on the Balinese cockfight. *Dædalus, 101*(1), 1–37.

Gibson, K. (2014). More than murder: Ethics and hunting in New Zealand. *Sociology of Sport Journal, 31*(4), 455–474.

Gibson, K. (2020). Animals, sport, and the environment. In B. Wilson & B. Millington (Eds.), *Sport and the environment* (pp. 103–121). London: Emerald.

Gilbert, M., & Gillett, J. (2012). Equine athletes and interspecies sport. *International Review for the Sociology of Sport, 47*(5), 632–643.

Gillespie, D. L., Leffler, A., & Lerner, E. (2002). If it weren't for my hobby, I'd have a life: Dog sports, serious leisure, and boundary negotiations. *Leisure Studies, 21*(3–4), 285–304.

Gillett, J., & Gilbert, M. (Eds.). (2014). *Sport, animals, and society.* London: Routledge.

Giraud, E. (2019). *What comes after entanglement?* Durham: Duke University Press

Green, K., Liston, K., Smith, A., & Bloyce, D. (2005). Violence, competition and the emergence and development of modern sports: Reflections on the Stokvis-Malcolm debate. *International Review for the Sociology of Sport, 40*(1), 119–124.

Haraway, D. J. (2003). *The companion species manifesto: Dogs, people, and significant otherness.* Chicago: Prickly Paradigm Press.

Haraway, D. J. (2008). *When species meet.* Minneapolis: University of Minnesota Press.

Hawley, F. (1989). Cockfight in the cotton: A moral crusade in microcosm. *Contemporary Crises, 13*(2), 129–144.

Hultsman, W. Z. (2012). Couple involvement in serious leisure: Examining participation in dog agility. *Leisure Studies, 31*(2), 231–253.

Ingold, T. (1994). *What is an animal?* London: Routledge.

Kalof, L., & Taylor, C. (2007). The discourse of dog fighting. *Humanity and Society, 31*(4), 319–333.

Kerr, G., Stirling, A., & Wilson, E. (2020). When the coach-athlete relationship influences vulnerability to sexual abuse of female artistic gymnasts. In R. Kerr, N. Ruchti-Barker, C. Stewart, & G. Kerr (Eds.), *Women's artistic gymnastics: Socio-cultural perspectives* (pp. 143–157). London: Routledge.

Kheel, M. (1999). An eco feminist critique of hunting. *Journal of the Philosophy of Sport, 23,* 30–44.

King, S., & Weedon, G. (2020). Embodiment is ecological: The metabolic lives of whey protein powder. *Body Society, 26*(1), 82–106.

Kuhl, G. (2019). Sharing a world with wolves: perspectives of educators working in wolf-focussed education. *Environmental Education Research, 25*(1), 1–15.

Levi-Strauss, C. (1966). *The savage mind.* Chicago: University of Chicago Press.

Locke, P. (2013). Explorations in ethnoelephantology: Social, historical, and ecological intersections between Asian elephants and humans. *Environment and Society: Advances in Research, 4*(1), 79–97.

Lynch, H. (2019). Esposito's affirmative biopolitics in multispecies homes. *European Journal of Social Theory*, 22(3), 364–381.

Malcolm, D. (2005). The emergence, codification and diffusion of sport: Theoretical and conceptual issues. *International Review for the Sociology of Sport*, 40(1), 115–118.

Malcolm, D. (2019). Elias on the development of modern sport: Empirical error, interpretive insight and conceptual clarification. In J. Haut, P. Dolan, D. Reiche, & R. Sánchez García (Eds.), *Excitement processes: Norbert Elias's unpublished works on sports, leisure, body, culture* (pp. 153–169). Wiesbaden: Springer.

Markuksela, V., & Valtonen, A. (2019). Dances with fish. *Leisure Studies*, 38(3), 353–366.

Markwell, K. (2019). Relating to reptiles: An autoethnographic account of animal-leisure relationships. *Leisure Studies*, 38(3), 241–352.

Merchant, S. (2020). Running with an "other": Landscape negotiation and inter-relationality in canicross. *Sport in Society*, 23(1), 11–23.

Morris, S. P. (2014). The ethics of interspecies sports. In J. Gillett & M. Gilbert (Eds.), *Sport, animals and society* (pp. 127–139). London: Routledge.

Nottle, C., & Young, J. (2019). Individuals, instinct and moralities: Exploring multi-species leisure using the serious leisure perspective. *Leisure Studies*, 38(3), 1–14.

Palmer, C. (2001). Taming the wild profusion of existing things? A study of Foucault, power, and human/animal relationships. *Environmental Ethics*, 23(4), 339–358.

Prouse, C. (2019). Of mosquitoes and mega events: Urban political ecologies of the more-than human city. In S. Darnell & R Millington (Eds.), *Sport, development and environmental sustainability* (pp. 113–129). London: Routledge.

Sanders, C. (1999). *Understanding dogs*. Philadelphia: Temple University Press.

Todd, Z. (2014). Fish pluralities: Human-animal relations and sites of engagement in Paulatuug, Arctic, Canada. *Inuit Studies*, 38(1–2), 217–238.

Van Dooren, T., Kirksey, E., & Münster, U. (2016). Multispecies studies: Cultivating arts of attentiveness. *Environmental Humanities*, 8(1), 1–23.

Von Essen, E., & Tickle, L. (2020). Leisure or labour: An identity crisis for modern hunting. *Sociologica Ruralis*, 60(1), 174–197.

Wade, M. (1990). Animal liberationism, ecocentrism, and the morality of sport hunting. *Journal of the Philosophy of Sport*, 17(1), 15–27.

Wacquant, L. (2005). Carnal connections: on embodiment, membership, and apprenticeship. *Qualitative Sociology*, 28(4), 445–471.

Warkentin, T. (2011). Interspecies etiquette in place: Ethical affordances in swim-with-dolphins programs. *Ethics & the Environment*, 16(1), 99–122.

Wilson, B., & Millington, B. (2020). Sport and the environment. In J. Scherer & B. Wilson (Eds.), *Sport and physical culture in Canadian society* (pp. 330–354). Toronto: Pearson.

Windeatt, P. (1982). *The hunt and the anti-hunt*. London: Pluto Press.

Wipper, A. (2000). The partnership: The horse-rider relationship in eventing. *Symbolic Interaction*, 23(1), 47–70.

Worden, S., & Darden, S. (1992). Knives and gaffs: Definitions in the deviant world of cockfighting. *Deviant Behavior: An Interdisciplinary Journal*, 13(3), 271–289.

Wright, S., Suchet-Pearson, S., Lloyd, K., Burarrwanga, L. L., & Burarrwanga, D. (2009). "That means the fish are fat": Sharing experiences of animals through Indigenous-owned tourism. *Current Issues in Tourism* 12(5–6), 505–527.

Young, K. (2017). The animal-sport complex. In S. E. Brown & O. Sefhia (Eds.), *Routledge handbook on deviance* (pp. 75–83). London: Routledge.

Young, K., & Gerber, B. (2014). "Necropsian" nights: Animal sport, civility, and the Calgary Stampede. In J. Gillett & M. Gilbert (Eds.), *Sport, animals, and society* (pp. 155–169). London: Routledge.

PART IV

LIFESPAN AND CAREERS

CHAPTER 32

SPORT, CHILDREN, AND SOCIALIZATION

KEN GREEN, SHARON WHEELER, AND PATRICK FOSS JOHANSEN

IN sport, as with many kinds of leisure, the people who continue to take part throughout their lives were usually introduced and became committed when they were children. Hence the significance of socialization and sport. There has been a long history of research on the topic since the advent of empirical studies in the 1950s (Coakley, 2007). Much initial investigation focused upon socialization *through* sport—the ways in which participation in organized, competitive, and physically vigorous activities, such as team games, were believed to be beneficial for the personal and social development of youngsters. While this aspect of socialization and sport will be touched upon in this chapter, the bulk of coverage is given over to issues and debates related to the socialization of children *into* sport.

The chapter concentrates on childhood, that is, the early years through to the ages at which children in most countries move from elementary to secondary school (around 11 to 13 years). In addition to providing a "natural" break, this period represents a stage at which children's leisure lives tend to be in "transition" (Zeijl, Poel, Bois-Reymond, Ravesloot, & Meulman, 2000), as they move from under the wings of their parents and into the zone of influence of friends and peers (in person and via social media). To help frame what follows, we begin with an introduction to the concept of socialization and why it matters to an understanding of sport.

What Is Socialization?

The term "socialization" alludes to "the influence of society on the development of the person, whereby society actually becomes part of the individual" (Roberts, 2009, p. 270)— in other words, the processes through which people acquire (either directly or indirectly, explicitly or implicitly, intentionally or unintentionally) and internalize the values, beliefs, expectations, knowledge, skills, and practices normative in their social groups. It amounts to young people learning the culture or ways of life of the networks (e.g., family, ethnic group, nation-state) into which they are born and live. Socialization becomes manifest in what we take for granted and think of as "natural" or "second nature"—what sociologists might call our (individual and group) habitus (see below).

The people and groups that pass on particular values and practices (intentionally or unintentionally, directly or indirectly) are said to be agents of socialization. Agents of socialization are characteristically subdivided into two groups: primary and secondary. Primary socialization refers to the initial and potentially most influential form of socialization experienced within the family, most notably from parents but also other caregivers and siblings. Secondary socialization, on the other hand, deals with those socializing agencies beyond the family—such as schools and friendship and peer groups—where young people experience additional formal and informal socialization processes. Other potentially significant secondary agents of sports socialization include sports clubs and modern social media.

Socialization is a more or less deliberate and conscious process depending upon the socializing agent(s). In families, primary socialization may be conscious, deliberate, and explicit as well as intuitive and implicit. In schools, secondary socialization is both formal (via the school curriculum) and informal (via the so-called hidden or informal curriculum). The secondary socializing effects of friendship groups tend to be informal, via imitation and peer-group norms.

ISSUES

Among the key issues in the area of sports socialization, we pick three: (1) the long-standing problematic of the *process* of socialization into sport, including the relative roles (and significance) of primary and secondary socializing agents and agencies; (2) the impact of socioeconomic divisions on the processes of socialization; and (3) the relationship between socialization and lifelong participation in sport.

How Are Children Socialized into Sport?

Primary Socialization in the Family

There are, of course, a variety of routes into sport: through the influence of family, schools, sports clubs, and friends and peers as well as the appeal of new activities (e.g., new forms of boarding and blading) and new facilities and amenities (e.g., commercial gyms and indoor adventure centers) (cf. Black, Johnston, Propper, & Shields, 2019). Crucial to an enduring attachment to sport, however, is likely to be socialization into sporting habits and dispositions in the family. Family cultures tend to be the source of many children's predispositions, and the role of parents tends to be profound (Birchwood, Roberts, & Pollock, 2008; Quarmby, 2016; Wheeler, 2011). Parents appear central to youngsters' internalization of some combination of coming to *value* sport, developing the necessary physical *skills* (what sociologists might call "physical capital"), possessing the relevant *knowledge* (sports-related "cultural capital" [Lenartowicz, 2016]), and establishing sporting *routines* (habits and practices).

Parents are the first point of socialization and remain the most prominent influence until around the transition to secondary schooling (Quarmby, 2016). There are a number of means by which parents shape or pattern the sporting behaviors of their children. The first and most obvious takes the form of parents *valuing* and *prioritizing* sport for their children (as well as themselves). Parental attitudes communicate beliefs regarding "what matters" and what is to be regarded as important and valuable for their children—their aspirations (Andersson, 2020). In this regard, parental involvement in children's organized sports has increased dramatically in the past 20 years or so (cf. Qunito Romani, 2019; Stefansen, Smette, & Strandbu, 2018) as more and more have come to view introducing their youngsters to structured activities, such as sport, to be part and parcel of "good parenting"—even when they have not been sports participants themselves or had negative experiences of sport when young (Wheeler & Green, 2012).

The second way in which parents (and, for that matter, siblings) shape children's sports socialization involves parents *modeling* sporting practices (cf. Strandbu, Bakken, & Stefansen, 2019). The term "role model" refers to those whose attitudes and behaviors (young) people are believed to not only admire but seek to imitate, whether consciously or subconsciously. At various times in children's lives, parents, teachers, peers, and sport stars, among others, are perceived or projected as role models for sports participation. While the empirical evidence regarding the significance of parental role modeling may appear somewhat equivocal (Wheeler, 2013), it seems that parents' sporting backgrounds (Harrington, 2009; Wheeler, 2011) and training habits (Strandbu, Bakken, et al., 2019) can influence the aspirations, strategies, and practices of parents in relation to their children's sport participation. However, it is important to note that this influence appears to be in terms of the type of activities parents introduce children to rather than introductions per se. Nevertheless, when parents' own training habits are part of a strong family sporting culture (Strandbu, Bakken, et al., 2019), this can be seen to increase the likelihood that their children will participate in organized sports in particular (Nielsen, Grønfeldt, Toftegaard-Støckel, & Andersen, 2012; Qunito Romani, 2019).

The third crucial way in which parents shape or pattern their children's sporting practices takes the form of *enabling* and *supporting*. When it comes to enabling participation, parents frequently provide the earliest opportunities and experiences in the shape of enrollment in sports clubs or organized physical activities (Wheeler, 2011). By way of sustaining their children's involvement in sport, parents typically provide different forms of logistical support, for instance, transporting youngsters to and from activities, helping them get ready, and preparing and paying for equipment and membership fees (cf. Wheeler & Green, 2019). In addition, and in order to sustain involvement, parents often introduce their children to several different types of sports so that they acquire diverse experiences—with all the associated benefits from ongoing participation believed to accrue (Wheeler, 2013)— during the so-called "sampling years" (ages 6 to 13) (Côté, Turnnidge, & Vierimaa, 2016). As well as providing youngsters with a taste of various sports and physical activities which may be crucial in developing the "wide sporting repertoires" which Roberts and Brodie (1992) found to be the key distinguishing characteristic of longer-running recreational sporting biographies, sampling is associated with the development of social networks which can serve to bind individuals to sport (Côté, Horton, MacDonald, & Wilkes, 2009), particularly among the middle classes (Neely & Holt, 2014).

Alongside this logistical assistance or "enabling," parents may supply emotional support, not only by being present at their children's sporting practices but also in furnishing motivational encouragement and dispensing feedback during and after the game or activity. While feedback is one of the key ways in which parents influence their children's experiences and enjoyment of sport, their self-perception, perceived competence, self-confidence, and the like (Johansen & Green, 2019), when parents "get it wrong"—typically by providing too much direction—children can feel pressured, and the resulting stress is related to dropout and burnout in sport (Fraser-Thomas & Côté, 2006; Wheeler, 2013).

With regard to parenting *practices* (the day-to-day things that parents do and say to their children), there is a wealth of empirical research demonstrating the ways in which parents or caregivers enable and support their children's sport participation though a variety of practices. Financial and logistical support appear particularly crucial to involvement in organized sporting activities (Nielsen et al., 2012; Wheeler & Green, 2019). Parenting *strategies*—the ways parents attempt to realize their aspirations for their children—are less well-researched than parenting practices but nevertheless appear to be equally important in securing children's longer-term attachments to sport (Bach, 2014; Wheeler, 2011). Common strategies include promoting commitment to sports participation by establishing participatory routines, monitoring progression, and intervening where obstacles emerge, as well as enabling children to sample a variety of sports (Wheeler, 2011). Whichever strategies and practices are employed, it is important to recognize that parental plans are influenced not only by the past as well as the present but also by assumptions about the future (Frønes, 1993) and future needs. Parental socialization of their children into sport appears one dimension of what contemporary (middle-class) parents believe are the challenges their children will face and what may be necessary in their preparation for "life" (Bach, 2014). In this regard, structural changes (in both the economy and leisure) have altered what adults think children need to be able to do in readiness for their future (Nomaguchi & Milkie, 2019).

Secondary Socialization in Schools

It is commonly assumed that schools, and physical education (PE) in particular, can and do play an important role in socializing youngsters into sport. Despite the prevalence of such beliefs, however, there remains a dearth of evidence, beyond anecdotal corroboration, demonstrating a "PE effect" on the socialization of children into sport (Green, 2014). Although some studies explore what makes school PE "meaningful" for children (for instance, social interaction, fun, challenge, and developing competence) (cf. Beni, Fletcher, & Ní Chróinín, 2017), the ostensible socialization effects of school PE are simply taken for granted. One of the very few studies to explore these socializing effects has suggested (counterintuitively, it must be said) that schools play little or no part in youngsters' sports socialization (cf. Pot, Verbeek, van der Zwan, & van Hilvoorde, 2016). Not only does PE appear not to have the widely touted positive impact on perceived ability, enjoyment, or participation outside school, but the competitive sporting environment wherein performance is prized and peer comparisons of ability are encouraged tend to impact negatively on many children's perceptions of sport (Parry, 2013, 2015). Indeed, school PE may well exacerbate nascent differences generated outside of school by subtly emphasizing performance over participation and reducing the enjoyment of those already less likely to be active (Parry,

2013, 2015). Even though PE in many elementary schools worldwide nowadays may be considerably less competitive than several decades ago (with competition kicking in mainly at
secondary school age via school sport, club sport, and the wider sports culture), PE remains
performance-oriented and, therefore, is as likely to alienate as engage.

Peers, on the other hand, influence the choice of specific (type of) sport (Pot et al.,
2016) because youngsters want to be (and remain) a part of friendship groups—friendship
matters to young people.

Secondary Socialization among Friends and Peers

A term commonly associated with socialization is "significant others"—people who have an
important influence on the values, attitudes, and practices of youngsters in relation to sport,
for example. In the case of children's sport, this might be teachers and adults in organized
play and sports settings. Beyond the influence of parents and family, taking up other sports
and continuing with them is often tied to significant others in the form of friends (typically same-sex friends in the case of children) but also peers more broadly. "Friend" refers
to those (usually peers) whose company children seek out (rather than being bound to, as
in the case of family members) and with whom they develop reciprocal emotional bonds.
Peers are youngsters' social equals—defined in terms of shared social status or characteristics, such as age, educational background, or sports club membership.

Being with friends and peers can enhance the sport experience (cf. Forsyth, Rowe,
Lowry, McNally, & Mutrie, 2011), which, in turn, reinforces and promotes friend and peer
interaction and socialization. While young children play at times, with friends, in places,
and at activities that are chosen and supervised by their parents (Roberts, 2016b), older
children begin choosing their friends while becoming increasingly subject to looser and
less obtrusive adult supervision than formerly—even meeting unsupervised. This occurs
on school playgrounds and, as they get older, on the streets, in parks, and in study/play/
bedrooms (Roberts, 2016b). By the early teenage years, adults have begun to lose control of
youngsters. In this manner, secondary socialization among friends and peers can and often
does challenge as well as reinforce primary socialization in the family and secondary socialization in school (Jones, 2009).

Because friends gradually come to occupy pride of place in children's leisure lives, other
leisure activities often tend to be subordinated to this priority. Older children view participation with friends as not only enabling but also motivational. As with family socialization, the mechanisms by which friends enable or discourage sports participation involve
not merely the transmission of attitudes and values but also "modeling" active or inactive
pursuits and providing psychological support or reinforcement for certain behaviors (Smith
& McDonough, 2008). It is not merely what their friends think about sport and do or do not
do in practice, however, that influences young people. It is also the opportunities that sport
(and, for that matter, any leisure practice) provides for making and sustaining friendships
and the ways in which young people's friendship groups facilitate links with other young
people sharing similar interests and situations. It is frequently commonality of activity or
interest that brings youngsters together (Carter, Bennetts, & Carter, 2003). Thus, sport is
often a site for the generation of friendships that sport then becomes a means of sustaining
(Neely & Holt, 2016). Indeed, one of the main motives among young people for engaging in

sport is the opportunity it provides for establishing and maintaining friendships (Brustad, Vilhjmalsson, & Fonseca, 2008; Hendry, Shucksmith, Love, & Glendenning, 1993), and "best" friendships in particular.

The Impact of Wider Socioeconomic Divisions on Socialization into Sport

Social Class

Social class remains the main form of socially structured inequality in modern societies and a key determinant of life chances (Roberts, 2009). The concept of class revolves around how people make their living: their market situation. Social class is not, however, reducible merely to occupation and income—it has social and cultural as well as economic dimensions. Thus, "class remains a fundamental organiser of social experience" (Roberts, 2008, p. 647). Because they are class-related rather than straightforwardly class-based (in a deterministic sense), there is scope for parenting cultures to mediate the effects on sports participation of social class. This nevertheless tends to be the exception rather than the rule in sporting terms (if not in parenting more generally; cf. Irwin & Elley, 2011). It is worthy of note, however, that while being a good parent is seen as crucial among parents themselves, just how to be a good parent is understood in different ways (Vincent & Maxwell, 2016). Middle-class parenting practices, for example, can vary across ethnic groups, not least in relation to education, sport, and culture. There is, for instance, a substantial literature on the ways in which African-heritage (e.g., African American) families encourage their children toward sport more than some other ethnic groups (cf. Shakib & Veliz, 2013).

Such caveats notwithstanding, middle-class parents are more likely to engage in the deliberate socialization of their children into valued cultural practices, such as sport and the arts (cf. Nielsen et al., 2012). Such "concerted cultivation" (Lareau, 2011) involves parents investing in their children in order to ensure that they have sufficient amounts—as well as the right kinds—of "cultural capital" to improve their life chances and life satisfaction (Lareau, 2011; Wheeler, 2018a). This investment has increasingly occurred at a younger age, with middle-class parents facilitating the acquisition of physical capital via so-called enrichment activities (Vincent & Ball, 2007) and "private enterprise PE" (Evans & Davies, 2010) during children's formative preschools years, which then lead to participation in organized sports activities during primary school years (Wheeler & Green, 2019). In short, 21st-century parents are sensitized to the ostensible need to provide plentiful opportunities for their children to engage with physical activity and sport as part of the so-called enrichment agenda. According to Stirrup, Sandford, and Duncombe (2015, p. 89):

> Growing pressure on parents to equip their children with the skills required for future success, coupled with an increased focus on providing quality learning experiences in the early years, has contributed to an upsurge in the enrolment of young children in formal (often privatised) activities.

These enrichment activities are influenced by the parents' own experiences, tastes, and values as much as by their aspirations in terms of the physical and cultural capital their children may need in order to lead well-rounded leisure lives in the future (Stirrup et al., 2015). Terms such as "involved" fathering (Gottzén, 2011; Kay, 2009a, 2009b) and "intensive," "professional," and "tiger" mothering (Chua, 2011; Guo, 2013; Hays, 1998; Vincent & Ball, 2007), as well as "helicopter" parenting (LeMoyne & Buchanan, 2011), have all been employed to make sense of contemporary middle-class parenting styles aimed at cultivating children's cultural capital in a deliberate and concerted manner.

By contrast, parents in lower socioeconomic strata are prone to adopt what has been termed laissez-faire or "natural growth" (Lareau, 2011) styles of parenting, amounting to a kind of "essential assistance" (Wheeler, 2018a). While this more "hands-off" (or permissive and democratic) style of parenting may afford working-class children more control over their leisure, it also tends to result in fewer opportunities to become socialized into structured activities such as sport (Wheeler, 2018b; Wheeler & Green, 2019; Wheeler, Green, & Thurston, 2019). While parents (especially in nuclear families) in the higher social class fractions control, direct, and regulate their children's engagement with sport (Stuij, 2015; Wheeler, 2013), among the working classes the socializing of children (and the resultant habitus) tends to be influenced more by the extended family, school PE teachers, and peers, "resulting in a broad range of less strictly ordered activities, undertaken at different places" (Stuij, 2015, p. 780). Hence, while both middle- and working-class children can and do acquire habituses in which sports and exercise play a greater or lesser role, differences arise largely as a consequence of the impact of significant socializing agents, such as parents (Stuij, 2015).

The socialization of children into sport in the family is important because differences in sport participation rates between sociodemographic groups, such as social classes, tend to be fixed by, then remain stable after, age 16 (Birchwood et al., 2008). All that said, we need to keep in mind that the effects of social class on sports socialization may be less pronounced than is often assumed (cf. Pot et al., 2016). Although children and young people (especially boys) on middle-class life trajectories continue to have higher levels of sports participation than working-class youngsters, the main social class differences are no longer whether young people play any sport, but how much, how many, and how often, as well as the general "styles" of participation—including whom individuals choose to play with, the clubs they belong to, and the centers they use (Coalter, 1999; Roberts, 2015). In sum, sport "is quite distinctive in largely attracting young people independently of their socio-economic background," and those engaged in sporting activities tend to be "less likely to be influenced by social origin" than many other leisure pursuits (Feinstein, Bynner, & Duckworth, 2005, p. 17).

Gender

Gender socialization refers to the ways in which boys and girls are introduced to, and more or less steeped in, what are seen as male- and female-appropriate values, attitudes, and behaviors. It is, in other words, the process by which boys learn to be boys and girls learn to be girls in relation to norms of femininity and masculinity. In sporting terms, gender socialization refers to the ways in which boys and girls are introduced to what are viewed as male- and female-appropriate activities (contact or noncontact play and games, for example), behaviors (such as aggressiveness and competitiveness), and practices (gender-appropriate clothing, for instance)—including those that might be seen as forming the initial preparation for later engagement with and adherence to sport.

It has long been known that girls' schedules tend to be more closely monitored and parental expectations more clearly stated in relation to daughters' participation in leisure activities, including sport (cf. Coakley & White, 1992). Nevertheless, as with social class, the impact of gender on children's and young people's leisure and sporting lifestyles has become blurred in recent decades as boys and girls from all social classes encounter a greater range of sporting activities. However, while children and young people as a whole are experiencing a broader diet of sports and physical activities at home and at school than previous generations, they continue by degrees to be introduced to various activities according to their sex. The upshot is that there remains a deal of continuity alongside the evident change in the sporting socialization of girls. Change is more visible in some cultures than others. Girls in many Nordic countries, for example, evidently lead sporting lives that to all intents and purposes are identical to those of boys (Green, Sigurjónsson, & Skille, 2019). This is due in no small measure to the manner in which Nordic parents socialize their offspring into sport. Like many parents, they provide the necessary resources (e.g., money, transportation, club membership) and encouragement for sports participation. (Transportation and company can be especially important for girls who are more likely to have less flexible expectations about away-from-home activities than their male counterparts.) One of the ways in which Nordic countries, such as Norway, differ somewhat in socialization is that the female parental role model for children (and girls especially) is increasingly likely to be a "sporty" mother who works for pay outside the home (Green, Thurston, Vaage, & Mordal-Moen, 2015). By contrast, continuities can be seen in some countries in Western Europe where gendered patterns of sports participation persist. While change is apparent, continuity is evident where girls remain less likely than their male counterparts to be socialized into competitive, physically intense, and contact activities, notwithstanding their increased involvement in indoor and recreational and newly emerging sports such as cheerleading, swimming, gymnastics, and dance (Wright, 2016).

Ethnicity

Despite the continued and widespread use of the term in the world of sport, the concept of "race" has no scientific validity, based, as it is, upon superficial, morphological differences in the form of observable physical features such as skin color, facial features, and hair texture. "Races" are social rather than biological constructions—ideologies that coincided with the 19th-century mania for classification alongside the social Darwinism associated with the empire building and colonialism of European powers. In short, the notion of "race" represents an ideological ex post facto rationalization of preferred views of the world and preferred practices (i.e., convenient justifications for the subjugation of peoples, such as slavery and ethnic cleansing). "Ethnicity," by contrast, is a far more useful concept with which to make sense of differences in cultures. Even though ethnic groups may share some physical characteristics (such as skin color) the term draws attention to cultural traditions and heritage (Coakley, 2004). More specifically, ethnicity focuses on membership of and identification with social groups or collectivities on the basis of country of origin, ancestry and history, family arrangements, language, religion, and culture alongside the shared values, beliefs, customs and traditions, and overall lifestyles these generate. Belonging to a particular ethnic group is therefore a matter of shared social experiences rather than shared genetic material. Focusing upon ways of life in the form of customs and traditions as well as values and beliefs also helps in exploring an important dimension of ethnicity (especially in relation to sport): acculturation, the process whereby people from one culture acquire or at least are constrained to engage with the way of life of another.

Ethnicity is an important aspect of socialization into sport. Nearly everything we do in terms of sports participation is ethnic—the product of one or another culture or cultures (capoeira in Brazil, cricket in England, baseball in the USA, Aussie rules in Australia, and bandy in Norway, for example). Thus, ethnicity is not simply a minority issue, even though it is usually treated as one—it is a facet of all sport (Roberts, 2016a). One of the big "take-home" messages, therefore, regarding the socialization of children into sport is the risk of ethnocentricity. Put another way, when it comes to understanding socialization into sport, allowance must be made for the possibility of a dearth of genuine interest in Western sports among some ethnic groups (in Muslim countries, for instance) where cultural, nonmaterial barriers to sport participation can prove highly resilient, irrespective of the existence of suitable preconditions for sports participation in the form of families' disposable income, "sport for all" policies, and suitable facilities (Birchwood et al., 2008).

Patterns of sports participation among ethnic groups highlight, above all, the significance of one particular aspect of ethnicity: religion and religiosity. The more emphasis is placed upon religion among particular ethnic groups, the lower the levels and rates of participation in sport tend to be. That said, it is the intersection between religion and gender in some ethnic groups that particularly impacts sports socialization. Girls and young women from ethnic minority groups tend to be constrained more by their gender than their ethnicity— or, rather, the interaction between the two—when it comes to engaging with leisure and sport. Muslim girls, in particular, face significant gender-specific barriers in the form of household and family responsibilities. Being a young Muslim woman and participating in sport challenges the boundaries of one's ethnic identity (Benn, 2005), not least because it draws attention to women behaving in an "unfeminine" manner when sport is not viewed as an expression of respectable femininity (Walseth, 2006, 2016). In this regard, sport is typically seen as antithetical to adhering to the norms for young South Asian Muslim women (Walseth, 2006, 2016).

Although socialization into (or, for that matter, away from) sport are shaped by structural factors such as ethnicity and social class, this tends to be mediated by parents and families. Here, opportunities in particular activities and encouragement in sport and physical activity are often promoted in the family, albeit within ethnic parameters (cf. Birchwood et al., 2008; Sabo & Veliz, 2008). Among Cuban Americans, for example, family plays a primary role in sport socialization, while neither school nor sport coaches are key socializing agents (Mercado & Bernthal, 2016). African Americans are also more likely than other ethnic groups to receive encouragement from family members and nonkin (Shakib & Veliz, 2013).

Socialization into Sport and Lifelong Participation

By age 16 very many young people have already begun to adopt some of the leisure practices that will become features of their adult leisure lifestyle (Roberts & Brodie, 1992). Hence the relevance of early life socialization. However, while socialization into sport in the family tends to be a necessary condition for ongoing participation, it may not be sufficient. Experiencing and participating in a diverse pattern of sports during childhood enhances the likelihood of sports participation among youth and adults (cf. Scheerder et al., 2006). Those who remain active in several sports throughout their teenage years and into their 20s are the ones most likely to remain sport participants as adults (Roberts & Brodie, 1992; Roberts, Minten, Chadwick, Lamb, & Brodie, 1991). At age 10, future "lifelong participants" are playing the largest number of sports on average. Up to age 15, they enlarge their ranges of sports, such that by age 16 they are playing three times as many sports as other youngsters. (Thereafter they maintain several sports in their repertoires; cf. Smith, this volume).

All things considered, childhood increasingly appears the really critical life stage for laying secure foundations for long-term careers in sport (cf. Birchwood et al., 2008; Quarmby & Dagkas, 2010). This is not because childhood sporting experiences are in any sense deterministic. People are not bound to become lifelong adherents to sport merely as a consequence of practicing an activity or acquiring a taste for sport during childhood:

> Rather, the situation is that unless people become involved in sport (or any leisure activity, for that matter) during childhood and youth, and remain involved through the youth life stage, they are unlikely to become involved later in their lives. (Roberts, Kovacheva, & Kabaivanov, 2020, p. 9)

In this regard, it is by no means self-evident that schools, friendship groups, sports clubs, and the like can be substitutes for the power of family socialization which operates daily throughout childhood (Roberts, 2016b).

APPROACHES

Studies of socialization and sport have been reasonably plentiful in the fields of anthropology, psychology, and sociology. While anthropological studies have focused on the role of play, games, and sports in the formation of value orientations in particular cultural contexts, the dominant theoretical perspectives in the study of socialization and sport have increasingly come from psychology and sociology.

Psychological Approaches

In the field of psychology, the concept of socialization has long been associated with the development of personality, with personality seen as preeminently a characteristic of the individual. While behaviorists have tended to implicitly view socialization as quasi-automatic reflex-like behaviors (Keel, 2016) (what sociologists would call habit or habitus), the mainstream developmental psychological view is that the acquired patterns of behaviors and dispositions that constitute personality traits result from some interplay between the biological organism and the social environment. Thus, a key problematic in developmental psychology is the relationship between innateness and the environmental influences and self-actualizing tendencies toward satisfying inherent needs and drives—what might be termed the relationship between socialization and youngsters' basic psychological needs. This involves treating the personality as the unfolding of inborn inherited patterns gradually impacted by the (socio-ecological) surroundings—in other words, heredity interacting with the social environment to form some kind of biopsychological makeup of personality.

Prominent in this line of inquiry have been ecological models, which explore the interactive effects of social and environmental surroundings. Interaction (as well as "competition") between personal, family, social, sociocultural, organizational, community, policy, and physical environmental factors is said to positively and/or negatively impact youngsters' engagement with sport and physical activity (King & Gonzalez, 2018). In the process, socio-ecological models endeavor to understand why young people may behave differently in different settings: in the family, at school, with friends, and during leisure. Keen to point out that no one socializing agency is necessarily superior, ecological approaches seek to establish which situations or environments are more significant than others in particular times and places. Ecological models are especially interested in intrapersonal factors (such as knowledge, attitudes, beliefs, and personality) as well as how interpersonal factors (interactions with others) can enhance or diminish participation and positively or negatively impact health behaviors. As we shall see, sociologists want to say that, as far as sports socialization is concerned, one institution—the family—is indeed preeminent. In this regard, developmental psychologists explore the ways in which children are introduced to values via sport through their interaction with adults, particularly parents. Thus, developmental psychology has tended to focus not so much on the mechanics of socialization as on the socialization effects of sport participation on the development of the personality. In particular, it has explored the potential for sport to have a positive impact upon children's moral and sociopsychological development, including promoting emotional maturity, self-regulation, autonomy, and compassion. The transmission of positive values between parents and children is often presented as the hallmark of successful socialization (Danioni, Barni, & Rosnati, 2017).

Where psychological studies of socialization have focused on processes they have often drawn on the work of Diane Baumrind (1971) in order to explore parenting approaches to childrearing, dividing "parenting styles" into authoritarian, authoritative, permissive, and uninvolved or neglectful—each with its supposedly distinctive patterns of parental behaviors or practices and communication. In this vein, parents' application of specific parenting styles has received much attention in youth sport in particular (cf. Harwood, & Knight, 2015, p. 201; Holt, Tamminen, Black, Mandigo, & Fox, 2009). Subsequently, developmental psychological approaches have extended the concept of parenting styles—and the "emotional climates" in which parents' attitudes and values are communicated to children—toward a model that includes parenting goals and parenting practices, on the basis that the emotional climate and associated parental behaviors are dependent upon the goals they have for their children's socialization. A wealth of psychologically oriented, predominately quantitative research in the 1980s and 1990s sought to establish which parental "variables"—for example, belief systems, role modeling, pressuring behaviors, and support and encouragement—were correlated with a range of child outcomes in sporting contexts.

Another conspicuous psychological model in sports socialization is positive youth development (PYD). In PYD, sport is treated as a vehicle for children's positive physical, psychological, and social development. It focuses on the so-called personal assets of childhood and youth, including confidence and competence, the development of which are believed to lead not only to long-term participation but also to significant and positive personal development (Côté et al., 2016). In terms of the actual process of socializing children into sport—and the facilitation and enhancement of sports participation and performance—the developmental model of sport participation holds sway (Côté & Vierimaa, 2014). The central tenet of this model is the ostensible need for diversity of sporting experiences during the sampling phase, mentioned earlier, as a precursor to and precondition for the "specializing stage," when youngsters commit to one or a few sports and develop the technical and tactical skills in the context of sporting competition.

The obvious overlap in terms of interests (e.g., the early models of family socialization whereby developmental psychologists highlighted the significance of both the orientations and practices of parents for children's sport participation) and ideas (e.g., habit) notwithstanding, there remain notable differences in the approaches of developmental psychology and sociology to making sense of the relationship between socialization and sport. These differences are often characterized in terms of a "biosocial dualism" wherein "the division between the 'natural child' of developmental psychology and the 'social child' of socialisation theory replicates a tendency in modern thought and practice to divide nature from culture" (Ryan, 2012, p. 439). Where developmental psychologists have tended to view socialization as a combination of biopsychological elements and social molding, sociological approaches are more concerned with dependency on learning as the hallmark of being human (Murphy, 2020). Sociologists are suspicious of what they see as a psychological tendency to view individuals in quasi-isolation from their sociohistorical contexts. For sociologists, viewing children's and young people's choices as other than social underplays the influence of primary and secondary socialization in framing young people's perceptions of what they can and cannot do and what they do and do not want to do.

Sociological Approaches

Unsurprisingly, then, it is a central ontological assumption in sociological approaches to socialization that people (and children par excellence) are fundamentally social beings: they are always and everywhere bound into networks of interdependency—with parents, siblings, teachers, friends, peers, and so forth. It is the web of social relations in which children live during their most impressionable phase that sociology focuses upon.

Early sociological research into socialization and sport was grounded in structural functionalism and, subsequently, forms of Marxism, neo-Marxism, and conflict theories more generally (Coakley, 2004). Functionalist approaches tended to view socialization as a process of learning particular roles through which people internalized shared values and orientations as well as appropriate skills, thereby enabling them to participate successfully in the social systems of which they were a part. Marxist approaches (and critical theories more widely) to sports socialization also focused on socialization as a process of internalizing particular values, albeit ones deemed inimical to the true interests of an alienated and exploited working class. Marxist and critical theorists have tended to focus on the significance of the material, economic organization of (capitalist) societies for the process of socialization generally and into sport in particular—both in terms of the opportunities and resources available to different social classes as well as the outcomes of sports socialization for youngsters' values, beliefs, and attitudes vis-à-vis the supposed "needs" of capitalist economies.

Contemporary sociological perspectives on socialization tend to be more Weberian insofar as they challenge the implicit notion of (sports) socialization as the mere internalization of external norms and youngsters as more than the passive recipients of adult and societal influences. In this vein, Weberian and interactionist approaches have criticized classical theories of socialization as too static and unidirectional, failing to recognize the dynamism inherent in socialization processes and, in particular, the significance of agency—insofar as people, including children, can be self-reflexive and able therefore to interpret and mediate socializing influences/agents (Coakley, 2004; Coakley & Pike, 2009). Seen from this perspective, socialization is a two-way street. Youngsters not only accept and adopt (sometimes unreflexively and routinely) adults' attempts at socialization; they also adapt adult messages and display resistance to conventional practices and expectations. Hence the view that the significance of early life socialization notwithstanding, children and young people are frequently active socializing agents in their own right, in part through the ways they interpret their parents' attitudes and behaviors (Andersson, 2020), but also insofar as they consciously choose from the range of activities they are exposed to at home, with friends, and in school. Young people's engagement with sport spills over into other domains of their lives, such as their friendship networks. As previously indicated, peer groups and sporting dispositions are likely to be mutually reinforcing as young people seek out for friendship those other young people who are most like them in the sense of sharing similar interests.

The influence of the classical sociologists can still be seen in sociological studies of socialization into sport in the ways research seeks to identify Durkheimian "social facts" (e.g., in the form and patterns of family sports participation) and the division of labor (e.g., the supposed roles of school PE and sports clubs in the sporting socialization of children); the continuing influence of Marx's material (economic) factors (e.g., class-related access to sporting resources, and patterns of socialization and participation); as well as concern for Weberian meaningful human action—the meanings and motives that children develop through the course of formal and informal socialization processes. Indeed, whatever contemporary sociological theoretical approach is adopted, some of the central tenets of functionalist, Marxist, and Weberian perspectives have become taken-for-granted assumptions (albeit in modified form) in studying socialization. Examples are the notion of agents of socialization, and socialization as the internalization of social norms of one kind or another, as well as the supposed functionality (for better—functionalist—or worse—Marxist) of the outcomes (a particular focus shared with developmental psychologists) of socialization into social systems.

Since the latter part of the 20th century, feminist theories of socialization have highlighted the ways in which systems of patriarchy (in the family and beyond) and heteronormativity have, until relatively recently, resulted in the exclusion of girls from traditionally masculine sports (such as team games). Feminist studies have highlighted the roles of primary (families) and secondary (schools and sports clubs) agents of socialization in reinforcing (although sometimes challenging) gender norms in the socialization of children into sport. Both families and schools stand accused of reproducing gender stereotypes—in the form of associations between humility, restraint, niceness, and femininity—which have had a negative impact on girls' involvement in sport, not least in entrenching gendered zones of play (Clarke & Paechter, 2007). For their part, schools are said to perpetuate gendered sports socialization through a legacy of single-sex PE teaching with sex-specific teachers, resulting in two (more or less) distinct PE subcultures, teaching differing activities, and holding differing views of what is appropriate for boys and girls in terms of particular activities (e.g., football and dance). More recently, postfeminist or third/fourth-wave feminism, "new" men's studies, and queer theory are among a raft of critical theories developing the study of gender socialization into and through sport (e.g., Mansfield, Caudwell, Wheaton, & Watson, 2018).

Perhaps the most influential, relatively recent sociological approach to socialization generally, and sport in particular, centers upon the concept of habitus. Coined variously by Pierre Bourdieu (1978, 1980, 1984) and Norbert Elias (2000, 2001), "habitus" can be defined as

> the durable and generalized disposition that suffuses a person's action throughout an entire domain of life or, in the extreme instance, throughout all of life—in which case the term comes to mean the whole manner, turn, cast, or mold of the personality. (Camic, 1986, quoted in Van Krieken, 1998, p. 47)

In other words, it amounts to the subconscious (pre)dispositions, ways of thinking, feeling, and acting, that lie largely beyond consciousness and which enable us to act routinely, without much, if any, thought, calculation, or reflection (Roberts, 2016a). On this view, "the real forces which govern us" (van Krieken, 1998, p. 47) are our habits or habitus (Camic, 1986), and it is because we tend not to be aware of the ways in which our seemingly free choices are influenced by our deep-seated predispositions (or second nature) that "the choices involved seem to be made naturally" (Tolonen, 2005, p. 356). The significance of early life socialization, and the resulting habitus, lies in the impact it has on young people's predispositions toward sport. It is important because "[a] habitus formed during childhood, then relevant capitals (tastes and skills) acquired during childhood and youth are likely foundations for 'serious' long-term leisure careers in the relevant fields [e.g., sport]" (Roberts, 2016a, p. 140).

In theoretical terms, the concept of habitus represents an attempt to bring together structure and agency. Youngsters are said to make sporting choices (about what they do, where, and with whom) and create their own sporting lives in the context of their acquired predispositions (embedded via socialization). Where young people acquire similar habituses (e.g., in working-class neighborhoods, as girls, and as part of minority ethnic communities), we talk of a group habitus. These group habituses are typically mediated by families, in the first instance, as everyday life is structured and constructed for children by their family habitus. Families from different social strata and ethnic groupings provide differing cultural contexts for children and play a part in constructing different childhood habituses and practices (Tomanović, 2004).

Sociological and developmental psychologists have utilized a diverse array of methods in studying socialization and sport. Developmental psychological studies favor, where feasible, experimental designs, interventions of one kind or another, and quantitative studies more generally in order to establish cause-and-effect relationships among variables. Such studies utilize quantitative methods and present correlational analyses but tend to provide relatively little information about the social processes and contexts in which people make participation decisions and in which participation is maintained on a day-to-day basis. Hence the reason that sociological studies have tended to explore processes, such as parenting, in greater depth using qualitative strategies in the form of case studies, ethnographies, and biographical research with semistructured interviews to the fore. Where the two disciplines part company, both theoretically and methodologically, is in the tendency for developmental psychologists to view social processes, such as socialization into sport, through an individual lens—to view the process of socialization in individual or psychological terms rather than social and structural ones. The focus remains on individual children, and their unfolding personalities and traits, rather than the social systems they are inevitably bound into and the structural dimension of these systems, such as social class, gender, and ethnic groups (Irwin, 2009).

Debates

Among the many and varied debates in the area of socialization and sport during childhood, several stand out. First, there is the concept of socialization itself. A second debate revolves around the growing involvement of parents and especially fathers in the sporting socialization of children (cf. Coakley, 2006). A third area of interest concerns claims made regarding socialization *through* sport.

Criticisms of Socialization as a Concept

The concept of socialization is often criticized in two broad ways. First, socialization is said to be far too static a concept, implying a once and for all occurrence rather than a process— in other words, something that is never total or complete but rather ongoing and developmental. In reality, socialization continues throughout the life course. However, while socialization does not end with adulthood and the habitus can and does develop, it is a domain assumption that it always does so from foundations laid early on during childhood and youth.

Second, and as we have seen, socialization is criticized for being too deterministic, failing to account for the ways in which (young) people mediate, interpret, adapt, and sometimes reject what they "learn" from their families, friends, and schools, for example. Whereas a term like "education" implies deliberate guidance, the term "socialization" is often taken to imply conditioned responses to various social influences. It is a gross oversimplification, however, to imagine that the social environment conditions or shapes young people any more than young people are entirely free to shape themselves. Socialization is neither a "homogenizing" nor an "all-embracing" process (Malcolm, 2008, p. 232). The relationship between young people and socializing agencies such as the family and school is best conceptualized as reciprocal and interactive and one that is, to some extent, contingent upon the former's interpretations of the influences of latter. In this regard, socialization theories have been criticized for, among other things, being too adult-centric (Buhler-Niederberger, 2010), failing to appreciate just what capable social actors children and young people typically are, not least in terms of their ability to mediate rather than simply imbibe socialization processes. This is why sociologists prefer to talk of "negotiation" between young people and others in their social networks in an attempt to convey the significance of young people's interpretations of the explicit and implicit "messages" they receive from the networks they are a part of. The fact that they do not simply conform to all the norms they are imbued with during primary and secondary socialization is evident in the numerous examples of young people negotiating and compromising on, even rejecting, particular behaviors (for example, sport and drinking alcohol) as well as embracing them. This is especially apparent when young people begin, more overtly, to construct their own identities from the material of early socialization.

The Growing Involvement of Parents in the Sporting Socialization of Children

The fact that sport is a central aspect of many parent-child relationships is likely to be a consequence of the normalization of proactive parenting, especially among the middle classes, resulting in a marked generational change in the role of sport in parenting (Stefansen et al., 2018; Wheeler, 2013) and family (McCarthy & Edwards, 2011). Parenting, it is said, is in the process of changing from a relationship to a set of tasks or practices which reflect the growing "responsibilization" of parents (McCarthy & Edwards, 2011) whereby they feel increasingly accountable for their children's life chances and well-being. This, in turn, raises expectations regarding what constitutes "good parenting" and "increase[s] the scope for moral evaluation of parents" in tune with the alleged "moral discourse of parenting obligations" (p. 143), not least in relation to the sports socialization of children. There is a growing expectation for parents, and fathers in particular (Kay, 2009a, 2009b), to be involved in their children's leisure activities (Vincent & Maxwell, 2016). Parental involvement in children's sports socialization has, in effect, become normalized, particularly among the middle classes and especially in Nordic countries such as Norway (Johansen & Green, 2019; Stefansen, Smette, & Strandbu, 2016; Stefansen et al., 2018). One aspect of the debate regarding the role of parents that has been receiving increased attention is the issue of whether some middle-class parents' investment in children's organized activities has "gone too far," with both parents and children being overscheduled (Qunito Romani, 2019), leading to undue pressure on parents logistically, financially, and emotionally and children's well-being and development potentially being compromised (Wheeler & Green, 2019).

Socialization through Sport

Sport is widely believed to be particularly beneficial for young people in a range of ways. Although sport is also recommended for its own sake, advocates have always claimed instrumental benefits, such as health and fitness, character development, and so on. The alleged consequences of socialization *through* sport and the structured experiences of competitive sports, in particular, are frequently portrayed as providing ideal contexts for adult-controlled socialization of children (Coakley, 2007). This functionalist conception of socialization—in which sports are seen as a vehicle for the inculcation of desirable values and attitudes regarding, for example, working as part of a team, conforming to rules, obeying authority, embracing competition and a competitive ethos, striving to achieve and be productive (Coakley, 2007)—is implicit in PYD approaches. However, many of the claims of instrumental benefits are often implausible and usually unproven (Roberts, 2016b). In truth, the link between sports participation and all manner of good outcomes is due mainly to the types of people who play rather than the effects of participation (Roberts, 2016b). Advocates deliberately overlook or, at best, simply miss the tension, negotiation, misunderstanding, and resistance that characterize lived sport experiences. All told, sports may be most accurately viewed as sites for socialization experiences rather than causes of specific socialization outcomes (Coakley, 2007).

CONCLUSION

Irrespective of preferred disciplinary approaches and favored theories within these, there is widespread agreement that socialization is a fundamental concept in the social sciences. Because childhood is an especially impressionable phase of life, young people's biographies and the early attachments (or otherwise) they form to sport appear to have a profound impact on their later life involvement. Specific sporting habits and more general predispositions toward being physically active tend to be deeply embedded or internalized during childhood and reinforced in youth (cf. Smith, this volume). And these early experiences have lasting effects: "[A]ll the major, recognised differences in adult rates of sports participation between socio-demographic groups are generated during childhood, via cultures that are transmitted through families. . . . [P]ost-childhood experiences play a relatively minor direct part in generating these differences" (Birchwood et al., 2008, p. 283). Nevertheless, sports participation is not a "once and for all time" phenomenon, and whether or not youngsters engage in sport and remain involved from childhood, through youth, and into adulthood is highly likely to depend upon the predispositions (habitus) to sport acquired through childhood socialization. This fixing of sports participation tends to occur in sports-active families. In the Nordic countries, for instance, the most plausible explanation of the relatively high rates of sports participation at all life stages lies in the norm for childhood socialization in sports-active households (Green et al., 2015). Hence, the continued relevance of family sport culture for young people's sports participation in the form of a prolonged socialization effect manifest in dispositions toward sports participation (Strandbu, Stefansen, Smette, & Sandvik, 2019). A general sporting habitus developed during childhood can become focused during youth (cf. Smith, this volume) as players become immersed in the social bonds and culture of a particular sport or sports (Roberts, 2016b). Youngsters not only become locked into sport by a desire to repeat the pleasures and satisfactions experienced during childhood; they also became bound into social networks—whether family or friends, and often both—in which sporting activity is seen as normal (Roberts & Brodie, 1992).

All in all, there is now a substantial body of evidence showing that the foundations for lifelong participation in sport are usually laid in childhood and youth in family contexts. Socialization into sport in the family may be reinforced by other experiences—for example, with friends. However, one thing is clear: participation is unlikely to endure into and through adulthood unless foundations have been laid in childhood in the family. It is here that sporting habitus—in the form of a propensity to play based on habit and enjoyment—takes root when childhood socialization makes physically active recreation a normal part of everyday life, for life (Roberts et al., 2020).

References

Andersson, E. (2020). Parent-created educational practices and conditions for players' political socialisation in competitive youth games: A player perspective on parents' behaviour in grassroots soccer. *Sport, Education and Society, 25*(4), 436–448.

Bach, D. (2014). Parenting among wealthy Danish families: A concerted civilising process. *EthnographyC Education, 9*(2), 224–237.

Baumrind, D. (1971). Current patterns of parental authority. Developmental Psychology, *4*(1, Pt.2), 1–103. doi:10.1037/h0030372.

Beni, S., Fletcher, T., & Ní Chróinín, D. (2017). Meaningful experiences in physical education and youth sport: A review of the literature. *Quest, 69*(3), 291–312.

Benn, T. (2005). Race and physical education, sport and dance. In K. Green & K. Hardman (Eds.), *Physical education: Essential issues* (pp. 197–219). London: Sage Publications.

Birchwood, D., Roberts, K., & Pollock, G. (2008). Explaining differences in sport participation rates among young adults: Evidence from the South Caucasus. *European Physical Education Review, 14*(3), 283–300.

Black, N., Johnston, D. W., Propper, C., & Shields, M. A. (2019). The effect of school sports facilities on physical activity, health and socioeconomic status in adulthood. *Social Science & Medicine, 220*, 120–128.

Bourdieu, P. (1978). Sport and social class. *Social Science Information, 17*(6), 819–840.

Bourdieu, P. (1980). *The logic of practice.* Cambridge, U.K.: Polity Press.

Bourdieu, P. (1984). *Distinction. A social critique of the judgement of taste.* London: Routledge.

Buhler-Niederberger, D. (2010). Introduction: childhood sociology—defining the state of the art and ensuring reflection. *Current Sociology, 58*(2), 155–164.

Brustad, R. J., Vilhjmalsson, R., & Fonseca, A. M. (2008). Organized sport and physical activity promotion. In A. L. Smith & S. J. H. Biddle (Eds.), *Youth physical activity and sedentary behavior.* (pp. 351–375). Champaign, IL: Human Kinetics.

Camic, C. (1986). The matter of habit. *American Journal of Sociology, 91*(5), 1039–1087.

Carter, D. S. G., Bennetts, C., & Carter, S. M. (2003). "We're not sheep": Illuminating the nature of the adolescent peer group in effecting lifestyle choice. *British Journal of Sociology of Education, 24*(2), 225–241.

Chua, A. (2011). *Battle hymn of the tiger mother.* London: Bloomsbury Publishing.

Clarke, S., & Paechter, C. (2007). "Why can't girls play football?" Gender dynamics and the playground. *Sport, Education and Society, 12*(3), 261–276.

Coakley, J. (2004). *Sport in society. Issues and controversies.* New York: McGraw-Hill.

Coakley, J. (2006). The good father: Parental expectations and youth sports. *Leisure Studies, 25*(2), 153–163.

Coakley, J. (2007). Socialization and sport. In G. Ritzer (Ed.), *The Blackwell encyclopedia of sociology* (pp. 4576–4580). London: Blackwell Publishing. http://www.blackwellreference.com/subscriber/tocnode?id=g9781405124331_chunk_g978140512433124_ss1-198.

Coakley, J., & Pike, E. (2009). *Sport in society: Issues and controversies*. Maidenhead, U.K.: McGraw-Hill Education.

Coakley, J., & White, A. (1992). Making decisions: Gender and sports participation among British adolescents. *Sociology of Sport Journal, 9*, 20–35.

Coalter, F. (1999). Sport and recreation in the United Kingdom: Flow with the flow or buck the trends? *Managing Leisure, 4*(1), 24–39.

Côté, J., Horton, S., MacDonald, D., & Wilkes, S. (2009). The benefits of sampling sports during childhood. *Physical Education and Health, 4*, 6–11.

Côté, J., Turnnidge, J., & Vierimaa, M. (2016). A personal assets approach to youth sport. In K. Green & A. Smith (Eds.), *The Routledge handbook of youth sport* (pp. 243–255). Oxford: Routledge.

Côté, J., & Vierimaa, M. (2014). The developmental model of sport participation: 15 years after its first conceptualization. *Science & Sports, 29*(Suppl.), S63–S69.

Danioni, F., Barni, D., & Rosnati, R. (2017). Transmitting sport values: The importance of parental involvement in children's sport activity. *European Journal of Psychology, 13*(1), 75–92.

Elias, N. (2000). *The civilizing process*. Oxford: Blackwell.

Elias, N. (2001). *The society of individuals*. New York: Continuum.

Evans, J., & Davies, B. (2010). Family, class and embodiment: Why school physical education makes so little difference to post-school participation patterns in physical activity. *International Journal of Qualitative Studies in Education, 23*(7), 765–784. doi:10.1080/09518398.2010.529473.

Feinstein, L., Bynner, J., & Duckworth, K. (2005). *Leisure contexts in adolescence and their effects on adult outcomes*. London: Centre for Research on the Wider Benefits of Learning, Institute of Education.

Forsyth, S., Rowe, D., Lowry, R., McNally, J., & Mutrie, N. (2011). "You don't have fun if you are not with your friends": What students say about participating in physical education. In A. MacPhail & M. O'Sullivan (Eds.), *Moving people, moving forward* (pp. 102–131). Proceedings of AIESEP 2011 International Conference, 22–25 June 2011. Limerick, Ireland: University of Limerick.

Fraser-Thomas, J., & Côté, J. (2006). Youth sports: Implementing findings and moving forward with research. *Athletic Insight, 8*(3), 12–27.

Frønes, I. (1993). Changing childhood. *Childhood, 1*(1), 1–2.

Gottzén, L. (2011). Involved fatherhood? Exploring the educational work of middle-class men. *Gender and Education, 23*, 619–634.

Green, K. (2014). Mission impossible? Reflections on the relationship between physical education, youth sport and lifelong participation. *Sport, Education & Society, 19*(4), 357–375.

Green, K., Sigurjónsson, T., & Skille, E. Å. (Eds.). (2019). *Sport in Scandinavia and the Nordic countries*. London: Routledge.

Green, K., Thurston, M., Vaage, O., & Mordal-Moen, K. (2015). Girls, young women and sport in Norway: A case study of sporting convergence amid favourable socio-economic conditions. *International Journal of Sports Policy and Politics, 7*(4), 531–550.

Guo, K. (2013). Ideals and realities in Chinese immigrant parenting: Tiger mother versus others. Journal of Family Studies, 19(1), 44–52. doi:10.5172/jfs.2013.19.1.44.

Harrington, M. (2009). Sport mad, good dads: Australian fathering through leisure and sport practices. In T. Kay (Ed.), *Fathering through sport and leisure* (pp. 51–72). Oxford: Routledge.

Harwood, C. G., & Knight, C. J. (2015). Parenting in youth sport: A position paper on parenting expertise. *Psychology of Sport and Exercise, 16*, 24–35.

Hendry, L. B., Shucksmith, J., Love, J. G., & Glendenning, A. (1993). *Young people's leisure and lifestyles*. London: Routledge.

Holt, N. L., Tamminen, K. A., Black, D. E., Mandigo, J. L., & Fox, K. R. (2009). Youth sport parenting styles and practices. *Journal of Sport & Exercise Psychology*, 31(1), 37–59.

Irwin, S. (2009). Locating where the action is: Quantitative and qualitative lenses on families, schooling and structures of social inequality. *Sociology*, 43(6), 1123–1140.

Irwin, S., & Elley, S. (2011). Concerted cultivation? Parenting values, education and class diversity. *Sociology*, 45(3), 480–495.

Johansen, P. F., & Green, K. (2019). "It's alpha omega for succeeding and thriving": Parents, children and sporting cultivation in Norway. *Sport, Education and Society*, 24(4), 427–440.

Jones, G. (2009). *Youth*. Cambridge, U.K.: Polity Press.

Kay, T. (2009a). Introduction: Fathering through sport and leisure. In T. Kay (Ed.), *Fathering through sport and leisure* (pp. 1–6). London: Routledge.

Kay, T. (2009b). The landscape of fathering. In T. Kay (Ed.), *Fathering through sport and leisure* (pp. 7–22). London: Routledge.

Keel, S. (2016). *Socialization: Parent-child interaction in everyday life*. London: Routledge.

King, K., & Gonzalez, G. B. (2018). Increasing physical activity using an ecological model. *ACSM's Health & Fitness Journal*, 22(4), 29–32.

Lareau, A. (2011). *Unequal childhoods: Class, race, and family life*. (2nd ed.). Berkeley: University of California Press.

LeMoyne, T., & Buchanan, T. (2011). Does "hovering" matter? Helicopter parenting and its effect on well-being. *Sociological Spectrum*, 31, 399–418.

Lenartowicz, M. (2016). Family leisure consumption and youth sport socialization in post-communist Poland: A perspective based on Bourdieu's class theory. *International Review for the Sociology of Sport*, 51(2), 219–237.

Malcolm, D. (2008). *The Sage dictionary of sports studies*. London: Sage Publications.

Mansfield, L., Caudwell, J., Wheaton, B., & Watson, B. (Eds.). (2018). *The Palgrave handbook of feminism and sport, leisure and physical education*. London: Palgrave Macmillan.

McCarthy, J. R., & Edwards, R. (2011). *Key concepts in family studies*. London: Sage Publications.

Mercado, H., & Bernthal, M. J. (2016). Hispanic subcultural sport socialization: An initial investigation. *Sport Marketing Quarterly*, 25(2), 103–114.

Murphy, P. (2020). *Reconfiguring figurational sociology: A radical critique from an insider perspective: A synopsis* (Unpublished manuscript).

Neely, K. C., & Holt, N. L. (2014). Parents' perspectives on the benefits of sport participation for young children. *Sport Psychologist*, 28(3), 255–268.

Neely, K., & Holt, N. L. (2016). Peer group experiences in youth sport. In K. Green & A. Smith (Eds.), *The Routledge handbook of youth sport*. (pp. 218–226). Oxford: Routledge.

Nielsen, G., Grønfeldt, V., Toftegaard-Støckel, J., & Andersen, L. B. (2012). Predisposed to participate? The influence of family socio-economic background on children's sports participation and daily amount of physical activity. *Sport in Society*, 15(1), 1–27.

Nomaguchi, K., & Milkie, M. A. (2019). What should children learn? Americans' changing socialization values, 1986–2018. Socius: Sociological Research for a Dynamic World, 5, 1–17. doi:10.1177/2378023119879016.

Parry, W. (2013). *Experiences of physical activity at age 10 in the 1970 British Cohort Study*. Working paper 2013/6. London: Institute of Education, University of London.

Parry, W. (2015). *Do active children become active adults? Investigating experiences of sport and exercise using the 1970 British Cohort Study* (Unpublished PhD thesis). Institute of Education, University College London.

Pot, N., Verbeek, J., van der Zwan, J., & van Hilvoorde, I. (2016). Socialisation into organised sports of young adolescents with a lower socio-economic status. *Sport, Education & Society, 21*(3), 319–338.

Quarmby, T. (2016). Parenting and youth sport. In K. Green & A. Smith (Eds.), *The Routledge handbook of youth sport* (pp. 209–217). Oxford: Routledge.

Quarmby, T., & Dagkas, S. (2010). Children's engagement in leisure time physical activity: Exploring family structure as a determinant. *Leisure Studies, 29*(1), 53–66.

Qunito Romani, A. (2019). Parental behaviour and children's sports participation: Evidence from a Danish longitudinal school study. *Sport, Education and Society, 25*(3), 332–347 doi:10.1080/13573322.2019.1577235.

Roberts, K. (2008). Extended review of "The way class works: Readings on school, family and the economy," edited by Lois Weis, New York, Routledge, 2008, xvii + 390 pp., £20.99 (paperback), ISBN 978-0-415-95708-3. *British Journal of Sociology of Education, 30*(5), 647–651.

Roberts, K. (2009). *Key concepts in sociology.* Basingstoke, U.K.: Palgrave MacMillan.

Roberts, K. (2015). Social class and leisure during recent recessions in Britain. *Leisure Studies, 34*(2), 131–149.

Roberts, K. (2016a). *Social theory, sport, leisure.* Abingdon, U.K.: Routledge.

Roberts, K. (2016b). Youth leisure as the context for youth sport. In K. Green & A. Smith (Eds.), *The Routledge handbook of youth sport* (pp. 18–25). Oxford: Routledge.

Roberts, K., & Brodie, D. (1992). *Inner-city sport: Who plays and what are the benefits?* Culemborg, Netherlands: Giordano Bruno.

Roberts, K., Kovacheva, S., & Kabaivanov, S. (2020). Careers in participant sport and other free time activities during youth and young adulthood in South and East Mediterranean countries. *Athens Journal of Sports, 7*, 1–16.

Roberts, K., Minten, J. H., Chadwick, C., Lamb, K. L., & Brodie, D. A. (1991). Sporting lives: A case study of leisure careers. *Loisir et Societe/Society and Leisure, 14*(1), 261–284.

Ryan, K. (2012). The new wave of childhood studies: Breaking the grip of bio-social dualism? *Childhood, 19*(4), 439–452.

Sabo, D., & Veliz, P. (2008). *Go out and play. Youth sports in America.* New York: Women's Sports Foundation.

Scheerder, J., Thomis, M., Vanreusel, B., Lefevre, J., Renson, R., Vanden Eynde, B., & Beunen, G. P. (2006). Sports participation among females from adolescence to adulthood: A longitudinal study. *International Review for the Sociology of Sport, 41*(3–4), 413–430.

Shakib, S., & Veliz, P. (2013). Race, sport and social support: A comparison between African American and white youths' perceptions of social support for sport participation. *International Review for the Sociology of Sport, 48*(3), 295–317.

Smith, A. L., & McDonough, M. H. (2008). Peers. In A. L. Smith & S. J. H. Biddle (Eds.), *Youth physical activity and sedentary behavior. Challenges and solutions* (pp. 295–320). Champaign: Human Kinetics.

Stefansen, K., Smette, I., & Strandbu, Å. (2016). "De må drive med noe": Idrettens mening i ungdomstida, fra foreldres perspektiv ["They must do something": The meaning of sports during youth, from parents' perspectives]. In Ø. Seippel, M. K. Sisjord, & Å. Strandbu (Eds.), *Ungdom og Idrett* (pp. 154–172). Oslo: Cappelen Damm akademisk.

Stefansen, K., Smette, I., & Strandbu, Å. (2018). Understanding the increase in parents' involvement in organized youth sports. *Sport, Education and Society, 23*(2), 162–172.

Stirrup, J., Sandford, R., & Duncombe, R. (2015). "Intensive mothering" in the early years: The cultivation and consolidation of (physical) capital. *Sport, Education and Society, 20*(1), 89–106.

Strandbu, Å., Bakken, A., & Stefansen, K. (2019). The continued importance of family sport culture for sport participation during the teenage years. *Sport Education and Society*, 25(8), 931–945. doi:10.1080/13573322.2019.1676221.

Strandbu, Å., Stefansen, K., Smette, I., & Sandvik, M. R. (2019). Young people's experiences of parental involvement in youth sport. *Sport, Education and Society*, 24(1), 66–77.

Stuij, M. (2015). Habitus and social class: A case study on socialisation into sports and exercise. *Sport, Education and Society*, 20(6), 780–798.

Tolonen, T. (2005). Locality and gendered capital of working-class youth. *Young*, 13(4), 343–61.

Tomanović, S. (2004). Family habitus as the cultural context for childhood. *Childhood*, 11(3), 339–360.

Van Krieken, R. (1998). *Norbert Elias*. London: Routledge.

Vincent, C., & Ball, S. J. (2007). Making up the middle-class child: Families, activities and class dispositions. *Sociology*, 41(6), 1061–1077.

Vincent, C., & Maxwell, C. (2016). Parenting priorities and pressures: Furthering understanding of "concerted cultivation." *Discourse: Studies in the Cultural Politics of Education*, 37(2), 269–281.

Walseth, K. (2006). Young Muslim women and sport: The impact of identity work. *Leisure Studies*, 25, 75–94.

Walseth, K. (2016). Sport, youth and religion. In K. Green & A. Smith (Eds.), *The Routledge handbook of youth sport* (pp. 297–307). Oxford: Routledge.

Wheeler, S. (2011). The significance of family culture for sports participation. *International Review for the Sociology of Sport*, 47(2), 235–252.

Wheeler, S. (2013). *Patterns of parenting, class relations and inequalities in education and leisure: A grounded theory* (Unpublished PhD thesis). University of Chester.

Wheeler, S. (2018a). "Essential assistance" versus "concerted cultivation": Theorising class-based patterns of parenting in Britain. *Pedagogy, Culture and Society*, 26(3), 327–344.

Wheeler, S. (2018b). The (re)production of (dis)advantage: Class-based variations in parental aspirations, strategies and practices in relation to children's primary education. *Education, 3–13*, 46(7), 755–769.

Wheeler, S., & Green, K. (2012). Parenting in relation to children's sports participation: Generational changes and potential implications. *Leisure Studies*, 33(3), 267–284.

Wheeler, S., & Green, K. (2019). "The helping, the fixtures, the kits, the gear, the gum shields, the food, the snacks, the waiting, the rain, the car rides": Social class, parenting and children's organised leisure. *Sport, Education and Society*, 24(8), 788–800.

Wheeler, S., Green, K., & Thurston, M. (2019). Social class and the emergent organised sporting habits of primary-aged children. *European Physical Education Review*, 25(1), 89–108.

Wright, J. (2016). Sexuality, gender and youth sport. In K. Green & A. Smith (Eds.), *The Routledge handbook of youth sport* (pp. 276–286). Oxford: Routledge.

Zeijl, E., Poel, Y. T., Bois-Reymond, M. D., Ravesloot, J., & Meulman, J. J. (2000). The role of parents and peers in the leisure activities of young adolescents. *Journal of Leisure research*, 32(3), 281–302.

CHAPTER 33

···

SPORT, YOUTH, AND ELITE DEVELOPMENT

···

ANDY SMITH

In the previous chapter, Green, Wheeler, and Johansen draw attention to the socialization of children (up to around age 13) into sport and review international evidence which points to the significance of children's networks of relations (or interdependencies) and associated habitus formation, and wider inequalities and sources of social division, in explaining children's differential engagement in sport. They argue that the development of specific sporting habits (e.g., playing particular sports) alongside more general predispositions toward being physically active have their roots in and become deeply embedded and internalized during childhood—especially among sports-active families. Recognizing the significance of childhood and socializing practices during this life stage for sport participation, this chapter examines changes in sport participation during the subsequent youth life stage (roughly 13 to 25 years). In so doing, it considers the changing nature of youth sport careers, how these are related to the extension, destandardization, and individualization of youth as a life stage, and the significance of leisure as the context for youth sport careers.

The chapter also considers the sporting experiences of those young people who embark upon elite sport careers from their early teenage years. Attention is drawn to the significance of family support, coaching practices, and elite sports cultures and structures for young people who pursue elite sport pathways, and some of the "costs" incurred in the process. These issues are discussed from largely sociological vantage points on the study of youth and the youth life stage.

Understanding Youth and the Youth Life Stage

It is now recognized that youth represents the life stage between childhood and adulthood, and that the precise chronological ages when youth starts and ends vary by time and place (France, Coffey, Roberts, & Waite, 2020; Roberts, 2016a). In the early 20th century, a theory of adolescence was proposed by the American psychologist, G. Stanley Hall (and subsequently incorporated into Freudian psychology), who argued that adolescence began with puberty and lasted until young people had come to terms with the impact that significant physiological changes and stress had on their emotions, identities, and lives (Roberts, 2016a). Since puberty was universal, adolescence was similarly regarded as a universal life stage which represents youth as encompassing a series of developmental stages which are to a large extent shaped, if not fixed, by changes in psychology or biology (France et al., 2020). This was, however, a view which came to be questioned by sociologists who have since proposed that "youth has always been socially constructed: that the ages when it begins and ends have varied by time and place, and often between social groups in the same places and at the same time" (Roberts, 2016a, p. 12).

In this regard, attempts to define youth are particularly difficult, and it is not adequate simply to conceptualize youth as a life stage that can be tied rigidly to "specific age ranges, nor can its end point be linked to specific activities, such as taking up paid work or having sexual relations" (Furlong, 2013, p. 1). Youth is perhaps most adequately recognized sociologically as a "period of semi-dependence that falls between the full dependency that characterizes childhood and the independence of adulthood" (p. 3), and which can very broadly be mapped, in chronological terms, onto the transitions experienced roughly by those ages 16 to 25, but also by youngsters in their mid-teens. It is this group which is the focus of this chapter.

Issues

Participant Youth Sport Careers

The concern with sport participation among young people, whether during youth or in their subsequent adult life stages, is long standing and exists in many countries globally. Whether related to concerns about physical or mental health, other social outcomes (including drug use and crime prevention), or the many priorities related to the promotion of sport for sport's sake, youth sport is now of significant interest to politicians, policymakers, other professionals, the media, and of course academic researchers. Most recently, interest in youth sport careers has also coincided "with a worldwide lengthening of the youth life-stage with upward movements in the typical ages of completing full-time education, commencing adult employment, and parenthood" (Roberts, Kovacheva, & Kabaivanov, 2020, p. 1), and with careers of varying lengths in activities such as sport and other means of spending leisure time.

We shall return to the significance of the lengthening youth life stage later. It is now well-established that recruitment into leisure sport participation is typically greatest during childhood but that the heaviest dropout, and drop-off, in participation—while common in all age groups—is often in youth, and many people fail to participate at all, or regularly, thereafter (e.g., Green, 2014; Haycock & Smith, 2014, 2016; Pot, Verbeek, van der Zwan, & van Hilvoorde, 2016; Roberts & Brodie, 1992; Roberts, Minten, Chadwick, Lamb, & Brodie, 1991; Roberts et al., 2020; Stuij, 2015). An important but often overlooked longitudinal study of U.K. adults' sport and leisure careers (Roberts & Brodie, 1992; Roberts et al., 1991) concluded that those who remained active in several (usually three or more) sports throughout their late teenage years and into their mid-20s were most likely to participate throughout young adulthood. The foundations of these groups' longer-running sport careers were laid during youth, and engagement in sport during their mid-30s was related to changes occurring in the youth life stage and other uses of leisure (Roberts & Brodie, 1992; Roberts et al., 1991). Other studies, also in the U.K., have since demonstrated that the extension of youth sport careers into adulthood depends on experiences acquired during childhood, in sports-active families, where significant investments of time, money, and attention (often from parents) are made in the sporting experiences of young people (e.g., Haycock & Smith, 2014; Quarmby & Dagkas, 2010)—an observation confirmed by studies of parental engagement in children's sport and leisure participation, especially in middle- and upper-middle-class families (e.g., Strandbu, Bakken, & Stefansen, 2019; Strandbu, Stefansen, Smette, & Sandvik, 2019; Wheeler & Green, 2012, 2019; Wheeler, Green, & Thurston, 2019).

Evidence from other countries, including Nordic countries such as Norway, suggests that childhood socialization in sporting families best explains sustained sporting careers in later life stages (Green, Thurston, & Vaage, 2015; Green, Thurston, Vaage, & Roberts, 2015; Green, Sigurjónsson, & Skille, 2019) and result from intensive parental cultivation of sporting experiences (Green, Thurston, Vaage, & Mordal-Moen, 2015; Johansen & Green, 2019). Sociodemographic group differences in sport participation rates have also been shown to be relatively fixed by and remained stable after age 16 among adults in the South Caucasus (Birchwood, Roberts, & Pollock, 2008). Most recently, Roberts et al. (2020) explored the sport careers of 15- to 29-year-olds living in five South and East Mediterranean countries (Algeria, Egypt, Lebanon, Morocco, and Tunisia). They reported that males had higher rates of sport participation than females, and that the differences between them were similar at ages 15 to 19 (21%) and 25 to 29 (18%). In all age groups, those with better-educated fathers also had the highest sport participation rates, but while the social class gap remained stable for females across age groups, for males it widened from 14% to 19%. This, they argued, was "due to highly educated fathers tending to have sons whose sport participation proved enduring from late-teens to late-20s," while the "sport careers of sons with less educated fathers proved more vulnerable as they progressed through youth and into young adulthood" (p. 5). Overall, the sons and daughters of highly educated fathers had the highest sport participation rates in all age groups and were more likely to have longer-running sport careers through youth and into young adulthood, while age-related declines in participation were observed among those in all the other social class groups (Roberts et al., 2020).

In light of these studies' findings, Roberts et al. (2020, p. 13) have argued that we now have persuasive evidence from several countries that "the foundations for enduring careers in participant sport are usually laid in childhood and early adolescence in specific family contexts" where parents and siblings are sports-active or the families encourage their children to play. They add that sport participation by older children and young people "can probably be boosted in school and community facilities and projects, but all the evidence now available suggests that participation is unlikely to endure into later life stages unless supportive foundations have been laid in childhood family cultures" (p. 13–14).

Among the key features of youth sport careers, and those of participants in later life stages, which have emerged over the past 30 years or so have been changes in the nature of participation and the activities undertaken during the transition from youth to young adulthood. While engagement in full versions of team sports (e.g., soccer, netball, rugby) remain popular until around the end of statutory schooling and thereafter among a significant committed minority of youth (and adults), for many others highly structured sporting activities become less organizationally convenient than their derivatives which have since become more popular (e.g., 5-a-side soccer) and become progressively less prominent features of sport careers (Coalter, 2013; Green, 2014; Haycock & Smith, 2014; Roberts & Brodie, 1992; Roberts et al., 2020). There has been a corresponding increase, observed in many countries, in young people's engagement in more flexible partner (e.g., squash, tennis, and badminton) and individually oriented (e.g., running, multi-gym, swimming) exercise or lifestyle activities and popular events such as parkrun and other so-called action sports (e.g., surfing, rock climbing, snowboarding) (e.g., Thorpe, 2016; Wheaton, Wheaton, 2019). These activities can can be accommodated within youth sport careers alongside broader changes in leisure lifestyles and can be more resilient to the challenges experienced during the transition to adulthood. As will become clear below, changes in the youth life stage can alter the context within which youth sport careers develop (or not) and their trajectories (Roberts, 2016a), but the construction of youth sport careers—which are of course continually shaped and reshaped by experiences of intersecting markers of social division (e.g., gender, ethnicity, class, age, sexuality) and the availability of provisions (e.g., facilities, facilitators)— appear critically related to experiences first encountered during childhood.

Elite Youth Sport Careers

The evidence cited above on youth sport careers comes largely from sociological investigations of participant sport in leisure and, to an extent, the associated role that schools and subjects such as physical education are believed to play in encouraging sport participation among the majority of young people who engage at recreational (leisure) but not elite or high-performance levels. It is clear, however, that for the minority of talented youngsters who do enter talent development and elite sport pathways when young, and who may go on to compete nationally and internationally, this career trajectory appears to be supported by many experiences similar to those who engage in participant leisure sport. Among the evidence-based attempts made by sports psychologists (though evidence can also be found in sociological studies) to explain the links between engagement in participant sport during childhood and adolescence, and subsequently in elite sport, include the Developmental Model of Sport Participation (e.g., Côté, 1999; Côté, Baker, & Abernethy, 2007; Côté & Viermaa, 2014). That model suggests the development of talented athletes can be divided broadly into three phases: (1) sampling (usually during childhood up to early teens), (2) specializing (often from around 13 to 15, where participation is limited to one or possibly two sports), and (3) investment (typically from mid-teens onward, with a focus on achieving elite performance in one sport). Although there can be important diversity in the initial construction of the early sport careers of elite athletes, during the sampling phase these athletes are typically involved in a range of sports, supported variously by significant others (especially parents, but also siblings, other family members, friends, coaches, and teachers), often for fun and enjoyment (e.g., Berg, Fuller, & Hitchinson, 2018; Côté, 1999; Côté et al., 2007; Côté & Viermaa, 2014; Fraser-Thomas, Côté, & Deakin, 2008; Stevenson, 1990a, 1990b). Indeed, as with their peers who engage only in participant leisure sport, for many elite athletes the richness and diversity of childhood sport socialization is often characterized by supportive sports-active families who often, but not always, help develop their intrinsic motivation and love of sport and support the development of the competencies and skills required for subsequent participation (Côté, 1999; Côté et al., 2007; Côté & Viermaa, 2014).

These early socializing practices can be reinforced further by youngsters' experiences of schooling, sometimes in state (or public) settings, but especially in the growth of private and independent fee-paying schools where significant investment is often made in attracting and developing talented athletes in the curriculum and/or extracurricular activity. The growth of so-called sport schools, for example, has occurred in several countries and continues to play a prominent role in their elite sport development strategies (Kristiansen & Houlihan, 2015). However, as the findings of a study on the social backgrounds of British athletes who competed at the London 2012 Olympic Games revealed, these schools disproportionately attract and benefit already advantaged middle-/upper-class youngsters who are more likely to enjoy the benefits of the positive childhood sport socialization experiences mentioned earlier (Smith, Haycock & Hulme, 2013). Thus, while the benefits and class-related advantages of attending sports schools and independent and private institutions will impact differentially on different groups of athletes competing in different sports, they are nevertheless perceived to play an important role in the specializing and investment phases, and particularly in supporting athlete development and their engagement in dual (sport and education) careers (see Aquilina & Henry, 2010; Berg et al., 2018).

Young athletes' engagement in the specializing, then investment, phases often continues to be supported by parents and families in leisure settings, alongside schooling. However, this tends to be complemented by a gradual engagement in local and national child and youth-based talent identification and development systems (TIDS), which have grown markedly in the past 30 years or so (Cobley, 2016; Vaeyens, Lenoir, Williams, & Philippaerts, 2008). These systems are perceived to be critical in supporting the transition from participant to more elite sport settings and in intensifying greater engagement in specialized competition and training intended to support national and international performance (Baker, Horton, Robertson-Wilson, & Wall, 2003; Cobley, 2016). For Cobley (2016, p. 478), two features characterize this intensification: "the identification of precocious young athletes earlier and earlier in their lives . . . [and] attempts to accelerate the youngsters' performance through provision of supposedly more optimal training conditions and environments." In this context, coaches and other specialist support staff become progressively more important in shaping the careers of elite youth athletes, and their experience of associated TIDS processes oriented toward maximizing individual and collective success (e.g., Baker et al., 2003; Berg et al., 2018; Cobley, 2016).

Coaches, along with significant others, often also play an important role in young athletes' decisions to specialize in a particular sport, which they do sometimes voluntarily through personal choice (supported by considerations of potential success and positive personal relations), but also through enforced decision-making (e.g., by being deselected from other sports, interpersonal conflict, other lifestyle considerations). For the minority of youngsters who go on to have longer-lasting elite sport careers, their subsequent engagement is sustained by varying indicators of success, which can in turn support the construction of reputable and valued athletic role identities (Stevenson, 1990a, 1990b) and/or engagement in disidentification as a means of resisting coach/managerial domination (Roderick, 2014), which develop throughout the course of their careers. Other reasons can be more pragmatic or convenient, including being in the right place at the right time, benefiting from changes in coaching staff and other personnel, the deselection of or injuries encountered by teammates, and so on (Stevenson, 1990a, 1990b). The initial (and subsequent) construction of elite sport careers is thus always a contingent process involving decisions and actions which are not always deliberate, conscious, or planned; they may, perhaps most commonly, be largely unintended and serendipitous, perceived more or less positively or negatively (Stevenson, 1990a, 1990b), but experienced always in the context of their interdependence with others (Roderick, 2006).

APPROACHES

Studies of sport, youth, and elite development have been undertaken from a variety of perspectives, including in the subdisciplinary fields of physiology, psychology, sport policy, sport management, sports coaching, and sociology. We shall focus here on sociological approaches (including those of Elias and Bourdieu) which have been applied to youth sport careers and which have, in turn, been informed by the work of sociologists whose research has been particularly influential in the related fields of youth studies and leisure (such as Roberts and Furlong).

Youth Figurations, Habitus, and Capital

In moving beyond the largely individual-oriented emphasis of psychological and developmental approaches, sociologists prefer to recognize how "youth has to be understood in its historical, social, political and cultural contexts" (France et al., 2020, p. 3). In so doing, it is critical that we move beyond conceptualizing youth solely as individuals, that is, as if they were closed self-contained entities isolated from society (what Elias called the *Homo clausus* portrayal of human beings), and should instead focus on viewing them as *Homines aperti*, as open pluralities of people bound together in dynamic networks of interdependency (Elias, 2012a, 2012b; van Krieken, 1998, 2019). For Elias, these networks (or power relationships) constitute the nexus of the figuration he described as "a structure of mutually oriented and dependent people" (Elias, 2012a, p. 525) and which he developed as a means of circumventing the unhelpful tendency to conceive of the individual (or agency) and society (or structure) as separate entities (Elias, 2012a; van Krieken, 1998, 2019). In this regard, individual and groups of (young) people are conceived as being embedded within dynamic figurations which enable and constrain action, and within which their habitus, or biopsychological structure, develops from birth throughout the rest of life.

Although most commonly associated with the work of Bourdieu (1984) and his related discussion of capital development, habitus was also central to the work of Elias (2012a, p. 406), who regarded it as embodied social learning, "an automatic, blindly functioning apparatus of self-control" which develops within the sociogenic (the broad contours of a figuration) and psychogenic (our individual and collective psychological orientations) dimensions of figurations, or dynamic interdependency networks (see also van Krieken, 1998, 2019). Conceptualizing habitus in this way reflected Elias's suggestion that over time external forms of regulation are gradually converted into forms of self-regulation, a process associated with the increasing size, complexity, and differentiation of interdependency networks (or figurations) which leads to greater individualization (van Krieken, 2019).

As Haycock and Smith (2014, 2016) and others (e.g., Birchwood et al., 2008; Green et al., this volume; Pot et al., 2016; Quarmby & Dagkas, 2010; Stuij, 2015) have noted, habitus formation and capital development are two dimensions of youth biographies which are among the key processes that need to be understood if we are to make adequate sociological sense of youth sport (and leisure) careers and the contexts in which these are enacted. Since childhood and youth are the more impressionable phases of habitus formation (van Krieken, 1998, 2019), it is unsurprising that—as we noted earlier—these are also life stages during which the foundations for subsequent sport careers are (or are not) laid and during which predispositions for sport participation are continually constructed, and reconstructed, in the context of our complex, historically produced and reproduced, networks of interdependence (Birchwood et al., 2008; Green et al., this volume; Haycock & Smith, 2014, 2016; Stuij, 2015). These life stages have also been shown to be critical in the transference (from parents initially, and later additional significant others) of important physical, social, cultural, and educational capital during childhood socialization, especially among those in sports-active and middle-class families (Birchwood et al., 2008; Haycock & Smith, 2016; Wheeler & Green, 2012, 2019; Wheeler et al., 2019). The accumulation of capital and habitus formation during childhood and youth thus provides the foundations upon which the necessary predispositions and tastes that underpin subsequent sport careers are based and have proven particularly efficacious for transmitting the kinds of values and norms of sport-supportive cultures needed for longer-term participation in sport (Birchwood et al., 2008; Haycock & Smith, 2014, 2016; Stuij, 2015).

The Youth Life Stage: Extended, Destandardized, and Individualized

To adequately understand the construction of youth sport careers it is essential we conceptualize young people in terms of their figurations or networks and recognize the significance of these for their biopsychosocial development, habitus formation, and socialization into sport (and, indeed, other leisure activities). It is critical also to understand how, over the past 50 years, the youth life stage in all Western countries and many others has been extended (though there remain significant variations in how long it lasts), destandardized, and individualized (see Roberts, 2016a). As Roberts has noted, for many (though not all) young people the youth life stage has extended in various ways, including in the lengthening and increasing complexity of education-to-work transitions and delays in the ages at which they marry and become parents. The destandardization, or reordering, of the life stage in post-industrial societies refers to how it is now uncommon for young people to follow what was previously regarded as a standard sequencing of life transitions, namely "completing education, then establishing yourself in employment, following which you became financially independent and able, with a partner, to maintain an independent household whereupon you could marry and become a parent" (p. 14). It is also now common, and acceptable, for young people to move back and forth between these transitions.

The third feature of the youth life stage in postindustrial societies is individualization, which has involved, among other things, an acceleration in the individualization of personal biographies, preferences, and lifestyles used to navigate one's life course (including in

relation to sport participation), albeit within the constraints imposed by long-standing social divisions which characterize our lives (Roberts, 2016a). This has been associated with the
wider individualization of life, the theory of which was developed by the sociologists Ulrich
Beck and Elisabeth Beck-Gernsheim (2002), and also by Elias, who regarded individualization as an important feature of the lengthening, increasing complexity, and differentiation
of our interdependency networks. For sociologists of youth like Furlong (Furlong et al.,
2017), Eliasian ideas about individualization are particularly helpful in providing the context for understanding youth as a transition to adulthood and for recognizing the centrality
of dynamic figurations in this process (see Woodman, Shildrick, & MacDonald, 2020).

As Roberts (2016a) has noted, these changes in the youth life stage are important for
understanding the development of youth sport careers, but they do not necessarily have
direct implications for these since they are relatively independent of wider shifts in youth
life stages, can continue to be constructed within them, and have themselves always been
individualized. This being said, the wider changes in the youth life stage do "alter the context in which youth sports careers develop (or do not develop)" (p. 16). And the changed
educational context—particularly through the prolongation of educational transitions
and growth of higher education participation—alongside wider changes in sports facility
provision are among the developments which are favorable for the development of long-
lasting sport careers, especially among those who are sufficiently predisposed to participate (Birchwood et al., 2008; Coalter, 2013; Haycock & Smith, 2016; Roberts, 2016a). The
problem for those wishing to promote lifelong sport participation via long-running sport
careers among young people, it is claimed, is "not recruitment but retention throughout
what is now a prolonged life stage during which individuals and peer groups are seeking
places to go and things to do" (Roberts, 2016a, p. 17). This brings us to the significance of
leisure for youth sport careers.

The Significance of Leisure for Youth Sport Careers

Locating youth sport careers in the context of young people's wider leisure lives, alongside
changes in the youth life stage, adds further explanatory power to sociological explanations
of youth and sport in at least two ways (Roberts, 2016b). First, it draws attention to how
young people who do not engage in sport, or do very little, are not simply becoming couch
potatoes. Second, unlike other forms of leisure (such as visiting pubs and bars), youth is not
typically the life stage during which large numbers of young people begin playing sport and
adopt long-running sport careers. Indeed, it is a stage when "drop-out from sport peaks and
the explanation lies in the greater appeal of other uses of leisure" (p. 18) which occur in the
context of, and the inequalities which characterize, participants' wider lives. Let us examine
these in turn.

As Roberts (2016b) has noted, youth is a life stage during which sport comes to compete
with other forms of leisure for time, money, and attention, often at the expense of—but
sometimes alongside—regular sport participation. It is a life stage when, for some young
people, peer-oriented activities such as eating and drinking out of the home, use of technology and new media, shopping, and engaging in sedentary and drug-oriented activities come to characterize their unfolding, increasingly individualized leisure lives, which
may involve sport indirectly but can often be at the expense of active sport participation
(Haycock & Smith, 2016; Hendry, Shucksmith, Love, & Glendenning, 1993; Roberts, 2016b;

Smith & Green, 2005). For others, engaging in popular commercialized, technology-based, home-centered, and peer-oriented leisure activities is not undertaken at the expense of sport participation. Rather, these activities are often accommodated within the busy leisure lives of youth (Haycock & Smith, 2016; Roberts, 2016b; Smith & Green, 2005). As Roberts (2016b, p. 21) has noted:

> Different sports compete for young people's loyalty, and all sports compete with other tastes and places that can act as sources of friends, identities and reputations. The choice is not be-tween sport and idleness. Sport has to compete in a market-place of leisure activities, styles and identities.

Thus, to adequately understand the sport careers of young people it is essential to recognize the increased appeal of other leisure activities during the youth life stage, since doing so will reveal how sport participation competes with many other activities within an already busy leisure marketplace in which the construction of young people's identities, reputations, and relationships are frequently prioritized and valued (Roberts, 2016b). It is a marketplace where young people typically experiment with different leisure activities, often in the company of peers, as they develop their leisure tastes, skills, and interests which provide the foundations for adult leisure (Hendry et al., 1993; Roberts, 2016b; Roberts & Brodie, 1992).

Given the increasing significance and appeal of leisure as an aspect of the wider transitions experienced during youth, it is perhaps unsurprising that youth is the life stage in which, for many young people, dropout from sport peaks and drop-off in participation begins to accelerate, while for a minority it becomes a secure foundation upon which their adult sport careers are based (e.g., Birchwood et al., 2008; Green, 2014; Roberts, 2016b; Roberts & Brodie, 1992; Roberts et al., 1991; Roberts et al., 2020). For those who embark upon elite sport careers during the youth life stage, it is often said that they necessarily forgo many of the leisure activities and experiences in which many of their peers engage in return for the chance of pursuing a career in sport. They are instead constrained to make a range of sacrifices in pursuit of apparently lucrative careers available in elite sport. These sacrifices include spending time away from family and friends, modifying dietary and other lifestyle practices, forgoing pursuit of educational qualifications, incurring financial costs to support training and competition, regulating their use of social media and other technologies, managing pain and injury, responding to routine public scrutiny of their work-based successes and failures, and many other sacrifices entailed in the "logic" of elite sports work (e.g., Berg et al., 2018; Platts & Smith, 2016; Roderick & Allen-Collinson, 2020; Roderick & Gibbons, 2015). Although these are sacrifices which aspirant youth elite athletes are prepared to take, they can come at significant personal cost and raise concerns of various kinds, some of which are considered next.

DEBATES

Unequal Youth Sport Careers

As we noted earlier, it has now been shown quite convincingly that childhood is the critical life stage during which the foundations of youth (and adult) sport careers are laid (or not), including for those young people who embark upon a career in elite sport. These foundations are, however, unequally laid and can be traced to the wider inequalities which characterize their familial situation and other experiences children may have during childhood. Here, those from more advantaged backgrounds are disproportionately more likely to benefit from living in sports-active and culturally omnivorous families than their disadvantaged peers. Indeed, unequal propensities for participating in sport are related especially to social inequalities that, to a large degree, are acquired and have their roots in childhood and family life (Birchwood et al., 2008; Green et al., this volume; Haycock & Smith, 2014; Quarmby & Dagkas, 2010; Wheeler & Green, 2019) and are reproduced in other settings, including leisure. The unequal home lives of children subsequently become translated into other forms of inequality, many of which persist across generations, and reinforce the likelihood of being able to develop (or not) youth sport careers. The significance of these inequalities for sport participation is clear, including in the U.K., where studies of sport participation have

> exhibited consistent correlations with aspects of social structure such [as] sex, level of education, age and social class. Even in times of increasing aggregate participation, the relationships between the rates of participation of these social groups remained relatively constant. An appropriate metaphor might be an escalator—although all were moving up, the relationship between the various steps on the escalator remained relatively constant—this applied both when participation was increasing and decreasing. (Coalter, 2013, p. 5)

Given the persistence of such socially structured and consistent correlations, it has been suggested that sport participation might be regarded as "epiphenomenal, a secondary set of social practices dependent on and reflecting more fundamental structures, values and processes" (Coalter, 2013, p. 18) associated with wider social inequalities which typically precede sport participation. The corrosive nature of social inequalities and their impact on sport participation and other activities have of course been of long-standing interest to sociologists and other social scientists, but there has been renewed debate and interest in these during the 21st century. This appears partly related to the wider emergence of what has been described as an "inequality paradigm" (Savage, 2016) in the social sciences. Most particularly, since the global recession in 2008, these inequalities have accelerated, widened, and deepened in ways that negatively impact many aspects of social life, including public health and well-being, among all social groups, and especially the most disadvantaged (cf. Marmot, Allen, Boyce, Goldblatt, & Morrison, 2020; Wilkinson & Pickett, 2010, 2018).

In many countries there continue to be significant inequalities in sport participation which are linked disproportionately to socioeconomic status and are amplified by social and health inequalities, including among youth, where the most disadvantaged, women, and some Black, minority, and ethnic groups are most likely to be inactive. These groups thus remain the targets of much international sport policy, many of which include among their preferred outcomes improvements in physical and mental health and well-being, personal and community development, increases in individual and population-level sport and physical activity participation, and elite sport success (Smith, Greenough, & Lovett, 2022). Whether these policy approaches will be successful in narrowing inequalities in sport participation and related areas will doubtless remain an important source of debate, as will the continued blurring between sport and other areas of social policy, especially public health, and what this suggests about the increasingly vulnerable and marginalized status of sport as a policy sector (Smith et al., 2022). If the best guide to the future is the past, then there appear to be very real grounds for caution about whether the current policy trajectories in many countries will have the intended impacts on encouraging sport participation (including among youth) and narrowing of inequalities for the benefit of health and well-being.

The Impacts of Elite Youth Sport Careers

As well as their long-standing interest in inequalities, whether in sport or other areas of social life, sociologists and other scientists (especially sports psychologists) have also focused on the impacts that engaging in elite sport careers have on the lives of young people, including in relation to early specialization and subsequent career transitions. It is not possible here to review this body of work, but especially since the 1990s there has been growing interest in and much debate about the consequences of young people's earlier and more intense involvement in elite sport settings.

One source of debate, noted earlier, has been the rapid growth of child- and youth-based TIDS and their impacts on young people's current and future engagement in elite sport and other aspects of their health and well-being. Indeed, it is not uncommon to hear concerns about the number and experiences of young people who "fail to make it" because they have spent much of their formative years engaged in TIDS or other academy sport structures, from which only a minority of participants eventually reach, and stay at, elite or high-performance levels (e.g., Cobley, 2016; Vaeyens et al., 2008). Among other things, this is typically the case because

> throughout adolescence, programmes offer age-group bands ending at youth or adult/senior ages (e.g., 18–21 years). Ultimately, this structure means that most recruits (perhaps up to 99 per cent of participants) will experience de-selection, withdrawal and dropout in childhood and youth, and it is rare that substantial numbers of athletes transfer across TID contexts. (Cobley, 2016, p. 479)

These TIDS also require young athletes to willingly conform, often when very young, to an institutionalized expectation that they will take serious risks with their health and accept the various "cultures of risk" Nixon (1992, 1993) and values which underpin what Hughes and Coakley (1991) term the "sport ethic" (see Malcolm & Pullen, this volume) which characterize many aspects of the elite sport workplace. These norms and values, it is claimed, are often accepted without question or qualification by aspiring youth athletes who, especially during the early stages of their working lives, are constrained to accept the prevailing values and cultures of their respective sports from important gatekeepers who to a large extent control access to the world of elite sport (Brackenridge, 2001; Platts & Smith, 2016; Roderick, 2006).

Youth frequently rationalize these sacrifices as necessary—especially during the early parts of their careers—to become an elite sports worker and to be accepted by powerful significant others (e.g., coaches, managers, performance directors, scientific support staff) (Brackenridge, 2001; Platts & Smith, 2016; Roderick, 2006). Yet there is now a wide and accumulating body of evidence which points to how young people pay a whole range of other personal costs which have been frequently identified by and continue to act as sources of concern among sociologists. Among these are youth-based experiences of physical and emotional abuse (e.g., McMahon & McGannon, 2020; Stirling & Kerr, 2007, 2008), sexual abuse and violence (e.g., Hartill, 2005, 2009; Kerr & Kerr, 2020; Sanderson & Weathers, 2020), and the prevalence of injury (e.g., Hastmann-Walch & Caine, 2015; Maffulli, Longon, Gougoulias, Loppini, & Denaro, 2010).

In the U.K., concern about the lack of duty of care which is thought to exist in sport was the subject of an independent review led by Baroness Grey-Thompson (2017). Focused on seven key themes underpinning duty of care matters in sport (education; transition; representation of the participant's voice; equality, diversity, and inclusion; safeguarding; mental welfare and safety; injury and medical issues), the review made a whole series of recommendations to improve the standard of duty of care in recreational and elite sport. Among these was the suggestion that government should create a sports ombudsman which "should have powers to hold national governing bodies (NGBs) to account for the Duty of Care they provide to all athletes, coaching staff and support staff, providing independent assurance and accountability to address many of the issues covered by this review" (p. 6). Supporting this, it was suggested that appropriate measures and key performance indicators should be introduced to determine the progress made in relation to duty of care, while a Duty of Care Charter was proposed as a necessary step through which the government should articulate how "participants, coaches and support staff can expect to be treated and where they can go if they need advice, support and guidance" (p. 6).

At the time of writing, none of these innovations have been implemented, yet there continue to be revelations regarding cultures of abuse and welfare concerns in sports, including British gymnastics (Roan, 2020), which clearly would benefit from the existence of a sports ombudsman rather than a process managed by associated funding agencies or the NGB itself. Gymnasts in New Zealand and other countries have similarly recalled experiences of psychological and physical abuse, depression and anxiety, and eating disorders (George, 2020). Indeed, the high-profile Netflix documentary *Athlete A*, which explores the case of Larry Nassar—the USA Gymnastics team doctor who abused hundreds of young women— provides yet further evidence, should it have been needed, that much more attention needs to be given the sporting cultures and practices experienced by all athletes, but especially young aspiring athletes who are particularly vulnerable to misuses of power in elite or high-performance sport settings. These cases will likely add further momentum to ongoing (and future) investigations of the harms and breaches in sport practices, including those involving young people, as concerns about duty of care and welfare in sport continue to occupy the agendas of researchers, investigative journalists, and other individuals and organizations committed to safeguarding the welfare of (youth) athletes.

CONCLUSION

Interest in the sporting careers of young people, and their other uses of leisure as aspects of youth lifestyles more broadly, is long standing and will likely continue in the future. There is now a growing community of sociologists, psychologists, and other social scientists working in youth studies and beyond who are variously committed to exploring the continuities and changes in young people's lives within countries and around the world. Indeed, sociologists in particular remain centrally interested in understanding how "transitions to adulthood have become longer, fuzzier and more complex" (Macdonald, Shildrick, & Woodman, 2019, p. 1), and how these and other profound social changes are impacting the lives of young people and intersecting with various inequalities. As MacDonald et al. have noted, recent and rapidly "changing socio-economic circumstances have had important implications for young people: new opportunities have been created, but inequality and marginalisation have increased and taken new forms" (p. 1), and these provide the dynamic contexts within which future investigations of youth sport careers will be undertaken. Recognizing how inequalities shape experiences of youth will doubtless be particularly significant as the implications of the COVID-19 pandemic are better understood. It is already apparent that the pandemic has not only exposed and amplified social inequalities (Marmot & Allen, 2020; Marmot et al., 2020) but has also had adverse and severe consequences for health and well-being, particularly among disadvantaged communities and Black and minority ethnic groups, as well as the educational and employment prospects of young people. As the research discussed earlier suggests, impacts on these features of the youth life stage will likely have important implications for the ways in which young people engage in sport (or not), and how this can be adequately understood with reference to their childhood and family-based experiences.

In the context of elite sport, as noted earlier, it is unambiguously clear that concerns about the health and welfare of young people will continue to occupy an important part of the research landscape in the sociology of sport and social sciences more broadly. These concerns will likely continue to exist in addition to those of researchers who have a greater interest in understanding the performance success of young athletes and how that success can be nurtured and maximized through TIDS, especially given that the prevailing elite sport policy context continues to emphasize, among other things, the early identification of talent and subsequent specialization of sporting performance. The degree to which the pursuit of performance-oriented goals can be undertaken effectively, while at the same time safeguarding the health and well-being of (young) athletes, might well be a productive area of research with important applied implications for those working in sport, whether as researchers, practitioners, or participants, and their significant others.

Regardless of which preferred research trajectories and priorities are pursued in the future, it is essential that this research recognizes the complexity and diversity of young people's lives, how their lives are shaped by their unavoidable interdependence with others, and how the inequalities which characterize these networks of relations actually provide the foundations upon which young unequal sporting lives exist.

REFERENCES

Aquilina, D., & Henry, I. (2010). Elite athletes and university education in Europe: A review of policy and practice in higher education in the European Union member states. *International Journal of Sport Policy and Politics, 2*(1), 25–47.

Baker, J., Horton, S., Robertson-Wilson, J., & Wall, M. (2003). Nurturing sport expertise: Factors influencing the development of elite athletes. *Journal of Sports Science and Medicine, 2*(1), 1–9.

Beck, U., & Beck-Gernsheim, E. (2002). *Individualization: Institutionalized individualism and its social and political consequences.* London: Sage.

Berg, B., Fuller, R., & Hitchinson, M. (2018). "But a champion comes out much, much later": A sport development case study of the 1968 U.S. Olympic team. *Sport Management Review*, *21*(4), 430–442.

Birchwood, D., Roberts, K., & Pollock, G. (2008). Explaining differences in sport participation rates among young adults: Evidence from the South Caucasus. *European Physical Education Review*, *14*(3), 283–300.

Bourdieu, P. (1984). *Distinction*. London: Routledge.

Brackenridge, C. (2001). *Spoilsports*. London: Routledge.

Coalter, F. (2013). Game plan and the Spirit Level: The class ceiling and the limits of sports policy? *International Journal of Sport Policy and Politics*, *5*(1), 3–19.

Cobley, S. (2016). Talent identification and development in youth sport. In K. Green & A. Smith (Eds.), *The Routledge handbook of youth sport* (pp. 476–91). London: Routledge.

Côté, J. (1999). The influence of the family in the development of talent in sport. *Sport Psychologist*, *13*(4), 395–417.

Côté, J., Baker, J., & Abernethy, B. (2007). Practice and play in the development of sport expertise. In G. Tenenbaum & R. Eklund (Eds.), *Handbook of sport psychology* (3rd ed.), (pp. 184–202). New York: Wiley.

Côté, J., & Viermaa, M., (2014). The developmental model of sport participation: 15 years after its first conceptualization. *Science and Sports*, *29(Suppl.)*, 563–569.

Elias, N. (2012a). *On the process of civilization*. Dublin: University College Dublin.

Elias, N. (2012b). *What is sociology?* Dublin: University College Dublin.

France, A., Coffey, J., Roberts, S., & Waite, C. (2020). *Youth sociology*. London: Red Globe Press.

Fraser-Thomas, J., Côté, J., & Deakin, J. (2008). Examining adolescent sport dropout and prolonged engagement from a developmental perspective. *Journal of Applied Sport Psychology*, *20*(3), 318–333.

Furlong, A. (2013). *Youth studies: An introduction*. London: Routledge.

Furlong, A., Goodwin, J., O'Connor, H., Hadfield, S., Hall, S., Lowden, K., & Plugor, R. (2017). *Young people in the labour market: Past, present, future*. London: Routledge.

George, Z. (2020, August 1). An insidious culture? New Zealand gymnastics rocked by allegations of psychological and physical abuse. *Stuff*. https://www.stuff.co.nz/sport/300071 427/an-insidious-culture-new-zealand-gymnastics-rocked-by-allegations-of-psychologi cal-and-physical-abuse.

Green, K. (2014). Mission impossible? Reflecting upon the relationship between physical education, youth sport and lifelong participation. *Sport, Education and Society*, *19*(4), 357–375.

Green, K., Sigurjónsson, T., & Skille, E. Å. (Eds.). (2019). *Sport in Scandinavia and the Nordic countries*. London: Routledge.

Green, K., Thurston, M., & Vaage, O. (2015). Isn't it good, Norwegian wood? Lifestyle and adventure sports participation among Norwegian youth. *Leisure Studies*, *34*(5), 529–546.

Green, K., Thurston, M., Vaage, O., & Mordal-Moen, K. (2015). Girls, young women and sport in Norway: A case study of sporting convergence amid favourable socio-economic conditions. *International Journal of Sports Policy and Politics*, *7*(4), 531–550.

Green, K., Thurston, M., Vaage, O., & Roberts, K. (2015). "We're on the right track, baby, we were born that way!" Exploring sports participation in Norway. *Sport, Education & Society*, *20*(3), 285–303.

Grey-Thompson, T. (2017). *Duty of care in sport: Independent report to government*. London: Department for Digital, Culture, Media and Sport.

Hartill, M. (2005). Sport and the sexually abused male child. *Sport, Education and Society*, 10(3), 287–304.

Hartill, M. (2009). The sexual abuse of boys in organized male sports. *Men and Masculinities*, 12(2), 225–249.

Hastmann-Walch, T., & Caine, D. (2015). Injury risk and long-term effects of injury in elite youth sports. In J. Baker, P. Safai, & J. Fraser-Thomas (Eds.), *Health and elite sport: Is high performance sport a healthy pursuit?* (pp. 65–80). London: Routledge.

Haycock, D., & A. Smith (2014). A family affair? Exploring the influence of childhood sports socialisation on young adults' leisure-sport careers in north-west England. *Leisure Studies*, 33(3), 285–304.

Haycock, D., & Smith, A. (2016). Youth sport and leisure careers. In K. Green & A. Smith (Eds.), *The Routledge handbook of youth sport* (pp. 42–54). London: Routledge.

Hendry, L., Shucksmith, J., Love, J., & Glendenning, A. (1993). *Young people's leisure and lifestyles*. London: Routledge.

Hughes, R., & Coakley, J. (1991). Positive deviance among athletes: The implications of overconformity to the sport ethic. *Sociology of Sport Journal*, 8(4), 307–325.

Johansen, P., & Green, K. (2019). "It's alpha omega for succeeding and thriving": Parents, children and sporting cultivation in Norway. *Sport, Education and Society*, 24(4), 427–440.

Kerr, R., & Kerr, G. (2020). Promoting athlete welfare: A proposal for an international surveillance system. *Sport Management Review*, 23(1), 95–103.

Kristiansen, E., & Houlihan, B. (2015). Developing young athletes: The role of private sport schools in the Norwegian sport system. *International Review for the Sociology of Sport*, 52(4), 447–469.

Macdonald, R., Shildrick, T., & Woodman, D. (2019). The future of youth research and the *Journal of Youth Studies*: Editorial statement. *Journal of Youth Studies*, 22(1), 1–6.

Maffulli, N., Longon, U., Gougoulias, N., Loppini, M., & Denaro, V. (2010). Long-term health outcomes of youth sports injuries. *British Journal of Sports Medicine*, 44(1), 21–25.

Marmot, M., & Allen, J. (2020). Covid-19: Exposing and amplifying inequalities. *Journal of Epidemiology and Community Health*, 74(9), 681–682.

Marmot, M., Allen, J., Boyce, T., Goldblatt, P., & Morrison, J. (2020). *Health equity in England: The Marmot Review 10 years on*. London: Institute of Health Equity.

McMahon, J., & McGannon, K. (2020). Acting out what is inside of us: Self-management strategies of an abused ex-athlete. *Sport Management Review*, 23(1), 28–38.

Nixon, H. L., II (1992). A social network analysis of influences on athletes to play with pain and injuries. *Journal of Sport and Social Issues*, 16(2), 127–135.

Nixon, II. L., II (1993). Accepting the risks of pain and injury in sport: Mediated cultural influences on playing hurt. *Sociology of Sport Journal*, 10(2), 183–196.

Platts, C., & Smith, A. (2016). Health, well-being and the "logic" of elite youth sports work. In K. Green & A. Smith (Eds.), *The Routledge handbook of youth sport* (pp. 492–504). London: Routledge.

Pot, N., Verbeek, J., van der Zwan, J., & van Hilvoorde, I. (2016). Socialisation into organised sports of young adolescents with a lower socio-economic status. *Sport, Education & Society*, 21(3), 319–338.

Quarmby, T., & Dagkas, S. (2010). Children's engagement in leisure time physical activity: Exploring family structure as a determinant. *Leisure Studies*, 29(1), 53–66.

Roan, D. (2020, August 1). Nile Wilson: British gymnasts are treated like "pieces of meat." BBC Sport. https://www.bbc.co.uk/sport/gymnastics/53727425.

Roberts, K. (2016a). Young people and social change. In K. Green & A. Smith (Eds.), *The Routledge handbook of youth sport* (pp. 10–17). London: Routledge.

Roberts, K. (2016b). Youth leisure as the context for youth sport. In K. Green & A. Smith (Eds.), *The Routledge handbook of youth sport* (pp. 18–25). London: Routledge.

Roberts, K., & Brodie, D. (1992). *Inner-city sport: Who plays and what are the benefits?* Culemborg, Netherlands: Giordano Bruno.

Roberts, K., Kovacheva, S., & Kabaivanov, S. (2020). Careers in participant sport and other free time activities during youth and young adulthood in South and East Mediterranean countries. *Athens Journal of Sports, 7*, 1–16.

Roberts, K., Minten, J., Chadwick, C., Lamb, K., & Brodie, D. (1991). Sporting lives: A case study of leisure careers. *Loisir et Societe/Society and Leisure, 14*(1), 261–284.

Roderick, M. (2006). *The work of professional football. A labour of love?* London: Routledge.

Roderick, M. (2014). From identification to dis-identification: Case studies of job loss in professional football. *Qualitative Research in Sport, Exercise and Health, 6*(2), 143–160.

Roderick, M., & Allen-Collinson, J. (2020). "I just want to be left alone": Novel sociological insights into dramaturgical demands on professional athletes. *Sociology of Sport Journal, 37*(2), 108–116.

Roderick, M., & Gibbons, B. (2015). "To thine own self be true": Sports work, mental illness and the problem of authenticity. In J. Baker, P. Safai, & J. Fraser-Thomas (Eds.), *Health and elite sport: Is high performance sport a healthy pursuit?* (pp. 149–162). London: Routledge.

Sanderson, J., & Weathers, M. (2020). Snapchat and child sexual abuse in sport: Protecting child athletes in the social media age. *Sport Management Review, 23*(1), 81–94.

Savage, M. (2016, June 2). Are we seeing a new "inequality paradigm" in social science? *LSE BPP*. https://blogs.lse.ac.uk/politicsandpolicy/are-we-seeing-a-new-inequality-paradigm-in-social-science/.

Smith, A., & Green, K. (2005). The place of sport and physical activity in young people's lives and its implications for health: Some sociological comments. *Journal of Youth Studies, 8*(2), 241–253.

Smith, A., Greenough, K., & Lovett, E. (2022). The politics and policy of community sport coaching. In B. Ives, L. Gale, P. Potrac, & L. Nelson (Eds.), *Community sport coaching: policy and practice* (pp. 7–24). London: Routledge.

Smith, A., Haycock, D., & Hulme, N. (2013). The Class of London 2012: Some sociological reflections on the social backgrounds of Team GB athletes. *Sociological Research Online, 18*(3), 158–162.

Stevenson, C. (1990a). The athletic career: Some contingencies of sport specialization. *Journal of Sport Behavior, 13*(2), 103–113.

Stevenson, C. (1990b). The early careers of international athletes. *Sociology of Sport Journal, 7*(3), 238–253.

Stirling, A., & Kerr, G. (2007). Elite female swimmers' experiences of emotional abuse across time. *Journal of Emotional Abuse, 7*(4), 89–113.

Stirling, A. & Kerr, G. (2008). Defining and categorizing emotional abuse in sport. *European Journal of Sport Science, 8*(4), 173–181.

Strandbu, Å., Bakken, A., & Stefansen, K. (2019). The continued importance of family sport culture for sport participation during the teenage years. *Sport Education and Society, 25*(8), 931–945.

Strandbu, Å., Stefansen, K., Smette, I., & Sandvik, M. R. (2019). Young people's experiences of parental involvement in youth sport. *Sport, Education and Society, 24*(1), 66–77,

Stuij, M. (2015). Habitus and social class: A case study on socialisation into sports and exercise. *Sport, Education and Society*, 20(6), 780–798.

Thorpe, H. (2016). Action sports for youth development: Critical insights for the SDP community. *International Journal of Sport Policy and Politics*, 8(1), 91–116.

Vaeyens, R., Lenoir, M., Williams, A. M., & Philippaerts, P. (2008). Talent identification and development programmes in sport: Current models and future directions. *Sports Medicine*, 38(9), 703–714.

van Krieken, R. (1998). *Norbert Elias*. London: Routledge.

van Krieken, R. (2019). Law and civilization: Norbert Elias as a regulation theorist. *Annual Review of Law and Social Science*, 15, 267–288.

Wheaton, B. (2019). Staying "stoked": Surfing, ageing and post-youth identities. *International Review for the Sociology of Sport*, 54(4), 387–409.

Wheeler, S., & Green, K. (2012). Parenting in relation to children's sports participation: Generational changes and potential implications. *Leisure Studies*, 33(3), 267–284.

Wheeler, S., & Green, K. (2019). "The helping, the fixtures, the kits, the gear, the gum shields, the food, the snacks, the waiting, the rain, the car rides": Social class, parenting and children's organised leisure. *Sport, Education and Society*, 24(8), 788–800.

Wheeler, S., Green, K., & Thurston, M. (2019). Social class and the emergent organised sporting habits of primary-aged children. *European Physical Education Review*, 25(1), 89–108.

Wilkinson, R., & Pickett, K. (2010). *The spirit level*. London: Penguin.

Wilkinson, R., & Pickett, K. (2018). *The inner level*. London: Allen Lane.

Woodman, D., Shildrick, T., & MacDonald, R. (2020). Inequality, continuity and change: Andy Furlong's legacy for youth studies. *Journal of Youth Studies*, 23(1), 1–11.

CHAPTER 34

....

SPORT, EDUCATION, AND OPPORTUNITY

....

RICHARD BAILEY AND IVA GLIBO

Most educational systems include sports within their curricula, often as a core feature of programs (Bailey, 2017; UNESCO, 2013). This implies that sports are good for young people in some way and ought to be taught to them. Yet sports remain a divisive topic among educationalists, with doubts raised about their compatibility with appropriate educational outcomes, the intrusion of external influences, and whether the sports field is a setting where all students can flourish. The value and values associated with sports in schools have become a contentious issue in the academic literature as well, with scholars questioning the often exuberant claims made by policymakers and advocacy groups (e.g., Coalter, 2007). They point to evidence that certain presentations of sports can lead to some students becoming isolated, marginalized, and alienated from diverse forms of health-enhancing physical activities. Theorists have described how real and symbolic boundaries have been drawn to limit access for ethnic minorities, girls, members of LGBTQ communities, and other disadvantaged groups (Cooky, 2009). Empirical researchers have corroborated these concepts with evidence of diminished levels of engagement in sports by girls, the socially marginalized, and excluded groups within society (Belcher et al., 2010). One significant exception to this pattern, at least in Western societies, is Black boys, who participate in school sports at higher rates than other subpopulations (Harrison, Harrison, & Moore, 2002). This seems to be because the notion of innate athleticism has become internalized as part of their ethnic identity (Shifrer, Pearson, Muller, & Wilkinson, 2015). This has been often accompanied by concomitant societal assumptions about Black boys' academic limitations.

Perhaps the loudest calls of concern have been those concerning gender, with girls being found to participate less frequently and intensely in sporting activities and reporting more negative attitudes to sports, relative to boys (Shifrer et al., 2015). Sports in school tend to rely on traditional notions of gender and the body, accentuating the relationship between gender and physicality. These notions are manifest in the formal, taught curriculum, in which boys and girls are taught separately or presented in different kinds of activity. They are also communicated through the hidden, "caught" curriculum shaped by teachers' norms, values, and beliefs about innate, gender-based physical and psychological differences, and subsequent behaviors of teachers and students in their schools and gyms (Hills, 2006).

For example, fieldwork involving female and male high school sports participation in the United States by Shakib and Dunbar (2002) found students of both sexes viewed girls' basketball as "less than" boys' basketball, with girls' basketball having lower social value, even when this school's girls' team ranked higher than the boys' team. This dynamic appears to be a global phenomenon, although gender differences in participation levels are greater in patriarchal than in nonpatriarchal societies (Deaner & Smith, 2013). Recent years have witnessed a growth in the developed world of girls playing sports and is seen in the range of sporting activities that girls play, although many girls continue to remain at the margins in their engagement with sport. Thus, the study of sporting opportunities in schools engages a topic where understanding the complexities of access and participation can offer both theoretical and practical rewards.

In this chapter, we consider the current position of sports in schools, focusing on the justifications and consequences of their inclusion and the extent to which they can provide adequate opportunities to meet the needs of all students. Sporting activities can take a variety of forms in schools, both curricular physical education and extracurricular, including before and after the compulsory school hours, during recess and lunch breaks, and in school-affiliated programs away from the school premises (Scheuer & Bailey, 2021). There is variation in terminology, too; the term "sport" (the United Kingdom and the Commonwealth) or "sports" (United States) is generally reserved for competitive, rule-based activities, while in Continental Europe, Asia, and elsewhere, those words are often synonymous with "physical activities" (Bailey, 2018a). Here, the focus is on the Anglophone usage, although links to the broader understanding will be made when relevant.

The chapter is organized into three parts. First, we present some perennial issues related to students' opportunities, including theoretical and empirical insights into sports in schools. Second, we consider a selection of theoretical approaches that have been employed in understanding these sporting experiences. This discussion draws on philosophical, sociological, and educational perspectives to understanding an inherently complex situation. Third, we consider some specific debates at the nexus of sport, education, and opportunities.

Issues

Sport and Education

Views of the relationship between sport and education tend to fall into three groups:

1. Sport is separate from social concerns and is consequently either an irrelevance or an alternative to education.
2. Sport contributes positively to social goals, including educational goals.
3. Sport is harmful to these social goals.

An explicit expression of the first position is that of the International Olympic Committee (Bach, 2020) that sport stands separate from everyday concerns. The founder of the modern Olympic Movement, Pierre de Coubertin, thought sport represents a democracy of ability, protected from the inequalities and inequities that plague the outside world. The second assertion is that the nature of sport means it has a distinctive capability to undermine some of the inequalities found in society. So, in practice, the first and second positions often merge into one. The third view is that the potentially exclusionary character of sport makes it inappropriate in the context of education. The philosopher Charles Bailey (1975) argued that there is a logical connection between winning and the demonstration of superiority over an opponent. As such, sports are incompatible with education tied to moral and social goals. Some sociologists have similarly described sport as an inherently competitive activity entailing distinct social relations, infused with aggressive masculinity and a relatively high tolerance of injury. On these latter points, Waddington (2000, p. 27) asserts, "The use of physical violence to a greater or lesser degree remains a central characteristic of modern sport." Thus, critics often suggest an inherent incompatibility between the brutish nature of sports and the civilizing ambitions of education. In contrast, others have argued that it is precisely the competitive ethos that gives sports their social value. The theologian Michael Novak (1967) claimed that the striving, failing, and play-like immersion of the players, on the one hand, and the justice and order of the competitions, on the other, jointly characterize sports. From this perspective, far from working against the aims of education, competitive sports can play a distinctive role in preparing students for capitalist society.

Each of these positions treats engagement in sports as entailing relatively homogeneous activities. Advocates routinely present claims of causal links between engaging with sporting activities and personal and social benefits (see Coalter, 2007 for examples). This assertion has been undermined by empirical findings that outcomes are dependent at least as much on teacher pedagogy and the associated social climate as the sporting activities themselves. Ample evidence suggests that participation in sport and physical activity can result in negative as well as positive outcomes (Bailey, Hillman, Arent, & Petitpas, 2013). Thus, it may be concluded that although participation in sporting contexts has a potential to promote positive, healthy development, this outcome is not a given and is likely to be realized only in association with many contextual factors.

The critics can be justifiably censored, too. Accounts of sports as arenas of violence and oppression seek to extrapolate concerns with contexts associated with a tiny minority of sports and their players to all sports participation. Yet every sport has unique characteristics that appeal to different interests, abilities, and expectations. As a result of matters such as these, the most reasonable answer to the question of whether sports can contribute to educational outcomes is "It depends." It depends on how sports participation is planned, presented, rewarded, and integrated into the goals of the wider school setting.

This raises another challenge, in that there is no common understanding of the relationship between educational goals and sporting activities (Bailey, 2018a). Systems identify different aims and outcomes, with consequent variation in terms of schemes of work, curricular content, and pedagogy. A comparative study of the curricula of the 37 member states of the Organisation for Economic Co-operation and Development found considerable variation in the organization of sporting activities within education systems (Bailey, 2017). UNESCO's (2013) *World-wide Survey of School Physical Education* revealed even greater diversity in how sport and physical education are conceived. The terminologies employed by educational systems give a clue to the situation, as "physical education" has become a generic term for an uneasy cluster of manifestations of the curricular area: "sports and health" (China); "sport" (Germany); "movement" (Netherlands); and "health and wellbeing" (Scotland).

Formal labels notwithstanding, there has been a clear tendency to push health and habitual physical activity in the forefront regarding both curriculum goals and content (Bailey 2017). For example, the Australian curriculum underwent a significant change, resulting in a new "Health and Physical Education" curriculum. This was partly driven by a widely held belief among the country's stakeholders that the existing approach, focused on competitive sports, was no longer fit for purpose and failed to respond adequately to the call to move more deliberately toward health-enhancing physical activities (Bailey, 2018a).

Recognition of the need for all curriculum areas to engage in some future-oriented thinking, responding to the social and cultural trends, is likely to affect children's lives as they grow up. In this context, links between schools and sport have become frequent foci of discussion (Bailey & Kirk, 2009). If physical education needs to take a public health role in coordinating and leading physical activity for all students, then sports are confronted with a challenge. By its nature, public health has a universalist character. It remains uncertain whether this is compatible with the world of sports, in which competitive structures typically mean the expulsion of increasing numbers of players (Bailey & Collins, 2013). However, the vast majority of young people do not play sports at elite levels. Indeed, there is emerging literature showing adapted frameworks of sports participation can be inclusive and support positive development (Bailey, 2018a).

When presented appropriately, some studies suggest, sports can play a valuable role within wide public health goals (see Bailey, 2018a for a summary). First, sports participation seems to provide the experiences underpinning later capabilities to engage in physical activities. Indeed, some have suggested the first 10 years or so help children overcome a "proficiency barrier" of skills that would otherwise exclude large groups of activities for lack of the necessary confidence and competence (Bailey & Collins, 2013). Second, sports may provide children with opportunities to acquire the psychological competencies to facilitate participation in physical activities later in life (Bailey et al., 2010). Third, positive sports experiences during childhood and adolescence may support the development of intrinsic motivation (Larson, 2000), which may, in turn, lead to increased motivation to be physically active later in life (Kilpatrick, Hebert, & Bartholomew, 2005). However, to reiterate a point made earlier, participation benefits are unlikely to result without appropriate planning, pedagogy, and philosophy. This implies a need for adequate and ongoing professional development, cross-sector professional conversations, and international dissemination of quality guidance, exemplars, and models.

Sport and Opportunities

In the previous section, we discussed some themes that have occupied theorists and practitioners working at the intersection of education and sport. This intersection has a long history. Even Coubertin famously took his inspiration from the team games he witnessed in English private schools. More recently, however, doubts have emerged about the continued relevance of competitive activities. The focus on many of these doubts relates to the exclusive character of sports at a time when almost all people working in education are calling for opportunities, inclusion, and engagement for everyone.

Most of the literature on educational and sporting opportunities is framed by discussions of equality (Evans, 2017). This goes beyond the widely known "equality of opportunity" theme that has shaped a great deal of sports scholarship over the years (Amade-Escot, 2016; Talbot, 1993). Discussions of inequality in sport encompass many lines of inquiry, including ethnicity and race, geography, social and economic status, and gender, which is arguably the most visible site of inequality in sport (Spaaij, Farquharson, & Marjoribanks, 2015).

We next review some of the fundamental principles that have characterized discussions of equality and inequality in society. We then move on to consider some of the perennial challenges facing sports, both in itself and as it relates to broader social processes. Many commentators have cautioned that, far from being a force driving opportunities in wider society, sport is a site of entrenched social inequalities (see, for example, Collins, 2014). According to this view, sports cannot help but reflect and even reinforce broader social structures. While there is evidence of sports acting as sites for equality and inclusion, they can also exclude and reproduce hierarchies and privilege. Criticisms are, perhaps, most clearly articulated in discussions of gender. A common argument is that sport reinforces rather than challenges patterns of inequality because it is organized by ideologies of patriarchy and hegemonic masculinity that serve to marginalize certain groups and justify the unbalanced distribution of resources (Coad, 2008).

Equality is both an attractive and a threatening concept within the contexts of sport, education, and society. Its appeal lies in "the comfort of commonality, the promise of impartiality, the hope of genuine meritocracy" (Peters, 1997, p. 1211). The threat is that equality can go too far and usurp individuality and meritocracy, and that the edict to treat people the same can slide into treating some people unjustly. Inequality—the state of not being equal, especially in status, rights, and opportunities—is a concept at the heart of social and sport policy. However, it is a concept prone to confusion in both academic and popular discussions as it can be understood in different ways. As a result, there are also many misunderstandings and disagreements. A key scholar on inequality, Anthony Atkinson (2015), argues that complete equality is unachievable. Atkinson's primary concern centers instead on reducing inequality below its current level. This goal is premised on a belief that present levels of inequality are intolerable and unsustainable.

Mount (2008) summarized different forms of equality and inequality as follows:

- Political (in)equality, which includes civic equality and equality before the law.
- (In)equality of opportunity, which is often called (in)equality of access or life chances.
- (In)equality of outcome or result, which primarily indicates (in)equality of income and wealth.
- (In)equality of treatment, which can be taken to include or at least help to generate (in)equality of agency and responsibility.
- (In)equality of membership in society.

This list clarifies similarities and differences in concerns between uses of (in)equality and helps identify the targets of policies. It is not suggested these are discrete categories, as, in reality, they are slippery, entangled, and connected at various points.

With a small number of high-profile exceptions, considerable movement toward political equality has been achieved in many countries (Atkinson, 2015). In this regard, a key driver has been the near-universal spread of democracy and its acceptance as the most desirable way of organizing a political community (Erman & Näsström, 2013). Democracy, it is often argued, is the best mechanism for achieving equal decision-making, and consequently it reflects equal consideration of the interests of all community members. While these ideals may not in practice be fully realized, the importance that democracy can place on issues of equality comes about from a combination of formal procedures, such as regular elections, and less tangible features, such as communal civil engagement, free media, and the exercise of basic rights (Dahl, 1989). While democracy is often taken as a condition of political equality, it does not exhaust the scope of equality. In particular, equality is usually associated with a broad set of civil, legal, and political rights, as well as equal treatment before the law (Erman & Näsström, 2013).

In sports, numerous political commitments made by key stakeholders and organizing bodies have asserted the principle of equal treatment within legal frameworks. High-profile declarations, such as UNESCO's (2015) International Charter of Physical Education, Physical Activity and Sport, offer rights-based references that orient policy- and decision-makers toward what are essentially proactive and positive discrimination-reduction procedures to redress long-standing political imbalances. In many countries, unequal status based on social divisions, especially gender and ethnicity, is illegal, and legislation has been used to prevent gender discrimination in most developed countries' educational sports systems. Antidiscrimination law was written into the founding structure of the European Union, with the Treaty of Amsterdam offering a broad conception of what may be considered discriminatory, including matters that called out gender inequities alongside all kinds of discrimination, particularly those based on actual or supposed ethnic origin (European Communities, 1997).

The distinction between equality of opportunity and equality of outcome has been one of the dominant debates in political philosophy. Liberal theorists characterize this debate as between the ideals of fairness and fair share (Fawcett, 2018). To use a sporting metaphor, in the race of life, equality of opportunity promises a level playing field, where each player can express and benefit from their talents; equality of outcome aims to ensure everyone finishes more or less at the same time. In practice, the distinction between the two forms of equality is less clear-cut. At least in terms of engagement, sports organizations typically aim to balance both aspirations. They most often seek to promote equality of opportunity by removing arbitrary obstacles that might prevent people from achieving heights their talents can reach (Galston, 1986). In this respect, equality of opportunity is bolstered by political equality and equality before the law. It is also an expression of equality premised on fairness and the freedom to pursue one's private interests without restrictions based on irrelevant contextual characteristics.

Action in favor of equality necessarily involves government interference, although the degree of intervention associated with promoting equality of outcome is much greater. Countless initiatives have been introduced to address continuing inequalities of both opportunity and outcome, especially those targeting gender. Unfortunately, sports continue to be arenas where marginalized groups experience overt and structural forms of discrimination (Cahn, 2015). Indeed, the manifestations of exclusions faced by women within sports continue to be diverse. Gender inequality is a persistent and resistant concern, magnified by the relatively low levels of physical activity and sport among girls and women. Studies report a clear trend of decreasing activity levels as girls get older and a widening disparity between girls' and boys' physical activity behaviors (Basterfield et al., 2015). The picture for sports participation is more positive in some developed countries. In the United States, for example, there has been a significant increase in the number of girls and women participating in sports over recent decades (Cooky, 2009). However, even in the United States, there are still many girls who do not participate because of limited opportunities, structural barriers, and gender ideologies, and their levels of participation do not match those of boys and men (Bailey, 2018a).

Equality of treatment, sometimes called equality of access, is less controversial as it seeks to ensure that all citizens are afforded full and equal access to public information and basic services, regardless of their situation, status, or ability (Gould, 1989). Yet, despite its intuitive persuasiveness as a social goal, there is considerable evidence that some groups can experience particular problems in accessing education, healthcare, and other fundamental services. However, in some countries such as the United Kingdom, equal access is warranted by the country's policies (see Talbot, 1993). Applied to sports, equality of treatment encompasses a range of concerns originating in a breakdown in political equality as it indicates a division between the letter of the law and its fair application. Talbot warns about this discrepancy, noting that anointing policies with the label of "equality of access" does not automatically imply the "equality of opportunity." The latter, which can entail much more nuanced issues, may vary due to taken-for-granted expectations and norms about gender, social class, ethnicity, and other constructions resulting in further forms of sexism and discrimination (Bourdieu, 1977). This, in turn, may prevent sport and physical education from being delivered to all groups equally. A marker of such unequal treatment may be seen in the evident differences between women and men at elite levels (Cooky et al., 2018), such as fewer high-level event opportunities for women, along with exclusion from competitions and less remuneration on entering adult "professionalized" ranks. All of these matters point toward females' unequal treatment and inequity of opportunities at different participation levels.

Finally, equality of membership is relatively intangible and is not typically included in discussions of equality (Mount, 2008). Yet the notion suggests an ideal in which all community members share a sense of citizenship and can identify shared values that, together, represent that community. There is ample evidence that many people, families, and groups in diverse societies are deprived of access to sporting opportunities, whether because of poverty or discrimination (Collins, 2014). This phenomenon, often called "social exclusion," indicates a basic social disadvantage and often entails relegation to the fringe of a community or specific sporting domains (Bailey, 2005). So, for example, sports participation in many countries is characterized by quite strict social and economic divisions, with the relatively wealthy and powerful doing some activities and the relatively poor and powerless doing others (Jarvie, 2011). For example, in the Commonwealth, girls in high school have traditionally been directed to netball (a version of basketball originally designed for girls), gymnastics, and dance, while boys have conventionally played soccer, cricket, and rugby union.

Equality is a concept that has been beset with charges of ambiguity (Mount, 2008). Indeed, it serves as a paradigm case of a "magic concept," concepts which are "very broad, normatively charged and lay claim to universal or near universal application" (Pollitt & Hupe, 2011, p. 643). They are defensible and allow little room for opposition, but are simultaneously so vague that they rarely address underlying problems. For this reason, the analysis in this chapter has been based on consideration of the five types of equality and inequality outlined earlier. The benefit of this more nuanced approach is that it helps make clear some of the claims made by different people and groups, and the associated goals that might follow from them. What becomes clear is that different claims carry with them often competing demands. It may indeed be the case that some of these conceptions are incommensurable or inconsistent with other values. Thus, calls for equality in any domain, in a very basic sense, can never be straightforward and require both the recognition and maintenance of at least basic standards to avoid arbitrary distinctions, which may be considerably entrenched, if they are to result in social change.

APPROACHES

As our consideration of issues has suggested, there is a notable tension between the enthusiastic views of advocates and the skepticism of sociologists toward sports' relationship to equality. While the former position often assumes sport somehow stands apart from economic and political travails, social scientists tend to locate sport as inseparable from wider society, sharing similar processes and problems, such as inequality, discrimination, and the development of ideological stances justifying them.

In considering the dynamics of inequality in sport, Donnelly (1996) traced a progression of reflection, reproduction, and resistance. The premise of the reflection thesis is that sport mirrors society. Sport is taken to be neutral about issues of equality, allowing both positive and negative outcomes. However, the fact that sports are part of society and, consequently, reflect it allows little more than description; it does not offer a satisfactory explanation. The reproduction thesis, inspired by Marxism and other critical stances, challenged the idea of sport as a passive reflection of wider society, replacing it with an account of sport as an active player in the maintenance of unequal relationships between different social groups. Some theorists interpreted this position as offering support for the view promoted by both policymakers and practitioners that sport could be a powerful setting for social integration.

There was, however, dissatisfaction with reflection and reproduction theses, and particularly their shared conception of people as relatively passive consumers of sport, unaware of the social forces producing and reproducing inequality (Donnelly, 2003). The resistance thesis portrayed sport as a "contested terrain" and people as active, reflexive agents who might simultaneously embrace sport as a valuable aspect of their lives while recognizing its potential use in the reproduction of inequality (Hargreaves, 1982). By highlighting agency, the resistance thesis supplements the notion of reproduction with a dialectical or interactive element in which "the tensions, negotiations, misunderstandings, and resistances characterizing the social relationships associated with a person's entry into and participation in [sport]" need to be taken into account and where the sport participant is seen "as an active agent, as someone with self-reflective abilities and creative potential, as someone seeking autonomy and affirmation of identities" (Coakley, 1993, p. 170).

Running in parallel with these more nuanced conceptions of relations has been an evolving understanding of levels of analysis of inequality. The first level is categorical analysis, which is concerned with identifying and explaining differences in characteristics and/or behaviors between categories of people, such as members of different social or ethnic groups. Within the context of school sport, analysis has traditionally been used to examine sports practices or preferences and the characteristics presumed to be associated with different groups. While categorical analysis focuses mainly on individual bases of inequality, distributive analysis is concerned with social structures; in other words, it addresses equality of opportunity, examining "who gets what, and why" in terms of "the numbers of programs, the funding, facilities, and opportunities for mobility to leadership positions" (Dewar, 1991, p. 19). Finally, relational analysis favors accounts of inequality in which negotiated social relations figure centrally. Shifting beyond discrete categories and the distribution of resources among those categories to consider whole sets of social relations, it examines these relationships in their social context (e.g., among men and women who belong to a certain social class and racial-ethnic grouping, in a particular time and place). In relational analysis, sport is an example of "cultural representations of social relations," beginning with "the assumption that sporting practices are historically produced, socially constructed and culturally defined to serve the interests and needs of powerful groups in a society" (p. 20). According to this perspective, sporting practices take certain forms representing the privileged positions of those with power, maintained so the position of the dominant appears natural and normal to the dominated. Also, since relational analysis is sensitive to contextual aspects of engagement, it is better able to accommodate multiple lines of inquiry, including social and economic status, ethnicity, and gender.

DEBATES

Values and Goals

Educational sport and physical education are typically concerned with the physical domain, including the development of psychomotor skills and the improvement of physical health and well-being. However, there is a near-universal consensus that their scope extends to many aspects of children's education. One common approach identifies physical education domains in terms of physical, affective, social, and cognitive aspects (Laker, 2000). Another model suggests the physical, lifestyle, affective, and cognitive development domains (Bailey et al., 2009) are central. However, any drawing of such broad domains leaves a great deal of space for interpretation about how they might contribute to generalized educational goals. Comparative studies have highlighted significant variation in the manifestation of sport and physical education around the world, reflecting different values associated with sport and physical education (Bailey, 2017; Leibinger, Hamar, & Dancs Szegner, 2007; UNESCO, 2013). Tensions may arise between values or between their interpretation at various levels of planning and oversight. It has been suggested by many scholars that physical education goals prioritizing sports performance are inconsistent with ambitions for health-enhancing physical activity (Skille & Solbakken, 2014), and a focus on competitive activities will intrinsically come at the expense of inclusivity (Waddington, 2000). Educational values can often be influenced by factors originating outside the educational system (Jie, 2016), and the most powerful force affecting sport and physical education has been concerns about health. The prevalence of obesity has increased substantially in children and adolescents in developed countries (Bailey et al., 2016). This has led many policymakers to place greater emphasis on the promotion of healthy lifestyles. For example, in reorganizing their whole curriculum, Scotland changed the status of physical education from a discrete subject to a part of the broader "Health and Wellbeing" key curricular areas (Horrell, Sproule, & Gray,

2012). The Korean government has expressed concerns about a range of health issues among children, including high rates of anxiety due to an uncertain future, addiction to internet games, declining physical strength, and rising obesity (Korea Institute for Curriculum and Evaluation, 2012).

Themes embracing concerns about health run through statements of goals in most curricula of developed countries. Responses to the inactivity and obesity "epidemics" have prompted changes in physical education curricula and the role of sport during, after, and away from schools. The Active Schools concept is an obvious manifestation of these changes, offering a model of schooling in which the promotion of students' health-enhancing physical activity becomes a primary goal of education; traditional settings for activity, such as physical education classes and school sports clubs, are supplemented by strategies like active transport to and from school, games and sports during recess periods, and activity-based homework (Scheuer, & Bailey, 2021). The extent to which these ideas become mainstream is uncertain; however, there is no doubt that connections between physical education and health education are now the norm in policy documents, and competitive sports have been pushed toward the margins (Michelini, 2015).

Status

Inherent in every school curriculum is some sort of assumption that some school subjects are more valuable than others. Bleazby (2015) discussed the often implicit assumptions that underpin what she called "the traditional curriculum hierarchy." According to this framework, "Tier 1 Subjects," such as mathematics, are located at the top, and "Tier 4 Subjects," including health and physical education, are at the bottom. For example, Lee and Cho (2014, p. 527) write, "PE is suffering from a low status, poor quality, lack of investment in facilities, and a curriculum that does not always engage with Korean young people." Furthermore, a survey by SHAPE America (2016) reported considerable variation of the status of physical education, including a wide diversity of state education legislative and regulatory activity and the resulting variety in policies and implementation approaches.

Low status has become a familiar refrain among commentators on physical education and sport in schools, and with it come restrictions in human and physical capital and senior management support. Certain themes reappear in international and comparative studies over the past two decades (e.g., Hardman & Marshall, 2001; Leibinger et al., 2007; UNESCO, 2013). These may be summarized as follows:

- Sport and physical education are generally low-status subjects.
- There are significant differences between the curriculum requirement and the implementation in schools, so even when sport and physical education are compulsory parts of the school curriculum, they are sometimes not taught.
- The greatest time allocation occurs when children are ages 9 to 14, and time allocated in schools declines as children get older, when sport and physical education either become optional courses or not available at all.
- Time for physical activities and sport is often extended through extracurricular activities; in some cases, this is very well-developed, in others much less so.

- Limits to funding and resourcing mean that many schools are unable to deliver a comprehensive or even coherent curriculum, and this is especially the case in the developing world.
- Specialist sport and physical education teachers during the elementary phase are rare, and in some cases teacher training for elementary teachers is extremely poor.
- Lack of equity, especially in terms of gender and disability, means that many children are marginalized from quality sport and physical education experiences or excluded completely.

The standard response to the often impoverished position of sport and physical education in schools has been to tie them to more valued themes. For example, the Korean government reevaluated its physical education curriculum after a good case had been made that physical activities could be effective vehicles for developing personal and social skills (Korea Institute for Curriculum and Evaluation, 2012). Most educational systems base their sport and physical education programs on judgments about the capability of regular physical activity to reduce the costs of noncommunicable diseases, such as obesity and Type II diabetes (Bailey, 2017). This is neither a new strategy nor a new set of claims. Indeed, Coubertin saw in sports palatable ways of toughening up the spoiled young men he saw in Europe at the end of the 19th century, as war beckoned. These strategies certainly made sense within the specific contexts in which they arose. However, the evidence behind such extrinsic justifications (lying outside of the activity itself, such as weight management and social skills training) is scant and studies have shown that such results are at best likely to be short-term "fixes" rather than long-term solutions. For this reason, many scholars have argued that what is needed to secure the place of sports and physical education in schools are *intrinsic* justifications, based on the nature of activities themselves (see McNamee & Bailey, 2009 for a review of these arguments). Here, some scholars have argued that sport and physical education belong at the core of schools' curricula because they develop knowledge, skills, and values that are inherently valuable for everybody (Bailey, 2018b). Others implicitly discard sports and focus their arguments on the intrinsic importance of movement in people's lives (Arnold, 1979). Observers seeing it in those terms often call for a sea-change in educational thinking about the nature of learners and their learning, which challenges cultural assumptions about the sovereignty of the intellectual in favor of a more balanced view in which the body and its movement are more properly recognized. Since more traditional views of the relationships here can be traced at least as far back as the Ancient Greeks, any meaningful change is likely to be hard-fought and face resistance.

CONCLUSION

Philosophers describe education as an essentially contested concept. There are multiple meanings attributed to education, which is often exacerbated by geography, tradition, and values. Much the same could be said for sports, as the term itself is used in a wide variety of ways. Thus, anyone seeking to engage in international or collaborative research first needs to make sure that the different accounts of what is actually under investigation are talking about the same thing! While on the face of it, this seems like a simple matter to overcome, in practice it has stymied the coherence of a research agenda on sport, education, and opportunity.

Nevertheless, as has been discussed in this chapter, there seem to be certain perennial concerns regarding the relationship between sports and education. Inequality of opportunity is one of the most pressing of these concerns. Evidence suggests that most educational systems reflect injustice based on assumptions and stereotypes about gender, ethnicity, sexuality, and social class, and that this is reflected in both policies and the treatment that certain groups experience. With their reliance on and celebration of the body, sports seem to magnify these inequalities, leading to certain groups finding themselves pushed to the margins of sporting opportunities in schools. This is a cause for great concern, as it means that not only are policymakers and practitioners confronted with the challenges of disaffection and disengagement from sporting activities, but the wider community will have to deal with the very real costs to both health and livelihood.

References

Amade-Escot, C. (2016). How gender order is enacted in physical education. In G. Doll-Tepper, K. Koenen, & R. Bailey (Eds.), *Sport, education and social policy: The state of the social science* (pp. 62–72). London: Routledge.

Arnold, P. (1979). *Meaning in movement, sport, and physical education*. London: Heinemann.

Atkinson, A. (2015). *Inequality*. Cambridge, MA: Harvard University Press.

Bach, T. (2020, January 10). Opening remarks to the 135th IOC Session. Lausanne: International Olympic Committee.

Bailey, C. (1975). Games, winning and education. *Cambridge Journal of Education, 5*(1), 40–50.

Bailey, R. (2005). Evaluating the relationship between physical education, sport and social inclusion. *Educational Review, 57*(1), 71–90.

Bailey, R. (2017). *Discussion paper on values, aims, and health and physical education towards 2030*. Paris: OECD.

Bailey, R. (2018a). Is sport good for us? In D. Parnell & P. Krustrup (Eds.), *Sport and health* (pp. 7–35). London: Routledge.

Bailey, R. (2018b). Sport, physical education, and educational worth. *Educational Review, 70*(1), 51–66.

Bailey, R., Armour, K., Kirk, D., Jess, M., Pickup, I., & Sandford, R. (2009). The educational benefits claimed for physical education and school sport. *Research Papers in Education, 24*(1), 1–27.

Bailey, R., & Callary, B. (2022). Sport education from a global perspective. In K. Petry & J. de Jong (Eds.), *Education in sport and physical activity: Future directions and global perspectives*. London: Routledge.

Bailey, R., & Collins, D. (2013). The standard model of talent development and its discontents. *Kinesiology Review, 2*(4), 248–259.

Bailey, R., Collins, D., Ford, P., MacNamara, A., Toms, M., & Pearce, G. (2010). *Participant development in sport*. Leeds: Sports Coach UK.

Bailey, R., Hillman, C., Arent, S., & Petitpas, A. (2013). Physical activity: An underestimated investment in human capital? *Journal of Physical Activity and Health, 10*, 289–308.

Bailey, R., Holzweg, M., Koenen, K., Glibo, I., Olosová, G., & De Roos, J. (2016). *The state of physical activity in Europe*. Paris: Think Tank Sport et Citoyenneté.

Bailey, R. P., & Kirk, D. (2009). *The Routledge reader of physical education*. London: Routledge.

Basterfield, L., Reilly, J., Pearce, M., Parkinson, K., Adamson, A., Reilly, J., & Vella, S. (2015). Longitudinal associations between sports participation, body composition and physical activity from childhood to adolescence. *Journal of Science and Medicine in Sport*, 18(2), 178–182.

Belcher, B., Berrigan, D., Dodd, K., Emken, B., Chou, C., & Spuijt-Metz, D. (2010). Physical activity in US youth. *Medicine and Science in Sports and Exercise*, 42(12), 2211.

Bleazby, J. (2015). Why some school subjects have a higher status than others. *Oxford Review of Education*, 41(5), 671–689.

Bourdieu, P. (1977). *Outline of a theory of practice*. Cambridge: Cambridge University Press.

Cahn, S. (2015). *Coming on strong*. Urbana: University of Illinois Press.

Coad, D. (2008). *The metrosexual*. New York: SUNY Press.

Coakley, J. (1993). Sport and socialization. *Exercise and Sport Sciences Reviews*, 21(1), 169–200.

Coalter, F. (2007). *A wider social role for sport*. London: Routledge.

Collins, M. (2014). *Sport and social exclusion*. London: Routledge.

Cooky, C. (2009). Girls just aren't interested. *Sociological Perspectives*, 52(2), 259–283.

Cooky, C., Messner, M., Musto, M., Rauscher, L., Begovic, M., & Oglesby, C. (2018). *No slam dunk*. New Brunswick, NJ: Rutgers University Press.

Dahl, R. (1989). *Democracy and its critics*. New Haven: Yale University Press.

Deaner, R., & Smith, B. (2013). Sex differences in sports across 50 societies. *Cross-Cultural Research*, 47(3), 268–309.

Dewar, A. (1991). Incorporation of resistance? *International Review for the Sociology of Sport*, 26(1), 15–23.

Donnelly, P. (1996). Approaches to social inequality in the sociology of sport. *Quest*, 48(2), 221–242.

Donnelly, P. (2003). Sport and social theory. In B. Houlihan (Ed.), *Sport and society* (pp. 11–27). London: Sage Publishing.

Erman, E., & Näsström, S. (2013). In search of political equality. In E. Erman & S. Nasstrom (Eds.), *Political equality in transnational democracy* (pp. 1–15). New York: Palgrave Macmillan.

European Communities. (1997). Treaty of Amsterdam amending the Treaty on European Union, the Treaties establishing the European Communities and certain related acts, as signed in Amsterdam on 2 October 1997. Luxembourg: Office for Official Publications of the European Communities.

Evans, J. (Ed.). (2017). *Equality, education, and physical education*. London: Routledge.

Fawcett, E. (2018). *Liberalism: The life of an idea*. Princeton, NJ: Princeton University Press.

Galston, W. (1986). Equality of opportunity and liberal theory. In F. S. Lucash (Ed.), *Justice and equality here and now* (pp. 89–107). Ithaca, NY: Cornell University Press.

Gould, M. (1989). Equality of access to education? *Modern Law Review*, 52(4), 540–550.

Hardman, K., & Marshall, J. (2001). World-wide survey on the state and status of physical education in schools. *Proceedings of the World Summit on Physical Education*, 15–37.

Hargreaves, J. (1982). Sport, culture and ideology. In J. Hargreaves (Ed.), *Sport, culture and ideology* (pp. 30–61). London: Routledge & Kegan Paul.

Harrison, L., Harrison, C., & Moore, L. (2002). African American racial identity and sport. *Sport, Education and Society*, 7(2), 121–133.

Hills, L. (2006). Playing the field(s). *Gender and Education*, 18(5), 539–556.

Horrell, A., Sproule, J., & Gray, S. (2012). Health and wellbeing: A policy context for physical education in Scotland. *Sport, Education and Society*, 17(2), 163–180.

Jarvie, G. (2011). Sport, social division and social inequality. *Sport Science Review*, 20(1–2), 95–109.

Jie, N. (2016). *Towards a framework of education policy analysis*. Singapore: Head Foundation.

Kilpatrick, M., Hebert, E., & Bartholomew, J. (2005). College students' motivation for physical activity. *Journal of American College Health*, 54(2), 87–94.

Korea Institute for Curriculum and Evaluation. (2012). *Revision of Korean national curriculum for character education*. Research Report, ORM2012- 46. Seoul: Yujin Culture.

Laker, A. (2000). *Beyond the boundaries of physical education*. London: Routledge.

Larson, R. W. (2000). Toward a psychology of positive youth development. *American Psychologist*, 55(1), 170–183.

Lee, K. C., & Cho, S. M. (2014). The Korean national curriculum for physical education: a shift from edge to central subject. *Physical Education and Sport Pedagogy*, 19(5), 522–532.

Leibinger, É., Hamar, P., & Dancs Szegner, H. (2007). Survey of the public educational system and structure of European countries from a physical education point of view. *Kinesiology*, 39(1), 85–96.

McNamee, M., & Bailey, R. P. (2009). Physical education and sport. In R. P. Bailey, D. Carr, R. Barrow, & C. McCarthy (Eds.), *Sage handbook of the philosophy of education* (pp. 467–480). London: Sage.

Michelini, E. (2015). Disqualification of sport in health-related promotion of physical activity: A global social phenomenon? *European Journal for Sport and Society*, 12(3), 257–280.

Mount, F, (2008). *Five types of inequality*. York, U.K.: Joseph Rowntree Foundation.

Novak, M. (1967) *The joy of sports: End zones, bases, baskets, balls and consecration of the American spirit*. New York: Basic Books.

Peters, C. J. (1997). Equality revisited. *Harvard Law Review*, 110(6), 1210–1264.

Pollitt, C., & Hupe, P. (2011). Talking about government: The role of magic concepts. *Public Management Review*, 13(5), 641–658.

Scheuer, C., & Bailey, R. P. (2021). The active school concept. In R. Bailey, J. Agans, J. Côté, & P. Tomporowski (Eds.), *Physical activity and sport during the first ten years of life: Multidisciplinary perspectives*. London: Routledge.

Shakib, S., & Dunbar, M. D. (2002). The social construction of female and male high school basketball participation: Reproducing the gender order through a two-tiered sporting institution. *Sociological Perspectives*, 45(4), 353–378.

SHAPE America. (2016). Shape of the nation. http:www.shapeamerica.org/shapeofnation.

Shifrer, D., Pearson, J., Muller, C., & Wilkinson, L. (2015). College-going benefits of high school sports participation. *Youth and Society*, 47(3), 295–318.

Skille, E., & Solbakken, T. (2014). The relationship between adolescent sport participation and lifelong participation in physical activity in Norway. *Scandinavian Sport Studies Forum*, 5, 25–45.

Spaaij, R., Farquharson, K., & Marjoribanks, T. (2015). Sport and social inequalities. *Sociology Compass*, 9(5), 400–411.

Talbot, M. (1993). A gendered physical education. In J. Evans (Ed.), *Equality, education and physical education* (pp. 74–89). London: Falmer Press.

UNESCO. (2013). *World-wide survey of school physical education*. Paris: UNESCO.

UNESCO. (2015). *Revised International Charter of Physical Education and Sport*. Paris: UNESCO.

Waddington, I. (2000). Sport and health. In J. Coakley & E. Dunning (Eds.), *Handbook of sports studies* (pp. 408–421). London: Sage.

CHAPTER 35

···

SPORT, SOCIAL MOBILITY, AND ELITE ATHLETES

···

RAMÓN SPAAIJ AND SUZANNE RYDER

POPULAR belief holds that sport offers those living in poverty or socioeconomic marginality considerable opportunities for upward social mobility. Media outlets such as *The Guardian* and the *Bleacher Report* have published "the greatest" (Dart, Doyle, & Hill, 2006) and "most inspiring" (Ferrari-King, 2014) rags-to-riches stories of how some boys or young men, with only the shirts on their backs, were able to launch stellar and highly lucrative sporting careers. Diego Maradona, Pelé, boxing champion Kassim Ouma, and mixed martial artist Bibiano Fernandes all seem to fit this storyline, as does the quote attributed to long-distance runner Emil Zátopek: "An athlete cannot run with money in his pockets. He must run with hope in his heart and dreams in his head" (GETVAL, 2017). Both researchers and critics, however, have dispelled this popular belief as being false or at least misleading (Eitzen, 2009). For example, Tom Farrey (2017), founder of the Aspen Institute's Sports & Society Program, has provided strong evidence for the rising gentrification of college sports in the United States, which have seen a decline in opportunities for disadvantaged students, even in the big-money sports of basketball and American football.

Social mobility is a vibrant topic of research in sociology at large. Social stratification is a structuring principle in sport (Bourdieu, 1978; Pociello, 1995; Sugden & Tomlinson, 2000), and it is therefore unsurprising that the relationship between sport participation and social mobility has attracted scholarly attention over the years, including some attempts to pull together some of the existing knowledge (Spaaij, 2011; Spaaij, Farquharson, & Marjoribanks, 2015). However, relatively little is known, by way of scientific research, as to who benefits, how, and under what circumstances. In this chapter, we will examine to what extent, and in what ways, sport provides a context within which elite athletes can improve their individual and collective social positions. We will first provide an overview of key issues and definitions in social mobility and their application to the career trajectories of athletes. This will be followed by a discussion of the different theoretical and methodological approaches that scholars have taken to the topic. This discussion is followed by a more in-depth examination of one of the most vibrant current debates in the field: gender bias and the professional career and mobility prospects of women athletes. This debate will be empirically illustrated through findings from the second author's research on professional women cyclists. These findings illustrate the tensions and some of the key debates concerning social mobility and sport. The concluding section of the chapter will reflect on the current status of research on athletes' struggles and achievements in advancing their social positions through elite playing careers in sport, and identify potentially fruitful directions and methods for future research.

Issues

Social mobility can be seen as a standard feature of modern societies (Bottero, 2005). It occurs when the correlation between one's origins and future destinations may be less than perfect (Hasenbalg & Silva, 2003; Hout, 2015). Although social mobility is a slippery and multidimensional concept, it may be broadly defined as "the movement or opportunities for movement between different social classes or occupational groups" (Aldridge, 2003, p. 189). The concept is strongly associated with educational attainment, occupational status, and earnings (Breen & Jonsson, 2005). People move both up and down in relation to others and their own origins (Hout, 2015). This is so-called vertical mobility, resulting in a relatively durable change to a person's or a group's position within the system of social stratification (Lipset & Bendix, 1992). In this chapter, we are concerned primarily with *relative* mobility, which refers to "movement of an individual between different social classes, regardless of changes in the distribution of the population between them" (Nunn, Johnson, Monro, Bickerstaffe, & Kelsey, 2007, p. 16).

A distinction can be made between *intergenerational* and *intragenerational* mobility. Intragenerational mobility refers to the movement of individuals between different social strata during their lifetime. In principle, this can be measured between any two points during their life (Nunn et al., 2007). In contrast, intergenerational mobility refers to the difference between the social positions of individuals at a particular point in their adult life (i.e., destination) with that of their parents (i.e., origins). Whereas intergenerational mobility is envisaged as transitions between social origins and destinations, intragenerational mobility tends to be approached from within a complete life-course perspective (Goldthorpe, 2003). Although the focus of this chapter is on the latter, it will also be seen that there tends to be a strong correlation between social origins and destinations. In this regard, Hout (2015, p. 27) argues that it is more appropriate to ask "how the conditions and circumstances of early life constrain adult success than to ask who is moving up and who is not. The focus on origins keeps the substantive issues of opportunity and fairness in focus."

How do these conceptualizations of social mobility apply to sport? The academic literature on the relationship between social mobility and sport participation suggests the possibility of accumulating wealth, social prestige, and cultural capital in and through sport exists, especially within the context of the global sports-industrial complex that is characterized by hypercommodification, professionalization, and mediatization (Maguire, 2005). However, as we will show, the relationship between sport and social mobility is complex and ambivalent. Moreover, the literature features some areas of contention and theoretical and methodological diversity that can make it difficult to make meaningful comparisons across studies or to come to an overarching, "generalizable" conclusion.

Recent decades have seen a growth in research on at least three aspects of the relationship between sport and social mobility: (1) gender and elite sport, (2) race, sport, and social mobility, and (3) career duration, termination, and postcareer transitions. Below we summarize select work from each of these areas in turn.

Gender, Sport, and Social Mobility

The social mobility of women in sport has been a topic of considerable research and is discussed in greater depth in the Debates section. In sport, access to available occupations, income, and prestige is primarily reserved for men. It largely remains true that men dominate the playing, coaching, managerial, and occupational aspects of sport (Ann & Rodriguez, 2000; Messner, 2007). Such evidence suggests that social mobility pathways in sport may be relatively limited for women, but there is also some evidence supporting the belief that female athletes benefit from athletic experiences beyond sport in various ways, including quality of life, academic performance, educational attainment, and economic earning power (Espinoza, 2009; Kane et al., 2007; LaVoi, Thul, & Wasend, 2018; Sabo & Veliz, 2008; Schultz, 2018). For example, LaVoi, Thul, Wasend, Barber et al. (2018) report that 94% of women executives played sport and that wages of athletes were 7% higher than for nonathletes. However, women's sport participation did not boost their employment numbers in the professional sport industry. There is an ongoing lack of women in leadership and management positions in many sports (Staurowsky et al., 2020). Factors that limit women to experience upward mobility within the sports industry include stereotypical hiring perceptions (i.e., employers looking for stereotypical leaders, in other words: masculine leaders), a hiring bias in regard to women's family obligations, the lack of mentors and role models, and workplace climates that perceive women as less competent than men in their jobs (Staurowsky et al., 2020). The presence of these barriers suggests that the mere participation in sport does not mean a proportional hiring reality for women in sport.

Finally, it is important to understand that girls are not a homogeneous group and that their participation and the associated benefits are distributed unevenly (Sabo & Veliz, 2008). This gap reflects wider socioeconomic inequalities that affect the capacity of families, schools, and communities to create equal opportunities for all children and young people to engage in sport (Sabo & Veliz, 2008). The population group that appears to benefit most from the positive correlation between sport participation and college completion (with educational attainment being important for subsequent socioeconomic status [SES]) are girls and women who identify as white and who have benefited from their family's generational social mobility (Biscomb, 2012). Troutman and Dufur (2007) found that white girls from higher SES families, living with both parents, and attending private, suburban, or rural schools (i.e., not attending urban schools) were the most likely to participate in sport. Their odds of completing a college degree were higher than the odds of girls who did not engage in interscholastic sport (Troutman & Dufur, 2007), but it is unknown if this difference in educational attainment can be attributed to their sport participation. Daughters of wealthier parents who value physical activity and share an interest in their daughters' participation report the highest levels of physical activity (Biddle, Whitehead, O'Donovan, & Nevill, 2005; LaVoi, Thul, Wasend, Barber et al., 2018). In contrast, in the United States, parents of girls from disadvantaged backgrounds are more likely to encourage their daughters to work outside the home or focus on school instead of participate in sport (LaVoi Thul, Wasend, Barber et al., 2018; Sabo & Veliz, 2008).

Race, Sport, and Mobility

The extent to which sport offers a realistic pathway for social mobility for racialized minorities, and particularly African American young men, has long occupied the hearts and minds of scholars of sport (e.g., Book, Henriksen, & Stambulova, 2020; Edwards, 2000; Hawkins, 2010). Hawkins, for example, argues that while, at the surface level, college sport offers African American student-athletes opportunities for mobility, in reality their bodies have been exploited as a valued commodity in generating wealth for predominantly white institutions. He shows how, among other critical findings, there have been no significant or enduring changes in African Americans' access to administrative positions. A similar absence from positions of power has been found among Black and minority ethnic (former) athletes in European soccer (Bradbury, 2013) and for Indigenous people in Australia (Hallinan & Judd, 2009).

Eminent sports sociologist Harry Edwards (2000, p. 9) echoes this critical perspective by stating that "the dynamics of black sports involvement, and the blind faith of black youths and their families in sport as a prime vehicle of self-realization and social-economic advancement, have combined to generate a complex of critical problems for black society." Yet he argues that, in the context of high levels of crime, incarceration, unemployment, and school dropout,

> exploiting black youths' overemphasis on sports participation and achievement may be our only remaining avenue for guiding increasing numbers of them out of circumstances that today lead to even more devastating destructiveness and a greater waste of human potential than that which I, and others, have long decried in connection with unrealistic black sports aspirations.

Edwards advises that

> all involved must learn to dream with their eyes open, always remaining fully cognizant of participation's pitfalls no less than its positive possibilities, of its potential as a dead end trap no less than its promise as a vehicle for outreach and advancement. (pp. 12–13)

More granular, empirically driven research suggests that race and gender intersect to produce more adverse outcomes for Black girls and women in sport. For example, Black male athletes from urban areas were four times more likely than nonathletes to be in college working toward bachelor's degrees, but for Black female athletes from urban areas, sport participation seemed to actually work against them, as they were far less likely to have high-status jobs (5%) after high school compared with nonathletes (59%) (Hanson & Kraus, 1998; Smith, 1992). The best route to upward social mobility for Black women is believed to be the one of education, which is stressed by their families and results in a socialization into self-sufficiency and leadership (Smith, 1995). The lower participation rates in sport and physical activity of this group of girls and the lack of family support make it difficult for them to experience socioeconomic benefits of sport.

Career Termination and Postcareer Transitions

In taking stock of the issues raised in some key studies that have garnered attention over the years, it is important to recognize that the majority of studies that found a correlation between sport and upward mobility have focused on elite athletes who had achieved professional status. Here, it should be kept in mind that for every athlete who achieves professional status, there are thousands who never reach elite or professional status (Leonard, 1996). The odds of becoming a professional athlete are low, and even after a rigorous selection process, a major league career may be brief. Just 2 of 10,000 males ages 15 to 39 reach professional athlete status (Leonard, 1996). Leonard found that the odds are better for high school athletes: the odds of a high school baseball player entering the major leagues are 0.002, roughly the same for football players and two times better than for basketball players.

A characteristic that distinguishes professional sports careers from most other careers is that players know (but do not necessarily accept) that the role is temporary; here exit is often involuntary, and the elite status conferred by the role is difficult to achieve after leaving the role (Drahota & Eitzen, 1998). Career termination is often one of the most significant and traumatic experience encountered by athletes (Taylor & Ogilvie, 2001). Many professional sport careers tend to be relatively short and compressed as the ability to compete at elite levels is often brief. As a result, Witnauer, Rogers, and Saint Onge's (2007, p. 382) study aptly characterizes baseball careers in the United States as ones that spend "an inevitably short time on a very slippery slope."

The turbulent and fragile nature of sports careers stresses the importance of establishing viable postcareer opportunities (Butt & Molnar, 2009; McCormack & Walseth, 2013). Upward mobility achieved during an athlete's career may be followed by downward mobility after retirement (Spaaij et al., 2015). Yet research on postcareer transition experiences and strategies, such as increased institutional investment in education, suggests that athletes are often so focused on establishing and maintaining a professional career that other aspects of identity and investment become of secondary importance. For example, Kelly and Hickey (2008) identified the tensions that Australian footballers face in trying to respond to the pressures and practices associated with undertaking education and training programs outside of football. They conclude:

> While time and access are recurring issues, by far their greatest obstacle to them achieving success in these arenas is their general lack of focus and commitment. Although many players genuinely attempt to engage in education and training practices, whenever these programmes clash with football, football is given priority. (p. 491)

A recent study by Schmidt, Torgler, and Jung (2017) examined the factors that influence young people's tendencies to choose a professional football career over a lower risk option. They found that such risk taking could be explained by potential benefits expected from this decision, as well as one's own assessments about the likelihood of achieving a professional career.

In the next section, we outline different theoretical and methodological approaches to the relationship between elite sport and social mobility.

APPROACHES

The relationship between social mobility and sport has been studied from different theoretical and methodological perspectives. In terms of theory, the first approach reflects a developmental model, wherein participation in sport is thought to contribute to performance in education and in the labor market (Mackin & Walther, 2012). Barron, Ewing, and Waddell (2000) refer to this as the "human-capital enhancement model," arguing that athletic involvement enhances productivity. From this perspective, sport participation can be conceptualized as a vehicle for intragenerational and intergenerational social mobility through mechanisms such as occupational status, income status, educational attainment, and social prestige (Eisen & Turner, 1992; Loy, 1972; Semyonov, 1986; Sohi & Yusuff, 1987). Athletic development can thus be viewed as a resource that can be converted into performance, wealth, and prestige. This resource may be seen as considerable, most particularly for athletes from marginalized backgrounds, such as, for example, disadvantaged aspiring athletes (Book et al., 2020). This developmental model has been verified empirically. Mackin and Walther (2012) found limited support for the developmental model, concluding that some sport participation increases the number of years of education that the athlete will complete and increases the probability of earning a college degree. Barron et al. (2000) reported some evidence that athletic participation directly affects wages and educational attainment. However, they hasten to add that "much of the effect of athletic participation on wages and educational attainment appears to reflect differences across individuals in ability or value of leisure" (p. 409).

Another approach, which comes in different variants, offers resistance to this received conventional wisdom. Building on social reproduction theory and neo-Marxism, one strand argues that the popular belief that sport offers a viable social mobility pathway is detrimental to disadvantaged athletes and community groups and reproduces their disadvantage (e.g., Anderson & White, 2017; Carrington, 1986). Here it is recognized that the relationship between sport and social mobility may be a zero-sum game as the time and energy invested in sport take away from time that could be spent on education, which, by virtually all accounts, offers a more feasible pathway to social mobility. Qualitative studies, such as Rodriguez and McDonald's (2013) study of Polynesians in Australia, illustrate this zero-sum approach well. They conclude that the main earning potential of working-class Polynesian men is between the ages of 20 and 50; if these years are spent "chasing the goal of being an elite athlete, this may come at the expense of acquiring other skills or experience" that are more likely to translate into economic capital (i.e., educational attainment and work experience) (p. 213). From this perspective, elite sport appears to primarily benefit those from relatively privileged backgrounds in terms of economic resources and educational attainment (Coakley, 2009). Aspiring athletes from disadvantaged backgrounds often face challenging realities that are summed up in a "sink or swim" narrative of risk, descent, and gain (Book et al., 2020). For example, Book et al. report on the career narratives of two African American elite athletes whose "pathway to professional sports focuses more upon their underserved communities, racial issues, and how these social factors presented a myriad of challenges they would overcome to reach the professional level" (p. 11). Quantitative studies, on the other hand, appear to have found little or no evidence of any negative effect of sport participation in terms of labor market outcomes or educational attainment (e.g., Barron et al., 2000; Mackin & Walther, 2012).

The collective evidence from research conducted from these different perspectives points in a similar direction with regard to the issues of equal opportunity and equality of outcome. As the developmental model suggests, sport participation can indeed serve to increase social mobility for various population groups. However, in many cases, access to social mobility opportunities and pathways in sport is moderated by race-ethnicity, gender, and SES. It appears that white males from middle-class backgrounds generally benefit most from professional sports careers (Sabo, Melnick, & Vanfossen, 1993), while there are fewer viable, well-paid career opportunities for women, racial and ethnic minorities, those from lower SES backgrounds, and those athletes at the intersections of these attributes (Leonard, 1996; Messner, 2007; Sabo et al., 1993). For example, research by Snellman, Silva, Frederick, and Putnam (2015) has found a growing "engagement gap" and a sharp increase in the class gap in involvement, whereby working-class students' access to and involvement in extracurricular sports activities, and hence their opportunities for associated social mobility outcomes, are diminishing. There are also significant differences in social mobility opportunities between the small number of high-paid, male-dominated sports such as football, baseball, basketball, and rugby, and other sports that are less well funded and broadcast (Eitle, 2005; Eitle & Eitle, 2002). This is demonstrated by, for example, Schotté's (2008) findings in a study of the economic precariousness of long-distance running in France.

Methodological Approaches

Reflecting the diversity of social mobility studies in general (Hout, 2015), conceptualization and measurement of social mobility in sport vary considerably across different studies. In their discussion of the quantitative literature, Macklin and Walther (2012) argue that the results are in part due to the variety of ways social mobility is operationalized, whether cross-sectional or longitudinal studies are conducted, and whether results are disaggregated by SES, race, gender, or other social factors. They highlight the need for nationally representative longitudinal studies to assess the effect of participation in sport on social mobility.

Research tends to take a quantitative and aggregated approach to social mobility (cf. Miller, 1998). Some studies define and measure social mobility by years of education, educational attainment, and earnings, while other research uses occupational attainment or subjective factors such as social prestige as proxy indicators. In quantitative studies, social origins have often been examined in relatively crude ways, reduced to broad social factors such as gender, race-ethnicity, and SES and, more occasionally, the intersections of these factors. Qualitative researchers argue that "hard" or aggregated indicators alone provide insufficient insight into how changes in SES are actually experienced by individuals. Spaaij's (2011, 2013) research draws on the biographical method of the French sociologist Daniel Bertaux (1981), who argues that life stories bring home the complexity of the sequences of cause and effect in human lives, emphasizing the evolving interconnection between individual actors and structural opportunities and constraints. Bertaux and Thompson (1997, pp. 15–16) argue that "objective resources . . . and constraints . . . are so much mediated by the *perceptions* that young people have of them that they remain ineffective and almost unreal as such." Similar qualitative methods that have been employed in this field of research include narrative analysis (Book et al., 2020) and ethnography (Rodriguez & McDonald, 2013; Schotté, 2008).

Another problem with much of the literature on the topic is that it typically adopts an individualistic perspective, where it examines only intragenerational mobility or, when it does look at intergenerational mobility, measures the family's social location by one of its members (i.e., the father alone). This approach appears to be out of step with advances in social mobility studies more broadly, where calls have been made to adopt a family-level perspective (e.g., Beller, 2009; Miller, 1998). This can be achieved by, for example, broadening the traditional view of intergenerational mobility, that is, father-to-son/daughter mobility, to include other (intergenerational) pathways within the family, such as female pathways of mobility (Miller, 1998).

In the remainder of this chapter, we elaborate on the intersection between social mobility and inequality in sport by examining in greater detail how gender moderates the relationship between social mobility and sport. The career prospects and experiences of women athletes have been receiving growing scholarly attention, and it is timely to synthesize this knowledge through the lens of social mobility. We do so by drawing on a combination of academic literature and primary data collected by the second author as part of her doctoral research. This research engages ethnography in examining the gender, labor, and power relations in the field of professional women's road cycling. The methods include participation in the Melbourne road racing scene, observations at the Women's World Tour (WWT) races, and semistructured interviews with elite/professional women cyclists. The data presented in this chapter are derived mostly from interviews and is presented using pseudonyms.

DEBATES

As noted in the previous section, the question of if—and if so, how and for whom—sport participation can lead to social mobility proves to be complex, with research pointing in different directions. It is clear, however, that the relationship between sport participation and academic achievement differs by gender, race, the particular sport one plays, and the achievement domain (Eitle, 2005). In the Issues section, we flagged gender, sport, and social mobility as a major area of research in this field. In this section, we elaborate on this thread by focusing on an increasingly prominent scholarly and public debate: professional women's sport and its opportunities for social mobility. We do so by examining, first, some of the key literature, and, second, a case study of elite women's road cycling.

Elite Women Athletes and Social Mobility

Sport development outcomes are complex and depend on many factors (Clark & Burnett, 2010). As discussed earlier, most social mobility opportunities in and through sport are destined for men, especially those with relatively high SES. Nonetheless, women are believed to benefit from sport participation, and some research suggests they may actually benefit more from experiences with sport than do men (e.g., Hanson & Kraus, 1998). Findings from a number of studies, such as those considered below, contribute to a better understanding of the complexities of sport and social mobility for women athletes.

In South Africa, most football players live in the context of poverty, and sport provides them an opportunity to escape harsh living conditions, especially for the talented individuals playing professionally (Clark & Burnett, 2010). Despite professional football not being a viable option for women in South Africa,[1] Clark and Burnett suggest that playing football gives some young women the opportunity to attend tertiary education as they receive sport scholarships, and with that, improve their chances for upward social mobility and break the cycle of poverty. Female footballers' dreams of social mobility also impact the decision for some to take their football skills abroad (Agergaard & Botelho, 2014). Playing abroad enhances footballers' social prestige in their home country because, for most people, leaving Central Africa is part of a larger migration dream. However, compared to male players, female players' attainment of prestige is not as widespread, and their sports careers often lack financial security or career structure (Agergaard & Botelho, 2014).

The problem of limited financial rewards in women's sport leaves many high-level competitors requiring extra income, often gained through supplemental employment. In Scotland, for example, many female football players require additional income from a job besides their competitive football career, restricting their economic mobility (Gilmore, 2008). The need for additional income clearly signals the lack of economic viability for these women, but in turn, their possibility of growing in a career outside of football might be limited by their time, energy, and money invested in football. This precarious situation leads many Scottish female football players to retire early, as they are not in a position to wait to be "forced" out (by either age or atrophy) as they need to make decisions earlier for their future professional careers beyond football (Gilmore, 2008). For female African migrant players, in addition to the limited financial rewards for their football labor, their opportunities for a postcareer professional occupation are restricted by their young age when they migrate. These women have not completed a level of schooling that allows them to study in the country where they play, which results in a lack of education (Agergaard & Botelho, 2014). Low educational attainment and language difficulties result in limited possibilities for pursuing a football coaching career, the main considered career option after their playing career is over (Agergaard & Botelho, 2014). For these women, playing football abroad might provide small economic benefits and locally attained social prestige, but their participation in elite football contributes little to their long-term social mobility.

For women athletes in China and the United States, things look slightly different. Jinxia's (2001) analysis of sportswomen and social mobility in China indicates that the mere status of being an elite athlete makes sportswomen a "state worker," which means that they acquire formal occupation status in terms of wage, city residence, and welfare benefits. After retiring from sport, many female athletes receive a job in either a sport or a nonsport field and thus a secure future and one that often results in upward social mobility (Jinxia, 2001). In the United States, Eisen and Turner (1992) found that Olympic athletes enjoyed increased social prestige. This is the result of an essentially guaranteed education (compulsory college attendance for intercollegiate athletes) and the fact that their athletic achievements helped most of them to gain employment (Eisen & Turner, 1992).

Elite Women's Road Cycling

Similar to the elite female athletes in Sohi and Yusuff's (1987) study and the active girls in the research by LaVoi, Thul, and Wasend (2018) and Troutman and Dufur (2007), elite women cyclists mostly originate from a higher social and economic class (see also Sirna, 2016). Where boots, a ball, and club membership generally suffice to develop football skills, to be allowed to race cyclists need to purchase a particular kind of bike with clip-in pedals, a helmet, and shoes with cleats. Besides paying for a membership license with a club and with representative cycling bodies, a rider must pay an entry fee for every race. The technological advancements of the bicycle might make riding and racing more enjoyable, but they can also influence who lines up at the start. Carbon frames are lighter; Shimano's Dura-Ace is the superior (and concomitantly costly) groupset (i.e., the brakes and gears); electronic shifting is faster; and MIPS technology (Multi-directional Impact Protection System) helmets reduce the impact on the brain should one crash. These are also among the most expensive options. The talented riders who can afford a lighter, better, and thus faster bike are more likely to win, draw the attention of the right people, and attract sponsorship and other opportunities. The road cycling culture requires a certain type of expensive clothing (using Lycra and other technologically advanced fabrics) and accessories that match one's bike. Bicycle maintenance, custom professional fittings, insurance, repairs from crashes, and transport add significant expenses. Elite-level cycling is expensive, and thus novice riders are generally reliant on their family's ability and willingness to financially support them in order to train and compete in the right races. In total, the requirements of competitive road racing often works strategically against the notion of sport as a great equalizer (Maguire, 2011; Sohi & Yusuff, 1987).

When riders make it to the elite level (i.e., competing in the WWT), these costs are often mostly covered by their professional cycling teams. The team functions as an employer, and riders sign labor contracts with them. However, as with many women's sports, there is little money to earn in elite women's road cycling. The most prestige race in the sport, the Tour de France, organized by the Amaury Sport Organisation ([ASO] 2020b), offers a 21-day stage race with a total prize money of €2,293,000. A stage winner wins €11,000, and the overall winner leaves with €500,000. The women's version of this race, La Course, is reduced to a one-day race with a total prize pot of €20,200; the winner goes home with €6,000 (ASO, 2020a). The minimum wage of third-tier male cyclists is set at €30,855 (Mitchell, 2020), but top World Tour men riders can have million-euro contracts. A minimum wage for WWT team riders was implemented by the UCI (2019), the international governing body of cycling, in 2020 and was set at €15,000. In 2020, there were only five WWT teams. The remaining teams are classified as Continental teams and do not have to pay their riders the minimum wage. Only 12% of the women's peloton earns more than €40,000 a year (The Cyclists' Alliance, 2019). This means that during their active cycling career, few elite women cyclists have the opportunity to save or invest money or build a retirement fund. Many, mostly non-European riders have to take out loans to make their dream of professional bike riding a reality and/or depend on their support network.

One point of focus within social mobility scholarship is the strong relationship with educational attainment. The women's peloton is highly educated. According to the 2019 Cyclists' Alliance Rider Survey, around 59% of female riders have a college degree or higher, and 32% are currently enrolled as a student (although 6% of these students also hold a second job).

The world of elite road cycling gives some the opportunity to combine their cycling career with their academic experience. This is illustrated by the following comments from Violet (pseudonym), who was in the midst of pursuing a business degree focused on sport:

> It's been good, it's applicable. I can see how it applies to the world that I live in. I actually did my internship with [my team] which was quite interesting, I got a little bit more of an insight inside the team. I worked with the marketing team, so I had to help them with the website and sort of help with the marketing and I guess awareness of [our] project. I did a little bit of data analysis and I wrote some blogs for them as well. All different little things I had to do. It was enjoyable, it was good. So, I got a lot out of it and [the internship] kind of brought to- gether a lot of [my course's] topics.

It is important to note that despite the high numbers of educated riders, the survey does not describe how or when these degrees were acquired. Cyclists interrupt their education, finish their study over many years, or burn out from the high demands of excelling in sport and school, as the following comments indicate:

> I nearly finished a science degree, but I have been doing it for ten years, like very slowly. (Lisa)

> After five years of studying—my Bachelor took me five years—I had to really recover from that. Combining elite sport and university . . . So, for two seasons I focused on [cyclo] cross, to really tone it down, but I got over trained and it's since this summer that I started riding on the road again, for the Giro [Rosa]. Sometimes I wonder how I did it, because I also lived in a student house and had a job. It was all too much really. (Ane)

Just as their education provides the cyclists with a safety net undergirding financial secu- rity, it also may lead them to justify a decision to pursue an elite cycling career. As Abigail reflects:

> It was not really a decision I had to think about. You only get one chance, you can only be a professional athlete for so many years and I am already . . . pretty old to be starting out, so it's really only a few years of my life, whereas I can sit at my desk and be an engineer for decades. (Abigail)

As Ann and Rodriguez (2000) point out, occupational opportunities in sport are dominated by men, and road cycling is no exception. Despite the announcement that two current professional cyclists, Anna van der Breggen and Chantal Blaak, became sports directors for their teams in 2021 and 2022, respectively (Cash, 2020), there are few women directors, managers, team owners, or race organizers. In other words, while these elite women cyclists do indeed gain specific cycling capital, this particular cultural capital does not often lead to higher-status occupational positions. Although many women cyclists work at jobs besides cycling, and cycling careers might leave space for education, the pattern in terms of social mobility is that this combination largely leads to the aforementioned zero-sum model. Reinforced is their finding that studying and working takes away from progressing as an elite cyclist, and full-time cycling takes away opportunities for earning and saving money and gaining work experience for a professional career. The following comments by cyclists Violet and Hannah illustrate this:

> Yeah, [my parents] helped me [financially] and I also had to get a loan to cover the other expenses, like visas, things like that; additional costs that I hadn't quite considered. I think

my scholarship was for $36,000 or something but my tuition was $48,000 but like covered a room and that sort of thing as well. (Violet)

The effects on my career have more been that I have stayed at the same workplace because of the security. Which has been fabulous, which just means you cannot progress, your career, as much as you might want to. I was working at the . . . Institute of Sport doing physical preparations so strength and conditioning and that sort of thing. Obviously, that is regarded quite highly as a career. I would've liked to have pursued that more but because of becoming the athlete, you only have a limited time you can actually be the athlete, so I made that choice. (Hannah)

Such setbacks in the course of a professional career, when combined with the lack of savings and potential debt, makes it difficult to advance socially, given that most women cyclists come from a middle-class status to begin with. This example reflects some of the complexities and limitations of the "sport as a vehicle for social mobility" thesis, as well as the "trade-off" between commitment to a sports career and alternative investment that may pay higher dividends postcareer. In the next section, we draw together some of the main findings of this chapter.

CONCLUSION

In his synthesis of trends and pressing questions in the study of social mobility, Hout (2015, p. 28) argues that the main question we should ask is "To what extent do the conditions and circumstances of early life constrain success in adulthood?" According to Hout and others, such as Hasenbalg and Silva (2003), focusing on the association between social origins and destinations gets us "closer to the ultimate questions of whether society offers opportunity and whether it does so fairly" (Hout, 2015, p. 28).

In this chapter, we have sought to adapt this question to sport by exploring whether sport offers opportunities for social mobility, and whether it does so fairly. The findings from both quantitative and qualitative studies presented in this chapter suggest that opportunities for advances in one's social mobility do in fact exist in sport, the key mechanisms being earnings, occupational status, educational attainment, and social prestige. However, it is evident from the literature that these opportunities and pathways are not distributed evenly. The available research shows that these factors moderate opportunities for social mobility in and through sport, whereby those from privileged backgrounds are more likely to benefit than persons from disadvantaged backgrounds.

Although there are some divergences and contradictions in the literature, there is now a considerable amount of evidence to support the argument that, on the whole, sport is not the social equalizer it is often considered to be, regardless of what high-profile rags-to-riches "success stories" may suggest. White males from middle-class backgrounds appear to benefit most from their experiences in professional sport, while there are fewer viable and durable mobility opportunities for those who are women, belong to racialized minorities, have initially lower SES, or for whom these characteristics intersect. Overall, this social stratification pattern is influenced by conditions and circumstances of early life, which shape disparities in access to sport participation opportunities from an early age. This brief case study of women's road cycling illustrates how these dynamics can vary across sports labor markets of different size, depending on both the economic opportunities within a sport and the resources required to enter the sport and to maintain a playing career.

Compared to the vibrancy of social mobility research at large, the study of social mobility in and through sport is a rather underexplored field of research in terms of both volume (of publications) and methodological innovation. Recent decades have seen a growth in research on three particular aspects of the association between sport and social mobility: (1) gender and elite sport, (2) race, sport, and social mobility, and (3) career duration, termination, and postcareer transitions. We expect that these three subfields, which intersect also with SES, will continue to produce new insights about the association between sport and social mobility in years to come. The study of transnational sports labor migration, a topic we have not discussed in this chapter, is another area that promises to deliver insights into the relationship between sport and social mobility, building on recent advances in the body of anthropological scholarship (e.g., Besnier, Calabrò, & Guinness, 2020). Yet, if we are to follow Hout's (2015) lead, we need to pursue further methodological innovation. Social origins have often been examined quantitatively in relatively crude ways in the literature, reduced to broad social factors such as gender, race-ethnicity, and SES and, more occasionally, the intersections of these factors. Incorporating intergenerational family effects or dynamics helps to broaden and deepen our conceptualization and measurement of social mobility. Moreover, there is room to bridge the divide between quantitative and qualitative approaches by designing mixed-methods studies that capture both measurement and meaning. Herein lie welcome opportunities for moving this field of research forward.

NOTE

1. In South Africa in particular, "lack of material resources such as sponsorships, facilities, coaches, equipment, transportation, professional leagues and to a lesser degree lack of nonmaterial resources such as media coverage and advertising, recognition and public support appear as important obstacles for women athletes" (Agergaard & Botelho, 2014, p. 524).

REFERENCES

Agergaard, S., & Botelho, V. (2014). The way out? African players' migration to Scandinavian women's football. *Sport in Society, 17*(4), 523–536.

Aldridge, S. (2003). The facts about social mobility: A survey of recent evidence on social mobility and its causes. *New Economy, 10*(4), 189–193.

Anderson, E., & White, A. (2017). *Sport, theory and social problems: A critical introduction.* London: Routledge.

Ann, L., & Rodriguez, S. (2000). Our sporting sisters: How male hegemony stratifies women in sport. *Women in Sport and Physical Activity Journal, 9*(1), 15–34.

ASO. (2020a). La course règlement particulier. https://netstorage.lequipe.fr/ASO/cycling_tff/reglement-2020.pdf.

ASO. (2020b). Tour de France réglement. https://netstorage.lequipe.fr/ASO/cycling_tdf/tdf20-reglement-fruk-bd.pdf

Barron, J. M., Ewing, B. T., & Waddell, G. R. (2000). The effects of high school athletic participation on education and labor market outcomes. *Review of Economics and Statistics 82*, 409–421.

Beller, E. (2009). Bringing intergenerational social mobility research into the twenty-first century: Why mothers matter. *American Sociological Review, 74*, 507–528.

Bertaux, D. (Ed.) (1981). *Biography and society: The life history approach in the social sciences*. London: Sage.

Bertaux, D., & Thompson, P. (1997). Introduction. In D. Bertaux & P. Thompson (Eds.), *Pathways to social class: A qualitative approach to social mobility* (pp. 1–31). Oxford: Clarendon Press.

Besnier, N., Calabrò, D. G., & Guinness, D. (Eds.). (2020). *Sport, migration, and gender in the neoliberal age*. London: Routledge.

Biddle, S. J., Whitehead, S. H., O'Donovan, T. M., & Nevill, M. E. (2005). Correlates of participation in physical activity for adolescent girls: A systematic review of recent literature. *Journal of Physical Activity and Health, 2*(4), 423–434.

Biscomb, K. (2012). Three generations of Lancashire women. *Asia-Pacific Journal of Health, Sport and Physical Education, 3*(3), 253–265.

Book, Jr., R., Henriksen, K., & Stambulova, N. (2020). Sink or swim: Career narratives of two African American athletes from underserved communities in the United States. *Qualitative Research in Sport, Exercise and Health, 13*(6). doi:10.1080/2159676X.2020.1787490.

Bottero, W. (2005). *Stratification: Social division and inequality*. London: Routledge.

Bourdieu, P. (1978). Sport and social class. *Social Science Information, 17*(6), 819–840.

Bradbury, S. (2013). Institutional racism, whiteness and the under-representation of minorities in leadership positions in football in Europe. *Sport in Society, 14*(3), 296–314.

Breen, R., & Jonsson, J. O. (2005). Inequality of opportunity in comparative perspective: Recent research on educational attainment and social mobility. *Annual Review of Sociology, 31*, 223–243.

Butt, J., & Molnar, G. (2009). Involuntary career termination in sport: A case study of the process of structurally induced failure. *Sport in Society, 12*(2), 240–257.

Carrington, B. (1986). Social mobility, ethnicity and sport. *British Journal of Sociology of Education, 7*(1), 3–18.

Cash, D. (2020, May). Van der Breggen will hang up the wheels in 2021, Blaak in 2022. Cycling Tips.https://cyclingtips.com/2020/05/van-der-breggen-will-hang-up-the-wheels-in-2021-blaak-in-2022/.

Clark, C., & Burnett, C. (2010). Upward social mobility through women's soccer: Psycho-social perspectives of sports. *African Journal for Physical Health Education, Recreation and Dance, 16*(1), 141–154.

Coakley, J. (2009). *Sports in society: Issues and controversies* (10th ed.). Boston: McGraw-Hill.

The Cyclists' Alliance. (2019). The Cyclists' Alliance rider survey 2019. https://cyclistsalliance.org/2019/12/rider-survey-2019/.

Dart, J., Doyle, P., & Hill, J. (2006, April 12). The greatest rags-to-riches stories ever. *The Guardian*. https://www.theguardian.com/football/2006/apr/12/theknowledge.sport.

Drahota, J. A., & Eitzen, D. S. (1998). The role exit of professional athletes. *Sociology of Sport Journal, 15*, 263–278.

Edwards, H. (2000). Crisis of Black athletes on the eve of the 21st century. *Society, 37*(3), 9–13.

Eisen, G., & Turner, D. (1992). Myth and reality: Social mobility of the American Olympic athletes. *International Review for the Sociology of Sport, 27*(2), 165–174.

Eitle, T. (2005). Do gender and race matter? Explaining the relationship between sports participation and achievement. *Sociological Spectrum*, 25(2), 177–195.

Eitle, T., & Eitle, D. (2002). Race, cultural capital, and the educational effects of sports participation. *Sociology of Education*, 75(2), 123–146.

Eitzen, D. S. (2009). *Fair and foul: Beyond the myths and paradoxes of sport*. Lanham, MD: Rowman & Littlefield.

Espinoza, C. (2009). Sports and the social mobility of women. *Revista de Ciencias del Ejercicio FOD*, 5(2), 62–74.

Farrey, T. (2017). The gentrification of college hoops. *The Undefeated*. https://theundefeated.com/features/gentrification-of-ncaa-division-1-college-basketball/ (accessed on July 20, 2020).

Ferrari-King, G. (2014, August 18). Most inspiring "from-rags-to-riches" sports stories. *Bleacher Report*.https://bleacherreport.com/articles/2163388-most-inspiring-from-rags-to-riches-sports-stories.

GETVAL. (2017). Runner Emil Zatopek. *Get Addicted to Sport Values (GETVAL)*. https://www.sportvalues.eu/runner-emil-zatopek/ (accessed on October 14, 2020).

Gilmore, O. (2008). *Leaving competitive sport: Scottish female athletes' experiences of sport career transitions* (Unpublished PhD thesis). University of Stirling.

Goldthorpe, J. (2003). The myth of education-based meritocracy. *New Economy*, 10(4), 234–239.

Guest, A., & Schneider, B. (2003). Adolescents' extracurricular participation in context: The mediating effects of schools, communities, and identity. *Sociology of Education*, 76(2), 89–109.

Hallinan, C., & Judd, B. (2009). Race relations, Indigenous Australia and the social impact of professional football. *Sport in Society*, 12(9), 1220–1235.

Hanson, S., & Kraus, R. (1998). Women, sports, and science: Do female athletes have an advantage? *Sociology of Education*, 71(2), 93–110.

Hasenbalg, C., & Silva N. V. (Eds.). (2003). *Origens e destinos*. Rio de Janeiro: Topbooks.

Hawkins, B. (2010). Economic recession, college athletics, and issues of diversity and inclusion: When White American sneezes, Black America catches pneumonia. *Journal of Intercollegiate Sport*, 3(1), 96–100.

Hawkins, B. (2013). *The new plantation: Black athletes, college sports, and predominantly white NCAA institutions*. New York: Palgrave Macmillan.

Hicket, C., & Kelly, P. (2008). Preparing to not be a footballer: Higher education and professional sport. *Sport, Education and Society*, 13(4), 477–494.

Hoberman, J. M. (1997). *Darwin's athletes: How sport has damaged Black America and preserved the myth of race*. Boston: Houghton Mifflin Harcourt.

Hout, M. (2015). A summary of what we know about social mobility. *Annals of the American Academy of Political and Social Science*, 657(1), 27–36.

Jinxia, D. (2001). Cultural changes: Mobility, stratification and sportswomen in the new China. *Sport in Society*, 4(3), 1–26.

Kane, M. J., LaVoi, N., Wiese-Bjornstal, D., Duncan, M., Nichols, J., Pettee, K., & Ainsworth, B. (2007). The 2007 Tucker Center research report: Developing physically active girls: An evidence-based multidisciplinary approach. Minneapolis, MN: Tucker Center for Research on Girls & Women in Sport.https://www.cehd.umn.edu/tuckercenter/library/docs/research/2007-Tucker-Center-Research-Report.pdf (accessed on October 3, 2020).

Kelly, P., & Hickey, C. (2008). Player welfare and privacy in the sports entertainment industry: Player development managers and risk management in Australia Football League clubs. *International Review for the Sociology of Sport, 43*(4), 383–398

LaVoi, N., Thul, C., & Wasend, M. (2018). Understanding girls in and through physical activity: Assets, identities and disparities. Minneapolis, MN: Tucker Center for Research on Girls & Women in Sport.https://z.umn.edu/tcrr-r3 (accessed August 9, 2020).

LaVoi, N., Thul, C., Wasend, M., Barber, H., Bar-Anderson, D., Buysse, J., . . . Wood, K. (2018). The 2018 Tucker Center research report: Developing physically active girls: An evidence-based multidisciplinary approach. Minneapolis, MN: Tucker Center for Research on Girls & Women in Sport. https://z.umn.edu/tcrr-r3 (accessed October 3, 2020).

Leonard, W. M. (1996). The odds of transiting from one level of sports participation to another. *Sociology of Sport Journal, 13*, 288–299.

Lipset, S. M., & Bendix, R. (1992). *Social mobility in industrial society.* New Brunswick, NJ: Transaction Publishers.

Loy, J. W. (1972). Social origins and occupational mobility patterns of a selected sample of American athletes. *International Review for the Sociology of Sport, 7*(1), 5–25.

Mackin, R. S., & Walther, C. S. (2012). Race, sport and social mobility: Horatio Alger in short pants? *International Review for the Sociology of Sport, 47*(6), 670–689.

Maguire, J. (2005). *Power and global sport: Zones of prestige, emulation and resistance.* London: Routledge.

Maguire, J. (2011). Power and global sport: Zones of prestige, emulation and resistance. *Sport in Society, 14*(7–8), 1010–1026.

McCormack, C., & Walseth, K. (2013). Combining elite women's soccer and education: Norway and the NCAA. *Soccer and Society, 14*(6), 887–897.

Messner, M. A. (2007). *Out of play: Critical essays on gender and sport.* New York: SUNY Press.

Miller, R. (1998). The limited concerns of social mobility research. *Current Sociology, 46*(4), 145–163.

Mitchell, M. (2020). How much do pro cyclists earn? Pro Cycling.https://www.procyclinguk.com/how-much-pro-cyclists-earn/.

Nunn, A., Johnson, S., Monro, S., Bickerstaffe, T., & Kelsey, S. (2007). *Factors influencing social mobility.* London: Department for Work and Pensions.

Pociello, C. (1995). *Les cultures sportives.* Paris: Presses Universitaires de France.

Rodriguez, L. & McDonald, B. (2013). After the whistle: Issues impacting on the health and wellbeing of Polynesian players off the field. *Asia-Pacific Journal of Health, Sport and Physical Education, 4*(3), 201–215.

Sabo, D., Melnick, M., & Vanfossen, B. (1993). High school athletic participation and postsecondary educational and occupational mobility: A focus on race and gender. *Sociology of Sport Journal, 10*(1), 44 56.

Sabo, D., & Veliz, P. (2008). *Go out and play: Youth sports in America.* East Meadow, NY: Women's Sports Foundation.

Schmidt, S., Torgler, B., & Jung, V. (2017). Perceived trade-off between education and sports career: Evidence from professional football. *Applied Economics, 49*(29), 2829–2850.

Schotté, M. (2008). La condition athlétique: Ethnographie du quotidien de coureurs professionnels immigrés. *Genéses, 71*(2), 84–105.

Schultz, J. (2018). *Women's sports: What everyone needs to know:* Oxford: Oxford University Press.

Semyonov, M. (1986). Occupational mobility through sport: The case of Israeli soccer. *International Review for the Sociology of Sport, 21*(1), 23–32.

Sirna, K. (2016). Road cycling over forty: Fitness, friends, and fondos. *Sociology of Sport Journal, 33*(3), 230–239.

Smith, Y. (1992). Women of color in society and sport. *Quest, 44*(2), 228–250.

Smith, Y. (1995). Women sports leaders and educators of color—their socialization and achievement. *Journal of Physical Education, Recreation & Dance, 66*(7), 28–33.

Snellman, K., Silva, J. M., Frederick, C. B., & Putnam, R. D. (2015). The engagement gap: Social mobility and extracurricular participation among American youth. *Annals of the American Academy of Political and Social Science, 657*(1), 194–207.

Sohi, A., & Yusuff, K. (1987). The socio-economic status of elite Nigerian athletes in perspective of social stratification and mobility. *International Review for the Sociology of Sport, 22*(4), 295–303.

Spaaij, R. (2011). *Sport and social mobility: Crossing boundaries.* London: Routledge.

Spaaij, R. (2013). Changing people's lives for the better? Social mobility through sport-based intervention programmes: Opportunities and constraints. *European Journal for Sport and Society, 10*(1), 53–73.

Spaaij, R., Farquharson, K., & Marjoribanks, T. (2015). Sport and social inequalities. *Sociology Compass, 9*(5), 400–411.

Staurowsky, E. J., Watanabe, N., Cooper, J., Cooky, C., Lough, N., Paule-Koba, A., Pharr, J., Williams, S., Cummings, S., Issokson-Silver, K., & Snyder, M. (2020). *Chasing equity: The triumphs, challenges, and opportunities in sports for girls and women.* New York: Women's Sports Foundation.

Sugden, J., & Tomlinson, A. (2000). Theorizing sport, social class and status. In J. Coakley & E. Dunning (Eds.), *Handbook of sports studies* (pp. 309–321). London: Sage.

Taylor, J., & Ogilvie, B. C. (2001). Career termination among athletes. In R. Singer, H. Hausenblas, & C. Janelle (Eds.), *Handbook of sport psychology* (2nd ed.), pp. 672–691. New York: Wiley & Sons.

Troutman, K., & Dufur, M. (2007). From high school jocks to college grads: Assessing the long-term effects of high school sport participation on females' educational attainment. *Youth & Society, 38*(4), 443–462.

UCI. (2019). Inside UCI: Women's professional road cycling enters a new dimension in 2020 [Press release].https://www.uci.org/inside-uci/press-releases/women's-professional-road-cycling-enters-a-new-dimension-in-2020.

Witnauer, W., Rogers, R., & Saint Onge, J. (2007). Major League Baseball career length in the twentieth century. *Population Research and Policy Review, 26*(4), 371–386.

CHAPTER 36

··

SPORT, LABOR, AND
MIGRATION

··

GYŐZŐ MOLNÁR

IT is reasonable to argue that the history of humans is, by and large, also the history of migrations. Why people migrated and still migrate, the development and decline of migratory routes/patterns, the multiplicity of conditions migrants faced in their original local and face in their new settings, and to what extent migrants may or may not assimilate into their new culture are essential to understanding the development of societies and people (Samers, 2010). Arguably, people have always migrated and will always migrate (de Haas, Castles, & Miller, 2020). However, there might be qualitative differences between pre-European extension wonderings and the premeditated movement (whether voluntary or forced) of people from an identified or identifiable location to target areas with specific purpose. In this chapter, migration refers to peoples' premeditated movements and is understood as a "multifaceted, highly complex phenomenon, touching many aspects of modern life" (Marshall, 2006, p. 3).

According to Stalker (1994, 2000), most migrations of today are associated with the idea of the international labor market, and so we can easily connect work (labor) and migration. In fact, there is a plethora of evidence showing that people frequently migrate for work-related reasons, either because of the availability of better work conditions in the target country or because of withering options in the domestic space (for recent statistics, see International Labour Organisation, 2020). While it is a sensible and well-versed approach to understand and explain migrations based on connections between people and economic capital, it is also limiting and places a dominant, if not exclusive, emphasis on the financial gains to be had through mobility. Such approaches have been supported by a range of theoretical perspectives, such as neo-imperialism theory, dependency theory, and world system theory (de Haas et al., 2020). While these are useful and we cannot deny the significance of financial gains, such monocausal depictions of the complex tapestry of global as well as local migrations may not capture all essential aspects of every migratory venture. A good case in point may be found in the recent waves of forced migration through the Mediterranean Sea to many European countries (Bierbach, 2019), many instances of which have been subject to controversial public narratives and are not directly connected to economic gains.

It might be reasonable to argue that such finance-driven approaches have always enjoyed prominence as, when we talk of migrations, we are often presented with statistics and maps (BBC, 2014) which portray how migrations play out in terms of influx, emigration, and net migrations. Based on those statistics, we can determine a country's role in the migratory process, which may be characterized as receiver, donor, or transitional. Such insight is useful for politicians and policymakers to assess their country's migratory status and decide whether it is best to shut down, restrict, or encourage migratory flows. In terms of governmental reactions to migrations, Samers (2010) notes the example of how fortifying the Spanish border at Ceuta and Melilla in 2005, as a consequence of increasing immigration from Morocco and a directive from the European Union, affected migratory patterns and experiences. To illustrate changes in migratory experiences, Samers refers to media reporting from 2007, describing the drowning of 47 illegal migrants. While this example is pertinent to understanding how migrations are and can be connected to nation-state and supranational organizations' politics, it also demonstrates that migrants are more than just mere numbers, statistical figures, or lines on a map who move across territories and oceans for a range of reasons. Therefore, to fully understand migration as both a process and an experience, going beyond a macro-analysis is essential.

Although adopting a migrant-centered approach to migration is desirable (Sinatti, 2019), it is not without challenges. There are contemporary examples wherein migration and its reduction were offered as a solution to overpopulation and/or, recently, to restore national security and national pride. Populist political parties have exploited public resentment of rising multiculturalism to blame the immigrant "other" for the various ills of their nation (Yılmaz, 2012). Recent populist political narratives have reduced migrants to mere numbers and turned them into what Adams (2000) calls the "absent referent" in relation to animals. It is the process, when applied to migration, through which the individual migrant, regardless of age, gender, race, religion, and so on, becomes an objective, depersonified number, with the resultant effect being rising tendencies for us to forget that, hidden within those statistical narratives, there are real people with real feelings, desires, and hopes. Such dehumanization, coupled with scapegoating, have played a significant role in the United Kingdom's Brexit referendum and, arguably, shifted the vote toward the "leave" side. It is then possible to argue that, in the recent and (at the time of writing) still ongoing Brexit debate and broader populist political context, migration has become much more than an economic cost-benefit question and has been elevated to the level of national security and identity. More important and, pertinent to the content of this chapter, contemporary, politicized migratory narratives demonstrate that (1) migration and related sociocultural issues are still relevant and capture the public's attention; (2) migrations are connected to and influenced by broader social, cultural, political, and economic processes; and (3) our understanding of migration and its multiple consequences requires continuous examination as our complex global-local sociocultural tapestries evolve. Sensitive to these matters, I offer an overview of sport labor migration research, focusing on issues, approaches, and debates.

ISSUES

One of the issues that relates to sport migration research is the general social perception of Western sports in many cultural domains. Similar to the majority of mainstream sociology textbooks and, in fact, mainstream sociology per se, we may decide to marginalize the importance of sport in relation to everyday life and reinforce the traditional and, I believe, dated thinking that sport is separate from society or, at best, sport mirrors society. These types of perceptions are anchored in assessments that underestimate the sociocultural significance of sport and related leisure activities and likely play a role in why the standing of sociology of sport, and other sport-focused subdisciplines, has tended to lag behind parent disciplines. This prejudice is perhaps also the reason, or one of the reasons, why the academic field that explores links between migration and sport began to emerge around the late 1980s to early 1990s, as opposed to the general migratory literature which may be dated to as early as the beginning of 1900s (see Ferenczi, 1929). While I cannot specifically pinpoint the beginning of general migratory research, Ferenczi's work indicates that it began long before we turned our attention to sport migrations.

We can hypothesize that one of the reasons for sport migratory research's relative infancy is the lack of sport-specific migrations in the early 1900s. This may appear to be a reasonable argument, but historical evidence suggests that sport and people traveled together even during those times (Lanfranchi & Taylor, 2001). In fact, pioneers of sport migration were instrumental in spreading and establishing sport across the globe (Fox, 2003). In relation to football, Lanfranchi and Taylor (2001, p. 3) noted that the migration of footballers was "fundamentally bound up with general migration patterns." Perhaps then we could argue that early sport migrations had little to no social significance and, thus, remained unnoticed or negligible. Again, we have evidence to suggest that as Western sports spread, they often had significant interactions with local cultures. Sometimes sport was a "good fit" from the outset, such as how rugby morphed into the everyday culture of many Pacific Island nations (Molnar & Kanemasu, 2014). At other times, sport's introduction caused a national uproar against the physically violent foreign practices that were spreading, much to the detriment of local values and cultural practices. A good example here is the Hungarian Parliament's reaction at the early sight of football-related violence (Handler, 1985). It very well may be that our general, traditionally held perception that sports are beneficial to society, and to anyone involved with them, is responsible for sport migratory research's relative infancy. Sports have been perceived and employed as social glue, rehabilitative tool, health-improving activity, creator and rebuilder of (national and other types of) identity, and, generally, an essential element in the development and maintenance of successful societies through social solidarity. Many governments, politicians, and political regimes used and still use sports for nation-building purposes (Bairner & Molnar, 2010; Molnar & Whigham, 2021). Yet we often have an uncritical, functionalist perception of modern, Western sports (Molnar & Kelly, 2013), which, I would argue, is responsible for the gap between the studies of sport and their parent disciplines, the lack of critical dominant narratives around sports, and the relative infancy of sport labor migration research.

Another issue in sport migration research has been the dominance of football-related work. When I contributed a chapter (Molnar & Faulkner, 2016) to the *Routledge Handbook on Football Studies*, the amount of work accumulated on football migration was overwhelming. The chapter did not adopt a systematic review approach, but in light of that work, I think it safe to say that football has dominated and still dominates sport migration research. The dominance of football in research carried out within the remit of social sciences was also recognized by the Research Excellence Framework 2014 (2015, p. 117) panel (a U.K.-based government organization responsible for accessing research excellence in universities), noting that "the sub-panel [Sport and Exercise Sciences, Leisure and Tourism] did express some concern that much of the focus of this research has become concentrated in only a few sports, most notably football." This observation, I think, is pertinent for future migration-centered researchers to consider. There is a clear need to decentralize football from migration studies and seek out opportunities to explore migratory tendencies and experiences in other sports and physical activities as well.

In addition to sport labor migration research having an almost unrelenting focus on football, there is a tendency for research to be monodisciplinary and for studies to be dominated by scatings in history, sociology, human geography, or anthropology. All of these disciplines have their traditions, strengths, and favored research paradigms, yet I think there is a need for engaging with multiple disciplines and theoretical perspectives simultaneously. Similar calls have been made in other areas of sport and physical activity studies, which herald both the challenges and benefits of theoretical and disciplinary diversification (Bouffard & Spencer-Cavaliere, 2016). In the field of migration studies, an example of going beyond disciplinary silos is represented by the work of Engh, Settler, and Agergaard (2017), who adopted an intersectionality-informed approach to their research in exploring the experiences of athletes in relation to their gender, race, and sport. Here, there is evidence of fruitful engagement with critical feminist and racialization theories, as Engh and colleagues made sense of the experiences of Nigerian female footballers in Scandinavian countries. This work is particularly pertinent as it does not simply demonstrate the advantages of employing intersectionality but also provides impetus for critically engaging current and emerging political narratives in Europe that tend to favor and envision white, patriarchal Christian values as dominant and favorable (Fernández-García & Luengo, 2018).

As another major trend in sport migration research has been the dominance of men, here too Engh et al.'s (2017) research, albeit indirectly, points toward the need to consider having more women on both sides of the migratory research platform, as researchers and participants. Male dominance is clear in relation to studying both athletes and types of sports given attention. With few exceptions, Kanemasu and Molnar (2019) note that men have dominated this field as researchers, which might, to some extent, explain the pre-occupation with football and male athletes. Women conducting research in the field of migration have not only begun to address this gender imbalance but have broadened the spectrum of migratory research. Examples include exploring handball (Agergaard, 2008), winter sports (Thorpe, 2014, 2017), as well as Japanese (Edwards, 2018) and Taiwanese (Jiang & Lee, 2016) women's sporting experiences. By engaging with different cultures, different sports, and intersectionality-informed approaches, women academics have helped the field diversify both theoretically as well as empirically.

Finally, in light of the needs identified by Spaaij et al.'s (2019) recent review of sport, refugees, and forced migration literature—to go beyond the dominance of instrumentalist approaches, to engage diverse innovative methods, to reconsider ethical relationships with research participants, and to decolonizing postures embedded in research—I suggest that a key issue for and ethical responsibility of academics interested in sport labor migration to ponder is their relation to research participants. Spaaij et al.'s findings, and my recent collaborative work (Kanemasu & Molnar, 2019), suggest that the inherent power imbalances in research, so often manifested between researchers and participants, are not well recognized, and neither are they well-articulated. Whether we consider power inequalities as Euro/Western-centric bias, neocolonial knowledge production, Western research paradigm reproduction or othering, they all point to the complexity of power matrices that envelop metropolitan epistemology-informed research and, thus, to the majority of research that has focused on sport labor migration. Gegeo (2001, p. 182) posed a pertinent question regarding Western knowledge systems and their relation to local knowledge(s) in the Pacific: "What good is political independence if we remain colonised epistemologically?" Indeed, researchers should consider their epistemic responsibility (Carlson, 2010) and as such continuously ponder: What is the point of future research around sport, labor, and migration if knowledge is predominantly generated from a uniform perspective that may arguably be in line with the viewing of research participants as exotic, foreign noble savages. Of course, some migrants do come from Western countries, but not all of them. However, we, researchers and academics (here I also include the majority of my previous work on sport labor migration), seem to apply the same straitjacketed approach to exploring and representing their experiences regardless of their culture and country of origin. In doing so, we remain in control of the entire research process and narrative, and we are often the ones reaping the benefits of the research's outcomes (Kanemasu & Molnar, 2019). These aspects of Western-practice-informed research create and maintain power imbalances that cannot be overcome by seeking and gaining informed consent in the traditional fashion (Spaaij et al., 2019). Kanemasu and Molnar (2019) noted that such practices, including disregard for inherent power differentials in research, have the tendency to reduce our participants to research commodities who, through our systematic and colonizing academic work, remain typecast due to our framings within the *sport research production complex* as oppressed, marginalized, and exploited.

APPROACHES

In this section, I briefly review what I consider to be key theoretical approaches and their relation to sport labor migration. For this purpose, I limit consideration to four main theories, namely Marxism, cultural studies, process sociology, and transnational mobility. While my selection and grouping of migration theories may appear truncated given that the theoretical field is much richer (Brettell & Hollifield, 2000), I, to some extent, follow Bale and Maguire's (1994) approach to theory identification. At the outset of sport labor migration research, Bale and Maguire identified four main theories: modernization, (neo-)imperialism, dependency, and world system theory. This grouping was useful and still provides valuable pointers to identify key theoretical threads and work embedded in them; however, sport migration research has progressed, which means that some of the previously separated theories now form an overlap and that there are new perspectives to consider. However, I would argue that many of the key theories that have been implemented in explaining sport migrations derive from or are connected to thinking that is embedded in classical roots, which, to some extent, informs the categories presented below.

Marxism-Informed Approaches

A Marxist view perceives sport as one of the tools of capitalism for exploiting and oppressing the proletariat. That is, Marxist scholars argue against the (functionalist) myth of sport that exists in contemporary societies cultivating a type of physical activity that is beneficial and mainly consists of play-like characteristics. Rather, they pose that sport and labor are structurally analogous, exploitative, and marginalizing (Rigauer, 1981). Marxists strictly distinguish between the features and functions of sport and play and argue that sport is essentially a product of capitalism (Brohm, 1978; Ingham, 2004; Ingham & Loy, 1973) that incorporates the achievement principle, result rationalization, specialization, bureaucratization, quantification, and an obsession with records (Guttmann, 1978). In this sense, athletes, just like other workers, sell the fruits of their labor and talent to the bourgeoisie for a wage. Here, the product is athletic performance that can be recorded, quantified, and evaluated. So, to add to Brohm's (1978) argument, sport is not only a prison of measured time but the penitentiary of capitalist production values, class struggles, and supply and demand.

To understand migration from a Marxist-informed perspective, academics engaged dependency (Baran, 1973) and world system (Wallerstein, 1974) theories as well as (neo-) imperialist explanations (Cashman, 1980; Mangan, 1986). These theories depict power imbalances between colonizers and colonized, and compartmentalize the countries of the world into certain (e.g., two or three) regions and support the idea of economic and political regionalization and movement of people from less to more developed geographic locations. Arguably, in relation to sport migration, Wallerstein's (1974) world system theory has been broadly used to explain the global flow of human capital from the periphery to the core. Specifically, the early work of Bale (1989, 2003) and Bale and Sang (1996) has pointed to some significant economic factors in athletic labor force migration. Bale (2003, p. 107) observed that "modern sport is a part of the entertainment industry [and] as profit and commercialisation have become increasingly prevalent in Western sport, so sport clubs have engaged in a number of geographical readjustments." One of these "geographical readjustments" has widened clubs' geographical area of recruitment, leading to an increasing flow of athletes from non-Western to Western countries, caused by financial differentials. To this category I would also add work carried out by scholars such as Poli (2006, 2010) and Darby (2013). This approach, and work embedded in it, has been useful to highlight migration trends, talent pipelines, global inequalities, and various forms of exploitation. In particular, Darby's (e.g., 2002, 2010, 2013) work has been influential in terms of revealing the exploitative potential of Global North–South economic power inequalities in terms of African footballers.

Cultural Studies–Informed Approaches

Cultural studies, an approach closely linked to Marxist tradition, is not defined or dominated by one methodological or theoretical position and is often considered to be a bricolage of disciplines and ideas (Hall, 1992). Cultural studies scholars focus on developing systematic and critical analysis of cultures and people's experience within (Hargreaves & McDonald, 2000). Culture is an ever-evolving tapestry of power matrices where people and their cultural values are in continuous conflict for domination. From this perspective, the main concern is to identify, explain, and challenge dominant and oppressive cultural practices (not that different from what was described in the previous subsection). Western sports are part of the dominant culture(s) and has moved from a local, national level to a global stage (Bairner, 2001). In this sense, sport has been influenced by and has impacted numerous cultures (see Klein, 1991) and has the tendency to reinforce global, cultural inequality and economic disparity, but can also act as a site of resistance.

A particularly useful review of existing sport migration literature has been conducted by Smith, Spaaij, and McDonald (2019) to explore present work that connects migration and cultural capital. They identified four key connections between migration and cultural capital: (1) participating in mainstream sports/physical activity has increased migrants' cultural capital and helped assimilation in the host environment; (2) participating in ethno-specific sports/physical activity has aided the reinforcement and preservation of migrants' original cultural identity; (3) migrants have also negotiated their cultural capital, which was essentially a balancing act between points 1 and 2, by both producing destination-country-specific cultural capital and maintaining their original ethnic identity; and (4) cultural capital can also act as a barrier to assimilation when, for instance, there is a clash between mainstream and ethnocultures. In addition to being thorough, Smith et al.'s (2019) review of 45 research papers indicated the importance of cultural studies in unpacking the complex connections between migrations and cultures and the applicability of concepts such as cultural capital and hegemony. To this category, I would add the work of Kanemasu and Molnar (2013, 2014), who in many instances employed Wallerstein's (2004) world system theory—a revised and updated conception that takes culture into consideration and expresses clear awareness of the cultural domination and oppression that is performed by core, metropolitan countries—to explain economic and cultural inequalities, as well as cultural resistance experienced and enacted by migrant Fijian rugby players during and after their professional career.

Process Sociology–Informed Approaches

This sociological approach is informed by the work of Norbert Elias and grew in popularity through the work of Eric Dunning and his students. This perspective views sport as part of long-term sociocultural processes which have been interconnectedly shaping our societies. According to process sociology, Western societies follow a civilizing process in their development that drives societies to become more civilized and less (physically) violent. The civilizing process can be interrupted by decivilizing spurts, creating decreased appreciation for values and practices previously upheld (Dunning, 2002). Modern sports and related migrations are an optimal example of such long-term global and cultural interchanges; that is, "sport is a significant touchstone of prevailing global, national and local patterns of interchange" (Maguire, 1999, p. 76). Therefore, the worldwide spread of modern sports, and people along with it, has been understood as part of long-term historical processes that began to emerge around the mid-19th century as part of Western industrialization (Elias & Dunning, 1986; Maguire, 1999). As modern sports diffused from England to other countries, mainly between the second half of the 19th and first half of the 20th centuries (Elias, 1986), the significance of sport-related migrations began first to manifest, then to increase. In essence, from this perspective migrations are considered as part of larger historical and sociocultural processes such as globalization and, thus, are complex, multifaceted experiences.

Writing from this perspective, Maguire (1994, 1995, 1996) has been both pioneering and influential. Maguire explored basketball, cricket, ice hockey, rugby, and football, thereby enriching the smorgasbord of sports to be considered as the foci of migratory research. He also introduced typologies to the field of sport migration. While those sport migrant categories and categorizations have been questioned (more on this in the next section), those have made a contribution to our understanding of different migrants and migrations (Molnar & Maguire, 2008). Another contribution of process sociology has been to theorize the globalization of sport and related migrations through the concept of diminishing contrasts and increasing varieties (Maguire, 1999). This approach has helped flesh out the phenomena of the global diffusion and differential popularization of sports. This concept depicts the sport-cultural interchanges between different nations, indicating two-way, interactive processes between Western and non-Western cultures. Western societies attempt to introduce and imprint specific values onto outsider groups, but a concurrent reaction comes from the outsider (non-Western) groups as well. "As a result of this cultural interchange, outsider, non-Western codes and customs began to permeate back into Western societies" (Maguire, 1999, p. 44). The form and degree of interaction between established and outsider societies (cf. Baran, 1973) depends on various factors, which are to be concurrently and case-specifically considered. For instance, dominant, Western nations introduced both the forms and the ethos of sport to outsider populations. These outsider, subordinate populations sometimes adopted only the sport or the ethos, and other times adopted both, depending on the culture of the specific subordinate population and its relations to the dominant groups. What is particularly useful here is not only the recognition of cultural exchanges through and within sport but also in recognizing the power matrices that develop between donor and host countries in an ever-transforming global context (Maguire, 2005).

Transnational Mobility–Informed Approaches

This approach emerged from the discipline of anthropology around the 1970s, when anthropologists began to more broadly embrace the concept and phenomenon of migration and extended their attention to metropolitan societies (Brettell & Hollifield, 2000). While this turn helped different theoretical explanations arise and advanced anthropological concerns in the analysis of world social order, the approach was often perceived to be more constraining than enabling. Consequently, a sense of dissatisfaction with applying macro-approaches to migration emerged. Brettell (2000, p. 104) argued that such macro-analyses did not perceive migrants "as active agents but as passive reactors manipulated by the world capitalist system." To overcome the limitations of previous approaches and, to some extent, the host-donor country binary, interpretations adopting transnationalist perspectives began to take center stage. The work of Glick Schiller, Basch, and Blanc (1992) and Basch, Glick Schiller, and Blanc (1994) is frequently cited as seminal in advancing meaningful debates around transnationalism and its connection to migration. These debates questioned the extent to which migrants' experiences and mobilities may still be reasonably considered through "uprooting" and "regrounding" concepts (Ahmed, Castaneda, Fortier, & Sheller, 2003) and not through more fluid interpretations of home and receiving environments. As a critique of the host-donor bipolar model of perceiving migration, transnationalist perspectives acknowledge that by relying on various global networks of technology, migrants often maintain their connections with their country of origin and previous host countries, thereby enhancing their ability to "move" freely between various geographic locations. In doing so, migrants may experience space, place, and mobility based on their individual circumstances and connections. Transnational mobility thus indicates a shift away from perceiving migrants as "bounded units" (Brettell, 2000), and while there is a clear recognition of the agency of the individual migrant, it is also considered that those actions are enveloped in national identity and international politics (Castles & Miller, 2009).

In relation to sport labor migration, this theoretical approach has been so far underutilized in comparison to other perspectives. However, there are good examples of engagement with transnationalism to explain sport-related mobility. Perhaps the most significant deployment of transnationalism has been made by Carter (e.g., 2007, 2011), who approached sport migrations from an anthropological perspective. While the importance of networks in explaining social mobility were also recognized by Poli (2006, 2010), and arguably Maguire also explored such aspects of migrations through the concept of social figurations, it was initially Carter's work that explicitly used this approach. The benefit of interpreting sport migration through this theoretical lens is that the spectrum of analysis is broadened. For instance, there is a clear move away from giving exclusive centrality to migrating athletes, and more attention is paid to other components of the migratory dynamics, such as family networks (Carter, 2007), along with recognizing that other sport professionals (e.g., coaches) can and have migrated to enhance their career. Importance is given too to people who engage with and experience migration, as opposed to depicting them as passive dupes in top-down processes and flows. Carter (2011, p. 11) offers an extensive critique of existing approaches to sport migration and suggests a research direction that is informed by anthropology and transnationalism with a view to bring about "a more dynamic articulated space in which theories about the cultural insinuation called 'sport' will become more nuanced and less blinded by presumptions of historical pre-eminence, cultural superiority . . . that reduce people to cardboard cut-outs." Given transnational mobility's emphasis on the individual's experience and how that is bound up in globalization, technological development, and cultural interchanges, transnational mobility–informed approaches have recently been gaining momentum in sport labor migration research (e.g., Engh & Agergaard, 2015; Faulkner, Molnar, & Kohe, 2019; Thorpe, 2014, 2017) and have the potential to become broadly recognized and utilized.

DEBATES

As typologies of migration in the realm of sport studies have received controversial attention and some typologies have been contested, in this section I explore debates that revolve around the use and significance of migration typologies in sport labor migration research. In doing so, I offer a brief overview of some of the migration typologies and note that if we recognize the utility of ideal-type description of migrants, then there is a need for a more extensive engagement with the general migration literature to draw upon already existing categories and concepts as opposed to (re)inventing sport specific ones.

The migration of workers (athletes) usually follows certain patterns. These patterns can create so-called talent/migratory pipelines, networks, or routes, through which individuals can move and/or be recruited. For example, Maguire, Jarvie, Mansfield, and Bradley (2002, p. 27) write that "after the people's revolution of 1989 and the subsequent 'opening up' of

Eastern Europe, Hungarians, Czechs, Slovakians and Romanians moved west—creating a talent pipeline." Such connections, regardless of what they are called, are essential between host and donor countries and are indicators of international migratory movements. By mapping migratory patterns we can also identify reasons for and motivational forces behind migrations. For instance, based on the example of post–Iron Curtain migrations, we could observe the development of migratory flows from East to West for work-related purposes, mostly for gaining economic benefits. Initially, many of these migrants embarked on their journey to profit from the reopening of borders (Wallace & Stola, 2001) and, thus, may be referred to as *target earners* with a view to return to their country of origin. The arrival of labor migrants in one country may in tandem contribute to the relative *de-skilling* of donor countries (Klein, 1991), as well as stimulating varied local reactions to the increased presence of foreign influx. Therefore, migrants' stories and experiences can be complex. Indeed, in many instances, they can be unpredictable, influenced by the fluidity of migration routes and wrapped up in local, regional, and global politics (de Haas et al., 2020). Additionally, the migratory intentions of individuals can, and often do, change. The many migrants' stories in Sorhaindo and Pattullo's (2009) collection reveal how some of the Dominican migrants may not have envisioned a long stay in their chosen host country, but then remained there for decades. This collection of stories also highlights that migration-related experiences often do not end with returning to the homeland and that migration may have a longer reach that includes returnees and retired athletes as well (see also Kanemasu & Molnar, 2014). Therefore, I would argue that to garner an initial and broad understanding of the complexity of migrations, certain migration patterns, practices, and motivational forces, the creation of migration typologies can be a useful heuristic device to provide a state-of-play representation. This is perhaps the reason why migration typologies have been developed since the 1950s and have multiple variants.

Petersen (1958) may be credited for one of the earliest migration typologies, including categories such as *primitive, impelled, forced, free,* and *mass.* Not long after, from an anthropological standpoint, de Gonzales (1961) identified types of laborers in the Caribbean region as *seasonal, nonseasonal, temporary, recurrent, continuous,* and *permanent.* In Du Toit's (1975) work we find references to *weekly commuters, seasonal/circular movers, permanently displaced,* and *sojourners.* In Tilly's (1990) history-informed writing there are mentions of *colonizing, coerced, circular, chain,* and *career* migrants. Düvel and Vogel (2006) developed their typologies on Polish migrants, and Iredale (2008) on professional migrants. This is only a small representation of the different typologies from the general migration literature, but what they all do is present an overview of migrations in a given era and geographic area, which is both beneficial and limiting. In relation to sport, it was Maguire (1996) who introduced typologies of migrant athletes, which helped map the field and included *pioneers, mercenaries, settlers, nomads,* and *returnees.* These categories were later contested by Magee and Sugden (2002), who introduced new types to explain their data. In a similar vein, Molnar and Maguire (2008) introduced a typology that was informed by primary evidence and previous general migration typologies, such as Tilly's (1990) work.

These classifications of migrants present in the literature reflect and reinforce certain patterns, motivational forces, and issues that surround the sphere of labor migration as well as the limitations of this approach. Consequently, when it concerns migration typologies, I would argue that they are a useful but not flawless way of approaching migrations. Typologies are useful to develop an initial understanding of specific areas of migration (e.g., sport and professional migrants or refuges); aid general assessment of migratory tendencies and issues; help shape migration-related policies; identify general issues that migrants and host, transit and donor countries may experience before, during, and after migrations; and serve as a springboard for future research inquiries. On the other hand, migration typologies can be overly rigid and simplistic representations of the fluidity and complexity of migratory experiences, dismissive of individual iteration of migratory stories, and bound to historical eras and geographic locations. Therefore, to successfully deploy typologies, I suggest that we continuously revisit existing categories and change/revise those as and when necessary; ensure that classifications are informed by appropriate primary and/or secondary evidence, develop connections between evidence and theory to underpin migration typologies, and clearly express that a typology is not another term for "absent referent," and neither are a migrant's experiences often "stuck" or wholly contained within one category but rather more typically can transition from one category to another(s) as their journey unfolds. With specific regard to sport-focused research, I would also suggest a greater level of engagement with the broader, general migratory literature, which features a more extensive history of carefully developing and effectively deploying migration typologies.

CONCLUSION

In sum, it can be observed that despite sports, migrations, and cultures being inherently interconnected long before academics took notice and saw evidence that the general migration literature could be more extensively utilized in sport migration research, the field began to demonstrate growth in the 1980s, developed a good deal of momentum in the 1990s, and has significantly broadened after 2000. Essentially, in the past four decades, researchers have generated an impressive and extensive body of literature. This literature has deployed a range of theories, used different sources of evidence and data collection methodologies, explored diverse sporting contexts, and considered the experiences of people from different national, gender, and cultural identity backgrounds. Hence, it is safe to say that what we have at present is a still-evolving but vibrant academic area that has made significant contributions to knowledge generation and increased our understanding of the sociocultural significance of sports, not only in Western societies but across the globe.

However, based on the issues, approaches, and debates I have presented, there are some shortcomings in the field, and thus careful consideration should be given within sport labor migration research to place more emphasis on broadening the array of sporting contexts that typically garner focus in migration research. Specifically, decentering football from the foci of sport labor migration research could be a useful strategy to consider, so that more space is allotted to other areas and activities. Accompanying this, there seems to be clear evidence about the benefits of adopting interdisciplinary approaches and decolonizing research practices. While interdisciplinary collaborative work may be considered complicated and demanding, as we can find it challenging to part with our disciplinary assumptions (Szostak, 2014), the benefits of such integrative approaches are multiple and "interdisciplinary conversations are productive and have the potential to address complex problems" (Bouffard & Spencer-Cavaliere, 2016, p. 11). I contend that the field of sport labor migration would greatly benefit from increasing interdisciplinary, collaborative research given that the subject is culturally complex and both empirically and epistemically diverse.

Epistemic diversity is particularly pertinent to take note of in relation to how we perceive and pursue research. Here, I heed the suggestions of Spaaij et al.'s (2019) review prompting future sport labor migration researchers to consider adopting more varied, ethically balanced, and responsible approaches. A key aspect of such a research approach would be that the researcher's voice does not reign supreme (Kanemasu & Molnar, 2019), and neither do academic texts distort, marginalize, or exclude the knowledge(s) and perspectives of our research participants (Ortner, 1995). To strive for research that is more participant-oriented and emancipatory is our epistemic responsibility, which is connected to our epistemic authority (Carlson, 2010). We researchers, academics, and journal editors have epistemic authority to define and identify what counts as acceptable and legitimate knowledge and are in a position to authoritatively speak of such knowledge. In this sense, and in supporting Spaaij et al.'s (2019) observation, it is our epistemic responsibility to recognize, reflect on, and systematically challenge traditional Western-based academic research practices that continuously marginalize, even silence, participants' words and their knowledge(s), which should be in a position to play a more central role in the work we produce.

In this light, I would encourage all researchers to continually revisit their own and others' work and ponder the pertinent and perennial questions posed by Ingham and Donnelly (1990, p. 58) in relation to the sociology of sport, which in its contemporary practice cuts across disciplines and subdisciplines: "Knowledge from whom and for whom? knowledge for what ends? whose interests influence the perception of what is really useful knowledge?" and "whose knowledge counts?" When we see these questions as guiding principles for research that focus on, in this case, labor migration, we can develop the potential to not only return to meaning but to return meaning to our work as social scientists (Alvesson, Gabriel, & Paulsen, 2017).

References

Adams, J. C. (2000). *The sexual politics of meat*. New York: Continuum.

Agergaard, S. (2008). Elite athletes as migrants in Danish women's handball. *International Review for the Sociology of Sport, 43*(1), 5–19.

Ahmed, S., Castaneda, C., Fortier, A.-M., & Sheller, M. (Eds.). (2003). *Uprootings/regroundings: Questions of home and migration*. Oxford: Berg.

Alvesson, M., Gabriel, Y., & Paulsen, R. (2017). *Return to meaning: A social science with something to say*. Oxford: Oxford University Press.

Bairner, A. (2001). *Sport, nationalism, and globalisation: European and American perspectives*. Albany: State University of New York Press.

Bairner, A., & Molnar, G. (Eds.). (2010). *Politics of the Olympics: A survey*. London: Routledge.

Bale, J. (1989). *Sports geography*. London: E. and F. N. Spon.

Bale, J. (2003). *Sports geography* (2nd ed.). London: Routledge.

Bale, J., & Maguire, J. (Eds.). (1994). *The global sports arena: Athletics talent migration in an interdependent world*. London: Frank Cass.

Bale, J., & Sang, J. (1996). *Kenyan running: Movement culture, geography and global change*. London: Frank Cass.

Baran, P. (1973). *The political economy of growth*. London: Penguin Books.

Basch, L., Glick Schiller, N., & Blanc, C. S. (1994). *Nations unbound: Transnational projects, postcolonial predicaments, and deterritorialized nation-states*. Utrecht: Gordon and Breach Publisher.

BBC. (2014, September 15). Mapping Mediterranean migration. https://www.bbc.co.uk/news/world-europe-24521614.

Bierbach, M. (2019). Migration to Europe in 2019: Facts and figures. *InfoMigrants*. https://www.infomigrants.net/en/post/21811/migration-to-europe-in-2019-facts-and-figures.

Bouffard, M., & Spencer-Cavaliere, N. (2016). Interdisciplinarity in adapted physical activity. *Quest, 68*, 4–14.

Brettell, C. B. (2000). Theorising migration in anthropology. In C. B. Brettell & J. F. Hollifield (Eds.), *Migration theory: Talking across disciplines* (pp. 97–135). London: Routledge.

Brettell, C. B., & Hollifield, J. F. (Eds). (2000). *Migration theory: Talking across disciplines*. London: Routledge.

Brohm, J.-M. (1978). *Sport: A prison of measured time*. London: Ink Links.

Carlson, L. (2010). Who's the expert? Rethinking authority in the face of intellectual disability. *Journal of Intellectual Disability Research, 45*(1), 58–65.

Carter, F. T. (2007). Family networks, state interventions and the experience of Cuban sport migration. *International Review for the Sociology of Sport, 45*(4), 371–390.

Carter, F. T. (2011). Replacing sport migrants: Moving beyond the institutional structures informing international migration. *International Review for the Sociology of Sport, 48*(1), 66–82.

Cashman, R. (1980). *Patrons, players and the crowd: The phenomenon of Indian cricket*. Bombay: Longman Orient.

Castles, S., & Miller, M. J. (2009). *The age of migration* (4th ed.). Basingstoke, U.K.: Palgrave Macmillan.

Darby, P. (2002). *Africa, football and FIFA: Politics, colonialism and resistance*. London: Frank Cass.

Darby, P. (2010). "Go outside": The history, economics and geography of Ghanaian football labour migration. *African Historical Review, 42*(1): 19–41.

Darby, P. (2013). Moving players, traversing perspectives: Global value chains, production networks and Ghanaian football labour migration. *Geoforum, 50*, 43–53.

de Gonzalez, N. L. S. (1961). Family organization in five types of migratory wage labor, *American Anthropologist, 63*, 1264–1280.

de Haas, H., Castles, S., & Miller, J. M. (2020). *The age of migration* (6th ed.). London: Red Globe Press.

Dunning, E. (2002). Figurational contribution to the sociological study of sport. In J. Maguire & K. Young (Eds.), *Theory, sport and society* (pp. 211–238). Oxford: Elsevier.

Du Toit, B. (1975). A decision-making model for the study of migration. In B. Du Toit & H. I. Safa (Eds.), *Migration and urbanization: Models and adaptive strategies* (pp. 49–74). The Hague: Mouton.

Düvell, F., & Vogel, D. (2006). Polish migrants: Tensions between sociological typologies and state categories. In A. Triandafyllidou (Ed.), *Contemporary Polish migration in Europe* (pp. 267–289). Lampeter, PA: Edwin Mellen Press.

Edwards, E. (2018). Migration and laws of contagion: Cultivating talent in Japanese women's soccer. *Japanese Studies, 38*(1), 39–56.

Elias, N. (1986). The genesis of sport as a sociological problem. In N. Elias & E. Dunning (Eds.), *Quest for excitement: Sport and leisure in the civilising process* (pp. 126–149). Oxford: Blackwell.

Elias, N., & Dunning, E. (Eds.). (1986). *Quest for excitement: Sport and leisure in the civilising process*. Oxford: Blackwell.

Engh, M. H., & Agergaard, S. (2015). Producing mobility through locality and visibility: Developing a transnational perspective on sports labour migration. *International Review for the Sociology of Sport, 50*(8), 974–992. https://doi.org/10.1177/1012690213509994.

Engh, M. H., Settler, F., & Agergaard, S. (2017). "The ball and rhythm in her blood": Racialized imaginaries and football migration from Nigeria to Scandinavia. *Ethnicities, 17*(1), 66–84.

Faulkner, C., Molnar, G., & Kohe, G. (2019). "I just go on Wi-Fi": Imagining worlds through professional basketball migrants' deployment of information and communication technology. *Journal of Sport and Social Issues, 43*(3), 195–218.

Ferenczi, I. (1929). *International migrations*. Vol. 1. New York: National Bureau of Economic Research.

Fernández-García, B., & Luengo, O. G. (2018). Populist parties in Western Europe: An analysis of the three core elements of populism. *Communication & Society, 31*(3), 57–76.

Fox, N. (2003). *Prophet or traitor? The Jimmy Hogan story*. Manchester, U.K.: Parrs Wood Press.

Gegeo, D. W. (2001). (Re)visioning knowledge transformation in the Pacific: A response to Subramani's "The Oceanic Imaginary." *The Contemporary Pacific, 13*(1), 178–183.

Glick Schiller, N., Basch, L., & Blanc, C. S. (Eds.). (1992). *Towards a transnational perspective on migration: Race, class, ethnicity and nationalism reconsidered*. New York: New York Academy of Sciences.

Guttmann, A. (1978). *From ritual to record*. New York: Columbia University Press.

Hall, S. (1992). The question of cultural identity. In S. Hall, D. Held, & A. McGrew (Eds.), *Modernity and its futures* (pp. 273–325). Cambridge, U.K.: Polity Press.

Handler, A. (1985). *From the ghetto to the games: Jewish athletes in Hungary*. Boulder, CO: East European Monographs.

Hargreaves, J., & McDonald, I. (2000). Cultural studies and the sociology of sport. In J. Coakley & E. Dunning (Eds.), *Handbook of sport studies* (pp. 48–61). London: Sage.

Ingham, A. G. (2004). The sportification process: A biographical analysis framed by the work of Marx, Weber, Durkheim and Freud. In R. Giulianotti (Ed.), *Sport and modern social theorists* (pp. 11–32). London: Palgrave.

Ingham, A. G., & Donnelly, P. (1990). Whose knowledge counts? The production of knowledge and issues of application in the sociology of sport. *Sociology of Sport Journal, 7*, 58–65.

Ingham, A. G., & Loy, J. W. (1973). The social system of sport: A humanistic perspective. *Quest, 19*(Winter), 3–23.

International Labour Organisation. (2020). *World employment and social outlook: Trends 2020*. Geneva: International Labour Office.

Iredale, R. (2008). The migration of professionals: Theories and typologies. *International Migration, 39*(5), 7–26.

Jiang, R.-S., & Lee, P.-C. (2016). An evolution of the migration of Taiwanese female basketball players: From the "American dream" to the "Chinese dream." *International Journal of the History of Sport, 33*(18), 2253–2270.

Kanemasu, Y., & Molnar, G. (2013). Collective identity and contested allegiance: A case of migrant professional Fijian rugby players. *Sport in Society, 16*(7), 863–882.

Kanemasu, Y., & Molnar, G. (2014). Life after rugby: Issues of being an "ex" in Fiji rugby. *International Journal of the History of Sport, 31*(11), 1389–1405.

Kanemasu, Y., & Molnar, G. (2019). "Representing" the voices of Fijian women rugby players: Limits and potentials of research as a transformative act. *International Review for the Sociology of Sport, 55*(4), 399–415.

Klein, A. M. (1991). *Sugarball: The American game, the Dominican dream*. New Haven, CT: Yale University Press.

Lanfranchi, P., & Taylor, M. (2001). *Moving with the ball: The migration of professional footballers*. Oxford: Berg.

Magee, J., & Sugden, J. (2002). The world at their feet: Professional football and labour migration. *Journal of Sport and Social Issues, 26*(4), 421–437.

Maguire, J. (1994). Preliminary observations on globalisation and the migration of sport labour. *Sociological Review, 42*(3), 452–480.

Maguire, J. (1995). Common ground? Links between sports history, sports geography and the sociology of sport. *Sporting Traditions, 12*(1), 1–25.

Maguire, J. (1996). Blade runners: Canadian migrants and global ice-hockey trials. *Journal of Sport and Social Issues, 20*(3), 335–360.

Maguire, J. (1999). *Global sport: Identities, societies, civilisations*. Cambridge, U.K.: Polity Press.

Maguire, J. (2005). *Power and global sport: Zones of prestige, emulation and resistance*. Oxford: Routledge.

Maguire, J., Jarvie, G., Mansfield, L., & Bradley, J. (2002). *Sport worlds: A sociological perspective*. Champaign, IL: Human Kinetics Publisher.

Mangan, J. A. (1986). *The games ethic and imperialism*. London: Viking.

Marshall, B. (Ed.). (2006). *Politics of migration: A survey*. London: Routledge.

Molnar, G., & Faulkner, C. (2016). Football related migrations. In J. Hughson, J. K. Moore, R. Spaaij, & J. Maguire (Eds.), *Routledge handbook of football studies* (pp. 151–162). Oxford: Routledge.

Molnar, G., & Kelly, J. (2013). *Sport, exercise and social theory*. London: Routledge.

Molnar, G. & Kanemasu, Y. (2014). Playing on the global periphery: Social scientific explorations of rugby in the Pacific Islands. *Asia Pacific Journal of Sport and Social Science, 3*(3), 175–185.

Molnar, G., & Maguire, J. (2008). Hungarian footballers on the move: Issues of and observations on the first migratory phase. *Sport in Society, 11*(1), 74–89.

Molnar, G., & Whigham, S. (2021). Radical right populist politics in Hungary: Reinventing the Magyars through sport. *International Review for the Sociology of Sport, 56*(1), 133–148. https://doi.org/10.1177/1012690219891656.

Ortner, S. B. (1995). Resistance and the problem of ethnographic refusal. *Comparative Studies in Society and History, 37*(1), 173–193.

Petersen, W. (1958). A general typology of migrations. *American Sociological Review, 23*(3), 256–266.

Poli, R. (2006). Migrations and trade of African football players: Historic, geographical and cultural aspects. *Africa Spectrum, 41*(3), 393–414.

Poli, R. (2010). African migrants in Asian and European football: Hopes and realities. *Soccer and Society, 13*(6), 1001–1011.

Research Excellence Framework. (2015). Research Excellence Framework 2014: Overview report by Main Panel C and Sub-panels 16 to 26. https://www.ref.ac.uk/2014/media/ref/content/expanel/member/Main%20Panel%20C%20overview%20report.pdf.

Rigauer, B. (1981). *Sport and work*. New York: Columbia University Press.

Samers, M. (2010). *Migration*. London: Routledge.

Sorhaindo, C., & Pattullo, P. (2009). *Home again: Stories of migration and return*. London: Papillote Press.

Sinatti, G. (2019). Return migration, entrepreneurship and development: Contrasting the economic growth perspective of Senegal's diaspora policy through a migrant-centred approach. *African Studies, 78*(4), 609–623.

Smith, R., Spaaij, R., & McDonald, B. (2019). Migrant integration and cultural capital in the context of sport and physical activity: A systematics review. *Journal of International Migration and Integration, 20*, 851–868.

Spaaij, R., Broerse, J., Oxford, S., Luguetti, C., McLachlan, F., McDonald, B., . . . Pankowiak, A. (2019). Sport, refugees, and forced migration: A critical review of the literature. *Frontiers in Sports and Active Living, 1*, 1–47.

Stalker, P. (1994). *The work of strangers: A survey of international labour migration*. Geneva: International Labour Office.

Stalker, P. (2000). *Workers without frontiers: The impact of globalisation on international migration*. Geneva: International Labour Office.

Szostak, R. (2014). Communicating complex concepts. In M. O'Rourke, S. Crowley, S. D. Eigenbrode, & J. D. Wulfhorst (Eds.), *Enhancing communication and collaboration in interdisciplinary research* (pp. 34–55). Los Angeles, CA: Sage.

Thorpe, H. (2014). *Transnational mobilities in action sport cultures*. Basingstoke, U.K.: Palgrave Macmillan.

Thorpe, H. (2017). "The endless winter": Transnational mobilities of skilled snow sport workers. *Journal of Ethnic and Migration Studies, 43*(3), 528–545.

Tilly, C. (1990). Transplanted networks. In V. Yans-McLaughlin (Ed.), *Immigration reconsidered: History, sociology, and politics* (pp. 79–95). Oxford: Oxford University Press.

Wallace, C., & Stola, D. (Eds.). (2001). *Patterns of migration in Central Europe*. Basingstoke, U.K.: Palgrave.

Wallerstein, I. (1974). *Modern world-system: Capitalist agriculture and the origins of the European world-economy in the sixteenth century*. London: Academic Press.

Wallerstein, I. (2004). *World-systems analysis: An introduction*. London: Duke University Press.

Yılmaz, F. (2012). Right-wing hegemony and immigration: How the populist far-right achieved hegemony through the immigration debate in Europe. *Current Sociology, 60*(3), 368–381.

CHAPTER 37

SPORT, ATHLETIC CAREERS, AND RETIREMENT

MARTIN RODERICK AND LAUREN M. KAMPERMAN

THE career trajectories of athletes as they unfold across their lifespans have always been at the heart of discussions for supporters, spectators, journalists, and commentators of sport. The twists and turns of athletes' sporting journeys have left their mark on the global history of sport. Here, narratives of success, tragedy, bravery, triumphing against the odds, and achieving redemption from past failure are all regular features (Smart, 2005). Even early forms of *organized* sport—horse racing, boxing, foot races—involved now celebrated figures who inspired the romanticized stories upon which the dominant narratives and values of sport are constructed (Colls, 2020; Guttmann, 2004). Athletes' careers have been the matter of endless public curiosity, and yet, in spite of the richness of these relational endeavors, examinations of athletes' life histories have only rarely been the subject of focused academic attention. This comparative marginalization is unusual since *work* and how it is organized and experienced is central among the traditional concerns of many social scientists (Strangleman & Warren, 2008). So, despite the enormous amount of popular attention paid to high-level athletes in particular, most of which debate levels of performance, there has been relatively little sociological and psychological scrutiny of their working lives and how they cope with the normalized workplace practices and conditions characteristic of sports industries.

In an attempt to establish a sense of coherence of the arc of an athlete's biography, sociologists and psychologists have turned to the idea of a "career" and connected transitions, turning points, and contingencies (Ball, 1976; Ingham, Blissmer, & Davidson, 1999). The concept of "career" has been associated traditionally with the idea of unilinear sequential progression through an occupation, usually one considered a "profession," such as medicine, law, academia, finance, in the life course of an individual (Abbott & Hrycak, 1990). Sociologists developed the study of careers in an attempt to understand the perspectives of the people involved. Focus was given to their personal experiences or subjective feelings, as well as concentrating on patterned sequences of passage (Hughes, 1958). Historically, sociological studies of careers necessarily focused on typical stages, status positions, or patterned sequences of events, be they for the politician, doctor, musician, or athlete (Becker, 1963; Wilensky, 1961). Careers, however, are not restricted to the smooth passage or transition from one status to another within a job; it is of course entirely possible to have a career in an avocation as well as a vocation (Goffman, 1961). Even so, sociology's early and key contribution to understanding vocational pursuits has been to suggest that it is possible to focus on *subjective* or personal careers (Hughes, 1958; Stebbins, 1970). The implication is that it is insufficient to examine solely objectively identifiable occupational patterns. Rather, the concept of career involves self-identity and reflects an individual's sense of who they are, who they wish to be, their hopes, dreams, fears, and frustrations (Young & Collin, 2000). Indeed, sociological understandings of career necessarily enable a back-and-forth conceptual movement between "subjective" and "objective" aspects of career (Goffman, 1961). Of great importance to an understanding of an individual's subjective career, however, are the turning points, transitions, contingencies, and situations that mark for any individual a change in their network of relationships with others, and which therefore signal a reevaluation of self (Strauss, 1962).

These traditional, sociological conceptual ideas feature substantially in both sociological and psychological examinations of sport, athletic careers, and retirement. There is now a large and growing body of sociological and psychological research, which has employed both quantitative and qualitative methodologies to conceptualize the career trajectories of athletes and key transitional passages in time. To characterize these developments, this chapter has three main objects: (1) to introduce and examine literature which has focused on the issues of retirement from high-level sport and the more contemporary topic of dual careers; (2) to outline and critically understand sociological and psychological approaches to explaining careers and career transitions in high-level sport; and (3) to outline three areas of debate, followed by a brief conclusion about this line of research and its future.

ISSUES

Retirement from Sport

The earliest academic literature on retirement from sport suggested that professional and elite athletes suffer from adjustment problems and that retirement from sport is a traumatic experience. The early works of Weinberg and Arond (1952), Mihovilovic (1968), Hill and Lowe (1974), and Ball (1976) all concur that retirement for many elite-level performers augments rather than diminishes adjustment problems such as alcoholism and forms of addiction and increases the "fear," and for some the likelihood, of poverty. Later literature linked with gerontology and thanatology tended to reinforce not only the idea that retirement from sport is traumatic but, also, that it is a kind of social death (Lerch, 1981; McPherson, 1980; Rosenberg, 1984). Gerontological studies are distinct from the earliest sociological studies in that the primary focus is on aging and on life satisfaction; it is this stimulating body of work from which disengagement as "loss" stems. In contrast to early attempts to comprehend retirement experiences, empirically grounded research from the 1980s started to indicate that athletes might not suffer from long-term adjustment problems to the extent previously reported. In fact, some athletes experienced a sense of rebirth (Allison & Meyer, 1988; Coakley, 1983; Curtis & Ennis, 1988; Koukouris, 1994; Swain, 1991).

Sport psychologists contributed importantly to the notion that high-level performers can experience adjustment crises when facing the end of their careers (Ogilvie & Taylor, 1993; Werther & Orlick, 1986). Much of the early psychological literature focused attention on role transitions and sought to construct coping strategies for athletes leaving high-level sport (Baillie & Danish, 1992; Grove, Lavallee, & Gordon, 1997; Sinclair & Orlick, 1993). It seems to be understood implicitly in this developing literature that those athletes who adjust positively tend to retire after they achieve what they perceive as their sport-related goal(s). For example, Sinclair and Orlick suggest that athletes who felt their retirement was largely due to declining performance subsequently experienced more difficulties connected with feelings of loss of status and a lack of confidence.

Issues of personal identity, career planning, and, in particular, support networks have been examined as factors that can affect retirement from sport (Ogilvie & Taylor, 1993; Park, Tod, & Lavallee, 2012). It is generally understood that career termination may lead retiring athletes to experience a sense of loss of personal competence and mastery, social recognition, and enjoyment (Park, Lavallee, & Tod, 2013). Additionally, athletes can often struggle with the loss of performance metrics/indicators that impact and influence their sense of self-worth and validity in their sport spaces (which interlinks with their overall sense of identity). Goal setting and goal achieving is so central to athlete experiences that when these performance indicators are gone, athletes often struggle to perform in the workplace due to the absence of similar indicators for measuring success (e.g., Wendling & Sagas, 2020).

Two key conclusions can be drawn from all this literature. First, originally focused on retirement from competitive sport, the end-of-career transition was approached as a singular event and compared to retirement from the workplace (Alfermann & Stambulova, 2007). For sport psychologists, however, this comparison was found to be flawed due to the non-sport-specific character of explanatory models (Stambulova, 2012; Stambulova, Ryba, & Henriksen, 2020). The decision to withdraw, the "relief" response, and the sense of loss which may be felt by athletes can be explained more adequately by understanding retirement, disengagement, and/or withdrawal as a social process and not as a singular event (Lavallee, 2005; Lavallee & Robinson, 2007; North & Lavallee, 2004). For example, Swain (1991) identifies the middle part of the career of athletes when they begin to take stock of their personal circumstances and become more self-reflexive about their profession and their own *self* in relation to it. Furthermore, athletes begin to comprehend the *demands* of the sports lifestyle in terms that are more objective; that is, they see their career evolution in more reality-congruent ways and "free" from dominant ideological contamination. Allison and Meyer (1988) suggest similarly that, unless the career of the elite athlete is terminated unexpectedly, they are likely to undergo conscious and unconscious processes of continual analysis and evaluation of the status of their career. In their study of athletic careers, these authors indicate that particular "catalytic" situations become watershed periods. Such a period in the career of the athlete may manifest as, for example, a rejection or demotion, a team transfer, funding and contract negotiations, a serious injury, or a reduced level of performance that may be stimulated by changing personal circumstances, such as greater responsibilities brought about by marriage or newly born children (Allison & Meyer, 1988).

The second key and popular conclusion is that a strong and exclusive athletic identity can lead to heightened stress and anxiety responses during times of career adjustment (Brewer & Petitpas, 2017; Lavallee, Gordon, & Grove, 1997; Mitchell et al., 2014). Studies of career transitions, and particularly studies of discontinuation and retirement, have expanded since the early 1980s. Over this period, a significant body of work has explored links between career withdrawal and matters of social/role identity. Broadly speaking, studies conclude that athletes experience a "loss of identity" when they report a strong commitment to their careers during fateful moments or at points of vulnerability, including the point at which they disengage from performance sport (Brewer & Petitpas, 2017; Lavallee et al., 1997; Ronkainen, Kavoura, & Ryba, 2016a). In short, athletes considered at risk of a more traumatic withdrawal from sport are those who associate *strongly* and often exclusively with the role and identity of "athlete." Therefore, beginning in the 1990s researchers pursued the idea of a strong athletic identity as an explanatory concept to help comprehend overly narrow lifestyle development, underdeveloped career planning, and emotional and psychological distress on retirement (Brown & Potrac, 2009; Grove, Fish, & Eklund, 2004; Ronkainen et al., 2016a).

The way sport psychologists have gone about investigating the strength of association between an athlete and their identification with their sporting performance has changed in important ways. The most consistent body of cognitive psychological research employed initially a psychometric instrument, the Athletic Identity Measurement Scale (AIMS), to measure "the degree to which an individual identifies with the athlete role" (Brewer, Van Raalte, & Linder, 1993, p. 237). AIMS is a 10-item questionnaire and has been embraced as the popular mechanism for studying athletic identity, examining the strength of the identification with the role of athlete, emotional responses to failure to fill the athlete role, and a lack of other distinct social roles in athletes' lives. In contrast to such traditional, cognitive examinations of athletic identity, measured as a sole product of psychological processes within an individual, sports psychologists have more recently turned to qualitative approaches in which athletic identity is theorized as constituted within cultural narratives and discourses available to the individual (Ronkainen, Kavoura, & Ryba, 2016b). So even though AIMS remains a popular methodological tool in sport transition research, qualitative athletic identity research has, since the early 2000s, undergone something of a shift from a post-positivist to a constructivist epistemology. Qualitative studies have increased significantly and moved the research focus from examining the relationship between athletic identity and variables, including adaptation to athletic retirement, career maturity, and burnout, to analyzing the powerful impact of sociocultural factors on athletic identity development (Ronkainen et al., 2016b).

In spite of the apparent epistemological developments, across the broad spectrum of research on the issue of retirement in both sport sociology and psychology there remains consistent reference to the notion of "high" or "strong" and exclusive athletic identity as a mechanism to explain in part the various ways athletes might experience forms of loss, trauma, or emotional distress (Ronkainen et al., 2016a; Ryba, Ronkainen, & Selänne, 2015). Methodological exploration of the quality and makeup of individual attachments to sport have been of less concern. Indeed, ideas about sport as a *labor of love* prevail, with scant attention to the nature or the strength of attachment. For example, an athlete's strong association with sport might result from the fact that the individual may have few alternative sources of either economic or *psychic* income, yet this singular means of making both ends meet might represent a deep-seated source of resentment toward the one activity on which an athlete's public sense of self might ultimately hang. Disengaging from sport might lead to a sense of loss and existential worry, raising the ineluctable question

What next? Simultaneously, however, disengagement might also represent for athletes a huge and complex source of liberation. For instance, no longer can their athletic bodies be expropriated for others' economic or symbolic gain. The problem with post-positivist analyses of identity is the lack of recognition of the sociological fact that the multiple and dynamic identifications of athletes are not fixed (Lawler, 2008). The stages of progression into all kinds of occupations, including sports work, necessitate often changing self-perceptions and identifications as athletes advance (Hickey & Roderick, 2017). A lacuna in studies of retirement from athletic careers therefore is an understanding of the various ways athletes come to understand themselves and their relationship to their profession throughout their sporting journey, and what this means as they (in)voluntarily step away from an activity that, to an extent, has sustained an important feature of their sense of self. Thus, talking simply of relative strengths of athletic identification overly diminishes more ethnographic accounts, which have revealed disillusionment (Robidoux, 2001), cynicism, and disidentification (Roderick, 2014), as well as a developing realism (Wacquant, 2001). Free from the delusions bound up in ideological accounts of what sport can be, the state of mind of athletes and their understandings of self, all of which result from athletes' persistent and inescapable experiences of nonnormative career turning points and contingencies, are significant in examinations of this progressively isolating transitional experience.

Dual Careers

In recent years, a new subsection of athlete career research has emerged: dual careers. Since the 1990s, interest around athletes combining sport with education or work has steadily increased due to recognition of the positive impacts of sport on individuals as well as on society (Guidotti, Cortis, & Capranica, 2015). In response to an expanding provision of schemes, in the early 2000s, the European Parliament (2003) commissioned a series of studies to research dual-career athletes across European Union member states (Amara, Aquilina, Henry, & PMP Consultants, 2004; INEUM Consulting & TAJ, 2008). The studies found that support for dual-career athletes differed greatly by country and that dual-career pathways did not have clear structures for facilitating success. In 2007, the European Commission (EC) produced "White Paper on Sport," which outlined sport-related challenges in EU member states. Within this text, specific focus was placed on sport having a societal role (public health, balanced lifestyle, social inclusion, etc.) and also the challenges that athletes face, especially balancing sport with education. The term "dual career" arose from these studies and is gradually becoming a popular way to describe athletes and systems where sport is combined with education or work. It is widely believed that combining sport with education leads to personal enrichment, expanding skillsets, and additional routes to career paths. Support of dual career pathways is further buoyed by the popular "whole person" approach to understanding and developing elite athletes, as seen in the Wylleman, Reints, and De Knop (2013b) holistic athlete career model, referenced later in this chapter.

Despite the terminology's growing use, there are varied definitions of what constitutes a dual career athlete. For example, an early key point of reference, the *Handbook of Best Practices in Dual Career of Athletes* from DC4AC (Dual Career for Athletes Centre) defines "dual career" as the "possibility for talented, professional and elite athletes to build an educational or job path simultaneously with a sport career" (Boboc et al., 2017, p. 5). The 2012 EU "Guidelines on Dual Careers of Athletes" also refers to having a dual career as combining sport with education or work (European Commission, 2012). In contrast, some definitions leave out those who pursue work or vocational pathways, instead insisting that a dual career must involve education (e.g., Wylleman, De Brandt, & Drefruyt, 2017). As such, the literature base primarily examines athlete experience from a student-athlete perspective, with minimal research related to dual career athletes who pursue job pathways instead of education. The same is true for dual career provision and practice, where student-athletes are the focus and there is little support available for athletes who pursue work pathways. This focus on education has served to create an additional gap in the research, as experiences of older dual career athletes (who are not within the typical age range of university students) are scarce within the dual career literature.

Leading authors in this field (for example, Aquilina, De Brandt, De Knop, Lavallee, Ryba, Stambulova, and Wylleman) have predominantly focused their work on athlete careers, with the aim of understanding the experiences and challenges of the dual career, and with particular interest in athlete retirement and transitions. Research on athletes' career development and transitions reveals the various challenges that athletes face (e.g., Debois, Ledon, Argiolas, & Rosnet, 2012; De Brandt, 2017; Gomez, Bradley, & Conway, 2018; Stambulova, Engström, Franck, Linnér, & Lindahl, 2015; Vickers, 2018) and point to a need for enhanced dual career systems with increased athlete support (Alfermann & Stambulova, 2007; Stambulova & Ryba, 2013; Vickers, 2018). Many transition studies examine individual athlete experiences and perspectives, which are often linked to particular sports or nations (Debois et al., 2012; Stambulova et al., 2015; Tekavc, Wylleman, & Cecić Erpič, 2015; Wylleman, Reints, & De Knop, 2013a). Collectively, this line of inquiry has highlighted that dual career athletes have specific demands and challenges, namely identity confusion and social and athletic challenges (Vickers, 2018), and suggest that the development of talented athletes should be holistic and gradual (De Brandt, 2017; European Commission, 2012).

The landscape of dual career research has been predominantly shaped by Eurocentric studies that have set the pace for the dual career space (Amara et al. 2004; Aquilina, 2013; Debois, Ledon, & Wylleman, 2015; De Knop, Wylleman, Van Hoecke, & Bollaert, 1999; Ryba, Stambulova, Ronkainen, Bundgaard, & Selänne, 2015b; Stambulova, 2009, 2012; Stambulova, Alfermann, Statler, & Côté, 2009; Stambulova & Ryba, 2013; Wylleman & Lavallee, 2004). Due to heavy investment from the EU and European Commission to produce dual career research and resources, European perspectives and populations dominate the space, showcasing homogeneity across the research. It is also notable that most dual career studies are nation-specific (e.g., Lupo, Tessitore, Capranica, Rauter, & Doupona-Topic, 2012; Stambulova et al., 2015; Wylleman, Reints, & De Knop, 2013a), which may be a response to several researchers calling for culturally specific approaches in career research, especially in sport psychology (e.g., Burnett, 2010; Lupo et al., 2015; Stambulova & Ryba, 2013). The European Commission (2012) guidelines for dual careers also appealed to national authorities to develop culturally aware policies. These nation-specific studies contribute to deeper understandings of dual career experiences.

However, there is a significant absence of demographically focused, or indeed intersectional research surrounding the multiple facets of athlete identity (i.e., race, ethnicity, disability, gender, sexuality, class, religion, etc.) as well as a focus on experiences of inclusion and exclusion in dual career spaces. Notably, the race or ethnicity of dual career athletes is rarely considered or reported in studies where athletes were interviewed or surveyed. For example, in a study on elite-level swimmers and basketball players, the age, education level, subject of study, and current occupation of each participant were recorded, but race and ethnicity were not recorded or considered (Tekavc et al., 2015). Similarly, a study on dual career elite male athletes did not record or consider the race or ethnicity of its participants (Debois et al., 2015). This is the norm for dual career research, but some exceptions lie in student-athlete studies, which are primarily focused on university-level athletes competing in the United States. The term "dual career" is rarely, if at all, used in American studies; instead they continue to separate student-athletes from other athletes mostly due to the strict rules around amateur athlete status in the United States, as regulated by the NCAA. Still, a limited number of studies highlight the experiences of individual athletes related to their identity characteristics (e.g., Fynes & Fisher, 2016; Sato, Hodge, & Eckert, 2017; Turk, 2018), and even fewer consider how the intersectionality of identities affects the athlete experience (e.g., Bernhard, 2014; Bruening, Armstrong, & Pastore, 2005; White, 2020). Future research should close this gap and highlight experiences of diverse athletes pursuing dual career pathways.

APPROACHES

The predominant research that exists on the two issues discussed, retirement and dual careers, stems largely from two broad disciplinary approaches: sociology and psychology. This section therefore outlines and examines substantive topics, conceptual models, and disciplinary contrasts from both approaches, highlighting key ideas, authors, and significant works in these fields.

Sociological Approaches to Athletic Careers

The construction and negotiation of the identity of athletes is a psychosocial problem that has long been at the core of social science research on the subject of athletic careers (Donnelly & Young, 1988; Messner, 1992; Theberge, 2000; Wacquant, 1998). Ethnographic studies of the careers of professional and high-level athletes have foregrounded sociological issues bound up with identity and the complexity of its formation and maintenance (Butler, 2017; Douglas & Carless, 2015; Howe, 2003; Kalman-Lamb, 2018; Parker, 2001; Robidoux, 2001; Wacquant, 1995). The constant battle for athletes with problems related to sense of self, their dignity "at work," and their struggles to retain—perhaps reclaim—some comprehension of authenticity in terms of their self-identities, and how these are blurred by the public nature of their performances, wear down athletes' emotional and physical resilience (Roderick & Allen-Collinson, 2020). Sociological studies illustrate how "prolympic" sporting *workplaces* are increasingly geared toward establishing the identities of workers via a mixture of discipline, techniques of surveillance, and power (Shogun, 1999). On this point, several studies make evident how athletes come to comply visibly with managerial "cultural" direction and rules (Manley, Palmer, & Roderick, 2012; McGillivray, Fearn, & McIntosh, 2005).

High-level and professional sport is commonly understood as a *labour of love* undertaken by "privileged" athletes (some of whom now achieve celebrity status) who steadfastly commit—and *sacrifice*—body and soul to achieve valorized ambitions (Roderick, 2006). It is a career often associated with recognition and glamour. Even so, the public nature of this body-focused performance trade can bleed into all relational aspects of the lives of athletes, who frequently report a loss of control of their everyday realities (Brownrigg, Burr, Bridger, & Locke, 2018). One outcome of the impact of these social processes is that, in time, a good number of athletes come to *disidentify* with values tied to team and work culture. Here, athletes inwardly harbor high levels of cynicism toward managerial powers in order to re-possess a sense of self-truth that, for some, comes to prevail over tensions between who they feel *they really are* and who they need to be "at work" (Roderick, 2014). The idea that athletes can be cynically disenchanted by their sport—and for some it is their profession—is somewhat surprising for those who come to believe what the dominant performance narrative tells us (Douglas & Carless, 2009): that sport as an industry offers an opportunity for certain individuals blessed with *God-given* talents to be imbued with a great deal of symbolic capital (Nesti, 2010).

Sociological research on high-level athletes has consistently revealed that the structures of professional sport are integral to stimulating psychosocial problems for individual athletes (Brownrigg et al., 2018; Douglas & Carless, 2015; Hoberman, 1992; Roderick, Smith, & Potrac, 2017). Sociological and anthropological studies of professional and high-level sport refer to cynically minded but reality-congruent athletes who *come to* recognize and accommodate the notion that they are "pieces of meat," "commodities," "just another number," and "not worth anything to anyone" (Robidoux, 2001; Roderick, 2006; Wacquant, 2001). Such explicit narratives of exploitation are, however, seldom articulated beyond a limited group of academics and are largely absent from serious media-led debate. The upshot and moral effects of careers in professional sport for athletes who repeatedly come through identity-arresting employment contingencies can include a diminished sense of dignity at work and a questionable sense of respect for colleagues (Roderick, 2006), the development of individualistic frames of reference (Parker, 2001), the devaluing of work responsibilities (Fry & Bloyce, 2017), and cynical and uncommitted relationships with managerial and leadership figures (Wacquant, 1995).

A key sociological issue for all athletes is that they struggle to develop any sense of who they are as well as what they have become. This is because all their work stems from others' *legitimatized* claims to control, survey, observe, and correct their working bodies (Manley et al., 2012; McMahon & Penney, 2013; Shogun, 1999). In short, elite athletes are celebrated, sensationalized, mortified, commodified, dehumanized (Hoberman, 1992). They are subject to constant observation, scrutiny, and correction in relation to their working bodies, their talent, and performances (Hatteberg, 2018; Manley, Roderick, & Parker, 2016). They are open to changing—often experimental—technological and medical (scientific) innovation and development (Manley & Williams, 2019; Miah, 2013). These largely structuralist, often Marxist-influenced examinations indicate that the enduring effect for athletes of dedication to their craft is the production of alienated, paratechnically dependent subjects who are unable openly to rationalize failure—or to employ ego defenses—other than in ways which reaffirm the hegemony of this achievement-oriented ideology (Ingham et al., 1999).

Lying at the heart of empirical, sociological studies is the recognition that exploitation is a fact of existence (Murphy & Waddington, 2007). Even so, as part of the language of accommodating their expendability, Wacquant (2001) claims that individual adaptation to the realities of corporeal manipulation is essential, as seen in the case of boxers, to reclaim a sense of personal integrity. In other quarters, Robidoux (2001, p. 162) argues that hockey players in Canada lack any effective forms of resistance to unfavorable labor circumstances; their only real emotional survival strategy is to "turn back into play what management has turned into work." A significant feature of these empirical studies is that athletes are embroiled in a form of "coerced affection," yet they are not blind to their use-value (Wacquant, 1995). Sociological and psychological studies demonstrate how the commitment of athletes to their *calling*, and their desire to remain active at the point of production, necessitates a complex mixture of rationalizing and suppressing their feelings of resentment to, most often, their coaches, sponsors, employers, and funders of their domination (Brownrigg et al., 2018; Fry, Bloyce, & Pritchard, 2015).

The notion of worker opposition has never found consistent expression in studies of high-level sport, even though athlete subjectivities, questions of vocational desire, and personal attitude have always been targeted by coaches (Parker, 2001; Roderick, 2006). In the few work-centered studies of careers in professional sport, there are clear and identifiable patterns of exploitation and *vocabularies of motive* for accommodating and continuing in such working conditions (Brown & Potrac, 2009; McGillivray et al., 2005). To an extent, academic attention is situated more often in the broader field of sport-related socialization and identity formation (Douglas & Carless, 2015; Theberge, 2000). What is happening in terms of athletes' lifeworld orientations, and athletes' subjective and *moral* careers, has been less well interpreted and articulated. Even though athletic careers have been the subject of such everyday, populist, and media scrutiny, and elite athletes inhabit public lives poised on the *fringes* of "normality," it remains the case that, as a subdiscipline, the sociology of sport has taken conceptual ideas from mainstream sociology more than it has given back original ways of theorizing "careers."

Sport Psychology Career-Transition Research

Sociological and anthropological studies of athletes' lives and careers, and their *working* conditions, are comparatively sparse but tend to target athletes' subjective experiences. Here the focus has been on what athletes think and feel about, as well as how they make sense of and give meaning to, the way their lives in their sporting roles unfold (Douglas & Carless, 2015; Robidoux, 2001). In contrast, studies are more abundant in the sport psychology literature. Here, fewer studies employ *in-depth* ethnographic approaches to fieldwork. Rather, the focus tends to be on conceptualizing athletes' careers as a series or sequence of transitions through relatively predictable, normative stages of performance sport (Alfermann & Stambulova, 2007; Wylleman & Lavallee, 2004; Wylleman & Reints, 2010). Athletic career scholarship in sports psychology consists of three major areas: (1) career development research focusing on descriptions of career stages; (2) career transition research that describes and explains transition processes and factors—usually the psychological demands—involved; and (3) career assistance aimed at helping athletes with various career problems in and outside of sport (North & Lavallee, 2004).

In all three areas, an athletic career is viewed as a developmental process, which includes career stages and transitions underpinned by a performance sport logic (Ryba, Ronkainen, et al., 2015; Stambulova, 2009, 2012). This literature has focused to date on the career development of Olympic and other elite performers. In contrast, research on the careers of professional athletes has largely been found in the domain of sociology. Reflecting initial sociological studies, early emphasis in sports psychology was placed on retirement—perhaps the key career transition—employing what Stambulova et al. (2009) refer to as nonsport frameworks. A good example can be found in the work of Swain (1991), who employed Schlossberg's (1981) model of transitions. Broadly speaking, the tendency has been for studies of athletic careers to focus centrally on two defining transitions: (1) the transition to serious sport (junior to senior levels of competition) and (2) the transition away from serious sport (retirement) (Stambulova et al., 2020; Wylleman, Alfermann, & Lavallee, 2004). Arguably, the key and most influential outcomes of this initial body of retirement research has clarified two facts. First, the termination of an athletic career should not be considered a single biographical episode, but rather must be conceptualized as a transitional *process* consisting of different stages unfolding over time (Douglas & Carless, 2009; Park et al., 2013). Second, the effects of disengaging from sport are not always inevitably negative, and the types of support which are offered make a difference in aiding the transitional process (Lavallee, 2005, 2019). Thus, research on withdrawal from high-level sport offered fundamental evidence for the development of subsequent conceptual models, which sought more general insight into how talented and high-level athletes cope with transitional processes across the lifespan of their athletic development, and, most important, not solely at the end of an athletic career (Stambulova et al., 2009; Wylleman & Reints, 2010).

In sports psychology, the foundation for all athletic career frameworks is built largely on empirical research examining the interconnections between career development and transitions (Stambulova et al., 2020). In their attempt to account for the broader athletic careers of athletes, career structure, and contextual content, athletic career (transition) models from the early 2000s (e.g., the lifespan model developed by Wylleman & Lavallee, 2004) involve an examination of various career stages—for example, initiation, development, perfection, maintenance, and discontinuation—and how they intersect with various layers of individual athletes' lives, namely at athletic, psychological, psychosocial, academic-vocational, financial, and legal levels. Thus lifespan models offer an understanding of the complexity of the range of demands that athletes encounter, and must deal and cope with, as they progress through athletic career turning points. Further, the models demonstrate how these demands must be integrated in varying ways as they experience career stages, statuses, demands, barriers, pathways, and outcomes (Wylleman et al., 2004, 2013b). In considering these dynamics, sport psychologists see it as essential to place emphasis on career transitional *demands* and coping processes at each developmental stage (Battochio & Stambulova, 2019; Battochio, Stambulova, & Schinke, 2016). Empirically grounded studies illustrate the point that an effective fit between an athlete's coping resources and strategies and the particularized transitional demands at play often leads to a higher probability of a successful transition into the next stage. On the other hand, evidence suggests that ineffective coping (inappropriate resources and coping strategies) often leads to a crisis transition, with much potential for negative consequences (Stambulova, 2009, 2012).

The identification of career demands appears to place sports psychologists consistently in line with dominant performance sport ideology because their role demands are more often anchored in optimizing athletic performance than they are in focusing on the *relational* dynamics at play (Battochio & Stambulova, 2019). Types of external and internal demands typically include adjustments to training loads, constant and increasing rates of travel, ever more intense competitions, struggles to allow for periods of physical and emotional rest, and mental challenges relating to coping with perceived organizational challenges (Battochio & Stambulova, 2019; Battochio et al., 2016; Park, Tod, & Lavallee, 2012; Stambulova, 2016. Because of these demands, few questions are typically raised by sports psychologists about the contrasting sociological demands of *being* an athlete and the existential worry bound up with maintaining a social identity as an athlete, with all the material and reputational threats that failure can bring about (Roderick & Allen-Collinson, 2020). In other words, the sport psychology vantage point typically brings little understanding of the relentless emotional demands of living up to expectations; of comprehending how athletes come to alter their *worldviews* of sport and the meanings they attach to sporting activity; of maintaining a public-facing reputation; of being the athlete that employers/funders expect (e.g., the required emotional labor); or of the fatigue of maintaining, season upon season, a moral social self in a career embedded in exploitative labor relations. A notable exception includes more recent studies of "athlete burnout." Here, most studies have been focused primarily on *stress* and are often survey-based (e.g., Sorkkila, Tolvanen, Aunola, & Ryba, 2019).

In summary, psychological knowledge of athletic careers is to date based almost exclusively on the identification of the coping processes and athletic performance demands of moving from one status position to the next (e.g., Battochio et al., 2016; Henriksen, Stambulova, & Roessler, 2010; Stambulova, 2015, 2016). What is lacking in the field of sports psychology is therefore a focused comprehension and explanation of *the social relations* of athletic career development.

As sport psychology research has unfolded, most particularly since the early 2000s, a greater emphasis has been placed on the development of more culturally sensitive frameworks that seek to grasp specific features of athletes' careers. Certainly there has been in this research line recently a need to pay attention to the notion of cultural praxis and for inquiry to embrace a "turn to culture" (Ryba, Stambulova, & Ronkainen, 2016; Stambulova & Ryba, 2013). For example, studies of athletic careers demonstrate a shift of analytical focus to the "whole person" situated in a more holistic understanding of performance sport environments. In real terms, however, the raison d'être of holistic models, similar in kind to long-established sociological studies of careers, is to examine individual people in their relational surroundings. For example, Stambulova (2016, p. 7) refer to contextualizing "athlete subjectivity in lived culture," while Ryba, Ronkainen, at al. (2015, p. 48) make reference to relations between athletic careers and "lives outside of sport." One of the outcomes for Ryba, Ronkainen, et al. is to push the notion of a *subjective career*, which they claim emphasizes individual experiences and can facilitate analyses of how athletes construct their lives embedded in sporting social situations. In contrast, the notion of subjective careers has long been featured in many sociological studies of high-level sport (Ball, 1976; Roderick, 2006).

Still, while largely remaining anchored in sport performance, the psychological field has seen a flourishing of approaches, models, and conceptual thinking, all with the aim of understanding and conceptualizing career development, transitions, and career assistance (Stambulova et al., 2020). There is a great deal of imaginative and insightful empirical research that offers thick descriptions of, for example, performance-oriented transitional demands and coping processes (Battochio & Stambulova, 2019; Battochio et al., 2016). Even so, there is little connection between this body of sports psychology research and more contemporary social science ways of conceptualizing approaches to "work," careers, and transitioning. As a field of inquiry, sports psychology seems reluctant to look for conceptual advances beyond the limits of (sport) psychology, and therefore has become unwittingly detached from contemporary advances and conceptual considerations in other academic (sub)disciplines from which it might benefit (e.g., Dean, 2005; Potter, 2015, 2020; Sennett, 1998; Umney & Kretsos, 2014). While attempting to step away from nonsport frameworks (Stambulova et al., 2009), sport psychologists have rarely looked beyond "objective," sequential ways of grasping athletic careers and post-positive methodologies (Stambulova, 2016) that, in wider social science fields, are recognized as narrow in scope, and thereby risk being dissociated from the real and complex frontline "work" and *whole person* experiences of athletes.

DEBATES

Literature examining athletic careers and the twin issues of retirement and dual careers is comparatively *passive* more than critical inasmuch as there are no standout theoretical or methodological debates or ethical dilemmas outlined in extant published work (Stambulova et al., 2020). Indeed, as mentioned previously, this body has largely extracted conceptual ideas from mainstream sociology and psychology more than it has given in return. Therefore, this section implicitly highlights conceptual challenges with this body of academic research and poses some potential areas of future growth.

There remains much debate about the tensions between the "professional" or "work" lives of athletes and their lives as "whole persons." Indeed, for periods in their career, an athlete may remain economically stable and "in work" (i.e., selected to perform), and their career may appear to onlookers to be coherent, "on track," and established, yet simultaneously they may feel disenchanted with their sporting lives, their feelings toward their performances, and untrusting of the interests of the people for whom they work: funders, sponsors, coaches, employers. Sociological studies indicate importantly that what might appear somewhat random from the perspective of an outsider is, in fact, structured logically from an athlete's point of view (Roderick, 2014). It seems important, therefore, to not confuse the matter of an athlete's feelings toward, for instance, the *ludic* elements of what it is they do, with their orientation to the production of performances that define their *work*. Social science approaches to conceptualizing athletic careers must therefore place an emphasis on the importance of comprehending the perspectives from which they are considered. Sociological and anthropological studies of the working lives of athletes militate against the notion of a normal career curve and challenge the idea of career continuity (Douglas & Carless, 2015; Kalman-Lamb, 2018; Nesti, 2010; Wacquant, 1998). Athletic careers have received a great deal of analysis, but there exists only limited theorizing of the coexistence in athletes' lives of opportunity, insecurity, flexibility, and uncertainty, and this is where scholars of athletic careers can make more original theoretical contributions. To date, little scholarly attention has been given to the way that athletes make sense of and deal with the micro-interactions bound up in passages of subjective vulnerability within a career in which unpredictability and precariousness are built-in and always pervasive features.

A second debate about the "problem" of the theorizing of the lives of high-level athletes, which has been only partially examined, is about the social construction of age. Anecdotal evidence from studies of retirement and athlete biographies indicates that athletes are profoundly cognizant of the way they live out their sporting lives under the eye of a culturally bound *time clock* (Faulkner, 1974). Indeed, while it is clear that all athletes who look to experience a career of any length develop culturally normed understandings about career stages and when progression and/or decline might or should come about, there remains much room for debate about emerging and differential sensitivities to the social relations of time (Roderick, 2006). Yet, in this space, there exists little scholarly examination of how athletes perceive and give meaning to the coming together of social, career, and biological timeframes, and how they structure the passage of time through amplified periods of insecurity and uncertainty, periods that often accompany changes in subjective conceptions of work and self.

A third overlooked area of debate concerns the way athletes come to commit to and openly demonstrate a commitment to their athletic career and how their commitment alters toward that career. There is currently little attention paid to the nature of "commitment" theoretically, and how changing commitments may affect athletes' frames of reference to vocational pursuits. As they invest time, money and emotion in their craft and their search for success, however defined, athletes become more committed to specific courses of action. There are a whole series of "formal" and "informal" commitments bound up in athletes' career paths, from formal employment and funding contracts to informal and symbolic promises to the "imaginary" communities which athletes represent. In both cases, athletes might feel committed and yet not be committed, or they may be fully committed without being aware of that commitment. What is sociologically important is the understanding that *the process of becoming committed* involves a whole series of commitments to other people, which influence the ways in which individuals acquire different frames of reference to their work and give meaning to vocational identities. Even so, commitments can "push" athletes in certain directions. So while the frames of reference acquired function to open career possibilities in particular situations, they can function simultaneously as *blindnesses* in others. Through the process of becoming committed to a vocational role, with all that is bound up in that *social* process, serious opportunities available in other occupations, career lines, and alternative self-conceptions may be neglected. At present, there exists little understanding of how the orientation of athletes to "work" is concurrently a way of seeing and also a way of not seeing.

Finally, there remain many debates to be resolved about the tensions and conflicts in an athletic career. As much evidence in this chapter has suggested, athletic careers must be thought of as reflecting the ways in which self-images and orientations are obtained by individuals throughout a "process of becoming" and how athletes may be directed and conflicted by the structure of available resources and opportunities. Individuals who occupy similar (a)vocations or who are categorized together in "occupational" typologies might come from varied backgrounds and have diverse statuses and yet have similar ways of making both ends meet for a wide range of reasons and in incomparable circumstances. To date, the structural features of athletes' lives have rarely been theorized in studies of athletic careers. Here, career status passages have often been identified without any overarching rationale about how such individual journeys and associated *transformations of self* result from the manifest intersection and circulation of social class, gender, sexuality, race, ethnicity, and disability influences and the unfolding of life chances. All social identities, including athletic identities, hinge on paradoxical combinations of sameness and difference (Lawler, 2008). No one has one exclusive identity, whether actively conscious of this or not; people identify with various groups. Rather than researching athletic identities in isolation or combining multiple identities in an *additive* way, future studies of athletic careers and transitions must work to resolve clearer ways to conceptualize the identities of all athletes as dynamic, interactive, and mutually constitutive, and seek out those features of personhood that athletes share, as well as what makes them unique.

Conclusion

Athletes' careers develop on the basis of contingently but not at all randomly ordered sequences of interaction with other people. Athletes' route to performance sport may seem as though they were on many occasions in the right place at the right time, a series of chance happenings. Sociologically and psychologically, however, it is possible to identify connections between all athletes who "make it" in relation to, for example, the types of people with whom they mix, the ways in which they learn to become committed to the role of athlete, their feelings of belonging associated with their achievements, and the subsequent formation of self-identities. Athletes' careers are beset by particular turning points, junctures, and episodes which mark decisive passages in their life history. Even so, contemporary "sport" militates against the notion of biographical continuity; their conditions of work do not provide any sports worker with a secure model for identifications. While sport psychologists have singled out formally ordered sequences of prescribed stages, the contingencies at issue in the process of becoming an athlete may relate to socioeconomic status, gender, ethnicity, and disability, as much as proximity to participatory opportunities, amount of treatment facilities available, and demonstrations of "passion." Of course, in other chapters in this volume, alternative career-related contingencies are examined in much greater depth, for example, the experience of injury, labour mobility, and the emotions. And despite occurring independently of each individual, and hence outlined separately in this volume, these are basic and common to all experiencing an athletic career. The life histories of athletes can be said to be structured, as one can identify the sorts of things that are systematically likely to happen, whether earlier or later. Sociologists and psychologists must explore more creative ways to better capture and theorize the enabling and constraining features of the network of relationships in which athletes are embedded as they evolve over time. There exists a pattern to the occupational experiences of people and how they view the world, and these experiences can be located within the overall structures of performance sport.

References

Abbott, A., & Hrycak, A. (1990). Measuring resemblance in sequence data: An optimal matching analysis of musicians' careers. *American Journal of Sociology, 96*(1), 144–185.

Alfermann, D., & Stambulova, N. B. (2007). Career transitions and career termination. In G. Tenenbaum & R. C. Eklund (Eds.) *Handbook of sport psychology* (pp. 712–736). New York: Wiley.

Allison, M. T., & Meyer, C. (1988). Career problems and retirement among elite athletes: The female tennis professional. *Sociology of Sport Journal*, 5(3), 212–222.

Amara, M., Aquilina, D., Henry, I., & PMP Consultants. (2004). *Education of elite young sportspersons in Europe.* Brussels: European Commission, DG Education and Culture.

Aquilina, D. (2013). A study of the relationship between elite athletes' educational development and sporting performance. International Journal of the History of Sport, 30(4), 374–392.

Baillie, P. H. F., & Danish, S. J. (1992). Understanding the career transition of athletes. *Sports Psychologist*, 6, 77–98.

Ball, D. W. (1976). Failure in sport. *American Sociological Review*, 41(4), 726–739.

Battochio, R. C., & Stambulova, N. (2019). Coping resources and strategies of Canadian ice-hockey players: An empirical National Hockey League career model. *International Journal of Sports Science & Coaching*, 14(6), 726–737.

Battochio, R. C., Stambulova, N., & Schinke, R. J. (2016). Stages and demands in the careers of Canadian National Hockey League players. *Journal of Sports Sciences*, 34(3), 278–288.

Bernhard, L. (2014). "Nowhere for me to go": Black female student-athlete experiences on a pre-dominantly white campus, *Journal for the Study of Sports and Athletes in Education*, 8(2), 67–76.

Boboc, D., Bardocz-Bencsik, M., Farkas, J., Kozsla, T., D'Angelo, C., Reverberi, E., & Corvino, C. (2017). *Handbook of best practices in dual career of athletes in countries implicated in the DC4AC project.* Brussels: European Commission.

Brewer, B. W., & Petitpas, A. J. (2017). Athletic identity foreclosure. *Current Opinion in Psychology*, 16, 118–122.

Brewer, B. W., Van Raalte, J. L., & Linder, D. E. (1993). Athletic identity: Hercules' muscles or Achilles heel? *International Journal of Sport Psychology*, 24, 237–254.

Brown, G., & Potrac, P. (2009). "You've not made the grade, son": De-selection and identity disruption in elite level youth football. *Football and Society*, 10(2), 142–159.

Brownrigg, A., Burr, V., Bridger, A., & Locke, A. (2018). "You shut up and go along with it": An interpretative phenomenological study of former professional footballers' experiences of addiction. *Qualitative Research in Sport, Exercise and Health*, 10(2), 238–255.

Bruening, J., Armstrong, K., & Pastore, D. (2005). Listening to the voices: The experiences of African American female student athletes. *Research Quarterly for Exercise and Sport*, 76(1), 82–100.

Burnett, C. (2010). Student versus athlete: Professional socialisation influx. *African Journal for Physical, Health Education, Recreation & Dance*, 16(1), 193–203.

Butler, D. (2017). *Women, horseracing and gender: Becoming "one of the lads."* London: Routledge.

Coakley, J. J. (1983). Leaving competitive sport. Retirement or rebirth. *Quest*, 35, 1–35.

Colls, R. (2020). *This sporting life: Sport and liberty in England, 1760–1960.* Oxford: Oxford University Press.

Curtis, J., & Ennis, R. (1988). Negative consequences of leaving competitive sport? Comparative findings of former elite-level hockey players. *Sociology of Sport Journal*, 5(2), 87–106.

Dean, D. (2005). Recruiting a self: Women performers and aesthetic labour. *Work, Employment and Society*, 19(4), 761–774.

Debois, N., Ledon, A., Argiolas, C., & Rosnet, E. (2012). A lifespan perspective on transitions during a top sports career: A case of an elite female fencer. *Psychology of Sport and Exercise*, 13, 660–668.

Debois, N., Ledon, A., & Wylleman, P. (2015). A lifespan perspective on the dual career of elite male athletes. *Psychology of Sport and Exercise, 21*, 15–26.

De Brandt, K. (2017). *A holistic perspective on student-athletes' dual career demands, competencies and outcomes.* Brussels: VUBPress.

De Knop, P., Wylleman, P., Van Hoecke, J., & Bollaert. L. (1999). A European approach to the management of the combination of academics and elite-level sport. *Perspectives: The Interdisciplinary Series of Physical Education and Sport Science: School Sports and Competition, 1*, 49–62.

Donnelly, P., & Young, K. (1988). The construction and confirmation of identity in sport subcultures. *Sociology of Sport Journal, 5*(3), 223–240.

Douglas, K., & Carless, D. (2009). Abandoning the performance narrative: Two women's stories of transition from professional sport. *Journal of Applied Sport Psychology, 21*, 213–230.

Douglas, K., & Carless, D. (2015). *Life story research in sport: Understanding the experiences of elite and professional athletes through narrative.* Abingdon, U.K.: Routledge.

European Commission. (2007). White paper on sport.http://eur-lex. europa.eu/legal-content/EN/TXT/PDF/?uri=CELEX:52007DC0391&from=EN.

European Commission. (2012). Guidelines on dual careers of athletes—Recommended policy actions in support of dual careers in high-performance sport. http://www.ua.gov. tr/docs/default-source/gen%C3%A7lik-program%C4%B1/dual-career-guidelines-(%C3%A7ift-kariyer- rehberi).pdf?sfvrsn=0.

European Parliament. (2003). *Combining sport and education: Support for athletes in the EU member states.* Luxembourg: European Parliament.

Faulkner, R. R. (1974). Coming of age in organizations: A comparative study of career contingencies of musicians and hockey players. In D. Ball & J. Loy (Eds.), *Sport and social order: Contributions to the sociology of sport* (pp. 525–556). Boston, Massachusetts: Addison-Wesley.

Fry, J., & Bloyce, D. (2017). "Life in the travelling circus": A study of loneliness, work stress, and money issues in touring professional golf. *Sociology of Sport Journal, 34*(2), 148–159.

Fry, J., Bloyce, D., & Pritchard, I. (2015). Professional golf—A license to spend money? Issues of money in the lives of touring professional golfers. *Journal of Sport and Social Issues, 39*(3), 179–201.

Fynes, J., & Fisher, L. (2016). Is authenticity and integrity possible for sexual minority athletes? Lesbian student-athlete experiences of U.S. NCAA Division I sport. *Women in Sport and Physical Activity Journal, 24*(1), 60–69.

Goffman, E. (1961). *Encounters: Two studies in the sociology of interaction.* Indianapolis: Bobbs-Merrill Company.

Gomez, J., Bradley, J., & P. Conway, P. (2018). The challenges of a high-performance student athlete. Irish Educational Studies, 37(3), 329–349.

Grove, R. J., Fish, M., & Eklund, R. C. (2004). Changes in athletic identity following team selection: Self-protection versus self-enhancement. *Journal of Applied Sport Psychology, 16*(1), 75—81.

Grove, R. J., Lavallee, D., & Gordon, S. (1997). Coping with retirement from sport: The influence of athletic identity. *Journal of Applied Sport Psychology, 9*(2), 191–203.

Guidotti, F., Cortis, C., & Capranica, L. (2015). Dual career of European student-athletes: A systematic literature review. *Kinesiologia Slovenica, 21*(3), 5–20.

Guttmann, A. (2004). *From ritual to record: The nature of modern sports.* New York: Columbia University Press.

Hatteberg, S. J. (2018). Under surveillance: Collegiate athletics as a total institution. *Sociology of Sport Journal, 35*(2), 149–158.

Henriksen, K., Stambulova, N., & Roessler, K. K. (2010). Holistic approach to athletic talent development environments: A successful sailing milieu. *Psychology of Sport and Exercise, 11*(3), 212–222.

Hickey, C., & Roderick, M. (2017). The presentation of possible selves in everyday life: The management of identity among transitioning professional athletes. *Sociology of Sport Journal, 34,* 270–280.

Hill, P., & Lowe, B. (1974). The inevitable metathesis of the retiring athlete. *International Review for Sport Sociology, 4,* 5–29.

Hoberman, J. (1992). *Mortal engines: The science of performance and the dehumanization of sport.* New York: Free Press.

Howe, D. (2003). *Sport, professionalism and pain: Ethnographies of injury and risk.* London: Routledge.

Hughes, E. C. (1958). *Men and their work.* Glencoe, IL: Free Press.

INEUM Consulting & TAJ. (2008). *European Commission Study on training of young sportsmen/women in Europe.* Brussels: European Commission.

Ingham, A. G., Blissmer, B. J., & Davidson, K. W. (1999). The expendable prolympic self: Going beyond the boundaries of the sociology and psychology of sport. *Sociology of Sport Journal, 16*(3), 236–268.

Kalman-Lamb, N. (2018). *Game misconduct: Injury, fandom, and the business of sport.* Halifax: Fernwood Publishing.

Koukouris, K. (1994). Constructed case studies: Athletes' perspectives of disengaging from organised competitive sport. *Sociology of Sport Journal, 11*(2), 114–139.

Lavallee, D. (2005). The effect of a life development intervention on sports career transition adjustment. *Sport Psychologist, 19,* 193–202.

Lavallee, D. (2019). Engagement in sport career transition planning enhances performance. *Journal of Loss and Trauma, 24*(1), 1–8.

Lavallee, D., Gordon, S., & Grove, J. R. (1997). Retirement from sport and the loss of athletic identity. *Journal of Personal and Interpersonal Loss, 2,* 129–147.

Lavallee, D., & Robinson, H. K. (2007). In pursuit of an identity: A qualitative exploration of retirement from women's artistic gymnastics, *Psychology of Sport and Exercise, 8,* 119–141.

Lawler, S. (2008). *Identity: Sociological perspectives.* London: Polity Press.

Lerch, S. (1981). The adjustment to retirement of professional baseball players. In S. L. Greendorfer & A. Yiannakis (Eds.), *Sociology of sport: Diverse perspectives* (pp. 138–148). West Point, NY: Leisure Press.

Lupo, C., Guidotti, F., Goncalves, C., Moreira, L., Doupona, M., Bellardini, H., Tonkonogi, M., Colln, A., & Capranica, L. (2015). Motivation towards dual career of European student athletes. *European Journal of Sport Science, 15*(2), 1–10.

Lupo, C., Tessitore, A., Capranica, L., Rauter, S., & Doupona-Topic, M. (2012). Motivation for a dual career: Italian and Slovenian student-athletes. *Kinesiologia Slovenica, 18*(3), 47–56.

Manley, A., Palmer, C., & Roderick, M. (2012). Disciplinary power, the oligopticon and rhizomatic surveillance in elite sports academies. *Surveillance & Society, 10*(3–4), 303–319.

Manley, A., Roderick, M., & Parker, A. (2016). Disciplinary mechanisms and the discourse of identity: The creation of "silence" in an elite sports academy. *Culture and Organization, 22*(3), 221–244.

Manley, A., & Williams, S. (2019). "We're not run on numbers, we're people, we're emotional people": Exploring the experiences and lived consequences of emerging technologies, organizational surveillance and control among elite professionals. *Organization.* doi:10.1177/1350508419890078.

McGillivray, D., Fearn, R., & McIntosh, A. (2005). Caught up in and by the beautiful game: A case of Scottish professional footballers. *Journal of Sport and Social Issues, 29*(1), 102–123.

McMahon, A., & Penney, D. (2013). (Self-)surveillance and (self-)regulation: Living by fat numbers within and beyond a sporting culture. *Qualitative Research in Sport, Exercise and Health, 5*(2), 157–178.

McPherson, B. D. (1980). Retirement from professional sport: The process and problems of occupational and psychological adjustment in sociology of sport. In proceedings of Sociological Symposium (No. 30, pp. 126–143). Blacksburg, VA: Sociological Symposium.

Messner, M. A. (1992). *Power at play.* Boston: Beacon Press.

Miah, A. (2013). *Genetically modified athletes: Biomedical ethics, gene doping and sport.* London: Routledge.

Mihovilovic, M. A. (1968). The status of former sportsmen. *International Review for Sport Sociology, 3,* 73–96.

Mitchell, T., Nesti, T., Richardson, D., Midgley, A., Eubank, M., & Littlewood, M. (2014). Exploring athletic identity in elite-level English youth football: A cross-sectional approach. *Journal of Sports Sciences, 32*(13), 1294–1299.

Murphy, P., & Waddington, I. (2007). Are elite athletes exploited? *Sport in Society, 10*(2), 239–255.

Nesti, M. (2010). *Psychology in football: Working with elite and professional players.* London: Routledge.

North, J., & Lavallee, D. (2004). The investigation of potential users of career transition services in the United Kingdom. *Psychology of Sport and Exercise, 5,* 77–84.

Ogilvie, B. C., & Taylor, J. (1993). Career termination issues among elite athletes. In R. N. Singer, M. Murphey, & L. K. Tennant (Eds.), *Handbook of research on sports psychology* (pp. 761–775). New York: Macmillan.

Park, S., Lavallee, D., & Tod, D. (2013). Athletes' career transition out of sport: A systematic review. *International Review of Sport and Exercise Psychology, 6*(1), 22–53.

Park, S., Tod, D., & Lavallee, D. (2012). Exploring the retirement from sport decision-making process based on the transtheoretical model. *Psychology of Sport and Exercise, 13*(4), 444–453.

Parker, A. (2001). Soccer, servitude and sub-cultural identity: Football traineeship and masculine construction. *Soccer and Society, 2*(1), 59–80.

Potter, J. (2015). *Crisis at work: Identity and the end of career.* Basingstoke: Palgrave Macmillan.

Potter, J. (2020). The ghost of the stable path: Stories of work-life change at the "end of career." *Work, Employment and Society, 34*(4), 571–586.

Robidoux, M. A. (2001). *Men at play: A working understanding of professional hockey.* Montreal: McGill-Queen's University Press.

Roderick, M. (2006). *The work of professional football: A labour of love?* London: Routledge.

Roderick, M. (2014). From identification to dis-identification: Case studies of job loss in professional football. *Qualitative Research in Sport, Exercise and Health, 6*(2), 143–160.

Roderick, M. & Allen-Collinson, J. (2020). "I just want to be left alone": Novel sociological insights into dramaturgical demands on professional athletes. *Sociology of Sport Journal, 37*(2), 108–116.

Roderick, M., Smith, A., & Potrac, P. (2017). The sociology of sports work, emotions and mental health: Scoping the field and future directions. *Sociology of Sport Journal, 34*(2), 99–107.

Ronkainen, N. J., Kavoura, A., & Ryba, T. V. (2016a). A meta-study of athletic identity research in sport psychology: Current status and future directions. *International Review of Sport and Exercise Psychology, 9*(1), 45–64.

Ronkainen, N. J., Kavoura, A., & Ryba, T. V. (2016b). Narrative and discursive perspectives on athletic identity: Past, present, and future. *Psychology of Sport and Exercise, 27*, 128–137.

Rosenberg, E. (1984). Athletic retirement as social death: Concepts and perspectives. In N. Theberge & P. Donnelly (Eds.), *Sport and the sociological imagination* (pp. 245–258). Fort Worth: Texas Christian University Press.

Ryba, T. V., Ronkainen, N. J., & Selänne, H. (2015). Elite athletic career as a context for life design. *Journal of Vocational Behavior, 88*, 47–55.

Ryba, T. V., Stambulova, N. B., & Ronkainen, N. J. (2016). The work of cultural transition: An emerging model. *Frontiers in Psychology, 7*, 427–440.

Ryba, T.V., Stambulova, N. B., Ronkainen, N. J., Bundgaard, J., & Selänne, H. (2015). Dual career pathways of transnational athletes. *Psychology of Sport and Exercise, 21*, 125–134.

Sato, T., Hodge, S., & Eckert, K. (2017). Experiences of Black student-athletes on a predominantly white university campus. *Journal for the Study of Sports and Athletes in Education, 11*(2), 104–124.

Schlossberg, N. K. (1981). A model for analyzing human adaption to transition. *Counseling Psychologist, 9*(2), 2–18.

Sennett, R. (1998). *The corrosion of character: The personal consequences of work in the new capitalism.* New York: W. W. Norton.

Shogun, D. (1999). *The making of high-performance athletes: Discipline, diversity, and ethics.* Toronto: University of Toronto Press.

Sinclair, D. A., & Orlick, T. (1993). Positive transitions from high-performance sport. *Sports Psychologist, 7*, 138–150.

Smart, B. (2005). *The sport star: Modern sport and the cultural economy of sporting celebrity.* London: Sage.

Sorkkila, M., Tolvanen, A., Aunola, K., & Ryba, T. V. (2019). The role of resilience in student-athletes' sport and school burnout and dropout: A longitudinal person-oriented study. *Scandinavian Journal of Medicine & Science in Sports, 29*, 1059–1067.

Stambulova, N. (2009). Talent development in sport: A career transitions perspective. In E. Tsung-Min Hung, R. Lidor, & D. Hackfort (Eds.), *Psychology of sport excellence* (pp. 63–74). Morgantown, WV: Fitness Information Technology.

Stambulova, N. (2012). Working with athletes in career transitions. In S. Hanton & S. Mellalieu (Eds.), *Professional practice in sport psychology: A review* (pp. 165–194). New York: Routledge.

Stambulova, N. (2016). Looking at the future of qualitative methodology through the prism of athlete career research. In B. Smith & A. Sparks (Eds.), *Handbook on qualitative research methods in sport and exercise* (pp. 450–460). London: Routledge.

Stambulova, N., Alfermann, D., Statler, T., & Côté, J. (2009). ISSP position stand: Career development and transitions of athletes. *International Journal of Sport and Exercise Psychology, 7*, 395–412.

Stambulova, N., Engström, C., Franck, A., Linnér, L., & Lindahl, K. (2015). Searching for an optimal balance: Dual career experiences of Swedish adolescent athletes. *Psychology of Sport and Exercise, 21*, 4–14.

Stambulova, N., & Ryba, T. V. (2013). *Athletes' careers across cultures*. London: Routledge.

Stambulova, N., Ryba, T. V., & Henriksen, K. (2020). Career development and transitions of athletes: The International Society of Sport Psychology position stand revisited. *International Journal of Sport and Exercise Psychology*, 19(4), 524–550.

Stebbins, R. A. (1970). Career: The subjective approach. *Sociological Quarterly*, 11(1), 32–49.

Strangleman, T. & Warren, T. (2008). Work and society: Sociological approaches, themes and methods. London: Routledge.

Strauss, A. (1962). Transformations of identity. In A. M. Rose (Ed.), *Human behaviour and social processes: An interactionist approach* (pp. 63–85). Henley, U.K.: Routledge.

Swain, D. A. (1991). Withdrawal from sport and Schlossberg's model of transitions. *Sociology of Sport Journal*, 8(2), 152–160.

Tekavc, J., Wylleman, P., & Cecić Erpič, S. (2015). Perceptions of dual career development among elite level swimmers and basketball players. *Psychology of Sport and Exercise*, 21, 27–41.

Theberge, N. (2000). *Higher goals: Women's ice hockey and the politics of gender*. Albany, NY: SUNY Press.

Turk, M. (2018). *A case study: Inclusion of student-athletes who identify as sexual minority at an NCAA Division I institution* (Unpublished PhD dissertation). University of Arkansas, Fayetteville.

Umney, C., & Kretsos, L. (2014). Creative labour and collective interaction: The working lives of young jazz musicians in London. *Work, Employment and Society*, 28(4), 571–588.

Vickers, E. (2018). *An examination of the dual career pathway and transitions UK student-athletes experience throughout university education* (Unpublished PhD dissertation). Liverpool John Moores University.

Wacquant, L. J. D. (1995). The pugilistic point of view: How boxers think and feel about their trade. *Theory and Society*, 24(4), 489–535.

Wacquant, L. J. D. (1998). A fleshpeddler at work: Power, pain, and profit in the prizefighting economy. *Theory and Society*, 27(1), 1–42.

Wacquant, L. J. D. (2001). Whores, slaves and stallions: Language of exploitation and accommodation among boxers. *Body and Society*, 7(2–3), 181–194.

Weinberg, S. K., & Arond, H. (1952). The occupational culture of the boxer. *American Journal of Sociology*, 57, 460–469.

Wendling, E., & Sagas, M. (2020). An application of the social cognitive career theory model of career self-management to college athletes' career planning for life after sport. *Frontiers in Psychology*, 11(9).

Werther, P., & Orlick, P. (1986). Retirement experiences of successful Olympic athletes. *International Journal of Sport Psychology*, 17(5), 337–363.

White, A. L. (2020). *The culture of learning disabilities, race and athletics: An examination of student-athlete experiences in predominantly white institutions of higher education's Division One college football programs* (Unpublished PhD dissertation). University of South Florida, Tampa.

Wilensky, H. L. (1961). Work, careers and social integration, *American Sociological Review*, 26, 521–539.

Wylleman, P., Alfermann, D., & Lavallee, D. (2004). Career transitions in sport: European perspectives. *Psychology of Sport and Exercise*, 5, 7–20.

Wylleman, P., De Brandt, K., & Drefruyt, S. (2017). GEES handbook for dual career support providers. http://kics.sport.vlaanderen/.../170301_GEES_Handbook.

Wylleman, P., & Lavallee, D. (2004). A developmental perspective on transitions faced by athletes. In M. Weiss (Ed.), *Developmental sport and exercise psychology: A lifespan perspective* (pp. 503–523). Morgantown, WV: Fitness Information Technology.

Wylleman, P., & Reints, A. (2010). A lifespan perspective on the career of talented and elite athletes: Perspectives on high-intensity sports. *Scandinavian Journal of Medicine & Science in Sports, 20*, 88–94.

Wylleman, P., Reints, A., & De Knop, P. (2013a). Athletes' careers in Belgium. A holistic perspective to understand and alleviate challenges occurring throughout the athletic and post-sport career. In N. B. Stambulova, & T. V. Ryba (Eds.), *Athletes' careers across cultures* (pp. 31–42). New York: Routledge.

Wylleman, P., Reints, A., & De Knop, P. (2013b). A developmental and holistic perspective on athletic career development. In P. Sotiaradou, & V. De Bosscher (Eds.), *Managing high performance sport* (pp. 159–182). New York: Routledge.

Young, R. A., & Collin, A. (2000). Introduction: Framing the future of career. In A Collin & R. A. Young (Eds.), *The future of career* (pp. 1–18). Cambridge: Cambridge University Press.

CHAPTER 38

....

SPORT, AGING, AND ADAPTATION

....

ELIZABETH C. J. PIKE, ELSPETH J. MATHIE, AND DANIEL D. BUCKLEY

"You are old, Father William," the young man said,
—"And your hair has become very white;
And yet you incessantly stand on your head—
—Do you think, at your age, it is right?"

"In my youth," Father William replied to his son,
—"I feared it might injure the brain;
But, now that I'm perfectly sure I have none,
—Why, I do it again and again."

"You are old," said the youth, "as I mentioned before,
—And have grown most uncommonly fat;
Yet you turned a back-somersault in at the door—
—Pray, what is the reason of that?"

"In my youth," said the sage, as he shook his grey locks,
—"I kept all my limbs very supple
By the use of this ointment—one shilling the box—
—Allow me to sell you a couple?"

—Lewis Carroll (1865, p. 45)

CARROLL's oft-quoted poem provides an example of the different ways that older adults might adapt to the aging process and the role that may be played by sporting and physical activities in later life. We see here the presentation of a "youthful" older self, alongside the perceptions of older adults from the perspective of a younger person and the health messages that often combine with these perceptions to constrain some lifestyle choices as people age. We will explore these issues, along with other aspects of aging and adaptation, in what follows.

It is well documented that the world's population is aging, with almost every country experiencing growth in the number and proportion of older persons. Globally in 2018, for the first time in history, persons 65 or above outnumbered children under 5. Population predictions suggest that by 2050, 16% of the world's population will be over 65 (25% in Europe and North America), which is up from 9% in 2019. The number of persons 80 years or over is projected to triple, from 143 million in 2019 to 426 million in 2050 (United Nations, 2019).

Population aging is likely to be one of the most significant social transformations of the 21st century, with implications for nearly all sectors of society, including the economy, infrastructure, and community relationships. At the same time, older adults are increasingly seen as contributors to development, with many countries likely to face fiscal and political pressures in relation to ensuring that there is appropriate health and social care for a growing older population (United Nations, 2020).

These demographic changes have implications for the provision and experiences of sport and physical activity. The benefits of physical activity for older adults are well documented (see Bangsbo et al., 2019), including improved functional capacity, brain health, cognitive function, and psychological and social well-being. However, also well documented is the fact that engagement in sporting activity declines with age in most societies (see Pike, 2019).

This chapter will focus on the intersection of aging and adaptation with specific attention to sport and physical activity. Parsons (1977) conceptualizes "adaptation" as one of four essential prerequisites to the continued existence of social systems—this is understood as having the flexibility to be able to change to suit different conditions so that the necessary resources are available to society. While Parsons's work is not without its critics, this concept may be helpful in understanding adaptation as a necessary process in aging societies. This chapter will consider this in a number of ways: how individuals adapt to the changing abilities of their body as they age, and what impact this has on their engagement with sporting activities; how sports are being adapted to accommodate the needs of older adults; how societies adapt to the changing demographics of aging populations, focusing on the role of sport and physical activity in these processes of adaptation; and how researchers need to adapt their methodologies to meet the needs of older adults. Particular attention will be given to debates regarding the sporting experiences and opportunities for older adults living with dementia.

Issues

When sports were first organized during the late 1800s and early 1900s, the dominant theories at the time emphasized the benefits of participation in organized physical activity for young people, while simultaneously reinforcing beliefs that old people (at that time, this meant those older than 40!) should avoid such vigorous activities because they had passed their prime and were facing inevitable and unavoidable physical decline (Coakley & Pike, 2014). This is illustrated in the words of Dostoyevsky (1986, p. 7), who stated, "I am forty years old now, and you know forty years is a whole lifetime; you know it is extreme old age."

By the early 21st century, there had been a move toward advocating "active aging," a celebrated notion that has become "the dominant discourse in policy, the media and health promotion messages, and language used in gerontological and sport science literatures which generally encourages people to remain physically, socially and mentally active as they age" (Gard & Dionigi, 2016, p. 739). While this suggests that there has been a fundamental shift in opinion regarding the capacity of the aging body, in reality much that is operant remains still grounded in a traditional "deficit" model of aging, which presents growing old as a period of inevitable decline, dominated by the experience of deficits, diseases, and other age-related problems (Pike, 2019). Physical activity is thus presented as a panacea for social problems, including the potential for sport and physical activity to address the perceived social and economic challenges of population aging and specifically the management of diseases associated with old age (Gard et al., 2017). The encouragement to engage in physical activity is, therefore, seen as a form of intervention to delay age-related decline and reduce the risk of developing chronic conditions (Tulle, 2008). Such messages are often grounded in neoliberal ideologies that emphasize taking responsibility for one's own health in order to avoid being a burden on society (Pike, 2011, 2019). This approach often overlooks the fact that some older people are unwilling or unable to participate in physical activity, the consequence of which may be that they are stigmatized, victimized, and their needs not fully considered in health policy and practice (Dionigi, 2017).

Aging and Adaptation: Older Adults

The factors enabling and constraining the involvement of older adults in sport and physical activity have been understood, in part, as an aging habitus (Dumas & Turner, 2006). This is identified as a set of shared dispositions among older adults that is distinctive from younger people, in particular considering how people take a different view of their world and the capabilities of their body as they grow older. A systematic review of the extant literature (Jenkin, Eime, Westerbeek, O'Sullivan, & van Uffelen, 2017) highlights the ways that individuals adapt to aging, and the impact this has on decisions and opportunities to engage in sport and physical activity. The most frequently reported determinant for older adults' participation in sport is their health, either as a positive outcome of or as a limiting factor to participation. The second most frequently mentioned theme is negotiating the aging process, either through the production of positive aging discourse or negotiating negative stereotypes of aging. Many older adults also mention the benefits of social and community connection through sport and physical activity.

Of course, it is also the case that these choices are determined by the various forms of capital available to older adults (Bourdieu, 1986). This may include access to economic capital, including costs of classes and equipment; cultural capital, including fear about doing sport in later life, and particularly medical concerns; social capital, such as a lack of confidence, embarrassment, and an absence of relevant older role models or companions; and symbolic capital, particularly in the form of advice from other people regarding what are deemed appropriate activities to do at an older age (see Pike, 2015).

Access to capital, and concerns about health and ageist stereotypes, appear to be particularly significant for older women as they try to adapt to their aging bodies and make choices about engagement in sport and physical activity. Women have longer life expectancies than men in all societies, a trend that has been described as the "feminization of aging," which also means they are more likely to experience a loss of relationships with partners, family, friends, and colleagues through bereavement and/or retirement, contributing to social exclusion and loss of the capital which may enable sporting activity (Featherstone &

Hepworth, 1991). Women are also often hampered by their experience of menopause, a process that reinforces perceptions about the fragility of the aging female body. This can lead to discouragement of physical effort in later years, which consequently obscures the actual benefits of exercise for menopausal women and reinforces ageist stereotypes (see Pike, 2010, 2019; Vertinsky & O'Brien Cousins, 2007). However, some older women have indicated that engagement in sport helps them to adapt to menopause and their aging bodies. As illustrated in the words of a female Masters swimmer, "I'm retired now, and hope to increase my exercising, as this really helps the side effects of the menopause and keeps my muscles flexible" (female, 60, club-level competitor, quoted in Pike, 2012, p. 503). This illustrates the complexities for older adults in trying to adapt to their aging bodies, and the need for sports and societies to also adapt to accommodate the needs of aging populations.

Aging and Adaptation: Sports

Evidence demonstrates that older adults are more likely to attend sporting activities which are adapted to meet their requirements and specific needs (Griffin, 2017). Where physical activities are designed *with* the participants rather than *for* the participants, this increases attendance and enjoyment (Armstrong & Morgan, 1998). This appears to be the case for both competitive and recreational sporting events.

In order to accommodate the needs of older adults wishing to participate in competitive sports into later life, a number of individual sports now hold age-segregated competitions. Swimming and track and field (athletics) have the longest histories of masters-level events. The first World Masters Athletics Championships were held in Toronto in 1975, and the first swimming championships were held in Tokyo in 1986 (Weir, Baker, & Horton, 2010). Both of the most recent events (at the time of writing) had attracted more than 4,000 competitors from over 80 countries at the World Masters Athletics Championships in Malaga, Spain, in 2018 and the World Masters Swimming Championship in Gwangju, South Korea, in 2019. Research demonstrates that adapting the structure of sports competitions to allow age-segregated competitions helps people to negotiate growing older. Participants indicate that they are able to "simultaneously resist, define and accept the ageing process" (Dionigi, Horton, & Baker, 2013, p. 385), and they understand that their performance is likely to decline while also enjoying the competition (see also Dionigi, 2010, 2011; Dionigi, Horton, & Baker, 2011; Dionigi & O'Flynn, 2007; Pike, 2012; Tulle, 2007).

Sports have also been adapted in other ways in order to accommodate the needs of older adults who may not wish to engage in activities that demand performance improvement. "Adapted" sports are defined as activities that are directed at those "who require adaptation for participation in the context of PA (physical activity)" (Carlier, Mainguet, & Delevoye-Turrell, 2016, p. 351). Various walking sports have been designed as modified versions of competitive activities which emphasize staying active, maintaining physical abilities so that people can remain active as they get older, as well as offering social experiences and connections (Cholerton, Breckon, Butt, & Quirk, 2019; Klostermann & Nagel, 2014). In particular, adapted walking sports have been found to offer a level of activity that caters to all abilities, allowing those with poorer health or mobility to participate (Cholerton et al., 2019) and so addressing the barriers of health and access to capital identified above (see Jenkin et al., 2017; Pike, 2015).

Aging and Adaptation: Society

As the global population ages, many societies are recognizing the need to adapt to these demographic changes. The United Nations' (2015) 2030 Agenda for Sustainable Development identifies the importance of supporting the needs of the globally increasing population of older people, and sport and physical activity are frequently identified as having a key role in addressing social changes needed for a globally aging population. When older people participate in sporting activities it may be seen to subvert the traditional "deficit" model of aging toward a more positive view that aging can be associated with a pleasurable lifestyle, including engagement in a range of activities in later life. This shift has been defined as a "heroic" model of aging, which defines aging as something to be fought and defeated, while conversely, giving in to aging is regarded as a failure (see Pike, 2018).

However, it is argued that neither of these societal models of aging fully reflects the views and experiences of older people (Reed, Cook, Childs, & Hall, 2003) and, indeed, that both views can be considered ageist (see Dionigi, 2008). Despite this, these models continue to inform much of the research and policy agendas that affect the lives of older people, and are even used as a strategy for marketing and/or regulating certain groups of the population, while marginalizing those who adopt alternative styles of aging (see Dionigi & Litchfield, 2018; Gard, et al., 2017). As Gard and Dionigi (2016) point out, governments increasingly see the sports industry as a driver of economic growth, and this includes promoting sporting activities to an increasing aging population. Indeed, Neilson (2006, p. 151) states that older adults are often viewed as a "blossoming consumer market," and Pike (2011, p. 221) has argued that "entrepreneurs continue to perpetuate a moral panic around the burgeoning aging population and present 'evidence' that physical activity provides a solution to the problem of these aging folk devils" in order to encourage older adults to purchase their age-defying products and sports club memberships.

It is proposed elsewhere that societies need to pay more attention to aging in ways that are meaningful to the individual, or what has been described as "authentic aging" (see Biggs, 2004; Ranzijn, 2010) or "everyday aging" (Pike, 2018). In particular, most societies need to encourage all citizens to adapt to thinking of themselves as members of aging societies in order to challenge the disenfranchisement of older adults from the societies in which they live. As Neilson (2006, p. 152) has noted, "it is not only the aged who live in ageing societies."

APPROACHES

We identified in the previous section that the early development of organized sports focused on younger people. The sociological understandings of sport have also tended to focus on studies of youth, and older people have traditionally been neglected in sociological studies of sport, and in social and policy research more widely. However, the emergence of "third age" societies (those where more than half of the population can expect to live to 70) has led to the development of the academic discipline of gerontology (see Pike, 2019).

Gerontologists study aging and later life, seeking to develop a framework that outlines "successful aging," or the process of growing older while maintaining high levels of physiological functioning, psychological satisfaction, and positive quality of life. Early gerontology took a predominantly biomedical approach, often overlooking the social, historical, political, and economic features of aging (Achenbaum, 1997). However, since the 1970s, greater attention has been given to the social construction and lived experience of aging (see Blaikie, 1999), including the role of sport and physical activity in becoming and being an older person.

When sociologists and social gerontologists have turned their attention to the provision and experiences of sport and physical activity for older adults, they have increasingly come to understand this through neoliberal ideologies. Neoliberalism helps us to understand the promotion of sport and physical activity for older adults as a way of encouraging (or obliging) people to take responsibility for their aging bodies in order to maintain health and functioning and to reduce the impact on the health and social care services (see Gard et al., 2017; Pike, 2011). This appears to be related to perceptions that increased life expectancy is problematic rather than a cause for celebration, and this has provided the foundations for older adults to be seen as a threat or risk to society (see Cavanagh, 2007; Pike, 2011). In this way, discourses emerge of "good" and "bad" ways to age. The "good" way to age is to be active and maintain an independent lifestyle into later life. The "bad" way to age is to remain socially (and economically) dependent (Hepworth, 1995). This is illustrated in the findings of the systematic review by Jenkin et al. (2017) that many older adults choose to engage in sport to address health issues and/or aging stereotypes, and in doing so are heralded as among those following a "good" way to age. Of course, much of this assumes that all older adults have the same opportunities and ability to be active and independent, which is not the case. In addition, the advice to be active is often "made according to professionally generated criteria—and which fit the circumstances of older people's lives imprecisely" (Cavanagh, 2007, p. 81). In particular, as we will discuss later in this section, too often lifestyle recommendations and definitions of physical activity are made from the perspective of younger people rather than understanding what it is that older adults actually want (see Pike, 2011).

Our research has largely been informed by the theoretical approach of Erving Goffman. A central tenet of Goffman's (1969) work is that identities are constructed through interactions between social actors and others in an ongoing dynamic social process, and identities need to be (re)negotiated and potentially adapted at various stages of the life cycle. Goffman (1963) developed the concept of stigma to explain what happens when these social interactions fail because people look or act in a way that deviates from social norms—for example, when the aging body appears and moves differently from the youthful body that is prevalent in images of sporting activities. This social theory is useful in understanding how stigmatization may challenge feelings of self-worth and identity, and how older adults may experience marginalization and discrimination which impacts their sports participation and experiences (see Pike, 2012).

In order to effectively research these issues, a further process of adaptation is required for researchers who need to adapt their methodological approach to be sensitive to the lived experiences of aging (Goodman, Froggatt, & Mathie, 2012; Luff, Ferreira, & Meyer, 2011). The focus on aging means that research is focusing on people who have lived a long time and so may have had a greater array of life experiences. This means recognizing that the older population is increasingly heterogeneous and not easy to categorize in ways that are meaningful (see Pike, 2012, 2014).

Sociological and social gerontological research of sporting activities in later life therefore tend to take multimethod approaches, as explained by Pike (2014), who draws on participant observation, interviews, written stories, and semiology "in order to understand the relationship between personal experience and the social and political landscape within which they are embedded" and so that research can be "an instrument of socio-political change" (Wray, 2014, p. 145). For example, adopting methods of participant observation, ethnography, and interviews is consistent with the theoretical approach of Goffman that views sociological inquiry as something that should be "done" by interacting with people's lives (see Birrell & Donnelly, 2004) and ensures that any interpretation of what constitutes "good" aging is from the perspective of older adults themselves (Pike, 2012).

Documentary analysis, including policy documents and other official reports, can also reveal important aspects of how aging is constructed in contemporary society (Pike, 2012). Furthermore, Pike (2013) argues that fictional narratives can be used as an important gerontological research resource for understanding how ideas about aging are normatively shaped by culture. Perhaps as important, such analysis can reveal how alternative images of aging may be constructed and made possible through literary fiction. This is also consistent with the work of Goffman (1959), who himself used a fictional analogy to understand human behavior in his concept of dramaturgy. In this, he describes the world as a stage on which people are "actors" with an "audience," explaining how they behave in public (or on the "front stage") and what they choose to hide about themselves by keeping some personal information "back stage"—some of which may be related to the aging process and the role of sporting activities to display a youthful self on the front stage while hiding aspects of the aging body on the back stage.

Pike's (2014) work also identifies the challenge of researching those with age-related health issues and often a sense of impending mortality. Sensitive, ethical issues surrounding research with people who are nearing the end of life have particular meaning in gerontological research (Haraldsdottir, Lloyd, & Dewing, 2019). It is argued elsewhere that the fear of death appears to have increased where religious belief has decreased, removing some of the potentially reassuring answers about death and the afterlife. Older people living in care homes, in particular, are rarely offered opportunities to discuss the end of life (Mathie et al., 2012). As a result, aging and dying become increasingly fearful and stigmatized (Pike, 2012). Some research participants find that discussing experiences of physical activity as they negotiate their aging bodies can be a distressing or depressing experience, illustrated by the comments of one woman who stated she was "in tears now thinking about the things I can't do any more" (quoted in Pike, 2014, p. 136). Another research participant in the same study died during the research journey. Pike explains:

> [W]hen these participants are in poor health, suffering pain, and even dying, this creates additional dilemmas for the researcher to consider, including their own sense of responsibility for, and emotional attachment to, the people whose lives they wish to represent. (p. 140)

In addition to older people being included as research participants, those with lived experience have increasingly been involved in shaping research design and priorities in England (U.K. Department of Health 2006; Wilson et al., 2018) and internationally (Boivin et al., 2010). The term "patient and public involvement" (PPI) is often used in the United Kingdom, while "public engagement" is more frequently used in Europe, the USA, and

Canada (Hoddinott et al., 2018). An important distinction is made between "research being carried out 'with' or 'by' members of the public (PPI) rather than 'to', 'about' or 'for' them" (that is, the participants) (INVOLVE, 2012). Recent guidance to this effect has been published as "UK Standards for Public Involvement" (National Institute for Health Research, 2019). The benefits of including those with lived experience (which may also involve gaining the perspectives of their carers) are enhanced quality and appropriateness of research, user-focused research objectives, and user-friendly recruitment strategies, while challenges include time and cost (Brett et al., 2014). Members of the public can be involved in research in a variety of ways, including consultation, collaboration, and user-controlled research (INVOLVE, 2012). The most common public involvement activity is being a member of a research steering committee and reviewing patient information leaflets to make them more user-friendly (Mathie et al., 2014). Coproduction approaches have recently become popular, with a growing emphasis on sharing of power, the inclusion of all perspectives, respecting and valuing diverse knowledge, and building and maintaining reciprocal relationships (Hickey et al., 2018). An underlying key to this kind of approach is to recognize those who are involved in research as PPI contributors by acknowledging their contributions and keeping them informed of progress and any changes made as a result of their input (Mathie et al., 2018).

While involving older people in the research process may provide some challenges, it is essential that involvement is not "tokenistic" and that a working partnership is promoted, valued, and integral (Dewar, 2005). Strategies to enhance effective involvement of older people include the choice of location, use of visualization and accessible communication, and building good communication and flexible approaches (Schilling & Gerhardus, 2017). Examples of such research include Di Lorito, Godfrey, and Dunlop's (2020) study, which included carers' views in shaping a randomized controlled trial on promoting activity for people living with dementia. An increasing amount of co-research is now being published, including research shaped by the voices of people living with dementia (Di Lorito et al., 2017; Mann & Hung, 2019; Swarbrick et al., 2019; Tanner, 2012). Mockford et al. (2016) share the benefits of involving people living with dementia as co-researchers, which include developing the research agenda and implementation. Along with the considerable benefits of such inclusion, there can be challenges, such as organizational difficulties in required background checks and difficulties of arranging payments, which can create delays in the research process.

In studies such as these that involve people living with dementia (either as participants or as public involvement), there are additional ethical considerations concerning mental capacity that relate to the legitimacy of garnering informed consent from those with cognitive impairment (Silbert & Scott, 2020; Thorogood, Mäki-Petäjä-Leinonen, Dalpé, Gastmans, & Gauthier, 2019). Further, it is important to acknowledge the distinction between participants and public involvement. While ethical probity and consent are needed for both mounting research and engaging participants, ethical approval is not needed for involving members of the public in shaping research in England (Health Research Authority, 2016), although ethical procedures must be followed (Pandya-Wood, Barron, & Elliott, 2017).

Safety, support, and involvement of carers and family members are key considerations to enable people living with dementia to take part in research (Rivett, 2017). Dewing (2007, 2008) discusses an approach of process consent to enable more people living with dementia to participate in research if they want to. This form of consent is ongoing and flexible, taking into consideration verbal, nonverbal, and behavioral indicators. Dewing (2007, 2008) takes an "inclusionary" approach to consent and emphasizes the person-centered relationship between researcher and participants. The voices of those living with dementia have often been absent from research (Bartlett, 2012) or represented by carers, even though carers and people living with dementia often have different perspectives and views.

Debates

There are approximately 50 million people living with dementia worldwide (World Health Organization, 2017). While dementia does not exclusively affect older adults, approximately 1 in 14 people over 65 will develop dementia, and the condition affects 1 in 6 people over 80. Dementia is one of the main causes of disability in later life (Prince et al., 2007). There is convincing evidence about the benefits of engaging in physical activity for adults living with dementia, including the potential for physical activity to reduce the risk of developing dementia and prevent decline as well as numerous social benefits (Ahlskog, Yonas, Graff-Radford, & Petersen, 2011; Livingston, Sommerlad, & Orgeta, 2017; Norton, Matthews, Barnes, Yaffe, & Brayne, 2014; Nuzum et al., 2020; Zhou, Fu, Hong, Wang, & Fang, 2017). Physical inactivity has been identified as one of 12 potential modifiable risk factors for dementia (Livingston et al., 2020). However, survey data indicates that older adults living with dementia find it particularly challenging to engage in many organized physical activities (Sport England, 2019).

Adults who are diagnosed with dementia before the age of 65 (known as "young-onset dementia") may have support needs different from those diagnosed in later years (Mayrhofer, Mathie, McKeown, Bunn, & Goodman, 2017). Those diagnosed with young-onset dementia have their own challenges, as they are still of employment age, possibly forced to take early retirement, and may have dependent children and older parents. To enable physical activity to continue, modifications such as "slow swimming" lanes or reduced memberships at leisure facilities have been suggested, as have community-based solutions, such as facilitating volunteer support to attend football matches or to accompany individuals swimming (Mayrhofer, Mathie, et al., 2020; Mayrhofer, Shora, et al., 2020).

Aging and Adaptation for People Living with Dementia: Older Adults

Older adults affected by dementia (those living with dementia and also their carers) have a higher risk of being socially isolated and lonely than other social groups, and they often report that they do not feel connected with their communities (Penninkilampi, Casey, Singh, & Brodaty, 2018). This is particularly the case for long-term-care residents, who may spend up to 65% of their time entirely alone in their residence (Evans, Garabedian, & Bray, 2019). This is attributed in part to the stigma associated with dementia, which means they have fewer opportunities to engage in social interaction, including sporting activities (Age UK, 2018; Alzheimer's Society, 2018; Nelson, Tomyn, Hampton, & McCabe, 2017). Evidence from the U.K. Alzheimer's Society (2019) suggests that nearly a third of people (29%) living with dementia are unable to spend time with their friends, although many (23%) feel that people openly avoid them because of their diagnosis. Furthermore, the Alzheimer's Society (2018) states that dementia has a detrimental effect on those who care for people living with dementia, with three in five carers indicating that their role as a carer has impacted their own health and well-being. Additionally, 68% of carers have stated they do not have enough social contact to meet their needs (NHS Digital, 2017).

There is emerging evidence that older adults living with dementia, and their carers, experience a shared benefit when engaging together in physical activity (Lowery et al., 2014; Quinn & Toms, 2019). Such initiatives provide people with the opportunities to socialize with others affected by the same condition, to improve their communication skills, and to reduce their sense of vulnerability, all of which facilitate adaptation to the diagnosis of dementia (Carone, Tischler, & Dening, 2016; Góngora et al., 2019; Kelly & Innes, 206; Kirk, Rasmussen, Overgaard, & Berntsen, 2018).

Aging and Adaptation for People Living with Dementia: Sports

In 2019, Sport England produced the *Dementia-Friendly Sport and Physical Activity Guide* (Alzheimer's Society, 2019), which indicates that, while there is evidence of the benefits of physical activity for older adults living with dementia, they often do not feel sufficiently connected to their communities to be able to participate in physical activity programs. The *Guide* provides information regarding the ways that sports can be adapted to better meet the needs of those affected by dementia. What is likely to support engagement is increasingly well understood. Key matters here include access to transport and facilities that are enabling. For example, a person living with dementia may have memory problems, have difficulty making decisions or following instructions, or have visuo-perceptual difficulties with distances, patterns, or reflections. Adapting sports activities and facilities can address these challenges by providing clear signage and offering dementia-friendly design with regard to color, flooring, and noise. Furthermore, having trained helpers available who have the ability to accommodate specific physical and cognitive needs helps to address the concerns of people living with dementia and lessens the likelihood of being stigmatized or excluded by staff and members of the public.

Evidence suggests that, when sport-based activities are adapted and combined with other activities, such as singing, dancing, and reminiscence, there is a significant positive short-term effect on people living with dementia (Brett, Traynor, & Stapley, 2016; Cohen-Mansfield, 2016). This supports evidence on the importance and effectiveness of a personalized approach to interventions and programs designed for people living with dementia (Charlesworth et al., 2016; Coll-Planas et al., 2017; Dempsey et al., 2014; Tolson & Schofield, 2012; Watchman & Tolson, 2015).

Reminiscence therapy helps those living with dementia to remember events, people, and places from their past. Often sports events are used as effective triggers for reminiscence, discussion, and activities (Arean et al., 1993; Lin, Dai, & Hwang, 2003). This approach has proven particularly "promising in improving the mood of people with dementia as well as the communication between them and their caregivers" (Huldtgren, Mertl, Vormann, & Geiger, 2017, p. 1). In the United Kingdom, the Sporting Memories Foundation uses individual and collective memories of sporting occasions and events as a basis for reminiscence for older adults living with dementia (Clark, Murphy, Jameson-Allen, & Wilkins, 2017). The Foundation's offerings are tailored to selected groups of people who share an interest in a particular sport or sporting event (Clark, Murphy, Jameson-Allen, & Wilkins, 2015). Griggs, Leflay, and Groves (2012) found that selected iconic sporting events could often be recalled quite clearly, with some participants experiencing an emotional response to past experiences that they were able to recollect. A number of professional football (soccer) clubs in the United Kingdom have adapted their facilities to invite people living with dementia onto the grounds to enjoy sport and engage in football reminiscence. Early evidence suggests that football reminiscence positively affects the lives of people living with dementia, serving to reduce social barriers within communities. This is particularly evident when reminiscence is combined with adapted physical activities such as walking football, a variation of association football that bans running and sliding tackles (Carone et al., 2016; Cho & Han, 2018; Schofield & Tolson, 2010; Tolson & Schofield, 2012). Furthermore, participants identify a sense of anticipation in advance of attending dementia-specific programs (Charlesworth et al., 2016).

Aging and Adaptation for People Living with Dementia: Society

In 2006, the World Health Organization responded to the aging population and the growing numbers living in urban areas with the Age-Friendly Cities initiative. The idea is to encourage active aging "by optimising opportunities for health, participation and security in order to enhance quality of life as people age" (World Health Organization, 2007, p. 1). Societal adaptations are challenged by the fact that people living with dementia are identified by some researchers as a hard-to-reach population (Field et al., 2019).

Many countries have now identified Dementia-Friendly Communities (DFCs) as an approach to community engagement that supports people affected by dementia to live well. DFCs are collaborations of local people and organizations, often geographically defined, and are formally recognized as working to the common aim of promoting dementia awareness and inclusion of people affected by dementia (Alzheimer's Disease International, 2015). They work to address the stigma and social exclusion, and at an individual level, they create opportunities for individuals to be active citizens and facilitate access to services and support (Alzheimer's Society, 2018; Heward, Innes, Cutler, & Hambidge, 2017). In England, a national evaluation of DFCs has revealed that while many include awareness raising and activity programs, activities often tend to segregate when they are designated for dementia-centered purposes (such as through dementia cafés), and as a consequence, there are slightly fewer opportunities for involvement as part of the wider community (for example, attending existing leisure facilities and sports) (Buckner et al., 2019). The online presence of DFCs has been variable; some websites are not always kept up to date, making it difficult for people to find and access information (Buckner et al., 2019). While DFCs have had varying resources for support, many relied on volunteers, and there has often been limited formal monitoring and evaluation of participants' performance and progress (Buckner et al., 2019). Further, study findings have suggested that DFCs in England tend to be found in areas of epidemiological-based need (Woodward et al., 2019). Nevertheless, much evidence has shown that DFCs have the potential to enable those living with dementia to continue to take part in physical exercise and everyday activities by improving transport facilities, adapting buildings and services, increasing public and community awareness, and providing appropriate support, such as through buddy systems. Research findings support the notion that effective DFCs need to be shaped and designed by those living with dementia and their carers (Dementia Engagement and Empowerment Project, 2015).

Conclusion

This chapter has identified a range of issues related to aging and adaptation. At the time of writing, most countries were navigating the global COVID-19 pandemic. The pandemic exposed a number of social inequalities that impact participation in sport, as well as health more widely, with older adults, including those living with dementia among the populations notably affected by government restrictions (Donnelly, Darnell, & Kidd, 2020). In particular, older adults and those with underlying health conditions were advised to self-isolate or shield themselves from wider society. This, in turn, reduced social interaction and increased social isolation for some members of the population who already experience isolation and loneliness. In particular, these messages also have the potential to "other" older adults and those with particular health conditions, reproducing limiting and stigmatizing messages regarding their vulnerability and marginalizing them from both the likelihood and the benefits of engagement in sport and physical activities (Evans et al., 2020). The long-term implications of the pandemic for older adults and their engagement in sport remains to be seen, but there is much potential for positive adaptation:

> Perhaps the recognition of inequality can lead to the reallocation of public and private funds. Perhaps the fragility or robustness of specific sports systems will lead to new ways of conceptualising how sport should be organised. Perhaps awareness of the difficulties faced by specific populations will lead us to reconsider the way in which sport and healthcare resources are utilised in new, more ethical and inclusive ways. Perhaps the intersection of the virus with environmental stresses and the recognition of the wastefulness of our previously globalised version of sport will lead us to rethink the very nature of sport and the sports "industry." (Evans et al., 2020, pp. 8–9)

In this chapter, we have argued that adaptation is multifaceted and multilevel if it is to be meaningful to older adults. The aging process requires multiple levels of adaptation to accommodate the needs of older adults in sport: older adults themselves often go through a personal process of adaptation learning to live with an aging body; sports have a responsibility to adapt to the needs of the growing older population; and societies need to adapt to ensuring all citizens think of themselves as members of an aging community.

In order to fully understand the lived experience of aging, researchers need to adapt their methodologies to be sensitive to and inclusive of those older adults whose lives and stories they wish to understand. We argue for a collective effort of academics, policymakers, practitioners, providers, civil society, and other stakeholders (including older persons themselves) to set "a new agenda of active and healthy ageing that can reduce the vulnerabilities and enhance the rights, capabilities and resilience of older persons, and thus fulfil the pledge of the 2030 Agenda to leave no one behind" (United Nations, 2015).

REFERENCES

Achenbaum, W. (1997). Critical gerontology. In A. Jamieson, S. Harper, & C. Victor (Eds.), *Critical approaches to ageing and later life* (pp. 16–26). Buckingham, U.K.: Open University Press.

Age UK. (2018). *All the lonely people: Loneliness in later life*. London: Age UK.

Ahlskog, J. E., Yonas, E. G., Graff-Radford, N. R., & Petersen, R. C. (2011). Physical exercise as a preventive or disease-modifying treatment of dementia and brain aging. *Mayo Clinic Proceedings, 86*(9), 876–884.

Alzheimer's Disease International. (2015). Dementia friendly communities: Key principles. https://www.alz.co.uk/adi/pdf/dfc-principles.pdf.

Alzheimer's Society. (2018). Tackling loneliness in people living with dementia. https://www.alzheimers.org.uk/blog/tackling-loneliness-people-living-dementia.

Alzheimer's Society. (2019). *Dementia-friendly sport and physical activity guide*. London: Alzheimer's Society.

Arean, P. A., Perri, M. G., Nezu, A. M., Schein, R. L., Christopher, F., & Joseph, T. X. (1993). Comparative effectiveness of social problem-solving therapy and reminiscence therapy as treatments for depression in older adults. *Journal of Consulting and Clinical Psychology, 61*(6), 1003–1010.

Armstrong, G. K., & Morgan, K. (1998). Stability and change in levels of habitual physical activity in later life. *Age and Ageing, 27*(3), 17–23.

Bangsbo, J., Blackwell, J., Boraxbekk, C.-J., Caserotti, P., Dela, F., Evans, A., . . . Viña, J. (2019). Copenhagen consensus statement 2019: Physical activity and ageing. *British Journal of Sports Medicine*. Advance online publication. doi:10.1136/bjsports-2018–100451.

Bartlett, R. (2012). Modifying the diary interview method to research the lives of people with dementia. *Qualitative Health Research, 22*(12), 1717–1726.

Biggs, S. (2004). In pursuit of successful identities and authentic ageing. In E. Tulle (Ed.), *Old age and agency* (pp. 143–162). New York: Nova Science Publishers.

Birrell, S., & Donnelly, P. (2004). Reclaiming Goffman: Erving Goffman's influence on the sociology of sport. In R. Guilianotti (Ed.), *Sport and modern social theorists* (pp. 49–64). Basingstoke, U.K.: Palgrave Macmillan.

Blaikie, A. (1999). *Ageing and popular culture*. Cambridge: Cambridge University Press.

Boivin, A., Currie, K., Fervers, B., Gracia, J., James, M., Marshal, C., . . . Burgers, J. (2010). Patient and public in clinical guidelines: International experiences and future perspectives. *Quality and Safety in Health Care, 19*(22), e22. doi:10.1136/qshc.2009.034835.

Bourdieu, P. (1986). *Distinction: A social critique of the judgement of taste*. London: Routledge.

Brett, J., Staniszewska, S., Mockford, C., Herron-Marx, S., Hughes, J., Tysall, C., & Suleman, R. (2014). Mapping the impact of patient and public involvement on health and social care research: A systematic review. *Health Expectations, 17*(5), 637–650.

Brett, L., Traynor, V., & Stapley, P. (2016). Effects of physical exercise on health and well-being of individuals living with a dementia in nursing homes: A systematic review. *Journal of the American Medical Directors Association, 17*(2), 104–116.

Buckner, S., Darlington, N., Woodward, M., Buswell, M., Mathie, E., Arthur, A., . . . Goodman, C. (2019). Dementia friendly communities in England: A scoping study. *International Journal of Geriatric Psychiatry. 34*, 1235– 1243. https://doi.org/10.1002/gps.5123.

Carlier, M., Mainguet, B., & Delevoye-Turrell, Y. (2016). Cognitive exercise through body movement: Using a fun and short neuropsychological tool to adapt physical activity and enhance pleasure in individuals suffering from mental illnesses. *Psychologie Francaise, 61*, 349–359.

Carone, L., Tischler, V., & Dening, T. (2016). Football and dementia: A qualitative investigation of a community based sports group for men with early onset dementia. *Dementia, 15*(6), 1358–1376.

Carroll, L. (1865). *Alice's adventures in wonderland*. London: The Thames.

Cavanagh, A. (2007). Taxonomies of anxiety: Risk, panics, paedophilia and the internet. *Electronic Journal of Sociology*. https://sociology.lightningpath.org/ejs-archives/2007/__cavanagh_taxonomies.pdf.

Charlesworth, G., Burnell, K., Crellin, N., Hoare, Z., Hoe, J., Knapp, M., . . . Orrell, M. (2016). Peer support and reminiscence therapy for people with dementia and their family carers: A factorial pragmatic randomised trial. *Journal of Neurosurgery and Psychiatry, 87*(11), 1218–1228.

Cho, C.-M., & Han, S.-J. (2018). The effect of reminiscence intervention on the elderly population: A systematic review. *International Journal of Elderly Welfare Promotion and Management, 2*(1), 33–38.

Cholerton, R., Breckon, J., Butt, J., & Quirk, H. (2019). Experiences influencing walking football initiation in 55- to 75-year-old adults: A qualitative study. *Journal of Aging and Physical Activity, 28*(4), 521–533.

Clark, M., Murphy, C., Jameson-Allen, T., & Wilkins, C. (2015). Sporting memories and the social inclusion of older people experiencing mental health problems. *Mental Health and Social Inclusion, 19*(4), 202–211.

Clark, M., Murphy, C., Jameson-Allen, T., & Wilkins, C. (2017). Sporting memories, dementia care and training staff in care homes. *Journal of Mental Health Training, Education and Practice, 12*(1), 55–66.

Coakley, J., & Pike, E. (2014). *Sports in society: Issues and controversies*. London: McGraw Hill/OU Press.

Cohen-Mansfield, J. (2016). Non-pharmacological interventions for agitation in dementia: Various strategies demonstrate effectiveness for care home residents: Further research in home settings is needed. *Evidence-Based Nursing, 19*(1), 31–31.

Coll-Planas, L., Watchman, K., Doménech, S., McGillivray, D., O'Donnell, H., & Tolson, D. (2017). Developing evidence for football (soccer) reminiscence interventions within long-term care: A co-operative approach applied in Scotland and Spain. *Journal of the American Medical Directors Association, 18*(4), 355–360.

Dementia Engagement and Empowerment Project. (2015). Involving people with dementia in creating dementia friendly communities. https://dementiavoices.org.uk/wp-content/uploads/2013/11/DEEP-Guide-Involving-people-with-dementia-in-Dementia-Friendly-Communities.pdf.

Dempsey, L., Murphy, K., Cooney, A., Casey, D., O'Shea, E., Devane, D., . . . Hunter, A. (2014). Reminiscence in dementia: A concept analysis. *Dementia*, 13(2), 176–192.

Dewar, B. J. (2005). Beyond tokenistic involvement of older people in research—A framework for future development and understanding. *Journal of Clinical Nursing*, 14(S1), 48–53.

Dewing, J. (2007). Participatory research: A method for process consent with persons who have dementia, *Dementia*, 6(1), 11–25.

Dewing, J. (2008). Process consent and research with older persons living with dementia. *Research Ethics*, 4(2), 59–64. https://doi.org/10.1177/174701610800400205.

Di Lorito, C., Birt, L., Poland, F., Csipke, E., Gove, D., Diaz-Ponce, & Orrell, M. (2017). A synthesis of the evidence on peer research with potentially vulnerable adults: How this relates to dementia. *International Journal of Geriatric Psychiatry*, 32(1), 58–67. doi:10.1002/gps.4577.

Di Lorito, C., Godfrey, M., & Dunlop, M. (2020). Adding to the knowledge on patient and public involvement: Reflections from an experience of co-research with carers of people with dementia. *Health Expectations*, 23, 691–706. https://doi.org/10.1111/hex.13049.

Dionigi, R. (2008). *Competing for life: Older people, sport and ageing*. Saarbrücken: Verlag Dr. Müller.

Dionigi, R. (2010). Masters sport as a strategy for managing the aging process. In J. Baker, S. Horton, & P. Weir (Eds.), *The masters athlete: Understanding the role of sport and exercise in optimizing aging* (pp. 137–156). London: Routledge.

Dionigi, R. (2011). Older athletes: Resisting and reinforcing discourses of sport and aging. In S. Spickard Prettyman & B. Lampman (Eds.), *Learning culture through sports: Perspectives on society and organized sports* (pp. 260–278). Lanham, MD: Rowman & Littlefield.

Dionigi, R. (2017). Leisure and recreation in the lives of older people. In M. Bernoth & D. Winkler (Eds.), *Healthy ageing and aged care in Australian communities* (pp. 204–220). Sydney: Oxford University Press.

Dionigi, R., Horton, S., & Baker, J. (2011). Seniors in sport: The experiences and practices of older World Masters Games competitors. *International Journal of Sport and Society*, 1(1), 55–68.

Dionigi, R., Horton, S., & Baker, J. (2013). Negotiations of the ageing process: Older adults' stories of sports participation. *Sport, Education and Society*, 18(3), 370–387.

Dionigi, R., & Litchfield, C. (2018). The mid-life "market" and the creation of sporting subcultures. In R. Dionigi & M. Gard (Eds.), *Sport and physical activity across the lifespan* (pp. 283–300). Basingstoke, U.K.: Palgrave MacMillan.

Dionigi, R., & O'Flynn, G. (2007). Performance discourses and old age: What does it mean to be an older athlete? *Sociology of Sport Journal* 24(4), 359–377.

Donnelly, P., Darnell, S., & Kidd, B. (2020). *Discussion paper: The implications of COVID-19 for community sport and sport for development*. Toronto: Centre for Sport Policy Studies, Faculty of Kinesiology and Physical Education, University of Toronto.

Dostoyevsky, F. (1986). *Notes from underground*. London: Penguin Classics.

Dumas, A., & Turner, B. (2006). Age and ageing: The social world of Foucault and Bourdieu. In J. Powell & A. Wahidin (Eds.), *Foucault and ageing* (pp. 145–155). New York: Nova Publishers.

Evans, A. B., Blackwell, J., Dolan, P., Fahlén, J., Hoekman, R., Lenneis, V., . . . Wilcock, L. (2020). Sport in the face of the COVID-19 pandemic: Towards an agenda for research in the sociology of sport. *European Journal for Sport and Society*, 17(2), 85–95. https://doi.org/10.1080/16138171.2020.1765100.

Evans, S. C., Garabedian, C., & Bray, J. (2019). "Now he sings": The My Musical Memories Reminiscence programme: Personalised interactive reminiscence sessions for people living with dementia. *Dementia, 18*(3), 1181–1198.

Featherstone, M., & Hepworth, M. (1991). The mask of ageing and the postmodern life course. In M. Featherstone, M. Hepworth, & B. Turner (Eds.), *The body: Social processes and cultural theory* (pp. 371–389). London: Sage.

Field, B., Mountain, G., Burgess, J., Di Bona, L., Kelleher, D., Mundy, J., & Wenborn, J. (2019). Recruiting hard to reach populations to studies: Breaking the silence: An example from a study that recruited people with dementia. *BMJ Open, 9*(11) 1–6.

Gard, M., & Dionigi, R. (2016). The world turned upside down: Sport, policy and ageing. *International Journal of Sport Policy and Politics, 8*(4), 737–743. doi:10.1080/19406940.2016.1186719.

Gard, M., Dionigi, R., Horton, S., Baker, J., Weir, P., & Dionigi, C. (2017). The normalization of sport for older people? *Annals of Leisure Research 20*(3), 253–272.

Goffman, E. (1959). *The presentation of self in everyday life.* New York: Anchor Books.

Goffman, E. (1963). *Stigma: Notes on the management of spoiled identity.* Harmondsworth, U.K.: Penguin.

Goffman, E. (1969). *Where the action is.* London: Penguin.

Goodman, C., Froggatt, K., & Mathie, E. (2012). *End of life care: Methods review 12.* London: NIHR School for Social Care Research.

Góngora Alonso, S., Hamrioui, S., de la Torre Díez, I., Motta Cruz, E., López-Coronado, M., & Franco, M. (2019). Social robots for people with aging and dementia: A systematic review of literature. *Telemedicine and e-Health, 25*(7), 533–540.

Griffin, M. (2017). Embodied learning and new physical activity in mid- and later life. *Qualitative Research in Sport, Exercise and Health, 9*(5), 554–567.

Griggs, G., Leflay, K. & Groves, M. (2012). "Just watching it again now still gives me goose bumps!": Examining the mental postcards of sport spectators. Sociology of Sport Journal, 29(1), 89–101.

Haraldsdottir, E., Lloyd, A., & Dewing, J. (2019). Relational ethics in palliative care research: Including a person-centred approach. *Palliative Care and Social Practice, 13*, 1–7. https://doi.org/10.1177/2632352419885384.

Health Research Authority. (2016). Public involvement: What do I need to do? https://www.invo.org.uk/posttypepublication/public-involvement-in-research-and-research-ethics-committee-review/.

Hepworth, M. (1995). Positive aging: What is the message? In R. Bunton, S. Nettleton, & R. Burrows (Eds.), *The sociology of health promotion: Critical analyses of consumption, lifestyle and risk* (pp. 176–190). London: Routledge.

Heward, M., Innes, A., Cutler, C., & Hambidge, S. (2017). Dementia-friendly communities: Challenges and strategies for achieving stakeholder involvement. *Health and Social Care in the Community, 25* (3), 858–867.

Hickey, G., Brearley, S., Coldham, T., Denegri, S., Green, G., Staniszewska, S., . . . Turner, K. (2018). *Guidance for co-producing a research project.* Southampton, U.K.: INVOLVE.

Hoddinott, P., Pollock, A., O'Cathain, A., Boyer, I., Taylor, J., MacDonald, C., . . . Donovan, J. L. (2018). How to incorporate patient and public perspectives into the design and conduct of research, *F1000Research, 7*(752), 1–33.

Huldtgren, A., Mertl, F., Vormann, A., & Geiger, C. (2017). Reminiscence of people with dementia mediated by multimedia artifacts. *Interacting with Computers, 29*(5), 679–696.

INVOLVE. (2012). *Briefing notes for researchers: Public involvement in NHS, public health and social care research*. Hampshire, U.K.: INVOLVE.

Jenkin, C., Eime, R., Westerbeek, H., O'Sullivan, G., & van Uffelen, J. (2017). Sport and ageing: A systematic review of the determinants and trends of participation in sport for older adults. *BMC Public Health, 17*, 976. doi:10.1186/s12889-017-4970-8.

Kirk, M., Rasmussen, K. W., Overgaard, S. B., & Berntsen, D. (2018). Five weeks of immersive reminiscence therapy improves autobiographical memory in Alzheimer's disease. *Memory, 27*(4), 1–14.

Klostermann, C., & Nagel, S. (2014). Changes in German sport participation: Historical trends in individual sports. *International Review for the Sociology of Sport, 49*(5), 609–634.

Lin, Y. C., Dai, Y. T., & Hwang, S. L. (2003). The effect of reminiscence on the elderly population: A systematic review. *Public Health Nursing, 20*(4), 297–306.

Livingston, G., Huntley, J., Sommerlad, A., Ames, D., Ballard, C., Banerjee, S., . . . Mukadam, N. (2020). Dementia prevention, intervention, and care: 2020 report of the Lancet Commission. *The Lancet, 396*, 413–446.

Livingston, G., Sommerlad, A., & Orgeta, V. (2017). Dementia prevention, intervention, and care. *Lancet, 390*, 2673–2734.

Lowery, D., Cerga-Pashoja, A., Iliffe, S., Thuné-Boyle, I., Griffin, M., Lee, J., . . . Warner, J. (2014). The effect of exercise on behavioural and psychological symptoms of dementia: The EVIDEM-E randomised controlled clinical trial. *International Journal of Geriatric Psychiatry, 29*(8), 819–827.

Luff, R., Ferreira, Z., & Meyer, J. (2011). *Care homes: Methods review 8*. London: NIHR School for Social Care Research.

Mann, J., & Hung, L. (2019). Co-research with people living with dementia for change. *Action Research, 17*(4), 573–590. https://doi.org/10.1177/1476750318787005.

Mathie, E., Goodman, C., Crang, C., Froggatt, K., Iliffe, S., Maththorpe, J., & Barclay, S. (2012). An uncertain future: The unchanging views of care home residents about living and dying. *Palliative Medicine, 26*(5), 734–743.

Mathie, E., Wilson, P., Poland, F., McNeilly, E., Howe, A., Staniszewska, S., . . . Goodman, C. (2014). Consumer involvement in health research: A UK scoping and survey. *International Journal of Consumer Studies, 38*(1), 35–44.

Mathie, E., Wythe, H., Munday, D., Millac, P., Rhodes, G., Roberts, N., . . . Jones, J. (2018). Reciprocal relationships and the importance of feedback in patient and public involvement: A mixed methods study. *Health Expectations, 21*(5), 899–908.

Mayrhofer, A., Mathie, E., McKeown, J., Bunn, F., & Goodman, C. (2017). Age-appropriate services for people diagnosed with young onset dementia (YOD): A systematic review: *Aging and Mental Health, 22*(8), 933–941.

Mayrhofer, A., Mathie, E., McKeown, J., Goodman, C., Irvine, L., Hall, N., & Walker, M. (2020). Young onset dementia: Public involvement in co-designing community-bases support. *Dementia, 19*(4), 1051–1066.

Mayrhofer, A., Shora, S., Tibbs, M.-A., Russell, S., Littlechild, B., & Goodman, C. (2020). Living with young onset dementia: Reflections on recent developments, current discourse, and implications for policy and practice, *Ageing and Society, 41*(11), 1–9.

Mockford, C., Murray, M., Seers, K., Oyebode, J., Grant, R., Boex, S., . . . Suleman, R. (2016). A SHARED study: The benefits and costs of setting up a health research study involving lay co-researchers and how we overcame the challenges. *Research Involvement and Engagement, 2*(8), 1–12.

National Institutes for Health Research. (2019). UK standards for public involvement, 2019. https://sites.google.com/nihr.ac.uk/pi-standards/home.

Neilson, B. (2006). Anti-ageing cultures, biopolitics and globalisation. *Cultic Studies Review*, *12*(2), 149–164.

Nelson, K., Tomyn, A., Hampton, I., & McCabe, M. (2017). How can we improve quality of life for aged care residents? *Australian Ageing Agenda, November*, 20.

NHS Digital. (2017). *Personal social services survey of adult carers in England, 2016–17*. London: NHS.

Norton, S., Matthews, F. E., Barnes, D. E., Yaffe, K., & Brayne, C. (2014). Potential for primary prevention of Alzheimer's disease: An analysis of population-based data. *The Lancet Neurology, 13*(8), 788–794.

Nuzum, H., Stickel, A., Corona, M., Zellar, M., Melrose, R., & Wilkins, S. S. (2020). Potential benefits of physical activity in MCI and dementia. *Behavioural Neurology*, Article ID 7807856, 1–10. https://www.ncbi.nlm.nih.gov/pmc/articles/PMC7037481/.

Pandya-Wood, R., Barron, D. S., & Elliott, J. (2017). A framework for public involvement at the design stage of NHS health and social care research: Time to develop ethically conscious standards. *Research Involvement and Engagement, 3*(6), 1–21.

Parsons, T. (1977). *The evolution of societies*. Englewood Cliffs, NJ: Prentice Hall.

Penninkilampi, R., Casey, A. N., Singh, M. F., & Brodaty, H. (2018). The association between social engagement, loneliness, and risk of dementia: A systematic review and meta-analysis. *Journal of Alzheimer's Disease, 66*(4), 1619–1633.

Pike, E. (2010). Growing old (dis)gracefully? The gender/ageing/exercise nexus. In E. Kennedy & P. Markula (Eds.), *Women and exercise: The body, health and consumerism* (pp. 180–196). London: Routledge.

Pike, E. (2011). The active aging agenda, old folk devils and a new moral panic. *Sociology of Sport Journal, 28*(2), 209–225.

Pike, E. (2012). Aquatic antiques: Swimming off this mortal coil? *International Review for the Sociology of Sport, 47*, 492–510.

Pike, E. (2013). The role of fiction in (mis)representing later life leisure activities. *Leisure Studies, 32*(1), 69–88.

Pike, E. (2014). Methodological issues in researching physical activity in later life. In A. Smith & I. Waddington (Eds.), *Doing real world research in sport studies* (pp. 131–140). London: Routledge.

Pike, E. (2015). Assessing the sociology of sport: On age and ability. *International Review for the Sociology of Sport, 50*(4–5), 570–574.

Pike, E. (2018). Outdoor adventurous sport: For all ages? In R. Dionigi & M. Gard (Eds.), *Sport and physical activity across the lifespan* (pp. 301–315). Basingstoke, U.K.: Palgrave Macmillan.

Pike, E. (2019). Aging, sports and society. In J. Maguire, K. Liston, & M. Falcous (Eds.), *The business and culture of sports* (pp. 231–251). Farmington Hills, MI: Macmillan.

Prince, M., Knapp, M., Albanese, E., Banerjee, S., Dhanasiri, S., Fernandez, J. L., . . . Stewart, R. (2007). *Dementia UK: Report to the Alzheimer's Society*. London: Kings College London and London School of Economics and Political Science.

Quinn C., & Toms, G. (2019). Influence of positive aspects of dementia caregiving on caregivers' well-being: A systematic review. *The Gerontologist, 59*(5), 584–596.

Ranzijn, R. (2010). Active ageing—Another way to oppress marginalized and disadvantaged elders? Aboriginal elders as a case study. *Journal of Health Psychology, 15*(5), 716–723.

Reed, J., Cook, G., Childs, S., & Hall, A. (2003). *Getting old is not for cowards.* York, U.K.: Joseph Rowntree Foundation.

Rivett, E. (2017). Research involving people with dementia: A literature review. *Working with Older People, 21*(2):107–114.

Schilling, I., & Gerhardus, A. (2017). Methods of involving older people in health research—A review of the literature. *International Journal of Environmental Research and Public Health, 14*(12), 1–20. https://doi.org/10.3390/ijerph14121476.

Schofield, I., & Tolson, D. (2010). *Scottish Football Museum reminiscence pilot project for people with dementia: A realistic evaluation.* Glasgow: School of Health Glasgow Caledonian University.

Silbert, B. S., & Scott, D. A. (2020). Informed consent in patients with frailty syndrome. *Anesthesia & Analgesia, 130*(6), 1474–1481.

Sport England. (2019). *Active lives adult survey.* London: Sport England.

Swarbrick, C. M., Doors, O., Scottish Dementia Working Group, Educate. Davis, K., & Keady, J. (2019). Visioning change: Co-producing a model of involvement and engagement in research (innovative practice). *Dementia, 18*(7–8), 3165–3172. https://doi.org/10.1177/14713 01216674559.

Tanner, D. (2012). Co-research with older people with dementia: Experience and reflections. *Journal of Mental Health, 21*(3), 296–306. doi:10.3109/09638237.2011.651658.

Thorogood, A., Mäki-Petäjä-Leinonen, A., Dalpé, G., Gastmans, C., & Gauthier, S. (2019). Openness, inclusion, and respect in dementia research. *The Lancet Neurology, 18*(2), 135–136.

Tolson, D., & Schofield, I. (2012). Football reminiscence for men with dementia: Lessons from a realistic evaluation. *Nursing Inquiry, 19*(1), 63–70.

Tulle, E. (2008). Acting Your Age? Sports Science and the Ageing Body. Journal of Aging Studies, 22(4), 340–347.

Tulle, E. (2007). Running to run: Embodiment, structure and agency amongst veteran elite runners. *Sociology, 41*(2), 329–346.

Tulle, E. (2008). Acting your age? Sports science and the ageing body. Journal of Aging Studies, 22(4), 340–347.

U.K. Department of Health. (2006). *Best research for best health: A new national health research strategy. The NHS contribution to health research in England.* London: Department of Health.

United Nations. (2015). Transforming our world: The 2030 agenda for sustainable development. https://sustainabledevelopment.un.org/post2015/transformingourworld/publication.

United Nations. (2019). 2019 revision of world population prospects. https://population.un.org/wpp/.

United Nations, Department of Economic and Social Affairs, Population Division. (2020). World population ageing (2019) (ST/ESA/SER.A/444). https://www.un.org/en/development/desa/population/publications/pdf/ageing/WorldPopulationAgeing2019-Report.pdf.

Vertinsky, P., & O'Brien Cousins, S. (2007). Acting your age: Gender, age and physical activity. In K. Young & P. White (Eds.), *Gender and sport in Canada* (pp. 155–193). Oxford: Oxford University Press.

Watchman, K., & Tolson, D. (2015). Football reminiscence for men with dementia in a care home: A 12-week pilot study in Scotland, final report. Alzheimer Scotland Centre for Policy and Practice. Hamilton: University of the West of Scotland.

Weir, P., Baker, J., & Horton, S. (2010). The emergence of masters sport: Participatory trends and historical development. In J. Baker, S. Horton, & P. Weir (Eds.), *The masters athlete: Understanding the role of sport and exercise in optimizing aging* (pp. 7–14). London: Routledge.

Wilson, P., Mathie, E., Poland, F., Keenan, J., Howe, A., Munday, D., . . . Goodman, C. (2018). How embedded is public involvement in mainstream health research in England a decade after policy implementation? A realist evaluation. *Journal of Health Services Research & Policy*, 23(2), 98–106. https://doi.org/10.1177/1355819617750688.

Woodward, M., Arthur, A., Darlington, N., Buckner, S., Killett, A., Thurman, J., . . . Goodman, C. (2019). The place for dementia friendly communities in England and its relationship with epidemiological need. *International Journal of Geriatric Psychiatry*, 34(1), 67–71.

World Health Organization. (2007). Global age-friendly cities: A guide. www.who.int/ageing/publications/Global_age_friendly_cities_Guide_English.pdf.

World Health Organization. (2017). *Global action plan on the public health response to dementia 2017–2025*. Geneva: World Health Organization.

Wray, S. (2014). Ageing, embodiment and physical activity: Some key methodological issues. In A. Smith & I. Waddington (Eds.), *Doing real world research in sport studies* (pp. 141–145). London: Routledge.

Zhou, Z., Fu, J., Hong, A., Wang, P., and Fang, Y. (2017). Association between exercise and the risk of dementia: Results from a nationwide longitudinal study in China. *BMJ Open*, 7(12), e017497. doi:10.1136/bmjopen-2017-017497.

CHAPTER 39

....

SPORT, LIFESTYLE, AND ALTERNATE PATHWAYS

....

HOLLY THORPE AND GUILLAUME DUMONT

THE term "action sports" broadly refers to a wide range of mostly individualized activities (i.e., surfing, skateboarding, BMX, climbing, parkour, snowboarding) that "differ—at least in their early phases of development—from organized, competitive, "achievement" sports cultures" (Thorpe & Wheaton, 2013, p. 341) (Booth & Thorpe, 2007; Kusz, 2007; Rinehart, 1998; Wheaton, 2004, 2010). While each action sport has its own unique history, identity, and development patterns (Wheaton, 2004), early participants allegedly touted antiestablishment and do-it-yourself philosophies, prioritized self-expression and creativity over competition, and subscribed to an "outsider identity relative to the organized sports establishment" (Kusz, 2007, p. 359; see also Beal, 1995). Despite varying terminology (i.e., alternative sports, extreme sports, lifestyle sports) (Cohen, Baluch, & Duffy, 2018), we use "action sports" in this chapter because it is a useful umbrella term that recognizes the varied ways of participating in these activities. Some participants pursue the most risky locations and progressive styles and maneuvers (and thus could be considered "extreme" in their engagement), while others are highly committed to everyday recreational participation (and thus could be considered "lifestyle" participants), and many more opt for more occasional, leisurely engagement.

Many have questioned what makes action sports distinctive. In their critical comparison between action sports and established sports, Booth and Thorpe (2007) identify differences in four key areas: participation, relationships with the environment, values, and presentation. In terms of participation, they explain that "rather than conceptualizing their participation in simple terms of victory or defeat, disciples of [action] sports tend to frame their involvement in terms of meeting personal challenges, testing themselves, and competing against themselves" (p. 188). They note that the objectives of action sports overlap with and extend into "special relationships with the environment" that are "quite different from those experienced in established sports, where the body acts on artificial, formally constituted spaces (e.g., courts, arenas, fields, ovals, tracks) in formally recognized times (e.g., start, finish)"; by contrast, action sports tend to "blur the boundaries between the body and the environment" (p. 189). Much of the early academic research focused on the specific values within action sports cultures. A foundational thinker on action sports, Rinehart

(2000, p. 506), defined them as "activities that either ideologically or practically provide alternatives to mainstream sports and mainstream values." In his later work with Sydnor, Rinehart was also among the first to examine the distinctive presentational styles developed in action sports, particularly events such as the X Games (Rinehart & Sydnor, 2003).

The past three decades have seen a plethora of research exploring the contexts and cultural formations within and across action sports. In this chapter we document key trends in these unique sporting cultures, with a particular focus on the lifestyle and career pursuits of action sport participants. This is an area that has received less scholarly attention but is revealing some of the key social, technological, and organizational transformations within the action sports culture and industry. Building upon our own and others research on action sport cultures, in this chapter we focus on key issues in this literature, including the highly mobile and alternative career paths carved out by those seeking to pursue this lifestyle, and the growing body of scholarship on action sport professionals (i.e., athletes, coaches, journalists, photographers, and social media producers) and transnational action sport migrants and volunteers. We conclude by mapping new lines of inquiry and key debates in the field of action sports studies.

ISSUES

Developing during a "historically unique conjuncture" of transnational mass communications, corporate sponsors, entertainment industries, and a growing affluent and young population, many action sports cultures "diffused around the world at a phenomenal rate" (Booth & Thorpe, 2007, p. 187). Action sports have grown to become a highly visible feature of popular culture: athletes appear on the covers of *Rolling Stone*, *Sports Illustrated*, and *FHM*, and they are regularly featured in advertisements for corporate sponsors such as Nike, Mountain Dew, American Express, and Apple. Previous estimates suggest that during the early 2000s there were more than 22 million Americans participating annually in the four most popular action sports—skateboarding, snowboarding, BMX riding, and surfing—with many participating on a regular basis and engaging in an array of other action sports (see Thorpe & Wheaton, 2011). Importantly, such numbers primarily consist of recreational participants; the number of competitive action sports athletes is very small in comparison. While the majority of early participants in action sports cultures were in their late teens and 20s, some have observed the increasing "graying" of action sports, with participants continuing (or taking up) these activities in later life (Wheaton, 2017b; Willing, Bennett, Piispa, & Green, 2019).

Reliable international statistics are rare, but participation in action sports appears to be growing in some Western and many Eastern (e.g., China, Japan, South Korea) and Middle Eastern countries (see Evers & Doering, 2019; Fok & O'Connor, 2020; Thorpe & Ahmad, 2015; Wheaton, 2010). According to Evers and Doering (2019, p. 343), while action sports have been dominated commercially and ideologically by late capitalist Western nations, "non-occidental cultures—such as those in Asia, Latin America, and Africa—also influence lifestyle sport institutions, commodities, values, and practices." Continuing, they argue that this influence "is expanding and is accelerating as the populations of non-occidental cultures champion their interests and perspectives" (p. 343). As these sports continue to gain popularity around the world, participants are demonstrating philosophical and cultural differences and various levels of skill and commitment.

The Commodification and Professionalization of Action Sports

The commercial or mainstream inclusion, particularly the shift from "alternative" to "mainstream" (or more commercialized forms of) sports, have been prevalent in the action sports literature (e.g., Beal & Weidman, 2003; Beal & Wilson, 2004; Donnelly, 1993; Humphreys, 1997, 2003; Rinehart, 2005; Wheaton, 2007; Wheaton & Thorpe, 2022). In one of the first in-depth investigations of the commercialization of action sports in the post-Fordist culture and economy, Humphreys (1997) examined the processes by which action sports such as skateboarding and snowboarding increasingly became controlled and defined by transnational corporations seeking to tap into the highly lucrative youth market. In his examination of participants' symbolic and political responses to the forces and constraints of the commercialization process, Humphreys presented the much-publicized case of the Norwegian snowboarder Terje Haakonsen's critique of the International Olympic Committee. Undoubtedly the world's best half-pipe rider at the time, Haakonsen refused to participate in the 1998 Winter Olympics because he believed that the IOC comprised a group of Mafia-like officials and that the event was tantamount to joining the army. Haakonsen publicly criticized the IOC's lack of understanding of snowboarding culture and protested against snowboarders being turned into "uniform-wearing, flag-bearing, walking logo[s]" (quoted in Mellegren, 1998, para. 8). Other snowboarders expressed similar sentiments. Yet Humphreys (2003) later lamented that such sentiments seemed to do nothing to stem the process of incorporation.

As action sports became incorporated into the mainstream via mega-events such as the X Games and the Olympics, they assumed many of the features of other modern sports, including corporate sponsorship, large prize monies, "rationalized systems of rules," hierarchical and individualistic star systems, win-at-all-costs values, and the creation of heroes, heroines, and "rebel" athletes who look like "walking corporate billboards" (Messner, 2002, p. 82). As Wheaton (2004, p. 14) and others have noted, debates on "selling out" relate not just to commodification but also to the appropriation of action sports ethos and ideologies, such as attitudes to risk, responsibility, freedom, and regulation, and repackaging and selling their values and lifestyles for mass consumption (see also Humphreys, 1997; Rinehart, 2000, 2008a, 2008b). Importantly, however, contemporary action sports participants are not simply victims of commercialization but active agents who continue to critically engage with the images and meanings circulated within their sporting cultures and within global consumer culture (Thorpe & Wheaton, 2013; Wheaton, 2004; Rinehart, 2008a, 2008b).

The inclusion of surfing, skateboarding, sport climbing, and BMX freestyle into the Tokyo 2020 Olympic Games, and the ongoing politics regarding the possible future inclusion of other action sports (i.e., parkour), have been highly controversial within the action sport communities (see Batuev & Robinson, 2019; Kilberth & Schwier, 2019; Puddle, Wheaton & Thorpe, 2019;Thorpe & Wheaton, 2011; Wheaton & Thorpe, 2022). As Wheaton and Thorpe (2018, 2019, 2021) have pointed out, attitudes toward Olympic inclusion vary considerably, younger participants and women being much more enthusiastic about the decision. In particular, they explain how women action sports participants are excited about the opportunities that such visibilities can offer to women as athletes, as well as for advancement to leadership positions, within these historically male-dominated sports (Wheaton & Thorpe, 2018; also see D'Orazio, 2020). The movement toward Olympic inclusion has also prompted major structural changes with implications at the global and national levels (Puddle, Wheaton, & Thorpe, 2018; Wheaton & Thorpe, 2016, 2022). These changes have considerable implications in the everyday lives of action sports athletes and committed participants (Thorpe & Dumont, 2019). It is the impact of these broader cultural transformations on the lifestyles and career paths of athletes and highly committed action sport participants that we turn to now.

Action Sport Athletic Careers: Alternative Professional Pathways

The action sports industry has historically consisted of companies providing technical goods necessary for performing these activities, a large variety of related products (i.e., clothes, shoes, bags), as well media content, events, and competitions (see Booth, 2005; Stranger, 2011; Thorpe, 2014). By successfully broadening the reach of these products beyond the niche of action sports participants, action sports companies such as Quicksilver, Billabong, Vans, Burton, and Rip Curl have become major retailers in sport-related apparel (Hough-Snee, 2020; Stranger, 2010; Thorpe, 2014). Nowadays, behind these giants, smaller action sport companies are following similar paths, seeking to extend their reach beyond core participants and diversifying their products to reach new consumer segments. Rooted in the efforts of dedicated participants who started designing and producing their skis, skateboards, snowboards, or climbing shoes in their garage, these companies have generated an array of new career opportunities (i.e., brand manager, communications officer, digital content specialist, team manager). Companies such as Black Diamond, Burton, Patagonia, and Quiksilver, with headquarters in Salt Lake City, Utah; Burlington, Vermont; and Ventura and Huntington Beach, California, respectively, attract action sports enthusiasts as employees by offering the opportunity to combine their passion for their sport with highly flexile working schedules (Stranger, 2011; Thorpe, 2011b).

Intimately tied with the growth and professionalization of this industry is athlete sponsorship. The commodification and dissemination of action sports are typically associated with a limited number of world-famous athletes whose names resonate with the brand of their sponsors. Professional skateboarders (e.g., Ryan Sheckler, Leticia Bufoni), surfers (e.g., Kelly Slater, Stephanie Gilmore), snowboarders (e.g., Shaun White, Chloe Kim), climbers (e.g., Chris Sharma, David Lama), BMX riders (e.g., Mat Hoffman) and other action sport athletes have benefited from the increasing commercialized forms of their activities. Some have achieved superstar status within and beyond the culture of their specific sports and are/were earning multimillion-dollar salaries from their sponsorship and advertisement deals combined with competition earnings.

Such support, however, is not equitably distributed across the most talented athletes, and resources have been more accessible to young, white male athletes (Das, 2020; Siber, 2017).

Whereas some action sportswomen are gaining high levels of media coverage and corpo-rate support, they tend to be those who embody and conform to a traditional heteronor-mative femininity. For example, world-champion surfer and self-proclaimed "surf feminist" Cori Schumacher (2016) has described the challenges for women in competitive surfing and in a homophobic, sexist surfing industry. Similarly, lisahunter (2016) and Thorpe, Toffoletti, and Bruce (2017) have illuminated the politics of who is made visible in surfing media and who remains invisible, and the strategies of different women to negotiate coverage in (mass and social) media and access to cultural and industry resources (i.e., sponsorships).

It would also be a mistake to assume that corporate- and national-level sponsorships and support flow evenly across different action sports and countries. Indeed, athletes from coun-tries with fewer financial resources to invest in new high-performance sport will continue to struggle to generate enough income to pursue their careers (Wheaton & Thorpe, 2016, 2022). Whereas some countries (e.g., Australia; see Ellmer & Rynne, 2019) are investing strongly in their current and future action sports athletes with facilities and support staff, in other countries athletes receive very little support from their national federations (see Wheaton & Thorpe, 2022 for a detailed discussion of national differences following Olympic inclusion). Furthermore, in some action sports such as sport climbing, corporate sponsorships and prize money are very low in comparison to other action sports, and thus future athletes in such sports may continue to struggle with how to finance their travel, living, and training expenses (Dumont, 2018a).

Yet it is important to note that not all athletes follow a competitive career path. As Ojala (2014), Snyder (2012), Woermann (2012) and Dumont (2017b) have described in snowboarding, skateboarding, freestyle skiing, and climbing, respectively, many action sport athletes pursue alternative career paths via media-based performances. Also, the rise of social media has enabled those pursuing media-based careers (as athletes, but also as photographers, writers, filmmakers, etc.) an important new forum to share their skills with their transnational communities and to build audiences via social media platforms (i.e., YouTube, Instagram, Facebook, Snapchat, TikTok) and thus gain and maintain sponsors based on their digital performances and success at connecting with hard-to-reach con-sumer groups (Dumont, 2017a, 2017b; Dupont, 2020; Gilchrist & Wheaton, 2013; Thorpe, 2014, 2017a). A good example of action sport athletes following a social media–based career strategy is Storror, a U.K.-based professional parkour team, who occasionally compete but spend most of their time traveling the world self-producing short films (e.g., *Roof Culture Asia*) and posting images and "stories" on Instagram, such that they have close to one million Instagram followers. They have created their own line of clothing that they market and sell via their social media accounts, and have attracted various corporate investors and advertisers who recognize the cultural and economic capital of their digital reach.

The alternative career strategies married with the entrepreneurial, self-branding, and marketing approaches being employed by some freestyle surfers (Evers, 2019a), street skaters (Dupont, 2020; Snyder, 2012), freestyle snowboarders (Ojala, 2014), climbers (Dumont, 2018a, 2018b; Rahikainen, 2020; Rahikainen & Toffoletti, 2021), wakeboarders (Parris, Troilo, Bouchet, & Welty Peachey, 2014), and parkour participants (Gilchrist & Wheaton, 2013), and their large international followings, suggest that there remains a crit-ical, highly creative value system evident at the core of action sport cultures and industries. Dumont (2018a), for instance, has argued that, to be recognized as a "valuable" athlete for sponsors and the audience, many professional rock climbers primarily build upon creative and symbol-making activities with the aim of making enough money to fund their lifestyle. Indeed, drawing parallels with the creative professions, he shows that their work is inextricably intertwined with achievement in highly creative activities and anchored in a complex system of communication aiming for the production and dissemination of experiences through media products. In the contemporary moment, for some action sport athletes and committed participants, becoming an "influencer" (using social media to document their action sports lifestyle) has become more profitable than performing at the top level.

Although action sport athletes are the very visible tip of the industry "iceberg," such a focus obscures the increased viability of several related professional roles, including as photographers, filmmakers, team managers, agents, coaches, and personal trainers (e.g., Dumont, 2015, 2016a, 2016b; Snyder, 2012, 2017; Thorpe & Dumont, 2019). These individuals are mostly hired as independent contractors by magazines, companies, and/ or sports federations. Their working relationships are often highly personal and based on connections within the sporting culture, before becoming progressively professionalized (Dumont, 2016a, 2016b; Ojala & Thorpe, 2015). While the opportunities for action sport coaches, agents, and managers (among other roles) are increasing as these sports become more institutionalized, action sports social networks and personal connections remain the main gatekeepers to access this unique labor market. Research also shows the role of racial considerations in accessing careers in the action sports industry. The doctoral research of Williams (2020), for instance, focuses on the career paths of Black and People of Color skateboarders in the United States and explores the lived experiences of professional skateboarders, photographers, editors, journalists, and company owners, with a focus on their experiences of race, racism, and racial politics at various stages in their careers.

Finally, the dramatic increase in action sport facilities has also brought a variety of work opportunities (e.g., Van Bottenburg & Salome, 2010), notably by supporting the rise of new professions and related certifications and programs. For instance, route setters for national and international climbing competitions must now undertake formal training leading to professional certifications. Additional examples are found in the work of the shapers in charge of designing and building park facilities for ski resorts and events of different kinds and in the creation of professional consultancy services helping in the conception and implementation of climbing gyms, skate parks, and bike parks. As Atencio, Beal, Wright, and McClain (2018) explain, the rise of urban skateparks in the United States has led to new social dynamics, with parents (particularly mothers) and community members taking on new (paid and unpaid) roles in managing and regulating these recreational sporting spaces. The opening of hundreds of action sport facilities (i.e., Woodward action sports camps, Windells) worldwide also fostered the emergence of more jobs related to teaching, training, and facility management. For those who are passionate about action sports, there are many ways to carve out a career in the industry and to sustain participation within the sporting cultures and communities they love.

Lifestyle Sport Migrants: "Living the Dream"

Action sports niche media (i.e., magazines, videos, and, more recently, social media) have long promoted, romanticized, and idealized the "dream" of traveling nationally and internationally in pursuit of new places for participation and connecting with "like-minded" enthusiasts (Ford & Brown, 2006; Ponting, 2009). In their efforts to "live the dream," some of the most fervent action sport enthusiasts follow the seasons (i.e., chasing swell and/or wind patterns and winter and/or summer seasons, depending on the sport), thus becoming what Maguire (1996, p. 339) termed "nomadic cosmopolitans" or what Thorpe (2011a, p. 119) refers to as "seasonal lifestyle sport migrants."

In her work on the transnational mobilities of action sport participants (i.e., athletes, tourists, and highly committed participants), Thorpe (2011a, 2014, 2017b) explored passionate snow sport migrants (i.e., skiers and snowboarders) who follow the winter between hemispheres. She explained that such mobilities typically commence when enthusiasts are in their late teens and early 20s, before they have taken on adult responsibilities (such as marriage, children, mortgages, long-term employment, and so on). During this time their commitment to their sporting culture becomes such that it organizes their whole lives. In this regard, she cites snowboarding journalist Jennifer Sherowski (2005, p. 160), who describes the commitment to this highly mobile lifestyle:

> The road starts calling—off to mountain towns and the assimilation into weird, transient tribes full of people who work night jobs cleaning toilets or handing you your coffee in the early mornings, all so they can shove a fistful of tips in their pocket and ride, their real motives betrayed by goggle tans or chins scuffed by Gore-Tex. In this world, people don't ask what you "do," they ask you where you work—knowing that what you do is snowboard, just like them, and any job you might have is simply a means for it.

As this comment suggests, many highly committed snowboarders and skiers are nomadic, traveling nationally and internationally to experience new terrain, meet new people, or "live the dream" of the endless winter. Often they work in low-paying jobs in hospitality and/or in the tourism economy ("night jobs cleaning toilets or handing you your coffee in the early mornings"), where the "best jobs" are those that allow for the most time on the snow. Similar patterns have been observed in highly committed climbers (Dumont, 2011; Rickly, 2016).

To facilitate and prolong their transnational action sport lifestyles, many pursue further training and education to obtain skilled employment in their sporting industries; some become highly proficient instructors, coaches, journalists, photographers, rental technicians, and/or competition judges (Thorpe, 2017b). As mentioned earlier, despite the skilled nature of many of these jobs, the majority are not high paying; they tend to be held by passionate action sport participants committed to the lifestyle rather than the economic rewards.

Importantly, the transnational mobilities of action sport migrants are facilitated and constrained by various factors, including work and travel visas, travel and accommodation costs, employment opportunities and wages, languages and exchange rates, and translocal relationships (see Thorpe, 2014). Action sport migrants develop an array of creative strategies in their efforts to maintain their highly mobile lifestyles, but often (not always) such lifestyles are curtailed as participants take on more adult responsibilities or experience the limits of the injured and/or aging body. Even as such lifestyles become less mobile, the number of back-to-back or consecutive seasons and the places traveled for their sport continue to be important symbols of cultural commitment, and thus a regular topic of conversation among core action sport participants. Of course, such lifestyle mobilities are highly privileged and not available to all, and in the context of the COVID-19 pandemic, many such highly mobile action sport lifestyles have come to an abrupt halt.

As action sport participants travel the world, some have been exposed to the extreme inequalities and injustices of other societies. Such travel experiences have prompted some to become more aware of the privileged nature of their own lifestyle (Thorpe, 2014). In response to such revelations, some are seeking to use their passion and skills to improve the lives of others (Thorpe & Rinehart, 2010, 2013); some pursue employment and volunteering opportunities in the subfield of Action Sports for Development and Peace. Thorpe and Chawanksy (2017) have explored the motivations, reflections, and embodied experiences of risk, reflexivity, and knowledge of predominantly white women action sports enthusiasts from the Global North and their work for a skateboarding NGO in Afghanistan. More critical research is needed to explore the emergent forms of labor (paid and unpaid) in nonprofit action sports for development organizations around the world and the (often neo-colonialist, imperialist) assumptions, motivations, and embodied practices involved in such initiatives that are typically founded, led, managed, and operated by privileged white action sport enthusiasts from the Global North for disadvantaged youth in the Global South.

APPROACHES

Since the mid-1990s, scholars from an array of disciplinary backgrounds (i.e., anthropology, architectural studies, geography, history, media studies, philosophy, psychology, sociology, youth studies) have employed various methodological and theoretical approaches to try to understand and explain the experiences of action sports participants within local, national, global, and virtual contexts and in historical and contemporary conditions. In this section we focus on theoretical tactics and qualitative research efforts that have been used to identify and explain the workings of power and politics within action sports cultures and, reflect, in that light, on the emphasis on ethnographic approaches.

Theoretical Approaches: The Focus on Identity Politics

Questions of power, inequality, and identity feature strongly in research on action sports cultures, especially gender politics. Researchers have examined the hypermasculinity celebrated among committed male athletes within climbing (Robinson, 2008), snowboarding (Anderson, 1999; Thorpe, 2010), surfing (Evers, 2006), and windsurfing (Wheaton, 2000) cultures, as well as the hierarchical power relations between these participants and groups of "other" men (i.e., gay men, older men, boys) and women within these cultures. For example, in her analysis of snowboarding masculinities, Thorpe (2010) reveals the dominance of the snowboarding "fratriarchy"—young, highly committed male snowboarders with close homosocial bonds with their peers—and the various physical and symbolic performances that work to reinforce their cultural positioning over younger boys, older men, and women.

Some have also investigated the multiple (and often contradictory) ways that women negotiate space within male-dominated action sports cultures such as adventure racing (Kay & Laberge, 2004), skateboarding (Pomerantz, Currie, & Kelly, 2004; Young & Dallaire, 2008), skydiving and snowboarding (Laurendeau & Sharara, 2008), snowboarding (Spowart,

Hughson & Shaw, 2008; Thorpe, 2008), surfing (Booth, 2002; Comer, 2010; Heywood, 2007; Knijnik, Horton, & Cruz, 2010; Olive, McCuaig, & Phillips, 2015; Roy, 2016), and windsurfing (Wheaton & Tomlinson, 1998). For example, Wheaton and Tomlinson revealed the multiple ways women negotiate space in the windsurfing culture, ranging from girlfriends and wives on the beach to the active and highly committed women in the waves who garner status and respect through displays of cultural commitment, physical prowess, and risk-taking. To facilitate their analyses of the complex gender practices, performances, and politics operating within action sports cultures, researchers have engaged an array of theoretical perspectives, including hegemonic masculinity, various strands of feminism (i.e., liberal, radical, and third-wave feminism), and poststructural feminist engagements in the work of Bourdieu, Deleuze and Guattari, and Foucault. In an overview of the feminist theoretical approaches to studying action sports, Thorpe (2018) acknowledges the important contributions of action sports scholars in advancing understandings of gender relations within informal sporting cultures with distinctive gendered dynamics and cultural histories.

Despite a growing number of theoretically sophisticated and empirically nuanced studies of the gender power relations and politics in local, national, and global contexts, there is a paucity of intersectional research that engages the various forms of identity-based politics operating within and across action sports cultures. Intersectional research is important for acknowledging the multiplicities of action sport participant identities and how gender, race, ethnicity, class, sexuality, nationality, age, religion, and/or socioeconomic variables may impact participant experiences differently. Some scholars have provided partial intersectional analyses of the youthful, privileged, white masculinity celebrated in action sports in North America (particularly skateboarding) (Brayton, 2005; Kusz, 2007; Yochim, 2010). More recently, Wheaton (2017a) has explored the cultural and racial politics of African American surfers, and Nemani and Thorpe (2016) have examined the experiences of "brown" (Māori and Pasifika) female bodyboarders in Aotearoa New Zealand. Others are exploring the colonial and indigenous histories and current politics and pedagogies of surfing in different parts of the world, including Hawaii (Walker, 2011), South Africa (Thompson, 2017), and Australia (Osmond, 2011).

The cultural politics within action sports communities—based on cultural commitment (i.e., the long-term adoption of a lifestyle that revolves around the requirements of the sport, such as weather, seasons, cultural events), physical prowess, or styles of participation—as well as among "outsider" groups and other sporting cultures, have gained considerable academic attention. Pierre Bourdieu's concepts of field, capital, practice, and habitus have been particularly popular among those seeking to explain how distinctions among individuals and groups expressed as differences in embodied tastes and styles, and as uses of cultural products and commodities, are practiced, performed, and regulated in various locations (e.g., skate parks, waves, mountains) (see Atencio, Beal, & Wilson 2009; Ford & Brown, 2006; Thorpe, 2011b; Uekusa, 2019). Some scholars have explained embodied dress and language practices, as well as displays of cultural commitment, physical prowess, and risk-taking, as contributing to the social construction and classification of group identities within action sports fields (e.g., Beal & Wilson, 2004; Robinson, 2008; Wheaton, 2003). Extending such theoretical frameworks, some have explored how cultural and symbolic capital within action sports industries leads (some) to access economic capital as sponsored athletes (Kay & Laberge, 2002; Thorpe, 2011b).

Others have investigated the cultural politics involved in negotiating space and access to physical, social, and economic resources within hierarchically organized sporting, cultural, or industry contexts. The power relations among different types of wave users (i.e., short-board surfers, body-boarders, long-boarders, Stand Up Paddle riders), and conflicts among surfers/wave-riders seeking to navigate space in the "line up" in local contexts, and thus regulate and control others' access to waves, have been particularly well documented (e.g., Ford & Brown, 2006; Nemani & Thorpe, 2016; Olivier, 2010; Uekusa, 2019; Waitt, 2008). Another focus of analysis has been the gender politics and hypermasculinity in high-risk natural environments, such as the backcountry for skiers (Stoddart, 2010) and snowboarders (Thorpe, 2011b) and big waves for surfers (Booth, 2011; Stranger, 2011). Some scholars have also drawn upon highly interdisciplinary approaches (e.g., cultural geography, architecture, urban studies) to describe the spatial politics practiced by action sports participants, especially skateboarders and parkour practitioners, in their attempts to challenge dominant meanings ascribed to public spaces in urban environments (e.g., Atkinson, 2009; Borden, 2003, 2019; Jones & Graves, 2000; Stratford, 2002). More recently, Olive's (2019, p. 39) work on the gendered politics of localism in surfing "enmeshed in the settler politics of place in Australia" provided an important contribution to action sports scholarship that focuses on place, identity, belonging, community, and contested histories around the past and present usage of natural environments (i.e., beaches) for sport and leisure.

Methodological Approaches: The Dominance of Ethnography

Qualitative research has been the dominant methodological approach to studying action sports for more than three decades. Within such work, ethnography has featured strongly, with participant observation, media analysis, and interviews among the most popular methodological tools. Many action sport researchers come to their projects as active participants, and their research methods often include long-term participation and close relationships within the field (Thorpe & Wheaton, 2013). Ethnography has proven highly beneficial for accessing the unique cultural knowledge (i.e., language, value systems) circulating among action sport participants, some of which is difficult to understand without sustained participation and cultural access. While some advocate strongly for the value of insider positioning (e.g., Borden, 2019; Dupont, 2014; Snyder, 2017), others recognize the benefits of more critical distance and note that one's location within the field is always dynamic and context-specific (Donnelly, 2006; Pavlidis & Olive, 2014; Thorpe & Wheaton, 2017). Such issues of "insider-outsider" status are brought to the fore when researchers travel beyond their local action sports communities. In their efforts to explore the global or transnational dimensions within and across local action sport cultures, some have developed transnational and multisite ethnographic methods (Canniford, 2005; Dumont, 2018a, 2018b; Puddle, 2019; Thorpe, 2014). Throughout such work, action sports scholars have engaged in discussion and debate around the benefits and challenges of insider-outsider positioning and have advocated the importance of reflexivity when working in action sport communities (Beal, 2019; Canniford, 2005; Dumont, 2018a; Olive, 2019; Olive & Thorpe, 2011; Wheaton, 2002). Adopting feminist approaches, some are exploring the possibilities for rethinking researcher politics, ethics, and positionality through collaborative ethnographic projects (Olive & Thorpe, 2017; Olive et al., 2016; Pavlidis & Olive, 2014).

Drawing inspiration from the affective and sensual turn in the social sciences and humanities, some action sports researchers have also moved toward more creative and embodied forms of research in their attempts to better understand and explain the athletic experience (Evers, 2006, 2016; lisahunter & Stoodley, 2020; Roy, 2014). In so doing, they are engaging a range of technologies (e.g., GoPro) to help capture more multisensual (i.e., visual, auditory, kinesthetic) perspectives on the action sports experience. Some scholars have written critical autoethnographies and ethnographic fiction to shed light on their own and others' lived and embodied action sports experiences, and draw attention to the various forms of power operating within the culture (Evers, 2006; Thorpe, 2011b).

As well as the extensive use of ethnographic methods in action sport studies, scholars have engaged in media-centered studies of diverse cultural artifacts (i.e., magazines, videos) (e.g., Booth, 2008; Brayton, 2005; Wheaton & Beal, 2003; Willing, Green, & Pavlidis, 2020). Among some groups of action sports researchers, media analysis alone (without active participation in the sporting culture) can draw some criticism. Such critiques are grounded in the lingering (and problematic) assumption that cultural insiders and those with lived experience are best positioned for studying them. Media analyses, in tandem with interviews and "ethnographic visits" (Sugden & Tomlinson, 2002), constitute a common multimethod approach for studying action sport cultures (Thorpe, 2012). Such approaches have risen as sustained cultural participation (long-term ethnography) is becoming more and more difficult as universities put limits on research funding and the length of projects. Beyond sociological approaches, historians have also engaged in rigorous examinations of the cultural changes within action sports (Booth, 1994; Osmond, 2011), some offering critical discussions of methodological challenges of studying the history of action sports (Booth, 2013; Booth & Thorpe, 2019; Phillips & Osmond, 2015).

More recently, the widespread use of social media across most facets of action sports has prompted many researchers (sociologists and historians) to incorporate digital methods into their toolkits. In so doing, action sport researchers took to adapting their qualitative tools for the online environment, mirroring the development of digital qualitative research across other disciplines (e.g., Markham & Baym, 2008; Pink et al., 2015). For instance, recent action sports research on social media usage among athletes and everyday participants has used digital platforms as a tool to gather information, a source of data, and an alternative mode of dissemination and sharing findings back to the community (Dumont, 2018b; Evers, 2019a; MacKay & Dallaire, 2012; Olive, 2013; Rahikainen, 2020). Such research has helped illuminate the persistence of power relationships, gendered inequalities, impression management, and new forms of digital and affective labor. While some of the early work has focused on digital contexts, other scholarship explores the complex blurring between the online and offline lives of action sport participants and communities (Olive, 2015; Puddle, 2019; Rahikainen & Toffoletti, 2021; Thorpe & Wheaton, 2021).

Finally, whereas ethnographic methods have had great value for studying the cultural dynamics within action sport cultures and identifying new research questions, the field remains limited in its understanding of the broader socioeconomic dynamics of the industry and the development of action sports on a global scale. A recent exception is an international online survey (disseminated in nine languages) conducted by Wheaton and Thorpe (2019) exploring action sport participant attitudes toward the inclusion of more action sports into the Olympic Games. Their work also signals another important trend of more action sports researchers working with sporting organizations to understand trends and developments and to guide practice and policy (Puddle, Wheaton & Thorpe, 2019; Thorpe & Wheaton, 2019; Wheaton & Thorpe, 2022). As action sports become increasingly institutionalized and professionalized, we should expect more quantitative and mixed-methods research, as well as partnerships between researchers, action sports businesses, and mainstream sports organizations. Inevitably, such relationships will require researchers to navigate complex ethical terrain and will require heightened reflexivity throughout such power-laden processes.

Debates

A topic that repeatedly comes to the fore in action sports communities (particularly when a high-profile athlete dies) is risk. Over recent years, action sport athletes have increasingly expressed concerns about the rising expectations from corporate sponsors to constantly push the boundaries of what is possible on a pair of skis, a skateboard, snowboard, surfboard, or climbing wall. The deaths (e.g., Hawaiian big-wave surfer Mark Foo, Canadian freestyle skier Sarah Burke, U.S. freestyle motocross rider Jeremy Lusk, U.S. skier and BASE-jumper Shane McConkey) and the life-threatening/-changing injuries of athletes such as top U.S. snowboarder Kevin Pearce (see *The Crash Reel* documentary) and U.S. BMX rider Dave Mirra have prompted many to (at least momentarily) critically consider the glorification of risk and the celebration of progression that remain at the core of their sporting cultures, but that are also strongly endorsed and (financially) encouraged by corporate sponsors.

For example, following Mirra's suicide in 2016, a postmortem diagnosed him as the first action sport athlete with chronic traumatic encephalopathy (a neurodegenerative disease resulting from multiple concussions that can lead to dementia, memory loss, and depression) (Roenigk, 2016). This diagnosis raised concerns across the action sports community about the long-term consequences of the "go hard or go home" mentality that underpins so much progression in these sporting cultures. In an interview in *Rolling Stone* magazine following Mirra's diagnosis, fellow BMX legend Mat Hoffman reflected critically on the high concussion rate: "[W]e ride until we crash. That's just the nature of the sport" (quoted in Hyde, 2016). Before his death, Mirra himself had commented on the overzealous drive in riders seeking the glory and big prizes: "I could see it in their eyes, man, they'll do whatever it takes to win. They'll die. Just like I would when I was younger. I would have died to win" (quoted in Hyde, 2016).

As we have discussed in our previous work (Thorpe & Dumont, 2019), with major corporations increasingly offering large sponsorships and advertising deals to (carefully selected) action sport stars, some athletes have also complained that extreme forms of individualism and egocentrism have become increasingly prevalent. Observing this shift in the early 2000s, U.S. Olympic silver medalist snowboarder Gretchen Bleiler believes the "industry pressure" and "ultrahigh" level of snowboarding abilities were creating an "extremely competitive atmosphere," such that, in their hunger to win, the younger generation was "changing the overall feel at the top of the half-pipe" (cited in Thorpe & Dumont, 2019, p. 1642). As signaled by both Mirra and Bleiler, many contemporary "up-and-comers" participate differently from past participants, and many opt for alternative schooling to give them the time and space to focus on their training and travel. In contrast to previous generations of action sport athletes, many of whom taught themselves and engaged in peer mentoring throughout their careers (Ojala & Thorpe, 2015), today's children and youth are increasingly training under the guidance of coaches in highly organized structures in which their sports offer the possibility of earning a profitable career (Ellmer & Rynne, 2019; Smits, 2019, 2020). The tragic suicide of British professional snowboarder Ellie Soutter on her 18th birthday brought to the fore the pressures on young action sports athletes and the often unacknowledged mental health issues that come with such expectations. Soutter's father spoke publicly on mental health concerns, head injuries, and the excessive pressure on young athletes: "She wanted to be the best. She didn't want to let anybody down. . . . There's a lot of pressure on children" (cited in Badshah, 2018).

Such cultural shifts and increasing pressures on athletes are gaining momentum as more action sports are included in the Olympic Games (Wheaton & Thorpe, 2022). One such example is the recent near-death injury incurred by the 11-year-old world number three, Nike-sponsored, skateboarding phenom Sky Brown while training with Tony Hawk on his private ramp. Although she was wearing a helmet, Brown's serious head injury (among various other injuries) should raise important questions about the normalization of the high risks being taken by increasingly young action sport athletes, and the ethics and responsibilities of adults (i.e., coaches, parents, agents) who are "supporting" preteen participants in their "careers" as both digital entrepreneurs and highly competitive athletes. As action sports become increasingly institutionalized and professionalized, younger athletes are training and competing at very high levels. They are expected to manage a wide array of (sometimes conflicting) pressures and expectations from parents, coaches, corporate sponsors (sometimes multimillion-dollar contracts), national sporting bodies, and digital audiences (often in the millions). Despite such high stakes and pressure on ever younger athletes, the organizational structures of action sports are evolving more slowly. Issues of athlete welfare and well-being, and particularly facilitating ethical and responsible young athlete support and development, need to be at the forefront of such developments (Smits, 2020).

Action Sports Lifestyles and the Environment

Another important topic is action sports' intersections with the environment. A number of researchers have discussed the close relationship action sport participants have with the natural environment and how it can lead to heightened "ecological sensibilities" (Olive, 2016) or "ecocentricity" (Brymer & Gray, 2010). Some scholars offer overly romantic views of action sport participants' environmental activism based on the deep "kinship with the natural world" that develops through athletes' sporting participation and how this influences their relationships with the environment (Brymer & Gray, 2010, p. 366; Hill & Abbott, 2009). Critical scholars, however, offer a more nuanced reading of action sport participants as "individualistic *and* part of a collectivity: they are hedonistic *and* reflexive consumers, often politically disengaged yet environmentally aware and/or active" (Wheaton, 2007, p. 298; see also Humberstone, 2011; Stoddart, 2012; Thorpe & Rinehart, 2010; 2013).

Action sports communities have long been involved in environmental initiatives, such as Surfers Against Sewage (Laviolette, 2006; Wheaton, 2007). Action sport athletes are increasingly getting involved with such initiatives, with some recognizing the environmental impacts of their highly mobile and consumptive careers. For example, professional U.S. snowboarder Jeremy Jones set up the nonprofit Protect Our Winters in 2007 after acknowledging the damage his own snow-chasing lifestyle was doing to the environment: "Let's be honest, pro snowboarders are fundamentally at odds with the environment. Their globetrotting ways are pretty damn detrimental to the globe and its increasingly fragile climate" (quoted in "Variables," 2008, p. 62). Today, Protect Our Winters has grown into an international nonprofit focused on activating passionate outdoors people and initiating legislation regarding climate change (Thorpe, 2014).

An increasing number of high-profile athletes across a range of action sports (i.e., climbing, surfing, skiing, snowboarding) use their social media accounts to speak publicly about their environmental concerns, to educate their followers about various events and campaigns, and to describe their own everyday efforts to reduce the impact of their lifestyles on the environment. Action sport companies and competitive leagues are also increasingly investing in climate change initiatives (e.g., the World Surf League's Pure One Ocean campaign). Despite widespread awareness campaigns and the use of professional action sport athletes as environmental ambassadors, however, few action sports corporations or competitive leagues are changing event structures (i.e., reducing events) or rethinking the high-carbon international travel practices of their athletes, staff, and spectators. The environmental contradictions in early action sports communities and industries are ever more evident in the contemporary context (Wheaton, 2020).

Although scholars have recognized the environmental sensibilities and politics within action sports communities, the environment is seen primarily as a backdrop for human activity. However, recently some scholars are embracing creative experimental methods and performance art to rethink human relationships with action sports and the environment. For instance, Evers (2019b) has drawn upon posthumanist and new materialist theory to explore the various connections and assemblages between the environment and surfing, with a focus on polluted waterways. Evers argues that we need to take a posthumanist, material-social approach to recognize how humans are entangled with more-than-human worlds—pollution, capitalism, and environmental crises—and develops what he refers to as "wet ethnography" to explore such assemblages in deeply embodied and affective ways. In so doing, Evers confronts the climate crisis in a manner that emphasizes the dynamism of nonhuman matter (waterways) and a need to move away from anthropocentric understandings of action sports. He also engages in an array of creative modes of dissemination (i.e., art exhibits, videos, website). Such research signals exciting theoretical and methodological innovations in action sports scholarship.

CONCLUSION

In this chapter we have examined the emergence of different career pathways for those working in the action sports cultural industries and how such opportunities are enabled and constrained by various cultural, technological, and organizational transformations. To conclude we offer some final reflections on areas requiring further attention and consideration, particularly the need for more theoretical and methodological innovation, the growing overspecialization within action sports studies, and studies focused on power relations within the action sports industry that enable careers for some, while limiting the opportunities for others.

Since the foundational work of a select group of critical sociohistorical scholars of sports during the mid- and late 1990s (e.g., Becky Beal, Douglas Booth, Peter Donnelly, Duncan Humphreys, Nancy Midol, Robert Rinehart, Belinda Wheaton, and Kevin Young), the subfield of action sports studies has continued to flourish and diversify. Researchers from various disciplinary backgrounds have been examining a plethora of action sports–related topics in an array of local, national, global, and virtual contexts, and publishing across the social science and humanities. But for scholarship to continue to develop in new and important ways, researchers need to critically reflect upon some of the methodological and theoretical assumptions underpinning their work. Rather than asking familiar questions in different contexts or drawing upon common theoretical and methodological approaches to reveal somewhat predictable findings, it is important to (re)imagine action sports research in new and socially valuable ways. Hopefully future action sports researchers will take their cue from Evers (2019b) and others (i.e., Rebecca Olive, Neftalie Williams, Indigo Willing) who are also pursuing creative forms of praxis. Through social media awareness campaigns (i.e., see Consent Is Rad, 2019), art exhibitions and documentaries (i.e., see Polluted Leisure, 2020), podcasts (Saltwater Library), media appearances, and a range of public engagements (see Cowan, 2020; Moving Oceans, 2020), some scholars are using research on action sports cultures to build public awareness and activate action sports communities on some of the most pressing social issues (e.g., Black Lives Matter, climate change, sexual violence). Action sports public intellectualism is on the rise and signals exciting new trends in researcher engagement and commitment to social change.

With action sports studies continuing to grow, scholars are gathering around and working on particular action sports. As the editors of *The Critical Surf Studies Reader* acknowledge, "the critical surfing studies field is currently undergoing a scholarly renaissance of sorts and . . . contributions to the field continue to emerge from diverse academic disciplines and wave-riding communities across the globe" (Hough-Snee & Sotelo Eastman, 2017, p. xi). Similar observations can be made in relation to critical skateboarding studies (see Lombard, 2016) and arguably a few other action sports (e.g., parkour). While it is exciting to see a growing, critical mass of scholars working on particular action sports, it is perhaps more important than ever for researchers to also be able to step back from their intimate relations with their sporting cultures and scholarship in the field to see similar and different trends across other action sports and the broader industry. Arguably, as the critical mass of action sports scholars grows and groups form around particular sports, there is also a risk of more insular (even repetitive) dialogues, with researchers working in their sporting silos rather than speaking across and back to the field more broadly. Therefore, it is important for researchers to continue to read widely across sporting cultures and to speak to one another (and others outside the field) about the key issues facing the subdiscipline and the past, present, and future directions of critical, socially impactful research within and beyond these unique sporting cultures.

In sum, understanding quickly evolving trends in action sports lifestyles and careers must be considered alongside cultural, technological, and environmental shifts. Insights into the creative, entrepreneurial, and innovative career paths of action sport athletes and committed participants will be further enhanced by working across disciplinary boundaries, particularly at the intersection of critical theory, work studies, creative industries, environment and sustainability studies, geography, and sport and physical cultural studies.

Furthermore, there is an urgent need for critical scholars to use their research to inform (and improve) the practices and policies of action sports organizations to better support the health and well-being of their young, emerging, elite, and retiring athletes, staff, and volunteers. With younger action sport athletes competing at international levels, garnering millions of online followers and seven-figure sponsorship and advertising deals, research is needed on the ethics and responsibilities of adults, organizations, and corporations in protecting young athlete welfare (Smit, 2020). Much more work is also needed on the experiences of BIPOC, LGBTQI+, and non-Western athletes and those working in the action sports industry. Such work is important in revealing the ongoing power inequalities in the action sports cultures and industries and the various forms of unpaid labor (i.e., volunteering, activism) among those engaging in action sports communities.

References

Anderson, K. (1999). Snowboarding: The construction of gender in an emerging sport. *Journal of Sport and Social Issues, 23*(1), 55–79.

Atencio, M., Beal, B., & Wilson, C. (2009). The distinction of risk: Urban skateboarding, street habitus and the construction of hierarchical gender relations. *Qualitative Research in Sport and Exercise, 1*(1), 3–20.

Atencio, M., Beal, B., Wright, E. M., & McClain, Z. N. (2018). *Moving boarders: Skateboarding and the changing landscape of urban youth sports.* Fayetteville, AR: University of Arkansas Press.

Atkinson, M. (2009). Parkour, anarcho-environmentalism, and poiesis. *Journal of Sport and Social Issues, 33*(2), 169–94.

Badshah, N. (2018). Ellie Soutter death: Father criticizes demands on young athletes. *The Guardian.* https://www.theguardian.com/uk-news/2018/jul/31/ellie-soutter-death-father-criticises-demands-on-young-athletes.

Batuev, M., & Robinson, L. (2019). Organizational evolution and the Olympic Games: The case of sport climbing. *Sport in Society, 22*(10), 1674–1690.

Beal, B. (1995). Disqualifying the official: An exploration of social resistance through the sub-culture of skateboarding. *Sociology of Sport Journal, 12*, 252–267.

Beal, B. (2019). Review: Skateboarding LA: Inside professional street skateboarding. *Contemporary Sociology, 48*(3), 352–354.

Beal, B., & Weidman, L. (2003). Authenticity in the skateboarding world. In R. E. Rinehart & S. Sydnor (Eds.), *To the extreme: Alternative sports, inside and out* (pp. 337–352). Albany: State University of New York Press.

Beal, B., & Wilson, C. (2004). "Chicks dig scars": Commercialisation and the transformations of skateboarders' identities. In B. Wheaton (Ed.), *Understanding lifestyle sports: Consumption, identity and difference* (pp. 31–54). New York: Routledge.

Booth, D. (1994). Surfing '60s: A case study in the history of pleasure and discipline. *Australian Historical Studies, 26*(103), 262–279.

Booth, D. (2002). From bikinis to boardshorts: Wahines and the paradoxes of the surfing culture. *Journal of Sport History, 28*(1), 3–22.

Booth, D. (2005). Paradoxes of material culture: The political economy of surfing. In J. Nauright & K. S. Schimmel (Eds), *The political economy of sport* (pp. 104–125). London: Palgrave Macmillan.

Booth, D. (2008). (Re)reading the surfers' bible: The affects of Tracks. *Continuum: Journal of Media and Cultural Studies, 22*(1), 17–35.

Booth, D. (2011). *Surfing: The Ultimate Guide.* Santa Barbara, CA: Greenwood Press.

Booth, D. (2013). History, culture, surfing: Exploring historiographical relationships. *Journal of Sport History, 40*(1), 3–20.

Booth, D., & Thorpe, H. (2007). The meaning of extreme. In D. Booth & H. Thorpe (Eds.), *The Berkshire encyclopedia of extreme sports* (pp. 181–197). Great Barrington, MA: Berkshire.

Booth, D., & Thorpe, H. (2019). Form and performance in oral history (narratives): Historiographical insights from surfing and snowboarding. *International Journal of the History of Sport, 36*(13–14), 1136–1156.

Borden, I. (2003). *Skateboarding, space and the city: Architecture and the body.* London: Berg.

Borden, I. (2019). *Skateboarding and the city. A complete history.* London: Bloomsbury Academic.

Brayton, S. (2005). "Back-lash": Revisiting the "white Negro" through skateboarding. *Sociology of Sport Journal, 22,* 356–372.

Brymer, E., & Gray, T. (2010). Developing an intimate "relationship" with nature through extreme sports participation. *Leisure/Loisir, 34*(4), 361–374.

Canniford, R. (2005). Moving shadows: Suggestions for ethnography in globalized cultures. *Qualitative Market Research: An International Journal, 8*(2), 204–219.

Cohen, R., Baluch, B., & Duffy, L. (2018). Defining extreme sport: Conceptions and misconceptions. *Frontiers in Psychology, 1–8.* https://doi.org/10.3389/fpsyg.2018.01974.

Comer, K. (2010). *Surfer girls in the new world order.* Durham, NC: Duke University Press.

Consent Is Rad. (2019). Skateism. https://www.skateism.com/consent-is-rad-is-rad/.

Cowan, J. (2020, June 18). How skateboarding can help fight racism. *New York Times.* https://www.nytimes.com/2020/06/18/us/usc-skateboarding-study.html.

Das, S. (2020). Top 10 richest extreme sports athletes of all time. *SportsShow.* https://sportsshow.net/richest-extreme-sports-athletes/.

Donnelly, M. (2006). Studying extreme sports: Beyond the core participants. *Journal of Sport and Social Issues, 30*(2), 219–224.

Donnelly, P. (1993). Subcultures in sport: Resilience and transformation. In A. Ingham & J. Loy (Eds.), *Sport in social development: Traditions, transitions and transformations* (pp. 119–145). Champaign, IL: Human Kinetics.

D'Orazio, D. (2020). Skateboarding's Olympic moment: The gendered contours of sportification. *Journal of Sport and Social Issues.* Advance online publication. https://doi.org/10.1177/0193723520928595.

Dumont, G. (2011). Antropologia multi-situada y Lifestyle Sports: Por un examen de la escalada a través de sus espacios [Multi-sited anthropology and lifestyle sports: Space and place in rock climbing]. *Perifèria: Revista de Recerca i Formació en Antropología, 14,* 1–16.

Dumont, G. (2015). Co-creation and new media: The entrepreneurial work of climbing photographers in digital times. *Anthropology of Work Review, 36*(1), 26–36.

Dumont, G. (2016a). Multi-layered labor: Entrepreneurship and professional versatility in rock climbing. *Ethnography, 17*(4), 440–459.

Dumont, G. (2016b). Understanding ethnographically athletes' perception and experience of sponsorship: The case of professional rock-climbing. *European Sport Management Quarterly, 16*(4), 525–542.

Dumont, G. (2017a). The beautiful and the damned: The work of new media production in professional rock climbing. *Journal of Sport and Social Issues, 41*(2), 99–117.

Dumont, G. (2017b). Relational labor, collaboration and professional rock climbing. In L. Hojrth, H. Horst, A. Galloway, & G. Bell (Eds.), *The Routledge companion to digital ethnography* (pp. 121–131). London: Routledge.

Dumont, G. (2018a). *Grimpeur professionnel: Le travail créateur sur le marché du sponsoring* [Professional climber: Creative work on the sponsoring labor market]. Paris: Ecole des Hautes Etudes en Sciences Sociales.

Dumont, G. (2018b). The labor of reputation building: Creating, developing and managing individual reputation. *Consumption Markets & Culture, 21*(6), 515–531.

Dupont, T. (2014). From core too consumer: The informal hierarchy of the skateboard scene. *Journal of Contemporary Ethnography, 43*(5), 556–581.

Dupont, T. (2020). Authentic subcultural identities and social media: American skateboarders and Instagram. *Deviant Behavior, 41*(5), 649–664.

Ellmer, E., & Rynne, S. (2019). Professionalisation of action sports in Australia. *Sport in Society, 22*(10), 1742–1757.

Evers, C. (2006). How to surf. *Journal of Sport and Social Issues, 30*(3), 229–243.

Evers, C. (2016). Researching action sport with a GoPro™ camera: An embodied and emotional mobile video tale of the sea, masculinity, and men-who-surf. In I. Wellard (Ed.), *Researching embodied sport: Exploring movement cultures* (pp. 145–162). London: Routledge.

Evers, C. (2019a). The gendered emotional labor of male professional freesurfers' digital media work. *Sport in Society, 22*(10), 1707–1723.

Evers, C. (2019b). Polluted leisure. *Leisure Sciences, 41*(5), 423–440.

Evers, C., & Doering, A. (2019). Lifestyle sports in East Asia. *Journal of Sport and Social Issues, 43*(5), 343–352.

Fok, C. Y. L., & O'Connor, P. (2020). Chinese women skateboarders in Hong Kong: A skatefeminism approach. *International Review for the Sociology of Sport.* Advance online publication. https://doi.org/10.1177/1012690220928735.

Ford, N., & Brown, D. (2006). *Surfing and social theory.* London: Routledge.

Gilchrist, P., & Wheaton, B. (2013). New media technologies in lifestyle sport. In B. Hutchins & D. Rowe (Eds.), *Digital media sport: Technology and power in the network society* (pp. 169–185). New York: Routledge.

Heywood, L. (2007). Third wave feminism, the global economy, and women's surfing: Sport as stealth feminism in girls' surf culture. In A. Harris (Ed.), *Next wave cultures: Feminism, subcultures, activism* (pp. 63–82). London: Routledge.

Hill, L., & Abbott, J. A. (2009). Representation, identity, and environmental action among Florida surfers. *Southeastern Geographer, 49*(2), 157–170.

Hough-Snee, D. (2020). Bob McKnight and Quicksilver: Surf shorts, stock exchanges, and bankruptcy. *Sport in Society.* Advance online publication. https://doi.org/10.1080/17430437.2020.1746015.

Hough-Snee, D., & Sotelo Eastman, A. (Eds.). (2017). *The critical surf studies reader.* Durham, NC: Duke University Press.

Humberstone, B. (2011). Embodiment and social action in nature-based sport: Spiritual spaces. *Leisure Studies, 30*(4), 495–512.

Humphreys, D. (1997). Shredheads go mainstream? Snowboarding and alternative youth. *International Review for the Sociology of Sport, 32*(2), 147–60.

Humphreys, D. (2003). Selling out snowboarding. In R. Rinehart & S. Sydnor (Eds.), *To the extreme: Alternative sports, inside and out* (pp. 407–428). Albany: New York State University Press.

Hyde, J. (2016, September 13). Dave Mirra's tragic legacy: CTE and extreme athletes. *Rolling Stone.* Retrieved fromhttps://www.rollingstone.com/sports/dave-mirras-suicide-cte-and-extreme-athletes-w438361.

Jones, S., & Graves, A. (2000). Power plays in public space: Skateboard parks as battlegrounds, gifts, and expression of self. *Landscape, 1–2,* 136–48.

Kay, J., & Laberge, S. (2002). The "new" corporate habitus in adventure racing. *International Review of the Sociology of Sport, 37*(1), 17–36.

Kilberth, V., & Schwier, J. (Eds.). (2019). *Skateboarding between subculture and the Olympics: A youth culture under pressure from commercialization and sportification.* Wetzlar: Transcript.

Knijnik, J., Horton, P., & Cruz, L. (2010). Rhizomatic bodies, gendered waves: Transitional femininities in Brazilian surf. *Sport in Society, 13*(7–8), 1170–1185.

Kusz, K. (2007). Whiteness and extreme sports. In D. Booth & H. Thorpe (Eds.), *Berkshire encyclopedia of extreme sport* (pp. 357–361). Great Barrington, MA: Berkshire Publishing.

Laurendeau, J., & Sharara, N. (2008). "Women could be every bit as good as guys": Reproductive and resistant agency between two "action" sports. *Journal of Sport and Social Issues, 32*(1), 24–47.

Laviolette, P. (2006). Green and extreme: Free-flowing through seascape and sewer. *Worldviews, 10*(2), 178–204.

lisahunter. (2016). Becoming visible: Visual narratives of "female" as a political position in surfing: The history, perpetuation, and disruption of patriocolonial pedagogies? In H. Thorpe & R. Olive (Eds.), *Women in action sport cultures* (pp. 319–348). Houndmills, U.K.: Palgrave.

lisahunter & Stoodley, L. (2020). Bluespace, senses, wellbeing and surfing: Prototype cyborg theory-methods. *Journal of Sport and Social Issues.* Advance online publication. https://doi.org/10.1177/0193723520928593.

Lombard, K. J. (Ed.). (2016). *Skateboarding: Subcultures, sites and shifts.* New York: Routledge.

MacKay, S., & Dallaire, C. (2012). Skirtboarder net-a-narratives: Young women creating their own skateboarding (re)presentations. *International Review for the Sociology of Sport, 48*(2), 171–195.

Maguire, J. (1996). Blade runners: Canadian migrants, ice hockey, and the global sports process. *Journal of Sport and Social Issues, 23*(3), 335–360.

Markham, A., & Baym, N. (2008). *Internet inquiry: Conversations about method.* Thousand Oaks, CA: Sage.

Mellegren, D. (1998, January 7). AP reports Terje boycotting Nagano? *SOL Snowboarding Online.* www.solsnowboarding.com/compete/terje.html.

Messner, M. (2002). *Taking the field.* Minneapolis: University of Minnesota Press.

Moving Oceans. (2020). About. https://movingoceans.com/about/.

Nemani, M., & Thorpe, H. (2016). The experiences of "brown" female bodyboarders: Negotiating multiple axes of marginality. In H. Thorpe & R. Olive (Eds.), *Women in action sport cultures: Identity, politics and experience* (pp. 213–234). Houndmills, U.K.: Palgrave Macmillan.

Ojala, A. L. (2014). Institutionalisation in professional freestyle snowboarding: Finnish professional riders' perceptions. *European Journal for Sport and Society, 11*(2), 103–126.

Ojala, A. L., & Thorpe, H. (2015). The role of the coach in action sports: Using a problem-based learning approach. *International Sport Coaching Journal, 2*(1), 64–71.

Olive, R. (2013). "Making friends with the neighbours": Blogging as a research method. *International Journal of Cultural Studies, 16*(1), 71–84.

Olive, R. (2015). Reframing surfing: Physical culture in online spaces. *Media International Australia, Incorporating Culture & Policy*, 155(1), 99–107.

Olive, R. (2016). Surfing, localism, place-based pedagogies and ecological sensibilities in Australia. In B. Humberstone, H. Prince, & K. Henderson (Eds.), *Routledge international handbook of outdoor studies* (pp. 501–510). New York: Routledge.

Olive, R. (2019). The trouble with newcomers: Women, localism and the politics of surfing. *Journal of Australian Studies*, 43(1), 39–54.

Olive, R., McCuaig, L., & Phillips, M. (2015). Women's recreational surfing: A patronizing experience. *Sport, Education and Society*, 20(2), 258–276.

Olive, R., & Thorpe, H. (2011). Negotiating the 'F-word' in the field: Doing feminist ethnography in action sport cultures. *Sociology of Sport Journal*, 28(4), 421–440.

Olive, R., & Thorpe, H. (2017). Feminist ethnography and physical culture: Towards reflexive, political, and collaborative methods. In M. Giardina & M. Donnelly (Eds.), *Physical culture: Ethnography and the body* (pp. 114–128). New York: Routledge.

Olive, R., Thorpe, H., Roy, G., Nemani, G., lisahunter, Wheaton, B., & Humberstone, B. (2016). Surfing together: Exploring the potential of a collaborative ethnographic moment. In H. Thorpe & R. Olive (Eds.), *Women in action sport cultures: Identity, politics and experience* (pp. 45–68). Houndmills, U.K.: Palgrave Macmillan.

Olivier, S. (2010). "Your wave, bro!" Virtue ethics and surfing. *Sport in Society*, 13(7–8), 1223–1233.

Osmond, G. (2011). Myth-making in Australian sport history: Re-evaluating Duke Kahanamoku's contribution to surfing. *Australian Historical Studies*, 42(2), 260–276.

Parris, D., Troilo, M., Bouchet, A., & Welty Peachey, J. (2014). Action sports athletes as entrepreneurs: Female professional wakeboarders, sponsorship, and branding. *Sport Management Review*, 17(4), 530–545.

Pavlidis, A., & Olive, R. (2014). On the track/in the bleachers: Authenticity and feminist ethnographic research in sport and physical cultural studies. *Sport in Society*, 17(2), 218–232.

Phillips, M. G., & Osmond, G. (2015). Australia's women surfers: History, methodology and the digital humanities. *Australian Historical Studies*, 46(2), 285–303.

Pink, S., Horst, H., Postill, J., Hjorth, L., Lewis, T., & Tacchi, J. (2015). *Digital ethnography: Principles and practice*. Thousand Oaks, CA: Sage.

Polluted Leisure. (2020). https://pollutedleisure.com/.

Pomerantz, S., Currie, D., & Kelly, D. (2004). Sk8er girls: Skateboarders, girlhood and feminism in motion. *Women's Studies International Forum*, 27, 547–557.

Ponting, J. (2009). Projecting paradise: The surf media and the hermeneutic circle in surfing tourism. *Tourism Analysis*, 14(2), 175–185.

Puddle, D. (2019). *Making the jump: Examining the glocalisation of parkour in Aotearoa New Zealand* (Unpublished PhD dissertation). University of Waikato, New Zealand. https://hdl. handle.net/10289/12712.

Puddle, D., Wheaton, B., & Thorpe, H. (2019). The glocalization of parkour: A New Zealand/ Aotearoa case study. *Sport in Society*, 22(10), 1724–1741.

Rahikainen, K. (2020). *What kind of example do you wanna set? Sponsored female climbers negotiating femininity in climbing and social media* (Unpublished PhD dissertation). University of New South Wales, Sydney.

Rahikainen, K., & Toffoletti, K. (2021). "I just don't wanna deal with the headache of people fighting over the internet: A study of sponsored female climbers' digital labor. *Sociology of Sport Journal*. https://doi.org/10.1123/ssj.2020-0177.

Rickly, J. (2016). Lifestyle mobilities: A politics of lifestyle rock climbing, *Mobilities*, 11(2), 243–263.

Rinehart, R. (1998). Inside of the outside: Pecking orders within alternative sport at ESPN's 1995 "The EXtreme Games." *Journal of Sport and Social Issues*, 22(4), 398–414.

Rinehart, R. (2000). Emerging/arriving sport: Alternatives to formal sports. In J. Coakley & E. Dunning (Eds.), *Handbook of sports studies* (pp. 504–519). London: Sage.

Rinehart, R. (2005). "Babes" and boards. *Journal of Sport and Social Issues*, 29(3), 232–255.

Rinehart, R. (2008a). ESPN's X Games, contests of opposition, resistance, co-option, and negotiation. In M. Atkinson & K. Young (Eds.), *Tribal play: Subcultural journeys through sport: Vol. 4. Research in the Sociology of Sport* (pp. 175–196). Bingley, U.K.: JAI.

Rinehart, R. E. (2008b). Exploiting a new generation: Corporate branding and the co-optation of action sport. In M. Giardina & M. Donnelly (Eds.), *Youth culture and sport: Identity, power, and politics* (pp. 71–90). London: Routledge.

Rinehart, R. E., & Snydor, S. (2003). *To the extreme: Alternative sports, Inside and out.* New York: State University of New York Press.

Robinson, V. (2008). *Everyday masculinities and extreme sport: Male identity and rock climbing,* New York: Berg.

Roenigk, A. (2016, May 24). Doctors say late BMX legend Dave Mirra had CTE. ESPN. http://www. espn.com/action/story/_/id/15614274/bmx-legend-dave-mirra-diagnosed-cte.

Roy, G. (2014). "Taking emotions seriously": Feeling female and becoming-surfer through UK surf space. *Emotion, Space and Society*, 12, 41–48.

Roy, G. (2016). *Coming* together and paddling *out*: Lesbian identities and British surfing spaces. In H. Thorpe & R. Olive (Eds), *Women in action sport cultures* (pp. 193–212). Houndmills, U.K.: Palgrave.

Schumacher, C. (2016). "My mother is a fish": From stealth feminism to surfeminism. In D. Zavalza Hough-Snee & A. Sotelo Eastman (Eds), *The Critical Surf Studies Reader* (pp. 284–304). Duke University Press.

Sherowski, H. (2005, April). What it means to be a snowboarder. *Transworld Snowboarding*, 160–169.

Siber, K. (2017, July 12). 8 top women athletes on the pay gap in action sports. *Outside Magazine.* https://www.outsideonline.com/2197102/8-women-athletes-how-they-make-living-sports.

Smits, F. (2019). Youth Dutch commercially sponsored kite surfers: Free as a bird? *Sport in Society*, 22(10), 1707–1723.

Smits, F. (2020). The well-being of adolescent high-performance action sport athletes: The case of young Dutch commercially sponsored kitesurfers. In M. Lang (Ed.), *The Routledge handbook of athlete welfare* (pp. 231–241). New York/London: Routledge.

Snyder, G. (2012). The city and the subculture career: Professional street skateboarding in LA. *Ethnography*, 13(3), 306–329.

Snyder, G. (2017). *Skateboarding LA: Inside professional street skateboarding.* New York: New York University Press.

Spowart, L., Hughson, J., & Shaw, S. (2008). Snowboarding moms carve out fresh tracks: Resisting traditional motherhood discourse? *Annals of Leisure Research*, 11(1–2), 187–204.

Stoddart, M. (2010). Constructing masculinized sportscapes: Skiing, gender and nature in British Columbia, Canada. *International Review for the Sociology of Sport*, 46(1), 108–124.

Stoddart, M. (2012). *Making meaning out of mountain: The political ecology of skiing.* Vancouver: UBC Press.

Stranger, M. (2010). Surface and substructure: Beneath surfing's commodified surface. *Sport in Society*, 13(7–8), 1117–1134.

Stranger, M. (2011). *Surfing life: Surface, substructure and the commodification of the sublime.* Surrey, U.K.: Ashgate.

Stratford, E. (2002). On the edge: A tale of skaters and urban governance. *Social and Cultural Geography, 3*(2), 193–206.

Sugden, J., & Tomlinson, A. (2002). Theory and method for a critical sociology of sport. In J. Sugden & A. Tomlinson (Eds.), *Power games: Theory and method for a critical sociology of sport* (pp. 240–266). London: Routledge.

Thompson, G. (2017). Pushing under the whitewash: Revisiting the making of South Africa's surfing sixties. In D. Hough-Snee & A. Sotelo Eastman (Eds.), *The critical surf studies reader* (pp. 155–176). Durham, NC: Duke University Press.

Thorpe, H. (2008). Foucault, technologies of self, and the media: Discourses of femininity in snowboarding culture. *Journal of Sport and Social Issues, 32*(2), 199–229.

Thorpe, H. (2010). Bourdieu, gender reflexivity and physical culture: A case of masculinities in the snowboarding field. *Journal of Sport and Social Issues, 34*(2), 176–214.

Thorpe, H. (2011a). "Have board, will travel": Global physical youth cultures and transnational mobility. In J. Maguire & M. Falcous (Eds.), *Sport and migration: Borders, boundaries and crossings* (pp. 112–126). London: Routledge.

Thorpe, H. (2011b). *Snowboarding bodies in theory and practice.* Basingstoke, U.K.: Palgrave Macmillan.

Thorpe, H. (2012). The ethnographic (i)nterview in the sports field: Towards a postmodern sensibility. In K. Young & M. Atkinson (Eds.), *Qualitative research on sport and physical culture* (pp. 51–78). Bingley, U.K.: Emerald Group Publishing.

Thorpe, H. (2014). *Transnational mobilities in action sport cultures.* Basingstoke, U.K.: Palgrave Macmillan.

Thorpe, H. (2017a). Action sports, social media, and new technologies: Towards a research agenda. *Communication and Sport, 5*(5), 554–578.

Thorpe, H. (2017b). "The endless winter": Transnational mobilities of skilled snow sport workers. *Journal of Ethnic and Migration Studies, 43*(3), 528–545.

Thorpe, H. (2018). Feminist views of action sports. In L. Mansfield, J. Caudwell, B. Wheaton, & B. Watson (Eds.), *Palgrave handbook of sport, leisure and physical education* (pp. 699–719). Houndmills, U.K.: Palgrave.

Thorpe, H., & Ahmad, N. (2015). Youth, action sports and political agency in the Middle East: Lessons from a grassroots parkour group in Gaza. *International Review for the Sociology of Sport, 50,* 678–704.

Thorpe, H., & Chawansky, M. (2017). The gendered experiences of women staff and volunteers in sport for development organizations. The case of transmigrant workers of Skateistan. *Journal of Sport Management, 31*(6), 546–561.

Thorpe, H., & Dumont, G. (2019). The professionalization of action sports: Mapping trends and future directions. *Sport in Society, 22*(10), 1639–1654.

Thorpe, H., & Rinehart, R. (2010). Alternative sport and affect: Non-representational theory examined. *Sport in Society, 13*(7/8), 1268–1291.

Thorpe, H., & Rinehart, R. (2013). Action sport NGOs in a neo-liberal context: The cases of Skateistan and Surf Aid International. *Journal of Sport & Social Issues, 37*(2), 115–141.

Thorpe, H., Toffoletti, K., & Bruce, T. (2017). Sportswomen and social media: Bringing third-wave feminism, postfeminism, and neoliberal feminism into conversation. *Journal of Sport and Social Issues, 41*(5), 359–383.

Thorpe, H., & Wheaton, B. (2011). "Generation X Games," action sports and the Olympic movement: Understanding the cultural politics of incorporation. *Sociology, 45*(5), 830–847.

Thorpe, H., & Wheaton, B. (2013). Dissecting action sports studies: Past, present and beyond. In D. L. Andrews & B. Carrington (Eds.), *A companion to sport* (pp. 341–358). Oxford: Wiley-Blackwell.

Thorpe, H., & Wheaton, B. (2017). The X Games: Redefining youth and sport. In A. C. Billings & L. A. Wenner (Eds.), *Sports, media and mega-events* (pp. 247–261). London: Routledge.

Thorpe, H., & Wheaton, B. (2019). The Olympic Games, Agenda 2020 and action sports: The promise, politics and performance of organizational change. *International Journal of Sport Policy and Politics, 11*(3), 465–483.

Thorpe, H., & Wheaton, B. (2021). Young Gazan refugees, sport and social media: Understanding migration as a process of becoming. *International Migration Review, 55*(3), 902–928.

Uekusa, S. (2019). Surfing with Bourdieu! A qualitative analysis of the fluid power relations among surfers in the line-ups. *Journal of Contemporary Ethnography, 48*(4), 538–562.

Van Bottenburg, M., & Salome, L. (2010). The indoorisation of outdoor sports: An exploration of the rise of lifestyle sports in artificial settings. *Leisure Studies, 29*(2), 143–160.

Variables: Protect Our Winters. (2008, April). *Transworld Snowboarding,* 62.

Waitt, G. (2008). "Killing waves": Surfing, space and gender. *Social and Cultural Geography, 9*(1), 75–94.

Walker, I. H. (2011). *Waves of resistance: Surfing and history in twentieth-century Hawaii.* Honolulu: University of Hawai'i Press.

Wheaton, B. (2000). "New lads"? Masculinities and the "new sport" participant. *Men and Masculinities, 2,* 434–456.

Wheaton, B. (2002). Babes on the beach, women in the surf: Researching gender, power and difference in the windsurfing culture. In J. Sugden & A. Tomlinson (Eds.), *Power games: A critical sociology of sport* (pp. 240–266). London: Routledge.

Wheaton, B. (2003). Windsurfing: A subculture of commitment. In R. Rinehart & S. Sydnor (Eds.), *To the extreme: Alternative sports, inside and out* (pp. 75–101). New York: State University of New York Press.

Wheaton, B. (2004). Selling out? The globalization and commercialization of lifestyle sports. In L. Allison (Ed.), *The global politics of sport: The role of global institutions in sport* (pp. 127–146). London: Routledge.

Wheaton, B. (2007). Identity, politics and the beach: Environmental activism in Surfers Against Sewage. *Leisure Studies, 26*(3), 279–302.

Wheaton, B. (2010). Introducing the consumption and representation of lifestyle sports. *Sport in Society, 13*(7–8), 1057–1081.

Wheaton, B. (2013). *The cultural politics of lifestyle sport.* London: Routledge.

Wheaton, B. (2017a). Space invaders in surfing's white tribe: Exploring surfing, race, and identity. In D. Hough-Snee & A. Sotelo Eastman (Eds.), *The critical surf studies reader* (pp. 177–195). Durham, NC: Duke University Press.

Wheaton, B. (2017b). Surfing through the life-course: Silver surfers' negotiation of ageing. *Annals of Leisure Research, 20*(1), 96–116.

Wheaton, B. (2020). Surfing and environmental sustainability. In B. Wilson & B. Millington (Eds.), *Sport and the environment* (pp. 157–178). Bingley, U.K.: Emerald Publishing.

Wheaton, B., & Beal, B. (2003). "Keeping it real": Sub-cultural media and discourses of authenticity in alternative sport. *International Review for the Sociology of Sport, 38,* 155–176.

Wheaton, B., & Thorpe, H. (2016). Youth perceptions of the Olympic Games: Attitudes towards action sports at the YOG and Olympic Games. *IOC Report.* https://library.olym

pic.org/Default/doc/SYRACUSE/165853/youth-perceptions-of-the-olympic-games-attitu des-towards-action-sports-at-the-yog-and-olympic-games-?_lg=en-GB.

Wheaton, B., & Thorpe, H. (2018). Action sports, the Olympic Games, and the opportunities and challenges of gender equity: The cases of surfing and skateboarding. *Journal of Sport and Social Issues*, 42(5), 315–342.

Wheaton, B., & Thorpe, H. (2019). Action sport media consumption trends across generations: Exploring the Olympic audience and the impact of action sports inclusion. *Communication and Sport*, 7(4), 415–445.

Wheaton, B., & Thorpe, H. (2022). *Action Sports and the Olympic Games: Past, Present, Future*. Routledge: New York.

Wheaton, B., & Tomlinson, A. (1998). The changing gender order in sport? The case of windsurfing subcultures. *Journal of Sport and Social Issues*, 22, 251–272.

Williams, N. (2020). *Colour in the lines: The racial politics and possibilities of US skateboarding culture* (Unpublished PhD thesis). University of Waikato, New Zealand.

Willing, I., Bennett, A., Piispa, M., & Green, B. (2019). Skateboarding and the "tired generation": Ageing in youth cultures and lifestyle sports. *Sociology*, 53(3), 503–518.

Willing, I., Green, B., & Pavlidis, A. (2020). The "boy scouts" and "bad boys" of skateboarding: A thematic analysis of *the bones brigade*. *Sport in Society*, 23(5), 832–846.

Woermann, N. (2012). On the slope is on the screen: Prosumption, social media practices, and scopic systems in the freeskiing subculture. *American Behavioral Scientist*, 56(4), 618–640.

Yochim, E. C. (2010). *Skate life: Re-imagining white masculinity*, Ann Arbor: University of Michigan Press.

Young, A., & Dallaire, C. (2008). Beware *#! sk8 at your own risk: The discourses of young female skateboarders. In M. Atkinson & K. Young (Eds.), *Tribal play: Subcultural journeys through sport* (pp. 235–254). Bingley, U.K.: JAI.

PART V

INCLUSION AND
EXCLUSION

CHAPTER 40

....

SPORT, SOCIAL INCLUSION, AND DEVELOPMENT

....

EMMA SHERRY AND KATHERINE RAW

THIS chapter examines the ways in which sport can contribute to social inclusion and individual or community development. Although there is no universally accepted definition of social inclusion, it can be broadly defined as "having the resources, opportunities and capabilities to learn, work, engage and have a voice" (Australian Social Inclusion Board, 2013). In the context of the global growth of sport for development (SFD)—both as an area of research and as a sector within the sport and development communities—the role that sport and associated activities can play in creating or contributing to more inclusive societies has been increasingly promoted and scrutinized. With a growing focus of high-income country governments on developing societies that are more inclusive and accepting of diversity, sport has been identified as a potentially impactful mechanism for social inclusion.

Globalization has seen wider movement of people, resulting in greater visibility of ethnic, racial, and religious diversity within and across communities. Additionally, social movements for access and equity for all, in the areas of people with a disability, gender, and sexual diversity, have brought about an increased focus on ensuring social inclusion. In considering such overlays of intersectionality, this chapter will discuss the different approaches to achieving social inclusion through sport, and how sport may provide opportunities to increase or enhance social inclusion and development. In particular, our treatment will consider different approaches to social inclusion and development experienced by different groups, as not all social groups experience the same discrimination in or exclusion from the sport system.

Social inclusion is a contested and complex concept that cannot be easily decoupled from its opposite: social exclusion. The chapter examines some of the key theories underpinning social inclusion and identifies how social inclusion can be understood as a development outcome or, more precisely, a long-term impact of SFD programs and initiatives. The role of governments in these efforts, via funding or policy direction, is also discussed.

The final section of the chapter overviews some of the ongoing debates within research examining sport, social inclusion, and development. The chapter will examine how sport programs and organizations are used by governments to facilitate social inclusion, and the outcomes of those initiatives for individuals and the broader community.

ISSUES

Social inclusion can be an outcome sought by a SFD program for a particular target community. Alternatively, it may be viewed as a mechanism to enable more diversity or representation in sport participation in mainstream organized sport. This section begins by outlining research that conceptualizes social inclusion as a development outcome, before discussing research that is focused on making traditional organized sport more socially inclusive.

Social Inclusion as a Development Outcome (Sport for Development)

In the SFD context, social inclusion is largely positioned as a development outcome being sought by the SFD program. SFD uses sport activities, programs, or events to create a platform for social inclusion, with the aim of creating more socially inclusive communities and mitigating socially excluding practices for particular groups in communities.

Social inclusion outcomes from targeted SFD programs are often reported in terms of improved social relationships (cf. Morgan & Parker, 2017), development of life skills (cf. Buelens, Theeboom, Vertonghen, & Martelaer, 2015), and an improved or increased sense of belonging (cf. Maxwell, Foley, Taylor, & Burton, 2013). Extant SFD research has recognized that sport is a vehicle capable of promoting social inclusion (Sherry, 2010; Welty Peachey & Sherry, 2016), and different programs have identified different outcomes with varying levels of success. One example of a program that has arguably created greater social inclusion for people with an intellectual disability is the Unified Sports program of the Special Olympics. This initiative aims to offer athletes an opportunity to connect with peers and local community by bringing together players with and without intellectual disabilities. Research into the program was conducted using individual interviews with 200 participants across five countries and determined that the initiative was able to positively contribute to social inclusion (McConkey, Dowling, Hassan, & Menke, 2013). Similarly, Maxwell and colleagues' (2013) investigation into the social inclusion of Muslim women in a community sport context found that the program was positively contributing to social inclusion. However, while the program supported social inclusion among Muslim participants, the findings also indicated that the program served to exclude non-Muslim participants (Maxwell et al., 2013). Findings such as these bring into question the aim of social inclusion programs in the SFD setting—social inclusion for whom?

Achieving the intangible aim of social inclusion is a challenge in SFD programs and events, as found in a case study of the Homeless World Cup, in which it was identified that organizers of this event faced difficulties in trying to promote social inclusion among participants. While the initiative largely positively impacted participants through reduced social isolation and exclusion and increased social capital, challenges arose when some participants' teams lost games by a large margin. For some, losing a game impacted negatively on their self-confidence, and their feelings of social exclusion were increased (Welty Peachey & Sherry, 2016). These findings illustrate the way in which such programs, even while largely successful, can have ambiguous outcomes and underscore the importance of careful program planning and implementation that account for potential barriers to successful inclusion (Green, 2008).

Dagkas and Armour (2012), in their study investigating sport for Muslim girls, identified proposed solutions for inclusion. These included using teaching techniques that help girls identify and address inequities that inhibit their opportunities for and/or enjoyment of physical activity and centering students' diverse needs and desires in physical education curricula to increase engagement and inclusion. Maintaining a good working relationship between schools and Muslim parents was also proposed as a solution to address tensions that was seen to increase participation in some schools. In three studies in three different developing countries, Kay (2013) found SFD programs were successful in attracting youth to education programs and transferring learning from sport into other contexts. Transferred learning included higher self-belief, confidence, communication skills, aspirations, decision-making skills, relationship skills, discipline, self-control, and collective action. Informality and increased reach to those "on the margins" were identified as special aspects that help to make sport beneficial for social inclusion (Kay, 2013).

Crabbe (2008) argues for a "developmental" rather than a "diversionary" approach to social inclusion in SFD, one which focuses on personal development rather than the reduction of a participant's behaviors or actions according to predefined outcomes. Crabbe asserts that a program can be considered successful when it offers social capital, and that long-term and deep engagement should be a key goal, as should "widening the horizons and aspirations of participants" (p. 27). Ekholm and Dahlstedt (2017, 2019) argue similarly, noting that it is difficult to assess the potential effectiveness of sport for social inclusion programs as the transfer of skills is often simply presumed to occur, rather than the transference of skills forming an essential element of program pedagogy. Ekholm and Dahlstedt (2017, 2019) found that many SFD programs take a neoliberal approach that targets individual choices and behavior; in so doing, conditions of segregation and inequality are actually normalized, thereby reinforcing the social hierarchies that created social problems and tensions in the first place.

In the Australian context, Gibbs and Block (2017) evaluated three types of sports participation models for refugee youth in Australia. They concluded that, rather than programming specifically focused on refugee youth cohorts, long-term programs that integrate participants into mainstream clubs were the ideal and had the most success in increasing participation for refugee youth. Success factors in such programs included fee subsidies, facilitating transport and communication, and having a designated liaison linking families to clubs (Gibbs & Block, 2017). Indeed, collaborations between sport clubs and community organizations were identified as key by Hermens, Super, Verkooijen, and Koelen (2015), who studied collaborations between youth work organizations and local sports clubs in the Netherlands. In this study, stakeholders' capacity to encourage vulnerable youth participation was cited as a barrier. The stakeholders called for funding to be made available specifically for projects targeting intersectional participants. They cited the need to establish a positive sociopedagogical climate, which views young people's engagement and inclusion in socially significant activities and their development of social relations with society and its institutions as central to positive youth development. In addition, they identified a need for boundary spanners, individuals who can manage the partnership between youth work organizations and sports clubs.

Research investigating social inclusion in the SFD context has identified the importance of coaches and volunteers (Buelens et al., 2015; Morgan & Parker, 2017) in creating spaces and environments that are safe, welcoming, and inclusive. Interpreting social inclusion through the concepts of recognition and acceptance, Morgan and Parker argue that sport-based programs have strong potential in this regard when participants are able to develop robust relationships with staff such as coaches, particularly when these relationships are built on "trust, recognition and developing self-worth" (p. 1028). The importance of coaches, volunteers, and support staff in making participants feel welcome, safe, and included appears to be key to a successful social inclusion–focused program.

The most common criticism of programs or initiatives focusing on social inclusion in SFD is that they are founded on a deficit model of the target group, thereby positioning the program participants as the social problem to be addressed rather than the broader social and structural inequalities they face (cf. Bustad & Andrews, 2017; Kelly, 2011; Spencer-Cavaliere, Thai, & Kingsley, 2017). Spencer-Cavaliere and colleagues, in their study of sport programming for youth with a disability, found that while practitioners seemed to value diversity and were willing to make environments inclusive, ableist beliefs still underpinned the continued justification of segregated settings. For example, segregation was viewed by practitioners as necessary to "support the participation of youth with impairments who were unable to 'keep up' in mainstream competitive sport" (p. 126) because practitioners often continued to equate ability with dominance, excellence, and competition between individuals, in line with the way sport is culturally understood. Further, participation in the segregated setting was described in terms of a "stepping stone" (p. 126) to mainstream sport participation, a conceptualization that is founded on the ableist understanding of impairment as inherently negative—a problem to be "fixed." Thus, while participants experienced some inclusion, they also experienced exclusion as a result of the culturally informed, ableist understanding of sporting ability, which served to position them as "[a] part of and apart from sport" (p. 120).

In a similar vein, Collison, Darnell, Giulianotti, and Howe (2017) argue that while youth are often targeted in sport for development and peace (SDP) projects, in practice, girls are often excluded, and the authors attribute this exclusion to cultural norms in the home country or within sport. Indeed, they suggest, "youth" in SDP initiatives is often code for "male youth." Culturally informed perceptions of the intervention participants impact the success of the program. For example, in some cases, sporting achievement was overvalued; in others, ethnic tensions made intercultural participation challenging. Thus, Collison and colleagues found that benefits of social inclusion in these SDP programs were limited to a minority, rather than a majority, of participants as a result of preexisting social and structural inequalities. Similarly, based on interviews with community sports coaches, managers, and partners in an SFD intervention in Sweden, Ekholm, Dahlstedt, and Rönnbäck (2019) found that girls from ethnic minorities were constructed as absent from sport-based intervention programs and were characterized in stereotypical ways, according to entrenched norms of gender and culture. Interviewees themselves perceived a need for female coaches as role models and the prioritization of girls' own voices and needs as they perceive them. The authors propose that girls' own perspectives on their needs regarding sport participation, but also about their lives more broadly, are essential to inform the design and implementation of sport-based intervention programs. Ultimately, however, the authors question the feasibility of segregated sport-based interventions for girls at all as they are not generally inclusive.

From this synopsis of the research literature, it can be argued that SFD initiatives can facilitate social inclusion; however, there are many design, implementation, and participant engagement challenges that need to be addressed for this to be successful.

Making Sport More Inclusive (Sport Development)

In both practice and research, much of the sport development (SD) focus in terms of social inclusion is on how traditional, organized sport can be made more safe, welcoming, and inclusive for all. Research that investigates diversity and inclusion in sport often focuses on a particular target or a socially excluded group, such as people with a disability (cf. Bantjes & Swartz, 2018; Inoue & Forneris, 2015; Jeanes et al., 2019), same-sex-attracted and gender-diverse people (cf. Buzuvis, 2011), women and girls (see, for example, Elling & Knoppers, 2004), immigrants and refugees (cf. Rich, Misener, & Dubeau, 2015), and ethnic and religious minorities (cf. Maxwell et al., 2013; Ratna, 2016).

Research by Collins and Kay (2014) examining an inclusion-focused SD program for Bangladeshi English Muslim girls identified several important design factors: a relaxed, informal style of delivery; the development of social relationships with coaches and peers; and the ability to integrate participants with different abilities. Participants in the program reported increased self-confidence, sporting ability, and interest in higher education. Collins and Kay argue that programs must be people-focused and, further, that the target group must be involved in the design if programs are to achieve their aim.

The requirement to engage directly with the excluded groups was identified by Dagkas (2018), who argues that it is essential to engage with culturally diverse young people and their families to design culturally relevant intervention programs, to ensure that program meets the specific needs of the target group. The aims of sport organizations to engender social inclusion and for initiatives to be community-led and empowering were also identified as key by Ratna (2016), who argues that sport organizations must understand the circumstances of their target groups, such as their feeling "othered" by popular representations that position them as deviant. Ratna further argues that sport organizations must address target groups' social needs, for example by respecting and accommodating cultural or religious beliefs in off-field socializing, reducing the pressure to "blend in" and recognizing that individuals may have a multiplicity of identities, including regional and national identities.

Intersectionality is also critical to any effective approach to advance inclusion. Intersectionality refers to the ways that individuals can be disadvantaged by multiple sources of oppression, such as their race, sexual orientation, religion, gender identity, and class. Here, Dagkas (2018, p. 72) argues that there is a pressing need to recognize that although some opportunities for participation in sport might appear to be accessible, "structural barriers such as language, type of activities and also mode of delivery of these activities" can render them inaccessible. Thus, Dagkas advocates for specific training for teachers, coaches, sports administrators, and organizers that takes into account the multiple and diverse sources of disadvantage that underpin participants' experiences of sport participation. Similarly, Corthouts et al. (2020), following their study of special initiatives implemented for specific target groups in European voluntary sports clubs, assert that a paid manager or "innovation champion" familiar with the problems associated with intersectionality could be a strong driver of social innovation. The authors found that there was unevenness in the development of initiatives targeting specific groups, such as women and girls, people from migrant backgrounds, and people with a disability, largely due to gaps in managerial, organizational, and environmental determinants, such as transformational leadership that values social inclusion, size of club, managerial structure, access to resources, and the size and complexity of the community. They argue that a "paid manager seems important for an organization to innovate" (p. 43) and assert that such a position might be eligible for public funding, which was found to be a positive influence on the capacity of clubs to implement social innovation initiatives. They conclude further that the position would pay for itself within a relatively short time by attracting new target groups.

In the Australian context, Frost, Lightbody, and Halabi (2013) concluded that rural Australian rules football clubs are increasingly adopting strategies and internal organizational practices to be more socially inclusive, despite retaining problematic aspects of stereotypical masculine culture. Central to the effectiveness of these strategies and practices has been the creation of "dense" social networks of acquaintances who interact often and include a greater range of people, matters which contribute to a sense of collective capability (Frost et al., 2013). Frost and colleagues found that when Australian regional football clubs were willing to make amendments to organizational structure and when they increased their strategic focus on becoming more socially inclusive by adopting proactive community building strategies, they became "nurturing resources that promote healthier, more resilient communities through expanded social inclusion" (p. 463). In contrast, Jeanes and colleagues (2019) found that some sporting organizations are unwilling to deal with the complexity required to enact policies aimed at including youth with disabilities. Participants in their study included club volunteers, SD workers, officers from state sporting associations and from the state-funded initiative providing opportunities to participate in sport for people with a disability, Access All Abilities. Here, some participants framed inclusion as "too difficult," not part of their "core business," and/or not compatible with sporting success in order to justify the maintenance of structures and practices that exclude disabled youth. At the club level, there was tension between the expectations of state sporting associations in terms of development and implementation of inclusion policies, and a club's enactment of those policies. Indeed, policy critics within the clubs viewed the ambition of inclusion as "unreasonable and unobtainable" (p. 998) and claimed that it could "detract from [the club's] core ambitions and aims focused primarily on on-field success" (p. 999). The authors identify challenging ableism, and the perceived tension between competitive success and universal participation that informs "responses to policies and . . . the values and beliefs held by clubs" (p. 1001), as central to achieving "transformational inclusion" (p. 986).

A key focus for SD programs seeking to improve inclusion has been on creating sport settings where participants who would normally be excluded can feel safe, welcome, and included. These outcomes focus on providing places and opportunities for underrepresented communities to participate and engage with mainstream sport, to change perceptions of mainstream community sport clubs and participants, and to build alliances with local communities (cf. McConkey et al., 2013). However, in his ethnographic fieldwork with Somali Australian youth at community soccer clubs, Spaaij (2015) points out that some barriers to social inclusion—such as gender, ethnicity, and religion—are more difficult to break down. He also noted that refugee youth in multiethnic clubs tended to experience less inclusion as they were required to fit in with the dominant group. In addition, Spaaij found that individuals with intersections of disadvantage—such as young Somali women—were provided with even fewer opportunities to participate.

As noted in the SFD context, criticisms of programs or initiatives aiming to achieve social inclusion in SFD most commonly point to the lack of attention to the structural issues that make social inclusion more challenging to address, including the inability of programming to properly mitigate or remove barriers to full participation by all. For example, Kelly (2011, p. 126) argues that while programs can have varying degrees of success in relation to themes of "sport for all," "social cohesion," "a pathway to work," and "giving voice," they have a limited impact on the structural factors that exclude marginalized youth. In fact, there is a risk of such interventions providing legitimacy for analyses that position the individual and their marginalization as the source of the problem because the focus is placed on the individual's deficits rather than on the structural inequalities that underpin marginalization. Collins and Haudenhuyse (2015) argue that sport-based measures for wider social inclusion of youth are completely inadequate as they cannot change the sociocultural contexts that marginalize and exclude young people. They note that "austerity measures" imposed by the Conservative–Liberal Democrat coalition government in the United Kingdom, which have resulted in vastly reduced government spending in social programming, have further entrenched structural inequality and warn that some sport interventions could be viewed as "generating social order in disadvantaged neighbourhoods" (p. 11). To help understand and address this, McDonald, Spaaij, and Dukic (2018) examined in what ways football facilitates forms of social inclusion for refugee and asylum seeker team members. The authors argue that participation in sport can enhance social inclusion, but caution that the trajectory of inclusion is neither linear nor straightforward. They note that most participants connected their participation on the team with wider social inclusion outcomes, such as those related to employment, education, and/or other nonsport areas of society (McDonald et al., 2018). Critics have identified that, in some instances, the social inclusion aspects of a particular sport event or program may wittingly or unwittingly take a neoliberal approach by focusing almost exclusively on making responsible, productive citizens out of those who face barriers to traditional forms of employment due to marginalization or discrimination. Thus, rather than addressing any social problems, neoliberalist instincts tend to construct marginalized individuals as problems, and efforts are focused on encouraging individuals to change in order to more readily fit the current social conditions and received norms (cf. Vanwynsberghe, Surborg, & Wyly, 2013).

APPROACHES

Defining Social Inclusion and Development

There is no clear or singular definition of social inclusion; indeed, a broad range of interpretations exists when it comes to defining and understanding this concept. Typically, social inclusion has been situated at the opposing end of the spectrum to social exclusion, which is a term used to describe circumstances that lead to individuals being prevented from participating in societal activities (Spaaij, 2012). As a result, explanations of social inclusion revolve around improved opportunities for free speech, decision-making, and access to various social institutions (Oxoby, 2009).

Historically, the roots of social inclusion have been linked with several European sociologists and trace back as far as Aristotle. Primarily originating in France in the early 18th century, initial notions of the concept were closely associated with political and cultural concerns that focused on "liberty, equality, and fraternity" (Sen, 2000, p. 24). Lenoir (1974) instigated more contemporary interest in the concept through his focus on "excluded" groups in the French population, for example, people with a disability, the elderly, substance abusers, delinquents, abused children, suicidal individuals, and single parents. Political dissemination of the concept occurred throughout Europe and the United Kingdom during the 1980s and 1990s, culminating in the Blair government's Social Exclusion Unit. In the Australian context, it was first popularized by the South Australian government in 2002 and nationally in 2008 with the establishment of a Social Inclusion Board (Gidley, Hampson, Wheeler, & Bereded-Samuel, 2010). The academic discourse surrounding social inclusion has followed a similar timeline, with research into the topic gaining momentum after the turn of the millennium (Wright & Stickley, 2013). More recently, research around social inclusion has moved to exploring its sources, impacts, and indicators in societal contexts.

A universally accepted definition of social inclusion has yet to be established; however, the Australian Social Inclusion Board (2013) defines it as "having the resources, opportunities and capabilities to learn, work, engage, and have a voice." From the outset, it is important to note that social inclusion and exclusion are closely related, and it is difficult to discuss social inclusion without also discussing social exclusion; these concepts can be viewed as two ends of a single dimension. Bailey (2005)—one of the first scholars to research the concept of sport, development, and social inclusion—listed a set of connected dimensions of social inclusion and exclusion: (1) spatial—proximity and the closing of social and economic distances; (2) relational—sense of belonging and acceptance; (3) functional—enhancement of knowledge, skills, and understanding; and (4) power—a change in the locus of control. Bailey writes:

> Claims made on behalf of participation in sporting activities suggest that it has the potential to, at least, contribute to the process of inclusion by: bringing individuals from a variety of social and economic backgrounds together in a shared interest in activities that are inherently valuable (spatial); offering a sense of belonging, to a team, a club, a program (relational); providing opportunities for the development of valued capabilities and competencies (functional); and increasing "community capital," by extending social networks, increased community cohesion and civic pride (power). (pp. 76–77)

Sport for development, then, is a term that has been used increasingly by researchers and practitioners alike to define the intentional use of sport (or sport-like activities) to bring about positive change in the lives of people and communities. In the context of this chapter, it is important to understand that social inclusion—or the amelioration of social exclusion—can be one of the more featured goals or outcomes that demonstrate impact of SFD programs and initiatives.

Theorizing Social Inclusion and Development

Current research suggests that social inclusion is founded on a dynamic interplay between structural and relational determinants (Ponic & Frisby, 2010; Yanicki, Kushner, & Reutter,

2015). However, the manner in which this interaction is interpreted varies from one inquiry to the next. For instance, Yanicki and colleagues explored the processes underlying the dynamic between social inclusion and exclusion, finding that the processes involved "just/unjust social relations and social structures enabling or constraining opportunities for participation" (p. 1). Analysis of the literature on social inclusion and exclusion has identified three discourses on different facets of these two concepts: recognition, capabilities, equality, and citizenship. By examining these discourses, the authors deduced that, in order to promote inclusion and hinder exclusion, social justice should be developed and social injustice minimized (Yanicki et al., 2015). Using a slightly different approach, Ponic and Frisby's (2010) study explored social inclusion processes in a community-based health promotion project. In six years of participatory action research, they identified four interdependent components of social inclusion: organizational, participatory, relational, and psychosocial. The organizational component incorporated the structures, standards, and practices of the organization. The participatory factor integrated the opportunities that were available and accessible to individuals. The relational element involved how participants engaged and behaved with one another. The psychosocial component involved the extent to which individuals felt accepted and recognized; this was closely determined by association with the other three factors (Ponic & Frisby, 2010).

Measuring Social Inclusion and Development: Methodological Challenges

A construct as complex and ill-defined as social inclusion makes measurement and research particularly challenging. In a meta-evaluation of social inclusion research, Collins, Henry, and Houlihan (1999) found only 11 studies which were sufficiently rigorous in their evaluation, and some studies did not even provide specific data, for example about participants' backgrounds, aims of programs, and methods for evaluation and measuring outcomes. Consequently, Coalter, Allison, and Taylor (2000, p. 14, emphasis in original) state:

> [T]he issue is not simply whether increased sports participation can be viewed as contributing to personal and community development and the reduction of social exclusion. Rather, the question relates to the *nature* of the contribution such participation can make to reducing the linked factors underpinning social exclusion.

In their case study of an SFD program for youth in the United Kingdom based on soccer and applied intervention mapping, Parnell, Pringle, Widdop, & Zwolinsky (2015) argue that partnering between academic institutions and sporting organizations is necessary to ensure that sport-based social inclusion programs can be implemented and evaluated effectively and are therefore successful. They point to a lack of expertise at the program level to develop and apply robust methods for monitoring and evaluation, which are essential to provide proof of return on investment to secure ongoing funding. They posit partnerships between institutions with expertise in these areas as a solution to the problem of inadequate monitoring and evaluation (Parnell et al., 2015). Indeed, the application of academic rigor and theoretically derived measurement may go a good way toward facilitating an evidence-based outcome assessment for sport initiatives that claim to enhance or contribute to social inclusion in their communities.

Indeed, much international research commonly recognizes that social environments and experiences have the power to influence the health and well-being of individuals (Begen & Turner-Cobb, 2015). Crabbe (2008) critiques the tendency to try to measure direct, concrete outcomes of sport-based social inclusion programs—such as measuring incarceration/ arrest rates or employment and education outcomes—and instead argues for a focus on relationships and a sense of belonging. It is for these reasons that research has hypothesized that at the center of an individual's social realm is the fundamental human need to belong (Baumeister & Leary, 1995), and that this need is critical to psychological and physical well-being (Begen & Turner-Cobb, 2015).

How the effects of social inclusion might be measured depends on the scope of outcomes being investigated and the context in which these might occur. A number of approaches and instruments have been adapted for use throughout inclusion research and, as such, a range of indicators exist. For example, the Social Inclusion Questionnaire Experience was adapted from the Poverty and Exclusion Survey and adopts a 75-item scale. A 62-item Social Inclusion Survey was also adapted for use and was originally developed using recommendations from clinical experts on schizophrenia (Baumgartner & Burns, 2013). Other inquiries have taken alternative approaches aimed at comparing levels of inclusion between different cultures and countries. One study, by Giambona and Vassallo (2013), measured inclusion across 27 European countries, using four indicators developed from European policy research. The indicators were primarily—but not exclusively—based on economic status and included poverty levels, deprivation of material possessions, employment levels, and the percentage of early school leavers.

Specifically in the SFD context, qualitative methods comprise the bulk of approaches (Schulenkorf, Sherry, & Rowe, 2016) and, as a result, the indicators of social inclusion are often self-reported by participants. The use of qualitative methods serves to provide detail and depth that can explain the underpinnings of participants' feelings of inclusion, fine detail that is essential if research is to uncover and explain the complex range of interrelated personal, cultural, social, and structural factors that contribute to social inclusion. Further, qualitative research approaches that give voice to participants respond directly to the ongoing call for programming that prioritizes participants' needs as they perceive them (cf. Ekholm et al., 2019; Frisby, 2011) and provides opportunities for their voices to be heard (cf. Rich et al., 2015). Qualitative approaches capture insights from a range of stakeholders, resulting in rich data that can reveal synergies and tensions of central importance to understanding inclusion from a range of perspectives, particularly when a multimodal approach using varied qualitative tactics is applied. For example, in Maxwell and colleagues' (2013) study mentioned earlier, facilitating the inclusion of Muslim women in community sport, interviews, focus groups, and examination of strategic documents were used to determine that social inclusion was occurring through increased sense of belonging, the building of social relationships, and leadership opportunities. Similarly, working in rural communities in Australia, Frost and colleagues (2013) used qualitative research methods, which interrogated written submissions to the state government's 2004 Inquiry into Country Football from a range of stakeholders, to demonstrate that community football clubs promoted social inclusion by developing trust, reciprocity, and social networks. These findings suggest that social inclusion and other social development indicators can be investigated with a range of mixed-methods and approaches.

A criticism of research in sport and social inclusion can be the privileging of certain voices over others. In the work of Gibbs and Block (2017), investigating social inclusion through sport for young people from refugee backgrounds in Australia, the authors interviewed representatives of nongovernmental organizations, local government, and sports clubs rather than refugee/asylum seeker participants. Given the repeated assertions regarding the importance of including participants in the development of interventions (Mohammadi, 2019; Rich et al., 2015), the exclusion of participants in such research contexts represents a significant oversight that has implications for the robustness and trustworthiness of the findings. Ensuring that the voice of the participant or target population is not only heard but privileged is key to ensuring the representation of those who are being excluded and to contribute to the broader social inclusion agenda of any sport initiative (Mohammadi, 2019).

DEBATES

One of the key debates in the area of sport and social inclusion is, first, whether sport can be truly socially inclusive, and if so, whether this inclusion is sustained outside of the sport context. Fehsenfeld's (2015) research found that while participants reported a sense of social cohesion and connectedness to others with similar experiences, that this did not extend to wider inclusion beyond the particular sporting context. Indeed, participants in programs outside of the particular target group felt excluded and disengaged (Fehsenfeld, 2015). The ability for social inclusion benefits to extend outside of the sport setting was likewise questioned by Southby (2013), who argues that football fandom offers significant social benefits to those with learning disabilities—such as a sense of belonging and a shared identity unrelated to disability. However, as relationships connected to fandom are "fleeting" and specific to sport, this sense of belonging is unlikely to translate into other forms of social inclusion, such as employment or other mainstream social spaces. Southby acknowledges there is a need for specific research in this area. In Australia, Rossi and Rynne (2013) question whether sport intervention programs for Indigenous communities are not simply neoliberal legacy products of "white guilt" that, because they are unable to address the structural inequalities that have resulted in exclusion, may actually serve to further entrench marginalization and welfare dependency. The authors argue that "it would be simply fallacious to suggest that a single programme (albeit an ongoing one) could singularly bring about a 'just' world" (p. 12). However, Rossi and Rynne suggest that while sport programs are not a panacea, because many individuals in these programs also view personal responsibility as desirable, they do "have the capacity to create opportunities *for* development" (p. 12, emphasis in original), which can be a first step in self-determination. That sports programs may be effective in providing the conditions for long-term change was also noted by Astbury, Knight, and Nichols (2005) in their evaluation of the Fairbridge Program, which works with disaffected young people. The authors noted that, while improvements gained in the program were not "maintained a year later, they were good predictors of the long-term behavioral improvements, which included better performance in jobs and education, stable housing arrangements, and having a positive attitude toward self and others" (p. 82). Astbury and colleagues argue that the long-term impacts were preceded by gains in personal skills, again suggesting that, while not a solution in themselves, sport programs can play a modest, valuable role in affecting positive change, in particular when participants' and programs' perceptions of desirable outcomes are aligned.

Frisby (2011) argues that programming for inclusion is most effective when it takes a citizen engagement approach that focuses clearly on participants' own perceived needs. Commonly, program providers have an inadequate knowledge of the participating cohort's specific needs in terms of inclusion, which can lead to participants being constructed according to stereotypical and poorly informed conceptualizations of culture and demography. In such circumstances, programming has limited outcomes beyond the duration of the program. Frisby's study examined practices that showed promise in achieving inclusion for migrant Chinese women in Canada. Civic engagement that promotes mutual learning was cited as key to successful programming; not only does it result in program providers' greater understanding of the cultural and personal experiences and needs of the target group, but it also provides opportunities for participants to better understand how to engage with physical activity programming. The study also identified a need to address paucities in government policy around access to leisure; the government policy routinely resulted in exclusion from leisure programming as a result of culturally founded perceptions about eligibility. For example, eligibility is based on household income, meaning that households comprising multiple generations—as is commonly the case for this participant cohort—are often ineligible. Also cited was a need to enhance community partnerships. Frisby's study found that, on arrival in their new country, participants routinely encountered immigration and culturally specific support services, but that improved collaboration was needed between these and other partners. Participants perceived community partners as sources of social support, which increased their sense of trust in the program's value. Frisby's findings about the need for mutual learning and a clear focus on participants' needs as they perceive them are echoed by Mohammidi (2019). Using a case study of a community cycling program for refugee women newly arrived in Germany, Mohammadi argues that in order to succeed, sports programs for social inclusion must be needs-based—for example, addressing gaps in knowledge or physical ability. Participants in the study experienced social recognition from learning to cycle—an activity with high cultural value in Germany. But, while they reported a feeling of belonging and an opportunity to befriend other asylum seekers and local residents, they did not foster strong connections, and, in fact, their social interactions were often limited to their time attending the program. In part, this was attributed to language deficits, as participants' novice grasp of German prevented the development of deep and long-lasting relationships. However, participants did cite participation in the program as having a positive effect on their language acquisition, and pilot-phase participants who went on to become volunteers in the next rounds of the project experienced greater inclusion as a result of both improved German-language skills and stronger social connections. The study concludes by noting that participants needed prolonged engagement with the program to maximize the possibility of "upward social mobility" (Mohammadi, 2019). Frisby (2011) asserts that, while outcomes achieved are important, the collective process of mutual generation of new ideas is potentially just as important, underscoring that ongoing outcomes are most likely to occur when programs are designed, developed, and implemented collectively by program providers and their participant cohorts.

The challenge of any single initiative to create or contribute to social inclusion at the community level or broader cannot be understated. Sport programs, events, and clubs can provide spaces and activities that are safe, welcoming, and inclusive. However, these programs—no matter how well designed or intentioned—will not be able to address the larger structural inequities that led to the social exclusion being experienced by the target communities.

Participant-Focused Design

A consistent theme in recent research has been the importance of participant-focused and, ideally, participant-led design of any social inclusion initiatives. Welty Peachey and Sherry (2016) argue that although well-designed sport programs can foster social inclusion for various groups—including the homeless and those from culturally and linguistically diverse backgrounds—and can include connecting to other services and social aspects outside sport, design flaws can mean that participants experience further exclusion and alienation. In addition, other factors—such as parental involvement— can determine whether ongoing effects take hold. Rich and colleagues (2015) examined a Canadian community sporting event for refugees and recent migrants that aimed to aid with acculturation. The authors concluded that the organization of the event, in which inclusion was prioritized, was effective in helping to achieve program outcomes. In this instance, the multicultural, celebratory setting meant that participants felt "comfortable maintaining and expressing their own ethnic distinctiveness and also value the interactions among ethnic groups" (p. 138). The study found that participants developed social networks, valued recognition, and, for volunteer participants, experienced improvements in human development, involvement, and engagement, and, in some cases, material well-being. The authors attribute some of the program's success to the fact that participants are involved in decision-making and that there is flexibility in the ways they can contribute, based on their skills, abilities, and needs.

"Nothing about us, without us" is a catch-cry of many marginalized or excluded people and communities. Although it has been recognized that sport can play a role in a broader social inclusion agenda and can provide spaces and places for people to develop relationships and a sense of belonging, too often these initiatives are built upon neoliberal logics and/or a deficit model view of the excluded community. By creating sport programs that have a top-down approach to "fixing" the target community, there is limited potential for social cohesion to be truly developed. Direct, authentic, and genuine engagement with excluded or marginalized communities can provide a more participant-focused and enabling approach to social inclusion that instead sees difference as a strength and facilitating inclusion as a two-way, or many-way, process.

Government and Policy

The role of government and policy that leverages the attractiveness of sport to the community to engender social inclusion has also been a focus of debate. As noted earlier, governments across the globe have attempted to use the attractive nature of sport as a mechanism to enhance social inclusion or address disadvantage in the community. Although these governments may be well intentioned, the funding of sport programs to enhance social inclusion cannot substantively address the underlying structural issues that created the social disconnect or exclusion. Földesi (2010) argues that exclusion in sport according to age, gender, socioeconomic status, and geographical location is largely due to governmental failures in implementing strategies that promote social inclusion. Even where the economic resources are available, they are too often not used effectively for inclusion (Földesi, 2010). Sport programs may be able to create a feeling of inclusion, but they cannot in themselves address the larger social issues, structures, and policies (Collins & Haudenhuyse, 2015).

As an example from the school or education setting, Smith (2009) assessed the United Kingdom's National Curriculum for Physical Education, which emphasizes inclusion. Smith argues that some school students with disabilities have developed positive experiences of physical education, particularly when they can choose the activities and those activities are less sport-based and more recreational, such as swimming and dance. However, as curricula are typically designed for able-bodied youth, and the range of activities offered to disabled youth is often limited, the possibilities for inclusion are likewise limited. Furthermore, Smith found that emphasizing inclusion has also alienated some students from their peers, thereby limiting their chances of having satisfying experiences in sport and physical education. Although these initiatives are well-intentioned and the aim is to create a more inclusive sport experience for students with a disability, without fundamentally addressing the inequities in the curricula or enacting a universal design approach to learning, certain student groups will continue to be excluded.

CONCLUSION

Social inclusion in and through sport has been the focus of research, government policy and initiatives, and sport programming in recent times. Social inclusion is a complex concept, and in the sport setting it is often conflated or confused with social capital. It is prudent to view social inclusion and social exclusion as the opposing ends of a spectrum. By understanding the mechanisms and structural reasons for exclusion, we can better understand the role that sport could play in creating spaces to play that are safe for and welcoming to all who want to participate.

Both the conceptualization and subsequent measurement of social inclusion remain varied and unstable, and clarifying these foundational matters will be an ongoing challenge for both research and practice. When sport organizations or SFD/SD initiatives aim to be more inclusive, those working toward that goal need to be both critically engaged and cautious in understanding what this means in practice. Is the result really "sport for all"? Do initiatives successfully provide specialist programs for targeted communities? Are initiatives based on universal access and designed for those with a disability? Do initiatives aim to achieve a reduction in discrimination, vilification, or objectification of gender, sexuality, race, or religion? Sport organizations—and those who wish to research them—need to ensure that they are clear on the aims, outcomes, and impacts of any social inclusion program or initiative so that these are designed in collaboration with those communities for which benefits are sought, and are consequently researched and evaluated in meaningful and useful ways.

To close, it is important to not let conceptual complexity or criticism of intention get in the way of the often robust good work that a well-designed and implemented sport program promoting social inclusion can deliver to its participants. There is no perfect sport organization culture, nor an ideal one-size-fits-all SFD or SD program, and thus constructive criticism of both approaches and evaluation should be used to enhance and improve attempts to create a more inclusive sport sector, not to discourage attempts to do so.

REFERENCES

Astbury, R., Knight, B., & Nichols, G. (2005). The contribution of sport-related interventions to the long-term development of disaffected young people: An evaluation of the Fairbridge Program. *Journal of Park & Recreation Administration, 23*(3), 82–99.

Australian Social Inclusion Board. (2013). Social inclusion in Australia: How Australia is faring. http://www.socialinclusion.gov.au/resources/how-australia-is-faring.

Bailey, R. (2005). Evaluating the relationship between physical education, sport and social inclusion. *Educational Review, 57*(1), 71–90. doi:10.1080/0013191042000274196.

Bantjes, J., & Swartz, L. (2018). Social inclusion through para sport: A critical reflection on the current state of play. *Physical Medicine and Rehabilitation Clinics of North America, 29*, 409–416.

Baumeister, R. F., & Leary, M. R. (1995). The need to belong: Desire for interpersonal attachments as a fundamental human motivation. *Psychological Bulletin, 117*(3), 497–529. https://doi.org/10.1037/0033-2909.117.3.497.

Baumgartner, J. N., & Burns, J. K. (2013). Measuring social inclusion—A key outcome in global mental health. *International Journal of Epidemiology, 43*(2), 354–364. https://doi.org/10.1093/ije/dyt224.

Begen, F. M., & Turner-Cobb, J. M. (2015). Benefits of belonging: Experimental manipulation of social inclusion to enhance psychological and physiological health parameters. *Psychology & Health, 30*(5), 568–582. https://doi.org/10.1080/08870446.2014.991734.

Buelens, E., Theeboom, M., Vertonghen, J., & Martelaer, K. D. (2015). Socially vulnerable youth and volunteering in sports: Analyzing a Brussels training program for young soccer coaches. *Social Inclusion, 3*(3), 82–97.

Bustad, J. J., & Andrews, D. L. (2017). Policing the void: Recreation, social inclusion and the Baltimore Police Athletic League. *Social Inclusion, 5*(2), 241–249.

Buzuvis, E. E. (2011). Transgender student-athletes and sex-segregated sport: Developing policies of inclusion for intercollegiate and interscholastic athletics. *Seton Hall Journal of Sports and Entertainment Law, 21*(1), 1–59.

Coalter, F., Allison, M., & Taylor, J. (2000). *The role of sport in regenerating deprived areas.* Edinburgh: Scottish Executive Central Research Unit.

Collins, M., & Haudenhuyse, R. (2015). Social exclusion and austerity policies in England: The role of sports in a new area of social polarisation and inequality? *Social Inclusion, 3*(3), 5–18.

Collins, M., Henry, I., & Houlihan, B. (1999). *Sport and social inclusion: A report to the Department of Culture, Media and Sport.* Loughborough, U.K.: Institute of Sport and Leisure Policy, Loughborough University.

Collins, M., & Kay, T. (2014). *Sport and social exclusion.* New York: Routledge.

Collison, H., Darnell, S., Giulianotti, R., & Howe, P. D. (2017). The inclusion conundrum: A critical account of youth and gender issues within and beyond sport for development and peace interventions. *Social Inclusion, 5*(2), 223–231.

Corthouts, J., Thibaut, E., Breuer, C., Feiler, S., James, M., Llopis-Goig, R., . . . Scheerder, J. (2020). Social inclusion in sports clubs across Europe: Determinants of social innovation. *Innovation: The European Journal of Social Science Research, 33*(1), 21–51.

Crabbe, T. (2008). A game of two halves: Understanding sport-based social inclusion. *Research in the Sociology of Sport, 5*, 15–31.

Dagkas, S. (2018). "Is social inclusion through PE, sport and PA still a rhetoric?" Evaluating the relationship between physical education, sport and social inclusion. *Educational Review, 70*(1), 67–74.

Dagkas, S., & Armour, K. (Eds.). (2012). *Inclusion and exclusion through youth sport.* New York: Routledge.

Ekholm, D., & Dahlstedt, M. (2017). Football for inclusion: Examining the pedagogic rationalities and the technologies of solidarity of a sports-based intervention in Sweden. *Social Inclusion, 5*(2), 232–240.

Ekholm, D., & Dahlstedt, M. (2019). Pedagogies of (de)liberation: Salvation and social inclusion by means of Midnight Football. *Sport, Education and Society, 26*(1), 58–71. doi:10.1080/13573322.2019.1694504.

Ekholm, D., Dahlstedt, M., & Rönnbäck, J. (2019). Problematizing the absent girl: Sport as a means of emancipation and social inclusion. *Sport in Society, 22*(6), 1043–1061.

Elling, A., & Knoppers, A. (2004). Sport, gender and ethnicity: Practises of symbolic inclusion/exclusion. *Journal of Youth and Adolescence, 34*(3), 257–268.

Fehsenfeld, M. (2015). Inclusion of outsiders through sport. *Physical Culture and Sport: Studies and Research, 65*, 31–40. doi:10.1515/pcssr-2015-0009.

Földesi, G. (2010). Social exclusion/inclusion in the context of Hungarian sport. *Physical Culture and Sport, 50*(1), 43–59.

Frisby, W. (2011). Promising physical activity inclusion practices for Chinese immigrant women in Vancouver, Canada. *Quest, 63*(1), 135–147.

Frost, L., Lightbody, M., & Halabi, A. (2013). Expanding social inclusion in community sports organizations: Evidence from rural Australian football clubs. *Journal of Sport Management, 27*(6), 453–466. https://doi.org/10.1123/jsm.27.6.453.

Giambona, F., & Vassallo, E. (2013). Composite indicator of social inclusion for European countries. *Social Indicators Research, 116*(1), 269–293. https://doi.org/10.1007/s11205-013-0274-2.

Gibbs, L., & Block, K. (2017). Promoting social inclusion through sport for refugee-background youth in Australia: Analysing different participation models. *Social Inclusion, 5*(2), 91–100.

Gidley, J., Hampson, G., Wheeler, L., & Bereded-Samuel, E. (2010). Social inclusion: Context, theory and practice. *Australasian Journal of University Community Engagement, 5*(1), 6–36. https://researchbank.rmit.edu.au/view/rmit:4909.

Green, B. C. (2008). Sport as an agent for social and personal change. In V. Girginov (Ed.), *Management of sports development* (pp. 129–145). Oxford: Taylor & Francis.

Hermens, N., Super, S., Verkooijen, K., & Koelen, M. (2015). Intersectoral action to enhance the social inclusion of socially vulnerable youth through sport: An exploration of the elements of successful partnerships between youth work organisations and local sports clubs. *Social Inclusion, 3*(3), 98–107.

Inoue, C., & Forneris, T. (2015). The role of Special Olympics in promoting social inclusion: An examination of stakeholder perceptions. *Journal of Sport for Development, 3*(5), 23–34.

Jeanes, R., Spaaij, R., Magee, J., Farquharson, K., Gorman, S., & Lusher, D. (2019). Developing participation opportunities for young people with disabilities? Policy enactment and social inclusion in Australian junior sport. *Sport in Society, 22*(6), 986–1004.

Kay, T. (2013). Sport and youth inclusion in the "majority world." In S. Dagkas & K. Armour (Eds.), *Inclusion and exclusion through youth sport* (pp. 218–232). London: Routledge.

Kelly, L. (2011). Social inclusion through sports-based interventions? *Critical Social Policy*, *31*(1), 126–150.

Lenoir, R. (1974). *Les exclus: Un français sur dix*. Paris: Seuil.

Maxwell, H., Foley, C., Taylor, T., & Burton, C. (2013). Social inclusion in community sport: A case study of Muslim women in Australia. *Journal of Sport Management*, *27*(6), 467–481.

McConkey, R., Dowling, S., Hassan, D., & Menke, S. (2013). Promoting social inclusion through Unified Sports for youth with intellectual disabilities: A five-nation study. *Journal of Intellectual Disability Research*, *57*(10), 923–935. https://doi.org/10.1111/j.1365-2788.2012.01587.x.

McDonald, B., Spaaij, R., & Dukic, D. (2018). Moments of social inclusion: Asylum seekers, football and solidarity. *Sport in Society*, *22*(6), 935–949.

Mohammadi, S. (2019). Social inclusion of newly arrived female asylum seekers and refugees through a community sport initiative: The case of Bike Bridge. *Sport in Society*, *22*(6), 1082–1099. https://doi.org/10.1080/17430437.2019.1565391.

Morgan, H., & Parker, A. (2017). Generating recognition, acceptance and social inclusion in marginalised youth populations: The potential of sports-based interventions. *Journal of Youth Studies*, *20*(8), 1028–1043.

Oxoby, R. (2009). Understanding social inclusion, social cohesion, and social capital. *International Journal of Social Economics*, *36*(12), 1133–1152. https://doi.org/10.1108/03068290910996963.

Parnell, D., Pringle, A., Widdop, P., & Zwolinsky, S. (2015). Understanding football as a vehicle for enhancing social inclusion. *Social Inclusion*, *3*(3), 158–166.

Ponic, P., & Frisby, W. (2010). Unpacking assumptions about inclusion in community-based health promotion: Perspectives of women living in poverty. *Qualitative Health Research*, *20*(11), 1519–1531. https://doi.org/10.1177/1049732310374303.

Ratna, A. (2016). "Getting inside the wicket": Strategies for the social inclusion of British Pakistani Muslim cricketers. *Journal of Policy Research in Tourism, Leisure and Events*, *8*(1), 1–17.

Rich, K., Misener, L., & Dubeau, D. (2015). "Community Cup, we are a big family": Examining social inclusion and acculturation of newcomers to Canada through a participatory sport event. *Social Inclusion*, *3*(3), 129–141.

Rossi, T., & Rynne, S. (2013). Sport development programmes for Indigenous Australians: Innovation, inclusion and development, or a product of "white guilt"? *Sport in Society*, *17*(8), 1030–1045. doi:10.1080/17430437.2013.838355.

Schulenkorf, N., Sherry, E., & Rowe, K. (2016). Sport-for-development: An integrated literature review. *Journal of Sport for Development*, *30*, 22 39. https://doi.org/10.1123/jsm.2014-0263.

Sen, A. (2000, June). Social exclusion: Concept, application and scrutiny. Social Development Papers No. 1. Asian Development Bank, Office of Environment and Social Development. https://www.adb.org/sites/default/files/publication/29778/social-exclusion.pdf.

Sherry, E. (2010). (Re)engaging marginalized groups through sport: The Homeless World Cup. *International Review for the Sociology of Sport*, *45*(1), 59–71. https://doi.org/10.1177/1012690209356988.

Smith, A. (2009). Disability and inclusion policy towards physical education and youth sport. In H. Fitzgerald (Ed.), *Disability and youth sport* (pp. 24–38). London: Routledge.

Southby, K. (2013). Social inclusion through football fandom: Opportunities for learning-disabled people. *Sport in Society*, *16*(10), 1386–1403.

Spaaij, R. (2012). Beyond the playing field: Experiences of sport, social capital, and integration among Somalis in Australia. *Ethnic and Racial Studies*, *35*(9), 1519–1538. https://doi.org/10.1080/01419870.2011.592205.

Spaaij, R. (2015). Refugee youth, belonging and community sport. *Leisure Studies*, *34*(3), 303–318.

Spencer-Cavaliere, N., Thai, J., & Kingsley, B. (2017). A part of and apart from sport: Practitioners' experiences coaching in segregated youth sport. *Social Inclusion*, *5*(2), 120–129.

Vanwynsberghe, R., Surborg, B., & Wyly, E. (2013). When the games come to town: Neoliberalism, mega-events and social inclusion in the Vancouver 2010 Winter Olympic Games. *International Journal of Urban and Regional Research*, *37*(6), 2074–2093.

Welty Peachey, J., & Sherry, E. (2016). Sport and social inclusion. In N. Schulenkorf, E. Sherry, & P. Phillips (Eds.), *Managing sport development: An international approach* (pp. 135–146). London: Routledge.

Wright, N., & Stickley, T. (2013). Concepts of social inclusion, exclusion and mental health: A review of the international literature. *Journal of Psychiatric and Mental Health Nursing*, *20*(1), 71–81. https://doi.org/10.1111/j.1365-2850.2012.01889.x.

Yanicki, S. M., Kushner, K. E., & Reutter, L. (2015). Social inclusion/exclusion as matters of social (in)justice: A call for nursing action. *Nursing Inquiry*, *22*(2), 121–133. https://doi.org/10.1111/nin.12076.

CHAPTER 41

SPORT, SOCIAL EXCLUSION, AND DISCRIMINATION

RUTH JEANES AND RYAN LUCAS

THIS chapter examines the relationship between sport, social exclusion, and discrimination. Social exclusion is broadly defined as a lack of opportunity to participate in key domains of society (Burchardt, Le Grand, Piachaud, Hills, & Grand, 2002), including cultural, political, social, and economic activities. It is a process inflicted on people as much as it is experienced (Hargie, Mitchell, & Somerville, 2017). Although public discourse presents sport as a great leveler that offers a common language for uniting people, an extensive body of research has continued to highlight that many groups are underrepresented as sport participants, volunteers, coaches, fans, and managers (Burton & LaVoi, 2016; Collins, 2004; Collins & Kay, 2014; Esmonde, Cooky, & Andrews, 2015; Shaw & Frisby, 2006; Spaaij, Magee, & Jeanes, 2014). Kay (2000a, p. 166) suggests that "from the humblest levels of mass participation through to the pinnacles of performance, participation profiles are skewed away from the less privileged sectors of our society." This observation remains pertinent two decades later. The rhetoric of "sport for all" that has dominated sports policies remains aspirational (Haycock & Smith, 2018). Spaaij, Magee, and Jeanes (2014, p. 3) propose that, by its nature, sport

> performs or at least condones the exclusion of some through its emphasis on performance and winning, and (over-)conformity to the norms of the sport ethos. Exclusionary processes in sports-related policies and practices are multiple and diverse, embedded as they are in existing ethnocentric, patriarchal and heteronormative systems.

Exposure to social exclusion contributes to poorer mental and physical health outcomes and lower educational attainment, as well as disengagement, lack of social connection, and greater feelings of vulnerability and lack of safety (Agulnik, 2002; Baum & Gleeson, 2010; Spandler, 2007). Social exclusion experienced within sports contexts can reinforce societal-level exclusion and have a detrimental effect on individuals and communities (Spaaij, Magee, & Jeanes, 2014).

This chapter considers the various mechanisms that contribute to the processes of exclusion within sport as well the impact of exclusionary experiences on individuals. Social exclusion is a contested and complex concept. The chapter unpacks this by examining some of the key theories underpinning social exclusion. The final section overviews some of the ongoing debates within research examining sport, social exclusion, and marginalization, particularly the persistence of social exclusion in sport, and raises questions as to whether, without radically reshaping the meanings, ideologies, and values that underpin it, sport can ever be socially inclusive.

Issues

Social exclusion within sport occurs due to a series of multifaceted and multilayered processes (Spaaij, Magee, & Jeanes, 2014). Within this section, we outline some of the key mechanisms of social exclusion and discuss how these impact participation. The section is split into three parts: the first outlines various sociocultural and individual-level mechanisms that contribute to exclusion; the second explores the structural, environmental, and institutional mechanisms that influence involvement in sport; and the third discusses exclusionary policies and sport. Within Global North societies in particular, damaging and discriminatory attitudes are among the most commonly cited reasons for individuals feeling excluded and unwelcome in sport (Hargie et al., 2017; Shields, Synnot, & Barr, 2012). Sport in Global North societies is dominated and regulated by white, middle-class, able-bodied, high-ability men (Spaaij, Farquharson, & Marjoribanks, 2015). A range of factors influence this, centered on patriarchy, wealth, heteronormativity, sporting traditions, and maintenance of the dominant hegemony (Kalman-Lamb, 2020), which leads to racist, homophobic, sexist, and ableist attitudes, which are prevalent in mainstream society, manifesting in sporting contexts and becoming powerful mechanisms of exclusion. The initial part of the section overviews these. While in reality the various mechanisms discussed interlink and influence participation experiences, we unpack these separately to illustrate the various exclusionary layers that exist within sport that work to exclude individuals outside of the dominant group.

Sport, Discriminatory Attitudes, and Social Exclusion

An ongoing body of research highlights that racist, sexist, ableist, and homophobic/transphobic attitudes exist at all levels of sport (Baker-Lewton, Sonn, Vincent, & Curnow, 2017; Brittain, Biscaia, & Gérard, 2020; Fink, 2016; Hargie et al., 2017; Symons, O'Sullivan, & Polman, 2017). Such attitudes contribute to individuals feeling unwelcome, devalued, demeaned, and unsafe within sporting contexts, as well as continuing to perpetuate the discriminatory beliefs that exist within broader society.

Racism is an enduring issue in sport (Hylton & Lawrence, 2016; Long, 2000; Reeves, Ponsford, & Gorman, 2015). It creates unwelcoming and even toxic environments for people of color, resulting in dropout and self-exclusion (D'Cruz, 2018; Love, Deeb, & Waller, 2019). Racism occurs at all levels of sport. Farquharson et al. (2019) showed how young people in Australian junior sport were regularly subjected to racist abuse from opposition players, spectators, and at times coaches. Examples of exclusionary practices included coaches using racist terminology to refer to Indigenous players, such as calling them "darkies," or assigning Western names to Asian players whose names were considered to be too difficult to pronounce.

Existing research points to the struggle facing the community and participants in elite sports in challenging racism. In Farquharson et al.'s (2019) study, if a junior player was subjected to racist abuse, the burden of proof lay with the player. Challenging the discrimination required taking the case to a tribunal, which was often a protracted and intimidating experience and frequently one that young players and their families were unwilling to subject themselves to. This left racism in community sport largely unchecked. There are numerous high-profile examples of elite athletes of color who have sought to challenge and make a stand against racism being unsupported by the sporting system and ultimately excluded from participating in their chosen sport (Hartmann, 2019; Kaufman, 2008). Recent examples include Colin Kaepernick, a professional U.S. football player who, since kneeling during the playing of the national anthem in public protest against racism in society, has been unable to secure a professional contract (Boykoff & Carrington, 2020), and Adam Goodes, an Indigenous Australian Rules footballer, who was subjected to extensive racial abuse from sporting crowds; the abuse was denied or ignored by the Australian Football League, resulting in Goodes's retirement from the game (Coram & Hallinan, 2017).

People of color are often accused of self-excluding from sport and choosing instead to establish mono-ethnic clubs and teams. Fletcher and Walle (2015) discuss Asian cricket leagues in the United Kingdom, and Spaaij (2012) cites Somalian soccer teams in Australia, as examples of supposed self-exclusion. However, self-exclusion is a complex concept that is "often a function of restricted opportunities to participate or a response to the experience of discrimination or moral rejection" (Spaaij, Magee, & Jeanes, 2014, p. 17). The assumed "choice" participants make to play in specific cultural and ethnic groups is instead the result of their poor experiences within mainstream sporting teams (Fletcher & Walle, 2015).

People with disabilities frequently cite negative attitudes as the most significant contributor to their experience of social exclusion and marginalization (Brittain, 2004; Misener & Darcy, 2014). Sport is inherently ableist; it privileges able bodies and devalues those bodies that cannot perform to normative standards (Brittain, Biscaia & Gerard, 2020). People with disabilities encounter patronizing and paternalistic attitudes that discourage participation, and an unwillingness by coaches and providers to accommodate difference, both of which lead to exclusion (Jeanes et al., 2018; Saxton, 2018; Suggs & Guthrie, 2017).

Policymakers within sport have sought to address the exclusion of people through the policy of mainstreaming. Under the guise of inclusion, able-bodied sport in most Global North countries has responsibility for developing opportunities for people with disabilities (Kitchin & Howe, 2014), on the assumption that this will create more opportunities for participation. Studies examining the realities of mainstreaming suggest that while it has in part led to a greater number of opportunities to participate in sport, it results in more nuanced experiences of exclusion for people with disabilities (Hammond, 2019; Thomas & Guett, 2014). Jeanes, Spaaij et al. (2019) highlight that within community sport, clubs frequently establish disability provision that is entirely separate from the everyday activities of the club. Players with disabilities train and play matches on days and times different from mainstream teams, are not invited to social activities, and are not celebrated in social media in the same way other teams are. While their state sporting associations suggest these clubs are inclusive, participants with disabilities suggest otherwise. They feel they are devalued, othered, and invisible within the club environment.

Homophobic and transphobic attitudes, another form of exclusion, have received less attention within research (Hargie et al., 2017; Storr, Robinson, Davies, Nicholas, & Collison, 2020). Spaaij et al. (2015, p. 401) suggest homophobic and transphobic discrimination occurs because "sport itself is organised by ideologies of patriarchy and heteronormativity . . . around discourses of hegemonic masculinity that value hyper masculine, heterosexual men." These discourses result in the normalization and tolerance of homophobia within sport, promoting attitudes and practices that are particularly exclusionary of gay men (Baiocco, Pistella, Salvati, Loverno, & Lucidi, 2018). There are very few openly gay professional male athletes, particularly within team sports. Professional male athletes who have come out tend to do so after they have retired, to limit potential negative impacts on their sporting careers (Ogawa, 2014).

While a number of recent studies suggest that homophobia is decreasing in sport (Bush, Anderson, & Carr, 2012; Magrath, 2016), others point to the ongoing use of homophobic language, particularly within community sport settings (Denison & Kitchen, 2015; Symons et al., 2017). Within schools, physical education is highlighted as a key setting where young people experience homophobic bullying that contributes to the normalizing of homophobic practices (Drury, Stride, Flintoff, & Williams, 2017). Unsurprisingly, homophobic sentiment contributes to LGBT+ young people feeling unsafe and unwelcome within sport and therefore participating less than their heterosexual peers (Cunningham, 2019).

Alongside more overt forms of homophobia, studies point to subtle micro-aggressions that occur in community sport contexts, reinforcing feelings of exclusion and marginalization among LGBT+ participants (Petty & Trussell, 2018). Trussell, Kovac, and Apgar (2018) discuss the experiences of same-sex parents whose children participate in community sport, suggesting that, although overall they find clubs welcoming, certain practices reinforce heteronormative ideals that "other" them within the club context. For example, these parents outlined how club-registration processes that assumed all children had a mother and a father could make them feel excluded when they asked for father and mother contact details alongside social events that targeted mothers and children or fathers and children.

There is a limited literature base exploring the experiences of transgender athletes (Elling-Machartzki, 2017; Hargie et al., 2017); however, available studies suggest transgender participants experience considerable feelings of disconnect and exclusion within mainstream sport settings. Key mechanisms of exclusion include negative transphobic attitudes and bullying and the deployment of rigid gender norms that segregate participants in sport, both matters which are particularly challenging for transitioning athletes. Inflexible policies suppress participation of transgender women in particular, in some sports, an issue discussed further later in the chapter (Elling-Machartzki, 2017; Jones, Arcelus, Bouman, & Haycraft, 2017). Hargie et al. (2017, p. 234) outline how transitioning women have been asked to leave women-only sport spaces, and how "transgender men, despite leaving 'femaleness' behind, still feel alienated by 'normal' male sporting cultures where masculinity is associated with athletic ability, transphobia and heteronormativity."

Racist, ableist, and homophobic/transphobic attitudes provide some of the most powerful and entrenched mechanisms contributing to social exclusion within sport. The chapter will now examine some of the structural mechanisms that intersect with these attitudes, creating further layers of exclusion for some individuals.

Structural, Environmental, and Institutional Mechanisms

Structural Mechanisms

Structural mechanisms of exclusion can operate both within and outside of sport, shaping participation and engagement. Within the sport literature, one of the most frequently discussed structural mechanisms influencing participation is poverty. Studies repeatedly show that young people and adults from low-income backgrounds participate less in organized and club-based sport than those with middle to high incomes (Collins & Kay, 2014; Vandermeerschen, Vos, & Scheerder, 2015). This is further influenced by factors such as gender, ethnicity, and disability, which intersect with poverty (Collins & Haudenhuyse, 2015). Collins and Haudenhuyse suggest that "poor young people are less likely to be club members, compete, and be coached" (p. 6) due to a lack of disposable income. Sport participation, even within community sport contexts, can be expensive, usually requiring some specialist equipment, clothing, registration fees, and competition fees, among other costs.

Collins (2004) and Collins and Kay (2014) have repeatedly argued that poverty is the single most influential factor contributing to social exclusion within sport contexts, suggesting that those on uncertain and low incomes are unlikely to use what financial resources they have on perceived luxury/optional items such as those required for sport. Beyond the obvious barriers presented by a lack of money, poverty influences the social exclusion process in other ways. Various studies suggest that children in low-income families are exposed to fewer sporting opportunities from an early age, both informally in the family context and formally through school and sport clubs, which affects the development of the fundamental movement skills that are essential for sport participation (Collins, 2013; Vandermeerschen et al., 2015) and prevents the development of sporting tastes and interests (Nielsen, Grønfeldt, Toftegaard-Støckel, & Andersen, 2012). Without the basic skills to engage in sport, along with believing that sport has little relevance in their lives, young people find themselves excluded from sporting contexts regardless of whether they acquire necessary income in adulthood.

Although poverty is a critical element of social exclusion, sport policies and processes have failed to address the systemic disadvantage faced by individuals and families on low incomes (Kay, 2000a; Widdop, King, Parnell, Cutts, & Millward, 2018). Policies generally favor subsidy approaches, but this does not mitigate the lack of exposure to sporting contexts in childhood (Collins & Kay, 2014). Furthermore, studies examining the experience of individuals and families seeking to access subsidies point to the ways these can contribute to the further marginalization and stigmatizing of individuals on low incomes (Ponic & Frisby, 2010). Participants in Frisby and Hoeber's (2002) research describe having to work through substantial administrative requirements to "prove" they merited financial support. They spoke of sport and recreation administrators making them feel like they were trying to cheat the system rather than individuals who genuinely required support.

Poverty has a profound impact on elite-sport participation (Collins & Buller, 2003). Although examples are often cited of elite athletes who have "made it" despite experiencing challenging and impoverished childhoods, these are the exception rather than the norm (Spaaij et al., 2015). While there may be an assumption, therefore, that talent is the main requirement for an elite athlete, considerable financial resources are essential to allow talented athletes to progress to the elite level (Kay, 2000b). Elite athletes in many sports tend to be middle class, have received considerable financial and emotional support from their family, and have often attended private schools that offer access to high-quality facilities and coaching from an early age (Smith, Haycock, & Hulme, 2013). The cost of additional coaching, equipment, medical support, and competition is heightened once young people move into talent-development squads (Collins & Buller, 2003); many sports require athletes to self-fund at the sub-elite level, and sometimes beyond, depending on the sport. There are additional challenges for talented athletes from low-income backgrounds if they do not succeed in their chosen sport, as they often have fewer resources, support networks, and alternative career pathways to rely on (Smith et al., 2013). This process is further mediated by gender, as women are less likely to gain financial rewards as elite athletes through either pay or sponsorship (except within a small number of sports), and so greater emphasis is placed on women to self-fund their elite pathway, which is not possible for those on low incomes (Koller, 2019).

Environmental Mechanisms

While poverty as a structural mechanism is inextricably connected with social exclusion in a sporting context, it is also connected to environmental factors, which we overview now. As Spaaij, Magee, and Jeanes (2014, p. 64) outline:

> Environmental perspectives have been utilized to demonstrate how location and, in particular, access to resources can lead to exclusion from particular sporting opportunities. This can manifest in various forms, from tangible exclusion due to a lack of adequate facilities within an individual's local area through to a perception of exclusion created from not feeling welcomed within a particular sporting space.

A lack of facilities and environmental resources to support participation is another powerful mechanism contributing to social exclusion. Neighborhoods deemed to be at a low socioeconomic level or disadvantaged tend to have fewer sporting facilities, and these may be poorly maintained (Collins & Haudenhuyse, 2015). Rosso's (2010) analysis of the growth of women's football in South Australia illustrates how a lack of facilities constrains women's participation in low-socioeconomic areas.

To attempt to address this particular mechanism of social exclusion in the United Kingdom, there has been a policy drive (e.g., Sport England, 2006) to develop sport and recreation facilities within areas characterized by economic deprivation. However, analysis suggests that providing facilities does not necessarily negate experiences of exclusion, the costs of using the facilities may not always reflect the disposable income levels in the area, and communities not used to participating in sport and recreation spaces may not consider the new facilities accessible (Taylor, 2001).

A lack of access to appropriate facilities is an important mechanism in the exclusion of people with disabilities from sport (Martin, 2013). While the introduction of various disability antidiscrimination laws in most Global North countries has ensured that the design of new buildings has to take access into consideration, there are still many sport and recreation facilities that remain inaccessible for people with physical disabilities (Calder, Sole, & Mulligan, 2018; Darcy, Lock, & Taylor, 2017). Particularly within community sporting clubs, changing rooms, toilets, and pitches may not have the necessary modifications to allow access. Often sporting contexts will facilitate only partial access, or sporting facilities them-selves may be accessible, but the clubrooms, bar, and catering facilities are not, resulting in people with physical disabilities being unable to participate in social activities that are important to fostering social connection and belonging within a sport (Jeanes, Spaaij, Magee, Farquharson, et al., 2019). Studies also point to various micro-practices that con-strain access for people with disabilities and contribute to feelings of exclusion. Mulligan, Miyahara, and Nichols-Dunsmuir (2017) found that swimmers with a disability who wished to use adapted changing facilities and toilets had to request a key from pool reception. In this study, participants discussed their frustration with this process, suggesting it marked them out as different and added an unnecessary layer of complexity to negotiating access.

Exclusion due to access issues is not simply the result of whether facilities are available. Individuals and communities may be granted only partial entry to sporting spaces, with traditions and ideologies regarding whose space it is dominating policies about who is granted access and to which spaces and resources (Pavlidis, 2018). Women, particularly within mixed-gender community sport clubs, are often allocated poorer sporting spaces than men (e.g., lesser-quality pitches) and are given more inconvenient training and com-petition times to use the facilities, and clubrooms are often dominated by memorabilia and images that celebrate only male athletic achievement (Spaaij, Knoppers, & Jeanes, 2020; Pavlidis, 2018). As the Approaches section will discuss, social exclusion occurs on a spec-trum, and these practices demonstrate the subtle ways in which some groups, though not fully excluded from sporting settings, are not fully included either, and as a result of this can feel devalued.

Studies in the Global South highlight that while a lack of facilities is a key issue in impoverished communities, certain groups cannot access facilities due to safety concerns (Oxford, 2017). Research conducted in African and South American contexts suggests that for girls and women in particular, playing sport in public spaces symbolizes an overt challenge to gender stereotypes that can render them vulnerable to community backlash and violence (Meier & Saavedra, 2009; Oxford, 2017). Access is therefore a complex mech-anism of social exclusion, interwoven with various other cultural and social factors.

Institutional Exclusion

Alongside policies, ingrained institutional practices contribute to exclusion within sport. Studies have illustrated how institutionalized beliefs and values, based on discriminatory attitudes, lead to inequities, particularly within the governance and management of sport (Claringbould & Knoppers, 2012; Knoppers & Anthonissen, 2008). For example, while women's and girls' participation in sport has increased exponentially over the past decade, women continue to be considerably underrepresented in coaching and leadership roles across many sports, particularly at the elite level (Norman, 2010; Walker & Bopp, 2011). Studies suggest that sexist attitudes, combined with institutional mechanisms of exclusion, result in women, even those who have participated at a high level, being positioned as less capable, skilled, and competent than their male counterparts (Norman, 2010). Stereotypical and sexist assumptions surrounding women's strengths and capabilities influence attitudes, leading to beliefs that women are better equipped to undertake caregiving and support roles rather than serving in leadership and management positions (Evans & Pfister, 2020). As a result, women remain heavily underrepresented in sport governance at global, international, and national levels (Burton, 2015).

In considering coaching roles specifically, recent research has highlighted the challenges for women in progressing through coach-education systems in sports that are not stereotypically feminine (de Haan & Knoppers, 2020). In soccer, for example, women are often subjected to heavily masculinized course content (e.g., videos that provide examples of male players), sexist and patronizing attitudes, and continual questioning of their skills and competencies (de Haan, Norman, La Voi, & Knoppers, 2020). Attitudinal and institutional mechanisms intertwine, leading women to question their own suitability to undertake leadership roles, resulting in many either dropping out or not engaging with management and coaching opportunities (Evans & Pfister, 2020).

Some studies have highlighted the ongoing role of institutionalized racism in excluding people of color from positions of power within sport, particularly in coaching and leadership roles (Norman, North, Hylton, Flintoff, & Rankin, 2014). Cashmore and Cleland (2011) point to the lack of Black managers, for example, within professional soccer in the United Kingdom, despite the high number of Black players. Similarly, several studies examining Indigenous Australian football players suggest stereotypes of Indigenous people as having "natural" flair and talent alongside perceptions of them being unreliable and lacking in organizational skills lead to few professional players being supported to advance in coaching roles (Apoifis, Marlin, & Bennie, 2018; Hallinan & Judd, 2009). As Spaaij et al. (2015, p. 404) summarize:

> [T]he myth of natural talent appears to be behind much of the discrimination and differential treatment experienced by Black athletes. Based on an ideology that situates Black peoples as physically gifted but mentally inferior, the myth of natural talent serves to justify the differential treatment meted out to Black athletes.

Exclusionary Policies and Sport

Policies form yet another structural mechanism of social exclusion within sports contexts. Historically, societal-level policies have been responsible for the exclusion of entire populations from certain sport contexts. Government policies within apartheid South Africa, for example, led to the exclusion of people of color from mainstream sporting opportunities (Brittain, 2011). These discriminatory policies are evident elsewhere. Until 1975, people of color were unable to enter the clubhouse at the famous Augusta Golf Course, home to the Masters Tournament, and until 1999 women were prevented from entering the "Long Room" within the pavilion at Lord's Cricket Ground during play. With the advent of policies aimed at challenging discrimination (e.g., disability discrimination legislation, sexual discrimination legislation), many of the overt policies contributing to exclusion in sport have been addressed (Oliver & Lusted, 2015). However, the exclusion of transgender and intersex athletes in recent years provides a contemporary example of the ongoing policy-based exclusion encountered by some individuals (Hargie et al., 2017).

The debates surrounding transgender and intersex inclusion have focused almost exclusively on the participation of transgender and intersex women, particularly at the elite level, where it is perceived that transgender and intersex women have an unfair advantage, despite the scientific evidence that this claim is contentious (Bianchi, 2017; Jones et al., 2017). Spaaij et al. (2015, p. 402) explain why exclusionary policies are mainly focused on women:

> A woman masquerading as a man is thought to have little chance of winning, and whether such a woman participates does not threaten the perceived fairness of competition. However, a man masquerading as a woman is expected to have an advantage, and his participation would threaten the evenness of the playing field. So sports care very much whether men participate as women, but not at all whether women participate as men.

This had led some sports to ban transgender women from participating in elite-level competition, particularly within team sports (e.g., Hannah Mouncey, a transgender women prevented by the Australian Football League from playing in the professional women's league). There have been similar consequences for intersex athletes, who are deemed to have an unfair advantage due to hormonal composition (Cooky & Dworkin, 2013) (e.g., Caster Semenya banned from international competition in 2019 by the International Amateur Athletics Federation unless she took medication to reduce her levels of testosterone).

APPROACHES

The first half of the chapter served to highlight the multiple ways in which sport is a context that contributes to the social exclusion of some individuals and communities. This section examines the various ways in which social exclusion as a concept is theorized and understood.

Defining Social Exclusion

Social exclusion is a contested concept open to multiple interpretations and definitions and various theories (Silver & Miller, 2003; Taket, Foster, & Cook, 2009). Levitas et al. (2007, p. 25) provide an overarching definition, based on analysis of multiple theoretical perspectives:

> Social exclusion is a complex and multi-dimensional process. It involves the lack, or denial, of resources, rights, goods and services, and the inability to participate in the normal relationships and activities, available to the majority of people in a society, whether in economic, social, cultural or political arenas. It affects both the quality of life of individuals and the equity and cohesion of society as a whole.

Historically, it has been linked to poverty and exclusion of individuals based on a lack of economic means and those who have fallen outside of the social security system (Taket et al., 2009). However, while acknowledging the powerful impact of poverty on shaping experiences of exclusion, as the proceeding section has illustrated, mechanisms of social exclusion extend beyond poverty alone; individuals can be excluded from multiple facets of life, including social, cultural, political, and economic. The most acute forms of social exclusion occur when multiple dimensions intersect.

Spaaij, Magee, and Jeanes (2014) assert that, alongside the structural and institutional mechanisms, there is also a moral dimension of social exclusion that is particularly prevalent within sporting contexts, whereby individuals are "rejected and stigmatised for being outside the norm" (Hargie et al., 2017, p. 234). This further reinforces that social exclusion at an individual level is not just associated with exclusion from economic structures; it is also "influenced by societal beliefs and structures which act to 'exclude' individuals based on personal characteristics" (Taket et al., 2009, p. 16). As illustrated, within sport in particular and society more broadly, the negative attitudes, judgments, and stigma attached to certain individuals, communities, and groups act as a powerful mechanism in the continuation of exclusion, contributing to the dynamics of self-exclusion.

Theorizing Social Exclusion

Contemporary theories conceptualize social exclusion as a relational concept resulting from the intersection of processes operating at macro, meso, and micro levels of society. Mathieson et al. (2008, p. 21) suggest that a relational perspective, fruitful in assessing the interplay between layers of exclusion, has two dimensions: "it focuses on exclusion as the rupture of relationships between people and the society resulting in a lack of social participation, social protection, social integration and power," and "a relational perspective points to exclusion as the product of unequal social relationships characterised by differential power i.e. the product of the way societies are organised."

Importantly, social exclusion is both a state experienced by individuals and a multidimensional process (Popay, 2010) and occurs across the individual, family, community, societal, and global levels. The positioning of process is important in highlighting that social exclusion is "inflicted on people as much as a condition experienced by people" (Hargie et al., 2017, p. 234). Acknowledging social exclusion as a multidimensional phenomenon prompts consideration of how "sociocultural, institutional and interpersonal mechanisms interlink to affect individual experiences" (Spaaij, Magee, & Jeanes, 2014, p. 166), encouraging a focus on how exclusion occurs, not just the experience of exclusion.

Typically, social exclusion is theorized as occurring on a continuum; it is rare for individuals to be fully included or excluded, and, as Spaaij, Magee, and Jeanes (2014) suggest, few people become absolutely excluded because links usually remain with some community members. Social exclusion, therefore, tends to occur in degrees. Here, Miliband (2006) and Levitas et al., (2007) utilize the concept of "deep exclusion" to refer to individuals who are excluded as a result of multiple and overlapping factors and processes. Furthermore, social inclusion and exclusion are not dualistic; individuals do not experience one or the other but may feel both simultaneously related to different contexts of their lives. Social exclusion can also be self-driven, as illustrated in the previous section, when certain individuals "choose" not to participate in sport contexts where they feel unwelcome, unsafe, marginalized, and demeaned. As Levitas (2006) suggests, it is imperative to critique and challenge the idea of choice in any form of exclusion. It is particularly important in a sporting context to challenge discourse that suggests certain groups aren't interested in sport and don't want to be coaches or leaders as incorrect assumptions that become justifications for not addressing broader mechanisms of exclusion.

Theorizing social exclusion as a process that is influenced by numerous practices shifts thinking away from the notion of exclusion as resulting from individual deficits such as a lack of character or limited skills leading to low employability (Levitas et al., 2007). However, social policy theorists have illustrated that responses to social exclusion are frequently deployed using deficit frameworks that focus on fixing individual cases rather than addressing the broader systemic mechanisms contributing to exclusion. Levitas (2005) suggests that within the United Kingdom there are three different policy responses to addressing social exclusion: (1) the redistributive model, which focuses on redistributing resources to those experiencing exclusion; (2) the social integrationist approach, which focuses on addressing access to employment and considers employment as the key to addressing exclusion and therefore fails to acknowledge the moral and social dimensions of exclusion; and (3) the moral underclass discourse (MUD), which seeks to fix the individual deficiencies of the those who are are excluded. MUD connects with broader neoliberal frameworks of government, entrenched within most Global North societies, which move responsibility for social welfare away from the government and instead position it as the responsibility of families and individuals (Deeming & Smyth, 2015). Families and individuals unable to take responsibility for their own welfare, within neoliberal contexts, become further stigmatized and demonized (Fullagar, 2009). Much of the sport-for-development literature critiques sport and social inclusion programs for operating from a MUD/neoliberal position, suggesting they fail to challenge broader structural inequalities (Darnell, Chawansky, Marchesseault, Holmes, & Hayhurst, 2018; Kelly, 2011). This is discussed further in the final section.

Theories of Social Exclusion and the Global South

As a concept that originated in Europe and has been largely deployed within policies in the Global North, the majority of conceptualizations of social exclusion are drawn from Global North understandings. Jeanes, Spaaij, Magee, and Kay (2019, p. 153) write:

> [I]n the Global North, social exclusion is usually associated with a marginalised minority who are unable to fully and equitably participate in "normal" activities. . . . [I]n contrast, within the Global South, the majority populations may live in poverty, be excluded from formal labour and receive little protection by the state.

Global North theorizations are potentially unhelpful in considering the experiences of individuals, communities, and societies within the Global South, particularly as colonization has created and maintained various forms of exclusion and led to the historical privileging of certain ethnic and racial groups over others (Hunter, 2004; McCalman & Smith, 2016).

Hence, acknowledgment of the powerful exclusionary mechanisms created by colonization is critical in theorizing social exclusion within a Global South context. Atkinson and Marlier (2010, p. 29) suggest:

> Indigenous peoples continue to live amid long-standing conflicts or hostility with governments, dominant population groups and industries. They have been subject to

displacement and dispossession of their lands and resources, marginalization, denial of their cultural right and of their voice in political processes.

Alongside a consideration of how colonization has contributed to and shaped experiences of social exclusion, scholars working in Global South contexts point to additional dimensions that are not privileged or highlighted in Global North scholarship (Mathieson et al., 2008).

Spaaij, Magee, and Jeanes (2014) suggest that four distinct themes emerge from Global South frameworks: (1) exclusion from civil and political rights, (2) lack of social recognition and human dignity, (3) violence and personal security, and (4) marginalization within global power relations. Global South understandings of social exclusion therefore have strong rights-based underpinnings that seek to illustrate how social exclusion occurs from a lack of access to fundamental human rights (van Wormer, 2005). The focus on violence and security, while certainly relevant in Global North contexts, is at the forefront of understanding exclusion in Global South contexts. Violence against women, children, diverse ethnicities, and cultures is a key mechanism in exclusionary processes in the Global South but is rarely considered in Global North theorizations (McIlwaine, 2013).

Measuring Social Exclusion: Methodological Challenges

Much of the literature examining social exclusion within sporting contexts has tended to utilize qualitative methodologies, examining specific case studies of the experiences of social exclusion within sporting contexts for particular individuals or communities. Usually studies will focus on one dimension of diversity and the impact this has on mechanisms, processes, and experiences of exclusion, for example, the influence of gender, disability, and ethnicity, and how these demographics shape experiences of exclusion within sport. A range of studies has also drawn on large-scale participation data to illustrate ongoing discrepancies in participation and how these are mediated by factors such as income, education, and key demographics (Haudenhuyse, 2018; Spaaij, Farquharson et al., 2014; Vandermeerschen et al., 2015). Such studies provide ongoing illustrations of which groups continue to be excluded within sport contexts and how contextual dynamics facilitate this.

However, within the social exclusion literature more broadly, the challenges of measuring social exclusion are well-documented (Levitas et al., 2007), and this constraint impacts studies within a sport context. Developing a set of indicators that can appropriately capture and track the complex ways in which individuals and communities are excluded remains a challenge. Therefore there is a disconnect between the theoretical definitions of social exclusion and what data it is empirically possible to collect (Atkinson & Marlier, 2010). Established frameworks include the Bristol Social Exclusion Matrix (Levitas et al., 2007), which measures individuals' access to resources, participation in economic, social, cultural, and political activities, and quality of life. A second established approach relies on the CASE framework (Burchardt & Vizard, 2007), which measures physical security, health, education, standard of living, productive and valued activities, individual, family, and social life participation, influence and voice, self-respect, and legal security. The CASE framework enables the capture of data that more readily align with Global South theories. Still, capturing data that measure social exclusion within society and sport specifically remains challenging. Mathieson et al. (2008, p. 48) point out that quantitative measures "fail to provide insights into what it means to experience exclusionary forces or to capture the wisdom of experience amongst people most severely affected." There is therefore a drive within social exclusion research, and within sports-related studies more broadly, to adopt mixed-methods approaches that capture data on indicators of social exclusion while also providing a narrative of experiences (van der Roest, Spaaij, & van Bottenburg, 2015).

DEBATES

Can Social Exclusion in Sport Be Addressed?

There is an extensive literature examining social exclusion within sport, and there are a number of ongoing debates and challenges. A key issue centers on consideration of whether social exclusion within sport can be addressed. As the previous chapter has illustrated, sport does have the potential to contribute to social inclusion agendas, but sport has to be delivered and engaged in particular ways to achieve these outcomes (Crabbe, 2007). Despite the policy rhetoric suggesting that sport is a level playing field, it is constructed around winning and losing—some will succeed; others will not. As a concept and a cultural arena, sport is not readily suited to embrace practices of inclusion because of the overriding emphasis on competition and winning (Spaaij, Farquharson et al., 2014). Debates are on-going as to whether social exclusion and marginalization within sporting contexts can ever fully be addressed without dramatically changing the meaning, values, and ideologies that shape sport in contemporary society (Gard, Dionigi, & Dionigi, 2018).

Marginalized Communities and Resistance to Social Exclusion in Sport

Reflecting this, it is valuable to explore the responses of policymakers and practitioners to the ways marginalized communities negotiate the mechanisms of social exclusion. As discussed in the Issues section, when faced with overt and discriminatory forms of exclu-sion, groups and communities frequently opt to self-exclude from mainstream sporting opportunities, establishing their own provision where they can shape opportunities to better suit their needs and regulate damaging and discriminatory practices. Examining the experiences of newly arrived migrants and refugees, Spaaij (2012) illustrates the preference of young men from these communities to form their own sporting groups and teams, finding that self-organized monocultural teams create a safe space that provides social connection and a sense of shared belonging, as opposed to the racist and exclusionary experiences they encounter in mainstream sport. However, minority groups establishing their own sporting cultures is usually viewed negatively by sport policymakers and practitioners (Jeanes, O'Connor, & Alfrey, 2015). In the case of newly arrived communities, self-organized mon-ocultural teams are viewed problematically by policymakers as communities resisting integration within their new communities (Adair, Taylor, & Darcy, 2010; Jeanes et al., 2015). While policymakers and practitioners acknowledge that sport in its current form is exclusionary, there is considerable unwillingness to change fundamental aspects of sport and sporting culture to promote greater levels of inclusion.

A growing body of research suggests that, if we are seeking to address exclusion, we should abandon attempts to change processes and practices within mainstream sport and instead look to better support alternative, nontraditional forms of participation that can ensure more inclusive experiences (Jeanes, Spaaij, Penney, et al., 2019). As highlighted above, many marginalized communities are bypassing traditional sport opportunities and instead opting to participate in informal, self-organized, and self-regulated participation opportunities (Jeanes, Spaaij, Penney, et al., 2019; Spracklen, Long, & Hylton, 2015). While much of the research examining sport and social exclusion has focused on the issues inherent in sport that require addressing, the rise of alternative, informal participation within traditional sports such as soccer and cricket points to the need to address exclusion by reframing and rethinking what sport is, rather than keep attempting to change systems and cultures within mainstream sport that have largely been resistant and where progress is slow. Informal, community-driven sport participation offers different platforms upon which social exclusion might more effectively be addressed (Gilchrist & Wheaton, 2017).

Social Exclusion in Sport, Structural Inequality, and the Challenge of Inclusion

Although numerous initiatives and programs have sought to address social exclusion within sport, often these fail to address the complex and interlinked structural, cultural, environmental, and social mechanisms that have been illustrated throughout the chapter as facilitating exclusion (Reid, 2017; Spaaij et al., 2013). Policies and approaches to addressing social exclusion in sport tend to focus on the level of access and the assumption that excluded groups simply need readily available opportunities to increase their engagement (Collins & Haudenhuyse, 2015). Policies aimed at tackling social exclusion are generally underpinned by neoliberal ideologies that position marginalized and excluded communities as deficient and in need of fixing rather than recognizing that the overarching problem lies within the structures, systems, and values inherent in sport (Gard, Dionigi, & Dionigi, 2018; Reid, 2017). Haudenhuyse (2018, p. 210) writes:

> [R]egarding sport-for-inclusion (and sport for all) policies, the implications are that policies risk becoming limited to merely raising participation rates of specific target/problem groups (through fixing the presumed personal deficits of such groups), thereby leaving the exclusionary mechanisms of such policies (and practices) largely under-examined.

For example, approaches seeking to increase women's engagement in leadership and management positions in sport focus on addressing women's self-confidence and increasing women's social networks, rather than addressing deep-rooted sexist attitudes and the prioritizing of masculinized leadership approaches that create exclusion (Knoppers & Anthonissen, 2008).

Those individuals experiencing acute or deep social exclusion are often overlooked within sport and social inclusion initiatives because they are considered too hard to engage, and sport and social policy programs are seen as unlikely to be able to achieve the positive outcomes that are necessary for securing ongoing funding (Kelly, 2011; Spaaij et al., 2013). Even if sport is inclusive and embracing of diversity, its capacity to address the deep-set inequalities that exist within society and create social exclusion remains limited; Collins and Haudenhuyse (2015, p. 13), for example, suggest that individualized social inclusion intervention and sport programs are limited by their "sheer inability to alter substantially the adverse socio-cultural contexts in which social exclusion occurs."

CONCLUSION

Sport is an important cultural arena within society that contributes to and perpetuates the social exclusion and marginalization of some groups and individuals. Exclusion occurs due to a complex array of interlinking mechanisms and is experienced in degrees. Social exclusion has numerous negative consequences for those individuals and communities impacted, including isolation, loneliness, fewer social networks, poorer physical and mental health, lower educational attainment, and lower perceptions of safety and security. In short, social exclusion leads to many fundamental human needs being unmet in the populations that are affected. For this reason, continuing to highlight and seek to address the social exclusion experienced within sporting contexts is important. There are several avenues that future research could productively explore.

A key area that is relatively unexplored is considering how sport and social policymakers, practitioners, and researchers can more effectively and productively engage with excluded communities and facilitate their input into how to address social exclusion (Reid, 2017). As highlighted in the Debates section, existing approaches formulated by policymakers tend to focus on neoliberal assumptions that seek to "fix" the individual and pay little attention to broader structural inequalities within society. Furthermore, attempts by marginalized communities to mitigate their own exclusion have been largely dismissed or viewed as problematic within sport and social policy.

Research is beginning to highlight the lack of engagement by policymakers and practitioners with excluded communities and recognizing that strategies to address exclusion need to be developed in consultation with those experiencing marginalization (Frisby & Millar, 2002). However, the voices of those socially excluded are still notably absent. Within Australia and Canada, for example, Indigenous peoples are often invisible in discussions that inform the development of policies aimed at supporting their social development and engagement in sport (Gardam, Giles, Rynne, & Hayhurst, 2018; Lucas, Jeanes, & Diamond, 2020). Again, this illustrates the importance of conceptualizing social exclusion as multilayered. Even when physically present in sport, marginalized groups are often rendered invisible within decision-making processes (Collins & Kay, 2014). While this form of exclusion is noted in discussions in the field, there has been limited engagement with how this problem could be addressed, making it an important area of focus for future research. Engaging those who are socially excluded from sport in developing and designing their own solutions and providing the opportunity to influence and shape policy is a critical aspect of challenging and addressing social exclusion moving forward.

A further challenge for researchers examining sport and social exclusion relates to some of the issues raised in the theoretical overview. Social exclusion is a contentious concept, and while it is important to acknowledge it as a multifaceted, multilayered process, this has resulted in a concept that at times is viewed as nebulous and unwieldy. It is challenging to operationalize research that examines the multiple facets contributing to social exclusion; this is evident in some of the sport and social exclusion research that tends to focus on certain facets of exclusion (e.g., attitudes or access) or focuses exclusively on poverty or views diversity in isolation. There remains a lack of research utilizing an intersectional lens that explores the multiple facets of exclusion that exist within sporting contexts (Haudenhuyse, 2018). An intersectional lens is increasingly important to, as Dagkas (2016, p. 223) says, examine "how various social identities intersect at the micro level of individuals' experience" and highlight "interlocking systems of hierarchies, domination and oppression and inequalities at the macro level." It is important, therefore, that future research examines the intersections and multiple layers of social exclusion within sport, and how these contribute to particular experiences. Developing more nuanced understandings of how identities and social exclusion mechanisms intersect and how this intersection impacts experiences of social exclusion is particularly important for developing more effective policies and solutions to addressing exclusion in the future.

References

Adair, D., Taylor, T., & Darcy, S. (2010). Managing ethnocultural and racial diversity in sport: Obstacles and opportunities. *Sport Management Review*, 13(4), 307–312.

Agulnik, P. (2002). *Understanding social exclusion*. Oxford: Oxford University Press.

Apoifis, N., Marlin, D., & Bennie, A. (2018). Noble athlete, savage coach: How racialised representations of Aboriginal athletes impede professional sport coaching opportunities for Aboriginal Australians. *International Review for the Sociology of Sport*, 53(7), 854–868.

Atkinson, A. B., & Marlier, E. (2010). *Analysing and measuring social inclusion in a global context*. New York: United Nations.

Baiocco, R., Pistella, J., Salvati, M., Ioverno, S., & Lucidi, F. (2018). Sports as a risk environment: Homophobia and bullying in a sample of gay and heterosexual men. *Journal of Gay & Lesbian Mental Health*, 22(4), 385–411.

Baker-Lewton, A., Sonn, C. C., Vincent, D. N., & Curnow, F. (2017). "I haven't lost hope of reaching out . . .": Exposing racism in sport by elevating counter narratives. *International Journal of Inclusive Education*, 21(11), 1097–1112.

Baum, S., & Gleeson, B. (2010). Space and place: Social exclusion in Australia's suburban heartlands. *Urban Policy and Research*, 28(2), 135–159.

Bianchi, A. (2017). Transgender women in sport. *Journal of the Philosophy of Sport*, 44(2), 229–242.

Boykoff, J., & Carrington, B. (2020). Sporting dissent: Colin Kaepernick, NFL activism, and media framing contests. *International Review for the Sociology of Sport*, 55(7), 829–849. 1012690219861594.

Brittain, I. (2004). Perceptions of disability and their impact upon involvement in sport for people with disabilities at all levels. *Journal of Sport and Social Issues*, 28(4), 429–452.

Brittain, I. (2011). South Africa, apartheid and the Paralympic Games. *Sport in Society*, *14*(9), 1165–1181.

Brittain, I., Biscaia, R., & Gérard, S. (2020). Ableism as a regulator of social practice and disabled peoples' self-determination to participate in sport and physical activity. *Leisure Studies*, *39*(2), 209–224.

Burchardt, T., Le Grand, J., Piachaud, D., Hills, J., & Grand, L. (2002). *Understanding social exclusion*. London: London School of Economics.

Burchardt, T., & Vizard, P. (2007). *Definition of equality and framework for measurement: Final recommendations of the Equalities Review Steering Group*. London: London School of Economics.

Burton, L. J. (2015). Underrepresentation of women in sport leadership: A review of research. *Sport Management Review*, *18*(2), 155–165.

Burton, L. J., & LaVoi, N. M. (2016). An ecological/multisystem approach to understanding and examining women coaches. In N. LaVoi (Ed.), *Women in sports coaching* (pp. 49–62). London: Routledge.

Bush, A., Anderson, E., & Carr, S. (2012). The declining existence of men's homophobia in British sport. *Journal for the Study of Sports and Athletes in Education*, *6*(1), 107–120.

Calder, A., Sole, G., & Mulligan, H. (2018). The accessibility of fitness centers for people with disabilities: A systematic review. *Disability and Health Journal*, *11*(4), 525–536.

Cashmore, E., & Cleland, J. (2011). Why aren't there more Black football managers? *Ethnic and Racial Studies*, *34*(9), 1594–1607.

Claringbould, I., & Knoppers, A. (2012). Paradoxical practices of gender in sport-related organizations. *Journal of Sport Management*, *26*(5), 404–416.

Collins, M. (2004). Sport, physical activity and social exclusion. *Journal of Sports Sciences*, *22*(8), 727–740.

Collins, M. (2013). Youth sport and UK sport policy. In A. Parker & D. Vinson (Eds.), *Youth sport, physical activity and play: Policy, intervention and participation* (pp. 13–27). London: Routledge.

Collins, M. F., & Buller, J. R. (2003). Social exclusion from high-performance sport: Are all talented young sports people being given an equal opportunity of reaching the Olympic podium? *Journal of Sport and Social Issues*, *27*(4), 420–442.

Collins, M., & Haudenhuyse, R. (2015). Social exclusion and austerity policies in England: The role of sports in a new area of social polarisation and inequality? *Social Inclusion*, *3*(3), 5–18.

Collins, M., & Kay, T. (2014). *Sport and social exclusion*. London: Routledge.

Cooky, C., & Dworkin, S. L. (2013). Policing the boundaries of sex: A critical examination of gender verification and the Caster Semenya controversy. *Journal of Sex Research*, *50*(2), 103–111.

Coram, S., & Hallinan, C. (2017). Critical race theory and the orthodoxy of race neutrality: Examining the denigration of Adam Goodes. *Australian Aboriginal Studies*, *2017*(1), 99–107.

Crabbe, T. (2007). Reaching the "hard to reach": Engagement, relationship building and social control in sport based social inclusion work. *International Journal of Sport Management and Marketing*, *2*(1–2), 27–40.

Cunningham, G. B. (2019). Understanding the experiences of LGBT athletes in sport: A multilevel model. In M. H. Anshel, T. A. Petrie, & J. A. Steinfeldt (Eds.), *APA handbook of sport and exercise psychology: Vol. 1. Sport psychology* (pp. 367–383). APA handbooks in psychology series. New York: American Psychological Association.

Dagkas, S. (2016). Problematizing social justice in health pedagogy and youth sport: Intersectionality of race, ethnicity, and class. *Research Quarterly for Exercise and Sport, 87*(3), 221–229.

Darcy, S., Lock, D., & Taylor, T. (2017). Enabling inclusive sport participation: Effects of disability and support needs on constraints to sport participation. *Leisure Sciences, 39*(1), 20–41.

Darnell, S. C., Chawansky, M., Marchesseault, D., Holmes, M., & Hayhurst, L. (2018). The state of play: Critical sociological insights into recent "sport for development and peace" research. *International Review for the Sociology of Sport, 53*(2), 133–151.

D'Cruz, G. (2018). Breaking bad: The booing of Adam Goodes and the politics of the Black sports celebrity in Australia. *Celebrity Studies, 9*(1), 131–138.

Deeming, C., & Smyth, P. (2015). Social investment after neoliberalism: Policy paradigms and political platforms. *Journal of Social Policy, 44*(2), 297–318.

de Haan, D., & Knoppers, A. (2020). Gendered discourses in coaching high-performance sport. *International Review for the Sociology of Sport, 55*(6), 631–646. https://doi.org/10.1177/1012690219829692.

de Haan, Norman, L., La Voi, N., & Knoppers, A. (2020) Elite women coaches in global football: A report. Executive Summary. https://www.sportanddev.org/sites/default/files/downloads/executive_summary_-_elite_women_coaches_in_global_football.pdf 14/07/2020.

Denison, E., & Kitchen, A. (2015). *Out on the fields: The first international study on homophobia in sport.* Repucom. e-book.

Drury, S., Stride, A., Flintoff, A., & Williams, S. (2017). Lesbian, gay, bisexual and transgender young people's experiences of PE and the implications for youth sport participation and engagement. In J. Long, T. Fletcher, & B. Watson (Eds.), *Sport, leisure and social justice* (pp. 84–97). London: Routledge.

Elling-Machartzki, A. (2017). Extraordinary body-self narratives: Sport and physical activity in the lives of transgender people. *Leisure Studies, 36*(2), 256–268.

Esmonde, K., Cooky, C., & Andrews, D. L. (2015). "It's supposed to be about the love of the game, not the love of Aaron Rodgers' eyes": Challenging the exclusions of women sports fans. *Sociology of Sport Journal, 32*(1), 22–48.

Evans, A. B., & Pfister, G. U. (2020). Women in sports leadership: A systematic narrative review. *International Review for the Sociology of Sport.* Advance online publication. doi:1012690220911842.

Farquharson, K., Spaaij, R., Gorman, S., Jeanes, R., Lusher, D., & Magee, J. (2019). Managing racism on the field in Australian junior sport. In P. Essed, K. Farquharson, K. Pillay, & E. White (Eds.), *Relating worlds of racism* (pp. 165–189). London: Palgrave Macmillan.

Fink, J. S. (2016). Hiding in plain sight: The embedded nature of sexism in sport. *Journal of Sport Management, 30*(1), 1–7.

Fletcher, T., & Walle, T. (2015). Negotiating their right to play: Asian-specific cricket teams and leagues in the UK and Norway. *Identities, 22*(2), 230–246.

Frisby, W., & Hoeber, L. (2002). Factors affecting the uptake of community recreation as health promotion for women on low incomes. *Canadian Journal of Public Health, 93*(2), 129–133.

Frisby, W., & Millar, S. (2002). The actualities of doing community development to promote the inclusion of low income populations in local sport and recreation. *European Sport Management Quarterly, 2*(3), 209–233.

Fullagar, S. (2009). *Governing healthy family lifestyles through discourses of risk and responsibility.* New York: Routledge.

Gard, M., Dionigi, R. A., & Dionigi, C. (2018). From a lucky few to the reluctant many: Interrogating the politics of sport for all. In R. A. Dionigi & M. Gard (Eds.), *Sport and physical activity across the lifespan: Critical perspectives* (pp. 67–89). London: Palgrave Macmillan.

Gardam, K. J., Giles, A. R., Rynne, S., & Hayhurst, L. M. (2018). A comparison of Indigenous sport for development policy directives in Canada and Australia. *Aboriginal Policy Studies, 7*(2), 29–46.

Gilchrist, P., & Wheaton, B. (2017). The social benefits of informal and lifestyle sports: A research agenda. *International Journal of Sport Policy and Politics, 9*(1), 1–10.

Hallinan, C., & Judd, B. (2009). Race relations, Indigenous Australia and the social impact of professional Australian football. *Sport in Society, 12*(9), 1220–1235.

Hammond, A. (2019). The mainstreaming of disability swimming in Australia, 1990–2016. *Sporting Traditions, 36*(1), 43–58.

Hargie, O. D., Mitchell, D. H., & Somerville, I. J. (2017). "People have a knack of making you feel excluded if they catch on to your difference": Transgender experiences of exclusion in sport. *International Review for the Sociology of Sport, 52*(2), 223–239.

Hartmann, D. (2019). The Olympic "revolt" of 1968 and its lessons for contemporary African American athletic activism. *European Journal of American Studies, 14*(1). https://doi.org/10.4000/ejas/14355.

Haudenhuyse, R. (2018). The impact of austerity on poverty and sport participation: Mind the knowledge gap. *International Journal of Sport Policy and Politics, 10*(1), 203–213.

Haycock, D., & Smith, A. (2018). Adult sport participation and life transitions: The significance of childhood and inequality. In R. A. Dionigi & M. Gard (Eds.), *Sport and physical activity across the lifespan* (pp. 195–210). London: Palgrave Macmillan.

Hunter, B. (2004). *Social exclusion, social capital, and Indigenous Australians: Measuring the social costs of unemployment*. Canberra: Australian National University.

Hylton, K., & Lawrence, S. (2016). "For your ears only!" Donald Sterling and backstage racism in sport. *Ethnic and Racial Studies, 39*(15), 2740–2757.

Jeanes, R., O'Connor, J., & Alfrey, L. (2015). Sport and the resettlement of young people from refugee backgrounds in Australia. *Journal of Sport and Social Issues, 39*(6), 480–500.

Jeanes, R., Spaaij, R., Magee, J., Farquharson, K., Gorman, S., & Lusher, D. (2018). "Yes we are inclusive": Examining provision for young people with disabilities in community sport clubs. *Sport Management Review, 21*(1), 38–50.

Jeanes, R., Spaaij, R., Magee, J., Farquharson, K., Gorman, S., & Lusher, D. (2019). Developing participation opportunities for young people with disabilities? Policy enactment and social inclusion in Australian junior sport. *Sport in Society, 22*(6), 986–1004.

Jeanes, R., Spaaij, R., Magee, J., & Kay, T. (2019). SDP and social exclusion. In H. Collison, S. Darnell, R. Giulianotti, & P. D. Howe (Eds.), *Routledge handbook of sport for development and peace* (pp. 152–161). London: Routledge.

Jeanes, R., Spaaij, R., Penney, D., & O'Connor, J. (2019). Managing informal sport participation: Tensions and opportunities. *International Journal of Sport Policy and Politics, 11*(1), 79–95.

Jones, B. A., Arcelus, J., Bouman, W. P., & Haycraft, E. (2017). Sport and transgender people: A systematic review of the literature relating to sport participation and competitive sport policies. *Sports Medicine, 47*(4), 701–716.

Kalman-Lamb, N. (2020). "I hate Christian Laettner" and the persistence of hegemonic masculinity and heteronormativity in sporting cultures. In R. Magrath, J. Cleland, & E. Anderson

(Eds.), *The Palgrave handbook of masculinity and sport* (pp. 241–260). New York: Palgrave Macmillan.

Kaufman, P. (2008). Boos, bans, and other backlash: The consequences of being an activist athlete. *Humanity & Society, 32*(3), 215–237.

Kay, T. (2000a). Leisure, gender and family: The influence of social policy. *Leisure Studies, 19*(4), 247–265.

Kay, T. (2000b). Sporting excellence: A family affair? *European Physical Education Review, 6*(2), 151–169.

Kelly, L. (2011). "Social inclusion" through sports-based interventions? *Critical Social Policy, 31*(1), 126–150.

Kitchin, P. J., & Howe, P. D. (2014). The mainstreaming of disability cricket in England and Wales: Integration "one game" at a time. *Sport Management Review, 17*(1), 65–77.

Knoppers, A., & Anthonissen, A. (2008). Gendered managerial discourses in sport organizations: Multiplicity and complexity. *Sex Roles, 58*(1–2), 93–103.

Koller, D. (2019). The new gender equity in elite women's sports. In N. Lough & A. Geurin (Eds.), *Routledge handbook of the business of women's sport* (pp. 217–227). London: Routledge.

Levitas, R. (2005). *The inclusive society? Social exclusion and New Labour*. Springer.

Levitas, R. (2006). The concept and measurement of social exclusion. In C. Pantazis, D. Gordon, & R. Levitas (Eds.), *Poverty and social exclusion in Britain* (pp. 123–160). Bristol, U.K.: Policy Press.

Levitas, R., Pantazis, C., Fahmy, E., Gordon, D., Lloyd-Reichling, E., & Patsios, D. (2007). *The multi-dimensional analysis of social exclusion*. Bristol, U.K.: University of Bristol.

Long, J. (2000). No racism here? A preliminary examination of sporting innocence. *Managing Leisure, 5*(3), 121–133.

Love, A., Deeb, A., & Waller, S. N. (2019). Social justice, sport and racism: A position statement. *Quest, 71*(2), 227–238.

Lucas, R., Jeanes, R., & Diamond, Z. (2020). Sport for development and Indigenous Australians: A critical research agenda for policy and practice. *Leisure Studies*. Advance online publication. doi:10.1080/02614367.2020.1808050.

Magrath, R. (2016). *Inclusive masculinities in contemporary football: Men in the beautiful game*. London: Routledge.

Martin, J. J. (2013). Benefits and barriers to physical activity for individuals with disabilities: A social-relational model of disability perspective. *Disability and Rehabilitation, 35*(24), 2030–2037.

Mathieson, J., Popay, J., Enoch, E., Escorel, S., Hernandez, M., Johnston, H., & Rispel, L. (2008). Social exclusion meaning, measurement and experience and links to health inequalities: A review of literature. WHO Social Exclusion Knowledge Network Background Paper 1. Geneva: World Health Organization.

McCalman, J., & Smith, L. (2016). Family and country: Accounting for fractured connections under colonisation in Victoria, Australia. *Journal of Population Research, 33*(1), 51–65.

McIlwaine, C. (2013). Urbanization and gender-based violence: Exploring the paradoxes in the Global South. *Environment and Urbanization, 25*(1), 65–79.

Meier, M., & Saavedra, M. (2009). Esther Phiri and the Moutawakel effect in Zambia: An analysis of the use of female role models in sport-for-development. *Sport in Society, 12*(9), 1158–1176.

Miliband, D. (2006). *Social exclusion: The next steps forward*. London: ODPM.

Misener, L., & Darcy, S. (2014). Managing disability sport: From athletes with disabilities to inclusive organisational perspectives. *Sport Management Review*, *17*(1), 1–7.

Mulligan, H., Miyahara, M., & Nichols-Dunsmuir, A. (2017). Multiple perspectives on accessibility to physical activity for people with long-term mobility impairment. *Scandinavian Journal of Disability Research*, *19*(4), 295–306.

Nielsen, G., Grønfeldt, V., Toftegaard-Støckel, J., & Andersen, L. B. (2012). Predisposed to participate? The influence of family socio-economic background on children's sports participation and daily amount of physical activity. *Sport in Society*, *15*(1), 1–27.

Norman, L. (2010). Feeling second best: Elite women coaches' experiences. *Sociology of Sport Journal*, *27*(1), 89–104.

Norman, L., North, J., Hylton, K., Flintoff, A., & Rankin, A. J. (2014). Sporting experiences and coaching aspirations among Black and minority ethnic (BME) groups: A report for Sports Coach UK. Project Report. Leeds: Sport Coach UK.

Ogawa, S. (2014). Participation, selection, and silence of gay athletes. In J. Hargreaves & E. Anderson (Eds.), *Routledge handbook of sport, gender and sexuality* (pp. 291–299). London: Routledge.

Oliver, P., & Lusted, J. (2015). Discrimination cases in grass-roots sport: Comparing Australian and English experiences. *Sport in Society*, *18*(5), 529–542.

Oxford, S. (2017). The social, cultural, and historical complexities that shape and constrain (gendered) space in an SDP organisation in Colombia. *Journal of Sport for Development*, *6*(10), 1–11.

Pavlidis, A. (2018). Making "space" for women and girls in sport: An agenda for Australian geography. *Geographical Research*, *56*(4), 343–352.

Petty, L., & Trussell, D. E. (2018). Experiences of identity development and sexual stigma for lesbian, gay, and bisexual young people in sport: "Just survive until you can be who you are." *Qualitative Research in Sport, Exercise and Health*, *10*(2), 176–189.

Ponic, P., & Frisby, W. (2010). Unpacking assumptions about inclusion in community-based health promotion: Perspectives of women living in poverty. *Qualitative Health Research*, *20*(11), 1519–1531.

Popay, J. (2010). Understanding and tackling social exclusion. *Journal of Research in Nursing*, *15*(4), 295–297.

Reeves, K., Ponsford, M., & Gorman, S. (2015). Codes combined: Managing expectations and policy responses to racism in sport. *Sport in Society*, *18*(5), 519–528.

Reid, G. (2017). A fairy-tale narrative for community sport? Exploring the politics of sport social enterprise. *International Journal of Sport Policy and Politics*, *9*(4), 597–611.

Russo, E. (2010). From informal recreation to a geography of achievement: Women's soccer in South Australia. *Geographical Research*, *48*(2), 181–196.

Saxton, M. (2018). Hard bodies: Exploring historical and cultural factors in disabled people's participation in exercise: Applying critical disability theory. *Sport in Society*, *21*(1), 22–39.

Shaw, S., & Frisby, W. (2006). Can gender equity be more equitable? Promoting an alternative frame for sport management research, education, and practice. *Journal of Sport Management*, *20*(4), 483–509.

Shields, N., Synnot, A. J., & Barr, M. (2012). Perceived barriers and facilitators to physical activity for children with disability: A systematic review. *British Journal of Sports Medicine*, *46*(14), 989–997.

Silver, H., & Miller, S. M. (2003). Social exclusion. *Indicators*, *2*(2), 5–21.

Smith, A., Haycock, D., & Hulme, N. (2013). The class of London 2012: Some sociological reflections on the social backgrounds of Team GB athletes. *Sociological Research Online*, *18*(3), 158–162.

Spaaij, R. (2012). Beyond the playing field: Experiences of sport, social capital, and integration among Somalis in Australia. *Ethnic and Racial Studies*, *35*(9), 1519–1538.

Spaaij, R., Farquharson, K., Magee, J., Jeanes, R., Lusher, D., & Gorman, S. (2014). A fair game for all? How community sports clubs in Australia deal with diversity. *Journal of Sport and Social Issues*, *38*(4), 346–365.

Spaaij, R., Farquharson, K., & Marjoribanks, T. (2015). Sport and social inequalities. *Sociology Compass*, *9*(5), 400–411.

Spaaij, R., Knoppers, A., & Jeanes, R. (2020). "We want more diversity but . . .": Resisting diversity in recreational sports clubs. *Sport Management Review*, *23*(3), 363–373.

Spaaij, R., Magee, J., & Jeanes, R. (2013). Urban youth, worklessness and sport: A comparison of sports-based employability programmes in Rotterdam and Stoke-on-Trent. *Urban Studies*, *50*(8), 1608–1624.

Spaaij, R., Magee, J., & Jeanes, R. (2014). *Sport and social exclusion in global society*. London: Routledge.

Spandler, H. (2007). From social exclusion to inclusion? A critique of the inclusion imperative in mental health. *Medical Sociology Online*, *2*(2), 3–16.

Sport England. (2006). Sport action zones: A key to transforming community participation. Sport England Research. https://sportengland-production-files.s3.eu-west-2.amazonaws.com/s3fs-public/sport-action-zones-evaluation-summary-report.pdf.

Spracklen, K., Long, J., & Hylton, K. (2015). Leisure opportunities and new migrant communities: Challenging the contribution of sport. *Leisure Studies*, *34*(1), 114–129.

Storr, R., Robinson, K., Davies, C., Nicholas, L., & Collison, A. (2020). *Game to play? Exploring the experiences and attitudes towards sport, exercise and physical activity amongst same sex attracted and gender diverse young people*. Sydney: Western Sydney University Publication.

Suggs, D. W., & Guthrie, J. L. (2017). Disabling prejudice: A case study of images of Paralympic athletes and attitudes toward people with disabilities. *International Journal of Sport Communication*, *10*(2), 258–276.

Symons, C. M., O'Sullivan, G. A., & Polman, R. (2017). The impacts of discriminatory experiences on lesbian, gay and bisexual people in sport. *Annals of Leisure Research*, *20*(4), 467–489.

Taket, A., Foster, N., & Cook, K. (2009). Understanding processes of social exclusion: Silence, silencing and shame. In A. Taket, B. Crisp, A Nevill, G. Lamaro, M. Graham, & S. Barter-Godfrey (Eds.), *Theorising social exclusion* (pp. 183–194). London: Routledge.

Taylor, P. (2001). Sports facility development and the role of forecasting: A retrospective on swimming in Sheffield. In C. Gratton & I. Henry (Eds.), *Sport in the city: The role of sport in economic and social regeneration* (pp. 214 –226). London: Routledge.

Thomas, N., & Guett, M. (2014). Fragmented, complex and cumbersome: A study of disability sport policy and provision in Europe. *International Journal of Sport Policy and Politics*, *6*(3), 389–406.

Trussell, D. E., Kovac, L., & Apgar, J. (2018). LGBTQ parents' experiences of community youth sport: Change your forms, change your (hetero) norms. *Sport Management Review*, *21*(1), 51–62.

Vandermeerschen, H., Vos, S., & Scheerder, J. (2015). Who's joining the club? Participation of socially vulnerable children and adolescents in club-organised sports. *Sport, Education and Society, 20*(8), 941–958.

van der Roest, J. W., Spaaij, R., & van Bottenburg, M. (2015). Mixed methods in emerging academic subdisciplines: The case of sport management. *Journal of Mixed Methods Research, 9*(1), 70–90.

van Wormer, K. (2005). Concepts for contemporary social work: Globalization, oppression, social exclusion, human rights, etc. *Social Work & Society, 3*(1), 1–10.

Walker, N. A., & Bopp, T. (2011). The underrepresentation of women in the male-dominated sport workplace: Perspectives of female coaches. *Journal of Workplace Rights, 15*(1), 47–64.

Widdop, P., King, N., Parnell, D., Cutts, D., & Millward, P. (2018). Austerity, policy and sport participation in England. *International Journal of Sport Policy and Politics, 10*(1), 7–24.

CHAPTER 42

....

SPORT, RACE, AND ETHNICITY

....

DARYL ADAIR

DISCUSSING "race" and ethnicity conjointly is often a pragmatic necessity in both society and sport, but it is also an exercise fraught with difficulty. These terms derive from long-standing discursive efforts to classify humans into visible groups (Tatz, 2009). The history of doing so involved the pseudo-scientific creation of hierarchies, with some "racial" or ethnic groups positioned as superior or inferior to others (Gates, 1997). Thus, the evolution of attitudes about these classifiers was not simply a quest to interpret distinctiveness; it was as much about "othering" people as either more or less valuable, with "the powerful producing the other as subordinate" (Jensen, 2011, p. 53). That said, the concepts of "race" and ethnicity have variances in both theory and praxis.

As this chapter reveals, embodied identities are a significant part of sport as a social practice. Athletic activities involve visceral competition, or at the least physical performance; thus the vitality and capability of the human body are commonly on public display. The spectacle of sport therefore involves athletic and aesthetic representations of the human condition (Blake, 1996). However, if we are to accept the metaphor of sport as theater, it is obvious that the stage prioritizes certain groups of actors, typecasts some into narrow roles, and closes the curtain on some. Indeed, historically the sporting stage has regularly been "unsporting" in respect of opportunities for racial and ethnic minorities the world over (Adair, 2011, 2012b; Adair & Rowe, 2010; Mangan & Ritchie, 2004; Nauright, Gobley, & Wiggins, 2014) That was, as we will see, a direct reflection of societal norms and values, with sport organized to entrench group differences and associated inequalities. This is a contrast to the more common aspiration for sport today, which is that physical culture ought to be a vehicle through which to bring together culturally and ancestrally diverse people in a welcoming way (Cunningham, 2019; Hallinan & Jackson, 2008; Stidder & Hayes, 2013). Of course, where societies remain diverse but discriminatory, sport still epitomizes exclusion rather than inclusion.

Today the theater of sport is more cosmopolitan than ever. Actors are still grouped according to attributes of gender, age, and (dis)ability, which speak to conventions around fair and reasonable athletic competition. The theater of sport no longer explicitly includes or excludes actors on the basis of ethnoracial background, nor are there punitively separate stages for people of different skin color. However, the directors of the sport play are overwhelmingly male and white, as are the owners of the playing troupe (Lu, Huang, Seshagiri, Park, & Griggs, 2020; Todaro, 2018). Indeed, those who bring televised versions of the play into living rooms are, no surprise, commonly also male and white (Lapchick, 2018; Lewis, Bell, Billings, & Brown, 2019). This speaks to three things. First, unlike the performing arts, the theater of sport separates male and female actors, where they perform on different stages, unequally so. Second, the theater of sport—both as play and as production—has principally been a demonstration of athletic manliness, featuring popularized expressions of masculinity. Third, although today's sporting stage is more cosmopolitan, the management of the playing troupe and its home theater, along with mediated representations of its spectacle, remain the bastion of white men.

ISSUES

Skin in the Game

Despite its widespread social currency, there is no biological basis to race (Yudell, Roberts, DeSalle, & Tishkoff, 2016). Consequently, the qualifier "race" is often deployed by social scientists to emphasize the (inequitable) social origins of the term and to counter the fallacy of biological determinism according to "race" (Graves, 2008). Put bluntly, "race" has involved mythopoeic perceptions about the virtues or otherwise of skin color, together with stereotypical assumptions about identity and status associated with corporeal, theological, and other forms of racial "positioning" (Hockey, 2018; Norwood, 2013). Colonial societies exemplified white dominance by subordinating Indigenous and colored peoples, using segregation or separatism to institutionalize inferiority—a process sometimes referred to as enforcing the "color line" (Reynolds & Lake, 2008).

The "color line" was given sharp relief in U.S. sports history: white pugilists typically refused to fight Black opponents, and (until 1908) the Heavyweight Championship of the World was for white boxers only (Moore, 2017). Concurrently, Black baseballers were obliged to play among themselves, eventually establishing "negro" leagues; they were barred (until 1947) from participation in whites-only Major League Baseball (Heaphy, 2015). During the last half of the 20th century, racist ideology toward Blacks was gradually disrupted: the 1950s–1960s American civil rights and South African anti-apartheid movements advocated for equality under the law for people of color. This coincided with political efforts to desegregate sport in both countries. In the NFL, for example, it took until 1962 for every team to open up to African American players; that followed years of antiracist agitation on the part of Black players, sportswriters, and fans (Moore, 2018; Smith, 1987). However, a postracial world was hardly ushered in; as we will see, "racial" ideology has continued to be a strident vehicle for bigotry and discrimination.

In recent times, greater intergroup diversity is confounding binary notions of "race" (Harris & Sim, 2002). "Mixed-race" families showcase the complexity of image and identity, especially when combined with a growing trend to self-identify with one or more "racial" groups, as exemplified today in the United States (Pew Research Center, 2015). In the context of sport, the 1997 declaration by golfer Tiger Woods about his complex ethnoracial identity was a pivotal moment in that direction. Woods described himself as "Cablinasian," a term intended to encompass his sense of mixed ancestry and nonbinary "racial" identity. For Woods, Cablinasian encompassed his "Caucasian, Black, Indian, and Asian heritages" and, to him, "was preferable to the inaccurate label, 'African American'" (Ibrahim, 2015, p. 29).

Kin in the Game

Like "race," ethnicity is also difficult to conceptualize. Typically, ethnic groups are associated with a shared sense of kinship and culture, which speaks to characteristics like ancestry, folklore, and language. Most commonly, groups deemed "ethnic" have minority status in a wider populace; "ethnics" join a new country as immigrants or self-identify as part of a locally born diaspora, often with a hybrid sense of "home" (Fenton, 2013). Compared to "race," personal engagement or otherwise with an ethnic group is generally more fluid, with individuals able to embed themselves in a cultural tradition in the absence of a primordial connection (Hale, 2004). That can be so, for example, when people convert to an ethnoreligious way of life, evincing a combination of faith, language, and homeland. Of course, in isolation, religion is not a guide to ethnicity; Catholics might as easily be connected with Irish or Italian roots, while Jews can be secular or devout. What all of these groups have in common is a sense of collective identity, however variable and imprecise that might be. Similarly, they may face accommodation, estrangement, or hostility by outsiders (Prentiss, 2003). Therefore, much like "race," ethnicity can be a focus of bigotry by others, but also a source of pride among group members.

Self-identifiable claims about ethnic identity are made visible "when group members display the ostensible referents that mark them as such" (Vine, 1997, p. 53). In that respect, sport has long been a vehicle for expressions of ethnic pride. For Italians in the United States, boxing became a key referent for their sense of achievement as an ethnic group, and several champion fighters—including the iconic Rocky Marciano—earned "symbolic capital as ['authentic'] Americans" (Gems, 2012, p. 493). Most poignant of all, sport and ethnic pride have resonated in response to pejorative labels. Jews are a salient example. Tatz (2009, p. 24) reminds us that "antisemitism included the 'truth' that the Jewish posture (and nature) was different, decadent and pathological." Yet the idea that Jews were physically "feeble" was countered by the reality that "nearly one-third of professional boxers" were Jewish in the 1920s and 1930s, while "Jews held 30 world titles between 1910 and 1940" (p. 24). Whether in boxing or a range of other sports, from baseball to basketball (Levine, 1993), "the image of the strong Jewish athlete" helped to break "the long-held stereotype of the bookish or weak Jew" (MJL, 2007).

Divides *between* ethnic groups have also featured in sport. A long-standing ethnosectarian rift is the "Old Firm" derby in Scottish soccer involving Glasgow Rangers (ostensibly British Protestant) and Glasgow Celtic (ostensibly Irish Catholic). Their on-field clashes have typically had more spiteful expressions off the pitch, where hardline fans are welded to diametrically opposed political, ethnonationalist, and sectarian discourses (Murray, 2003). Sport in the Middle East, meanwhile, has featured an even more complex mix of tribal loyalties. Well-known Arab-Israeli geopolitical divides tend to overshadow the potency of underlying sectarian tensions within those regions. In a discussion of domestic soccer in Arab countries, Al Ganideh (2020) explains that competition between local teams is more than mere rivalry; games are fiercely sectarian and ideological, reproducing conflicts between various religious communities and political groups. Similarly, in a discussion of Hebrew sport, Kaufman and Galily (2009) emphasize that Zionist sports unions had an overtly sectarian ideological mission in the first half of the 20th century, with their separatist sensibilities consolidated after the establishment of the Israeli state in 1948. It is some irony, therefore, that today "Israeli national teams are no longer represented only by Jews—they include Arabs and naturalized non-Jewish Israeli players" (p. 1025).

APPROACHES

Founders

Critical research into sport, race, and ethnicity is relatively recent. The germinal works of C. L. R. James (1963) on the aesthetics and culture of West Indian cricket and Harry Edwards (1969) on the case for Black athlete activism in the United States stand as beacons. Importantly, both of these publications involved personal reflections by Black intellectuals. In that respect, the books derived authenticity on the back of these authors' lived experiences. James, an Afro-Trinidadian historian, social theorist, and public commentator, shared a passion for West Indian cricket along with a determination to give voice to the international pan-African diaspora. For him, sport was evolving to be a more positive interracial force: he understood that athletic competitions were contested sociocultural spaces, but he observed that sport was now providing improved opportunities for people of all colors to coexist under a common set of rules and a similar ethos of "fair play." West Indies cricket, which had begun as a symbol of white colonial autocracy, had, over time, been reinvented as a display of Black athletic dominance in the Caribbean (Dixit, 2018; Hartmann, 2003). James was not suggesting that sport was a panacea for (male) racial inequality, but via the prism of cricket he had observed prospects for a more equitable alignment of racially contested spaces. One of the legacies of James's voluminous writings on cricket is his insistence that sport was worthy of intellectual inquiry—an all too radical position for him and others at the time.

Edwards, writing from the USA, was intimately aware of the rising status of African American athletes in that country, but for him this was little consolation in a society where people of color were systematically subjugated. For that reason, Edwards saw in sport an opportunity for Black athletes to advocate on behalf of communities of color. This initially involved his leadership of United Students for Action, a protest group at San Jose University (where he taught sociology), which put forward demands to turn around the mistreatment of the institution's Black athletes. Edwards was articulate, calculating, and imposing, combining his experience as an athlete with the critical thinking of an academic. He was instrumental in galvanizing an "increasing involvement of African American athletes in the Civil Rights Movement," which gave credence to the "controversial practice of using sport to [try to] achieve racial equality" (Wiggins, 2014, p. 261).

Concurrently, Edwards was instrumental in the establishment of the Olympic Project for Human Rights, which, in essence, called for a Black boycott of the 1968 Mexico City

Olympic Games or, at the very least, to use international exposure from the Games to high-light racial inequality in America. Edwards (1979, p. 2) later acknowledged the immense challenge of bringing any of this to fruition, though he noted that his principal problem was "Black America's highly illusionary perspective on sports." He lamented that "Black people had been brainwashed" about the virtues of sport in their lives, so the idea of using this adored cultural practice in an adversarial manner seemed "ludicrous," "treasonous," even "*unthinkable*" (p. 2). Whereas James saw within sport some prospects for reconfiguring intergroup relationships, Edwards took a more adversarial position by insisting that sport instead provided an illusion of progress for Black people. The few who "made it" in ath-letic pursuits were a tiny minority of a wider African American community that was subjugated. Yet sport remained a tantalizing attraction, with athletic purists—whatever their skin color—uncomfortable with explicit efforts to use sport to advocate political dissent (Edwards, 1969).

Within the Olympic Project for Human Rights there was discussion about protest strategy: an Olympic boycott never took place, and, despite Edwards's wishes, African American athletes took part in celebratory medal ceremonies featuring the Stars and Stripes and the "Star-Spangled Banner" (Wiggins, 2014). A notable exception was winning sprinters Tommie Smith and John Carlos on the medal stand in solemn repose, without shoes, one arm raised, wearing a black glove; they sought to convey a message about U.S. racism, African American poverty, and a need for Black empowerment. After this display, Smith and Carlos were ordered home by Olympic authorities; at the time their symbolic dissent was widely considered heinous (Bass, 2004). For Edwards, the "Black Power Salute" offered a tangible, even if frustratingly exceptional, moment for sport to be used as a site for the ne-gotiation of equitable norms and rules in wider society (Henderson, 2008). The mantra that "sport and politics should not mix" largely persisted in the United States, but Edwards and a growing cohort of athlete-focused activists continued their fight, and by 1971 were able to point to some "improvement in the overall racial situation in the sports arena" (Edwards, 1971, p. 32). Thus, much like James, Edwards was indeed interested in the sports field as a site for the pursuit of racial equity.

Developers

One of the principal tasks of sport scholars has been to document and, as appropriate, rec-ognize the accomplishments of people of color and ethnic minorities in sport, especially given long-standing constraints to their participation (Porter, 1995, 2004). That enterprise continues today, especially among historians charged with the task of investigating and interpreting change over time (Kirwin, 2005; Wiggins, 2008). Given that the groups under focus have been subjugated or marginalized, there have been growing efforts to seek out the voices of contemporaries. Oral history therefore emerged as a crucial method. For example, Fussman (2007), in pursuing the impact of Jackie Robinson's breaking of the color bar (in 1947), interviewed some 100 retired Major League baseballers about Robinson's legacy for both the American game and wider society. In a similar vein, Henderson (2013), when conducting a retrospective analysis of Black activism and U.S. sport, drew upon the oral testimony of more than 40 athletes.

No surprise, though, that the most abundant scholarly focus has been contemporary sport policy, practice, and experience—which is the domain of the social sciences. What have been the most significant developments? In terms of sport sociology, Carrington (2013, p. 389) asserts that, from the early 1960s to the mid-1990s, the field was mainly characterized by the task of "measuring" racism in sport: racial disparities in salary, unequal opportunities in leadership roles, relative absence from managerial positions, and so on. All of that was important. But there were significant gaps. In the United States, for example, Native Americans were often overlooked in scholarship that focused, almost exclusively, on African Americans, while Latino communities, which were especially prominent in baseball, failed to capture much academic interest. However, from the mid-1990s onward the international sports studies research field evolved to include a wider spectrum of "minority" communities. Historians helped to catalyze this, such as with Tatz's (1995a, 1995b) work on the racial politics of Indigenous Australians in sport, along with anthropologists such as King and Springwood (2001a, 2001b), whose field research included critiques of the cultural appropriation of Native American mascots in U.S. professional and college sports.

A further developmental weakness was identified. Questions of equity in sport studies had focused principally on the economic and policy concerns of nonwhite *male* athletes: what the college scholarship opportunities were, whether player salaries were fair, discussions about affirmative action for Black coaches, and so on. While such questions remained critical, there were calls to frame sports studies research more equitably—as a topic of concern for all genders (Hall, 1988). Change was afoot. For example, a special issue of the *Journal of Sport History* was devoted to "ethnicity, gender, and sport in diverse historical contexts," which featured papers on masculinities and femininities in the context of minority diaspora experiences (Borish & Gems, 2000). There had also been pointed efforts to redress the relative absence of research into women from minority backgrounds: how, for example, had the U.S. Title IX influenced their athletic participation in educational institutions (Abney & Richey, 1992)?

Demographic changes in the wake of increased global migration proved significant to the developmental role of sport in society. For example, during the last quarter of the 20th century, the genesis of multicultural policy in ethnoracially diverse countries like Australia, Britain, and Canada catalyzed discussion about how, and indeed whether, sport was meeting the needs of a growing volume of culturally diverse constituents. Multiculturalism, as an embryonic form of public policy, reflected a move away from assimilationist approaches to ethnic ancestry and toward a more hybrid and inclusive sense of civic identity. In its ideal form, multiculturalism combined the freedom for ethnic minorities to connect proactively with their heritage, while they, in turn, respected the laws, norms, and values of the nation of which they were a part (Ashcroft & Bevir, 2017; Jupp, 1997; Wayland, 1997). From the perspective of sport, early efforts to engage migrants in sport had typified the assimilationist approach: new arrivals were expected to blend in with existing organizational norms and structures or were simply ignored, serving to marginalize them (Taylor & Toohey, 1995, 1998). As we will see, avowedly *multicultural* sport policies took longer to evolve.

Innovators

Sports studies has undergone incremental conceptual shifts. A spark was ignited in the early 1990s when feminist sport-focused academics made a clarion call for action, combining a demand for research into ethnoracial minorities along with theoretical innovation to better enable that. While materialist critiques had typified research about distributive injustices in sport for minorities, feminist scholars now advocated a stronger emphasis on relational approaches. A key to this was the cultural turn in social research, which emphasized both lived experience and human agency: women of color were, from that perspective, not simply passive participants within a white-controlled sport system (Birrell, 1989; Smith, 1992). Indeed, in a vein similar to the new breed of social historians, there was now a concerted realization that the voices of "ordinary" people—in this case women of color and minority-group females—matter to the investigative process.

What remained, of course, was the application of research techniques to enable these calls to action. Testimonials, whether oral (via interview) or textual (via journaling) had long been the stock in trade of qualitative scholars in fields like social psychology and ethnography, but these tools were not typical of the materialist tradition in sport studies. However, practice-oriented scholars in sport sociology had begun to develop more intimate and reflexive relationships with respondents who, in the new cultural milieu, were not mere objects but active partners in the investigative process (Carrington, Chivers, & Williams, 1987; Scraton, Caudwell, & Holland, 2005; Sterkenburg & Knoppers, 2004). That approach has been mirrored by scholars engaged in sport for development, with action research and fieldwork methods featuring in projects that involve sport as a tool for improved social outcomes. There are, of course, complexities associated with qualitative scholarship involving people of color, ethnic minorities, and various vulnerable populations, so researchers are rightfully confronted with questions about their positionality, capacity, authenticity, and so on, along with concerns about neocolonialism in the guise of "aid" (Darnell & Hayhurst, 2011; Sugden, Adair, Schulenkorf, & Frawley, 2019).

Another key trend has been scholarship taking hybrid approaches, combining interests in race and/or ethnicity with evaluations of how these areas have been indelibly shaped by other sociocultural factors, such as gender, sexuality, ableism, ageism, and citizenship (Andrew, 1995; Crenshaw, 1991). Arguably, this innovation was provoked by the African American scholar Patricia Collins (1990) in her potent tome *Black Feminist Thought*. Prior to the cultural turn in sports studies, the first wave of scholars principally focused on physical activity as a site that was normatively male and heterosexual and featured able-bodied competitors. That materialist approach singled out class relationships among men in sport, along with questions about the exercise of power by men in authority (Brohm, 1978; Morgan, 1994; Stone, 1971). A second wave of scholars then rightfully advocated for a gender lens and, while women were their initial focus, laid the foundations for writers in other areas, such as queer studies, body culture studies, postcolonialism, and so on, who then enabled these genres to be pursued within race/ethnicity contexts (Bale & Cronin, 2003; Caudwell, 2006; Cole, 1993; Friedman & van Ingen, 2011). That, in turn, encouraged more diverse contributions to sport studies, featuring a growing acceptance of multidimensional experiences via the emerging intersectional research paradigm, with race and/or ethnicity explicitly combined with concurrent experiences, such as sexuality, socioeconomic status, age, and religion (Anderson & McCormack, 2010; Flintoff, Fitzgerald, & Scraton, 2008; Watson & Scraton, 2012).

Disruptors

Postpositivist sensibilities have certainly impacted the social science and humanities in recent decades. In particular, postmodern thinking and language have disrupted traditional forms of scholarly evaluation and communication, questioning disciplinary boundaries, metanarratives, and the idealism of objectivity in the social and physical sciences (Best & Kellner, 1991). In terms of sport studies, this involved researchers seeing themselves as participants rather than objective observers, which overturned the pretense of the "innocent" author. As Rail (2002, p. 198) has put it, postmodernism is "guided by multiple voices" and the input of "ordinary people." Postmodern scholarship has, in that sense, complemented intersectional research, especially as both genres pursue the experiences of people who have been subjugated; they also focus on the fluidity and hybridity of individual and group identities. However, in terms of sport research practice, intersectionality has been more easily adopted; postmodernism has had a more disruptive, though nonetheless creative, impact on the conceptual status quo (Bale & Christensen, 2004; Phillips & Munslow, 2012). Indeed, in terms of research into race/ethnicity and sport, postmodern perspectives have emerged in a raft of areas, such as the deconstruction of racialized masculinities and femininities, discourses underpinning the racial stereotyping of Black athlete celebrities, and the cultivation of postmodern masculinities to de-deconstruct ethnicities in Australian soccer (Andrews, 1996; Carniel, 2008; Leonard, 2004; de Oca, 2012).

However, in terms of sport and race scholarship, the most important disruptor to conventional research has arguably been critical race theory (CRT). This approach arose in the late 20th century, prompted by Black legal scholars who asserted that the American legal system was not, as often asserted, fair to everyone, but was instead part of a societywide system of white supremacy that enabled the routine subjugation of Blacks (Bell, 1995; Crenshaw, 1989; Taylor, 1998). Although the civil rights movement had established the principle of equality for all under the law, in practice the application of that law—along with various rules and norms in American society—were still marshaled to protect white privilege and oppress Blacks (Sensoy & DiAngelo, 2017).

Sport sociologists have engaged prolifically with CRT as a theoretical framework, asserting that sport is not, as conservatives tout, "color blind" but instead deeply rooted in a wider (from a Western perspective) system of white supremacy (Hylton, 2012). As Hylton (2008, p. 23) has deftly put it, CRT has a radical imperative: its goal is to resist "the passive reproduction of established practices, knowledge and resources" that marginalize rather than centralize the question of "race," racism, and racial logic in sport. Conceptually, while CRT aligns with postmodernism's commitment to hear alternative voices, the deliberative approach of CRT moves the researcher into the position of advocate. Hylton and others, much like the founders of CRT, are firmly committed to a cause (Cooper, Nwadike, & Macaulay, 2017; Hawkins, Carter-Francique, & Cooper, 2016; Hylton, 2005, 2010; Kochanek & Erickson, 2019).

This moves them away from postmodern positions that presuppose value relativism and distrust claims to truth (Wiltshire, 2018). Racism, CRT scholars aver, is very real and systematic, and thus it ought not be limited to the status of "one perspective" by relativists (Singer, 2005). In effect, therefore, CRT serves to disrupt the distrust about deliberation that underpins postmodernism, though that relativist paradigm had itself disrupted confidence in the modernist worldview of positivism and objectivity.

In that respect, CRT is more closely aligned with critical realism (Lopez & Potter, 2001; Sousa, 2010), a philosophy of knowledge which asserts "that it is possible for social science to refine and improve its knowledge about the real world over time" and, to do so, make claims that are justifiable yet incomplete in that knowledge is "historical, contingent, and changing" (Archer et al., 2016, p. 7). In a sport studies context, critical realism has attracted scholars interested in transformative change, often using fieldwork to explore goals like improved intergroup (i.e., ethnic minority and majority) relations (Sugden, 2010, 2015) and the social integration of migrants (Ley, Karus, Wiesbauer, Barrio, & Spaaij, 2021; Luguetti, Singehebhuye, & Spaaij, 2020).

DEBATES

Insiders and Outsiders

There remain many topics of debate within scholarship around race/ethnicity in sport, but there is scope within this section to outline only some of the unresolved or most pressing issues. To begin, we explore the question of authenticity in scholarship: Are those within a social group best placed to conduct research about that community? Can outsiders make legitimate and significant contributions? The cultural turn in social science research has underscored the importance of investigator positionality. From that perspective, authors ought to write themselves into their text, being overt about their worldview, social background, and relevant experience, all of this helping to address questions of framing, authenticity, and expertise (Bourke, 2014; Fisher, 2014; Mason-Bish, 2019).

In a sport and race context, critical responses to two books provide a window into the challenges (and possibilities) of insider/outsider research. As mentioned previously, the African American scholar Harry Edwards (1969) had controversially insisted that the playing field was too often deemed to be a space beyond racial critique, and that sport successes offered an illusion of wider progress for Black people. Nearly 30 years later, the white American scholar John Hoberman (1997a) made similar assessments in his controversial book *Darwin's Athletes: How Sport Has Damaged Black America and Preserved the Myth of Race*. But Hoberman went further: he asserted that the overrepresentation of African Americans in sports like basketball and football was a consequence of the "hoops dream" phenomenon. This was not simply the dream of dribbling out of poverty; it also spoke to racial stereotyping: according to convention, to be Black was to be "physically adept" but "intellectually weak" compared to whites.

While Edwards's efforts to politicize and radicalize sport were roundly applauded by critics (Brooks & Althouse, 2013; Thompson, 1971), Hoberman's efforts to counter the convention that sport was overwhelmingly beneficial to African Americans was almost universally castigated, often with hostility (Hoberman, 1997b, 1998; Shropshire & Smith, 1998). Part of Hoberman's critique was that Black academics had too often been cheerleaders for Black accomplishments in sport without deeply considering its mythopoeic attributes. He singled out Edwards as the foremost exception to that trend (Hoberman, 1997a). Three years later, though, Edwards remarked that Hoberman's critique was flawed; he countered that the volume and success of Blacks in sport need not be traded off against the need for more African American contributions in other walks of life (Leonard, 2000). Hoberman, meanwhile, felt that his position as a white academic was central to the hostile response he received from Black scholars. Unlike researchers influenced by the cultural turn, Hoberman had not thought through how to write himself into the narrative or to demonstrate his authenticity as a critic by way of engaging with Black scholars throughout the research process. While acknowledging in retrospect that he might have been more active in these ways, Hoberman (1997a) still felt that individuals outside a group have the potential to offer novel insights *because* they are interested in the welfare of others yet *have not* faced their experiences. The Edwards-Hoberman cases are salient because author positioning has now become more important than ever, while the question of insider/outsider perspectives remains a subject of debate.

Racial Stereotyping

Around the Western world, as people of color became more prominent in elite-level sport, they often impressed by way of performance. The influence of class and status meant that minority groups tended to have scant representation in "expensive" sports like golf, yachting, and motor racing, which were dominated by affluent whites. However, in activities where equipment was not costly or was provided gratis by being part of a team, people of color came to have a substantial—even dominant—on-field presence by the late 20th century. Whether in basketball, track and field, or American or Australian Rules football, Black athletes appeared in unprecedented numbers and with substantial impact (Bale & Sang, 1996; Gorman et al., 2016; McKissack, 1999; Ross, 2016). Social researchers explained that people of color were benefiting from increased opportunities to play; racism had certainly not evaporated from sport, but segregation or exclusion on the basis of race had now become exceptional, not routine (Burnett, 2019; Robinson, 2017).

Black acumen in high-profile sports spurred theories about why this was so. One thing seemed obvious: athletes from minority groups, such as those who are African American, Aboriginal, and Māori, were drawn to sports that rewarded talent irrespective of skin color. This is not to suggest an absence of inequality in playing ranks, but the presence of athletes of color provided role models in minority communities. Aside from environmental influences (nurture), some pundits offered biological explanations (nature). Prior to Hoberman's (1997a) criticism about racial stereotyping of African American (male) capabilities, some Black scholars had themselves pointed out that athletes of color were being typecast as "naturally" suited to physical activity but less suited to mental activity—the so-called brawn-versus-brain dichotomy (Sammons, 1994; Smith, 1995). Racial folklore was at the core of attitudes about what people were capable of according to "race." For example, in the 1990s, champion (white) golfer Jack Nicklaus mused that the reason there were not more African American golfers playing at the highest level is because Blacks have "different muscles that react in different ways" (quoted in Hatfield, 1996, p. 38). Then along came golfers of color who took home major titles: the Indo-Fijian Vijay Singh, the Māori Michael Campbell, and the Black (albeit ethnoracially diverse) American player Tiger Woods.

In the past two decades, social researchers have tackled the persistence of racial folklore in sport, as well as its impact. Such discourses work to marginalize people of color (as with the Nicklaus example) or position them as biologically "gifted"—depending on the sport in question. In Australia, for instance, it is common for Indigenous boys to believe they are "born to play" either Australian Rules or rugby league football but are, by virtue of *being* Indigenous, unsuited to academic pursuits. That is not only a question of external stereotyping; glorification of Black athleticism is widely believed—and commonly celebrated—within Indigenous communities (Adair, 2012a; Godwell, 2000; Williams, 2017). Recently, Indigenous Australian Rules footballers have moved to counter the "Black magic" myth by emphasizing that extremely hard work and thousands of hours of practice are needed for sporting success (Adair & Stronach, 2011). Two icons of the game, Adam Goodes and Michael O'Loughlin, have also responded by setting up an educational foundation for Indigenous youth (Osborne, 2019). The message is that success comes in many forms and that academic achievement is as important as athletic acumen (Evans, Wilson, Dalton, & Georgakis, 2015).

Beyond racial folklore, the rise to prominence (and in some cases dominance) by athletes of color, especially in track and field, has attracted growing scholarly interest—among sociologists and sports scientists—but remains highly controversial (Entine, 2008; St Louis, 2004). One of the dangers in all of this is to conflate population genetics with "race." There is an old joke that if someone wants to be an Olympic champion, they ought to choose their parents wisely. To that extent, it makes no sense to speak of common athletic acumen among the "African race"—whether among those on the continent or their transatlantic descendants. In very crude terms, the typical somatotype and gait of a West African runner is very different from that of an East African runner; one is anatomically well positioned to sprint (Pitsiladis, Davis, & Johnson, 2011), while the other is well suited for distance running (Onywera, 2009). That is a product of heredity, not "race" (Cerit, 2020; MacArthur & North, 2005). Of course, physiology is only ever part of an explanation for acumen or otherwise—environmental influences are also crucial (Irving, Charlton, Morrison, Facey, & Buchanan, 2013; Taylor, 2016). This is where stereotype deficits have an impact. Hoberman worried about the unintended consequences of the African American obsession with sport; others have since pointed out that whites are now less likely to pursue athletic activities where, they believe, Blacks are "naturally" better than they (Azzarito & Harrison, 2008; Walton & Butryn, 2006) Racial stereotyping, in various forms, therefore remains a significant topic of discussion.

Athlete Advocacy: Antiracism and Social Justice

In an age of the 24-hour news cycle and social media, athletes have never been in a better position to leverage their profile in the interests of solidarity with a cause. The year 2020 proved pivotal when many American athletes—colored and white—took a stand against racial injustice by taking a knee in solemn protest. This action was not new; it had been championed by NFL player Colin Kaepernick back in 2016. That action was vehemently opposed by President Trump and other white nationalists (Boykoff & Carrington, 2020; Dickerson & Hodler, 2020). What changed in 2020 was that an African American man, George Floyd, was murdered by a white policeman, and, in tragic irony, the officer used a knee to suffocate Floyd. The murder was captured on video and shared globally, to widespread horror. Athletes around the world, like other concerned people, were determined to provide a symbolic demonstration of their distress and support for antiracism. The Black Lives Matter movement became a wider part of the discourse of contemporary sport (Evans, Agergaard, Campbell, Hylton, & Lenneis, 2017).

American sports bodies, some of which had a checkered history around questions of racial equality, mostly chimed in (Hylton, 2020). Some athletes, while stating they supported the right to protest, decided not to take a knee, which—to skeptics—called into question their sincerity (Bailey, 2020). Yet there were also wildly unexpected reforms: for instance, the typically conservative NASCAR organization decreed that the Confederate flag, long associated with white supremacy, would no longer be welcome at race tracks (Almasy, 2020). Elsewhere, though, the International Olympic Committee equivocated about what athlete advocates might say or do at the Tokyo Games. The IOC concluded that the playing field and the podium were not appropriate places for statements or symbolism that went beyond the sportive nature of the event (O'Shea, Adair, Maxwell, & Stronach, 2020). Advocacy groups such as Global Athlete argue that the athlete voice is a human right and that the IOC should not be trying to silence sportspeople on a matter of conscience (DeGeorge, 2020). The IOC has, however, resisted modifying its stand to provide guidelines about athlete expression. Yet for those advocating unfettered speech there may be unintended consequences: athletes devoted to MAGA and white nationalism, among other possibilities (Maese, 2021). All of this is difficult and will be a subject for ongoing debate.

CONCLUSION

This chapter underscores the complex and often imprecise nature of "race" and ethnicity in sport. There have been important changes, many continuities, and new challenges. The playing field is now much more open to people of color and ethnic minorities. Indeed, the theater of sport has never been more cosmopolitan. But racism and bigotry toward athlete "others" has hardly disappeared from stadiums, despite dissuasive efforts by sporting bodies and security personnel. In the United Kingdom, for example, the Football Association (2021) recently pleaded with spectators to respect the desire of players on the English men's team to take a knee as an expression of solidarity with global antiracism sentiments. For some fans in English football, this symbolism triggered antagonism rather than empathy, with flagrant booing a measure of their displeasure.

Of course, historically, the theater of sport has long provided an opportunity to either adore or abuse athlete actors. Some of that is itself theatrical, with crowds applauding or booing in repertoire, in tune with the ebb and flow of the sports play. Yet there are individuals and groups for whom the sporting stage is an opportunity, through the use of gesture, commentary, or chant, to express revulsion toward "others" they deem worthy of contempt—simply for "existing." From that bigoted and perverse perspective, many athletes are fair game for abuse *because* they are Black, Brown, Asian, Muslim, and so on.

Beyond the sports field, social media, which connects athletes with fans around the world, is a source of both adulation and vilification. Social media platforms have yet to adequately address the problem of trolling, let alone bigotry and hatred toward others on the basis of attributes like "race," ethnicity, gender, and so on. Whereas athletes once flooded to social media to promote their team, sport, and personal brand, many are now cautious about the risk of being subjected to existential abuse.

Finally, and perhaps most important, people of color are still vastly underrepresented in managerial, administrative, and broadcasting roles. The world of sport, especially that conceived in the West, was devised by and for white men—not just as athletes but as administrators, promoters, scribes, and commentators. While the playing field has become more colorful, the organization, business, and mediatization of sport still represent what might be called a white ceiling, something that few without that privilege rise through. If sport is ever to really "mirror" society, as is often claimed, then plenty of change lies ahead.

References

Abney, R., & Richey, D. L. (1992). Opportunities for minority women in sport—The impact of Title IX. *Journal of Physical Education, Recreation & Dance, 63*(3), 56–59. doi:10.1080/07303084.1992.10604137.

Adair, D. (2011). *Sport, race, and ethnicity: Narratives of difference and diversity.* Morgantown, WV: Fitness Information Technology.

Adair, D. (2012a). Ancestral footprints: Assumptions of "natural" athleticism among indigenous Australians. *Journal of Australian Indigenous Studies, 15*(2), 23–35.

Adair, D. (2012b). *Sport: Race, ethnicity and identity. Beyond boundaries.* Abingdon, U.K.: Taylor and Francis. doi:10.4324/9780203717981.

Adair, D., & Rowe, D. (2010). Beyond boundaries? "Race," ethnicity and identity in sport. *International Review for the Sociology of Sport, 45*(3), 251–257. doi:10.1177/1012690210378798.

Adair, D., & Stronach, M. (2011). Natural-born athletes? Australian Aboriginal people and the double-edged lure of professional sport. In J. Long & K. Spracklen (Eds.), *Sport and challenges to racism* (pp. 117–134). London: Palgrave Macmillan. doi:10.1057/9780230305892_8.

Almasy, S. (2020, June 11). NASCAR bans Confederate flags at all races, events. *CNN.* https://edition.cnn.com/2020/06/10/us/nascar-bans-confederate-flag-spt-trnd/index.html.

Anderson, E., & McCormack, M. (2010). Intersectionality, critical race theory, and American sporting oppression: Examining Black and gay male athletes. *Journal of Homosexuality, 57*(8), 949–967. doi:10.1080/00918369.2010.503502.

Andrew, C. (1995). Ethnicities, citizenship and feminisms: Theorizing the political practices of intersectionality. *Nationalism and Ethnic Politics, 1*(3), 64–81. doi:10.1080/13537119508428439.

Andrews, D. L. (1996). The fact(s) of Michael Jordan's Blackness: Excavating a floating racial signifier. *Sociology of Sport Journal, 13*(2), 125–158. doi:10.1123/ssj.13.2.125.

Archer, M., Decoteau, C., Gorski, P., Little, D., Porpora, D., Rutzou, T., . . . Vandenberghe, F. (2016). What is critical realism? *Perspectives, 2*(38), 4–9.

Ashcroft, R. T., & Bevir, M. (2017). Multiculturalism in contemporary Britain: Policy, law and theory. *Critical Review of International Social and Political Philosophy, 21*(1), 1–21. doi:10.1080/13698230.2017.1398443.

Azzarito, L., & Harrison, L. (2008). White men can't jump. *International Review for the Sociology of Sport, 43*(4), 347–364. doi:10.1177/1012690208099871.

Bailey, A. (2020, July 24). Giants reliever Sam Coonrod explains why he didn't kneel for Black Lives Matter moment before opener. *USA Today.* https://www.usatoday.com/story/sports/mlb/2020/07/24/sam-coonrod-giants-reliever-why-he-didnt-kneel-blm-moment/5500442002/.

Bale, J., & Christensen, M. K. (2004). *Post-Olympism: Questioning sport in the twenty-first century.* Oxford: Berg.

Bale, J., & Cronin, M. (2003). *Sport and postcolonialism.* Oxford: Berg.

Bale, J., & Sang, J. (1996). *Kenyan running: Movement culture, geography, and global change.* London: Frank Cass.

Bass, A. (2004). *Not the triumph but the struggle: The 1968 Olympics and the making of the Black athlete.* Minnesota: University of Minnesota Press.

Bell, D. A. (1995). Who's afraid of critical race theory? *University of Illinois Law Review, 1995*(4), 893–910.

Best, S., & Kellner, D. (1991). *Postmodern theory, critical interrogations.* Basingstoke, U.K.: Macmillan.

Birrell, S. (1989). Racial relations theories and sport: Suggestions for a more critical analysis. *Sociology of Sport Journal, 6*(3), 212–227. doi:10.1123/ssj.6.3.212.

Blake, A. (1996). *The body language: The meaning of modern sport.* London: Lawrence & Wishart.

Borish, L. J., & Gems, G. R. (2000). Introduction: Ethnicity, gender, and sport in diverse historical contexts. *Journal of Sport History, 27*(3), 377–381.

Bourke, B. (2014). Positionality: Reflecting on the research process. *Qualitative Sociology, 19*(4), 471–495.

Boykoff, J., & Carrington, B. (2020). Sporting dissent: Colin Kaepernick, NFL activism, and media framing contests. *International Review for the Sociology of Sport, 55*(7), 829–849. doi:10.1177/1012690219861594.

Brohm, J.-M. (1978). *Sport, a prison of measured time: Essays.* London: Ink Links.

Brooks, D., & Althouse, R. (2013). Revolt of the Black athlete. *Journal for the Study of Sports and Athletes in Education, 3*(2), 195–214. doi:10.1179/ssa.2009.3.2.195.

Burnett, C. (2019). Value of sport in post-apartheid South Africa. *South African Journal for Research in Sport, Physical Education and Recreation, 41*(2), 11–27. doi:10.10520/ejc-1756e78f5d.

Carniel, J. (2008). Sheilas, wogs and metrosexuals: Masculinity, ethnicity and Australian soccer. *Soccer & Society, 10*(1), 73–83. doi:10.1080/14660970802472676.

Carrington, B. (2013). The critical sociology of race and sport: The first fifty years. *Annual Review of Sociology, 39*(1), 379–398. doi:10.1146/annurev-soc-071811-145528.

Carrington, B., Chivers, T., & Williams, T. (1987). Gender, leisure and sport: A case-study of young people of South Asian descent. *Leisure Studies, 6*(3), 265–279. doi:10.1080/02614368700390211.

Caudwell, J. (2006). *Sport, sexualities and queer/theory.* Oxford: Routledge. doi:10.4324/9780203020098.

Cerit, M. (2020). Genetics and athletic performance. *Research in Physical Education, Sport and Health, 9*(2), 65–76. doi:10.46733/pesh20920065c.

Cole, C. L. (1993). Resisting the canon: Feminist cultural studies, sport, and technologies of the body. *Journal of Sport & Social Issues, 17*(2), 77–97. doi:10.1177/019372359301700202.

Collins, P. H. (1990). *Black feminist thought: Knowledge, consciousness, and the politics of empowerment.* Cambridge, MA: Unwin Hyman.

Cooper, J. N., Nwadike, A., & Macaulay, C. (2017). A critical race theory analysis of big-time college sports: Implications for culturally responsive and race-conscious sport leadership. *Journal of Issues in Intercollegiate Athletics, 10,* 204–233.

Crenshaw, K. (1989). Demarginalizing the intersection of race and sex: A Black feminist critique of antidiscrimination doctrine, feminist theory and antiracist politics. *University of Chicago Legal Forum, 1*(8), 139 167.

Crenshaw, K. (1991). Mapping the margins: Intersectionality, identity politics, and violence against women of color. *Stanford Law Review, 43*(6), 1241–1299. doi:10.2307/1229039.

Cunningham, G. B. (2019). *Diversity and inclusion in sport organizations: A multilevel perspective* (4th ed.). New York: Routledge.

Darnell, S. C., & Hayhurst, L. M. C. (2011). Sport for decolonization. *Progress in Development Studies, 11*(3), 183–196. doi:10.1177/146499341001100301.

DeGeorge, M. (2020, June 14). Global athlete calls on IOC to "immediately abolish" ban on kneeling. *Swimming World.* https://www.swimmingworldmagazine.com/news/global-athlete-calls-on-ioc-to-immediately-abolish-olympic-ban-on-kneeling/.

de Oca, J. M. (2012). White domestic goddess on a postmodern plantation: Charity and commodity racism in *The Blind Side*. *Sociology of Sport Journal, 29*(2), 131–150. doi:10.1123/ssj.29.2.131.

Dickerson, N., & Hodler, M. (2020). "Real men stand for our nation": Constructions of an American nation and anti-Kaepernick memes. *Journal of Sport and Social Issues, 45*, 329–357. doi:10.1177/0193723520950537.

Dixit, P. (2018). Decolonial strategies in world politics: C. L. R. James and the writing and playing of cricket. *Globalizations, 15*(3), 1–13. doi:10.1080/14747731.2018.1424284.

Edwards, H. (1969). *The revolt of the Black athlete*. New York: Free Press.

Edwards, H. (1971). The sources of the Black athlete's superiority. *The Black Scholar, 3*(3), 32–41. doi:10.1080/00064246.1971.11431195.

Edwards, H. (1979). The Olympic Project for Human Rights: An assessment ten years later. *The Black Scholar, 10*(6–7), 2–8. doi:10.1080/00064246.1979.11414041.

Entine, J. (2008). *Taboo: Why Black athletes dominate sports and why we're afraid to talk about it*. New York: Public Affairs.

Evans, A. B., Agergaard, S., Campbell, P. I., Hylton, K., & Lenneis, V. (2017). "Black Lives Matter": Sport, race and ethnicity in challenging times. *European Journal for Sport and Society, 17*(4), 289–300. doi:10.1080/16138171.2020.1833499.

Evans, J. R., Wilson, R., Dalton, B., & Georgakis, S. (2015). Indigenous participation in Australian sport: The perils of the "Panacea" proposition. *Cosmopolitan Civil Societies: An Interdisciplinary Journal, 7*(1), 53–79. doi:10.5130/ccs.v7i1.4232.

Fenton, S. (2013). *Ethnicity* (2nd ed.). Hoboken, NJ: Wiley.

Fisher, K. T. (2014). Positionality, subjectivity, and race in transnational and transcultural geographical research. *Gender, Place & Culture, 22*(4), 456–473. doi:10.1080/0966369x.2013.879097.

Flintoff, A., Fitzgerald, H., & Scraton, S. (2008). The challenges of intersectionality: Researching difference in physical education. *International Studies in Sociology of Education, 18*(2), 73–85. doi:10.1080/09620210802351300.

Football Association. (2021, June 12). A message to England supporters. https://www.thefa.com/news/2021/jun/12/a-message-to-england-supporters-20210611.

Friedman, M. T., & van Ingen, C. (2011). Bodies in space: Spatializing physical cultural studies. *Sociology of Sport Journal, 28*(1), 85–105. doi:10.1123/ssj.28.1.85.

Fussman, C. (2007). *After Jackie: Pride, prejudice, and baseball's forgotten heroes: An oral history*. New York: ESPN Books.

Ganideh, S. F. A. (2020). Demystifying Arabs: Is soccer Arab societies' "crystal ball"? *National Identities, 23*(5), 531–553. doi:10.1080/14608944.2020.1830265.

Gates, E. N. (1997). *The concept of race in natural and social science*. London: Routledge.

Gems, G. R. (2012). Sport and the Italian American quest for whiteness. *Sport in History, 32*(4), 479–503. doi:10.1080/17460263.2012.738610.

Godwell, D. (2000). Playing the game: Is sport as good for race relations as we'd like to think? *Australian Aboriginal Studies, 1–2*, 12–19.

Gorman, S., Judd, B., Reeves, K., Osmond, G., Klugman, M., & McCarthy, G. (2016). Aboriginal rules: The Black history of Australian football. *International Journal of the History of Sport, 32*(16), 1947–1962. doi:10.1080/09523367.2015.1124861.

Graves, J. L. (2008). *The emperor's new clothes: Biological theories of race at the millennium*. New Brunswick, NJ: Rutgers University Press.

Hale, H. E. (2004). Explaining ethnicity. *Comparative Political Studies, 37*(4), 458–485. doi:10.1177/0010414003262906.

Hall, M. A. (1988). The discourse of gender and sport: From femininity to feminism. *Sociology of Sport Journal, 5*(4), 330–340. doi:10.1123/ssj.5.4.330.

Hallinan, C., & Jackson, S. J. (2008). *Social and cultural diversity in a sporting world.* Bingley, U.K.: Emerald Group Publishing.

Harris, D. R., & Sim, J. J. (2002). Who is multiracial? Assessing the complexity of lived race. *American Sociological Review, 4*(67), 614–627. doi:10.2307/3088948.

Hartmann, D. (2003). What can we learn from sport if we take sport seriously as a racial force? Lessons from C. L. R. James's *Beyond a Boundary. Ethnic and Racial Studies, 26*(3), 451–483. doi:10.1080/0141987032000067282.

Hatfield, D. (1996). The Jack Nicklaus syndrome. *The Humanist, 56*(4), 38.

Hawkins, B. J., Carter-Francique, A. R., & Cooper, J. N. (2016). *Critical race theory: Black athletic sporting experiences in the United States.* New York: Palgrave Macmillan.

Heaphy, L. A. (2015). *The Negro leagues, 1869-1960.* Jefferson, NC: McFarland.

Henderson, S. (2008). Crossing the line: Sport and the limits of civil rights protest. *International Journal of the History of Sport, 26*(1), 101–121. doi:10.1080/09523360802500576.

Henderson, S. (2013). *Sidelined: How American sports challenged the Black freedom struggle.* Lexington: University Press of Kentucky.

Hoberman, J. M. (1997a). *Darwin's athletes: How sport has damaged Black America and preserved the myth of race.* Boston: Mariner Books.

Hoberman, J. M. (1997b). How not to misread "Darwin's Athletes": A response to Jeffrey T. Sammons. *Journal of Sport History, 24*(3), 389–396.

Hoberman, J. M. (1998). Response to three reviews of "Darwin's Athletes." *Social Science Quarterly, 79*(4), 898–903.

Hockey, K. M., & Horrell, D. G. (2018). *Ethnicity, race, religion: Identities and ideologies in early Jewish and Christian texts, and in modern biblical interpretation.* New York: Bloomsbury Publishing.

Hylton, K. (2005). "Race," sport and leisure: Lessons from critical race theory. *Leisure Studies, 24*(1), 81–98. doi:10.1080/02614360412331313494.

Hylton, K. (2008). *"Race" and sport.* London: Routledge. doi:10.4324/9780203893678.

Hylton, K. (2010). How a turn to critical race theory can contribute to our understanding of "race," racism and anti-racism in sport. *International Review for the Sociology of Sport, 45,* 335–354. doi:10.1177/1012690210371045.

Hylton, K. (2012). Talk the talk, walk the walk: Defining critical race theory in research. *Race, Ethnicity and Education, 15*(1), 23–41. doi:10.1080/13613324.2012.638862.

Hylton, K. (2020). Black Lives Matter in sport. . . ? *Equality, Diversity and Inclusion: An International Journal.* Advance online publication. doi:10.1108/edi-07-2020-0185.

Ibrahim, H. (2015). Toward Black and multiracial "kinship" after 1997, or how a race man became "Cablinasian." *The Black Scholar, 39*(3–4), 23–31. doi:10.1080/00064246.2009.11413495.

Irving, R., Charlton, V., Morrison, E., Facey, A., & Buchanan, O. (2013). Demographic characteristics of world class Jamaican sprinters. *Scientific World Journal, 2013,* 1–5. doi:10.1155/2013/670217. https://www.hindawi.com/journals/tswj/2013/670217/.

James, C. L. R. (1963). *Beyond a boundary.* London: Vintage.

Jensen, S. Q. (2011). Othering, identity formation and agency. *Qualitative Studies, 2*(2), 63–78. doi:10.7146/qs.v2i2.5510.

Jupp, J. (1997). Immigration and national identity: Multiculturalism. In G. Stokes (Ed.), *The politics of identity in Australia* (pp. 132–144). Cambridge: Cambridge University Press.

Kaufman, H., & Galily, Y. (2009). Sport, Zionist ideology and the state of Israel. *Sport in Society, 12*(8), 1013–1027. doi:10.1080/17430430903076316.

King, C. R., & Springwood, C. F. (2001a). *Beyond the cheers: Race as spectacle in college sport.* New York: State University of New York Press.

King, C. R., & Springwood, C. F. (2001b). *Team spirits: The Native American mascots controversy.* Lincoln: University of Nebraska Press.

Kirwin, B. (2005). *Out of the shadows: African American baseball from the Cuban Giants to Jackie Robinson.* Lincoln: University of Nebraska Press.

Kochanek, J., & Erickson, K. (2019). Interrogating positive youth development through sport using critical race theory. *Quest, 72*(2), 1–17. doi:10.1080/00336297.2019.1641728.

Lapchick, R. (2018, May 2). The 2018 Associated Press sports editors racial and gender report card. *ESPN.* https://www.espn.com/espn/story/_/id/23382605/espn-leads-way-hiring-practices-sports-media.

Leonard, D. (2000, April 20). The decline of the Black athlete: An online exclusive extended interview with Harry Edwards. *Colorlines.* https://www.colorlines.com/articles/decline-black-athletean-online-exclusive-extended-interview-harry-edwards.

Leonard, D. J. (2004). The next M.J. or the next O.J.? Kobe Bryant, race, and the absurdity of colorblind rhetoric. *Journal of Sport & Social Issues, 28*(3), 284–313. doi:10.1177/0193723504267546.

Levine, P. (1993). *Ellis Island to Ebbets Field: Sport and the American Jewish experience.* New York: Oxford University Press.

Lewis, M., Bell, T. R., Billings, A. C., & Brown, K. A. (2019). White sportscasters, Black athletes: Race and ESPN's coverage of college football's national signing day. *Howard Journal of Communications, 31*(4), 1–14. doi:10.1080/10646175.2019.1608482.

Ley, C., Karus, F., Wiesbauer, L., Barrio, M. R., & Spaaij, R. (2021). Health, integration and agency: Sport participation experiences of asylum seekers. *Journal of Refugee Studies, 34*(4), 4140–4160. doi:10.1093/jrs/feaa081.

Lopez, J., & Potter, G. (2001). *After postmodernism: An introduction to critical realism.* London: Athlone Press.

Lu, D., Huang, J., Seshagiri, A., Park, H., & Griggs, T. (2020, September 9). Faces of power: 80% are white, even as U.S. becomes more diverse. *New York Times.*https://www.nytimes.com/interactive/2020/09/09/us/powerful-people-race-us.html.

Luguetti, C., Singehebhuye, L., & Spaaij, R. (2020). Towards a culturally relevant sport pedagogy: Lessons learned from African Australian refugee-background coaches in grassroots football. *Sport, Education and Society, 27*(4), 1–13. doi:10.1080/13573322.2020.1865905.

MacArthur, D. G., & North, K. N. (2005). Genes and human elite athletic performance. *Human Genetics, 116*(5), 331–339. doi:10.1007/s00439-005-1261-8.

Maese, R. (2021, January 15). Klete Keller, Olympic gold medal winner, charged for role in capitol riots. *Washington Post.* https://www.washingtonpost.com/sports/2021/01/12/klete-keller-olympic-swimmer-capitol-trump/.

Mangan, J. A., & Ritchie, A. (2004). *Ethnicity, sport, identity: Struggles for status.* London: Frank Cass.

Mason-Bish, H. (2019). The elite delusion: Reflexivity, identity and positionality in qualitative research. *Qualitative Research, 19*(3), 263–276. doi:10.1177/1468794118770078.

McKissack, F. (1999). *Black hoops: The history of African-Americans in basketball.* New York: Scholastic Press.

MJL. (2007, December 16). Jews and sports.https://www.myjewishlearning.com/article/jews-sports/.

Moore, L. (2017). *I fight for a living: Boxing and the battle for Black manhood, 1880–1915.* Champaign: University of Illinois Press.

Moore, L. (2018, September 12). The NFL and a history of Black protest. *AAIHS.*https://www.aaihs.org/the-nfl-and-a-history-of-black-protest/.

Morgan, W. J. (1994). *Leftist theories of sport: A critique and reconstruction.* Urbana-Champagne: University of Illinois Press.

Murray, W. J. (2003). *Bhoys, bears and bigotry: Rangers, Celtic and the Old Firm in the new age of globalised football.* Edinburgh: Mainstream.

Nauright, J., Gobley, A. G., & Wiggins, D. K. (2014). *Beyond C. L. R. James: Shifting boundaries of race and ethnicity in sports.* Fayetteville: University of Arkansas Press.

Norwood, K. J. (2013). *Color matters: Skin tone bias and the myth of a postracial America.* London: Routledge.

Onywera, V. O. (2009). East African runners: Their genetics, lifestyle and athletic prowess. *Medicine and Sport Science, 54,* 102–109. doi:10.1159/000235699.

Osborne, S. (2019). Go Foundation creates student "ecosystem." *Independent Education, 49*(2), 12–13.

O'Shea, M., Adair, D., Maxwell, H., & Stronach, M. (2020, September 18). The Olympics strive for political neutrality. So, how will they deal with surging athlete activism? *The Conversation.* https://theconversation.com/the-olympics-strive-for-political-neutrality-so-how-will-they-deal-with-surging-athlete-activism-144951.

Pew Research Center. (2015). Multiracial in America: Proud, diverse and growing in numbers.https://www.pewresearch.org/wp-content/uploads/sites/3/2015/06/2015-06-11_multiracial-in-america_final-updated.pdf.

Phillips, M. G., & Munslow, A. (2012). *Deconstructing sport history: A postmodern analysis.* Albany: State University of New York Press.

Pitsiladis, Y., Davis, A., & Johnson, D. (2011). The science of speed: Determinants of performance in the 100m sprint. *International Journal of Sports Science & Coaching, 6*(3), 495–498. doi:10.1260/1747-9541.6.3.495.

Porter, D. L. (1995). *African-American sports greats: A biographical dictionary.* Westport, CT: Greenwood Press.

Porter, D. L. (2004). *Latino and African American athletes today: A biographical dictionary.* Westport, CT: Greenwood Press.

Prentiss, C. R. (2003). *Religion and the creation of race and ethnicity: An introduction.* New York: NYU Press.

Rail, G. (2002). Postmodernism and sport studies. In J. A. Maguire & K. Young (Eds.), *Theory, sport and society* (pp. 179–207). Bingley, U.K.: Emerald.

Reynolds, H., & Lake, M. (2008). *Drawing the global colour line.* Melbourne: Melbourne University Publishing.

Robinson, R. L. (2017). *More than just a game: The impact of sports on racial segregation in one southern town* (Unpublished PhD thesis). University of Alabama, Tuscaloosa.

Ross, C. (2016). *Mavericks, money, and men: The AFL, Black players, and the evolution of modern football.* Philadelphia, PA: Temple University Press.

Sammons, J. T. (1994). "Race" and sport: A critical, historical examination. *Journal of Sport History, 21*(3), 203–278.

Scraton, S., Caudwell, J., & Holland, S. (2005). "Bend it like Patel": Centring "race," ethnicity and gender in feminist analysis of women's football in England. *International Review for the Sociology of Sport, 40*(1), 71–88. doi:10.1177/1012690205052169.

Sensoy, O., & DiAngelo, R. (2017). *Is everyone really equal? An introduction to key concepts in social justice education* (2nd ed.). New York: Teachers College Press.

Shropshire, K., & Smith, E. (1998). The Tarzan syndrome. *Journal of Sport & Social Issues, 22*(1), 103–112. doi:10.1177/019372398022001009.

Singer, J. N. (2005). Addressing epistemological racism in sport management research. *Journal of Sport Management, 19*(4), 464–479. doi:10.1123/jsm.19.4.464.

Smith, E. (1995). The self-fulfilling prophecy: Genetically superior African American athletes. *Journal of Sport History, 21*(2), 139–164.

Smith, T. G. (1987). Civil rights on the gridiron: The Kennedy administration and the desegregation of the Washington Redskins. In P. Miller & D. Wiggins (Eds.), *Sport and the color line: Black athletes and race relations in twentieth century America* (pp. 189–208). New York: Routledge. doi:10.4324/9780203497456-19.

Smith, Y. R. (1992). Women of color in society and sport. *Quest, 44*(2), 228–250. doi:10.1080/00336297.1992.10484052.

Sousa, F. J. (2010). Metatheories in research: Positivism, postmodernism, and critical realism. In A. G. Woodside (Ed.), *Organizational culture, business-to-business relationships, and interfirm networks* (pp. 455–503). Bingley, U.K.: Emerald.

Sterkenburg, J. van, & Knoppers, A. (2004). Dominant discourses about race/ethnicity and gender in sport practice and performance. *International Review for the Sociology of Sport, 39*(3), 301–321. doi:10.1177/1012690204045598.

St Louis, B. (2004). Sport and common-sense racial science. *Leisure Studies, 23*(1), 31–46. doi:10.1080/0261436042000182308.

Stidder, G., & Hayes, S. (2013). *Equity and inclusion in physical education and sport* (2nd ed.). New York: Routledge.

Stone, G. P. (1971). *Games, sport, and power*. Boston: E. P. Dutton.

Sugden, J. (2010). Critical left-realism and sport interventions in divided societies. *International Review for the Sociology of Sport, 45*(3), 258–272. doi:10.1177/1012690210374525.

Sugden, J. (2015). Assessing the sociology of sport: On the capacities and limits of using sport to promote social change. *International Review for the Sociology of Sport, 50*(4–5), 606–611. doi:10.1177/1012690214555166.

Sugden, J. T., Adair, D., Schulenkorf, N., & Frawley, S. (2019). Exploring sport and intergroup relations in Fiji: Guidance for researchers undertaking short-term ethnography. *Sociology of Sport Journal, 36*(4), 1–12. doi:10.1123/ssj.2018-0165.

Tatz, C. (1995a). *Obstacle race: Aborigines in sport*. Kensington: UNSW Press.

Tatz, C. (1995b). Racism and sport in Australia. *Race & Class, 36*(4), 43–54. doi:10.1177/030639689503600403.

Tatz, C. (2009). Coming to terms: "Race," ethnicity, identity and Aboriginality in sport. *Australian Aboriginal Studies, 2009*(2), 15–31.

Taylor, E. (1998). A primer on critical race theory: Who are the critical race theorists and what are they saying? *Journal of Blacks in Higher Education*, (19), 122–124.

Taylor, O. W. (2016). It's culture, not genes: Explaining why Jamaican sprinters are the fastest humans on earth. *Caribbean Quarterly, 61*(1), 23–41. doi:10.1080/00086495.2015.11672546.

Taylor, T., & Toohey, K. (1995). Ethnic barriers to sports participation. *Australian Parks & Recreation, 31*(2), 32–36.

Taylor, T., & Toohey, K. (1998). Negotiating cultural diversity for women in sport: From assimilation to multiculturalism. *Race Ethnicity and Education, 1*(1), 75–90. doi:10.1080/1361332980010106.

Thompson, R. (1971). Book reviews: *The Revolt of the Black Athlete* by Harry Edwards. *Race & Class, 12*(4), 507–508. doi:10.1177/030639687101200416.

Todaro, P. (2018, January 12). The NFL: How the hegemonic elite are ruining the greatest sport on Earth. Global Critical Media Literacy Project. https://gcml.org/nfl-hegemonic-elite-ruining-greatest-sport-earth/.

Vine, V. T. L. (1997). Conceptualizing "ethnicity" and "ethnic conflict": A controversy revisited. *Studies in Comparative International Development, 32*(2), 45–75. doi:10.1007/bf02687324.

Walton, T. A., & Butryn, T. M. (2006). Policing the race: U.S. men's distance running and the crisis of whiteness. *Sociology of Sport Journal, 23*(1), 1–28. doi:10.1123/ssj.23.1.1.

Watson, B., & Scraton, S. J. (2012). Leisure studies and intersectionality. *Leisure Studies, 32*(1), 35–47. doi:10.1080/02614367.2012.707677.

Wayland, S. V. (1997). Immigration, multiculturalism and national identity in Canada. *International Journal on Minority and Group Rights, 5*(1), 33–58. doi:10.1163/15718119720907408.

Wiggins, D. K. (2008). *Out of the shadows: A biographical history of African American athletes.* Fayetteville: University of Arkansas Press.

Wiggins, D. K. (2014). "The struggle that must be": Harry Edwards, sport and the fight for racial equality. *International Journal of the History of Sport, 31*(7), 760–777. doi:10.1080/09523367.2014.890431.

Williams, J. (2017). A figurational analysis of how Indigenous students encounter racialization in physical education and school sport. *European Physical Education Review, 24*(1), 76–96. doi:10.1177/1356336x16667372.

Wiltshire, G. (2018). A case for critical realism in the pursuit of interdisciplinarity and impact. *Qualitative Research in Sport, Exercise and Health, 10*(5), 1–18. doi:10.1080/2159676x.2018.1467482.

Yudell, M., Roberts, D., DeSalle, R., & Tishkoff, S. (2016). Taking race out of human genetics. *Science, 351*(6273), 564–565. doi:10.1126/science.aac4951.

CHAPTER 43

....

SPORT, INDIGENEITY, AND NATIVE IDENTITIES

....

TARA KEEGAN AND JENNIFER GUILIANO

THE United Nations Permanent Forum on Indigenous Issues (n.d.) notes that there are "an estimated 370 million people spread across 70 countries worldwide" who define themselves as Native American, First Peoples, First Nations, Indigenous, Metis, as well as those who use tribal, clan, or family specific names. Indigeneity generally is situated within a complicated framing of political, legal, and cultural sovereignty, self-determination, legal and governmental recognition, and linguistic and cultural expression. Indigenous peoples articulate themselves in relationship to land and its use; kinship, family, and community; traditional and contemporary knowledge; as well as history and ceremony (Byrd & Rothberg, 2011). Contemporary framings of indigeneity, both conceptually and in its material realities, have been shaped by the forces of global colonialism, imperialism, and modernity, which have largely forced Indigenous peoples into conflicts over land use, capitalism, citizenship, and social, political, and cultural autonomy. From the loss of millions of acres of land to forced assimilation and cultural and physical genocide, Indigenous peoples have not only faced the challenges of non-Indigenous expansion but have been resilient in preserving communal and traditional knowledges and ways of life.

Studies of Indigenous peoples longitudinally illustrate the vital importance of sport—not contained only to matters surrounding competition, recreation, entertainment, religion, or fitness, but as a product of these contexts and more. This chapter poses that to accurately understand contemporary Indigenous cultures and sport we should look to the historical study of sport to understand the way contemporary sporting societies are manifested through historical sporting practices. Indigenous scholar Nick Estes (Lower Brule Sioux) (2019, p. 14) has explained:

> Indigenous notions of time consider the present to be structured entirely by our past and by our ancestors. There is no separation between past and present, meaning that an alternative future is also determined by our understanding of our past. Our history is the future.

Studying Indigenous sport on Indigenous terms means acknowledging this conception of time. It also requires recognition that studying Indigenous sport is increasingly interdisciplinary within the academy and is reliant on frameworks and insights drawn from literature, history, sociology, and Native American, Indigenous, and First Nations studies (O'Bonsawin, 2017b). Part of how we understand contemporary culture is through its history.

Indigenous sport, therefore, should be understood as both *part of* and *outside of* the mainstream parameters more typically associated with Euro-American sports. After a brief explanation of Native sport prior to colonization, these parameters often take as their starting point the domination of British sporting ideals, followed quickly by explorations of the 19th century and the rise of industrialization, immigration, and American expansion (Gems, Borish, & Pfister, 2008). Where the Euro-American sports paradigm does apply, Indigenous sport histories allow us to credit Indigenous peoples for their critical inventions, developments, and victories in a realm that sought to exclude or appropriate them. Indigenous sport histories offer a competing vision of sport and American territorial expansion before the United States initiated its imperial project around the globe. They also offer insight into women's sports stories centuries before, and disconnected from, the U.S. Title IX context (Walton-Fisette, 2018). Such studies reveal inventions of sporting practices in North America long before the arrival of white settler society and mesh with studies of racism and resistance that reach beyond the better-known structural racism that Black athletes have experienced in American sports (Welch, Siegele, Smith, & Hardin, 2021). In these ways, studies of Indigenous experiences stand to expand scholars' knowledge of issues already at stake in sports scholarship and offer critical examples and implications for those concerned with the role of sport in society. Indigenous sport, as we argue in this chapter, is inextricably interwoven with who Indigenous people are and how they view the world. As such, sport is not merely play but is also a way to consider the richness of Indigenous society before and after colonialism.

A few notes on terminology are warranted as we begin this chapter. The terms "Indian," "Native," and "Indigenous" are all utilized in sport scholarship and discussions of indigeneity more generally. As we largely focus on sport in the lands that became the United States, we use these terms to describe Indigenous peoples there, unless examples call for more particularized characterizations to aid accuracy. In such cases, we use tribal names. In Canada, the terms "First Nations" and "Aboriginal" are common in titles and scholarship, so Canadian examples include those instead of their counterparts in the American context. Similarly, where we touch on Indigenous sport in Australia—another major site of relevant literature—"Aboriginal" reflects common practice.

We also wish to note for readers that we recognize these terms are fraught socially, culturally, and politically for Indigenous peoples and are inextricably tied to colonization and identity. In contrast to many sport histories written in 1970s and 1980s which sought to define what constitutes sport and who "athletes" were, consideration here of Indigenous sporting practices requires us to interrogate these terms critically (Adelman, 1990; Cahn, 1994; Gems, 1997; Levine, 1994; Riess, 2015; Ruck, 1987). As physical games and contests have long permeated Indigenous life, and as they remain connected in many cases to ritual, religion, and ceremony, the people engaged in these activities might not foremost consider themselves athletes. This is often in spite of observers outside of their immediate communities who likely would. Early Euro-American explorers definitely articulated this stance (Culin, 1975; Krus, 2011). As we sketch sport's relationship to indigeneity and Native identity, we acknowledge the imperfection and imprecision of these terms and the political and cultural weight they carry for Indigenous peoples.

ISSUES

In this chapter, we consider how sport connects to Indigenous and non-Indigenous society. While there is a significant need to explore Indigenous sport globally, we focus primarily on the U.S. contexts, which serve as major sites of sporting practices both historically and contemporarily. The chronicling of sport within the lands that became the continental United States generally starts in the early 18th century with dice and card games, cockfighting, horse racing, and bare-knuckle boxing (Gorn, 2012; Riess, 1999, 2011; Sparks, 1992). White men dominate these narratives with few, if any, mentions of Indigenous participation. Yet games, particularly dice and horse racing, were essential activities within Indigenous diplomatic, political, economic, and social exchanges (Belanger, 2011). Indigenous peoples of the U.S. Southwest and Plains leveraged running and horse-racing as both sport and matters of survival. Ute, Crow, Bannock, Shoshone, Diné, and other tribal communities acquired horses from Spanish colonizers and used them to develop and expand the trade networks of 18th-century Mexico (Mitchell, 2020). Horse races between both friendly and hostile communities were common within Apache and Gros Venture communities. Racers and attendees alike would boast of their prowess as racers and as warriors. Racehorses were valuable commodities, and thieves would seek to steal them. Gambling on sport, along with the sports themselves, were threats to colonizers who saw them as immoral and a sign of weakness of character (DeBoer, 2001; Pasquaretta, 2003; Weiner, 2018). Games of chance and games of skill like horse racing, though, allowed Indigenous individuals to assert their wealth, demonstrate strategic thinking, and highlight both cooperative and competitive skill sets (Mitchell, 2020). Today we see similar concerns about gambling in Indigenous communities, yet they have been reframed around discourses of Indigenous sovereignty (Edwards, 2020; Nicoll, 2018; Rand & Light, 2019). More than 350 Native casinos in the United States offer organized gaming on tribal lands; these casinos largely arose after the 1987 Supreme Court decision in *California v. Cabazon Band of Mission Indians*, which spurred tribal establishment of casino businesses.

The identification of precontact Indigenous sporting practices as religious, spiritual, or local customs rather than sporting activities has shaped the ways in which cultural histories have been written; largely precontact Indigenous scholarship is the domain of anthropologists and archaeologists, while postcontact sport is the space of historians and sociologists. This division has encouraged a bias toward written archival evidence rather than the more expansive Indigenous archive of oral histories and material cultures that would be needed to engage with precontact Indigenous sporting practices. It has also highlighted the framing of "modernity" as a key element of sport in the United States. Mel Adelman (1997, pp. 70–71), for example, noted in his discussion of harness racing that "pre-modern" sport has "either non-existent or at best informal and sporadic" organization, that rules were "simple, unwritten and based upon local customs and traditions," and that competition was "locally meaningful" with "no chance for national reputation." Adelman clearly did not conceptualize how sovereign Indigenous nations and their sporting competitions were, in fact, national events between competing communities. While this may seem like a minor distinction, the framing of modernity as a key aspect tied to organized rules, published guides, specialized roles and equipment, and published records would have a long-term impact by marginalizing Indigenous sports as local play rather than part of national sporting stories. Thus, Winnebago players, for example, who would share their successes in war before play to intimidate opponents, are recognized merely for participating in local games rather than in competitive sport against other nations. This marginalization would also encourage scholars and the general public to frame Indigenous sports, even in the 19th and 20th centuries, as static representations unshaped by changes in sporting practices. In the dominant view, "modern" sports emerged in the mid- to late 19th century as urbanization, industrialization, and immigration reshaped American life. As a result, Indigenous communities were largely ignored within featured narratives. This would also encourage sport scholars to subtly reinforce the mistaken public perception that Indigenous sport was something relegated to the past rather than part of contemporary sporting culture (Clevenger, 2020).

Indigenous communities did have organized rules and specialized roles and kept records of their sporting practices. These rules, roles, and records were situated within an Indigenous worldview that appeared unfamiliar to white explorers and the sport scholars who followed. From artistic renderings to oral stories of sporting successes, to elaborate ceremonial clothing for spiritual advisors and physical objects handed down within families and communities, what sport historians once saw as "premodern," Indigenous scholars understand as rich sporting practices that took place in cities, small towns, and rural communities. In part, the focus on the modern, primarily white sports of swimming, golf, and bicycling aligned neatly with the changing world of 19th-century America which encouraged order, rules, and the production of records that attested to the success of the colonial project and nation-building. The antithesis of the modern sporting world of the 19th and 20th centuries (particularly basketball, baseball, and American football), Indigenous sports and their histories existed both prior to and well after the onslaught of British, French, Spanish, and American sporting cultures. The narrative of both Indigenous removal, which justified physically forcing Indigenous peoples from the eastern United States onto reservations from the 1820s on, and the belief that Indigenous peoples had disappeared, died off, or otherwise been eradicated from the United States, encouraged the sense that sport was by, for, and about white male Americans. The U.S. project of colonial and imperial expansion, both domestically and internationally, often was tied to the exportation of these modern sports which reproduced racial, gendered, and social hierarchies (Davis, 2013; Gems, 2004, 2006; Guthrie-Shimizu, 2012; Klein, 1991).

In considering scholarly study of sport and indigeneity, then, we argue that the concentration on "modern sports" and the athletes who play those games has fetishized Western concepts and frameworks of competitive athletics that are tied to capitalism and commercialism rather than Indigenous values. By refocusing on Indigenous sport, we center the lived experiences of Indigenous peoples. This allows us to challenge the notion that sport must be tied to capitalism, consumption, mass media, regulation, and commercial forms of play (MacLean, 2019). Recentering the values of Indigenous sport as tied to individual experiences, communal expression and belonging, familial and kinship relationship, and tribal autonomy and authority allows us to understand that Indigenous sport serves as an expression of religious, communal, and cultural ways of knowing. These understandings are viewed as grounded in the local contexts of athletes and their games and as active processes always being negotiated. This revisionism allows us to also consider these histories as vital elements of contemporary Indigenous peoples (O'Bonsawin, 2010, 2017a; Phillips, Field, O'Bonsawin, & Forsyth, 2019). The important rise of decolonial approaches to sport is breaking down the bifurcation between history and contemporary Indigenous life. Thus, Brooklyn Nets basketball player Kyrie Irving's (Standing Rock Sioux) use of sage to purify the court prior to play can be read not just as an act of initiating connection to his ancestors and his spirituality; it can also be read as intervention into white sporting practices (Fernandez, 2020). Irving's sageing, like the prayers, blessings, and rituals offered by other athletes prior to play, allows us to understand that telling one's own history, and for non-Indigenous scholars ethically engaging with descendent communities, is a key element to fully capturing the variety of Indigenous sporting pasts that complicate articulations of professional, collegiate and youth sport and issues of sporting culture as primarily white cultural practices.

Scholarly inquiry about situating Indigenous participation within white sporting cultures has been a relatively recent concern in sport studies. Fueled in the 1990s and early 2000s by scholars with concern over issues about the representation of Indigenous peoples in the mass media, much debate focused on the long-standing entrenched use of Native mascots in American sport. This was stimulated by both university-based diversification of student populations that brought Indigenous students to campuses that "branded" their sports teams with Native mascots and the influence of the Indigenous rights movements of the mid-20th century. Here, Indigenous activism over the harms inherent in appropriating Native images and characterization in logos, branding, and mascot performances in both collegiate and professional sports encouraged scholarly inquiry about how these practices came to be and their residual harm in the contemporary context (Davis, 1993; Farnell, 2004; Hofmann, 2005; Kim-Prieto et al., 2010; King, Staurowsky, Baca, Davis, & Pewewardy, 2002; Rosenstein, 1997).

King and Springwood's (2001) *Team Spirits: The Native American Mascot Controversy* revealed much about the evolution and employment of Indigenous stereotypes in fashioning mascots for collegiate and professional teams. Case studies interrogated the use of Native mascots by the National Football League's Washington football team and Major League Baseball's Cleveland Indians and Atlanta Braves (Staurowsky, 1998, 2000). These were accompanied by studies of Native mascots as used by Miami University (Guiliano, 2002) and the University of North Dakota (Tovares, 2002), as well as comparative multisite studies that explored how multiple schools founded and profited from their Native athletic identities (Guiliano, 2015; Taylor, 2005). All of these studies have identified problematic, negative, and even outright racist forms of sporting cultures associated with the use of these mascots and merge seamlessly with the findings of social scientists who have documented concerns over issues of equity and representation that were raised by the use of stereotyped Native team mascots (Baca, 2004; Connolly, 2000; Fryberg & Markus, 2003; Fryberg, Markus, Oyserman, & Stone, 2008; LaRocque, 2001, 2004).

Collectively, these studies identified that the use of Native mascots, brands, and identities negatively affects Native children's sense of self-worth. Not only did Native students identify feeling worse about themselves, but Native mascotry also impacted Black, Asian, Latinx, and white students who were exposed to these stereotypes. In tandem, legal scholars established a track of scholarship exploring branding, mascotry, and the law (Brown, 2002; Clarkson, 2003; Hemmer, 2008). Studying society through the lens of law suggests a way to understand how cultural values, moral stances, and social systems are entwined with systems of power. Legal studies on mascotry, and their application to branding in particular, have centered on whether these representations can be copyrighted, whether they are inherently derogatory, and whether the evidence for the right of use is held by Natives or by white universities.

The use of derogatory terminology in relation to Asian identity pitted free speech advocates against those who sought to more strictly apply right of use and brought Native mascotry to the attention of Susan Shown Harjo (2017) and other Native anti-mascotry advocates who saw the case as a crucible for a future Native-based suit. Who has the right to claim copyright on a racialized identity? Who could profit from the sale of goods associated with that identity? In 2017, the Supreme Court ruled in *Matal v. Tam* that rejecting trademarks based on being derogatory went against First Amendment protections. Interestingly, although the ruling was thought to bolster pro-mascot groups, since that time teams, including the Washington football team, the Cleveland baseball team, the Atlanta baseball team, and many high schools and elementary schools, have altered or outright discarded their use of Native names, imagery, and branding. Importantly, to be meaningful, studies about the dynamics behind and effects of sport mascotry must increasingly embrace the inherently interdisciplinary nature of such inquiry. Often required are fluencies in humanistic and social science and legal approaches to understand the full sociocultural impacts and policy options in the use, abuse, mediation, and remediation of Indigenous sport mascots.

Despite the recent moves away from Indigenous naming, branding, and mascots at both professional and amateur levels, there is a continuing unwillingness to consider the more than 50-year debate over the appropriation of Native identity for the purposes of sport mascotry and the reliance on anchoring institutional identity as part of a larger colonial legacy of ignoring Indigenous sovereignty. The National Collegiate Athletic Association (2005) continues to use "tribal" approval to avoid grappling with scholarship that clearly demonstrates the negative impact of Indigenous mascots on Native and non-Native students. Their posture also allows universities and teams to leverage their financial resources to gain tribal support—as was the case with Florida State University (2005) and the University of Utah (2020).

APPROACHES

As we turn to common approaches in the scholarly study of sport and indigeneity, we begin with exploring how scholars have approached Indigenous sport from Native worldviews, an approach that represents a divergence from framing sport within white sporting frameworks. This has obvious effects on both understandings and characterizations of Native experiences *in* and *with* sport. Works engaging Indigenous sport history are notable for their increasing emphasis on Native-produced sources and local knowledges and their continuing efforts to locate essential developments in national and international sporting stories with Native participants. Sociologists, anthropologists, and historians share commitments to proper consultation and usage of Indigenous ways of knowing, the pattern of increased production by Indigenous academics, and the utilization of local examples as vantage points to larger issues. This commitment to self-reflexive methodologies guards against colonial perspectives inadvertently shaping the emergent research agenda.

Writing Native Sports Stories Individually and Communally

The study of Indigenous sport, which includes individual and communal sporting practices, should begin by exploring Native sporting stories located in Native spaces. While those spaces intersect with wider competitive or nationally/internationally organized networks, Indigenous athleticism and sport does not draw its meaning from engagement with the values of competition, capitalism, and individual success that were part and parcel of modernity. This focus highlights Native sporting traditions outside of mainstream sports cultures and is aligned with the rise of the "New Indian History" of the 1970s–1990s, which emphasized Indigenous agency and perspective (Axtell, 1981, 1992; Grinde & Johansen, 1994; White, 1991).

Regularly combining anthropological, ethnohistorical, and archival sources, works that explore Native sporting stories expand the very scope of sport as they relay the many meanings of sporting activities in Native cultures past and present. Joseph B. Oxendine's (1995) *American Indian Sports Heritage* stemmed from his participation in a sports workshop on the Pine Ridge Reservation of the Oglala Lakota in South Dakota. Oxendine sought to reveal the sport practices of Native people in their own contexts as well as in their understandings of experiences with colonizers. In his view, this would rekindle interest, pride, and self-esteem among the would-be athletes he met (p. ix). *American Indian Sports Heritage* established a timeline of Native invention, participation, influence, and excellence in sport that is still utilized today.

The 2005 edited collection *Native Athletes in Sport and Society: A Reader* (King, 2005) offers commentary on a variety of Native sports and athletic figures, building on Oxendine's provocation and also expanding engagement (in certain chapters) with theories of identity and race. The collection offers biographical interpretations of notable historical figures and careers (Louis Francis Sockalexis, George Howard Johnson, Tommy Yarr, SuAnne Big Crow, the Thorpe family) and fleshes out the contributions that Native people have made to American sports and to Indigenous communities mostly in the United States. Another edited collection, *The Native American Identity in Sports* (Salamone, 2013), focuses on Native identity and engages with issues such as Native public health initiatives, sports tourism, mascots, and boarding schools. Explorations of boxing, tennis, specific Olympic events, Seminole alligator wrestling, and *toka*, a Tohono O'odham women's sporting tradition, share a language of concern about identifying Indigenous participation in sport and focus on identity, community-building, representation, and reclamation. Collectively, these studies identify meanings, contexts, and settings of Native sport through case studies at the local level. They also represent interdisciplinary approaches to examining Indigenous sports, making good cases that the issues at stake require considerations of identity, politics, and society.

Western sports adapted to Native purposes and perspectives provide a different angle from which to understand some of the same issues that Oxendine introduced, from resistance to colonialism to community-building, athletic stardom, and Indigenous modernity. Especially in the United States, reservation basketball ("Rez Ball") looms large in this body of work. Basketball, requiring relatively low-cost facilities and equipment, grew immensely in popularity on reservations, in working-class urban neighborhoods, and at schools throughout the 20th century. Rez Ball is known for its fast pace and aggressive tactics. Native players—both men and women and boys and girls—developed unique styles of play and team dynamics that led not only to growing popularity but also to communal pride. Success in state- and national-level tournaments is highly prized not only as demonstrations of sporting success but also as sites of generational knowledge transfer (Cummins, Anderson, & Briggs, 2005; Peavy & Smith, 2008). Native authors and artists have featured Rez Ball and basketball players in a wide range of media, from Stephen Graham Jones's (2020) works of horror to former WNBA player Natalie Diaz's (2019) creative autobiographical essay that opens *Bodies Built for Game*, an edited collection of sports writing across genres and communities. Scholars and journalists in communication with Native players have also featured Rez Ball stories in recent publications that explicate contemporary issues related to reservation poverty, public health, and culture (Davies, 2020; Klein, 2020; Powell, 2019). This array of genres reflects the place of basketball in many Native societies in the United States as a tool and site for self-discovery, expression, growth, and belonging.

Recovering Native Sports Stories within White Institutions

Much research that considers Indigenous-specific contexts for sport prior to the mid-20th century depends on sources and stories from colonial archives and government-operated "Indian boarding schools" (typically called "residential schools" in Canada). Certainly, both voluntary and forced attendance at these schools at the end of the 19th century and through the early to mid-20th century sculpted a shared Indigenous experience in *settler colonial* countries. Settler colonialism, as readers might know, is a form of colonialism in which individuals charged with settling lands aim to eradicate Native peoples and cultures from established settler societies (Wolfe, 2006). Boarding school sports provided settings in which Native students could forge meaningful relationships with one another and could match or beat the talent of white competitors "at their own games." As John Bloom (2000) argued, students, administrators, coaches, teams, and the media articulated and struggled with sport and its role within Indian education.

Scholars have examined ways in which sports at boarding schools became active sites of resistance by Native students (Child, 1998; Deloria, 2004). These examinations are particularly important as the United States, Canada, Australia, and New Zealand continue to reckon with the injustices and legacies of forced residential schooling that relied on cultural genocide (Truth and Reconciliation Committee of Canada, 2015). In 2021, Canada's historical residential school system again dominated the media after a group from the Tk'emlups te Secwepemc First Nation unearthed an unmarked mass grave containing the bodies of 215 children at the site of the former Kamloops Indian Residential School in British Columbia (Austen, 2021). Understanding the destructive goals and abusive policies at government-operated schools may accelerate policies to benefit the survivors. Understanding former students' perspectives and agency, however, requires examinations of their personal choices and experiences at and memories of attending the schools. Sports were important activities for many former attendees.

Boarding school athletic programs became nationally and internationally famous for their athletes and accomplishments. The earliest athletic programs to gain this type of fame were at Carlisle Indian Industrial School in Pennsylvania. Here, track and field and gridiron football programs produced Olympians and professional athletes and drew significant resources to the school (Bloom, 2000; Jenkins, 2008; Sheinkin, 2017). A robust scholarly literature has also focused on programs at Haskell Institute in Lawrence, Kansas, that, although founded in 1884, became a sports powerhouse in the early 20th century. Research on the Haskell Institute emphasizes the way that white viewers received Native American athletes and the success of all-Native teams and how the teams influenced national sports in the 1920s (Low, 2003; Schmidt, 2001).

Though most research has focused on male teams and athletes, more recent scholarship has traced stories about Haskell's girls' programs, revealing how experiences for female participants in sport were gendered. While men received financial and material support from boarding school administrators, women received fewer material benefits from their sporting participation. Instead, their sporting experiences were about establishing female companionship and support systems (Eby, 2019).

Other important cultural histories, such as those by Michael Oriard (1993, 2001) which explore popular press and football, illustrate how sport was tied to racialized spectacle and the experiences of individual athletes and Native boarding school teams. Together, they unearth a rich set of archival sources that other scholars can explore to help mesh understandings of the experiences of Native athletes with larger received narratives of baseball and football as modern sports that too often fail to consider Indigenous experience. Scattered research on early 20th-century baseball players—some biographies and some that consider a cohort of early Major League Baseball players—illustrate themes of exclusion, racism, and American ambivalence toward Native athletes (Bruchac, 2008; Crawford, 2004; Powers-Beck, 2001, 2004; Rice, 2019; Rubinfeld, 2007; Wise & Farnsworth, 2007). Balancing analysis of media representation with Native perspectives is an approach widely visible in work that focuses on specific athletes and white-controlled sports institutions in which Native athletes participated (Bauer & Delsahut, 2020; Bauer, Delsahut, & Leconte, 2020; Bloom, 2000; Delsahut, 2019; Oxendine, 1995).

Sport-Specific Approaches

Certain sports that originate with Indigenous communities in North America have long been popular and important in Native society. Running, lacrosse, horseback sports, and surfing are perhaps the best examples. Each offers a lens to examine the many contexts in which these sports have been located to explore historical and present politics of inclusion/exclusion, identity, assimilation, and self-determination.

Running

The study of Indigenous running—particularly on the North American continent—reveals the diversity of meanings the sport holds in Native communities. These redefine what falls into the category of "sport," both generally and in the modern context. In the borderlands spanning the lands that became northwestern Mexico and the southwestern United States, running factored centrally into daily life and sacred ceremonies. It was also central to all facets of Raramuri society in lands that became northern Mexico (Dyreson, 2004; Keegan, 2016; McDougall, 2010). After contact with Europeans, messenger-runners coordinated resistance movements, such as the 1680 Pueblo Revolt against the Spanish in New Mexico and the 1763 war known as "Pontiac's Rebellion" in the Great Lakes region against the British (Brasseaux & Leblanc, 1982; Liebmann, 2012; Nabokov, 1981). In South America, the *chasqui* network, which delivered communication via relay running, tied together the Inca Empire and traversed the sophisticated road and bridge system the Incas built. Matthew Sakiestewa Gilbert (2010, 2012, 2018) (Hopi) has recently explored community dynamics among runners of the Hopi Nation who attended schools, ran in American marathons, or ran in Hopiland. Gilbert's work reveals how Native sporting traditions serve Native communities, influence broader popular culture, situate racist stereotyping, and forge national identity. His work illustrates Indigenous people forging intersectional identities and influencing Native and mainstream cultures and societies.

Lacrosse

Research on Indigenous lacrosse, or related variations of stick and ball games, considers the disconnect between the public perception of lacrosse as a white prep school pastime and its long standing as a cultural staple of numerous Indigenous communities. A good deal of attention has been focused on the Great Lakes region in the United States and Canada (Downey, 2018; Vennum, 2007, 2008). Allan Downey (2018) (Dakelh, Nak'azdli Whut'en) provided a long history of lacrosse in *The Creator's Game: Lacrosse, Identity, and Indigenous Nationhood*. Downey used lacrosse as a lens to examine First Nations' experiences before and during "Canada's colonial age," from 1860 to 1990. This work traces the evolution of the sport through its mainstream appropriation in the late 19th century as white Canadians claimed lacrosse as grounds for the production and performance of proper Victorian manhood, a category that excluded Indigenous individuals.

Responding to such appropriation, Indigenous communities and competitive teams worked to reclaim lacrosse as their own by positioning it as a sport for a "modern" era. Indeed, professional competition with non-Indigenous teams was a hallmark of the growth of Native participation in "modern" U.S. sporting culture. As Dr. Dan Henhawk (Wozniak, 2020) (Mohawk) has observed, today's "modern version of lacrosse is reflective of current mindsets related to sport, yet many would argue it still has its roots based in Indigenous philosophies." Henhawk adds, "The challenge, however, is making sense of historical knowledge in the present that hasn't been influenced through colonization." Here too, achieving this objective requires engaging interdisciplinary approaches. Recent research on lacrosse has displayed great dynamism in the fields of sport history and studies of media and sport. Collaborations have examined stick ball sports among various Indigenous communities and explored themes of community, kinship, and gender (Welch, Siegele, & Hardin, 2017; Welch, Siegele, Smith, & Hardin, 2019). Contemporary Indigenous participation in lacrosse is perhaps best known by the Iroquois Nationals men's lacrosse team, which represents the Haudenosaunee Confederacy in international competitions (Siebel, 2020).

Other Notable Sports

Ball sports and running are not the only sports important in Indigenous society. Horses have long been a part of the iconic imagery and performances of the American West, including cowboy and Indian narratives. Across the Plains, Native communities adopted horses and became expert riders long before the arrival of Anglos in their homelands. Thus, not surprisingly, equestrian sports have long entailed diverse meanings in Native communities, ranging from performances of male honor to entertainment. Native Americans and Indigenous people have competed and performed with horses in both their own communities and in rodeos (Chavis, 1993; Mellis, 2003; Mitchell, 2020; Wolman & Smith, 2020). Indigenous equestrians and the rodeos they have been featured in have garnered broad appeal, competing from time to time overseas (Mannik, 2006).

Surfing, a Kanaka Maoli (Indigenous Hawaiian) sport, has received broad attention, much of it stimulated by the study of Duke Paoa Kahanamoku, who popularized He'e nalu, the Indigenous conception and practice of wave-riding (Davis, 2015; Lemarié, 2016; Osmond, 2006, 2011). *Waves of Resistance: Surfing and History in Twentieth-Century Hawaii* (Walker, 2011), *Empire in Waves: A Political History of Surfing* (Gonzalez, 2015), and *The Critical Surf Studies Reader* (Hough-Snee & Sotelo Eastman, 2017) showcase surfing's role in Indigenous society with attention to social, cultural, and economic changes.

Continued Indigenous participation and excellence in these sports and others are highly visible indicators of Indigenous modernity that blend community goals and the structures of the Western competitive athletic circuits. Collectively, studies of these sports seek to address the erasure of Native participants in enduring perceptions. Sport-specific approaches have showcased Native authority, sources, and engagement and helped to reframe certain sports as Indigenous inventions with a wider set of meanings than competition and entertainment as those categories are understood in the 21st century.

Oral testimony, interviews, reinterpretation of historical objects, and the inclusion of art, literature, and song have reshaped the cultural record of Indigenous and non-Indigenous sporting worlds. Undoubtedly there remain "hidden stories" of Indigenous athletes at critical moments in their experience of sport in settler nations. Continuing to collect and deconstruct these will enrich broader understandings of sports as products of the labors of diverse contributing groups. The blending of little recognized "recovered narratives" of Indigenous sport experience with new archival accountings can be important resources for those seeking to reframe and correct long-entrenched (mis)understandings of Indigenous sporting societies.

DEBATES

Studies of Indigenous sports constitute a growing field ripe with salient questions about scope and positionality. Who gets to write about Indigenous sport, what evidence is used, and how sport relates to Indigenous experience undergird contemporary debates about how inquiry regarding Indigenous peoples and sport might be best approached. Such matters are necessarily seated in the long, but comparatively little chronicled, story of sport in Native American, Indigenous, and First Nations communities. For decades, inquiry into Indigenous experience, not only about sport, has struggled to receive recognition and be broadly valued in scholarly communities, be they sport history, sociology of sport, cultural studies, or journalism. Key challenges remain in mounting serious scholarly inquiry that is accountable to contemporary Indigenous communities. What is the best approach to research Indigenous peoples? How do we accurately engage with their sporting cultures? What constitutes getting the story right? Meaningful study entails interrogating questions over who does the research, frames inquiry, interprets findings, and ultimately writes the tale of Indigenous sport and society.

Global Indigeneity

In his foreword to *Native Games: Indigenous Peoples and Sports in the Post-Colonial World*, Brendan Hokowhitu (2016, p. xvii) (Māori, Ngāti Pūkenga) writes:

> [A]ny analysis of indigeneity and sport must firstly be cognizant of "local knowledges" and place, the dispossessing nature of colonialism, the role sport played in assimilating the indigenous population within the nation state, the complexity that is the indigenous athlete within the nation state, the complexity that is the indigenous athlete as both indigenous hero and dupe, the possibilities that sport holds as a spectacle of indigenous resistance and, more than anything, the relationship between sport and indigenous postcolonial corporeality.

Interrogating such a list of concerns is essential in ongoing examinations of Indigenous sport in society, a field that, while growing globally, has garnered scholarly attention most particularly in Australia, New Zealand, and Canada (Forsyth & Giles, 2013; Hallinan & Judd, 2016). Sociologists and sports studies scholars necessarily engage with understanding Indigenous sport within both Indigenous communities and colonial systems, but in doing so must consider more centrally the active legacies of these histories and how revelatory knowledge may be leveraged into increased empowerment and leadership for Indigenous individuals participating in national and community sports today. Placing emphasis on the local prioritizes knowledge rooted in indigeneity. Sociologists and Indigenous studies scholars focused on sports have explored what is needed to increase Indigenous leadership and management within sports organizations and help national institutions in fostering Indigenous self-determination through sport (Burnett, 2013; Heine, 2013; Skille, 2014; Wikaire & Newman, 2014).

Rethinking What Sport Is and Who Tells Its Story

Contemporary Native athletes who compete often speak of their relationship to sport as generational knowledge transfer (Ali Christie, 2013). Others, like professional soccer player Madison Hammond (Navajo, San Felipe), note that their success as a professional athlete provides an opportunity for tribal youth to see others with similar backgrounds and experiences succeed (Evans, 2020). Studies of Native experiences with sport offer the opportunity to consider a variety of structural obligations between Indigenous communities and settler-colonial governments, be they treaty-based, legal, or cultural. There is ample space for scholars to reinterpret colonial records by incorporating Native knowledge, interpretations, and sources. However, this necessarily requires recognition that Native ways of knowing may challenge notions of sport as pleasurable, civilizing, and capitalist. Importantly, scholarship that moves beyond the U.S. context to consider other national and even global sporting experiences has provided a space for rethinking sport's history and its cultural impacts.

In Canada, where an organization called the Aboriginal Sport Circle acts as a governing body and advocate for Indigenous sports, and where the government has formally acknowledged the need for "truth and reconciliation" regarding national policies that constituted cultural genocide, approaches to new scholarly work have facilitated more comprehensive and inclusive understandings. *Aboriginal Peoples and Sport in Canada*, edited by Janice Forsyth and Audrey R. Giles (2013), features studies that utilize sport to ground examinations of issues ranging from public health in Aboriginal communities to ongoing resistance to colonial structures and self-determination for Aboriginal people.

In *Aboriginal Sports Coaches, Community, and Culture*, Demelza Marlin, Nicholas Apoifis, and Andrew Bennie (2020) have collected stories from Indigenous coaches and mentors throughout Australia to challenge narrow definitions of who participates in Indigenous sport. Grappling with Australia's history of settler colonialism, the volume argues for a more expansive understanding of sport to move beyond athletes and coaches to consider a spectrum of individuals involved in sport culture. Australia-based researchers Chris Hallinan and Barry Judd (2016) engage similar concerns in research that explores the representation and accomplishments of Aboriginal athletes in Australia in their *Indigenous People, Race Relations and Australian Sport*, which is derived from a special issue of *Sport in Society*. Hallinan and Judd (2013) also edited *Native Games: Indigenous Peoples and Sports in the Post-Colonial World*, which is one of few works that take a global approach to examining Indigenous sport traditions and perspectives.

Consistently, the most fruitful contributions come from interdisciplinary inquiry that spans the humanities and social sciences. Over the past decade, these works from across the globe indicate several important trends. Contributions come from Indigenous people, people of Indigenous descent, and non-Indigenous researchers working directly with Indigenous communities. Most authors have not rejected the structure of Western sport, but centrally examine its intersection with Indigenous notions and needs of sport.

As well, it is important to recognize that it is not just scholars who undertake the work of increasing the visibility and articulating the importance of Indigenous sports and Indigenous histories. In 2019, the streaming service Netflix released *Basketball or Nothing*, which follows the Navajo Nation Chinle High School boys' basketball team, who find meaning and build community through high-level "Rez Ball" basketball (Howley, 2019). The Chinle Wildcats' cross-country team was the focus of another documentary, *Racing the Rez* (Truglio, 2012). New York filmmaker Henry Lu (2010) directed *Run to the East*, which presents running as an empowering force in students' lives as they pursue opportunities among the demands and stressors of reservation life and poverty. All of these films simultaneously expose social ills and celebrate sport—and Indigenous athletes—and aim to produce an "authentic" account of their subjects through the documentary format. Digital forms of media beyond films have also challenged the dominance of sport history written by and for sport history audiences. The *Grounded Podcast with Dinée Dorame* explores the intersection of "running, community, land, and culture" (Dorame, n.d.). The host, Dinée Dorame, is a citizen of the Navajo Nation and of Indigenous Mexican and Yaqui descent.

Such enterprises suggest that there is considerable public appetite for content about Native American and Indigenous sporting traditions and modern athletes. It also suggests the need for sport scholars to apply their work across academic boundaries. There are stories all over the world, at every level of sport, and in corners of society that do not constitute the popular notion of *sport* at all, and other stories that do transmit conventional images of sport but include Indigenous protagonists, perspectives, and priorities. In a variety of formats and with Indigenous voices at the helm, Indigenous sports stories can reach public audiences and readers in the academy and beyond with a greater range of approaches and contexts. This diversity allows for the received and embedded focus on "modernity," the achievement of individual athletes like Jim Thorpe, and the dominance of football, basketball, and baseball as sites of study to be unsettled and dissipated. Such "disruption" provides a wider variety of cultural understandings about sporting experiences, both across sports and across Indigenous communities, but it also serves to stimulate scholars to address the dramatic imbalances in framing Indigenous sport in a more resilient and more veridical way than has been the case with much mainstream scholarship that has focused on male, heteronormative sporting experiences.

Conclusion

As we close our consideration of sport, indigeneity, and Native identities, it is important to note that the long view on understanding Indigenous sporting experiences offers three main interventions. First, understanding Indigenous sport necessarily will entail challenging the primacy of textual printed sources as the main form of scholarly evidence by bringing to bear culturally sensitive and inclusive approaches. This means not only including evidence from oral history and interviews but also requires the engaged reading of material and physical culture objects like sporting equipment, artistic renderings, and song.

Second, Indigenous sporting experiences offer complex narratives that challenge dominant sporting narratives as white, urban, and tied to the muscular Christianity at the turn of the 20th century. Indigenous sport is deeply tied to cultural, spiritual, and religious practices that are built on family, kinship, and community. Non-Indigenous sport scholars must reckon with their own positionality that might make certain parts of sport unknowable to all but those who are part of that community.

Finally, Indigenous sport studies posits that meaningful accountings inherently require consideration of contemporary Indigenous peoples and their abilities to contribute to and lead research into their sporting practices. There is tremendous potential for new research into Indigenous sporting practices and cross-Indigenous sporting traditions. That work, though, can occur only when sport scholars, their associations, and their publication outlets recognize the need to support and publish Natives writing about their own sports.

References

Adelman, M. L. (1990). *A sporting time: New York City and the rise of modern athletics, 1820–70.* Champaign, IL: Illini Books.

Adelman, M. L. (1997). Harness racing: The first modern American sport, 1825–1870. In S. A. Reiss (Ed.), *Major problems in American sport history: Documents and essays* (pp. 70–81). New York: Wadsworth Publishing.

Ali Christie, A. (2013). *American Indian collegiate athletes: Accessing education through sport* (Unpublished PhD dissertation). University of Arizona.

Austen, I. (2021, May 28). "Horrible history": Mass grave of Indigenous children reported in Canada. *New York Times*. https://www.nytimes.com/2021/05/28/world/canada/kamloops-mass-grave-residential-schools.html.

Axtell, J. (1981). The English colonial impact on Indian culture. In J. Axtell (Ed.), *The European and the Indian: Essays in the ethnohistory of colonial North America* (pp. 245–271). Oxford: Oxford University Press.

Axtell, J. (1992). *Beyond 1492: Encounters in colonial North America*. Oxford: Oxford University Press.

Baca, L. R. (2004). Native images in schools and the racially hostile environment. *Journal of Sport and Social Issues, 28*(1), 71–78.

Bauer, T., & Delsahut, F. (2020). Jim Thorpe—All American: A thin Hollywood line of truth? *International Journal of the History of Sport, 37*(10), 1–13.

Bauer, T., Delsahut, F., & Leconte, M. P. (2020). Sporting Indianness: Challenging the cinematic representation of Native American athletes. *Sport in Society, 24*(5), 1–17.

Belanger, Y. D. (2011). Toward an innovative understanding of North American Indigenous gaming in historical perspective. In Y. Belanger (Ed.), *First Nations gaming in Canada* (pp. 10–34). Winnipeg: University of Manitoba Press.

Bloom, J. (2000). *To show what an Indian can do: Sports at Native American boarding schools*. Minneapolis: University of Minnesota Press.

Brasseaux, C. A., & Leblanc, M. J. (1982). Franco-Indian diplomacy in the Mississippi Valley 1754–1763: Prelude to Pontiac's uprising? *Journal de La Société Des Américanistes, 68*(1), 59–70.

Brown, K. A. (2002). Native American team names and mascots: Disparaging and insensitive or just a part of the game? *Sports Law Journal, 9*, 115–263.

Bruchac, J. (2008). *Jim Thorpe: Original All-American*. New York: Penguin.

Burnett, C. (2013). Paradigm lost: Indigenous games and neoliberalism in the South African context. In C. Hallinan & B. Judd (Eds.), *Native games: Indigenous peoples and sports in the post-colonial world* (pp. 205–227). Ediburgh: Emerald Group Publishing.

Byrd, J. A., & Rothberg, M. (2011). Between subalternity and indigeneity: Critical categories for postcolonial studies. *Interventions, 13*(1), 1–12. https://doi.org/10.1080/1369801X.2011.545574.

Cahn, S. K. (1994). *Coming on strong: Gender and sexuality in twentieth-century women's sport*. New York: Free Press.

California v. Cabazon Band of Indians, 480 U.S. 202 (1987), No. 85-1708 (United States Supreme Court February 25, 1987). https://supreme.justia.com/cases/federal/us/480/202/.

Chavis, B. (1993). All-Indian rodeo: A transformation of Western Apache tribal warfare and culture. *Wicazo Sa Review, 9*(1), 4–11.

Child, B. J. (1998). *Boarding school seasons: American Indian families, 1900–1940*. Lincoln: University of Nebraska Press.

Clarkson, G. (2003). Racial imagery and Native Americans: A first look at the empirical evidence behind the Indian mascot controversy. *Cardozo Journal of International & Comparative Literature, 11*, 393–411.

Clevenger, S. M. (2020). Transtemporal sport histories; or, rethinking the "invention" of American basketball. *Sport in Society, 23*(5), 959–974. https://doi.org/10.1080/17430437.2019.1597855.

Connolly, M. R. (2000). What's in a name? A historical look at Native American–related nicknames and symbols at three US universities. *Journal of Higher Education 71*(5), 515–547.

Crawford, B. (2004). *All American: The rise and fall of Jim Thorpe.* New York: John Wiley & Sons.

Culin, S. (1975). *Games of the North American Indians.* Washington DC: Courier Corporation.

Cummins, A. M., Anderson, C., & Briggs, G. (2005). Women's basketball on the Navajo Nation: The Shiprock Cardinals, 1960–1980. In C. R. King (Ed.), *Native athletes in sport and society: A reader* (pp. 143–169). Lincoln: University of Nebraska Press.

Davies, W. (2020). *Native hoops: The rise of American Indian basketball, 1895–1970.* Lawrence: University Press of Kansas.

Davis, D. (2015). *Waterman: The life and times of Duke Kahanamoku.* Lincoln: University of Nebraska Press.

Davis, J. M. (2013). Cockfight nationalism: Blood sport and the moral politics of American empire and nation building. *American Quarterly, 65*(3), 549–574.

Davis, L. R. (1993). *Protest against the use of Native American mascots: A challenge to traditional American identity.* ARENA Institute for Sport and Social Analysis.

DeBoer, W. R. (2001). Of dice and women: Gambling and exchange in Native North America. *Journal of Archaeological Method and Theory, 8*(3), 215–268. https://doi.org/10.1023/A:101166 3123339.

Deloria, P. J. (2004). *Indians in unexpected places.* Lawrence: University Press of Kansas.

Delsahut, F. (2019). The revoking and returning of Jim Thorpe's Olympics awards: 70 years of Native-American sports protest? *Sport in Society, 22*(11), 1769–1782. https://doi.org/10.1080/17430437.2019.1625551.

Diaz, N. (Ed.). (2019). *Bodies built for game: The Prairie Schooner anthology of contemporary sportswriting.* Lincoln: University of Nebraska Press.

Dorame, D. (n.d.). *Grounded podcast.* https://groundedpod.com/.

Downey, A. (2018). *The creator's game: Lacrosse, identity, and Indigenous nationhood* (reprint ed.). Vancouver: UBC Press.

Dyreson, M. (2004). The foot runners conquer Mexico and Texas: Endurance racing, "Indigenismo," and nationalism. *Journal of Sport History, 31*(1), 1–31.

Eby, B. (2019). *Building bodies, (un)making empire: Gender, sport, and colonialism in the United States, 1880–1930* (Unpublished PhD dissertation). University of Illinois at Urbana-Champaign. http://hdl.handle.net/2142/105606.

Edwards, W. (2020). The future of indigenous sovereignty and the paths for Native development in the United States. In W. Edwards (Ed.), *Sovereignty and land rights of Indigenous peoples in the United States* (pp. 111–131). New York: Springer.

Estes, N. (2019). *Our history is the future: Standing Rock versus the Dakota Access Pipeline, and the long tradition of Indigenous resistance.* New York. Verso.

Evans, J. (2020, October 28). OL Reign's Madison Hammond is the NWSL's first Indigenous player. *Spokesman-Review.* https://www.spokesman.com/stories/2020/oct/28/ol-reigns-madison-hammond-is-the-nwsls-first-indig/.

Farnell, B. (2004). The fancy dance of racializing discourse. *Journal of Sport and Social Issues, 28*(1), 30.

Fernandez, G. (2020, December 19). Kyrie Irving explains why he burned sage around TD Garden court prior to Nets preseason game against Celtics. CBS Sports. https://www.cbssports.com/nba/news/kyrie-irving-explains-why-he-burned-sage-around-td-garden-court-prior-to-nets-preseason-game-against-celtics/.

Florida State University. (2005). Relationship with the Seminole Tribe of Florida. University Communications. https://unicomm.fsu.edu/messages/relationship-seminole-tribe-florida/.

Forsyth, J. E., & Giles, A. R. (Eds.). (2013). *Aboriginal peoples and sport in Canada: Historical foundations and contemporary issues*. Vancouver: UBC Press.

Fryberg, S. A., & Markus, H. R. (2003). On being American Indian: Current and possible selves. *Self and Identity, 2*(4), 325–344.

Fryberg, S. A., Markus, H. R., Oyserman, D., & Stone, J. M. (2008). Of warrior chiefs and Indian princesses: The psychological consequences of American Indian mascots. *Basic and Applied Social Psychology, 30*(3), 208–218.

Gems, G. R. (1997). *Windy City wars: Labor, leisure, and sport in the making of Chicago*. New York City: Scarecrow Press.

Gems, G. R. (2004). The athletic crusade: Sport and colonialism in the Philippines. *International Journal of the History of Sport, 21*(1), 1–15. https://doi.org/10.1080/095233604 12331305983.

Gems, G. R. (2005). Negotiating a Native American identity through sport: Assimilation, adaptation, and the role of the trickster. In C. R. King (Ed.), *Native athletes in sport and society* (pp. 1–21). Lincoln: University of Nebraska Press.

Gems, G. R. (2006). Sport, colonialism, and United States imperialism. *Journal of Sport History, 33*(1), 3–25.

Gems, G. R., Borish, L. J., & Pfister, G. (2008). *Sports in American history: From colonization to globalization*. Champaign, IL: Human Kinetics.

Gilbert, M. S. (2010). Hopi footraces and American marathons, 1912–1930. *American Quarterly, 62*(1), 77–101.

Gilbert, M. S. (2012). Marathoner Louis Tewanima and the continuity of Hopi running, 1908–1912. *Western Historical Quarterly, 43*(3), 325–346.

Gilbert, M. S. (2018). *Hopi runners: Crossing the terrain between Indian and American*. Lawrence: University of Kansas Press.

Gonzalez, V. V. (2015). Empire in waves: A political history of surfing. *Journal of American History, 101*(4), 1239–1240.

Gorn, E. J. (2012). *The manly art: Bare-knuckle prize fighting in America*. Ithaca, NY: Cornell University Press.

Grinde, D. A., & Johansen, B. E. (1994). *Ecocide of Native America: Environmental destruction of Indian lands and peoples*. Santa Fe, NM: Clear Light.

Guiliano, J. (2015). *Indian spectacle: College mascots and the anxiety of modern America*. New Brunswick, NJ: Rutgers University Press.

Guiliano, J. E. (2002). *Red card: The role of Native Americans as sports mascots at Miami University* (Unpublished PhD dissertation). Miami University.

Guthrie-Shimizu, S. (2012). *Transpacific field of dreams: How baseball linked the United States and Japan in Peace and War*. Chapel Hill: University of North Carolina Press.

Hallinan, C., & Judd, B. (Eds.). (2013). *Native games: Indigenous peoples and sports in the postcolonial world*. Bingley, UK: Emerald Group Publishing.

Hallinan, C., & Judd, B. (Eds.). (2016). *Indigenous people, race relations and Australian sport*. New York City, NY: Routledge.

Harjo, S. S. (2017, December 15). Offensive mascots belong in museums and history books. *Indianz*. https://www.indianz.com/News/2017/12/15/suzan-shown-harjo-offensive-mascots-belo.asp.

Heine, M. K. (2013). No "museum piece": Aboriginal games and cultural contestation in sub-arctic Canada. In C. Hallinan & B. Judd (Eds.), *Native games: Indigenous peoples and sports in the post-colonial world* (pp. 1–19). Bingley, UK: Emerald Group Publishing.

Hemmer, J. J. (2008). Exploitation of American Indian symbols: A First Amendment analysis. *American Indian Quarterly, 32*(2), 121–140.

Hofmann, S. (2005). The elimination of Indigenous mascots, logos, and nicknames: Organizing on college campuses. *American Indian Quarterly, 29*(1–2), 156–177.

Hokowhitu, B. (2016). Foreword. In C. Hallinan & B. Judd (Eds.), *Native games: Indigenous peoples and sports in the post-colonial world.* (pp. xv–xxi). New York City: Emerald Group Publishing.

Hough-Snee, D. Z., & Sotelo Eastman, A. (2017). *The critical surf studies reader.* Durham, NC: Duke University Press.

Howley, M. (Director). (2019). *Basketball or nothing* [Streaming]. *Netflix.* https://www.netflix.com/title/80245353.

Jenkins, S. (2008). *The real All Americans: The team that changed a game, a people, a nation.* Anchor Books.

Jones, S. G. (2020). *The only good Indians.* Gallery/Saga Press.

Keegan, T. (2016). *Runners of a different race: North American Indigenous athletes and national identities in the early twentieth century* (Unpublished PhD dissertation). University of Oregon.

Kim-Prieto, C., Goldstein, L. A., Okazaki, S., Dimler, M., Gumbs, L., Harris, R. D., Moran, L., & Smith, J. A. (2010). Effect of exposure to American Indian sports mascots on stereotyping. *Journal of Applied Social Psychology, 40,* 534–553. https://doi.org/10.1111/j.1559-1816.2010.00586.x.

King, C. R. (Ed.). (2005). *Native athletes in sport and society: A reader.* Lincoln: University of Nebraska Press.

King, C. R., & Springwood, C. F. (Eds.). (2001). *Team spirits: The Native American mascots controversy.* Lincoln: University of Nebraska Press.

King, C. R., Staurowsky, E. J., Baca, L., Davis, L. R., & Pewewardy, C. (2002). Of polls and race prejudice: *Sports Illustrated*'s errant "Indian wars." *Journal of Sport and Social Issues, 26*(4), 381–402.

Klein, A. (1991). Sport and culture as contested terrain: Americanization in the Caribbean. *Sociology of Sport Journal, 8*(1), 79–85. https://journals.humankinetics.com/view/journals/ssj/8/1/article-p79.xml.

Klein, A. (2020). *Lakota hoops: Life and basketball on Pine Ridge Indian Reservation.* New Brunswick, NJ: Rutgers University Press.

Krus, A. M. (2011). Bridging history and prehistory: The possible antiquity of a Native American ballgame. *Native South, 4,* 136–145. https://doi.org/doi:10.1353/nso.2011.0004.

LaRocque, A. R. (2001). *The effect of cultural affiliation on attitudes, beliefs, and reactions to the Fighting Sioux nickname issue between Northern Plains American Indian and majority culture college students* (Unpublished master's thesis). University of North Dakota.

LaRocque, A. R. (2004). *Psychological distress between American Indian and majority culture college students regarding the use of the Fighting Sioux nickname and logo* (Unpublished PhD dissertation). University of North Dakota.

Lemarié, J. (2016). Debating on cultural performances of Hawaiian surfing in the 19th century. *Journal de La Société Des Océanistes, 142–143,* 159–174. https://doi.org/10.4000/jso.7625.

Levine, P. (1994). *Ellis Island to Ebbets Field: Sport and the American-Jewish experience*. Oxford, UK: Oxford University Press.

Liebmann, M. (2012). *Revolt: An archaeological history of Pueblo resistance and revitalization in 17th century New Mexico*. Tucson: University of Arizona Press.

Low, D. (2003). Boarding school resistance narratives: Haskell runaway and ghost stories. *Studies in American Indian Literatures, 15*(2), 106–118.

Lu, H. (Producer). (2010). *Run to the east* [film]. Moxie Pictures. https://runtotheeast.com/.

MacLean, M. (2019). Engaging (with) indigeneity: Decolonization and Indigenous/ indigenizing sport history. *Journal of Sport History, 46*(2), 189–207. https://doi.org/10.5406/jsporthistory.46.2.0189.

Mannik, L. (2006). *Canadian Indian cowboys in Australia: Representation, rodeo, and the RCMP at the Royal Easter Show, 1939*. Calgary: University of Calgary Press.

Marlin, D., Apoifis, N., & Bennie, A. (2020). *Aboriginal sports coaches, community, and culture*. Springer.

Matal v. Tam, No. 15-1293 (2017), (United States Supreme Court June 19, 2017).

McDougall, C. (2010). *Born to run: The hidden tribe, the ultra-runners, and the greatest race the world has never seen*. Profile Books.

Mellis, A. F. (2003). *Riding buffaloes and broncos: Rodeo and Native traditions in the Northern Great Plains*. Norman: University of Oklahoma Press.

Mitchell, P. (2020). "A horse-race is the same all the world over": The cultural context of horse racing in Native North America. *International Journal of the History of Sport, 37*(3–4), 337–356. https://doi.org/10.1080/09523367.2020.1758672.

Nabokov, P. (1981). *Indian running*. Capra Press.

National Collegiate Athletic Association. (2005). Guidelines for use of Native American mascots at championship events. *NCAA*. http://fs.ncaa.org/Docs/PressArchive/2005/Announcements/NCAA%2BExecutive%2BCommittee%2BIssues%2BGuidelines%2Bfor%2BUse%2Bof%2BNative%2BAmerican%2BMascots%2Bat%2BChampionship%2BEvents.html.

Nicoll, F. (2018). Beyond the figure of the problem gambler: Locating race and sovereignty struggles in everyday cultural spaces of gambling. *Journal of Legal & Social Policy, 30*, 127–149.

O'Bonsawin, C. M. (2010). "No Olympics on stolen native land": Contesting Olympic narratives and asserting indigenous rights within the discourse of the 2010 Vancouver Games. *Sport in Society, 13*(1), 143–156.

O'Bonsawin, C. M. (2017a). Humor, irony, and Indigenous peoples: A re-reading of the historical record of the 1904 St. Louis Olympic championship. *Sport History Review, 48*(2), 168–184.

O'Bonsawin, C. (2017b). "Ready to step up and hold the front line": Transitioning from sport history to Indigenous studies, and back again. *International Journal of the History of Sport, 34*(5–6), 420–426. https://doi.org/10.1080/09523367.2017.1378184.

Oriard, M. (1993). *Reading football: How the popular press created an American spectacle*. Chapel Hill: University of North Carolina Press.

Oriard, M. (2001). *King football: Sport and spectacle in the golden age of radio and newsreels, movies and magazines, the weekly and the daily press*. Chapel Hill: University of North Carolina Press.

Osmond, G. (2006). "Putting up your Dukes": Statues, social memory and Duke Paoa Kahanamoku. *International Journal of the History of Sport, 23*(1), 82–103.

Osmond, G. (2011). Myth-making in Australian sport history: Re-evaluating Duke Kahanamoku's contribution to surfing. *Australian Historical Studies*, 42(2), 260–276.

Oxendine, J. B. (1995). *American Indian sports heritage*. Lincoln: University of Nebraska Press.

Pasquaretta, P. (2003). *Gambling and survival in Native North America*. Tucson: University of Arizona Press.

Peavy, L. S., & Smith, U. (2008). *Full-court quest: The girls from Fort Shaw Indian School, basketball champions of the world*. Norman: University of Oklahoma Press.

Phillips, M. G., Field, R., O'Bonsawin, C., & Forsyth, J. (2019). Indigenous resurgence, regeneration, and decolonization through sport history. *Journal of Sport History*, 46(2), 143–156.

Powell, M. (2019). *Canyon dreams: A basketball season on the Navajo Nation*. Blue Rider Press.

Powers-Beck, J. (2001). "Chief": The American Indian integration of baseball, 1897–1945. *American Indian Quarterly*, 25(4), 508–538.

Powers-Beck, J. P. (2004). *The American Indian integration of baseball*. Lincoln: University of Nebraska Press.

Rand, K. R., & Light, S. A. (2019). Gambling on authenticity: Gaming, the noble savage, and the not-so-new Indian. *Great Plains Quarterly*, 39(1), 91–92.

Rice, E. (2019). *Baseball's first Indian: The story of Penobscot legend Louis Sockalexis*. Down East Books.

Riess, S. A. (1999). *Touching base: Professional baseball and American culture in the progressive era* (rev. ed.). Champaign: University of Illinois Press.

Riess, S. A. (2011). *The sport of kings and the kings of crime: Horse racing, politics, and organized crime in New York 1865–1913*. Syracuse, NY: Syracuse University Press.

Riess, S. A. (2015). *Sports in America from colonial times to the twenty-first century: An encyclopedia*. Taylor and Francis.

Rosenstein, J. (Producer). (1997). *In whose honor?* [Documentary]. New Day Films.

Rubinfeld, M. (2007). The mythical Jim Thorpe: Re/presenting the twentieth century American Indian. In C. R. King (Ed.), *Native Americans and sport in North America* (pp. 48–70). Routledge.

Ruck, R. (1987). *Sandlot seasons: Sport in Black Pittsburgh*. Champaign: University of Illinois Press.

Salamone, F. A. (Ed.). (2013). *The Native American identity in sports: Creating and preserving a culture*. Scarecrow Press.

Schmidt, R. (2001). Lords of the prairie: Haskell Indian School football, 1919–1930. *Journal of Sport History*, 28(3), 403–426.

Sheinkin, S. (2017). *Undefeated: Jim Thorpe and the Carlisle Indian School football team*. Macmillan.

Siebel, D. (2020, September 8). World lacrosse announces teams for men's lacrosse competition at TWG 2022; Iroquois Nationals accept invitation to compete. World Lacrosse. http://worldlacrosse.sport/article/world-lacrosse-announces-teams-for-mens-lacrosse-competition-at-twg-2022-iroquois-nationals-accept-invitation-to-compete/.

Skille, E. (2014). Lassoing and reindeer racing versus "universal" sports: Various routes to Sámi identity through sports. In C. Hallinan & B. Judd (Eds.), *Native games: Indigenous peoples and sports in the post-colonial world* (pp. 21–41). Emerald Group Publishing.

Sparks, R. J. (1992). Gentleman's sport: Horse racing in antebellum Charleston. *South Carolina Historical Magazine*, 93(1), 15–30.

Staurowsky, E. J. (1998). An act of honor or exploitation? The Cleveland Indians' use of the Louis Francis Sockalexis story. *Sociology of Sport Journal*, 15, 299–316.

Staurowsky, E. J. (2000). The Cleveland "Indians": A case study in American Indian cultural dispossession. *Sociology of Sport Journal, 17*(4), 307–330.

Taylor, M. (2005). *Native American images as sports team mascots from Chief Wahoo to Chief Illiniwek* (Unpublished PhD dissertation). Syracuse University Press.

Tovares, R. (2002). Mascot matters: Race, history, and the University of North Dakota's "Fighting Sioux" logo. *Journal of Communication Inquiry, 26*(1), 76–94.

Truglio, B. (Producer). (2012). *Racing the rez* [film]. Wolf Hill Films and Vision Maker Media.

Truth and Reconciliation Committee of Canada. (2015). Truth and Reconciliation Committee Reports. https://nctr.ca/records/reports/.

United Nations Permanent Forum on Indigenous Issues. (n.d.). Indigenous peoples, Indigenous voices fact sheet. https://unstats.un.org/UNSD/geoinfo/UNGEGN/docs/26th-gegn-docs/UN%20PFII%20session_factsheet1.pdf.

University of Utah. (2020). Ute Indian Tribe and University of Utah renew athletics naming agreement. @theU. https://attheu.utah.edu/athletics/ute-indian-tribe-and-university-of-utah-renew-athletics-naming-agreement/.

Vennum, T. (2007). *Lacrosse legends of the first Americans* (illustrated ed.). Baltimore, MD: Johns Hopkins University Press.

Vennum, T. (2008). *American Indian lacrosse: Little brother of war* (illustrated ed.). Baltimore, MD: Johns Hopkins University Press.

Walker, I. H. (2011). *Waves of resistance: Surfing and history in twentieth-century Hawai`i*. Honolulu: University of Hawaii Press.

Walton-Fisette, T. (2018). Metaphorically "taking a knee": Pausing, reflecting, acting. *Sociology of Sport Journal, 35*(4), 293–300. https://doi.org/10.1123/ssj.2018-0024.

Weiner, R. S. (2018). Sociopolitical, ceremonial, and economic aspects of gambling in ancient North America: A case study of Chaco Canyon. *American Antiquity, 83*(1), 34.

Welch, N. M., Siegele, J., & Hardin, R. (2017). For the sga-du-gi (community): Modern day Cherokee stickball. *American Indian Culture and Research Journal, 41*(2), 93–114.

Welch, N. M., Siegele, J., Smith, Z. T., & Hardin, R. (2019). Making herstory: Cherokee women's stickball. *Annals of Leisure Research, 24*(1), 1–21.

Welch, N. M., Siegele, J., Smith, Z. T., & Hardin, R. (2021). Making herstory: Cherokee women's stickball. *Annals of Leisure Research, 24*(1), 51–71. https://doi.org/10.1080/11745 398.2019.1652104.

White, R. (1991). *The middle ground: Indians, empires, and republics in the Great Lakes Region, 1650–1815*. Cambridge University Press.

Wikaire, R. K., & Newman, J. I. (2014). Neoliberalism as neocolonialism? Considerations on the marketisation of Waka Ama in Aotearoa/New Zealand. In C. Hallinan & B. Judd (Eds.), *Native games: Indigenous peoples and sports in the post-colonial world* (pp. 59–83). Emerald Group Publishing.

Wise, B., & Farnsworth, B. (2007). *Louis Sockalexis: Native American baseball pioneer*. Lee & Low Books.

Wolfe, P. (2006). Settler colonialism and the elimination of the Native. *Journal of Genocide Research, 8*(4), 387–409.

Wolman, D., & Smith, J. (2020). *Aloha rodeo: Three Hawaiian cowboys, the world's greatest rodeo, and a hidden history of the American West*. William Morrow Paperbacks.

Wozniak, B. (2020). Indigenous Scholar decolonizes sport by returning to a land-based way of learning. *University of Manitoa News*. https://news.umanitoba.ca/indigenous-scholar-deco lonizes-sport-by-returning-to-a-land-based-way-of-learning/.

CHAPTER 44

....

SPORT, BODILY IDEALS, AND OBESITY

....

PIRKKO MARKULA

In a November 2019 *New York Times* commentary, Mary Cain, a former teenage American distance-running protégé, provided an emotional confession of her struggles with her body weight when training with the renowned coach Alberto Salazar of the Nike Oregon Project. Due to persistent requests by Salazar to lose yet more weight, among other abusive coaching behaviors, Cain claimed that she did not reach her performance potential and was left emotionally scarred and with low self-confidence. She finally left the group. Cain's revelations caused the distance-running community to further condemn the coaching practices of Salazar, who was already banned from coaching due to drug charges. As a result, the Nike Oregon Project folded.

While not all weight-related issues in sport conclude as dramatically as Cain's story, controlling body size remains a central part of achieving successful sport performance. Battles such as Cain's are typically accepted as part of the process of advancing sport performance for elite athletes, and weight loss is increasingly seen as an integral part of training for recreational athletes. Highly visible elite athletes' bodies are also presented as inspirations for many ordinary citizens who may struggle with body weight problems. In addition to elite sport, the fitness industry offers diverse commercial options to those seeking to control the size and shape of their bodies.

In a TV advertisement, "Rachel" is heard telling her emotional story of changing from someone who is fat and "so sad" to someone who is thin and fit after joining Good Life Gym. From "not loving herself" and hiding her overweight body, she advised others "to just start" exercising to see how their fitness level and self-confidence would improve with reduced body size. Rachel's new 126-pounds-lighter body is posited to have enabled her to feel empowered both physically and mentally and to love herself. The significance of her story is, then, that successfully diminishing one's body shape is the path to self-love and better physical health.

Such stories abound globally: sport and exercise are commonly advertised as weapons to battle the raising rates of being overweight and obese. In this chapter, I highlight the contradictory position that physical activity occupies in the fight against the so-called obesity epidemic and a concurrent means for breeding obsession with extreme thinness. This position,

I demonstrate, is supported by a cultural body ideal that prescribes a thin appearance as the normative body shape. As the slender, fit body characterizes sport and physical activity, it has been harnessed to serve the medicalized health outcomes that many have come to believe can be visibly seen based on the casual assessment of body size.

Issues

Obesity and Overweight as Health Problems

Governmental health-promotion programs treat physical activity primarily as a medicine to prevent costly illnesses (e.g., Markula & Chikinda, 2016; Pullen & Malcolm, 2018). To reach large populations, they rely on clearly articulated physical activity guidelines for citizens to follow on their own volition. For example, the Canadian Physical Activity Guidelines for 18- to 64-year-olds recommend 150 minutes of weekly moderate- to vigorous-intensity aerobic activity with additional muscle and bone strengthening activities twice a week to achieve health benefits such as reduced risk of premature death from heart disease, stroke, certain types of cancer, Type 2 diabetes, osteoporosis, and being overweight and obese (Canadian Society for Exercise Physiology, 2022). In these campaigns, being overweight or obese is included in the list of illnesses cited as risks to health, a concept that is rather narrowly defined as the absence of illness. Indeed, Statistics Canada (2019) reports that in 2018, 26.8% of Canadians 18 and older (roughly 7.3 million adults) were classified as obese, and another 9.9 million (36.3%) were classified as overweight. This means, the report emphasizes, the total population with an increased risk of diabetes, high blood pressure, and heart disease due to excess weight is 63.1%. In the European Union, the corresponding figure in 2014 was 53% (Harjunen, 2019).

The data for these reports, following the recommendation by the World Health Organization, are based on Body Mass Index (BMI, which is the ratio of weight in kilograms divided by the square of height in meters in relation to height). An individual's health is considered to be optimal in the "normal range" of the BMI (18.5–24.9). One is judged to be overweight with a BMI above 25 and obese with a BMI above 30. Despite significant critique (e.g., of whether BMI is an appropriate measure of actual fat content), the use of the BMI has persisted as it is easily measurable without expensive equipment. Some critics argue that the posing of BMI as a reliable measure for something that it does not directly measure is a social construction (Campos, 2004; Harjunen, 2019; Oliver, 2006). In other words, rather than serving as a biomedical tool, BMI has become a political and economic tool for targeted health-promotion strategies used to determine the distribution of (commercialized) healthcare service funding. As well, governmental funding of elite sports may now be linked to broader understandings of sports as health-promotion vehicles (e.g., Mansfield, 2016; Weed, 2016). For example, the Sport for Life Society is an independent national governing organization with federal funding from Sport Canada. It promotes lifelong involvement in recreational or elite sport through eight stages of "physical literacy" that are to provide "a clear path to better sport, greater health, and higher achievement" (Sport for Life, 2020).

In addition to public health campaigns, physical activity is sold commercially as a weight-loss tool by numerous fitness industry services. Indeed, a whole sector of various health and fitness clubs and studios stimulate their profit goals by promising effective weight loss, a narrative reinforced by reality television programs promoting high-intensity exercise as a fast way to reduce body size. For example, the program *The Biggest Loser* displays obese and overweight contestants competing to lose weight with the help of perfect-looking, fit personal trainers and a rather grueling exercise regime during a 10-week season; it has had ongoing success in the highly competitive TV market. The industry premise concerning weight loss differs in key ways from the emphasis that governmental physical activity programs place on illness prevention. Instead of physical disease, the industry approach to weight loss is predominantly promoted against the backdrop of a socially constructed thin body ideal. This body ideal is strongly gendered: men's lean body ideal centers on a large, muscular upper body and visible abdominals, whereas women are expected, first and fore-most, to build thin, toned, and youthful-looking bodies without visible muscularity. These ideals are sold through various marketing channels throughout legacy and new media. Their strategies tightly intertwine health and appearance into the aesthetics of the healthy-looking body (Markula & Kennedy, 2011). Here, the fit, thin body is sold as a requirement for good looks and a necessary requirement of self-love. Rachel's story, discussed at the beginning of this chapter, exemplifies this strategy. Establishing the "looking good—feeling good" maxim masks the reliance on the social construction of the ideal body by drawing on scientific logics from physiology and medicine to maximize weight loss.

Thinness as a Health Problem

While the risks of obesity and overweight tend to dominate public discussion, problems that come with weight loss have received significantly less attention. When the slender body is established as a socially desirable norm, thinness is typically considered unproblematic. An excessive quest for thinness, however, is an essential element of diagnoses for a class of illnesses generally characterized as eating disorders. The prevalence of these conditions tends to be much smaller than the incidents of obesity and being overweight. For example, the National Initiative for Eating Disorders Canada (2018) reports that approximately 1 million Canadians meet the diagnostic criteria for an eating disorder such as anorexia nervosa, bulimia nervosa, binge eating disorder (BED), avoidance restrictive food intake disorder (ARFID), and otherwise specified feeding and eating disorder (OSFED). In the United Kingdom, between 1.25 and 3.4 million people are affected by an eating disorder; 10% are diagnosed as anorexia, 40% as bulimia, and the rest as BED or OSFED (Priory, 2018). In the United States, about 30 million people have been diagnosed with eating disorders (National Association of Anorexia Nervosa and Associated Disorders, 2020). While these numbers appear relatively small in comparison to overweight, the eating disorder or-ganizations emphasize that the majority of cases are never diagnosed. In addition, eating disorders have the highest mortality rate of any psychiatric disorder (National Initiative for Eating Disorders Canada, 2018; National Association of Anorexia Nervosa and Associated Disorders, 2020; Priory, 2018). Notably, the majority of people affected by eating disorders are girls and women, with dancers and athletes like Cain, whose case was introduced at the beginning of the chapter, most particularly at risk (Arcelus, Witcomb, & Mitchell, 2014;

Bratland-Sanda & Sundgot-Borgen, 2013). Medical scientists have identified a related sport-specific condition previously known as the female athlete triad, currently renamed relative energy deficiency in sport (RED-S) (Thorpe & Clarke, 2020).

The female athlete triad refers to the three interrelated risks of bone mineral loss, disordered eating, and amenorrhea (chronic loss of menstruation) in sportswomen (Thorpe, 2016). Diagnoses of RED-S recognize the considerable risks associated with low energy availability due to underfueling that, relative to the energy expenditure required for sport performance, leads to significant hormonal changes triggering the loss of menstruation and bone mineral. As Thorpe and Clark (2020) note, collectively these symptoms have both acute and chronic implications for injury rates, psychological well-being, and the health of skeletal, reproductive, cardiovascular, immunological, and gastrointestinal systems. Their evidence makes clear that not only sportswomen but an increasing number of recreational exercising women display symptoms of RED-S.

In summary, physical activity has been established as one of the primary tools for weight loss in the world, where obesity and overweight are statistically increasing. Although not necessarily curing the ills related to excess weight, physical activity has been endorsed broadly in governmental health-promotion campaigns. At the same time, one of the most successful selling points for the commercial fitness industry has been the promise of weight loss. While intertwined with health, their marketing relies strongly on the normative thin and toned aesthetics of a body ideal and situating this as resulting from a regular exercise regime. This body ideal is socially constructed and, as such, does not correspond to the physical and genetic makeup of most people (e.g., Bordo, 2004; Markula, 1995) This social construction, and its offset with reality, interacts with the narrowly defined feminine thin and toned body ideal. In addition, Western women's fashion privileges highly exposed bodies that are more visible in public than men's bodies. In this context, many women feel significant pressure to lose weight regardless of their actual body size. Consequently, body dissatisfaction is rampant among women across all ages (Kilpela, Becker, Wesley, & Stewart, 2015). This has led to avoidable but serious conditions, such as eating disorders and RED-S. Thus, rather than facilitating healthy outcomes, such dynamics have often fueled dangerous illnesses and costly medical intervention.

It is clear that while publicly promoted and sanctioned, the quest for thinness does not necessarily result in purely positive physical or mental well-being and may cause substantial harms. Several research approaches have been used to explain the perseverance of the normative thin body ideal in a constellation where social constructions of health, bodies, and identities are tightly interwoven with medical and physiological understandings of health.

APPROACHES

Sociocultural researchers of the physically active body approach the problematic issues of body size from several theoretical perspectives. They propose to illustrate how the biomedical issues of health and illness are also deeply embedded in relations of social and cultural power. A significant amount of research locates both the obese/overweight body and normative thin body as parts of the political-economic landscape of health in contemporary society. There are two major theoretical approaches, critical theory and Foucauldian-inspired research on biopower, that highlight how body size, particularly, has become a serious health and moral problem in many societies.

Approaches from Critical Theory: The Ideological Construction of Body Size

From the perspective of critical-cultural theory, obesity is constructed as a moral problem to stigmatize a portion of the population that does not conform with the dominant ideological constructions of healthy citizenship. In this context, overweight individuals have not taken personal responsibility to properly take care of their health and, thus, present a risk population in society. Labeled "healthism," this normative ideal posits absence of illness as an individual's moral duty and, thus, a part of one's self-identity as a normal, good citizen. Healthism establishes fat bodies as out of control, dangerous, at risk, and threats to the economy and, as such, condemns obesity as immoral behavior (e.g., Harjunen, 2019). Drawing on this perspective, the "obesity critics" reconstruct "the obesity epidemic" as a moral rather than purely a biomedical health problem. They further argue that the epidemiological, physiological, and medical view of (ill) health as an individual's problem is supported by "the media, educational institutions, health and fitness practitioners, and public health officials" (Rail, 2012, p. 234). To reveal the social construction of obesity as a moral problem, critics challenge the dominant biomedical research claims of causality between BMI and such diseases as cardiovascular disease (e.g., Harjunen, 2019). They further point to very low correlations (instead of causality) between obesity and mortality rates (Campos, Saguy, Ernsberger, Oliver, & Gaesser, 2006; Oliver, 2005; Rail, 2012). For example, there is evidence that the healthiest people are in the overweight BMI category of 25–30 (Harjunen, 2019). Against this context, such prominent obesity critics as Gard and Wright (2005) and Rail (2012) contest the taken-for-granted notions of obesity as an illness that can be cured through weight loss and exercise. While BMIs may have increased, these critics demonstrate, the boundaries of obesity are socially constructed when mainstream obesity scientists, bariatric surgeons, the fitness and weight loss industries, insurance companies, and the pharmaceutical industry all profit from constructing it as a disease (Campos, 2004; Gard & Wright, 2005; Oliver, 2005; Rail, 2012). Consequently, the "obesity epidemic" emerges as a tangled web of interests of various beneficiaries. In addition, there is evidence that sociocultural factors that determine individuals' lifestyles have a strong influence on BMI (i.e., people have higher BMIs due to poverty). As such, obesity or being overweight is not entirely an individual's choice, nor is it cured by an individual diligently dieting and exercising, but is a result of social inequality with low socioeconomic status strongly associated with obesity (e.g., Evans, Rich, Davies, & Allwood, 2008; Rail, 2012). Within the cultural context of Westernized countries, women, in particular, are stigmatized as obese/overweight due to cultural standards of femininity that hold them "to a more rigid standard of body size" compared to men (Rail, 2012, p. 238; see also Harjunen, 2019).

Seen through the lens of healthism, Harjunen (2019) summarizes, obesity might be considered a social disease defined by social norms. When social aspects are used to reinforce the medicalization of fatness as a cause for increased risk of illness, the obesity epidemic has effectively spread as a global "moral panic" about fatness (Rail, 2012). Harjunen further observes that the obesity epidemic makes "fat people" an easily recognizable group with a clear identity category. Although the obese deviate from the "normal" body and can thus be stigmatized by moral panic, they can also exemplify nonconformity and thus resist the dominant ideologies of healthism that render a healthy lifestyle (e.g., weight loss and exercise) as an individual responsibility. As a marginalized group oppressed by the dominant biomedical obesity epidemic discourse, "fat activists" fight to reveal the ideologies that reproduce a fat stigma (Rinaldi, Rice, & Friedman, 2019). Fat activism, alongside fat studies, continues to address the complexities of resisting capitalist society logics where healthism medicalizes and individualizes obesity into an illness.

Riley and Evans (2018) further complicate the relationship between resistance and compliance by connecting healthism with a "postfeminist sensibility" that has modified the concept of individual agency to mean self-transformation toward the normative ideal. This transformation is now framed as empowerment: women and girls choose to diet and exercise to obtain "sexy," attractive bodies. Instead of hard work, this process is associated with pleasure and fun that is taken on voluntarily in the name of living a good life. Rachel's story of finding self-confidence through this type of transformation in the Good Life Gym can demonstrate how healthism works together with the gendered postfeminist sensibility in the commercial fitness industry context. Similar trends have been detected in sport, where women athletes now find empowerment from selling their sexualized bodies. For example, sportswomen's media often depict sexualized presentations as a free choice that the athletes themselves cherish (e.g., Toffoletti, Thorpe, Francombe-Webb, 2018). These texts skillfully combine the feminist notion of sport as empowering to advance gendered ideologies supporting women's oppression in the male-dominated sport industry. In this sense, paradoxically, women's continued oppression by selling their sexualized, slender bodies is celebrated as empowering.

In the fitness industry, masculine domination operates through the ideological construction of the body ideal. Critical feminist researchers (e.g., Dworkin & Wachs, 2009; Maguire & Mansfield, 1998; Markula, 1995; Markula & Kennedy, 2011) have long critiqued the fitness industry for its singular emphasis on the impossible feminine body ideal that is more likely to cause mental (e.g., body dissatisfaction) and physical (eating disorders, injuries) ill health than improve fitness. Based on the ideological construction of the masculine body as naturally strong and the feminine body as "weak" but attractive, the fit body is built along strictly gendered lines whereby the feminine body ideal now appears as a somewhat "boyish" lanky, thin figure with tightly toned musculature. Consequently, critical feminists point out, such a beauty ideal is socially constructed along ideological lines instead of being the "natural" feminine figure. As a shape that is impossible for most to realize, this ideal is oppressive to most women, who are persuaded to devote numerous hours, much energy and worry, and often significant amounts of money to a useless pursuit. In a patriarchal society, the ideal is effectively maintained by male control of the neoliberal fitness industry and media. Aligned with the obesity critics, critical feminist researchers argue that exercising women can resist the ideological construction of the ideal body by building muscular bodies, engaging in sport instead of fitness, focusing on enjoying exercise, or openly questioning the fit ideal presented in the media (Markula & Kennedy, 2011). However, women's exercise experiences continue to be contradictory: despite numerous resistant strategies, not much has changed in the way the fitness industry operates or promotes itself. Similar to the postfeminist representations of sportswomen, the fitness industry continues to advance itself through an open celebration of thin, often sexualized bodies that are deemed as both healthy and beautiful (e.g., Markula & Kennedy, 2011).

Approaches from Foucauldian Theory: Disciplined Bodies in Power Relations

Critical scholars tend to reconstruct the obesity epidemic as sustained by the ideology of healthism in a way that individualizes a moral imperative to strive for normal weight through diet and exercise. Adopting a different starting point, Foucauldian researchers focus on how a dominant power/knowledge nexus supports medicalization within capitalist conditions. Unlike ideologies that are assumed to be carefully orchestrated to support dominant groups in society (e.g., wealthy, white men), Foucault (1978) conceptualized power as consisting of relations between forces. In his thought system, power is not purely repressive, but is practiced by both the mastered and the masters. Consequently, everyone is engaged in power relations, yet with differing degrees of potential affect. Instead of ideologies, the power relations are sustained by strategic uses of knowledge, some of which dominate and others that are marginalized. Individual selves and bodies are then formed by the combined effects of dominant power relations and knowledges.

Foucault (1978) further identified two main forms of power in current society: (1) biopower and (2) anatomo-political power. Biopower functions by administering and controlling the lives of a large multiplicity of people. For example, governmental physical activity promotion is aimed at populations at large who are expected to take responsibility to live more effective and productive lives through tightly controlled and measurable physical activity outcomes (Markula & Pringle, 2006). These campaigns, nevertheless, are considered to improve life and as such are practiced by both "the mastered and masters" in the name of health. This message, some researchers argue, is distributed by "biopedagogies" supported by the dominant medical knowledge (Evans, Rich, Allwood, & Davies, 2008; Wright & Harwood, 2009). For example, governmental campaigns regarding the health risks of obesity operate as biopedagogies to teach populations to manage their bodies appropriately against the risks of illness associated with overweight. As conveyers of biopedagogies, medical and physical activity experts occupy a central role in controlling the knowledge base, the "truth," about obesity risks (Rail, 2012). As thinness is considered less of a health risk, the fit ideal is sustained through a specific knowledge and power mechanism that Foucault (1978) labeled "anatomo-political power."

Anatomo-politics (Foucault, 1978, 1991) functions by disciplining bodies to normalcy, for example to the ideal fit body, through the effective use of space, time, and exercise practices. More specifically, individuals learn to operate in enclosed, purpose-built spaces that efficiently partition them to provide a useful and functional evaluation of the "workforce" in each enclosure. For example, the gym or health club can operate as such a purpose-built space to exercise (Markula & Pringle, 2006). The activities in these spaces are further controlled by the efficient use of detailed, correct training timetables (Markula & Pringle, 2006). According to Foucault, controlling space and time creates a machinery that manifests in the actual movements, a series of exercises that effectively educate the body through added intensity and increasingly more complex exercises (e.g., Markula & Pringle, 2006).

In this process, fit bodies become docile bodies: obedient individuals who unquestioningly and efficiently work toward the ideal body. The visibility in exercise spaces reinforces this quest by making a certain body shape appear normal. Any deviation from the correct use of time, exercise performance, and body shape become clearly observable and are deemed "abnormal." In this environment, every exercising body aims to adhere to normalcy as closely as possible. Therefore, an assumed constant surveillance, for example, by an instructor or a coach and fellow exercisers, athletes, or students, characterizes these spaces (e.g., Konoval, Denison, & Mills, 2019; Markula, 1995; Mills & Denison, 2018). Foucault (1991) described this kind of disciplinary space as a Panopticon, following Bentham's design for prisons, where all prisoners in their cells are visible while the guards remain invisible in an isolated, central tower. Invisible power can also be felt in enclosed physical activity spaces where the controlling "gaze" assumed by others encourages self-surveillance of one's body shape (Markula & Pringle, 2006).

Currently, the anatomo-political and biopolitical power arrangements appear to function simultaneously by rendering the ideal fit body also a healthy body. This aesthetics of the healthy-looking body further assists endorsement of the idea that health is determined based on the look of the body (Markula & Kennedy, 2011). At the same time, the healthy-looking body ideal is supported by a combined reading of such dominant knowledges as medicine (thin body as healthy body) and psychology (self-esteem and self-confidence deriving from thinness) and reinforced by consumerism (using exercise services to obtain the healthy-looking body) and the effective use of the media (old and new) to endorse the singular representation of the thin body. In this reading, everyone, including media producers, fitness center owners and managers, instructors, and participants within the power relations, draw on the dominant knowledges to sustain the operation of the fitness-media industry complex.

Rail (2012) discusses the "Obesity Clinic" as a place that employs a similarly naturalized combination of biopower supported by biomedicine and a panoptic formation supported by biocultural knowledges and bioeconomics that produce certain types of dieting and exercise practices. These forces meld together in defining how bodies are judged as abnormal based on their size. Unlike a clearly defined enclosure, Rail pictures the Obesity Clinic as a space without borders, one that now permeates all our living spaces. She concludes, "As a global and all-pervading entity, the Obesity Clinic uses biopedagogies and re/produces the obesity discourse by involving multiple points of collusion with variously positioned obesity entrepreneurs" (p. 241).

Like critical theorists, Foucault (1988a) discussed the role of individuals within power relations. Instead of individual agency to resist ideological control to change one's marginalized position, however, he endorsed active self-creation that can challenge the disciplinary knowledge base. For Foucault, individuals actively construct a self through problematization of the knowledge/power nexus. Through this process, which Foucault labeled "the technologies of the self," individuals are able to make sense of the moral codes of sport and fitness (e.g., the imperative of thinness, hypermasculinity) and construct their sporting or exercising selves accordingly (e.g., Crocket, 2016; MacKay & Dallaire, 2013; Pringle & Hickey, 2010; Thorpe, 2008). Constructing a new self, one aligned with the existing moral codes, however, does not necessarily change the dominant knowledge/power nexus. In his later work, Foucault (1988b) began to formulate an "ethics of care" based on which an individual, after the process of problematization, engages in "practices of freedom" to create a self "outside" of the moral codes. This critical attitude can result in shifting, for example, the substance or goal of exercise away from the aesthetics of the healthy-looking body (Markula & Pringle, 2006).

DEBATES

Much previous research has effectively critiqued the one-sided governmental health strategy that, while designed to improve well-being, also serves as an economic and social tool to marginalize and stigmatize a segment of the population. These scholars have further illustrated how the healthist construction of illness prevention as an individual responsibility to diet and exercise for weight loss supports this marginalization. In such a neoliberal context, critical scholars argue, the focus on the individual's duty to take care of their health masks the narratives used to fuel the profiteering of medical, diet, nutrition, or food industries—aptly named "Obesity Inc." by Rail (2012)—that structure the obesity epidemic. Embedded in this, the notion of the obesity epidemic has also a distinctly gendered dimension: women's bodies are visually judged overweight more consistently due to the more narrowly defined feminine body ideal. When judged on their appearance, women commonly suffer from body dissatisfaction, with serious consequences such as eating disorders. Foucauldian researchers have demonstrated how women have been turned into docile bodies who do not question the quest for the ideal body. Similar to Obesity Inc., the fitness industry, along with related media industries, profits from the imperative to build a thin, healthy-looking body. If critical research has exposed the body ideal as socially constructed and oppressive, what can be done to change this? Is cultural transformation possible by using the existing theoretical and methodological tools? If not, what are other possible ways to problematize and then change the dominant body ideal? I offer two recent approaches, new materialism and Deleuzian poststructuralism, as alternative perspectives to obesity, thinness, and the ideal body. These research orientations problematize social construction as the primary way of understanding the body politics of inequality, marginalization, and resistance.

While not a unified theoretical approach, new materialism rejects what is defined as the cultural, linguistic, interpretive, or representational turn in the social sciences and humanities (e.g., Barad, 2003, 2007; Coole & Frost, 2010; Fox & Alldred, 2017; Markula, 2019; Seigworth & Gregg, 2010; St. Pierre, Jackson, & Mazzei, 2016). This turn privileges humanist (radical) (social) constructivism according to which culture, human behavior, the body, ideas, values, and organizations are socially constructed (Markula, 2019). Marxist-derived critical theory, particularly, is criticized for relying on the social construction (e.g., Coole & Frost, 2010) of, for example, the obese body as a representation of healthist and gendered ideologies. Social constructionism, the new materialists argue, tends to be embedded in binary constructions such as a masculine versus a feminine body, an obese versus a thin body, a healthy versus an unhealthy body. New materialists find these binaries to be a limited set of analytical tools and argue for new onto-epistemological positions that include material objects and their environments as integral aspects of inquiry. Coole and Frost (2010, p. 6), for example, advocate that mere social analysis is "inadequate for thinking about matter, materiality, and politics in ways that do justice to the contemporary context of biopolitics and global political economy." From this point of view, the material human body, nonhuman objects, and their environments create a field of force relations that intra-acts with human actors, their ideas, values, and politics (Barad, 2003). Consequently, the social world of power relations is put in motion by human and nonhuman actors, both of which have to be accounted for in order to fully understand the world that is constantly in flux (e.g., Coole & Frost, 2010; Fox & Alldred, 2016; Markula, 2019; Tuin & Dolphijn, 2012).

It can be difficult to envision a new materialist project regarding body size. It has become evident, however, that analyzing the ideological construction of body size and individuals' resistance to it does not account for the complexity of force relations in the world, and thus no significant change has resulted from researching only this element of our lives. New materialism, thus, can offer one option for transformative research for alternatives to the negative social constructions of large bodies and the unwarranted celebration of thin bodies. However, new materialist projects begin by illustrating how the fat-thin binary, in the first place, has become a necessary element of biopolitics in the current world. I offer Deleuze's (1995) work on control society as a tool to analyze how the current emerging conditions of digitalization can cloud the interrelationship of material and nonmaterial conditions of different sized bodies that are then harnessed to serve Obesity Inc.

Expanding on Foucault's insights on power relations, Deleuze (1995) observed that we are shifting from a disciplinary society into a society where control permeates every aspect of life. Technological developments, particularly digital media technology, have made controlling bodies more effective than spatial control through permanent, stable institutions such as schools, hospitals, or governments. The digitalized world enables modulations of rapid shifts in power relations at local and global levels. The fast fluctuations of stock markets as responses to global crises now impact people's everyday lives at multiple levels, from employment to health benefits, child care, education possibilities, and exercise facility closures. We are also constantly aware of numerous global developments—that we appear to have no control over—through unlimited (social) media access. Digitalization also compresses information, distance, and time up to the point where we tend to immerse ourselves entirely in the virtual world: we shop online, we communicate online, and, as demonstrated during the COVID-19 pandemic, we increasingly work online and even exercise online. The access to these digital services, however, is manipulated by codes through which we are now identified as "dividuals" rather than individuals (Deleuze, 1995, p. 180). When cut off from the surrounding real world, the body as a visible marker of identity becomes potentially less relevant, yet there are various ways to expose one's body to the global virtual world through numerous social media channels that now carry a plethora of messages celebrating and condemning either fatness or thinness. In this world of instant communication, individuals' lives are controlled even more strictly than before.

In her work, Rail (2012, p. 241) hints at these developments when she conceptualizes the Obesity Clinic as "an evasive and invisible system of order." Here, instead of a clearly established and materialized location of disciplinary control, the Obesity Clinic "involves a form of architecture without structure" that nevertheless tightly controls overweight through various channels (p. 241). In my work, I have located the obesity epidemic within this context by demonstrating how the panic of overweight is effectively driven by both old and new media campaigns that provide global statistical comparisons by coding, storing, and distributing biological information on obesity (Markula, 2008). The bodies coded as obese are then exposed to the control of a global media gaze unlimited by distance or time.

To fight these new forms of control, Deleuze (1995) emphasized the importance of first recognizing the type of control, detailing how it works, and then identifying "new weapons" to prepare for the battle. Instead of a revolution that would only replace the control society with another form of control, Deleuze was interested in how to live with the control without entirely submitting to its numbing effects. To this point, I have earlier argued that "[w]hile it is important to understand the effects of globalised digital communication technology that promotes endless interaction with (numerical) information," it is nonetheless evident that "control does not vanish even if this technology disappears" (Markula, 2008, p. 64). As researchers, it is important that we capture the often small, fast outbursts of resistance in our everyday environments, whether on- or offline, in order to focus on "how the body harnessed by global capitalism might create the 'vacuoles of noncommunication' at the level of local events" (p. 64).

From a new materialist perspective, analyses of everyday lived experiences are essential for understanding the interplay of material and nonmaterial elements (e.g., Fox & Alldred, 2016). In their local-level analysis of the micro-context of everyday life, Fox, Bissell, Peacock, and Blackburn (2018) used a new materialist approach to examine the production of fat and slim bodies in the United Kingdom. They interviewed 45 adult participants with various BMI scores to consider how individual bodies, food, shopping, and money affect and are affected by social ideas, formations, industrial production, economic relations, and governmental policies. In this context, they conceptualize obesity as an assemblage of various material and nonmaterial relations in the world. Their analysis reveals how the larger obesity assemblage manifests in two micro assemblages, the "becoming-fat" body and the "becoming-slim(mer)" body. The becoming-fat body was produced in relation to individuals' desire for food, but also the availability of certain foods and tastes manufactured for "a fattening body" (p. 117). The becoming-slimmer body was an attempt to move away from consuming such foods. Food remained a predominant element of "slimming" as the participants spent time learning to classify some foods as "unhealthy" and others as "a route to health based on their capacities to reduce or increase weight" (p. 121). Not only food, but such activities as yo-yo dieting or joining slimming clubs were integral to the process of becoming a slimmer body. The researchers summarized that "the becoming-slim(mer) assemblage was a struggle for control of a body between the desire to lose weight and powerful opposing forces deriving from food, food retailers and industry, family and other relations in the obesity-assemblage" (p. 121). In addition to individual weight management, consequently, it is important to examine how food production, distribution, and retailing produces obesity. These are manifest in consumer-supermarket relations to reflect "the marketised character of global industrialised food production, processing and distribution" (p. 122). Such food production "is dominated by a small number of large, multinational agribusiness corporations that have a global reach" and "an economic and scientific orientation towards feeding mass populations rather than local communities" (p. 122). Squeezed between such powerful relations, these researchers demonstrated, current individualized approaches addressing obesity and overweight have proven quite ineffective. Consequently, changing the obesity-assemblage requires providing financial incentives to local and regional ecological agriculture instead of multinational food corporations and the global marketization of food production.

To further investigate how local-level material and nonmaterial elements intertwine, I have experimented with how a very specific event, a group fitness class, may present opportunities for thinking differently about thinness in the very appearance-oriented fitness industry. In my ongoing project (Markula, 2011, 2014), I have sought ways to instruct group fitness classes with an emphasis different from the aesthetics of the healthy-looking, thin body. My project draws on Deleuze's (2006) reading of Foucault's work to highlight, particularly, how poststructuralism can inform the study of the moving body. In his discussion of Foucault's texts, Deleuze pictured knowledge assembled from visible, "non-discursive" and articulable, "discursive" elements (p. 27). The visible elements are comprised of material bodies, their practices, and their environments, whereas the articulable elements refer to how we talk about, conceptualize, and think about bodies, practices, or environments. The material bodies doing certain types of practices in a specific environment thus comprise specific practical knowledge of physical activity. The articulable elements assemble with the visible, material elements to specify "an interpretation" of what we "see" taking place. For example, we know about training physically active bodies through a combination of such "sciences" as physiology, psychology, and medicine that can act as the articulable elements for exercise. In addition, as Deleuze pointed out, there are educational, ethical, aesthetic, and political articulations that shape our interpretations of how to exercise. The visible and the articulable knowledges do not exist without each other and thus comprise equally crucial aspects of each formation. To fully analyze how the articulable and the visible interact, scholars must account for relations of power that, in different contexts, facilitate different knowledge formations. Consequently, how we come to know about, learn, and practice bodily movements is always determined through dominant knowledges in certain relations of power. I have aimed to identify what dominant knowledges support the aesthetics of the healthy-looking body as a substance of (women's) fitness and how I may be able to use this knowledge differently to create more ethical ways to instruct fitness classes (Markula, 2014). It is important to note that I cannot change the substance of my fitness classes purely through articulation (e.g., not mentioning body shaping in my class). I have to concomitantly change the exercises to align with a different substance (i.e., optimal function for everyday life settings). Consequently, both articulable knowledges as well as movement practices (the visible knowledges) need to be assembled differently to create a group fitness class that departs from such practices as body sculpting that currently dominate the commercial fitness industry.

Conclusion

The social construction of body size has become a timely and important topic in sociocultural research on sport, exercise, and physical activity. Currently, critical analyses of the ideological construction of the obese as unhealthy body have dominated the field. This work further demonstrates a binary that reinforces the aesthetic preference for thinness and relegates fatness as necessarily diseased, abject, and unattractive. In effectively arguing against body politics that assigns building the ideal body entirely as an individual's responsibility in the world where economic conditions and political decisions disadvantage certain groups, critical researchers have demonstrated the discrimination embedded in current obesity campaigns as well as in the overt celebration of thin, fit bodies. Despite this criticism, the thin ideal continues to animate the prominent obesity-prevention campaigns as well as the (women's) fitness and sport industries, as demonstrated by Rachel's success and Cain's failure that opened this chapter.

While a critique of the neoliberal conditions that produce these oppressive body politics is imperative, there is a pressing need to suggest ways to change the singular body ideal. As one solution, new materialist research suggests examinations of how material (bodies, nutrients, exercise practices) and nonmaterial (ideas, knowledges, politics) elements intertwine to produce the current conditions. After mapping all these elements, it becomes possible to suggest ways to harness their power to create social change. To do this, new materialist researchers look for local contexts where individuals' everyday experiences can be analyzed through diverse (qualitative) methods. While semi-structured interviews have dominated social science research, there is a need for a wider variety of research tools to tap into the digitalized contexts of contemporary control and individuals' creative "resistance" to their dominance.

It is important to examine how both the nonmaterial and material aspects shape sport, body ideals, and obesity to obtain a fuller understanding of the physically active human body as a central element of our existence. While the look of the body, notably influenced by judgments of its size, currently occupies a central role in how we classify bodies into healthy-unhealthy, thin-fat, masculine-feminine, dominant-marginalized, and are used to then normalize a certain type of body as morally good, such binaries also limit both our vision and the possibilities for transformation. To consider how multiple different types of bodies can contribute to social and cultural life, it is important to explore the body's potential as a social and cultural, as well as material, force for positive change.

References

Arcelus, J., Witcomb, G. L., & Mitchell, A. (2014). Prevalence of eating disorders amongst dancers: A systemic review and meta-analysis. *European Eating Disorders Review, 22*(2), 92–101.

Barad, K. (2003). Posthumanist performativity: Toward an understanding of how matter comes to matter. *Signs, 28*(3), 802–831.

Barad, K. (2007). *Meeting the universe halfway.* Durham, NC: Duke University Press.

Bordo, S. (2004). *Unbearable weight: Feminism, Western culture, and the body.* Oakland: University of California Press.

Bratland-Sanda, S., & Sundgot-Borgen, J. (2013). Eating disorders in athletes: Overview of prevalence, risk factors and recommendations for prevention and treatment. *European Journal of Sport Science, 13*(5), 499–508.

Cain, M. (2019, November). I was the fastest girl in America, until I joined Nike. *New York Times.* https://www.nytimes.com/2019/11/07/opinion/nike-running-mary-cain.html?refe rringSource=articleShare.

Campos, P. (2004). *The obesity myth: Why America's obsession with weight is hazardous to your health.* New York: Penguin Books.

Campos, P., Saguy, A., Ernsberger, P., Oliver, E., & Gaesser, G. (2006). The epidemiology of overweight and obesity: Public health crisis or moral panic? *International Journal of Epidemiology, 35*(1), 55–60.

Canadian Society for Exercise Physiology. (2022). 24-hour movement guidelines. www.cse pguidelines.ca.

Coole, D., & Frost, S. (2010). Introduction to new materialisms. In D. Coole & S. Frost (Eds.), *New materialism: Ontology, agency, and politics* (pp. 1–43). Durham, NC: Duke University Press.

Crocket, H. (2016). Problematizing Foucauldian ethics: A review of the technologies of the self in sociology of sport since 2003. *Journal of Sport and Social Issues, 41*(1), 21–41.

Deleuze, G. (1995). Postscript on control societies. In M. Joughin (Ed.), *Negotiations* (pp. 177–182). New York: Columbia University Press.

Deleuze, G. (2006). *Foucault*. London: Continuum.

Dworkin, S. L., & Wachs, F. L. (2009). *Body panic: Gender, health, and the selling of fitness.* New York: New York University Press.

Evans, J., Rich, E., Allwood, R., & Davies, B. (2008). Body pedagogies, policy, health and gender. *British Educational Research Journal, 34*(3), 387–402.

Evans, J., Rich, E., Davies, B., & Allwood, R. (2008). *Education, disordered eating and obesity discourse: Fat fabrications.* London: Routledge.

Foucault, M. (1978). *The history of sexuality: Vol. 1. An introduction.* London: Penguin Books.

Foucault, M. (1988a). Technologies of the self. In L. H. Martin, H. Gutman, & P. H. Hutton (Eds.), Technologies of the self: A seminar with Michel Foucault (pp. 16–49). Amherst, MA: The University of Massachusetts Press.

Foucault, M. (1988b). An aesthetics of existence. In L. D. Kritzman (Ed.), Michel Foucault politics, philosophy, culture: Interviews and other writing 1977–1984 (pp. 47–53). London: Routledge.

Foucault, M. (1991). *Discipline and punish: The birth of the prison.* London: Penguin Books.

Fox, N., & Alldred, P. (2016). *Sociology and the new materialism: Theory, research, action.* Thousand Oaks, CA: Sage.

Fox, N., Bissell, P., Peacock, M., & Blackburn, J. (2018). The micropolitics of obesity: Materialism, markets and food sovereignty. *Sociology, 52*(1), 111–127.

Gard, M., & Wright, J. (2005). *The obesity epidemic: Science, morality and ideology.* London: Routledge.

Harjunen, H. (2019). *The neoliberal bodies and gendered fat body: The fat body in focus.* Abingdon, U.K.: Routledge.

Kilpela, L. S., Becker, C. B., Wesley, N., & Stewart, T. (2015). Body image in adult women: Moving beyond the younger years. Advances in Eating Disorders: Theory, Research and Practice, 3(2), 144–164.

Konoval, T., Denison, J., & Mills, J. P. (2019). The cyclical relationship between physiology and discipline: One endurance running coach's experiences problematizing disciplinary practices. *Sports Coaching Review, 8,* 124–148.

Maguire, J., & Mansfield, L. (1998). "No-body's perfect": Women, aerobics, and the body beautiful. *Sociology of Sport Journal, 15*(2), 109–137.

Mansfield, L. (2016). Resourcefulness, reciprocity and reflexivity: The three Rs of partnership in sport for public health research. *International Journal of Sport Policy and Politics, 8*(4), 713–729.

Markula, P. (1995). Firm but shapely, fit but sexy, strong but thin: The postmodern aerobicizing female bodies. *Sociology of Sport Journal, 12,* 424–453.

Markula, P. (2008). Governing obese bodies in a control society. *Junctures, 11,* 53–66.

Markula, P. (2011). "Folding": A feminist intervention in mindful fitness. In E. Kennedy & P. Markula (Eds.), *Women and exercise: The body, health and consumerism* (pp. 60–78). New York: Routledge.

Markula, P. (2014). The moving body and social change. *Cultural Studies—Critical Methodologies, 14,* 471–482.

Markula, P. (2019). What is new about new materialism for sport sociology? Reflections on body, movement, and culture. *Sociology of Sport Journal, 36,* 1–11.

Markula, P., & Chikinda, J. (2016). Group fitness instructors as local level health promoters: A Foucauldian analysis of the politics of health/fitness dynamic. *International Journal of Sport Policy and Politics, 8*(4), 625–646.

Markula, P., & Kennedy, E. (2011). Introduction: Beyond binaries: Contemporary approaches to women and exercise. In E. Kennedy & P. Markula (Eds.), *Women and exercise: The body, health and consumerism* (pp. 1–26). New York: Routledge.

Markula, P., & Pringle, R. (2006). *Foucault, sport, and exercise: Power, knowledge and transforming the self.* London: Routledge.

MacKay, S., & Dallaire, C. (2013). Skirtboarders.com: Skateboarding women and self-formation as ethical subjects. *Sociology of Sport Journal, 30,* 173–196.

Mills, J. P., & Denison, J. (2018). How power moves: A Foucauldian analysis on [in]effective coaching. *International Review for the Sociology of Sport, 53,* 296–312.

National Association of Anorexia Nervosa and Associated Disorders. (2020, January). Eating disorder statistics. https://anad.org/education-and-awareness/about-eating-disorders/eating-disorders-statistics/.

National Initiative for Eating Disorders Canada. (2018). About eating disorders in Canada. https://nied.ca/about-eating-disorders-in-canada/.

Oliver, J. E. (2006). *Fat politics: The real story behind America's obesity epidemic.* Oxford: Oxford University Press.

Pringle, R., & Hickey, C. (2010). Negotiating masculinities via the moral problematization of sport. *Sociology of Sport Journal, 27,* 115–139.

Priory. (2018). Eating disorder statistics. https://www.priorygroup.com/eating-disorders/eating-disorder-statistics.

Pullen, E., & Malcolm, D. (2018). Assessing the side effects of the "exercise pill": The paradox of physical activity health promotion. *Qualitative Research in Sport, Exercise and Health, 10*(4), 493–504.

Rail, G. (2012). The birth of the obesity clinic: Confessions of the flesh, biopedagogies and physical culture. *Sociology of Sport Journal, 29,* 227–253.

Riley, S., & Evans, A. (2018). Lean light fit and tight: Fitblr blogs and the postfeminist transformation imperative. In K. Toffoletti, H. Thorpe, & J. Francombe-Webb (Eds.), *New sporting femininities: Embodied politics in postfeminist times* (pp. 207–230). London: Palgrave.

Rinaldi, J., Rice, C., & Friedman, M. (2019). Introduction. In M. Friedman, C. Rice, & J. Rinaldi (Eds.), *Thickening fat: Fat bodies, intersectionality, and social justice* (pp. 1–12). New York: Routledge.

Seigworth, G. J., & Gregg, M. (2010). An inventory of shimmers. In M. Gregg & G. J. Seigworth (Eds.), *The affect theory reader* (pp. 1–25). Durham, NC: Duke University Press.

Sport for Life. (2020). Long term development. https://sportforlife.ca/long-term-development/.

Statistics Canada. (2019, June 25). Overweight and obese adults. https://www150.statcan.gc.ca/n1/en/pub/82-625-x/2019001/article/00005-eng.pdf?st=8GZa54YX.

St. Pierre, E. A., Jackson, A. Y., & Mazzei, L. A. (2016). New empiricisms and new materialisms: Conditions for new inquiry. *Cultural Studies—Critical Methodologies, 16*(2), 99–110.

Toffoletti, K., Thorpe, H., & Francombe-Webb, J. (Eds.). (2018). *New sporting femininities: Embodied politics in postfeminist times*. London: Palgrave.

Thorpe, H. (2008). Foucault, technologies of self, and the media: Discourses of femininity in snowboarding culture. *Journal of Sport & Social Issues, 32*, 199–229.

Thorpe, H. (2016). Athletic women's experiences of amenorrhea: Biomedical technologies, somatic ethics and embodied subjectivities. *Sociology of Sport Journal, 33*, 1–13.

Thorpe, H., & Clarke, M. (2020). Gut feminism, new materialisms and sportwomen's embodied health: The case of RED-S in endurance athletes. *Qualitative Research in Sport, Exercise and Health, 12*(1), 1–17. doi:10.1080/2159676X.2019.1631879.

Tuin, I. V. D., & Dolphijn, R. (2012). New materialism: Interviews & cartographies. Open Humanities Press.

Weed, M. (2016). Should we privilege sport for health? The comparative effectiveness of UK government investment in sport as a public health intervention. *International Journal of Sport Policy and Politics, 8*(4), 559–576.

Wright, J., & Harwood, V. (2009). *Biopolitics and the "obesity epidemic": Governing bodies*. London: Routledge.

CHAPTER 45

··

SPORT, DISABILITY, AND INCLUSION

··

IAN BRITTAIN AND MATEJ CHRISTIAENS

I<small>T</small> is estimated that 10% to 15% of the world's population has a disability, which approximates to 1 billion disabled people around the world (World Health Organization & World Bank, 2018). The probability of becoming disabled is higher than might be expected: around 25% of today's 20-year-olds become disabled before they retire (U.S. Social Security Administration, 2019). Despite such a significant proportion of the population being considered as having a disability, disabled people have historically been marginalized and excluded from the rest of society based on the perception that they are, as a result of their impairments, different from the norm (Oliver & Barnes, 2012).

While over the past 30 years, the life chances and opportunities for many disabled people in society have dramatically changed, the pace of change has not been uniform; many disabled people remain institutionalized and discriminated against and continue to experience social isolation and limited access to sport (Filmer, 2005; Loeb, Eide, Jelsma, Toni, & Maart, 2008; Watermeyer, Swartz, Lorenzo, Schneider, & Priestley, 2006). As a result, the enormous benefits of physical activity that have been widely recognized for the non-disabled population are currently not experienced by the entire population. Sport also serves a more practical purpose, which often forms the basis for government interest in sport. For example, research has shown that regular physical activity is key to preventing and treating noncommunicable diseases such as heart disease, stroke, diabetes, and cancer and regulating weight, while also being instrumental in alleviating depression and contributing to a positive sense of well-being (Kruk, 2007; Mammen & Faulkner, 2013; Winzer, Woitek, & Linke, 2018). Additionally, sport is used as a tool to achieve broader social objectives, such as tackling crime and drug use (Cameron & MacDougall, 2000; Crabbe, 2000; Smith & Waddington, 2004), peacemaking and peacekeeping (Parry, 2012) and promoting diversity and social inclusion (Kelly, 2010; Spaaij et al., 2016). The idea of using sport as a vehicle to increase the inclusion of disabled people into the wider society has been going on since the 1940s, when Ludwig Guttmann introduced sport as part of the rehabilitation regime for spinally injured servicemen and women from World War II at Stoke Mandeville Hospital in the United Kingdom (Brittain, 2016).

This chapter, split into three sections, will interrogate this idea further. In the first section (Issues), we will look at some of the reasons why greater inclusion of disabled people in the wider society might be necessary. In the second section (Approaches), we will look at some of the models and theories pertaining to disability that seek to explain and create an improved understanding of human behavior with respect to disability. In the third section (Debates), we will outline some of the issues that may arise when trying to use sport as a vehicle for greater inclusion of disabled people in the wider society.

ISSUES

The Genesis of Sport, Disability, and Inclusion

The Paralympic Movement itself and its precursor, the Stoke Mandeville Games, were founded partly on the idea that disability sport could help disabled people navigate the problems they generally faced within society on a day-to-day basis (Brittain, 2016). Indeed, Sir Ludwig Guttmann (1976, pp. 12–13), internationally recognized founder of the modern-day Paralympic Movement, highlighted three main areas in which participation in sport could benefit disabled people. We examine each of these in the following subsections.

Sport as a Curative Factor

According to Guttmann, sport represents the most natural form of remedial exercise and can be used to successfully complement other forms of remedial/rehabilitative exercise. Sport, it was posited, can be invaluable in restoring the overall fitness, including strength, speed, coordination, and endurance, of someone who has received a disabling injury.

The Recreational and Psychological Value of Sport

Guttmann claims that the big advantage of sport for disabled people over other remedial exercises lies within its recreational value. He also points out that much of the restorative power of sport is lost if the disabled person does not enjoy their participation in it. As long as enjoyment is derived from the activity, then sport can help develop an active mind, self-confidence, self-dignity, self-discipline, competitive spirit, and camaraderie, all of which are essential in helping to overcome the often all-consuming depression that can occur with sudden traumatic disability.

Sport as a Means of Social Reintegration

There are certain sports in which disabled people are capable of competing alongside their non-disabled peers (e.g., archery, bowls, and table tennis), something that Neroli Fairhall of New Zealand proved when she competed from a wheelchair in archery at the 1976 Olympic Games in Montreal. It was Guttmann's contention that this tangible interaction between disabled and non-disabled individuals helps create a better understanding between them and aids in the social reintegration of disabled people through the medium of sport.

The International Paralympic Committee and Inclusion

Founded in 1989, the International Paralympic Committee (IPC) leans heavily on these original three principles of Guttmann's, especially the third, concerning social reintegration. Indeed, in their latest strategic plan (2019–2022), the IPC's vision statement clearly links the movement to the idea of increasing societal inclusion: "Make for an inclusive world through Para sport" (International Paralympic Committee, 2019, p. 6). This overarching vision is further reinforced in the IPC's Strategic Priority 3, to "drive a cultural shift through Para sport for a truly inclusive society" (p. 14). Despite the fact that the word "inclusion" is used eight times in their 22-page strategic plan, what the IPC does not do at any point is define what they actually mean by inclusion. The closest they get is to state, "The Paralympic Movement must use its global position and influence, together with its events and activities, to challenge the stigma attached to disability, empower social transformation and make for a more inclusive society for all" (p. 15). However, even this is not really a definition of what inclusion should look like. Rather, the statement speaks to some of the processes that need to be undertaken to move toward inclusion. It should be noted, however, that it is often the case that even in policies designed to promote inclusion in other areas of society, rarely, if ever, do we see definitions of what true inclusion means or looks like in practice. Obviously, such ambiguities can contribute to confusion and misunderstanding, and even enable deliberate misinterpretation of the goals of inclusion policies by those asked to enact them (see further consideration of this dynamic in the Debates section).

Why Are Disabled People Excluded from Society?

Before going further, it is worthwhile to underline why inclusion policies for disabled people are even necessary. Why and how are disabled people excluded in the first place? To a large extent, disabled people are still viewed by many as a "class or category" (Dunn and Sherrill, 1996), with little appreciation or understanding of the unique nature of each person, regardless of their impairment. The definition of disability within a particular society can potentially say a good deal about how that society perceives, and thus treats, disability and disabled people. The following dictionary definition of the term "disability" (*Oxford Illustrated Dictionary*, 1998, p. 230), which is common in many societies, clearly pathologizes disability by representing it as biologically situated and produced:

> **Disability,** *n.*—1. A physical incapacity; either congenital or caused by injury, disease, etc., esp. when limiting a person's ability to work.

Definitions of disability such as this form the basis for what most often constitutes conventional views of disability. The implications of this, and the larger contested terrain about this foundational definitional issue, are considered in more detail in the Debates section.

   Still, in order to explain why disabled people are excluded from society, it is important to highlight the way many disabled people are treated and viewed by the wider non-disabled society. Here, the adaptation of Galtung's (1990) Triangle of Violence, shown below in Figure 45.1, highlights some of the ways in which disabled people have historically been "victims" of various kinds of "violence" or discrimination around the world. For the purposes of this

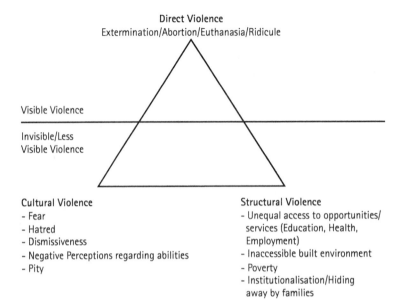

Direct Violence
Extermination/Abortion/Euthanasia/Ridicule

Visible Violence

Invisible/Less
Visible Violence

Cultural Violence
- Fear
- Hatred
- Dismissiveness
- Negative Perceptions regarding abilities
- Pity

Structural Violence
- Unequal access to opportunities/
  services (Education, Health,
  Employment)
- Inaccessible built environment
- Poverty
- Institutionalisation/Hiding
  away by families

FIGURE 45.1 Disability and the triangle of violence (adapted from Johan Galtung, 1990)

chapter, the following definition of violence put forward by the World Health Organization (2010) will anchor our considerations:

> the intentional use of physical force or power, threatened or actual, against oneself, another person, or against a group or community, that either results in or has a high likelihood of resulting in injury, death, psychological harm, maldevelopment, or deprivation.

As can be seen in the adaptation of Galtung's Triangle, violence can range from more visible and direct forms of violence, such as the deliberate killing of disabled babies and children in Ghana (Kassah, Kassah, & Agbota, 2012), to less visible and less direct forms of violence, which includes negative attitudes toward disabled people (Livneh, 1982), facilitating an inaccessible environment (Banda-Chalwe, Nitz, & de Jonge, 2014), and/or the creation of social structures that prevent access to key forms of social capital, such as education and employment (Brittain, Biscaia, & Gerard, 2020). The combined effect of direct, cultural, and structural violence against disabled people is social exclusion. A brief explanation of each form of violence is given below.

Direct Violence

Extermination of disabled people has occurred throughout history, beginning in ancient times, for a variety of reasons, including a religious belief that disabled people were evil. For example, Kassah et al. (2012, p. 690) claim that "disabled children in some communities in Ghana are often killed or ritualistically returned to the world of their ancestors." As well, modern genetic engineers or eugenicists have claimed that there is a need to exterminate anything that (or presumably anyone who) might interfere with ideal or "normal" development of the human body, a posture that was put into practice, for example, in Nazi Germany (Mitchell & Snyder, 2003).

While less severe, sanctioned ridicule can be seen as direct violence. For example, ridicule played a role in earlier societies, most particularly during the medieval period, when court jesters, many of whom were individuals with different appearances or mental functions (e.g., dwarfs, hunchbacks), were frequently subject to ridicule and taunting because they were disabled in some way that some found offensive. A more recent example of this exercise of violence may be seen in so-called Freak Shows (Shakespeare, 1994) that occurred between the 17th and 20th centuries in the United Kingdom and other countries, in which people whose bodily appearance widely varied from accepted norms for appearance were put on show for the paying public's amusement. Shakespeare claims that this is a clear example of the way that many "human beings were seen as non-human" (p. 287). And even in contemporary times, when one might think that such aggressions would not be tolerated, disabled individuals frequently have to endure rude, ignorant, and offensive comments. Indeed, our language is full of expressions that poke fun through sharp words (e.g., "cripple," "retard") used to characterize those with a variety of impairments (Siperstein, Pociask, & Collins, 2010).

Although the more extreme forms of visible direct violence, such as extermination, may not be anywhere near as prevalent today in responding to disabled people (although this is not to say that it does not still happen in more isolated areas or in individual cases), other forms of visible violence, such as abortion and even euthanasia, still occur, often legally, within society, even though both of these latter practices have understandably come under heavy criticism from a number of different sources (cf. Davis, 2004).

Structural Violence

In addition to commonly recognized issues, such as poverty (Banks, Kuper, & Polack, 2017) and an inaccessible built environment (Stephens et al., 2017), there are myriad issues that fall under the heading of structural violence. Up until the early 1900s, it was very common to institutionalize any individual who deviated significantly from the norm. Although, at the time, this was often viewed as the humane thing to do, many have acknowledged that housing disabled people in institutions was done, in no small part, to protect the non-disabled from those with disabilities (Barnes, 1994). In Japan, Hayashi and Okuhira (2001) claim that, as recently as the 1980s, Japanese society did not perceive confining disabled people in institutions for life as a human rights violation. As one example of how disabled people were perceived within Japanese society at that time, they state that "a standard practice in these institutions was to give hysterectomies to women who menstruate, in order to make the staff's work easier. Disabled women were simply not regarded as 'women' (p. 857).

The hiding away by families of family members who are disabled can occur as a result of a variety of cultural and/or religious reasons. For example, the central precept of Buddhism revolves around "karma," whereby actions in this life dictate the level of existence in the next. At a conceptual level, this often means that disability is seen as a punishment for bad actions committed in previous lives. Disabled people, especially in rural areas, in Cambodia, a Buddhist nation, are therefore often hidden by their families, who are afraid for their reputation in the community, a dynamic which has been linked to the culturally embedded Asian idea of "losing face" (Yan, Accordino, Boutin, & Wilson, 2014).

Crawford (2004) attributes similar behaviors in Kenya to myths that surround the passing on of "bad blood." Such myths embrace a notion of contagion or being tarnished by disability, which is similar to the idea of karma and plays a key part in impacting the way many disabled people are differentially treated in Kenya in comparison to those who are not disabled. In the Kenyan context, non-disabled family members of disabled people may also be deemed to be tainted by the "curse" of disability, resulting in whole families being treated differently or even shunned.

A very recent example of unequal access to services occurred during the COVID-19 pandemic in the United Kingdom and the USA, where there were numerous reports about the reinforcement and application of ableist normative values in treating disabled people infected with the virus. For example, disabled people infected with the virus were deprioritized in gaining access to ventilators in favor of non-disabled patients (Goggin & Ellis, 2020).

Cultural Violence

Emotional responses to disability, such as fear, hatred, dismissiveness, or pity, can have major impacts upon the way people within non-disabled society interact with disabled people. Brittain (2016) clearly demonstrates this with the case of Danny, who found that, after losing his right arm in a car accident, many of his close friends suddenly found it very hard to be in his company. Their reaction is in line with Hogan's (1999) contention that an acquired disability, such as the one Danny's accident led to, can result in a massive change in social status from the perspective of those in the newly disabled person's social network. The reaction of Danny's friends to his acquired impairment clearly demonstrates this effect. Their lack of understanding and possible fear of the visible difference of anyone who does not conform to societal norms of physicality may well have underpinned their reactions. Danny is still fully ambulatory, with all his visual and intellectual faculties intact. He simply has one arm less than the majority of people.

It might be assumed that negative perceptions with regard to disability are relevant to non-disabled individuals only when dealing with or discussing disabled people. However, the power and reach of the perceptions of disability that are embedded in a medical model (see Approaches section) are such that they can inform disabled people's own discourses about people with different or more severe impairments in much the same way as they do for the non-disabled community. This kind of occurrence has been reported by Hunt (1966, quoted in Sherrill, 1986, pp. 23–24) who stated that "people with less stigmatized disabilities are often quite prejudiced against individuals who are more stigmatized." This (unfortunately ironic) dynamic then plays a part in reinforcing, re-creating, and naturalizing negative perceptions of disability and their continued use in society, by both disabled and non-disabled people. It can also lead to the formulation and reinforcement of a "hierarchy of disability," as reported by Tringo (1970), or a "hierarchy of impairments," reported by Deal (2003). In each hierarchical notion, those whose impairments more closely align with the normative values of the society they live in are positioned at the top of the hierarchy, and those whose impairments fall the furthest from those normative values are placed at the bottom of the hierarchy.

Implications for Inclusion

The varied ways that violence can be inflicted upon disabled people are both considerable and impactful. In what follows, we consider some of the implications of such treatment of disabled people on their prospects for inclusion within wider society. We offer some select, albeit certainly not exhaustive, examples as illustrations of repercussions that can be broadly felt.

The Economic and Social Position of Disabled People

Disabled people are far less likely to be hired than their non-disabled counterparts, and those who do get hired are likely to be employed in poorly paid, low-status positions. As a consequence, a far larger proportion of disabled people tend to be associated with low economic status (Saxton, 2018). According to Goodley (2014), the current global economic climate, which is now being exacerbated by the COVID-19 pandemic, has led the United Kingdom and other countries to narrow the definition they use for "disability" in order to restrict access to welfare benefits as a way to cut national budgets. It has been further noted that disabled people in the United Kingdom are enduring "nine times the burden of cuts compared to the average citizen, with people with the most severe disabilities being hit a staggering nineteen times harder" (Ryan, 2019, p. 3). Work is central to industrial societies due to the fact that gainful employment not only produces the goods to support life but also helps to create some of the social relationships necessary for a satisfactory life. The difficulties of finding paid work for disabled people can exacerbate social isolation and makes inclusion in other areas of society, including sport, a major challenge.

Accessibility of the Built Environment

Because the built environment in which we all have to live our lives is, on the whole, designed, constructed, paid for, and operated by those within the non-disabled majority, it is, more often than not, built only with their needs in mind (Imrie & Thomas, 2008). This often leads to a great many accessibility issues for people with a wide variety of impairments. However, when accessibility is taken into account and adaptations such as ramps are added to buildings, it is not just disabled people who benefit. For example, ramps make access far easier and more dignified for parents with small children in pushchairs and the elderly who may struggle with steps.

Non-Disabled Social Interactions with Disabled People

Perceptions of disability embodied in the medical model (explained in the Approaches section) may form the basis for how many non-disabled people act toward a disabled person and what they might say when discussing disabled people with others (Shakespeare, 1994).

Fear of difference and societal "norms" for bodily functions may cause many people to shun disabled people without even getting to know them first (Dovidio, Pagotto, & Hebl, 2011).

Self-Confidence and Self-Image

The social interactions that non-disabled people have with disabled people, highlighted above, can have a major impact upon disabled people's self-confidence and self-image. When constantly confronted with negative perceptions about their abilities to carry out tasks that most people take for granted, and also being bombarded with media images of "physical perfection" that most of the general public cannot live up to, it is little wonder that many disabled people suffer from low self-esteem. Seymour (1989, quoted in Hargreaves, 2000, p. 185) sums this up when she states:

> [T]he body in which I live is visible to others, it is the object of social attention. I learn about my body from the impressions I see my body make on other people. These interactions with others provide critical visual data for my self-knowledge.

This socially imposed feeling of worthlessness and low self-esteem brought on by the reaction of others to obvious physical difference can have very strong and long-term effects upon disabled people and are key factors contributing to the likelihood of internalized ableism (explained in more detail below).

These are just a few examples of the impacts of the perceptions of disability embodied in the medical model. Without the financial wherewithal to take part in various activities and compounded by a hostile built environment and unwelcoming reactions by many within the non-disabled population, it is easy to see how inclusion within the wider society can be an extremely difficult proposition for many disabled people. Overcoming these culturally embedded negative perceptions of disabled people is essential to improving their inclusion within the wider community and their everyday life.

APPROACHES

The Theory behind the Problem

Models and theories pertaining to disability represent a range of systematized structural approaches that seek to explain phenomena by referencing abstractions in a given system and their mechanisms. At a foundational level, the goal of such models and theories is to create an improved understanding of human behavior (Llewellyn & Hogan, 2000). As such, they are analytical tools that facilitate "seeing" and "understanding" disability and can serve to explain the treatment of disabled people within society and, further, explain how and why discrimination might occur (Smart, 2009). However, it is important to keep in mind that any given model cannot by itself comprise a social theory of disability and, as such, cannot explain disability in totality. A brief explanation follows of six such theories: the medical, social, relational, affirmative, and human rights models of disability and ableism.

Medical Model

This model was developed in the 20th century and took root in a well-established medical framework (Howe, 2008). A key cornerstone of the medical framework is the "normalized" body, which is culturally, ideologically, and politically based. By placing the normalized body at the center, the medical model focuses on bodily abnormality, disorder, or deficiency and how this causes functional limitations, called disability (Barnes & Mercer, 2010; Harris, Cox, & Smith, 1971). Because a biological approach is used, the general view is that the problems that disabled people face are the result of their physical and/or mental impairment. Thus, problems faced by disabled people lie within them and their impairments and are independent of the wider sociocultural, physical, and political environments. As a result, the only rational course of action that can be imagined is medical treatment or intervention in order to correct the "problem" with the individual (World Health Organization, 2002). This has created not only an environment that promotes the differential treatment of disabled people but also one that devalues the worth and citizenship of disabled people (Scullion, 2010). At its core, inequality is deeply embedded in the medical model.

Social Model

The social model was developed by the disability rights movement in the 1970s in response to the negative implications of the medical model (Union of the Physically Impaired Against Segregation, 1976). The social model inspired a move away from the traditional medical model that viewed impairments as disabling and toward a standpoint that viewed societal responses to disability as oppression. Indeed, the social model argues that it is environmental barriers and social attitudes toward disabled people that actually "disable" (Goodley, 2014; Shakespeare & Watson, 2002). As such, this model recognizes that there are deeply rooted prejudices against disabled people and that society is organized in ways that exclude them. The social model highlights that the only segregating factors are those that have been manufactured by and naturalized through a social system governed by a non-disabled logic (Shapiro, Pitts, Hums, & Calloway, 2012). Rather than pursuing a strategy of medical cure or rehabilitation, this perspective takes the view that if people's attitudes were to change, and public policy legislated that environmental barriers should be removed, then many of the problems associated with disability would disappear (Shakespeare & Watson, 2002).

Relational Model

In contrast to the social and medical models, the relational model considers lived experience, psycho-emotional well-being, social oppression, impairment, and the body as simultaneously biological, cultural, and social (Thomas, 2007). It acknowledges that social oppression emerges not from the individual's mind but instead out of relationships with structures and human beings. The model introduces "impairment effects," which refer to the restriction of activity in the lives of disabled people that arise directly from their impairments (Thomas, 2007). However, such effects can spread beyond restrictions caused just by biology to the social sphere and can result in social and psycho-emotional oppression through paternalistic and other oppressive attitudes. The relational model provides insights into how people with an impairment can be socially oppressed and how their psychosocial well-being can be damaged during interactions in ways that limit sporting options and a physically active lifestyle, even when structural barriers are absent (Smith, 2013a, 2013b).

Human Rights Model

The human rights model argues that society should acknowledge the value of all persons based on their inherent human worth, rather than basing value on a person's ability to contribute to society (Degener, 2017; Steint, 2007). In this sense, the human rights model places the individual center stage in all decisions affecting them and focuses on the inherent dignity of human existence, and thus human beings, because of their inherent self-worth. Such a posture makes a good case for the rights of individuals to make their own personal identities. Therefore, the human rights model brings to the fore a person's medical characteristics only when absolutely necessary as a matter of justice. The human rights model of disability concerns itself with a wide swathe of human rights. Its interlocking concerns for political, civil, economic, and cultural rights may be seen as underpinning a broad roadmap for change (Smith & Bundon, 2018). In embracing this vantage point, the United Nations (2006) Convention on the Rights of Persons with Disabilities can be viewed as the codification of the human rights model. The Convention is a visionary law designed to create a more just society through eight principles: (1) respect for inherent dignity, individual autonomy including the freedom to make one's own choices, and independence of persons; (2) nondiscrimination; (3) full and effective participation and inclusion in society; (4) respect for difference and acceptance of disabled people as part of human diversity and humanity; (5) equality of opportunity; (6) accessibility; (7) equality between men and women; and (8) respect for the evolving capacities of disabled children and the right of disabled children to preserve their identities (Misener & Darcy, 2014, p. 3).

Affirmative Model

Both the medical and social models are based on the notion of disability as "tragedy," as each views disabled people as victims of circumstances (whether biological or societal). These tragedy models try to avoid, eradicate, or normalize disability by all possible means based on the assumption that disabled people want to be like the non-disabled, even if this entails the often wholesale rejection of their own identities. The affirmative model, which arose out of disability culture, considers such models to be disabling in themselves and proposes an oppositional approach based on a "nontragic" view of disability. It does so by shifting the focus to the celebration of diversity. The affirmative model acknowledges the positive identities that disabled people have and embraces their rights to be the way they are, that is, "to be equal but different" (French & Swain, 2004).

Ableism

Ableism is perhaps the newest addition to the armory of those researchers working in the disability studies field and is applicable to multiple contexts, including race, gender, and sexuality, thereby facilitating consideration of intersectional dynamics that may be helpful in gaining real-life understandings. However, in the context of disability, ableism tends to focus on the deeply rooted prejudicial attitudes and discriminatory behaviors that are manifested toward disabled people (Wolbring, 2012). Here, embedded assumptions and practices are seen to promote differential and unequal treatment based on received views of presumed differences. In this sense, ableism can be viewed as the embodiment of the medical model. Similarly to the medical model, a cornerstone of ableism is normalcy, which is closely associated with one's understanding of normal ability and the rights and benefits afforded to persons deemed "normal" by a particular society. In this sense, ableism is concerned with the resultant power relationships derived from the imposition of normative values as a mechanism for maintaining the power of one group over another, with those who best fit these construed norms holding power over those who diverge from them. Yet, what comes to be deemed normal is, of course, culturally, socially, and value-based and associated with abilities that are normatively framed in understandings of one's physical or intellectual capacities.

In this context, any deviations from such embedded norms, often created by non-disabled society, are deemed undesirable. This has resulted in a structural network of beliefs, processes, and practices that support the assumption that it is "better" not to have a disability than to have one. Further, it entails the belief that it is "better" to do things in the same ways that non-disabled people do. This includes the perception that disabled people are "assumed to be helpless, dependent, asexual, economically unproductive, physically limited and emotionally immature" (Hahn, 1986, p. 130). Such viewpoints have resulted in a paternalism that has allowed society to express "sincere sympathy" to people with disabilities, while at the same time keeping them in subordinate positions. The structural nature of ableism has resulted in "internalized ableism," the process by which disabled people come to believe the assumptions and value the practices embedded within an ableist approach to disability (Kearney, Brittain, & Kipnis, 2019). Ableism, therefore, devalues disabled people and results in segregation, social isolation, and social policies that limit opportunities for full societal participation.

These models and theories of disability provide different perspectives on disability and may aid in understanding societal behavior and attitudes toward disabled people. Having discussed some of the key theories underpinning disability, we now turn to some of the critical debates around the intersectionality of disability and sport.

DEBATES

Perhaps one of the key issues in trying to connect disability, sport, and inclusion is what is actually meant by the term and concept "inclusion." What should inclusion look like in practice? One of the key problems with the inclusion agenda is that policymakers rarely, if ever, define what they mean by the term. This leaves those responsible for interpreting and operationalizing policy recommendations with an enormous amount of wiggle room in defining inclusion a way that suits their needs (i.e., minimal disruption and effort) rather than in a way that suits those it is designed to "include" (i.e., disabled people).

What Do We Mean by Inclusion?

At its most basic, inclusion is the state of being included or having the opportunity to take part. However, in reality, it is far more complicated than that, entailing diverse ideas and values about equality, equity, fairness, and distributive justice and how to best achieve these. An example of equality in a sporting context might be as simple as the notion that everyone on a team gets the same shirt to wear (of exactly the same size). In this way, no one can claim to have been treated differently. Yet, in reality, the shirt may actually fit only a small number of the team members. What is lacking from this view of equality is a sense of equity and fairness. If all team members are given the same shirt, but in a size that suits each individual member of the team, then it can be claimed that everyone has been included in an equal and equitable manner. However, fairness isn't just about everyone getting the same thing. In the end, it is about all people getting what they need in order to achieve their life goals, as well as those goals common to the society they live in. True inclusion, therefore, is about valuing all individuals, giving equal access and opportunity to all, and removing discrimination and other barriers to involvement. The larger goal is to ensure that all people feel a sense of belonging, as well as feeling respected and valued for who they are (Miller & Katz, 2002).

Differing Interpretations of Inclusion

It has been argued that there is no clear definition of the term "inclusion" (Collins, 1997; Ito, 1999; Thomas, 2004). This leads to one of the key issues in sport and disability policy in that inclusion is often explained using vague terminology that is broadly interpretable. For example, inclusion is often used as a generic term encompassing all underrepresented groups (e.g., age, gender, sexuality, etc. as well as disability). This is illustrated by the latest sport strategy in England "to get more people from every background regularly and meaningfully involved in sport" (Sport England, 2016). While this statement incapsulates the ideology of inclusion, it does not explain what meaningful participation looks like for disabled people in the sport sector. In this state of affairs, there is also an overarching assumption that stakeholders know exactly what is meant by inclusion. By failing to make clear what inclusion actually means, the IPC and international and national policymakers have unfortunately cleared the path for those who are charged with implementing inclusion policy within society, such as community sport clubs, to interpret inclusion in ways that best fit their own needs rather than the needs of disabled people (Christiaens, 2018).

The understandings of inclusion that have developed in the sport landscape undergird two important debates about sport and disability. The first debate is about who should be considered to be included. Is inclusion about including only those with mild disabilities who can achieve non-disabled standards and can potentially adapt themselves to a non-disabled environment, or is inclusion about all disabled people, even those with severe disabilities

Table 45.1 Community Sports Clubs' Approaches to Inclusion

	Placement		Opportunity
	Parallel inclusion	*Full inclusion*	*Choice*
Outcome			
Approaches	Barrier removal.[1]	Able inclusion.[2]	Achieving both parallel and
Adopted	Creation of	Barrier removal.[1]	full inclusion.
	opportunity.[3]	Creation of	Valuing disability sport clubs
		opportunity.[3]	as equal.
		Creation of identity.	

Notes: 1. When focused on physical barrier removal, this does not address structural ableism in the club. 2. Ableist discourse in which only people with a disability who are similar to people without a disability are accepted. 3. Creation of opportunities can result in segregated participation which is considered to be ableist.

who might need additional support and changes to be made? The second foundational debate is whether inclusion is more about access to opportunity or placement within a non-disabled setting. While the answers to such debates remain elusive, according to Christiaens (2018), the answer that people, and the organizations they represent, formulate will guide the operationalization of inclusion in the field of sport and disability.

An illustration of how such "cloudy" matters may play out in the context of community sport can be seen in Table 45.1. Here, in a study of local community sport clubs, ableism was shown to play a key role in the way that senior managers, coaches, and disabled people shaped their understandings of inclusion and how inclusion was differentially operationalized in different clubs and sports organizations (Christiaens & Brittain, 2021).

Broadly speaking, there were three outcomes that stakeholders strove toward: (1) parallel inclusion, (2) full inclusion, and (3) choice. The first two focus on a strategy of placement, moving disabled people into a non-disabled setting. Parallel inclusion seeks to achieve inclusion by organizing a separate activity for disabled people within the non-disabled environment. In contrast, full inclusion welcomes disabled people to take part in activities alongside non-disabled people. The strategy of choice focuses on access to participation, independent of where and with whom this takes place, and allows disabled people free choice and access.

Furthermore, it is possible to distinguish between five strategies that stakeholders utilize to achieve inclusion. These strategies are not mutually exclusive and can occur at the same time and will lead to one of the outcomes discussed above.

Able Inclusion

This is a restrictive approach to inclusion based on assumptions underlying the medical model and ableism. In essence, only those who are deemed capable of meeting non-disabled norms, usually persons with mild disabilities, are considered for inclusion. Such an approach creates extra barriers to participation and reinforces the ableist idea that disabled people must "overcome" their disability to take part in sport. This approach establishes the notion of the "able-disabled," those disabled people who manage to achieve a level of sports participation that is deemed acceptable by non-disabled standards (Kearney et al., 2019).

Barrier Removal

This approach to inclusion focuses on the removal of (mainly) physical barriers (e.g., by installing a ramp, an accessible toilet, parking spaces near entries) and is often the only consideration for community clubs to consider themselves "inclusive." This focus on removing physical barriers has its roots within the social model of disability (Owens, 2015) but often results in overlooking other issues such as attitudinal barriers and structural ableism.

Creation of Opportunity

This approach to inclusion is founded on a broader understanding of the social model of disability and aims to overcome social barriers and create social change. In this sense, new opportunities are created for disabled people to take part within a non-disabled setting (e.g., inclusive learn-to-swim programs). However, when not carefully thought out this can result in segregation and exclusion within the non-disabled environment.

Creation of Identity

This approach is foundationally concerned with embracing the positive identities of disabled people as embedded in the affirmative model of disability (French & Swain, 2004). At its starting point are the similarities between disabled and non-disabled athletes (i.e., the athletic activity they take part in such as being a sprinter or thrower). This approach to inclusion moves beyond the social model of disability and is rooted within the affirmative model. It embraces the fact that people identify with and want to be with others who take part in similar activities.

Equity in Sport Participation

This last approach toward inclusion celebrates diversity. It has as a starting point the needs and wants of disabled people. This means striving toward both parallel and full inclusion, while at the same time valuing sport participation in a non-disabled setting as equal to participation in a disabled-only setting (Misener & Darcy, 2014). A good example of such an approach is seen in the "hybrid" sport club that embraces the fusion of a non-disabled and a disabled sport club, an approach that allows for easy transitions and interactions between the two.

In sum, the approach that community clubs take toward inclusion impacts whether disabled people feel both welcome and able to participate within that environment. Obviously, the choice of approach also shapes attitudes that club members may come to have about the broader sport landscape. Research indicates that, irrespective of policy intent, the way inclusion policy is understood by those who have to operationalize it is often underpinned by an ableist view of disability (Jeanes et al., 2018). Time and time again, this has unfortunately resulted in approaches being taken that best suit the needs of the non-disabled rather than those of disabled people. To some extent, this has been both delusional and dysfunctional. Non-disabled organizers may come away with the sense that they have been successful in being inclusive without having to make too much of an effort to do so or to confirm that their approach was truly inclusive to those who wish to be included (Christiaens, 2018). As a result, the desired increase in sports participation for disabled people may not materialize, and disabled sportspersons may come to internalize ableist ideas, thus maintaining structural ableism within society.

What Does This Mean for the Paralympic Movement and Its Vision for a More Inclusive Society?

Before we answer this question, we would like to make it very clear that we truly believe that the Paralympics Games are currently the only truly global platform from which to start a debate around issues of disability in the wider society due to their media coverage and increasing profile within the world of sport. However, that media coverage is unevenly distributed among countries, access to TV and/or the internet may vary greatly both between and within countries (Pearce & Rice, 2013). Therefore, raising awareness of the Paralympic Movement and its broader aims may prove more difficult in some countries than in others. In addition, the quality of coverage may vary depending upon the training of media personnel with regard to how to best present disability and disability sport. Without disability awareness training, the "overcoming disability" supercrip narrative is often dominant, which can undermine the intended message (Silva & Howe, 2012). Countries are also at very different stages of development with regard to disability/human rights, which can impact how, and indeed whether parasport and disabled people more generally receive any kind of recognition. This is often, but not always, related to country's current state of economic development (Brittain, 2019). A selection of further questions and issues around sport, disability, and inclusion as they relate to the Paralympic Games is discussed next.

Disability Rights Policies as a Games Legacy

A recent development in several Paralympic Games host countries has been the introduction of new laws or policies designed to prevent disability discrimination. In Brazil in the lead-up to the Rio 2016 Paralympic Games, the Inclusion of People with Disabilities Act was passed into law (International Paralympic Committee, 2015). The Act eliminates accessibility barriers in transport, housing, services, education, sport, and the exercise of citizenship. The new law also states that 2.7% of the gross revenues from federal lotteries should be invested in sport, up from the current level of 2%. Of this investment, the Brazilian Olympic Committee will receive 63% and the Brazilian Paralympic Committee 37%, which is a significant increase as the latter received only 15% prior to the Act being implemented (Brittain, 2016). Another example may be seen in Japan in the lead-up to the Tokyo 2020 Games. In 2013, the Japanese government brought into force the Act on the Elimination of Discrimination against Persons with Disabilities in order to bring the country into line with the requirements of the UN Convention, which the Japanese government ratified in January 2014 (Shirasawa, 2014). Clearly, only time will tell whether these laws are actually legally enforced, but at the very least having such the law on the books gives disabled people and the organizations that represent them in Brazil and Japan a legal basis upon which to fight discrimination that did not exist prior to the Paralympic Games taking place in these countries. Regardless of any lingering imperfections, these changes clearly move a step closer to inclusion than previously.

Who Decides If Inclusion Has Occurred?

There is a saying that history is always written by the victor (in the case of war) or the powerful. This is true of many situations in life, including the perceived outcomes of legacy claims made after a Paralympic Games has taken place. According to Brittain and Beacom (2016), a joint U.K. Government and Mayor of London (2013) report published in July 2013, nearly a year after the London Paralympic Games had ended, cited the following headline achievement under the chapter "The Legacy of the Paralympics": "81% of people surveyed thought that the Games had a positive effect on how disabled people are viewed by the British public."

However, research by the charity Scope (2013) published at around the same time reported findings that differed markedly from the upbeat government report. After interviewing approximately 1,000 disabled people, Scope concluded:

- 81% of disabled people said that attitudes toward them hadn't improved in the past 12 months.
- 22% said that things had actually got worse.
- 17% reported they have experienced either hostile or threatening behavior or have even been attacked.

Although the contrasting viewpoints are somewhat worrying, they are perhaps not surprising given that the U.K. government had spent nearly 10 billion pounds to host the Olympic and Paralympic Games and had promised numerous legacies in return. Their need to claim success was especially pressing following the global economic crash of 2008. The contrast does, however, highlight the difficulties and complexities for the Paralympic Movement of actually achieving the goals embraced in its vision statement.

Greater Inclusion for All Disabled People?

Particularly apparent when reading the comments by disabled people's organizations and disabled individuals regarding the London 2012 Paralympic Games is the disconnect they feel with both Paralympians and society in general. Walker (2012) has observed, "The Paralympics showcases the amazing achievements and triumphs of a tiny percentage of disabled people—just as the Olympics demonstrates what a tiny percentage of 'able-bodied' people are able to achieve." Certainly, some Paralympians have become celebrities as a result of the media coverage they received for their sporting successes from the Games. However, the apparent inability of some people to differentiate between Paralympians and the average disabled person has caused more problems than it solves. As Bush, Silk, Porter, and

Howe (2013, p. 635) note, Seb, a 16-year-old with cerebral palsy, "already sensed the disappointment lurking behind people's eyes when he told them he was not training for a future Paralympics. People would now expect this, yet he was more worried about the day-to-day struggles of being disabled."

Brittain (2016) reports that research carried out by the Australian Paralympic Committee, which interviewed spectators at disability sports events in that country, appear to confirm that it is only spectators' attitudes toward the actual athletes and not those about the disabled population as a whole that are changed. It should also be noted that not all impairment groups get to participate in the Paralympic Games, which raises some foundational questions of how excluded groups can gain greater recognition within the wider society when they don't have access to this important playing field.

Sports Mega-Events Do Not Take Place in a Vacuum

Sports mega-events are often promoted for the lasting positive legacies they can offer to communities. But sports mega-events are subject to a whole host of complex social, economic, and political dynamics. As a result, it can be extremely challenging to effectively plan for any kind of real legacy to occur or be long-lasting. This includes legacies that facilitate increased inclusion of disabled people in the wider society. Such dynamics can work for or against the legacy process in unexpected ways. Both the London 2012 and Rio 2016 Games were impacted heavily by economics and politics following the global economic crash of 2008. It led the U.K. government to introduce financial austerity policies that appeared to impact the most marginalized people in society, including disabled people, the hardest (Ryan, 2019). Due to the political and economic turmoil in Brazil, Rio ended up in a situation where they were three days from canceling the Paralympic Games because the budget had already been spent to cure problems with the Olympic Games (Brittain & Mataruna, 2018). A more recent outside influence on sports mega-events is the COVID-19 pandemic, which has caused the postponement of the Tokyo 2020 Games, with continuing uncertainty that they will ever actually happen.

CONCLUSION

Physical activity and sport are important in the lives of disabled people and bring physical, social, and emotional benefits. However, as demonstrated throughout this chapter, disabled people still face challenges to gaining access to sporting opportunities. This is the result of how disability is viewed within society. Disability remains a culturally embedded phenomenon, often shaped by religious and societal beliefs in addition to societal values and norms. This has resulted in societies developing different "coping" mechanisms to deal with people who are perceived to be different from the "norm," often resulting in the differential treatment of disabled people. Such perspectives of disability also impact the way a non-disabled society interacts with disabled people, illustrated by being hidden away by families, ending up in poverty, or deprioritized for emergency help, as demonstrated during the COVID-19 outbreak.

This chapter has attempted to provide an overview of the most important models and theories of disability: the medical, social, relational, affirmative, and human rights models of disability and ableism. We have illustrated how these models and theories are useful in helping us to understand the underlying reasons for the differential treatment of disabled people and the various understandings and approaches to inclusion. These models and theories provide perspectives on disability, for example, revealing how society is organized in a disabling way, and can provide guidance to policymakers who adopt the underlying philosophies into legislation (e.g., barrier removal legislation). While legislation is not a sufficient factor in and of itself to produce inclusion, it is nevertheless an essential aspect.

We argued that while inclusion has been uncritically accepted and considered an unambiguously good and desirable policy, the operationalization of inclusion is more troublesome. The sport sector remains dominated by an ableist culture that sometimes makes it difficult and/or unpleasant for disabled people to engage within the non-disabled sport landscape. That is not to say there are no positive movements. Indeed, there are actors who embrace a transformative belief system that strives toward equality through the creation of a mutual identity based on the sport one participates in. While such views are not new (e.g., Guttmann's view on archery), they can instigate important change in how disabled people are treated within sport.

In conclusion, then, although we firmly believe that the Paralympic Games and Movement have a key role to play in the greater inclusion of disabled people within society, we have highlighted the complexity of the issues at play. The potential for the Games and Movement to increase inclusion is clearly apparent, but there are numerous interconnected issues to be overcome to achieve inclusion goals, some of which can be planned for by organizers (e.g., providing a clear explanation of what constitutes inclusion) and others that are completely beyond their control (e.g., the global economic crash of 2008 or the COVID-19 pandemic). However, by providing an impetus for discussing issues of disability, involving a wide audience, and providing an opportunity for disabled athletes to eliminate some of the social stereotypes regarding their abilities, the Paralympic Games are currently the most important and far-reaching platform available. With their inspiration, experiences for disabled people participating in sport might improve at all levels. The data and arguments presented in this chapter offer some initial insights into disability and sport issues and emphasize that there is still much work to be done to enhance the experiences of disabled people in the sport sector.

References

Banda-Chalwe, M., Nitz, J. C., & de Jonge, D. (2014). Impact of inaccessible spaces on community participation of people with mobility limitations in Zambia. *African Journal of Disability*, 3(1), 33–49.

Banks, L. M., Kuper, H., & Polack, S. (2017). Poverty and disability in low- and middle-income countries: A systematic review. *PLoS ONE*, 12(12). https://doi.org/10.1371/journal.pone.0189996.

Barnes, C. (1994). *Disabled people in Britain and discrimination* (2nd ed.). London: Hurst & Co.

Barnes, C., & Mercer, G. (2010). *Exploring disability* (2nd ed.). Cambridge, U.K.: Polity Press.

Brittain, I. (2016). *The Paralympic Games explained* (2nd ed.). Routledge.

Brittain, I. (2019). The impact of resource inequality upon participation and success at the summer and winter Paralympic Games. *Journal of the Nippon Foundation Paralympic Research Group, 12*(September), 41–67. https://www.jstage.jst.go.jp/article/parasapo/12/0/ 12_41/_article/-char/ja.

Brittain, I., & Beacom, A. (2016). Leveraging the London 2012 Paralympic Games: What legacy for people with disabilities? *Journal of Sport and Social Issues, 40*(6), 499–521.

Brittain, I., Biscaia, R., & Gerard, S. (2020). Ableism as a regulator of social practice and people with disabilities' self-determination to participate in sport and physical activity. *Leisure Studies, 39*(2), 209–224.

Brittain, I., & Mataruna, L. (2018). The Rio 2016 Paralympic Games. In I. Brittain & A. Beacom (Eds.), *The Palgrave handbook of Paralympic studies* (pp. 531–550). Palgrave-Macmillan.

Bush, A., Silk, M., Porter, J., & Howe, P. D. (2013). Disability [sport] and discourse: Stories within the Paralympic legacy. *Reflective Practice, 14*, 632–647.

Cameron, M., & MacDougall, C. (2000). Crime prevention through sport and physical activity. *Crime and Criminal Justice, 165*, 1–6.

Christiaens, M. (2018). *Towards mainstreaming: A principle-practice gap in the UK sports sector* (Unpublished PhD dissertation). Coventry University.

Christiaens, M. & Brittain, I. (2021). The complexities of implementing inclusion policies for disabled people in UK non-disabled voluntary community sports clubs. *European Sport Management Quarterly*, 1–21. https://doi.org/10.1080/23750472.2021.1985595.

Collins, D. (1997). *Conference report: National disability sport conference*. London: Kings Fund Centre.

Crabbe, T. (2000). A sporting chance? Using sport to tackle drug use and crime. *Drugs: Education, Prevention and Policy, 7*(4), 381–391. http://curve.coventry.ac.uk/open/ items/90fff1fa-cca3-48cf-81e3-f11551f63978/1/.

Crawford, J. (2004). *Constraints of elite athletes with disabilities in Kenya* (Unpublished master's thesis). University of Illinois at Urbana-Champaign.

Davis, A. (2004). Commentary: A disabled person's perspective on euthanasia. *Disability Studies Quarterly, 24*(3). https://dsq-sds.org/article/view/512/689.

Deal, M. (2003). Disabled people's attitudes toward other impairment groups: A hierarchy of impairments. *Disability & Society, 18*(7), 897–910.

Degener, T. (2017). A new human rights model of disability. In V. la Fina, R. Cera, & G. Palmisano (Eds.), *The United Nations Convention on the rights of persons with disabilities* (pp. 41–59). Springer.

Dovidio, J. F., Pagotto, L., & Hebl, M. R. (2011). Implicit attitudes and discrimination against people with physical disabilities. In R. Wiener & S. Willborn (Eds.), *Disability and aging discrimination* (pp. 157–183). Springer.

Dunn, J. M., & Sherrill, C. (1996). Movement and its implication for individuals with disabilities. *Quest, 48*(3), 378–391.

Filmer, D. (2005, December). Disability, poverty, and schooling in developing countries: results from 11 household surveys. World Bank Policy Research Working Paper No. 3794. Washington, DC.

French, S., & Swain, J. (2004). Whose tragedy? Towards a personal non-tragedy view of disability. In S. French & J. Swain (Eds.), *Disabling barriers—enabling environments* (pp. 34–40). Sage.

Galtung, J. (1990). Cultural violence. *Journal of Peace Research, 27*(3), 290–302.

Goggin, G., & Ellis, K. (2020). Disability, communication, and life itself in the COVID-19 pandemic. *Health Sociology Review*, 29(2), 168–176.

Goodley, D. (2014). *Dis/Ability studies: Theorising disablism and ableism*. Routledge.

Guttmann, L. (1976). *Textbook of sport for the disabled*. Aylesbury, U.K.: HM and M Publishers.

Hahn, H. (1986). Public support for rehabilitation programs. *Disability, Handicap & Society*, 1(2), 121–137.

Hargreaves, J. (2000). *Heroines of sport: The politics of difference and identity*. Routledge.

Harris, A., Cox, E., & Smith, C. (1971). Handicapped and impaired in Great Britain: Part 1. Office of Population Censuses and Surveys. London: H.M.S.O.

Hayashi, R., & Okuhira, M. (2001). The disability rights movement in Japan: Past, present and future. *Disability & Society*, 16(6), 855–869.

Hogan, A. (1999). Carving out a space to act: Acquired impairment and contested identity. In M. Corker & S. French (Eds.), *Disability discourse* (pp. 79–91). Buckingham, U.K.: Open University Press.

Howe, D. (2008). *The cultural politics of the Paralympic movement: Through an anthropological lens*. Routledge.

Hunt, P. (Ed.). (1966). *Stigma: The experience of disability*. London: Chapman.

Imrie, R., & Thomas, H. (2008). The interrelationships between environment and disability. *Local Environment*, 13(6), 477–483.

International Paralympic Committee. (2015). New law hailed as a landmark in Brazil. http://www.paralympic.org/news/new-law-hailed-landmark-brazil.

International Paralympic Committee. (2019). Strategic plan (2019–2022). https://www.paralympic.org/sites/default/files/document/190704145051100_2019_07+IPC+Strategic+Plan_web.pdf.

Ito, C. (1999). *Inclusion confusion*. Williamsburg: William & Mary School of Education.

Jeanes, R., Spaaij, R., Magee, J., Farquharson, K., Gorman, S., & Lusher, D. (2018). "Yes we are inclusive": Examining provision for young people with disabilities in community sport clubs. *Sport Management Review*, 21(1), 1–13.

Kassah, A. K., Kassah, B. L. L., & Agbota, T. K. (2012). Abuse of disabled children in Ghana. *Disability & Society*, 27(5), 689–701.

Kearney, S., Brittain, I., & Kipnis, E. (2019). "Superdisabilities" vs "disabilities"? Theorizing the role of ableism in (mis)representational mythology of disability in the marketplace. *Consumption Markets & Culture*, 22(5–6), 545–567.

Kelly, L. (2010). "Social inclusion" through sports-based interventions? *Critical Social Policy*, 31(1), 126–150.

Kruk, J. (2007). Physical activity in the prevention of the most frequent chronic diseases: An analysis of the recent evidence. *Asian Pacific Journal of Cancer Prevention*, 8(3), 325–338.

Livneh, H. (1982). On the origins of negative attitudes toward people with disabilities. *Rehabilitation Literature*, 43, 338–347.

Llewellyn, A., & Hogan, K. (2000). The use and abuse of models of disability. *Disability & Society*, 15(1), 157–166.

Loeb, M., Eide, A. H., Jelsma, J., Toni, M., & Maart, S. (2008). Poverty and disability in East and West Cape provinces, South Africa. *Disability and Society*, 23(4), 311–321.

Mammen, G., & Faulkner, G. (2013). Physical activity and the prevention of depression: A systematic review of prospective studies. *American Journal of Preventive Medicine*, 45(5), 649–657.

Miller, F. A., & Katz, J. H. (2002). *Inclusion breakthrough: Unleashing the real power of diversity*. Berrett-Koehler.

Misener, L., & Darcy, S. (2014). Managing disability sport: From athletes with disabilities to inclusive organisational perspectives. *Sport Management Review, 17*, 1–7.

Mitchell, D., & Snyder, S. (2003). The eugenic Atlantic: Race, disability, and the making of an international eugenic science, 1800–1945. *Disability & Society, 18*(7), 843–864.

Oliver, M., & Barnes, C. (2012). *The new politics of disablement*. Palgrave Macmillan.

Oxford Illustrated Dictionary. (1998). Oxford University Press.

Owens, J. (2015). Exploring the critiques of the social model of disability: The transformative possibility of Arendt's notion of power. *Sociology of Health & Illness, 37*(3), 385–403.

Parry, J. (2012). The power of sport in peacemaking and peacekeeping. *Sport in Society, 15*(6), 775–787.

Pearce, K. E., & Rice, R. E. (2013). Digital divides from access to activities: Comparing mobile and personal computer internet users. *Journal of Communication, 63*(4), 721–744.

Ryan, F. (2019). *Crippled: Austerity and the demonization of disabled people*. Verso.

Saxton, M. (2018). Hard bodies: Exploring historical and cultural factors in disabled people's participation in exercise: Applying critical disability theory. *Sport in Society, 21*(1), 22–39.

Scope. (2013). Paralympics legacy in balance as attitudes fail to improve. https://www.politicshome.com/members/article/paralympics-legacy-in-balance-as-attitudes-fail-to-improve.

Scullion, P. A. (2010). Models of disability: Their influence in nursing and potential role in challenging discrimination. *Journal of Advanced Nursing, 66*(3), 697–707.

Seymour, W. (1989). *Body alterations*. Unwin Hyman.

Shakespeare, T. (1994). Cultural representation of disabled people: Dustbins for disavowal? *Disability & Society, 9*(3), 283–299.

Shakespeare, T., & Watson, N. (2002). The social model of disability: An outdated ideology? *Research in Social Science and Disability, 2*, 9–28.

Shapiro, D., Pitts, B., Hums, M., & Calloway, J. (2012). Infusing disability sport into the sport management curriculum. *Sport Management International Journal, 8*(1), 101–118.

Sherrill, C. (Ed.). (1986). *Sport and disabled athletes*. Champaign, IL: Human Kinetics.

Shirasawa, M. (2014, October 2). The long road to disability rights in Japan. *Nippon*. https://www.nippon.com/en/currents/d00133/.

Silva, C., & Howe, D. (2012). The (in)validity of supercrip representation of Paralympian athletes. *Journal of Sport & Social Issues, 36*, 174–193.

Siperstein, G. N., Pociask, S. E., & Collins, M. A. (2010). Sticks, stones, and stigma: A study of students' use of the derogatory term "retard." *Intellectual and Developmental Disabilities, 48*(2), 126–134.

Smart, J. (2009). The power of models of disability. *Journal of Rehabilitation, 75*, 3–11.

Smith, A., & Waddington, I. (2004). Using "sport in the community schemes" to tackle crime and drug use among young people: Some policy issues and problems. *European Physical Education Review, 10*(3), 279–298.

Smith, B. (2013a). Disability, sport and men's narratives of health: A qualitative study. *Health Psychology, 32*(1), 110–119.

Smith, B. (2013b). Sporting spinal cord injuries, social relations, and rehabilitation narratives: An ethnographic creative non-fiction of becoming disabled through sport. *Sociology of Sport Journal, 30*(2), 132–152.

Smith, B., & Bundon, A. (2018). Disability models: Explaining and understanding disability sport in different ways. In I. Brittain & A. Beacom (Eds.), *The Palgrave handbook of Paralympic studies* (pp. 15–34). Palgrave Macmillan.

Spaaij, R., Magee, J., Farquharson, K., Gorman, S., Jeanes, R., Lusher, D., & Storr, R. (2016). Diversity work in community sport organizations: Commitment, resistance and institutional change. *International Review for the Sociology of Sport, 51*, 1–18.

Sport England. (2016). Towards an active nation: Strategy 2016–2021. https://sportengland-production-files.s3.eu-west-2.amazonaws.com/s3fs-public/sport-england-towards-an-active-nation.pdf.

Steint, M. A. (2007). Disability human rights. *William & Mary Law School Scholarship Repository: Faculty Publications, 264*, 1–49.

Stephens, L., Spalding, K., Aslam, H., Scott, H., Ruddick, S., Young, N. L., & McKeever, P. (2017). Inaccessible childhoods: Evaluating accessibility in homes, schools and neighbourhoods with disabled children. *Children's Geographies, 15*(5), 583–599.

Thomas, C. (2007). *Sociologies of disability and illness: Contested ideas in disability studies and medical sociology*. Palgrave Macmillan.

Thomas, N. (2004). *An examination of the disability sport policy network in England: A case study of the English Federation of Disability Sport and mainstreaming in seven sports* (Unpublished doctoral dissertation). Loughborough University.

Tringo, J. L. (1970). The hierarchy of preference toward disability groups. *Journal of Special Education, 4*(3), 295–306.

U.K. Government & Mayor of London Office. (2013). Inspired by 2012: The legacy from the London 2012 Olympic and Paralympic Games. https://www.gov.uk/government/uploads/system/uploads/attachment_data/file/224148/2901179_OlympicLegacy_acc.pdf.

Union of the Physically Impaired Against Segregation. (1976). Fundamental principles of disability. https://disabledpeoplesarchive.com/wp-content/uploads/sites/39/2021/01/001-FundamentalPrinciplesOfDisability-UPIAS-DA-22Nov1975.pdf.

United Nations. (2006). United Nations Convention on the rights of persons with disabilities. https://www.un.org/development/desa/disabilities/convention-on-the-rights-of-persons-with-disabilities.html.

U.S. Social Security Administration. (2019). Disability benefits. No. 05-10029. https://www.ssa.gov/pubs/EN-05-10029.pdf.

Walker, S. W. (2012). And so begins demonisation's subtle new post-Paralympic form. *Black Triangle Campaign*. https://blacktrianglecampaign.org/2012/09/03/and-so-begins-demonisations-subtle-new-post-paralympic-form-skwalker1964-blog/

Watermeyer, B., Swartz, L., Lorenzo, T., Schneider, M., & Priestley, M. (2006) *Disability and social change: A South African agenda*. Cape Town: HSRC Press.

Winzer, B., Woitek, F., & Linke, A. (2018). Physical activity in the prevention and treatment of coronary artery disease. *Journal of the American Heart Association, 7*(4), 1–16.

Wolbring, G. (2012). Expanding ableism: Taking down the ghettoization of impact of disability studies scholars. *Societies, 2*(4), 75–83.

World Health Organization. (2002). Towards a common language for functioning. Disability and Health ICF. http://www.who.int/classifications/icf/training/icfbeginnersguide.pdf.

World Health Organization. (2010). Definition and typology of violence. https://www.who.int/groups/violence-prevention-alliance/approach

World Health Organization & World Bank. (2018). Disability and health: Key facts. http://www.who.int/en/news-room/fact-sheets/detail/disability-and-health.

Yan, K. K., Accordino, M. P., Boutin, D. L., & Wilson, K. B. (2014). Disability and the Asian culture. *Journal of Applied Rehabilitation Counseling, 45*(2), 4–8.

CHAPTER 46

....

SPORT, MASCULINITIES, AND HETERONORMATIVITY

....

RORY MAGRATH AND ERIC ANDERSON

MEN'S competitive team sports have traditionally been a social institution principally organized around the political project of defining certain forms of masculinity as acceptable, while simultaneously denigrating other, often posited as weaker, forms of masculinity (Curry, 1991). Sport associates boys and men with masculine dominance by constructing identities and sculpting their bodies to align with dominant notions of masculine embodiment and expression. Accordingly, boys and men who participate in competitive sports, and particularly team sports, have long been expected to exhibit, value, and reproduce traditional notions of masculinity (Anderson & Magrath, 2019). Central to this process has been the deployment of homophobia, which has pervaded men's team sports to a high degree (Hekma, 1998; Pronger, 1990; Wolf-Wendel, Toma, & Morphew, 2001), so much so that, in the 20th century, very few gay and bisexual athletes came out of the closet, at any level of play.

Over the past three decades, however, attitudes toward homosexuality have improved considerably across the Western world (Keleher & Smith, 2012; Twenge, Sherman, & Wells, 2016; Watt & Elliot, 2019). Additionally, despite frequent claims to the contrary, much in sport in recent years has also undergone a significant transformation with regard to equality, diversity, and inclusion. Indeed, a plethora of scholarly works—both in the United States and the United Kingdom—have countered outdated assumptions that team sports continue to act as a bastion of homophobia (Adams & Anderson, 2012; Anderson, Magrath, & Bullingham, 2016). For example, numerous studies have documented increased acceptance of gay athletes at all levels of competition, alongside growing support for their social and legal equality (Anderson, 2011b; Cashmore & Cleland, 2012; Magrath, 2017a, 2018).

As sporting cultures continue to embrace social change, there has been a significant increase in elite-level lesbian, gay, and bisexual (hereafter LGB) athletes who have publicly come out of the closet (Billings & Moscowitz, 2018; White, Magrath, & Morales, 2021). Rather than rejection and ostracism from sport—as has historically been the case—these athletes have been embraced, celebrated, and propelled to stardom as symbols of sport's ongoing transformation toward inclusion. Gay male athletes such as Jason Collins, Michael Sam, John Amaechi, and Robbie Rogers all represent evidence of this change. While this change has not occurred universally—for example, overall numbers of "out" bisexual athletes remain disproportionally low (Magrath, Anderson, & Cleland, 2017) and issues for trans athletes remain subject to more complex challenges (Anderson & Travers, 2017)—there are many markers that the sports industry has nonetheless evolved from its toxic past into a default position seemingly of acceptance and inclusion (Magrath, 2021).

In this chapter, we explore the historical relationship between sport, masculinity, and sexuality. We first discuss sport's role in masculinizing boys and men during the process of industrialization, before outlining its cultural significance in the 1980s—when cultural homophobia in the Western world reached an apex. We then present a range of research documenting how, since the turn of the millennium, sport has become increasingly inclusive of sexual minorities.

In the next sections, we outline how the decline of cultural homophobia has facilitated a paradigm shift: where Connell's hegemonic masculinity was once the dominant theoretical perspective, changing patterns of masculinity have resulted in scholars turning to Anderson's conceptions about inclusive masculinity. Finally, we discuss some of the ongoing debates in the field of masculinity and sport—including underresearched areas—before concluding with some directions for future research.

ISSUES

The Foundations of Sport, Masculinity, and Homophobia

Although the invention of machinery and transportation necessary for industrialization began in the early 1700s, the antecedents of most of today's sporting culture can be traced to the years of the second Industrial Revolution: the mid-1800s through early 1900s. It was around this time that the organization, regulation, and codification of most dominant sports occurred (Guttmann, 1978). At that time, sport—largely men's competitive team sports—was thought to instill the qualities of discipline and obedience necessary in dangerous occupations (Rigauer, 1981). Factory workers, in particular, were required to sacrifice their time and health for the sake of earning wages at a level required to support their dependent families. Predictably, in service to industrialized interests, participation in sport was thus taught to boys to reinforce the value of self-sacrifice (Anderson, 2009).

Importantly, the gender segregation conventions of that time enabled sport also to play an important role in "masculinizing"—and "remasculinizing"—boys. Given the emergence of an apparent "crisis" of masculinity (Anderson & Magrath, 2019)—characterized by fears that boys were becoming overly feminized due to an overbearing mother and absent father—men were forced to demonstrate the vibrancy of their heterosexuality by aligning their "gendered behaviors with an idealized and narrow definition of masculinity" (McCormack & Anderson, 2014, p. 114). According to Kimmel (1994), idealized attributes here included repressing pain, concealing feminine and homo(sexual) desires and behaviors, all the while committing acts of violence against oneself and others. Sport, therefore, was a solution to a perceived social problem. Sports historian Neil Carter's (2006, p. 5) seminal work, *The Football Manager*, for instance, argues that sport provided a "clear hierarchical structure, autocratic tendencies, traditional notions of masculinity and the need for discipline." Early modern sport was, perhaps unsurprisingly, epitomized by high levels of violence from participants and spectators alike (Young, 2019).

Because of sport's historical role in facilitating normative masculine ideals, men who played sport were not thought likely—or even possible—to be gay. Thus, sport has served to privilege not all men, but specifically heterosexual men (Anderson, 2009). The exclusion of gay men and women (the latter's participation was denounced as uncivilized) has historically led sport to promote and celebrate an orthodox form of masculinity (Anderson, 2009).

Sport and Heteronormative Masculinity

Academic investigations of sport and masculinity expanded in the 1980s and 1990s. It was during this time that Dunning (1986, p. 79) famously labeled sport a "male preserve," while Messner and Sabo (1990) described it as an institution created by men, for men. At this time a broad range of inquiry began to focus on how sport contributed to a socially desired gendered identity, and the received presentation of the athletic male body as an idealized and orthodox symbol of a dominant form of masculinity (Kimmel, 1994).

Male athletic subcultures have served to reinforce an ideology of male superiority by way of projecting hegemonic ideals. Indeed, it has traditionally been through participation in competitive team sports. Whitson (1990, p. 19), for example, argued that "demonstrating the physical and psychological attributes associated with success in athletic contests has . . . become an important requirement for status in most adolescent and preadolescent male peer groups." Thus, he argues, sport has provided the opportunity for boys to *become* men.

This apparent "becoming" would be typically characterized through displays of "fighting spirit" and a determination for sporting success. According to Pronger (1990), it might also include the demeaning of nonaggressive play as feminine. Sabo and Runfola's (1980) seminal text, *Jock: Sports and Male Identity,* details the aggressive and abusive nature of team sport athletes. Athletes who successfully embody these abusive characteristics have typically been referred to—in the United States, at least—as "jocks."

This included the subordination of women; Harry's (1995) research on U.S. male college students found widespread sexist and misogynistic attitudes. Moreover, Curry's (1991) ethnographic research on male locker rooms found that talk about women was dominated by sexual conquests and objectification. This talk was also essential to the establishment of "real men." These behaviors begin at a young age. Fine's (1987) research on Little League baseball shows that preadolescent boys must learn that they should feel (or express) sexual desire for girls. This is normally through the objectification of girls and women, by sharing pinups and pornography and by presenting themselves as sexually active.

Sport, Masculinity, and the "Awful '80s"

As we examined in the previous section, sport has typically played a central role in socializing boys and men into a heteronormative environment. It is thus unsurprising that this reflected the broader cultural context. Indeed, the partial decriminalization of homosexuality in the United Kingdom in 1967[1] —and its removal from the American Psychiatric Association's list of mental illnesses in 1973—resulted in a steady growth of homosexual visibility in Western cultures. By the mid-1980s, however, the advent of a new—deadly—virus, HIV, became closely associated with the gay community. The virus killed tens of thousands of gay men, and this drew increased attention to homosexuals' existence in larger numbers in the general population than earlier recognized (Anderson, 2009).

As a backlash built against the spread of HIV, the growing influence of fundamentalist Christian movements stirred up hatred against the gay community. Equally, this became entangled with the strong conservative politics of the times. This was especially palpable in the United States, with ex–movie star Ronald Reagan's Republican presidency. Reagan's silence on the issue was indicative of his administration's contempt for homosexuality (Bosia, 2013). Similar trends also emerged in the United Kingdom, with Reagan's closest ally, Margaret Thatcher, and her Conservative government's treatment of homosexuality as a threat to traditional British family values. This was best evidenced by the introduction of Section 28 in 1988, which prohibited the promotion of homosexuality in schools—effectively erasing any discussions whatsoever (McCormack, 2012).

Evidencing the broader cultural antipathy toward homosexuality around this time, social attitude surveys also demonstrate an increase in intolerant attitudes. The British Social Attitude Survey, for example, showed that the number of adults who believed same-sex sex was either "always wrong" or "mostly wrong" increased almost 15%—from 62% to 76%—between 1983 (when it was first asked) and 1987 (Watt & Elliot, 2019). In the United States, these figures were even higher: Twenge et al.'s (2016) analysis of the data show that, in 1988, around 80% of adults believed homosexuality was "always wrong." These data led Anderson (2009, p. 89) to conclude that "1987 or 1988 seems to be the apex of homophobia in both countries."

Owing to this toxic environment, sport at this time became an increasingly important site for boys and men to exhibit extreme forms of masculinity—serving to reduce the likelihood of being socially perceived as gay. Accordingly, research conducted around this time also confirmed sport's hostility to the gay community. Curry (1991, p. 130) found that, among the heterosexual athletes he sampled, "[n]ot only is being homosexual forbidden, but tolerance of homosexuality is theoretically off limits as well." Similarly, Pronger (1990) wrote that the gay men he interviewed—all of whom were closeted—were "uncomfortable" with team sports and avoided them when possible. And in the Netherlands, Hekma (1998, p. 2) found that "gay men who are seen as queer and effeminate are granted no space whatsoever in what is generally considered to be a masculine preserve and macho enterprise."

Elite-level athletes who came out during this time were, predictably, low in number. This was because, as Barret (1993, p. 161) wrote, "[m]ost gay professional athletes keep their gay lives carefully hidden out of a fear that coming out will destroy their ability to maintain their careers." Those who did come out around this time received abuse from spectators, faced rejection from teammates, and found their career in tatters. This is likely best evidenced by British soccer player Justin Fashanu, who, after coming out in 1990, saw his career deteriorate—eventually culminating in his suicide in 1998 (Magrath, 2017a). Thus, as we approached the end of the millennium, sport across the world continued to act as an adverse, dangerous, and inhospitable cultural milieu for LGB athletes.

Sport and Inclusivity in the 21st Century

Since the turn of the millennium, however, cultural attitudes toward homosexuality across the Western world have improved considerably. Drawing once again on social attitude surveys, we are, as Keleher and Smith (2012, p. 1324) argued, "witnessing a sweeping change in attitudes toward lesbians and gay men." For example, around 66% of American adults now believe that homosexuality should be accepted by society (Twenge et al., 2016). Support for this view is seen as well in the most recent figures from U.K. adults, which shows that those who believe that same-sex sex is "always wrong" is only 12%. Data from the Pew Research Center (2013) have also consistently documented the advance of positive attitudes toward homosexuality across numerous Western countries. LGB people also now enjoy greater legal privileges than ever before. Since the Netherlands became the first country to legalize same-sex marriage, in 2001, around 30 countries around the world now recognize same-sex unions. This includes most of the world's most powerful nations, including the United States, Australia, Germany, Italy, Canada, and France. In 2019, Taiwan became the first Asian country to permit same-sex marriage.

Despite frequent claims that sport is slower than wider society to embrace social change (e.g. Butterworth, 2006), the shift toward inclusivity has also been paralleled in the industry. In the first-ever research with "out" gay athletes in mainstream, educationally based sport, Anderson (2002) showed that these athletes had broadly positive experiences. Prior to disclosing their sexuality to teammates, these athletes reported that they were anxious about being socially excluded, verbally abused, and physically beaten. After coming out, however, these concerns were not realized for the majority of the sample; these gay athletes instead regretted not coming out sooner. When this research was replicated almost a decade later, Anderson (2011b) found even greater levels of social inclusion for gay athletes. This included a reduction of the "Don't ask, don't tell" culture, inclusion of gay athletes in the team's social activities, and the acceptance of same-sex partners at these events. Since Anderson's pioneering studies on the inclusion of gay male athletes, there has been a growing body of research documenting similar levels of inclusion in a variety of sports (Adams & Anderson, 2012; Anderson et al., 2016; Letts, 2021).

Support from heterosexual peers for the presence of LGB people in sport has also improved considerably. Bush, Anderson, and Carr (2012), for example, found that while athletic identity was connected with homophobia among undergraduate sports students upon arrival at university, that link eroded for those students upon leaving British higher education. Elsewhere, Anderson's (2011a) research with a university soccer team in the American Midwest showed that these young, athletic men were supportive of gay rights, eschewed violence both on and off the sports field, and enjoyed a close emotional bond with one another across gender identities. Magrath's (2019a) research with working-class university soccer players documented similar levels of positivity and support; these men also shared a unique bond in that both their academic and athletic lives centered around soccer, allowing them to create a close-knit "support bubble."

Research with elite-level heterosexual athletes also documents high levels of support for LGB counterparts. Magrath's (2017a) research with elite young soccer players found that, unlike older research emanating from this level of play (e.g., Parker, 1996), these players were broadly supportive of homosexuality in sport and society and espoused positive attitudes toward equal rights for same-sex marriage. Magrath, Anderson, and Roberts (2015, p. 819) contend that, without direct contact with a gay teammate, this research "serves as a roadmap for when one of their teammates actually does come out." Such positivity is also evident in the increased number of elite-level straight athletes willing to place on record their public support for LGB rights (Cleland & Magrath, 2020).

Even research on sports fandom—a demographic which has traditionally been stigmatized as homophobic—shows increasingly that tolerant attitudes toward homosexuality have become commonplace. Cashmore and Cleland's (2012) large-scale quantitative research found that 93% of fans were supportive of homosexuality in British soccer. These fans believed that a player's on-field performance should be the only significant criterion on which they are judged. Magrath (2018) also found that, despite some of his sample engaging in chanting that featured animus toward homosexuality, they still maintained positive attitudes. And in the first-ever research with gay male sports fans, Magrath (2021) shows that, despite concerns over soccer being a heteronormative environment, these fans felt that stadia had transformed into a more inclusive and safe space in recent years.

Similar findings are also evident in netnographic research on sports fandom. Indeed, despite the anonymity of online fan forums, Cleland's (2015) analysis of soccer found largely positive discussions of gay athletes; the few posts containing homophobic sentiment were actively challenged by other users (Cleland, Magrath, & Kian, 2018). However, these findings are typically dependent on the sport under discussion. For example, in the context of American football, Kian, Clavio, Vincent, and Shaw (2011) found homophobic posts went largely uncontested.

Finally, we note the effect of mainstream sports media in changing representations of homosexuality in sport. While sports media has traditionally erased discussions of male homosexuality, more recent analyses have become increasingly positive in their coverage of elite LGB athletes (Magrath, 2019b), including NBA center Jason Collins (Billings & Moscowitz, 2018), American football player (now retired) Michael Sam (Cassidy, 2017), and British diver Tom Daley (Magrath, Cleland, & Anderson, 2017). Accordingly, Kian, Anderson, and Shipka (2015, p. 634) argue that "the institution of sport, and the sport media industry itself, are both adopting more inclusive perspectives concerning gay men." These increasingly positive dispositions have also extended to the sports journalism workplace, which, despite remaining an overwhelmingly heteronormative environment, has been shown to be an inclusive space (Magrath, 2020). As this cultural landscape for LGB people continues to change, so too have the field's dominant theoretical perspectives—as the next sections of this chapter now addresses.

APPROACHES

Hegemonic Masculinity

The first paradigmatic heurism for understanding the social stratification of masculinity has been Raewyn Connell's (1995) concept[2] of hegemonic masculinity. Developed in the early 1980s, Connell's (1987) work moved away from the simplicity of sex-role theory, recognizing the plurality of masculinities. From a social constructionist perspective, hegemonic masculinity articulates two social processes. The first concerns how all men apparently benefit from patriarchy. In her influential text, *Masculinities,* Connell (1995, p. 77)—famously—describes this as the "configuration of gender practice which embodies the currently accepted answer to the problem of the legitimacy of patriarchy." Lacking empirical evidence, however—as well as criticisms that Connell's theorizing underestimates the complexity of patriarchy—has resulted in many scholars' failure to engage in this element of the theory. Even adherents of this theory argue that its patriarchal aspect is not borne out by scholars (Connell & Messerschmidt, 2005). Scholars have instead focused on Connell's other theoretical contribution: conceptualizing how multiple masculinities are stratified within an intramasculine hierarchy.

This hierarchy, Connell argues, is predicated on a gender order, where certain men are privileged over others (and *all* men maintain power over *all* women). By conceptualizing this intramasculine hierarchy, Connell in 1987 and then again in 1995 (p. 77) argued that an archetype—or *hegemonic* form—of masculinity is "culturally exalted above all other" and is the "most honoured and desired" form of masculinity (Connell, 2000, p. 10). Those who most closely embody this exalted form are afforded the most social capital. Underneath this exist three other categories: (1) *complicit*—this represents the vast majority of men who, despite having little connection with the hegemonic form of masculinity, still benefit from it in some way; (2) *marginalized*—this is said to categorize men subordinated by their race or class; and (3) *subordinate*—this refers to gay (or effeminate) men, who, according to Connell (1995, p. 79), typify "the most conspicuous" form of subordinate masculinity. Accordingly, in this model, homophobia is a particularly effective weapon to stratify men in deference to a hegemonic mode of heteromasculine dominance.

While the intramasculine hierarchy has been a model with great utility, hegemonic masculinity fails to accurately account for what occurs in a macro or even local culture of decreased levels of cultural homophobia—which we considered in the previous. Further, Connell's model permits only one form of masculinity to reside atop a social hierarchy. It also fails to explain the social processes in an environment in which more than one version of masculinity has legitimacy (Anderson, 2009).

In their reformulation of hegemonic masculinity, Connell and Messerschmidt (2005) reaffirm that it presupposes the subordination of nonhegemonic masculinities and that it continues to be predicated upon one dominating—that is, hegemonic—archetype of masculinity. While the attributes of this archetype can change, an essential component is that other masculinities will be hierarchically stratified in relation to it. Accordingly, hegemonic masculinity is incapable of explaining empirical research that documents multiple masculinities of legitimate cultural value (Anderson & McCormack, 2015; Magrath, 2017a; Magrath & Scoats, 2019; McCormack, 2012; Robinson, White, & Anderson, 2019).

Such dynamics were not an issue in the 1980s, when Connell developed her work, or in the 1990s, when it was widely taken up in the literature. Indeed, at this time gay men faced extreme social marginalization (Herek, 1988)—especially in the conservative environments of sport (Curry, 1991; Pronger, 1990). But Connell's theorizing has continued to face significant critique. Moller (2007) argues that the wide endorsement of hegemonic masculinity as a theoretical concept has frequently led scholars to interpret patterns of hegemonic masculinity too easily. In other words, rather than *explaining* masculinity patterns, the concept's dominance actually *obscures* them. There are also definitional issues with the concept's central archetypes—*complicit, marginalized,* and *subordinate*—which are only loosely explained in Connell's work. And even after Connell and Messerschmidt's (2005) reformulation of the concept, it continued to lack theoretical specificity, thus leaving little to distinguish it from the paradigm of social constructionism more broadly (Anderson & Magrath, 2019).

Perhaps most important, however, the decline of cultural homophobia over the past two decades—as we outlined in more detail in previous sections—means that the heurism of hegemonic masculinity fails to account for the varying masculinities that researchers have found flourishing without hierarchy or hegemony in numerous sporting (and nonsporting) contexts.

Inclusive Masculinity Theory

Given the changing nature of masculinities across most of the Western world in recent years, numerous scholars have critiqued hegemonic masculinity's effectiveness in capturing the social dynamics of young men (Demetriou, 2001; Hearn, 2004; Howson, 2006; Moller, 2007). One of the most promising means of theorizing this shift has been through Eric Anderson's (2009) inclusive masculinity theory. While Anderson's early research cited Connell's scholarship (e.g., Anderson, 2002), he found her work increasingly incapable of explaining the reduction of homophobia, increased inclusivity of sexual minorities, and the reduction of homophobic discourse. Antecedents of this research emerged in Anderson's (2005, p. 337) research on American cheerleading, where he documented "two contrasting and competing forms of normative masculinity . . . orthodox [and] inclusive."

Central to Anderson's theorizing is the concept of *homohysteria,* which seeks to explain the power dynamics of heterosexual masculinities within a historical frame. It is best defined as a "homosexually-panicked culture in which suspicion [of homosexuality] permeates" (Anderson, 2011a, p. 83). Anderson further argues that, in order for a culture of homohysteria to exist, three social factors must coincide: (1) mass cultural awareness of homosexuality, (2) a cultural zeitgeist of disapproval toward homosexuality, and (3) cultural disapproval of men's femininity, as displaying these behaviors becomes closely associated with homosexuality.

In a Feminist Forum debate in the *Sex Roles* journal, McCormack and Anderson (2014) discuss three conditions through which a culture historically moves: (1) *homoerasure*—describing a severely homophobic culture but one which fails to recognize the existence of homosexuality as a static part of their population; (2) *homohysteria*—a combination of the acceptance of and antipathy toward homosexuality, such as Western cultures in the 1980s (e.g. Watt & Elliot, 2019); and (3) *inclusivity*—a culture in which homosexual stigma is minimal, and men are not required to alter their expression of masculinity (Anderson & McCormack, 2015).

Since its evolution in the field over a decade ago, inclusive masculinity theory—and its associated concept, homohysteria—has been prolific in its theorizing of contemporary masculinities. It has been used in hundreds of separate academic studies—primarily in sport, but also in other settings such as education (McCormack, 2012), the media (Kian et al., 2015), and the workplace (Magrath, 2020). It has, therefore emerged into a more adaptable heuristic tool in explaining the contemporary stratification of Western men. With this flexibility, it has helped to move standpoints from vertical (in Connell's model of masculinity) to horizontal (in Anderson's theory), as homophobia continues to decline. It has been so widely employed that Borkowska (2020, p. 412) has argued that the most recent phase of masculinities research—the "third phase"—should be described as "Andersonian" because this work has "moved away from the hierarchical order of social relations where men attempt to distance themselves from femininity or position themselves within the orthodox ideologies of manhood."

Evidencing these softer versions of masculinity, heterosexual boys and men are no longer bound by the rigid gendered practices of previous generations (e.g., Williams, 1985). Anderson and McCormack (2015, p. 223), for example, document how young, university-age men are able to engage in "prolonged acts of homosocial tactility—namely cuddling and spooning," without the threat of homophobic policing (see also Anderson, 2011a). Moreover, in research with 145 British university men, 89% had kissed another man on the lips. Aside from a show of celebration among sporting men, such displays were seen as simply demonstrations of love and affection for one's close friends (Anderson, Adams, & Rivers, 2012). Drummond, Filiault, Anderson, and Jeffries (2015) showed that while the figure was reportedly less in the Australian university context—only approximately 33% of those sampled—this assessment was still significantly higher than documented in previous research. And in the United States, while 40% of undergraduate men had kissed another man on the cheek, only 10% had done so on the lips (Anderson, Ripley, & McCormack, 2019). Academic work has documented an expansion of heterosexual men's same-sex sexual activity and, thus, a decline of the "one-time rule of homosexuality" (e.g., Anderson, 2008; Scoats, Joseph, & Anderson, 2018).

An extension of gendered male behaviors is notable in the development of emotionally open and intimate friendships—labeled by Robinson et al. (2019) the "bromance." Interestingly, men in this research even prioritized their bromantic over their romantic relationships. This was because bromances were deemed to have fewer boundaries and be more free of judgment, thus allowing men to "push the margins of traditional masculinity" (p. 864). While most research on the bromance has been restricted to university friendships, Magrath and Scoats (2019) show that these friendship bonds frequently continue years after graduation.

As with Connell's theorizing, inclusive masculinity theory has also received critique from masculinity scholars. These have (1) mostly involved nonempirically validated statements that homophobia has not or is not declining or (2) that the continued presence of heterosexism is just as extreme in its negative affect on people as overt homophobia or (3) that inclusive masculinity theory is not globally generalizable and (4) that it does not account for patriarchy.

In 2016, Anderson and McCormack (2018) addressed these critiques in the *Journal of Gender Studies*. Here, they utilized numerous, international studies to refute (1) and showed that declining homophobia over the past three decades was sustained and profound. They also refuted (2) by drawing on a range of qualitative studies to show that gay (and bisexual) men's lives are dramatically improved compared to those who lived in the 1980s due to the decline of hostile attitudes (see Anderson & McCormack, 2016). Since these critiques, the theory has been applied in multiple international settings, including works in Asia (Hu, 2018) and Africa (Hamdi, Lachheb, & Anderson, 2017). This work includes quantitative data, as well (Piedra, García-Pérez, & Channon, 2017). Finally, Anderson and McCormack (2018) agree that (4) inclusive masculinity theory does not account for the reproduction of patriarchy, noting that, indeed, this was not at its creation, nor is it now, the purpose of the theory (see also Anderson & Magrath, 2019).

Debates

So far, this chapter has outlined how the relationship between sport, masculinity, and sexuality has undergone considerable change. However, there remain a number of debates and unresolved issues in the field, most of which center around the extent to which homophobia has declined in contemporary sport. Equality, diversity, and inclusion organizations—such as Stonewall (the United Kingdom's most notable LGBT rights charity), the National LGBTQ Task Force (one of the largest advocacy organizations in the United States), and numerous sporting equivalents (e.g., Kick It Out, Pride Sports, Football v. Homophobia)—frequently produce reports claiming that LGBT-phobia and discrimination remain endemic in sporting culture. In 2015, a project declaring itself "the first international study conducted into homophobia in sport" claimed that there were "few positive signs in any country that LGB people are welcome and safe playing team sport." This study was retrospectively published in 2020 in the *Sexuality Research and Social Policy* journal (Denison, Jeanes, Faulkner, & O'Brien, 2020).

McCormack (2020, p. 101) argues that such findings must be treated with caution because "significant flaws in the rigour of the research in the reports exist, in both methods and analysis. Overly generalised claims are then made." Some of these flaws—as has been previously identified by Anderson et al. (2016)—include no age or jokester controls (particularly on internet surveys), which has been shown to elevate levels of discrimination (see Li, Follingstad, Campe, & Chahal, 2020); counting retrospective accounts of homophobia as current; targeting participants through associations that provide support for LGB people; collapsing and conflating transgender, gay male, bisexual, and lesbian results (see Sullivan, 2020); or making claims that pathologize LGBT people without comparing them to heterosexuals. Such studies are therefore best described as "'hearts and minds' stud[ies] of perceptions and fears, not necessarily reflecting empirical realities" (Anderson et al., 2016, p. 5).

Other critiques of work documenting sport's changing relationship with masculinity and sexuality have pointed out that findings are primarily restricted to young, white, middle-class, university-educated men in the Anglo-American contexts studied (e.g., Adams & Anderson, 2012; Anderson, 2011a; Magrath & Scoats, 2019). While critiques based on race, class, and level of education may have initially appeared to be accurate, more recent findings beyond these demographics—in both sport and society more broadly—have shown comparable levels of inclusivity (e.g., Cashmore & Cleland, 2012; Magrath, 2017a, 2017b). Outside of sport, recent research with working-class boys and men (e.g., Blanchard, McCormack, & Peterson, 2015; Roberts, 2018) also documents positive attitudes toward homosexuality, as well as softer and more inclusive forms of masculinity compared to older research (e.g., Nayak & Kehily, 1996). While research with nonwhite men in Anglo-American contexts has shown improved attitudes (e.g., Morales, 2018), other research still documents generally more conservative attitudes among these groups of men (Magrath, 2017b; Magrath, Batten, Anderson, & White, 2020; Southall, Anderson, Nagel, Polite, & Southall, 2011).

The social trend of declining homophobia is also evident among older generations of men (Twenge et al., 2016; Watt & Elliot, 2019). Other research has indicated that there is both a generational and a cohort effect, occurring simultaneously (Keleher & Smith, 2012). Interestingly, however, despite evidence of attitudinal change across age cohorts, there remains an absence of contemporary research that examines the performance and construction of masculinity among men whose adolescence occurred in the 1960s and 1970s or for men over 40. Only research by Anderson and Fidler (2018), which focuses explicitly on men over 65, provides any insight into this cohort's acceptance of homosexuality—which, in comparison to younger men, is found to be severely more conservative and highly homophobic. More substantial research into these age cohorts is lacking, however, and is thus required to develop the field of study further.

We note that while sport has undergone significant changes in respect to declining homophobia, it still remains a largely heteronormative environment. Indeed, the macho culture of the locker room—and sports as a whole—has resulted in the need for LGB individuals to adapt their behaviors. White et al.'s (2021) analysis of gay male athletes' coming-out stories on Outsports, for example, documents how, prior to coming out, they espoused an identity predicated on masculine stereotypes. Magrath's (2021) research on gay male fans shows that they adopt a "straight image" while in stadia in order to reduce the risk of homosexual suspicion. Nevertheless, it is important to acknowledge that heteronormativity, despite its implicit privileging of heterosexuality, does not equate to homophobia. However, while this dynamic remains difficult to tackle, research is needed to assess how much this could be a contributory factor in the relative lack of elite-level LGB athletes.

Alongside this, however, Anderson et al. (2016) also propose a number of hypotheses to explain the lack of out, elite-level male athletes (see also Ogawa, 2014). These include (1) the *silence* hypothesis—that gay male athletes *do* exist but simply remain closeted during their athletic careers (or longer); (2) the *nonparticipation* or *nonexistent* hypothesis—that gay men simply avoid sports and prefer instead to participate in other locales; (3) the *international* hypothesis—that gay athletes' participation in international competitions, which are held in countries where attitudes toward homosexuality remain conservative in comparison to the West, make coming out a problematic proposition (as we discuss in the next section); and (4) the *generational* hypothesis—where younger athletes are put off coming out due to concerns that influential figures within their organization (most of whom are older) may espouse less progressive attitudes toward homosexuality.

Global Challenges

Earlier in this chapter we noted how the majority of research on sport, masculinity, and sexuality is predominantly restricted to studies in the United Kingdom and the United States, and, to a lesser degree, Australia and Canada. While social attitude survey data continue to show that attitudes toward homosexuality across the Western world are improving, some sports research in Europe continues to observe homophobic attitudes and/or behaviors. In research with Spain's first-ever out gay team sport athlete, Victor Gutiérrez, Vilanova, Soler, and Anderson (2018) found general acceptance, but also the continued presence of discriminatory language. In Italy, Baiocco, Pistella, Salvati, Ioverno, and Lucidi (2018) concluded that gay men reported more frequent bullying and were, therefore, more likely to drop out of participation in sport. And Kaelberer (2020) argues that tackling endemic homophobia has yet to be a priority in German sport. This is thus important evidence that declining homophobia is an uneven social process.

We also know from some, albeit largely anecdotal, examples and a paucity of scholarly research that other countries' cultural disapproval of homosexuality is paralleled across much of the sports world. The 2018 FIFA (men's) soccer World Cup in Russia, for example, saw the Mexican Football Federation fined and threatened with expulsion for their fans' continued use of the word "puto," a homophobic epithet referring to a male sex worker (see Rodriguez, 2017). The previous year saw Russian politicians' claims that the virtual soccer game *FIFA* should be banned due to its apparently illegal promotion of "gay propaganda" in the form of a rainbow-colored kit in support of English sport's antihomophobia movement. July 2020 also saw Russian politicians seeking to ban same-sex marriage after a constitutional change that defined marriage as a male-female union only.

Outside of Europe and North America, while there is some evidence of changing notions of gender (e.g., Hasan, Aggleton, & Persson, 2018; Hu, 2018), research on sport, masculinity, and sexuality is scant. However, we know that LGB people face significant challenges in countries that are socially conservative or are entrenched in religiosity. For example, Hamdi, Lachheb, and Anderson's (2017, p. 688) examination of gay athletes in Tunisia concluded, "Same-sex sexual relations are religiously taboo and legally prohibited. There is [therefore] no public discourse about homosexuality in sport in this context." Other notable publications include Shang and Gill's (2012) research on LGB athletes in Taiwan, which shows continued evidence of hostile sporting cultures and de facto sanctioned normalization of homophobic language. More recently, research in Hong Kong, China, and Taiwan has shown that sports coaches were more likely to espouse positive attitudes toward homosexuality if they had worked with an LGB athlete (Tseng & Kim-Wai Sum, 2021).

These studies are therefore an important reminder that declining cultural homophobia can vary according to gender, age, education, religion, race, geography, socioeconomic status, and other variables (Keleher & Smith, 2012). These studies also serve as a reminder of the importance of further research investigating the contemporary relationship between *global* sport, masculinities, and sexualities. For instance, while some research has started to examine attitudes toward homosexuality in sport outside the West, we know little about changing (or not) patterns of masculinity—and whether or not this has also followed a more inclusive trend. The importance of this research cannot be overestimated, and we therefore call on scholars to include this in their future research agendas.

Conclusion

As we have evidenced throughout this chapter, there has been an undeniable shift toward the acceptance and inclusivity of sexual minorities in contemporary sports culture in Anglo-American societies, where sport was once seen as one of the last refuges of homophobia (e.g., Curry, 1991; Hekma, 1998; Pronger, 1990). Attitudes toward homosexuality in the sports industry—and society more broadly—have improved exponentially over the past two decades (Keleher & Smith, 2012; Twenge et al., 2016; Watt & Elliot, 2019). Indeed, where sport once embraced its intolerance of homosexuality, it is now proud of its increased commitment to equality, diversity, and inclusion (Letts, 2021). Indeed, one need only examine the treatment of athletes such as Israel Folau and Manny Pacquiao, both of whom have been widely condemned for their anti-LGB comments in recent years, or conversely, the praising of so many athletes who have come out publicly (White et al., 2021). So far, however, most of the research documenting increased acceptance and declining tolerance for homophobia has been restricted to Western nations. As the previous section examined, matters outside of these nations are often more complex, and further investigation into sociocultural dynamics undergirding masculinity and sexuality is required.

Research has also examined a whole range of competitive sports across the Western world: rugby, soccer, dance, horse racing, football, wrestling, cross country, and cheerleading, to name but a few. Less is known, however, about a multitude of other sports, most particularly individual sports as well as those which continue to be cast as more feminine-appropriate terrains. Additionally, while we must acknowledge and unequivocally accept the positive change which has occurred in recent years, we must also remain cautious. We know little about how contemporary masculinity might intersect with other important factors—such as disability, for example. There are numerous areas which require further exploration in order to achieve data saturation, such as the construction of masculinity among older generations of men, particularly those from nonwhite backgrounds. We also know little about how other cultural, economic, and political factors influence matters—particularly in the context of Trumpism (in the United States) and Brexit (in the United Kingdom).

There are also, perhaps, more nuanced challenges we continue to face. Indeed, in areas where attitudes have undoubtedly changed are more implicit microaggressions which are, oftentimes, harder to tackle. Needed interrogation might include focusing on homosexually themed (or homophobic) language, irrespective of its intentions, and assessing the heteronormative environment that remains omnipresent but unspoken and rarely acknowledged in many sporting contexts (Magrath, 2020). Indeed, while there is undoubtedly evidence of considerable improvements in the sporting climate, intransigent issues such as these still remain. There is, therefore, more research needed to further explore the ever-changing relationship between sport, masculinity, and sexuality.

Over a decade ago, Anderson (2009, p. 160) appealed to "graduate students and young scholars . . . [to] investigate the intersection of inclusive masculinities in other arenas." While this appeal was answered, as evidenced by the substantial body of work cited in this chapter, we again reiterate the call for further research. We reach out to graduate students and young scholars, but also to established senior scholars in the field to help to paint a broader and more accurate picture of contemporary masculinities across the world. Perhaps most important, we also call on scholars to be led by impartial and rigorous methodological procedures, to be led by data, not by entrenched agendas or personal dispositions. This is important not only for the academic world but also for policymakers, as confronting these issues without predisposed biases helps to further develop sport into a more inclusive environment.

NOTES

1. The recommendations of the Wolfenden Report were only implemented in England and Wales, and referred to consenting men over the age of 21. The law did not apply in Scotland until 1980, and Northern Ireland in 1982.

2. Outsports.com is typically recognized as the world's prominent website and resource for LGBT issues in sport.

References

Adams, A., & Anderson, E. (2012). Exploring the relationship between homosexuality and sport among the teammates of a small, midwestern Catholic college soccer team. *Sport, Education and Society*, 17(3), 347–363.

Anderson, E. (2002). Openly gay athletes: Contesting hegemonic masculinity in a homophobic environment. *Gender and Society*, 16(6), 860–877.

Anderson, E. (2005). Orthodox and inclusive masculinity: Competing masculinities among heterosexual men in a feminized terrain. *Sociological Perspectives*, 48(3), 337–355.

Anderson, E. (2008). "Being masculine is not about who you sleep with": Heterosexual athletes contesting masculinity and the one-time rule of homosexuality. *Sex Roles*, 58(1–2), 104–115.

Anderson, E. (2009). *Inclusive masculinity: The changing nature of masculinities*. London: Routledge.

Anderson, E. (2011a). Inclusive masculinities of university soccer players in the American Midwest. *Gender and Education*, 23(6), 729–744.

Anderson, E. (2011b). Updating the outcome: Gay athletes, straight teams, and coming out in educationally based sport teams. *Gender and Society*, 25(2), 250–268.

Anderson, E., Adams, A., & Rivers, I. (2012). "I kiss them because I love them": The emergence of heterosexual men kissing in British institutes of education. *Archives of Sexual Behavior*, 41(2), 421–430.

Anderson, E., & Fidler, C. O. (2018). Elderly British men: Homohysteria and orthodox masculinities. *Journal of Gender Studies*, 27(3), 248–259.

Anderson, E., & Magrath, R. (2019). *Men and masculinities*. London: Routledge.

Anderson, E., & McCormack, M. (2015). Cuddling and spooning: Heteromasculinity and homosocial intimacy tactility among student-athletes. *Men and Masculinities*, 18(2), 214–230.

Anderson, E., & McCormack, M. (2016). *The changing dynamics of bisexual men's lives: Social research perspectives*. New York: Palgrave.

Anderson, E., & McCormack, M. (2018). Inclusive masculinity theory: Overview, reflection and refinement. *Journal of Gender Studies*, 27(5), 547–561.

Anderson, E., Magrath, R., & Bullingham, R. (2016). *Out in sport: The experiences of openly gay and lesbian athletes in competitive sport*. London: Routledge.

Anderson, E., Ripley, M., & McCormack, M. (2019). A mixed-method study of same-sex kissing among college-attending heterosexual men in the US. *Sexuality and Culture*, 23(1), 26–44.

Anderson, E., & Travers, A. (Eds.). (2017). *Transgender athletes in competitive sport*. London: Routledge.

Baiocco, R., Pistella, J., Salvati, M., Ioverno, S., & Lucidi, F. (2018). Sports as a risk environment: Homophobia and bullying in a sample of gay and heterosexual men. *Journal of Gay and Lesbian Mental Health*, 22(4), 385–411.

Barret, R. L. (1993). The homosexual athlete. In L. Diamant (Ed.), *Homosexual issues in the workplace* (pp. 161–170). New York: Routledge.

Billings, A. C., & Moscowitz, L. (2018). *Media and the coming out of gay male athletes in American team sports*. New York: Peter Lang.

Blanchard, C., McCormack, M., & Peterson, G. T. (2015). Inclusive masculinities in a working-class sixth form in northeast England. *Journal of Contemporary Ethnography, 46*(3), 310–333.

Borkowska, K. (2020). Approaches to studying masculinity: A nonlinear perspective of theoretical paradigms. *Men and Masculinities, 23*(3-4), 409–424.

Bosia, M. J. (2013). Why states act: Homophobia and crisis. In M. L. Weiss & M. J. Bosia (Eds.), *Global homophobia: States, movements, and the politics of oppression* (pp. 30–54). Chicago: University of Illinois Press.

Bush, A., Anderson, E., & Carr, S. (2012). The declining existence of men's homophobia in British sport. *Journal for the Study of Sports and Athletes in Education, 6*(1), 107–120.

Butterworth, M. L. (2006). Pitchers and catchers: Mike Piazza and the discourse of gay identity in the national pastime. *Journal of Sport and Social Issues, 30*(2), 138–157.

Carter, N. (2006). *The football manager: A history*. London: Routledge.

Cashmore, E., & Cleland, J. (2012). Fans, homophobia and masculinities in association football: Evidence of a more inclusive environment. *British Journal of Sociology, 63*(2), 370–387.

Cassidy, W. P. (2017). *Sports journalism and coming out stories: Jason Collins and Michael Sam*. New York: Springer.

Cleland, J. (2015). Discussing homosexuality on association football fans message boards: A changing cultural context. *International Review for the Sociology of Sport, 50*(2), 125–140.

Cleland, J., & Magrath, R. (2020). Association football, masculinity, and sexuality: An evolving relationship. In R. Magrath, J. Cleland, & E. Anderson (Eds.), *Palgrave handbook of masculinity and sport* (pp. 341–357). Basingstoke, U.K.: Palgrave.

Cleland, J., Magrath, R., & Kian, E. M. (2018). The internet as a site of decreasing cultural homophobia in association football: An online response by fans to the coming out of Thomas Hitzlsperger. *Men and Masculinities, 21*(1), 91–111.

Connell, R. W. (1987). *Gender and power*. Cambridge, U.K.: Polity Press.

Connell, R. W. (1995). *Masculinities* (2nd ed). Cambridge, U.K.: Polity Press.

Connell, R. W. (2000). *The men and the boys*. Cambridge, U.K.: Polity Press.

Connell, R. W., & Messerschmidt, J. (2005). Hegemonic masculinity: Rethinking the concept. *Gender and Society, 19*(6), 829–859.

Curry, T. (1991). Fraternal bonding in the locker room: A profeminist analysis of talk about competition and women. *Sociology of Sport Journal, 8*(2), 119–135.

Demetriou, D. Z. (2001). Connell's concept of hegemonic masculinity: A critique. *Theory and Society, 30*(3), 337–361.

Denison, E., Jeanes, R., Faulkner, N., & O'Brien, K. S. (2020). The relationship between "coming out" as lesbian, gay, or bisexual and experiences of homophobic behaviour in youth team sports. *Sexuality Research and Social Policy*. Advance online publication. https://doi-org.electra.lmu.edu/10.1007/s13178-020-00499-x.

Dunning, E. (1986). Sport as a male preserve: Notes on the social sources of masculine identity and its transformations. *Theory, Culture and Society, 3*(1), 79–90.

Drummond, M. J., Filiault, S. M., Anderson, E., & Jeffries, D. (2015). Homosocial intimacy among Australian undergraduate men. *Journal of Sociology, 51*(3), 643–656.

Fine, G. A. (1987). *With the boys: Little league baseball and preadolescent culture*. Chicago, IL: University of Chicago Press.

Guttmann, A. (1978). *From ritual to record: The nature of modern sports*. New York: Columbia University Press.

Hamdi, N., Lachheb, M., & Anderson, E. (2017). Masculinity, homosexuality and sport in an Islamic state of increasing homohysteria. *Journal of Gender Studies, 26*(6), 688–701.

Harry, J. (1995). Sports ideology, attitudes toward women, and anti-homosexual attitudes. *Sex Roles, 32*(1–2), 109–116.

Hasan, M. K., Aggleton, P., & Persson, A. (2018). The makings of a man: Social generational masculinities in Bangladesh. Journal of Gender Studies, 27(3), 347–361.

Hearn, J. (2004). From hegemonic masculinity to the hegemony of men. *Feminist Studies, 5*(1), 49–72.

Hekma, G. (1998). "As long as they don't make an issue of It . . . " Gay men and lesbians in organized sports in the Netherlands. Journal of Homosexuality, 35(1), 1–23.

Herek, G. M. (1988). Heterosexuals' attitudes toward lesbians and gay men: Correlates and gender differences. *Journal of Sex Research, 25*(4), 451–477.

Howson, R. (2006). *Challenging hegemonic masculinity*. London: Routledge.

Hu, L. (2018). Is masculinity 'deteriorating' in China? Changes of masculinity representation in Chinese film posters from 1951 to 2016. Journal of Gender Studies, 27(3), 335–346.

Kaelberer, M. (2020). Inclusive masculinities, homosexuality and homophobia in German professional soccer. Sexuality and Culture, 24(3), 796–808.

Keleher, A., & Smith, E. R. A. N. (2012). Growing support for gay and lesbian equality since 1990. *Journal of Homosexuality, 59*(9), 1307–1236.

Kian, E. M., Anderson, E., & Shipka, D. (2015). "I am happy to start the conversation": Examining sport media framing of Jason Collins' coming out and playing in the NBA. *Sexualities, 18*(5–6), 618–640.

Kian, E. M., Clavio, G., Vincent, J., & Shaw, S. D. (2011). Homophobic and sexist yet uncontested: Examining football fan postings on internet message boards. *Journal of Homosexuality, 58*(5), 680–699.

Kimmel, M. S. (1994). Masculinity as homophobia: Fear, shame and silence in the construction of gender identity. In H. Brod & M. Kaufman (Eds.), *Theorizing masculinities* (pp. 119–141). Thousand Oaks, CA: Sage.

Letts, D. (2021). Sexual minority prevalence and attitudes within the British horseracing industry. *International Review for the Sociology of Sport, 56*(6), 823-841.

Li, C. R., Follingstad, D. R., Campe, M. I., & Chahal, J. K. (2020). Identifying invalid responders in a campus climate survey: Types, impact on data, and best indicators. *Journal of Interpersonal Violence*. Advance online publication. doi:10.1177/0886260520918588.

Magrath, R. (2017a). *Inclusive masculinities in contemporary football: Men in the beautiful game*. London: Routledge.

Magrath, R. (2017b). The intersection of race, religion and homophobia in British football. *International Review for the Sociology of Sport, 52*(4), 411–429.

Magrath, R. (2018). "To try and gain an advantage for my team": Homophobic and homosexually themed language among English football fans. *Sociology, 52*(4), 709–726.

Magrath, R. (2019a). Inclusive masculinities of working-class university footballers in the South of England. *Sport in Society*. Advance online publication. doi:10.1080/17430437.2019.1672157.

Magrath, R. (Ed.). (2019b). *LGBT athletes in the sports media*. Basingstoke, U.K.: Palgrave.

Magrath, R. (2020). "Progress . . . slowly, but surely": The sports media workplace, gay sports journalists, and LGBT media representation in sport. *Journalism Studies, 21*(2), 254–270.

Magrath, R. (2021). Gay male football fans' experiences: Authenticity, belonging and conditional acceptance. Sociology, 55(5), 978–994.

Magrath, R., Anderson, E., & Roberts, S. (2015). On the doorstep of equality: Attitudes toward gay athletes among academy-level footballers. *International Review for the Sociology of Sport, 50*(7), 804–821.

Magrath, R., Batten, J., Anderson, E., & White, A. J. (2020). Examining attitudes towards homosexuality among young, athletic BME men in the UK. *Sport in Society*. Advance online publication. https://doi.org/10.1080/17430437.2020.1844183.

Magrath, R., Cleland, J., & Anderson, E. (2017). Bisexual erasure in the British print media: Representation of Tom Daley's coming out. *Journal of Bisexuality*, 17(3), 300–317.

Magrath, R., & Scoats, R. (2019). Young men's friendships: Inclusive masculinities in a post-university setting. *Journal of Gender Studies*, 28(1), 45–56.

McCormack, M. (2012). *The declining significance of homophobia: How teenage boys are redefining masculinity and homophobia*. Oxford: Oxford University Press.

McCormack, M. (2020). Advocacy research on homophobia in education: Claims-making, trauma construction and the politics of evidence. *Sociology*, 54(1), 89–106.

McCormack, M., & Anderson, E. (2014). The influence of declining homophobia on men's gender in the United States: An argument for the study of homohysteria. *Sex Roles*, 71(3–4), 109–120.

Messner, M. A., & Sabo, D. F. (1990). Introduction: Toward a critical feminist reappraisal of sport, men, and the gender order. In M. A. Messner & D. F. Sabo (Eds.), *Sport, men, and the gender order: Critical feminist perspectives* (pp. 1–15). Champaign, IL: Human Kinetics.

Moller, M. (2007). Exploiting patterns: A critique of hegemonic masculinities. *Journal of Gender Studies*, 16(3), 263–276.

Morales, L. E. (2018). The impact of gay friendly cultures on religious expression: A study of inclusive attitudes and behaviours among religious adolescent American male athletes. *Journal of Gender Studies*, 27(3), 323–334.

Nayak, A., & Kehily, M. J. (1996). Playing it straight: Masculinities, homophobias and schooling. *Journal of Gender Studies*, 5(2), 211–230.

Ogawa, S. (2014). 100 missing men: Participation, selection, and silence of gay athletes. In J. Hargreaves & E. Anderson (Eds.), *Routledge handbook of sport, gender and sexuality* (pp. 291–299). London: Routledge.

Parker, A. (1996). *Chasing the "big-time": Football apprenticeship in the 1990s* (Unpublished doctoral dissertation). University of Warwick.

Pew Research Center. (2013, June 4). The Global Divide on Homosexuality. https://www.pewresearch.org/global/2013/06/04/the-global-divide-on-homosexuality/.

Piedra, J., García-Pérez, R., & Channon, A. G. (2017). Between homohysteria and inclusivity: Tolerance towards sexual diversity in sport. *Sexuality & Culture*, 21(4), 1018–1039.

Pronger, B. (1990). *The arena of masculinity: Sports, homosexuality, and the meaning of sex*. New York: St. Martin's Press.

Rigauer, B. (1981). *Sport and work*. New York: Columbia University Press.

Roberts, S. (2018). *Young working-class men in transition*. London: Routledge.

Robinson, S., White, A. J., & Anderson, E. (2019). Privileging the bromance: A critical appraisal of romantic and bromantic relationships. *Men and Masculinities*, 22(5), 850–871.

Rodriguez, N. S. (2017). # FIFAputos: A Twitter textual analysis over "Puto" at the 2014 World Cup. Communication and Sport, 5(6), 712–731.

Sabo, D. F., & Runfola, R. (1980). *Jock: Sports and male identity*. Englewood Cliffs, NJ: Prentice-Hall.

Scoats, R., Joseph, L. J., & Anderson, E. (2018). "I don't mind watching him cum": Heterosexual men, threesomes, and the erosion of the one-time rule of homosexuality. *Sexualities*, 21(1–2), 30–48.

Shang, Y. T., & Gill, D. (2012). Athletes' perceptions of the sport climate for athletes with non-gender-congruent gender expressions and non-heterosexual sexual orientations in Taiwan. *Journal for the Study of Sports and Athletes in Education, 6*(1), 67–82.

Southall, R. M., Anderson, E., Nagel, M. S., Polite, F. G., & Southall, C. (2011). An investigation of ethnicity as a variable related to US male college athletes' sexual-orientation behaviours and attitudes. *Ethnic and Racial studies, 34*(2), 293–313.

Sullivan, A. (2020). Sex and the census: Why surveys should not conflate sex and gender identity. *International Journal of Social Research Methodology, 23*(5), 517–524.

Tseng, Y. H., & Kim-Wai Sum, R. (2021). The attitudes of collegiate coaches toward gay and lesbian athletes in Taiwan, Hong Kong and China. *International Review for the Sociology of Sport, 56*(3), 416–435.

Twenge, J. M., Sherman, R. A., & Wells, B. E. (2016). Changes in American adults' reported same-sex sexual experiences and attitudes. *Archives of Sexual Behavior, 45*(7), 1713–1730.

Vilanova, A., Soler, S., & Anderson, E. (2018). Examining the experiences of the first openly gay male team sport athlete in Spain. *International Review for the Sociology of Sport, 55*(1), 22–37.

Watt, L., & Elliot, M. (2019). Homonegativity in Britain: Changing attitudes towards same-sex sex relationships. *Journal of Sex Research, 56*(9), 1101–1114.

White, A. J., Magrath, R., & Morales, L. E. (2021). Gay male athletes' coming-out stories on Outsports.com. *International Review for the Sociology of Sport, 56*(7), 1017–1034.

Whitson, D. (1990). Sport in the social construction of masculinity. In M. A. Messner & D. F. Sabo (Ed.), *Sport, men, and the gender order: Critical feminist perspectives* (pp. 19–29). Champaign, IL: Human Kinetics.

Williams, D. G. (1985). Gender, masculinity-femininity, and emotional intimacy in same-sex friendship. *Sex Roles, 12*(5–6), 587–600.

Wolf-Wendel, L., Toma, D., & Morphew, C. (2001). How much difference is too much difference? Journal of College Student Development, 42(5), 465–479.

Young, K. (2019). *Sport, violence and society* (2nd ed). London: Routledge.

CHAPTER 47

···

SPORT, FEMININITIES, AND HETERONORMATIVITY

···

CHERYL COOKY

On December 12, 2020, Sarah Fuller, an American female collegiate football player, made history in the United States as the "first woman" to score in the Power 5 college conference when she successfully kicked a field goal during a game against the University of Tennessee. This history-making moment went viral on social media in the United States, with notable celebrities, famous athletes, and politicians all congratulating Fuller, including American tennis legend and women's sports advocate Billie Jean King, who referred to Fuller as a "trailblazer" (Kinney, 2020). While other women have played college football, including Katie Hnida, who played for the University of Colorado in 1999 and was raped by one of her teammates (Luther, 2016; Reilly, 2005), Fuller drew attention not for making history as much as for playing in a sport that has been historically and culturally linked to hegemonic masculinity. Both Fuller's gender as well as the gendered dimensions of the sport of American gridiron football helped shape the public and media reaction and response. Certainly, not all who posted on social media celebrated this trailblazing accomplishment. As feminist media studies scholar Sarah Banet-Weiser (2018) argued, popular feminism circulates alongside popular misogyny. Some social media posts dismissed Fuller's accomplishment as an achievement easily attained by a high school (male) football player and found it to be a "stunt" (Kinney, 2020) rather than, as the coach explained, the realities of fielding a football team during a pandemic.

Fuller's achievement and the corresponding response speak to the ways in which cultural meanings of gender have shaped access and opportunity, as well as acceptance and inclusion, for women athletes. Modern sports have developed in the United States (and other Global North cultures) as a context for socializing boys and men into culturally accepted norms, behaviors, and beliefs that define masculinity in a way that scholars have characterized as "hegemonic masculinity" (see Magrath & Anderson, in this volume). This context has been central to women's lived experiences as well as academic theorizing on sport. While boys' and men's participation in sports reaffirms cultural expectations for their gender, girls' and women's sport participation challenges cultural proscriptions of femininity, particularly in those sports at the "center of sports" (Messner, 2002), such as American gridiron football, basketball, ice hockey, and baseball. Thus, girls' and women's access, opportunity, acceptance, and inclusion in sports have been defined and shaped by these gendered dynamics. Moreover, sport itself reproduces the gender binary in ways that reaffirm "natural" differences between men and women through its organizational structure as a sex-segregated institution.

This chapter explores the intersections of sport, femininities, and heteronormativity, with a primary focus on contemporary U.S. sporting cultures, practices, and meanings. The chapter begins with a brief overview of the gendered context of sport in the United States, with a particular focus on the development of modern sport. The role of sport in reaffirming and challenging gendered ideologies is considered. The second section highlights several foundational approaches used by feminist sports studies scholars to understand and explain the experiences and meanings of sportswomen and women's sports, including Connell's structural theories of gender, intersectional theories of domination and oppression, and postfeminisms. The third section provides insight into three ways heteronormative femininity shapes women's sports to illustrate how historical dynamics and persisting gender ideologies produce particular experiences and meanings in women's sports.

ISSUES

The Gendered Context of Sport

In the United States, modern sports emerged during the late 19th and early 20th century, a time characterized by massive social changes to key structures, including the economy, work, family, and education. These changes were precipitated by urbanization and industrialization, coupled with shifting gendered power relations (cf. Cahn, 1994; Messner, 1988). Specifically, according to Messner, the development of modern American organized sports corresponded with two crises of masculinity. The first occurred in the early to middle part of the 20th century, when sport developed as a "male-created homosocial cultural sphere that provided men with psychological separation from the perceived feminization of society while also providing dramatic symbolic proof of the 'natural superiority' of men over women" (Messner, 2010, p. 35). The second crisis of masculinity occurred during the post–World War II era. Messner (1988) argues the rise of mass spectator sports corresponded with an economic shift from entrepreneurial capitalism to corporate capitalism, which produced the docile consumer. There was also a decline in the centrality of physical prowess in the labor market and military; this was a decline that was not accompanied by a similar decline in the psychological need for ideological gender difference. As such, spectator sports, which symbolically illustrated the strength, virility, dominance, and power of the male body, rose in prominence to culturally reassert and reaffirm "natural" gender differences and men's dominance over women (Messner, 1988). Thus, throughout the 20th century, "sport was clearly one of the less contested, core institutions in which heterosexual men's embodied power was enabled and celebrated in ways that supported and naturalized patriarchal beliefs in male superiority and female inferiority and dependence" (Messner, 2002, p. xx).

Contributing to the first crisis of masculinity, the women's suffrage movement gained momentum and women's enrollment in colleges was on the rise. White middle-class women increasingly began participating in lawn tennis and bicycling as leisure activities, challenging

Victorian notions of femininity and women's "natural" frailty (Cooky, 2017; Messner, 2002). These societal changes were a part of wider societal shifts in gender relations. Homosocial organizations, such as the Boy Scouts and the YMCA, youth sport organizations such as Little League baseball and the Playground Movement were established to take over the role of socializing boys into masculine roles in hopes of combating the influences of an increasingly feminized social world (Cahn, 1994; Cooky, 2017; Messner, 1992). Thus, boys and men, mostly white and middle class, were encouraged to participate in sports in order to learn the values, behaviors, and expectations associated with hegemonic masculinity.

During the second crisis of masculinity, white women physical educators and opponents of women's athletic competition had sidelined women's sports into select women's universities and high schools (Cooky, 2017; Cooky & Messner, 2018) or in leagues such as the Amateur Athletic Union or the All American Girls' Baseball League (which emerged during World War II in response to male athletes' deployment overseas, and was disbanded several years after the end of the war). Despite their differing perspectives on women's athleticism and physicality, both groups had to assuage the societal fears of mannishness among women (white, middle-class) athletes (Cahn, 1994). White women physical educators promoted a wholesome image of girls and women who play sports and structured physical activity to highlight conventional femininity. In contrast to this, the organizers of women's sports leagues chose to market female athletes' (hetero)sexual appeal (Cahn, 1994; Cooky, 2017; Gregg & Taylor, 2019; Messner, 2002).

Both approaches to promoting women's sports relied upon heteronormative femininity and emphasized sportswomen conforming to gendered expectations, despite their participation in a hypermasculinized social space. Opportunities to participate in sports differed for working-class women, immigrant women, and women of color, who, due to racialized and classed ideologies, were not subject to the culturally dominant definitions of womanhood (Cooky, 2017; Smith-Rosenberg, 1985). For example, within African American sporting communities, Black women athletes often experienced encouragement and support in competitive athletics that was absent in white affluent sporting communities. Specifically, Black women's participation in sport was believed to create visibility for the larger civil rights movement and was supported and celebrated as symbolic of this (Cahn, 1994; Himes Gissendander, 1994). Moreover, unlike historically white educational institutions, many historically Black colleges and universities endorsed intercollegiate sport for women (Gilreath, Zupin, & Judge, 2017). This was in large part due to the role that Black female physical educators played in interscholastic and intercollegiate women's sports competition (Cahn, 1994; Gilreath et al., 2017). Thus, Black women's participation in sport was viewed differently in African American communities, with greater acceptance of an "active femininity" (Himes Gissendander, 1994, p. 88). This was in part due to the differing economic realities for Black women, who were more likely to participate in the workforce and perform manual labor. As a result, the restrictive feminine ideals were altered or ignored in many African American communities (p. 89) Given Jim Crow laws and the racial segregation of educational institutions in the United States, however, the positive influence of Black female physical educators was limited to Black colleges and high schools (Cahn, 1994).

This brief overview (see also Cooky, 2017) illustrates how girls' and women's inclusion in sports has historically been connected to dominant gendered (and racialized) social relations. Societal crises of masculinity and expectations for girls and women (specifically white, affluent women) to adhere to heteronormative femininity, in part due to fears of the "masculinizing" effects of physicality, competition, and athleticism, shaped the modern development of women's sports in the United States. Intersectional approaches to understanding the gendered historical context of sport are central to discussions of heteronormative femininity, as heteronormative femininity is not only constructed relative to heteronormative/hegemonic masculinity, but it is also constructed upon whiteness and circulated through white, male-dominated sports institutions and cultures. As the following sections will demonstrate, this historical gendered legacy regarding the development of modern sports in the United States continues throughout the late 20th and early 21st centuries.

Reaffirming/Challenging Heteronormative Femininities in Sports

The historical foundations of modern sports help to locate the contemporary arrangements in sports cultures. Given the gendered dimensions of sports organizations, institutions, and cultures, feminist sports studies scholars explore the ways in which sportswomen's presence in athletic and sporting spaces reaffirms and/or challenges broader societal gender and sexual ideologies. On the one hand, women's presence in an institution that has historically been organized to establish, reaffirm, and reproduce hegemonic masculinity has the potential to challenge or disrupt dominant cultural definitions of femininity that link women with characteristics and qualities viewed as antithetical to sporting practices, such as cooperation, physical frailty, and submission (Heywood & Dworkin, 2003). Feminist scholars have argued, however, that much of the potential for such challenges or disruptions to lead to meaningful changes in gendered norms, meanings, expectations or social institutions/ structures will be contained to primarily marginalized sporting spaces (Messner, 2002). This is due to the way sports in the United States (and in many other countries) have been and continue to be a cultural site wherein hegemonic masculinity is displayed and celebrated and are an institution dominated and controlled by men.

While Title IX (federal legislation that prohibits educational institutions from discriminating on the basis of sex) passed in the United States in 1972, expanded opportunities for young girls and women, and helped shift gendered cultural expectations particularly for girls and women, increased opportunities to participate in sports did not fundamentally change the gendered structural arrangements of sport or in the wider society (Cooky, 2009; Cooky & La Voi, 2012). As Bryson (1994, p. 48) argues, sport is "basic to maintain masculine hegemony in that sport crucially privileges males and inferiorizes women." Women, and specifically white, middle-class girls, did indeed experience opportunities on a scale not enjoyed by generations prior. But women's sports is directly controlled by men: women are largely absent from key decision-making/leadership positions in sports organizations, governing bodies such as the International Olympic Committee, and sports media. In contrast, the way sport is culturally defined means that boys and men are encouraged in their participation (Bryson, 1994; Cooky, 2009). Even when women successfully challenge male definitions and male control of sport, the result is that women's sport is very often either ignored or trivialized:

[I]t does become clear that where women do achieve what men see as significant performances, these are likely to be ignored and forgotten. If threat is too great, they may be excluded from the arena entirely. Only in this way can men maintain their power and sustain the view . . . that "virtually all women's sport is second rate." (Clancy, 1985, p. 2, quoted in Bryson, 1994, p. 57)

As Bryson continues, "Thus, we must recognize the ignoring of women's sport as not merely a passive and inadvertent act. It is a dynamic process and one which is invoked to protect hegemonic masculinity" (1994, p. 57). In other words, participation itself, whether as athletes, as coaches, as leaders, or as sports reporters/producers, does not alone challenge masculine domination; women's sports talents and achievements become marginalized through a series of diverse mechanisms.

One mechanism through which women's sports are marginalized is vividly on display in the media coverage of women's sports. Messner (1988) has argued it is imperative to examine the media frameworks for women athletes to better understand the contradictory meanings of women's sports. In the context of American organized sports, this mechanism includes facilitating the marginalization of women's sports by not covering women's sports events or female athletes, by trivializing women's achievements by sexualizing female athletes, and by framing female athletes in gendered domestic roles of heterosexually married mothers or men's / male athletes' wives. Messner finds that gender ideologies are simultaneously reaffirmed and challenged in sport media coverage of female athletes and women's sports and has characterized the place of female athletes as a "contested ideological terrain."

Bruce (2013, 2016) systematically examined over 30 years of research in gender, media, and sport and identified several major patterns regarding the ways in which sportswomen are covered and represented by sports media. In addition to patterns of trivialization and marginalization, Bruce charts how compulsory heterosexuality leads to the privileging of sportswomen who are able to successfully conform to cultural expectations for heterosexual women, such as girlfriend, wife, or mother, while simultaneously silencing lesbian identities. Other patterns and key mechanisms identified by Bruce, such as "appropriate" femininity and sexualization, also illustrate the ways in which heterosexuality is linked with conventional femininity in sport media's representation of sportswomen. Bruce makes a compelling case that cultural anxieties about the potential for nonnormative sexualities in sports, and women's sports in particular, have served to shape sportswomen's embodiment, lived experiences, cultural representations, and meanings as well as opportunities and access.

Underlying the foundations of women's sports in the United States (and in other Western and Global North cultures) is homophobia. That homophobia continues to be a pervasive ideology in sports and in the wider society suggests that challenging the gendered boundaries corresponds with challenging sexual boundaries. In other words, the often presumed lesbianism of women who play sport, whether valid or not, has undergirded the character and likelihood of women's athletic and sport participation (Blinde & Taub, 1992; Griffin, 1998). The "antidote" is found in the common expectation for sportswomen to conform to compulsory heterosexuality (Bruce, 2013; Kolnes, 1995). This is supported by regular cultural cues for them to be portrayed as sexually desirable to men, as men's girlfriends or wives, or as heterosexual mothers, thereby offering reassurance of the heterosexuality and heteronormative femininity of sportswomen. It has become clear that stereotypes and fears about the "masculinization" of women in sport, noted in the previous section, were not simply about gender; rather these stereotypes tapped into cultural anxieties regarding the sexual orientation of sportswomen (Cahn, 1994; Lenskyj, 2013).

Approaches

Sport and the Gender Order

In *Gender and Power*, feminist scholar R. W. Connell (1987) departs from classical social theory to argue that institutions are not gender-neutral, although they may appear that way to social actors. Connell advocates for theorizing all social institutions as gendered. In other words, gender relations are present in all institutions; therefore all institutions are gendered. Moreover, social institutions and organizations are structured in ways that reflect, re-create, and naturalize gender hierarchies in society. Connell referred to this as the "gender order." Gender regimes (institutions) reproduce the gender order of a particular society within a particular historical moment. Connell set forth the concept of "structural inventories" as foundational to a methodology that could be used to study the state of play of gender regimes within particular institutions. While a full discussion of structural inventories is beyond the scope of this chapter, they provide a framework for understanding how the gender order is constituted in any given historical moment in a particular society.

Within the study of sport, Messner (2002, p. xx) has applied the concept of structural inventories and Connell's notion of core and peripheral institutions to theorize sport as a gendered institution that is not "fully consistent or coherent." In his book *Taking the Field*, Messner provides a conceptual framework for understanding sports in the United States at the turn of the 21st century. He makes a compelling case that many of the elements of sport, particularly those at the "center," continue to be patriarchal, with men (and the corporations that profit from sports, also run by men) in control. This "core" of sport is comprised of the "sport-media-commercial complex that organizes, promotes, and profits from big-time college and professional American gridiron football, basketball, baseball, hockey, and boxing" (p. xxi). Its combination of practices, values, principles, and organizing ethos then "trickles down" to school-based sports and youth sports. At the periphery are those sports not fully incorporated or included in the sports-media-commercial complex, including women's sports. Messner suggests that because women's sports are not fully integrated into the sports-media-commercial complex that it is able to engage in a "range (sometimes even subversive) of meanings, identities, and relationships around issues of gender and sexuality" (p. xxi). Messner continues, "Examining the gender regime of sport, then, becomes a complex process of exploring the different kinds of spaces within sport, how these spaces are variously occupied, given meaning, and contested" (p. xxi). By drawing on Connell's theories and focusing on such dynamics, Messner provides scholars a perspective from which to analyze how and in what ways the "center of sports" may be challenged by the increasing numbers of women playing sport post-Title IX and the increased presence of LGBTQ athletes in sports contexts.

In addition to structural theories of sport, Connell's theorization of multiple masculinities/femininities has been influential in feminist sport studies. While Connell's focus was specifically on masculinities, many feminist sports studies scholars have utilized the notion of hegemonic masculinity as a contextual framework to understand and analyze women's sports, including the experiences of women athletes as well as the media coverage of women's sports (in comparison to men's). Connell argues that the interplay of various masculinities (hegemonic, subordinated, marginalized, etc.) is an important part of understanding how patriarchal social order operates. Given that hegemonic masculinity is centered on men's global domination of women and because there is no form of femininity that is organized around women's domination of men, Connell argues that the concept of hegemonic femininity cannot exist. Instead Connell used the term "emphasized femininity" to refer to the ideologically dominant constructions of femininity (frail, weak, submissive, irrational, dependent, emotional, caregiving, etc.). Pyke and Johnson (2003) critiqued Connell for the failure to consider the ways in which the matrix of domination (Collins, 2009) operates to privilege certain forms of femininity over others. For example, based on their research regarding the ways in which Asian American women "do gender" in contemporary U.S. culture, Pyke and Johnson suggest that white, middle-class, heterosexual femininity should be seen as hegemonic in this regard. Krane (cf. 2001) has also applied the concept of hegemonic femininity to her analysis of gender, sport, and sexuality and has found utility in the concept for explaining the consequences of nonconformity to hegemonic femininity, which include sexist and heterosexist discrimination.

Emphasized Femininity and Stealth Feminism

Connell's conceptualization of emphasized femininity has been fruitfully applied to the study of women athletes, and hegemonic masculinity has informed the ways in which feminist sports studies scholars interpret and understand wider gendered dynamics that shape women's sports participation and its corresponding cultural meanings. Although emphasized femininity is antithetical to sport participation, given the discursive relationship between sport, athleticism, and masculinity, many sport studies scholars have found the concept to be relevant for understanding how female athletes/female-identified athletes negotiate the contradictory expectations of athleticism and femininity. Research in this area demonstrated that for adolescent girls (specifically white, economically privileged), who often experience peer pressure to conform to cultural expectations, the accomplishment of emphasized femininity on the sporting field is important in the construction of gendered identities (Adams, Schmitke, & Franklin, 2005; Malcolm, 2003). Moreover, expectations to conform to emphasized femininity are not solely experienced by adolescent athletes. Professional female athletes were found to embrace a "heterosexy" image in the public presentation of self. This image was celebrated by some feminist sports studies scholars (Heywood & Dworkin, 2003) and admonished by others (Griffin, 1998).

In their book *Built to Win: The Female Athlete as Cultural Icon*, Heywood and Dworkin (2003, p. 5) offer a dialogue between the critical approaches of academic feminist analyses of sport, which tend to focus on the "darker side" of girls' and women's sports participation (such as eating disorders, playing through pain, overtraining) and the "let's go" rhetoric of mass-media advocacy. As I've noted elsewhere, Heywood and Dworkin made "a sustained argument for both individual development and collective action, for the cultivation of traditionally masculine characteristics as well as traditionally feminine ones, for women's and men's participation in both the 'male sport' model and the more participatory 'female' version, for engagement with and critique of the media as well as recognition of its more affirmative potentialities" (Cooky, 2018, p. 144). They offer a third-wave feminist analysis of gender and sport that suggests women's sports participation can be understood as a form of "stealth feminism." Stealth feminism, according to Heywood and Dworkin, allows girls and women to advocate for equality in opportunity and condition without having to use the "f-word":

> [T]he newly iconic image of the female athlete is one of the few sites of resistance against this trend [essentialist notions of sex/gender difference]. The image is one of the few spaces where, unlike elsewhere in the media, female masculinity is validated rather than ignored or repressed with a too-easy-insistence on essential sexual difference. (p. 45)

Heywood and Dworkin suggest cultural images and texts of female athletes be read through the lens of third-wave feminism, which allows for the contradictions inherent in discursive and representational frameworks of female athletes without the need to resolve these contradictions or tensions.

Intersectionality

Sports studies scholars have drawn on theories of intersectionality to examine the experiences and representations of Black sportswomen (cf. Carter-Francique, 2020; Carter-Francique & Richardson, 2016; Cooky, Wachs, Messner, & Dworkin, 2010). Intersectionality (cf. Collins, 2009; Crenshaw, 1991) asserts that Black women simultaneously experience racism and sexism, thus social/legal theories must account for the interlocking nature of oppression. Collins (2009), in her book *Black Feminist Thought*, builds upon feminist standpoint theories to argue for Black women's epistemic privilege. Intersectional perspectives explain how forms of domination and oppression operate simultaneously in a web of crosscutting relationships, which Collins refers to as the matrix of domination. According to Collins:

> Intersectionality refers to particular forms of intersecting oppressions, for example, intersections of race and gender, or of sexuality and nation. Intersecting paradigms remind us that oppression cannot be reduced to one fundamental type, and that oppressions work together in producing injustice. In contrast, the matrix of domination refers to how these intersecting oppressions are actually organized. (p. 21)

The matrix of domination takes into account how various forms of oppression (e.g., race, class, gender, sexuality) interlock. As such, "both/and perspectives," rather than "either/or perspectives," of social locations are used to understand the ways in which individuals (and social institutions) are situated within interlocking forms of privilege/dominance and oppression/subordination (Collins, 2009; Cooky et. al., 2010).

Moreover, Collins (2009) has argued that dominant groups control social institutions in society, such as schools, the media, and popular culture, which produce "controlling images" that are rife with stereotypes about subordinated groups. These controlling images are not passively accepted by marginalized groups, as there are cultures of resistance within subordinated communities (Collins, 2009). Collins also notes there are segments of subordinated communities that internalize and perpetuate dominant ideologies.

Intersectional frameworks have been central in examining how heteronormative sporting femininities are racialized and classed. For example, the masculinization of female athletes historically has operated to "other" women of color (Cahn, 1994; Schultz, 2005). Moreover, racialized meanings shape the ways sportswomen are represented by sports media, particularly how whiteness and white privilege inform those representations (Douglas, 2005, 2012). This is considered in further depth in the sections below.

Postfeminisms and New Sporting Femininities

By the 2010s, feminist sports studies scholars had increasingly shifted analytical focus from the cultural meanings of female/female-identified athletes and their participation in sport toward the very meanings of feminism itself and the role that the increased visibility of feminism in popular culture and the media played in understandings of sports, femininities, and sexuality. The scholarship in this area draws on feminist conversations on postfeminism and the forces of neoliberalism (Gill, 2007; McRobbie, 2009; Rottenberg, 2014) to understand the intersections of femininity, sports, and "sports feminism" (Toffoletti, Francombe-Webb, & Thorpe, 2018). These approaches attempt to move beyond both academic and popular meanings of postfeminism, which suggest postfeminism as signaling the demise of feminism, and respond by focusing analytical attention on the ways in which women's sports experiences and cultural discourses are constituted in and in relation to broader feminist interventions (Toffoletti et al., 2018). In their introduction to *New Sporting Femininities: Embodied Politics in Postfeminist Times,* feminist sports studies scholars Kim Toffoletti, Jessica Francombe-Webb, and Holly Thorpe advocate for postfeminism as a "move forward feminist thinking about women's participation and representation in sport and physical activity" (p. 7). As they explain:

> Whereas once the discussion about women's relationships to sport, leisure and fitness was largely framed in terms of their exclusion, marginalization, trivialization, sexualization, and objectification under patriarchy, researchers of sport and physical cultures are now faced with new conceptual challenges. Namely, it is becoming increasingly difficult to speak about female athletes and women who participate in physical activity as objects of a patriarchal economy in a postfeminist and neoliberal context that characterizes women as active and knowing agents in the making of their own identities. (p. 7)

The analytical framework of "new sporting femininities" follows earlier feminist sports studies scholarship (e.g., Birrell & Cole, 1994; Hargreaves, 1994) in its concern with challenging essentialist notions of femininity and gender binaries in sports and the wider culture that limit the fluidity of gendered subjectivities and nonnormative sexualities and identities (Toffoletti et al., 2018). While not unique to postfeminist interrogations of sport, feminist sports studies scholars situate this concern within the postfeminist neoliberal context to focus on how narratives of women's equality and empowerment often overlook both intersectional identities and cultural, ethnic, and national contexts (Toffoletti et al., 2018). Moreover, according to Toffoletti et al., it is this postfeminist context that compels feminist sports studies scholars to develop new concepts, frameworks, and analytical lenses. New sporting femininities provide a framework for feminist sports studies scholars to interrogate the contradictory meanings through which feminism is simultaneously understood as both a relic of the past and a reemergent force.

Debates

As illustrated thus far, women's sport experiences in the United States have been shaped by conventional notions of femininity and dominant discourses of gender/sexuality. Given the historical linkages between sport, physicality, and masculinity, a focus of much of the feminist sports studies scholarship explores the paradoxes and contradictions sportswomen must navigate given this context. Moreover, the sociocultural expectations for heteronormative femininity are often at odds with sports, which are built upon ideological notions of natural gender difference. This presents gender-specific cultural pressures, challenges, and barriers for sportswomen, as well as for the institutions that are involved in the organization and promotion of women's sports. Cultural anxieties regarding sportswomen's sexuality, as well as the pervasiveness of homophobia in sports specifically and American culture more broadly, contribute to the gendered context of women's sports within which sportswomen and women's sports organizations must necessarily navigate. The remainder of this chapter will explore three ways heteronormative femininities shape women's sports. While the pathways considered are not intended to be exhaustive, the treatment provides a brief overview which helps to illustrate how historical dynamics and persistent gender ideologies produce particular experiences and meanings in women's sports.

Sex Testing in Sports

The policies and practices by which sports governing bodies determine eligibility for women's athletic events illustrate how Westernized notions of the sex/gender binary and of heteronormative femininity, along with histories of colonialism, nationalism, and scientific racism, shape the material and discursive contexts of women's sport (Hoad, 2010; Nyong'o, 2010). While sex testing policies have shifted since the emergence of the modern Olympic Games at the turn of the 20th century (cf. Pieper, 2014, 2016; Schultz, 2011), the justification and legitimation for sex testing are rooted in ideologies of essentialized difference and upheld through the sex/gender binary of international athletic competition (Cooky & Dworkin, 2013; Nyong'o, 2010). Bodies are the products of historically specific practices and thus are shaped by and through relations of power (Bordo, 1994; Fausto-Sterling, 2000) and are simultaneously produced by and constitutive of social meanings (Butler, 1993). These processes, as located within physical contexts such as sports, highlight the ways in which sport reaffirms the sex/gender binary as inherent, natural, and inevitable (Cole, 2000; Cooky, Dycus, & Dworkin, 2013; Kane, 1995; Travers, 2008).

One example of the oppressive impacts of sex testing occurred during the World Track and Field Championships in August 2009, held in Berlin. At the event, South African track and field athlete Caster Semenya won the 800-meter race. Media reports stated that the International Association of Athletics Federations (IAAF) requested the tests because of Semenya's "deep voice, muscular build and rapid improvement in times" (Associated Press, 2009, para. 7). The general secretary of the IAAF stated that Semenya underwent gender verification testing because of "ambiguity" regarding her sex. Feminist scholars argue this "ambiguity" was in part due to the imposition of Westernized notions of heteronormative femininity upon Semenya's bodily subjectivity (Cooky et al., 2013). Indeed, Human Rights Watch (2020) has observed the historically disproportionate targeting of women from the Global South for sex testing and gender verification protocols. Moreover, "Western scientific classifications of sex/gender are not 'objective' or 'value free' accounts of raced and gendered bodies but are themselves imbued with cultural meanings and informed by the socio-political contexts" (Cooky et al., 2013, p. 47). Thus, the linkage between athleticism and masculinity seems clearly very much dependent upon the co-constitution of gender and race (Magubane, 2014; Dworkin, Swarr, & Cooky, 2013).

Promotional Cultures of Women's Sports

As discussed in the first section, the historical linkage between sports/athleticism and masculinity has served to create a paradox for sportswomen and those involved in the promotion and marketing of women's sports. The presumed masculinizing aspects of sport participation, along with the corresponding cultural expectations for women to adhere to heteronormative femininity along with cultural anxieties over the "mannish lesbian" (Cahn, 1994), shape promotional cultures of women's sports. Throughout the 20th century, those involved in promoting women's sports, and in particular women's commercialized sports, have emphasized heteronormative femininity and focused on enhancing the (hetero)sexual appeal of women athletes. One of the first major professional sports leagues for women in the United States was the All-American Girls Baseball League (AAGBL). Organized by Major League Baseball owner Phillip K. Wrigley as a way to bridge the gap in professional sports as a result of the influx of men enlisting to serve in World War II, women baseball players attended mandatory etiquette classes and charm schools and were expected to wear makeup, and emphasis was placed on players maintaining an "attractive" appearance (Gregg & Taylor, 2019). This strategy of emphasizing women athletes' attractiveness and adherence to heteronormative femininity would continue throughout the late 20th and into the 21st century in the United States in both the Women's National Basketball Association ([WNBA]; Banet-Weiser, 1999; McDonald, 2012) and women's professional soccer leagues (Allison, 2018).

During the WNBA's inaugural season in 1997, the league's marquee players were selected in part based on their physical attractiveness, heterosexual relationships, and adherence to heteronormative femininity (Banet-Weiser, 1999; McDonald, 2000). Lisa Leslie of the Los Angeles Sparks, who would become a WNBA champion and MVP (besides earning other accolades), was one of the women selected as a marquee player for the league. This was in part due to her successful modeling career and, later, her role as a mother. During the first few years of the league, the WNBA's marketing strategy revolved around highlighting the heterosexual, emphasized femininity of WNBA players, as models, mothers, or the girl-next-door (Banet-Weiser, 1999). Nearly a decade after the league's formation, it would continue this marketing strategy while ignoring the league's significant lesbian fan base. For example, the "Have You Seen Her" campaign from the 2006–2007 season featured players in both hetero-sexy and stereotypically glamourous ways (McDonald, 2012). Similar to the mandatory etiquette classes and emphasis on the AAGBL players maintaining an attractive appearance, the WNBA offered seminars for players like the one that provided advice on makeup application (McDonald, 2012). In this way, "the WNBA marketing accounts thus help reaffirm heteronormativity via institutionalized practices that 'legitimize and privilege heterosexuality and heterosexual relationships as fundamental and natural within society'" (Cohen 1997, as cited in McDonald, 2012, p. 212). Although the WNBA as a league emphasizes heteronormative femininity, heterosexual families, and conventional (i.e., white) beauty norms in its marketing and promotional campaigns, individual teams have actively acknowledged and addressed the significant segment of the fanbase that identifies as lesbian (McDonald, 2012). McDonald argues that such attempts facilitate lesbian visibility in a league that reproduces and reaffirms heteronormativity while also doing so in ways that situate "lesbian concerns as commensurable with the market and domesticity" (2012, p. 220).

Feminist sports sociologist Rachel Allison's (2018) rich ethnographic research on the professional women's soccer league in the United States found similar dynamics at play in the marketing and promotion of women's professional soccer. Allison found that both corporate sponsors and the league itself had vacillated between highlighting either the athleticism and talent or the (hetero)sexual appeal of the players. While not overtly sexual in its promotional strategies, some teams in the league believed emphasizing the "glamour" of the players and their (heteronormative) feminine beauty would be a way to enhance the public image of women's soccer. Allison describes one team whose leadership believed "highlighting feminine beauty was an acceptable way to 'bring a little something' to the public image of women's soccer" (p. 119). Allison suggests the emphasis on "glamour" served to distance the league from lesbian sexuality while simultaneously reinforcing its youthfulness, whiteness, and heterosexuality in ways understood to be compatible with (and not opposed to) appreciation for players' on-field talents.

Media Representations of Sportswomen

As discussed earlier, women's participation in sport, and in particular team sport, is frequently accompanied by a questioning of their (hetero)sexuality (Cahn, 1994; Griffin, 1998). Sportswomen in masculine-identified contact sports such as basketball confront cultural assumptions regarding their lack of femininity, and thus their lack of heterosexuality (Banet-Weiser, 1999). These cultural assumptions shape media representations of sportswomen and women's sports. Moreover, negotiating the contradictions of women's sport participation differs for Black female athletes, who are both hypersexualized and are perceived to not confirm with culturally dominant notions of white femininity (for discussion, see Cooky & Rauscher, 2016).

In contrast with the cultural imagery of white female athletes, which reproduces the "good white girl construct" (cf. McDonald, 2009), or representations of white female athletes as men's wives, as mothers, and as citizens (Banet-Weiser, 1999; McDonald, 2000, 2009), the cultural imagery of female athletes of color often reproduces "controlling images" (Collins, 2009; Douglas, 2012). Feminist sports studies scholars have noted that a Black sportswoman is at risk of becoming a "fallen hero" at the slightest indiscretion, such as wearing a provocative tennis outfit or not having "fixed" hair (Cooky & Rauscher, 2016). This body of research has demonstrated how sport media portrays Black female athletes as "young ladies of class" (Cooky et al., 2010, p. 153), "racially neutralized American goddess[es]" (Meân, 2013, p. 79), aesthetically beautiful and feminine (Meân, 2013), and sexually attractive to men (Collins,

2005). Sports media also have exhibited a tendency to portray Black female athletes as "bad girls" (McDonald & Cooky, 2013, p. 199), "nappy headed ho's" (Cooky et al., 2010; p. 140), "sexually grotesque" (McKay & Johnson, 2008, p. 500), animalistic (Schultz, 2005), and "too muscular" (Cooky et al., 2013). Given the ways in which heteronormative femininities are racialized, Black sportswomen transgress white, Westernized boundaries of traditional femininity and "decency" (Schultz, 2005, p. 342). Thus, *how* female athletes are represented in media and the differences in the ways in which cultural representations are racialized can be particularly problematic. Here, a prevalent tendency is that representations of white female athletes serve to uphold heteronormativity and white privilege, while media representations of Black female athletes serve to reproduce racist discourses about both Black women athletes and Black women in general (Cooky & Rauscher, 2016).

CONCLUSION

This chapter illustrates how women's sport experiences, particularly those in the United States, have been shaped by heteronormative femininities. Given the historical linkages between sport, physicality, and masculinity, much of the feminist sports studies scholarship has explored the paradoxes and contradictions faced by sportswomen. Moreover, the sociocultural expectations for heteronormative femininity are often at odds with sports cultures and contexts, which are built upon dominant ideological notions of natural gender difference. This presents gender-specific cultural pressures, challenges, and barriers for sportswomen, as well as for the institutions that are involved in the organization and promotion of women's sports. Cultural anxieties regarding sportswomen's sexuality and the continued pervasiveness of homophobia in sports specifically and American culture more broadly, as well as systemic forms of racism, contribute to the gendered context of women's sports by which sportswomen and women's sports organizations navigate. Key issues at play here include how heteronormative femininity produces and is produced by sex testing in sports, the promotional cultures that contextualize the meanings and value of women's sports, and the tendencies evident in media coverage of women's sports. Each of these three areas illustrates the tensions that sport as a masculine-identified, male-dominated institution creates for sporting femininities. These tensions are indicative of how historical dynamics and persisting gender ideologies produce particular experiences and meanings in women's sports not only in the United States but in much of the Global North.

REFERENCES

Adams, N., Schmitke, A., & Franklin, A. (2005). Tomboys, dykes and girly girls: Interrogating the subjectivities of adolescent female athletes. *Women's Studies Quarterly, 33*(1–2), 17–34.

Allison, R. (2018). Kicking center: Gender and the selling of women's professional soccer. New Brunswick, NJ: Rutgers University Press.

Associated Press. (2009, September 16). IAAF: Semenya decision in November. *ESPN.* http://sports.espn.go.com/olu/trackandfield/news/story?id=4464405#correx.

Banet-Weiser, S. (1999). Hoop dreams: Professional basketball and the politics of race and gender. *Journal of Sport and Social Issues, 23*, 403–420.

Banet-Weiser, S. (2018). *Empowered: Popular feminism and popular misogyny.* Durham, NC: Duke University Press.

Blinde, E. M., & Taub, D. E. (1992). Homophobia and women's sports: The disempowerment of athletes. *Sociological Focus, 25*, 151–166.

Birrell, S., & Cole, C. (1994). *Women, sport and culture.* Champaign, IL: Human Kinetics.

Bordo, S. (1994). *Unbearable weight: Feminism, Western culture and the body.* Berkeley: University of California Press.

Bruce, T. (2013). Reflections on communication and sport: On women and femininities. *Communication & Sport, 1*(1–2), 125–137.

Bruce, T. (2016). New rules for new times: Sportswomen and media representation in the third wave. *Sex Roles, 74*, 361–376.

Bryson, L. (1994). Sport and the maintenance of masculine hegemony. In S. Birrell & C. L. .Cole (Eds.) *Women, Sport, and Culture,* (pp. 40–64). Champaign, IL: Human Kinetics.

Butler, J. (1993). *Bodies that matter: On the discursive limits of sex.* New York: Routledge.

Cahn, S. (1994). *Coming on strong: Gender and sexuality in twentieth century women's sport.* New York: Free Press.

Carter-Francique, A. R. (2020). Intersectionality and the influence of stereotypes for Black women in college sport. In V. L. Farmer & E. S. W. Farmer (Eds.), *Critical race theory in the academy* (pp. 453–480). Charlottee: Information Age Publishing.

Carter-Francique, A. R., & Richardson, F. M. (2016). Controlling media, controlling access: The role of sport media on Black women's sport participation. *Race, Class, and Gender, 23*(1), 7–33.

Cole, C. L. (2000). One chromosome too many? In K. Schaffer & S. Smith (Eds.), *The Olympics at the millennium: Power, politics and the games* (pp. 128–146). New Brunswick, NJ: Rutgers University Press.

Collins, P. H. (2005). *Black sexual politics: African Americans, gender and the new racism.* New York: Routledge.

Collins, P. H. (2009). *Black feminist thought: Knowledge, consciousness, and the politics of empowerment.* New York: Routledge.

Connell, R. W. (1987). *Gender and power.* Stanford, CA: Stanford University Press.

Cooky, C. (2009). "Girls just aren't interested": The social construction of interest in girls' sport. *Sociological Perspectives, 52*, 259–284.

Cooky, C. (2017). Women, sports, and activism. In H. McCammon, V. Taylor, J. Reger, & R. Einwohner (Eds.), *The Oxford handbook of US women's social movement activism* (pp. 602–622). New York: Oxford University Press.

Cooky, C. (2018). Gender, sport, and media between the mid-1980s and early 2000s: Developments, trajectories and transformations. In L. Mansfield, J. Caudwell, B. Wheaton, and B. Watson (Eds.), The Palgrave handbook of feminism and sport, leisure, and physical education (pp. 133–148). London: Palgrave Handbooks.

Cooky, C., & Dworkin, S. L. (2013). Policing the boundaries of sex: A critical examination of gender verification and the Caster Semenya controversy. *Journal of Sex Research, 50*, 103–111.

Cooky, C., Dycus, R., & Dworkin, S. L. (2013). "What makes a woman a woman?" vs. "our first lady of sport": A comparative analysis of Caster Semenya in U.S. and South African news media. *Journal of Sport and Social Issues, 37*, 31–56.

Cooky, C., & LaVoi, N. M. (2012). The unfinished revolution in women's sport. *Contexts: Understanding People in Their Social Worlds, 11*, 42–46.

Cooky, C. & Messner, M. A. (2018). No Slam Dunk: Gender, Sport, and the Unevenness of Social Change. New Brunswick, NJ: Rutgers University Press.

Cooky, C., & Rauscher, L. (2016). Girls and the racialization of female bodies in sports contexts. In M. A. Messner & M. Musto (Eds.), *Child's play: Sport in kids' worlds* (pp. 61–81). New Brunswick, NJ: Rutgers University Press.

Cooky, C., Wachs, F. L., Messner, M. A., & Dworkin, S. L. (2010). It's not about the game: Don Imus, race, class, gender and sexuality in contemporary media. *Sociology of Sport Journal, 27*, 139–159.

Crenshaw, K. (1991). Mapping the margins: Intersectionality, identity politics, and violence against women of color. Stanford Law Review, 6, 1241–1299.

Douglas, D. D. (2005). Venus, Serena and the Women's Tennis Association: When and where race enters. *Sociology of Sport Journal, 22*, 256–282.

Douglas, D. D. (2012). Venus, Serena, and the inconspicuous consumption of Blackness: A commentary on surveillance, race talk, and new racism(s). *Journal of Black Studies, 43*, 127–145.

Dworkin, S. L., Swarr, A. L., & Cooky, C. (2013). (In)Justice in sport: The treatment of South African track star Caster Semenya. *Feminist Studies, 39*(1), 40–69.

Fausto-Sterling, A. (2000). *Sexing the body: Gender politics and the construction of sexuality.* New York: Basic Books.

Gill, R. (2007). *Gender and the media.* Cambridge, U.K.: Polity Press.

Gilreath, E. L., Zupin, D., & Judge, L. W. (2017). From field days to Olympic gold: How Black women revitalized track and field in the United States. *The Physical Educator, 74*, 359–376.

Gregg, E. A., & Taylor, E. (2019). History and evolution of women's sports. In N. Lough & A. N. Guerin (Eds.), *The Routledge handbook of the business of women's sport* (pp. 11–22). New York: Routledge.

Griffin, P. (1998). *Strong women, deep closets: Lesbians and homophobia in sport.* Champaign, IL: Human Kinetics Publishers.

Hargreaves, J. (1994). *Sporting females: Critical issues in the history and sociology of women's sports.* London: Routledge.

Heywood, L., & Dworkin, S. L. (2003). *Built to win: The female athlete as cultural icon.* Minneapolis: University of Minnesota Press.

Himes Gissendander, C. (1994). African-American women and competitive sport, 1920–1960. In S. Birrell & C. L. Cole (Eds.), *Women, sport and culture* (pp. 81–92). Champaign, IL: Human Kinetics.

Hoad, N. (2010). "Run, Caster Semenya, run!" Nativism and the translations of gender variance. *Safundi: The Journal of South African and American Studies, 11*, 398–405.

Human Rights Watch. (2020, December 4). "They're chasing us away from sport": Human rights violations in sex testing of elite women athletes. https://www.hrw.org/report/2020/12/04/theyre-chasing-us-away-sport/human-rights-violations-sex-testing-elite-women.

Kane, M. J. (1995). Resistance/transformation of the oppositional binary: Exposing sport as a continuum. *Journal of Sport and Social Issues, 19*, 191–218.

Kinney, E. (2020, December 8). Sarah Fuller's impact will outlast online hate. Los Angeles Loyolan. https://www.laloyolan.com/sports/sarah-fullers-impact-will-outlast-the-online-hate/article_9ffa93b9-9c91-53c2-8ea3-e88befc982c0.html

Kolnes, L. J. (1995). Heterosexuality as an organizing principle in women's sport. *International Review for the Sociology of Sport, 30*, 61–77.

Krane, V. (2001). We can be athletic and feminine, but do we want to? Challenging hegemonic femininity in women's sport. *Quest, 53*, 115–133.

Lenskyj, H. J. (2013). Reflections on communication and sport: On heteronormativity and gender identities. *Communication & Sport, 1*(1–2), 138–150.

Luther, J. (2016). *Unsportsmanlike conduct: College football and the politics of rape.* New York: Edge of Sports/Akashic Books.

Magubane, Z. (2014). Spectacles and scholarship: Caster Semenya, intersex studies, and the problem of race in feminist theory. *Signs: Journal of Women and Culture in Society, 39*(3), 761–785.

Malcolm, N. L. (2003). Constructing female athleticism: A study of girls' recreational softball. *American Behavioral Scientist, 46*(10), 1387–1404.

McDonald, M. G. (2000). The marketing of the Women's National Basketball Association and the making of postfeminism. *International Review for the Sociology of Sport, 35*, 35–47.

McDonald, M. G. (2009). Dialogues on whiteness, leisure and (anti)racism. *Journal of Leisure Research, 41*, 5–21.

McDonald, M. G. (2012). Out-of-bounds plays: The Women's National Basketball Association and the neoliberal imaginings of sexuality. In D. L. Andrews & M. L. Silk (Eds.), Sport and neoliberalism: Politics, consumption, and culture (pp. 211-224). Philadelphia, PA: Temple University Press.

McDonald, M. G., & Cooky, C. (2013). Interrogating discourses about the WNBA" "bad girls": Intersectionality and the politics of representation. In L. A. Wenner (Ed.), Fallen sports heroes, media, and celebrity culture (pp. 193–207). New York: Peter Lang.

McKay, J., & Johnson, H. (2008). Pornographic eroticism and sexual grotesquerie in representations of African-American sportswomen. *Social Identities, 14*, 491–504.

McRobbie, A. (2009). *The aftermath of feminism: Gender, culture, and social change.* London: Sage Publishing.

Meân, L. J. (2013). On track, off track, on Oprah: The framing of Marion Jones as golden girl and American fraud. In L. Wenner (Ed.), *Fallen sports heroes, media, and celebrity culture* (pp. 77–91). New York: Peter Lang.

Messner, M. A. (1988). Sports and male domination: The female athlete as contested ideological terrain. *Sociology of Sport Journal, 5*(2), 197–211.

Messner, M. A. (1992). *Power at play: Sports and the problem of masculinity.* Boston: Beacon Press.

Messner, M. A. (2002). *Taking the field: Women, men and sports.* Minneapolis: University of Minnesota Press.

Messner, M. A. (2010). *Out of play: Critical essays on gender and sport.* Albany, NY: SUNY Press.

Nyong'o, T. (2010). The unforgivable transgression of being Caster Semenya. *Women & Performance: A Journal of Feminist Theory, 20*, 95–100.

Pieper, L. P. (2014). Sex testing and the maintenance of Western femininity in international sport. *International Journal of the History of Sport, 31*(13), 1557–1576.

Pieper, L. P. (2016). *Sex testing: Gender policing in women's sports.* Champaign: University of Illinois Press.

Pyke, K. D., & Johnson, D. L. (2003). Asian American women and racialized femininities. *Gender & Society, 17*(1), 33–53.

Reilly, R. (2005, January 20). Another victim at Colorado. *Sports Illustrated.* https://www.si.com/more-sports/2005/01/20/hnida.

Rottenberg, C. (2014). The rise of neoliberal feminism. *Cultural Studies, 28*(3), 418–437.

Schultz, J. (2005). Reading the catsuit: Serena Williams and the production of Blackness at the 2002 U. S. Open. *Journal of Sport and Social Issues, 29,* 338–357.

Schultz, J. (2011). Caster Semenya and the question of "too": Sex testing in elite women's sport and the issue of advantage. *Quest, 63,* 228–243.

Smith Rosenberg, C. (1985). *Disorderly conduct: Visions of gender in Victorian America.* New York: Oxford University Press.

Toffoletti, K., Francombe-Webb, J., & Thorpe, H. (Eds.). (2018). *New sporting femininities: Embodied politics in postfeminist times.* London: Palgrave Macmillan.

Travers, A. (2008). The sport nexus and gender injustice. *Studies in Social Justice, 2,* 79–101.

CHAPTER 48

SPORT, TRANSGENDER ATHLETES, AND NONBINARY EXPERIENCE

TRAVERS

SINCE Renée Richards's successful quest to compete in events sponsored by the Women's Tennis Association in 1977 (Birrell & Cole, 1990; Pieper, 2017), transgender people and people who either identify outside the binary sex system or who are biomedically difficult to classify according to this system have emerged as polemic figures in sport policy debates, scholarly research, and media discourse.

Questions around participation center on widely accepted beliefs that there are only two sexes and that boys and men, in general, have an athletic advantage over girls and women. These taken-for-granted beliefs inform a particular moral panic around the participation of both transgender women and hyperandrogenous (HG) women—women whose natural levels of testosterone are higher than the threshold for female eligibility identified by the International Amateur Athletics Federation (IAAF) and the International Olympic Committee (IOC). Transgender, nonbinary, and HG women athletes create a crisis for modern sport. By "transgender" or "trans," I refer to people who do not identify with the binary sex category assigned to them at birth, whether they identify as male or female or neither. "Nonbinary" refers to people who identify outside the sex/gender binary and includes people who may nor may not also identify as trans.

To date, the IAAF and IOC—and the many international and national amateur and professional sport associations and organizations that look to these organizations to set sport policy—have struggled to address this crisis by developing a succession of female eligibility policies. The current IAAF and IOC policy rests on a testosterone threshold as a boundary biomedical marker for women, resulting in the inextricable linkage of issues relating to transgender participation, the participation of HG women, and World Anti-Doping Agency (WADA) regulations.

Central debates about "fairness" (Cunningham & Pickett, 2018; Lucas-Carr & Krane, 2012) in women's sport concern the "physiological equivalency" (Gleaves & Lehrbach, 2016) of transgender and HG women with cisgender women. Trans women often experience extreme hostility from cisgender women competitors in elite sport on this basis (Fischer & McClearen, 2019). Policies that enable the participation of transgender men, in contrast, are less controversial because of the presumed deficiencies of athletes who are assigned female at birth. Jones, Arcelus, Bouman, and Haycraft (2017) note, however, that trans men are as likely as trans women to be excluded from sport participation, even as they are presumed to be at a disadvantage against cisgender men. Very little explicit research has been conducted with nonbinary athletes, but the sex-segregated and/or sex-differentiated structure of most sport and physical recreation spaces and activities means that, for the most part, nonbinary people have literally no place to play (Travers, 2016, 2018).

ISSUES

Barriers to Sport Participation

According to a report by the Williams Institute (Flores, Herman, Gates, & Brown, 2016), 0.42% of the population in the United States identifies as transgender. Hellen (2009) observes that the majority of transgender children are invisible, and it is reasonable to assume that many remain so throughout their lives. Although a number of trans athletes competing in elite amateur and professional sport have become known to sporting organizations and the general public, we have to assume that this is just the tip of the iceberg and that people of all ages who would now be understood as trans and/or nonbinary have had complicated relationships and experiences throughout the era of modern sport.

Two U.S. transgender athletes, Mack Beggs and Molly Cameron, had profoundly complicated experiences with sport participation because of rules governing their sport at the time (Harper, 2019). As a high school wrestler and a trans boy, Beggs won the Texas Girls State Wrestling Championship in 2017 and 2018. Even though he was taking testosterone—a hormone that is central to commonsense understandings of male athletic advantage and female eligibility policies—Beggs was denied the opportunity to wrestle in the boys' competition because state requirements stipulated assigned sex at birth. Unfortunately, but unsurprisingly, he experienced toxic hostility and harassment from the parents of his competitors.

Cameron competed in women's cyclocross while on hormone therapy in 2004. Her success prompted complaints from her competitors and resulted in her being banned from further women's competitions and directed to race against men, in part because she was not in compliance with the surgical requirement in place. Cameron quit for several years and stopped taking hormones at some point. She returned to the sport in 2015 with the intention of competing in the men's division but was initially told she was ineligible because of the female sex marker on her racing and driver's licenses. She was ultimately permitted to enter the men's race, but her difficulties participating in either category speak to the struggles trans and nonbinary people have with sport participation. In her own words, "Sports aren't really fair, you know, but we have a men's category and a women's category, and somehow you have to shoehorn trans and intersex people into those two categories" (quoted in Harper, 2019, p. 23).

Transgender people have competed in a wide range of elite sport competitions. While Caitlyn Jenner won a gold medal in the men's decathlon in 1976, however, only one no posttransition transgender athlete, Laurel Hubbard, weightlifting in the 2020 Olympic games, has competed in the Olympic Games to date. Comparatively little is known about nonbinary athletes in elite amateur or professional sport. Layshia Clarendon of the WNBA is the first athlete in a major professional sport to publicly announce their nonbinary identity (Feinberg, 2021). They did so in January 2021, via a news story about having undergone "top" surgery (removal of breast tissue and masculine chest reconstruction). In a far cry from its early efforts to distance itself from female masculinity and lesbianism (McDonald, 2008), WNBA Commissioner Cathy Engelbert issued a statement in support of Clarendon and nonbinary people in general via her Twitter account.

While considerable attention has been paid to trans athletes in elite amateur and professional sport (see, for example, Fischer & McClearen, 2019), an increasing body of literature documents issues relating to the experiences of trans and nonbinary athletes in a range of contexts, from recreational to highly competitive. Much of this literature identifies participation in sport as a fundamental human right and therefore a requirement of social justice (Jones et al., 2017), mental and physical health (Klein, Krane, & Paule-Koba, 2018; Lucas-Carr & Krane, 2012), and social inclusion (Cohen & Semerjian, 2008; Cunningham, Buzuvis, & Mosier, 2018; Elling-Machartzki, 2017; Tagg, 2012).

Research on the experiences of trans and nonbinary people in sport identifies a number of barriers to full participation, focusing chiefly on the sex-segregated/sex-differentiated character of sport, with special attention to difficulties in accessing and using appropriate changing rooms (Herrick & Duncan, 2020; Lewis & Johnson, 2011; Muchicko, Lepp, & Barkley, 2014), the requirement for accurate identity documents, experiences of discrimination and alienation, the ignorance of organizations and leaders about the existence and needs of trans people, as well as gender dysphoria and self-exclusion (Pérez-Samaniego, Fuentes-Miguel, Pereira-García, López-Cañada, & Devís-Devís, 2019).

The difficulty experienced by nonbinary participants or trans men and women who do not "pass," that is, who are not gender-conforming, is cited as a significant limitation to policies that seek to integrate trans participants into existing sex-based frameworks. In a systematic review of eight research studies published between 2005 and 2015 and 31 international and national policies relating to transgender participation, Jones et al. (2017) found that trans people have mostly negative experiences in competitive sport and that policies related to transgender participation are, on the whole, not evidence based. They go on to specify that trans people's negative experiences, in local, community-based as well as more elite contexts, are shaped by discriminatory policies based on questionable science, sex-segregated and unwelcoming changing facilities, and the failure of organizations and institutions to support trans participants. A metasynthesis of 12 qualitative studies relating to the experiences of trans people in physical activity and sport (Pérez-Samaniego et al., 2019) produced similar findings. While research to date overwhelmingly documents barriers to and negative experiences with sport participation, there is evidence that sport can be a source of enjoyment, mental and/or physical health benefits, and even empowerment for trans people (Fletcher, 2020; Herrick, Rocchi, & Couture, 2020; Travers & Deri, 2011).

Pérez-Samaniego et al. (2019) reference Travers's (2006) distinction between "gender-conforming" and "gender-transforming" transgender participants to note that it is easier, although still often difficult, for gender-conforming trans people with binary identities to participate in sport, in comparison to those with nonbinary identities or whose gender is not "intelligible" (Butler, 1993) to others. Caudwell (2014) astutely describes this distinction among trans people as binary and simplistic. Nonetheless, it provides an incisive measure when used to assess policies and social practice rather than participants.

Gender-conforming transgender participation policies seek to accommodate trans people within existing sporting institutions and cultures, while gender-transforming policies require sporting institutions and cultures to change. The former, unsurprisingly, is much easier to achieve than the latter because modern sport is, at its foundations, a white supremacist, hetero-patriarchal, and wealth-generating constellation of institutions, spaces, and social practices.

Sport, Gender, and Power

Today's sporting environments are an outgrowth of the precedents established as modern sport emerged in Europe and its colonies in the late 19th and early 20th centuries as a hetero-patriarchal "civilizing" project (Carter, 2008) that represented a backlash against the increasing power of middle- and upper-class white women (Bullough & Bullough, 1993). Sport was designed to emphasize sex difference, to socialize boys and men into orthodox heteromasculinity (Hargreaves, 2013; Pronger, 1990), and to further the goal of white middle- and upper-class morality and leadership within colonial projects (Carrington & Mcdonald, 2009; Collins, 2013; Hill Collins, 2004). A model of sport as a "comparative test" (Gleaves & Lehrbach, 2016, p. 312) with formal rules and quantifiable results amenable to betting and newspaper coverage reflected the related emergence of sport with capitalism (Collins, 2013). As Gleaves and Lehrbach (2016, p. 317) emphasize, "The vision of sport underlying it is a rather recent one located in a specific time (post–Industrial Revolution) and culture (Western) and rooted in patriarchal, masculine values of non-relation, aggression, and oppositional achievement." Sports play a central role in gendering citizenship as male (and white and heterosexual) (Burstyn, 1999; Travers, 2008), and trans and nonbinary athletes threaten this social, economic, and political system with disarray, whether as individuals they are interested in doing so or not.

Sport is organized around a sex binary that is ideological rather than naturally occurring (Dreger, 1998; Fausto-Sterling, 2000; Fine, 2017), an ideology central to and integrated within a Eurocentric, white supremacist, colonial, and hetero-patriarchal assemblage of power (Collins, 2013). Unpacking this assemblage (Higginbotham, 1992; Puar, 2007; Weheliye, 2014; Wynter, 2003) is crucial for understanding the experiences of trans athletes and policy debates about the terms of inclusion. Western colonialism encoded binary sex differentiation and male superiority as marks of "civilization," whereas other gender systems and gender equality were regarded as primitive (Nyong'o, 2010).

Girls and women were purposefully excluded from modern sport from the outset (Hargreaves, 1994), but activism by sportswomen forced a degree of inclusion. While sport participation has widened radically, sport continues to play a central role in reinforcing the two-sex system. The role of sport in naturalizing hierarchies of bodies and producing gendered and racialized norms cannot be overstated (Douglas, 2003, 2012; Pape, 2017).

Sex Segregation

The sex segregation of sport and sex differentiation of activities within the same sport (for example, gymnastics and figure skating) or different rules (for example, in basketball, golf, and volleyball) play an important role in normalizing gender inequality by packaging, showcasing, and emphasizing differences between male and female bodies to celebrate masculine superiority and justify extensive opportunity structures and disproportionate patterns of remuneration for male athletes (Burstyn, 1999; Travers, 2013). In spite of evidence of overlapping performances (cf. Kane, 1995; McDonagh & Pappano, 2008; Ring, 2009), mainstream sporting policies continue to lean heavily on a trope of white, female frailty and male athletic superiority (Dowling, 2000). Understood in this light, gendered networks for resource distribution associated with mainstream sport depend on fierce patrol of borders. This speaks to the many obstacles to participation experienced by trans and nonbinary athletes.

Unfair Advantage

Concerns about transgender participation in sport tend to crystallize around assumptions that transgender women have an "unfair advantage" over cisgender women as a result of past exposure to "male" levels of testosterone (Cavanagh & Sykes, 2006; McArdle, 2008). The human right of transgender people to participate in all aspects of society, although far from universally affirmed and experienced, is often seen by sports organizations and the wider public to be justifiably limited by presumptions of male athletic advantage retained by trans women. Debates about inclusion typically center on the extent to which hormone therapy for trans women effectively achieves "physiological equivalency" (Gleaves & Lehrbach, 2016) with cisgender women.

Sex Testing

Assumptions about binary sex difference and female inferiority that animate female eligibility policies have been put under the microscope by human rights and science-based challenges to each succeeding practice of sex-verification testing for women athletes (Kirby & Huebner, 2002; Pieper, 2016; Wells, 2020), with the overwhelming consensus that sex is *not* binary and sex testing is fundamentally flawed. The practice of mandatory sex testing for *all* women athletes was abandoned by the IAAF in 1992 and the IOC in 2000; however, selective testing of "suspicious" women athletes continues. Instead of the genetic technique of sex testing abandoned in 1999, the "new paradigm of sex testing" (Vilain, Betancurt, Bueno-Guerra, & Martinez-Patiño, 2017) reflected in IAAF and IOC female eligibility policies is based on measuring functional testosterone levels and impacts trans and HG women as well as women who contravene WADA regulations by taking testosterone to improve athletic performance.

Policy Evolution

2004 Stockholm Consensus

In 2004, some transgender athletes gained the right to inclusion at the highest levels of amateur sport. The Stockholm Consensus required trans athletes to undergo genital reassignment surgery and two years of testosterone suppression treatment and provide national identity documents proving legal recognition of their affirmed sex. In a testament to the leadership of the IOC in making sport policy, many international and national sporting bodies developed identical policies. The Stockholm Consensus was widely criticized by critical feminist sport scholars (Griffin & Carroll, 2010; Sykes, 2006) on the grounds that genitals are irrelevant to athletic performance, surgery is expensive and invasive, and legal documents are unequally available, depending on nationality.

2011 IAAF and 2012 IOC Consensus Statement on Hyperandrogenism

The IAAF's selective practice of sex testing was most dramatically evident in the case of South African runner Castor Semenya, whose "masculine" appearance became a subject of concern among competitors and sporting officials when she won the 800-meter race at the 2009 World Championships of Athletics in Berlin (Nyong'o, 2010). The 2011 Consensus Statement on Hyperandrogenism was a response to Semenya as well as Indian runner Santhi Soundarajan, whose silver medal at the 2006 Asian Games was stripped after IAAF officials requested a sex test (Sanchez, Martinez-Patino, & Vilain, 2013). The policy requires HG women to undergo testosterone suppression treatment to compete. While on testosterone suppression, Semenya won a silver medal in the 800-meter event at the 2012 Olympics (Harper, 2019; Wells, 2020). Semenya, Soundarajan, and other HG women are diagnosed as having "differences of sexual development (DSD)" (American Psychiatric Association, 2013), a term that has replaced the former diagnosis of persons with "intersex" conditions.

As a result of Dutee Chand's 2015 challenge of the provisions of the 2011 Consensus Statement on Hyperandrogenism, the Court of Arbitration for Sport (CAS) suspended it for two years (Harper, 2019). The CAS ruling stipulated that new evidence supporting the link between testosterone and athletic performance had to be provided by the IAAF within that time frame if Chand and other HG women are to be barred from competing. During this interval, Semenya and other affected athletes were able to compete without medical intervention. Subsequently, at the 2016 Olympics, Semenya won a gold medal in her signature event, the 800 meter. The silver and bronze medals also went to Black women from African countries, who became subject to resentful claims about their "unfair advantage" from white competitors, claims that mainstream media chose to amplify (Wente, 2019). Prejudice and hostility from other competitors and sport media continue to surround Semenya and other (often racialized) female athletes deemed too muscular to be "normal" women. A number of scholars draw attention to the extent to which selective sex testing is disproportionately deployed against Black and brown women from the Global South (Dworkin, Swarr, & Cooky, 2013; Fischer & McClearen, 2019; Lenskyj, 2018; Magubane, 2014; Nyong'o, 2010; Pape, 2017; Pieper, 2016).

2015 IOC Consensus Meeting on Sex Reassignment and Hyperandrogenism

Challenges to the Stockholm Consensus also played a role in producing changes to female eligibility policies. The 2015 Consensus Statement on Sex Reassignment and Hyperandrogenism formally linked transgender women with HG women via a uniform female eligibility policy. Two challenges to the Stockholm Consensus were pivotal in producing a change in transgender participation policy. These were the 2011 National

Collegiate Athletics Association (NCAA) policy on transgender participation and the challenge by Chris Mosier, a duathlete and triathlete from the USA who was initially barred from competing in the 2016 World Duathlon championships, to the surgical requirement of the Stockholm Consensus (Harper, 2019).[1]

In their influential 2010 report, "On the Team: Equal Opportunity for Transgender Student Athletes," Griffin and Carroll recommended against genital surgery as a participation requirement for transgender athletes. They instead recommended that trans women athletes be allowed to compete in their affirmed gender category if they had taken hormone blockers to forgo natal "male" puberty or after one year of hormone therapy if they had not. This protocol for participation in college-level athletics was adopted by the NCAA in 2011.

The 2015 Consensus Statement stipulated that trans women are to follow a hormone regime that negates the supposed performance-enhancing effects of testosterone, with no corresponding requirements for trans men to participate in men's sports. These regulations also required all participants in women's events to have functional testosterone levels below 10 nmols/L. The 2015 Consensus—and its 2018 update, which I elaborate below—formally link trans and HG sportswomen. The accepted practice of testing the urine of all competitors at elite amateur events immediately following competition in order to comply with WADA regulations is now linked with the policing of female eligibility (Foddy & Savulescu, 2011; Henne, 2015). The new Consensus took effect at the 2016 Summer Olympics.

2015 Suspension of Hyperandrogenism Rules/2018 Testosterone Level Modification

In 2018, the IAAF provided the CAS with what it claimed was new research proving the performance-enhancing impact of naturally higher than "normal" testosterone levels in women and used this evidence to produce new rules on hyperandrogynism. The new rule required HG women to medically suppress their testosterone levels to less than 5 nmol/L, rather than the 10 nmol/L specified previously. Although this represented a more stringent standard, it applied only to running events from 400 meters to the mile. Women with higher levels of testosterone but who are diagnosed as androgen insensitive, meaning their bodies are incapable of mobilizing testosterone, were not restricted by this regulation. The CAS accepted this evidence, and the new regulations went into effect at the IAAF level in November 2018. A related change to the rules for trans women that sets the eligibility threshold at less than 5 nmol/L across the board, rather than just for certain events, was to go into effect after the 2020 Tokyo Olympic Games (postponed to 2021 due to COVID-19) (Vilain et al., 2017).

The new rules explicitly targeted the 800-meter event and the three women from African countries who dominated it at that time: Semenya, Margaret Wambui, and Francine Niyonsaba. In order to continue competing, all three have been subjected to selective sex testing and forced to undergo unnecessary and invasive medical treatment (Pieper, 2016; Wells, 2020). Citing the negative effects on her health that resulted from being forced to undergo testosterone therapy for five years, Semenya appealed the CAS ruling to the Supreme Court of Switzerland. In a 2–1 decision, the court upheld the 2018 female eligibility policy. In response, Semenya announced her intention to compete in the 200-meter, a race not restricted by the ruling, rather than subject her body to unnecessary medical treatment

(Dunbar & Imray, 2020), but ultimately decided not to compete in 2020 Olympics (Sky Sports, 2021). Critical scholarship continues to contest what is considered to be simplistic correlative evidence between testosterone levels and athletic performance (Jordan-Young & Karkazis, 2019).

2020 World Rugby Ban on the Participation of Transgender Women

In contrast to the improving policy landscapes for trans athletes at elite international levels and national and recreational levels in a number of countries at the time, the World Rugby Federation stunned the sports world in November 2020 by banning trans women from participation in international women's competition, claiming that their superior size and strength as a result of "male" puberty puts cisgender women at risk (World Rugby, 2020). The ban has produced considerable opposition from a number of national rugby organizations, Rugby Canada (2020) and the USA Rugby (2020) among them, as well as from sport policy think tanks and advocacy organizations for women and LGBT athletes. For example, in a joint statement, Canadian Women & Sport and the Canadian Centre for Ethics in Sport (2020) announced their strong opposition to the ban on the grounds that it discriminates against trans athletes, denies trans and gender-diverse women the benefits of sport, is not based on peer-reviewed scientific evidence, excludes nonbinary participants assigned male at birth, and privileges the safety and well-being of cisgender athletes over the evidence-based harm this will cause to trans athletes. The letter refers to recommendations from the Canadian Trans Inclusion in Sport Expert Working Group (2016) that prioritize creating inclusive rather than restrictive environments for trans participants.

2021 Framework on Fairness, Inclusion, and Non-Discrimination on the Basis of Gender Identity and Sex Variations

During the 2020 summer Olympic Games (held in 2021), Laurel Hubbard competed in the sport of weightlifting as the first openly transgender woman in Olympic history to do so. She may be the last – at least in this sport, for some time –as conflicts over appropriate criteria for female eligibility in elite sport have recently produced a reactive shift in sport policy. In November of 2021, the IOC announced a new policy in the form of the Framework on Fairness, Inclusion, and Non -Discrimination on the Basis of Gender Identity and Sex Variation, identity and sex variations..

The new IOC policy acknowledges that the so-called scientific evidence about the effect of higher average levels of testosterone among men that was used to support a policy revision for both transgender and HG women that required them to reduce their testosterone levels to 5 nmols, as opposed to the previous 10 nmols, was, as its critics had insisted all along (Dreger, 1998, 2010; Fausto-Sterling, 2000, 2020; Fine, 2017; Jordan-Young & Karkazis, 2019), lacking in scientific veracity (Pielke, 2021). While the new IOC policy is refreshing in that it rules out medically unnecessary treatment and acknowledges the harms to women athletes that have resulted from past regulations, it is deeply concerning for other reasons. The new policy supports a sport-by-sport assessment that allows the IOC to abdicate any role it has ever had to support the human rights of transgender athletes. It is now up to individual sport associations and federations to do the dirty work of drawing boundaries between 'real' and 'unreal' girls and women. The scientific evidence produced in support of such assessments remains epistemologically suspect as it supports a sporting framework based on assumptions of male athletic superiority. The harm that such assessments will produce has already been materialized with the aforementioned World Rugby's 2020 ban on the participation of transgender women in international 'female' rugby competitions on the basis of the claim that the trans women retain vestigial strength that makes their participation unsafe for their cisgender counterparts.

Seemingly following the IOC's lead, in January 2022 the U.S. National Collegiate Athletic Association (NCAA) announced a new policy for transgender participation, replacing the leading-edge transgender inclusive policy it adopted in 2011 with one that relies on sport-by-sport evidence-based decision-making about the extent to which transgender women purportedly have an unfair advantage as a result of their being assigned male at birth. The new policy enables banning transgender women from so-called "gender-affected" sports. The recent success of NCAA swimmer, Lia Thomas, a transgender woman who has been breaking records, has "sparked debate" (Athlete Ally & Mosier, C., 2022; Dutton, 2021).

Taking the lead in this new framework approach, the IOC formally acknowledged the insufficiency of the science behind testosterone regulations, apologized for unnecessary and harmful interventions required by its past female eligibility policies, and outsourced determinations surrounding female eligibility to individual sport associations. How this will play out in practice remains to be seen, but the example of World Rugby's 2020 exclusion of transgender women entirely, as spoken to above, gives considerable cause for concern.

Summative Assessment on the State of Policy Play

Taken as a whole, transgender participation policies to date remain "gender conforming" in that they are limited, for the most part, to trans people who are "intelligible" (Butler, 1993) according to binary sex categories. Trans and nonbinary people who do not or cannot conform to such categories or who are unable to access trans-affirming healthcare are often left out, pushed out, or self-excluded (Hargie, Mitchell, & Somerville, 2017) when it comes to sport. Nonbinary athletes typically have few options as even so-called mixed-sex sports typically apply sex-based criteria for the purposes of registration, role differentiation, and/or quotas for male and female players on the basis of assumed male advantage (Phipps, 2019).

It is simplistic but instructive to speak of two classes of transgender people in the process of emerging on the basis of access to/desire for medicalized transition or lack thereof (Travers, 2018). Barriers to accessing the affirming healthcare that ameliorates gender dysphoria and aids assimilation—whether that is the desired goal or not—include citizenship, poverty, racism, lack of health insurance, lack of family support, geographic inaccessibility, binary nonconformity, mental health issues/trauma, and coming to understand oneself as trans too late to redirect puberty. There is also evidence to indicate that some trans kids who would not otherwise choose to medically transition do so in order to participate in sport (Ehrensaft, 2016; Travers, 2018). While most sport policy has yet to show coherent progress in taking issues like these into consideration, it is encouraging that there have been some recent steps taken to begin to confront the issues at play.

Presently, participation policies for trans people of all ages, at recreational and competitive levels, vary considerable throughout the world, not just by country but by province/state or city. Human rights discourses have been effective in achieving policy changes to enable trans youth to participate in accordance with their affirmed gender identity without requiring medical treatment in a handful of school districts and provinces/states in Canada and the United States. For example, the U.S. LGBT Sports Foundation (2021) has developed the All 50 model policy for sport participation on this basis that corresponds with policies in 15 states. This represents a step forward for binary-based trans students, but it falls short by lacking provisions for nonbinary trans youth and recommendations for overhauling the sex-segregated structure of most high school sport. The Trans Inclusion in Sport Expert Working Group (2016), facilitated by the Canadian Centre for Ethics in Sport, makes recommendations similar to the All 50 policy but goes beyond it in a significant way by advising that sport and physical recreation be restructured to provide all-gender programs and address safety concerns via skill and size categories rather than gender.

While transgender people have had some success in gaining recognition and advancing their human rights in the collection of nations known colloquially as 'the West,' in the past decade, a well-financed reactionary movement is attempting to roll back these gains. A constellation of white supremacist, conservative, and hetero-patriarchal organizations and movements are in collusion with so-called 'gender critical feminists' (Butler, 2021) to resist feminist and gender-inclusive challenges to traditional gender and sexual hierarchies by targeting trans girls and women – more so than trans boys, trans men, and non-binary people – for surveillance and exclusion. In the past several years, bills designed to delegitimize and exclude trans girls and young women in particular in sport have been introduced in many U.S. state legislatures and signed into law in eleven U.S. states (Sharrow, 2022; Sharrow, Schultz, Pieper, Baeth, & Lieberman, 2021).

APPROACHES

Competing Epistemologies

The experience of transgender participants is profoundly linked to policy debates about female eligibility at the highest levels of sport. These policy debates are sites for competing claims about the nature of sex differentiation as it relates to athletic ability and the possibilities for physiological equivalency between trans, HG, and cisgender women. Here, I provide a brief overview of three epistemological vantage points in the scholarly literature: those of *positivists*, *critical feminists,* and *feminist science scholars.*

Positivists

Positivists advance a "medical/biological perspective" (Martínková, 2020) and work in "natural" science fields that include the science of sex development, exercise physiology, and sport performance. They rely on a positivist epistemology and the scientific method to make claims about differences between male and female bodies and the possibilities for physiological equivalency between trans, HG, and cisgender women. Of these studies, those that reflect and reinforce ideological beliefs about sex difference and female athletic inferiority (Handelsman, Hirschberg, & Bermon, 2018; Harper, Kolliari-Turner et al., 2018) and the utility of medical intervention dominate in terms of influencing policy at the highest levels of sport. In fact, the most influential studies are not only referred to in policy debates and legal proceedings but are frequently formally or informally commissioned by the IAAF and/or IOC to justify participation rules that have already been established (Jordan-Young & Karkazis, 2019).

One of the studies that has been influential in shaping recent policy on transgender women was conducted by Joanna Harper, a trans woman herself and a member of the expert team that presented evidence in the 2015 case brought by Chand and the 2018 case brought by Semenya. A former competitive runner, Harper noticed a drop-off in her own athletic performance posttransition and contacted seven other trans women to ask them to report on their race times, pre- and posttransition. This data led Harper (2019) to conclude that trans women experience significant drops in performance as a result of testosterone suppression. A number of critics, however, note flaws with the study that include small sample size, unverified data, and inconsistent race conditions (Jones et al., 2017). Still, Harper's study is widely accepted as evidence of the effectiveness of hormone therapy in achieving physiological equivalence between trans and cisgender women. A minority discourse in the literature, however, claims to demonstrate that trans women who undergo natal male puberty retain advantages that even years of hormone therapy cannot mitigate (Devine, 2019; Hilton & Lundberg, 2020; Sutherland, Wassersug, & Rosenberg, 2017).

Critical Feminists

Critical feminists work in fields related to the social sciences and humanities and view sex/gender systems as socially constructed and maintained as part of hetero-patriarchal relations of power. This scholarship is variously theoretically informed by poststructuralism, queer theory, cultural studies, trans studies, disability studies, postcolonial theory, and critical race theory/Black feminism. Critical feminist analyses of trans experiences in sport and rules relating to female eligibility (Fischer & McClearen, 2019; Wells & Darnell, 2014) view modern sport as reflecting and reinforcing intersecting relations of power and the unequal distribution of cultural and material resources.

Critical feminism relies on a hybrid of critical and social constructionist epistemologies and primarily—but not exclusively—qualitative methods. Such scholarship has documented the extent to which lack of opportunity for girls and women to develop athletic ability is linked to purportedly "natural" sex differences in athletic performance (Ring, 2009; Young, 2005). Critical feminists dispute both the validity of the evidence relating to sexually dimorphic biomarkers between men and women and related assumptions of male athletic superiority. There is a subset of critical feminist scholarship that targets the sex segregation of sport as itself reflecting and reproducing gender inequality (Bianchi, 2017, 2019; Cohen & Semerjian, 2008; Dowling, 2000; Kane, 1995; Love, 2017; McDonagh & Pappano, 2008; Travers, 2008, 2011, 2013, 2018).

Positivists and critical feminists are limited in their capacity to engage with each other because of lack of overlap in disciplinary expertise and political antipathy. For critical feminists, there is no controlling for culture in the scientific method. Still, critical feminists are typically unable to refute the claims of the positivists on their own terms. This is not only because of their disparate epistemologies and methodologies but also because of the disparate relations of power between the two "fields." Positivists receive much greater legitimacy—and research funding—as their "ways of knowing" are widely taken for granted and privileged over the qualitative and interpretive approaches of much critical feminist scholarship. In spite of this, critical feminist scholarship has combined with feminist activism to challenge the unjust exclusion of girls and women from sport, establish gender equity as a foundational principle of access to sport in many countries, and end the practice of sex-verification testing for all women athletes in elite competitions.

Feminist Science Scholars

Feminist science scholars combine expertise in the natural sciences in general and/or the science of sex development with a critical feminist material analysis of science as a set of institutions and social processes that are embedded in relations of power. This latter field includes feminist science studies (Rivers, 2019) and new materialism (Van der Tuin, 2011). Feminist science scholars subject so-called scientific studies of sex difference to scrutiny to determine the extent to which scientific procedures and standards have been adhered to. In doing so, they often uncover Eurocentric, hetero-patriarchal assumptions operating under the surface to animate research questions, the scope of scientific inquiry, and the findings of studies themselves. In subjecting the Tanner Scale of "normal" binary pubertal development to critical analysis, for example, Gill-Peterson (2014, 2018) draws our attention to the colonial context within which the discipline of endocrinology emerged. The very science of hormone systems and sex difference and measurement is grounded in Eurocentric norms. These norms were violently imposed on Indigenous populations through colonial conquest and on Black people via the transatlantic slave trade. As sex testing verifies, these norms continue to do violence (Henne, 2015).

Feminist science scholars (see, for example, Fine, 2017; Barad, 2007, 2015; Fausto-Sterling, 2000, 2020; Grosz, 1994, 2017; Haraway, 1997; Willey, 2016) are "tricksters" (Haraway, 1991) because they fully understand and speak the language of the positivists *and* value the insights of critical feminists. As such, they are particularly adept at identifying the *social* decisions and interpretations reflected in the studies that are deployed to support dimorphic sex biomarkers and causal relationships between functional testosterone levels and athletic performance.

Notably, feminist science scholars make three interventions that are relevant to the participation of trans and HG women in sport: first, that there is no clear line of demarcation between male and female bodies; second, that gendered overlaps in hormone levels and athletic performance regularly occur (Fausto-Sterling, 2020; Jordan-Young & Karkazis, 2019); and third, that the case for pinpointing testosterone levels as indicators of athletic performance and therefore the basis for determining female eligibility has yet to be scientifically proven. Henne (2015, p. 7) locates the focus of this intervention as "the biopolitics of athlete citizenship," observing that "scientific tools have been deployed to scrutinize athletes' bodies in order to protect ideological beliefs."

What feminist science scholars and positivists have in common regarding female eligibility policies is the terms of the debate: both focus on the question of physiological equivalency. In spite of their extraordinary meta-expertise, however, feminist science scholars remain, so far, only marginally included (feminized) in policy debates about female eligibility. We see this most notably in the devaluation of the work of Jordan-Young and Karkazis (2019) that contests positivist claims that higher endogenous testosterone is causally linked to athletic advantage. Jordan-Young and Karkazis emphasize that their work reinforces the empiricist method in that it seeks to demonstrate that studies of sex differentiation are not actually empirical but rather ideological. They approached their work on testosterone by conducting "a network analysis of social neuroendocrinology research" (p. 20) that purported to produce facts about the relationship between testosterone levels and athletic ability. Their review revealed not only inconsistencies in methods and analysis but inconsistent and contradictory findings across studies. From this perspective, sex testing reflects the biopolitical management of athlete citizens to prop up ideologies of sex (and race) difference (Henne, 2015) and is a form of "violence to make materially specific bodies coincide with a particular sex" (Linghede, 2018, p. 576).

Studies commissioned by the IAAF and the IOC that supported the link between testosterone and athletic performance were privileged by the CAS, in spite of being scientifically flawed; the study the IAAF drew on to support the 2018 rules on hyperandrogenism (Wiik et al., 2019) had yet to be peer reviewed, a foundational requirement of positivist science, when presented to the CAS. At the same time, peer-reviewed studies that disrupted the assumed causal connection between testosterone and athletic performance and male versus female statistical norms were ignored (Pape, 2019). Feminist science scholars draw attention to the frequent failure of positivist studies of so-called sex differences to adhere to the scientific procedures that grant them their aura of power and legitimacy (Jordan-Young, 2010). Jordan-Young and Karkazis (2019, pp. 10–11) describe this as "scientism—the elevation of scientific values, evidence, and authority above all others," observing, "Scientism also promotes forms of authority in which something is a 'fact' or is 'scientific' because a scientist says it is, not because it meets any particular criterion of method."

Where feminist science has succeeded is in the increasing acknowledgment among positivists and IAAF and IOC policymakers that sex is a continuum rather than a binary and that boundaries between those who are eligible and those who are ineligible to compete in women's events are somewhat arbitrary. Positivists and policymakers, however, manage an ongoing form of cognitive dissonance between this ontological premise and the prevailing logic of sport to assert the scientific veracity of male athletic superiority and hence the need to protect cisgender women from male-coded trans women and HG interlopers, while subscribing to the view of DSD as pathological rather than reflecting human sex variation. Beyond superficially acknowledging that sex is far more complex than the female eligibility policies they support encode, positivists dismiss feminist science scholars by accusing them of not understanding science. Harper (2019), for example, makes veiled criticisms of Jordan-Young and Karkazis on the basis of their expertise in disciplines outside the natural scientists, and yet Harper's (2015) very influential study comparing pre- and posttransition performance among trans women is not published in a "real science" journal at all but rather in the *Journal of Sporting Cultures and Identities*.

DEBATES

There are two central, interrelated questions that drive policy debates about the participation of trans and nonbinary people in sport: (1) Do trans girls and women have an unfair advantage over cisgender girls and women? (2) If so, does testosterone suppression therapy mitigate this advantage over a certain period of time?

Physiological Equivalence?

The debate about whether or not trans women possess an unfair advantage overlaps profoundly with debates about the appropriateness of imposing hormonal suppression treatment on HG women athletes (Vilain et al., 2017). These debates come down to efforts to isolate, measure, and control for embodied "male advantage." In other words, what is it about the "male" body that makes it athletically superior, and correspondingly, what is it that the "female" body lacks that requires and justifies the enclosure of women's competition as a protected category for gender equity reasons? Past regimes of sex testing were considered unscientific by leaders in related fields for decades prior to being abandoned (Pieper, 2016; Wells, 2020).

The assumption that trans women have an unfair advantage rests on the widely held belief that men as an aggregate are athletically superior to women as an aggregate. In spite of commonsense assumptions that boys and girls, as binary aggregates, are dimorphic in athletic ability seemingly from the womb, the majority scientific consensus is that male puberty, and the accompanying divergence in terms of average testosterone levels, marks the point at which the "two" sexes diverge (Vilain et al., 2017). Trans women who undergo natal male puberty, according to accepted wisdom, therefore need testosterone suppression treatment to achieve physiological equivalency with cisgender women. A number of studies purport to demonstrate the success of testosterone suppression (Harper, 2015; Vilain et al., 2017) in achieving this. Debates relating to unfair advantage hinge, first, on scientific claims that testosterone level is a sexually dimorphic biomarker (Harper, 2019; Harper et al., 2018) and *the* causal factor driving both maleness and athletic advantage that can be measured via scientific tests administered on the body, and second, on what constitutes a "fair" versus an "unfair" advantage.

Positivists insist that research studies provide evidence of the causal relationship between testosterone levels and athletic performance via "normal" ranges in functional testosterone that diverge not in individual male and female bodies, because there is too much variation therein, but in statistical terms. A number of scholars point to consistent evidence that, in comparable events, men outperform women on average (Foddy & Savulescu, 2011; Vilain et al., 2017). Critical feminist and feminist science scholars emphasize that the gap between women's and men's performances has significantly decreased as access to sport participation and training has increased, and therefore point to the difficulty in isolating biological from cultural factors, factors feminist science scholars view as always and inevitably entangled (Grosz, 2017; Haraway, 1997).

Feminist scientists (Dreger, 1998, 2010; Fausto-Sterling, 2020; Fine, 2017) have subjected studies purported to prove dimorphic sex difference to rigorous analysis to determine the extent to which they meet scientific criteria and found them fundamentally flawed. Jordan-Young and Karkazis (2019) took this approach to read across multiple studies on testosterone and concluded that studies often report findings that are inadequately supported by the evidence and are often inconsistent with or contradict each other or are conducted in ways that prevent comparison. They conclude that assumptions about the causal relationship between testosterone and athletic performance shape the studies far more than the studies support this finding and that the relationship of sport governing bodies at the highest level to the research is also problematic. Jordan-Young and Karkazis (2019, p. 164) describe the circular argument underpinning the hyperandrogenism rule as practicing "opportunistic epistemology—reverse engineering that starts with a course of action, a policy, or a conclusion and searches for evidence to support it."

Critics (Jordan-Young & Karkazis, 2019; Pape, 2017; Pieper, 2016; Wells, 2020) of the rules governing HG women question the validity of research that correlates increases in athletic performance in cisgender athletes who were given very large doses of exogenous testosterone, via doping, with the impact of endogenous (naturally occurring) testosterone levels. Jordan-Young and Karkazis (2019) also cite research that demonstrates considerable overlap in testosterone levels among men and women, studies that show no clear connection between testosterone levels and winning, and studies that demonstrate that the socially mediated experience of participating in competition itself raises testosterone levels.

There is a disturbing racial subtext to the targeting of HG women that goes beyond the salient fact that the majority of women targeted are Black and brown women from the Global South. This is most evident in Harper's unsubstantiated claims that intersex athletes have dominated women's events since the 1930s and that the disproportionate number of Black and brown women from the Global South targeted for selective sex testing reflects "inbreeding" in those regions. To justify the change in female eligibility regulations from 10 to 5 nmol/Ls of functional testosterone, Harper (2019, p. 196) cites the increased race times of Wambui, Niyonsaba, and Semenya after the CAS suspended the 2015 Consensus and their gold-silver-bronze performance in the 800 meters at the 2016 Olympics. Harper claims that women with intersex conditions are disproportionately successful in women's sport, specifically claiming their overrepresentation on the podium in Olympic women's events. In keeping with the view of people with intersex conditions as abnormal and pathological, Harper explains DSD as resulting from "consanguinity," a practice she claims has fallen out of favor in the West but remains common in rural regions of the Global South (p. 98). This inaccurate claim is racist and consistent with the white supremacist "Black gender ideology" (Hill Collins, 2004) that views Black people as hypersexual and more primitive. According to Foddy and Savulescu (2011, p. 1185), "the natural range of variation in testosterone and testosterone sensitivity suggests that a great many athletes have a genetic testosterone advantage without having an intersex condition."

Unfair Advantage?

With regard to transgender women, a minority of research insists that hormonal suppression therapy for trans women who underwent natal male puberty does not result in physiological equivalency. This means that at least some of the advantage cannot be ameliorated. Devine (2019) and Hilton and Lundberg (2020) claim that trans women retain advantages related to exposure to "male" levels of testosterone even after years of hormone therapy. Devine reviews studies on testosterone doping to conclude that this advantage persists decades after doping ceases. Based on these findings, he claims that trans women retain similar benefits even after years of testosterone suppression. He explains this residual advantage as based on "muscle memory," claiming that tissues that have been exposed to high levels of testosterone, whether through doping or male puberty, retain their strength-building capacity, even long after the higher levels of testosterone are out of their system. Hilton and Lundberg assert the basic premise that men are bigger, stronger, and faster than women. Indeed, they consider the biological factors underpinning athletic performance to be "unequivocally established" and focus on the role of testosterone in driving the development of secondary sex characteristics in males. They base their claim that separate competitions for transgender women are necessary for safety reasons based on longitudinal studies of transgender women who are not athletes. Interestingly, however, one of the cross-sectional studies they report on puts trans women in the 90th percentile for women in terms of size and muscle mass, still within the so-called female range. The authors code this, however, as male advantage and therefore unfair.

While Sutherland et al. (2017) accept findings that hormone therapy adequately reduces the strength of trans women, they claim that the testosterone-fueled sexually dimorphic skeletal growth and formation associated with "male" puberty provides trans women with an "osteological advantage" that is retained even after hormonal transition. The authors recognize the cultural and biological complexity of the sex binary but state that "there are anatomical and biomechanical reasons to believe that a post-pubertal MtF transsexual, who is fully female according to the laws of her country, may still be outside the range of normal variation for phenotypical females" and that an alternative to including them in women's competitions is required (Sutherland et al., 2017, p. 176).

Sutherland et al. (2017) further claim that the current hormonally based categories for sport participation fail to address unfair advantages that Renée Richards in tennis, Michelle Dumaresq in mountain biking, and Kristen Worley in cycling would have benefited from when competing against women. Interestingly, they claim that the typical female elbow makes it difficult, biomechanically, to throw a ball properly, aka, "throwing like a girl." Critical feminist scholarship has shown, however, that proper throwing mechanics are disproportionately taught to boys (Young, 2005) and that, when using the nondominant arm, boys and girls throw in a similarly ineffective way. In contrast, Harper (2019) claims that trans women may actually be at a disadvantage when competing against cisgender women because cisgender women produce testosterone with both their ovaries and their adrenal glands, whereas trans women who rely on their adrenal glands alone produce less testosterone.

Critics of the new rules governing female eligibility point to the reality that distinguishing between natural advantages that are fair versus unfair—not to mention between forms of technological mediation that are legal versus illegal, or the considerable impact of socioeconomic factors on athletic success—is a *social* rather than a biomedical decision (Bianchi, 2019; Butryn, 2003; Fischer & McClearen, 2019; Gleaves & Lehrbach, 2016; Henne, 2015). If, for example, higher than normal natural levels of functional testosterone are deemed to confer an unfair advantage, why are men who have testosterone levels higher than the norm not regulated?

CONCLUSION

Current policies for female eligibility in sport are predominantly "gender conforming" (Travers, 2006) in that they require no restructuring of sport and reflect efforts to contain scientific and social justice challenges to the Eurocentric, hetero-patriarchal sex/gender system that is encoded in and reinforced by modern sport. But the regulatory challenges posed by transgender and HG women have sparked scholarly debate about new ways of organizing sport, some of which have the potential to be "gender transforming" (Travers, 2006). This last section includes a brief overview.

Beyond Sex?

Scholars who contest the potential for physiological equivalence between trans and cisgender women (Devine, 2019; Hilton & Lundberg, 2020; Richardson & Chen, 2020) propose a number of solutions. Richardson and Chen recommend that women's competitions be subdivided and a new category introduced for trans women only, thereby establishing the women's category proper as a cisgender one. While they do not address HG women, it is conceivable that they would exclude HG women from the women's category as well. The proposal to segregate trans women is a minority one that is met with strong opposition on the basis of human rights as well as arguments in favor of physiological equivalence (Jones, Arcelus, Bouman, & Haycraft, 2020). Sutherland et al. (2017), propose multiple categories for competition based on hormone levels (functional testosterone) and osteology (skeletal structures) that confer different degrees of advantage.

Critical feminists and feminist science scholars argue that gender self-determination as a basis for participation is the most socially just way of including trans and HG women in the current sport system. Gleaves and Lerbach (2016), for example, view gender as a meaningful narrative category rather than a biological one and suggest, therefore, that those for whom the narrative category of "woman" is meaningful should participate in that category, regardless of biology. Instead of the historically situated "comparative test" narrative that dominates modern sport, they recommend shifting the narrative to an equally valid and more socially just one, that of gender self-determination. They suggest that this shift will provide trans and HG women with the opportunity to contribute to a narrative of inclusion that will have a broader impact in terms of social justice for trans and gender-nonconforming people in society more broadly. Other scholars similarly emphasize the need to balance concerns with fairness with concerns about inclusivity, emphasizing that inclusivity is just as, if not more, important (Buzuvis, 2018; Fletcher, 2020; Teetzel, 2014).

McDonagh and Pappano (2008) and Travers (2008) view sex segregation in sport as reinforcing gender inequality more broadly but propose a modified restructuring of sport. McDonagh and Pappano make a distinction between "voluntary" and "coercive" sex segregation for girls and women and argue that the former should be maintained because it promotes the participation and comfort of girls and women, while the latter should be abolished because it reinforces male dominance. Similarly, but with the explicit intent of supporting trans inclusion, Travers advocates for the abolition of all male-only sex-segregated sporting spaces while retaining girl- and women-only sporting spaces with trans-inclusive boundaries. This builds on Travers's (2006) vision of "queering sport" away from rigid binary sex categories. Martînková (2020) proposes a modification in the form of "unisex" sport as a gender-inclusive addition and perhaps eventual replacement for sex-segregated sport. Unisex sport, according to Martînková, has the potential to break down assumptions about athletic sex difference by rendering overlaps in performance visible.

Reconfiguring Sport

A small body of scholarship advocates for a more radical reenvisioning of sport beyond sex segregation entirely (Bianchi, 2017, 2019; Kane, 1995; Pronger, 1990, 1999; Rothblatt, 1995; McDonagh & Pappano, 2008; Tännsjö, 2000; Travers, 2008, 2011, 2013) and is a burgeoning although fragmented area of inquiry, as evidenced by frequent failures to cite previous scholarship. In 1995, Rothblatt recommended the abolition of sex-segregated sport as a requirement of gender justice. Tännsjö (2000) claimed the abolition of sex categories will give the most elite women athletes an opportunity to show their abilities to the fullest, insisting that sports is about competition, and if there are some sports where some men dominate all women, so be it. Bianchi (2017) proposes replacing the binary sex organization of sport with a "handicap system" based on a "skills thesis" (Bianchi, 2019), noting this precedent in weight classes for boxing and wrestling and skill level in golf, partially duplicating an argument raised by previous scholars (Pronger, 1990; Travers, 2008). Under the logic of this alternative to sex-based sport, scholarship emphasizes that all elite athletes are anomalies anyway in terms of exceptional natural abilities. Rather than designating some natural abilities as fair and others unfair, sport categories should be organized according to the various abilities that confer advantage (height, weight, age, level of functional testosterone [Tamburrini & Tännsjö, 2005], perhaps even osteology [Sutherland et al., 2017]) to provide more genuinely "level playing fields" for competition.

In a move consistent with a post-/transhumanist vision of humans as inevitably techno-logically mediated (Butryn, 2003; Gill-Peterson, 2014; Haraway, 1991, 1997, 2016), Sutherland et al. (2017) and Tamburrini and Tännsjö (2005) recommend permitting athletes to employ a range of technologies, from doping to surgical modification, to alter their bodies to impact athletic performance. For Tamburrini and Tännsjö, this includes enabling cisgender women to "become the new Amazons" by increasing functional testosterone to "male" levels.

Current female eligibility policies privilege the participation of cisgender women over trans and HG women and, via the criteria for their inclusion, place trans and HG women in morally abject proximity (Pérez-Samaniego, Fuentes-Miguel, Pereira-Garcîa, & Devîs-Devîs, 2016) to athletes who dope, whose own abjection is equally arbitrary (Butryn, 2003). Within this context, opportunities for transgender participation in sport are disproportionately available to trans men and women with binary identities and the socioeconomic privilege required to access affirming medical care.

Social justice for transgender and nonbinary people is inconsistent with exclusion from sport. Measures to achieve inclusion, however, must be situated within a larger struggle to resist a "sport nexus" (Burstyn, 1999; Travers, 2008) wherein sport participation and the benefits of sport are striated and shaped by an assemblage of forces that include global capitalism and the international division of labor, white supremacy, colonialism, and cisgender hetero-patriarchy. Proposals for socially just transgender inclusion in sport, whether via reform or radical restructuring, require a more equal disciplinary footing between positivists, critical feminists, and critical feminist science scholars.

ACKNOWLEDGMENTS

Thanks to Cassandra Wells for reviewing the section on policy evolution for accuracy, Marina Khonina for assistance in compiling an up-to-date list of relevant literature, and Lawrence Wenner for his patience and encouragement.

NOTE

1. Mosier went on to compete at the world championships but failed to earn a spot at the 2016 Olympics.

REFERENCES

American Psychiatric Association. (2013). *DSM-V: Diagnostic and statistical manual of mental disorders*. Arlington, VA: American Psychiatric Association.

Athlete A., & Mosier, C. (2022, January 20). Athlete Ally & Chris Mosier respond to NCAA new trans inclusion policy. https://www.athleteally.org/athlete-ally-mosier-respond-ncaa-new-trans-policy/.

Barad, K. (2007). *Meeting the universe halfway: Quantum physics and the entanglement of matter and meaning*. Durham, NC: Duke University Press.

Barad, K. (2015). Transmaterialities: Trans*/matter/realities and queer political imaginings. *GLQ*, *21*(2–3), 387–422.

Bianchi, A. (2017) Transgender women in sport. *Journal of the Philosophy of Sport*, *44*(2), 229–242. doi:10.1080/00948705.2017.1317602.

Bianchi, A. (2019). Something's got to give: Reconsidering the justification for a gender divide in sport. *Philosophies*, *4*(23), 229–242. doi:10.3390/philosophies4020023.

Birrell, S., & Cole, C. L. (1990). Double fault: Renée Richards and the construction and naturalization of difference. *Sociology of Sport Journal*, *7*(1), 1–21.

Bullough, V., & Bullough, B. (1993). *Cross dressing, sex and gender*. Philadelphia: University of Pennsylvania Press.

Burstyn, V. (1999). *The rites of men: Manhood, politics and the culture of sport*. Toronto: University of Toronto Press.

Butler, J. (1993). *Bodies that matter: On the discursive limits of sex*. New York: Routledge.

Butryn, T. (2003). Posthuman podiums: Cyborg narratives of elite track and field. *Sociology of Sport Journal*, 20(1), 17–39.

Buzuvis, E. E. (2018). Challenging gender in single-sex spaces: Lessons from a feminist softball league. Duke Law. http://lcp.law.duke.edu/.

Canadian Women & Sport and the Canadian Centre for Ethics in Sport. (2020). Canadian Women & Sport and the Canadian Centre for Ethics in Sport strongly oppose the ban on transgender women athletes by World Rugby. https://womenandsport.ca/?s=rugby.

Carrington, B., & McDonald, I. (2009). *Marxism, cultural politics and sport*. London: Routledge.

Carter, T. F. (2008). *The quality of home runs: The passion, language, and politics of Cuban baseball*. Oxford: Blackwell.

Caudwell, J. (2014). [Transgender] young men: Gendered subjectivities and the physically active body. *Sport, Education and Society*, 19(4), 398–414. doi:10.1080/13573322.2012.672320.

Cavanagh, S., & Sykes, H. (2006). Transexual bodies at the Olympics: The International Olympic Committee's policy on transsexual athletes at the 2004 Athens Summer Games. *Body & Society*, 12(3), 75–102.

Cohen, J., & Semerjian, T. (2008). The collision of trans-experience and the politics of women's ice hockey. *International Journal of Transgenderism*, 10(3), 133–145.

Collins, T. (2013). *Sport in capitalist society: A short history*. New York: Routledge.

Cunningham, G. B., Buzuvis, E., & Mosier, C. (2018). Inclusive spaces and locker rooms for transgender athletes. *Kinesiology Review*, 7, 365–374.

Cunningham, G. B., & Pickett, A. C. (2018). Trans prejudice in sport: Differences from LGB prejudice, the influence of gender, and changes over time. *Sex Roles: A Journal of Research*, 78(3–4), 220–227. https://doi.org/10.1007/s11199-017-0791-6

Devine, J. W. (2019). Gender, steroids, and fairness in sport. *Sport, Ethics and Philosophy*, 13(2), 161–169.

Douglas, D. D. (2003). Venus, Serena and the Women's Tennis Association: When and where race enters. *Sociology of Sport Journal*, 22, 256–282.

Douglas, D. D. (2012). Venus, Serena, and the inconspicuous consumption of Blackness: A commentary on surveillance, race talk, and new racism(s). *Journal of Black Studies*, 43, 127–145.

Dowling, C. (2000). *The frailty myth*. New York: Random House.

Dreger, A. D. (1998). *Hermaphrodites and the medical invention of sex*. Cambridge, MA: Harvard University Press.

Dreger, A. (2010). *Sex typing for sport*. Hastings Center Report, 40(2), 22–24.

Dunbar, G., & Imray, G. (2020, September 8). Caster Semenya loses bid to have IAAF testosterone regulations overturned. *CBC*. https://www.cbc.ca/sports/olympics/summer/trackandfield/caster-semenya-appeal-testosterone-rules-dismissed-1.5715936.

Dutton, J. (2021, August 12). Who is Lia Thomas? Trans swimmer breaking college records sparks debate. Newsweek. https://www.newsweek.com/trans-swimmer-breaking-college-records-sparks-debate-1657354.

Dworkin, S. L., Swarr, A. L., & Cooky, C. (2013). (In)Justice in sport: The treatment of South African track star Caster Semenya. *Feminist Studies*, 39(1), 40–69.

Ehrensaft, D. (2016). *Gender born, gender made: Raising healthy gender nonconforming kids*. New York: The Experiment.

Elling-Machartzki, A. (2017). Extraordinary body-self narratives: Sport and physical activity in the lives of transgender people. *Leisure Studies*, 36(2), 256–268.

Fausto-Sterling, A. (2000). *Sexing the body: Gender politics and the construction of sexuality.* New York: Basic Books.

Fausto-Sterling, A. (2020). *Sexing the body: Gender politics and the construction of sexuality* (updated ed.). New York: Basic Books.

Feinberg, D. (2021, January 29). WNBA's Layshia Clarendon has surgery to remove breasts. *AP News.* https://apnews.com/article/sports-new-york-media-social-media-layshia-clarendon-11c5c8ff46a1c81baae97856cabebe0a.

Fine, C. R. (2017). *Testosterone Rex: Myths of sex, science, and society.* New York: W. W. Norton.

Fischer, M., & McClearen, J. (2019). Transgender athletes and the queer art of athletic failure. *Communication & Sport, 7,* 1–21.

Fletcher, D. (2020). The positive impact of trans inclusion in team sports men's roller derby. In R. Magrath, J. Cleland, & E. Anderson (Eds.), *The Palgrave handbook of masculinity and sport* (pp. 171–187). London: Palgrave Macmillan.

Flores, A. R., Herman, J. L., Gates, G. J., & Brown, T. N. T. (2016). How many adults identify as transgender in the United States? Williams Institute, UCLA School of Law. https://williamsinstitute.law.ucla.edu/publications/trans-adults-united-states/.

Foddy, B., & Savulescu, J. (2011). Time to re-evaluate gender segregation in athletics? *British Journal of Sports Medicine, 45,* 1184–1188.

Gill-Peterson, J. (2014). The technical capacities of the body: Assembling race, technology, and transgender. *Transgender Studies Quarterly, 1*(3), 402–418.

Gill-Peterson, J. (2018). *Histories of the transgender child.* Minneapolis: University of Minnesota Press.

Gleaves, J., & Lehrbach, T. (2016). Beyond fairness: The ethics of inclusion for transgender and intersex athletes. *Journal of the Philosophy of Sport, 43*(2), 311–326.

Griffin, P., & Carroll, H. J. (2010). On the team: Equal opportunity for transgender student athletes. *Women's Sport Foundation and National Center for Lesbian Rights.* https://www.nclrights.org/get-help/resource/on-the-team-equal-opportunities-for-transgender-student-athletes/.

Grosz, E. (1994). *Volatile bodies: Towards a corporeal feminism.* Bloomington: Indiana University Press.

Grosz, E. (2017). *The incorporeal: Ontology, ethics, and the limits of materialism.* New York: Columbia University Press.

Handelsman, D. J., Hirschberg, A. L., & Bermon, S. (2018). Circulating testosterone as the hormonal basis of sex differences in athletic performance. *Endocrine Reviews, 39,* 803–829.

Haraway, D. J. (1991). *Simians, cyborgs, and women: The reinvention of nature.* London: Free Association Books.

Haraway, D. J. (1997). *Modest witness @second millennium: Femaleman meets onco-mouse: Feminism and technoscience.* New York: Routledge.

Haraway, D. J. (2016). *Staying with the trouble: Making kin in the Chthulcene.* Durham, NC: Duke University Press.

Hargie, O. D., Mitchell, W. D. H., & Somerville, I. J. A. (2017). "People have a knack of making you feel excluded if they catch on to your difference": Transgender experiences of exclusion in sport. *International Review for the Sociology of Sport, 52*(2), 223–239.

Hargreaves, J. (1994). *Sporting females: Critical issues in the history and sociology of women's sports.* London: Routledge.

Hargreaves, J. (2013). Gender equality in Olympic sport: A brief history of women's setbacks and successes at the Summer Olympic Games. *Aspetar Sports Medicine Journal, 2*(1), 80–86.

Harper, J. (2015). Race times for transgender athletes. *Journal of Sporting Cultures and Identities*, 6(1), 1–9.

Harper, J. (2019). *Sporting gender: The history, science and stories of transgender and intersex athletes*. Lanham, MD: Rowman & Littlefield.

Harper, J., Lima, G., Kolliari-Turner, A., Malinsky, F. R., Wang, G., Martinez-Patino, M. J., . . . Pitsiladis, Y. P. (2018). The fluidity of gender and implications for the biology of inclusion for transgender and intersex athletes. *International Federation of Sports Medicine*, 7(12), 467–472.

Hellen, M. (2009). Transgendered children in schools. *Liminalis*, 3, 81–99.

Henne, K. E. (2015). *Testing for athlete citizenship: Regulating doping and sex in sport*. New Brunswick, NJ: Rutgers University Press.

Herrick, S. C., & Duncan, L. R. (2020). Locker-room experiences among LGBTQ+ adults. *Journal of Sport and Exercise Psychology*, 42, 227–239.

Herrick, S. C., Rocchi, M. A., & Couture, A. L. (2020). A case study exploring the experiences of a transgender athlete in synchronized skating, a subdiscipline of figure skating. *Journal of Sport and Social Issues*, 44(5), 421–449.

Higginbotham, E. B. (1992). African American women's history and the metalanguage of race. *Signs*, 17(2), 251–274.

Hill Collins, P. (2004). *Black sexual politics: African Americans, gender, and the new racism*. London: Routledge.

Hilton, E. N., & Lundberg, T. R. (2020). Transgender women in the female category of sport: Perspectives on testosterone suppression and performance advantage. *Sports Medicine*, 51(2), 199–214. https://doi.org/10.1007/s40279-020-01389-3 .

Jones, B. A., Arcelus, J., Bouman, W. P., & Haycraft, E. (2017). Sport and transgender people: A systematic review of the literature relating to sport participation and competitive sport policies. *Sports Medicine*, 47, 701–716.

Jones, B. A., Arcelus, J., Bouman, W. P., & Haycraft, E. (2020). Authors' reply to Richardson and Chen: Comment on "Sport and transgender people: A systematic review of the literature relating to sport participation and competitive sport policies." *Sports Medicine*, 50, 1861–1862.

Jordan-Young, R. (2010). *Brain storm: The flaws in the science of sex difference*. Cambridge, MA: Harvard University Press.

Jordan-Young, R. M., & Karkazis, K. (2019). *Testosterone: An unauthorized biography*. Boston: Harvard University Press.

Kirby, S., & Huebner, J. (2002). Talking about sex: Biology and the social interpretations of sex in sport. *Canadian Woman Studies*, 21(3), 36–43.

Kane, M. J. (1995). Resistance/transformation of the oppositional binary: Exposing sport as a continuum. *Journal of Sport and Social Issues*, 19, 191–218.

Klein, A., Krane, V., & Paule-Koba, A. L. (2018). Bodily changes and performance effects in a transitioning transgender college athlete. *Qualitative Research in Sport, Exercise and Health*, 10(5), 555–569.

Lenskyj, H. J. (2018). *Gender, athletes' rights, and the Court of Arbitration for Sport*. Bingley, U.K.: Emerald Publishing.

Lewis, S., & Johnson, C. (2011). "But it's not that easy": Negotiating (trans)gender expressions in leisure spaces. *Leisure/Loisir*, 35(2), 115–132.

LGBT Sports Foundation. (2021). "All 50" Policy. www.transathlete.com.

Linghede, E. (2018). The promise of glitching bodies in sport: A posthumanist exploration of an intersex phenomenon. *Qualitative Research in Sport, Exercise and Health, 10*(5), 570–584. doi:10.1080/2159676X.2018.1479980.

Love, A. (2017). The tenuous inclusion of transgender athletes in sport. In E. Anderson & A. Travers (Eds.), *Transgender athletes in competitive sport* (pp. 194–205). London: Routledge,

Lucas-Carr, C., & Krane, V. (2012). Troubling sport or troubled by sport. *Journal for the Study of Sport and Athletes in Education, 6*(1), 21–44.

Magubane, Z. (2014). Spectacles and scholarship: Caster Semenya, intersex studies, and the problem of race in feminist theory. *Signs, 39*(3), 761–785.

Martínková, I. (2020). Unisex sports: Challenging the binary. *Journal of the Philosophy of Sport, 47*(2), 248–265. doi:10.1080/00948705.2020.1768861.

McArdle, D. (2008). Swallows and Amazons, or the sporting exception to the gender recognition act. *Social & Legal Studies, 17*(1), 39–57.

McDonagh, E., & Pappano, L. (2008). *Playing with the boys: Why separate is not equal in sports.* New York: Oxford University Press.

McDonald, M. G. (2008). Rethinking resistance: The queer play of the Women's National Basketball Association, visibility politics and late capitalism, *Leisure Studies, 27*(1), 77–93. doi:10.1080/02614360701687776.

Muchicko, M. M., Lepp, A., & Barkley, J. E. (2014). Peer victimization, social support and leisure-time physical activity in transgender and cisgender individuals. *Leisure, 38*(3–4), 295–308.

Nyong'o, T. (2010). The unforgivable transgression of being Caster Semenya. *Women & Performance: A Journal of Feminist Theory, 20*, 95–100.

Pape, M. (2017). The fairest of them all: Gender-determining institutions and the science of sex testing. *Gender Panic, Gender Policy, Advances in Gender Research, 24*, 177–200.

Pape, M. (2019). Expertise and nonbinary bodies: Sex, gender and the case of Dutee Chand. *Body & Society, 25*(4), 3–28.

Pérez-Samaniego, V., Fuentes-Miguel, J. Pereira-García, S., López-Cañada, E., & Devís-Devís, J. (2016). Abjection and alterity in the imagining of transgender in physical education and sport: A pedagogical approach in higher education. *Sport, Education and Society, 21*(7), 985–1002.

Pérez-Samaniego, V., Fuentes-Miguel, J. Pereira-García, S., López-Cañada, E., & Devís-Devís, J. (2019). Experiences of trans persons in physical activity and sport: A qualitative meta-synthesis. *Sport Management Review, 22*, 439–451.

Phipps, C. (2019). Thinking beyond the binary: Barriers to trans* participation in university sport. *International Review for the Sociology of Sport, 56*(1), 81–96.

Pieper, L. P. (2016). *Sex testing: Gender policing in women's sports.* Champaign: University of Illinois Press.

Pieper, L. P. (2017). Advantage Renée? Renée Richards and women's tennis. In E. Anderson & A. Travers (Eds.), *Transgender athletes in competitive sport* (pp. 13–22). New York: Routledge.

Pronger, B. (1990). *The arena of masculinity: Sports, homosexuality, and the meaning of sex.* Toronto: Summerhill Press.

Pronger, B. (1999). Outta my endzone: Sport and the territorial anus. *Journal of Sport & Social Issues, 23*(4), 373–389.

Puar, J. (2007). *Terrorist assemblages: Homonationalism in queer times.* Durham, NC: Duke University Press.

Richardson, A., & Chen, M. A. (2020). Comment on "Sport and transgender people: A systematic review of the literature relating to sport participation and competitive sport policies." *Sports Medicine, 50*, 1857–1859. https://doi.org/10.1007/s40279-020-01323-7.

Ring, J. (2009). *Stolen bases: Why American girls don't play baseball.* Urbana: University of Illinois Press.

Ring, J. (2013). "Invisible women in America's national pastime" . . . or, "She's good. It's history, man." *Journal of Sport & Social Issues, 37*(1), 57–77.

Rivers, D. L. (2019). Cartographies of feminist science studies. *Women's Studies, 48*(3), 177–185. doi:10.1080/00497878.2019.1603980.

Rothblatt, M. (1995). *The apartheid of sex: A manifesto on the freedom of gender.* New York: Crown.

Rugby Canada. (2020). Rugby Canada provides update on feedback to proposed transgender guidelines. https://rugby.ca/en/news/2020/09/rugby-canada-provides-update-on-feedback-to-proposed-transgender-guidelines.

Sanchez, F., Martinez-Patino, M. & Vilain, E. (2013). The new policy on hyperandrogenism in elite female athletes is not about "sex testing." *Journal of Sex Research, 50*(2), 112–115.

Sharrow, E. A. (2022). Personal communication.

Sharrow, E., Schultz, J., Pieper, L. P., Anna Baeth, A., & Lieberman, A. (2021, July 26). States are still trying to ban trans youths from sports. Here's what you need to know. The Washington Post. https://www.washingtonpost.com/politics/2021/07/26/states-are-still-trying-ban-trans-youths-sports-heres-what-you-need-know/.

Sky Sports. (2021). Tokyo 2020: Caster Semenya confirms she will not attempt 200m Olympics qualification. https://www.skysports.com/more-sports/olympics/news/29175/12276210/tokyo-2020-caster-semenya-confirms-she-will-not-attempt-200m-olympics-qualification.

Sutherland, M. A. B., Wassersug, R. J., & Rosenberg, K. R. (2017). From transsexuals to transhumans in elite athletics: The implications of osteology (and other issues) in leveling the playing field. In E. Anderson, & A. Travers (Eds.), *Transgender athletes and competitive sport* (pp. 173–193). London: Taylor & Francis.

Sykes, H. (2006). Transsexual and transgender policies in sport. *Women in Sport and Physical Activity Journal, 15*(1), 3–13.

Tagg, B. (2012). Transgender netballers: Ethical issues and lived realities. *Sociology of Sport Journal, 29*(2), 151–167.

Tamburrini, C., & Tännsjö, T. (2005). The genetic design of a new Amazon. In C. Tamburrini & T. Tännsjö (Eds.), *Genetic technology and sport: Ethical questions* (pp. 181–198). New York: Routledge.

Tännsjö, T. (2000). Against sexual discrimination in sports. In T. Tännsjö & C. M. Tamburrini (Eds.), *Values in sport: Elitism, nationalism, gender equality and the scientific manufacture of winners* (pp. 101–115). New York: Taylor & Francis.

Teetzel, S. (2014). The onus of inclusivity: Sport policies and the enforcement of the women's category in sport. *Journal of the Philosophy of Sport, 41*(1), 113–127. doi:10.1080/00948705.2013.858394.

Trans Inclusion in Sport Expert Working Group. (2016). Creating inclusive environments for trans participants in Canadian sport: Guidance for sport organizations. Canadian Centre for Ethics in Sport. https://cces.ca/sites/default/files/content/docs/pdf/cces-transinclusionpolicyguidance-e.pdf.

Travers, A. (2006). Queering sport: Lesbian softball leagues and the transgender challenge. *International Review for the Sociology of Sport, 41*(3–4), 431–446.

Travers, A. (2008). The sport nexus and gender injustice. *Studies in Social Justice Journal, 2*(1), 79–101.

Travers, A. (2011). Women's ski jumping, the 2010 Olympic Games, and the deafening silence of sex segregation, whiteness and wealth. *Journal of Sport & Social Issues, 35*(2), 126–145.

Travers, A. (2013). Thinking the unthinkable: Imagining an "un-American," girl-friendly, women- and trans-inclusive alternative for baseball. *Journal of Sport and Social Issues, 37*(1), 78–96.

Travers, A. (2016). Transgender and gender nonconforming kids and the binary requirements of sport participation in North America. In M. Messner & M. Musto (Eds.), *Child's play: Sport in kids' worlds* (pp. 179–201). New Brunswick, NJ: Rutgers University Press.

Travers, A. (2018). *The trans generation: How trans kids (and their parents) are creating a gender revolution.* New York: NYU Press.

Travers, A., & Deri, J. (2011). Transgender inclusion and the changing face of lesbian softball leagues. *International Review for the Sociology of Sport, 46*(4): 488–507.

USA Rugby. (2020). USA rugby response to updated world rugby transgender athlete policy. https://www.usa.rugby/2020/10/usa-rugby-response-to-updated-world-rugby-transgender-athlete-policy/.

Van der Tuin, I. (2011). New feminist materialisms. *Women's Studies International Forum, 34*, 271–277.

Vilain, E., Betancurt, J. O., Bueno-Guerra, N., & Martinez-Patiño, M. J. (2017). Transgender athletes in elite sport competitions: Equity and inclusivity. In E. Anderson, & A. Travers, (Eds.), *Transgender athletes and competitive sport* (pp. 156–170). London: Taylor & Francis.

Weheliye, A. (2014). *Habeas viscus: Racializing assemblages, biopolitics and Black feminist theories of the human.* Durham, NC: Duke University Press.

Wells, C. J. (2020). *On the resiliency of sex testing in sport* (Unpublished PhD dissertation). University of British Columbia.

Wells, C., & Darnell, S. C. (2014). Caster Semenya, gender verification and the politics of fairness in an online track and field community. *Sociology of Sport Journal, 31*(1), 44–65.

Wente, M. (2019, May 2). The case of Caster Semenya: How do you compete against testosterone? *The Globe & Mail.* https://www.theglobeandmail.com/opinion/article-the-case-of-caster-semenya-how-do-you-compete-against-testosterone/.

Wiik, A., Lundberg, T. R., Rullman, E., Andersson, D. P., Holmberg, M., Mandić, . . . Gustafsson, T. (2019). Muscle strength, size and composition following 12 months of gender-affirming treatment in transgender individuals: Retained advantage for the transwomen. *Journal of Clinical Endocrinology & Metabolism, 105*(3), e805–e813. https://doi.org/10.1210/clinem/dgz247.

Willey, A. (2016). *Undoing monogamy: The politics of science and the possibilities of biology.* Durham, NC: Duke University Press.

World Rugby. (2020). Transgender guidelines. https://www.world.rugby/the-game/player-welfare/guidelines/transgender.

Wynter, S. (2003). Unsettling the coloniality of being/power/truth/freedom: Towards the human, after man, its overrepresentation—An argument. *New Centennial Review, 3*, 257–337.

Young, I. M. (2005). *On female body experience: "Throwing like a girl" and other essays.* New York: Oxford University Press.

PART VI

··

SPECTATOR
ENGAGEMENT
AND MEDIA

··

CHAPTER 49

···

SPORT, HEROES, AND CELEBRITIES

···

BARRY SMART

From classical antiquity to the present day, successful, high-profile athletes have been accorded iconic status, regarded as heroic figures, considered legends in their field, heralded as stars, and, in more recent commercially commodified and media-saturated times, treated as celebrities (Smart, 2005, 2013). What such terms signify, how, if at all, they are to be differentiated from one another, and whether their attribution to particular sporting figures is warranted, are matters that need to be carefully considered. As Whannel (2002, p. 40) has argued, "the concepts of hero and star, celebrity and personality, are often confused and any notional boundaries between them blurred," which makes critical reflection and analysis of such terms necessary. For example, U.S. tennis player Serena Williams is described as a sports and style icon, a feminist hero, a tennis legend, and a celebrity. Indeed, while each description may be merited, the respective terms are not synonyms. In this chapter, I will critically engage with the question of what it means to be accorded the status of sporting "hero" and treated as a "celebrity," and to that end will consider the complex processes that have transformed the identity, status, public profile, and lives of athletes we have come to know through their achievements in sporting contexts.

Heroes and narratives on heroic sporting figures are very much a product of their time (Holt & Mangan, 1996). The pantheon of sports history provides numerous examples of athletes and players in a variety of sporting fields who have been accorded the status of hero and treated as celebrities. Such designations are generally bound up with the quality of sporting performances and achievements, but the character, personality, or "charisma" of individuals accorded status as heroes or celebrities may be influential factors. In addition, their contributions to matters beyond the domain of sport, as well as their expression and representation of wider concerns, causes, and campaigns, may come into play. The prevailing social, economic, and political contexts, current events, the cultural zeitgeist or mood of the times, as well as the circumstances and controversies of everyday life, may all influence how the deeds, actions, and achievements of individuals, including sporting figures, are recognized, described, valued, and consecrated.[1]

In the treatment that follows, I will begin with a consideration of the overriding issues in play by briefly identifying a few of the athletes from the pantheon of sports history who have been accorded the status of "hero" and/or have been treated as celebrities, as social life as a whole became transformed by the development of consumer capitalism and the increasing "production and consumption of images" and, in turn, facilitated sport becoming imbued with the values of commerce and a culture of entertainment and spectacle (Lasch, 1979, p. 122). After framing this larger backdrop, the focus will shift to a consideration of the qualities and characteristics associated with the construction of contemporary sports celebrity. This will be followed by a section considering the approaches that have guided inquiry about sporting heroes and celebrities, including "the plight of the fallen sports hero" (Wenner, 2013, p. 9). I will conclude by making the case for genuine heroes in sport being those athletes who have shown they are prepared to risk their popularity by using the public profile, media access, and celebrity that their sporting success has provided to address significant, and often controversial, social and political concerns. Opportunities to speak out and support causes and campaigns may arise from athletes' participation in sporting events themselves or through the multiplicity of diverse media platforms and corporate promotional engagements, which allow athletes to influence events well beyond sport.

ISSUES

 It was in the closing decades of the 19th century, primarily in England and America, that formally constituted and rule-governed modern sports first emerged and, along with growing public and press interest in sports matches and events, began to dramatically transform what it meant to be an athlete or player. In this period the English cricketer W. G. Grace (1848–1915) became very popular. Grace was a brilliant if belligerent "amateur" cricketer who attracted crowds of people on and off the field of play, a late Victorian and Edwardian personality, a character who has been described as "heroic" and also as "sport's first celebrity" (Massie, 2015). Grace was playing in a transitional era, at a time of "great transformation" (Polanyi, 1944/2001), when commercialism and professionalism were beginning to reconfigure a number of sports in England and America. He was also notable for being a pioneer in the promotional game, endorsing "a variety of products for money, some related to cricket, others with no connection at all, such as Coleman's Mustard" (Polley, 1998, p. 122).

 The boxing champion John L. Sullivan (1858–1918) emerged in this same time period to become America's first sporting hero, its first sports "superstar" (Klein, 2013). Sullivan's public profile and reputation benefited from growing sports press coverage of his considerable boxing exhibition tours across America. He reveled in the company of entertainers and show business figures and supplemented his income from fighting with product advertising and his appearing in stage plays. In many respects, it is appropriate to regard Sullivan too as "a transitional figure, a cultural hero who reflected many of the strains and uncertainties of an America in the throes of 'modernization'" (Isenberg, 1994, p. 383).

 By the early 20th century a growing number of sporting figures were receiving increasing attention from the public and the media. The combination of successful competitive endeavors, character attributes, and public personae caused them to be regarded as heroes. In some instances their media visibility and increasing assimilation into the world of entertainment caused them to be treated as celebrities, and in a few cases the unfair treatment and struggles they faced in the course of their sporting careers led them to be associated with political campaigns against social injustices and forms of discrimination. Here one might consider as examples such celebrated American sporting figures of the time as "Babe" Didrikson Zaharias, Jesse Owens, and Jackie Robinson.

Zaharias (1911–1956) was truly an all-rounder who, undeterred by the sexism she faced, excelled at golf, basketball, baseball, and track and field, winning three medals at the 1932 Olympic Games in Los Angeles. Notwithstanding the discrimination that he encountered, Owens (1913–1980), an African American sprinter and long jumper, won four gold medals at the 1936 Olympics, but like 17 other African American Olympians was not, as their Caucasian counterparts were, invited to the White House to be congratulated by President Franklin D. Roosevelt (Smart, 2018). Robinson (1919–1972) also suffered from racial abuse as he broke the color barrier in 1947, becoming the first African American to play Major League Baseball.

The subsequent development of professionalization and commercialization in the course of the 20th century, as well as innovations in communications media, accelerated the transformation of sport and, in turn, the public profile, status, and lives of successful players. In the 21st century the economy and culture of sport are inextricably articulated with the logic of late modern consumer capitalism (Smart, 2007) and fueled by media globalization and marketing (Wenner, 1998, 2015). Commercial and financial matters now intrude into virtually every aspect of elite sport. Sport is firmly embedded in the corporate world. As Jackson (2012, p. 101) observes, sport is "a valuable cultural commodity within the sport/media/promotional cultural context," and successful athletes, with their international profiles and cultural capital, are frequent and prominent players within global consumer capitalism's promotional culture. Athletes routinely employ financial advisors, agents, and media personnel as they seek to pursue their careers, raise their profiles, and prioritize and advance their personal interests on and off the field of play (Giulianotti & Numerato, 2018). In short, as Andrews and Jackson (2001, p. 7) recognize, "the sport celebrity is effectively a multitextual and multi-platform promotional entity." As the articulation of sport with consumer culture has intensified, an increasing number of celebrity athletes with a global profile have been able to "multiply their in-play earnings through commercial work as brand signs and endorsement vehicles" (Giulianotti & Numerato, 2018, p. 234).

Two notable contemporary sporting celebrities who have been beneficiaries of such developments are Swiss tennis player Roger Federer and Brazilian footballer Neymar da Silva Santos Júnior, better known simply as Neymar. In different ways their careers bring to the forefront "the importance of the body and embodied performance to the construction and maintenance of sport celebrityhood" (Andrews, Lopes, & Jackson, 2016, p. 421). The way they play their respective sports exemplifies the distinctive characteristics of their national cultures. In the case of Federer, the qualities he brings to the court, notably physical agility and endurance, mastery and poise, along with "self-control, reserve, inner-discipline and calm . . . have Protestant ethic affinities," reflecting his roots in the "Reformation town of Basel" (Carroll, 2020, p. 289). In a comparable manner, when he plays for club or country, Neymar exhibits "a mastery of the techniques of corporal improvisation" that is associated with an aesthetic style of football expressive of Brazilian identity (Andrews et al., 2016, p. 429).

In their discussion of Neymar's sporting celebrity, Andrews et al. (2016, p, 432) note that his public persona is "articulated according to, and through, neoliberal logics." Neymar is represented, especially in popular media and in marketing discourses generated by the multiplicity of endorsement relationships he is involved in, as embodying such values as individualism, self-interest, and competition. In sum, Neymar is portrayed "as the epitome of neoliberal personhood" (p. 433). The representation of other sports heroes and celebrities in this manner serves to naturalize and normalize neoliberal values and assumptions and embed them in everyday life. In terms of his tennis tournament record (20 Grand Slam singles titles) and standing within his sport, Federer is arguably in a different league than Neymar. However, like Neymar, Federer has a lucrative endorsement portfolio and is represented as the embodiment of neoliberal attributes and values ("#3 Roger Federer," 2020). Federer too is regarded as "more than [a] sporting star and celebrity" (Carroll, 2020, p. 289) and has been credited with "athletic instances of heroism" (Morgan, 2013, p. 25).

On what grounds has Federer been accorded the status "hero"? What is it about his sporting actions that has warranted the description "heroism"? In his observations on Federer's physical and personal qualities, Carroll (2020, pp. 288–289) emphasizes the importance of character and in particular sobriety, composure, application, and humility. For Carroll, sport is not "just about successful performance"; what is central is "the conjunction of vocation, excellence, and character" (p. 290). Federer is described as "more than the exalted king of tennis and lead role model for excellence in his craft, and for good sportsmanship. . . . He is a hero" (p. 289). It is the vocation-like way that Federer plays the game and succeeds, his display of virtues, which leads Carroll to identify him as a hero.

Where Carroll places emphasis on character in considering Federer's status as a sporting hero, Morgan (2013, p. 29) focuses on Federer's embodied performance and actions, on his "heroic movements" on court. Morgan cites a 2006 *New York Times Magazine* article about Federer and, in particular, an account of his 2005 U.S. Open final against Andre Agassi. The article, "Roger Federer as Religious Experience" (Wallace, 2006, para. 1–5), refers to the spectator's uplifting experience of the athletic and aesthetic qualities Federer expresses in his game, the memorable "Federer moments." One such moment of athletic prowess is at the heart of Morgan's view of Federer's heroism. It is a magnificent shot Federer played, an almost impossible forehand, which wins the point and demonstrates each of the features Morgan associates with heroic action, namely decisiveness, response to uncontrolled events, practical intelligence, and that the action is met with enthusiastic acclaim.

Although the focus of Morgan's (2013, p. 28) account is on Federer and his athletic heroism, there is a recognition of the importance of character in his discussion of tennis player Arthur Ashe, the first, and to date only, African American to win the U.S. Open and Wimbledon singles events. In particular, Morgan makes reference to the character Ashe displayed and the heroism he demonstrated off court, working in the inner city with AIDS victims and disadvantaged young people. As Wenner (2013, p. 8) recognizes, "Sports not only build character, they reveal it."

APPROACHES

When giving consideration to the approaches that have been used in the study of heroism and celebrity in sport, it is important to understand what the key terms represent, what they signify. Precisely what is meant when reference is made to heroes in the 21st century? (Kinsella, Ritchie, & Igou, 2015). And most particularly, what is a sporting hero and what does sporting celebrity entail (Rojek, 2001)? The issues involved in thinking about what a hero is today are complex, especially in respect of sport, where the cultural significance attributed to athletes and their performances is vulnerable to media amplification, which may be disproportionate (Wenner, 2013).

The notion of the hero has a long and very complex history. Its genealogical threads can be found in mythical figures of classical antiquity, thematic preoccupations of modern European philosophers such as David Hume and Jean-Jacques Rousseau, Thomas Carlyle's admiration of "great individuals," sociologist Max Weber's identification of those endowed with charismatic qualities, and a multitude of literary and popular cultural fictional figures represented as exemplifying heroic attributes and qualities (Franco, Allison, Kinsella, Kohen, & Langdon, 2018; Whannel, 2002).

In their psychological study of lay conceptions of hero features, designed as a contribution to the refinement of "heroism into a scientific concept," Kinsella et al. (2015, p. 114) reflect on the "sheer variety of heroes." They comment that in the wake of "disasters those who rescue and rebuild communities are considered heroic," and to that they add, in a somewhat disparaging manner, that "[c]elebrities and sports stars are often presented as heroes in the media" (pp. 2–3). Kinsella et al. identify a number of character traits which they find to be central to lay notions of heroism. Their research revealed that heroes are considered brave, moral, courageous, protective, dedicated, honest, altruistic, selfless, determined, lifesavers, inspiring, and helpful. For them, heroes are "individuals who choose to take physical risks," qualities which signify forms of "social heroism . . . heroic action in the service of ideals."(pp. 2–3). Some of these qualities, but not by any means all, may in some measure be displayed by athletes in the course of their careers (Franco et al., 2018, p. 387).

Two categories of hero are distinguished by Zimbardo (2009) in his critical reflections on the psychological dynamics of the Stanford Prison Experiment. First are those exceptional individuals, "a special breed," who rebel, resist, or oppose powerful forces, engage in "daring deeds," and "organize their lives around a humanitarian cause" (p xiii). Second, in contrast, are the more ordinary heroes, who are "heroes of the moment, of the situation, who act decisively when the call to service is sounded" (p. xiii). In total, Zimbardo goes so far as to identify 12 types of hero, including civil, scientific, religious, political, and military figures, martyrs, adventurers, and whistleblowers, but significantly no reference is made to sporting figures. Is there any respect in which the designation "hero" would be apposite for athletes? Might the expression "heroes *of* the moment" capture the temporal, event- and performance-based respects in which the accolade is often ascribed to athletes, as well as the frequency with which sporting heroes are made in and through media representations? Or would "heroes *for* the moment" be a more appropriate expression?

In his social and cultural analysis of mediated sport Whannel (2002, p. 41) outlines the complex history of the term "hero" and reminds readers that the heroic has been "problematised" in various ways. He argues that with the increasing prominence of media communications and images in the modern world it is "stars" rather than heroes that sport now produces. In many respects, "celebrity" represents a more appropriate description of high-profile successful sporting figures than the media-manufactured designation "hero." Being famous was once associated with exceptional achievements or great deeds, but increasing media coverage of sport has led to many sporting figures being known and celebrated merely for being well-known household names, marketable faces, and "brands." The media can construct influential narratives and images that make individuals well known and popular, they "can make a celebrity," but as Boorstin (1963, p. 58) argues, those so represented, those "mass produced to satisfy the market," are not heroes.

Lasch (1991), noting the commercial and media transformations of sport into spectacle and entertainment, offers important critical observations on the sporting hero-celebrity nexus. In a manner that bears close comparison with Boorstin's analysis, Lasch (1991, pp. 118–119) argues that it is "difficult to think of the athlete as a local or national hero," for athletes and players are now professional entertainers pursuing their personal interests, generally concerned with maximizing their financial rewards, and an increasing number of them "become media celebrities and supplement their salaries with endorsements that often exceed the salaries themselves." Increasingly exposed to and transformed by an "entertainment ethic" that routinely informs its media coverage, sport, in Lasch's view, has been subjected to degradation, as its rituals and dramas are reduced to and rendered as "spectacle" (p. 122).

Indeed, there are many examples of the ways sport and sporting figures have embraced the values and rituals of entertainment. These include athletes striking theatrical poses, as was the case with sprinter Usain Bolt's "To Di World" pose and long-distance runner Mo Farah's "Mobot pose" (Kessell, 2012). Today it is not surprising that sporting figures increasingly celebrate successes in choreographed fashion. In doing so they effectively display themselves as self-conscious "entertainers" or "stars," cognizant that they are "performing" in a mediated cultural environment, where they need to play to both local and global audiences, who not only spectate at live events but may engage with others about these performances on digital and social media platforms. As well, long standing in this environment, celebrated sporting figures are routinely featured in explicitly entertainment-orientated contexts, for example on television panels and chat and reality shows, where celebrity status is a prerequisite for invitation and is, in turn, reaffirmed and amplified by performance in such settings.

With the commercialization of sport and the increase in endorsement and sponsorship opportunities for high-profile star athletes, marketable "image" has been imbued with significant financial value. As a consequence, legally protected rights were established in the form of image rights in the United Kingdom, personality rights in the European Union, and publicity rights in the United States (Blackshaw, 2019). In some instances, successful high-profile players have progressed beyond being merely marketable products to become celebrity brands. Good examples here include former NBA icon Michael Jordan, former England international association footballer David Beckham, golfer Tiger Woods, and tennis players Venus Williams ("the most marketable female athlete in the US") and Serena Williams ("the highest earning women's athlete of all-time in all sports . . . [whose] sponsors [include] Nike, Wilson, Gatorade and OPI Products") (Neilsen Sports, 2014, pp. 23, 25; see also Smart, 2005). Nurtured by cultural intermediaries in the promotional and publicity fields of advertising and public relations, sports celebrities have become increasingly reliant upon agents and specialist media advisors, who help "shape and protect their clients' images" (Ruxin, 2010, p. 15).

In considering the rise of the sport star, important parallels can be drawn between the cultural function of celebrity and religion. Many of the qualities attributed to contemporary celebrities are considered by Rojek (2012) to bear a striking similarity to those ascribed to religious figures. Insofar as the commodified appeal of celebrities is articulated with a performance culture that promotes and excites worship and ecstasy, Rojek argues that "religiosity permeates the production, exchange and consumption of celebrity culture" (p. 121). The parallels that Rojek identifies are endorsed by Verner Møller (2017, p. 55), who notes that narratives about sporting celebrities frequently invoke religious ideas and concepts. Such tendencies are evident, for example, when the Portuguese international association footballer Cristiano Ronaldo is described as having "God-given talent" or the return of England international association footballer Robbie Fowler to the Liverpool Football Club in 2006 is popularly referred to as "the Second Coming." Møller (2017, p, 55) provides a further striking example of the extent of sport-religion affinities:

> the foundation of the Iglesia Maradoniana, a church founded . . . to worship arguably the world's best ever football player Diego Maradona. . . . Maradona is probably the only sport star who has become so directly sanctified, but many athletes have been idolised as demigods by their fans.

A significant characteristic of sport stars, or idols as Møller (2017) also refers to them, is the charismatic effect they have on us. The charismatic effect, or impression made on people, is "a situational experience . . . between the person (*who in situ appears charismatic*) and the role he enacts in front of a receptive listener or audience" (p. 58, emphasis added). Møller contends that sport provides an appropriately appealing social form in which people may confidently place their trust and that they can relate to and identify with athletes whose reputations and statuses are associated with authentic achievements in competitive events and matches.

Sporting figures derive authenticity from the public performative character and quality of their play, "the seeming visceral, dramatic immediacy of . . . [their] sport practice" (Andrews & Jackson, 2001, p. 8). As Carroll (2020, p. 288) observes, "sport provides a very public stage on which to observe and judge character performing under extreme pressure." It is athletes' demonstration of sublime skill and flair, "gifts of the body and spirit . . . not accessible to everybody," and their ability to "perform miracles" that produces the effect of "charisma" (Weber, 1970, pp. 245, 249). Consider the following three examples.

Olympic and World Championship gold medal–winning sprinter Usain Bolt, who at the Rio Olympics smiled at the camera while winning the 100-meters semifinal (Sweney, 2016) and joked with a fellow competitor 30 meters from the finishing line in the process of winning his 200-meters semifinal event (Lovett, 2016).

Manchester United footballer Eric Cantona's incomparable style, appearance, and striking performances on the field of play: "he had an aura about him . . . he oozed charisma and genius in equal measure" (UEFA, 2019).

The greatest and most charismatic of sporting figures, World Heavyweight Boxing Champion Muhammad Ali, who would acknowledge ringside commentators and encourage crowd chants in the course of title fights, most memorably encouraging the "Ali boma ye" chant when he fought George Foreman in Kinshasa, Zaire (Mailer, 1975, pp. 187, 198, 202; Nack, 2007).

As I have argued elsewhere, this charisma effect is vulnerable. It is always at risk and has to be continually reaffirmed by the *genuine* quality of exceptional sporting performances, demonstrated over and over again in competition, and can be tarnished by doubts and suspicions about achievements. When exceptional performances are revealed as being fueled by performance-enhancing drugs or helped by unethical play, authenticity is destroyed and charisma along with it (Smart, 2005, cf. pp. 30–31, 195–196).

While our spirits might be lifted by outstanding play by sporting heroes, we are, as Morgan (2013, p. 24) observes, "just as often morally troubled by heroes who fail us." The history of sport reveals a catalogue of fallen heroes (Wenner, 2013). Sporting figures are not always honest competitors, as the match-fixing scandals in Major League Baseball (1919), British football (1964), and test cricket (India vs. South Africa 1999–2000) confirm (Huggins, 2018; Paulden, 2016). Alongside the long history of match-fixing in sport there is the no less significant matter of the use of performance-enhancing drugs (Rosen, 2008). There are numerous examples. Sprinter Ben Johnson was found to have used an illegal steroid drug, stanozolol, when he "won" the 100-meter race at the 1988 Seoul Summer Olympic Games. Cricketer Shoaib Akhtar was found guilty in 2006 of using the steroid nandrolone, and tennis player Maria Sharapova failed a drug test at the Australian Open in 2016. The most noteworthy example concerns the American cyclist Lance Armstrong. In 2012 he was found by the United States Anti-Doping Agency to have engaged in doping and was stripped of his seven Tour de France titles (Macur, 2012). After years of denial Armstrong finally admitted, in a television interview with Oprah Winfrey, that he had used performance-enhancing drugs when winning his seven titles (Carroll, 2013). Such sporting moments serve as a reminder of the importance of authenticity and ethical integrity in sport.

Sport history is "littered with scandal," and each instance of a sporting hero falling from grace tarnishes the reputation of the individual involved and risks damaging their sport (Wenner, 2013, p. 3). In turn, the associated media-orchestrated "morality plays" may call into question the authenticity of other sports performances (p. 4). Without doubt, media reporting has played a pivotal role in the making and unmaking of sporting heroes and will continue to do so. In addition, character is particularly important, as the contributions of the sporting heroes considered below demonstrate.

DEBATES

Outstanding sporting performances and achievements, amplified by media visibility and the enhanced public profiles that this brings, have commonly led successful sporting figures to be accorded star status. Such media treatment brings celebrity status, and athletes become attractive and financially well-rewarded endorsement vehicles for the promotion of local and global brand identities through product marketing campaigns. The close articulation of sport with entertainment media and business, with what one analyst has termed "Sportsbiz" (Aris, 1990, p. xi), makes the designation of successful, high-profile athletes as stars and/or celebrities seem appropriate and uncontroversial. However, the anointing of individual athletes as heroes for outstanding performances and achievements, in a sense for doing what it is they have trained and practiced for, and are exceptionally well rewarded for, on and off the field of play, is open to contestation (Morgan, 2013). Athletes may display dedication and determination in games, at times be a source of inspiration, and be physically committed and engaged, even perhaps at times taking risks in the course of competitive action, but do their endeavors genuinely qualify as "heroism," as conduct upholding ideals or a humanitarian cause (Franco et al., 2018; Zimbardo, 2009)?

If a veridical notion of heroism is rarely, if ever, appropriate for describing what takes place in sports competition, are there any other sport-related respects in which it might be appropriate to designate sporting figures as heroes? Are there any respects in which sporting figures meet Zimbardo's (2009) criteria for true heroism, perhaps through rebellion or opposition to powerful forces, exceptional conduct in support of a humanitarian cause, or by decisive action in support of others? As well as furnishing athletes with a public profile as stars and celebrities, the combination of sporting success and media amplification has made it possible for outstanding performers to demonstrate their character by using platforms that their sporting prowess delivers to take stands on important social and political issues. Today, there are increasing opportunities for athletes to have a public voice for particular causes and campaigns. There are more moments where they may emulate Muhammed Ali's 1967 refusal to be drafted into the U.S. military during the Vietnam War, telling reporters, "I ain't got no quarrel with them Vietcong" (quoted in Remnick, 2000, p. 287). Rare moments, such as when African American athletes Tommie Smith and John Carlos protested against U.S. racism and injustice against African Americans by raising black gloved fists in a "Black Power salute" at the 1968 Olympic Games, have become more commonplace (Boykoff, 2016).

Here, there are a number of comparable contemporary examples that warrant consideration. In 2016, for the final preseason and 16 regular season games, Colin Kaepernick, a National Football League quarterback, refused to stand and later knelt, "taking a knee," during the playing of the U.S. national anthem before games "as a protest against social injustice, especially the deaths of African-Americans at the hands of police" in the United States (Branch, 2017). Speaking after a game Kaepernick commented:

> I am not going to stand up to show pride in a flag for a country that oppresses black people and people of color. . . . To me, this is bigger than football, and it would be selfish on my part to look the other way. There are bodies in the street and people . . . getting away with murder. (quoted in Branch, 2017, para. 64)

In 2017, Kaepernick opted out of his contract with the San Francisco 49ers and became a free agent. He would not compromise his views or commit to end his kneeling protests during the playing of the national anthem before matches, and in consequence owners would not sign him. Unsigned and effectively blackballed because of his political views, he was not able to get back into the game and later filed a grievance procedure against the NFL's team owners, finally reaching a settlement in early 2019 (Graham, 2019).

The NFL has a very significant place within American culture. With every game it reaffirms a specific set of values. As summarized in an essay by Baltimore Ravens head coach John Harbaugh (2015, para. 6), "Football is hard. It's tough. It demands discipline. It teaches obedience. It builds character. Football is a metaphor for life." Kaepernick's conduct certainly demonstrated strength of character and self-discipline. However, it did not show sufficient obedience to the values of a system that has continued to oppress African Americans and other people of color. As a result, his protest prompted the expression of very significant differences of opinion, reflecting disagreements over inequalities and injustices in society (and where it might be appropriate to hear them), and confirming, in a wider sense than Harbaugh had in mind, that football may well be a metaphor for life. For example, while U.S. President Donald Trump described kneeling during the national anthem as "a total disrespect of our heritage" (BBC, 2018), *Mother Jones* described Kaepernick as a hero, "a good and righteous man," for protesting against police brutality and racial oppression (Endicott, 2019). Showing the complexities at play, premier sports marketer Nike creatively appropriated cultural capital from the protests and responses to Kaepernick's actions by building a controversial and financially very successful politically tinged marketing campaign. The Nike "Dream Crazy" campaign, with the slogan "Believe in something. Even if it means sacrificing everything," delivered record engagement with the brand and boosted product sales, along with the former quarterback's emerging status as an unconventional sporting hero (Abad-Santos, 2018; Yip, 2018).

A closely related example of a player demonstrating their character and using their public profile in a politically progressive manner is provided by U.S. Women's national football (soccer) team (USWNT) co-captain Megan Rapinoe, a leading sporting figure who has publicly supported LGBTQ and minority rights. Rapinoe, who has consistently campaigned against racism and homophobia, took a knee in solidarity with Kaepernick's protest before a match against the Chicago Red Stars in 2016. She stated that it was her "patriotic duty . . . [to] be a support and an ally to Kaepernick, bringing attention to the issues that he was talking about" (BBC, 2017, para. 2; Marks, 2019). In interviews on CNN and in the magazine *Eight by Eight* in 2019, Rapinoe was asked about the prospect, after the Women's World Cup in France, of the team being invited to the White House to meet President Trump. Here she made very clear that she would not be going and that every team member she had asked shared her view (Hirshey, 2019). In the interview on CNN's *Anderson Cooper 360°* program on July 9 Rapinoe explained why:

> I don't think anyone on the team has any interest in lending the platform that we have worked so hard to build, the things that we fight for and the way that we live our life—I don't think that we want that to be co-opted or corrupted by this administration.

In answer to the question "What is your message to the president?," Rapinoe replied:

> I think that I would say that your message is excluding people, you're excluding me, you're excluding people that look like me, you're excluding people of color you're excluding, you know, Americans that maybe support you. I think that we need to have a reckoning with the message that you have and what you are saying about "Make America Great Again"—I think that you are harking back to an era that was not great for everyone. It might have been great for a few people and maybe America's great for a few people right now but it's not great for enough Americans in this world and I think that we have a responsibility, each and every one of us. You have an incredible responsibility as, you know, the chief of this country, to take care of every single person and you need to do better for everyone. (CNN, 2019)

After the team won the Women's World Cup tournament in France, the USWNT received a private invitation from the White House to visit. This led Rapinoe to reiterate her views and encourage teammates to take a similar stand (Kelly, 2019; West, 2019). The invitation was declined.

Rapinoe has subsequently been portrayed as "a new-age American hero" (Fishwick, 2019), "America's newest hero" (Brady, 2019), and has been described by *Mother Jones* as one of their heroes for the 2010s (Liss-Schultz, 2019). In September 2019 she won FIFA's "Player of the Year" award, in December the Ballon d'Or as the "World's Best Player," and was also named *Sports Illustrated* "Sportsperson of the Year." Nike (2019), in recognition of Rapinoe's cultural capital, created a pair of Mercurial commemorative boots, "one-of-a-kind boots for a one-of-a-kind player . . . not to be sold at retail." In her acceptance speech at FIFA's The Best awards ceremony, Rapinoe demonstrated once more why she has been described as a heroic figure. She used the platform that her sporting success had provided to speak out against sexism, racism, and homophobia. Notably, she focused on the death of an Iranian woman, Sahar Khodayari, who, rather than face six months in prison for trying to enter a football stadium to watch a match, set herself on fire outside the courtroom and later died. In accepting her award, Rapinoe also expressed support for LGBTQ players, as well as for the campaigns against racism by footballers Raheem Sterling and Kalidou Koulibaly and the struggle for equal pay in the game (Guardian Sport, 2019).

As these cases vividly illustrate, Kaepernick and Rapinoe demonstrated key attributes of heroism, including bravery, moral courage, dedication, determination, and selflessness. They engaged in courses of action "in the service of ideals" (Franco et al., 2018, p. 387), showed themselves to be exceptional individuals, were prepared to rebel and take on powerful forces, demonstrated the ability to act decisively and "organize their lives around a humanitarian cause" (Zimbardo, 2009, p. xiii). In short, they utilized the platforms their sporting profiles provided and demonstrated heroism.

Another related and comparable example of a player using their sporting reputation and profile to pursue a cause is worth considering here. As Rapinoe acknowledged in her FIFA award acceptance comments, Manchester City and England association footballer Raheem Sterling has confronted and overcome negative and offensive tabloid media reports and has consistently spoken out about racism. On Instagram, Sterling posted comments about differences in the media reporting of Black and white players and has fronted the Premier League's "No Room for Racism" campaign (Mance, 2019). As with Kaepernick, and in a different way Rapinoe, a 2018 Nike advertising promotion recognized the cultural capital value of Sterling's stance against racism and made him the face of its new marketing campaign, with his comment "Speaking up doesn't always make life easier. But easy never changed anything" as its key pitch.

Sterling was also selected to front a Gillette advertising campaign which focused on toxic masculinity in sport. The campaign advertisement "Made of what matters" features Sterling commenting:

> If someone asks you what you're made of don't just tell them, show them . . . and show them whatever our rivalries, whatever our differences, we stand shoulder to shoulder against all forms of prejudice so it's got no place to grow, because when we show our best side we don't just play the game, we change it. (Gillette UK, 2020)

The actions of Kaepernick, Rapinoe, and Sterling illustrate how a prominent public sporting profile can provide a platform for effective creative campaigning against prejudice and discrimination. Indeed, some corporations are recognizing the value of integrity and aligning themselves with political struggles against injustices. The Nike campaigns fronted by Kaepernick and Sterling, and Nike's celebration of Rapinoe and all that she represents, lend support to Møller's (2017, p. 52) judgment that, notwithstanding problems and difficulties that might arise in the course of athletic careers, "as long as they are committed to what they do . . . and their performances transcend the capabilities of ordinary people," sporting figures can continue to have an emotional effect and impact on us and "maintain their appeal and marketing value."

CONCLUSION

Does it matter whether high-profile sporting figures, in the public eye as a consequence of outstanding playing success and associated media representations, are described as heroes? Athletes and players who have a record of successful performance and achievement frequently are identified as stars in their sporting fields, increasingly assimilated into the world of entertainment, treated as celebrities, and described as icons or legends in media reports. Media hyperbole and amplification elevate many sporting figures to heroes *of* the moment or heroes *for* the moment. However, there are other sporting figures who use the public platform and profile their sporting successes have provided to engage in significant progressive campaigns and political struggles. While the actions of Kaepernick, Rapinoe, and Sterling are relatively exceptional, they do genuinely represent some of the features associated with heroism and heroic actions.[2] Perhaps the best response to the question "What is it to be a modern-day sporting hero?" is that the answer lies beyond sport. Heroism resides in the actions sporting figures engage in as citizens, in using their voices, their reputations, and their profiles to draw attention to discrimination and prejudice, inequalities and injustices in social and political life.

The significance of Kaepernick's 2016 protest against systemic racism, oppression, social injustice, and the deaths of African Americans at the hands of the police has become more apparent over time. Nowhere has this been more evident than in the protests following the death in 2020 of a 46-year-old African American, George Floyd, who died after a white police officer knelt on his neck for 8 minutes and 46 seconds while three other officers looked on. The subsequent expressions of outrage and anger led to demonstrations and support for the Black Lives Matter movement in the United States, including notable support by some U.S. National Guard troops and police, who had been called out to control crowds in American cities, taking the knee in support of demonstrators across the nation. The need for change had become so evident that NFL commissioner Roger Goodell reversed his long-standing stance, acknowledging the NFL had been wrong to ban players taking the knee. Drew Brees, a white star New Orleans Saints quarterback, reversed his opposition to players protesting against systemic racial injustice by taking the knee. Beyond sports, some Democratic representatives in the U.S. Congress knelt at the Capitol in Washington to honor George Floyd. Across the world, there have been comparable demonstrations and expressions of support, with Bundesliga and Premier League footballers taking the knee in training and before matches and crowds of demonstrators in cities (e.g. London, Madrid, Rome) doing likewise. As a journalist in the United Kingdom reported, taking the knee "has become an international symbol of opposition to racism" (Sherwood, 2020, para. 7).

The media will continue to eulogize the athletic and playing achievements of sporting figures and persist in describing their feats as "heroic," but such designations ring increasingly hollow in the context of a world made precarious by unaddressed social injustices and inequalities, a viral pandemic, and a climate emergency. It is those sporting figures who are deploying their cultural capital to give voice to such concerns, campaigning to positively transform the lives of citizens around the world, who may truly warrant the designation "hero."

Notes

1. In 2020, as countries around the world confronted a pandemic, COVID-19, and medical, health, and care workers everywhere displayed dedication, bravery, and a willingness to put their lives on the line every day, week in and week out for months, the very idea of designating contemporary sporting figures as "heroes" for their play, their performances and successes in matches and events, for which they are richly rewarded with lucrative club contracts, prize money, sponsorship, and endorsement contracts, seemed at the very least highly inappropriate and insensitive, if not offensive. As Pope Francis stated in his Palm Sunday Mass on April 5, 2020, "[T]he real heroes . . . are not famous, rich and successful people; rather they are those who are giving themselves in order to serve others" (quoted in Pepper, 2020).

2. Another comparable sporting figure who warrants inclusion in this context is Marcus Rashford, the Manchester United and England association footballer. In the 2020 Covid-19 lockdown, with schools closed, Rashford used his sporting profile and celebrity status to help raise funds for struggling families and campaigned for the UK Conservative government to extend its food voucher scheme for children eligible for free school meals. When the government cancelled the scheme over the summer holidays Rashford wrote an open letter to the government and succeeded in getting the scheme restored. Rashford made tackling food poverty in Britain a prominent issue and his partnership with the food distribution charity FairShare reportedly raised over £20 million. Later in 2020 he was awarded an MBE (Member of the Order of the British Empire) in recognition of his campaigning work and fund raising for vulnerable children in the UK during the pandemic (Olusoga & Olusoga, 2020).

References

Abad-Santos, A. (2018, September 24). Nike's Colin Kaepernick ad sparked a boycott—and earned $6 billion for Nike. *Vox.* https://www.vox.com/2018/9/24/17895704/nike-colin-kae pernick-boycott-6-billion.

Andrews, D. L., & Jackson, S. J. (2001). Introduction: Sport celebrities, public culture and private experience. In S. J. Jackson & D. L. Andrews (Eds.), *Sport stars: The cultural politics of sporting celebrity* (pp. 1–19). London: Routledge.

Andrews, D. L., Lopes, V. B., & Jackson, S. J. (2016). Neymar: Sport celebrity and performative cultural politics. In P. D. Marshall & S. Redmond (Eds.), *A companion to celebrity* (pp. 421–439). Chichester, U.K.: John Wiley & Sons.

Aris, S. (1990). *Sportsbiz: Inside the sports business.* London: Hutchinson.

BBC. (2017, September 29). Trump NFL row: Megan Rapinoe on why she backed Colin Kaepernick. https://www.bbc.co.uk/sport/football/41440504.

BBC. (2018, May 24). Trump: NFL kneelers "maybe shouldn't be in country." https://www.bbc. co.uk/news/world-us-canada-44232979.

Blackshaw I. (2019) Understanding sports image rights. *WIPO World Intellectual Property Organization.* https://www.wipo.int/ip-outreach/en/ipday/2019/understanding_sports_image_rights.html.

Boorstin, D. J. (1963). *The image, or what happened to the American dream.* Harmondsworth, U.K.: Penguin.

Boykoff, J. (2016). *Power games: A political history of the Olympics.* London: Verso.

Brady, M. (2019, July 14). Megan Rapinoe: Why is America's newest hero so polarising? *BBC.* https://www.bbc.co.uk/news/world-us-canada-48969342.

Branch, J. (2017, September 7). The awakening of Colin Kaepernick. *New York Times.* https://www.nytimes.com/2017/09/07/sports/colin-kaepernick-nfl-protests.html.

Carroll, J. (2020). Is the vocation paradigm under threat? *Journal of Sociology, 56*(3), 282–296. https://journals.sagepub.com/doi/abs/10.1177/1440783320905667#.

Carroll, R. (2013, January 18). Lance Armstrong admits doping in Oprah Winfrey interview. *The Guardian.* https://www.theguardian.com/sport/2013/jan/18/lance-armstrong-admits-doping-oprah-winfrey.

CNN. (2019, July 9). Rapinoe's message to Trump: You need to do better for everyone. *YouTube.* https://www.youtube.com/watch?v=8X5ixs8Nsdo.

Endicott, M. (2019, December 30). Heroes of the 2010s: Colin Kaepernick. *Mother Jones.* https://www.motherjones.com/politics/2019/12/heroes-of-the-2010s-colin-kaepernick/.

Fishwick, S. (2019, July 2). How Megan Rapinoe became a new-age American hero. *Evening Standard.* https://www.standard.co.uk/lifestyle/london-life/who-is-megan-rapinoe-usa-football-a4180281.html.

Franco, Z. E., Allison, S. T., Kinsella, E. L., Kohen, A., & Langdon, M. (2018). Heroism research: A review of theories, methods, challenges and trends. *Journal of Humanistic Psychology, 58*(4), 382–396.

Graham, B. A. (2019, February 15). Colin Kaepernick reaches settlement with NFL over kneeling protest fallout. *The Guardian.* https://www.theguardian.com/sport/2019/feb/15/colin-kaepernick-reaches-settlement-with-nfl-over-kneeling-protest-fallout.

Gillette UK. (2020, February 6). Gillette: Raheem Sterling made of what matters. *YouTube.* https://www.youtube.com/watch?v=GnaChQh5Slo.

Giulianotti, R., & Numerato, D. (2018). Global sport and consumer culture: An introduction. *Journal of Consumer Culture, 18*(2), 229–240.

Guardian Sport. (2019, September 23). Megan Rapinoe speaks out against racism and homophobia in FIFA speech. *The Guardian.* https://www.theguardian.com/football/2019/sep/23/megan-rapinoe-fifa-best-awards-football-speech.

Harbaugh, J. (2015, April 22). Why football matters. *Home Teams Online.* https://www.hometeamsonline.com/teams/Default.asp?u=GHHS&s=football&p=custom&pagename=Why+football+matters+by+John+Harbaugh.

Hirshey, D. (2019). Megan Rapinoe: The visionary. *Eight by Eight.* https://www.8by8mag.com/megan-rapinoe-visionary/.

Holt, R., & Mangan, J. A. (Eds.). (1996). *European heroes: Myth, identity, sport.* London: Frank Cass.

Huggins, M. (2018). Match-fixing: A historical perspective. *International Journal of the History of Sport, 35*(2–3), 123–140.

Isenberg, M. T. (1994). *John L. Sullivan and his America.* Chicago: University of Illinois Press.

Jackson, S. J. (2012). Reflections on communications and sport: On advertising and promotional culture. *Communication & Sport 1*(1–2), 100–112.

Kelly, C. (2019, July 10). Megan Rapinoe to Trump: "Your message is excluding people." *CNN Politics.*   https://edition.cnn.com/2019/07/09/politics/megan-rapinoe-anderson-cooper-trump-cnntv/index.html.

Kessell A. (2012, August 12). London 2012: Mo Farah honoured by Usain Bolt "Mobot" tribute. *The Guardian.* https://www.theguardian.com/sport/2012/aug/12/london-2012-mo-farah-usain-bolt-tribute.

Kinsella, E. L., Ritchie, T. D., & Igou, E. R. (2015). Zeroing in on heroes: A prototype analysis of hero features. *Journal of Personality and Social Psychology, 108*(1), 114–127.

Klein, C. (2013). *Strong boy: The life and times of John L. Sullivan, America's first sports hero.* Guilford, CT: Lyons Press.

Lasch, C. (1991). *The culture of narcissism: American life in an age of diminishing expectations.* London: W. W. Norton.

Liss-Schultz, N. (2019, December 31). Heroes of the 2010s: Megan Rapinoe. *Mother Jones.* https://www.motherjones.com/media/2019/12/heroes-of-the-2010s-megan-rapinoe/.

Lovett, S. (2016, August 18). Rio 2016: Usain Bolt laughs his way to 200m final as he jokes with Andre de Grasse 30m from the finish line. *The Independent.* https://www.independent.co.uk/sport/olympics/rio-2016-usain-bolt-laughs-his-way-to-200m-final-as-he-jokes-with-andre-de-grasse-30m-before-the-a7197221.html.

Macur, J. (2012, October 22). Lance Armstrong is stripped of his 7 Tour de France titles. *New York Times.* https://www.nytimes.com/2012/10/23/sports/cycling/armstrong-stripped-of-his-7-tour-de-france-titles.html.

Mailer, N. (1975). *The Fight.* London: Penguin.

Mance, H. (2019, May 30). Raheem Sterling: The England football star who took on the racists. *Financial Times.* https://www.ft.com/content/4822b158-819c-11e9-9935-ad75bb96c849.

Marks, A. (2019, June 26). Why US Soccer's Megan Rapinoe is the hero we need now. *Rolling Stone.*   https://www.rollingstone.com/culture/culture-news/megan-rapinoe-us-womens-soccer-donald-trump-852589/.

Massie, A. (2015, October 10). Sport's first celebrity: W. G. Grace. *The Spectator.* https://www.spectator.co.uk/2015/10/sports-first-celebrity-w-g-grace/.

Møller, V. (2017). Sport, religion, and charisma. *Sport, Ethics and Philosophy, 11*(1), 52–62.

Morgan, W. J. (2013). Athletic heroic acts and living on the moral edge. In L. A. Wenner (Ed.), *Fallen sports heroes, media and celebrity culture* (pp. 24–35). New York: Peter Lang.

Nack, W. (2007, December 28). Ali was simply "The Greatest." *ESPN.* https://www.espn.com/sports/boxing/ali/news/story?id=3171301.

Nielsen Sports. (2014). Women and sport: Insights into the growing rise and importance of female fans and female athletes. http://nielsensports.com/wp-content/uploads/2014/09/Women-and-Sport-Repucom.pdf.

Nike. (2019, December 2). Commemorative boots for Megan Rapinoe. *Nike News.* https://news.nike.com/footwear/rapinoe.

Olusoga, D. & Olusoga, P. (2020, December 22). What Marcus Rashford's campaign for hungry children tells us about the footballer – and Britain. The Guardian. https://www.theguardian.com/lifeandstyle/2020/dec/22/what-marcus-rashfords-campaign-for-hungry-children-tells-us-about-the-footballer-and-britain.

Paulden, T. (2016, June 6). Smashing the racket. *Significance.* https://rss.onlinelibrary.wiley.com/doi/10.1111/j.1740-9713.2016.00914.x.

Pepper, D. (2020, April 9). Let's remember the pope's call to honour the heroes of this pandemic. *The Tablet*. https://www.thetablet.co.uk/blogs/1/1401/let-s-remember-the-pope-s-call-to-honour-the-heroes-of-this-pandemic.

Polanyi, K. (1944/2001). *The great transformation: The political and economic origins of our time*. Boston: Beacon Press.

Polley, M. (1998). *Moving the goalposts: A history of sport and society since 1945*. London: Routledge.

Remnick, D. (2000). *King of the world: Muhammad Ali and the rise of an American hero*. London: Picador.

#3 Roger Federer. (2020, April 6). *Forbes*. https://www.forbes.com/profile/roger-federer/.

Rojek, C. (2001). *Celebrity*. London: Reaktion Books

Rojek, C. (2012). *Fame attack: The inflation of celebrity and its consequences*. London: Bloomsbury.

Rosen, D. M. (2008). *Dope: A history of performance enhancement in sports from the nineteenth century to today*. London: Praeger.

Ruxin, R. H. (2010). *An athletes' guide to agents*. London: Jones and Bartlett.

Sherwood, H. (2020, June 6). NFL's decision to permit players' anti-racist kneeling protest enrages Trump. *The Guardian*. https://www.theguardian.com/us-news/2020/jun/06/nfl-decision-to-permit-kneeling-protest-by-players-enrages-donald-trump.

Smart, B. (2005). *The sport star: Modern sport and the cultural economy of sporting celebrity*. London: Sage.

Smart, B. (2007). Not playing around: Global capitalism, modern sport and consumer culture. *Global Networks, 7*(2), 113–134.

Smart, B. (2013). Global sporting icons: Consuming signs of economic and cultural transformation. In D. L. Andrews & B. Carrington (Eds.), *Blackwell companion to sport* (pp. 513–531). Wiley-Blackwell.

Smart, B. (2018). Consuming Olympism: Consumer culture, sport star sponsorship and the commercialization of the Olympics. *Journal of Consumer Culture, 18*(2), 241–260.

Sweney, M. (2016, August 27). The defining image of Rio 2016 was Usain Bolt smiling at the camera. *The Guardian*. https://www.theguardian.com/media/2016/aug/27/rio-2016-usain-bolt-getty-images-dawn-airey-bbc.

UEFA. (2019, August 27). All hail King Eric: An inspiration on and off the pitch, https://www.uefa.com/uefachampionsleague/news/0254-0e99d91e4113-8022b8fa9961-1000--all-hail-king-eric-an-inspiration-on-and-off-the-pitch/.

Wallace, D. F. (2006, August 20). Roger Federer as religious experience. *New York Times Magazine*. https://www.nytimes.com/2006/08/20/sports/playmagazine/20federer.html.

Whannel, G. (2002). *Media sport stars: Masculinities and moralities*. London: Routledge.

Weber, M. (1970). *From Max Weber: Essays in sociology* (H. H. Gerth & C. Wright Mills, Eds.). London: Routledge.

Wenner L. A. (1998). Playing the mediasport game. In L. A. Wenner (Ed.), *MediaSport* (pp. 3–13). London: Routledge.

Wenner L. A. (2013). The fallen sports hero in the age of mediated celebrityhood. In L. A. Wenner (Ed.), *Fallen sports heroes, media and celebrity culture* (pp. 3–16). New York: Peter Lang.

West, J. (2019, December 9). USWNT received private invite from White House to visit after World Cup. *Sports Illustrated*. https://www.8by8mag.com/megan-rapinoe-visionary/.

Yip, T. (2018, September 14). Colin Kaepernick: Hero or villain? *Psychology Today*. https://www.psychologytoday.com/gb/blog/stumbling-towards-diversity/201809/colin-kaepernick-hero-or-villain.

Zimbardo, P. (2009). *The Lucifer effect: How good people turn evil*. London: Rider.

CHAPTER 50

SPORT, SPECTATORSHIP, AND FANDOM

KEVIN DIXON

THE late 19th century signified a golden age in the inauguration of professional sports with a growing proportion of athletes prepared to take their place as sport professionals who look to exchange sporting ability for cold hard cash. The inauguration of this nascent practice led to another. As Wray Vamplew reminds readers of his 1988 book, *Pay Up and Play the Game*, it soon became apparent that far more people were interested in spectating as opposed to competing in sport, and this disposition has remained strong across time. As the number of professional sports have increased, so has the spread of sport spectators, or "sports fans" as they are otherwise known. In fact, according to the *World Sport Encyclopaedia* there are over 8,000 indigenous sports and games, and each has a dedicated fan base (Liponski, 2003).

The term "fan" as it is used in this chapter is derived from the word "fanatic," emphasizing a certain devotion to a specific object of interest. When directly related to sport, fandom is paradoxically considered to be both a form of serious leisure and a frivolous popular pastime. It has been considered frivolous inasmuch as the unbridled enjoyment, carnivalesque atmosphere (both created and consumed by fans), and the embracing of lusory and sometimes nonsensical logic clearly distinguish sports fandom from more serious endeavors. Conversely, however, as those of us who have experienced sport fandom cultures know, being a sports fan can be extremely serious. Let us take one moment to ask, why?

Certainly, sport results are important to fans, but we should remember that fandom goes deeper than this. It can mean more than following the fortunes of a sport, individual, or team. It is bound up with our identity and desire for belonging. It speaks to our love of space, our sense of rivalries, character, and masculinities. It traverses issues such as globalization, media production and consumption, neoliberalism, commercialization, and consumerism. So, while it may, at first glance, appear to be an insignificant but pleasurable pastime, it is important to remember that fandom contributes to understandings and sensibilities about our societies, ourselves, and others in multiple ways and to varying degrees. So much so, in fact, that academics have studied the various facets related to this phenomenon for over 40 years.

Contributions from scholars across diverse disciplines demonstrate the importance of sports fandom and highlight its breadth of impact on the lives of the general populace, not only on those who are fans. Across time, scholars have focused attention on subjects such as sport fandom violence, including sociological approaches, which examine the social and cultural dimensions of sport violence (Williams, Dunning, & Murphy, 1984), and ethological and psychological approaches, which to varying degrees attempt to understand violence and aggression as natural features of animal or human interaction (Kerr, 1994; Marsh, 1982). Other studies have explored the discriminatory features of sport fandom cultures, including racism (Kilvington & Price, 2017), homophobia (Cashmore & Cleland, 2012), xenophobia (Maguire & Poulton, 1999), and sexism (Dunn, 2014; Pope, 2017). Additional work has taken into account sport fan cultures as sites for the promotion of masculinities (Bairner, 1999) and hooliganism (Gibbons, Dixon, & Braye, 2008), as well as identifying cognitive, behavioral, and affective dimensions of fandom (Waters, Burke, & Buning, 2011; Wenner & Gantz, 1998). Each of these threads have proven valuable in aiding and advancing our understanding of fan cultures, and this chapter complements this work by emphasizing sociological issues, approaches, and debates relating to the maintenance and evolution of sport fandom cultures.

ISSUES

Fans as Consumers

The question of whether sports fans can be defined as consumers remains a contested feature within sociological literature. While it has not gone unnoticed that sports have reaped the "benefits" of commercial enterprise (Giulianotti, 1999, 2002; Horne, 2006; Manzenreiter & Horne, 2004), there remains a stubborn denial among many that sports fans can or should be labeled consumers at all. Instead, scholars have often tended to preserve romanticized notions of fandom orthodoxy, positioning fans and consumers at opposing ends of theoretical dichotomies that downgrade certain consumer activities and celebrate forms of perceived "traditional" loyalty (Dixon, 2013a). For instance, Clarke (1978) writes of "genuine" and "other" types of fans; Boyle and Haynes (2000) have distinguished between "traditional" and "modern" fans, and Nash (2000) between "core" and "corporate" fans. While different terminology is used by these authors and others, the premise remains largely the same. As a result, judgments are often made regarding the professed authenticity of one's fandom practice, and they are based on the perceived motives of sporting interest and related sport consumption.

Similar arguments have been raised in sport typologies which attempt to conceptually account for the complexities of fandom practice that dichotomies cannot reach. Typologies can be either psychological (e.g., Wann, Melnick, Russell, & Pease, 2001), placing sport fandom in the context of identification and social identity, or sociological (e.g., Giulianotti, 2002), placing fandom in the context of a wider social framework. In either instance, theorists believe that fandom is textured, that it is lived differently by agents, and therefore a composite of factors and dimensions can be used to categorize fan types (van Driel, Gantz, & Lewis, 2019).

However, not all scholars agree with the conceptual segregation of fandom types. Garry Crawford (2004), for instance, explains that typologies are useful in the sense that they draw attention to the vast and varied ways that fandom can be practiced. However, despite their all-encompassing manner, taxonomies tend to spend too much time attempting to segregate and compartmentalize fandom types into idealistic but ultimately unrealistic components. The result tends to be that typologies, much like the theoretical dichotomies that preceded them, are theoretically rigid, inflexible, and unyielding and do not represent or fully explain the complexities and contradictions apparent in the lives of sports fans (Davis, 2015; Gibbons & Dixon, 2010; Sturm, 2020).

Cut to the bone, the scholarly search for fandom types tends to contrast "good supporters, with bad consumers" (Mehus, 2010, p. 897). Bad consumers have frequently been cast in the role of affluent, distant, and rational individuals whose motives for attending live sports and remaining "loyal" ought not to be assumed, given that competition for consumer attention is constant in neoliberal societies. Conversely, "good supporters," often associated with working-class cultures, are described as those with strong emotional connections to the team, athlete, and/or geographical location associated with athletic performance, and are thought to be bound together by group loyalties.

So-called good supporters or traditional fans are often portrayed as irrational and yet predictable beings in that they are thought to blindly follow group conventions and are "loyal to the core." Ironically however, this primes them for consumption. I state that this is ironic because despite their assumed working-class status and assumed outward promotion of the anticonsumerist message, they are just as susceptible to advertising and marketing as other fans.

Perceived traditional acts of fandom practice, for example match or performance attendance, require fans to consume in multiple ways. Most obviously, they must buy tickets and spend time and perhaps money at the event. In addition to this, it is not inconceivable to suggest that those attending the event may also purchase merchandise and take part in other consumption activities, such as contributing to internet discussions about sport. In fact, the former increases the probability of the latter. Think about it. Purchasing kits, tickets, paraphernalia, ephemera, and related gifts, watching television, subscribing to sport networks, reading news and books, listening to sport-related music, admiring sport-related art, playing computer games, acquiring match-day food and drink, traveling to the event, gambling, celebrating, commiserating, communicating with others (online or otherwise), and many other actions besides, are all, in the end, acts of consumption. After all, according to Warde (2005, p. 137), consumption is "a process where agents engage in appropriation or appreciation, whether for utilitarian, expressive or contemplative purposes, of goods, services, information or ambience, whether purchased or not, over which the individual has discretion." In other words, consumption infiltrates every level of fan practice to such an extent that affiliation to sport is impossible without it. With this in mind, I encourage readers of this chapter to visualize sports fans as both products and constituents of cultures in which consumption is of paramount importance.

The Market, Disneyization, and Sport Fandom

To borrow a phrase from Lash and Urry's 1994 book, *Economies and Signs of Space*, in late modern life "the economy is increasingly culturally inflected . . . and culture is more and more economically inflected" (p. 64). Concomitantly, as sport and sports-affiliated institutions have developed in accordance with consumer society, corporate values have infiltrated and altered the everyday sport fan experience. That is to say that experiences of sport fans are becoming more dependent on the consumption of official brands, pies, hotdogs, programs, and wider consumer experiences, which infiltrate, invade, and eventually embody perceptions of "authentic" practice. In other words, the boundaries between fan cultures, the economy, and marketing strategies are now blurred.

Alan Bryman's (2004) concept of Disneyization can help us to think through the ways in which market forces penetrate sport cultures in the manner I've described. He argues that Disney theme parks exemplify the omnipresence of a series of increasingly common procedures (underpinned by neoliberal philosophy) that aim to ensure the satisfaction of consumers whilst offering new strategies for selling in post-Fordist times. More specifically, the Disneyization thesis, as it has become known, gives heightened credence to the influencing power of marketing procedures which generally take into consideration four main components that encourage variety, choice, and differentiation. Those components are (1) theming, (2) hybrid consumption, (3) emotional performative labor, and (4) merchandising, and it is argued that over time all have merged seamlessly into the experiences of sports fans. Let me explain further.

Theming draws on the assumption that consumer enjoyment of or dislike for a service is only partially conditioned by the objective quality of the service itself. The "servicescape" (e.g., the contrived environment and ambience or the manner in which a service is delivered) is also thought to be a crucial factor of the consuming experience (Pine & Gilmore, 1999). Thus, theming is part of a strategy of differentiation that is deployed in order to allow agents to lose themselves in a contrived experience that will encourage consumption. In sport fandom, theming experiences are found in affiliated "sports bars," the themed promotion of food and drink by competing leisure providers (e.g., match-day specials), the themed match-day executive packages on sale at sports grounds (e.g., executive boxes), themed weddings or other special occasions that can be connected to sporting institutions, and the targeted marketing appeals of sports clubs and sponsors that aim to build a global fandom audience (through, for example, the sale of themed brands).

Hybrid consumption refers to the merging of various forms of consumption associated with different institutional spheres. Those forms of consumption become interlocked in a deliberate attempt to create a "destination" that will hold consumer attention and encourage agents to spend more time and money than they otherwise might. For instance, sports stadia are known to include food courts, beer gardens, video arcades, ATM machines, and gambling terminals, as well as providing prematch entertainment and other consumption elements (Ritzer & Stillman, 2001). Watching sport at the venue is only part of the experience. I discuss some of the more recent advancements in hybrid consumption options (related to developments in digital technology) later in this chapter.

Merchandising alludes to the promotion of goods bearing copyright images and logos. It is a form of franchising that leverages additional uses from existing well-known images. While merchandising may not be exclusively related to the late modern period, the variation and volume of products that are produced and sold by sports clubs and governing bodies under the conditions of market exchange have increased significantly (Dixon 2013a). Other scholars, such as Horne (2006), Crawford (2003, 2007), and Giulianotti (1999), are in agreement with this position; they suggest that even those fans who perceive authenticity to exist outside of the commercial sphere tend to be catered to by museums, stores selling classic club shirts, and video streams of old/classic games or other forms of memorabilia.

Finally, *emotional labor* is used by Bryman to refer to a specific delivery of service that, if implemented effectively, can offer a source of differentiation. It is a means of distinguishing services that are otherwise identical in order to make the consumer experience memorable, and the customer more likely to return. In Disney theme parks, for instance, employees are akin to performers who invest their time and energy to ensure that customers have a positive emotional experience. This logic is supported by research indicating that customers judge the success of any commercial exchange not only on the quality of the product but on the quality of service as well (Henkoff, 1994; Solomon, 1998). On this basis, Bryman suggests that fostering emotional labor to satisfy the needs of sovereign customers has become a crucial component of the framework of most businesses in the leisure sector. However, for fans of sport this concept does not translate exactly as described above for the following reasons.

Sports fans have a confused view of who ought to embody emotional labor. Sport professionals (as representatives of sport institutions) are thought to have a duty to display in their performances an emotional intensity which is admired and celebrated when it is embodied and disparaged when it is perceived to be lacking (Dixon, 2014b). However, despite this, there is little evidence to suggest that such attitudes do indeed impact customer relations with a sports club in a sense that aligns with the Disneyization thesis. For instance, while Bryman (2004, p. 105) suggests that "as many as two thirds of customers stop purchasing a service or product due to dissatisfaction with an employee," it seems unlikely that many sports fans would curb spending habits due to the negative attitudes about star performers. The likelihood is greater (given the global status of the player) that a disinterested and emotionally superfluous globally recognized sports star would benefit rather than harm (e.g., financially speaking) business relations with fans.

In other words, there tends to be an emotional differentiation between regular consumer practices and consumption as sports fans. This offset reinforces the point that sports fans possess a form of emotional labor that has surprising potential to imprison them into a cycle of consumerist activity. As Giulianotti (2005, p. 397) has written, "supporters do not understand themselves as possessing simple market choices between clubs." From this view, many fans do not act as rational consumers at all. Rather, consumption can be more accurately likened to an enduring form of compulsion based on emotional ties.

Sport Consumption and the Symbolic Expression of Fans

It is worth reminding ourselves that there is more to everyday sport consumption than economic exchange. Rather, the consumption of sport can be partially, if not entirely experiential. For the sports fan, acts of consumption are so much more than a means to an end. There is a human face to consumption, and this is reflected in the connection that fans come to have toward particularized commodities through processes of defetishization. Broadly speaking, this means that certain kinds of commodities may attract deep communal significance or personal attachment to sports fans in ways that extend far beyond installed meanings at the point of production (Sayer, 1997; Watts, 2014. In the 1990 book *Common Culture*, Paul Willis provides examples of this when he discusses the creative potential of consumption. He briefly quotes Wolverhampton Wanderers soccer fan, Steve, who describes the "necessary" collection of paraphernalia he possesses: "I mean my bedroom is painted all gold and black. I've got a big flag on one wall and a big picture of the team on the other . . . newspaper clippings on one wall too and the scarf hung up on the wardrobe" (p. 114).

As Willis (1990) describes it, Steve's bedroom is a temple to the Wolves, with inanimate objects taking on a social atmosphere. Similar observations are noted by King (2011) when he discusses the extraordinary power that objects can wield over the imagination of sports fans once they have been charged with collective emotion and memory, often by showcasing the club badge or other sports symbols. Willis has described such affective attachments and creativity of meaning to commodities of mass culture as "grounded aesthetics," a concept that acknowledges how capitalist culture has almost unwittingly provided for agents tools for further symbolic expression. Commerce and consumption, he asserts, have helped to release an explosion of everyday symbolic life and activity. Thus, it is now common for the sports fan to conceive of consumption as an activity that extends the material purchase, reflecting instead, a way of thinking and a mindset in which sport, consumption, and practice are inseparable. When considered collectively, the *issues* that I have raised in this section indirectly inform the *approaches* toward the sociology of sport fandom that are outlined next.

Approaches

Theorizing Sports Fandom

Over the past 40 years academics have grappled with the complex nature of sport fandom as it has developed and transformed in line with wider social changes. This period has witnessed an epochal shift from manufacturing to service-based economies and the unconstrained growth of consumer society, the latter contributing significantly to what has been termed "the endless quest for authenticity" in relation to academic interpretations of sport fandom practice (Gibbons & Dixon, 2010). As I explained earlier, academics have begun to shift their focus away from dichotomy and typology creation that sets out to compartmentalize fandom types and have instead begun to rethink how we ought to theoretically conceptualize sport fandom.

John Williams (2007) was perhaps the first to explicitly criticize much of the existing work in this field. He was critical of the use of what he termed "macro theories," those theories that centralize the role of structure in the maintenance of fandom cultures. Williams suggests that, within such approaches, the role of structure is exaggerated and that this often leads to the romanticizing of "tradition." The implication here is that macro-theories fail to position fans in the new social contexts of late modernity, where agents are assumed to be more reflexive than reactive. Conversely, however, Williams is also critical of those authors who favor micro-theories, that is, those theories that position fans as free agents with individual autonomy. He asserts that such approaches often negate and underestimate the importance of continuity, place, and community in sport fan cultures.

Given that criticisms are cast on either side of the macro (structure) or micro (agency) spectrum, Williams proposed that the meso (middle ground) approach would likely offer solutions to the theoretical problems that he identifies. For example, while macro considerations suggest that social structures compel agents to engage in social maneuvers, and micro paradigms tend to assume that individuality is the root of all action, the meso level can provide a link between the two (Kirchberg, 2007). Below, I consider some of the theoretical approaches to sport fandom that are situated at the meso level.

Sport Fan Habitus

Sports fans are not born with a sports fan gene which determines sporting allegiance and consumptive "taste." The reality is more mundane, but ever more complex. As a social construction, fandom is embraced by agents as they interact with one another across time. In his seminal book, *The Logic of Practice*, Pierre Bourdieu (1990) likens such processes of autonomization to learning the rules of an arbitrary game. He expresses his thoughts in the following way:

> In a game, the field (the pitch or board on which it is played, the rules, the outcomes at stake etc.) is clearly seen for what it is, an arbitrary social construct. . . . By contrast, in the social fields, which are the products of a long, slow process of autonomization, and are therefore, so to speak, games "in themselves" and not "for themselves," one does not embark on a game by a conscious act, one is born into the game, with the game; and the relation of investment, *illusio*, investment is made more total and unconditional by the fact that it is unaware of what it is. (p. 67)

Following this logic, Bourdieu's central theoretical concept, *habitus*, seeks to explain how our sensibilities, dispositions, sense of self, and that of others is learned and then internalized through implicit and explicit teachings. When applied to sport cultures, the "love" or emotional connection that fans feel for sports teams and sports stars is learned through social interactions, and this can take various forms. Wheeler and Green (2014), for instance, indicate that family mentors are often pivotal in the inauguration of sports fandom practice. Concomitantly, I have previously highlighted how the consumption of sport-related goods can be implicit within this learning process too, as agents develop their fandom habitus (Dixon 2013b).

For instance, according to McCracken (1986), it is through exchange rituals that emotional connections to material objects are formed. Thus, in keeping with Bourdieu's habitus, children are often subjected to sporting merchandise by significant others who purposefully offer gifts containing meaningful and emotive properties that the gift-giver wishes the receiver to absorb. Once embedded over time, consumption choices become naturalized into early adulthood and beyond. As agents mature (often in the role of parents, aunties, uncles, and grandparents), the receiver inevitably becomes the gift-giver and begins to influence the consumer choices of succeeding generations of sport fans. Throughout this cycle, consumption is sustained through the perceived emotional congruence that exists between the fan, market products, and the object of fandom. In any instance, it is mentors (whoever they may be) that sustain the recursive nature of practice where students inevitably become teachers, the mentored become mentors, and this allows "tradition" to continue across time and space.

Sports Fans as Reflexive Agents

To avoid misrepresenting Bourdieu's concept of habitus as a deterministic model that solely reproduces form across time and space, it is worth reinforcing the notion that habitus is always subject to change as agents progress through the life course. Writing in 1992, Bourdieu reminds critics of this theoretical construct that it is not the fate that some people have read into it (Bourdieu & Wacquant, 1992). He explains that being the product of history, habitus is an open system of dispositions that is constantly subjected to experiences and therefore constantly affected by them in a way that reinforces or modifies its structure. In other words, cultural fields, such as sports fandom, appear stable but are in fact continuously in flux as people shape and react to emerging social circumstances and trends, with reflexivity as much the habitual outcome of field requirements as of any other disposition (Sweetman, 2003).

In previous work I have argued that sports fans are indeed reflexive thinkers, and that during the life course they are presented with various options to reproduce social action, or else change behavior (Dixon, 2013b). And while they are influenced by the consumption of core knowledge gathered through one's childhood habitus, they are capable of consuming new knowledge of distant or estranged practices via interaction with others. For instance, when studying the genesis of sport fandom, I have uncovered examples where sport fandom has been introduced to agents with no prior interest in sport by husbands or wives, from chance competition wins, via engagement with computer games, or by following celebrity athletes, and it is worth noting that these trends appear timeless (Dixon, 2013a).

In the 1970s, scholars observed that it was not uncommon for children to socialize their parents in a process known as reverse socialization (Ritzer, Kammeyer, & Yetman, 1979). More recently, two studies involving former fans of National Hockey League teams have highlighted how children and grandchildren can reignite or initiate interest in sports teams for adults (Hyatt, 2007; Hyatt & Foster, 2015). And similarly, a 2014 study into consumptive relationships that children have with soccer teams found that children could influence the consumptive behaviors of the significant adults in their lives too (Thomson & Williams, 2014). Thus, while agents are constrained by childhood habitus, it is important to note that they are not imprisoned by it. Habitus can be fluid as agents react to life events and experiences. There are, however, some limits to the extent of reflexivity. As an example, let us consider the experiences of female sports fans.

Approaches toward the Marginalization of Female Fans

It is accepted that inequalities on account of gender exist in sport fan communities (Crawford, 2003; Pope, 2010; Wenner, 2021). Female sports fans are not only marginalized by their contemporaries within sport cultures and in the media (Wenner, 2008, 2010, 2012), but historically speaking, they have also been marginalized by academics. Stacey Pope (2013) has highlighted how female fans have long been an underrepresented population, and even when they are cited in research, they are compared unfavorably with male peers, who are more likely to be labeled as "authentic" (Pope, 2017). Adding contextual flavor to this, Garry Crawford (2001) argues that female fans, in direct contrast to male fans, are largely illustrated as screaming groupies, motivated by the chance to see or touch a male idol. Others, such as Mewett and Toffoletti (2012), have even suggested that some academic writings can accentuate perceptions of second-class fandom by focusing on female fans as synthetic, consumer fans.

Rather than investigating how fandom is practiced and the theoretical implications of this, some studies have been content to explain away the presence of female fans as a side effect of what became known as the bourgeoisification of contemporary sport in the 1990s (Jones & Lawrence, 2000; Nash, 2000, 2001; Pfister, Lenneis, & Mintert, 2013; Williams & Perkins, 1998). However, stigmatizing female sports fans in such a way has left a void in our theoretical understandings. In 2015 I set out to address this issue by explaining what appears to be a continued cultural marginalization of female sports fans from the perspective of Anthony Giddens's (1982) *Structuration Theory*.

I argued that Giddens provides us with a useful way of thinking about the production and reproduction of marginalization or subordination of agents within fan cultures (Dixon, 2015). Theorizing at the meso level, he does not favor structure or agency in his explanation of the constitution of society. Rather, he argues that it is through the duality of structure that cultural practice is produced and reproduced across time. In other words, Giddens (1982) proposes that the structural properties of social systems do not exist outside of agency. Instead, they are implicated in its production and reproduction through everyday routine interactions. He explains that across time, routine interaction informs a sense of "practical consciousness" which involves tacit modes of knowing how to behave in the context of social life (p. 33).

Furthermore, Giddens accepts that in the constitution of society, not all actors are equal. Rather, they are "positioned" based on perceived authority within a cultural space. Authority can involve the ownership and use of material and allocative resources, but equally, it can relate directly to genetic composition where agents can be "positioned" according to, for example, their race or, in this instance, their sex and gender. The key point to take from Giddens is that it is through routine interaction and one's "practical consciousness" that the recursive nature of dominance and subordination is upheld. Thus, he explains how social practices and issues of dominance and subordination have a broad spatial and temporal extension because they are acknowledged and largely followed by agents in their everyday routines.

In the context of my 2015 research, which focused attention on a sample of female sport fans, I have argued that the structuration process (particularly the production and reproduction of cultural "norms" that suppress female fans) occur through the performance of routine encounters of all agents and not solely as the result of imposed autocratic systems of male supremacy. For instance, in the research, participants were able to draw on a history of seemingly trivial encounters to explain the general positioning of females within sport fan cultures. Such trivial encounters were described as the sites from which the rules of practice are learned and authoritative/subordinate positioning is determined.

For example, participants who were exposed to sport cultures as children expressed an initial acceptance into the fold with fond recollections of introductions into sport cultures and an unhindered passage to developing a practical consciousness of fan practice. Sport fandom for preadolescent girls was widely perceived to be "cute," and yet participants reported that this attitude markedly changed in later childhood. For instance, one participant explained that "it was like someone turned a switch and you were expected to do woman things" (quoted in Dixon, 2015, p. 642); another stated, "[F]or some reason it's perfectly OK for little girls to support football teams, everyone thinks it's adorable . . . but for an adult woman it's not always accepted in the same spirit" (p. 641).

Far from blaming men for the lack of acceptance, participants were clear that resistance to this notion is reinforced by fellow females too. One fan spoke of being teased by other girls for her love of sport; another spoke of resistance to involvement in sport cultures from matriarchal figures and the emergence of a brand new "gender-centric" practical consciousness that adolescent girls were expected to adopt and embrace. Thus, in the manner that Giddens explains, participants described a process of informal teachings accompanied by the reflexive monitoring of self and others that heavily influenced subcultural subordination.

As adults, female sports fans were aware that assumptions were made about levels of knowledgeability based entirely on gender. Knowledge and expertise of female fans was not always recognized or rewarded across the social spectrum. For instance, one participant explained that in the company of female peers (outside of football culture) the ability to "talk football" holds little value and is disparaged, while another described a process in which females are viewed with skepticism by male fans.

In order to overcome skepticism and take their place as "authentic" fans, some participants reported employing a tactic that would involve joining in "masculine" banter, becoming one of the lads, and outcasting the behavior of fellow female fans who did not blend in with the status quo, or indeed those who refused to comply. This illustrates an unintended consequence for female sports fans in the system of structuration. After all, "fitting in" with masculine culture does not necessarily challenge inequality of practice in a way that will benefit all female fans. This demonstrates the multifaceted nature of dominance and subordination across time and space in light of the duality of structure.

DEBATES

Sports Consumers or Prosumers?

Advancements in technology have always influenced the way sport is consumed. For instance, in 1921 Major League Baseball was presented to fans beyond its "traditional" audience via the medium of radio. According to Hayden (2004), while purists were not sold on the use of this medium, it exposed a new generation of fans to some of the century's greatest plays. In fact, he explains how radio elevated baseball into its national pastime status and players into celebrities.

Television took this further still. In the USA, professional baseball, football, and hockey matches were first televised in 1939–1940, and the doomsayers predicted the beginning of the end for match-day attendance, though the reality was somewhat different. More media attention increased interest and demand for domestic and global audiences. But now, in our screen-laden societies which have provided the conditions for new digital media environments to thrive, sports fans are more active than ever before in their media engagement. Every day they fluidly navigate, manipulate, and reproduce media sports content (Sanderson, 2011; Sanderson & Kassing, 2014; Sturm, 2020). In other words, they are "prosumers" who produce as well as consume the information that defines them.

User-generated content powers the social media universe, and sports fans are now presented with myriad sophisticated digital tools, techniques, and devices for capturing, sharing, and disseminating sport-related content. Hutchins (2019) refers to this as the "mobile media sport moment"; for Lawrence and Crawford (2019) this represents the "hyperdigitalisation of sports fandom." Both of these neologisms capture the cultural importance of increased digital literacy, connectivity, and networking, which in effect has enabled the accelerated naturalization of the widespread use of technological developments.

Whether consuming sport at the event (Sandvoss, 2003), at the pub (Dixon, 2014a, Weed, 2008), at the fan park (Wenner & Billings, 2017), or at any other space, for that matter, fans often carry with them a second screen. The second screen is thought to be a revolutionary adaptation to fandom cultures as it not only allows for concurrent communication with others in the immediate physical vicinity but also allows for synchronous and asynchronous communications with physically dispersed fans who share space anywhere in the digital ether. According to numerous scholars, this nascent routine is redefining how fandom is practiced (Blaszka, Burch, Frederick, Clavio, & Walsh, 2012; Hutchins, 2019; Hutchins, Li, & Rowe, 2019; Sturm, 2020).

So where is sport fandom headed? As we move beyond Web 2.0, presumably to Web 3.0, digital technologies will continue to influence all aspects of our lives. For sure, new technologies will act as a conduit through which we can choose to engage with sport, but the future is not yet certain, largely because we (as prosumers) will accept, modify, or reject technological offers presented to us at any time by our capitalist masters. Of course, we can see the likely outcomes of short-term cultural change by eyeballing current patterns in fan behavior. Below, I provide a synopsis of some of the emerging questions that are likely to stimulate sport fandom debates into the future.

What Will Fans Demand from Sports Personalities in the Social Media Age?

Sports stars were once aloof personalities, distant figures observed from the terraces and on television, or those people fans read about in the print media and possibly in autobiographies. But with the advancement of digital technologies, including sophisticated social media and video-sharing platforms, the expectations of and demands placed on celebrity athletes by fans are changing shape. In fact, celebrity professional athletes are not the only stars glistening in the social media galaxy.

As an example, in October 2015, the online video-tracking firm Tubular Labs reported that there were more than 17,000 YouTube channels with more than 100,000 subscribers, and nearly 1,500 with more than 1 million (Dredge, 2016). In the world of sport, YouTubers, as they are known (a person/personality who uploads, produces, or appears in videos on YouTube channels), are incredibly popular. As father to one soccer-obsessed nine-year-old, I have been introduced to personalities such as Tekkerz Kid, also known as Lorenzo Greer, a 12-year-old aspiring soccer player currently affiliated with Birmingham City pre-academy (1.5 million subscribers); F2 Freestylers, also known as Billy Wingrove and Jeremy Lynch, former semiprofessional soccer players (and soccer fans) who present best match play tutorials, football entertainment, and banter (11.3 million subscribers); and SV2, also known as Abisola Emmanuel Balogun, an Arsenal FC fan who "specializes" in producing videos that feature soccer challenges (1.23 million subscribers). And, of course, other YouTube personalities are available!

But what, if anything at all, can professional sports persons and their affiliated agents and institutions learn from YouTubers? According to Stuart Dredge (2016), columnist for *The Guardian* newspaper, the answer is simple: while YouTubers may be less polished than mainstream sports stars, they are "real," "authentic," relatable, and therefore marketable. This logic is beginning to resonate with professional sports stars too. In 2014, Derek Jeter, former professional baseball player for the New York Yankees, explained how professional sports stars have emerged from a position of skepticism toward mainstream media (often considered ripe with manipulation) to embrace the unfiltered authenticity of social media platforms and other modes of internet-based communications. With this in mind, Jeter helped to develop the website The Players Tribune, on which celebrity athletes could share what they really think and feel about issues that are important to them and so communicate with their fans directly. Since its inception, players have used this platform to discuss transfers, disputes, and sensitive subjects such as mental health, racism, and sexuality. This is only one example of the many new modes of communication for the sports star and the emergence of the authentic voice of the celebrity athlete. (For studies relating to the use of social media by athletes see Grimmer & Clavio, 2019; Korzynski & Paniagua, 2016; Toffoletti & Thorpe, 2018.)

As athletes engage with social media, they are creating more new and intimate avenues to interact with sports fans, and with this, cultural expectations of celebrity athletes are evolving. Fans are not necessarily looking for sports stars with the morals of a saint, or those devoid of opinion. Instead there is a growing expectation that sports stars should be "real" people who are true to their core beliefs and convictions—while maintaining high levels of sporting performance.

What Is the Future for Televised Sport in the Lives of Sports Fans?

As more sport content is made available online, the allure of the pay-TV model that has been so successful for telecommunications companies across multiple sports has been impacted, according to the 2019 Grabyo "OTT Video Trends Report," which examines the viewing preferences of consumers in multiple countries. Overall, 53% of surveyed consumers stated that they watch sport regularly, and 45% watch sport more than any other form of content. This is not unusual, of course, but it is the medium through which sports broadcasts are being increasingly consumed by fans that is the newsworthy feature.

Among sports fans, there is a growing popularity of over-the-top (OTT) channels. Here I am referring to streaming services that are delivered over the internet (rather than traditional broadcast platforms), reaching across national copyright jurisdictions. For example, services such as Tencent Video, DAZN, Amazon Prime Video, and others are now intervening in coverage rights, and this is changing how live sport is experienced and shared across television, computer, game console, tablet, and smartphone screens (Hutchins et al., 2019). In the United Kingdom, the tech giant Amazon has cautiously entered into the football rights market by purchasing the rights to stream a small proportion of FA Premier

League matches, making this available to all Amazon Prime service subscribers. Amazon is already involved in live sports provision in the USA. In 2017, Amazon replaced Twitter by paying a reported U.S.$50 million for nonexclusive digital streaming rights to the NFL's *Thursday Night Football*, and then in 2018 paid an estimated U.S.$130 million to secure rights for an additional two seasons (Hutchins et al., 2019). For the sports fan, the attraction of premium sport that can be accessed across multiple devises with no lock-in contracts is obvious. The payoff for companies such as Amazon is obvious too. They intend to use premium sport to grow and secure their predominant place in the global consumer market.

The investment from OTT operators in recent years signifies both the continued popularity of television viewing and the growth of internet-based communications infrastructure, with implications for the structure of rights markets and media systems that have long been built around national and regional territories (Evans, Losifidis, & Smith, 2013). For instance, broadcasting corporations must consider whether to compete or collaborate with other providers and distributors in the digital technology and telecommunications sectors across the world. For sports fans, the provisioning and therefore the choices of live sports viewing has become vast. While this is ultimately good news for the fan who chooses to consume live sport via screens, some scholars (Kringstad, Solberg, & Jakobsen, 2018; Wallrafen, Pawlowski, & Deutscher, 2018) suggest that this could have implications for live attendance at sports events.

What Is the Future for the Live Sport Experience?

In some elite-level sports, a paradoxical situation is emerging where, on one hand, the number of associated sports fans is growing and, on the other, stadium attendance is declining. According to Deloitte (2019a) (a multinational professional services network that, as a proportion of their portfolio, conducts research into trends in sports business), emerging patterns in digital sports consumption should be considered a key factor for declining live sport audiences. In their "Digital and Media Trends" survey of 2019, the following was highlighted. As live ticket prices have continued to rise, fans have built comfortable "digital nests" at home with enormous TV screens, surround-sound, and access to 24/7 games and commentary. They can also watch on the go, getting updates from social media and live-streaming apps rather than committing three hours to watch a game in real time.

Of course, technology can be both the cause of a problem and its solution. You've heard the phrase "If you can't beat them, join them." Well, that's the attitude of many chief information officers and chief marketing officers at professional sports clubs that intend to use digital technologies to increase stadium attendance and encourage fans to spend money in the process. By digitizing the customer journey from ticketing to postgame and beyond, sports clubs are getting closer to fans, and this, in theory, could enable them to develop more personalized experiences for fans while making more money for the club in the process (Deloitte, 2019b). The aim is to differentiate and deliver an engaging fan experience by using next-generation marketing techniques that treat fans individually. As explained in Deloitte's (2019b) paper, "The Stadium Experience," this is where the CIO and CMO can collaborate to sell more tickets, drive more concessions, and deliver more personalized experiences that deepen fans' relationships with their clubs.

In this regard, augmented and virtual reality experiences are options that sporting institutions are beginning to explore in order to build relationships with fans in new ways

(Brousseau & Kelp-Stebbins, 2020; Hertzog, Sakurai, Hirota, & Nojima, 2020). Put simply, this is where fans use their mobile phones (or other compatible digital devices) within stadiums to interact with the live surroundings. For example, by pointing a mobile phone camera at the field of play in MLB baseball or NBA basketball games, interactive features such as dynamic statistics and probabilities can be revealed in real time. Beyond this, mobile apps can be used to guide fans to stadiums via GPS, to locate their seats, to browse exclusive interviews with players, and to purchase various consumables.

The aim of embedding augmented reality features into sports stadia is to stimulate fans in new ways by enabling them to get ever closer to the sporting action, while simultaneously assisting institutions in their goal of getting closer to the fans (Goebert & Greenhalgh, 2020). Thus, in stadia of the future it is likely that digital technologies will be used to drive fan experiences for mutual reward. In theory at least, digital stadia will be capable of providing an individualized fan experience while driving greater revenue.

Conclusion

This chapter has positioned fans as consumers above all else. Key arguments suggest that, over time, neoliberal capitalist markets have increasingly influenced sports fan cultures, habitus, and the perception of the "authentic" fandom experience. But far from acting as cultural dupes, this treatment in this chapter has acknowledged the reflexivity of sports fans and their role in the ongoing evolution of sport fandom cultures. For example, the global increase in digital literacy and access to communication devices across the world has propelled cultures of prosumption to new heights, and this has stimulated academics to ask new questions about the various ways that sport fandom is practiced and the consequences that this brings.

In the future, it is likely that researchers will explore new digital relationships between fans and sports stars. Where stars were once socially removed, visible only via choreographed and diluted "traditional" media guest appearances, they are now more personally immersed and engaged, albeit in digital format. In the world of live televised sport broadcasting, other avenues for investigation include the implications of new commercial offerings to fans from OTT platforms. And at the stadium, the integration of augmented reality, though in its infancy, is likely to be an important evolution in the future of fandom cultures for researchers to consider.

For over 40 years professional sports fandom has provided scholars with many issues, approaches, and debates to ponder. While it is impossible to see into the future, as social scientists we can say with some certainty that evolutions in sports fandom practice will continue to both fascinate us and illumine the relationships that underlie the sport spectating experience.

References

Bairner, A. (1999). Soccer, masculinity and violence in Northern Ireland: Between hooliganism and terrorism. *Men and Masculinities, 1*, 284–301.

Blaszka, M., Burch L., Frederick E. L., Clavio, G., & Walsh, P. (2012). #WorldSeries: An empirical examination of a Twitter hashtag during a major sporting event. *International Journal of Sport Communication, 5,* 435–543.

Bourdieu, P. (1990). *The logic of practice.* Cambridge, U.K.: Polity Press.

Bourdieu, P., & Wacquant, L. (1992). *An invitation to reflexive sociology.* Cambridge, U.K.: Polity.

Boyle, R., & Haynes, R. (2000). Sport, the Media, and Popular Culture. Harlow: Pearson Education.

Brousseau, M., & Kelp-Stebbins, K. (2020). On ice or on air? How an egregious glowing hockey puck crossed the line into augmented reality. *Sport in Society.* doi:10.1080/17430437.2020.1807956.

Bryman, A. (2004). *The Disneyization of society.* London: Sage.

Cashmore, E., & Cleland, J. (2012). Fans, homophobia and masculinities in association football: Evidence of a more inclusive environment. *British Journal of Sociology, 63,* 370–387.

Clarke, J. (1978). Football and working class fans: Traditions and change. In R. Ingham (Ed.), *Football hooliganism: The wider context* (pp. 37–60). London: Inter-Action.

Crawford, G. (2001). Characteristics of a British ice hockey audience: Major findings of the 1998 and 1999 Manchester Storm ice hockey club supporter surveys. *International Review for the Sociology of Sport, 36*(1), 71–81.

Crawford, G. (2003). The career of the sport supporter: The case of the Manchester Storm. *Sociology, 37,* 219–237.

Crawford, G. (2004). *Consuming sport: Fans, sport and culture.* London: Routledge.

Crawford, G. (2007). Consumption of sport. In G. Ritzer (Ed.), *The Blackwell encyclopedia of sociology* (vol. 2) (p. 716). London: Blackwell Reference.

Davis, L. (2015). Football fandom and authenticity: A critical discussion of historical and contemporary perspectives. *Soccer & Society, 16*(2–3), 422–436.

Deloitte. (2019a, October). Digital and media trends survey (13th ed.).https://www2.deloitte.com/us/en/insights/industry/technology/digital-media-trends-consumption-habits-survey.html.

Deloitte. (2019b, February). The stadium experience.https://www2.deloitte.com/us/en/pages/technology-media-and-telecommunications/articles/stadium-experience-fan-satisfaction-survey.html.

Dixon, K. (2013a). *Consuming football in late modern life.* London: Ashgate.

Dixon, K. (2013b). Learning the game: Football fandom culture and the origins of practice. *International Review for the Sociology of Sport, 48*(3), 334–348.

Dixon, K. (2014a). The football fan and the pub: An enduring relationship. *International Review for the Sociology of Sport, 49*(3/4), 382–399.

Dixon, K. (2014b). Football fandom and Disneyization in late modern life. *Leisure Studies, 33*(1), 1 21.

Dixon, K. (2015). A woman's place recurring: Structuration, football fandom and sub-cultural subservience. *Sport in Society, 18*(6), 636–651.

Dredge, S. (2016, February 3). Why are YouTube stars so popular? *The Guardian.* https://www.theguardian.com/technology/2016/feb/03/why-youtube-stars-popular-zoella.

Dunn, C. (2014). *Female football fans: Community, identity and sexism.* Basingstoke, U.K.: Palgrave.

Evans, T., Losifidis, P., & Smith, P. (2013). *The political economy of televised sports rights.* Basingstoke, U.K.: Palgrave Macmillan.

Gibbons, T., & Dixon, K. (2010). "Surf's up!" A call to take English soccer fan interactions on the internet more seriously. *Soccer & Society, 11*(5), 599–613.

Gibbons, T., Dixon, K., & Braye, S. (2008). "The way it was": An account of soccer violence in the 1980s. *Soccer & Society, 9*(1), 28–41.

Giddens, A. (1982). *Profiles and critiques in social theory.* London: Macmillan.

Giulianotti, R. (1999). *Football: A sociology of the global game.* Cambridge, U.K.: Polity.

Giulianotti, R. (2002). Supporters, followers, fans, and flaneurs: A taxonomy of spectator identities in football. *Journal of Sport and Social Issues, 26,* 25–46.

Giulianotti, R. (2005). Sport spectators and the social consequences of commodification: Critical perspectives from Scottish football. *Journal of Sport and Social Issues, 29*(4), 386–410.

Goebert, C., & Greenhalgh, G. (2020). A new reality: Fans' perceptions of augmented reality readiness in sports marketing. *Computers in Human Behaviour, 106.* https://doi.org/10.1016/j.chb.2019.10631.

Grabyo. (2019). OTT video trends report. https://about.grabyo.com/ott-video-trends-2019/.

Grimmer, C., & Clavio, G. (2019). Sport pro = Twitter pro? How soccer stars use Twitter at the height of their career. *International Journal of Sport Management and Marketing, 19*(3–4), 161–183.

Hayden, T. (2004). Empowering sports fans with technology. *Computer, 37*(9), 106–107.

Henkoff, R. (1994, October 3). Finding, training and keeping the best service workers. Fortune, 52–58.

Hertzog, C., Sakurai, S., Hirota, K., & Nojima, T. (2020). Towards augmented reality displays for sports spectators: A preliminary study. Paper presented at the 13th Conference of the International Sports Engineering Association. https://www.researchgate.net/publication/342210248_Toward_Augmented_Reality_Displays_for_Sports_Spectators_A_Preliminary_Study.

Horne, J. (2006). *Sport in consumer culture.* Basingstoke, U.K.: Palgrave.

Hutchins, B. (2019). Mobile media sport: The case for building a mobile media and communications research agenda. *Communication & Sport, 7*(4), 466–487.

Hutchins, B., Li, B., & Rowe, D. (2019). Over-the-top sport: Live streaming services, changing coverage rights markets, and the growth of media sport portals. *Media, Culture & Society, 41*(7), 975–994.

Hyatt, C. G. (2007). Who do I root for now? The impact of franchise relocation on the loyal fans left behind: A case study of Hartford Whalers fans. *Journal of Sport Behaviour, 30*(1), 1–20.

Hyatt, C. G., & Foster, W. M. (2015). Using identity work theory to understand the de-escalation of fandom: A study of former fans of National Hockey League teams. *Journal of Sport Management, 29*(4), 443–460.

Jeter, D. (2014, October 1). The start of something new. *The Players Tribune.* https://www.theplayerstribune.com/en-us/articles/introducing-derek-jeter.

Jones, I., & Lawrence, L. (2000). Identity and gender in sport and media fandom: An exploratory comparison of fans attending football matches and *Star Trek* conventions. In S. Scraton & B. Watson (Eds.), *Sport, leisure identities and gendered spaces* (pp. 1–30). Brighton, U.K.: LSA.

Kerr, J. (1994). *Understanding soccer hooliganism.* Maidenhead, U.K.: McGraw-Hill.

Kilvington, D., & Price, J. (2017). Tackling social media abuse? Critically assessing English football's response to online racism. *Communication and Sport, 7*(1), 64–79.

King. A. (2011). The badge. *Soccer & Society, 12*(2), 74–75.

Kirchberg, V. (2007). Cultural consumption analysis: Beyond structure and agency. *Cultural Sociology, 1*(1), 115–136.

Korzynski, P., & Paniagua, J. (2016). Score a tweet and post a goal: Social media recipes for sports stars. *Business Horizons, 59*, 185–192.

Kringstad, M., Solberg, H., & Jakobsen, T. (2018). Does live broadcasting reduce stadium attendance? The case of Norwegian football. *Sport, Business and Management: An International Journal, 8*(1), 67–81.

Lash, S., & Urry, J. (1994). *Economies of signs and space.* London: Sage.

Lawrence, S., & Crawford, G. (Eds.). (2019). *Digital football cultures: Fandom, identities and resistance.* London: Routledge.

Liponski, W. (2003). *World sport encyclopedia.* St. Paul, MN: MBI.

Manzenreiter, W., & Horne, J. (2004). *Football goes east: Business, culture, and the peoples' game in China, Japan, and South Korea.* London: Routledge.

Marsh, P. (1982). Social order on the British soccer terraces. *International Social Sciences Journal, 34*, 247–256.

McCracken, G. (1986). Culture and consumption: A theoretical account of the structure and movement of the cultural meaning of consumer goods. *Journal of Consumer Research, 13*(1), 71–84.

Mehus, I. (2010). The diffused audience of football. *Continuum: Journal of Media & Cultural Studies, 24*(6), 897–903.

Mewett, P., & Toffoletti, K. (2012). Finding footy: Female fan socialisation and Australian Rules Football. *Sport in Society, 14*, 670–684.

Nash, R. (2000). The sociology of English football in the 1990's: Fandom, business and future research. *Football Studies, 3*(1), 49–62.

Nash, R. (2001). English football fan groups in the 1990s: Class, representation and fan power. *Soccer & Society, 2*(1), 39–58.

Pfister, G., Lenneis, V., & Mintert, S. (2013). Female fans of men's football—A case study in Denmark. *Soccer and Society, 14*(6), 850–871.

Pine, B., & Gilmore, J. (1999). *The experience economy: Work is theatre and every business is a stage.* Boston: Harvard Business School Press.

Pope, S. (2010). *Female fandom in an English "sports city": A sociological study of female spectating and consumption around sport* (Unpublished PhD thesis). University of Leicester.

Pope, S. (2013). The love of my life: The meaning and importance of sport for female fans. *Journal of Sport and Social Issues, 37*(2), 176–195.

Pope, S. (2017). *The feminization of sports fandom: A sociological study.* London: Routledge.

Ritzer, G., Kammeyer, K. C. W., & Yetman, N. R. (1979). *Sociology: Experiencing a changing society.* Boston: Allyn & Bacon.

Ritzer, G., & Stillman, T. (2001). The modern Las Vegas Casino Hotel: The paradigmatic new means of consumption. *Management, 4*, 83–99.

Sanderson, J. (2011). *It's a whole new ball game: How social media is changing sports.* New York: Hampton Press.

Sanderson, J., & Kassing, J. (2014). New media and the evolution of fan-athlete interaction. In A. Billings & M. Hardin (Eds.), *Routledge handbook of sport and new media* (pp. 225–236). New York: Routledge.

Sandvoss, C. (2003). *A game of two halves: Football, television and globalization.* London: Routledge.

Sayer, A. (1997). The dialectic of culture and economy. In R. Lee & J. Wills (Eds.), *Geographies of economics* (pp. 16–26). London: Arnold.

Solomon, M. (1998). Dressing the part: The role of costume in the staging of the servicescape. In J. F. Sherry, Jr (Ed.), Servicescapes: The concept of place in contemporary markets (pp. 81–108). Lincolnwood, IL: NTC Business Books.

Sturm, D. (2020) Fans as e-participants? Utopia/dystopia visions for the future of digital sport fandom. Convergence. Advance online publication. doi:10.1177/13548565220907096.

Sweetman, P. (2003). Twenty-first century dis-ease? Habitual reflexivity or the reflexive habitus. Sociological Review, 51, 528–549.

Thomson, E., & Williams, R. (2014). Children as football fans: An exploratory study of team and player connections. Young Consumers, 15(4), 323–341.

Toffoletti, K., & Thorpe, H. (2018). The athletic labour of femininity: The branding and consumption of global celebrity sportswomen on Instagram. Journal of Consumer Culture, 18(2), 298–316.

Vamplew, W. (1998). Pay up and play the game: Professional sport in Britain 1875–1914. Cambridge: Cambridge University Press.

van Driel, I., Gantz, W., & Lewis, N. (2019). Unpacking what it means to be—or not be—a fan. Communication & Sport, 7(5), 611–626.

Wallrafen, T., Pawlowski, T., & Deutscher, C. (2018). Substitution in Sports: The case of lower division football attendance. Journal of Sports Economics, 20(3) 319–345.

Wann, D., Melnick, M., Russell, G., & Pease, D. (2001). Sports fans: The psychology and social impact of spectators. New York: Routledge.

Warde, A. (2005). Consumption and theories of practice. Journal of Consumer Culture, 5(2), 131–153.

Watts, M. (2014). Commodities. In P. Cloke, P. Crang, & M. Goodwin (Eds.), Introducing human geographies (3rd ed.) (pp. 391–412). London: Arnold.

Weed, M. (2008). Exploring the sport spectator experience: Virtual football spectatorship in the pub. Soccer & Society, 9(2), 189–197.

Wenner, L. A. (2008). Playing dirty: On reading media texts and the sports fan in commercialised settings. In L. W. Hugenberg, P. Haridakis, & A. Earnheardt (Eds.), Sports mania: Essays on fandom and the media in the 21st century (pp. 13–32). Jefferson, NC: McFarland.

Wenner, L. A. (2010). Gendered sports dirt: Interrogating sex and the single beer commercial. In H. Hundley & A. C. Billings (Eds.), Examining identity in sports media (pp. 87–107). Thousand Oaks, CA: Sage.

Wenner, L. A. (2012). Reading the commodified female sports fan: Interrogating strategic dirt and characterization in commercial narratives. In K. Toffoletti & P. Mewitt (Eds.), Sport and its female fans (pp. 131–151). London: Routledge.

Wenner, L. A. (2021). Media, sports, and society. In E. Pike (Ed.), Handbook of research on sports and society (pp. 111–126). Cheltenham, U.K.: Edward Elgar.

Wenner, L. A., & Billings, A. C. (Eds.). (2017). Sport, media, and mega-events. London: Routledge.

Wenner, L. A., & Gantz, W. (1998). Watching sports on television: Audience experience, gender, fanship, and marriage. In L. A. Wenner (Ed.), MediaSport (pp. 233–251). London: Routledge.

Wheeler, S., & Green, K. (2014). Parenting in relation to children's sports participation: Generational changes and potential implications. Leisure Studies, 33(3), 267–284.

Willis, P. (1990). Common culture: Symbolic work at play in the everyday cultures of the young. Milton Keynes, U.K.: Open University Press.

Williams, J. (2007). Rethinking sports fandom: The case of European soccer. Leisure Studies, 26(2), 127–146.

Williams, J., Dunning, E., & Murphy, P. (1984). *Hooligans abroad: The behaviour and control of English fans in continental Europe* (2nd ed.). London: Routledge.

Williams, J., & Perkins, S. (1998). Ticket pricing, football business, and excluded football fans: Research on the "new economics" of football match attendance in England. In Sir Norman Chester Centre for Football Research, *Report to the football task force.* Leicester: University of Leicester.

CHAPTER 51

....

SPORT, FAN VIOLENCE, AND HOOLIGANISM

....

JOHN WILLIAMS

SCHOLARS in Europe have long debated the nature and causes of fan violence and hooliganism at sporting events. It is broadly accepted, however—and on both sides of the Atlantic—that the umbrella term "hooliganism" should include small-scale, frustration and alcohol- or drug-assisted disturbances in sporting contexts, as well as more planned, collective activity (Ostrowsky, 2018). Distinctions are usefully drawn here between "stages" or categories of fan hooliganism. For example, scholars have distinguished between individual and collective violence, spontaneous and more organized incidents, and instrumental and more expressive forms of sports fan disorder (Spaaij, 2014). These highly expressive variants may include missile throwing; abuse aimed at officials, players, and coaches; clashes between fans and police inside the stadium; and postmatch confrontations between rival fans and/ or with the police (Ward, 2002). Most professional team sports almost everywhere in the world have instances of fan disorder to report. Baseball, basketball, and ice hockey crowds in both North America and Europe have all had their moments (Roberts & Benjamin, 2000; Rosenfeld, 1997; Russell & Arms, 1998; Swenson, 2012; Valantinė, Grigaliūnaitė, & Danilevičienė, 2017). Even genteel cricket (Malcolm, 1999) and virtual eSports (Knight, Hartman, & Bennett, 2020) are not immune to incidents of serious spectator problems. However, in many European and South American countries over the past four decades, it is football (soccer), in particular, that has experienced a shift from more spontaneous, ad hoc, event-focused episodes of crowd disorder to much more serious, organized, and institutionalized forms of aggressive or violent hooliganism (Dunning, Murphy, Waddington, & Astrinakis, 2002; Spaaij, 2014).

The important distinction drawn here between spontaneous and organized violence also denotes that collective fan hooliganism in Europe and in much of South America is often only loosely connected to the sporting event itself. Fan "trouble" at football can happen before or after the game, away from the stadium, or at almost any time fans choose to assemble (Collins, 2008). As a result, it is now generally agreed that the main focus for hooligan scholarship in these areas is on distinctive, liminal football fan groups or gangs— sometimes described in England as "firms" (Redhead, 2015a) and in other parts of the world, such as in Italy and Spain, as members of *ultras* groups (Scalia, 2009), as *barras in*

Argentina (Trejo, Murzi, & Nassar, 2019), and as the warrior *torcidas organizadas* in Brazil (Newson et al., 2018). Women may be involved on the margins of some violent hooligan groups, but they typically have only a limited role in physical exchanges. Indeed, discouraging women's participation in fan fighting around the world allows men to display the kind of hypermasculine, macho identities that guarantee recognition and respect among other hooligans and *ultras* (Pitti, 2019; Selmer, 2004). These forms of gendered exclusion have not, however, discouraged intrepid female researchers from exploring the life-world of the contemporary football hooligan (cf. Poulton, 2012).

The collective violence and aggression of male hooligans at football is primarily targeted at identifiable rival peers (Giulianotti, 1999; Roversi, 1991; Spaaij & Anderson, 2010). The specific structural divisions and the cultural textures and fissures that underpin and inform collective football fan violence and its motivation serve as broader "fault lines" in this respect. They make up the wider local frameworks for accentuating or shaping clashes at sports events between rival groups in different countries and locales. In Zimbabwe, for example, socioethnic tensions underwrite the violent rivalry between fans of Dynamos and Highlanders FC (Ncube & Munoriyarwa, 2018). In the Balkans today, political, ethnic, and national divisions still provoke or enhance serious football disorders (Neilson, 2013; Sack & Suster, 2000; Sindbæk, 2013), while in parts of the old Eastern Europe the strains of new nationhood, high unemployment, and the reemergence of old ethnic divisions in extremist political clothing continue to feed both youth alienation and hooligan outbreaks (Piotrowski, 2006). Spaaij (2006) has also shown how fan violence in Spanish soccer is inextricably intertwined with domestic and political nationalisms, while Guschwan (2007) identifies the central role of students and politics in shaping Italian *ultras* cultures. As Eric Dunning (2010, pp. 23–24) puts it:

> [T]he problem [football hooliganism] is contoured and fuelled . . . by what one might call the major fault lines of a particular country. In England, that means by class and regional inequalities and differences; in Scotland and Northern Ireland, religious sectarianism; in Spain, the partly language-based sub-nationalisms of the Catalans, Castilians and Basques; in Italy, city-based particularism and perhaps the division between North and South as expressed in the formation of the Northern League; and in Germany, relations between the generations and those between East and West.

In Europe and South America, recent academic investigations into the sports hooligan question have typically been ethnographic or interview-based, relying mainly for their theoretical purchase on sociological, anthropological, or, more occasionally, sociopsychological insights into the deeper meanings of fan disorder and the structures of fan subcultures (Armstrong, 1998; Giulianotti, 1999; Murphy, Williams, & Dunning, 1991; Pearson, 2009). Often, such studies focus on personal identity strains, the construction of hegemonic masculinities, the pleasures of transgression, and the internal solidarities of fan groups as "family" rather than, necessarily, on the relationship between such fans and the sport, or sports clubs, they follow.

A rather different social science tradition, coupled with more limited and more spontaneous fan problems in North America, has perhaps encouraged the use there of more psychology-driven experimental techniques around individual fans and occasionally rather pathological, psychological perspectives on crowds, approaches that lean more toward descriptive and classificatory models (Lanter, 2011). North American scholars also seem to have taken more of a multidisciplinary approach compared to those typically on offer in Europe, while addressing aggressive fan rivalries in college sport as well as those at the professional sports level. In such accounts, overly strong team identification is often regarded as *the* key psychological trigger for aggression or disorder, especially because of how it confronts situational threats to personal/social identity when a favored team suffers setbacks. Sport spectators, particularly those who identify excessively with their club, might display a willingness to engage in both hostile and instrumental aggressive acts toward opposing teams and officials (Pradhan, Lee, Snycerski, & Laraway, 2021). According to Branscombe and Wann (1991), North American male sports fans, most notably those who are unwilling or unable to reduce the strength of that identification in the face of negative on-field outcomes, may resort to excessive alcohol use and/or aggressive acts to cope with the stress brought on by this situationally perceived threat. Real violence or destructive hooliganism may result.

ISSUES

Back in the late 1970s, when academic exchange was rather less prevalent, typically less productive, and certainly less possible than the era of globalization has since allowed, a little-known (to British eyes) North American sports academic, Alan Roadburg, from the Department of Sociology at Dalhousie University in Nova Scotia, visited the United Kingdom to analyze the disorderliness of British football crowds. Roadburg attended football matches in Britain in order to make some, still highly pertinent, observations on the differences between British football fan cultures and North American sports fan equivalents—especially soccer—an analysis which was later the main theme of an important, but little discussed, paper he published in the prestigious *British Journal of Sociology* (Roadburg, 1980). British football was, at the time, mired in one of its postwar fan hooliganism crises, and Roadburg tried to explain to audiences on both sides of the Atlantic why this was the case and why North American sport had largely "escaped" similar problems. He was hoping to shed light on what was, at that time, a major research lacuna. Based on his experiences, Roadburg identified three main sources of difference.

First, football in Britain had evolved over a lengthy period of probably at least 600 years, from its wild and violent folk forms fought out among working people in pastoral settings, through the codification period in the mid-19th century in the elite English public schools, and eventually into organized professional contests across Britain in the late 19th and early 20th centuries. Then, early professional matches were played out in rudimentary stadia by symbolic representatives of working people in neighboring industrial towns and cities (Dunning, Murphy, & Williams, 1988). In North America, by contrast, sporting contests were still relatively new, and professional soccer, especially, had been "commercially guided," as Roadburg put it, in just a single decade. The average British football fan, Roadburg pointed out, was much more likely than his (*sic*) North American counterpart to identify with the game as a deeply rooted facet of place, heritage, and masculine culture. Club support in Britain was often fixed via peer, family, or religious affiliations and was both reflective and expressive of tribalized and masculinized local rivalries, especially with near neighbors and other "outsiders."

Second, Roadburg pointed out that the layout and location of sports stadia in Britain and North America at this time bore little comparison. In Britain, most football stadia had archaic and embattled facilities and were still typically locked into tightly packed residential areas, urban spaces reached by fans mainly by public transport or on foot. In North America, by contrast, sports stadia were more modern and located in out-of-town complexes, normatively accessed by private car. Crucially, most British football fans still paid low ticket prices to *stand* to watch fixtures in a communally participatory mode, while North American sports fans paid more to sit in relative comfort. Moreover, ranks of visiting fans were—and still are—a constitutive feature of British sport stadia, particularly for football. Tradition, and distance between sporting franchises, meant that little of the European-style practice of fan segregation and ritualized in-stadium rivalries then existed in North America. As a result, once inside the British stadium, Roadburg reported, one tends to feel a much greater sense of oppositional risk and discomforting excitement compared to North American sporting venues. To emphasize these points, he quoted the lauded British journalist, author, and playwright Arthur Hopcraft (1971, p. 162), who pithily described the standing terraces in British soccer stadia around this period as "[h]ideously uncomfortable. The steps are as greasy as a school playground lavatory in the rain. The air is rancid with beer and onions and belching and worse. The language is a gross purple of obscenity." In this kind of setting, the typical young male, working-class British football fan of the early 1980s stood with others and saw his club as an extension of himself. Once the "crowd psychology" develops, the referee, local police, innocent bystanders, and public or private property could all become extensions of the opposition (Roadburg, 1980, p. 273).

Third, and finally, Roadburg argued that his experience of attending British soccer matches quickly confirmed the crucial age, gender, and class distinctions in operation there compared with most North American sport. The relative absence of women and small children from sections of British football stadia and the classed vernacular and style of the aggressive young working-class men who made up a substantial proportion of the typical crowd, and who looked on their club as a "possession to be defended," meant that soccer there lacked the "family" rhetoric and declassed "cooler" practices of much North American professional sport (Roadburg, 1980, p. 274). He argued that American soccer might attract up to 40% of its audience from female followers—the famed ranks of "soccer moms"—and that while a large proportion of the active, substantially male, working-class, and notably more engaged *crowd* for football in Britain had probably played the sport at one time; the more socially mixed *audience* for soccer and other sports in North America was probably less likely to have done the same.

Roadburg's work, even 40 years on, serves as a useful reminder of the importance for social scientists of observational social experience—the underutilized comparative personal case study—as a potentially vital part of the academic toolkit. His account of British football culture in 1980 was, necessarily, drawn with broad brush strokes, and it occasionally used concepts—around crowd psychology, for example—more familiar to North American traditions. But much of it rang true for the period and it opened up possibilities for future comparative research, perhaps relying more on sociological categorizations and theories. Sadly, however, rather too little work of this kind resulted, though recently there has been much insightful ethnographic research comparing different football hooligan cultures across Europe (Spaaij, 2006, 2007). Much has also changed since Roadburg's unique analysis in terms of the staging, marketing, and crowd management typical of elite

British football clubs. The Hillsborough Stadium disaster of 1989, for example, forced the elite British game to modernize stadia, remove standing areas, revisit crowd management techniques, and market the sport to a very different kind of fan (Taylor, 1991; Williams, 2006, 2014). However, I would contend that, both structurally and culturally, much of what Roadburg described in 1980 also remains, very broadly, similar today.

North American academics have continued to argue—rather like Roadburg—that comparisons between the patterns and causes of North American sports fan disorder and the gang-like structures more typically identified in soccer hooliganism formations in Britain, Europe, and parts of South America provide for real anomalies. Here, the case is often made that highly episodic bouts of "spontaneous" small-scale sports fan violence and the much larger "celebration" riots that seem to be more a feature of North American sports culture than elsewhere have very different meanings and causes compared to the collective fan violence seemingly ingrained in and around European and South American football. Yet, in a society in which there are high levels of serious interpersonal violence, the intriguing question about the relative absence of American sports hooligans remained (Wann, Melnick, Russell, & Pease, 2001). Nevertheless, the Canadian-based British sports sociologist Kevin Young (2002, 2012) presented thoughtful evidence that normatively patterned forms of fan disorder at North American sport were underreported, and had been becoming increasingly routinized, even though their manifestation might be rather different from that at football matches in Europe. Young argued that incidents of fan-to-fan aggression at North American sports events tended to occur inside stadia—collective fighting *outside* seems to be more of a European and South American trait—and to involve individuals or small groups of supporters in relatively spontaneous and expressive lower-level forms of deviance, such as assault, drunken and disorderly behavior, bouts of small-scale frustration violence, and relatively minor confrontations with the police (Young, 2002, p. 9). All these occur in European and South American sporting contexts too, of course, but they seem very different in nature from the organized confrontations staged around football in many of those locations. Moreover, partly because of the favorable comparisons often made with the spectacular group hooliganism still regularly experienced elsewhere, North American sport has managed to maintain its commercially attractive image of a "family-friendly" entertainment-centered activity, involving a level of consumption-based cosmopolitanism which is generally more accommodating of relatively friendly, not aggressive, fan rivalries. In both age and gender terms and in terms of its managed fan relations, much North American sport spectating features the sensibilities of the socially mixed crowds more typical of elite rugby matches in England and other European locations rather than those attached to urban football clubs. Respectability and behavior characterized by placidity and family-based good order are not typical depictions of most European football crowds, even today. But football has certainly changed in Europe over the past four decades—and perhaps especially so in England.

APPROACHES

Recent North American research on the impact of sports branding suggests that marketeers can influence self-identification and the way fans might negatively perceive opposing teams and their supporters. As Jay Coakley (2001, p. 109) has argued, violent media hype around sporting events means that "spectators are more likely to perceive violence during the event itself, and they are more likely to be violent themselves." Using neutral words such as "rivalry" in promotional material, rather than more inflammatory terms, it is argued can help college sports fans in North America understand the competitive relationship with a rival team, without increasing feelings of overt animosity and deviance. Obtaining "buy-in" from influential fans can further promote rivalry, rather than hate, to the rest of the fan base (Havard, Wann, & Grieve, 2018). This strong focus on managing self-identity and on fan dysfunctionality in some comparative studies has produced a portrait of a "typical" North American hooligan sports fans as a younger, lower-class, less educated, single male, often from a violent background, who may be attracted by violent sports, drink beer, and consume sports media (Mustonen, Arms, & Russell, 1996; Wakefield & Wann, 2006).

North American fan hooliganism, therefore, is liable to involve excessive drinking, high levels of noxious complaining, and confrontational behavior, usually at the level of small groups or individuals (Wakefield & Wann, 2006). Indeed, the role of drink has been especially highlighted in recent accounts. Parrott and Eckhardt (2018), for example, describe their "I-Cubed" theory of when excessive alcohol use is likely to lead to aggression among North American sports fans. This typically involves (1) instigating factors—provocations that might push someone to behave aggressively; (2) impelling factors, dispositional variables—a history of aggressive behavior, anger, irritability, or other negative mood states; and (3) inhibitory factors—the capacity of individuals to resist an aggressive response in the face of instigating and impelling factors. Alcohol remains important in some European football hooligan cultures too, of course, but less so in parts of southern Europe and South America. However, in some Scandinavian locations, heavy drinking has been associated with *friendly* football fandom rather than violence (Peitersen, 2009). Mixing alcohol with drugs, however, has become increasingly valued as a sign of distinction, a means of suppressing fear, and for stimulating the adrenalin "buzz" among organized hooligan gangs in parts of northern Europe. According to Treadwell and Ayres (2015), for example, today's committed English football hooligans may use the complementary consumption of cocaine and alcohol in sporting and other contexts to fulfill three main functions: (1) the facilitation, when required or demanded, of extreme violence against rival fan groups; (2) the acquisition of "time out" and the experience of a "controlled loss of control" as a leisure release from what is both a stressful and a bleakly unsatisfying "normal" life; and (3) the construction of a sought-after, culturally prized, hypermasculine identity.

Early Theories about Football Hooliganism

All this may seem a long way from early sociological theories about fan hooliganism in Britain, but many of these early accounts also emphasized a subcultural-like stress on the creative, "problem-solving" dimensions of aggressive youth formations at sport. These early approaches stressed, for example, the "magical" renewal on the football terraces of traditional local working-class solidarities, long dissipated by spatial and occupational dislocation (Clarke, 1978; Robins, 1984). Football fans' territorial struggles were interpreted then as a distorted way of reinventing prized forms of traditional, collective masculine dignity, once expressed via place heritage and articulated through involvement in localized heavy manual labor. Such functions have not completely disappeared, especially at smaller clubs (Mainwaring & Clark, 2012). The Marxist sociologist Ian Taylor (1971) argued that English football had also commercialized and spectacularized in the 1960s in ways which further alienated its lower-working-class supporter rump. For Taylor, early hooliganism provided "voice," a means of reasserting through displacement some sort of participatory control over a rapidly changing, increasingly commodified and distant, sport (Taylor, 1971; Whannel, 2005). Taylor (1987) argued later that it was actually the *fragmentation* of class solidarities in Britain, under bellicose and racist neoliberal political regimes in Britain, that produced in the 1980s new, more aggressive, highly nationalistic and increasingly aestheticized versions of English football hooligan gangs. Such formations were epitomized by the emergence of the style-conscious *and* violent football "casual" (Thornton, 2003).

In their work in the late 1980s, the so-called Leicester school of sociologists in the United Kingdom focused less on style, the situational aspects of hooligan behavior, or speculations about recent changes in British working-class life and the game. Instead, they drew on the "civilizing process" theories of Norbert Elias (Elias & Dunning, 1966; Dunning, Murphy, & Williams, 1986, Dunning et al., 1988), and the sociology of the American scholar Gerald Suttles (1968, 1972), particularly his accounts of the social ecology of Chicago ghetto communities. Here, trendlines in the urban sociology of North America and in European class analysis seemed briefly to meld. The routine socialization of young lower-working-class male football hooligans in Britain approximated, it was argued, the structural patterns of gender differentiation and aggressive "segmental bonding" identified by Suttles in lower-class neighborhoods in Chicago, and they mirrored the relative lack of social incorporation such experiences implied. Here was a territorialized social formation characteristic of lower-class male street culture that existed in most developed societies. It was highly conducive to the production of hegemonic masculinities via hierarchical male street gangs and an emotional commitment to the pleasurable arousal and "buzz" of disorder and violence as a source of status and excitement for young men in otherwise unrewarding and unexciting societies (Dunning et al., 1988). As "respectable" upper-working-class men began deserting football stadia as fans in Britain in the 1960s and 1970s, and as youth culture began to dissolve traditional cross-generational working-class solidarities at football and elsewhere, so we saw increased evidence of younger male fans from lower-class communities taking charge of sections of the standing terraces in football stadia, basking in the media attention they provoked, and fighting, pleasurably and proprietorially, over "their" space.

The transatlantic difference here, of course, was that young men from the neighborhoods in North America studied by Suttles were probably not *active* sports fans at all in the way that their counterparts in the United Kingdom were a constituent feature of fandom at many football clubs. Indeed, this begs an obvious question today about celebration rioters in the USA: Are they sports fans or opportunity-seeking outsiders, otherwise excluded marginals, who latch on to jubilant sports crowds as a moment for exercising their own forms of "control" via police baiting, violent disorder, and looting (Rosenfeld, 1997)? Indeed, has the success of professional American sport, arguably, been its effective *exclusion* of those marginal youths who are most likely to be committed to oppositional collective violence? Certainly, groups of young lower-class (mainly white) males have long been key figures in northern and eastern European soccer cultures, and they have often been involved in its most serious bouts of hooliganism. Moreover, young English football fans' increasingly disorderly adventures abroad in Continental Europe in the 1970s and 1980s triggered defensive responses in domestic fan cultures in other European countries, where organized hooliganism had featured relatively little before the 1970s but would now grow in importance (Spaaij, 2007; Williams, Dunning, & Murphy, 1984).

Violence or Nonviolence?

These sorts of structural, class-based accounts of the roots of violent hooliganism proposed by the Leicester school were challenged, although they actually have more in common with the concerns of their critics than is sometimes recognized (Bairner, 2006). As social class began to fade as a reliable and defining marker of social difference and masculine identity formation in late modernity, so it was claimed that fan hooliganism was less delineated by such *structural* solidarities defending prescribed class traditions, but was more a celebration of transgressive forms of cross-class male hedonistic camaraderie and belonging. In this view, the research focus on fan violence had been overplayed. Instead, hooliganism is variegated and highly ritualized, underpinned by young men from socially incorporated backgrounds seeking out opportunities for honor contests, for comradeship and adventure in order to stave off existential crises of meaninglessness and boredom (Armstrong, 1998). Hooligan personas here are constituted mainly as open cultural choices, identity possibilities from a "basket of selves" ("organizer," "joker," "fashion victim," "thief," "fighter," etc.) made available to self-selecting members of hooligan firms (Giulianotti & Armstrong, 2002, p. 218). In such socio-anthropological and similar accounts, much soccer hooligan activity is actually about performing satisfying and entertaining collective nonviolent rituals—scuffling confrontations, street posturing, and public expressions of performative masculinities—more than it is about demonstrating classed solidarities and a prowess for serious violence (Marsh, 1978). Indeed, Giulianotti and Armstrong (2002, p. 217) claimed that, in Britain at least, "hooligans do not engage in confrontations with the intention of seriously harming their opponents." Instead, showing one's "gameness" in sports crowd confrontations is often less about inflicting damage or appearing fearless than it is showing the discipline and will needed to perform adequately when one is afraid (Collins, 1995, pp. 189–190; Treadwell & Ayres, 2015).

For the social psychologist, John Kerr (1994, 2005), the social background of those involved in fan hooliganism—their class roots—is also rather less important than the ways in which some male fans conform to rule expectations in one context but can revert to real violence in others. Here, something different from class masculinities, ritual, and belonging is at stake. Emotionally, Kerr argues, there are a number of "meta-motivational states" any of us can inhabit, "reversals" which can be triggered by frustration, saturation, or contingent events (i.e., changes in some aspect of the person or the person's environment). Violent confrontations at sports events and elsewhere may be initiated as part of a search for high levels of emotional arousal which can be experienced as pleasant and exciting. For thrill-seeking fans such as these, regularly engaging in violence and disorder at sports events is enjoyable, but only within a protective frame, a context which is "risky" but also offers relative safety. The police are usually close at hand to ensure hooligan fights are not unregulated and prolonged. However, at the extreme end, Kerr warns that some men (who, exactly?) may become addicted to real sports violence, thus seeking out more and more extreme risks. Indeed, although the level of organization of hooligan groups can often be exaggerated

(Giulianotti & Armstrong, 2002, p. 216), these feted leaders, or "top lads," can become national figures in hooligan circles, men for whom repeated involvement in sports fan violence is reinforced by positive emotional feedback loops, thus reducing possibilities for
their engaging in different, emotionally rewarding experiences. Perhaps these are the men
who, in Latvia, Russia, Poland, and other eastern European countries today, have largely
deserted the sports stadium in favor of organized bare-knuckle fights, held in fields between
identified teams according to set rules and with no third party present to adjudicate and
ensure "fair play"? These contests are usually filmed for online consumption. Fighters in
Poland are mostly fans trained in martial arts, and some may even seek out a more managed
and professional route for their talents, as hooligan firms from different countries take part
in the annual official Team Fight Championship competition in Riga. Such groups may still
be part of fan culture, but opportunities for fights at football today are increasingly rare, and
if they do occur, they take place strictly outside stadia (Kossakowski, 2017).

Of course, injuries and even fan fatalities *do* occur at football, especially perhaps in those
countries in South America and southern Europe where general levels of violence are high,
where sporting hooliganism dramatizes political upheaval or deep-seated political, ethnic,
or religious difference, or where local sociopolitical or criminal power struggles develop
around hooligan formations (Newson et al., 2018; Williams & Vannucci, 2020). Although
members of *barras* in Argentina, for example, can be socially marginalized, their older
leaders are often highly influential and are normatively socially integrated into football
clubs, unions, and political parties. Some fan leaders in Argentina even establish contacts in
higher political circles, thus making them vulnerable to attack by both enemies and insiders
and even, routinely, to murder (Trejo et al., 2019). Although numbers of hooligan-related
deaths in northern Europe are actually incredibly low, involvement in some soccer hooligan firms in both Europe and South America may well reflect local family traditions and
is often implicated, instrumentally, in career activity in criminal markets around drugs and
other trades. Indeed, for both Trejo et al. in Argentina and Treadwell and Ayres (2015, p. 68)
in England, extreme and risky behavior as sports fans often blurs into illicit or corrupt
and criminal activity elsewhere, rather more than it does the pursuit of Armstrong's low-
violence ritual satisfactions, or even the psychologically generated "reversals" of the sort
suggested by Kerr. In this sense, "[f]ootball hooliganism, for the most part, seems to be part
of a constellation of anti-social behaviors that also includes criminal offending" (Piquero,
Jennings, & Farrington, 2015, p. 113).

Policing and Crowd Management

While agreement on causation, motivation, and the nature of sports fan violence and disorder has proved somewhat elusive—or at least contentious—so attention has moved across
the globe to the impact of different styles of *policing* and *crowd management* on the behavior of fans. This stretches from the challenges of developing a "culture of accommodation" between police and troublesome fans at Australian A-League soccer (Warren & Hay,
2009, p. 134), to a focus on the militarization of the management of sports mega-events in
the USA and England (Giulianotti, 2011; Schimmel, 2006), to the complexities of policing
sports crowds in violent areas of Brazil (Raspaud & da Cunha Bastos, 2013) and the covert police "surveillance creep" aimed at football fans in Scotland (Atkinson, McBride, &

Moore, 2020). The recent work of crowd psychologists has focused on the predispositions or motivations of crowd members in relation to the crucial contextual *interaction* between the police and fans in large sports crowds (Jury & Scott, 2011; Stott, Hoggart, & Pearson, 2012; Stott & Reicher, 1998). Indeed, for authors such as these, as crowd conflict spreads and involves larger numbers of people, violent predispositions as an explanation of violent conduct become increasingly marginal. Using a version of their elaborated social identity model, these authors argue that a perceived hostile response to *all* fans by the police, or the failure of police to deal effectively with the hooligan hardcore, can help transform the collective identity of the mass of the crowd. Fans who may typically eschew violence and disorder might, then, see themselves as sharing a common fate with others, including committed hooligans. Here, disorder and resistance can be seen as a legitimate response among non-hooligan fans to overtly threatening or incompetent policing. Indeed, the hypermanagement of sterile, late modern stadium spaces designed to eliminate all risk can mean generally intolerant and inflexible approaches to policing and stewarding which may criminalize routine forms of fandom and can fuse hooligan and non-hooligan fans in their opposition to such excessive control (Brick, 2000; Waiton, 2014; Williams, 2001).

More recently, Martha Newson and her colleagues (2018) have extended this approach by drawing on evolutionary psychology to argue that, for some sports fans, this kind of collective "social fusion" can generate a deeply rooted human sense of belonging that connects self with others, and the group with stadium or territory. This visceral "oneness" with the group and place can lead to highly intense in-group solidarities and behaviors, the most renowned of which is football violence. But why does this produce violent hooliganism among some sports fans, in some cultures, and in some sports, but not in others? This, Newson (2019, p. 436) tantalizingly admits, remains a frustratingly "open" question. Stott and Reicher's (1998) work, in particular, is a useful reminder, however, that oppressive social control and heavy-handed policy is likely to stimulate—or in this case even spread— the crowd disorder it is designed to reduce (Bebber, 2012). It also alludes to the fact that non-hooligans are not always as distinctive from, or as opposed to, hooligans and their activities as official bodies might sometimes wish to contend. Hooligan groups may sometimes be identified by other young fans as offering valued protection in their defense of local masculine honor, as well as a useful source of excitement and entertainment when the sport itself fails to ignite fan passions (Rookwood & Pearson, 2011).

DEBATES

Marketing personnel, chief executive officers, television executives, politicians, and many non-hooligan fans around European and South American football have long publicly envied the successes of North American sport in marginalizing, or even outlawing, collective sports stadium fan disorder and violent hooliganism. Over the past 30 years or so, it has been the British who have perhaps tried hardest to follow key aspects of the highly managed, neoliberal American sporting model, and with some success, as evidenced by the reduced crowd problems and the growing commercial power and global popularity today of the English Premier League (Williams, 2007; 2017). But it is no easy matter to shape a late modern sporting experience which is organic, highly partisan, rigorously inclusive, *and* nonviolent, while also being responsive to the wide range of motivations and expectations that different types of spectators, of different genders, ages, ethnicities, and sociocultural backgrounds, bring to attending collective sporting events. In short, a key debate here remains the challenge of how to shape sporting locales as truly open and democratic but nonviolent, public spaces—as accommodating "venues of extremes" (Frosdick, 1996)—in an era in which our experience of the "other" in leisure and sport is increasingly limited. Much social life today is typically played out in silos, along the lines of ethnic, spatial, and economic inequalities and difference.

In terms of analyzing existing deviant sports fan cultures, perhaps the recent British ethnographic work of criminologists Ayres and Treadwell (2012; Treadwell & Ayres, 2015) offers some of the richest and most sophisticated insight into the wide range of emotional and material rewards and the considerable pleasures and deep camaraderie on offer in the contemporary, late modern football hooligan firm. They also do so without underplaying the very real violence which it sometimes delivers, while also stressing the importance of sociality and belonging inside the hooligan nexus. The ritual shaming of opponents is a central ambition of all hooligan formations, of course, but the capacity to deliver serious violence, when required, is also vital to maintain credible masculine "face." Anthony King's (1995) earlier sociological work was more ambitious in scope, but it similarly weighed up the framing importance in football hooligan encounters of key structural *background factors* (the social makeup of fans and the wider sociopolitical context). Crucially, too, it considered the effects of *fan memory* on hooligan behavior ("What is our history with these opposing fans, or peoples?") while, at the same time, evaluating the impact of immediate, on the ground *triggers* or *thresholds,* which are often identified by fans as appropriate cues for violence or, alternatively, constitute signals which effectively rule it out. Thus, we might begin to understand why organized or more spontaneous sports hooliganism may be anticipated on some occasions, but does not always occur, and vice versa. King is also keenly aware of the importance of the "cultural scripts" which circulate around collective hooligan activity. Even young men enmeshed inside violent hooligan formations have lives elsewhere, and they spend much more time *talking* about hooligan events than actually fighting. Talk is, in itself, deeply satisfying in identity terms, and it may be at least as important as direct involvement in violent or disorderly activity.

However, the Dutch sociologist Ramon Spaaij (2007, 2008) has, arguably, done more than most to try to settle some key debates around the connections between spontaneity and planned aggression in fan conflict. He has done so by attempting to meld different approaches into a single explanatory framework, one that also traverses the Atlantic. His latest attempt at a "socio-ecological model" (Spaaij, 2014, p. 153), for example, makes claims for some interdisciplinary coherence by not privileging any specific approach, instead emphasizing that insights from different disciplines are not mutually exclusive but rather "contribute different pieces of the same puzzle." Some of this work tends toward the descriptive listing of constituent features rather than offering an entirely convincing integrative whole, but it *is* a more holistic approach to conceptualizing fan hooliganism, one which "brings together distal and proximate causes of soccer fan violence" (Spaaij & Anderson, 2010, p. 563). Like a more complex version of the social realist approach of King (1995), this later work at least argues for an object-adequate, multilevel analytical model. It is one that (1) advances economic, political, cultural, and social factors as key framing macro-level influences; 2) sees local fan cultures and identities as the lived habitus of fan groups at the mid-level; and 3) recognizes individual and collective fan violence and disorder as the ground floor, micro-level output. In this sort of account, the familiar structure/agency debate around sports crowd disorder is addressed by including moderating influences which can shape developments at the level of habitus. These include match-related triggers (contentious officials' decisions, player violence, etc.), interventions by agents of social control (the provocative actions of police and crowd stewards), the impacts of place and space effects (stadium architecture and atmosphere), and the positive or negative effects of communications (e.g., by the media and among and between rival fan groups).

The ultimate aim here is to establish a new connectivity between the European sports violence research tradition, broadly rooted in structural concerns, ethnography, and socio-anthropology, and the experimental and more statistical approaches which explore the psychological triggers of individual and collective sports fan violence, more common perhaps in North America. Such a synthesis holds much promise in being able to interpret aspects of the interpersonal experience of disorder and violence, set against macro-social structures, while also acknowledging the importance of the "collective mind" as it is understood through the lens of social identification theory and habitus (Spaaij & Anderson, 2010, p. 575). The model may appear all-encompassing, lacking analytical fine-tuning—for example, how, when, and under what conditions do different elements of the model have greater or lesser impact—but it accommodates explanatory accounts from different disciplines of instances of both spontaneous and planned sports hooliganism in a way which at least attempts to capture some of their commonalities, their diversity, and their overall complexity.

CONCLUSION

So what exactly have we learned in the 40-year period since Alan Roadburg's pioneering work in Britain back in 1980? *First*, unsurprisingly perhaps, the past four decades have exhibited patterns of both continuity and change. We can probably confirm that more spontaneous, individualized forms of fan violence and disorder still tend to define sporting hooliganism in North America, compared to the more organized, collective hooligan fan subcultures that feature, particularly at football, in other parts of the world.

Second, English football has had its own "revolution" since 1992, effectively evading addressing deeper structural issues by eagerly following the path of marketized North American sport. Roadburg would barely recognize it today. Elite football stadia, particularly in England but also around Europe, have been part of a wider, forced program of modernization. New stadia have been built and relocated, and seats and CCTV systems have replaced the participatory, carnivalesque, and anonymized spectacle of standing areas of the 1980s, a move which, for one American scholar, has produced the dramatic transformation of the stadium and the English game in the public imagination, "from a dystopic hell to a utopic promise for the future" (Robinson, 2010, p. 1012). Memories of more disorderly times, at least in accounts such as this, are simply wallowing in hegemonic masculine nostalgia (Dart, 2008).

Certainly, football venues in England have become less violent and also less hostile to female and minority ethnic fans (Cleland and Cashmore, 2016; Pope, 2011). The same may not always be true elsewhere in Europe (Gould and Williams, 2011). Spectator attendance in England has been growing again since the hooligan crisis years of the 1980s. New stadium surveillance systems have been made mandatory, and the seats, marketing, and rising ticket pricing of the new English Premier League have served to gentrify, sanitize, and pacify stadium spaces, serving older, more mixed audiences, but also ensuring social exclusion and the type of "securitization" of the supporter experience that has not been to the satisfaction of all fans (Brick, 2000; Giulianotti, 2005; Williams, 2001, 2006). Critics argue that many English soccer stadia today risk becoming inauthentic or "placeless" sites, arenas where, typically, little happens spontaneously, autonomously, or accidentally (Bale, 2000; Duke, 2002; Sandvoss, 2003). According to this view, this new generation of sports stadia lacks place identity and offers too little scope for the collective expression of human emotions. It also threatens the ontological security still on offer at more traditional, smaller venues (Mainwaring & Clark, 2012).

These elite stadia today are rational, but tame, sporting landscapes. They are now regarded by many young, working-class fans—including, of course, many hooligans—as the antitheses of spaces of open access, excitement, and freedom. Instead, they are experienced as material and symbolic expressions of authoritarian control and restraint (Giulianotti, 2011; Redhead, 2015b; Waiton, 2014). Indeed, around Europe today fan groups have organized to oppose the overregulation and overcommodification of the stadium experience, as part of a popular Against Modern Football movement (Guschwan, 2007; Perasović & Mustapić, 2018). Nevertheless, football in Britain is now widely perceived internationally— if slightly erroneously—to have overcome its once deep-seated problems with hooligans. It has been transformed, via its new pricing regimes, its customer-focused ethos, and the sort of micro-management and mass surveillance techniques characteristic of the contemporary neoliberal state. Partly as a result, some excluded hooligan fans in Britain have relocated their allegiances and violent proclivities from sport to the street political activities of the Far Right (Allen, 2019).

Third, instances of more spontaneous fan disorder can occur in any team sport setting, especially when club identification is intense, frustrations are not effectively managed, and alcohol is freely available. Here, drunken arguments, missile throwing, crowd protests— and even some sports riots—seem common features across many cultures and continents, rooted as they often are in demonstrations of hegemonic masculinity, the psychology of frustration, social identity effects, or crowd fusion influences. Few of these ideas were part of the theoretical landscape for scholars such as Roadburg when he first visited British football stadia more than 40 years ago. Nor, really, *fourth*, was preplanned, highly organized football fan hooliganism of the type which developed into its mature form in England from the early 1980s. Today, hooligan groups around the world are, of course, well versed in the use of the internet and social media to celebrate their alleged conquests and promote and arrange future confrontations (Spaaij, 2011). Women remain marginal figures in hooligan circles, but we have learned that membership for men in established hooligan groups is about much more than simply manning up for battle: belonging, identity, comradeship, hedonism, social meaning, and honor are all in play.

Fifth, fan hooliganism is not a static phenomenon, and explanations which may have seemed perfectly adequate more than 40 years ago inevitably require some refinement today. Pointing to the significance of the structural features which underpin organized sports crowd violence—as Roadburg and others have done—probably underplays the more fluid nature of today's class identities and late modern masculine identity construction, and also the crucial importance of situational factors—perhaps particularly policing strategies—for provoking hooliganism. We must also consider the impact on fandom of processes of media amplification (Poulton, 2005, 2006).

Sixth, local or national political, ethnic, and other distinctions, as we have seen, are the "contextual processes" that can feed and help shape fan conflicts staged, over time, around football and other sports (Braun & Vliegenthart, 2008, p. 813). In short, we risk plenty by understating the significance of national, cultural, or sociopolitical effects.

Arguably, one thing *has* remained a near constant since Roadburg's work, even as homophobia has been decreasing, women's team sport has become globally more possible and more popular, and the management of sports fan disorder has changed over time. It is that fan disorder, in its various guises, continues to articulate, reinforce, and celebrate forms of aggressive hegemonic heteromasculinity. Although its roots are much more widely spread and are resilient, ideals of hegemonic masculinity remain perpetually built around some conveniently mediated "narrative myths" about sport, including portraying "being tough," "being competitive," "winning against all odds," "making a sacrifice play," and assuming a "winner takes all" mentality as equating to true (male) sporting heroism (Burstyn, 1999; English, 2017, p. 186). It might be idealistic, and even possibly misleading, to suggest, as the sports philosopher Coleen English (2017, p. 195) has recently done, that, "[p]utting respect above victory easily fits within sport when hegemonic masculinity is absent." But reducing some of the narrow, hypercompetitive, macho, heteronormative dimensions of elite sporting practice is perhaps worth aiming for in the longer term for its potential positive impact *off* the field, pitch, and court. Meanwhile, episodes of individual, and particularly collective, male fan violence—even when occurring away from the stadium—are increasingly being recorded and commodified, sold online as virtual entertainment packages, for mass global audiences of young men. Bread and circuses, indeed.

References

Allen, C. (2019). The Football Lads Alliance and Democratic Football Lads Alliance: An insight into the dynamism and diversification of Britain's counter-jihad movement. *Social Movement Studies* 18(5), 639–646.

Armstrong, G. (1998). *Football hooligans: Knowing the score.* Oxford: Berg.

Atkinson, C., McBride, M., & Moore, A. (2020). Pitched! Informants and the covert policing of football fans in Scotland. *Policing and Society*, 31(7), 863–877. doi:10.1080/10439463.2020.1795168.

Ayres, T., & Treadwell J. (2012). Bars, drugs and soccer thugs: Alcohol, cocaine use and violence in the NTE among English soccer firms. *Criminology and Criminal Justice*, 12(1), 83–100.

Bairner, A. (2006). The Leicester School and the study of football hooliganism. *Sport in Society*, 9(4), 583–598.

Bale, J. (2000). The changing face of soccer: Stadium and communities. *Soccer and Society*, 1(1), 91–101.

Bebber, B. (2012). *Violence and racism in soccer: Politics and cultural conflict in British society 1968–1998.* London: Pickering and Chatto.

Branscombe, N., & Wann, D. (1991). The positive social and self-concept consequences of sports team identification. *Journal of Sport and Social Issues, 15*(2), 115–127.

Braun, R., & Vliegenthart, R. (2008). The contentious fans: The impact of repression, media coverage, grievances and aggressive play on supporters' violence. *International Sociology, 23*(6), 796–818.

Brick, C. (2000). Taking offence: Modern moralities and the perception of the football fan. *Soccer and Society, 1*(1), 158–172.

Burstyn, V. (1999). *The rites of men: Manhood, politics, and the culture of sport.* Toronto: University of Toronto Press.

Clarke, J. (1978). Football and working-class fans: Tradition and change. In R. Ingham (Ed.), *Football hooliganism: The wider context* (pp. 37–60). London: Interaction.

Cleland, J., & Cashmore, E. (2016). Football fans' views of violence in British football: Evidence of a sanitized and gentrified culture. *Journal of Sport and Social Issues, 40*(2), 124–142.

Coakley, J. J. (2001). *Sport in society: Issues and controversies* (7th ed.). New York: McGraw-Hill.

Collins, R. (1995). Gewelddadig conflict en sociale organisatie [Violent conflict and social organization]. In J. Goudsblom, B. van Heerikhuizen, & J. Heilbron (Eds.), *Hoofdstukken uit de sociologie* (pp. 185–202). Amsterdam: Amsterdam University Press.

Collins, R. (2008). *Violence: A micro-sociological theory.* Princeton, NJ: Princeton University Press.

Dart, J. (2008). Confessional tales from former soccer hooligans: A nostalgic narcissistic wallow in soccer violence. *Soccer and Society, 9*(1), 42–55.

Duke, V. (2002). Local tradition versus globalisation: Resistance to the McDonaldisation and Disneyisation of professional soccer in England. *Soccer Studies, 5*(1), 5–23.

Dunning, E. (2010). Civilizing sports: Figurational sociology and the sociology of sport. In E. Smith (Ed.), *Sociology of sport and social theory* (pp. 15–25). Champaign, IL: Human Kinetics.

Dunning, E., Murphy, P., Waddington, I., & Astrinakis, A. (Eds.). (2002). *Fighting fans: Football hooliganism as a world phenomenon.* Dublin: University College Dublin Press.

Dunning, E., Murphy, P., & Williams, J. (1986). Spectator violence at football matches: Towards a sociological explanation. *British Journal of Sociology, 37,* 221–224.

Dunning, E., Murphy, P., & Williams, J. (1988). *The roots of soccer hooliganism.* London: RKP.

Elias, N., & Dunning, E. (1966). Dynamics of group sports with special reference to football. *British Journal of Sociology, 17*(4), 388–402.

English, C. (2017). Toward sport reform: Hegemonic masculinity and reconceptualizing competition. *Journal of the Philosophy of Sport, 44*(2), 183–198.

Frosdick, S. (1996). Venues of extremes. *International Magazine of Arena Construction and Management, Winter,* 26–30.

Giulianotti, R. (1999). *Football: A sociology of the global game.* Cambridge, U.K.: Polity Press.

Giulianotti, R. (2005). Sport spectators and the social consequences of commodification. *Journal of Sport & Social Issues, 29*(4), 386–410.

Giulianotti, R. (2011). Sport mega-events, urban football carnivals and securitised commodification: The case of the English Premier League. *Urban Studies, 48*(15), 3293–3310.

Giulianotti, R., & Armstrong, G. (2002). Avenues of contestation: Football hooligans running and ruling urban spaces. *Social Anthropology, 10*(2), 211–238.

Gould, D., & Williams J. (2011). After Heysel: How Italy lost the soccer "peace." *Soccer and Society, 12*(5), 586–601.

Guschwan, M. (2007). Riot in the curve: Soccer fans in twenty-first century Italy. *Soccer and Society, 8*(2–3), 250–266.

Havard, C., Wann, D., & Grieve, F. (2018). Rivalry versus hate: Measuring the influence of promotional titles and logos on fan rival perceptions. *Journal of Applied Management, 10*(2), 1–18.

Hopcraft, A. (1971). *The football man.* Harmondsworth, U.K.: Penguin.

Jury, J., & Scott, C. (2011). Contextualising the crowd in contemporary social science. *Contemporary Social Science, 6*(3), 275–288.

Kerr, J. (1994). *Understanding soccer hooliganism.* Buckingham, U.K.: Open University Press.

Kerr, J. (2005). *Rethinking aggression and violence in sport.* London: Routledge.

King, A. (1995). Outline of a practical theory of football violence. *Sociology, 29,* 635–641.

Kossakowski, R. (2017). Where are the hooligans? Dimensions of football fandom in Poland. *International Review for the Sociology of Sport, 52*(6), 693–711.

Knight, R., Hartman, K., & Bennett, A. (2020). Gun violence, eSports, and global crises: A proposed model for sport crisis communication practitioners. *Journal of Global Sport Management, 5*(2), 223–241.

Lanter, J. (2011). Spectator identification with the team and celebratory sports crowd violence. *Journal of Sport Behaviour, 34*(3), 268–280.

Marsh, P. (1978). *Aggro: The illusion of violence.* London: Dent.

Mainwaring, E., & Clark, T. (2012). We're shit and we know we are: Identity, place and ontological security in lower league soccer in England. *Soccer and Society, 13*(1), 107–123.

Malcolm, D. (1999). Cricket spectator disorder: Myths and historical evidence. *Sports Historian, 19*(1), 16–37.

Murphy, P., Williams, J., & Dunning, E. (1991). *Football on trial.* London: RKP.

Mustonen, A., Arms, R., & Russell, G. (1996). Predictors of sports spectators' proclivity for riotous behaviour in Finland and Canada. *Personality and Individual Difference, 21*(4), 519–525.

Neilson, C. (2013). Stronger than the state? Football hooliganism, political extremism and the Gay Pride parades in Serbia. *Sport in Society, 16*(3), 1038–1053.

Newson, M. (2019). Football, fan violence, and identity fusion. *International Review for the Sociology of Sport, 54*(4), 431–444.

Newson, M., Bortolini T., Buhrmester, M., Ricardo da Silva, S., Nicássio Queiroga da Aquino, J., & Whitehouse, H. (2018). Brazil's football warriors: Social bonding and inter-group violence. *Evolution and Human Behavior, 39,* 675–683.

Ncube, L., & Munoriyarwa, A. (2018). See no evil, hear no evil and speak no evil? The press, violence and hooliganism at the Battle of Zimbabwe. *Soccer & Society, 19*(5–6), 842–857.

Ostrowsky, M. (2018). Sports fans, alcohol use, and violent behavior: A sociological review. *Trauma, Violence and Abuse, 19*(4), 406–419.

Parrott, D., & Eckhardt, I. (2018). Effects of alcohol on human aggression. *Current Opinion in Psychology, 19,* 1–5.

Pearson, G. (2009). The researcher as hooligan: Where "participant" observation means breaking the law. *International Journal of Social Research Methodology, 12*(3), 243–255.

Peitersen, B. (2009). Supporter culture in Denmark: The legacy of the World's Best Supporters. *Soccer & Society, 10*(3–4), 374–385.

Perasović, P., & Mustapić, M. (2018). Carnival supporters, hooligans, and the "Against Modern Football" movement: Life within the ultras subculture in the Croatian context. *Sport in Society, 21*(6), 960–976.

Piotrowski, P. (2006). Coping with football-related hooliganism: Healing symptoms versus cause prevention. *Journal of Applied Psychology, 36*(3), 629–643.

Piquero, A., Jennings, W., & Farrington, D. (2015). The life-course offending trajectories of football hooligans. *European Journal of Criminology, 12*(1), 113–125.

Pitti, I. (2019). Being women in a male preserve: An ethnography of female football ultras. *Journal of Gender Studies, 28*(3), 318–329.

Pope, S. (2011). Like pulling down Durham Cathedral and building a brothel: Women as new consumer fans? *International Review for the Sociology of Sport, 46*(4), 471–487.

Poulton, E. (2005). English media representation of football-related disorder: "Brutal, short-hand and simplifying"? *Sport in Society, 8*(1), 27–47.

Poulton, E. (2006). "Fantasy football hooliganism" in popular media. *Media, Culture & Society, 29*(1), 151–164.

Poulton, E. (2012). "If you had the balls, you'd be one of us!" Doing gendered research: Methodological reflections on being a female researcher in the hyper-masculine subculture of "football hooliganism." *Sociological Research Online, 17*(4), 1–13.

Pradhan, S., Lee, N., Snycerski, S., & Laraway, S. (2021). Alcoholics fanonymous: The relationships between reasons for drinking, aggression, and team identification in sports fans. *International Journal of Sport and Exercise Psychology, 19*(4), 626–649. doi:10.1080/1612197X.2019.1674904.

Raspaud, M., & da Cunha Bastos, F. (2013). Torcedores de futebol: Violence and public policies in Brazil before the 2014 FIFA World Cup. *Sport in Society, 16*(2), 192–204.

Redhead, S. (2015a). The firm: Towards a study of 400 football gangs. *Sport in Society, 18*(3), 329–346.

Redhead, S. (2015b). The last of the working-class subcultures to die? Real tales of football hooligans in the global media age. In M. Hopkins & J. Treadwell (Eds.), *Football hooliganism, fan behaviour and crime* (pp. 127–153). Basingstoke, U.K.: Palgrave Macmillan.

Roadburg, A. (1980) Factors precipitating fan violence: A comparison of professional soccer in Britain and North America. *British Journal of Sociology, 31*(2), 265–276.

Roberts, J., & Benjamin, C. (2000). Spectator violence in sport: A North American perspective. *European Journal on Criminal Policy and Research, 8*, 163–181.

Robins, D. (1984). *We hate humans.* Harmondsworth, U.K.: Penguin.

Robinson, J. (2010). The place of the stadium: English football beyond the fans. *Sport in Society, 13*(6), 1012–1026.

Rookwood, J., and Pearson, G. (2011). The hoolifan: Positive fan attitudes to soccer hooliganism. *International Review for the Sociology of Sport, 47*(2), 149–164.

Rosenfeld, M. (1997). Celebration, politics, selective looting and riots: A micro level study of the Bulls Riot of 1992 in Chicago. *Social Problems, 44*(4), 483–502.

Roversi, A. (1991). Football violence in Italy. *International Review for the Sociology of Sport, 26*(4), 311–330.

Russell, G., & Arms, R. (1998). Toward a social psychological profile of would-be rioters. *Aggressive Behavior, 24*, 219–226.

Sack, A., & Suster, Z. (2000). Soccer and Croatian nationalism: A prelude to war. *Journal of Sport and Social Issues, 24*(3), 305–320.

Sandvoss, C. (2003). *A game of two halves: Soccer fandom, TV and globalisation.* London: Routledge.

Scalia, V. (2009). Just a few rogues? Football *ultras*, clubs and politics in contemporary Italy. *International Review for the Sociology of Sport, 44*(1), 41–53.

Schimmel, K. (2006). Deep play: Sports mega-events and urban social conditions in the USA. *Sociological Review*, 54(2), 160–174.

Selmer, N. (2004). *Watching the boys play: Frauen als fußballfans*. Kassel: Agon-Sportverlag.

Sindbæk, T. (2013). A Croatian champion with a Croatian name: National identity and uses of history in Croatian football culture—the case of Dinamo Zagreb. *Sport in Society*, 16(8), 1009–1024.

Spaaij, R. (2006). *Understanding football hooliganism: A comparison of six Western European football clubs*. Amsterdam: Amsterdam University Press.

Spaaij, R. (2007). Soccer hooliganism as a transnational phenomenon. *International Journal of the History of Sport*, 24(4), 411–431.

Spaaij, R. (2008). Men like us, boys like them: Violence, masculinity and collective identity in soccer hooliganism. *Journal of Sport and Social Issues*, 32(4), 369–392.

Spaaij, R. (2011). Mindless thugs running riot? Mainstream, alternative and online media representations of football crowd violence. *Media International Australia*, 140(1), 126–136.

Spaaij, R. (2014). Sports crowd violence: An interdisciplinary synthesis. *Aggression and Violent Behavior*, 19, 146–155.

Spaaij, R., & Anderson, E. (2010). Soccer fan violence: A holistic approach. *International Sociology*, 25(4), 561–579.

Stott, C., Hoggart, J., & Pearson, G. (2012). Keeping the peace: social identity, procedural justice and the policing of soccer crowds. *British Journal of Criminology*, 52(2), 381–399.

Stott, C., & Reicher, S. (1998). How conflict escalates: The inter-group dynamics of collective football crowd "violence." *Sociology*, 32(2), 353–377.

Suttles, G. (1968). *The social order of the slum: Ethnicity and territoriality in the inner city*. Chicago: University of Chicago Press.

Suttles, G. (1972). *The social construction of communities*. Chicago: University of Chicago Press.

Swenson, S. (2012). Unsportsmanlike conduct: The duty placed on stadium owners to protect against fan violence. *Marquette Sports Law Review*, 23(1), 135–153.

Taylor, I. (1971). Football mad: A speculative sociology of football hooliganism. In E. Dunning (Ed.), *The sociology of sport: A selection of readings* (pp. 352–377). London: Frank Cass.

Taylor, I. (1987). Putting the boot into a working-class sport: British soccer after Bradford and Brussels. *Sociology of Sport Journal*, 4(2), 171–191.

Taylor, I. (1991). English soccer in the 1990s: Taking Hillsborough seriously. In J. Williams & S. Wagg (Eds.), *British football and social change* (pp. 3–24). Leicester, U.K.: Leicester University Press.

Thornton, P. (2003). *Casuals: Football fighting and fashion: The story of a terrace cult*. London: Milo Books.

Treadwell, J., & Ayres, T. (2015). Taking Prada and powder: Cocaine use and supply among the football hooligan firm. In M. Hopkins & J. Treadwell (Eds.), *Football hooliganism, fan behaviour and crime* (pp. 49–70). Basingstoke, U.K.: Palgrave Macmillan.

Trejo, F., Murzi, D., & Nassar, B. (2019). Violence and death in Argentinean soccer in the new millennium: Who is involved and what is at stake? *International Review for the Sociology of Sport*, 54(7), 837–854.

Valantinė, I., Grigaliūnaitė, I., & Danilevičienė., L. (2017). Impact of basketball fan behaviour on the organisation's brand. *Baltic Journal of Sport and Health Sciences*, 1(104), 47–54.

Waiton, S. (2014). Football fans in an age of intolerance. In M. Hopkins & J. Treadwell (Eds.), *Football hooliganism, fan behaviour and crime* (pp. 201–221). Basingstoke, U.K.: Palgrave Macmillan.

Wakefield, K., & Wann, D. (2006). An examination of dysfunctional sports fans. *Journal of Leisure Research, 38*(2), 168–186.

Wann, D., Melnick, M., Russell, G., & Pease, D. (2001). *Sport fans: The psychology and social impact of spectators*. New York: Routledge.

Ward, R. (2002). Fan violence: Social problem or moral panic? *Aggression and Violent Behaviour, 7*, 453–475.

Warren, I., & Hay, R. (2009). "Fencing them in": The A-League, policing and the dilemma of public order. *Soccer & Society, 10*(1), 124–141.

Whannel, G. (2005). Pregnant with anticipation: The pre-history of television sport and the politics of recycling and preservation. *International Journal of Cultural Studies, 8*(4), 405–426.

Williams, J. (2001). The cost of safety in risk societies. *Journal of Forensic Psychiatry, 12*(1), 1–7.

Williams, J. (2006). Protect me from what I want: Soccer fandom, celebrity cultures and "new" soccer in England. *Soccer and Society, 7*(1), 96–114.

Williams, J. (2007). Rethinking sports fandom: The case of European soccer. *Leisure Studies, 26*(2), 127–146.

Williams, J. (2014). Justice for the 96? Hillsborough, politics and English football. In M. Hopkins & J. Treadwell (Eds.), *Football hooliganism, fan behaviour and crime* (pp. 273–295). Basingstoke, U.K.: Palgrave Macmillan.

Williams, J. (2017). Game changer? The English Premier League, big money and world football. In R. Elliott (Ed.), *The English Premier League: A socio-cultural analysis* (pp. 163–184). London: Routledge.

Williams, J., Dunning E., & Murphy, P. (1984) *Hooligans abroad*. London: RKP.

Williams, J., & Vannucci, N. (2020). English hooligans and Italian ultras sport, culture and national policy narratives. *International Journal of Sport Policy and Politics, 12*(1), 73–89.

Young, K. (2002). Standard deviations: An update on North American sports crowd disorder. *Sociology of Sport Journal, 19*, 237–275.

Young, K. (2012). *Sport, violence and society*. New York: Routledge.

CHAPTER 52

··

SPORT, GAMBLING, AND MATCH-FIXING

··

MINHYEOK TAK

ALTHOUGH they share a long history, today sport and gambling are more interconnected and more visible than ever before. Football (soccer) fans witness European clubs playing with gambling brand logos on their jerseys. In English football, half of 20 Premier League clubs and 17 of 24 Championship clubs had jersey sponsorship deals with betting companies in the 2019–2020 season. In the United States, the long-standing anti–sports betting stance of major leagues seems to have been renounced following the Supreme Court's ruling in May 2018 which granted each state the right to decide on legalization of sports betting in their jurisdiction (Holden & Schuster, 2019). In Scandinavian and East Asian countries with state-sanctioned betting operators, the revenues are earmarked to finance public sport provision (Vinberg, Durbeej, & Rosendahl, 2020). In Africa, worrying numbers of youth are alleged to bet on sports leagues in the Global North using transnational betting companies whose logos appear as part of the branding of high-profile teams (Mwesigwa, 2018). No matter how one engages with sport and regardless of level of competition, today's reality is that nobody is free from the influence of gambling. Within and around sporting domains, we are both targeted as consumers (hence potential at-risk gamblers) and beneficiaries of the symbiotic relationship between sports and gambling industries.

The foregoing changes did not emerge out of nowhere. Underneath the landscape of what is called "gamblization" or "gamblification" of sport lie various social forces at work on different levels. For example, the changing global political economy of the 1970s brought fiscal crises to states which, in turn, deregulated gambling and its advertising as an alternative form of revenue generation (Cosgrave & Klassen, 2001). The rise of internet technology created borderless gambling markets filled by legal and illegal operators armed with excessive marketing strategies (Forrest, 2012b). Sports organizations in financial difficulties have increasingly embraced betting as another stream of income. Hence, the ubiquity of gambling provision and promotion that we are experiencing in both physical and digital spaces is a logical consequence of the liberalization of gambling in political, regulatory, and cultural respects.

The growing influence of gambling on sport simultaneously creates opportunities and challenges (Villeneuve & Diaconu, 2011). On the one hand, sport organizations earn additional revenue from betting sponsorships and/or public subsidies from state-run sports gambling. The overall popularity of sports, as seen in levels of viewership, for example, also partially depends on the availability of betting as a secondary way of consuming sports as "content." On the other hand, sports betting, as a type of gambling, brings about social harms, such as gambling addiction and match-fixing. The purpose of this chapter is to offer a critical overview of the social and political background of the close relationship of sports and gambling today, as well as the regulations, issues, and discourses that come with this new social arrangement.

This chapter consists of three main sections. The next section explores the on-and-off relationship between sport and gambling in history. This brief historical review suggests that underlying sociopolitical considerations have governed the distance between the two social institutions. It also illuminates various ways in which they interact and relevant issues that merit social scientific inquiries. In a subsequent section, the focus shifts to the issue of integrity as a consequence of the contemporary solidification of the sport-gambling nexus. Here, four main academic approaches to the problem of match-fixing are presented. The last main section considers ongoing debates over the discourse of sport integrity, such as the influence that gambling has on sport ethics and the politics around policy measures for sport integrity. The chapter concludes with a brief summary and discussion of potential directions for research.

Issues

Both sport and gambling have been popular activities throughout human history (Guttmann, 1986). Their popularity may derive from the nature of the activities that, arguably, symbolize skill and chance, respectively. The combination of the two (aleatory engagement with agonistic competition) can amplify the pleasure of both through additional thrills of risk taking and the fun of calculating skill factors. However, this form of entertainment has often been challenged, or even banned, at various points in history because of the problems it presents to the social order. This has led to a pendulum-like history of their relationship (Tak, Sam, & Jackson, 2018b).

In ancient Rome, betting was a regular feature of public spectacles in the circuses and amphitheaters (Futrell, 2006; Harris, 1972). These gladiatorial combats had rules, umpires, and odds makers, and spectators followed and wagered on particular gladiators according to their "career stats" (Fagan, 2006; Futrell, 2006, pp. 86–87). However, the medieval era reveals early attempts to control gambling activities (Reith, 1999). In Britain, a large number of edicts and decrees were issued to forbid gambling to protect human resources for labor and the military from the social ills caused by gambling (Munting, 1996; Reith, 1999).

By the late 17th century in Britain, betting and human competitive events were reunited. Pugilism (prizefighting) and pedestrianism (footraces) experienced a boom as gambling events under the auspices of the aristocracy (Guttmann, 1986). Gambling also stimulated the formalization of rules, especially in cricket, golf, and boxing (Vamplew, 2007). However, their cohabitation created what Villeneuve and Diaconu (2011, p. 6) describe as "the twin dynamics of ethics and money." Gambling gave sports more popularity and financial gains. However, simultaneously, gambling put at risk the social legitimacy of sports because of the many social harms it entailed, including addiction, the degradation of the work ethic, and match-fixing (Tak, Sam, & Jackson, 2018a).

Thus, within the capitalist social order of the late 19th century, some of the financially viable sports tried to dissociate from gambling (Adelman, 1990; Clapson, 1992; McDaniel, Mason, & Kinney, 2004; McKelvey, 2004). For example, English football continued attempts to outlaw betting on the sport in the early 20th century (Huggins, 2013). On the other side of the Atlantic, similar endeavors were being made to ban gambling on baseball as part of the project to make that sport the national pastime (Shernock, 2014). This hard-line policy of football and baseball may represent the directions that 20th-century sports have pursued. Sport generally stood for values which were embraced by industrial capitalism (e.g., sobriety, self-denial, discipline, development) yet incompatible with gambling (Riess, 1995). During the 20th century, therefore, gambling was generally kept at bay from sports in most countries.

However, sport and gambling remarried in the mid- to late 20th century with a series of changes in the global political economy. After World War II, the Keynesian state of America, European welfare states, and developing nations elsewhere enjoyed high growth rates (Arrighi, 1994). However, their institutional basis (e.g., social security, employment, income policies) began to collapse with the advent of what Strange (1986) termed "casino capitalism," by which she meant the unpredictable and volatile global financial environment that occurred after the abandonment of the fixed exchange rate system in 1973. Having experienced stagflation and fiscal crises, the planner states per se were under pressure to restructure themselves for continuous accumulation (Harvey, 2006). Neoliberalism was the states' response to this crisis, and its specific manifestations (e.g., deregulation, the privatization of public service, and the flexibility of the labor market) created new space for capital accumulation or cost-cutting (Cosgrave, 2006; Harvey, 2006). According to Cosgrave, the legalization of gambling is a form of risk management of these late-capitalist states.

In this light, the contemporary legalization of sports betting can be understood as a part of the states' strategies to fill the revenue gap. In practice, since the last quarter of the 20th century, sports betting has been legalized in many countries around the world (Cosgrave & Klassen, 2001; Goodman, 1995; Hoye, 2006; Seelig & Seelig, 1998). Given that sports betting had always been available, albeit flying under the radar, this contemporary legislation was not making something out of nothing. Rather, such legislative efforts brought an existing cultural practice within the taxable, regulative remits of official government activities. This current reunion of sports and gambling arises in two major forms: gambling on sport and gambling promotion through sport. As Villeneuve and Diaconu's (2011) twin dynamics of ethics and money indicates, these two key interfaces bring important streams of revenue (money) to sport organizations and governments, but also create conditions for societal problems (ethics) by undermining integrity and stimulating public health issues.

The first interface, gambling on sport, is the more fundamental form of association between the two because the act of wagering directly concerns the content (process and result) of a sporting contest itself. Legalized sports betting assumes two major models: state monopoly and open-market models. The state monopoly model normally adopts an exclusive licensing system, whereby the business is consigned to a statutory (e.g., TAB in New Zealand) or private (e.g., Sports TOTO in South Korea) corporation (Villeneuve & Diaconu, 2011). This model is employed to raise public funds and take closer control over the supply, consumption, and side effects of gambling (Forrest, 2012a). Thus, monopolistic suppliers target their domestic markets, offer traditional types of betting, and provide relatively lower payout rates (e.g., Sports TOTO in South Korea: 84%). On the other hand, the open-market model has been adopted in the United Kingdom, Ireland, and Australia and in tax havens such as Gibraltar. These jurisdictions issue multiple licenses to qualified private operators that tend to offer far higher payout rates (over 90%) and branch out into other overseas markets (Boniface et al., 2012).

All this raises a key question: What do sport governing bodies gain from offering their matches for gambling? In theory, there is no direct, corresponding return for the use of sport for betting. Put simply, betting companies need no legal permission from sport governing bodies whose matches are used for betting (Edelman, 2018). This is because sport has been historically reluctant to be associated with gambling but also because there are no property rights for publicly available information about sports matches (Holden & Schuster, 2019). Nonetheless, sport governing bodies often try to secure some financial returns, in the form of "integrity fees," with the justification that betting on their sports increases costs for integrity maintenance (Hoye, 2006). Within domestic contexts, most public models allocate a certain ratio of betting revenues to sports organizations (e.g., South Korean Sports TOTO: approximately U.S.$1.3 billion annually) (Korea Sports Promotion Foundation, 2020).

In free market systems, the advent of live betting has opened the possibility for sports organizations to seek compensation from betting companies, albeit indirectly. In order to offer in-play betting, bookmakers need more accurate, reliable, real-time data feeds which are not always available publicly (Ramsey, 2018). Thus, betting companies subscribe to multiple data providers that exclusively distribute official match information and statistics of certain sports tournaments and leagues. Such data feed contracts among sports, data, and betting industries act as an alternative way for sports organizations to secure fees for the use of their events for gambling. In any case, sport's connection with betting tends not to be immediate, but rather mediated through governments, or data companies that may help to obscure the straight, commercial links between sport and gambling.

Without doubt, the most direct cost of expanded sports betting is the increased risk to the integrity of sport (Tak et al., 2018b). Match-fixing is hardly new in human sporting history (Stephens, 2020). The problem is that attempts at match manipulation have become more frequent and institutionalized since the start of the 21st century due to a range of factors, including the advancement of technologies (Griffiths, 2003). As sports betting has migrated online, hyperglobalized betting markets have emerged where one can bet with any operator on any match in the world (Sorbonne-ICSS, 2014b). Within the transnational online markets, both legal and illegal betting operators are vying for dominance by offering extremely high payout rates and risky product lines, such as single bets (wagering on the result of one match) (Forrest, 2012a). Such easy-to-guess (hence, easy-to-fix) bets attract not only punters but also match-fixers (Sorbonne-ICSS, 2014a). Moreover, increased total volumes of betting have facilitated more favorable conditions for fixers to operate in, because large bets for match-fixing are less noticeable (Forrest, 2012a). Meanwhile, the fierce market competition among bookmakers has also led them to introduce lower levels of local, even grassroots events to their marketplace, exposing more vulnerable sports to the risk of match-fixing (Gainsbury, 2012). As a result, now we more frequently hear of match-fixing scandals and confirmed cases from across the globe.

The second interface of the sport-gambling nexus is gambling promotion through sport (i.e., betting sponsorship and advertisement). The types and degrees of advertising vary from one jurisdiction to another as regulations differ. In the United Kingdom, for example, betting commercials appear during live sports broadcasts before 9 p.m., with companies spending around £234 million on television advertising in 2017 (Miller, 2018). Cassidy and Ovenden's (2017) study shows that three sampled episodes of BBC's *Match of the Day*, a household name for football highlights programs, contain 764 instances of gambling advertising in total (more than 250 instances per episode). Behind this lies the introduction of the Gambling Act 2005, which eased advertising regulations for expected revenue growth in the United Kingdom (Light, 2007). In contrast, as of 2019, Italy has imposed a complete ban on gambling promotion activities, including advertising, sponsorships, marketing, commercial communications, and even influencer marketing on social media, despite the potential loss of U.S.$140 million worth of annual contributions from gambling companies (Menmuir, 2019; Nicholson, 2018).

Sponsorship and advertising are key sources of revenue for sport, most especially in territories with laissez-faire betting markets such as the United Kingdom and Australia. For instance, the total amount of betting sponsorship for the 2019–2020 English Premier League football was worth £68.6 million (the highest single deal was £10 million). Though still sizable, it constitutes only about 20% of the League's total shirt sponsorship deals (£349.1 million) (Cole, 2019). More important is the fact that the lower in the league table (likely to be less wealthy), the more likely a team is to be dependent on betting sponsorship. This does not mean top-flight, lucrative clubs have no betting sponsors (Lopez-Gonzalez & Griffiths, 2018), but the higher-ranking clubs can afford not to have betting logos on their shirts, but rather somewhere less explicit.

The most serious consequences of liberalized betting advertising have come from the social harms stimulated by problem gambling, leading to a growing public health issue (Hing, Russell, Vitartas, & Lamont, 2016). It remains a moot point as to whether sport acts as a gateway to problem gambling—for example, to what extent sports spectatorship and viewership amid gambling advertising leads to problem gambling. However, studies suggest that sports betting itself is one of the gambling formats that can be linked to problem gambling and that the proportion of sports punters among problem gamblers is increasing (Commonwealth of Australia, Parliamentary Joint Select Committee on Gambling Reform, 2011; Gainsbury et al., 2015; Hing et al., 2016). Also, it seems undeniable that betting advertising in and around sporting venues (shirts sponsorship, banners, hanging billboards, perimeter advertising, postmatch interview background) normalize gambling activities among the vulnerable populations (Hing, Vitartas, & Lamont, 2013; Jones, Pinder, & Robinson, 2020). Young children in particular are likely to accept betting as an integral part of sporting culture (Djohari, Weston, Cassidy, Wemyss, & Thomas, 2019; Gainsbury, Delfabbro, King, & Hing, 2016). According to Lopez-Gonzalez, Griffiths, Jimenez-Murcia, and Estevez (2020), sport sponsorship and excessive marketing is a result of the competition between bookmakers; offering almost identical products (the same matches on the same day with the same odds), promotional activities are the only way to distinguish themselves from their rivals.

Well aware of such concerns, the betting industry has introduced several voluntary measures. For example, the Gambling Industry Code of Advertising in the United Kingdom prohibits gambling suppliers from presenting their logos or other promotional material on any commercial merchandising for children (U.K. Gambling Commission, 2020). However, children are, nevertheless, exposed to the logos as long as players' shirts are emblazoned with them. Another voluntary restriction the United Kingdom has put in place is a whistle-to-whistle ban, whereby no betting adverts are permitted during live sport coverage before the 9 p.m. watershed (Purves & Critchlow, 2019). However, many are skeptical about its effect because betting firms have already begun to invest five times more money in marketing on social media which are relatively underregulated (Gainsbury et al., 2016; Miller, 2018). Furthermore, a recent study suggests that the majority of gambling references made during television broadcasts (e.g., branded pitch peripheries and team jerseys) are exempt from the whistle-to-whistle ban, while only 2% of the references appearing in the adverts during commercial breaks are directly affected by the ban (Purves, Critchlow, Morgan, Stead, & Dobbie, 2020). In the end, self-regulative measures, such as the U.K. Gambling Industry Code and whistle-to-whistle ban, are likely to work as another form of publicity "under the thinly veiled guise of a social responsibility message" (Davies, 2020).

In addition, within the globalized sports and gambling markets, gambling advertising in one place has had far-reaching impacts in other places. In the Global South, transnational betting operators expose their presence in the broadcast sporting games of the Global North by sponsoring high-flying teams to target specific emerging regional audiences (Lopez-Gonzalez & Griffiths, 2018). For example, SportPesa, a Kenyan bookmaker, and other foreign bookies offering bets in Africa (e.g., Betway) sponsor the English Premier League clubs. In sub-Saharan Africa, young people's participation in sports betting has emerged as a serious issue (Owuor, 2019; see also Akanle & Fageyinbo, 2015; Olaore, Adejare, & Udofia, 2020). Despite other potential factors behind this problem (e.g., the increased use of smartphones, high unemployment rates, etc.), one notable contributing factor stems from bookmakers exploiting top sports leagues as a global billboard, while selling risky products to the most vulnerable groups of people in underdeveloped regions (Bunn, Mtema, Songo, & Udedi, 2020). Putting this in perspective, it might be difficult for sports teams opting to serve as global billboards for gambling to claim they have no responsibility for the consequences on the other side of the world.

To summarize, the two interfaces between sport and gambling seem to constitute what is today called the "gamblization" of sport (McMullan, 2011). While the general usage of this term has been more concerned with gambling promotion through sport and resultant public health issues (Milner, Hing, Vitartas, & Lamon, 2013), it also implicitly points to "the increasing colonisation of sport culture by gambling operators" (Lopez-Gonzalez, Guerrero-Solé, & Griffiths, 2018, p. 239), which has been made available by the legal provision of sports betting (as a first interface). However, if we locate this phenomenon within the larger historical context of the on-and-off relationship of sports and gambling, the gamblification of sport may be seen as not a phenomenon isolated to the present time but rather another "remarriage," one arranged by states' legal framework and advanced through marketing tactics of business interests within the global political economy. In the next section, focus narrows to consider match-fixing and review a variety of approaches to the problem.

APPROACHES

Motivations for rigging a sports match vary from sporting advantage (e.g., to take on easier opponents in the next round) to life opportunities (e.g., university admission) and threats from criminals (Tak, Sam, & Choi, 2020). As betting markets grow, however, gambling has emerged as the most dominant motivation. Gambling-motivated match-fixers carry out operations in both sporting and betting areas. They bet on certain results of a match in betting markets, while simultaneously recruiting athletes and/or referees to engineer the results on which they bet (Tak et al., 2018b). Therefore, previous research on gambling-motivated match-fixing has developed perspectives on the various areas that connect betting markets and local sporting environments. This section reviews approaches to research situated in four distinct, but related, realms: (1) rational choice, (2) investigative journalism, (3) sociocultural, and (4) political sociology. However, it is important to acknowledge that there are other approaches (legal, historical, philosophical, governance, etc.) that can also help explain how match-fixing operates. Thus, some of these perspectives are incorporated into the discussion of the four approaches considered in this section.

Rational-Choice Approaches

A major stream of match-fixing research is aligned with a rational-choice approach. David Forrest (Forrest & Simmons, 2003), a forerunner of this approach, adapted Ehrlich's (1996) economic model of crime to examine match-fixing. His applied model shows how individuals engage in a cost-benefit analysis as part of their decision-making process to take part in match-fixing (Forrest, 2012a; Lastra, Bell, & Bond, 2016). In this equation, individuals are assumed to decide to get involved when expected benefits (monetary gains) surpass expected costs (including loss of future income, loss of glory and reputation, and moral unease and shame) (Forrest, 2012a). The strength of this approach is not only in the clarity of the model but also its contextualization within the global sports and betting markets, thus pointing toward "where risks of occurrence may be highest" (p. 18). For example, sports leagues in financial difficulties, yet attracting disproportionately higher volumes of bets, are vulnerable because athletes in those leagues have not much to lose (less pay, less glory, and shame), while the size of bribe (expected benefits) can be large (Forrest, 2012b; Rodenberg, Sackmann, & Groer, 2016).

Mirroring its disciplinary background in economics, rational-choice scholars understand match-fixing from the perspective of betting operators. In this view, although manipulation takes place on the sporting field or court, it is on the betting market that money is swindled. Thus, the primary victims are betting customers and, by extension, betting operators (Forrest, 2012b). That is, sports betting, if it is on football, is a 90-minute-long investment product, and match-fixing is "a financial crime" that disturbs the economic transactions (p. 99). By looking beyond what happens on the sporting field and linking it to rarely known logics of betting, this approach helps us overcome somewhat naïve ethical views that often ignore the structural influence of betting markets over sporting individuals. However, the framing of betting companies as the victims of match-fixing can have the effect of obscuring the fact that the danger of match-fixing is generated by sports gambling itself, and thus it preempts potential challenges to the legitimacy of commercial sports gambling (Tak, 2018).

Investigative Journalism Approaches

The next great stride in match-fixing research was made by what can be termed an investigative journalism approach. As is the case with other forms of corruption or crime, the surreptitious nature of match-fixing requires access to closed circles of people. Hill's (2008, 2009, 2010, 2015) fieldwork across several countries (e.g., Malaysia, Singapore, and Russia) pioneered this line of approach by securing informant groups, including prosecutors, odds traders, corruptors, and players involved in match-fixing. The biggest contribution of this approach is the discovery of how match-fixing is organized between fixing groups and sporting individuals from solid in situ empirical evidence. For instance, Hill (2009, 2013) classified those involved in fixing schemes into separate roles and functions and identified their motivations in a way similar to how a team of detectives configures a flow chart of a crime on a bulletin board. According to Hill (2009), successful fixing rings normally employ a bridge-type network to induce athletes into their plans with a view to building trust. Also, Hill (2015) debunked some of the anecdotal myths around match-fixing, such as the argument that match-fixing is more frequent among early-career players in their early 20s. Noting that 51% of match-fixing is committed by players over 29 compared to 18.2% for those under 25, he maintains that individual motivations are related more to senior players' fear of diminishing career prospects (Hill, 2015).

Hill's interpretation of individuals' motives echoes the behavioral assumption of rational-choice approaches. On this account, his investigative journalism approach can be considered an offshoot of the rational-choice perspective. However, the difference is seen in their relative foci. Rational-choice academics focus on the motivations within the betting markets, whereas Hill's approach concentrates on the criminal activities that connect the motivations in the betting markets to vulnerable individuals in the sporting domain. The approach's attention to general conditions of match-fixing allows for wider generalizability and impact. By contrast, it hardly considers any "cultural" influences that may make particular sporting environments more susceptible to the effect of "common conditions" (Hill, 2010). In this regard, a sociocultural perspective, addressed next, can complement the first two approaches as it takes into account "the subtleties of human reasons for action" (Schmidt, 2006, p. 103).

Sociocultural Approaches

Given their focus on micro settings, sociocultural approaches tend to adopt in-depth, qualitative case study methods (Numerato, 2016). For example, Lee (2008, 2017), Tzeng and Lee (2021), and Tzeng, Lee, and Tzeng (2020) zoomed in on the betting syndicate–athletes relationship within five match-fixing scandals in Taiwanese professional baseball. Though the unit of analysis parallels Hill's (fixing rings–athletes links), this approach places greater emphasis on social norms that are deep-rooted in the society—such as Wulun (Mencius's 'Five Cardinal Relationships') and codes of brotherhood (Tzeng & Lee, 2021; Tzeng et al., 2020). According to these studies, such norms are usually manifested positively as social capital for "mutual help" and social cohesion, but they also materialize negatively as "soft coercion" in hierarchical social settings (Tzeng & Lee, 2021, pp. 11–12). Therefore, match-fixing occurs oddly "in the name of righteousness and loyalty" and is justified as "help, regardless of whether the behaviour is right or wrong" (Tzeng et al., 2020, pp. 1, 6).

Cases of match-fixing in Confucianist societies display some unique patterns. For example, as opposed to Hill's finding, "project managers" (intermediaries) on the team need much less time and effort to coax their teammates into match-fixing because the ball players are already organized into a homogeneous body (cf. Han, 2020). Also, Taiwanese baseball players often agree to fix for nothing based on the long-term code of "thick-and-thin" brotherhood (Tzeng et al., 2020). Another difference found in the East Asian cases is that players value "reputation among their fellows" when asked to partake, perhaps more than "reputation in society" (Tzeng & Lee, 2021, p. 12), revealing the cultural uniqueness where "relationship maintenance is in itself both an end and a means" (Tzeng et al., 2020, p. 12).

However, attributing match-fixing to general societal belief systems may be extending the lens of analysis too far. The moral codes based on Confucianism may not be direct causal sources for match-fixing, but perhaps constitute the foundation for other corruption, and even other positive cultural constructs. Also, this approach's stress on the particular can risk underestimating common denominators. For example, athletes' match-fixing participation for free might not reflect the cultural feature of prioritizing brotherhood over monetary interests, but could possibly mean "long overdue repayment." As one of Tzeng and Lee's (2021, p. 12) informants states, some players get involved because they feel "an enduring debt of gratitude" in the long-term relationship. In other words, the social norms may not work outside or separately from the general patterns of match-fixing, but rather can be integrated as a factor that lowers the costs of mobilizing athletes in the rational-choice model.

Political Sociology Approaches

The last point of entry can be called a political sociology approach in that it focuses on the power relations and interests around the regulatory regimes of sports betting. Informed by institutional theories (e.g., Offe, 2006), Tak (2018), Tak et al. (2018a), Moriconi (2018) and Moriconi and Almeida (2019) have tried to capture how the contemporary combination of sports and gambling generates institutional conditions for match-fixing. According to Tak (2018), legal sports betting is akin to relocating sports on the gambling table around which governments, sports organizations, betting operators, and media/data companies run the business and benefit from the revenues. Considering the historical relationship between sports and gambling, this approach posits that more fundamental risks are built into the combination of sports and betting itself. This is because, first, the remarriage of sports and gambling creates "an artificial market that can place as much monetary value on losing as winning" (p. 789). Second, far from other types of gambling, sports betting is betting on human beings with agency who cannot be completely insulated from outside influence (Tak, 2018). These two conditions have inherent, root causal power for match-fixing which can be triggered by, for example, the irregular factors in transnational betting markets. Therefore, this view sees match-fixing as an inescapable byproduct of sports betting.

Most particularly, Tak (2018) demonstrates why match-fixing is an institutional failure, not a failure of individuals, by comparing football betting and motorboat race betting. The former is representative of general sports, while the latter is equivalent to racing sports for gambling (e.g., horse racing). According to Tak, despite being subject to betting, football maintains its social legitimacy as a sport by its social activities independent of betting, whereas motorboat racing is perceived as an inadvisable social pursuit because it is sustained only for the purpose of gambling. On the other hand, because motorboat racing proclaims itself a "betting sport," it almost completely insulates its racers from outside influence, while football exposes its players to outside influence on the grounds that it is a sport, despite the fact that it is de facto a betting sport. From this, Tak argues that match-fixing originates from the loophole created by football's institutional prioritization of "social legit-imacy" at the expense of tighter insulation of athletes. Tak goes on to suggest that to make up for the institutional loophole, the stakeholders fall back on individual levels of morality. One example of this is the emphasis placed on individualized discourses of sport integrity.

Such a perspective explores beyond the visible culprits such as illegal betting operators, criminal organizations, and on-field athletes to hold the powerful stakeholders responsible for creating the fundamental risks of match-fixing. However, many would argue that unless we can eradicate all existing betting activities simultaneously, there is no point in criticizing legal sports-betting regimes because match-fixing would have propagated further via il-legal betting. Legal regulatory regimes might be the only way to curb its spread despite the unavoidable side effects. In this regard, it might be fair to say that the political sociology approach uncovers the hardly observable institutional causal source of match-fixing, but has less explanatory power about the reality, the construction of which relies heavily upon the commercial activities of the major stakeholders of sports betting regimes.

All four approaches have contributed to enhancing our understanding of match-fixing. However, it is also important to remember that each approach potentially represents par-ticular groups of interests because their relative foci (sport vs. gambling), different par-adigmatic assumptions (positivist, interpretivist, and critical realist) and methodological approaches inevitably delimit their scope (Tak et al., 2018b). While scholars using these approaches may agree that the transnational betting markets fuel the potential for match-fixing, they likely disagree on where the potential for change and solutions exist. The rational-choice approach's definition of match-fixing as a financial crime castigates match-fixers and on-field individuals, while exempting the sports-betting regimes from the re-sponsibility of creating institutionalized loopholes. In contrast, the sociocultural approach focuses on the foundational value system in a society, but this can dilute individual levels of responsibility by imputing individuals' misbehavior to the culture that normalizes it. On the other hand, the political sociology approach points to the combination of sports and betting as the origin of the problem on the grounds that they prepare the very condition for match-fixing, profit from it, and shift the blame for its side effects to individuals. That is, the academic approaches to the issue of match-fixing form a debate where the issue is framed in favor of certain groups, while disadvantaging other groups of interests.

These perspectives not only apply to the diagnosis of match-fixing issues but further expand into illuminating other issues around sports betting. In the next section, we move on to reviewing some ongoing debates concerning integrity issues around sports betting and match-fixing.

DEBATES

Match-fixing has been widely described as a threat to the integrity of sport. However, sport integrity is a complex and multifaceted notion (Kihl, 2019). There is no common definition, other than general understandings of it as referring to something positive, implicitly linked to core ethical values such as honesty, fairness, trust, transparency, and the like (Gardiner, Parry, & Robinson, 2017; Manoli, Bandura, & Downward, 2020). Moreover, the conception of sport integrity has been reformulated as a policy packaging brand to incorporate many other ethical issues in sport, such as those concerning doping, abuse, and corruption. More diverse cases of breaching integrity may give more clues, but they also intimate that this elusive ideal cannot prove its presence without its conspicuous absence. In other words, the only way to comprehend sport integrity is by studying its absence (Kihl, 2019). In this regard, rather than trying to advance some absolute definitions of sport integrity, it might be more useful to review different and often conflicting perspectives of the concept. Given the diverse stakeholders that populate sports and betting industries, integrity discourses about match-fixing necessarily contain political dimensions. Accordingly, this section considers key debates over who defines sport integrity and who may be framed as potential perpetrators or guardians of sport integrity.

A brief review of recent literature on sport integrity reveals several features integral to integrity discourses. First, sport integrity is a normative conception that connotes what is right, good, and advanced and what is not (Gardiner et al., 2017; Kihl, 2019). Second, sport integrity is often categorized into "on-field integrity," concerning sporting competition itself, and "off-field integrity," relating to how to organize and manage the competition on the field (Archer, 2016; Masters, 2015). While on-field integrity indicates what Archer (2016, p. 122) refers to as "a virtue of the sport itself," off-field integrity might be applicable to any other organizations (managerial integrity). Third, sport integrity can be imposed upon both individuals (individual responsibility) and any structural levels beyond individuals (institutional, organizational responsibility) (Archer, 2016; Gardiner et al., 2017; Kihl, 2019). This last distinction is different from the second one in that individual responsibility can be applied to both on-field and off-field individuals separately, while the institutional responsibility can also mean both: one that is to ensure on-field integrity and the other that focuses on off-field management practices. All three aspects seem applicable to match-fixing-related integrity discourses and policies.

These characteristics raise important questions concerning the integrity discourses around match-fixing and sports betting. First, if sport integrity is a normative conception, who judges what is right and what is wrong? There is no doubt that match-fixing itself is not a moral and ethical thing to do. However, the ethical discourse of why match-fixing is wrong can be constructed in differing ways according to who articulates it. Thus, it is important to examine whose conceptualization of sport integrity is advanced. Second, it might be ideal to think that integrity is the duty of both individuals and institutions (also of both on-field and off-field). For example, individuals are required to play with integrity on the field, while sound institutional structures should also be prepared for on-field individuals to play with integrity (Kihl, 2019). However, when match-fixing occurs, the duty of individuals and that of institutions are not equally scrutinized due perhaps to the power imbalance between the two entities (Tak et al., 2018a).

When it comes to the definition of sport integrity, the betting industry contends that sport integrity is not only the fundamental condition for sport but is also vital for their own industry (iGamingBusiness, 2020). Simply put, if there is no trust in the transparency of sports matches (i.e., no manipulation), people will not purchase their betting products and betting industries will collapse. For that reason, the betting industry has invested as much in anti-match-fixing campaigns as sports organizations have. In their view, sport integrity is a common interest for both sports and betting industries and can even be further refined for the purpose of betting (just like the rules of 19th-century cricket and boxing).

However, the integrity code of practice in sport is not always identical to and often is incompatible with one that is required for betting (Tak et al., 2018a). This is because sport has long established its own traditions and social practices independently of gambling. For example, in professional team sports such as football and basketball, fielding or benching key players is a common concern for both sports fans and punters. However, their interpretations differ because in sporting contexts, the team management of a single match is understood in terms of the team's season-long plans, whereas in the betting markets, each individual game is a short-term financial product. Therefore, while benching key starting players can be a tactical decision in sporting contexts, the same decision can arouse suspicion about the game's integrity in betting markets. Although punters consider sporting strategies in their investment, when sport is subject to betting and the financial support from gambling businesses, sporting competitions cannot help accommodating the view of betting customers (Tak et al., 2018a).

One consequence of this inflation of *betting* interests has been bans on sharing inside information. As mentioned in the previous section, the betting industry sees sports betting as a kind of stock market. Along this line of thinking, sports players, coaches, supporting staff, and officials (and their families) can have access to information that is key to predicting whether the stock price goes up or down (who wins a match), such as who is playing and who is injured (Hosmer-Henner, 2010). Even if these people did not bet, information from them can be used and sold in betting markets (Forrest, 2013). Therefore, in many countries, sharing of inside information is prohibited by match-fixing-related regulations of sports organizations and/or by criminal codes. This is reasonable from the perspective of the gambling industry. However, it is also a restriction that is imposed only for the purpose of betting. For example, Daniel Sturridge, an English professional footballer, received a four-month ban and £150,000 fine for charges alleging that he had talked about his transfer possibility (passed on inside information, in regulatory terms) to his brother (BBC, 2020). The point is not whether Sturridge actually "instructed his brother" to bet (BBC, 2020), but rather the fact that football players cannot freely discuss their future career decision with significant others as long as their moves on and off the field are subject to gambling. This incident shows how the gamblified sport is reformulating its code of ethics to protect and accommodate revenues from betting under the name of sport integrity.

In addition, what used to be regarded as a practice of sportspersonship can have a different implication within betting contexts. Nic Coward (2009), a former CEO of the British Horseracing Authority, offers as an example the episode of the 1969 Ryder Cup. In that golf tournament, Jack Nicklaus (American team member) finished the final hole one shot ahead and conceded a short putt to Tony Jacklin (British counterpart) who otherwise would have had to putt the final stroke under great pressure. With the tournament tied accordingly, Nicklaus said to Jacklin on the green, "I don't think you would have missed it, but I wasn't going to give you the chance, either" (quoted in Owen, 2016). Reminiscing about this scene as one of the greatest sporting moments, Coward (2009) asked, "Imagine if something similar were to happen at Celtic Manor next year, with millions staked on the competition." With millions of dollars staked on one putt, golfers could not easily do what they believe a man of integrity would do. While fans are the audience of a performance, punters are short-term stakeholders of a performance. When punters are influential stakeholders, the highest level of integrity code of conduct might be to break the tie and clearly determine the winners and losers of their bets. That is, this integrity for betting is at odds with the integrity of sport. As Coward stresses, perhaps "there is no place for sporting gestures when there is money on it."

Another possible unit of analysis through which to examine how the integrity discourse is deployed is to consider how match-fixing countermeasures are put in place. This is because the policy remedies are developed and implemented by networks of the major stakeholders: governments, sports governing bodies, betting companies, and law enforcement agencies at local, national, and international levels (see Macolin Convention, 2020). As with other policy areas, the development of such measures are underpinned by functionalist, rational-choice reasoning, such that a policy measure is a means to an end (i.e., protecting sport integrity) (Linder & Peters, 1989). However, political sociology approaches to policy instrumentation view policy tools as channels through which powerful actors project their perspectives and ideas (Lascoumes & Le Galès, 2007). From this perspective, their problem-solving activities concomitantly define the nature of the problem—that is, who is culpable for the problem and who is capable of solving the problem (Tak et al., 2018a).

A case in point can be found in betting monitoring systems that are designed to detect irregular betting patterns. This instrument developed from the risk management practices of bookmakers who had long traced winning customers' betting patterns to hedge their own risks. As match-fixing has become commonplace, this traditional risk management strategy has extended into observing real-time abnormal concentration of bets (money) on unlikely events and sharing information across the industry and with sports governing bodies (Forrest & McHale, 2019). This has further developed into gathering intelligence, including profiling suspicious athletes and referees and their on- and off-field track record (e.g., whether they have appeared in suspicious matches before) (Forrest & McHale, 2015). Such comprehensive activities have raised alarms about suspicious matches, and the evidence they provide has been used by the Court of Arbitration for Sport (Carpenter, 2018). This type of monitoring program is mostly run by trade associations of betting companies (e.g., International Betting Integrity Association—private operators; Global Lottery Monitoring System—public providers) and data service providers (Genius Sport, Sportradar, etc.). Moreover, these actors collaborate with each other and, more important, with national and international sports organizations. There are various collaborative policy frameworks for sport integrity (e.g., the International Olympic Committee's Integrity Betting Intelligence System), and short-term collaborative monitoring centers have been established for particular sporting events (e.g., the Olympic Games and FIFA World Cup).

This technology-based countermeasure surely contributes to preventing match-fixing by making match-fixing attempts more costly in evading surveillance (Forrest & McHale, 2019). However, this policy measure frames on-field actors as the *object* of monitoring, while the betting industry has come into the legitimate social arena as a key *subject* of monitoring (Tak, Choi, & Sam, 2021). Such co-optation of betting into the public policy networks helps betting companies build positive images and relieve public antipathy that stems from the social harms their addictive products create (Tak et al., 2018a). Moreover, since betting data has become critical in detecting match-fixing, betting companies should not be foes any longer, but friends. Their changed status from the producer of a socially stigmatized product to a legitimate partner of integrity initiatives has the effect of depoliticizing the controversial business of sports betting and forestalling some important questions as to the legitimacy of sports betting and the appropriateness of sports relying on money from the socially harmful activity, about which 20th-century sports have long been concerned (Tak et al., 2018a).

Thus, despite the seemingly straightforward discussion about protecting sport integrity, when it comes to determining whose interests are best served, the debate quickly becomes contested terrain. Therefore, it is important to guard against taking the ethical discourse at face value and further interrogate which versions of sport integrity are articulated in whose terms. Here, we need to consider "whether they are essentially about safeguarding the integrity of sport as is proclaimed on the surface; or about protecting the very interests of key stakeholders who live off the rhetoric of sport's integrity" (Tak et al., 2018a, p. 44).

Conclusion

This chapter has presented a critical overview of the history, regulations, approaches, and discourses around sports gambling and match-fixing. Having reviewed the on-and-off relationship between sport and gambling, the treatment has highlighted how the inherent trade-offs between ethics and money operate behind the long-standing history. The analysis has also considered how the political economy of casino capitalism has served to bring about the contemporary marriage between the two, creating two main interfaces that entail regulatory issues in relation to sport integrity and public health. In turn, the four major approaches to match-fixing have revealed that the problem, like many others, is inextricably linked with various interests and anchored at different societal levels, and thus the varied approaches inevitably work to the advantage of certain groups. Such political dimensions are more obvious in advancing the policy discourse of sport integrity. Therefore, considerations in this chapter touched on how a sporting code of integrity has been subtly transmuted into a way to meet the demand of betting.

These dynamics from the power relations of diverse stakeholders, various social forces, technological aspects, and the converged domains of sports and gambling seem to provide fertile ground for several future research agendas in the study of sport and society. As for the integrity issues, regional case studies on match-fixing continue to be conducted and published, enriching empirical data and perspectives. However, there is a relative dearth of empirical investigations into the role and significance of the stakeholders (especially in betting industries) in the anti-match-fixing policy initiatives. Many collaborative frameworks for sport integrity now take the form of "private authorities" wherein the possibility of abusing public power by private interests can be overshadowed by the positive connotation of "cooperation" for public good. Approaches from political science and public policy studies can provide fruitful theories and concepts, while other integrity regulatory frameworks (such as for doping) can offer valuable points of comparison for investigation (see Geeraert & Drieskens, 2021).

In relation to the public health concerns, prevalence studies (e.g., using a problem gambling severity index) have often spotlighted sports betting as another source of gambling addiction (e.g., Gainsbury et al., 2015; Hing et al., 2016). However, the seemingly objective and value-free prevalence studies necessarily demarcate "a minority of 'pathological' individuals" from "a majority of the population who gamble 'responsibly'" (Reith, 2013, p. 721), thus running the risk of situating the cause of problem gambling in the anomalous individual as opposed to the wider structural processes and relationships that legitimize gambling (Reith, 2013; Young, 2013). In this respect, one area that deserves closer socio-logical examination might be the role of sporting factors in the legitimation of the inten-sive production and consumption of gambling commodity (Reith, 2013). For instance, we might ask whether sports function as a softer medium of gambling in policy and industry discourses of liberalizing the gambling practice, in the same way that sports sponsorship is used to dilute the negative image of what is regarded as a "sin" product. More broadly, we might also examine how the technological innovations in gambling provision change the way we engage in sport for better or worse (see McGee, 2020).

With respect to regulatory issues of sports betting, it might be worth paying attention to American states that have been developing, and are in the process of implementing, leg-islation. The power relations between stakeholders in the United States are different from those in Europe and even between its states. This variance can provide real-time social experimental settings for different regulatory models to be compared with respect to how the inherent trade-offs between money and ethics are conflicting and reconciled, and how legal, social, and cultural instruments are utilized to minimize the challenges to the legiti-macy of sport.

REFERENCES

Adelman, M. (1990). *A sporting time: New York City and the rise of modern athletics.* Urbana: University of Illinois Press.

Akanle, O., & Fageyinbo, T. K. (2015). Football betting in Nigeria. *Miscellanea Anthropologica et Sociologica, 16*(4), 46–63.

Archer, A. (2016). On sporting integrity. *Sport, Ethics and Philosophy, 10*(2), 117–131.

Arrighi, G. (1994). *The long twentieth century: Money, power, and the origins of our times.* London: Verso Books.

BBC. (2020, March 2). Daniel Sturridge "devastated" by four-month ban for breaching betting rules. https://www.bbc.co.uk/sport/football/51712017.

Boniface, P., Lacarriere, S., Verschuuren, P., Tuaillon, A., Forrest, D., Icard, J. M., & Wang, X. (2012). *Sports betting and corruption: How to preserve the integrity of sport.* Study. Paris: French Institute of International and Strategic Relations and associated institutes.

Bunn, C., Mtema, O., Songo, J., & Udedi, M. (2020). The growth of sports betting in Malawi: Corporate strategies, public space and public health. *Public Health, 184,* 95–101.

Carpenter, K. (2018, January 15). Match-fixing life ban for elite football referee upheld by the CAS. *Captivate Legal Sports.* http://captivatelegalsports.com/analysis-publications/match-fixing-life-ban-for-elite-football-referee-upheld-by-the-cas/.

Cassidy, R., & Ovenden, N. (2017). Frequency, duration and medium of advertisements for gambling and other risky products in commercial and public service broadcasts of English Premier League football. SocArXiv. https://osf.io/preprints/socarxiv/f6bu8/.

Clapson, M. (1992). *A bit of a flutter: Popular gambling and English society, c. 1823–1961.* Manchester, U.K.: Manchester University Press.

Cole, O. (2019, August 16). Shirt sponsorship deals with gambling operators will bring Premier League clubs £68.6 million in 2019/20 season. *Casino Guardian.* http://www.casinoguardian.co.uk/2019/08/16/shirt-sponsorship-deals-with-gambling-operators-will-bring-premier-league-clubs-68-6-million-in-2019-20-season/.

Commonwealth of Australia, Parliamentary Joint Select Committee on Gambling Reform. (2011, December). Interactive and online gambling and gambling advertising (Second report). https://www.aph.gov.au/Parliamentary_Business/Committees/Joint/Former_Committees/gamblingreform/completedinquires/2010-13/interactiveonlinegamblingadvertising/report/index.

Cosgrave, J. F. (2006). Editor's introduction: Gambling, risk, and late capitalism. In J. F. Cosgrave (Ed.), The sociology of risk and gambling reader (pp. 1–24). New York: Taylor & Francis.

Cosgrave, J. F., & Klassen, T. R. (2001). Gambling against the state: The state and the legitimation of gambling. Current Sociology, 49(5), 1–15.

Coward, N. (2009, September 22). Ground has shifted on betting and the law must catch up. The Guardian. https://www.theguardian.com/sport/blog/2009/sep/22/sport-betting-regulations-law.

Davies, Rob. (2020, May 10). Gambling firms' social messages are "thinly veiled" adverts, say MPs. The Guardian. https://www.theguardian.com/world/2020/may/10/gambling-firms-social-messages-are-thinly-veiled-adverts-say-mps.

Djohari, N., Weston, G., Cassidy, R., Wemyss, M., & Thomas, S. (2019). Recall and awareness of gambling advertising and sponsorship in sport in the UK: A study of young people and adults. Harm Reduction Journal, 16(24), 1–12.

Edelman, M. (2018). Lack of integrity: Rebutting the myth that US commercial sports leagues have an intellectual property right to sports gambling proceeds. New York University Journal of Law & Business., 15(1), 1–17.

Ehrlich, I. (1996). Crime, punishment, and the market for offenses. Journal of Economic Perspectives, 10(1), 43–67.

Fagan, G. G. (2006). Leisure. In D. Porter (Ed.), A companion to the Roman Empire (pp. 369–384). Malden, MA: Blackwell Publishing.

Forrest, D. (2012a). Betting and the integrity of sport. In P. M. Anderson, I. S. Blackshaw, P. C. R. Siekmann, & J. Soek (Eds.), Sports betting: Law and policy (pp. 14–26). The Hague: Asser Press.

Forrest, D. (2012b). The threat to football from betting-related corruption. International Journal of Sport Finance, 7(2), 99–116.

Forrest, D. (2013). Match fixing: An economics perspective. In M. R. Haberfeld & D. Sheehan (Eds.), Match-fixing in international sports (pp. 177–198). London: Springer International Publishing.

Forrest, D., & McHale, I. G. (2015). An evaluation of Sportradar's fraud detection system. Sportradar. https://integrity.sportradar.com/wp-content/uploads/sites/22/2018/11/Sportradar-Integrity-Services_University-of-Liverpool_An-Evaluation-of-the-FDS.pdf.

Forrest, D., & McHale, I. G. (2019). Using statistics to detect match fixing in sport. IMA Journal of Management Mathematics, 30(4), 431–449.

Forrest, D., & Simmons, R. (2003). Sport and gambling. Oxford Review of Economic Policy, 19(4), 598–611.

Futrell, A. (2006). The Roman games: A sourcebook. Oxford: Wiley-Blackwell.

Gainsbury, S. (2012). Internet gambling: Current research findings and implications. New York: Springer.

Gainsbury, S. M., Delfabbro, P., King, D. L., & Hing, N. (2016). An exploratory study of gambling operators' use of social media and the latent messages conveyed. Journal of Gambling Studies, 32(1), 125–141.

Gainsbury, S. M., Russell, A., Hing, N., Wood, R., Lubman, D., & Blaszczynski, A. (2015). How the internet is changing gambling: Findings from an Australian prevalence survey. *Journal of Gambling Studies, 31*(1), 1–15.

Gardiner, S., Parry, J., & Robinson, S. (2017). Integrity and the corruption debate in sport: Where is the integrity? *European Sport Management Quarterly, 17*(1), 6–23.

Geeraert, A., & Drieskens, E. (2021). The dynamics of de-delegation: A principal-agent explanation of the reversal of private authority in international sport governance. *Public Administration, 99*(1), 156–170.

Goodman, R. (1995). *The luck business: The devastating consequences and broken promises of America's gambling explosion.* New York: Free Press.

Griffiths, M. (2003). Internet gambling: Issues, concerns, and recommendation. *Cyber Psychology & Behavior, 6*(6), 557–568.

Guttmann, A. (1986). *Sports spectators.* New York: Columbia University Press.

Han, S. (2020). Match-fixing under the state monopoly sports betting system: A case study of the 2011 K-League scandal. *Crime, Law and Social Change, 74*(1), 97–113.

Harris, H. A. (1972). *Sport in Greece and Rome.* Ithaca, NY: Cornell University Press.

Harvey, D. (2006). *Spaces of global capitalism.* London: Verso.

Hill, D. (2008). *The fix: Soccer and organized crime.* Toronto: McClelland & Stewart.

Hill, D. (2009). How gambling corruptors fix football matches. *European Sport Management Quarterly, 9*(4), 411–432.

Hill, D. (2010). A critical mass of corruption: Why some football leagues have more match-fixing than others. *International Journal of Sports Marketing & Sponsorship, 11*(3), 221–235.

Hill, D. (2013). *The insider's guide to match-fixing in football.* Toronto: Anne McDermid & Associates.

Hill, D. (2015). Jumping into fixing. *Trends in Organized Crime, 18*(3), 212–228.

Hing, N., Russell, A. M., Vitartas, P., & Lamont, M. (2016). Demographic, behavioural and normative risk factors for gambling problems amongst sports bettors. *Journal of Gambling Studies, 32*(2), 625–641.

Hing, N., Vitartas, P., & Lamont, M. (2013). Gambling sponsorship of sport: An exploratory study of links with gambling attitudes and intentions. *International Gambling Studies, 13*(3), 281–301.

Holden, J., & Schuster, M. (2019). The sham of integrity fees in sports betting. *New York University Journal of Law & Business, 16*(1), 31–73.

Hosmer-Henner, A. (2010). Preventing game fixing: Sports books as information markets. *Gaming Law Review and Economics, 14*(1), 31–38.

Hoye, R. (2006). Sports betting policy and product fees. Implications for Australian sports organisations. *Annals of Leisure Research, 9*(3–4), 155–172.

Huggins, M. (2013). Association football, betting, and British society in the 1930s: The strange case of the 1936 "Pools War." *Sport History Review, 44*(2), 99–119.

iGamingBusiness. (2020, June 5). Kindred: Match-fixing threatens "fundamental idea of sports." https://www.igamingbusiness.com/news/kindred-match-fixing-threatens-fundamental-idea-sports.

Jones, C., Pinder, R., & Robinson, G. (2020). Gambling sponsorship and advertising in British football: A critical account. *Sport, Ethics and Philosophy, 14*(2), 163–175.

Kihl, L. A. (2019). Sport integrity systems: A proposed framework. In D. Shilbury & L. Ferkins (Eds.), *Routledge handbook of sport governance* (pp. 395–409). Abingdon, U.K.: Routledge.

Korea Sports Promotion Foundation. (2020). 2019 Annual sales report. https://www.kspo.or.kr/kspo/main/contents.do?menuNo=200146.

Lascoumes, P., & Le Galès, P. (2007). Introduction: Understanding public policy through its instruments—from the nature of instruments to the sociology of public policy instrumentation. *Governance, 20*(1), 1–21.

Lastra, R., Bell, P., & Bond, C. (2016). Sports betting–motivated corruption in Australia: An under-studied phenomenon. *International Journal of Social Science Research, 4*(1), 61–82.

Lee, P. C. (2008). Managing a corrupted sporting system: The governance of professional baseball in Taiwan and the gambling scandal of 1997. *European Sport Management Quarterly, 8*(1), 45–66.

Lee, P. C. (2017). Understanding the match-fixing scandals of professional baseball in Taiwan: An exploratory study of a Confucianism-oriented society. *European Sport Management Quarterly, 17*(1), 45–66.

Light, R. (2007). The Gambling Act 2005: Regulatory containment and market control. *Modern Law Review, 70*(4), 626–653.

Linder, S. H., & Peters, B. G. (1989). Instruments of government: Perceptions and contexts. *Journal of Public Policy, 9*(1), 35–58.

Lopez-Gonzalez, H., & Griffiths, M. D. (2018). Betting, forex trading, and fantasy gaming sponsorships—a responsible marketing inquiry into the "gamblification" of English football. *International Journal of Mental Health and Addiction, 16*(2), 404–419.

Lopez-Gonzalez, H., Griffiths, M. D., Jimenez-Murcia, S., & Estevez, A. (2020). The perceived influence of sports betting marketing techniques on disordered gamblers in treatment. *European Sport Management Quarterly, 20*(4), 421–439.

Lopez-Gonzalez, H., Guerrero-Solé, F., & Griffiths, M. D. (2018). A content analysis of how "normal" sports betting behaviour is represented in gambling advertising. *Addiction Research & Theory, 26*(3), 238–247.

Macolin Convention. (2020). The convention on the manipulation of sports competitions (the Macolin Convention). Council of Europe. https://www.coe.int/en/web/sport/t-mc.

Manoli, A. E., Bandura, C., & Downward, P. (2020). Perceptions of integrity in sport: Insights into people's relationship with sport. *International Journal of Sport Policy and Politics, 12*(2), 207–220.

Masters, A. (2015). Corruption in sport: From the playing field to the field of policy. *Policy and Society, 34*(2), 111–123.

McDaniel, S. R., Mason, D. S., & Kinney, L. (2004). Sponsorship of sporting events to promote alcohol, tobacco and lotteries. In T. Slack (Ed.), *The commercialisation of sport* (pp. 288–306). New York: Routledge.

McGee, D. (2020). On the normalisation of online sports gambling among young adult men in the UK: A public health perspective. *Public Health, 184,* 89–94.

McKelvey, S. M. (2004). U.S. professional sport organisation policies shift to embrace legalised gambling entities: A roll of the dice? *Journal of Legal Aspects of Sport, 14*(1), 23–45.

McMullan, J. (2011, June 28). Submission to the Joint Select Committee on Gambling Reform: Inquiry into interactive and online gambling and gambling advertising. *Parliament of Australia.* http://www.aph.gov.au/DocumentStore.ashx?id=40e3c180-5666-4084-92c6-0e51b62d7d0b.

Menmuir, T. (2019, April 30). AGCOM lays out stark reality of Italian advertising ban. *SBC News.* https://sbcnews.co.uk/europe/2019/04/30/agcom-stark-reality-italian-advertising-ban/.

Miller, G. (2018, November 28). Gambling companies spend £1.2 billion marketing online, five times more than on television ads. *European Gaming.* https://europeangaming.eu/por tal/press-releases/2018/11/28/33678/gambling-companies-spend-1-2-billion-marketing-onl ine-five-times-more-than-on-television-ads/.

Milner, L., Hing, N., Vitartas, P., & Lamont, M. (2013). Embedded gambling promotion in Australian football broadcasts: An exploratory study. *Communication, Politics & Culture,* 46(2), 177–198.

Moriconi, M. (2018). The official football match-fixing prevention discourse as a cognitive limitation (the cases of Iberian countries). *Soccer & Society,* 19(2), 271–287.

Moriconi, M., & Almeida, J. P. (2019). Portuguese fight against match-fixing: Which policies and what ethic? *Journal of Global Sport Management,* 4(1), 79–96.

Munting, R. (1996). *An economic and social history of gambling in Britain and the USA.* London: Manchester University Press.

Mwesigwa, D. (2018). Football betting among the youths in Lira municipality: Will livelihoods improve? *International Journal of Development and Sustainability,* 7(4), 1299–1316.

Nicholson, P. (2018, July 6). Serie A says betting sponsorship ban will destabilise Italian football's economic model. *Inside World Football.* http://www.insideworldfootball.com/ 2018/07/06/serie-says-betting-sponsorship-ban-will-destabilise-italian-footballs-econo mic-model/.

Numerato, D. (2016). Corruption and public secrecy: An ethnography of football match-fixing. *Current Sociology,* 64(5), 699–717.

Offe, C. (2006). Political institutions and social power: Conceptual explorations. In I. Shapiro, S. Skowronek, & D. Galvin (Eds.), *Rethinking political institutions* (pp. 9–31). New York: New York University Press.

Olaore, G. O., Adejare, B. O., & Udofia, E. E. (2020). The nexus between the increasing involvement of youth in betting games and unemployment: The Nigerian perspective. *Journal of Humanities and Applied Social Sciences.* Advance online publication. doi:10.1108/ JHASS-02-2020-0026.

Owen, D. (2016, September 30). Now, about that famous Ryder Cup concession. *Golf Digest.* https://www.golfdigest.com/story/now-about-that-famous-ryder-cup-concession.

Owuor, V. O. (2019, November 24). The uncomfortable link between smartphones and the rise in gambling with Africa's youth. *Quartz Africa.* https://qz.com/africa/1754902/smar tphones-are-driving-sports-betting-with-young-africans/.

Purves, R., & Critchlow, N. (2019, November 7). Gambling and sport: How bookmakers win in voluntary "whistle-to-whistle" advert ban. *The Conversation.* https://theconversation. com/gambling-and-sport-how-bookmakers-win-in-voluntary-whistle-to-whistle-advert-ban-125692.

Purves, R. I., Critchlow, N., Morgan, A., Stead, M., & Dobbie, F. (2020). Examining the frequency and nature of gambling marketing in televised broadcasts of professional sporting events in the United Kingdom. *Public Health,* 184, 71–78.

Ramsey, E. (2018, March 22). "Data monopoly" key to leagues' desired control over US sports betting. *Legal Sports Report.* https://www.legalsportsreport.com/19047/data-monopoly-key-to-leagues-controlling-sports-betting/.

Reith, G. (1999). *The age of chance: Gambling in Western culture.* London: Routledge.

Reith, G. (2013). Techno economic systems and excessive consumption: A political economy of "pathological" gambling. *British Journal of Sociology,* 64(4), 717–738.

Riess, S. A. (1995). *Sport in industrial America, 1850–1920.* Wheeling, IL: Harlan Davidson.

Rodenberg, R. M., Sackmann, J., & Groer, C. (2016). Tennis integrity: A sports law analytics review. *International Sports Law Journal, 16*(1–2), 67–81.

Schmidt, V. A. (2006). Institutionalism. In C. Hay, M. Lister, & D. Marsh (Eds.), *The state: Theories and issues* (pp. 98–117). Basingstoke, U.K.: Palgrave.

Seelig, M. Y., & Seelig, J. H. (1998). "Place your bets!" On gambling, government and society. *Canadian Public Policy, 24*(1), 91–106.

Shernock, V. E. (2014). *Baseball as a microcosm of American west society: 1990–1935* (Unpublished doctoral dissertation). Humboldt State University, Arcata, CA.

Sorbonne-ICSS. (2014a). Guiding principles for protecting the integrity of sports Competitions. Sorbonne-ICSS Research Programme on Ethics and Sports. https://theicss.org/2019/01/01/guiding-principles-for-protecting-the-integrity-of-sports-competitors.

Sorbonne-ICSS. (2014b). Protecting the integrity of sport competition: The last bet for modern sport. Sorbonne-ICSS Research Programme on Ethics and Sports Integrity. https://theicss.org/2019/02/20/protecting-the-integrity-of-sport-competition-the-last-bet-for-modern-sport.

Stephens, S. (2020). Cheating and gaming the system in ancient athletics. *Journal of the Philosophy of Sport, 47*(3), 391–402.

Strange, S. (1986). *Casino capitalism.* New York: Blackwell.

Tak, M. (2018). Too big to jail: Match-fixing, institutional failure and the shifting of responsibility. *International Review for the Sociology of Sport, 53*(7), 788–806.

Tak, M., Choi, C. H., & Sam, M. P. (2021). Odds-wise view: Whose ideas prevail in the global integrity campaigns against match-fixing? *International Review for the Sociology of Sport.* Advance online publication. doi: 10.1177/10126902211045681.

Tak, M., Sam, M. P., & Choi, C. H. (2020). Too much at stake to uphold sport integrity? High-performance athletes' involvement in match-fixing. *Crime, Law and Social Change, 74*(1), 27–44.

Tak, M., Sam, M. P., & Jackson, S. J. (2018a). The politics of countermeasures against match-fixing in sport: A political sociology approach to policy instruments. *International Review for the Sociology of Sport, 53*(1), 30–48.

Tak, M., Sam, M. P., & Jackson, S. J. (2018b). The problems and causes of match-fixing: Are legal sports betting regimes to blame? *Journal of Criminological Research, Policy and Practice, 4*(1), 73–87.

Tzeng, C.-C., & Lee, P.-C. (2021). Understanding match-fixing from the perspective of social capital: A case study of Taiwan's professional baseball system. *International Review for the Sociology of Sport, 56*(4), 558–577.

Tzeng, C. C., Lee, P. C., & Tzeng, G. H. (2020). It's not all about money: The code of brotherhood has a role to play in match-fixing. *Sport in Society, 23*(12), 1926–1944.

U.K. Gambling Commission. (2020). Advertising/marketing rules and regulations. https://www.gamblingcommission.gov.uk/for-gambling-businesses/Compliance/General-compliance/Social-responsibility/Advertising-marketing-rules-and-regulations.aspx.

Vamplew, W. (2007). Playing with the rules: Influences on the development of regulation in sport. *International Journal of the History of Sport, 24*(7), 843–871.

Villeneuve, J., & Diaconu, M. (2011). Integrating betting in the governance of sport: Financial opportunities and ethical challenges. *Sport & EU Review, 3*(1), 5–27.

Vinberg, M., Durbeej, N., & Rosendahl, I. (2020). Gambling and gambling problem among elite athletes and their professional coaches: Findings from a Swedish total population survey of participants in four sports. *International Gambling Studies, 20*(2), 262–281.

Young, M. (2013). "Following the money": The political economy of gambling research. *Addiction Research & Theory, 21*(1), 17–18.

CHAPTER 53

....

SPORT, JOURNALISM, AND SOCIAL REPRODUCTION

....

DAVID ROWE AND RAYMOND BOYLE

SPORTS journalism came into being when organized sport began to take shape in the 18th century. In the first instance, its principal task was to report in print what had happened: a fairly dry, technical account of play during a sport contest and its quantifiable outcome for those in the pre-broadcast era who had to rely on print description. As the intersecting sport and media fields developed in modernity, sports journalism became more elaborate (Boyle, 2006). Play description and score information were accompanied by analysis and atmosphere-setting, as genres of sports journalism developed to satisfy readerships that wanted a word picture to be painted, alongside the dramatic sports photography that brought action and personality to visual life. Evocative sports journalism could give to readers a sense of "having been there," just like, for example, war or travel reporting. When broadcast media—first audio and then audio-visual—provided even richer mediated simulations of being at the event and featured their own journalists in news, current affairs, and discussion programming, print sports journalists had to provide an enhanced service. This could take the form of fine-grained coverage of sports clubs and of the growing ranks of sport stars and celebrities or more elaborate proto-literary treatments of sport. Some journalists, especially in the United States, were accorded the elevated status of the sportswriter. Sports journalism in its various forms grew with the "media sports cultural complex" (Rowe, 2004), supplying copy and commentary at levels that ranged from gossip about athlete injuries, news about player conduct and movement between clubs, to sometimes sophisticated analysis of the operations and ethics of sport organizations, which occasionally reflected upon matters of wider social and cultural significance.

Many years ago, one of the authors (Rowe, 1992) proposed a taxonomy of sports journalism that sought to capture these modes of sports writing. The four proposed categories included the two largely descriptivist modes of "hard" and "soft" sport news (categories that are familiar in other journalistic rounds). The third mode, "orthodox rhetoric," involves fulminating against or, more soberly, critiquing aspects of the institution of sport, but tending to isolate it from its social context and to ignore the journalist's own subject position. The fourth, "reflexive analysis," recognizes more extensively the culture and society that have produced the institution of sport and the potential complicity of the sports journalist in, by turns, endorsing, shaping, and challenging it. This chapter contends that, despite major changes to sports journalism in the 21st century, especially economically and technologically (Boyle, 2017), and to its place within sport culture, there are enduring concerns about the role played by sports journalism in reproducing, contesting, and changing the institution of sport. By extension, the analysis focuses on sports journalism's contribution to the wider sociocultural formation. This critical appraisal takes sports journalism seriously, instead of simply dismissing it as the "toy department of the news media" (Rowe, 2007). Our examination considers how sports journalism is practiced, by whom, and its relationships with other forms of knowledge work and with its audiences. It asks how important sports journalism might be to the making and unmaking of a social world that extends from local communities to global assemblages. In so doing, sports journalism's generation and circulation of social mythologies and ideologies are assessed in relation to obstructing, questioning, and/or advancing progressive social change.

ISSUES

This part of the chapter will focus on some of the key issues that exist around sports journalism, initially with regard to how it gets made and the pressures arising from accommodating both familiar work routines and organizational power structures. As noted earlier, sports journalism has been a constant companion of professional sport since its inception in the 18th century and consolidation in the 19th. The key processual forces affecting sport during this time—commercialization, internationalization, and various forms of political and cultural nationalism—have also changed sports journalism (Boyle & Haynes, 2009; Rowe, 2004). These processes register at two broad levels. First, and specifically before the advent of radio and television, it is important to remember that sports journalism was crucial to establishing the central narratives that became associated with sport. In essence, the sports journalist helps to relay, construct, and often embellish the sporting event and the narratives involving the range of actors that were part of sport as a cultural and, increasingly, commercial activity. Heroes and villains were created, drawing from sport, amplified by journalism, but then feeding back into the myths that became deeply embedded in sporting narratives and, indeed, playing an important part in its ongoing intergenerational popular appeal (Steen, 2014).

Roles and Institutional Demands

This role—establishing and reinforcing the narratives surrounding sport—has evolved over the decades as broadcasting transformed professional sport, not least through television becoming elite sport's core funder and financial underwriter. These discourses surrounding sport often have wider social, cultural, and political connotations that, we suggest, are more widely recognized in contemporary sports journalism than in some of its earlier iterations, which tended to treat sport as inhabiting an apolitical world. This "original" position is more difficult to sustain at a time when, for example, there is intense interest in political protests by sportspeople over such issues as gender equality, LGBTIQ+ rights, stigmatization of disability, ethnoreligious discrimination, and violence against Black people (cf. Jackson, Trevisan, Pullen, & Silk, 2020). It is now impossible, for example, for sports journalists not to take a stance on protocols for political protest and demonstration at the Olympics (Dryden, 2020) or on the National Basketball Association postponing games in protest at the police shootings of African American men (such as Jacob Blake in Wisconsin in August 2020) and drawing criticism from U.S. President Donald Trump for politicizing sport (Kalinic, 2020).

Self-reflection on the profession of sports journalism among practitioners remains, though, partial and largely fleeting, leading us to the second area of impact. If sport itself has been transformed, then so, too, have the institutions within which sports journalists ply their trade. There is a tendency to group journalists in a homogeneous manner, but it is an occupation that ranges widely across news and entertainment. Even within journalistic genres, the category of sports journalist masks a multitude of experiences, values, and practices, often driven by the nature of the media organization to which they belong (Boyle, 2006). Newspaper sports journalists working at what is still recognizable in, say, the U.K. media market as tabloid journalism, have an agenda quite different from those who work for what used to be the broadsheet end of the market (now increasingly called "compact," as most "quality" newspapers shrink in size but resist the negative connotations of the word "tabloid") (Rowe, 2011). Traditionally, tabloid sports journalists have little autonomy and are driven by the news agenda and demands of the sports editor (Boyle, 2006). Any senior sportswriter or columnist on a tabloid is under pressure to provoke and be controversial, their job being to create news and to shape the agenda rather than simply to offer considered reflection or analysis. This task has always been important to the circulation-based marketplace where competition is dependent on the mass sale of inexpensive newspapers, but has become imperative in an increasingly digital marketplace that aims to maximize clicks and encourage readers to pay to go behind paywalls (Bradshaw & Minogue, 2020).

Organizational Dynamics and Pressures

How a sports journalist represents the institution of sport and its social relations and structures is closely determined by their place in the media organization and the forces brought to bear on it. For example, if a sports journalist works for a dedicated sports rights holder, such as Sky Sports or BT Sports in the United Kingdom, then they are less likely to be stringently critical of the sports that they are broadcasting and more accustomed to seeing their role as, in part, to promote their organization and its relationship with the particular sports for which the company holds significant broadcast rights (Lambert, 2018). Hence, because working for an organization holding exclusive rights often delivers greater access for sports journalists to key players, coaches, and so forth, there are clear disincentives to stray too far into any rigorous, complicated investigation of the sports which they (and their employers) have a vested interest in promoting and, to a significant extent, in protecting. Of course, the reverse may be the case if, for example, their employer has lost the broadcast rights to a rival media organization. We contend, however, that this is something of a balancing act for any journalist and, indeed, media rights holder. If they are perceived as too compliant, then viewing fans may become annoyed and take to social media platforms to vent their disapproval of the coverage (Bradshaw & Minogue, 2020). The worst outcome in these circumstances for both journalist and media organization in "pay TV" is "churn": terminating a broadcast subscription. The growth of social media, as we note below, has made this relationship between the journalist of a rights-holding organization and the sport organization itself more complex and conflicting than in previous decades.

As suggested earlier, in recent years, driven in part by the proliferation of organizations covering elite sport and the attendant online chatter among fans and various stakeholders who are now part of this environment, it has become harder for sport to be represented as a cultural form immune from wider social, economic, and political influences. Debates around sporting ethics, cheating, and the impact of money on the players and structures of elite sport are all enjoying a higher profile (Sugden & Tomlinson, 2016). This journalistic coverage and engagement, as also noted, is often uneven in its intensity across media outlets, and in the case of, say, sport-related corruption, such stories are more likely to be driven by non-sports journalists, not uncommonly to the chagrin of their sporting colleagues. Thus, the "reflexive analysis" mode described earlier still occupies only a relatively small part of the hinterland of sports journalism and its sizable media presence.

There is no shortage of evidence to reinforce the argument that, broadly speaking, sports journalism's relationship with sport is one that is characterized by attempts to insulate both sport and journalism from playing any part in the wider constitution of social formations (Horky & Nieland, 2013). However, journalistic spaces that highlight the deeply embedded role that sport plays in wider aspects of society and culture can be found among the extensive sports media chatter (Boyle, 2019). With regard to how sports journalism addresses key social issues regarding class, "race," gender, sexuality, and so on, and their intersectional relationships, we need to be careful not to overstate the changes that have taken place in recent years—but change there has been, however limited. The position of women in sport media is a case in point.

Changing Political Dynamics

Two examples from the U.K. media environment highlight how media outlets and their associated sports journalism both respond to and also shape broader shifts in society, in this instance with regard to gender equity. The British Broadcasting Corporation has in recent years, not least under its director of sport, Barbara Slater, increasingly championed the profile of women's sport, and of association football (soccer) in particular. Driven by its public service remit and in the interest of what can be called "cultural citizenship" (Scherer & Rowe, 2014), while in a highly competitive sports rights environment, the organization, working with sports governing bodies, has increased media coverage of women's sport. For example, 2019 saw BBC Sport (2019) promote #changethegame, a summer of women's sports coverage across all its media sites. Using its multiplatform coverage of the FIFA Women's World Cup in France as the anchor point, the BBC carried newly commissioned documentaries about women in sport, as well as live coverage, fronted by female presenters such as Alex Scott.

The considerable marketing strength of the BBC was also used to promote this sport content. The BBC drew one of its largest television audiences of the year when 11.7 million watched the England versus USA World Cup semifinal (Waterson, 2019). It also carried the Netball World Cup in July of that year, as well as offering extensive coverage of women's golf across the BBC's various outlets. Under its 50:50 equality program, the BBC (2019, p. 19) has been increasing the number of female journalists and female on-screen contributors working in its sport coverage, rising from 15% in 2018 to 43% in some key programs such as *BBC Sportsday* in the following year. Importantly, this improvement has also extended to more female journalists covering men's sport. Again, it is necessary to be cautious about overstating the overall change in sports media coverage, and examples of sexist sports journalism are not hard to find (Bradshaw & Minogue, 2020). However, the lead taken by the BBC to engage seriously with women's sport, and its commitment to the wider representation of onscreen female broadcast journalists, is to be welcomed, and would have been difficult to envisage even a decade ago. There is little doubt that the public service broadcasting remit of the BBC has been central to this shift in representation, as is the case with Channel 4 in the United Kingdom via its increasingly progressive coverage of Paralympic sport (Pullen, Jackson, & Silk, 2020; Tate, 2016).

While newspaper sports journalism—and, of course, most of this content is now also online—has been slower to embrace wider social change in women's sport, there have been some encouraging examples of improvement in this regard. The *Daily Telegraph*, a conservative U.K. broadsheet newspaper, for primarily commercial reasons has sought to widen its audience by giving a higher profile to women's sport and female sports journalists. March 2019 saw the paper launch a dedicated section of its sports print section and website covering women's sport under its first female sports editor, Anna Kessel, and her deputy editor, Vicki Hodges. *Telegraph Women's Sport* (*TWS*) has announced (Kessel, 2020) a number of high-profile female columnists, including athlete Dina Asher-Smith and tennis coach Judy Murray, emphasizing that athletics and tennis would be important areas to cover, as well as, of course, women's association football.

Significantly, *TWS* also recruited female sports journalists not simply to work on women's sport (this practice arguably creates something of a female sport "ghetto") but across all its sports and platforms. The *Daily Telegraph* now covers around 29% (Kessel, 2020) more stories on women's sport than any other U.K. newspaper, and in the summer of 2019, its website led with a women's sport story almost every other day. One might legitimately ask why it has taken so long for the media to begin significantly raising the visibility of women's sport and to offer opportunities to female journalists. In truth, it has been an incremental process and, while relatively small, these remain important interventions in sports journalism in the United Kingdom and beyond. They reveal how sports journalism's historical reproduction of its own organizational gender inequality paralleled sport's social profile as a male-dominated social institution. For this reason, more female sports journalists covering more women and girls in sport clearly signals to media audiences that sport is not only a man's world, and normalizes the activities of women by placing value on them in both sport and media (including those within other male-dominated institutions, such as the military; cf. Tamir, Yarchi, & Galily, 2017).

Sociotechnical Change, the Sporting Product, and Its Audiences

The last issue that we wish to highlight in this section is whether sociotechnical change—especially the rise of sports organization media units, direct communication by athletes, social media, and citizen journalism—are redefining audiences and rendering sports journalism redundant. A significant trend within the sport-media relationship has been growing awareness among sporting bodies of the value of their media rights. An increased capacity to develop digital infrastructure delivering content directly to consumers, and the realization that media sports consumption patterns are continually evolving, present new challenges as well as opportunities. Greater vertical integration of the media sport product, with those who generate the "sport media content" also distributing and selling it, might be more profitable than selling media rights to media companies. Such a rearrangement may become increasingly prevalent given that global digital disruption to sport and media business models has caused the plateauing and even the fall of the value of media sports rights (Hutchins, Li, & Rowe, 2019; Hutchins & Rowe, 2012)—not to mention the COVID-19 crisis—with the additional advantage of allowing greater image control.

This more fluid and complex media environment has resulted in branding and brand management issues becoming more central in media sport debates and, in short, has helped fuel an ongoing battle for control over sports content and the narratives that surround it. This process typically has a commercial dimension. The rise of sports public relations is, of course, not new. But the more complex digital landscape, populated by an increasing number of platforms through which to deliver content and communicate with a potentially international sporting audience, has arisen only in the past decade or so (Boyle & Haynes, 2018). At the same time, as noted, we have seen the decline in print media value (newspapers and magazines), in some cases partially offset by the development of an online presence and revenue stream, in pursuit of audiences and advertisers who have moved online. Newspaper sports journalists are no longer simply print journalists (and haven't been so for many years) and are now required to work across multiple platforms. Even those reporters for whom print remains of deep importance (the "ink on the fingers" tradition) must cultivate an online brand image (and audience following) on platforms such as Twitter, Instagram, and Facebook, as well as develop new communicative skills in areas such as television, video, radio, photography, and blogging (Hutchins & Rowe, 2012).

What is especially difficult for the professional sports journalist to maintain in this environment is their reputation for having the "inside track" on sports reporting, when so much live sport content is available on various platforms, and athletes, clubs, sports, sponsors, and rights-holding media are all active in a digital space. Competition is intense in seeking to reach and communicate with an audience that is fragmented and often distracted by many other cultural attractions. That audience is itself operating in the same communicative space, with fans interacting via online, social, and mobile media alongside "citizen sports journalists," that is, those who may practice journalism in some form without being a professional journalist, while making some claim of equivalence to "legacy" media professionals (Allan, 2013). Within this mix, access to key sports organizations and personnel for the sports journalist has become a major challenge, and any taken-for-granted notion of discursive legitimacy among the audience is often challenged, not least in the loosely regulated online space of Twitter. Nonetheless, those sports journalists who work hard at seeking out distinctive content and offer stimulating insights and reflections on sport still have value and cachet within this more competitive and dynamic communicative milieu. In the United Kingdom, one such example (more are presented in the next section) is David Conn (2018), an investigative sports journalist who works at *The Guardian* newspaper. He has written across the sports sector, specifically on football and its commercial and business dimensions, as well as on corruption and sport.

Indeed, such tendencies are seen in the rise of subscription-based online sports journalism websites such as *The Athletic* (2020), which has (in part) marketed itself on its ability to deliver distinctive long-form journalism that is not readily available in other sectors of the media. In the United Kingdom, *The Athletic* has "poached" a number of high-profile sports journalists from newspapers, retaining dedicated "beat" journalists covering football teams across the United Kingdom and offering more analysis and background pieces on clubs (Buzzelli, Gentile, Billings, & Sadri, 2020; Mayhew, 2019). At present in the United Kingdom, its focus is on association football coverage, but depending on the success of *The Athletic*'s business model, coverage of other sports may be extended. These issues of organization, communication, and politics necessarily confront sports journalism as an important historical component of the media sports cultural complex that must engage with the 21st-century digital landscape. What approaches should be adopted to achieve a critical-analytical understanding of its present conditions and future prospects?

Approaches

All approaches to sports journalism, in broad terms, must take account of the relationship between the sport and media fields and their impact on other societal fields. According to the sociological theory of Pierre Bourdieu (1984/2010), sports journalism is at the confluence of the two closely related fields of sport and media, but its systematic analysis in the context of this chapter emanates from a third field, that of (higher) education. These fields interact in a range of ways: sometimes converging, as conceived in Wenner's (1998) influential concept of "MediaSport," and in other ways differentiated in terms of their orientations to sport, its mediation and analysis. Any attempt at classification of approaches to sports journalism in its social context is necessarily a process of simplification in some respects, but it is nonetheless useful in illuminating its various strands. In broad terms, and following a classic tripartite analytical structure, different degrees of emphasis are placed on how sports journalism is produced, what it means in its various forms, and on its potential and actual effects. Overlaying such analyses are theoretical perspectives that are more or less critical of sports journalism's processes, mythologies, and ideologies, key elements of which are elaborated next.

Professional Work Cultures

Sports journalism is, historically, a craft (Hutchins & Rowe, 2012, Chapter 6), an occupation, or, in a grander view, a "profession" dedicated to the mediation of sport for a range of publics: sport fans, the general populace, key institutions such as the state, sports organizations themselves, and, finally, for other journalists, not all of whom are specialists in sport. For over two centuries, sports journalists have reported on formal sporting contests and, as the sport and media industries developed along parallel and then intersecting pathways, on all manner of sport-related issues. From a sociological perspective, an immediate area of interest concerns the social character of this increasingly institutionalized phenomenon.

Professional sports journalists have typically worked within news media organizations in the generation and sale of sports media information and narrative. Their sociodemographic characteristics, therefore, come into focus—the most notable of which have been gender and "race"/ethnicity. Critiques of sports journalists have tended to echo those directed at the historical institution of sport itself, arguing that sport developed as a bastion of white masculinity in modernity (Hardin, Dodd, & Lauffer, 2006). It thereby attracted media personnel whose gender profile resembled that of the dominant males they were covering— and, indeed, often identified with them in a manner that could be described as hero worship. In its foundational Anglo-American markets, the ethnocultural diversity of this workforce was highly circumscribed (cf. Rowe, 2004, Chapter 2) because of compounding intersectional disadvantage.

Professional sports journalism can be practiced in different contexts, ranging from inside the large sports newsrooms of media companies where "staffers" can be found to the cafés, coworking spaces, and home offices occupied by "freelancers." Given that the latter are generally trying to sell their sport stories for publication and broadcast by the former, we will concentrate here on the sports journalism created in, or passing through, formal media organizations. Sports journalists operate within the media field to illuminate those aspects of the sport field that they deem to be newsworthy.

Approaching Gender

Historically, as noted, the institutions of both sport and media have resembled each other in the respect that their male domination produced a masculinist culture. Sports organizations were mostly—and largely still are—run by men, remunerating and/or managing the forms of sport that were most prized by the media, such as the male-dominated football codes, basketball, baseball, cricket, and, to a lesser degree, tennis and golf. Large multisport events like the FIFA World Cup and the Olympics have also been mostly male-dominated. It is not surprising, then, that sports journalists would also be men, often covering women's sports, while the reverse is infrequently seen.

Indeed, female sports journalists, historically a small minority, were almost exclusively confined to women's sports, especially those, like figure skating, gymnastics, or artistic (formerly synchronized) swimming, that emphasized the aesthetic dimensions of sport performance. By contrast, women have rarely been empowered to comment on men's sport and, if they have done so, have tended to be assigned the role of discussing the non-sporting aspects of the spectacle assumed to be of greater interest to other women (Horky & Nieland, 2013). In this way, sports journalism was a key means of reproducing gender inequality in the fields that it straddled, contributing to its naturalization through the pronounced demarcation of who plays the highest status forms of sport and gets to speak and write about it.

It is useful to examine the gendered hierarchies embedded in the organizations that have avoiding repetition produced mediated sports discourse. In newspapers—the first places where sports journalism was practiced—the sports desk developed as a semi-autonomous entity presided over by a male, usually Anglo-Celtic editor (in the Anglosphere). Most of the journalists who were hired were men, and most of the sports that they covered were male-dominated. As noted earlier, there have been attempts by some commercial media organizations to employ female sports editors and journalists, not least because of the logic of sport media market expansion. Public service broadcasters such as the BBC and the Australian Broadcasting Corporation have also taken significant steps to diversify their sports journalism workforce, at least along gender lines (Scherer and Rowe, 2014). Indeed, there is now a growing number of prominent female sports journalists, such as Clare Balding, Sally Jenkins, Lisa Salters, Alison Mitchell, Jacquelin Magnay, Tracey Holmes, Cindy Brunson, and Ines Sainz.

Nonetheless, in more traditional societies such as Poland, where the socially conservative legacy of Catholicism is still felt, the inequitable gender order is still evident in sports journalism in terms of occupational levels, sexualized conduct, and lack of accommodation of the structural demands of many women's lives as primary caregivers (Organista & Mazur, 2019). In the terms proposed by Italian political theorist Antonio Gramsci (Anderson, 2016), these organizational inequalities reflect the ways in which hegemonic values—in this case masculinist—have shaped the occupational culture of sports journalism by their insinuation into practical consciousness in ways that simulate "consent." They obdurately resist change by persistent attachment to myths that draw on the discourse of sport itself as a meritocratic space in which achievement translates into reward distributed on a "level playing field." Gramsci, though, argued that "winning consent" is never an automatic process, while within a Bourdieusian framework sport media's "field of struggles" (Bourdieu & Wacquant, 1992, p. 101) has experienced intensified contestation over once-unspoken principles underlying the allocation of social, economic, and cultural capital and the construction of the *habitus* (embodied, mental, and related dispositions; see Bennett, Carter, Gayo, Kelly, & Noble, 2020) of the sports journalist.

Analyzing Change on the "Sports Beat"

It cannot, though, be assumed that a change in the demographic composition of sports journalism personnel will automatically or uniformly alter what they produce unless occupational expectations and routines also change (Lowes, 1999). Sports journalism's labor force may change—the passage of time and its attendant social, political, economic, technological, and environmental transformations leave little choice in that respect—but its outcomes are uncertain. It might be anticipated that, for example, the recruitment of more journalists who are women, of color, LGBTIQ+, and so on would result in a corresponding diversification of the modes of sports journalism. Still, a number of contingent elements influence sports journalistic texts, including dominant occupational norms that impose limits on innovation, the rate of turnover of its practitioners, and wider changes to the working environment and sociocultural role of media sport. For these reasons, an important approach involves analyzing the structural and processual factors that influence the making of sports journalism.

Over the past century, the "sports beat" has witnessed, and been a party to, a substantial repositioning of sport in society and culture. Sports journalists first focused on the local reporting of sport contests, their scope expanding accordingly via the parallel development of sport and media into national, regional, international, and global domains. Initially, sports journalists were positioned mostly as *reporters*, predominantly charged with the task of recording what had occurred during sports events in written texts with accompanying photographs, including quite basic information such as sport scores. But as the media developed in a manner that demanded wider and deeper audience engagement, sports journalists (as noted earlier) were increasingly required to provide overarching narratives, offer evocative vignettes of key sporting moments, and reflect or provoke debates and controversies to attract the attention of readers.

The progressive development of broadcasting eroded the discursive duopoly involving those who saw sport contests with their own eyes as a leisure activity and told their immediate social groups about them, as opposed to those who were there in a professional capacity and were employed to disseminate their accounts to expanding publics across and even beyond countries. Broadcasting, especially television, brought dispersed audiences closer to sport, meaning that sports journalists were required to assert their professional advantage as superior sports analysts and as occupational actors whose access to the institution and its secrets could not be matched by everyday sport consumers. These developments helped create the more prestigious and well-remunerated figure of the sportswriter, whose cultural capital derived from a combination of sport-related knowledge and communicative excellence that was even judged by cultural critics to be high-status "literature." The much disparaged "jobbing" sports journalist, however, has been stereotyped—sometimes with justification—as less educated, narrower in origin, restricted in vision, and tending to be star-struck and gossip-hungry (Boyle, Rowe, & Whannel, 2010).

Unlike elite sportswriters, columnists, and commentators, though, working sports journalists are usually required to interact on a regular basis with professional sportspeople, entering their working spaces, such as stadia and locker rooms, and seeking to build relationships with them in order to elicit on-the-record interview comments, off-the-record insights, and "scoops." In this respect, they are not so different from journalists on other rounds, including politics and business, who must cultivate their sources. Like those journalists they can also suffer from being "frozen out" if considered to be hostile by their subjects, and as the labor force shrinks and work tasks proliferate, they generally rely on a restricted number of regular, friendly sources (Tiffen et al., 2014). As knowledge workers, sports journalists are in the business of generating, interpreting, and distributing a wide range of "data," including the physical condition of athletes, the financial health of clubs, the governance conduct of associations, and the feelings of fans. This is a wide remit, and it is not surprising that many practitioners will focus on a limited range of matters, having made the assumption (as mentioned below with regard to misconduct in Australian rugby league) that their audiences wish primarily to be entertained rather than, say, discomfited by the scandals (Rowe & Palmer, this volume) produced by investigative reporting.

Interrogating Received Power and Critical Engagement

Media organizations, as part of the institution of the media employing sports journalists, are constantly required to make judgments about their actual and implied audiences, what they might like or dislike, want or reject, and so on. As noted, historically they have largely conceived and addressed audiences as men like themselves. In this collective imagining of the sports fan, sports journalists are inevitably involved in the symbolic representation and reproduction of society. They can be regarded to some degree as "cultural intermediaries" (Maguire & Matthews, 2012), working at the meeting place of sport, media, and audience, and taking positions on issues relating to sport, culture, and society. Journalists constantly make assumptions about their audiences, in some ways distinguishing themselves from fans by claiming to be objective, expert observers of sport, and in other ways self-presenting as the typical fan, and so able to channel their attitudes and emotions in a manner that might unkindly be called ventriloquism. In discharging both functions, sports journalists render aspects of the institution of sport and its social roles. For example, having invested in sport in an occupational sense, many sports reporters may uncritically accept the heroic mythologies generated by peak sports bodies like the International Olympic Committee and FIFA, reinforcing and sharing their claims to global social benevolence, and ignoring or excusing their failures regarding governance, economic exploitation, social equity, and so on (Naha & Hassan, 2019).

Indeed, many sports journalists, as discussed earlier, have often accepted the fallacy of the separation of sport and politics, and consequently have been reluctant to ask uncomfortable questions about the sport-society nexus (Boyle, 2019). The texts they have produced are often criticized for social stereotyping and marginalization of various kinds, including that based on class, gender, "race," ethnicity, sexuality, ability, and age (Weedon, Wilson, Yoon, & Lawson, 2016). Given the wide reach of such media representations, sports journalism of this kind can be seen to contribute to hegemonic structures that naturalize social inequalities by mobilizing sport's mythologies and ideologies in ways that constitute functionalist justifications of an inequitable status quo.

More critical forms of sports journalism are urgently required, then, as old repressive orthodoxies come under challenge. A striking case is that of the role of the "take a knee" protest, which originated in sport and became a notable visual-corporeal symbol of the Black Lives Matter movement. The response of many sports journalists to Colin Kaepernick's 2016 antiracism protest in the U.S. National Football League was unsupportive or negative (Serazio, 2019), but the gesture was subsequently embraced by many sport organizations and sportspeople, especially after the violent death of George Floyd at the hands of Minneapolis police in May 2020 (Zaru, 2020).

As a result, it can be suggested that mainstream sports journalism reluctantly followed rather than enthusiastically led this change in social disposition toward racialized violence, just as it has struggled to come to terms with the issues that prompted protests and demonstrations within sport in general (Broussard, 2019). While we should not overgeneralize about the social attitudes of professional sports journalists, especially as they are gradually becoming more diverse and, in some ways, socially progressive, their craft can hardly be said to have been at the forefront of social change in sport and beyond.

The various methods employed by critical sport researchers and scholars each illuminate a different aspect of its structures and practices: organizational and labor studies are instructive about the conditions under which media sport texts are produced; discursive and textual studies interrogate, explicate, and critique those texts as interventions in reproduction, change, and contestation in sport and society; and ethnographic studies of media sport audiences, including their relationships with sports journalists, provide the necessary detailed information regarding how the texts generated by sports journalism are used, accepted, rejected, or modified in the everyday lives of social subjects.

In this chapter we have given considerable attention to the first area—the production of sports journalism—because we are interested primarily here in current debates not only about the sociocultural role of sports journalism but in what form, if at all, it can survive in the age of the "prosumer," the citizen journalist, and the digital networker (Boyle,

2019) within what was once simply called the audience. Those debates provide pointers to the overall trajectory of contemporary sports journalism.

DEBATES

Discussions regarding sports journalism, as we have seen, have tended to focus on occupational status, labor force composition, textual quality, audience relationships, ideological meanings, and social consequences. Sports journalism has long been controversial for a number of reasons, such as its struggle for legitimacy in a domain of popular culture where any fan can claim expertise. What sets a sports journalist apart, in terms of command of cultural capital, from a reader, listener, or viewer who in most cases has strong opinions about a sporting subject? In asking who should be recruited to a club and who sacked, game tactics, ticket prices, the design of sportswear, and so on, what discursive authority can a sport journalist mobilize?

In pondering such questions, one of the authors (Rowe) is often struck by the lack of respect for the "beat" sports journalists who cover his hometown football club, Plymouth Argyle. Part of the large British newspaper group, Reach PLC, Plymouth Live (2020) is a website that generates a constant stream of stories about the club in a dedicated section, each of which has a facility for barely moderated comments from readers. Virtually all newspapers now enable readers to comment on various sport stories, creating fora for relatively small proportions of active commenters to post their opinions (Ksiazek, 2018), many of which are unflattering to the journalist who wrote the story. This is a very different audience feedback arrangement from the classic physical newspaper forum, which requires a "letter to the editor" involving a media gatekeeper who selects only a few reader comments for publication, appearing after some delay in a later edition.

Thus, in essential ways, the 21st-century sports journalist operating in a digital environment must share their stories with reader-commenters whose remarks can be posted in the same online space within minutes of their publication. From the perspective of the new digital economy, the more comments a story elicits, the stronger the evidence of reader engagement, irrespective of how favorable, thoughtful, or insulting those comments may be—not least those directed toward sports journalists. (Notably, in August 2020 Reach PLC introduced a new commenting system in part to dissuade such incivility.)

The key issue here is the evolving status of the professional sports journalist. Indeed, the very fact that they are paid and have greater prominence in a recognized publication can be a source of reader resentment. This is an endemic problem challenging the entrenched historical legitimacy of the professional sports corps and can be exacerbated in cases where supporters have taken control of a sports club. These "executive fans" acquire organizational expertise and make a material investment in sport (Ruddock, Hutchins, & Rowe, 2010), and in some respects can claim to have a deeper knowledge of sport than an "outsider" journalist.

In such instances, the sport fan spans the boundaries between owner, producer, and consumer, with some also responsible for media communication. Here, the sports journalist is left in an even more awkward position than the usual one of being required to be both a sport fan and an independent "fourth estate" observer. As noted, there have long been obstacles to local sports journalists looking too closely and critically at the sports clubs and sportspeople with whom they frequently interact. Further, any investigative journalism directed at a local sports organization owned and run by fans—such as those related to governance—is likely to be regarded as almost treasonous.

At a much larger scale, this has been a continuing structural problem for sports journalists covering national and international sports organizations. As a result, they commonly leave the "dirty work" to journalists on rounds which do not require cultivating sport sources and relationships (Rowe, 2004). Those sports journalists who have specialized in critical investigative work—such as Hajo Seppelt on state-sponsored athlete doping (Brown, 2016), David Walsh (2013) on cyclist Lance Armstrong and his taking of performance-enhancing drugs, Declan Hill (2010) on match-fixing, or the late Andrew Jennings (2010; Jennings & Sambrook, 2000) on corruption in the IOC and FIFA—have encountered legal and illegal intimidation and threats from sports organizations, individuals, and their associates. Some fans themselves may also resent the exposure of sport's "dirty secrets."

Others who have moved into the area without being sports journalists as such, like Anas Aremeyaw Anas in his exposure of corruption in association football in West Africa and Kenya (BBC, 2018), experience similar treatment arising from their "excursions" into the field. However, importantly, such investigator outsiders can move on to other areas more easily than specialist sports journalists, who may not find an alternative 'round' in which to practice their craft. Notably, like other parts of the news media, sports journalism has become increasingly dangerous in South America, the Middle East, and other world regions (Sparre, 2019).

Lovability and Legitimacy in Sports Journalism

The sports press, therefore, can be regarded as "unlovable" in Michael Schudson's (2008) terms in more than one sense. Schudson conceives the necessary unlovability of the press as related in part to asking difficult questions and pursuing unpopular truths integral to the remit of the fourth estate. But they can become even less lovable when regarded as sycophantic or corrupt. When sports journalists are instrumental in "breaking" a big story that extends well beyond the sport field—for example, in 2015 FIFA governance abuses dominated the print, broadcast, online, and mobile news agenda for a period, even in countries where association football is not the dominant sport (Rowe, 2017)—the cultural capital that would seemingly accrue from holding major institutions to account does not automatically confer social status on them. Instead, as is the case with other disciplines of journalism, bearing bad news can lead to their disparagement (being called "muckrakers") or, at least, a denial of recognition that it took rigorous journalistic inquiry to break the story.

Indeed, editors themselves may intervene to maintain the strictly entertaining side of the sports pages, as occurred when Garry Linnell, editor of the Sydney *Daily Telegraph* tabloid, pledged to cover only positive stories on the back (main sport) page during a period when the scandalous conduct of rugby league players dominated media headlines. Linnell claimed that he adopted this policy of creating a "scandal-free zone" because "covering rugby league had become a 'crime beat' and his readers were sick of it" (Patching, 2014, pp. 17–18), an example of the negotiation of sport discourse between journalists and readers (Waterhouse-Watson, 2013). One way of handling this problem, and the frequent accusations that sports journalists lack the necessary credentials to write about sport if they have not played it at the highest level, is to hire current or former players to provide (sometimes "ghosted" or heavily edited) copy or to commentate in broadcast media. These "insiders" may be more "lovable" for fans than most sports journalists. Yet, while lauded for their heroics on the field (especially for national teams), their routine use in the role serves to undermine the necessity of traditional training and experience in the news media to qualify as a sports journalist. For example, the BBC's highest paid employee is the former England footballer Gary Lineker, who presents and appears in many programs on television and radio and writes newspaper columns, without having any formal journalism training or prior experience. Arguably, Lineker does much that can be described as sports journalism, thereby indicating the porosity of the occupation.

Indeed, as digitization has opened up multiple entry points for communication and "legacy" media organizations shrink in size and influence, sports journalists must compete with many others in the cultural and creative industries. This change in the structure of the industry fosters the kind of income and status inequality that is characteristic of other areas of cultural production, like rock music and film, where a small group of celebrities/stars is very well remunerated and a much larger, precarious population of cultural workers struggles to make a living (Oakley & O'Connor, 2015). To be an established sportswriter or commentator in the "quality" media (such as up-market newspapers and public service broadcasters) is to possess the more prestigious cultural capital, while the tabloid media have their own star system based on the recognition of sports journalists with longevity who occupy a position in the media sport field that is—or at least appears to be—closer to the "everyday" sports fan. Orbiting around these stars of sports journalism are many minor constellations in the "field of struggles," as Bourdieu describes it, where once relatively stable positions are constantly shifting.

Competing Legacies

The main debates now taking place around sports journalism are not entirely new (Bradshaw & Minogue, 2020), but they are more complicated and intense. They question what sports journalism is or ought to be, and how it should relate to the sport field. Journalism in general has had to distinguish itself from public relations in a mediated world where image and crisis management are crucial to the health and future of both sport and media organizations and their personnel.

As noted, the Black Lives Matter movement—alongside other phenomena pertaining to corporate social responsibility around sex and gender oppression, human trafficking, fair trade, and so on—has pushed many sports organizations to take public political positions (such as in the case of the 2022 Russian invasion of Ukraine) that they have been historically reluctant to adopt. Increasingly, they are joined in this task by sports journalists who, for reasons of conviction or self-interest, have previously repeated the mantra "Sport and politics don't mix." Many older sports journalists of limited demographic diversity are ill-equipped for this role, but it is cruelly ironic that, at the historical moment where younger, more diverse sports journalists are poised to penetrate the media field, it is being deconstructed by a range of social, cultural, economic, and technological factors.

A more palatable irony is that it is increasingly difficult for sports journalism to discharge its traditional socially reproductive function of justifying a range of inequalities as natural and even desirable while trying to connect with audiences that are increasingly polarized and that, despite the most sophisticated algorithms, are more difficult to know. The crisis of sports journalism is replicated across societies and its institutions, but it is more acute because, for too long, many of its practitioners believed in its heroic myths and the fiction that sport offered sanctuary from the troubled world that it tried, unsuccessfully, to hold at bay.

CONCLUSION

In early 2020, as the COVID-19 pandemic took hold, most sports events around the world were canceled. Sports journalists had no live sports to discuss, and many were forced to address the crisis that had befallen sport and, indeed, to reflect on sport's place in society. The sudden seizing-up of the global sport machine created something of a void in the working lives of sports journalists and in the leisure lives of sport spectators.

While the former looked for topics to cover that did not depend on current sport contests, the latter searched the media for sport-related content. Many found *The Last Dance* (2020) compelling. This is a 10-part documentary series about the Chicago Bulls basketball team in the last decade of the 20th century, featuring the sport's most famous figure, Michael Jordan. The series was shown on cable on ESPN (with some episodes on the ABC network) in the United States and on Netflix worldwide. A senior ESPN writer, Howard Bryant (2020), questioned key issues about the series in an article admirably published on the ESPN website. He cited concerns that *The Last Dance* could be seen as a "Jordan-brand vehicle instead of independent documentary journalism," given that close associates of his were among the executive producers and that "Jordan and the NBA jointly own the footage." Bryant lamented that it showed the weakness of "public journalism" and the domination of "public space" by "private interest," and that "athletes have decided that the best way to control their message is to control the medium." Bryant asserted, "This generation has entered into the media space not to preserve public journalism but to destroy it, to not be questioned." Around the same time, a journalist working for AFL Media, the largest sport media platform in Australia and owned by its largest sport (Australian Rules Football), was stood down for tweeting an Instagram post by a player's wife revealing that she had breached the strict COVID-19 protocols that enabled games to be played. He was reinstated only after deleting the tweet and apologizing for being unaware of an editorial decision not to name family members in such circumstances. This action by a media arm claiming to be independent of its owner reveals the obvious ethical threat to sports journalists posed by taking them "in house" (Heinrich, 2020).

This is a troubled vantage point from which to consider the next stage of research into sports journalism. It reveals the need to examine in detail the erosion of essential parts of sports journalism that have, however imperfectly, defined the sport-media nexus in the public sphere (Gripsrud, Moe, Molander, & Murdock, 2010). That much of the world would watch *The Last Dance* on Netflix, one of the media industry disruptors (along with Google, Facebook, etc.) that has significantly weakened the news media's capacity to support journalism, highlights the urgent need to analyze the political economy of sports journalism.

Reinvention or Retreat?

These changing structural dynamics should be a key priority area for social scientific inquiry, accompanied by a focus on the size and diversity of sports journalism's labor force. Understanding the evolving modes in which sports journalism comes to be practiced in "legacy" and new digital media, and the changing ways in which its audiences are contacted, informed, and entertained, is essential to the future mediated sport research agenda. Such research should be combined with critical discourse analysis of media sports texts and pay close attention to the too often unmined ethical dimensions of the sports narratives, mythologies, and implicit or explicit ideologies that are inevitably generated by the media sports cultural complex.

How sports journalism can engage with the major social issues with which sport is necessarily entangled will be both of key concern to researchers and a clear sign of its future relevance. There has been an apparently decisive shift in the disposition of the sport and media fields regarding the expected critical role of sports journalism. It is hoped that the possibilities for its reinvention will not be frustrated by the economically induced depletion of sports journalism's labor force at precisely the time that it can render a more valuable service to the cultural citizenship needs and rights of its current and potential audiences.

REFERENCES

Allan, S. (2013). *Citizen witnessing: Revisioning journalism in times of crisis.* Cambridge, U.K.: Polity.

Anderson, B. (2016). What Gramsci can tell sport communication scholars about how civic leaders sell sports to their communities: A look at the Braves' move to Atlanta. *International Journal of Sport Communication, 9*(3), 261–277.

The Athletic. (2020). https://theathletic.com/.

BBC. (2018, June 19). Betraying the game: Anas Aremeyaw Anas investigates football in Africa. https://www.bbc.com/news/world-africa-44535318.

BBC. (2019). 50:50 Project report 2019. http://downloads.bbc.co.uk/aboutthebbc/reports/reports/5050-may-2019.pdf.

BBC Sport. (2019, May 1). #changethegame: BBC Sport launches women's summer of sport season. https://www.bbc.com/sport/48078252.

Bennett, T., Carter, D., Gayo, M., Kelly, M., & Noble, G. (Eds.). (2020). *Fields, capitals, habitus: Australian culture, inequalities and social divisions.* London: Routledge

Bourdieu, P. (1984/2010). *Distinction: A social critique of the judgement of taste.* London: Routledge.

Bourdieu, P., & Wacquant, L. J. D. (1992). *An invitation to reflexive sociology.* Cambridge, U.K.: Polity.

Boyle, R. (2006). *Sports journalism: Contexts and issues.* London: Sage.

Boyle, R. (2017). Sports journalism: Changing journalism practice and digital media. *Digital Journalism, 5*(5), 493–495.

Boyle, R. (2019). *Changing sports journalism practice in the age of digital media.* London: Routledge.

Boyle, R., & Haynes, R. (2009). *Power play: Sport, the media and popular culture* (2nd ed.). Edinburgh: Edinburgh University Press.

Boyle, R., and Haynes, R. (2018). Sport, the media and strategic communications management. In D. Hassan (Ed.), *Managing sport business: An introduction* (pp. 478–501). London: Routledge.

Boyle, R., Rowe, D., & Whannel, G. (2010). "Delight in trivial controversy?" Questions for sports journalism. In S. Allan (Ed.), *Routledge companion to news and journalism* (pp. 245–255). London: Routledge.

Bradshaw, T., & Minogue, D. (2020). *Sports journalism: The state of play*. London: Routledge.

Broussard, R. (2019). *A field theory analysis of sports journalists' coverage of social justice protests in sports* (Unpublished PhD thesis). University of Alabama, Tuscaloosa. https://ir.ua.edu/bitstream/handle/123456789/6497/file_1.pdf?sequence=1&isAllowed=y.

Brown, A. (2016, April 29). Interview: Hajo Seppelt on how collusion in sport continues. *The Sports Integrity Initiative*. https://www.sportsintegrityinitiative.com/interview-hajo-seppelt-on-how-collusion-in-sport-continues/.

Bryant, H. (2020, June 28). What "The Last Dance" reveals about Michael Jordan's legacy. *ESPN*. https://www.espn.com/nba/story/_/id/29365615/what-last-dance-reveals-michael-jordan-legacy.

Buzzelli, N. R., Gentile, P., Billings, A. C., & Sadri, S. R. (2020). Poaching the news producers: *The Athletic*'s effect on sports in hometown newspapers. *Journalism Studies*, 21(11), 1514–1530.

Conn, D. (2018). *The fall of the house of FIFA*. London: Yellow Jersey Press.

Dryden, N. (2020, August 21). Athletes should not be gagged in exchange for Olympic dream. *Play the Game*.https://playthegame.org/news/comments/2020/1008_athletes-should-not-be-gagged-in-exchange-for-olympic-dream/.

Gripsrud, J., Moe, H., Molander, A., & Murdock, G. (Eds.). (2010). *The idea of the public sphere: A reader*. Lanham, MD: Lexington Books.

Hardin, M., Dodd, J., & Lauffer, K. (2006). Passing it on: Reinforcement of male hegemony in sports journalism textbooks. *Mass Communication and Society*, 9(4), 429–446.

Heinrich, S. (2020, August 5) Fundamental defects of AFL's in-house media arm laid bare. *The Guardian Australia*.https://www.theguardian.com/sport/2020/aug/05/fundamental-defects-of-afls-in-house-media-arm-laid-bare.

Hill, D. (2010). *The fix: Soccer and organized crime*. Toronto: McClelland & Stewart.

Horky, T., & Nieland, J.-U. (Eds.). (2013). *International sports press survey 2011*. Hamburg: Horky Sport & Communication.

Hutchins, B., Li, B., & Rowe, D. (2019). Over-the-top sport: Live streaming services, changing coverage rights markets, and the growth of media sport portals. *Media, Culture and Society*, 41(7): 975–994.

Hutchins, B., & Rowe, D. (2012). *Sport beyond television: The internet, digital media and the rise of networked media sport*. New York: Routledge.

Jackson, D., Trevisan, F., Pullen, E., & Silk, M. (Eds.). (2020). Special issue on sport communication and social justice. *Communication & Sport*, 8(4–5).

Jennings, A. (2010). *The dirty game: Uncovering the scandal at FIFA*. London: Arrow.

Jennings, A. with Sambrook, C. (2000). *The great Olympic swindle: When the world wanted its games back*. London: Simon & Schuster.

Kalinic, D. (2020, August 28). Donald Trump says NBA has become a "political organization," adds jab about TV ratings drop. *Sporting News*. https://www.sportingnews.com/us/nba/news/donald-trump-nba-political-organization/3tdrno1xoowg15vi9kknyg4rj.

Kessel, A. (2020, March 18). *Telegraph* women's sport's approach is rewriting script on sports coverage, and making it relevant for 21st century audience. *Daily Telegraph*. Retrieved from https://www.telegraph.co.uk/womens-sport/2020/03/18/telegraph-womens-sports-appro ach-rewriting-script-sports-coverage/.

Ksiazek, T. B. (2018). Commenting on the news: Explaining the degree and quality of user comments on news websites. *Journalism Studies, 19*(5), 650–673.

Lambert, C. M. (2018). *Digital sports journalism*. London: Routledge.

The Last Dance. (2020). J. Hehir (Director). ESPN, U.S.

Lowes, M. D. (1999). *Inside the sports pages: Work routines, professional ideologies and the manufacture of sports news*. Toronto: University of Toronto Press.

Maguire, J. S., & Matthews, J. (2012). Are we all cultural intermediaries now? An introduction to cultural intermediaries in context. *European Journal of Cultural Studies, 15*(5), 551–562.

Mayhew, F. (2019, August 5). *The Athletic* UK: Full list of staff poached from national and regional press. *Press Gazette*. https://pressgazette.co.uk/the-athletic-uk-full-list-of-staff/.

Naha, S., & Hassan, D. (Eds.). (2019). *Ethical concerns in sport governance*. Abingdon, U.K.: Routledge.

Oakley, K., & O'Connor, J. (Eds.). (2015). *Routledge companion to the cultural industries*. London: Routledge.

Organista, N., & Mazur, Z. (2019). "You either stop reacting or you don't survive. There's no other way": The work experiences of Polish women sports journalists. *Feminist Media Studies, 20*(8), 1110–1127.

Patching, R. (2014). *The private lives of Australian cricket stars: A study of newspaper coverage 1945-2010* (Unpublished PhD thesis). Bond University. https://pure.bond.edu.au/ws/port alfiles/portal/36233235/Roger_Patching_Thesis_1_.pdf.

Plymouth Live. (2020). https://www.plymouthherald.co.uk/all-about/plymouth-argyle.

Pullen, E., Jackson, D., & Silk, M. (2020). Watching disability: UK audience perceptions of the Paralympics, equality, and social change. *European Journal of Communication, 35*(5), 469–483.

Rowe, D. (1992). Modes of sports writing. In P. Dahlgren & C. Sparks (Eds.), *Journalism and popular culture* (pp. 96–112). London: Sage.

Rowe, D. (2004). *Sport, culture and the media: The unruly trinity* (2nd ed.). Maidenhead, U.K.: Open University Press, McGraw-Hill Education.

Rowe, D. (2007). Sports journalism: Still the "toy department" of the news media? *Journalism: Theory, Practice & Criticism, 8*(4), 385–405.

Rowe, D. (2011). Obituary for the newspaper? Tracking the tabloid. *Journalism: Theory, Practice & Criticism, 12*(4), 449–466.

Rowe, D. (2017). Sports journalism and the FIFA scandal: Personalization, co-optation, investigation. *Communication and Sport, 5*(5), 515–533.

Ruddock, A., Hutchins, B., & Rowe, D. (2010). Contradictions in media sport culture: "MyFootballClub" and the reinscription of football supporter traditions through online media. *European Journal of Cultural Studies, 13*(3), 323–339.

Scherer, J., & Rowe, D. (Eds.). (2014). *Sport, public broadcasting, and cultural citizenship: Signal lost?* London: Routledge.

Schudson, M. (2008). *Why democracies need an unlovable press*. Cambridge, U.K.: Polity Press.

Serazio, M. (2019). *The power of sports: Media and spectacle in American culture*. New York: NYU Press.

Sparre, K. (2019, April 15). Journalists investigating sports corruption exposed to many kinds of risks. *Play the Game*. https://www.playthegame.org/news/news-articles/2019/0561_jour nalists-investigating-sports-corruption-exposed-to-many-kinds-of-risks/.

Steen, R. (2014). *Sports journalism: A multimedia primer*. London: Routledge.

Sugden, J., & Tomlinson, A. (2016). *Football, corruption and lies: Revisiting "Badfellas," the book FIFA tried to ban*. London: Routledge.

Tamir, I., Yarchi, M., & Galily, Y. (2017). Women, sport and the media: Key elements at play in the shaping of the practice of women in sports journalism in Israel. *Communications*, 42(4), 441–464.

Tate, G. (2016, September 18). Why Channel 4 has proved itself a brilliant Paralympics broad caster. *Daily Telegraph*. https://www.telegraph.co.uk/tv/2016/09/18/channel-4-has-proved-itself-a-brilliant-paralympics-broadcaster/.

Tiffen, R., Jones, P., Rowe, D., Aalberg, T., Coen, S., Curran, J., . . . Soroka, S. (2014). Sources in the news: A comparative study. *Journalism Studies*, 15(4), 374–391.

Walsh, D. (2013). *Seven deadly sins: My pursuit of Lance Armstrong*. London: Simon & Schuster.

Waterhouse-Watson, D. (2013). *Athletes, sexual assault, and trials by media: Narrative immu nity*. London: Routledge.

Waterson, J. (2019, July 3). England's World Cup defeat to USA watched by 11.7 million viewers. *The Guardian*. https://www.theguardian.com/media/2019/jul/03/england-world-cup-def eat-to-usa-watched-by-117m-tv-viewers.

Weedon, G., Wilson, B., Yoon, L., & Lawson, S. (2016). Where's all the "good" sports jour nalism? Sports media research, the sociology of sport, and the question of quality sports reporting. *International Review for the Sociology of Sport*, 53(6), 639–667.

Wenner, L. A. (Ed.). (1998). *MediaSport*. London: Routledge.

Zaru, D. (2020, June). An "eerie" parallel of two knees: George Floyd's death renews debate on Kaepernick protest. *ABC News*. https://abcnews.go.com/US/eerie-parallel-knees-george-floyds-death-renews-debate/story?id=70981946.

CHAPTER 54

··

SPORT, TELEVISION, AND STRUCTURATION

··

ANDREW C. BILLINGS AND NICHOLAS R. BUZZELLI

THE relationship between sport and television has always been a symbiotic one; television seeks mass viewership, and sports fandom enacts moments in which interest in the outcome far exceeds the capacity of any stadium. A half-century ago, Real (1975, p. 31) argued that the U.S.-based Super Bowl was a perfect television product for three reasons: (1) ritualized mass activity, (2) specific cultural value conveyance, and (3) the advancement of "mythic spectacle." Such tenets still hold true about the relationship between sport and television today and are certainly not exclusive to any one nation. In fact, as the rights fees for conveying sports mega-events to the world have expanded exponentially (Hutchins & Rowe, 2013), the power of the televised product has an even more expansive role in the constitution of what we still reference as MediaSport (Wenner, 1998). Even the mainstreaming of the internet, with its popular social and user-generated media correlates, cannot displace the role of television, as most sports fans view the large majority of their sports products via their television sets, even if flatter, larger, and at higher definition than ever before. As Jones (2022) explains, live sports consistently provide the largest audiences, including 95 of the top 100 U.S. television audiences of 2021.

However, the relationship between sport and television has, by necessity, changed in a variety of ways. Televised sport originally involved simply adding cameras and announcers to a sporting contest that would take place anyway. Today's television sports production, though, involves a host of decisions and strategies. Television influences much about how sports are framed and understood. This arguably has an even larger impact than the production choices that television producers make. Couldry and Hepp (2013) explain that the notion of mediatization centers on how nonmediated cultural processes take on the logics of media. Mediatization is most evident when we notice that a sporting event has been changed in ways to accommodate its television coverage. Still, it is important to remember that, in mediatization dynamics, media do not *cause* societal opinions to shift, nor is the converse causality, whereby cultural values *cause* media treatment to be what it is in explicit ways, entirely the case. Rather, both sides involved in this media and cultural values dance co-construct one another (Hepp, Hajarvard, & Lundby, 2015). Frandsen (2019, p. 3) argues that mediatization processes are essential to the understanding of the cultural analysis of sport, an important shift that demands an "analytical refocusing" to truly understand the complex web of impacts that media has wrought across contemporary life.

To advance this focus, we draw on the theoretical concept of structuration, which illuminates the degree to which "the structural properties of social systems are both the medium and the outcome of the practices that constitute those systems" (Giddens, 1979, p. 69). As Dixon (2015) contends, structuration proves useful in understanding how marginalized groups are suppressed in light of routines endemic within sport and its mediation. The focus in the dynamics at play in this chapter will highlight the classic "agent-structure" debate in Giddens's (1976) work, showing that "social practices ordered through time and space" (Giddens, 1984, p. 2) are largely functions of events and forces that are operant well before the spectating fan's consumption of sports media takes place (Ogden & Rose, 2005). More specifically, this chapter will focus on sport televisual structures (cf. Whitson, 1986) in terms of the issues they advance (or thwart), the theoretical approaches best suited for exploring these structures, and the debates currently percolating within the symbiotic relationship between sport and television, even as digital structures continue to alter partitions long in place between what it means to be a media producer versus a consumer.

ISSUES

Given that structuration functions as a framework in which agency interacts with structural constraints on decisions that are made (Giddens, 1984), social systems become central to understanding the roles that power, economics, and form play in the character of televised sport. In understanding how sports structures play key roles in how television renders presentation and narratives, three main forms become initial springboards for understanding how larger debates reveal themselves in our considerations later in the chapter: (1) contest formatting structures, (2) contest development structures, and (3) contextual cue structures. Each, in turn, will be considered next.

Contest Formatting Structures

There are a variety of ways that sporting events are parsed and sold via television to the masses through the use of contest formatting, including (1) within game structures, (2) across game structures, and (3) across era structures. Regarding the first classification, within-game structures each have a temporality endemic to how singular events unfold (Halone & Billings, 2010). As witnessed in how a go-ahead goal in soccer is inarguably deemed more crucial in the 88th minute than in the 18th, urgency and perceived immediacy are reflected in televisual coverage by building tension on the structural characteristics of the game itself. In golf, competition in major tournaments feature a variety of structural imperatives (Saturday is "moving day," and a conventional media saying is that the event does not really start until the back nine holes on Sunday) to blunt the ephemerality of the singular shot being observed and its relationship (or lack thereof) to predicting the tournament winner. Television coverage often works within and extends these kinds of established structures, allowing for prolonged breaks at halftime or inserting shorter commercial breaks when players change sides after odd-numbered games in tennis. Likewise, television places new structures on the progression of live events. Most renderings of basketball, for instance, feature two forms of timeouts: media timeouts and team-allocated timeouts. The former are more hardwired as they are preprogrammed, meaning the latter become more malleable, building around the media breaks; a team desiring a timeout may wait until the next media break instead of using one of their own.

A second type of contest formatting structure pertains to longitudinal competitions: schedules, series, playoff brackets, or other constructs that organizers have established to contextualize individual contests. Thus, a Game 7 in a best-of-seven series is given primacy, as is a Grand Slam competition in golf or tennis, or a World Cup event, whether in soccer, rugby, cricket, volleyball, or other sports. Results accrue in these contexts to show whether one qualifies for higher level competition, such as a playoff, or whether an individual or team advances in their quest toward a championship. Televisual structures play an intriguing role here, as elevating the importance of an event is integrally linked to fashioning sport contests into more economically desirable products, both for the sporting body and for the media. Certainly, a World Cup Final is of much higher value than a World Cup qualifier, and an Olympic medal final is exponentially more intriguing to the masses than an Olympic qualifier.

Still, much everyday sport does not take place amid the immediate winnowing of competition toward a championship. Televised sport is particularly useful to the business of filling hours in broadcasters' daily programming schedules. Thus, even though there are only so many sporting events that one would anoint as "pinnacle," television executives are often willing to pay a good deal to secure a larger number of games/contests that will fill their airtime. In an equation in which more games equate to more dollars, strategies are regularly fashioned to advance the reach of the sporting product and to maximize profit, sometimes pushing aside evident health risks. For example, in the United States, football is rightly debated as a public health crisis (Bell, Applequist, & Dotson-Pierson, 2019) in light of the dangers associated with concussions. Still, we see television rights holders working to persuade teams and players to add a 17th game to the regular season and an additional pair of playoff teams because doing so would result in a billion-dollar bonus (Maske, 2019). Similarly, the men's FIFA World Cup has expanded four different times, to the point that now 48 nations participate, with added games correlating with additional rights fees that can be generated. Television can also fashion pseudo-sporting events, such as player drafts or draws to see brackets/groups for major sporting events, into revenue-generating hours of "special" programming. Hence, these types of structural adjustments are used to advance both interest and profit generation by expanding the broadcast calendars for sports chosen to be featured. Sports fans' seemingly insatiable desire for sporting content is easily matched only by the leagues' and television networks' desire to profit from that insatiability. As such, sports marketers now seek to provide content not only during a sport's "season" but also in the off-season, as evidence suggests that 95% of sports fans now engage content that facilitates interacting with or commenting about their favorite sports, teams, or athletes throughout the year ("Say Goodbye to the Off-Season," 2020).

Finally, contest formatting structures include making connections among "eras" that may be used for generational and historical comparison of players, teams, and their exploits in different epochs of sport. For example, televised sports feature multigenerational appeals (see Cote, 1999), much as grandparents might share their own insights of sports history and figures of the past with their grandchildren. One of the reasons for the proliferation of television sports talk programs, featuring banter and the viewpoints of "experts," is because they are cheap to produce. These programs are important because they stimulate the great debates of the past, generating interest and rewarding one's longitudinal knowledge as a fan (Nylund, 2007). Whether constructing your personal all-time starting 11 for the World Cup or debating the relative greatness of Tiger Woods versus Jack Nicklaus, these cross-era comparisons become appealing as they underscore the permanence of sports structures that have existed, in many cases, for at least a century and sometimes much longer. Even though televised sport has a relatively short history, regular tropes in television narratives reinforce the longevity, stability, and everlasting importance of sporting achievement. This can disadvantage less-established sports. Thus, one can immerse oneself in debate about the relative skill sets of baseball's Babe Ruth and Mike Trout in a manner that most women's sports, for instance, cannot because of the systematic exclusion of female athletes in earlier times. Because of this, sports television features a structural bias, highlighting the established at the expense of the new.

Contest Development Structures

In contrast to formatting structures, development structures occur during the game and are designed to elevate the drama for the television viewing audience (e.g., *ABC's Wide World of Sports* opening that included "The *thrill* of victory and the *agony* of defeat"). For instance, one structure pertains to whether an outcome is seen as contestable as opposed to perfunctory. Television prides itself on its agenda-setting powers (McCombs & Shaw, 1972), even going so far as congratulating itself for the primacy of games being showcased (e.g., *Game of the Week* or a promoting a "can't miss" matchup). Priority is given to featuring elite, evenly matched sides that generate interest by virtue of unpredictable, but hopefully close, outcomes. In doing so, such television structures work to elevate developed sport institutions, where a stable and broad fan base has been built, over those sports, leagues, and games in emergent or even embryonic stages. Thus, the FIFA Men's World Cup now has a greater number of challengers than the FIFA Women's World Cup, largely because the men's variant has been granted vastly more resources (and television money) than the women's event. As a result, an upset of a top-ranked team by a lower-ranked team is more likely to occur in the men's game as opposed to the women's, which more easily aids network programmers in publicizing the value of close competition and serving to remind viewers of the depth of quality in the men's game. Similarly, men's international basketball was once a game where Americans held elite dominance (the 1992 "Dream Team" won its Summer Olympic games by an average of 43.8 points). Now that the rest of the world has developed competitive strengths in basketball, games are closer, more appealing, and draw substantially more global interest.

Hence, contest development structures advance elements of dramatic tension, long found to be required to create a good television product (Bryant, Comiskey, & Zillmann, 1977; Bryant, Rockwell, & Owens, 1994). In doing so, the ebb and flow of the game, defined by lead changes and unpredictability, becomes the defining trademark of quality sports network programming. Moreover, the establishment of a history of close competitions forms lasting rivalries, which have been established as key predictors of viewer enjoyment (Raney & Kinnally, 2009). When tuning in to a sports event, one knows that the goal is for a victor to emerge, but the framing of the rivalry is key to fans' decision to watch and likelihood of being engaged.

Contextual Cue Structures

Finally, contextual cue structures help the uninitiated invest in a televised sporting event in which they would initially have had little rooting interest, such as a fan opting to root for a player because a televised cue was offered showing that they shared a hometown or po-litical interest. As such, contextual cue structures function as mechanisms for interpreting how a televised sports product is evaluated by using a series of heuristics to determine whether an unfolding narrative is noteworthy or remarkable in some manner. A common heuristic is the favorite-versus-underdog dichotomy. For instance, an underdog U.S. team defeat of a powerhouse Brazil team in men's soccer would be noteworthy, as would Brazil defeating the United States in men's basketball; the inverse in both cases would be seen as perfunctory. Likewise, narratives unfold in other dichotomies: Serena Williams battling Naomi Osaka in a tennis final would be seen as "stalwart versus the up-and-comer" be-cause of the age and track record differences between the two champions. FC Barcelona competing against FC Porto would feature a dichotomy of their financial resources, with the former holding a considerable advantage. Until recently, the two NBA teams in Los Angeles—the Lakers and the Clippers—featured a dichotomy of winning versus losing cultures. Television utilizes such contrasts because it provides useful heuristics through which the casual or moderate fan can develop more passionate interests. Televisual narrative tendencies build on the prospect (although not the likelihood) of seeing the "impossible" become possible. Depending on their identities and dispositions, fans can develop affinities by choosing to support teams because of their historical dominance, be-cause they are poorly sourced "underdogs," because they feature celebritized or skillful star players, or for many other reasons.

Regardless of the dichotomy at play (noting that many times simultaneous heuristics are functioning within the same contest), these contextual cues become more formalized over time, with television tending to privilege the established structures over newer ones unless and until a deviation appears to have a chance of occurring. The reason here is largely a self-evident dynamic: the symbiotic relationship between sport and television is one that aims to preserve success and reduce risk in seeking pathways to strong ratings, thereby avoiding upsetting the "apple cart" of structures undergirding the profitable dynamic between sport and television that has been in place for decades.

APPROACHES

Within the television space, the overwhelming majority of what people consume involves not just a nonfiction/documentary rendering of sport but a live athletic contest that is presumed to be less scripted because of its immediacy. Because of this, the vast majority of research inquiry about sports television production and narratives has been centered on questions of selection, including who/what gets shown (or not), what stories are advanced (or not), and what descriptions/themes are applied to athletes (or not). These types of questions are often advanced through media theories that focus on media exposure, salience, and description.

Theoretical Approaches to Sport on Television

Social Identity and Self-Categorization Approaches

Because of the inherent "us versus them" nature of athletic competition, sports television is often the facilitator of these tensions, as fans witness sports television through the "oscillating poles of love and hate" (Bruce, 2017, p. 100). As sport fanship pertains to both love of a favored team/player and disdain for the opposing team/player, sports television—even with national announcers desiring fanship agnosticism in their portrayal of these tensions—nevertheless amplifies the perceiving groupings, as sport ultimately subdivides into "winners, losers, and the ones who watch" (Bachman, 2018, p. 7).

Social identity theory (Tajfel & Turner, 1986) is built around the psychology of such ingroups and outgroups, highlighting how one's affiliation alters one's perception, either with upward contacts (positive associations that heighten self-esteem) or downward comparisons (disassociations with groups in which people see little of themselves represented; Taylor & Lobel, 1989). Building upon the notion of who one is/wants to be versus who one is not/does not desire to be is the correlative theory of self-categorization (Turner, Hogg, Oakes, Reicher, & Wetherell, 1987). Largely a theory that can be unpacked as "social identity of the group," self-categorization shows that groups can function with the same affiliations and disaffiliations that individuals do.

Televised sport, therefore, is the mechanism for these connections and fissures to be cemented. As Voci (2006, p. 86) finds in a study of a soccer team:

> The more the in-group was perceived as homogeneous and, at the same time, distinct from the out-group, the more the self was depersonalized . . . the more the self was depersonalized— that is, the more the self was perceived as different from the out-group and similar to other in-group members—the stronger were group phenomena.

While most studies in this genre focus on affiliations that occur within live sporting competitions (e.g., Kraszewski, 2008), Keaton and Gearhart (2014) found that anger (elevated above happiness or sadness) was linked to self-categorization tendencies. Such affiliations are often interwoven within other ingroup affiliations such as national identity (Devlin, Billings, & Brown, 2017) and now are manifest in social media comments of fans who desire second-screen interaction to find affiliation with other like-minded kindred spirits (Fan, Billings, Zhu, & Yu, 2020). Wann (2006, p. 332) characterizes such interests as fan identification, articulated as "the extent to which a fan feels a psychological connection to a team and the team's performances." These permeate virtually all forms of how sports television is received, partly because the sport-based in-group affiliation is one of the most intractable of all connections; the team one prefers as a child is quite often the one preferred later in life (Wann & Grieve, 2005).

Agenda-Setting Approaches

Important to understanding the effects of exposure to media more broadly, agenda-setting theory (McCombs & Shaw, 1972) has become an important lens for understanding sports television programming. Built on Cohen's (1963, p. 13) claim that media "may not be successful much of the time in telling people what to think, but it is stunningly successful in telling its (audience) what to think about", agenda-setting begat further constructs, including second-level agenda-setting (including elements of attribute salience; McCombs, Llamas, Lopez-Escobar, & Rey, 1997) and third-level agenda-setting (including the ability of media to influence feelings about a network of topics rather than a singular issue; McCombs, Shaw, & Weaver, 2014) and the relationship of media choices on agenda-building (including media consumers and public policymakers as media values translate to public agendas; Rogers & Dearing, 1988). At the core of all of these related agenda-setting concerns is the notion of thought transfer. If, for example, network sports news programs cover female athletes and contests less than 5% of the time (as both Cooky, Messner, & Musto [2015] and Billings & Young [2015] have found to be the case), the audience receives much reinforcement to see men's sports as more important and, by the same token, value women's sports less. Such concerns have even been applied to analyzing the words attached to the athletes themselves. If, for example, an athlete is continually complimented for their speed and reprimanded for a perceived lack of commitment, such content can help set an agenda for the audience that, generally, both speed and commitment are essential factors to athletic success—and that, in the particular, the athlete only possesses the former of these components and falls short of the conventional agenda.

Fewer studies have employed agenda-setting within sports television than some of the other theories listed here, at least in part because of the holistic nature of the live sports broadcast. If, for instance, a soccer match lasts 90 minutes of active time, a television broadcast is likely to show every second of that time. Thus, such transmissions tend to be analyzed more within framing mechanisms than with agenda-setting. Still, sports television is analyzed when producer choices must be made to determine which athletic events are shown and which will not air. This is most prominent within the Olympics, since there is enough athletic competition within those 17 days to show 24 hours per day for roughly nine months (Billings, Angelini, & MacArthur, 2017). This results in the television network's making decisions about what to highlight, what to divert to internet or less popular channels, and what to ignore entirely (Arth, Hou, Rush, & Angelini, 2019). Still, studies have focused on network decisions about which live sports to highlight to the widest markets (Fortunato, 2008), and scholars have often used agenda-setting as the core element in which framing mechanisms, the approach next discussed, will unfurl (Angelini & Billings, 2010).

Framing Approaches

Conjoined in the conception of agenda-setting is the also popular theoretical mechanism of framing, advanced by Goffman (1974) and then formalized into popularity by Gitlin (1980). Based on the postulate that "media frames are persistent patterns of cognition, interpretation, and presentation, of selection, emphasis, and exclusion," framing is applied to media to understand the degree to which "symbol-handlers routinely [organize] discourse, whether verbal or visual" (p. 7). Within sports, this can involve the prioritization of one theme over another, such as highlighting the parentage of one athlete while lamenting the lack of experience in another. As Wenner (2006, p. 49) underscored, "the games we play and the public stories we weave about them tell stories about social priorities, actions, and distractions". Framing thus becomes the mechanism not only for ascribing power to what is said and/or shown but also for what is muted, unselected, or unmentioned (Entman, 1993). As Gamson (1989, p. 158) has noted, "the informational content of news reports is less important than the interpretive commentary that surrounds it." Framing in sports television becomes particularly pertinent in cases where the viewing audience is witnessing a sport, athlete, or event with which they are unfamiliar; then the framing is not just influential but seminal as the first glimpse one might have of an athlete, team, or nation (Scheufele, 1999).

From the onset of key works such as Real's (1975), the case is made that these frames supersede the game (Wenner, 1994). Framing has more recently been interrogated to explore how core issues of identity unfold within televised sport, including portrayals of race (Lewis, Bell, Billings, & Brown, 2020; van Lienden & van Sterkenburg, 2022) and gender (Cummins, Ortiz, & Rankine, 2019; Xu, Billings, & Fan, 2018). Televised sport framing also shapes perceptions about often silenced groups, such as those participating in adapted sports (Solves, Pappous, Rius, & Kohe, 2019) or victims of domestic violence (Spencer & Limperos, 2020). In sum, frames function as heuristics that sports fans, sometimes overtly but more often subconsciously, utilize to navigate not only the sports world but society as a whole.

Uses and Gratifications Approaches

Adopting a different tack, uses and gratifications (Katz, Blumler, & Gurevitch, 1973) is still debated as to whether it is best labeled as a theory or an approach (because of its general lack of falsifiability). Nevertheless, scholars who adopt uses and gratifications approaches tend to focus on the viewer/consumer as an active participant in the selection and consumption of content (O'Donohoe, 1994), a noteworthy departure from the previous models of thinking that assumed a television viewer was a passive recipient of content. Within sports, this often pertains to the plethora of choices provided in the televised realm alone as, in the 1960s and 1970s, it was often the case that there was, at most, one form of sports programming on at all times, making the uses and gratification choice a simple one: sports versus non-sports. Over time, uses and gratification scholars have uncovered the byzantine cognitive paths that lead viewers to prioritize one type of programming over another. Earlier scholarship in this area (Gantz & Wenner, 1991, 1995) focused merely on the selection of a certain type of media that can bolster enjoyment, excitement, socialization, or any number of delineated aims. More recent studies illustrate how these needs can be layered and even combined with other media devices. Television is still considered the optimal primary/consumption screen (Billings, Brown-Devlin, Brown, & Devlin, 2019), even as a plethora of social media options have become available to satisfy gratifications that television was not built to readily provide, such as interacting with other fans, attaining additional information about sporting contests, or vetting sports news and information (Spinda & Puckette, 2018).

Cultivation Theory and Critical Approaches

Hall (2000, p. 51) argues that it is useful to think of media processes via "linked but distinctive moments—production, circulation, distribution/consumption, reproduction." Sports television functions as a prime example of what Hall then articulates as encoding and decoding, as media cannot be viewed as a "raw" rendering but, rather, must "become a 'story' before it can become a *communicative event*" (p. 52).

Thus, one final set of theoretical approaches influencing the study of sport and television involves cultivation theory (Gerbner, Gross, Morgan, & Signorielli, 1986) as well as critical studies. Within the former theoretical lens, cultivation theorists posit that media (particularly heavy consumption of media of a given genre/context) leads to beliefs that media depictions function in documentary form, becoming the reality one expects when venturing away from media. Cultivation theorists argue for a thought-shaping function of television that is exceedingly effective at shaping the heuristics one uses to determine stances on social issues (Gerbner, Gross, Morgan, Signorielli, & Shanahan, 2002). Thus, taking into account that agenda-setting serves to focus audience priorities, cultivation perspectives would be that the sports world becomes the primary habitat for heavy sports viewers, watching sports television far more frequently than witnessing athletic competition in person. While Potter (1991) cautions against the tendency to infer cause/effect relationships, it does appear that when one is an avid sports viewer, one in many ways becomes the embodiment of the cultivated heavy viewer, when "people simply internalize content from a medium with which they spend so much time" (Shanahan & Morgan, 1999, p. 173).

In essential ways, critical approaches recognize and build on this dynamic, often focusing on how discourses are shaped by sports television products. Grano and Zagacki (2011), for example, show how media coverage of a football game was used to assuage guilt about how America responded to New Orleans during Hurricane Katrina. Butterworth (2005) showed how televised baseball served to suppress dissent about the war on terror. Wenner (2007) highlights how communicative dirt theory proves useful in studying the transfer of meaning and context from sphere to sphere. Whereas most of the earlier considered approaches tend to adopt empirical methodologies to extract parsimonious answers to key questions about sports television, most critical approaches seek to interrogate more complex meanings within these television narratives, often revealing layers in televisual discourse that invoke political and cultural practices within a mediated sports broadcast.

Methodological Approaches to Studying Sport on Television

It is fair to say that a robust number of methodologies have been used to extract understandings of sports television. It is also fair to argue that content analyses outnumber the rest of these methodologies collectively. Focus on content analysis is partly natural; Wenner (2015) contends it is often a function of researchers doing the "easy things first." Nevertheless, content analyses also seem to thrive for other reasons, partly their sheer mass (exponentially growing in sports offerings in the cable and satellite television expansion) and partly because of their utility for longitudinal results. For example, troubling depictions of Black quarterbacks in American football (Rada, 1996) were found to have lessened a decade later (Byrd & Utsler, 2007). Similarly, changes in the amount of clock-time devoted to women athletes have been revealed via longitudinal content analyses, revealing an up-swing in the Olympics (Billings et al., 2017) and downturns in local and national sports news programs (Cooky et al., 2015).

Still, other methodologies have revealed considerable understandings of how sports telecasts are rendered and ultimately perceived. Within critical work, Oates (2007) illuminated the eroticism endemic in NFL draft coverage, while Hodler and Lucas-Carr (2015) revealed how women athlete narratives often differ from the narratives advanced about their men counterparts. Political economy has proved a useful heuristic within many of these studies; to wit, Phillips and Hutchins (2003) assessed the political-economic dynamics of Rugby League to show how power structures are reproduced in media.

Meanwhile, most empirical investigations of sports television that do not use content analysis tend to employ either experimental or survey methodologies. Experimental research has shown how sports television can amplify elements such as suspense (Bryant et al., 1994) or violence (Raney & Kinnally, 2009) to bolster enjoyment. Meanwhile, survey methodologies show how unique the sports television product is in terms of motivations and pre- and post-viewing rituals (Gantz, Wang, Bryant, & Potter, 2006), while also highlighting the degree to which watching international sports on television fosters amplified feelings for one's own country (Billings, Brown, & Brown-Devlin, 2015). Use of advanced statistical models such as structural equation modeling aids in identifying relationships in such survey data.

Nevertheless, qualitative work has functioned to reveal schisms in how television broadcasts are regarded by people of differing identities. For example, Whiteside and Hardin (2011) have used focus group techniques to uncover the social expectations and gender roles that make viewing sports a more difficult objective to obtain for women than for men; McCarthy, Jones, and Potrac (2003) used these same focus group approaches to show how Black groups were more likely than white groups to identify racial stereotyping.

DEBATES

Of course, even when armed with a robust set of theories and methodologies to explore sports television, many debates remain unresolved. Such schisms often revolve around notions of economic viability versus utopian equity, but also typically pit many structures of hegemonic entrenchment (most notably the elevation of white, male, monied interests) against more progressive stances for inclusion. These debates affect many things: production conventions, narrative focus and themes, the values and behaviors that are celebrated or frowned upon, and the basic ways that audience members approach sport on television. Such impacts are examined below, as we consider the ways in which the forces of structuration in televised sport interplay to affect social meanings and impact.

Which Sports Get Prioritized

The marriage of the conventions of television sports production with sports fans' desires defines a mutually beneficial relationship that continues to persist a half-century after Real's recognition of television and sports' continued symbiosis (cf. Wenner & Billings, 2017). As the relationship between sport and television has flourished and grown in the marketplace, the structures endemic within the relationship have remained relatively constant.

Nowhere is this more the case than in considering issues of gender equity. Coverage of women's sports (other than the biennial Olympics and quadrennial World Cup) on television pales in comparison to the attention given to men's sports. When there is live coverage of women's sporting contests, it is often relegated to less prominent outlets or scheduling and features less polished production values without marquee-level announcers (Musto, Cooky, & Messner, 2017). Further, women's sports continue to be almost wholly neglected in sports news/synopsis programs (Cooky et al., 2015). Crosset (1995) is among many who point to women's historical and continuing outsider status within sport to explain why women do not receive the media attention and access that would be equitable. In considering the paucity and quality of the coverage of women's sports on television, path dependency theory (see Markovits & Hellerman, 2001) contends that when channels for mass consumption were much more limited than they are today, societies tacitly decided who or what was worthy of attention. Such a framework provides a particularly useful lens to begin to understand the hard-wired structures that have systematically disenfranchised women's sports. As Markovits and Hellerman contend:

> Whichever sport entered a country's sport space first and managed to do so in the key period between 1870 and 1930, the crucial decades of industrial proliferation and establishment of modern mass societies, continues to possess a major advantage to this day. Put differently, the contingent trajectory, of sport culture—what social scientists would call its "path depend-ence"—is very high. (p. 15)

Within the structure that Markovits and Hellerman advance, women's sports are not necessarily excluded from television structures as much as men's sports are retained as valuable relics of the television sports zeitgeist. Novak and Billings (2012) show how path dependency has made soccer a difficult sell to mainstream American audiences and helps explain why the coverage of women in the mediated sports space between 1870 and 1930 was close to nil. As such, Giddens's (1984) arguments and evidence about how the powers of structure function as pseudo-state laws help explain an entrenched male hierarchy in which women's golf must occupy only the space left after men's golf is preserved, or where the Women's National Basketball Association games are scheduled in the "off-season," months that men's National Basketball Association does not value or occupy. Such inherent disadvantages make any sport seeking new television space a challenging prospect as one must make the case that the lesser known product (often lacking the contest formatting structures, contest development structures, and contextual cue structures that the established sports possess) is a demonstrably better gambit to propose to a television executive struggling to achieve mass audiences in a time of increasingly fragmented niche media audiences (see Benoit & Billings, 2020).

The interconnected structures that function as heuristics for televised production and reproduction (see Giddens, 1979) also illuminate how issues of race and ethnicity unfold in the narrative spaces for sport on television. Ogden and Rose (2005), for instance, make a compelling case for televised structural barriers leading to decreased participation of African American fans in baseball, citing examples of structuring factors such as advertising that tends to promote African American basketball players over baseball players and the tendencies for crowd shots in Major League Baseball game broadcasts to focus on African American fans only 2% of the time. Such tendencies reinforce complex messages about the African American athlete's "place" in sport. While touting that Black athletes can find a home in sports, basketball is shown to be a "natural" home, while a home in baseball is established as less appropriate in the cultural imagination.

Structuration in sports also comes about through the heuristics of "stacking," which Loy and McElvogue (1970) initially applied to race-dictated position assignments in sport. Research confirms that racial and ethnic groups receive messages that a certain sport or even position within that sport is more appropriate than others, such as a Black athlete being slated into a position where physicality is prioritized over leadership (Eitzen & Furst, 1989). Similarly, an athlete of Hispanic origin might select soccer over American football due to these structured cues, or might opt for a middle infield position in baseball over a corner infield position, as they see more people that look like them in those positions. Billings et al. (2017) show how an inherently multiracial product, like the Summer Olympics, can nevertheless be configured with siloed competitions. For example, we have often seen Caucasian and Asian competitors winning medals for swimming, where Black athletes are little seen, or, conversely, Black athletes winning more medals for sprinting or basketball than Caucasian or Asian athletes. Stacking, and the reproduction of it in television coverage of sport, also can cue women and nonbinary athletes that sport may not provide a safe place for them (Cooky & Messner, 2018; Dworkin, Swarr, & Cooky, 2013). Similarly, nations may decide to prioritize competing in those Olympic events in which prior broadcasts have celebrated their athletes succeeding, such as Chinese success in table tennis or Norwegian success in biathlon. Such pigeonholing is reinforced by television coverage, regaling a nation's "proud history" of accomplishment in a particular sport while, at the same time, excluding success narratives for other events.

How Sports Are Played and Rendered

The tensions between who holds power and how the public interest is served can influence the manner in which athletes perform their sports. Television has a finite bandwidth (of programming minutes minus the commercial breaks integral to private licensees' profit generation and increasingly supporting nationalized systems), and its framing tendencies (Goffman, 1974) as revealed in selection, emphasis, and exclusion (Gitlin, 1980) can overtly and covertly alter reception and interpretation. For instance, if a basketball game is synopsized in a matter of seconds on a news program, viewers quickly conclude that dramatic slam dunks are preferred over fundamentally sound layups. Similarly, seeing an athlete celebrating profusely and hearing an announcer elongating a call to great dramatic effect can bolster the chances that a soccer goal is replayed, archived, and savored. Metrics in baseball affirm that "a walk is as good as a hit," but any baseball player or fan can attest to television's priorities in celebrating the latter far more than the former, and both pale against the "big blast" of a home run, even a meaningless one in a losing effort.

Even if fans are unfamiliar with the concept of mediatization, most are cognizant of the role television plays in shaping the broadcasts they watch. For instance, most fans on the U.S. East Coast recognize that the teams involved did not decide 9 p.m. Eastern Time was the optimal start time for a Major League Baseball World Series game, but that television dictated that decision and people must adjust because of the financial realities of television seeking a Pacific Coast audience barely arriving home from work. Similarly, many fans struggle with the expanded length of games but may separate out the reasons for delays that occur because of strategy (endless pitching changes in baseball, constant coach-called timeouts at the end of a basketball game) and those delays that occur because of television (such as returning from a commercial break to an American football game for one play and then having a television timeout dictate that another break commence). In sum, sports fans largely consider the demands made by structuring television (even when it annoys them) to be part and parcel of what it means to follow their favored teams or sports. Indeed, fans have become acculturated to understanding that such elements are necessarily "baked into the cake" that constitutes modern sport television.

Nevertheless, there are other elements of how television sporting events get rendered that a majority of fans appear to be less aware of. For instance, in the U.S. Summer Olympic telecast, over 95% of the coverage focuses on just five events: swimming, gymnastics, track and field, diving, and beach volleyball (Billings et al., 2017). However, when U.S. viewers were surveyed as to the percentage of Olympic medals won by the American team, average responses more closely matched the mediatized version of NBC's telecast (in which Americans won nearly 30% of all the medals in these five sports) than the reality of the Olympics holistically (in which Americans more typically have won 11% to 13% of the medals; Billings, 2008). In a related example from NBC's Olympic coverage, a famous moment of the 1996 Summer Olympics—a one-legged vault landed for a perfect 10 by injured American gymnast Kerri Strug—was shown *before* the American team secured the gold medal, although her vault actually occurred *after* the Americans were mathematically assured of the medal (Billings, 2008). This production strategy most certainly cast Strug's performance as an even more heightened dramatic moment, but could be seen as manipulative to Olympic fans who may have found out the "altered reality" of the production chronology after the fact.

In all, the fact that television shapes when, how, and how much sports are shown likely does not surprise the average sports fan. However, the extent to which television dictates the time, pace of play, and manner in which sporting contests unfold is likely little recognized, as the inner forces of the political economy of sport is seldom revealed by broadcasters and rarely considered beyond the interrogations of academic inquiry (Szymanski, 2010).

What Gets *Valued*

The two previous sections identify how sports television influences what is prioritized and played, so it is likely no surprise that each of these functions as an antecedent to what is valued within the sports sphere. There are even instances in which the relationship between television and sport becomes so intermingled that it is difficult to determine where sport ends and television begins. For instance, many of the key sports awards an athlete or team can receive are largely dictated by media considerations and requirements. These include many honors of historic significance, such as Hall of Fame inductions and Player of the Year trophies.

In televisual renderings, these become more an exercise in stimulating collective memory through the replay of video highlights than a fresh assessment of athletic skill and performance (Parsons & Stern, 2012). Indeed, some awards are not only decided by media representatives (Sherman, 2017) but have become television products in their own right. For instance, the hour-long media production that culminates in announcing the winner of U.S. college football's Heisman Trophy is an example of a media-created event that was not televised at all until the 1980s; it is also a program reliant on common frames that advance the (re)production of racial tendencies (cf. Cranmer, Bowman, Chory, & Weber, 2014). At the same time, it is some of these same media inventions that can help the sports world move beyond its traditional parameters of event coverage and expand both their comfort zones and product inventory. For example, ESPN's ESPY Awards are staged at least in part to help the network program a month (July) that historically is lean in offerings other than baseball games ("ESPY Awards Switched to July," 2001). Nevertheless, these awards frequently have been used to challenge societal norms, including movements against racial inequalities in the justice system (Frederick, Pegoraro, & Sanderson, 2019) and for the acceptance of difference, including trans athletes, in sport (Brady, 2016).

How Televised Sports Are *Received*

Whannel (2002, p. 3) contends that "[t]he power of the media has always been a source of concern, yet the inherent reflex to blame media for a broad array of ills "betrays an unwillingness to face up to the multi-factorial complexity of cause and effect in the social world." Thus, as Whannel articulates, the study of audience orientations to televised sport and its effects has been an integral part of understanding sports television (see also Gantz, 1981). Much attention has been given to the motivations that fans have for viewing and behaviors that audience members engage in while they view sports. Raney (2006) illustrates the complexity of such motivations in articulating three primary drivers of sports media consumption: emotional (with subcategories of entertainment, eustress, self-esteem, and escape), cognitive (with subcategories of learning and aesthetic), and behavioral (with subcategories of release, companionship, group affiliation, family and economics).

Because of the expansive nature of what constitutes sport on television, much of the audience experience reinforces observations in John Donne's poem "No Man Is an Island": that no form of sports content is an island, and that the audience receives only part of what could be rendered—a framed, idyllic version of the comprehensive sport product, suitable for mass enjoyment. Indeed, as Whannel (1992, p. 104) contends, "the ways in which television structures, handles, its 'raw' materials demonstrates the privileged place occupied by presentation and the space constructed in the text for the setting up and framing of sport."

Hence, because of this framing, certain elements of sports broadcasts that are privileged shape the understandings that are made by audiences. This is true whether that content framing infers that men watch sports differently than women (Gantz & Wenner, 1991, 1995) or that the televisual desires to manufacture and heighten drama bolsters enjoyment (Bryant et al., 1994). Enjoyment is combined with other elements of motivation such as arousal and eustress (see Raney, 2006) to form a television product designed to be too tantalizing to turn off. Much sport on television is consequently received much as media producers intended, and thus coverage is spiked with suspense (Peterson & Raney, 2008) and aggression in ways that reinforce audiences' valuing such elements as part and parcel of the sports entertainment package (Raney & Depalma, 2006). Indeed, much research has supported the notion that no other televised media product is valued as much as live sports (Gantz et al., 2006). The value placed on television sport has fueled an insatiability for the most avid fans. When heightened drama and suspense are combined with the social pleasures that come from viewing sports with others, this has helped to make the televised sport rendering particularly valued, even in a digitized society that otherwise values convenience over firsthand live media consumption (Gantz et al., 2006).

Indeed, live sports remain unusual in that viewing is time-shifted just 3% of the time (Crupi, 2019) which, depending on the metric employed, is either one-10th or one-20th of the amount of time-shifting that occurs when viewing fictional narrative programming on television.

Nearly three decades ago, Whannel (1992, p. 6) argued that "the production of entertainment is both a cultural-ideological and an economic practice." Those factors have always benefited sports, resulting in billion-dollar revenues for single-nation sports leagues and elevating athletes to uber-celebrity status. There is currently little use in denying that sports have become the last consistent form of television content that viewers are willing to prioritize in real time, even when that means watching commercials. Sports viewers do so for a variety of reasons, such as seeking to bear witness to something in real time (Benoit & Billings, 2020) and increasingly to interact socially (both face-to-face and through social media) with others who have similarly prioritized viewing the live sports event (Kim, Song, & Lee, 2018).

Given these factors, it seems fair to query whether television needs dictate sporting values more than reflecting them to the masses. Sports television seemingly requires the formatting, development, and cue structures articulated in the Issues portion of this chapter. Because of these presumed needs to advance an appealing (and economically viable) product, there is a "tail wagging the dog" phenomenon at play, where sports television becomes the broader, more powerful entity over sport writ large. Regardless of where one resides on such an equation, one is admitting the obvious: sports television remains a powerful, prioritized business within world cultures.

CONCLUSION

In 2007, *Wired* declared, "The TV is dead. Long live the TV" (Borland & Hansen, 2007, para. 1). Despite myriad media influences and platforms that could potentially or collectively challenge the preeminence of sport television, this chapter highlights the degree to which such attempts could prove futile. Devices may change and funding mechanisms may shift, but the desire for millions to gather and witness a live sporting contest on the big screen appears as strong as ever, echoing Real's (1975) claim of a perfect marriage between the two.

This chapter has outlined the reasons for sports television's ascension and then entrenchment as the dominant vehicle within which sports fans advance their motivations and fuel their desires. The contest formatting structures, contest development structures, and contextual cue structures are all mechanisms that television facilitates and profits from utilizing. The approaches used to study these dynamics lean to media content's theoretical frameworks (framing, agenda-setting) and methodologies (content analyses). Yet such approaches are not remotely exclusive, and there has been a rise of increasingly robust and revealing ways to study the effects of television sports production and content toward understanding the complex interrelationships at play. Finally, the debates considered here highlight the power embedded within the sports-television partnership, often to the detriment of women's sports and other challengers to the established order. It is difficult to understate both the depth and breadth of sport television, and the tentacles it has long wielded are likely to be the subject of many future scholarly examinations because of the concepts infused within the structuration of sports television: dominance and power.

References

Angelini, J. R., & Billings, A. C. (2010). An agenda that sets the frames: Gender, language, and NBC's Americanized Olympic telecast. *Journal of Language and Social Psychology, 29*(3), 63–385.

Arth, Z. W., Hou, J., Rush, S. W., & Angelini, J. R. (2019). (Broad)casting a wider net: Clocking men and women in the primetime and non-primetime coverage of the 2018 Winter Olympics. *Communication & Sport, 7*(5), 565–587.

Bachman, F. (2018). *Us against you.* New York: Atria Books.

Bell, T. R., Applequist, J., & Dotson-Pierson, C. (2019). *CTE, media, and the NFL: Framing a public health crisis as a football epidemic.* Lanham, MD: Lexington.

Benoit, W. L., & Billings, A. C. (2020). *The rise and fall of mass communication.* New York: Peter Lang.

Billings, A. C. (2008). *Olympic media: Inside the biggest show on television.* London: Routledge.

Billings, A. C., Angelini, J. R., & MacArthur, P. J. (2017). *Olympic television: Broadcasting the biggest show on Earth.* London: Routledge.

Billings, A. C., Brown, K. A., & Brown-Devlin, N. B. (2015). Sports draped in the American flag: Impact of the 2014 Winter Olympic telecast on nationalized attitudes. *Mass Communication & Society, 18*(4), 377–398.

Billings, A. C., Brown-Devlin, N., Brown, K. A., & Devlin, M. B. (2019). When 18 days of coverage is not enough: A six-nation composite of motivations for mobile media use in the 2018 Winter Olympic Games. *Mass Communication & Society, 22*(4), 535–557.

Billings, A. C., & Young, B. D. (2015). Comparing flagship news programs: Women's sport coverage in ESPN's *SportsCenter* and FOX Sports 1's *FOX Sports Live. ElectronicNews, 9*(1), 3–16.

Borland, J., & Hansen, E. (2007, April 6). The TV is dead. Long live the TV. *Wired.* https://www.wired.com/2007/04/tvhistory-0406/.

Brady, A. (2016). Keeping away from the Kardashians: Celebrity worth and the re-masculinising of Caitlyn Jenner. *Celebrity Studies, 7*(1), 115–118.

Bruce, T. (2017). The Rugby World Cup experience: Interrogating the oscillating poles of love and hate. In L. A. Wenner and A. C. Billings (Eds.), *Sport, media, and mega-events* (pp. 100–114). London: Routledge.

Bryant, J., Comisky, P., & Zillmann, D. (1977). Drama in sports commentary. *Journal of Communication, 27,* 140–149.

Bryant, J., Rockwell, S. C., & Owens, J. W. (1994). "Buzzer beaters" and "barn burners": The effects of enjoyment of watching the game go "down to the wire." *Journal of Sport & Social Issues, 18*(4), 326–339.

Butterworth, M. L. (2005). Ritual in the "church of baseball": Suppressing the discourse of democracy after 9/11. *Communication & Critical/Cultural Studies, 2*(2), 107–129.

Byrd, J., & Utsler, M. (2007). Is stereotypical coverage of African-American athletes as "dead as disco"? An analysis of NFL quarterbacks in the pages of *Sports Illustrated*. *Journal of Sports Media, 2*(1), 1–28.

Cohen, B. C. (1963). *The press and foreign policy*. Princeton, NJ: Princeton University Press.

Cooky, C., & Messner, M. A. (2018). *No slam dunk: Gender, sport, and the unevenness of social change*. New Brunswick, NJ: Rutgers University Press.

Cooky, C., Messner, M. A., & Musto, M. (2015). "It's dude time!" A quarter century of excluding women's sports in televised news and highlight shows. *Communication & Sport, 3*(3), 261–287.

Cote, J. (1999). The influence of family in sports: A review. *International Journal of Sport Psychology, 21*, 328–354.

Couldry, N., & Hepp, A. (2013). Conceptualizing mediatization: Contexts, traditions, arguments. *Communication Theory, 23*(2), 191–202.

Cranmer, G. A., Bowman, N. D., Chory, R. M., & Weber, K. D. (2014). Race as an antecedent condition in the framing of Heisman finalists. *Howard Journal of Communications, 25*(2), 171–191.

Crosset, T. W. (1995). *Outsiders in the clubhouse: The world of women's professional golf*. Albany: State University of New York Press.

Crupi, A. (2019, November 14). As the pay TV bundle unravels, advertisers should stick to sports. *Advertising Age*. https://adage.com/article/media/pay-tv-bundle-unravels-advertisers-should-stick-sports/2214956.

Cummins, R. G., Ortiz, M., & Rankine, A. (2019). "Elevator eyes" in sports broadcasting: Visual objectification of male and female sports reporters. *Communication & Sport, 7*(6), 789–810.

Devlin, M. B., Billings, A. C., & Brown, K. A. (2017). Interwoven statesmanship and sports fandom: World Cup consumption antecedents through joint lenses of nationalism and fanship. *Communication & Sport, 5*(2), 186–204.

Dixon, K. (2015). A woman's place recurring: Structuration, football fandom and sub-cultural subservience. *Sport in Society, 18*(6), 636–651.

Dworkin, S. L., Swarr, A. L., & Cooky, C. (2013). (In)justice in sport: The treatment of South African track star Caster Semenya. *Feminist Studies, 39*(1), 40–69.

Eitzen, D. S., & Furst, D. (1989). Racial bias in women's collegiate basketball. *Journal of Sport & Social Issues, 13*, 46–51.

Entman, R. M. (1993). Framing: Toward clarification of a fractured paradigm. *Journal of Communication, 43*(4), 51–58.

ESPY awards switched to July. (2001, October 18). *Kitsap Sun*. https://products.kitsapsun.com/archive/2001/10-18/0018_espn__espy_awards_switched_to_jul.html.

Fan, M., Billings, A. C., Zhu, X., & Yu, P. (2020). Twitter-based BIRGing: Big data analysis of English National Team fans during the 2018 FIFA World Cup. *Communication & Sport, 8*(3), 317–345.

Fortunato, J. (2008). NFL agenda-setting: The NFL programming schedule: A study of agenda-setting. *Journal of Sports Media, 3*(1), 27–49.

Frandsen, K. (2019). *Sport and mediatization*. London: Routledge.

Frederick, E. L., Pegoraro, A., & Sanderson, J. (2019). Divided and united: Perceptions of athlete activism at the ESPY's. *Sport in Society, 22*(12), 1919–1936.

Gamson, W. A. (1989). News as framing: Comments on Graber. *American Behavioral Scientist, 33*(2), 157–161.

Gantz, W. (1981). An exploration of viewing motives and behaviors associated with television sports. *Journal of Broadcasting, 25*, 263–275.

Gantz, W., Wang, Z., Bryant, P., & Potter, R. F. (2006). Sports versus all comers: Comparing TV sports fans with fans of other programming genres. *Journal of Broadcasting & Electronic Media, 50*(1), 95–118.

Gantz, W., & Wenner, L. A. (1991). Men, women, and sports: Audience experiences and effects. *Journal of Broadcasting & Electronic Media, 35,* 233–243.

Gantz, W., & Wenner, L. A. (1995). Fanship and the television sports viewing experiences. *Sociology of Sport Journal, 12*(1), 56–74.

Gerbner, G., Gross, L., Morgan, M., & Signorielli, N. (1986). Living with television: The dynamics of the cultivation process. In J. Bryant & D. Zillmann (Eds.), *Perspectives on media effects* (pp. 17–40). Hillsdale, NJ: LEA.

Gerbner, G., Gross, L., Morgan, M., Signorielli, N., & Shanahan, J. (2002). Growing up with television: The cultivation perspective. In J. Bryant & D. Zillmann (Eds.), *Media effects: Advances in theory and research* (pp. 43–67). Hillsdale, NJ: LEA.

Giddens, A. (1976). *New rules of sociological method.* London: Hutchinson.

Giddens, A. (1979). *Central problems in social theory.* Berkeley: University of California.

Giddens, A. (1984). *The constitution of society: Outline of the theory of structuration.* Berkeley: University of California Press.

Gitlin, T. (1980). *The whole world is watching: Mass media in the making and unmaking of the new left.* Berkeley: University of California Press.

Goffman, E. (1974). *Frame analysis: An essay on the organization of experience.* Cambridge, MA: Harvard University Press.

Grano, D. A., & Zagacki, K. S. (2011). Cleansing the Superdome: The paradox of purity and post-Katrina guilt. *Quarterly Journal of Speech, 97*(2), 201–223.

Hall, S. (2000). Encoding/decoding. In P. Marris & S. Thornham (Eds.), *Media studies: A reader* (2nd ed.) (pp. 57–64). New York: NYU Press.

Halone, K. K., & Billings, A. C. (2010). The temporal nature of racialized sport consumption. *American Behavioral Scientist, 53*(11), 1645–1668.

Hepp, A., Hajarvard, S., & Lundby, K. (2015). Mediatization: Theorizing the interplay between media, culture and society. *Media, Culture & Society, 37*(2), 314–324.

Hodler, M. R., & Lucas-Carr, C. (2015). "The mother of all comebacks": A critical analysis of the fitspirational comeback narrative of Dara Torres. *Communication & Sport, 4*(4), 442–459.

Hutchins, B., & Rowe, D. (2013). *Digital media sport: Technology, power, and culture in the network society.* London: Routledge.

Jones, R. (2022, January 10). Study: NFL makes up 75 of top 100 most-watched U.S. broadcasts in 2021. *Sports Pro Media.* https://www.sportspromedia.com/news/nfl-most-watched-broadcasts-super-bowl-tampa-bay-bucs-brady-viewership/.

Katz, E., Blumler, J. G., & Gurevitch, M. (1973). Uses and gratifications research. *Public Opinion Quarterly, 37*(4), 509–523.

Keaton, S.A., & Gearhart, C.C. (2014). Identity formation, identity strength, and self-categorization as predictors of affective and psychological outcomes: A model reflecting sport team fans' responses to highlights and lowlights of a college football season. *Communication & Sport, 2*(4), 363–385.

Kim, J., Song, H., & Lee, S. (2018). Extrovert and lonely individuals' social TV viewing experiences: A mediating and moderating role of social presence. *Mass Communication & Society, 21*(1), 50–70.

Kraszewski, J. (2008). Pittsburgh in Fort Worth: Football bars, sports television, sports fandom, and the management of home. *Journal of Sport & Social Issues, 32*(2), 139–157.

Lewis, M., Bell, T., Billings, A. C., & Brown, K. A. (2020). White sportscasters, Black athletes: Race and ESPN's coverage of college football's National Signing Day. *Howard Journal of Communications, 31*(4), 337–350.

Loy, J. W., & McElvogue, J. F. (1970). Racial segregation in American sport. *International Review of Sport Sociology, 5*, 5–24.

Markovits, A. S., & Hellerman, S. (2001). *Offside: Soccer and American exceptionalism.* Princeton, NJ: Princeton University Press.

Maske, M. (2019, November 13). A 17-game NFL season is becoming more likely as league, players make progress on labor deal. *Washington Post.* https://www.washingtonpost.com/sports/2019/11/13/game-nfl-season-is-becoming-more-likely-league-players-make-progress-labor-deal/.

McCarthy, D., Jones, R. L., & Potrac, P. (2003). Constructing images and interpreting realities: The case of the Black soccer player on television. *International Review for the Sociology of Sport, 38*(2), 217–238.

McCombs, M. E., Llamas, J. P., Lopez-Escobar, E., & Rey, F. (1997). Candidate's images in Spanish elections: Second-level agenda-setting effects. *Journalism & Mass Communication Quarterly, 74*(4), 703–717.

McCombs, M. E., & Shaw, D. L. (1972). The agenda setting function of the mass media. *Public Opinion Quarterly, 36*, 176–187.

McCombs, M. E., Shaw, D. L., & Weaver, D. H. (2014). New directions in agenda-setting theory and research. *Mass Communication & Society, 17*(6), 781–802.

Musto, M., Cooky, C., & Messner, M. (2017). "From fizzle to sizzle": Televised sports news and the production of gender-bland sexism. *Gender & Society, 31*(5), 573–596.

Novak, D. R., & Billings, A. C. (2012). The fervent, the ambivalent, and the great gap between: American print media coverage of the 2010 FIFA World Cup. *International Journal of Sport Communication, 5*(1), 35–50.

Nylund, D. (2007). *Beer, babes, and balls: Masculinity and sports talk radio.* Albany, NY: SUNY.

Oates, T. P. (2007). The erotic gaze in the NFL draft. *Communication and Critical/Cultural Studies, 4*(1), 74–90.

O'Donohoe, S. (1994). Advertising uses and gratifications. *European Journal of Marketing, 28*(8–9), 52–75.

Ogden, D., & Rose, R. A. (2005). Using Giddens's structuration theory to examine the waning participation of African Americans in baseball. *Journal of Black Studies, 35*(4), 225–245.

Parsons, N. L., & Stern, M. J. (2012). There's no dying in baseball: Cultural valorization, collective memory, and induction into the Baseball Hall of Fame. *Sociology of Sport Journal, 29*(1), 62–88.

Peterson, E. M. & Raney, A. A. (2008). Reconceptualizing and reexamining suspense as a predictor of mediated sports enjoyment. *Journal of Broadcasting & Electronic Media, 52*(4), 544–562.

Phillips, M. G., & Hutchins, B. (2003). Losing control of the ball: The political economy of football and the media in Australia. *Journal of Sport & Social Issues, 27*(3), 215–232.

Potter, W. J. (1991). The linearity assumption in cultivation research. *Human Communication Research, 17*, 562–584.

Rada, J. A. (1996). Color blind-sided: Racial bias in network television's coverage of professional football games. *Howard Journal of Communications, 7*(3), 231–239.

Raney, A. A. (2006). Why we watch and enjoy mediated sports. In J. Bryant & A. Raney (Eds.), *Handbook of sports and media* (pp. 313–329). Mahwah, NJ: Lawrence Erlbaum Associates.

Raney, A. A., & Depalma, A. (2006). The effect of viewing varying levels of aggressive sports programming on enjoyment, mood, and perceived violence. *Mass Communication & Society, 9,* 321–338.

Raney, A. A., & Kinnally, W. (2009). Examining perceived violence in and enjoyment of televised rivalry sports contests. *Mass Communication & Society, 12*(3), 311–331.

Real, M. R. (1975). Super Bowl: Mythic spectacle. *Journal of Communication, 25*(1), 31–43.

Rogers, E., & Dearing, J. (1988). Agenda-setting research: Where has it been, where is it going? *Communication Yearbook, 11,* 555–594.

Say goodbye to the offseason. (2020). Deloitte Perspectives. https://www2.deloitte.com/us/en/pages/technology-media-and-telecommunications/articles/developing-sports-marketing-strategies-year-round.html.

Scheufele, D. A. (1999). Framing as a theory of media effects. *Journal of Communication, 49,* 103–122.

Shanahan, J. G., & Morgan, M. (1999). *Television and its viewers: Cultivation theory and research.* Cambridge: Cambridge University Press.

Sherman, E. (2017, January 12). For the last time, journalists shouldn't pick Hall of Fame winners. *Poynter.* https://www.poynter.org/ethics-trust/2017/for-the-last-time-journalists-shouldnt-pick-hall-of-fame-winners/.

Solves, J., Pappous, A., Rius, I., & Kohe, G. Z. (2019). Framing the Paralympic Games: A mixed-methods analysis of Spanish media coverage of the Beijing 2008 and London 2012 Paralympic Games. *Communication & Sport, 7*(6), 729–751.

Spencer, E. A., & Limperos, A. M. (2020). ESPN's coverage of intimate partner violence in the National Football League. *Communication & Sport, 8*(1), 3–25.

Spinda, J. S. W., & Puckette, S. (2018). Just a snap: Fan uses and gratifications for following sports Snapchat. *Communication & Sport, 6*(5), 627–649.

Szymanski, S. (2010). The political economy of sport. In S. Szymanski (Ed.), *The comparative economics of sport* (pp. 79–86). London: Palgrave Macmillan.

Tajfel, H., & Turner, J. C. (1986). The social identity theory of inter-group behavior. In S. Worchel & L. W. Austin (Eds.), *Psychology of intergroup relations.* Chicago: Nelson-Hall.

Taylor, S. E., & Lobel, M. (1989). Social comparison activity under threat: Downward evaluation and upward contacts. *Psychological Review, 96*(4), 569–575.

Turner, J. C., Hogg, M. A., Oakes, P. J., Reicher, S. D., & Wetherell, M. S. (1987). *Rediscovering the social group: A self-categorization theory.* Oxford: Blackwell.

van Lienden, A., & van Sterkenburg, J. (2022). Prejudice in the people's game: A content analysis of race/ethnicity in Polish televised football. *Communication & Sport, 10*(2), 313–333. https://journals.sagepub.com/doi/full/10.1177/2167479520939486.

Voci, A. (2006). Relevance of social categories, depersonalization and group processes: Two field tests of self-categorization theory. *European Journal of Social Psychology, 36*(1), 73–90.

Wann, D. L. (2006). Understanding the positive social psychological benefits of sport team identification: The team identification–social psychological health model. *Group Dynamics: Theory, Research, and Practice, 10,* 272–296.

Wann, D. L., & Grieve, F. G. (2005). Biased evaluations of in-group and out-group spectator behavior at sporting events: The importance of team identification and threats to social identity. *Journal of Social Psychology, 145*(5), 531–545.

Wenner, L. A. (1994). The Dream Team, communicative dirt, and the marketing of synergy: USA Basketball and cross-merchandising in television commercials. *Journal of Sport & Social Issues, 18*(1), 27–47.

Wenner, L. A. (Ed.). (1998). *Mediasport*. London: Routledge.

Wenner, L. A. (2006). Sport and media through the super glass mirror: Placing blame, breast beating, and a gaze into the future. In A. A. Raney and J. Bryant (Eds.), *The handbook of sports and media* (pp. 47–63). Mahwah, NJ: Lawrence Erlbaum Associates.

Wenner, L. A. (2007). Towards a dirty theory of narrative ethics. Prolegomenon on media, sport and commodity value. *International Journal of Media and Cultural Politics, 3*, 111–129.

Wenner, L. A. (2015). Communication and sport, where art thou? Epistemological reflections on the moment and field(s) of play. *Communication & Sport, 3*(3), 247–260.

Wenner, L. A., & Billings, A. C. (2017). *Sport, media, and mega-events*. London: Routledge.

Whannel, G. (1992). *Fields in vision: Television sport and cultural transformation*. London: Routledge.

Whannel, G. (2002). *Media sport stars: Masculinities and moralities*. London: Routledge.

Whiteside, E., & Hardin, M. (2011). Women (not) watching women: Leisure time, television, and implications for televised coverage of women's sports. *Communication, Culture & Critique, 4*, 122–143.

Whitson, D. (1986). Structure, agency and the sociology of sport debates. *Theory, Culture & Society, 3*(1), 99–107.

Xu, Q., Billings, A. C., & Fan, M. (2018). When women fail to "hold up more than half the sky": Gendered frames of CCTV's coverage of gymnastics at the 2016 Summer Olympics. *Communication & Sport, 6*(2), 154–174.

CHAPTER 55

....

SPORT, FILM, AND THE CULTURAL IMAGINARY

....

SEÁN CROSSON

THE nomination of the motor racing–themed production *Ford v Ferrari* (2019) for the Best Film Oscar at the 2019 Academy Awards marked a recent and high-profile reminder of the prominence of sport cinema in contemporary film and popular culture. Though the film did not win the award (one of four nominations it received), it did receive Academy Awards for Best Film Editing and Best Sound Editing, speaking to the dynamic and sophisticated use of both sound and visual editing that has become synonymous today with mainstream sports films. However, while the film enjoyed both critical and commercial success (taking in U.S.$225.5 million at the international box office alone before its release on DVD and via streaming platforms),[1] its critical reception also revealed salient features regarding sport cinema. First, the film was not always described as a sports film, despite the fact that its lead protagonists are motor racing drivers and its most dynamic sequences feature motor racing. On IMDb (the Internet Movie Database, the largest online database of film releases), the film is initially categorized on the landing page as "Action, Biography, Drama"[2]—but not in terms of sport. Indeed, the film's original title de-emphasizes its sporting connection—though this was highlighted more clearly in some European territories where the film was released under the alternative title *Le Mans '66*, referring to the celebrated French motor race featured prominently in the film. Furthermore, where sport was acknowledged, the film was frequently categorized as a "racing film" (Debruge, 2019; Hammond, 2019; Mithaiwala, 2019) rather than in terms of sport cinema, indicating the variability with which films featuring sport are described. In addition, a considerable portion of commentary inspired by the film focused not so much on the particulars of the film itself or its depiction of sport, but rather the complex and contested events that it drew inspiration from: the combative and competitive relationship between the Ford and Ferrari motor companies in the 1960s. As noted by *Forbes.com* contributor Chuck Tannert (2019, para. 3) following the film's release:

> The story begins in the early 1960s. U.S. purchasing habits changed as the Baby Boomer generation came of age. For the first time in history, youth were more important to American business' bottom line than their parents. Boomers had lots of disposable income to spend on items such as cars, clothes and homes, and unlike their "a penny saved is a penny earned"

parents, who had lived through the Great Depression and World War II, they were looking for something unique from a new vehicle. They wanted cars that were sportier and sexier, valuing speed and performance over comfort and reliability. They wanted sports cars, a fact that was not lost on the executives at Ford Motor Co.

Tannert's discussion and that of other commentators who responded to the film (e.g., Brody, 2019; CBS News, 2019) reveals a further recurring feature of the discourse surrounding sport cinema: these films are in many cases not primarily about sport. Sport provides a seductive and engaging cultural form to draw viewers to works telling other stories, stories that may be revealing with regard to larger and more complex societal issues, including questions of race, class, gender, or the changing economic or social structures of the society concerned. As such, sports films can be highly influential texts shaping audience understandings and appreciations of their social and cultural imaginary (Ardolino, 1988; Crawford, 1988; Dickerson, 1991; Mosher, 1983). It is this potential of sport cinema that has been a recurring concern of scholarship engaged with the topic, and this chapter will chart some of major issues, approaches, and debates that have featured in research of the area.

Issues

Sport Cinema: "Box Office Poison" or Cinema's Most Enduring Topic?

Throughout the history of the cinema, sport has been one of the most popular subjects featured. Zucker and Babich (1987) list over 2,000 relevant films in their index of sports cinema. With the advent of the internet and online indexing tools, IMDb categorizes in a recent search (July 31, 2020) 4,238 feature films under the "sport" category—and this does not include television productions (fiction, nonfiction, and serial) produced internationally that have featured sport.[3] Sports films have also enjoyed considerable box office success and critical acclaim, including such seminal productions as *Rocky* (1976), *Raging Bull* (1980), and more recent Academy Award winners *Million Dollar Baby* (2004), *The Blind Side* (2009), *The Fighter* (2010), and *Ford v Ferrari* (2019).

However, despite the popularity of sports fiction on film (the principal focus of this chapter),[4] research regarding the area has been slow to develop (Dickerson, 1991, p. 5; Poulton & Roderick, 2008, p. 107). The limited critical engagement with the topic until recent decades can be partly attributed to the low standing that sport cinema has had historically. Sports films have often been perceived as "box office poison" (Carlson, 1998, p. 361; Jones, 2005, p. 30) or less critically significant, with King and Leonard (2006, p. 1) arguing that even where films "about athletes or those set in sporting worlds may prove popular and even profitable . . . they do not rise to the level of critical significance, much less art."

Contributing to the poor reception critically of sport in film has been the heavy reliance of sports films on clichés. In his analysis of baseball films, Good (1996, p. 22) provided details on some of the most prominent of these, including the mythical status of the ballpark; the fatherly team manager; the presence of dual contrasting female leads, one pure, one tempting; and "raw rookies and worn-out veterans." Many, if not all, of these clichés recur across sport cinema, regardless of which sport is featured. Furthermore, films featuring sport have been criticized for frequently suffering from overly familiar scenarios and "nauseating sentimentality" (Sarris, 1980, p. 50). An obvious example of such a "familiar scenario" is the big game, race, or fight finish found at the climax of a considerable number of sports films.

Sport Cinema Beginnings

Despite this uncertain history, sport is nonetheless one of the oldest and most enduring topics found in the cinema. As a widespread cultural practice with a considerable following internationally, sport had a vital role in popularizing the new medium in its earliest years. Included in the program at the first public screening to a paying audience (sometimes referred to as "the birth of cinema" [Austin, 1996, p. 1; Jarvis, 2006, p. 49]) of short films by French film pioneers the Lumière brothers on December 28 1895 at Salon Indien du Grand Café in Paris were several that had sporting associations. Furthermore, the Catalogue-lumiere.com lists 62 productions in the "sport" genre, including actuality films featuring boxing, cycling, horseracing, gymnastics, various martial arts, tennis, boules, swimming, wrestling, rugby, rowing, athletics, skiing, and football.

As well as providing a recognizable popular cultural practice, sport also exhibited a defining feature of cinema: movement. It is these traits that contributed to sport being one of the most popular subjects in this new art form from its very earliest days. While the new moving-image technology may have attracted audiences for its novelty at the first screenings, it was sport, and particularly boxing in the United States (as evident in the large number of boxing-themed films produced by American film pioneer Thomas Edison's company), that ensured the continuing popularity of cinema in its first decade of production (Betts, 1974, p. 243). McKernan (1996, p. 110) identifies in the early boxing films "the very birth of American cinema realism and drama, newsfilm and fakery, commercialism, populism, professionalism, two protagonists battling within the perfect staging, the ring." The first feature-length films, the first use of actors, and the first commercial cinema exhibitions in the United States were all of boxing films (Streible, 2008). Furthermore, these early films were influential texts, particularly as vehicles for the inculcation and affirmation of American values to immigrants (Irish Americans and Italian Americans in particular prominently represented), facilitating their assimilation into American society (Jowett, 1976; Sklar, 1976).

Sport provided many of the ingredients that would be key to the sustainability of cinema: a captive audience, drama in a confined space (hence the popularity of boxing films in the early years), and strong characters to identify with and dislike. Indeed, one could argue that the rudiments of mainstream fiction film practice were all evident within the earliest sports film productions. However, as cinema developed and coalesced into specific forms and genres, the requirements and expectations of each brought both possibilities and challenges for filmmakers wishing to include sport in their work. These filmmakers (and above all those focused on producing fiction film) were challenged in recreating or communicating what has long been a crucial factor in the appeal of spectator sport: unpredictability, or what Whannel (2000, p. 295) refers to as sport's "uncertainty." As American film critic Andrew Sarris (1980, p. 50) has observed, "Sports are now. Movies are then. Sports are news. Movies are fables." This shortcoming of sport cinema became all the more apparent as popular media forms such as the radio and later television provided live coverage of sporting events.

The Evolving Focus of Sport Cinema

While cinema has evolved technically to allow for more dynamic depictions of sport—often informed by live television coverage—the focus of sport cinema has moved from the field of play to the lives of sporting protagonists. As a consequence, what we may describe as sport cinema may actually feature limited minutes of sport action; this is not to diminish the importance of these sequences, however, and they are often crucial to character and plot determination and resolution. As noted by Cummins (2006, p. 186) (describing fiction productions by ESPN):

> [T]he network has learned what novelists, playwrights, and Hollywood film and television producers have known for years, that sport serves as an ideal backdrop for telling other stories. . . . Racism, sexism, social inequality, the splintering of the American family—all of these issues have been addressed in countless fictional narratives that revolve around sports.

We will return to some of these themes identified by Cummins later in this chapter. However, television is also hugely indebted to cinema with regard to the narrative and aesthetic presentation of sport. Sport cinema defined the contours of subsequent depictions of sport, particularly through its popularization of "confrontainment" (Holly, 1994, cited in Hess-Lüttich, 2007, p. 1365)—that is, providing entertainment on the basis of confrontation—but also in the manner in which broadcast media "strives to place sports events within a dramatic framework for audience interpretation" (Sullivan, 2006, p. 137). The key ingredients in ensuring the appeal of televised sport are defining features of mainstream drama. As Wood and Benigni (2006, p. 154) observe, "the enjoyment of sports is contingent upon several factors, including *drama . . . interesting characters . . . conflict . . .* and *satisfying resolutions,*" and the ability of sport to provide all these elements has contributed to the endurance and popularity of sporting subjects since the earliest days of the cinema.

APPROACHES

There is a growing body of research engaged with sport cinema across a range of disciplines and informed by a variety of critical approaches and concerns. While some quantitative analysis of the area has been undertaken (Pearson, Curtis, Haney, & Zhang, 2003), qualitative studies have predominated. Research of sport cinema has evolved considerably over the past 40 years, from a point at which the topic was largely ignored (particularly within film studies) to its current status as the subject of increasing attention. Despite sport being one of the earliest subjects of film, in both nonfiction and fiction forms, academic engagement with these representations was slow to develop, partly due to the path that critical and theoretical approaches to film took from early in the 20th century. Indeed, because of film's initial consideration as a "lower" form of entertainment, in part because of its associ-ation with perceived "lesser" sports such as boxing, much of the early writings on film were concerned with advocating for a degree of respectability for this new cultural form and identifying its distinguishing features. Proponents argued for film's particularity as a form with a separate aesthetic of its own, rather than a format primarily used for adapting more established arts such as literature and theater, or representing popular cultural forms such as sport (cf. Monaco, 2000, pp. 391–394; also Lindsay, 1915; Münsterberg, 1916).

Researching Sport Cinema: From History to Genre

The second half of the 20th century was a particularly productive period for the develop-ment of critical and theoretical approaches to film. Facilitated by the popularization of film festivals and societies and the increasing acceptance of film internationally as an academic discipline, a broad and varied range of approaches to film developed, drawing inspiration from developments more generally in academia in diverse areas such as historical studies, psychoanalytic analysis, linguistics, cognitive psychology, social anthropology, Marxism, and feminism. Under the influence of both poststructuralism and ideological criticism, a movement is evident in scholarship of sport cinema from initial historical studies of the area to examinations of the role of sport cinema in articulating and influencing the so-cial imaginary (cf. Crosson, 2013, pp. 23–29; also Altman, 1999; Barthes, 1977; Monaco, 2000). Early engagements with the area in the work of film historians Manchel (1980) and Bergan (1982) mapped its historical development, identifying key texts and some of the re-curring themes. Bergan in particular stressed the role sport cinema can play in affirming societal beliefs and values, a focus that was further developed by Mosher (1983, pp. 15–16), who identified "the narrative of the quest" motif in particular as central to films featuring sport and the manner in which relevant texts serve "universal human needs." Bergan's and Mosher's respective approaches anticipated a broader turn in theoretical approaches to film, influenced by developments in media studies and cultural studies, as scholars increasingly examined the function and meanings of sport cinema texts (Miller, 1990; Tudor, 1997).

Sport Cinema Studies: A Growing Field of Scholarship

Whannel's (2000, p. 293) remark that "while there has been much discussion of indi-vidual films, there is no scholarly overview of sport in the cinema" preceded two decades of increased scholarship, including monograph studies by Baker (2003), Crosson (2013), Babington (2014), Lieberman (2014), Sheppard (2020), Bonzel (2020), and Friedman (2020); dedicated journal issues (*Sport in Society* 2008, *11*[2–3]; *Studies in Eastern European Cinema* 2017, *8*[1]); and collections (Briley, Schoenecke, & Carmichael, 2008; Crosson, 2020; King & Leonard, 2006; Poulton & Roderick, 2009); as well as non-English-language overviews of the area by Romaguera i Ramió (2003), Camy and Camy (2016), and Garioni (2017).

The increased engagement with sports films reflects the larger evolution of critical engagements with sport media, and similar critical tools and concerns are evident within the discourse specific to sport cinema. Poulton and Roderick's (2008, p. 108) contention (referring to work by Boyle, Millington, & Vertinsky, 2006; Miller, 1990, 1994; Poulton,

2006; Redhead, 2007; Rowe, 1998, 2004; Tomlinson, 1996, 1999) that "scholars from the sociology of sport appear to have given sport in film more critical attention than their film studies counterparts" responds to the predominant focus of scholarship to date (including in film studies) on how sport cinema engages with and impacts discourses long of interest to sociologists, including questions of race, gender, and social class. Sport cinema has also attracted the interest of scholars in the fields of sports management (Pearson & Lam, 2015), nursing (DiBartolo & Seldomridge, 2009; Wilson, Blake, Taylor, & Hannings, 2013), medicine (Alexander, Lenahan, & Pavlov, 1999), and psychology (Butler, Zaromb, Lyle, & Roediger, 2009; Núñez & Garcia, 2014), though principally in studies examining the potential use of relevant sport film texts in educational contexts. However, these studies are also revealing in their analysis of the employment of sports films in classes considering themes such as gender and diversity (Núñez & Garcia, 2014), a theme that has also been the subject of critical attention in studies of sport cinema.

Scholars have also sought to delineate the distinctive features of a sports fiction genre (whether in film or literature), though these attempts have encountered considerable challenges. Cummins (2006, p. 187) observes—drawing on work by Burns (1987), Dickerson (1991), Oriard (1982), and Zucker and Babich (1987):

> Virtually every scholar who has attempted to define sports fiction has been faced with a myriad of highly problematic questions. For example, is the mere presence of sports in a narrative enough to justify inclusion as sports fiction, or must sports be central to the storyline? To that end, how large a role must sports play in a narrative before it is considered a central element? In addition, should all forms of athletic competition be included, or only organized sports?

While Cummins lists several potential avenues toward defining what sports fiction might refer to, he ultimately declines the challenge, admitting that his intervention will do "little to clarify whether sports films exist as a distinct genre" (p. 188). In common with Cummins, for much of the 20th century, this question was either sidestepped or largely ignored in critical literature. This is evident in the omission entirely of sport from Gehring's *Handbook of American Film Genres* published in 1988. Subsequent studies have somewhat addressed this omission, including Lopez's (1993) *Film by Genre,* and focused overviews of sport cinema, including those by Wallenfeldt (1989), Williams (2006), Didinger and Macnow (2009), Camy and Camy (2016), and Friedman (2020), as well as recognition by the American Film Institute in 2008 of "Sports" as one of the 10 classic film genres. However, doubts still persist as to how we might define the area, with Whannel (2008, pp. 196–197) denying that a sport cinema genre exists at all, positing instead that sport is "simply a topic, which links a set of otherwise diverse texts."

A crucial determinant of genre recognizability is critical commentary regarding individual films; as Altman (1999, pp. 124, 127) observes, "Our terms and our concepts derive not so much from cinema itself, but from those who represent cinema to us. . . . In short, critics and not studios lie at the origin of most generic language." However, Babington (2014) attributes sport cinema's seeming absence in critical discourse for decades to its hybridity and the inclusion by critics of films featuring sport often in other genres, ranging from the romantic comedy to the musical, the history film, the art film, and many more besides. Indeed, he lists in total 27 subcategories within which sports films have been found (pp. 12–14), a list that is by no means exhaustive and does not include the subgenres associated with individual sports, very evident in many critical engagements with sport on film. Hence we have to date focused critical studies of popular sports in the cinema, including American football (Oriard, 2001; Vogan, 2014), baseball (Briley, 2011; Dickerson, 1991; Good, 1996), cycling (Bennett, 2019), boxing (Grindon, 2011; Streible, 2008; Vogan, 2020), association football (Glynn, 2018), cricket (Glynn, 2020), Gaelic games (Crosson, 2019), ice hockey (Cermak, 2017), and surfing (Engle, 2015).

Scholars have attempted to bring some order to this very broad range of areas by finding dominant categories within sport cinema. Mosher (1983, pp. 15–19) identified four principal archetypal patterns—comedy, tragedy, romance, and satire—in the sports film, each of which responds to quite different audience expectations. Cashmore (2000, pp. 132–139) adopted an approach similar to Mosher's when he described three prominent subgenres to sport cinema, namely the dramatic/biographical, the comedy/fantasy, and the documentary. Most recently Friedman (2020, pp. 15–16) defined sport cinema in terms of eight "master narratives that help to define the genre": "Individual salvation/redemption/renewal," "Team unity," "Generational mentorship," "Pathway out of poverty," "Small-town heroes," "Moral victories," "Miracle wins," and "Beleaguered everyman quest."

While the differing approaches to the categorization of sport cinema may suggest uncertainty regarding the genre, this uncertainty is not unique to films featuring sport (Bordwell & Thompson, 2010, pp. 328–329). Furthermore, the development of the classification of genres in cinema history has often been characterized by considerable change and variation (Crosson, 2013, pp. 55–60; Neale, 2000, pp. 231–257). This has led commentators to move beyond attempting to define genre according to a limited number of prerequisites, with Jim Collins (1993, pp. 242–263) proposing "genericity" as more appropriate to the reflexivity and textual awareness apparent in recent genre films. Rick Altman (1999, pp. 62–65) has suggested the term "genrification" to reflect the continuing construction and reconstruction of genre in film whereby "the constitution of *film* cycles and genres is a never-ceasing process, closely tied to the capitalist need for product differentiation." David Rowe (1998, p. 351) recognizes the changing and evolving nature of the sports genre in particular, arguing that "to claim that sports films may constitute a genre (perhaps with a range of subgenres) it would be necessary to establish the existence of some shifting yet patterned relationships within or between subject matter, presentation, narrative, and affect." Taking this as his starting point, Rowe suggests a

> common basis to nondocumentary or instruction-based sports films as a genre (or, more cautiously, as a "complex of sub genres"), underpinning a panoply of formal, substantive, and stylistic variations: that all films that deal centrally with sports are at some level allegorical, that they address the question of the dual existence of the social and sporting worlds as problematic, and that they are preoccupied with the extent to which (idealized) sports can transcend or are bound by existing (and corrupting) social relations. (pp. 351–352)

Rowe's analysis here points to a recurring concern of critical engagements with sport cinema: how films connect with and inform broader social relations and understandings. This concern has been at the center of ongoing debates regarding the area and individual sports film texts.

Debates

Sport Cinema: More Than Films about Sport

As summarized above, scholars of sport cinema have identified and examined the manner in which representative films have connected with wider questions and concerns in the time of their production and release. While Dickerson (1991, p. 153) contends that Hollywood sports films mirror "the changes of the culture that gives birth to the films," for Baker (2003, p. 2) these films also "contribute to the contested process of defining social identities." Informed by influential work in the broader cultural studies and communication studies fields (including Hall, 1973/1980; Morley, 1980) studies of sport cinema have engaged with the role relevant texts have had in either affirming and influencing dominant values and their acceptance or (occasionally) the potential of individual texts for progressive, alternative, or oppositional readings, what Mathia Diawara (2004) described (in relation to African American audiences) as "resisting spectatorship." Relevant work has considered a broad range of topics in relation to sport cinema, including nostalgia (Kibby, 1998; Nilsson, 2000; Paino, 2001; Springwood, 1996), religion (Ardolino, 2003; Crosson, 2017; Roubach, 2007), and youth and aging (Cummins, 2006; Good, 1996; Tudor, 1997). However, the most prominent and recurring debates have concerned questions of race (Denzin, 2002; Free, 2012; Giardina & McCarthy, 2005; Regester, 2003; Sheppard, 2020), gender (Kibby, 1998; Lieberman, 2014; Lindner, 2011; Nilsson, 2000), social class (Bowden, 1994; Crosson, 2013; Grindon, 1996, 2011; Hill, 2005), and nationalism (Bonzel, 2020; Crosson, 2020; Miller, 1990; Sobchack, 1997).

Race and the Sports Film

Reflecting the dominance of American sport cinema, the majority of critical work on the topic of race has been focused on the depiction of African American athletes, though some research has also been undertaken examining the depiction of Native American characters and other ethnic identities (cf. Crosson, 2013, pp. 125–156; also King, 2006; Ransom, 2014). The critical discourse regarding race and sport cinema is part of a wider engagement with the depiction of race in *MediaSport* (Wenner, 1998) as "a key site of contemporary corporeal display and consequently of racial signification" (Grainger, Newman, & Andrews, 2006, p. 447).

A recurring concern across analyses of sport cinema is the often problematic depictions of minorities. Good (1996, p. 140), referring to the depiction of minorities in baseball films, contends that these productions "often mistreat the player by giving him certain childish or uncivilised traits." He offers the example of *The Bingo Long Traveling All Stars & Motor Kings* (1976) to illustrate this practice, evident in this production in the manner in which African American characters are depicted in a comical manner. While depictions of African Americans have undoubtedly evolved, particularly after the civil rights movement in the 1960s and the legislative changes that followed, a wide range of scholars have nonetheless observed a lack of real progress in representations of African Americans athletes, who continue to be depicted in subservient or stereotypical positions. Baker (2003), Good (1996), and Crosson (2013) have all highlighted how, even in films that depict minorities in leading or prominent roles—including *Cool Runnings* (1993), *The Air Up There* (1994), *Jerry Maguire* (1996), *Hardball* (2001), *Radio* (2003), *Bring It On: All or Nothing* (2006), *The Love Guru* (2008)—these roles continue to support and "reinforce White superiority" (Cummins, 2006, p. 193). Crosson (2013. p. 83) identifies, for example, the continuing depiction of African Americans in one of the most commercially successful of all sports films, *The Blind Side* (2009), "as untrustworthy, violent and sexually aggressive . . . neglectful of their own social responsibilities in contrast to members of the dominant White community." In one of the most recent studies of the subject, Sheppard (2020, p. 10) is critical of the way sport cinema "subsumes the significance of race" even in texts where race is clearly a prominent issue. She adopts an innovative "black body genre" approach to the subject, contending that "sports films centralize Black athletes' corporeal performance as a spectacle, such that blackness is realized, mitigated, succumbed to, and disavowed via cinema's regimes of representation" (p. 8).

While the majority of critical engagements with the question of race in sport cinema have raised concerns regarding the problematic positioning of minority characters, Babington (2014, p. 70) sees relevant films as the result of compromises "imposed by their historical moment" that "need to be understood as the condition of their existence." There has also been a recognition of the possibility of oppositional readings given the polysemic nature of mainstream cinema. Baker (2003), for example, describes how two early boxing-themed films featuring African American boxers, *Spirit of Youth* (1938) and *Keep Punching* (1939) (works which ostensibly conform to "dominant discourses of self-formation and segregation"), "reverse the race film convention of casting dark-skinned blacks as the criminal heavies" by placing characters suggesting "whiteness" in these roles, thereby invoking "the racial barriers that were a historical reality" for African Americans. As a result, these films allow for alternative and potentially progressive readings within narratives that nonetheless did not contradict "the bourgeois values endorsed by the Hollywood pictures" screened at the time (pp. 111–112). The potential for such contrary readings of conventional texts has also been identified with regard to representations of women in sport cinema.

Gender and the Sports Film

One of the most prominent debates returned to repeatedly in academic studies of sport cinema—and indeed sports fiction more generally—concerns the depiction of gender. Baker (2003, p. 3) argues that "to some degree every sports film is about gender," and Crosson (2013, p. 104) contends that "film has had an important role to play in affirming the prominence of men in sport, with male physicality a prominent feature in many films." This focus is evident in the popularity (in terms of both numbers produced and commercial appeal) of the sports biopic, evident from as early as 1940 with the release of *Knute Rockne, All American*, the biopic of the legendary American football coach. Dickerson (1991), Good (1996), and Briley (2011) have each highlighted the 1940s and 1950s as a particularly prolific period for this subgenre; popular successes include *The Pride of the Yankees* (1942), *The Stratton Story* (1949), and *Jim Thorpe—All-American* (1951), all of which feature male protagonists and their heroic efforts to overcome considerable obstacles to achieve sporting (and personal) success.

Dickerson (1991, p. 43) has connected the popularity of these productions with ideological needs in the post–World War II period. An important development in these years was the increasing empowerment of women and their greater involvement in roles previously the preserve of men, a pattern accelerated during the war. A relevant cinematic response to this change was the MGM production *National Velvet*, released in 1944, prior to the end of the war. In its depiction of a female jockey winning the Aintree Grand National against the odds (and the rules), *National Velvet* reflected a paradigm shift more broadly in American society (Crosson, 2013, pp. 110–114).

Partly as a response to the growing women's movement and to women's increasingly active roles more generally in society, from the 1950s onward women began to feature more frequently in prominent roles in sport films; relevant productions include *Hard, Fast and Beautiful!* (1951), *Pat and Mike* (1952), *Ice Castles* (1978), and *The Main Event* (1979). Indeed, women now began to appear in roles and to possess qualities perceived historically as masculine, such as authority, strength, aggression, force, and intellect. While these films continued to be in the minority, the representations of women found therein often suggest the tensions inherent in placing strong females in contexts that have historically been predominantly the preserve of men and the need to manage the threat these women presented to patriarchy (Crosson, 2013, pp. 103–124; Tudor, 1997, pp. 80–81).

The increasing empowerment of women in the 1970s and 1980s has also contributed to what Dickerson (1991, p. 119) describes as a "return of mythbuilding," evident in the popularity of sports biopics focused on male athletes, including *Eight Men Out* (1988), *The Babe* (1992), and *Rudy* (1993)—all films concerning legendary figures in American sports history and sharing a nostalgia to varying degrees for a time prior to the women's liberation movement of the late 1960s. Further relevant examples include *Raging Bull* (1980), a work Pam Cook (1982) views as suffused with a nostalgia for a strong robust masculinity and traditional patriarchal culture, and *Cinderella Man* (2005). The theme of recuperating American masculinity is central to many of the most prominent sports films of recent decades: *The Rookie* (2002), *Invincible* (2006), *The Fighter* (2010), *Rush* (2013), and recent Oscar winner *Ford v Ferrari* (2019). While there are notable recent exceptions that feature women prominently—including *I, Tonya* (2017) and *Battle of the Sexes* (2017)—the vast majority of sports films continue to focus primarily on male athletes.

In most of these films, Tudor (1997, p. 79) contends, women's roles are "relative to the male athlete-hero," occupying principally supporting parts. Tudor summarizes these traditional roles as "mother, spectator, cheerleader, booster" (p. 94), findings supported by Good (1996) in his analysis of baseball-themed films, from *Pride of the Yankees* (1942) to *The Natural* (1986) and *Field of Dreams* (1989). Representations of women in sport cinema have clearly evolved, as women's roles more generally in society have evolved over the 20th and into the 21st century. However, scholars have contended that what may ostensibly appear to be progressive representations of female athletes in sports films (including prominent productions *A League of Their Own* [1992], *Bend It Like Beckham* [2002], and *Million Dollar Baby* [2004]) may actually disguise a conservative ideology concerned ultimately with the maintenance of patriarchy (Boyle et al., 2006; Lieberman, 2014). Crosson (2013, pp. 103–124) argues that the threat such strong women may pose to patriarchy is contained in three principle means in the sports film: in the often negative, or comic, portrayal of women in positions of authority; by positioning leading sporting females clearly under the guidance (and authority) of men; or by the sexual objectification of women for principally male gratification.

There is some recognition among scholars of the progressive potential of strong female characters in sport cinema. Lindner (2011, p. 337) has contended, referring in particular to boxing films featuring female lead protagonists (a subgenre that includes *The Opponent* [2000], *Million Dollar Baby* [2004], and *Die Boxerin* [2004]), that while mainstream sport cinema affirms the "generally hetero-normative representational context of cinematic fiction," it can also occasionally point "to ways in which filmic depictions of female athleticism might destabilise normative understandings of gender and the gendered body," a position also evident in Caudwell's (2008) analysis of *Girlfight* (2000). However, while Lieberman (2014, p. 168) also notes the potential of sport cinema to "challenge, create and celebrate women's accomplishments and imagine new possibilities," she laments that this feature has "yet to become common."

Social Class

Scholarship has engaged with the depiction of social class in sport cinema emerging from a variety of national contexts, though the American experience has attracted most sustained attention. The American sports film has been viewed as playing a central role in the promotion of a particular version of ideal masculinity, indelibly associated with the American Dream, and defined by Baker (2003, p. 49) as the "heroic individual" who "overcomes obstacles and achieves success through determination, self-reliance, and hard work" (see also Crosson, 2013, pp. 103–124). This feature is informed by a central aspect of sport in the United States; as noted by Tudor (1997, p. xx), "the notion of individualism heavily marks the discourse of North-American athletics." Scholars have observed the importance of this theme across American sport cinema (Englert, 2018; Lichtenfeld, 2014; Whannel, 2008) where individual responsibility is invoked regardless of the challenges characters may encounter, including with regard to race, gender, or social class. Repeatedly in sport cinema we witness working-class characters overcome considerable obstacles through sport to realize at least a part of the American Dream, particularly in those films depicting boxing.

Boxing has been one of the most popular sports featured in sport cinema; Leger Grindon (1996, p. 54) could count "well over 150 feature-length fiction productions since 1930" in his essay on the topic, and this number has increased substantially since then. These films have provided an ambiguous yet revelatory insight into sport and social class in the United States, often focusing on the dark and corrupt aspects of this sport, but also seeing in it an opportunity for those marginalized and less fortunate to realize the American Dream. However, as Bergan (1982, p. 35) observes, boxing films "hardly ever question the social conditions that help to produce this phenomenon." Rather, individual responsibility and achievement are foregrounded repeatedly. Frequently in the boxing film the decline of the boxer is related primarily to a personal weakness rather than social factors; this can sometimes be the boxer's pride or insecurity (as in *Champion* [1949] and *Raging Bull* [1980]) or a boxer's fondness for the good life and all that it brings, including alcohol (as evident in *The Champ* [1931] and *The Great John L* [1945]) (Baker, 1997, 2003; Crosson, 2013; Grindon, 2011).

Boxing films have enjoyed considerable commercial and critical success, including, in the 21st century, David O. Russell's Oscar-winning *The Fighter* (2010) and the relaunch of the *Rocky* franchise in the related sequel productions, the Oscar-nominated *Creed* (2015) and *Creed II* (2018). That relaunch reflected the influence and popularity of *Rocky* (1976), a film that, more than any other, defined and popularized the contours of sport cinema since its release in 1976, popularizing the figure of the working-class sporting hero in its eponymous lead character and the American Dream trajectory at the heart of the film (Crosson, 2013, pp. 93–98). However, critics have accused the film of implicit (if not explicit) racism in its contrasting of a sympathetic underdog working-class white character with a wealthy and excessive African American, the heavyweight champion Apollo Creed (Leab, 1979; Tomasulo, 2007; Wilkinson, 1984), in a work that elevates white ethnic immigrant identity (Italian American) as an acceptable cipher for WASP identity, while disavowing (and legitimating) white privilege (Jacobson, 2006). The film has also been viewed as a neoconservative backlash against the various social and civil rights movements that marked the 1960s (Elmwood, 2008; Jordan, 2003; Nystrom, 2009). Grant Wiedenfeld (2016) challenges these readings of *Rocky*, viewing the film more positively. Drawing on Bakhtin's theory of the carnivalesque and Northrop Frye's classification of literature, Wiedenfeld regards *Rocky* as a carnivalesque low mimetic comedy that embodies "progressive ideals for race and class under the general theme of respect" (p. 168).

Sport Cinema beyond Hollywood

The focus of sport cinema scholarship to date has been predominantly on the American experience, the source of most relevant texts. However, increasing attention has been given to the place of sport cinema in other contexts and its role in the articulation and representation of national identities. This research has built upon the extensive research considering the place of sport more broadly with regard to national culture (e.g., Bairner, 2001; Bale, 1986; Dolan & Connolly, 2017; Holt, 1990; Porter & Smith, 2004), while scholars have also noted the important influence the mass media (including the cinema) has had in the popularization of sport and affirming its political significance (Billig, 1995, pp. 120–126; O'Boyle & Free, 2020). The increasing (if still underdeveloped) focus of research on specific national contexts responds to the role sport cinema may play in affirming (and occasionally contesting) central tenets underpinning conceptions of national identity while also revealing the much more extensive experience and practice of sport cinema beyond the American and Anglophone context.

Indeed, in some countries Indigenous sports films have been among the most popular at the local box office: in Norway, *Flåklypa Grand Prix* (*Pinchcliffe Grand Prix*, 1975); Russia, Движение вверх (*Going Vertical*, AKA *Three Seconds*, 2017); Spain, *Campeones* (*Champions*, 2018); and India, *Dangal* (2016). These films often reflect the influence of the predominant trajectory found in American sport cinema, summarized by Rowe (1998, p. 355) as one in which "all manner of social, structural, and cultural conflicts and divisions are resolved through the fantastic agency of sports." However, they can also reveal cynicism and pessimism regarding that trajectory, as evident in films as various *as The Loneliness of the Long Distance Runner* (United Kingdom, 1962), *Boxer a smrt* (*The Boxer and Death*) (Czechoslovakia, 1962), and *Offside* (Iran, 2006). Studies of sport cinema have to date focused on a wide array of national contexts, including Spain (Ashton, 2013; Rodríguez Díaz, 2010; Romaguera i Ramió, 2003), Germany (Bonzel, 2006; McDougall, 2017), Australia (Crosson, 2013, pp. 143–150; Miller, 1990, 1994), Belgium (Biltereyst & Vande Winkel, 2020), Britain (Jones, 2005), France (Jouan-Westlund, 2006; Place-Verghnes, 2007), Italy (Buscemi, 2020; Garioni, 2017), Taiwan (Lin, 2020), Ethiopia (Thomas, 2020), Latvia (Brūveris, 2016), Brazil (Capraro & Vargas, 2020), New Zealand (Henley, 2020), Ireland (Crosson, 2019), Sweden (Dahlén, 2020), Hungary (Cunningham, 2004; Fodor, 2017), and India (Crosson, 2013, pp. 150–156). While responding to the salient features apparent in each context considered (or exemplary text analyzed), these studies individually and collectively reveal the ongoing significance of the relationship between sport cinema and national identity.

Conclusion

Much as sport has developed as a key and highly influential aspect of popular culture, so too sport cinema has responded and magnified central aspects of sport's appeal. Indeed, sport is one of the oldest, most enduring and popular topics featured in film, such that identifying and defining the parameters of a distinctive sports film genre has presented considerable challenges. However, due both to the low regard with which sports films were held for much of the 20th century and the focus of scholars on identifying distinctive traits of film itself as an art form, scholarship of sport cinema was slow to develop. The emergence of this critical discourse over the past 40 years has involved a broad range of disciplines and areas, with the influence of cultural studies particularly evident in relevant scholarship. As scholars of cultural studies have argued, film plays a critical role as a mediator of social relations through the naturalization of cultural and societal norms (Boyle et al., 2006, p, 110; Croteau & Hoynes, 2003; Schirato & Webb, 2004). This contention has informed the focus of research on the role and influence of sport cinema texts in articulating and informing broader discourses, including with regard to race, gender, social class, and national identity.

While there has been considerable recent scholarship of the genre—including four relevant monographs in 2020—there remains much potential for further research. The American experience has understandably attracted most attention as the source of the majority of sports films. However, research of sport cinema is underdeveloped with regard to other contexts, despite the popularity of sport on film internationally and the distinctive nature of its portrayal in specific national and regional contexts, both in terms of sports depicted (for example, association football in Europe) and singular narrative and aesthetic elements that may feature.

Furthermore, the impact on sports films of the changing nature of cinema itself, due to declining audiences, new technologies (a process accelerated by the COVID-19 pandemic), and the contemporary convergence culture (Jenkins, 2006), requires further study. Sports dramas are now an increasing and popular component of television programming, including for dedicated sports channels more familiarly engaged with live sporting events (Brown & Bryant, 2006, pp. 78–80, 97–98). The success of such fiction-based content eventually led to the establishment of ESPN Films (previously known as ESPN Original Entertainment) in March 2008, dedicated to the production and distribution of sport films (ESPN Press Room, 2008). ESPN Films lists over 100 productions, including TV series as well as fiction and nonfiction works. While these have had limited box office success, they have attracted huge audiences on television and streaming platforms, including the Academy Award–winning documentary mini-series (which also had a limited theatrical release) *O.J.: Made in America*, which had an audience in excess of 35 million in the United States alone (The Futon Critic, 2016).

ESPN is a subsidiary of the Walt Disney Company, one of the most prominent producers of sports-themed films, with over 60 produced to date (Disney Movies List, n.d.). Another Disney subsidiary is 20th Century Studios, coproducer and distributor of the film with which we began this chapter, *Ford v Ferrari*. Sport cinema is now part of the contemporary convergence culture in which major film studios are but one component of giant conglomerates with businesses that expand well beyond film productions, and may include publishing, television, merchandising, internet concerns, and in some prominent instances (as with Disney) sporting interests. The long-term impact of these developments on the content and reception of sport cinema is still to be determined; what is clear, however, is that sports drama will continue to occupy a prominent and influential place in popular culture for many years to come.

NOTES

1. Further information on the box office returns of the film is available here: https://web. archive.org/web/20191118055744/https://www.boxofficemojo.com/release/rl990348801/.
2. The film's listing is available here: https://www.imdb.com/title/tt1950186/.
3. This search is possible on IMDb at the following link: https://www.imdb.com/search/ title/?title_type=feature&genres=sport (search undertaken on July 31, 2020).
4. While this chapter focuses primarily on sports fiction, it is also important to acknowledge the significance and popularity of documentary depictions of sport. Sport has been a frequent subject of documentary from the emergence of the form in the 1920s. Some of the most influential and innovative documentaries ever produced have featured sport prominently, including Dziga Vertov's *Man with a Movie Camera* (1929), Jean Vigo's *Taris, roi de l'eau (Jean Taris, Swimming Champion*, 1931), Leni Riefenstahl's *Olympia* (1938), and Kon Ichikawa's *Tokyo Olympia* (1965). This continues to be the case today, and the popular and critical success of recent productions such as *Senna* (2010) and the television series *Sunderland 'til I Die* (2018–2020) and *The Last Dance* (2020) indicates the continuing relevance of the documentary approach—in both theatrically released productions and the televisual/online experience. Sports documentaries have enjoyed not just significant commercial success and popularity with audiences but also considerable critical acclaim, with sports-themed productions winning the Best Documentary feature Academy Award in 2017 (*O.J.: Made in America* [2016]), 2018 (*Icarus* [2017]), and 2019 (*Free Solo* [2018]) (Sheppard & Vogan, 2020, p. 1).

REFERENCES

Alexander, M., Lenahan, P., & Pavlov. A. (Eds.), (1999). *Cinemeducation: A comprehensive guide to using film in medical education*. London: CRC Press.

Altman, R. (1999). *Film/genre*. London: BFI Publishing.

American Film Institute. (2008). America's 10 greatest films in 10 classic genres. *AFI.* https://web.archive.org/web/20190202004049/https://www.afi.com/10top10/.

Ardolino, F. (1988). *Bull Durham, Field of Dreams,* and *Eight Men Out. Journal of Popular Film and Television, 18*(2), 43–51.

Ardolino, F. (2003). From Christ-like folk hero to bumbling Bacchus: Filmic images of Babe Ruth, 1920–1992. In S. C. Wood & J. D. Pincus (Eds.), *Reel baseball: Essays and interviews on the national pastime, Hollywood and American culture* (pp. 107–119). Jefferson, NC: McFarland & Company.

Ashton, T. (2013). *Soccer in Spain: Politics, literature and film.* Lanham, MD: Scarecrow Press.

Austin, G. (1996). *Contemporary French cinema.* Manchester, U.K.: Manchester University Press.

Babington, B. (2014). *The sports film: Games people play.* London: Wallflower Press.

Bairner, A. (2001). *Sport, nationalism, and globalization.* New York: State University of New York Press.

Baker, A. (1997). A left/right combination: Populism and depression era boxing films. In A. Baker & T. Boyd (Eds.), *Out of bounds: Sports, media, and the politics of identity* (pp. 161–174). Bloomington: Indiana University Press.

Baker, A. (2003). *Contesting identities: Sports in American film* Champaign: University of Illinois Press.

Bale, J. (1986). Sport and national identity: A geographical view. *British Journal of Sports History, 3*(1), 18–41.

Barthes, R. (1977). *Image-music-text* (Stephen Heath, Trans.). London: Fontana Press.

Bennett, B. (2019). *Cycling and cinema.* London: Goldsmiths Press.

Bergan, R. (1982). *Sports in the movies.* Orange, NJ: Proteus.

Betts, J. R. (1974). *America's sporting heritage: 1850–1950.* Boston: Addison-Wesley.

Billig, M. (1995). *Banal nationalism.* London: Sage Publications.

Biltereyst, D., & Vande Winkel, R. (2020). Sport films and "banal" nationalism in interwar Belgium: Flandria film, mythomoteurs and the cult of the "Flandriens." In S. Crosson (Ed.), *Sport, film, and national culture* (pp. 79–92). New York: Routledge.

Bonzel, K. (2006). Soccer to the rescue: How the *Miracle of Berne* gave Germans back their identity—twice. *Sporting Traditions, 22*(2), 1–12.

Bonzel, K. (2020). *National pastimes: Cinema, sports, and nation (sports, media, and society).* Lincoln: University of Nebraska Press.

Bordwell, D., & Thompson, K. (2010). *Film art: An introduction* (9th ed.). New York: McGraw-Hill.

Bowden, M. (1994). Jerusalem, Dover Beach, and Kings Cross: Imagined places as metaphors of the British class struggle in *Chariots of Fire* and *The Loneliness of the Long Distance Runner.* In S. C. Aitken & L. E. Zonn (Eds.), *Place, power, situation and spectacle: Geography of film* (pp. 69–100). Lanham, MD: Rowman & Littlefield.

Boyle, E., Millington, B., & Vertinsky, P. (2006). Representing the female pugilist: Narratives of race, gender, and disability in *Million Dollar Baby. Sociology of Sport Journal, 23*(2), 99–116.

Briley, R. (2011). *The baseball film in postwar America: A critical study, 1948–1962.* Jefferson, NC: McFarland & Company.

Briley, R., Schoenecke, M. K. & Carmichael, D. A. (Eds.). (2008). *All-stars and movie stars: Sports in film and history.* Lexington: University Press of Kentucky.

Brody, R. (2019, November 19). The airbrushed racing history of "Ford v Ferrari." *The New Yorker.* https://www.newyorker.com/culture/the-front-row/the-airbrushed-racing-history-of-ford-v-ferrari.

Brown, D. & Bryant, J. (2006). Sports Content on U.S. Television. In A. A. Raney & J. Bryant (Eds.), *Handbook of sports and media* (pp. 77–104). Mahwah, NJ: Lawrence Erlbaum Associates.

Brūveris, K. (2016). Sport, cinema and the national imaginary in Dream Team: 1935. *Studies in Eastern European Cinema*, 8(1), 49–61.

Burns, G. (1987). *The sports pages: A critical bibliography of twentieth-century American novels and stories featuring baseball, basketball, football, and other athletic pursuits*. Lanham, MD: The Scarecrow Press.

Buscemi, F. (2020). Primo Carnera, propaganda and Mussolini's international legitimisation: the boxer who was a passport for fascism. In S. Crosson (Ed.), *Sport, film, and national culture* (pp. 126–143). New York: Routledge.

Butler, A. C., Zaromb, F. M., Lyle, K. B., & Roediger, H. L. (2009). Using popular films to enhance classroom learning: The good, the bad, and the interesting. *Psychological Sciences*, 20(9), 1161–1168.

Camy, J., & Camy, G. (2016). *Sport et cinéma*. Paris: Éditions du Bailli de Suffren.

Capraro, A. M., & Vargas, P. P. I. (2020). Football, national culture and politics in Brazil in 1970: *O Ano em Que Meus Pais Saíram de Férias (The Year My Parents Went on Vacation)*. In S. Crosson (Ed.), *Sport, film, and national Culture* (pp. 195–205). New York: Routledge.

Carlson, L. H. (1998). Review of *Diamonds in the Dark*: America, baseball, and the movies. *Journal of Sport History*, 25(2), 360–362.

Cashmore, E. (2000). *Sports culture: An A–Z guide*. New York: Routledge.

Caudwell, J. (2008). *Girlfight*: Boxing women. *Sport in Society*, 11(2–3), 227–239.

CBS News. (2019, November 9). "Ford v Ferrari" looks at a racing rivalry that "transcends sport." https://www.cbsnews.com/news/ford-v-ferrari-movie-greatest-car-racing-rivalry-in-history-to-play-out-on-big-screen/.

Cermak, I. (2017). *The cinema of hockey: Four decades of the game on screen*. Jefferson, NC: McFarland & Company.

Collins, J. (1993). Genericity in the nineties: Eclectic irony and the new sincerity. In J. Collins, H. Radner, & A. Preacher (Eds.), *Film theory goes to the movies* (pp. 242–263). New York: Routledge.

Cook, P. (1982). Masculinity in crisis? *Screen*, 23(3–4), 39–46.

Crawford, S. A. (1988). The sport film—Its cultural significance. *Journal of Physical Education, Recreation & Dance*, 59(6), 45–49.

Crosson, S. (2013). *Sport and film*. New York: Routledge.

Crosson, S. (2017). Sport and Christianity in American cinema: "The beloved grew fat and kicked" (Deuteronomy 32:15). In A. Adogame, N. J. Watson, & A. Parker (Eds.), *Global perspectives on sports and Christianity* (pp. 225–242). New York: Routledge.

Crosson, S. (2019). *Gaelic Games on film: From silent films to Hollywood hurling, horror and the emergence of Irish cinema*. Cork: Cork University Press.

Crosson, S. (Ed.). (2020). *Sport, film, and national culture*. New York: Routledge.

Croteau, D., & Hoynes, W. (2003). *Media society: Industries, images and audiences*. Thousand Oaks, CA: Pine Forge Press.

Cummins, R. G. (2006). Sports fiction: Critical and empirical perspectives. In A. A. Raney & J. Bryant (Eds.), *Handbook of sports and media* (pp. 131–146). Mahwah, NJ: Lawrence Erlbaum Associates.

Cunningham, J. (2004). *Hungarian Cinema: From coffee house to multiplex*. London: Wallflower Press.

Dahlén, P. (2020). Sport and national culture in Swedish film. In S. Crosson (Ed.), *Sport, film, and national culture* (pp. 94–111). New York: Routledge.

Debruge, P. (2019, August 30). Christian Bale and Matt Damon in "Ford v Ferrari." *Variety*. https://variety.com/2019/film/reviews/ford-v-ferrari-review-1203319686/.

Denzin, N. D. (2002). *Reading race: Hollywood and the cinema of racial violence*. London: Sage.

Diawara, M. (2004). Black spectatorship: Problems of identification and resistance. In L. Braudy & M. Cohen (Eds.), *Film theory and criticism* (6th ed.) (pp. 892–893). New York: Oxford University Press.

DiBartolo, M. C., & Seldomridge, L. A. (2009). Cinemeducation: Teaching end-of-life issues using feature films. *Journal of Gerotological Nursing, 35*(8), 30–36.

Dickerson, G. E. (1991). *The cinema of baseball: Images of America, 1929–1989*. Westport, CT: Meckler.

Didinger, R., & Macnow, G. (2009). *The ultimate book of sports movies: Featuring the 100 greatest sports films of all time*. Philadelphia, PA: Running Press.

Disney Movies List. (n.d.) List of Disney sports movies. https://disneymovieslist.com/list-of-disney-sports-movies/.

Dolan, P., & Connolly, J. (Eds.). (2017). *Sport and national identities: Globalization and conflict*. New York: Routledge.

Elmwood, V. A. (2008). "Just some bum from the neighborhood": The resolution of post–civil rights tension and heavyweight public sphere discourse in *Rocky*. In R. Briley, M. K. Schoenecke, & D. A. Carmichael (Eds.), *All-stars and movie stars: Sports in film and history* (pp. 172–198). Lexington: University Press of Kentucky.

Engle, J. (2015). *Surfing in the movies: A critical history*. Jefferson, NC: McFarland & Company.

Englert, B. (2018). The Hollywood sports film—Visualizing hidden and familiar aspects of American sport. *Historical Social Research/Historische Sozialforschung, 43*(2), 165–180.

ESPN Press Room. (2008, March 3). ESPN Films established. https://espnpressroom.com/us/press-releases/2008/03/espn-films-established/.

Fodor, P. (2017). Erasing, rewriting, and propaganda in the Hungarian sport films of the 1950s. *Hungarian Historical Review, 6*(2), 328–354.

Free, M. (2012, July 7–9). Envy, jealousy, guilt and the construction of whiteness in contemporary Hollywood sport films. Paper presented at the Images of Whiteness Conference, Mansfield College, Oxford University. https://dspace.mic.ul.ie/bitstream/handle/10395/2463/Free%2C%20M.%20%282012%29%20Envy%2C%20Jealousy%2C%20Guilt%20and%20the....pdf?sequence=2&isAllowed=y.

Friedman, L. D. (2020). *Sports movies (Quick takes: Movies and popular culture)*. New Brunswick, NJ: Rutgers University Press.

The Futon Critic. (2016). ESPN Films' "O.J.: Made in America" seen by more than 35 million people. http://www.thefutoncritic.com/ratings/2016/06/27/espn films-oj-made-in-amer ica-seen-by-more-than-35-million-people-592114/20160627espn01/.

Garioni, C. (2017). *Fuori campo—Il cinema racconta lo sport*. Rome: Delos Digital.

Gehring, W. D. (1988). *Handbook of American Film Genres*. New York: Greenwood.

Giardina, M. D., & McCarthy, C. (2005). The popular racial order of urban America: Sport, identity, and the politics of culture. *Cultural Studies ↔ Critical Methodologies, 5*(2), 145–173.

Glynn, S. (2018). *The British football film*. Basingstoke, U.K.: Palgrave Macmillan.

Glynn, S. (2020). Cricket, film, and British national identity: On a sticky wicket? In S. Crosson (Ed.), *Sport, film, and national culture* (pp. 161–174). New York: Routledge.

Good, H. (1996). *Diamonds in the dark: America, baseball, and the movies*. Lanham, MD: Scarecrow Press.

Grainger, A., Newman, J., & Andrews, D. (2006). Sport, the media and the construction of race. In A. Raney & B. Jennings (Eds.), *Handbook of sports and media* (pp. 447–467). Mahwah, NJ: Lawrence Erlbaum Associates.

Grindon, L. (1996). Body and soul: The structure of meaning in the boxing film genre. *Cinema Journal*, 35(4), 54–69.

Grindon, L. (2011). *Knockout: The boxer and boxing in American cinema*. Jackson: University Press of Mississippi.

Hall, S. (1973/1980). Encoding/decoding. In S. Hall, D. Hobson, A. Lowe, & P. Willis (Eds.), *Culture, media, language* (pp. 128–38). London: Hutchinson.

Hammond, P. (2019, November 12). Matt Damon and Christian Bale excel in race picture with a winning formula. *Deadline*. https://deadline.com/video/ford-v-ferrari-review-matt-damon-christian-bale-james-mangold/.

Henley, M. (2020). Netball and national identity in Aotearoa New Zealand cinema newsreels 1930–1959: "There's a new life in the sporting world." In S. Crosson (Ed.), *Sport, film, and national culture* (pp. 177–194). New York: Routledge.

Hess-Lüttich, E. W. B. (2007). (Pseudo-)argumentation in TV-debates. *Journal of Pragmatics*, 39(8), 1360–1370.

Hill, J. (2005). Sport stripped bare: Deconstructing working-class masculinity in "This Sporting Life." *Men and Masculinities*, 7(4), 405–423.

Holly, W. (1994). Confrontainment: Politik als schaukampf im fernsehen. In L. Bosshart & W. Hoffman-Riem (Eds.), *Medienlust und mediennutz: Unterhaltung als öffentliche kommunikation* (pp. 421–434). München: Ölschläger.

Holt, R. (1990). *Sport and the British: A modern history*. New York: Oxford University Press.

Jacobson, M. F. (2006). *Roots too: White ethnic revival in post–civil rights America*. Cambridge, MA: Harvard University Press.

Jarvis, B. (2006). New York, 9/11. In C. Lindner (Ed.), *Urban space and cityscapes: Perspectives from modern and contemporary culture* (pp. 49–63). New York: Routledge.

Jenkins, H. (2006). *Convergence culture: Where old and new media collide*. New York: New York University Press.

Jones, G. (2005). "Down on the floor and give me ten sit-ups": British sports feature film. *Film & History*, 35(2), 29–40.

Jordan, C. (2003). *Movies and the Reagan presidency: Success and ethics*. Westport, CT: Praeger.

Jouan-Westlund, A. (2006). L'imaginaire populaire Franco-Américain dans *les Triplettes De Belleville*. *The French Review*, 79(6), 1195–1205.

Jowett, G. (1976). *Film: The democratic art*. Boston: Little, Brown and Co.

Kibby, M. D. (1998). Nostalgia for the masculine: Onward to the past in sports films of the eighties. *Canadian Journal of Film Studies*, 7(1), 16–28.

King, C. R. (2006). Vanishing points: Reframing Indianness in recent sport documentaries. In C. R. King and D. J. Leonard (Eds.), *Visual economies of/in motion: Sport and film (cultural critique)* (pp. 121–134). Frankfurt am Main: Peter Lang.

King, C. R., & Leonard, D. J. (Eds.). (2006). *Visual economies of/in motion: Sport and film (cultural critique)*. Frankfurt am Main: Peter Lang.

Leab, D. J. (1979). The blue collar ethnic in bicentennial America: *Rocky* (1976). In J. E. O'Connor & M. A. Jackson (Eds.), *American history/American film: Interpreting the Hollywood image* (pp. 257–272). New York: Ungar.

Lichtenfeld, E. (2014). "I, of the tiger": Self and self-obsession in the *Rocky* series. In C. Holmlund (Ed.), *The ultimate Stallone reader: Sylvester Stallone as star, icon, auteur* (pp. 75–97). London: Wallflower Press.

Lieberman, V. (2014). *Sports heroines on film: A critical study of cinematic women athletes, coaches and owners.* Jefferson, NC: McFarland & Company.

Lin, T.-Y. (2020). Reconstructing Taiwanese national identity in the sports film: Small nation, sports and cultural heterogeneity. In S. Crosson (Ed.), *Sport, film, and national culture* (pp. 224–236). New York: Routledge.

Lindner, K. (2011). Bodies in action: Female athleticism on the cinema screen. *Feminist Media Studies, 11*(3), 321–345.

Lindsay, V. (1915). *Art of the moving picture.* New York: Macmillan.

Lopez, D. (1993). *Film by genre.* Jefferson. N.C.: McFarland & Co.

Manchel, F. (1980). *Great sports movies.* New York: Franklin Watts.

McDougall, A. (2017). Eyes on the ball: Screening football in East German cinema. *Studies in Eastern European Cinema, 8*(1), 4–18.

McKernan, L. (1996). Sport and the first films. In C. Williams (Ed.), *Cinema: The beginnings and the future* (pp. 107–116). London: University of Westminster Press.

Miller, T. (1990). The dawn of an imagined community: Australian sport on film. *Sporting Traditions, 7*(1), 48–59.

Miller, T. (1994). Film. In W. Vamplew, K. Moore, J. O'Hara, R. Cashman, & I. F. Jobling (Eds.), *The Oxford companion to Australian sport* (2nd ed.) (pp. 163–165). Melbourne: Oxford University Press.

Mithaiwala, M. (2019, September 24). Why "Ford v Ferrari's" title is different in Europe (& why it's bad). *Screen Rant.* https://screenrant.com/ford-ferrari-title-le-mans-66-bad-why/.

Monaco, J. (2000). *How to read a film: The world of movies, media and multimedia, language, history, theory.* New York: Oxford University Press.

Morley, D. (1980). *The nationwide audience structure and decoding.* Television Monograph No. 11. London: British Film Institute.

Mosher, S. D. (1983). The white dreams of God: The mythology of sport films. *Arena Review, 7*(2), 15–19.

Münsterberg, H. (1916). *The photoplay: A psychological study.* New York: D. Appleton and Co.

Neale, S. (2000). *Genre and Hollywood.* London: Routledge.

Nilsson, J. (2000). Take me back to the ball game: Nostalgia and hegemonic masculinity in *Field of Dreams. Canadian Review of American Studies, 30*(1), 52–72

Núñez, M. T., & Garcia, A. J. (2014). Analyzing and teaching diversity and gender with a case study. *International Journal of Humanities and Social Science, 4*(9), 70–77.

Nystrom, D. (2009). *Hard hats, rednecks, and macho men: Class in 1970s American cinema.* New York: Oxford University Press.

O'Boyle, N., & Free, M. (2020). Introduction. In N. O'Boyle & M. Free (Eds.), *Sport, the media and Ireland: Interdisciplinary perspectives* (pp. 1–25). Cork: Cork University Press.

Oriard, M. (1982). *Dreaming of heroes: American sports fiction, 1868–1980.* Chicago: Nelson-Hall.

Oriard, M. (2001). *King football: Sport and spectacle in the golden age of radio and newsreels, movies and magazines, the weekly and the daily press.* Chapel Hill: University of North Carolina Press.

Paino, T. D. (2001). *Hoosiers* in a different light: Forces of change v. the power of nostalgia. *Journal of Sport History, 28*(1), 63–80.

Pearson, D. W., Curtis, R. L., Haney, C. A., & Zhang, J. J. (2003). Sport films: Social dimensions over time, 1930–1995. *Journal of Sport and Social Issues, 27*(2), 145–161.

Pearson, D. W., & Lam, E. T. C. (2015). Sport theme feature film analysis: A complimentary instructional technique within sport management. *Journal of Physical Education and Sports Management, 2*(2), 26–40.

Place-Verghnes, F. (2007). Douce France? *Les triplettes de Belleville*, de Sylvain Chomet. In P. Floquet (Ed.), *CinémAction: "CinémAnimationS"* (pp. 97–103). Paris: Corlet.

Porter, D., & Smith, A. (Eds.). (2004). *Sport and national identity in the post-war world.* New York: Routledge.

Poulton, E. (2006). "Lights, camera, aggro!" Readings of "celluloid hooliganism." *Sport in Society, 9*(3), 403–422.

Poulton, E., & Roderick, M. (2008). Introducing sport in films. *Sport in Society, 11*(2–3), 107–116.

Poulton, E., & Roderick, M. (Eds.). (2009). *Sport in films.* New York: Routledge.

Ransom, A. J. (2014). Bollywood goes to the stadium: Gender, national identity, and sport film in Hindi. *Journal of Film and Video, 66*(4), 34–49.

Redhead, S. (2007). This sporting life: The realism of the football factory. *Soccer and Society, 8*(1), 90–108.

Regester, C. (2003). From the gridiron and the boxing ring to the cinema screen: The African American athlete in pre-1950 cinema. *Sport in Society, 6*(2–3), 269–292.

Rodríguez Díaz, Á. (2010). Spain's social values through film: Films about sports. In P. Dine & S. Crosson (Eds.), *Sport, representation and evolving identities in Europe* (pp. 119–140). Frankfurt am Main: Peter Lang.

Romaguera i Ramió, J. (2003). *Presencia del deporte en el cine español, un primer inventario.* Sevilla: Fundación Andalucía Olímpica y Consejo Superior de Deportes.

Roubach, S. (2007). In the name of the father, the daughter and Eddie Scrap: Trinitarian theology in *Million Dollar Baby. Journal of Religion and Film, 11*(1). https://digitalcommons. unomaha.edu/jrf/vol11/iss1/2/.

Rowe, D. (1998). If you film it, will they come? Sports on film. *Journal of Sport & Social Issues, 22*(4), 350–359.

Rowe, D. (2004). *Sport, culture and the media* (2nd ed.). Berkshire, U.K.: Open University Press.

Sarris, A. (1980). Why sports movies don't work. *Film Comment, 16*(6), 49–53.

Schirato, T., & Webb, J. (2004). *Reading the visual.* Sydney: Allen & Unwin.

Sheppard, S. N. (2020). *Sporting Blackness: Race, embodiment, and critical muscle memory on screen.* Berkeley: University of California Press.

Sheppard, S. N., & Vogan, T. (Eds.). (2020). *Sporting realities: Critical readings of the sports documentary.* Lincoln: University of Nebraska Press.

Sklar, R. (1976). *Movie-made America: A cultural history of American movies.* London: Vintage.

Sobchack, V. (1997). Baseball in the post-American cinema, or life in the minor leagues. In A. Baker & T. Boyd (Eds.), *Out of bounds: Sports, media and the politics of identity* (pp. 175–198). Bloomington: Indiana University Press.

Springwood, C. F. (1996). *Cooperstown to Dyersville: A geography of baseball.* Boulder, CO: Westview Press.

Streible, D. (2008). *Fight pictures: A history of boxing and early cinema.* Berkeley: University of California Press.

Sullivan, D. B. (2006). Broadcast television and the game of packaging sports. In A. A. Raney & J. Bryant (Eds.), *Handbook of sports and media* (pp. 131–146). Mahwah, NJ: Lawrence Erlbaum Associates.

Tannert, C. (2019, November 14). "Ford vs. Ferrari": The real story behind the most bitter rivalry in auto racing. *Forbes*. https://www.forbes.com/wheels/news/ford-vs-ferrari-the-real-story-behind-the-most-bitter-rivalry-in-auto-racing/.

Thomas, M. W. (2020). Contesting visions of Ethiopia in two Amharic sports films: Between film festivals and local commercial cinema. In S. Crosson (Ed.), *Sport, film, and national culture* (pp. 206–223). New York: Routledge.

Tomasulo, F. P. (2007). 1976: Movies and cultural contradictions. In L. D. Friedman (Ed.), *American cinema of the 1970s: Themes and variations* (pp. 157–181). Oxford: Berg.

Tomlinson, A. (1996). Sports movies and the study of sport—comments on teaching and the hermeneutic. In J. O'Neill, E. Murdoch, & S. Fleming (Eds.), *Physical education, sport and leisure: A collection of working papers* (pp. 57–76). Eastbourne, U.K.: Chelsea School Research Centre.

Tomlinson, A. (1999). Images of sport—Situating *Chariots of Fire*. In A. Tomlinson (Ed.), *The game's up: Essays in the cultural analysis of sport, leisure and popular culture* (pp. 233–246). Aldershot, U.K.: Arena, Ashgate Publishing.

Tudor, D. V. (1997). *Hollywood's vision of team sports: Heroes, race, and gender*. New York: Garland Publishing.

Vogan, T. (2014). *Keepers of the flame: NFL Films and the rise of sports media*. Urbana: University of Illinois Press.

Vogan, T. (2020). *The boxing film: A cultural and transmedia history (screening sports)*. New Brunswick, NJ: Rutgers University Press.

Wallenfeldt, J. H. (1989). *Sports movies*. New York: CineBooks.

Wenner, L. A. (Ed.). (1998) *MediaSport*. New York: Routledge.

Whannel, G. (2000). Sport and the media. In J. Coakley & E. Dunning (Eds.), *Handbook of sports studies* (pp. 291–308). London: Sage.

Whannel, G. (2008). Winning and losing respect: Narratives of identity in sport films. *Sport in Society*, 11(2–3), 195–208.

Wiedenfeld, G. (2016). The conservative backlash argument controverted: Carnivalesque, comedy, and respect in *Rocky. Critical Studies in Media Communication*, 33(2), 168–180.

Wilkinson, R. (1984). *American tough: The tough-guy tradition and American character*. Westport, CT: Greenwood.

Williams, R. (2006). *Sports cinema—100 movies: The best of Hollywood's athletic heroes, losers, myths, and misfits*. Pompton Plains, NJ: Limelight Editions.

Wilson, A. H., Blake, B. J., Taylor, G. A., & Hannings, G. (2013). Cinemeducation: Teaching family assessment skills using full-length movies. *Public Health Nursing*, 30(3), 239–245.

Wood, C., & Benigni, V. (2006). The coverage of sports on cable TV. In A. A. Raney & J. Bryant (Eds.), *Handbook of sports and media* (pp. 147–169). Mahwah, NJ: Lawrence Erlbaum Associates.

Zucker, H. M., & Babich, L. J. (1987) *Sports films: A complete reference*. Jefferson, NC: McFarland & Company.

Filmography

Abbott, E., & Greenhut, R. (Producers), & Marshall, P. (Director). (1992). *A league of their own* [Motion Picture]. USA: Parkway Productions.

Ackerley, T., Robbie, M., Rogers, S., & Unkeless, Bryan (Producers), & Gillespie, C. (Director). (2017). *I, Tonya* [Motion Picture]. USA: LuckyChap Entertainment; Clubhouse Pictures; AI Film.

Arias-Salgado, G., Lebret, A., Longoria, Á., & Manso, L. (Producers), & Fesser, J. (Director). (2018). *Campeones (Champions)* [Motion Picture]. Spain: Películas Pendelton; Morena Films; Movistar+; TVE.

Aufiero, D., Hoberman, D., Lieberman, T., Kavanaugh, R., Tamasy, P., & Wahlberg, M. (Producers), & Russell, D. O. (Director). (2010). *The fighter* [Motion Picture]. USA: Closest to the Hole Productions; Mandeville Films; Relativity Media; Protozoa Pictures.

Bandík, E., & Canky, V. (Producers), & Solan, P. (Director). (1963). *Boxer a smrt (the boxer and death)* [Motion Picture]. Czechoslovakia: Studio Umeleckých Filmu Praha.

Barber, G., De Luca, M., & Myers, M. (Producers), & Schnabel, M. (Director). (2008). *The love guru* [Motion Picture]. USA: Spyglass Entertainment.

Berman, P. S. (Producer), & Brown, C. (Director). (1944). *National velvet* [Motion Picture]. USA: Metro-Goldwyn-Mayer.

Bevan, T., Fellner, E., & Gay-Rees, J. (Producers), & Kapadia, A. (Director). (2010). *Senna* [Motion Picture]. UK/France: StudioCanal; Working Title Films; Midfield Films.

Caprino, I. (Producer), & Caprino, I. (Director). (1975). *Flåklypa Grand Prix (The Pinchcliffe Grand Prix)* [Motion Picture]. Norway: Caprino Studios.

Chadha, G., & Nayare, D. (Producers), & Chadha, G. (Director). (2002). *Bend it like Beckham* [Motion Picture]. UK/USA/Germany: Kintop Pictures; Bend It Films; Roc Media; Road Movies Filmproduktion.

Chernin, P., Topping, J., & Mangold, J. (Producers), & Mangold, J. (Director). (2019). *Ford v Ferrari* [Motion Picture]. USA: 20th Century Studios.

Ciardi, M., Gray, G., & Johnson, M. (Producers), & Hancock, J. L. (Director). (2002). *The rookie* [Motion Picture]. USA: Walt Disney Pictures.

Clein, J., & Mead, E. (Producers), & Clein, J. (Director). (1939). *Keep punching* [Motion Picture]. USA: M.C. Pictures, Inc.

Coblenz, W., & Finnegan, B. (Producers), & Hiller, A. (Director). (1992). *The Babe* [Motion Picture]. USA: Universal Pictures.

Cogan, D., & Fogel, B. (Producers), & Fogel, B. (Director). (2017). *Icarus* [Motion Picture]. USA: Alex Productions; Diamond Docs; Impact Partners.

Colson, C., Boyle, D., & Graf, R. (Producers), & Faris, V. & Dayton, J. (Directors). (2017). *Battle of the sexes* [Motion Picture]. USA/UK: TSG Entertainment; Decibel Films; Cloud Eight Films.

Cook, N. A., & Young, C. (Producers), & Lupino, I., & Anderson, J. (Directors). (1951). *Hard, fast and beautiful!* [Motion Picture]. USA: RKO Radio Pictures.

Cort, R. W., Field, T., & Swedlin, R. (Producers), & Glaser, P. M. (Director). (1994) *The air up there* [Motion Picture]. USA: Hollywood Pictures; Interscope Communications; PolyGram Filmed Entertainment; Nomura Babcock & Brown.

Crowe, C., Brooks, J. L., Mark, L., & Sakai, R. (Producers), & Crowe, C. (Director). (1996). *Jerry Maguire* [Motion Picture]. USA: TriStar Pictures; Gracie Films; Vinyl Films.

Cummings, J. (Producer), & Wood, S. (Director). (1949). *The Stratton story* [Motion Picture]. USA: Metro-Goldwyn-Mayer.

Dill, S., & Hayes, E. (Producers), & Chai Vasarhelyi, E., & Chin, J. (Directors). (2018). *Free solo* [Motion Picture]. USA: Little Monster Films; Itinerant Media; Parkes+MacDonald; Image Nation; National Geographic Documentary Films.

Eastwood, C., Ruddy, A. S., Rosenberg, T., & Haggis, P. (Producers), & Eastwood, C. (Director). (2004). *Million dollar baby* [Motion Picture]. USA: Lakeshore Entertainment; Malpaso Productions.

Eaton, A., Fellner, E., Oliver, B., Morgan, P., Grazer, B., & Howard, R. (Producers), & Howard, R. (Director). (2013). *Rush* [Motion Picture]. USA/UK/Germany: Cross Creek Pictures; Exclusive Media; Working Title Films; Imagine Entertainment; Revolution Films.

Edelman, E., & Waterlow, C. (Producers), & Edelman, E. (Director). (2016). *O.J.: Made in America* [Documentary series]. USA: ESPN Films; Laylow Films.

Fellows, R., & Wallis, H. B. (Producers), & Bacon, L., & Howard, W. K. (Directors). (1940). *Knute Rockne, all American.* [Motion Picture]. USA: Warner Bros.

Franfilmdis (Producer), & Vigo, J. (Director). (1931). *Taris, roi de l'eau (Jean Taris, swimming champion)* [Motion Picture]. France: Franfilmdis.

Freeman, E. (Producer), & Curtiz, M. (Director). (1951). *Jim Thorpe—all-American* [Motion Picture]. USA: Warner Bros.

Fried, R. N., & Woods, C. (Producers), & Anspaugh, D. (Director). (1993). *Rudy* [Motion Picture]. USA: Tristar Pictures.

Gains, H., Robbins, B., & Tollin, M. (Producers), & Tollin, M. (Director). (2003). *Radio* [Motion Picture]. USA: Columbia Pictures; Revolution Studios; Tollin/Robbins Productions.

Golder, L. (Producer), & Fraser, H. L. (Director). (1938). *Spirit of youth* [Motion Picture]. USA: Globe Pictures Corp.

Goldwyn, S., & Cameron Menzies, W. (Producers), & Wood, S. (Director). (1942). *The pride of the Yankees* [Motion Picture]. USA: Samuel Goldwyn Productions.

Gordon, L., & Gordon, C. (Producers), & Robinson, P. A. (Director). (1989). *Field of dreams* [Motion Picture]. USA: Gordon Company.

Gordy, B., & Cohen, R. (Producers), & Badham, J. (Director). (1976). *The Bingo Long Traveling All-Stars & Motor Kings* [Motion Picture]. USA: Motown Productions.

Grant, J. E., & Mastroly, F. R. (Producers), & Tuttle, F. (Director). (1945). *The great John L.* [Motion Picture]. USA: Bing Crosby Productions.

Gray, G., & Ciardi, M. (Producers), & Core, E. (Director). (2006). *Invincible* [Motion Picture]. USA: Walt Disney Pictures.

Green, S., Griffin, M., & Renzi, M. (Producers), & Kusama, K. (Director). (2000). *Girlfight* [Motion Picture]. USA: Green/Renzi; Independent Film Channel (IFC).

Grollmann, C., Heckenbücker, C., & Trentmann, J. (Producers), & Deus, C. (Director). (2004). *Die Boxerin* [Motion Picture]. Germany: Credofilm; CH Media Berlin Brandenburg GmbH & Co. KG; Deutsche Film- und Fernsehakademie Berlin (DFFB); Fieber Film; Zweites Deutsches Fernsehen (ZDF).

Howard, R., Marshall, P., & Grazer, B. (Producers), & Howard, R. (Director). (2005). *Cinderella man* [Motion Picture]. USA: Miramax Films; Imagine Entertainment; Parkway Productions.

Jarecki, E., & Simpson, P. (Producers), & Jarecki, E. (Director). (2000). *The opponent* [Motion Picture]. USA: Edgewood Films; Think Tank Films.

Johnson, B, Kosove, A., & Netter, G. (Producers), & Hancock, J. L. (Director). (2009). *The blind side* [Motion Picture]. USA: Alcon Entertainment.

Johnson, M. (Producer), & Levinson, B. (Director). (1986). *The natural* [Motion Picture]. USA: Delphi II Productions.

Kemeny, J. (Producer), & Wrye, D. (Director). (1978). *Ice castles* [Motion Picture]. USA: Columbia Pictures.

Khan, A., Rao, K., & Roy Kapur, S. (Producers), & Tiwari, N. (Director). (2016). *Dangal* [Motion Picture]. India: Aamir Khan Productions; Walt Disney Pictures India.

Kramer, S. (Producer), & Robson, M. (Director). (1949). *Champion* [Motion Picture]. USA: Screen Plays; Stanley Kramer Productions.

Missel, R., & Rosenman, H. (Producers), & Zieff, H. (Director). (1979). *The main event* [Motion Picture]. USA: First Artists; Barwood Films.

Nides, T., Robbins, B., & Tollin, M. (Producers), & Robbins, B. (Director). (2001). *Hardball* [Motion Picture]. USA: Fireworks Pictures; Nides/McCormick Productions; Tollin/Robbins Productions.

Panahi, J. (Producer), & Panahi, J. (Director). (2006). *Offside* [Motion Picture]. Iran: Jafar Panahi Film Productions.

Pearlman, L., & Turner, L. (Executive Producers), & Judd, M., McIver, J., Kinross, C., Klasmer, I., Mallion, T., Donneky, A., Oldham, A., Parkin. A., & Soutar, D. (Directors). (2018–2020). *Sunderland 'til I die* [Documentary series]. UK: Fulwell 73.

Pillsbury, S. (Producer), & Sayles, J. (Director). (1988). *Eight men out* [Motion Picture]. USA: Orion Pictures Corporation.

Richardson, T. (Producer), & Richardson, T. (Director). (1962). *The loneliness of the long distance runner* [Motion Picture]. UK: Woodfall Film Productions; Seven Arts.

Riefenstahl, L. (Producer), & Riefenstahl, L. (Director). (1938). *Olympia* [Motion Picture]. Germany: Olympia-Film.

Roessell, D. (Producer), & Rash, S. (Director). (2006). *Bring it on: All or nothing* [Motion Picture]. USA: Beacon Pictures.

Steel, D., Landau, S. B., & Bydalek, J. (Producers), & Turteltaub, J. (Director). (1993). *Cool runnings* [Motion Picture]. USA: Walt Disney Pictures.

Taguchi, S. (Producer), & Ichikawa, K. (Director). (1965). 東京オリンピック *(Tokyo Olympiad)* [Motion Picture]. Japan: Organizing Committee for the Games of the XVIII Olympiad.

Tollin, M., & Polk, C. (Producers), & Hehir, J. (Director). (2020). *The last dance* [Documentary series]. USA: ESPN Films; Netflix; Mandalay Sports Media; NBA Entertainment.

Vereshchagin, L., Zlatopolskiy, A. Mikhalkov, N., Vasilyev, V., Yakovleva, E., Gurevich, S., & Utkin, A. (Producers). (2017). Движение вверх *(Going vertical)* (AKA *Three seconds*) [Motion Picture]. Russia: Three T Productions; Russia-1; Cinema Foundation.

Vidor, K., Rapf, H., & Thalberg, I. (Producers), & Vidor, K. (Director). (1931). *The champ* [Motion Picture]. USA: Metro-Goldwyn-Mayer.

VUFKU (Producer), & Vertov, D. (Director). (1929) *Chelovek s kino-apparatom (Man with a movie camera)* [Motion Picture] Soviet Union: VUFKU.

Weingarten, L. (Producer), & Cukor, G. (Director). (1952). *Pat and Mike* [Motion Picture]. USA: Metro-Goldwyn-Mayer.

Winkler, I., & Chartoff, R. (Producers), & Avildsen, J. G. (Director). (1976). *Rocky* [Motion Picture]. USA: Chartoff-Winkler Productions.

Winkler, I., & Chartoff, R. (Producers), & Scorsese, M. (Director). (1980) *Raging bull* [Motion Picture]. USA: United Artists.

Winkler, I., Chartoff, R., Winkler, C., Winkler, D., King-Templeton, K., & Stallone, S. (Producers), & Caple Jr., S. (Director). (2018). *Creed II* [Motion Picture]. USA: Metro-Goldwyn-Mayer Pictures; New Line Cinema; Chartoff-Winkler Productions.

Winkler, I., Chartoff, R., Winkler, C., Winkler, D., King-Templeton, K., & Stallone, S. (Producers), & Coogler, R. (Director). (2015). *Creed* [Motion Picture]. USA: Metro-Goldwyn-Mayer Pictures; New Line Cinema; Chartoff-Winkler Productions.

CHAPTER 56

....

SPORT, ADVERTISING, AND PROMOTIONAL CULTURE

....

STEVEN J. JACKSON

SPORT has emerged as one of the most powerful cultural forces in human history. From global mega-events, such as the Olympic Games and FIFA World Cup, to high-profile celebrity athletes like LeBron James and Serena Williams and popular consumer brands like Nike, sport is highly visible, popular, and influential. From an economic standpoint, estimates indicate that the global sports industry, its infrastructure, events, manufacturing, retail, and promotion, is worth as much as U.S.$700 billion per year, which is equivalent to 1% of the world's GDP (Klynveld Peat Marwick Goerdeler, 2016).

Arguably, sport's economic and cultural value as a commodity is due to its unique features and pivotal position within the media-sports-cultural complex (Rowe, 1999). This complex includes the entire entourage of sport personnel, sport organizations, media conglomerates, and corporate sponsors that, in combination, have transformed how sport is structured, produced, represented, and consumed. Moreover, this complex has played a fundamental role in incorporating sport within what Whitson (1998, p. 59) describes as a circuit of "global promotional culture." According to Whitson, global promotional culture involves maximization of revenue generation through (1) merchandising, (2) sponsorship and marketing of celebrity athletes who elevate the visibility of brands, and (3) the consolidation of ownership, combined with the integration of media technologies and platforms, in order to saturate the global landscapes of consumption.

With respect to advertising and promotional culture, contemporary sport is simultaneously an entertainment commodity and a cultural theme through which corporations seek to reach consumers. Hence, not only is sport a commodity that can be bought and sold in the form of live and media broadcast events; it is also a strategic cultural vehicle that corporations and their brands use to attract fans and consumers. It is within this context that we need to understand how and why sport features so prominently within contemporary advertising and promotional culture (Wernick, 1991). For example, before the COVID-19 pandemic, the World Advertising Research Center (2020) report on sport sponsorship investment estimated a global corporate spend of U.S.$48 billion. A key question then is: What are the unique features of sport that elevate its value and appeal to both advertisers and consumers? While there are no simple answers to this question, we do know that beyond the fact that it is one of human history's oldest cultural practices, sport is valued because (1) it attracts large, devoted, and global audiences; (2) it is cheaper to produce and translates well across languages; (3) it represents human drama and emotion in its purest form, where real athletes demonstrate the limits of the body; (4) it provides us with narratives of heroes, celebrities, and villains (Andrews & Jackson, 2001; Wenner, 2013; Whannel, 2002); and (5) it is associated with positive images of youth, health, and nationhood (Rowe, 1996). However, it is also important to note that the values of sport align seamlessly with those of the idealized version of consumer capitalism; that is, it is based on competition, achievement, efficiency, technology, and meritocracy.

This chapter is divided into three main sections. First, it outlines some key issues related to the social and economic impact of advertising on society: a basic understanding of when, why, and how advertising emerged as an industry. Highlighted are the unique features of sport that make it an attractive theme or vehicle within the broader realm of promotional culture, and in this light, a brief analysis considers how Nike operates as an image-based company. Second, the chapter explores some of the common theoretical approaches used within advertising theory and, in turn, offers the circuit of culture as one framework for understanding the complex interrelationships between production, representation, consumption, and regulation of commodities. Third, the analysis focuses on two key debates related to sport, advertising, and consumer culture, followed by a brief conclusion.

ISSUES

In order to understand the contemporary status of sport, advertising, and promotional culture it is essential to have some understanding of the origins and development of advertising and its links with consumer capitalism. Prior to the 1700s, sharing information about commodities, events, or services was denoted by the term *advertisen,* the Middle English word meaning "to notify." The advent of the Industrial Revolution (1760–1840) brought about fundamental changes in where and how people lived, the nature of the work they engaged in, and how they consumed. Beyond a rural-urban shift in populations, there were new forms of transportation, increased specialization of labor, and technological innovations that enabled mass production of commodities on a scale previously unimaginable.

The result was the emergence of a unique cultural-economic conjuncture where there was an ever-expanding surplus of commodities within an emerging capitalist system. This was, arguably, the historical moment representing the birth of advertising as an economic and cultural industry whose primary aim was to stimulate consumption. However, beyond its role in driving consumption (Featherstone, 1991; Miller, 1995), advertising underpinned, legitimated, and naturalized consumer capitalism as *the* dominant way of life (Bell, 1976; Ewen, 1976; Lury, 1996). Consequently, it has altered people's relationships with commodities and, in turn, the very basis of social identity (Cronin, 2000; Goldman, 1992; Kellner, 1995; Kilbourne, 1999). With respect to the latter point, over time our relationship with commodities has changed in two fundamental and interrelated ways. First, the sheer volume of commodities available has created opportunities for infinite consumption. Second has been a shift in how and why we consume commodities, from use value (function) to exchange value (relative trade worth) to symbolic value (status), such that consumption now represents a form of distinction, lifestyle, and identity. In combination, these two elementary changes have led to what has been described as the insatiable age, when "the seemingly boundless desire for consumer goods has become one of our society's most defining features" (Lewis, 2013, p. 54). In sum, advertising is much more than a basic form of communication that informs consumers about the nature, value, and use of products and services; rather, it has had a transformational impact on the global economy, lifestyles, identities, and, as will be later discussed, sustainability and the environment.

As previously noted, there is a wide range of characteristics that make sport a unique cultural theme for advertising, one that spans industries as varied as automobiles, technology, alcohol, and fashion. Here, the case of Adidas and the African American music group Run DMC is instructive. In 1986, Run DMC released a song titled "My Adidas." The song and the band's image, including their Adidas shoes and tracksuits, resonated with a new and emerging African American urban youth demographic. This was evident when the band's manager invited Adidas executive Angelo Anastasio to a concert at Madison Square Garden. Anastasio was shocked to see thousands of fans holding up their Adidas apparel during the song (Warnett, 2016) and eventually signed Run DMC to a million-dollar sponsorship deal. "My Adidas" was a watershed moment for the articulation of youth identity, hip-hop music, urban fashion, product placement, and a global sports brand that not only continues to influence popular culture but provided a new model for advertising and promotional culture.

If we want to understand some of the key issues related to sport, culture, and advertising within contemporary society, it would be difficult to find a better example than Nike. With a 2022 valuation of U.S.$34.7 billion, Nike is not the biggest corporation in the world, yet it remains the target of its competitors and the envy of larger companies for its ability to secure brand visibility and media coverage. In many ways, Nike defies description. Beyond being a popular and successful global corporation and sports brand, Nike is a business model, a cultural icon, a commodity sign, an athletic philosophy, a cultural contradiction, and the target of social justice activists. Summing up the polarized view of the brand, Goldman and Papson (1998, p. 2) state, "Nike has become the sign some people love to love and the sign others love to hate." Moreover, they offer insights into Nike's general advertising strategy that may explain its ability to navigate the challenging terrain of contemporary consumers. According to Goldman and Papson, Nike advertising is generally created and presented in one of two formats. The first is a motivational ethos that focuses on themes such as personal transcendence, achievement, and authenticity. This is arguably the predominant format and features both celebrity athletes and everyday people in ways that inspire others through representations of diversity or overcoming adversity or via performances that capture the purity and integrity of sport. Examples of recent Nike motivational ethos advertisements include "Dream Crazy" (with Colin Kaepernick) and "Dream Crazier" (with Serena Williams), "Find Your Greatness," and "What Are Little Girls Made Of." The second format of Nike advertising utilizes a sense of self-awareness that speaks "to savvy and jaded viewers about the glossy, staged exultations of one brand or another that daily assault us" (p. 3). This type of ad incorporates the "knowing wink," a strategy whereby Nike acknowledges that it knows that consumers know that Nike is trying to sell them something, so it is best to admit it and have fun with it. Examples of this format include classics such as NBA star Penny Hardaway and "Lil Penny," "Urban Hide and Seek," and "Musical Chairs" at a basketball game. In combination, Nike's two formats enable the company and its longtime advertising and creative agency, Wieden & Kennedy, to produce an "an advertising discourse that is able to present itself as legitimate public discourse" (p. 3).

Over the past three decades a growing body of critical sport studies literature has examined Nike advertising (and other media representations) and its role in representing various social identities, including gender, race, sexuality, and national identity. Most of these analyses acknowledge the utility of critically reading and interrogating sport, including events, celebrities, and advertising, as social texts that offer "unique points of access to the constitutive meanings and power relations of the larger world we inhabit" (Birrell & McDonald, 2000, p. 3). For example, critical textual analyses of Nike advertisements have examined gender with respect to representing or resisting stereotypes (Arsenault & Fawzy, 2001; Cole & Hribar, 1995; Davis & Delano, 1992; Duquin, 1989; Dworkin & Messner, 2002; Grow, 2006, 2008; Helstein, 2003; LaFrance, 1998; Lucas, 2000; Messner, 2002; Shao, Desmarais, & Weaver, 2014; Wenner, 1991; White & Gillett, 1994; Worsching, 2000).

Generally speaking, these Nike ads are intended to empower girls and women to participate in sport and physical activity, although things don't always go according to plan. For example, in 1995, in conjunction with ad agency Wieden & Kennedy and based on research from the Women's Sport Foundation, Nike released a 30-second commercial titled "If You Let Me Play." In a format reminiscent of a public service announcement, 19 girls appear voicing a range of messages about how playing sport will empower them by enhancing their self-esteem and confidence and improving their health and well-being. The commercial received positive feedback from many corners, including feminists. However, according to Lucas (2000, p. 155), although the commercial aims to increase girls' participation in sports, "the basic structure of the text . . . reinforces and contributes to dominant ideologies by normalizing the idea that girls need permission to play sports." A few scenes in the ad raised concerns. For example, midway through the commercial one young girl pictured sitting on a swing looks into the camera and says, "If you let me play I'll be more likely to leave a man who beats me." While the intention was likely to reinforce the empowering nature of sport participation, critics questioned why a young girl should know or even be thinking about such a terrible thing. Still, the advertisement highlights several key features of Nike advertising, including the fact that they undertake research, monitor social trends, and engage in shock advertising.

There has also been a substantial body of critical literature related to Nike advertisements and race (cf. Andrews, 1996; Carrington, 2001; Cole, 1996; Cole & Andrews, 1996; Dyson, 1993; Fresco, 2020; McKay, 1995; Müller, van Zoonen, & de Roode, 2008; Spencer, 2004; Wilson & Sparks, 1996). In 2018, Nike celebrated the 30th anniversary of its original "Just Do It" campaign by releasing the "Dream Crazy" advertisement featuring controversial National Football League quarterback Colin Kaepernick (Intravia, Piquero, Piquero, & Byers, 2020). By thus aligning its brand with the Black Lives Matter movement, Nike demonstrated its commitment to engaging with contemporary cultural politics and being provocative.

To put the "Dream Crazy" campaign in context, in 2016 Kaepernick was a quarterback for the San Francisco 49ers football team. In a symbolic gesture of protest against racial injustice, police brutality, and systematic oppression of African Americans, he chose to sit rather than stand during the national anthem before a preseason game. For the remainder of the season he engaged in a silent protest by "taking a knee." Public reaction to Kaepernick's display was divided. While he received some support, he was condemned as disrespectful and anti-American by others. By September 2017 Kaepernick's protest had inspired a wider movement, prompting President Donald Trump to enter the debate, declaring that his actions were a "total disrespect of our heritage . . . a total disrespect of everything that we stand for," and that NFL owners should fire players who kneel during the national anthem (Associated Press, 2017). The next season Kaepernick became a free agent but remained unsigned by any NFL team. In response, he filed a grievance accusing NFL owners of collusion to exclude him from the league, although this was withdrawn after reaching a confidential agreement.

On September 3, 2018, Kaepernick tweeted a print ad that featured his image, the words "Believe in something. Even it means sacrificing everything," and the hashtag "Just Do It." Two days later, Nike released a two-minute video advertisement for the campaign that broadened Kaepernick's political protest to incorporate other celebrity athletes and wider issues of social justice. For example, the ad features basketball star LeBron James, tennis legend Serena Williams, and Kenyan runner Eliud Kipchoge, each accompanied by inspirational narratives about overcoming adversity and becoming world champions. Amid these celebrity athletes are images of less famous sportspeople, including wheelchair basketball player Megan Blunk, LGBTQ skateboarder Lacey Baker, and Muslim female boxer Zeina Nassar wearing a branded hijab, enabling Nike to demonstrate its commitment to diversity and inclusion. Judging by the swift and fervent public reaction, the advertisement achieved its objective. On the one hand, some longtime brand fans rebuked Kaepernick's perceived unpatriotic stance by sharing a #NikeBoycott hashtag on Twitter and burning their Nike apparel, and there were reports that the company's stock price dropped 3.2% (Mitra, 2019). However, this type of negative reaction was both limited and short-lived. The "Dream Crazy" campaign received enormous attention across a range of media platforms, sales surged, and Nike eventually won the 2019 Emmy award for Outstanding Advertisement (Mitra, 2019). This is Nike at its best in terms of the production and representation of a promotional campaign that articulates its brand and the motivational ethos of celebrity and everyday athletes and demonstrates being a progressive company through political activism. Some scholars, however, have offered alternative readings of the advertisement. For example, Hoffmann, Nyborg, Averhoff, and Olesen (2020) note that Nike strategically avoids any anti-American sentiment by having Kaepernick narrate the commercial, yet never showing any images of his actual protests. Instead, the commercial displays a series of individual athletes, each confronting their own challenges. The focus on the individual and individualism is a cornerstone of Nike advertising, evident in other campaigns linked to race and featuring celebrity athletes Michael Jordan, Tiger Woods, Serena Williams, and Kobe Bryant.

Ultimately, Nike advertising is about more than just selling shoes, as it "gives voice to important cultural contradictions that define our era [and represents] . . . a newly unfolding stage of commodity culture mixed with cultural politics" (Goldman & Papson, 1998, p. 3). While there is no denying that Nike embraces cultural politics, as highlighted in the "Dream Crazy" advertisement, the real contradiction lies in how the company itself operates. Arguably, the entire business model, brand, and promotional culture of Nike represent an illusion that masks the exploitation, tyranny, and limits of capitalism, dynamics explored later, in the Debates section.

Next, this chapter presents a brief overview of some of the theoretical and methodological approaches used in advertising and promotional culture research.

APPROACHES

Over the past century, advertising has been characterized in myriad ways. Indeed, the vast array of theoretical perspectives that range from Marxism to poststructuralism and postmodernism has led to advertising being varyingly described as "a system of organised magic" (Williams, 1980, p. 186), a "hidden persuader" and form of subliminal seduction (Key, 1972, 1989; Packard, 1960), a form of myth making (Barthes, 1972), a cultural field (Bourdieu, 1984), a science (see Rothenberg, 1999), a cultural economy (Lash & Urry, 1994; McFall, 2004; Sinclair, 1987), a sphere of ideology (Goldman, 1992; Williamson, 1978), and the most influential institution of socialization in modern society (Jhally, 1990). This section briefly outlines some of the theoretical and methodological approaches used in the scholarly analysis of advertising and presents one example of the cultural economy approach. Specifically, the "circuit of culture" model is offered as a constructive way to understand the complex interrelationships between the production, representation, consumption, and regulation of sport advertising.

Advertising Theory: Manipulation, Ideology, Semiotics, and Cultural Economy

For most social theorists advertising plays a central role in communicating ideology that influences both what and how people consume, how they experience the world, and ultimately their social identity. Early scholars viewed advertising as playing a crucial ideological role by creating false needs for individuals, who learn to seek fulfillment through consumption. Emerging in the late 1970s, critical, including Marxist, analyses aligned with the Frankfurt school (c.f. Horkheimer & Adorno, 1973, p. 37) viewed advertising as "emblematic of capitalist societies, the visible manifestation or materialisation of the capitalist logics of exploitation, alienation and reification." For example, one of the earliest works that extended the Frankfurt school perspective was Raymond Williams's (1980) essay "Advertising: The Magic System." Drawing on Marx's understanding of commodity fetishism, Williams argues that advertising exists as a "magic system" transforming commodities into glamorous signifiers that represent an imaginary world. To this extent, his analogy of advertising as magic foreshadowed other Marxist and semiotic critiques of advertising as a system of persuasion laden with images and emotions as part of a highly symbolic representational process.

Persuasion has been an enduring and pervasive theme in the critical analysis of advertising, as represented in works such as Packard's (1960) *The Hidden Persuaders* and Key's (1972, 1989) analyses of subliminal seduction. However, with the exception of Ewen's (1976) *Captains of Consciousness,* most tended to view advertising as a mechanism of manipulation and false consciousness rather than as part of a new socioeconomic system that fundamentally changed the relationship between people, commodities, and consumption.

Perhaps the single largest body of critical literature on advertising, including sport-related advertising, has its roots in textual and semiotic analysis. Early research, for example, Judith Williamson's (1978) *Decoding Advertising,* drew on elements of Marx to highlight the ideological role of advertising as part of the economic imperatives of capitalism through symbolic representation. Communications scholar Sut Jhally (1990) and colleagues (Leiss, Kline, & Jhally, 1990) extended Williamson's (1978) arguments by focusing on Marx's concept of commodity fetishism in order to illustrate how advertising mediates a range of relationships, including those between people and objects, use and symbol, symbolism and power, and communication and satisfaction. Notably, Jhally (1984) conceptualized the term "sport/media complex," which he later reconceptualized as "sport/media/promotional culture nexus" (Jhally, 1989), as a way to highlight the powerful links between various sectors of sport, including media and advertising, and how they operate as part of the overall process of capital accumulation. For Jhally (1990), advertising is the most influential institution of socialization in modern society, existing as a discourse through and about objects.

Overall, these approaches have provided some valuable insights with respect to the relationship between advertising and ideology. A limitation of much of the early critical work on advertising is that it overlooked the pivotal location and influence of advertising within the broader cultural economy. In response, recent scholars have demonstrated the value of the "circuit of culture" (du Gay, 1997) as a framework to better comprehend the complex and interrelated moments of production, representation, identity, consumption, and regulation.

Advertising, the New Cultural Economy, and the Circuit of Culture

Over the past two decades a cultural economic framework has emerged to challenge some of the reductionist conjectures of neo-Marxist and Fordist textual critiques of contemporary advertising by examining the cultures and contexts of production within the advertising industry (Cronin, 2000, 2004; du Gay & Pryke, 2002; McFall, 2002; Nixon, 2003). These developments acknowledge the importance of advertising in sustaining the power of capitalism and commodity relations, but they refuse to reduce advertising solely to the macro-economic sphere. In relation to these developments, a growing body of research has focused on illuminating the cultures of advertising production, with a focus on explicating the cultural practices and institutions of the advertising industry, including the subjective aspects of commercial production (see du Gay, 1997; Featherstone, 1991; Negus, 2002). For example, there is increasing recognition of the role and influence of advertising agencies and practitioners who

> play a pivotal role as cultural intermediaries in articulating production with consumption. This articulation of production and consumption itself constitutes a determinant moment in the circuit of culture: the moment of circulation. What is important about the moment of circulation is that it both articulates production with consumption, and draws consumption back into the process of production. (Nixon, 1997, p. 181)

The term "cultural intermediaries" was introduced by Pierre Bourdieu (1984, p. 359) and generally refers to "occupations involving presentation and representation . . . providing symbolic goods and services." With respect to the advertising industry, cultural intermediaries possess a certain amount of cultural authority and symbolic expertise in making commodities and brands meaningful, and in turn shaping the nature of consumption (Beck, 2003; Moor, 2008; Wright, 2005).

The circuit of culture model presented in Figure 56.1 is adapted from previous work (du Gay, Hall, Janes, Mackay, & Negus, 1997; Johnson, 1986–1987) that sought to trace the key moments and relationships within the production, representation, consumption, and regulation of commodities. The model highlights the strategic location of advertising and promotional culture at the "pivotal position between production and consumption" (Leslie, 1995, p. 402) in order to help us "explore how [a commodity] is represented, what social identities are associated with it, how it is produced and consumed, and what mechanisms regulate its distribution" (du Gay et al., 1997, p. 3). Beyond this, the model is helpful in the critical analysis of advertising set in sporting contexts because it (1) reveals the relationships between sectors and agents and between public and private interests that are otherwise not explicitly visible, (2) locates sport commodities and brands within particular sociohistorical and political economic contexts, (3) allows us to trace the life of a sport commodity or brand as it moves throughout the circuit, and (4) shows how regulation, whether state or other, may enable or constrain the power of consumers and citizens, and also serve as a tool of resistance.

Perhaps the best way to illustrate the utility of the model is to briefly overview some specific research related to sport, advertising, and promotional culture. One of the key lines of sport advertising research that has employed the circuit of culture model is the analysis of corporate nationalism. The concept of corporate nationalism refers to how "the nation and national culture have become principal (albeit perhaps unwilling) accomplices as global capitalism seeks to, quite literally, capitalize upon the nation as a source of collective identification and differentiation" (Silk, Andrews, & Cole, 2005, p. 7). Highlighting the role of advertising as both a form of cultural communication and cultural colonization, Jackson (2004, p. 20) further conceptualizes corporate nationalism as "the process by which corporations (both local and global) use the currency of 'the nation,' that is, its symbols, images, stereotypes, collective identities and memories as part of their overall branding strategy." Over the past 20 years, scholars have used different definitions, theories, and methods to analyze corporate nationalism as it relates to a diverse range of case studies, including the NBA in Britain (Falcous & Maguire, 2005), the Women's United Soccer Association (Giardina & Metz, 2004), transnational sport corporations in China (Slack,

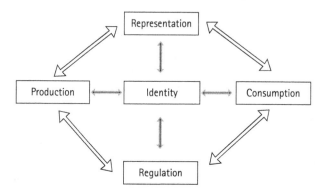

FIGURE 56.1 Circuit of Culture Model

Silk, & Hong, 2005), Guinness Beer branding in Ireland, Great Britain, and Africa (Amis, 2005), Molson Beer and national/masculine identity in Canada (Jackson, 2014), Nike and Asics advertising in Japan (Kobayashi, 2012a, 2012b; Kobayashi, Jackson, & Sam, 2017; Kobayashi, Sam, & Jackson, 2017), America's Cup Yacht racing (John & Jackson, 2011), and New Zealand rugby (Jackson, Batty, & Scherer, 2001; Jackson & Hokowhitu, 2002; Scherer & Jackson, 2007, 2008, 2010).

While space limitations prohibit a comprehensive analysis of how the circuit of culture operates, one good example of its application in the context of sport advertising research may be found in the work of Scherer and Jackson (2008). Their case study of the production of Adidas-sponsored advertising for the New Zealand All Blacks highlights the value of a systematic analysis, particularly in relation to production and representation. For example, with respect to the moment of production, they pose a series of questions that help frame their analysis: What were the sociohistorical and political-economic contexts of production? Who were the key decision-makers, and what were their marketing aims and objectives? Who was the target market? How did the producers integrate global and local initiatives?

To answer these questions, Scherer and Jackson (2008) offer a brief history of the professionalization of rugby, including the roles of three national governing bodies (South Africa, New Zealand, and Australia), as well as those of their broadcast media partners and corporate sponsors. They describe how the sport of rugby was able to turn professional in 1995 after signing a historic 10-year television deal with Rupert Murdoch's SKY TV. That global broadcast deal attracted corporate sponsors who saw an opportunity to access an emerging sport, reach a wider international audience, and thereby gain greater brand exposure. Consequently, in 1999 Adidas signed a five-year sponsorship deal with New Zealand Rugby estimated to be worth between U.S.$75 million and U.S.$100 million and, in the process, displaced local brand Canterbury, which had sponsored the All Blacks for 75 years. One might wonder why a global sport company would make such a huge investment in a relatively minor sport such as rugby, and a team representing a small national market of 4 million people. The answer, in part, was revealed in Adidas's (2000) own sponsorship documents:

> The All Blacks certainly transcend the game of rugby itself—with people in countries where rugby isn't even played having heard of the All Blacks. Partnered with a giant sports marketing company in Adidas, the All Blacks have the potential to one day become a true global sporting icon in the same league as the likes of Manchester United, Brazil Soccer, Chicago Bulls.

This sentiment was echoed by Saatchi & Saatchi, the advertising agency responsible for producing the initial Adidas promotional campaign: "[T]he All Blacks can deliver something to their brand that no other team or individual can in sport" (Primal Team, 1999, pp. 22–23). In short, the All Blacks offered something unique that Adidas believed could be leveraged for the global marketplace.

In securing the All Blacks sponsorship deal Adidas was confronted with two immediate challenges: (1) How could they, a foreign company, localize their brand in order to win over New Zealand consumers? and (2) How could they maximize the cultural value of the All Blacks for the global marketplace? To answer these questions Scherer and Jackson (2008) reviewed media coverage and corporate documents, conducted interviews with cultural intermediaries, and engaged in critical textual analysis of advertising campaigns. In effect, they were applying the circuit of culture model to explore the production and representation of a sport brand. Through a series of analyses they were able to demonstrate how Adidas navigated the global-local nexus by aligning their brand with local cultural values (Jackson et al., 2001, Scherer & Jackson, 2007, 2008), while simultaneously drawing upon the unique identity and mystique of the All Blacks to advance their global corporate ambitions (Scherer & Jackson, 2013). With respect to the latter, one particular advertising campaign is worth noting. As part of their original brand launch in 1999, Adidas incorporated the Ka Mate haka, a traditional Māori pregame challenge, into an advertisement titled "Black." According to Howard Greive, Saatchi & Saatchi's creative director, "We knew that if we could just show people what it is like to be confronted by a haka and to watch the All Blacks play their game—then you don't have to manufacture anything . . . and that's because it's authentic" (Primal Team, 1999, p. 23). In-depth analysis of the commercial, including information about its production, representation, and consumption, is offered elsewhere (Scherer & Jackson, 2010), but it is worth noting here that this 60-second commercial had a budget of U.S.$20 million, involved over 75 media specialists using a range of advanced technologies, and was based on footage secured by shooting a live rugby match. In short, the process of capturing authenticity was a very complex manufacturing process.

The overall set of partnerships between New Zealand Rugby, SKY TV, Adidas, and Saatchi advertising exemplifies the sport/media/promotional culture nexus, that is, the complex of entertainment sport, technology, and symbolic representation that collaborates to maximize audiences and consumption, enhance brand profile, and ultimately secure profits. This powerful nexus configures the ownership, structure, processes, representations, and capital accumulation of sport. Given this power, we might ask whether and how this influence is regulated, and likewise, how citizens/consumers can challenge and resist when negative effects emerge. Here, one particular aspect of the public response to the Adidas "Black" advertisement is insightful as it highlights how, despite the planning, consultation, and even the best of intentions, the aims and objectives of corporate advertising are never guaranteed, nor without resistance.

On June 11, 2000, the front page of New Zealand's *Sunday News* displayed the headline "$1.5m for Haka." The article explained that members of the Māori tribe Ngāti Toa had filed an intellectual property case against Adidas and New Zealand Rugby, arguing that they "deserve a large slice of the US$120 million Adidas sponsorship of NZ rugby, because the sportswear giant uses Māori imagery in its branding" (Reid, 2000, p. 1). Central to the legal argument was reference to an ancestor of the Ngāti Toa tribe who created the specific Ka Mate haka used in the advertisement (Jackson & Hokowhitu, 2002). Ultimately, the legal case was dismissed, although it did result in social change. For example, in 2011, the New Zealand Rugby Union signed an agreement with Ngāti Toa acknowledging the ancestral origins of the Ka Mate haka, and in 2014 the Ka Mate Attribution Bill was officially signed in Parliament. While neither of these formal agreements provides international intellectual property rights protection, they demonstrate that within the overall circuit of culture, and despite the power of global corporations and their advertising armatures, there are opportunities for resistance.

Resistance can take many forms, including citizen/consumer brand choice and boycotts, but it can also emerge in the form of regulation, one of the key dynamics operant within the circuit of culture. The next section considers further examples of resistance and regulation in framing two key debates related to contemporary sport-anchored advertising.

DEBATES

The world of sport, advertising, and promotional culture is a contested terrain, a battlefield of competing ideologies and interests. This section focuses on two contemporary debates related to sport advertising. The first, concerning Nike and labor exploitation, illustrates political-economic tensions. The second, concerning the regulation of alcohol advertising and sponsorship of sport, illustrates struggles over public policy.

Nike Advertising and the Illusion of an Exploitative Business Model

The Issues section referred to one of the most successful global corporations in history, Nike, and in particular its advertising and promotional culture. There is no doubt that Nike is successful in terms of generating revenue, global brand profile, consumer loyalty, and its virtual omnipresence within contemporary popular culture. Yet a key debate led by critics and activists asserts that Nike's success is built upon the exploitation of offshore sweatshop labor. In response, Nike contends that production costs are cheaper outside of North America; that it provides jobs for people in poor countries who need them, thereby elevating their standard of living; that it enforces a strict code of conduct regarding working conditions and worker rights in factories; and strikingly, that its labor costs need to be minimized in order for the company to afford the high cost of sponsoring celebrity athletes. To consider this debate one must understand that Nike and its image rely on a basic, but powerful, illusion—a mirage that is made transparent by examining its operations via the circuit of culture model. Here, the model is used to reveal the true nature of the relationships between Nike's production and representation and its impact on consumption and social experience/identity within the context of a largely unregulated consumer-capitalist environment.

The history of Nike has been well-documented (Strasser & Becklund; 1993; Goldman & Papson, 1998; Katz, 1994), but it is worth remembering that the idea for the company was based on an essay written by cofounder Phil Knight for an MBA course at Stanford University in the 1960s. The basic operating principle was the creation of a business that sourced cheap labor to reduce production costs, thus shifting the corporate focus to branding and marketing. From its 1960s forerunner, Blue Ribbon Sports, that sourced its product from Japan's Onitsuka/Tiger corporation, Nike's basic operating principle remains the same today. As a result, Nike represents what Goldman and Papson (1998, p. 4) refer to as a "hollowed corporation", where "the production process is broken up, farmed out, and spatially dispersed." In short, Nike (2020, p. 1) doesn't really "produce" anything, and this is confirmed in its own annual report:

> Our principal business activity is the design, development and worldwide marketing and selling of athletic footwear, apparel, equipment, accessories and services. NIKE is the largest seller of athletic footwear and apparel in the world. We sell our products directly to consumers through NIKE-owned retail stores and digital platforms (which we refer to collectively as our "NIKE Direct" operations) and to retail accounts and a mix of independent distributors, licensees and sales representatives in virtually all countries around the world. We also offer interactive consumer experiences through our digital platforms. Virtually all of our products are manufactured by independent contractors. Nearly all footwear and apparel products are produced outside the United States, while equipment products are produced both in the United States and abroad.

In 2020, Nike operated in 41 countries, with 533 factories and 1,100 retail outlets, and employed over 1 million workers. Today, about 44% of Nike products are made in Vietnam, 19% in China, and the remainder is spread across a range of countries, including Thailand and Indonesia. Clearly, Nike's focus remains on sourcing cheap labor so that it can invest its resources in its advertising, sponsorship, and promotional culture. Nike is an image company whose trademark logo is its primary asset. As Marshall and Morreale (2018, p. 139) note:

> More than the technology of design, the Nike Swoosh defines the very identity of Nike internationally. In the hollowed-out globalized corporation, the brand . . . is not only the identity of the company, it is what the company protects, upholds, manages, and ultimately disseminates.

Looking at Nike through the lens of the circuit of culture model (see Figure 56.1) illuminates some of the wider relations of production that tend to be forgotten. As mentioned earlier, the company does not produce anything; instead it outsources its production to independent factories located in distant countries where wages are low, working conditions are challenging, and labor rights are absent or limited. Yet we tend to know very little about where, how, or by whom Nike products are produced. Rather, what the public sees is the representation of the Nike brand through its advertising and sponsorship of celebrity athletes and major sporting events. This is where Nike invests its time, effort, and money—it is also the key to its illusion.

From its earliest days, Nike invested in elite athletes, such as Michael Jordan, who, in his rookie 1984–1985 NBA year, signed a U.S.$3 million, five-year contract, which pales by today's standards. According to *Forbes* magazine's annual list of the highest paid athletes and their corporate sponsorships, in 2020, the top 10 Nike-sponsored athletes were Michael Jordan (U.S.$60m/year), Tiger Woods (U.S.$100m/5 years), Rafael Nadal (U.S.$50m/5 years), Rory McIlroy (U.S.$100m, 10 years), Cristiano Rinaldo (U.S.$105m/ 5 years), LeBron James (U.S.$30m/year plus shares), Maria Sharapova (U.S.$70m/8 years), Kevin Durant (U.S.$285m/10 years), Kobe Bryant (U.S.$75m/5 years), and Serena Williams (U.S.$18m/year). Supporting these sponsorship contracts requires Nike to invest, on average, U.S.$219 million per year, for just its top 10 stars. The contrast between the cost of these sponsorships and the average wages of factory workers who actually produce Nike products is striking. In simple terms, some Nike celebrity athletes earn more in one hour than production workers earn in a year. Ironically, people from poorer nations, including Nike factory employees, may be just as eager to own or display the brand because they identify with celebrity athlete ambassadors or as a way of enhancing their status as part of their own identity construction (Bick & Chiper, 2007). This highlights the power of the illusion, one set in the contradiction and immorality of Nike's business model. In short, in order to secure profits for its shareholders, Nike uses the symbolic power of sport, celebrity athletes, and contemporary social justice issues that resonate with consumers as part of its advertising and promotional culture, while at the same time exploiting vulnerable and desperate foreign workers, many of whom are women.

Since the 1980s, Nike has been the target of social activists in labor and antiglobalization movements who have tried to hold the company to account for its unethical corporate ethos (Boje & Khan, 2009; Knight & Greenberg, 2002; Lund-Thomsen & Coe, 2015; Sage, 2010). There have been countless media exposés, including documentaries such as Michael Moore's *The Big One* (Glynn & Moore, 1997) and Jim Keady's (2004) *Behind the Swoosh*, along with U.S. college student protests demanding that their sport teams' apparel is sweatshop-free. Yet Nike has generally managed to navigate these complaints through both its promotional culture and its public relations strategy. As previously noted, Nike regularly creates advertisements that address issues of social justice and inequality. In addition, they have a formalized Corporate Social Responsibility program that covers everything from pay equity and labor rights to sustainability and the environment. With respect to labor rights, Nike takes every opportunity to highlight its Code of Conduct for production factories, which promotes a minimum age for workers, safe working conditions, fair wages, and worker rights. Unfortunately, despite all of the rhetoric that appears on their website and in official publications, it is very difficult to secure independent confirmation that the Code is being followed (Stabile, 2000). This is because "Nike" factories are located overseas, operated by independent subcontractors governed by different sets of laws, including labor regulations, and it is very difficult for human rights monitors to gain access for random inspections. Beyond this, Nike engages in what is referred to as "corporate writing" and "story branding" (Boje, 2000; Boje & Khan, 2009), where the entire complex of advertising, marketing, public relations, and even annual reports is part of a sophisticated and highly integrated corporate promotional culture. To this extent, Nike's Corporate Social Responsibility program is an integral part of its overall advertising and sponsorship.

Two final points are relevant and highlight both the success and the immorality of Nike's business model. First, despite all of the public criticism and social activism that targets the company for its sweatshop labor violations, few celebrity athletes have spoken up. This silence may simply be due to their sponsorship contract prohibiting them from making public statements about Nike factories. Nevertheless, given the profile and influence of star athletes who, over the years, have championed a wide range of social causes, including gender equality, homophobia, and most recently Black Lives Matter, it is curious that these athletes remain silent about labor exploitation.

And Nike adds insult to injury by avoiding the payment of taxes. For example, up until 2015, Nike Europe, based in the Netherlands, earned about U.S.$10 billion in revenue per year. However, Nike did not pay taxes on this amount (Hopkins & Bowers, 2017). Instead, Nike Europe, operating as a subsidiary, was required to pay a U.S.$9 billion "trademark fee" to Nike International, which is headquartered in Bermuda—a strategic location because it is a low-tax or tax-free zone. As a result, in 2015 Nike Europe paid tax on only U.S.$1 billion (Hopkins & Bowers, 2017), thereby increasing Nike's profits and power while simultaneously depriving nation-states of significant tax revenue that would support health, education, and other initiatives.

Sadly, the situation has gotten worse. Nike has now shifted its intellectual property from Nike International Ltd. to a new subsidiary, Nike Innovate CV. The new subsidiary has no documented location, allowing Nike to avoid paying its fair share of tax, although this is currently under investigation (Hopkins & Bowers, 2017).

Sport, Alcohol Advertising, and Regulation

Another debate gaining increasing attention relates to the role and regulation of alcohol advertising and sponsorship in sport. Once considered a "sin" product like tobacco and gambling, alcohol has established itself as a legitimate, respected, and even highly celebrated cultural commodity. Yet concerns remain about the negative impact of alcohol on society. For example, according to the World Health Organization (2018), 3 million, or 5.3%, of all annual deaths are attributable to alcohol. Moreover, consumption of alcohol is linked to a range of other social problems, including accidents, work absenteeism, violence, and addiction.

Within the context of sport, alcohol holds a rather contentious position. On the one hand, sport and alcohol have enjoyed a long and mutually reinforcing relationship (Collins & Vamplew, 2002). Today the alcohol industry's global investment in sport has reached U.S.$764 million per year, with the world's top five beer companies accounting for 75%, or U.S.$576 million (Sports Market Intelligence, 2018). The alcohol industry targets sport for reasons previously cited in this chapter, including its global popularity and links with youth and masculinity. This is despite the obvious cultural irony of a product that is detrimental to health and human performance being associated with sport (Wenner, 1991).

On the other hand, scholars, health practitioners, and policymakers have raised concerns about the overall impact of alcohol on sport. First and foremost, critics note that alcohol has saturated sport, both figuratively and financially, to such an extent that the relationship is best described as naturalized—rarely is alcohol perceived as a drug. The concerns extend to issues related to health, the reproduction of hegemonic masculinity (Gee & Jackson, 2017), and the role of advertising and sponsorship in driving a harmful culture of consumption among both athletes and fans (Cody & Jackson, 2016; Gee, 2020; Jones, 2010; O'Brien & Kypri, 2008; Palmer, 2011; Wenner & Jackson, 2009).

With respect to health and consumption, O'Brien and Kypri (2008) found that athletes and teams sponsored by alcohol companies were more likely to engage in hazardous drinking behavior, in part due to the practice of supplying the product as part of the sponsorship contract. More specifically, in relation to sport and alcohol advertising, concerns have been directed at its role in the reproduction of hegemonic masculinity and associated forms of oppression, including sexism and homophobia (Gee, 2015; Messner, Dunbar, & Hunt, 2004). In response to these concerns, some nation-states have sought to regulate or even ban alcohol sponsorship of sport. For example, the World Health Organization's (2011) survey of 106 countries found that while 44% had no policy on alcohol sponsorship of sport, 31.8% had some form of regulation, including total bans (14.4%), partial bans (12.8%), and self-regulation (5%).

One nation that has led efforts to regulate alcohol advertising and sponsorship of sport is France. In 1991, France introduced Loi Evin, which includes a ban on alcohol-related advertising or sponsorship that targets young people, is screened on television or in cinemas, and/or is associated with cultural or sporting events. There are mixed views on the success of Loi Evin (Rigaud & Craplet, 2004), but according to Dr. Mick Loftus, an antidrink campaigner and a former president of Ireland's Gaelic Athletics Association, "It has had a huge impact on the consumption of alcohol in France. . . . In 1960, the average adult in France consumed 30 litres of alcohol. Today, that figure is down to 13.5 litres and it's mainly thanks to Loi Evin" (quoted in "How to Tackle," 2013). A number of other nations have tried to adopt some of the key principles of Loi Evin, but this has largely occurred within the context of a system of self-regulation. In effect, self-regulation means that the alcohol industry, and its media and promotional partners, implement and adjudicate their own codes of practice. Generally, this involves establishment of an advertising standards authority, including an agency responsible for soliciting and evaluating public complaints. While this certainly enables the alcohol industry to claim that it is operating ethically and responsibly, the reality is that they maintain enormous power and control over the promotion and distribution of a publicly available drug.

Here, the case of New Zealand is instructive. In 2010, a New Zealand Law Commission (2010) report titled "Alcohol in Our Lives: Curbing the Harm" acknowledged that the nation had a binge-drinking problem and identified a range of potential solutions, including greater restrictions on alcohol advertising and sponsorship of cultural and sporting events (Cody & Jackson, 2016). Subsequently, in 2014, the New Zealand Ministry of Health established a Forum on Alcohol Advertising and Sponsorship. Following a review of 242 submissions that spanned the sport, health, alcohol, and media sectors, the Forum's final report proposed 14 recommendations aimed at reducing the exposure of youth to alcohol advertising and sponsorship (Gee, Batty, & Millar, 2021). With specific reference to sport, Recommendations 1 and 2 stated, "Ban alcohol sponsorship of all streamed and broadcast sport" and "Ban alcohol sponsorship of sports [long term]," respectively (New Zealand Ministry of Health, 2014, p. 3). More than six years later, not a single Forum recommendation has been discussed, let alone implemented, by government. Clearly, there is a range of factors for any government to consider, including the fact that some sports are very dependent on alcohol sponsorship for their survival. However, given the lobbying power of the alcohol industry, it is equally, if not more likely that they have managed to limit the terms and narrative of the debate in order to protect their interests. No doubt, this debate will continue, given the strength of the sport-alcohol nexus (Palmer, 2011) and its articulation within the broader sport-media-cultural complex.

CONCLUSION

This chapter has provided a select overview of the nature and state of sport, advertising, and promotional culture. Emphasis was placed on outlining when, how, and why advertising, as both a cultural practice and an economic industry, emerged. Moreover, the unique and strategic role of sport as a cultural theme and vehicle within advertising was delineated in order to help explain how and why media companies aggressively compete for broadcast rights to particular events and, in turn, how this attracts corporate sponsors.

It is the cultural and economic value of sport as a commodity that explains, for example, why America's NBC network paid U.S.$7.65 billion for the broadcast rights to screen the Olympic Games from 2022 to 2032. Likewise, it explains why, in combination, CBS, Fox, and NBC networks paid U.S.$27 billion for the rights to NFL broadcasts from 2013 to 2022. Where then does this "value" come from? The answer, in part, lies within the sport-media-cultural complex. For example, the corporate cost of one minute of advertising during the Super Bowl is about U.S.$10 million, and given that there is almost an hour of commercial time available, this equates to a yield of nearly half a billion dollars in potential advertising revenue during this annual spectacle. Corporate advertisers are willing to pay these extravagant costs because they are confident that many consumers will be watching, thus ensuring that their strategically placed commercials will elevate their brand profile and potentially translate into future sales. This raises an important but often misunderstood aspect of the sport-media promotional complex. As McQueen (1977, pp. 10–11, emphasis added) notes:

> To make sense of the media it is essential to get the relationship between the media and advertising the right way round: commercial mass media are not news and features backed up by advertising; on the contrary the . . . media are advertisements which carry news, features and entertainment in *order to capture audiences for advertisers.*

In other words, while media certainly screen advertisements, in real economic transactional terms, the media effectively sells the potential audience to corporate sponsors.

Using increasingly sophisticated tools, media, advertising, and corporate sponsors are able to identify, track, and target consumers by collating detailed information. What is even more disturbing is that technology companies such as Google, Facebook, Apple, and Amazon, which, combined, are worth over U.S.$5 trillion, have the legal right to sell our information. Indeed, our privacy has now been commodified and privatized. Notably, all of these companies have interests, either direct or indirect, in sport. It is beyond the scope of this chapter to forecast the implications of an increasingly consolidated global media-corporate landscape on the future of both consumer society and sport. However, if current trends are any indication, it is probable that vested interests will work to ensure that capitalism, despite all of its limitations and impending threats, maintains its hegemony. The reason that capitalism is a threat is because it is an economic and ideological system based on consumption and profit; that is, its inertia is propelled by the unending production of commodities regardless of human need.

As a consequence, the world is depleting its natural resources at an unprecedented rate, resulting in a range of problems, including climate change, that threaten the planet and human existence. Over 20 years ago, Sut Jhally's (1997) documentary *Advertising and the End of the World* offered a prescient warning about the relationship between advertising, consumer capitalism, and environmental sustainability. Sadly, despite greater public awareness about climate change and a raft of green initiatives, state and corporate policies have done little to change the pursuit of capital accumulation. While sport, and its associated advertising and promotional culture, may play a relatively small part in the overall scheme of the global economy and environmental sustainability, given its popularity we might ask what responsibility it has and whether it has the potential to serve as a model for positive change.

REFERENCES

Adidas. (2000). 1999/2000 All Blacks sponsorship. Unpublished manuscript. Wellington, New Zealand.

Amis, J. (2005). Beyond sport: Imaging and re-imaging a global brand. In M. L. Silk, D. L. Andrews, & C. L. Cole (Eds.), *Sport and corporate nationalisms* (pp. 143–165). Oxford: Berg.

Andrews, D. L. (1996). The fact(s) of Michael Jordan's Blackness: Excavating a floating racial signifier. *Sociology of Sport Journal, 13*(2), 125–158.

Andrews, D. L., & Jackson, S. J. (2001). *Sport stars: The politics of sporting celebrity.* London: Routledge.

Arsenault, D., & Fawzy, T. (2001). Just buy it: Nike advertising aimed at *Glamour* readers: A critical feminist analysis. *Journal of Critical Postmodern Organisational Science, 1*(3), 80–81.

Associated Press. (2017, September 23). Trump says N.F.L. players should be fired for anthem protests. *New York Times.* https://www.nytimes.com/2017/09/23/sports/trump-nfl-colin-kaepernick-.html.

Barthes, R. (1972). *Mythologies.* New York: Oxford University Press.

Beck, A. (2003) *Cultural work: Understanding the cultural industries.* London: Routledge.

Bell, D. (1976). *The cultural contradictions of capitalism.* New York: Harper and Row.

Bick, P. B., & Chiper, S. (2007). Swoosh identity: Recontextualizations in Haiti and Romania. *Visual Communication, 6*(1), 5–18.

Birrell, S., & McDonald, M. (2000). *Reading sport: Critical essays on power and representation.* Boston: Northeastern University Press.

Boje, D. M. (2000). Nike corporate writing of academic, business, and cultural practices. *Management Communication Quarterly, 14,* 507–516.

Boje, D. M., & Khan, F. R. (2009). Story-branding by empire entrepreneurs: Nike, child labour, and Pakistan's soccer ball industry. *Journal of Small Business & Entrepreneurship, 22*(1), 9–24.

Bourdieu, P. (1984). *Distinction.* London: Routledge.

Carrington, B. (2001). Postmodern Blackness and the celebrity sports star: Ian Wright, "race," and English identity. In D. L. Andrews & S. J. Jackson (Eds.), *Sport stars: The cultural politics of sporting celebrity* (pp. 102–123). London: Routledge.

Cody, K., & Jackson, S. (2016). The contested terrain of alcohol sponsorship of sport in New Zealand. *International Review for the Sociology of Sport, 51*(4), 375–393.

Cole, C. (1996). American Jordan: P.L.A.Y., consensus and punishment. *Sociology of Sport Journal, 13*(4), 366–397.

Cole, C., & Andrews, D. L. (1996). Look—It's NBA Showtime! Visions of race in the popular imaginary, *Cultural Studies Annual, 1*(1), 141–181.

Cole, C. L., & Hribar, A. (1995). Celebrity feminism: Nike style post-Fordism, transcendence, and consumer power. *Sociology of Sport Journal, 12*(4), 347–369.

Collins, T., & Vamplew, W. (2002). *Mud, sweat and beers: A cultural history of sport and alcohol.* Oxford: Berg.

Cronin, A. (2000). *Advertising and consumer citizenship: Gender, images and rights.* London: Routledge.

Cronin, A. (2004). *Advertising myths: The strange half-lives of images and commodities.* London: Routledge.

Davis, L., & Delano, L. (1992). Fixing the boundaries of physical gender: Side effects of anti-drug campaigns in athletics. *Sociology of Sport Journal, 9*(1), 1–19.

du Gay, P. (Ed.). (1997). *Production of culture: Cultures of production.* London: Sage.

du Gay, P., Hall, S., Janes, L., Mackay, H., & Negus, K. (1997). *Doing cultural studies: The story of the Sony Walkman.* London: Sage.

du Gay, P., & Pryke, M. (2002). *Cultural economy: Cultural analysis and commercial life.* London: Sage.

Duquin, M. (1989). Fashion and fitness: Images in women's magazine advertisements. *Arena Review, 13*(2), 97–109.

Dworkin, S. L., & Messner, M. (2002). Just do what? Sport, bodies and gender In A. Scraton & A. Flintoff (Eds.), *Gender and sport: A reader* (pp. 17–29). London: Routledge.

Dyson, M. E. (1993). Be like Mike? Michael Jordan and the pedagogy of the oppressed. *Cultural Studies, 7*(1), 64–72.

Ewen, S. (1976). *Captains of consciousness: Advertising and the social roots of consumer culture.* New York: McGraw-Hill.

Falcous, M., & Maguire, J. (2005). Making it local? National Basketball Association expansion and English basketball subcultures. In M. L. Silk, D. L. Andrews, & C. L. Cole (Eds.), *Sport and corporate nationalisms* (pp. 13–34). Oxford: Berg.

Featherstone, M. (1991). *Postmodernism and consumer culture.* London: Sage.

Fresco, E. (2020). In LeBron James' promotional skin: Self-branded athletes and fans' immaterial labour. *Journal of Consumer Culture, 20*(4), 440–456.

Gee, S. (2015). Sexual ornament or spiritual trainer? Envisioning and marketing to a female audience through the NHL's "Inside the Warrior" advertising campaign. *Communication & Sport, 3*(2), 142–167.

Gee, S. (Ed.). (2020). *Sport, alcohol and social inquiry: A global cocktail.* Bingley, U.K.: Emerald Publishing.

Gee, S., Batty, R., & Millar, P. (2021). Alcohol sponsorship and New Zealand regional rugby unions: Crisis point or business as usual? *International Journal of the Sociology of Leisure, 4*(2), 155–175.

Gee, S., & Jackson, S. J. (2017). *Sport, promotional culture and the crisis of masculinity.* London: Palgrave Macmillan.

Giardina, M. D., & Metz, J. L. (2004). All-American girls? Corporatizing national identity and cultural citizenship with/in the WUSA. In M. L. Silk, D. L. Andrews, & C. L. Cole (Eds.), *Sport and corporate nationalisms* (pp. 109–126). Oxford: Berg.

Glynn, K. (Producer), & Moore, M. (Director). (1997). *The big one* [film]. Los Angeles, CA: Miramax Films.

Goldman, R. (1992). *Reading ads socially.* London: Routledge.

Goldman, R., & Papson, S. (1998) *Nike culture: The sign of the swoosh.* London: Sage.

Grow, J. M. (2006). Stories of community: The first ten years of Nike women's advertising. *American Journal of Semiotics, 22*(1–4), 167–196.

Grow, J. M. (2008). The gender of branding: Early Nike women's advertising as a feminist anti-narrative. *Women's Studies in Communication, 31*(3), 312–343.

Helstein, M. (2003). That's who I want to be. *Journal of Sport and Social Issues, 27*(3), 276–292.

Hoffmann, J., Nyborg, K., Averhoff, C., & Olesen, S. (2020). The contingency of corporate political advocacy: Nike's "Dream Crazy" campaign with Colin Kaepernick. *Public Relations Inquiry, 9*(2), 155–175.

Hopkins, N., & Bowers, S. (2017, November 6). Revealed: How Nike stays one step ahead of the taxman *The Guardian.* https://www.theguardian.com/news/2017/nov/06/nike-tax-paradise-papers.

Horkheimer, M., & Adorno, T. (1973). *The dialectic of enlightenment*. London: Allen Lane.

How to tackle the drink link to sport? Just ask the French. (2013, June). Alcohol Ireland. https://alcoholireland.ie/how-to-tackle-the-drink-link-to-sport-just-ask-the-french.

Intravia, J., Piquero, A. R., Leeper Piquero, N., & Byers, B. (2020). Just do it? An examination of race on attitudes associated with Nike's advertisement featuring Colin Kaepernick. *Deviant Behavior*, 41(10), 1221–1231.

Jackson, S. J. (2004). Reading New Zealand within the new global order: Sport and the visualisation of national identity. *International Sport Studies*, 26(1), 13–29.

Jackson, S. J. (2014). Globalisation, corporate nationalism and masculinity in Canada: Sport, Molson Beer advertising and consumer citizenship. *Sport in Society*, 17(7), 901–916.

Jackson, S. J., Batty, R., & Scherer, J. (2001). Transnational sport marketing at the global/local nexus: The adidasification of the New Zealand All Blacks. *International Journal of Sports Marketing and Sponsorship*, 3(2), 185–201.

Jackson, S. J., & Hokowhitu, B. (2002). Sport, tribes and technology: The New Zealand All Blacks Haka and the politics of identity. *Journal of Sport and Social Issues*, 26(1), 125–139.

Jhally, S. (1984). The spectacle of accumulation: Material and cultural factors in the evolution of the sports/media complex. *Insurgent Sociologist*, 12(3), 41–57.

Jhally, S. (1989). Cultural studies and the sport/media complex. In L. Wenner (Ed.), *Media, sports and society*, (pp. 70–93). Newbury Park, CA: Sage.

Jhally, S. (1990). *The codes of advertising: Fetishism and the political economy of meaning in the consumer society*. London: Routledge.

Jhally, S. (Director & Producer). (1997). *Advertising and the end of the world* [DVD]. Northampton, MA: Media Education Foundation.

John, A., & Jackson, S. J. (2011). Call me loyal: Globalization, corporate nationalism and the America's Cup. *International Review for the Sociology of Sport*, 46(4), 399–417.

Johnson, R. (1986-1987). What is cultural studies anyway? *Social Text*, 16, 38–80.

Jones, S. C. (2010). When does alcohol sponsorship of sport become sports sponsorship of alcohol? A case study of developments in sport in Australia. *International Journal of Sports Marketing and Sponsorship*, 11(3), 67–78.

Katz, D. (1994). *Just do it: The Nike spirit in the corporate world*. Holbrook, MA: Adams Publishing.

Keady, J. (Producer). (2004). *Behind the swoosh* [film]. Asbury Park, NJ: Educating for Justice Films.

Kellner, D. (1995). *Media culture: Cultural studies, identity and politics between the modern and the postmodern*. London: Routledge.

Key, W. B. (1972). *Subliminal seduction: Ad media's manipulation of a not so innocent America*. Englewood Cliffs, NJ: Prentice-Hall.

Key, W. B. (1989). *The age of manipulation*. Lanham, Maryland: Madison Books.

Kilbourne, J. (1999). *Can't buy me love: How advertising changes the way we think and feel*. New York: Touchstone.

Knight, G., & Greenberg, J. (2002). Promotionalism and subpolitics: Nike and its labor critics. *Management Communication Quarterly*, 15(4), 541–570.

Kobayashi, K. (2012a). Corporate nationalism and glocalization of Nike advertising in "Asia": Production and representation practices of cultural intermediaries. *Sociology of Sport Journal*, 29(1), 42–61.

Kobayashi, K. (2012b). Globalization, corporate nationalism and Japanese cultural intermediaries: Representation of Bukatsu through Nike advertising at the global-local nexus. *International Review for the Sociology of Sport, 47*(6), 724–742.

Kobayashi, K., Jackson, S. J., & Sam, M. P. (2017). Globalization, creative alliance and self-Orientalism: Negotiating Japanese identity within Asics global advertising production. *International Journal of Cultural Studies, 13*(5), 511–529.

Kobayashi, K., Sam, M. P., & Jackson, S. J. (2017). Multiple dimensions of mediation within transnational advertising production: Cultural intermediaries as shapers of emerging cultural capital. *Consumption Markets & Culture, 21*(2), 129–146.

Klynveld Peat Marwick Goerdeler (KPGM). (2016). The business of sports: Playing to win as the game unfurls. Report. Confederation of Indian Industry, Mumbai.

LaFrance, M. (1998). Colonising the feminine: Nike's intersections of post-feminism and hyperconsumption. In G. Rail (Ed.), *Sport and postmodern times* (pp. 117–139). Albany, NY: SUNY Press.

Lash, S., & Urry, J. (1994). *Economies of signs and space.* London: Sage.

Leiss, W., Kline, S., & Jhally, S. (1990). *Social communication in advertising: Persons, products and images of well-being* (2nd ed.). London: Routledge.

Leslie, D. A. (1995). Global scan: The globalization of advertising agencies, concepts, and campaigns. *Economic Geography, 71*(4), 402–425.

Lewis, J. (2013). *Beyond consumer capitalism: Media and the limits to imagination.* Cambridge, U.K.: Polity Press.

Lucas, S. (2000). Nike's commercial solution: Girls, sneakers, and salvation. *International Review for the Sociology of Sport, 35*(2), 149–164.

Lund-Thomsen, P., & Coe, N. M. (2015). Corporate social responsibility and labour agency: The case of Nike in Pakistan. *Journal of Economic Geography, 15*(2), 275–296.

Lury, C. (1996). *Consumer culture.* Cambridge, U.K.: Polity.

Marshall, D. P., & Morreale, J. (2018). *Advertising and promotional culture: Case histories.* London: Palgrave Macmillan.

McFall, L. (2002). What about the old cultural intermediaries? An historical review of advertising producers. *Cultural Studies, 16*(4), 532–52.

McFall, L. (2004). *Advertising: A cultural economy: Culture, representation, and identities.* London: Sage Publications.

McKay, J. (1995). "Just do it": Corporate sports slogans and the political economy of "enlightened racism." *Discourse: Studies in the Cultural Politics of Education, 16*(2), 191–201.

McQueen, H. (1977). *Australia's media monopolies.* Victoria, Australia: Camberwell.

Messner, M. (2002). *Taking the field: Women, men and sports.* Minneapolis: University of Minnesota Press.

Messner, M. A., Dunbar, M., & Hunt, D. (2004). The televised sports manhood formula. In D. Rowe (Ed.), *Sport, culture and the media: Critical readings* (pp. 229–245). Berkshire, U.K.: Open University Press.

Miller, D. (1995). *Acknowledging consumption: A review of new studies.* London: Routledge.

Mitra, M. (2019, September 16). Nike won its first "outstanding commercial" Emmy in 17 years for an ad featuring Colin Kaepernick. *CNBC.* https://www.cnbc.com/2019/09/16/nike-wins-emmy-for-ad-featuring-colin-kaepernick.html.

Moor, L. (2008). Branding consultants as cultural intermediaries. *Sociological Review, 56*(3), 408–428.

Müller, F., van Zoonen, L., & de Roode, L. (2008). We can't "Just do it" alone! An analysis of Nike's (potential) contributions to anti-racism in soccer. *Media Culture & Society, 30*(1), 23–38.

Negus, K. (2002). The work of cultural intermediaries and the enduring distance between production and consumption. *Cultural Studies, 16*(4), 501–515.

New Zealand Law Commission. (2010). Alcohol in our lives: Curbing the harm. A report on the review of the regulatory framework for the sale and supply of liquor. Report 114. Wellington: New Zealand Law Commission.

New Zealand Ministry of Health. (2014). Ministerial forum on alcohol advertising and sponsorship: Recommendations on alcohol advertising and sponsorship. Wellington: New Zealand Ministry of Health.

Nike. (2020). U.S. Securities and Exchange Commission Form 10-K. https://s1.q4cdn.com/806093406/files/doc_financials/2020/ar/NKE-FY20-10K.pdf.

Nixon, S. (1997). Circulating culture. In P. du Gay (Ed.), *Production of culture: Cultures of production* (pp. 177–234). London: Sage.

Nixon, S. (2003). *Advertising cultures: Gender, commerce and creativity.* London: Sage.

O'Brien, K. S., & Kypri, K. (2008). Alcohol industry sponsorship and hazardous drinking among sportspeople. *Addiction, 103*(12), 1961–1966.

Packard, V. (1960). *The hidden persuaders.* London: Penguin.

Palmer, C. (2011). Key themes and research agendas in the sport-alcohol nexus. *Journal of Sport & Social Issues, 35*(2), 168–185.

Primal Team. (1999, October). *Admedia, 14*(9), 22–23.

Reid, N. (2000, June 11). $1.5m for Haka. *Sunday News,* 1.

Rigaud, A., & Craplet, M. (2004). The Loi Evin: A French exception. *The Globe, 1*(2), 33–36.

Rothenberg, R. (1999, March 29). The advertising century. *Advertising Age,* 9–16.

Rowe, D. (1996). The global love-match: Sport and television. *Media, Culture and Society, 18*(4), 565–582.

Rowe, D. (1999). *Sport, culture and the media: The unruly trinity.* Buckingham, U.K.: Open University Press. Sage, G. (2010). *Globalizing sport: How organisations, corporations, media and politics are changing sports.* Boulder, CO: Paradigm Publishers.

Scherer, J., & Jackson, S. (2007). Sports advertising, cultural production and corporate nationalism at the global-local nexus: Branding the New Zealand All Blacks. *Sport in Society, 10*(2), 268–284.

Scherer, J., & Jackson, S. (2008). Cultural studies and the circuit of culture: Advertising, promotional culture and the New Zealand All Blacks. *Cultural Studies/Critical Methodologies, 8*(4), 507–526.

Scherer, J., & Jackson, S. J. (2010). *Sport, globalisation and corporate nationalism: The new cultural economy of the New Zealand All Blacks.* Oxford: Peter Lang Publishers.

Scherer, J., & Jackson, S. J. (2013). *The contested terrain of the New Zealand All Blacks: Rugby, commerce, and cultural politics in the age of globalisation.* Oxford: Peter Lang Publishers.

Shao, Y., Desmarais, F., & Weaver, C. K. (2014). Chinese advertising practitioners' conceptualisation of gender representation. *International Journal of Advertising, 33*(2), 329–350.

Silk, M., Andrews, D. L., & Cole, C. (2005). *Corporate nationalism: Sport, cultural identity and transnational marketing.* Oxford: Berg.

Sinclair, J. (1987). *Images incorporated: Advertising as industry and ideology.* London: Croom Helm.

Slack, T., Silk, M. L., & Hong, F. (2005). Cultural contradictions/contradicting culture: Transnational corporations and the penetration of the Chinese market. In M. L. Silk, D. L. Andrews, & C. L. Cole (Eds.), *Sport and corporate nationalisms* (pp. 253–274). Oxford: Berg.

Spencer, N. (2004). Sister act VI: Venus and Serena Williams at Indian Wells: "Sincere fictions" and white racism. *Journal of Sport and Social Issues, 28*(2), 115–135.

Sports Market Intelligence. (2018). SportCal sponsorship sector report: Alcoholic beverages. London: SportsCal.

Stabile, C. (2000). Nike, social responsibility and the hidden abode of production. *Critical Studies in Media Communication, 17*(2), 186–204.

Strasser, J. B., & Becklund, L. (1993). *Swoosh: The unauthorized story of Nike and the men who played there.* New York: Harper Collins.

WARC. (2020). WARC sports sponsorship investment report. London.

Warnett, G. (2016, May). How Run-DMC earned their Adidas stripes. *Mr Porter.* https://www.mrporter.com/en-us/journal/lifestyle/how-run-dmc-earned-their-adidas-stripes-826882.

Wenner, L. A. (1991). One part alcohol, one part sport, one part dirt, stir gently: Beer commercials and television sports. In L. R. Vande Berg & L. A. Wenner (Eds.), *Television criticism: Approaches and applications* (pp. 388–407). New York: Longman.

Wenner, L. A. (Ed.). (2013). *Fallen sports heroes, media, and celebrity culture.* Oxford: Peter Lang.

Wenner, L. A., & Jackson, S. J. (Eds.). (2009). *Sport, beer, and gender: Promotional culture and contemporary social life.* Zurich: Peter Lang Publishers.

Wernick, A. (1991). *Advertising, ideology and symbolic expression.* London: Sage.

Whannel, G. (2002). *Media sport stars: Masculinities and moralities.* London: Routledge.

White, P., & Gillett, J. (1994). Reading the muscular body: A critical decoding of advertisements in *Flex* magazine. *Sociology of Sport Journal, 11*(1), 18–39.

Whitson, D. (1998). Circuits of promotion: Media, marketing and the globalization of sport. In L. A. Wenner (Ed.), *MediaSport* (pp. 57–72). London: Routledge.

Williams, R. (1980). *Problems in materialism and culture.* London: NLB.

Williamson, J. (1978). *Decoding advertisements: Ideology and meaning in advertising.* London: Marion Boyars.

Wilson, B., & Sparks, R. (1996). "It's gotta be the shoes": Youth, race, and sneaker commercials. *Sociology of Sport Journal, 13*(4), 398–427.

World Advertising Research Center. (2020). *Global Ad Trends: Sport Sponsorship Investment.* London, U.K.: Ascential.

World Health Organization. (2011). *Global status report on alcohol and health.* Geneva: World Health Organization.

World Health Organization. (2018). *Global status report on alcohol and health.* Geneva: World Health Organization.

Worsching, M. (2000). Sporting metaphors and the enactment of hegemonic masculinity: Sport and advertising in the German newsmagazine *Der Spiegel. Journal of Popular Culture, 34*(3), 59–86.

Wright, D. (2005). Mediating production and consumption: Cultural capital and "cultural workers." *British Journal of Sociology, 56*(1), 105–121.

CHAPTER 57

··

SPORT, DIGITAL MEDIA, AND SOCIAL MEDIA

··

JIMMY SANDERSON

SOCIAL media and digital technologies are firmly embedded within sport (Sanderson, 2017; Sanderson, Zimmerman, Stokowski, & Fridley, 2020). These technologies have exerted significant influence on a variety of sport stakeholders, including athletes (Hayes, Filo, Geurin, & Riot, 2020; Sanderson, Browning, & DeHay, 2020), coaches (Harvey, Atkinson, & Hyndman, 2020; Smith, Smith, & Blazka, 2017), sport organizations (Abeza, O'Reilly, & Seguin, 2019; Kautz, Schaffrath, & Gang, 2020), sport media entities (Hutchins & Sanderson, 2017; Tang & Cooper, 2018), sport journalists (Hanusch & Nölleke, 2019; Hull, 2017), and fans (Lewis, Brown, Hakim, Billings, & Blakey, 2020; MacPherson & Kerr, 2019). As these technologies have permeated the sport industry, they have introduced a number of opportunities and challenges for sport stakeholders (Na, Kunkel, & Doyle, 2020; Sanderson, 2018b).

For instance, with social media, athletes have a media platform wherein they can share their thoughts at any time with a vast audience (Geurin-Eagleman & Burch, 2016; Toffoletti & Thorpe, 2018). This capability has given rise to personal branding and marketing opportunities for them (Park, Williams, & Son, 2020). Athletes also utilize these platforms to engage in social justice and advocacy issues (Galily, 2019; Schmittel & Sanderson, 2015) and to expose issues within their organization (Callihan, 2020). Conversely, social media also function as digital archives that can be mined and sourced by other social media users. Consequently, several athletes have had key athletic accomplishments tarnished by old social media content resurfacing from when the athlete was in their teenage years (Kilgore, 2018; Young, 2018).

As social and digital technologies continue to advance within society as well as the sport sector, it is crucial to examine their impact. That is, social and digital media technologies contribute to many organizational conflicts (e.g., a player posts something that team management considers inappropriate), provide a platform for abusive behavior from fans toward athletes and media figures, and function as a space for athletes and other sport stakeholders to engage in social justice and advocacy. These technologies also change rapidly, and athletes are frequently early adopters. Thus, sport organizational personnel must be continually learning and assessing how athlete trends will impact their organizations.

For instance, children use social and digital technology at increasingly younger ages, which makes them vulnerable to abuse (Sanderson & Weathers, 2020) and contributes to their creation of digital repositories that can be mined in the future. Certainly, there are benefits that come from marketing initiatives and athletes' ability to take more control over self-presentation and use these platforms to facilitate social change and advocacy.

However, there also is a need to grapple with additional ways that social and digital technologies are being utilized and how sports communication scholarship can help address diverse problematic issues that may arise. Indeed, social media and digital technologies are often accepted as overwhelmingly beneficial for sport organizations and sporting participants, with platform marketing and personal branding features extolled. Yet there are a host of issues that arise from the massive social and digital technology consumption occurring in sport. Social and digital technologies provide voluminous amounts of discourse that can help both researchers and sport practitioners understand topics such as athlete mental health, privacy, social change, and gender, race, political, and sexuality issues in sport. Researchers investigating these issues must adopt critical and reflective approaches that problematize social and digital technologies and may question the often taken-for-granted assumptions regarding their value. For example, Sanderson and Weathers (2020) examined how coach perpetrators utilized Snapchat to facilitate child sexual abuse with minors. In doing so, their analysis raised important questions about safeguarding athletes who are growing up socialized to a digital world. These and other implications arising from the proliferation of social and digital technologies in sport will be examined in this chapter. This chapter also includes a discussion of how scholarship and research can assist in addressing these key issues. The chapter concludes with some matters in need of further attention and directions for future research efforts.

ISSUES

The literature on social and digital technologies in sport has experienced significant growth over the past decade and, at present, shows no signs of slowing. Although there are a number of research strands that might be highlighted here, this chapter will focus on the following topics as most pressing on the scholarly agenda: (1) social media and athlete identity and self-presentation, (2) social media and privacy, and (3) social media and abuse.

Social Media and Athlete Identity and Self-Presentation

Arguably, one of the most significant shifts that social media has introduced into sport is the capability for athletes to have more control over their public self-presentation and identity expression (Lebel & Danylchuk, 2012; Sanderson, 2011a). While athletes certainly had ways to disseminate their preferred or alternate identities prior to the advent of social media, these avenues were often limited. Through social and digital technologies, athletes engage in a variety of self-presentation strategies and express identity in varied ways (Geurin-Eagleman & Burch, 2016; Toffoletti & Thorpe, 2018).

Athletes' self-presentation also can influence their brand image and consumer perceptions (Na et al., 2020). Other research has noted that social media can help to increase the representation of traditionally marginalized groups in sport by facilitating and stimulating more coverage and attention of group concerns in online spaces and garnering the attention of mainstream media (Litchfield & Kavanagh, 2019). Still, in some cases, athletes may self-present in ways that reflect and reinforce traditional gender norms (Weathers et al., 2014; Smith & Sanderson, 2015). Further, some athletes also may feel pressure to self-present in ways they believe audiences want to see them or in a manner that will minimize negative audience feedback (Geurin, 2017).

Athletes' self-presentation via social and digital technology also has created friction with sport organizational personnel (Sanderson, 2014). Additionally, in the emergent days of social media, athletes appeared to be somewhat reticent to speak up about social and political topics. This initial stage has morphed to where many athletes now speak up about issues such as racism, police brutality, and other social justice concerns (Galily, 2019; Hyat, Galily, & Samuel-Azran, 2020). Whereas these expressions may create conflict with fans (Frederick, Sanderson, & Schlereth, 2017), many sport organizations are also in the midst of adapting to social change and increasingly appear to be more supportive of athletes' identity expressions, even if that alienates some fans and sponsors.

As social media becomes more ensconced in sport, vast amounts of data are being created by athletes and sport consumers that benefit social media companies. Sport organization personnel also have sought ways to regulate and manage athletes' social media use. Additionally, with children increasing their consumption of social media from increasingly younger ages, vast data repositories are being created that can be publicly mined.

Social Media and Privacy

Concerns about privacy have been intertwined with social media since its inception (Debatin, Lovejoy, Horn, & Hughes, 2009). Within sport, concerns about privacy were raised early in the literature (Sanderson, 2009), as athletes were subjected to people posting their whereabouts and activities and capturing private behavior to disseminate for public consumption. As social and digital media platforms have evolved and become staples of the sport industry, one aspect of privacy that is increasingly important to consider is data protection. This area includes social media users such as athletes, along with how social media entities such as Facebook and Instagram employ algorithms. On one hand, algorithms derived from social media provide sport organizations with efficiently narrow data on sport consumers, yet on the other hand, they may create skewed perceptions of the audience.

Rowe (2014) cautioned about the role of the capitalist marketplace in thinking about the need to temper unfettered enthusiasm around Twitter, while Hutchins (2014) posited a need to consider how the primacy of commodification concerns evident on social media platforms such as Twitter affect discourse and priorities. Indeed, it is important to recognize that social media companies such as Facebook, Twitter, and Instagram clearly profit from the traffic that sport audiences offer. These audiences, collectively, provide a host of insights to sport organizations that they can then use to tailor marketing campaigns and other organizational initiatives to advantage their marketplace position. In addition, as sport organizations adopt more mobile and digital-only practices such as ticketing and concessions (Marquez, Cianfrone, & Kellison, 2020), access to and protection of consumer information will be important considerations in evaluating these practices.

As athletes have adopted social media in large numbers, sport organizational personnel (e.g., coaches, athletic directors, and marketers) have seen a corresponding reduction in control over messaging (Sanderson, 2011a). Via social and digital media, athletes essentially have media platforms that enable them to reach large audiences at any time. Consequently, there have been a number of challenging public relations issues that have arisen from things athletes have posted on social media, or even disclosed during video game streaming (Evans, 2018). Perhaps in an effort to alleviate the number and severity of public relations incidents, sport organizations have adopted policies to manage and regulate social media use, particularly at the intercollegiate level in the United States (Sanderson, 2011b; Sanderson, Snyder, Hull, & Gramlich, 2015). These social media policies are strongly related to privacy as they raise questions about the degree to which an organization should be able to regulate and monitor what an athlete posts on social media (Sanderson, 2011b; Sanderson, Snyder, et al., 2015). Scholars also have observed that privacy boundaries relating to social media are unclear to athletes (Sanderson & Browning, 2013) and that athletes desire training and education about social media (Sanderson, Browning, & Schmittel, 2015).

One particular trend that illustrates negative repercussions for athletes as it pertains to social and digital technologies is the mining of archived content, which, when publicly exposed, often at inopportune times for athletes, can cause complex problems. For instance, as he was being named Most Outstanding Player during the 2018 NCAA Final Four, Villanova University men's basketball player Dante DiVincenzo was confronted with media reports documenting tweets from 2011 that contained rap lyrics that used the "n" word (Owens, 2018). DiVincenzo deleted his Twitter account and Villanova men's basketball released a tweet indicating that DiVincenzo's account had been hacked (Owens, 2018). Nonetheless, he was subjected to questions about an old social media post instead of being asked to talk about winning such a prestigious award or his team winning the National Championship. Similar incidents have happened to University of Oklahoma football player Kyler Murray on the night he won the 2018 Heisman Trophy (Young, 2018), Major League Baseball pitcher Josh Hader as he was pitching in the 2018 MLB All-Star Game (Kilgore, 2018), and University of Wyoming football player Josh Allen as he was being considered for the 2018 National Football League Draft (Kirshner, 2018).

These incidents illustrate privacy dilemmas inherent in social media for athletes. On one hand, an argument may be made that social media exists for public consumption and there is no expectation of privacy. On the other hand, it needs to be asked to what degree athletes should be judged for social media posts made years in the past? Additionally, there seem to be ethical complexities associated with those who mine the athlete's social media history looking for content to publicly expose. Indeed, using social media does entail risk, and users, including high-profile users such as athletes, certainly need to exercise restraint in what they post. However, given the increase in young children using social media, by the time an athlete reaches the age when college recruitment or professional sports becomes realistic, they may have an archive spanning a decade or more. It also is important to consider what kind of education athletes are given about their social media usage when they are younger. Some athletes may be given little education or receive little parental/guardian oversight and guidance about their social media use. Consequently, these athletes may operate under the premise that their social media content is being viewed only by friends and cannot be accessed by others. Given indicants that athletes desire social media education (Sanderson, Browning, et al., 2015), and because the risks inherent in social and digital technology use are considerable (Sanderson, 2018b), education is a critical endeavor.

Athletes can also be victims of abuse on social media (Kassing & Sanderson, 2015; Sanderson, Browning et al., 2020). Thus, another important issue to consider centers on virtual forms of abuse that athletes experience from fans as well as from more trusted individuals such as coaches.

Social Media and Abuse

Social and digital media are largely unregulated spaces, domains that are predicated on notions of freedom of speech and audience, or user-generated content (Litchfield, Kavanagh, Osborne, & Jones, 2018). While these technologies can be used for healthy and positive purposes, they also have created "the presence of unbridled, unexamined, and often unpunished abuse which can reach individuals not only in real-time, but can further be re-read, re-posted, and re-visited" (p. 155). Kavanagh and Jones (2014, p. 156) conceptualized abuse that occurs in virtual spaces as virtual maltreatment, which they defined as "[d]irect or non-direct online communication that is stated in an aggressive, exploitative, manipulative, threatening or lewd manner and is designed to elicit fear, emotional or psychological upset, distress, alarm, or feelings of inferiority" (see also Kavanagh, Jones, & Sheppard-Marks, 2016, p. 788).

Litchfield et al. (2018) further classified virtual abuse in four broad forms—physical, sexual, emotional, and discriminatory—which can be further parsed into discrimination based on gender, race, sexual orientation, religion, and/or disability. Athletes can be direct victims of virtual abuse or can be victimized indirectly by being "talked about" (p. 156). Further, social media platforms such as Twitter offer a space where social restrictions are abandoned. Thus, people may engage in abusive communication online, whereas they would not do so offline (Suler, 2004), a difference often attributed to the anonymity offered by these media (Litchfield et al., 2018). Indeed, social media platforms provide a "fertile space for abuse to occur" and normalize toxic behavior such as demeaning and belittling those who are perceived to deviate from social norms and ideals (p. 166). As a result, some scholars suggest that the proliferation of vitriol published online has become a major social issue (Kavanagh et al., 2016).

Sexual abuse may also occur through social and digital technology. Sanderson and Weathers (2020) examined how youth athletes experienced virtual maltreatment and sexually abusive behaviors from coaches using Snapchat. They found that these coaches employed Snapchat to facilitate grooming for more aggressive sexual contact and behaviors. Conversations would begin innocently, then progress to more sexually explicit topics. The authors also found that some coaches created fake profiles, posing and posting as children to request that victims send them nude pictures and videos. Additional findings in this research included coaches using Snapchat's geolocation feature to track victims' whereabouts and approach them. Perpetrators preferred Snapchat as a locus of communication, given perceptions that content disappears shortly after a recipient opens it. Sanderson and Weathers suggested that there was a need for sport organizations to work to protect children by developing and enforcing clear policies regarding coach-athlete communication.

Issues of self-presentation/identity, privacy, and abuse represent just a fraction of topics pertaining to social and digital media. Indeed, there are a number of compelling and needed directions for researchers to traverse, particularly as social media continues to evolve at a rapid pace. The following section reviews some methods and theoretical approaches that researchers can take to more critically examine the intersection of sport and social and digital media.

APPROACHES

Just as there are a multitude of areas wherein sport and social and digital technologies can be examined, there are a corresponding number of theoretical directions and approaches that scholars have employed. One of the primary concerns about social and digital media research in the sport communication literature has been an overreliance on descriptive research and content analyses (Hardin, 2014). As noted earlier, some scholars have argued for a stronger focus on commodification and the nature of capitalist forces that underpin social media channels and consumption related to sport (Hutchins, 2014; Rowe, 2014).

Still, a good deal of research that continues to be submitted and published in this area centers on attributes of social media content and messaging (Sanderson, 2018a). Certainly, it is important to understand how sport stakeholders may be fashioning strategic content. Unfortunately, the continued disproportionate focus on social media content analysis perpetuates two problematic outcomes: (1) limited research that does not advance broader understandings of content creation and its impacts and (2) missing out on opportunities to more critically examine the discursive dynamics at play in social media content. For example, there is extant research about how athletes self-present via a number of social media platforms (cf. Geurrin-Eagleman & Burch, 2016; Xu & Armstrong, 2019). It seems prudent that, rather than searching for a sport segment that has not been looked at for self-presentation (e.g., National Hockey League goalies) or jumping onto emergent social media platforms such as TikTok, researchers would be better served by looking at the implications of self-presentation on social media. For example, wrestling with the question of whether athletes are really "free" to self-present on social media by using tactics that would integrate identity politics research or other critical approaches can help advance important knowledge about whether social media is as liberating for identity as many advocates believe it to be.

Self-presentation research also could go beyond descriptive, thematic analyses by looking at the actual discourse of athletes and other sport stakeholders on social and digital media. For instance, rather than looking at a list of themes that reflect what kinds of things an athlete, coach, or broadcaster is conveying on social media, it would be beneficial to examine the discourse within these messages and responses to more fully understand their impact. Sveinson and Hoeber (2020) utilized critical discourse analysis to investigate social media responses to MLB player Kevin Pillar uttering a homophobic slur after striking out. They noted how the discourse functioned to both legitimize and condemn the use of homophobic slurs in sport and observed that the discourse illustrated the need for cultural changes within sport organizations and fan groups to promote more inclusivity. This research aligns with other scholarship that has found social media discourse can signal cultural changes in sport audiences around topics such as gender (Sanderson & Gramlich, 2016).

Indeed, the application of more culturally and critically engaged analytic tactics, such as critical discourse analysis, is needed to understand the contemporary sport environment at deeper levels. Further, given that sport competition stopped for a considerable period of time during the global pandemic and the debates surrounding return to play, along with social unrest in the United States relating to police brutality and systemic racism, there is a prime opportunity to more fully interrogate social media intersections with sport through discursive rather than less contextualized descriptive analysis. As one illustrative example for study, consider this tweet posted by the Tampa Bay Rays on July 24, 2020, prior to the start of their first post-COVID-19 game: "Today is Opening Day which means it's a great day to arrest the killers of Breonna Taylor" (quoted in Dedaj, 2020, para. 3). This one tweet generated a significant amount of discourse that would be useful in understanding the social climate in the United States related to racism and police brutality, and the role of sport and politics. Moreover, such a tweet represents a dramatic shift for sport organizations in their content strategy, as they have historically avoided making statements about political or social justice topics. Thus, examining the underlying factors leading to sport organizations embracing social and political topics as part of their social media strategy clearly needs deconstruction and, thus, would be a fruitful avenue to explore.

Privacy frameworks such as Petronio's (1991) community privacy management (CPM) theory hold great promise for examining social and digital technologies within sport. While research has utilized CPM theory to examine social media policies for athletes (Sanderson, 2011b; Sanderson, Snyder et al., 2015), there are other contexts where this perspective could be illuminating. Consider video game consumption and the growth of athletes participating in video game streams (Sanderson, Browning, et al., 2020). When athletes (or others, for that matter) participate in video game streams, should their conversations be considered private? Do they have an expectation of privacy when gaming? As one example, NASCAR driver Kyle Larson was fired by Chip Ganassi Racing after he used the "n" word while participating in a video game stream (Li, 2020). Other research has found that athletes often play video games with fans and with athletes they are facing in competition (Sanderson, Browning, et al., 2020), conditions that raise intriguing questions about privacy and boundaries. For instance, if an athlete criticizes a coach on a video game stream (Cowley, 2020; Evans, 2018), should the athlete be disciplined for making that statement? Using alternative frameworks such as CPM can help to further our understanding of digital boundaries and the contours of essential strategies such as dissent as they are employed on digital and social media.

Humanistic, qualitative approaches also are needed in more abundance to further our understanding of the impact of social and digital technology in sport. Most particularly, engaging different sport stakeholders to understand their experiences with social and digital media can provide insight that is often unattainable from merely examining social media content. Hayes, Filo, Geurin, and Riot (2020) examined athletes' use of social media during major sporting events. They found some athletes reported that being able to use social media helped them stay connected to friends and family, which subsequently helped them feel less stress during competition. Such findings counter dominant narratives about athlete consumption of social media, which is often framed as being largely a distraction. Hayes et al. also noted that such information can help better inform social media education for athletes.

There is a need as well for more savvy tactics to explore the use of social and digital technologies in inflicting abuse on athlete and other actors in the sporting community (Sanderson & Weathers, 2020). Although such examinations may be uncomfortable and certainly shine a light on the "dark" side of sports (Sanderson & Weathers, 2020), such endeavors are necessary to understand the need for the safeguarding of athletes, in terms of both their physical and mental health. For instance, at the time of this writing, one of the more emergent and popular social media platforms is TikTok. While there is likely to be a goodly amount of research forthcoming from sport management scholars that explores how sport organization, athletes, and other sport stakeholders use TikTok for marketing and branding, more critical analysis is needed on how this platform might function as a form of abuse.

As something new is always blooming around the corner, keeping pace with the endless array of topics needing investigation with regard to sport and digital technology can be daunting. Clearly, there are a number of approaches and frameworks that can be used. Whereas content and descriptive analyses have been predominant in the literature to this point, the preceding assessment serves to call for moving beyond the heretofore extensive reliance on content analysis and illustrates the myriad ways that we can understand key issues about social and digital technology in sport without examining content at all. Further, even when content is examined, a good case may be made that such analyses should move beyond description (Hardin, 2014) and employ more critically and culturally sensitive discursive approaches (Sveinson & Hoeber, 2020) that attend to the meaning of content rather than merely its classification.

Debates

Moving forward, there are a number of unresolved issues pertaining to social and digital media and identity/self-presentation, privacy, and athlete abuse. This section highlights some of these topics and discusses how researchers might advance the literature by attending to these issues. First, with regard to identity and self-presentation, there is a growing trend of athletes and sport figures using secret or alternate social media accounts, known as "burner accounts." These are operated by individuals without overtly disclosing their identity, which arguably plays a role in prompting them to divulge information that they might not otherwise share from their verified personal accounts. For example, National Basketball Association player Kevin Durant has openly admitted to using burner accounts on Twitter to respond to criticism directed at him from other social media users (Gartland, 2020). Durant's operation of a burner account was first discovered in 2017 after he elected to join the Golden State Warriors as a free agent (Gartland, 2020). Burner accounts also have implications for other sport figures. In one notable case in 2018, Philadelphia 76ers President Bryan Colangelo stepped down from his position after it was reported that he was operating Twitter burner accounts that disseminated criticism of current 76ers players (Detrick, 2018). Additionally, these burner accounts disclosed health information about injured 76ers players, raising questions about potential violations of the Health Insurance Portability and Accountability Act. It was later discovered that Colangelo's wife was operating the burner accounts (Detrick, 2018).

These examples highlight important implications pertaining to self-presentation and athlete identity expression via social media. Specifically, these constructs need to be addressed through consideration about how athletes and other sport stakeholders may be using burner accounts to communicate in more "authentic" ways to share more unvarnished, "honest" sentiments than are typically seen on their verified accounts. Indeed, uncovering holistic understandings of self-presentation and identity expression may involve a more nuanced approach of diverse alternate social media pathways. Clearly, while athletes self-present in very scripted ways via their identifiable "branded" accounts, some may engage in less scripted self-presentation via burner accounts that may be more revealing. Inquiries into the evolution of self-presentation and identity expression also need to consider the growth of fake Instagram accounts, or "finstas" (Kang & Wei, 2020). These accounts too are used to portray content that users wish to keep off their identified accounts.

Whereas users may believe these burner accounts cannot be traced, as Durant's case illustrates, their authorship can be uncovered. As an additional example, in 2018 seven University of Kansas rowers were suspended for operating finstas (Goodwin, 2018). With respect to "infractions" such as the Colangelo case, there are organizational implications that need examination as well. For instance, what kind of safeguards do sport organizations implement to prevent sensitive information, such as health data, from being disclosed via social media? In addition, it may be necessary to look at interpersonal relationships and how they factor into burner accounts. Sport organizations have historically tried to safeguard information, yet burner accounts make it possible for organizational members—and, as the Colangelo case illustrates, their family members—to divulge sensitive information.

One factor that may help explain the use of burner or other alternative accounts is the desire for privacy. Indeed, some athletes and sport figures may perceive that these accounts provide a format to share more of their authentic self, without a perceived fear of repercussions.

Another fruitful area to explore further pertains to the growth of digital technology applications that are heavily utilized in youth sports (Sanderson & Baerg, 2020). Parents and coaches are confronted with a host of applications that can help measure a variety of statistics in sports such as baseball, softball, and soccer. Some of this technology now includes GPS tracking and advanced biometric measuring, features which are marketed to parents and children to optimize athletic performance. The growth of reliance on and the mainstreaming of these technologies and their massive accumulation and repurposing of data suggest a need to critically assess how these technologies are altering or reconfiguring the youth sports experience (Sanderson & Baerg, 2020).

Another important area to examine centers on how athletes and other sport figures are judged for content they post on social and digital media, including material posted in the past. One notable illustration involves Houston Rockets General Manager Daryl Morey, who in October 2019 tweeted a graphic that indicated support for Hong Kong protestors (Botte, 2020). Shortly after this tweet was sent, the NBA experienced an international crisis as the Chinese government and Chinese-owned businesses began dissolving sponsorships and other partnerships (Botte, 2020). The NBA responded by deflecting the impact of Morey's tweet and expressing support for China and the league's Chinese consumers.

However, the economic fallout of Morey's tweet for the NBA is calculated to be as much as U.S.$200 million (Botte, 2020). The tweet also brought in a host of political actors, such as U.S. Senator Ted Cruz, who criticized the NBA for appearing to pander to China, positioning the NBA's response in apparently acquiescing to a communist regime against the backdrop of the league's support for those protesting police brutality in the United States (Dawson, 2019).

Key issues about athlete abuse and social media need further sorting. There remains much to be examined to better understand how athletes can be safeguarded, protected, and educated. A brief example will help to illustrate this claim. In their study of how coaches used Snapchat to engage in sexual abuse, one of Sanderson and Weathers's (2020) key findings was that the coaches were using fake accounts, pretending to be children to engage their victims. It is crucial that efforts be made to better educate young athletes and their parents about these practices. In addition to educating young athletes and parents on this behavior and how it might manifest, it would seem prudent for social media entities like Snapchat to take a more proactive role to mitigate the prevalence of these behaviors. Twitter has made some efforts to curb abusive behavior (Newton, 2018), although there has been criticism that these measures do not go far enough and still perpetuate abusive and bullying behaviors (Lorenz, 2018).

Finally, there is a need for continued programming and education to help athletes deal with abusive messages they may receive on social media. Researchers have noted that athletes can experience problematic psychological outcomes when viewing such messages (David et al., 2018). Accordingly, it is imperative that sport organizations continue to provide mental health resources, including counseling, to help athletes deal with receiving these kinds of messages. It also is crucial that such behavior be more clearly identified as constituting abuse (Kavanagh & Jones, 2014; Sanderson, Zimmerman et al., 2020). Although some of these messages have been attributed to maladaptive forms of fandom (Sanderson & Truax, 2014; Sanderson, Zimmerman et al., 2020), the content of many of these messages has the potential to inflict considerable harm. Thus, by clearly recognizing and labeling this type of content as abuse, it may be possible to increase public awareness and prompt sport organizations to be more proactive in taking firm stands that such behavior will not be tolerated. As a side effect, they will have fewer public relations crises to contend with.

Conclusion

The growth of digital and social technologies in sport over the past decade has been significant. These technologies now seem to penetrate essentially every area of sport. They also change rapidly, which can make it challenging for both sport organizational personnel and researchers to keep pace. However, with challenges comes opportunities, and there are many fruitful avenues that can be traversed in looking at the impact of social and digital technologies on sport as they pertain to self-presentation and identity expression, privacy, and athlete abuse.

First, as has been noted by other scholars (Hardin, 2014), it is important that much of the work in these areas be examined absent content and thematic analyses. Again, these content-centered approaches do have value, but they do not sufficiently address why athletes and other sport stakeholders engage in certain practices through digital and social technology, and the effects of these practices. For example, rather than a content analysis from an athlete's burner account, it would be beneficial to engage athletes to reflect about why they use burner accounts. Interview methodologies would help to better understand the lived experiences of athletes in utilizing these accounts and more significantly inform our understanding of self-presentation and identity expression.

Second, critical analyses are needed about identity expression and the implications that come with these portrayals. For instance, looking at the discourse employed by athletes and coaches across digital and social media would help to understand things like athlete activism beyond merely acknowledging that social media audiences tend to confirm or challenge what athletes have said. Critical discourse analysis methods (Sveinson & Hoeber, 2020) seem particularly useful here, as they can help illustrate how word choice and language further our understanding of topics like racism and police brutality and the role of sport and sport stakeholders in addressing these societal issues.

Third, critical analyses are warranted to look at aspects of surveillance and judgment of athletes and sport figures. For instance, what are the implications of sport organizations utilizing facial recognition technology? Should fans be given opportunities to consent to entering venues when this technology is being used? Assessing the protection and safeguarding of data also warrants further discussion and analysis. With respect to judgment and evaluation of athletes and sport figures and their use of social and digital technology, privacy boundaries and expectations are paramount topics to consider. When an athlete participates in a video game stream on a platform like Twitch, should their comments be considered public? If a sports figure criticizes an organizational member on a video game stream or social media post, how should such dissent be viewed? It also will be imperative to look at political and financial ramifications from social and digital content. Morey's tweet may be the most costly social media message ever transmitted given the loss of sponsorships the NBA experienced (Botte, 2020). Yet this tweet also opened up significant media discourse about the role of sport and politics and the handling of international crises. Indeed, such research at the intersection of social and digital media content with political and economic forces would not only advance understanding of this nexus with sport but would illustrate its cultural potency.

With respect to athlete abuse, it will be crucial to continue to explore how this behavior occurs, how it impacts athletes, and how sport organizations can better support athletes. Researchers must continue to analyze reports of how social and digital media may be used to enact abuse (Sanderson & Weathers, 2020) along with designing education and interventions that can help to minimize its prevalence. Researchers could utilize approaches similar to those taken by McMahon, Knight, and McGannon (2018), who employed narrative pedagogy to educate parents about abuse. Working with community sport organizations such as youth sport associations and NGOs can be instrumental in helping scholarship be applied more consistently in an area where it is severely needed. Future endeavors here would benefit from engaging athletes and other sport figures to better understand how they process abusive messages and deal with abuse (David et al., 2018).

As sport and digital technology continues to advance, so too must scholarship. As more holistic research efforts are undertaken to explore beyond the description of content, the impacts of social and digital technologies on sport can be more broadly assessed. As this occurs, the research in this area will grow more diverse and inclusive of the impact these technologies have and will help us to further understand central issues such as self-presentation, identity expression, privacy, and athlete well-being.

REFERENCES

Abeza, G., O'Reilly, N., & Seguin, B. (2019). Social media in relationship marketing: The perspective of professional sport managers in the MLB, NBA, NFL, and NHL. *Communication & Sport, 7,* 80–109.

Botte, P. (2020, January 30). Daryl Morey's Hong Kong tweet cost NBA $150–200 million. *New York Post.* https://nypost.com/2020/01/30/daryl-morey-hong-kong-tweet-cost-nba-150-200-million/.

Callihan, S. (2020, June 23). Breaking: WVU DC Vic Koenning placed on admirative leave. *Fan Nation.* https://www.si.com/college/westvirginia/football/breaking-wvu-dc-vic-koenning-placed-on-administrative-leave.

Cowley, J. (2020, July 21). Bulls rookie Daniel Gafford does no favors for his coach on Twitch. *NBC Sports.* https://www.nbcsports.com/chicago/bulls/bulls-coach-jim-boylen-defended-daniel-gafford-nba-2k20-twitch-stream.

David, J. L., Powless, M. D., Hyman, J. E., Purnell, D. M., Steinfeldt, J. A., & Fisher, S. (2018). College student athletes and social media: The psychological impacts of Twitter use. *International Journal of Sport Communication, 11,* 163–186.

Dawson, P. (2019, October 7). Rockets GM Daryl Morey's controversial tweet sparks reactions from Ted Cruz, Beto O' Rourke, others. *Houston Chronicle.* https://www.houstonchronicle.com/sports/rockets/article/Daryl-Morey-tweet-Rockets-Fertitta-Hong-Kong-China-14497866.php.

Debatin, B., Lovejoy, J. P., Horn, A. K., & Hughes, B. N. (2009). Facebook and online privacy: Attitudes, behaviors, and unintended consequences. *Journal of Computer-Mediated Communication, 15,* 83–108.

Dedaj, P. (2020, July 24). Tampa Bay Rays call for arrest of officers involved in Breonna Taylor's shooting death. *Fox News.* https://www.foxnews.com/sports/rays-tweet-arrest-fatal-shooting-breonna-taylor-opening-day.

Detrick, B. (2018, May 29). The curious case of Bryan Colangelo and the secret Twitter account. *The Ringer.* https://www.theringer.com/nba/2018/5/29/17406750/bryan-colangelo-philadelphia-76ers-twitter-joel-embiid-anonymous-markelle-fultz.

Evans, J. (2018, September 4). Padres' Wil Myers apologizes to manager Andy Green for comments made in Fortnite stream. *USA Today.*http://www.usatoday.com/story/sports/mlb/padres/2018/09/03/wil-myers-apologizes-fortnite-stream-comments-andy-green/1188565002/.

Frederick, E., Sanderson, J., & Schlereth, N. (2017). Kick these kids off the team and take away their scholarships: Facebook and perceptions of athlete activism at the University of Missouri. *Journal of Issues in Intercollegiate Athletics, 10,* 17–34.

Galily, Y. (2019). "Shut up and dribble!?" Athletes activism in the age of twittersphere: The case of LeBron James. *Technology in Society, 58,* 1–4.

Gartland, D. (2020, February 6). Kevin Durant still uses a burner account to respond to haters online. *Sports Illustrated.* https://www.si.com/nba/2020/02/06/kevin-durant-burner-account-matt-barnes-video.

Geurin, A. N. (2017). Elite female athletes' perceptions of new media use relating to their careers: A qualitative analysis. *Journal of Sport Management, 31*, 345–359.

Geurin-Eagleman, A., & Burch, L. (2016). Communicating via photographs: A gendered analysis of Olympic athletes' visual self-presentation on Instagram. *Sport Management Review, 19*, 133–145.

Goodwin, S. (2018, April 22). Seven Kansas rowers suspended amid social media scandal. *University Daily Kansan.* https://www.kansan.com/sports/seven-kansas-rowers-suspen ded-amid-social-media-scandal/article_6be7c8c4-4676-11e8-8a56-13d66c809639.html.

Hanusch, F., & Nölleke, D. (2019). Journalistic homophily on social media: Exploring journalists' interactions with each other on Twitter. *Digital Journalism, 7*, 22–44.

Hardin, M. (2014). Moving beyond description: Putting Twitter in (theoretical) context. *Communication & Sport, 2*, 113–116.

Harvey, S., Atkinson, O., & Hyndman, B. P. (2020). An investigation into sport coaches Twitter use. *Journal of Teaching in Physical Education.* Advance online publication. doi:10.1123/jtpe.2019-0283.

Hayes, M., Filo, K., Geurin, A., & Riot, C. (2020). An exploration of the distractions inherent to social media use among athletes. *Sport Management Review, 23*, 852–868.

Hayes, M., Filo, K., Riot, C., & Geurin, A. (2019). Athlete perceptions of social media benefits and challenges during major sporting events. *International Journal of Sport Communication, 12*, 449–481.

Hull, K. (2017). An examination of women's sports coverage on the Twitter accounts of local television sports broadcasters. *Communication & Sport, 5*, 471–491.

Hutchins, B. (2014). Twitter: Follow the money and look beyond sports. *Communication & Sport, 2*, 122–126.

Hutchins, B., & Sanderson, J. (2017). The flow of sports television: Olympic media, social networking services, and multi-screen viewing. *Media International Australia, 164*, 32–43.

Hyat, T., Galily, Y., & Samuel-Arzan, T. (2020). Can celebrity athletes burst the echo chamber bubble? The case of LeBron James and Lady Gaga. *International Review for the Sociology of Sport, 55*, 900–914.

Kang, J., & Wei, L. (2020). Let me be at my funniest: Instagram users' motivations for using Finsta (a.k.a. fake Instagram). *Social Science Journal, 57*, 58–71.

Kassing, J. W., & Sanderson, J. (2015). Playing in the new media game or riding the virtual bench: Confirming and disconfirming membership in the community of sport. *Journal of Sport & Social Issues, 39*, 3–18.

Kautz, F., Schaffrath, M., & Gang, A. C. (2020). Identifying the different approaches in use of social media outlets: A case study of German professional sports teams. *International Journal of Sport Communication, 13*, 239–261.

Kavanagh, E. J., & Jones, I. (2014). #cyberviolence. Developing a typology for understanding virtual maltreatment in sport. In D. Rhind & C. Brackenridge (Eds.), *Researching and enhancing athlete welfare* (pp. 34–43). London: Brunel University Press.

Kavanagh, E., Jones, I., & Sheppard-Marks. L. (2016). Towards typologies of virtual maltreatment: Sport, digital cultures and dark leisure. *Leisure Studies, 35*, 783–796.

Kilgore, A. (2018, July 18). Ugly tweets from Brewers' Josh Hader surface during MLB All-Star game. *Washington Post.* https://www.washingtonpost.com/sports/ugly-tweets-from-brew ers-josh-hader-surface-during-mlb-all-star-game/2018/07/18/7de58772-8a42-11e8-a345-a1bf7847b375_story.html.

Kirshner, A. (2018, April 27). Josh Allen's deleted tweets didn't keep the Bills from trading up to draft him. *SBNation.* https://www.sbnation.com/nfl/2018/4/26/17284170/josh-allen-dele ted-tweets-draft.

Lebel, K., & Danylchuk, (2012). How tweet it is: A gendered analysis of professional tennis players' self-presentation on Twitter. *International Journal of Sport Communication, 5,* 461–480.

Lewis, M., Brown, K. A., Hakim, S. D., Billings, A. C., & Blakey, C. H. (2020). Looking for information in all the right places? Outlet types of social media information and National Basketball Association fan desires. *International Journal of Sport Communication, 13,* 200–220.

Li, D. K. (2020, April 14). NASCAR star Kyle Larson fired by his team after saying N-word during virtual race. *NBC News.* https://www.nbcnews.com/news/us-news/nascar-star-kyle-larson-fired-his-team-after-saying-n-n1183611.

Litchfield, C., & Kavanagh, E. (2019). Twitter, Team GB and the Australian Olympic Team: Representations of gender in social media spaces. *Sport in Society, 22,* 1148–1164.

Litchfield, C., Kavanagh, E., Osborne, J., & Jones, I. (2018). Social media and the politics of gender, race and identity: The case of Serena Williams. *European Journal for Sport and Society, 15,* 154–170.

Lorenz, T. (2018, September 4). Twitter's new features aren't what users asked for. *The Atlantic.* https://www.theatlantic.com/technology/archive/2018/09/twitter-keeps-rolling-out-featu res-but-not-the-ones-that-matter/569296/.

MacPherson, E., & Kerr, G. (2019). Sport fans' responses on social media to professional athletes' norm violations. *International Journal of Sport and Exercise Psychology.* Advance online publication. doi:10.1080/1612197X.2019.162383.

Marquez, A., Cianfrone, B. A., & Kellison, T. (2020). Factors affecting spectators' adoption of digital ticketing: The case of interscholastic sports. *International Journal of Sports Marketing and Sponsorship, 21,* 527–541.

McMahon, J., Knight, C. J., & McGannon, K. R. (2018). Educating parents of children in sport about abuse using narrative pedagogy. *Sociology of Sport Journal, 35,* 314–323.

Na, S., Kunkel, T., & Doyle. J. (2020). Exploring athlete brand image development on social media: The role of signalling through source credibility. *European Sport Management Quarterly, 20,* 88–108.

Newton, C. (2018, May 15). Twitter will hide more bad tweets in conversations and searches. *The Verge.* https://www.theverge.com/2018/5/15/17352962/twitter-abuse-changes-ranking-tweets-conversations-search.

Owens, J. (2018, April 3). Donte DiVincenzo deletes Twitter account after past tweets surface. *Yahoo Sports.* https://sports.yahoo.com/donte-divincenzos-ncaa-mop-performance-shi nes-light-unfortunate-twitter-history-050759580.html.

Park. J., Williams, A., & Son, S. (2020). Social media as a personal branding tool: A qualitative study of student-athletes' perceptions and behaviors. *Journal of Athlete Development and Experience, 2,* 51–68.

Petronio, S. (1991). Communication boundary management: A theoretical model of managing disclosure of private information between martial couples. *Communication Theory, 1,* 311–335.

Rowe, D. (2014). Following the followers: Researchers' labour lost in the Twittersphere? *Communication & Sport, 2,* 117–121.

Sanderson, J. (2009). Professional athletes' shrinking privacy boundaries: Fans, ICTs, and athlete monitoring. *International Journal of Sport Communication, 2,* 240–256.

Sanderson, J. (2011a). *It's a whole new ball game: How social media is changing sports.* New York: Hampton Press.

Sanderson, J. (2011b). To tweet or not to tweet . . .: Exploring Division I athletic departments' social media policies. *International Journal of Sport Communication, 4,* 492–513.

Sanderson, J. (2014). Just warming up: Logan Morrison, Twitter, athlete identity, and building the brand. In B. Brummett & A. W. Ishak (Eds.), *Sport and identity: New agendas in communication* (pp. 208–223). New York: Routledge.

Sanderson, J. (2017). Sport as social media networking studies. In A. C. Billings (Ed.), *Sport communication: Defining the field* (pp. 281–295). New York: Routledge.

Sanderson, J. (2018a). Guarding against quick and easy: Tightening up qualitative sport and social media research. In A. Bundon (Ed.), *Digital qualitative research in sport* (pp. 80–92). New York: Routledge.

Sanderson, J. (2018b). Think twice before you post: Issues student-athletes face on social media. *New Directions for Student Services, 163,* 81–92.

Sanderson, J., & Baerg, A. (2020). Youth baseball and data analytics: Quantifying risk management and producing neoliberal responsible citizenship through the GameChanger app. *Communication and Sport, 8,* 72–91.

Sanderson, J., & Browning, B. (2013). Training versus monitoring: A qualitative examination of athletic department practices regarding student-athletes and Twitter. *Qualitative Research Reports in Communication, 14,* 105–111.

Sanderson, J., Browning, B., & DeHay, H. (2020). "It's the universal language": Investigating student-athletes' use of and motivations for playing Fortnite. *Journal of Issues in Intercollegiate Athletics, 13,* 22–44.

Sanderson, J., Browning, B., & Schmittel, A. (2015). Education on the digital terrain: A case study exploring college athletes' perceptions of social media education. *International Journal of Sport Communication, 8,* 103–124.

Sanderson, J., & Gramlich, K. (2016). "You go girl!" Twitter and conversations about sport culture and gender. *Sociology of Sport Journal, 33,* 113–123.

Sanderson, J., Snyder, E., Hull, D., & Gramlich, K. (2015). Social media policies within NCAA member institutions: Evolving technology and its impact on policy. *Journal of Issues in Intercollegiate Athletics, 8,* 50–73.

Sanderson, J., & Truax, C. (2014). "I hate you man!" Exploring maladaptive parasocial interaction expressions to college athletes via Twitter. *Journal of Issues in Intercollegiate Athletics, 7,* 333–351.

Sanderson, J., & Weathers M. (2020). Snapchat and child sexual abuse in sport: Protecting child athletes in the social media age. *Sport Management Review, 23,* 81–94.

Sanderson, J., Zimmerman, M., Stokowski, S., & Fridley, A. (2020). "You had one job!": A case study of maladaptive parasocial interaction and athlete maltreatment in virtual spaces. *International Journal of Sport Communication, 13,* 221–238.

Schmittel, A., & Sanderson, J. (2015). Talking about Trayvon in 140 characters: Exploring NFL players' tweets about the George Zimmerman verdict. *Journal of Sport & Social Issues, 39,* 332–345.

Smith, L. R., & Sanderson, J. (2015). I'm going to Instagram it! An analysis of athlete self-presentation on Instagram. *Journal of Broadcasting & Electronic Media, 59,* 342–358.

Smith, L. R., Smith, K. D., & Blazka, M. (2017). Follow me, what's the harm? Considerations of catfishing and utilizing fake online personas on social media. *Journal of Legal Aspects of Sport, 27,* 32–45.

Suler, J. (2004). The online disinhibition effect. *Cyber Psychology & Behavior, 7,* 321–326.

Sveinson, K., & Hoeber, L. (2020). "So begins the demise of #Superman from Metropolis": Consumers' Twitter reactions to an athlete's transgression. *Sport Management Review.* Advance online publication. doi:10.1016/j.smr.2020.03.001.

Tang, T., & Cooper, R. (2018). The most social games: Predictors of social media uses during the 2016 Rio Olympics. *Communication & Sport, 6,* 308–330.

Toffoletti, K., & Thorpe, H. (2018). Female athletes' self-representation on social media: A feminist analysis of neoliberal marketing strategies in "economies of visibility." *Feminism & Psychology, 28,* 11–31.

Weathers, M., Sanderson, J., Matthey, P., Grevious, A., Tehan, M., & Warren, S. (2014). The tweet life of Erin and Kirk: A gendered analysis of sports broadcasters' self-presentation on Twitter. *Journal of Sports Media, 9,* 1–24.

Xu, Q., & Armstrong, C. L. (2019). #SELFIES at the 2016 Rio Olympics: Comparing self-representations of male and female athletes from the U.S. and China. *Journal of Broadcasting & Electronic Media, 63,* 322–338.

Young, R. (2018, December 8). Kyler Murray apologizes after old homophobic tweets surface hours after he wins Heisman Trophy. *Yahoo Sports.* https://sports.yahoo.com/several-old-homophobic-tweets-kyler-murray-surface-hours-wins-heisman-tropohy-052857060.html.

INDEX

For the benefit of digital users, indexed terms that span two pages (e.g., 52–53) may, on occasion, appear on only one of those pages.

Note: Page numbers followed by *f* indicate a figure on the corresponding page. Page numbers followed by *t* indicate a table on the corresponding page.